Comprehensive

GO!

Learn | Practice | Succeed

Microsoft® Office 365®

PowerPoint™ 2019

D1651364

Shelley Gaskin | Nancy Graviett

Series Editor: Shelley Gaskin

Pearson

VP Courseware Portfolio Management: Andrew Gilfillan
Executive Portfolio Manager: Jenifer Niles
Team Lead, Content Production: Laura Burgess
Content Producer: Shannon LeMay-Finn
Development Editor: Cheryl Slavik
Portfolio Management Assistant: Bridget Daly
Director of Product Marketing: Brad Parkins
Director of Field Marketing: Jonathan Cottrell
Product Marketing Manager: Heather Taylor
Field Marketing Manager: Bob Nisbet
Product Marketing Assistant: Liz Bennett
Field Marketing Assistant: Derrica Moser
Senior Operations Specialist: Diane Peirano

Senior Art Director: Mary Seiner
Interior and Cover Design: Pearson CSC
Cover Photo: Jag_cz/Shutterstock, everything possible/Shutterstock
Senior Product Model Manager: Eric Hakanson
Manager, Digital Studio: Heather Darby
Digital Content Producer, MyLab IT: Becca Golden
Course Producer, MyLab IT: Amanda Losonsky
Digital Studio Producer: Tanika Henderson
Full-Service Project Management: Pearson CSC, Katie Ostler
Composition: Pearson CSC
Printer/Binder: LSC Communications, Inc.
Cover Printer: Phoenix Color/Hagerstown

Library of Congress Cataloging-in-Publication Data

On file with the Library of Congress.

01 19

ISBN-10: 0-13-544105-6
ISBN-13: 978-0-13-544105-3

Brief Contents

Table of Contents

About the Authors

Shelley Gaskin, Series Editor, is a professor in the Business and Computer Technology Division at Pasadena City College in Pasadena, California. She holds a bachelor's degree in Business Administration from Robert Morris College (Pennsylvania), a master's degree in Business from Northern Illinois University, and a doctorate in Adult and Community Education from Ball State University (Indiana). Before joining Pasadena City College, she spent 12 years in the computer industry, where she was a systems analyst, sales representative, and director of Customer Education with Unisys Corporation. She also worked for Ernst & Young on the development of large systems applications for their clients. She has written and developed training materials for custom systems applications in both the public and private sector, and has also written and edited numerous computer application textbooks.

This book is dedicated to my husband Fred, and to my students, who inspire me every day.

Nancy Graviett is a professor and department chair in Business Technology at St. Charles Community College in Cottleville, Missouri. She holds a bachelor's degree in marketing and a master's degree in business education from the University of Missouri and has completed a certificate in online education. Nancy has authored textbooks on WordPerfect, Google, Microsoft Outlook, and Microsoft Access.

This book is dedicated to my husband, Dave, and my children, Matthew and Andrea. I cannot thank my family enough for the love and support they share everyday.

GO! with Microsoft PowerPoint 2019 Comprehensive

Introducing seamless digital instruction, practice, and assessment

Using GO! with MyLab IT has never been better! With the integrated etext and pre-built learning modules, instructors can assign learning easily and students can get started quickly.

➡ **Proven content and pedagogical approach of *guided instruction*, *guided practice*, and *mastery*** is effective for all types of learners and all types of course delivery—face-to-face in the classroom, online, and hybrid.

➡ **Students learn Microsoft Office skills by creating practical projects** they will see in their academic and professional lives.

➡ **With GO! MyLab IT students can learn, practice, and assess live or in authentic simulations of Microsoft Office.**

- **Microsoft Office autograded Grader** projects for the instructional, mastery, and assessment projects allow students to work live in Excel, Word, Access, or PPT so that during each step of the learning process, they can receive immediate, autograded feedback!

- **Microsoft Office authentic simulations** allow students to practice what they are learning in a safe environment with learning aids for instant help—*Read*, *Watch*, or *Practice*. Authentic simulations can also be used for assessment without learning aids.

What's New?

- The **book (print or etext) is the student's guide** to completing all autograded Grader projects for instruction, practice, and assessment.

- The **GO! *Learn How* videos**, integrated in the etext, give students an instructor-led, step-by-step guide through the A & B projects.

- **Improved business case connection** throughout the instruction so students always understand the *what* and *why*.

- **Mac tips** 💻 are woven into the instruction for each project so Mac students can proceed successfully.

  - All text and Grader projects created and tested by the authors on both a Mac and a PC.

  - Content not limited by Mac compatibility! Everything students need to know for MOS exams, Excel, and Access that are not possible on the Mac are still covered!

- **MyLab IT Prebuilt Learning modules** make course setup a snap. The modules are based on research and customer use, and can be easily customized to meet your course requirements.

- **Critical Thinking assessments and badges** expand coverage of Employability Skills.

- **New combined Office Features and Windows chapter** with Grader projects and auto-graded Windows projects for a fast and concise overview of these important features. Shorter and easier to assign.

- **Regular content updates to stay current with Office 365** updates and new features:
  - New *Semester Updates* for the etext and Grader projects through MyLab IT
  - New *Lessons on the GO!* to help you teach new features

What's New for Grader Projects

- **Autograded *Integrated Projects*** covering Word, Excel, Access, and PPT.
- Projects **A & B Grader reports now include *Learning Aids*** for immediate remediation.
- Autograded Critical Thinking Quizzes and Badges
  - Critical Thinking Modules include a Capstone and Quiz that enable students to earn a Critical Thinking Badge
  - Critical Thinking quizzes for the A & B instructional projects
- A **final output image** is provided so students can visualize what their solution should look like.
- **Mac Compatibility:** All Grader projects are built for PC and Mac users, excluding Access. Only projects that have features not supported on the Mac are not 100% compatible.

What's New for Simulations

- Simulations are updated by the authors for improved reinforcement of the software navigation in each instructional project—as always, they are matched one-to-one with the text Activities.
- *Student Action Visualization* provides an immediate playback for review by students and instructors when there's a question about why an action is marked as incorrect.

The Program

The GO! series has been used for over 17 years to teach students Microsoft Office successfully because of the *Quality of Instruction*, *Ease of Implementation*, and *Excellence in Assessment*. Using the hallmark Microsoft Procedural Syntax and Teachable Moment approach, students understand how to navigate the Microsoft Office ribbon so they don't get lost, and they get additional instruction and tips *when* they need them. Learning by doing is a great approach for skill-based learning, and creating a real-world document, spreadsheet, presentation, or database puts the skills in context for effective learning!

To improve student results, we recommend pairing the text content with **MyLab IT,** which is the teaching and learning platform that empowers you to reach every student. By combining trusted author content with digital tools and a flexible platform, MyLab personalizes the learning experience and will help your students learn and retain key course concepts while developing skills that future employers are seeking in their candidates.

Solving Teaching and Learning Challenges

The GO! series continues to evolve based on author interaction and experience with real students. GO! is written to ensure students know where they are going, how to get there, and why. Today's software is cloud based and changes frequently, so students need to know how the software functions so they can adapt quickly.

Each chapter is written with two instructional projects organized around **student learning outcomes** and **numbered objectives,** so that students understand what they will learn and be able to do when they finish the chapter. The **project approach** clusters the learning objectives around the projects rather than around the software features. This tested pedagogical approach teaches students to solve real problems as they practice and learn the software features. By using the textbook (print or digital), students can complete the A & B instructional projects as autograded Grader projects in MyLab IT. The *Learn How* videos, integrated in the etext or learning modules, give students an instructor-led, step-by-step guide through the project. This unique approach enhances learning and engages students because they receive immediate feedback. Additionally, students can practice the skills they are learning in the MyLab IT simulations, where they also get immediate feedback and help when needed! Both *Graders* and *Simulations* are available in assessment form so that students can demonstrate mastery.

The **Clear Instruction** in the project steps is written following *Microsoft Procedural Syntax* to guide students where to go and *then* what to do, so they never get lost! With the **Teachable Moment** approach, students learn important concepts when they need to as they work through the instructional projects. No long paragraphs of text. And with the integrated etext in MyLab IT, students can access their book anywhere, anytime.

The page design drives effective learning; textbook pages are clean and uncluttered, with screenshots that validate the student's actions and engage visual learners. Important information is boxed within the text so that students won't miss or skip the *Mac Tips*, *Another Way*, *By Touch*, *Note, Alert*, or *More Knowledge* details. **Color-Coded Steps** guide students through the projects with colors coded by project and the **End-of-Project Icon** helps students know when they have completed the project, which is especially useful in self-paced or online environments.

Students can engage in a wide variety of end-of-chapter projects where they apply what they learned in outcomes-based, problem-solving, and critical thinking projects—many of which require students to create a complete project from scratch.

Within the GO! etext and MyLab IT, students also have access to the *GO! Learn How* training videos, the *GO! to Work* videos (which demonstrate how Microsoft Office is used in a variety of jobs), the GO! for Job Success videos (which teach essential employability skills), and the *Where We're Going* videos, which provide a clear and concise overview of the instructional projects to ensure student success!

This complete, highly effective offering ensures students can learn the skills they need to succeed!

Developing Employability Skills

For students to succeed in a rapidly changing job market, they should be aware of their career options and how to go about developing a variety of skills. With MyLab IT and GO! we focus on developing these skills in the following ways:

High-Demand Office Skills are taught to help students gain these skills and prepare for the Microsoft Office Specialist (MOS) certification exams. The MOS objectives are covered throughout the content and highlighted with the MOS icons.

Essential Employability Skills are taught throughout the chapters using GO! for Job Success Videos and discussions, along with the new Critical Thinking badge students can earn by successfully completing the Critical Thinking Modules.

Employability Skills Matrix (ESM)								
	Grader Projects	Project K	Project M	Project O Group Project	Critical Thinking Projects and Badge	GO! To Work and Job Success Videos	MOS Practice Exams	MOS Badges
Critical Thinking	x	x	x		x		x	x
Communication	x			x		x		
Collaboration				x		x		
Knowledge Application and Analysis	x	x	x		x		x	x
Social Responsibility						x		

Getting Started with Microsoft PowerPoint

◀ Real-World Projects and GO! To Work Videos

The projects in GO! help you learn skills you'll need in the workforce and everyday life. And the GO! to Work videos give you insight into how people in a variety of jobs put Microsoft Office into action every day.

◀ Projects in GO! are real-world projects you create from start to finish, so that you are using the software features and skills as you will on the job and in everyday life.

◀ GO! to Work videos feature people from a variety of real jobs explaining how they use Microsoft Office every day to help you see the relevance of learning these programs.

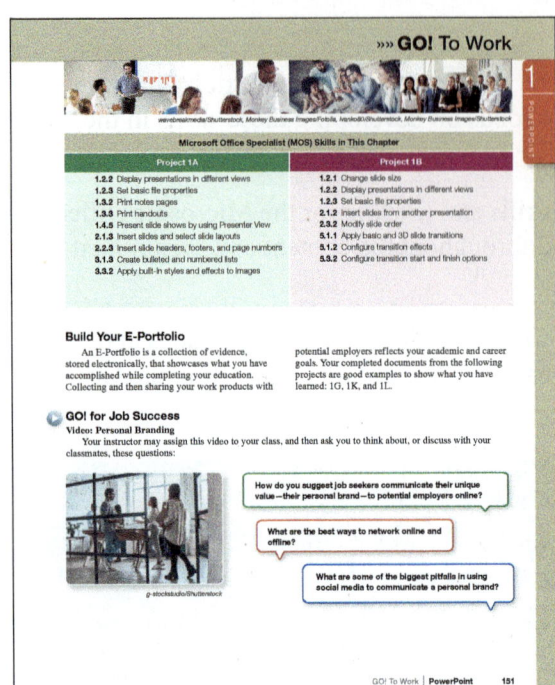

◀ GO! for Job Success Videos and Discussions

Important professional skills you need to succeed in a work environment, such as Accepting Criticism, Customer Service, and Interview Skills, are covered in a video with discussion questions or an overall discussion topic. These are must-have skills.

◀ Skills Badging

Within MyLab IT 2019, you can earn digital badges that demonstrate mastery of specific skills related to Office 2019 or Critical Thinking. These badges can be easily shared across social networks, such as LinkedIn, leading to real opportunities to connect with potential employers.

Applied Learning Opportunities

Throughout the chapters there are two projects for instruction, two for review, and a variety of outcomes-based projects to demonstrate mastery, critical thinking, and problem solving. In addition, within MyLab IT, GO! Learn How videos walk students through the A & B instructional project objectives. Grader projects and simulations provide hands-on instruction, training, and assessment.

▼ Live-in-the-Application Grader Projects

The MyLab IT Grader projects are autograded so students receive immediate feedback on their work. By completing these projects, students gain real-world context as they work live in the application, to learn and demonstrate an understanding of how to perform specific skills to complete a project.

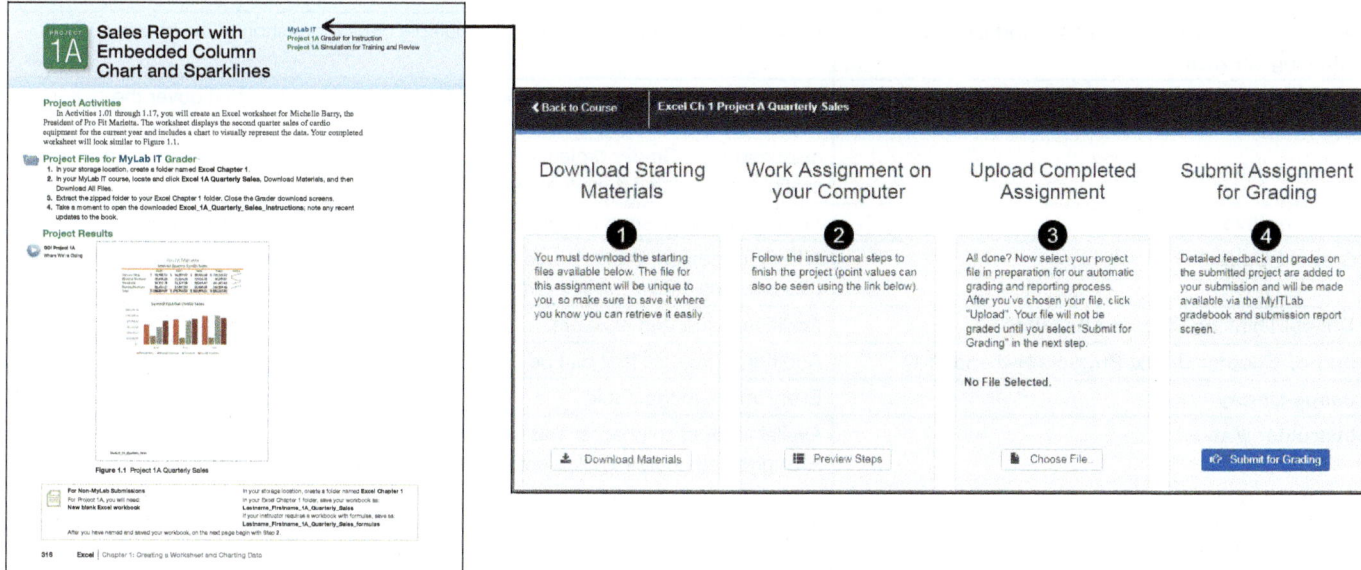

▼ Microsoft Office Simulations

The realistic and hi-fidelity simulations help students feel like they are working in the real Microsoft applications and enable them to explore, use 96% of Microsoft methods, and do so without penalty.

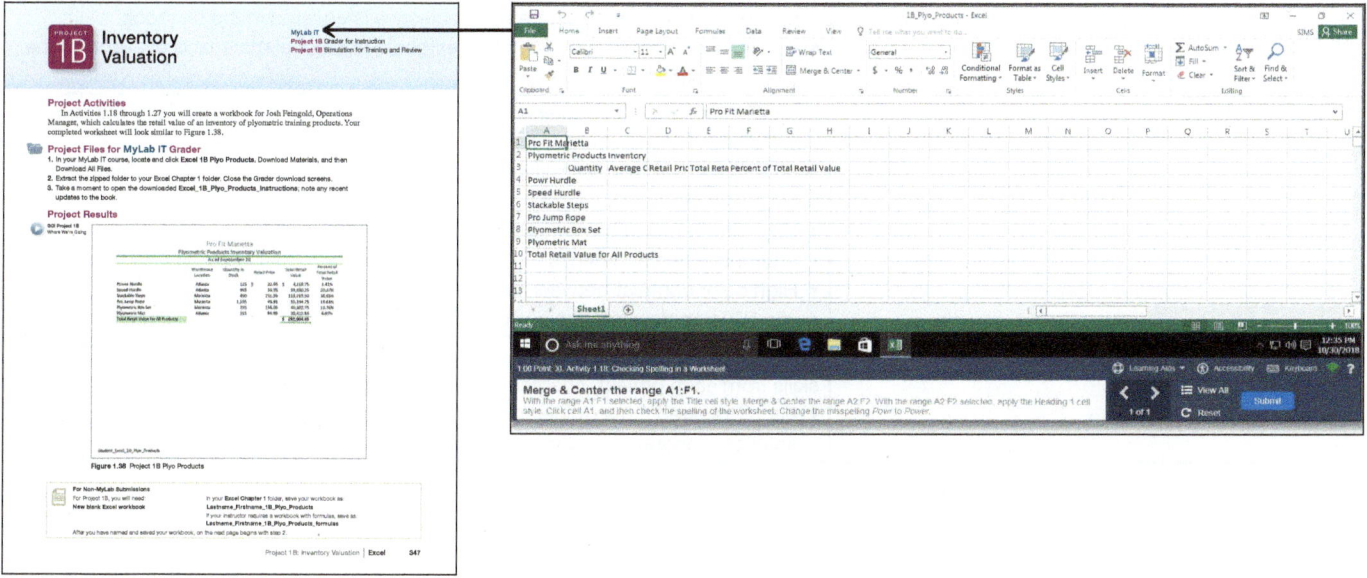

Instructor Teaching Resources

This program comes with the following teaching resources.

Resources available to instructors at www.pearsonhighered.com/go	Features of the Resources
Annotated Instructor Edition Tabs	Available for each chapter and include: • Suggested course implementation strategies and resources for the instructional portion of the chapter • Suggested strategies and resources for the Review, Practice, and Assessment portion of the chapter • Teaching tips
Annotated Solution Files	Annotated solution files in PDF feature callouts to enable easy grading.
Answer Keys for Chapter, MOS, and Critical Thinking Quizzes	Answer keys for each matching and multiple choice question in the chapter.
Application Capstones	Capstone projects for Word, Excel, Access, and PowerPoint that cover the objectives from all three chapters of each application. These are available as autograded Grader projects in MyLab IT, where students can also earn a proficiency badge if they score 90% or higher.
Collaborative Team Project	An optional exercise to assign to students to learn to work in groups.
Content Updates	A living document that features any changes in content based on Microsoft Office 365 changes as well as any errata.
Critical Thinking Quiz and Answers	Additional quiz and answers.
End-of-Chapter Online Projects H-J and M-O	Additional projects that can be assigned at instructor discretion.
Image Library	Every image in the book.
Instructor Manual	Available for each chapter and includes: • Suggested course implementation strategies and resources for the instructional portion of the chapter • Suggested strategies and resources for the Review, Practice, and Assessment portion of the chapter • Objectives • Teaching notes • Discussion questions
List of Objectives and Outcomes	Available for each chapter to help you determine what to assign • Includes every project and identifies which outcomes, objectives, and skills are included from the chapter
Lessons on the GO!	Projects created to teach new features added to Office 365. Available online only.
MOS Mapping and Additional Content	Based on the Office 2019 MOS Objectives • Includes a full guide of where each objective is covered in the textbook. • For any content not covered in the textbook, additional material is available in the Online Appendix document.
PowerPoint Presentations	PowerPoints for each chapter cover key topics, feature key images from the text, and include detailed speaker notes in addition to the slide content. PowerPoints meet accessibility standards for students with disabilities. Features include, but are not limited to: • Keyboard and screen reader access • Alternative text for images • High color contrast between background and foreground colors Audio PPTs contain spoken audio within traditional PowerPoint presentations.
Prepared Exams by Project, Chapter, and Application	An optional exercise that can be used to assess students' ability to perform the skills from each project, chapter, or across all chapters in an application • Each Prepared Exam folder includes the needed data files, instruction file, solution, annotated solution, and scorecard.

Resources available to instructors at www.pearsonhighered.com/go	Features of the Resources
Scorecards and Rubrics	Scorecards allow for easy scoring when hand-grading projects with definitive solutions. Rubrics are for projects without a definitive solution. These are available in Microsoft Word format, enabling instructors to customize the assignments for their classes.
Scripted Lectures	A lecture guide that provides the actions and language to help instructors demonstrate skills from the chapter.
Skills and Procedures Summary Charts	Concise list of key skills, including software icon and keyboard shortcut.
Solution Files, Solution File PDFs, and Solution Files with Formulas (Excel only)	Available for all exercises with definitive solutions.
Student Assignment Trackers	Document with a grid of suggested student deliverables per chapter that can be provided to students with columns for Due Date, Possible Points, and Actual Points.
Student Data Files	Files that students need to complete projects that are not delivered as Grader projects in MyLab IT.
Syllabus Template	Syllabus templates set up for 8-week, 12-week, and 16-week courses.
TestGen and Test Bank	TestGen enables instructors to: • Customize, save, and generate classroom tests • Edit, add, or delete questions from the Test Item Files • Analyze test results • Organize a database of tests and student results. The Test Gen contains approximately 75–100 total questions per chapter, made up of multiple-choice, fill-in-the blank, true/false, and matching. Questions include these annotations: • Correct answer • Difficulty level • Learning objective Alternative versions of the Test Bank are available for the following LMS: Blackboard CE/Vista, Blackboard, Desire2Learn, Moodle, Sakai, and Canvas.
Transition Guide	A detailed spreadsheet that provides a clear mapping of content from GO! Microsoft Office 2016 to GO! Microsoft Office 365, 2019 Edition.

Reviewers of the GO! Series

Carmen Montanez	Allan Hancock College	Therese ONeil	Indiana University of Pennsylvania
Jody Derry	Allan Hancock College	Bradley Howard	Itawamba Community College
Roberta McDonald	Anoka-Ramsey Community College	Edna Tull	Itawamba Community College
Paula Ruby	Arkansas State University	Pamela Larkin	Jefferson Community and Technical College
Buffie Schmidt	Augusta University	Sonya Shockley	Madisonville Community College
Julie Lewis	Baker College	Jeanne Canale	Middlesex Community College
Melanie Israel	Beal College	John Meir	Midlands Technical College
Suzanne Marks	Bellevue College	Robert Huyck	Mohawk Valley Community College
Ellen Glazer	Broward College	Mike Maesar	Montana Tech
Charline Nixon	Calhoun Community College	Julio Cuz	Moreno Valley College
Joseph Cash	California State University, Stanislaus	Lynn Wermers	North Shore Community College
Shaun Sides	Catawba Valley Community College	Angela Mott	Northeast Mississippi Community College
Linda Friedel	Central Arizona College	Connie Johnson	Owensboro Community & Technical College
Vicky Semple	Central Piedmont Community College	Kungwen Chu	Purdue University Northwest
Amanda Davis	Chattanooga State Community College	Kuan Chen	Purdue University Northwest
Randall George	Clarion University of Pennsylvania	Janette Nichols	Randolph Community College
Beth Zboran	Clarion University of Pennsylvania	Steven Zhang	Roane State Community College
Lee Southard	College of Coastal Georgia	Elizabeth Drake	Santa Fe College
Susan Mazzola	College of the Sequoias	Sandy Keeter	Seminole State
Vicki Brooks	Columbia College	Pat Dennis	South Plains College
Leasa Richards-Mealy	Columbia College	Tamara Dawson	Southern Nazarene University
Heidi Eaton	Elgin Community College	Richard Celli	SUNY Delhi
Ed Pearson	Friends University	Lois Blais	Walters State Community College
Nancy Woolridge	Fullerton College	Frederick MacCormack	Wilmington University
Wayne Way	Galveston College	Jessica Brown	Wilmington University
Leslie Martin	Gaston College	Doreen Palucci	Wilmington University
Don VanOeveren	Grand Rapids Community College	Rebecca Anderson	Zane State College

Microsoft Office Features and Windows 10 File Management

PROJECT 1A

Outcomes
Use the features common across all Microsoft Office applications to create and save a Microsoft Word document.

Objectives
1. Explore Microsoft Office
2. Create a Folder for File Storage
3. Download and Extract Zipped Files, Enter and Edit Text in an Office Application, and use Editor to Check Documents
4. Perform Office Commands and Apply Office Formatting
5. Finalize an Office Document
6. Use the Office Help Features

PROJECT 1B

Outcomes
Use Windows 10 features and the File Explorer program to manage files and folders.

Objectives
7. Explore Windows 10
8. Prepare to Work with Folders and Files
9. Use File Explorer to Extract Zipped Files and to Display Locations, Folders, and Files
10. Start Programs and Open Data Files
11. Create, Rename, and Copy Files and Folders

Petar Djordjevic/Shutterstock

In This Chapter

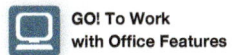 **GO! To Work**
with Office Features

In this chapter, you will practice using the features of Microsoft Office that work similarly across Word, Excel, Access, and PowerPoint. These features include performing commands, adding document properties, applying formatting to text, and searching for Office commands quickly. You will also practice using the file management features of Windows 10 so that you can create folders, save files, and find your documents easily.

The projects in this chapter relate to the **Bell Orchid Hotels**, headquartered in Boston, and which own and operate restaurants, resorts, and business-oriented hotels. Resort property locations are in popular destinations, including Honolulu, Orlando, San Diego, and Santa Barbara. The resorts offer deluxe accommodations and a wide array of dining options. Other Bell Orchid hotels are located in major business centers and offer the latest technology in their meeting facilities. Bell Orchid offers extensive educational opportunities for employees. The company plans to open new properties and update existing properties over the next decade.

Chef Notes

Project Activities

In Activities 1.01 through 1.19, you will create a handout for the Executive Chef at Skyline Metro Grill to give to her staff at a meeting where they will develop new menu ideas for wedding rehearsal dinners. The restaurant is located within Bell Orchid's San Diego resort hotel. Your completed notes will look similar to Figure 1.1.

Project Files for **MyLab IT Grader**

1. For Project 1A, you will start with a blank Word document, and then you will learn how to create a folder for your **MyLab IT** files as you work through the Project instruction. At the appropriate point in the Project, you will be instructed to download your files from your **MyLab IT** course.

Project Results

GO! Project 1A

Where We're Going

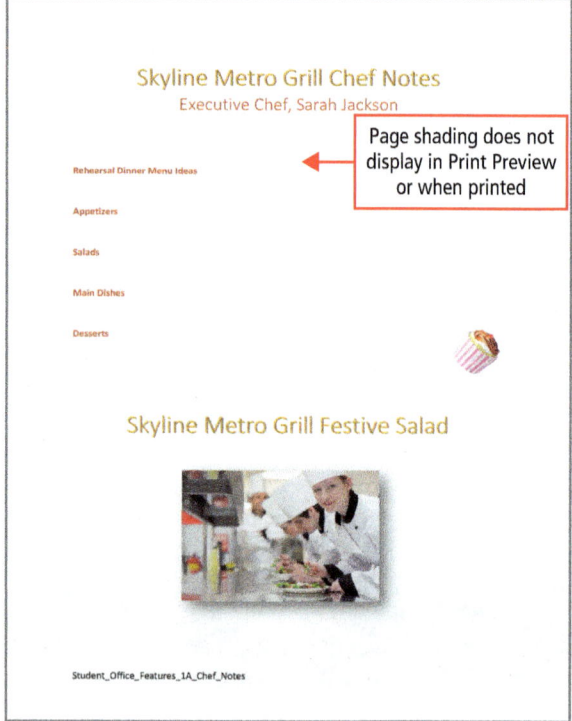

Figure 1.1 (Wavebreakmedia/Shutterstock)

 For Non-MyLab Submissions   **Start with a blank Word document**

For Project 1A, you will begin with a blank Word document and then learn how to create a folder and save a Word document as you work through the Project instruction.

NOTE   If You Are Using a Touch Screen

 Tap an item to click it.

 Press and hold for a few seconds to right-click; release when the information or commands display.

 Touch the screen with two or more fingers and then pinch together to zoom out or stretch your fingers apart to zoom in.

 Slide your finger on the screen to scroll—slide left to scroll right and slide right to scroll left.

 Slide to rearrange—similar to dragging with a mouse.

 Swipe to select—slide an item a short distance with a quick movement—to select an item and bring up commands, if any.

Objective 1   Explore Microsoft Office

ALERT   Because Office 365 is a cloud-based subscription service that receives continuous updates, you may encounter some variations in what appears on your screen and what is shown in this instruction. Microsoft Office 365 is fully installed on your PC or Mac; no internet access is necessary to create or edit documents. When you *are* connected to the internet, you will receive monthly upgrades and new features, so you always have the latest versions of Office apps as soon as they are available. Your subscription gives you continuous free access to the latest innovations and refinements.

ALERT   Is Your Screen More Colorful and a Different Size Than the Figures in This Textbook?

Your installation of Microsoft Office may use the default Colorful theme, where the ribbon in each application is a vibrant color and the title bar displays with white text. In this textbook, figures shown use the White theme, but you can be assured that all the commands are the same. You can keep your Colorful theme, or if you prefer, you can change your theme to White to match the figures here. To do so, open any application and display a new document. On the ribbon, click the File tab, and then on the left, click Options. With General selected on the left, under Personalize your copy of Microsoft Office, click the Office Theme arrow, and then click White. Change the Office Background to No Background. (In macOS, display the menu bar, click the application name—Word, Excel, and so on—click Preferences, and then click General. Under Personalize, click the Office Theme arrow to select either Colorful or Classic.)

Additionally, the figures in this book were captured using a screen resolution of 1280 x 768. If that is not your screen resolution, your screen will closely resemble, but not match, the figures shown. To view or change your screen's resolution, on the desktop, right-click in a blank area, click Display settings, click the Resolution arrow, and then select the resolution you want.

GO! Learn How
Video OF1-1

The term ***desktop application*** or ***desktop app*** refers to a computer program that is installed on your PC and that requires a computer operating system such as Microsoft Windows to run. The programs in Office 365 and in Microsoft Office 2019 are considered to be desktop apps. A desktop app typically has hundreds of features and takes time to learn.

Activity 1.01 | Exploring Microsoft Office

1 On the computer you are using, start Microsoft Word, and then compare your screen with Figure 1.2.

Depending on which operating system you are using and how your computer is set up, you might start Word from the taskbar or from the Start menu. On an Apple Mac computer, you might start the program from the Dock.

On the left, the Home tab is active in this view, referred to as ***Backstage view***, which is a centralized space for all your file management tasks such as opening, saving, printing, publishing, or sharing a file—all the things you can do *with* a file. In macOS the File tab is on the menu bar.

Documents that you have recently opened, if any, display under the Recent tab. You can also click the Pinned tab to see documents you have pinned there, or you can click the Shared with Me tab to see documents that have been shared with you by others.

On the left, you can click New to find a ***template***—a preformatted document that you can use as a starting point and then change to suit your needs. Or you can click Open to navigate to your files and folders. You can also look at Account information, give feedback to Microsoft, or look at the Word Options dialog box.

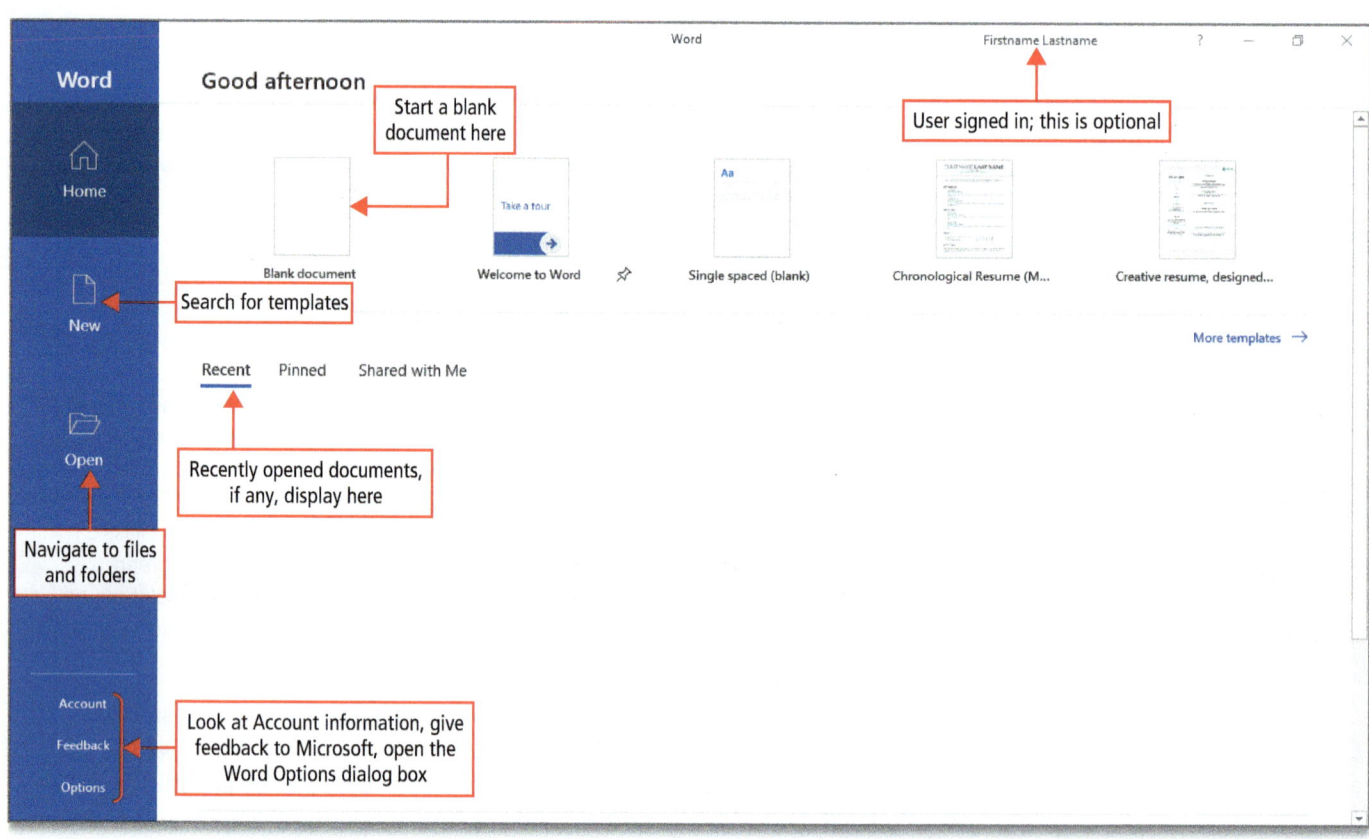

Figure 1.2

2 ▸ Click **Blank document**. Compare your screen with Figure 1.3, and then take a moment to study the description of the screen elements in the table in Figure 1.4.

NOTE   Displaying the Full Ribbon

If your full ribbon does not display, click any tab, and then at the right end of the ribbon, click ⊞ to pin the ribbon to keep it open while you work.

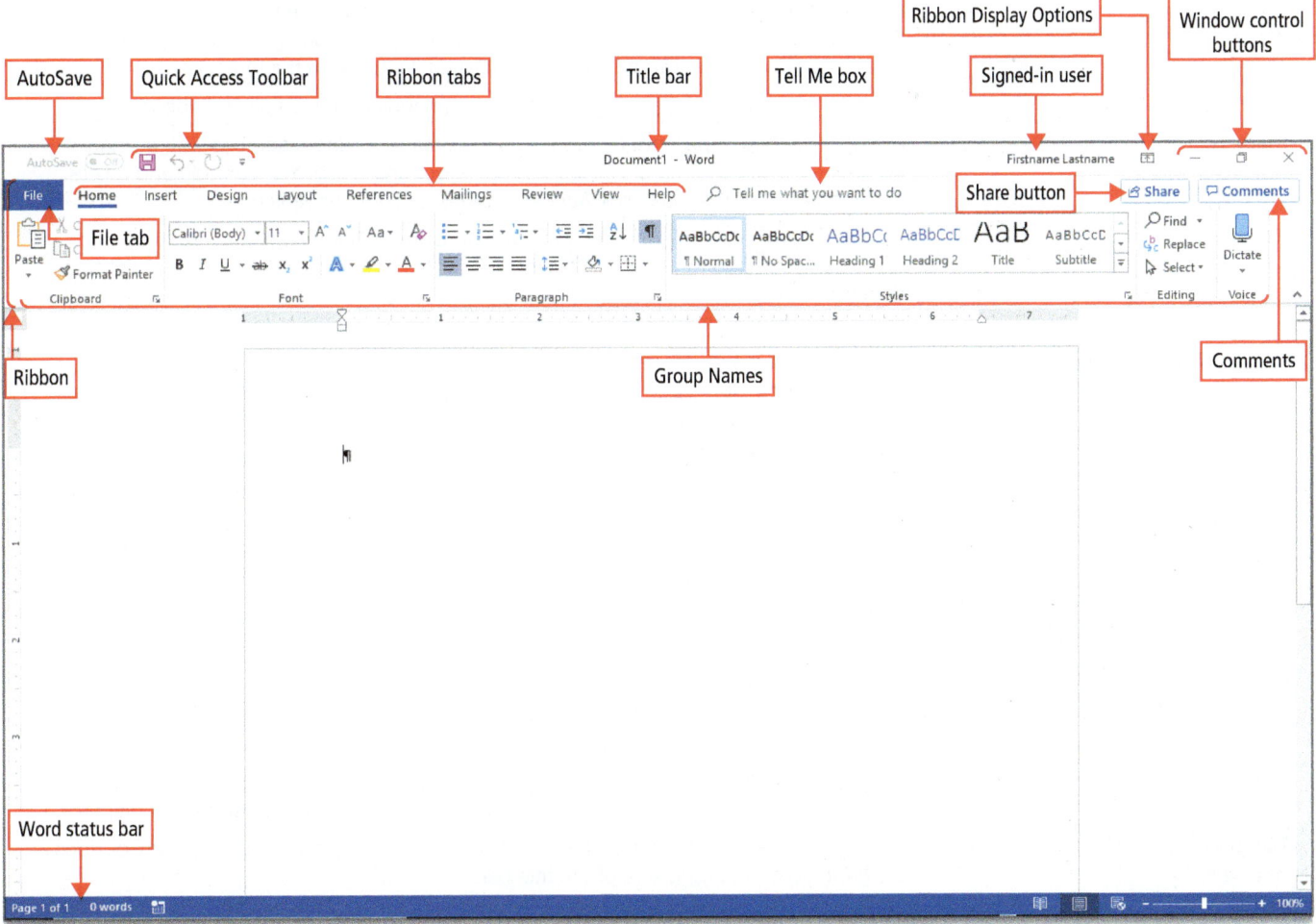

Figure 1.3

Screen Element	Description
AutoSave (off unless your document is saved to OneDrive using an Office 365 subscription)	Saves your document every few seconds so you don't have to. On a Windows system, AutoSave is available in Word, Excel, and PowerPoint for Office 365 subscribers. AutoSave is enabled only when a file is stored on OneDrive, OneDrive for Business, or SharePoint Online. Changes to your document are saved to the cloud as you are working, and if other people are working on the same file, AutoSave lets them see your changes in a matter of seconds.
Comments	Displays a short menu from which you can add a comment to your document or view other comments already in the document.
File tab	Displays Microsoft Office Backstage view, which is a centralized space for all your file management tasks such as opening, saving, printing, publishing, or sharing a file—all the things you can do *with* a file. (In macOS the File tab is on the menu bar.)
Group names	Indicate the name of the groups of related commands on the displayed ribbon tab.
Quick Access Toolbar	Displays buttons to perform frequently used commands and resources with a single click. The default commands include Save, Undo, and Redo. You can add and delete buttons to customize the Quick Access Toolbar for your convenience.
Ribbon	Displays a group of task-oriented tabs that contain the commands, styles, and resources you need to work in Microsoft Office desktop apps. The look of your ribbon depends on your screen resolution. A high resolution will display more individual items and button names on the ribbon.
Ribbon Display Options	Displays three ways you can display the ribbon: Auto-hide Ribbon, Show Tabs, or Show Tabs and Commands; typically, you will want to use Show Tabs and Commands, especially while you are learning Office.
Ribbon tabs	Display the names of the task-oriented tabs relevant to the open document.
Share	Opens the Share dialog box from which you can save your file to the cloud—your OneDrive—and then share it with others so you can collaborate. Here you can also email the Office file or a PDF of the file directly from Outlook if you are using Outlook to view and send email. A *dialog box* enables you to make decisions about an individual object or topic.
Signed-in user	Identifies the user who is signed in to Office.
Status bar	Displays file information on the left; on the right displays buttons for Read Mode, Print Layout, and Web Layout views; on the far right edge, displays Zoom controls.
Tell me what you want to do	Provides a search feature for Microsoft Office commands that you activate by typing what you are looking for in the *Tell me what you want to do* area. As you type, every keystroke refines the results so that you can click the command as soon as it displays.
Title bar	Displays the name of the file and the name of the program; the window control buttons are grouped on the right side of the title bar.
Window control buttons	Displays buttons for commands to Minimize, Restore Down, or Close the window.

Figure 1.4

GO! Learn How
Video OF1-2

Objective 2   Create a Folder for File Storage

A *location* is any disk drive, folder, or other place in which you can store files and folders. A *file* is information stored on a computer under a single name. A *folder* is a container in which you store files. Where you store your files depends on how and where you use your data. For example, for your college classes, you might decide to store your work on a removable USB flash drive so that you can carry your files to different locations and access your files on different computers.

If you do most of your work on a single computer, for example your home desktop system or your laptop computer that you take with you to school or work, then you can store your files in one of the folders on your hard drive provided by your Windows operating system—Documents, Music, Pictures, or Videos.

The best place to store files if you want them to be available anytime, anywhere, from almost any device is on your *OneDrive*, which is Microsoft's free *cloud storage* for anyone with a free Microsoft account. Cloud storage refers to online storage of data so that you can access your data from different places and devices. *Cloud computing* refers to applications and services that are accessed over the internet, rather than to applications that are installed on your local computer.

Besides being able to access your documents from any device or location, OneDrive also offers *AutoSave*, which saves your document every few seconds, so you don't have to. On a Windows system, AutoSave is available in Word, Excel, and PowerPoint for Office 365 subscribers. Changes to your document are saved to the cloud as you are working, and if other people are working on the same file—referred to as *real-time co-authoring*—AutoSave lets them see your changes in a matter of seconds.

If you have an *Office 365* subscription—one of the versions of Microsoft Office to which you subscribe for an annual fee or download for free with your college *.edu* address—your storage capacity on OneDrive is a terabyte or more, which is more than most individuals would ever require. Many colleges provide students with free Office 365 subscriptions. The advantage of subscribing to Office 365 is that you receive monthly updates with new features.

Because many people now have multiple computing devices—desktop, laptop, tablet, smartphone—it is common to store data *in the cloud* so that it is always available. *Synchronization*, also called *syncing*—pronounced SINK-ing—is the process of updating computer files that are in two or more locations according to specific rules. So, if you create and save a Word document on your OneDrive using your laptop, you can open and edit that document on your tablet in OneDrive. When you close the document again, the file is properly updated to reflect your changes. Your OneDrive account will guide you in setting options for syncing files to your specifications. You can open and edit Office files by using Office apps available on a variety of device platforms, including iOS, Android, in a web browser, and in Windows.

MORE KNOWLEDGE **Creating a Microsoft Account**

Use a free Microsoft account to sign in to Microsoft Office so that you can work on different PCs and use your free OneDrive cloud storage. If you already sign in to a Windows PC or tablet, or you sign in to Xbox Live, Outlook.com, or OneDrive, use that account to sign in to Office. To create a new Microsoft account, in your browser, search for *sign up for a Microsoft account*. You can use any email address as the user name for your new Microsoft account—including addresses from Outlook.com or Gmail.

Activity 1.02 | Creating a Folder for File Storage

Your computer's operating system, either Windows or macOS, helps you to create and maintain a logical folder structure, so always take the time to name your files and folders consistently.

NOTE **This Activity is for Windows PC users. Mac users refer to the document *Creating a Folder for File Storage on a Mac*.**

Mac users can refer to the document Creating a Folder for File Storage on a Mac available within **MyLab IT** or, for non-MyLab users, your instructor can provide this document to you from the Instructor Resource Center.

In this Activity, you will create a folder in the storage location you have chosen to use for your files, and then you will save your file. This example will use the Documents folder on the PC at which you are working. If you prefer to store on your OneDrive or on a USB flash drive, you can use similar steps.

1 Decide where you are going to store your files for this Project.

As the first step in saving a file, determine where you want to save the file, and if necessary, insert a storage device.

2 ▸ At the top of your screen, in the title bar, notice that *Document1 – Word* displays.

The Blank option on the opening screen of an Office program displays a new unsaved file with a default name—*Document1, Presentation1*, and so on. As you create your file, your work is temporarily stored in the computer's memory until you initiate a Save command, at which time you must choose a file name and a location in which to save your file.

3 ▸ In the upper left corner of your screen, click the **File tab** to display **Backstage** view, and then on the left, if necessary, click **Info**. Compare your screen with Figure 1.5.

Recall that Backstage view is a centralized space that groups commands related to *file management*; that is why the tab is labeled *File*. File management commands include opening, saving, printing, or sharing a file. The ***Backstage tabs***—*Info, New, Open, Save, Save As, Print, Share, Export,* and *Close*—display along the left side. The tabs group file-related tasks together.

Here, the ***Info tab*** displays information—*info*—about the current file, and file management commands display under Info. For example, if you click the Protect Document button, a list of options that you can set for this file that relate to who can open or edit the document displays.

On the right, you can also examine the ***document properties***. Document properties, also known as ***metadata***, are details about a file that describe or identify it, such as the title, author name, subject, and keywords that identify the document's topic or contents.

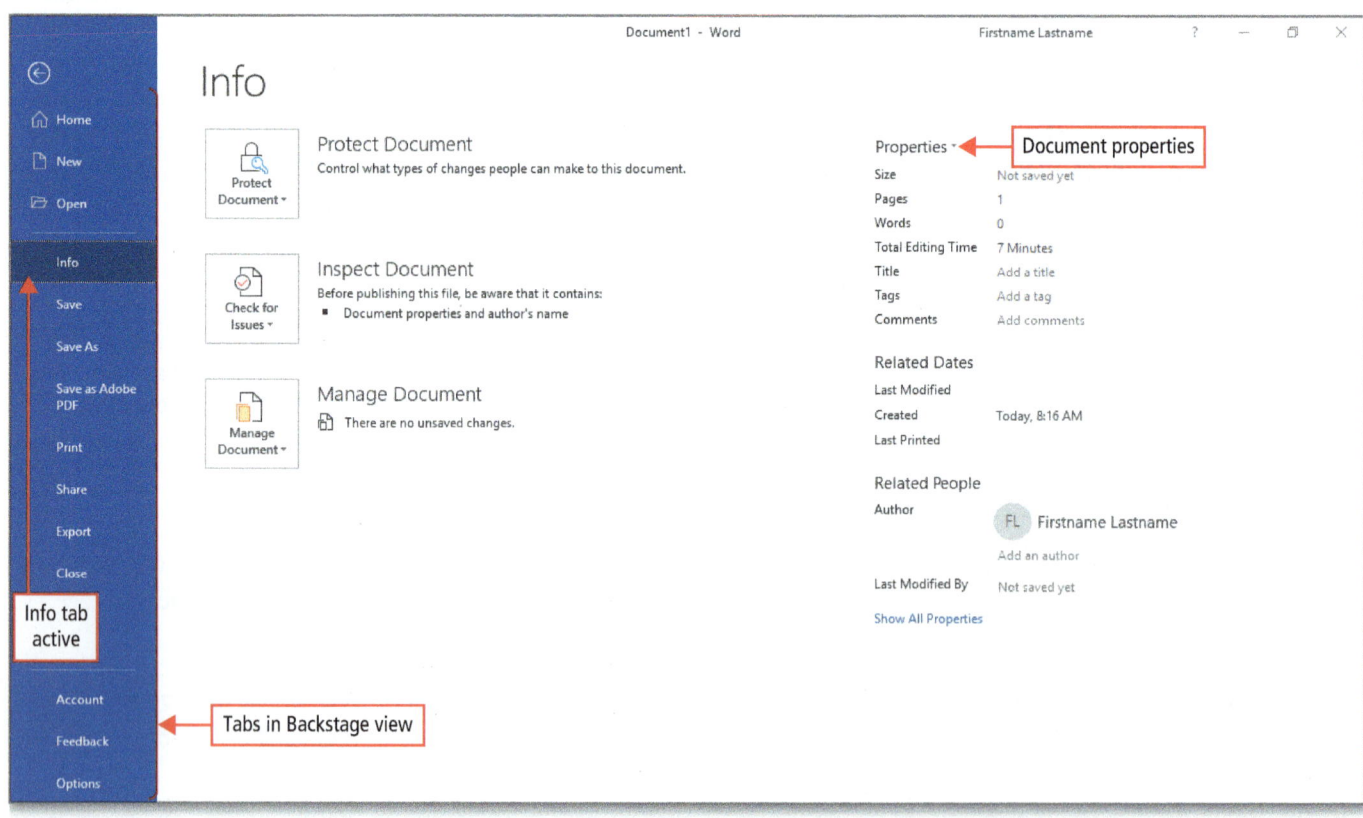

Figure 1.5

4 ▸ On the left, click **Save As**, and notice that, if you are signed into Office with a Microsoft account, one option for storing your files is your **OneDrive**. Compare your screen with Figure 1.6.

When you are saving something for the first time, for example a new Word document, the Save and Save As commands are identical. That is, the Save As commands will display if you click Save or if you click Save As.

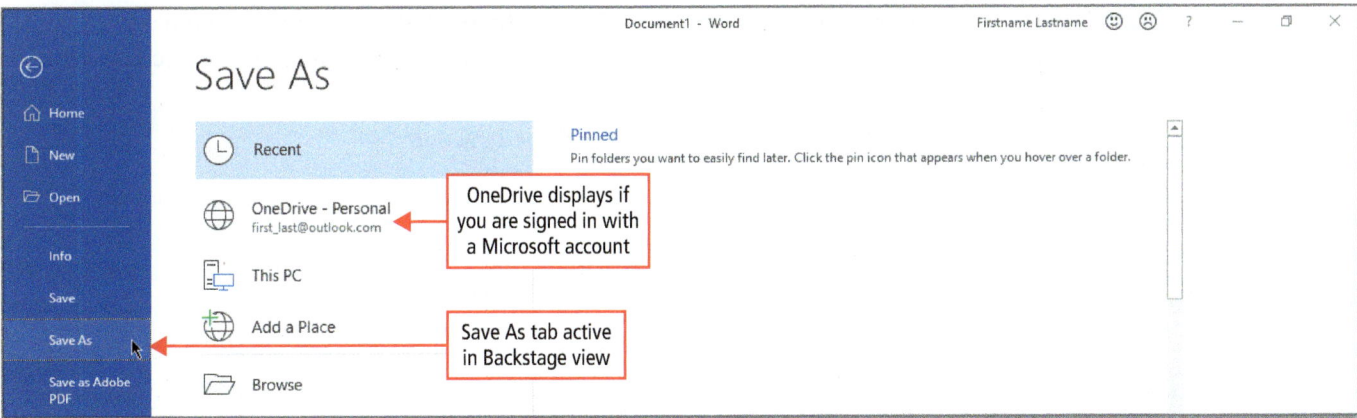

Figure 1.6

NOTE   Saving After Your File Is Named

After you name and save a file, the Save command on the Quick Access Toolbar saves any changes you make to the file without displaying Backstage view. The Save As command enables you to name and save a *new* file based on the current one—in a location that you choose. After you name and save the new document, the original document closes, and the new document—based on the original one—displays.

---

5 To store your Word file in the **Documents** folder on your PC, click **Browse** to display the **Save As** dialog box. On the left, in the **navigation pane**, scroll down; if necessary click **>** to expand This PC, and then click **Documents**. Compare your screen with Figure 1.7.

In the Save As dialog box, you must indicate the name you want for the file and the location where you want to save the file. When working with your own data, it is good practice to pause at this point and determine the logical name and location for your file.

In the Save As dialog box, a *toolbar* displays, which is a row, column, or block of buttons or icons, that displays across the top of a window and that contains commands for tasks you perform with a single click.

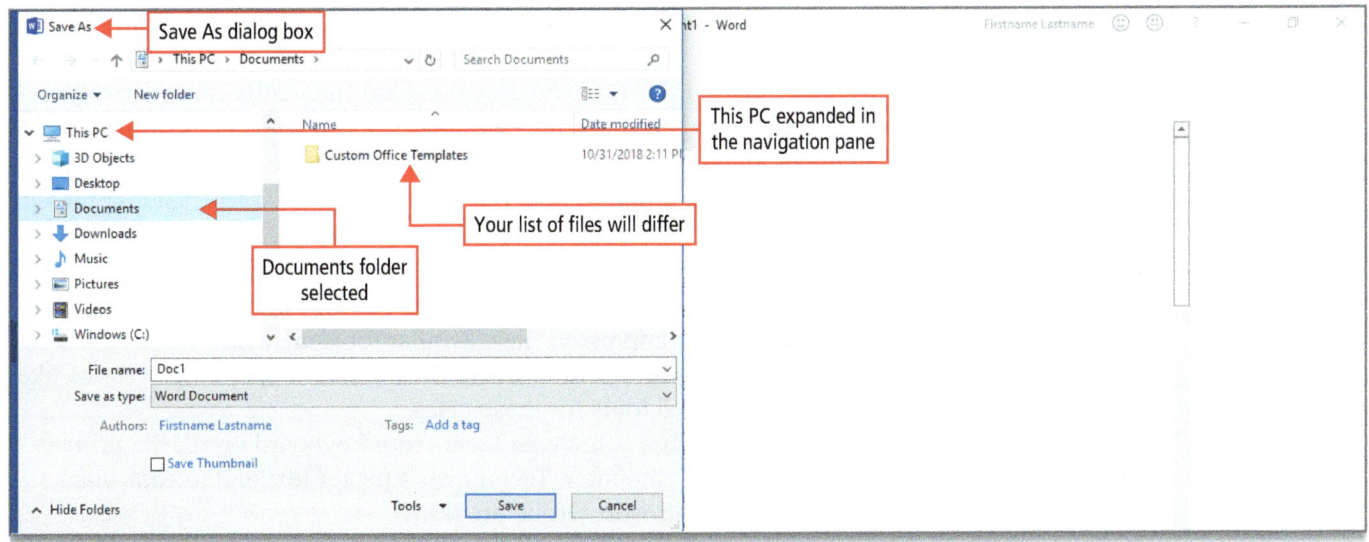

Figure 1.7

6 On the toolbar, click **New folder**.

In the file list, Windows creates a new folder, and the text *New folder* is selected.

7 Type **Office Features Chapter 1** and press `Enter`. In the **file list**, double-click the name of your new folder to open it and display its name in the **address bar**. Compare your screen with Figure 1.8.

In Windows-based programs, the `Enter` key confirms an action.

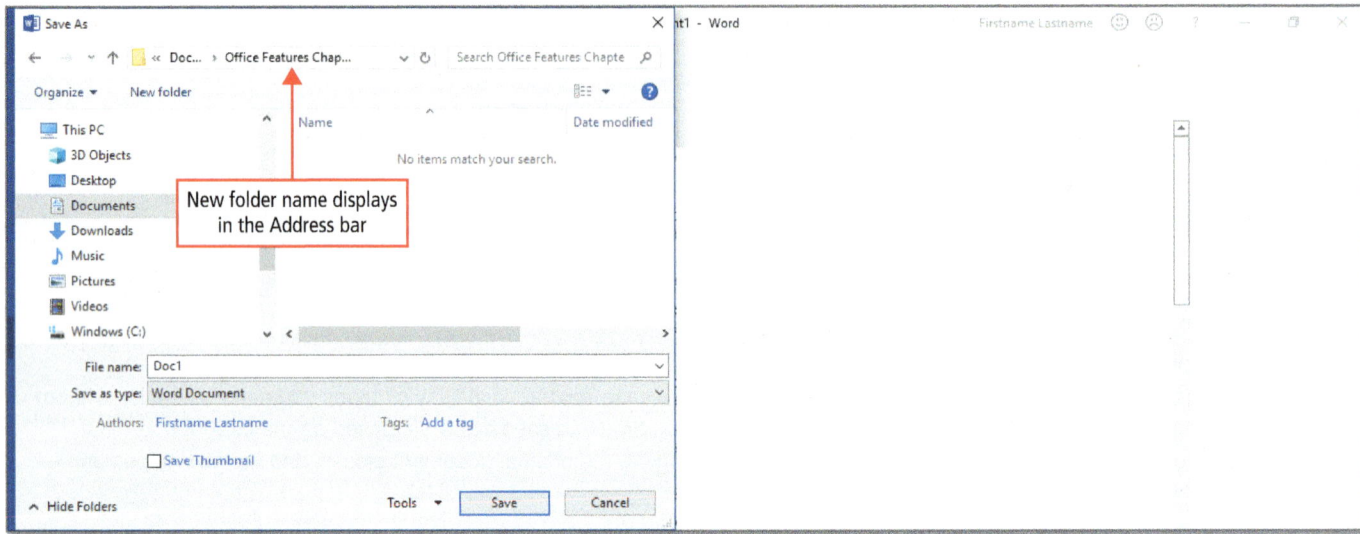

New folder name displays in the Address bar

Figure 1.8

8 In the lower right corner of the **Save As** dialog box, click **Cancel**. In the upper left corner of Backstage view, click the **Back** arrow ⊖.

9 In the upper right corner of the Word window, click **Close** ☒. If prompted to save your changes, click Don't Save. Close any other open windows or programs.

Objective 3	Download and Extract Zipped Files, Enter and Edit Text in an Office Application, and Use Editor to Check Documents

GO! Learn How

Video OF1-3

Download refers to the action of transferring or copying a file from another location—such as a cloud storage location, your college's Learning Management System, or from an internet site like **MyLab IT**—to your computer. Files that you download are frequently **compressed files**, which are files that have been reduced in size, take up less storage space, and can be transferred to other computers faster than uncompressed files.

A compressed folder might contain a group of files that were combined into one compressed folder, which makes it easier to share a group of files. To **extract** means to decompress, or pull out, files from a compressed form. The terms **zip** and **unzip** refer to the process of compressing (zipping) and extracting (unzipping). Windows 10 includes **Compressed Folder Tools**, available on the ribbon, to assist you in extracting compressed files. Similar tools are available in macOS. You do not need to install a separate program to zip or unzip files; modern operating systems like Windows and macOS provide sophisticated tools for these tasks.

All programs in Microsoft Office require some typed text. Your keyboard is still the primary method of entering information into your computer. Techniques to enter text and to **edit**—make changes to—text are similar across all Microsoft Office programs.

For Non-MyLab Submissions

Start Word and click Blank document. Click the File tab, on the left click Save As, click Browse, and then navigate to your **Office Features Chapter 1 folder.** At the bottom of the **Save As** dialog box, in the **File name** box, using your own name, name the file **Lastname_Firstname_Office_Features_1A_Chef_Notes** and then click Save. Then, move to Step 3 in Activity 1.03.

---

1 Sign in to your **MyLab IT** course. Locate and click the Grader project **Office Features 1A Chef Notes**, click **Download Materials**, and then click **Download All Files**. Using the Chrome browser (if you are using a different browser see notes below), extract the zipped folder to your **Office Features Chapter 1 folder** as follows (or use your favorite method to download and extract files):

- In the lower left, next to the downloaded zipped folder, click the small **arrow**, and then click **Show in folder**. The zipped folder displays in *File Explorer*—the Windows program that displays the contents of locations, folders, and files on your computer—in the Downloads folder. (Unless you have changed default settings, downloaded files go to the Downloads folder on your computer.)
- With the zipped folder selected, on the ribbon, under **Compressed Folder Tools**, click the **Extract tab**, and then at the right end of the ribbon, click **Extract all** (you may have to wait a few seconds for the command to become active).
- In the displayed **Extract Compressed (Zipped) Folders** dialog box, click **Browse**. In the **Select a destination** dialog box, use the navigation pane on the left to navigate to your **Office Features Chapter 1 folder**, and double-click its name to open the folder and display its name in the **Address bar**.
- In the lower right, click **Select Folder**, and then in the lower right, click **Extract**; when complete, a new File Explorer window displays showing the extracted files in your chapter folder. Take a moment to open **Office_Features_1A_Chef_Notes_Instructions**; note any recent updates to the book.
- **Close** ⊠ both File Explorer windows, close any open documents, and then close the Grader download screens. You can also close **MyLab IT** and, if open, your Learning Management system.

> **NOTE**   **Using the Edge Browser or Firefox Browser to Extract Files**
>
> Microsoft Edge: At the bottom, click Open, click Extract all, click Browse, navigate to and open your Chapter folder, click Select Folder, click Extract.
> Firefox: In the displayed dialog box, click OK, click Extract all, click Browse, navigate to and open your Chapter folder, click Select Folder, and then click Extract.

> 🖥 **MAC TIP**   Using the Chrome browser, in **MyLab IT**, after you click Download Materials, in the lower left, to the right of the zipped folder, click the arrow. Click Open. Click the blue folder containing the unzipped files. Use Finder commands to move or copy the files to your Office Features Chapter 1 folder.

2 On the Windows taskbar, click **File Explorer** 📁. Navigate to your **Office Features Chapter 1 folder**, and then double-click the Word file you downloaded from **MyLab IT** that displays your name—**Student_Office_Features_1A_Chef_Notes**. In this empty Word document, if necessary, at the top, click **Enable Editing**.

> 🖥 **MAC TIP**   When the Word application is not open, on the Dock, use the macOS Finder commands to locate your Word document. When the Word application is open, use the File tab on the menu bar.

3 On the ribbon, on the **Home tab**, in the **Paragraph group**, if necessary, click **Show/Hide** ¶ so that it is active—shaded. On the **View tab**, if necessary, in the **Show group**, select the **Ruler** check box so that rulers display below the ribbon and on the left side of your window, and then redisplay the **Home tab**.

The *insertion point*—a blinking vertical line that indicates where text or graphics will be inserted—displays. In Office programs, the mouse *pointer*—any symbol that displays on your screen in response to moving your mouse device—displays in different shapes depending on the task you are performing and the area of the screen to which you are pointing.

When you press Enter, Spacebar, or Tab on your keyboard, characters display to represent these keystrokes. These screen characters do not print and are referred to as *formatting marks* or *nonprinting characters*.

When working in Word, display the rulers so that you can see how margin settings affect your document and how text and objects align. Additionally, if you set a tab stop or an indent, its location is visible on the ruler.

NOTE   Activating Show/Hide in Word Documents

When Show/Hide is active—the button is shaded—formatting marks display. Because formatting marks guide your eye in a document—like a map and road signs guide you along a highway—these marks will display throughout this instruction. Expert Word users keep these marks displayed while creating documents.

4 Type **Skyline Grille Info** and notice how the insertion point moves to the right as you type. Point slightly to the right of the letter *e* in *Grille* and click to place the insertion point there. Compare your screen with Figure 1.9.

A *paragraph symbol* (¶) indicates the end of a paragraph and displays each time you press Enter. This is a type of formatting mark and does not print.

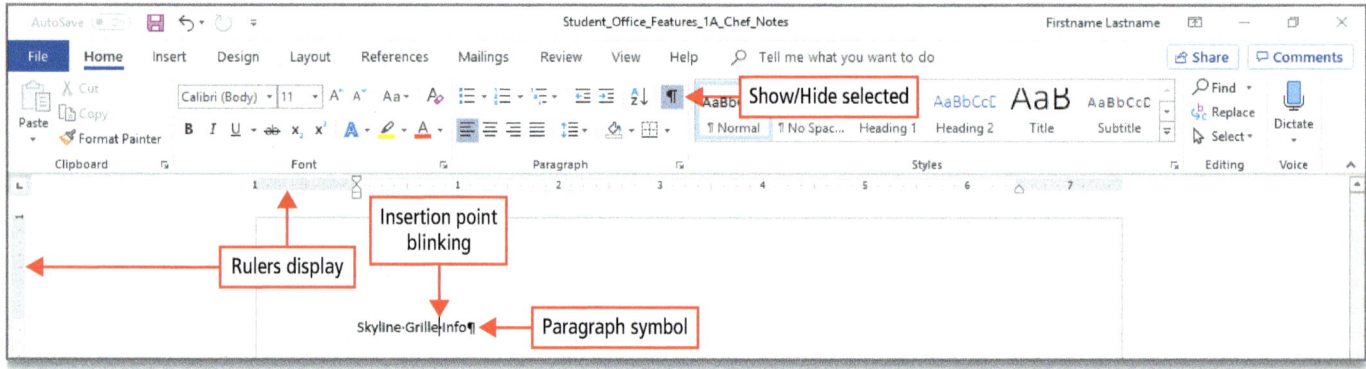

Figure 1.9

5 On your keyboard, locate and then press the Backspace key one time to delete the letter *e*.

Pressing Backspace removes a character to the left of the insertion point.

6 Press → one time to place the insertion point to the left of the *I* in *Info*. Type **Chef** and then press Spacebar one time.

By *default*, when you type text in an Office program, existing text moves to the right to make space for new typing. Default refers to the current selection or setting that is automatically used by a program unless you specify otherwise.

7 Press Del four times to delete *Info* and then type **Notes**

Pressing Del removes a character to the right of the insertion point.

8 With your insertion point blinking after the word *Notes*, on your keyboard, hold down the Ctrl key. While holding down Ctrl, press ← three times to move the insertion point to the beginning of the word *Grill*.

> This is a ***keyboard shortcut***—a key or combination of keys that performs a task that would otherwise require a mouse. This keyboard shortcut moves the insertion point to the beginning of the previous word.
>
> A keyboard shortcut is indicated as Ctrl + ← (or some other combination of keys) to indicate that you hold down the first key while pressing the second key. A keyboard shortcut can also include three keys, in which case you hold down the first two and then press the third. For example, Ctrl + Shift + ← selects one word to the left.

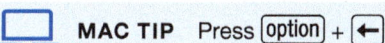 **MAC TIP** Press option + ←.

9 With the insertion point blinking at the beginning of the word *Grill*, type **Metro** and press Spacebar one time.

10 Click to place the insertion point after the letter *s* in *Notes* and then press Enter one time. With the insertion point blinking, type the following and include the spelling error: **Exective Chef, Madison Dunham** (If Word autocorrects *Exective* to *Executive*, delete *u* in the word.)

11 With your mouse, point slightly to the left of the *M* in *Madison*, hold down the left mouse button, and then ***drag***—hold down the left mouse button while moving your mouse—to the right to select the text *Madison Dunham* but not the paragraph mark following it, and then release the mouse button. Compare your screen with Figure 1.10.

> The ***mini toolbar*** displays commands that are commonly used with the selected object, which places common commands close to your pointer. When you move the pointer away from the mini toolbar, it fades from view.
>
> ***Selecting*** refers to highlighting—by dragging or clicking with your mouse—areas of text or data or graphics so that the selection can be edited, formatted, copied, or moved. The action of dragging includes releasing the left mouse button at the end of the area you want to select.
>
> The Office programs recognize a selected area as one unit to which you can make changes. Selecting text may require some practice. If you are not satisfied with your result, click anywhere outside of the selection, and then begin again.

MAC TIP The mini toolbar may not display; use ribbon commands.

BY TOUCH Tap once on *Madison* to display the gripper—a small circle that acts as a handle—directly below the word. This establishes the start gripper. If necessary, with your finger, drag the gripper to the beginning of the word. Then drag the gripper to the end of *Dunham* to select the text and display the end gripper.

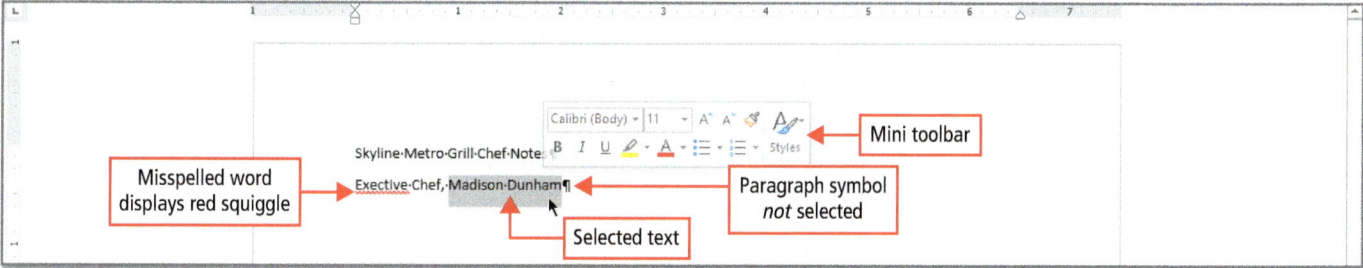

Figure 1.10

12 ▶ With the text *Madison Dunham* selected, type **Sarah Jackson**

In any Windows-based program, such as the Microsoft Office programs, selected text is deleted and then replaced when you begin to type new text. You will save time by developing good techniques for selecting and then editing or replacing selected text, which is easier than pressing ⌫Backspace or ⌦Del numerous times to delete text.

Activity 1.04 | Checking Spelling

ALERT   The Display of Spelling Suggestions Varies Among Office Versions

Depending on your version of Office (Office 365 or Office 2019), you may see variations in how the spelling checking displays suggestions for corrections. You will still be able to follow the screen prompts to select the correct spelling.

Microsoft Office has a dictionary of words against which all entered text is checked. In Word and PowerPoint, words that are not in the dictionary display a red squiggle, indicating a possible misspelled word, a proper name, or an unusual word—none of which are in the Office dictionary. In Excel and Access, you can initiate a check of the spelling, but red squiggles do not display.

1 ▶ Notice that the misspelled word *Exective* displays with a red squiggle.

2 ▶ Point to *Exective* and then **right-click**—click your right mouse button one time.

A ***shortcut menu*** displays, which displays commands and options relevant to the selected text or object. These are ***context-sensitive commands*** because they relate to the item you right-clicked. These are also referred to as ***context menus***. Here, the shortcut menu displays commands related to the misspelled word.

🖚 **BY TOUCH**   Tap and hold a moment—when a square displays around the misspelled word, release your finger to display the shortcut menu.

3 ▶ Press ⎋Esc two times to cancel the shortcut menus, and then in the lower left corner of your screen, on the status bar, click the **Proofing** icon 🔲, which displays an *X* because some errors are detected. In the **Editor** pane that displays on the right, if necessary, click the Results button, and then under **Suggestions**, to the right of *Executive*, click ☑, and then compare your screen with Figure 1.11.

The Editor pane displays on the right. ***Editor***, according to Microsoft, is your digital writing assistant in Word and also in Outlook. Editor displays misspellings, grammatical mistakes, and writing style issues as you type by marking red squiggles for spelling, blue double underlines for grammar, and dotted underlines for writing style issues.

Here you have many more options for checking spelling than you have on the shortcut menu. The suggested correct word, *Executive*, displays under Suggestions. The displayed menu provides additional options for the suggestion. For example, you can have the word read aloud, hear it spelled out, change all occurrences in the document, or add to AutoCorrect options.

In the Editor pane, you can ignore the word one time or in all occurrences, change the word to the suggested word, select a different suggestion, or add a word to the dictionary against which Word checks.

🖥 **MAC TIP**   In the Spelling and Grammar dialog box, click Executive, and then click Change. The Editor pane is not available on a Mac.

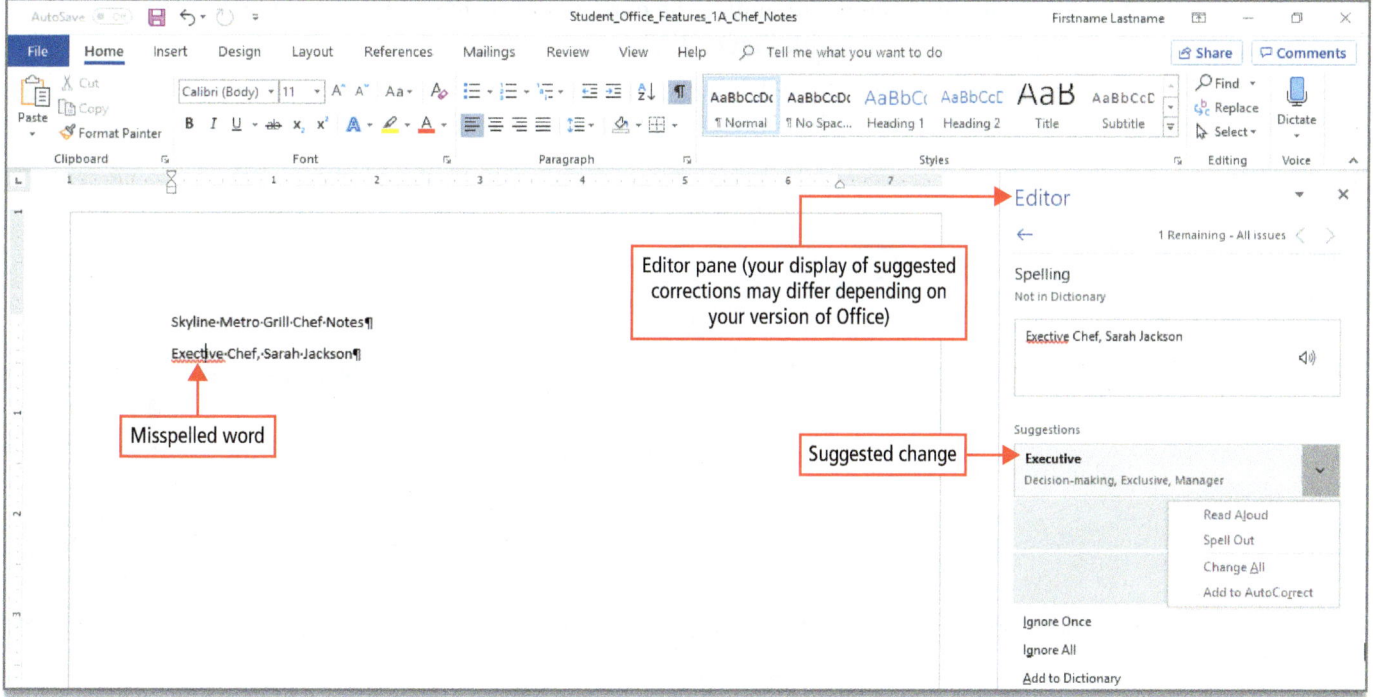

Figure 1.11

🔄 **ANOTHER WAY**   Press F7 to display the Editor pane; or, on the Review tab, in the Proofing group, you can check your document for Spelling.

4 ▶ In the **Editor** pane, under **Suggestions**, click *Executive* to correct the spelling. In the message box that displays, click **OK**.

5 ▶ If necessary **Close** the **Editor** pane by clicking ☒ in the upper right corner.

Objective 4   **Perform Office Commands and Apply Office Formatting**

GO! Learn How
Video OF1-4

Formatting refers to applying Office commands to make your document easy to read and to add visual touches and design elements to make your document inviting to the reader. This process establishes the overall appearance of text, graphics, and pages in your document.

Activity 1.05 │ **Performing Commands from a Dialog Box**

1.2.4

In a dialog box, you make decisions about an individual object or topic. In some dialog boxes, you can make multiple decisions in one place.

1 ▶ On the ribbon, click the **Design tab**, and then in the **Page Background group**, click **Page Color**.

2 At the bottom of the menu, notice the command **Fill Effects** followed by an **ellipsis** (. . .). Compare your screen with Figure 1.12.

An *ellipsis* is a set of three dots indicating incompleteness. An ellipsis following a command name indicates that a dialog box will display when you click the command.

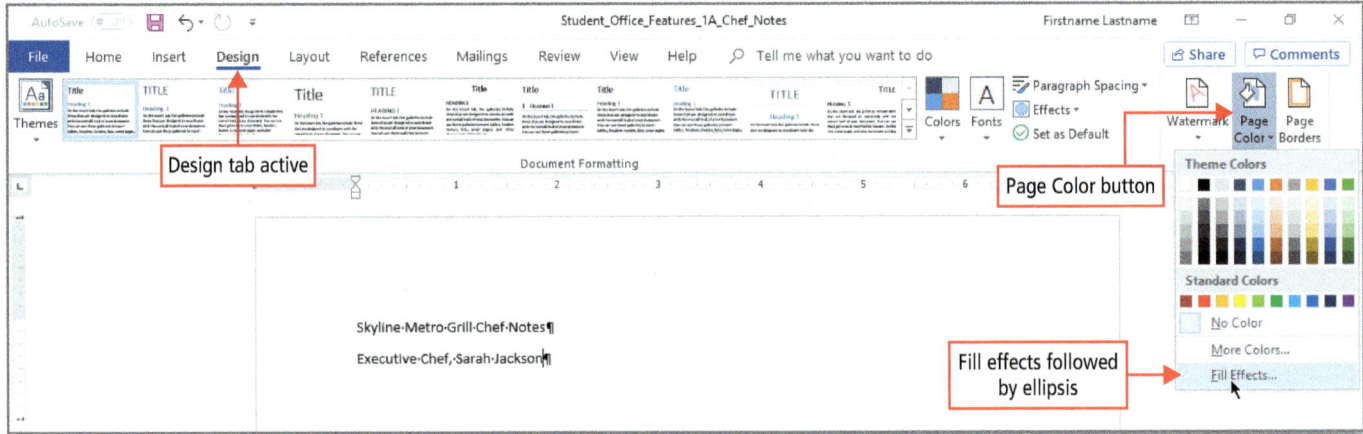

Figure 1.12

3 Click **Fill Effects** to display the **Fill Effects** dialog box. Compare your screen with Figure 1.13.

Fill is the inside color of a page or object. Here, the dialog box displays a set of tabs across the top from which you can display different sets of options. Some dialog boxes display the option group names on the left. The Gradient tab is active. In a *gradient fill*, one color fades into another.

MAC TIP Click More Colors to display the Colors dialog box.

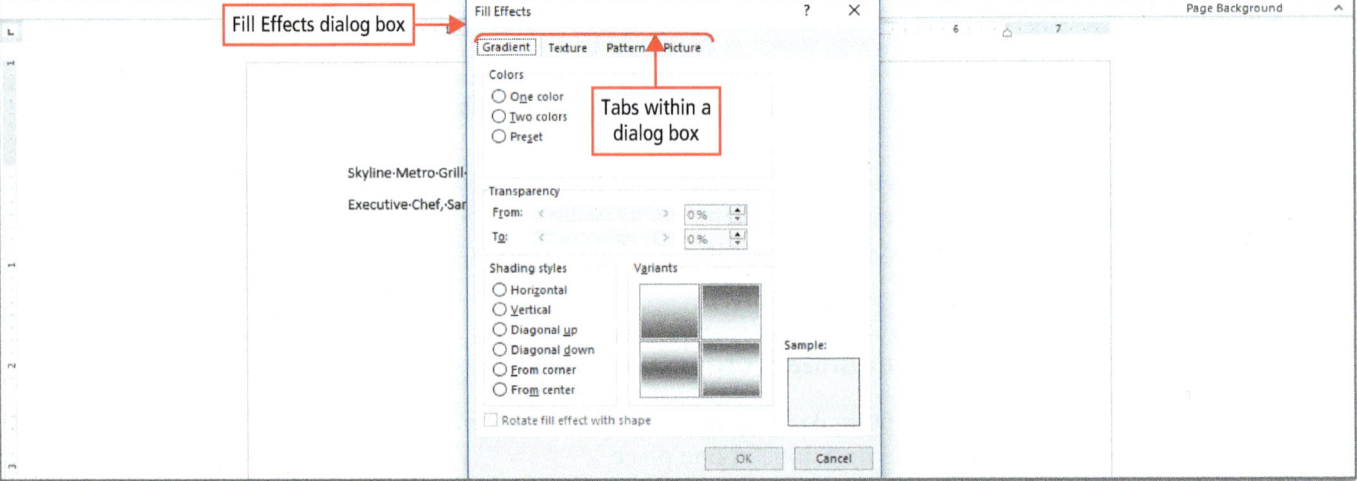

Figure 1.13

4 Under **Colors**, click the **One color** option button.

The dialog box displays settings related to the *One color* option. An ***option button*** is a round button that enables you to make one choice among two or more options.

5 Click the **Color 1 arrow**—the arrow under the text *Color 1*—and then in the eighth column, point to the second color to display a ScreenTip with the name of the color.

When you click an arrow in a dialog box, additional options display. A ***ScreenTip*** displays useful information about mouse actions, such as pointing to screen elements or dragging.

6 Click the color, and then notice that the fill color displays in the **Color 1** box. In the **Dark Light** bar, click the **Light arrow** as many times as necessary until the scroll box is all the way to the right—or drag the scroll box all the way to the right. Under **Shading styles**, click the **From corner** option button. Under **Variants**, click the **upper right variant**. Compare your screen with Figure 1.14.

This dialog box is a good example of the many different elements you may encounter in a dialog box. Here you have option buttons, an arrow that displays a menu, a slider bar, and graphic options that you can select.

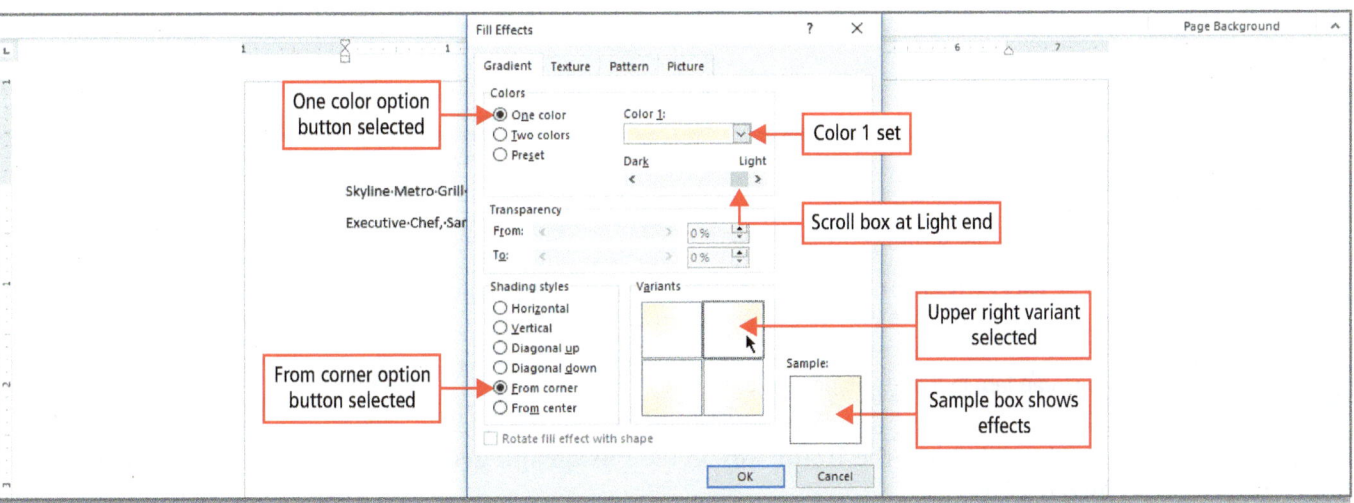

Figure 1.14

7 At the bottom of the dialog box, click **OK**, and notice the subtle page color.

In Word, the gold shading page color will not print—even on a color printer—unless you set specific options to do so. However, a subtle background page color is effective if people will be reading the document on a screen. Microsoft's research indicates that two-thirds of people who open Word documents on a screen never print or edit them; they only read them.

1 ▶ Point to the *S* in *Skyline*, and then drag down and to the right to select both paragraphs of text and include the paragraph marks. On the mini toolbar, click **Styles**, and then *point to* but do not click **Title**. Compare your screen with Figure 1.15.

A *style* is a group of formatting commands, such as font, font size, font color, paragraph alignment, and line spacing that can be applied to a paragraph with one command.

Live Preview is a technology that shows the result of applying an editing or formatting change as you point to possible results—before you actually apply it.

💻 **MAC TIP** The mini toolbar and Live Preview are not available; use ribbon commands.

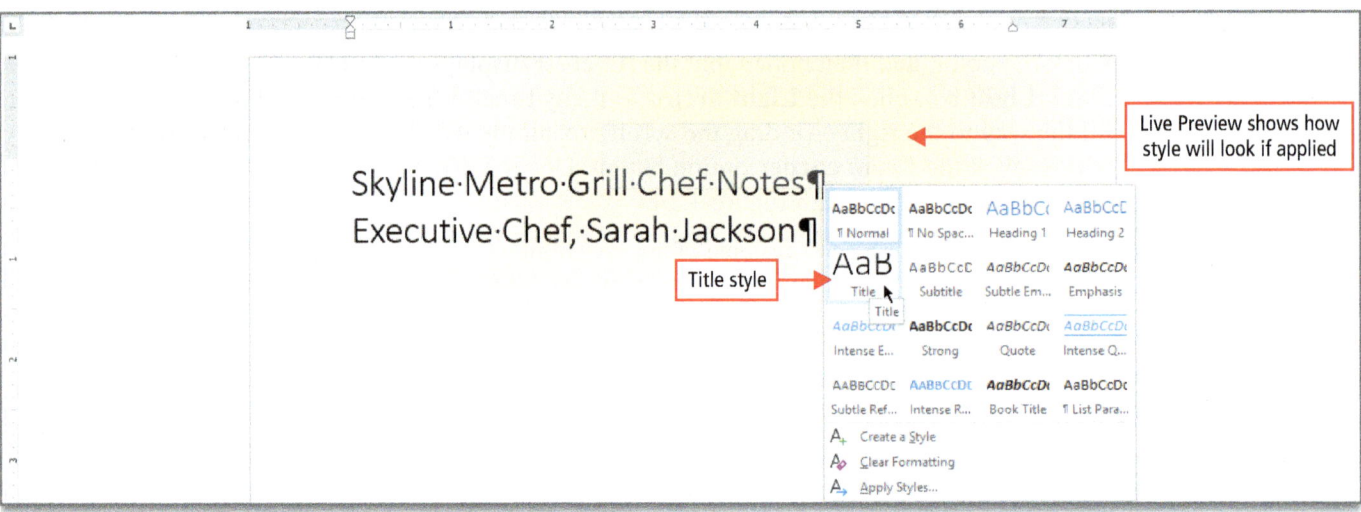

Figure 1.15

2 ▶ In the **Styles** gallery, click **Title**.

A *gallery* is an Office feature that displays a list of potential results.

💻 **MAC TIP** On the Home tab, in the Styles gallery, click Title.

3 ▶ On the ribbon, on the **Home tab**, in the **Paragraph group**, click **Center** 🔳 to center the two paragraphs.

Alignment refers to the placement of paragraph text relative to the left and right margins. *Center alignment* refers to text that is centered horizontally between the left and right margins. You can also align text at the left margin, which is the default alignment for text in Word, or at the right.

🔄 **ANOTHER WAY** Press ⌨Ctrl + ⌨E to use the Center command.

💻 **MAC TIP** Press ⌨command ⌘ + ⌨E to use the Center command.

4 ▶ With the two paragraphs still selected, on the **Home tab**, in the **Font Group**, click **Text Effects and Typography** 🅰⎘ to display a gallery.

5 ▶ In the second row, click the first effect. Click anywhere to *deselect*—cancel the selection—the text and notice the text effect.

6 Because this effect might be difficult to read, in the upper left corner of your screen, on the **Quick Access Toolbar**, click **Undo** 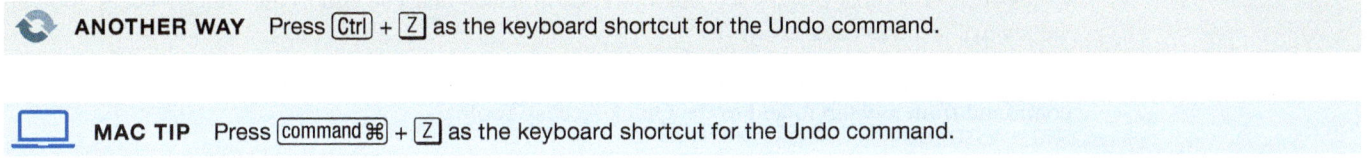.

The *Undo* command reverses your last action.

ANOTHER WAY Press `Ctrl` + `Z` as the keyboard shortcut for the Undo command.

MAC TIP Press `command ⌘` + `Z` as the keyboard shortcut for the Undo command.

7 Select the two paragraphs of text again, display the **Text Effects and Typography** gallery again, and then in the first row, click the fifth effect. Click anywhere to deselect the text and notice the text effect. Compare your screen with Figure 1.16.

As you progress in your study of Microsoft Office, you will practice using many dialog boxes and commands to apply interesting effects such as this to your Word documents, Excel worksheets, Access database objects, and PowerPoint slides.

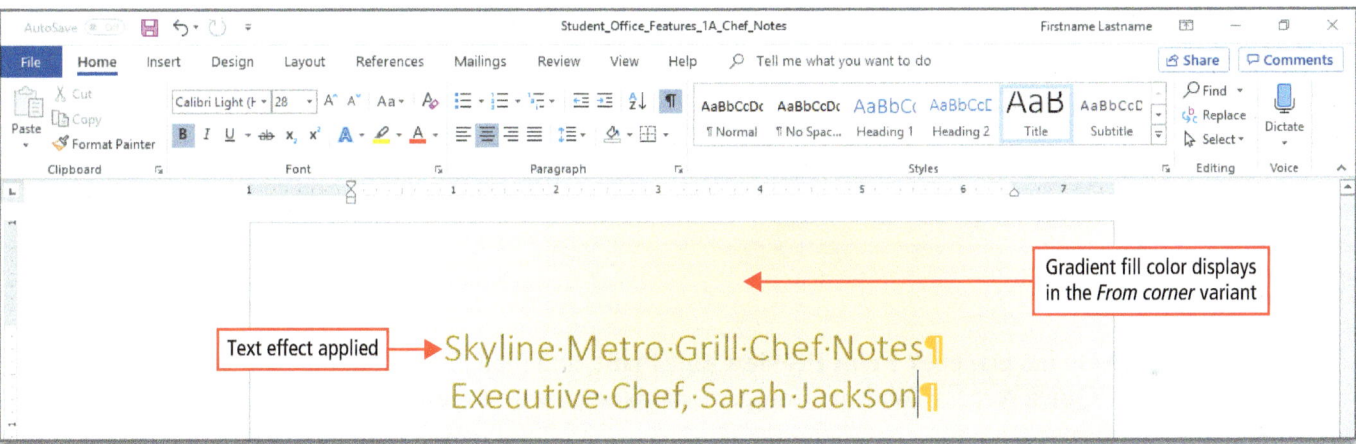

Figure 1.16

Activity 1.07 | Performing Commands from and Customizing the Quick Access Toolbar

The ribbon that displays across the top of the program window groups commands in the way that you would most logically use them. The ribbon in each Office program is slightly different, but all contain the same three elements: *tabs*, *groups*, and *commands*.

Tabs display across the top of the ribbon, and each tab relates to a type of activity; for example, laying out a page. Groups are sets of related commands for specific tasks. Commands—instructions to computer programs—are arranged in groups and might display as a button, a menu, or a box in which you type information.

You can also minimize the ribbon so only the tab names display, which is useful when working on a smaller screen such as a tablet computer where you want to maximize your screen viewing area.

1 In the upper left corner of your screen, above the ribbon, locate the **Quick Access Toolbar**.

Recall that the Quick Access Toolbar contains commands that you use frequently. By default, only the commands Save, Undo, and Redo display, but you can add and delete commands to suit your needs. Possibly the computer at which you are working already has additional commands added to the Quick Access Toolbar.

2 At the end of the **Quick Access Toolbar**, click the **Customize Quick Access Toolbar** button, and then compare your screen with Figure 1.17.

A list of commands that Office users commonly add to their Quick Access Toolbar displays, including New, Open, Email, Quick Print, and Print Preview and Print. Commands already on the Quick Access Toolbar display a check mark. Commands that you add to the Quick Access Toolbar are always just one click away.

Here you can also display the More Commands dialog box, from which you can select any command from any tab to add to the Quick Access Toolbar.

BY TOUCH Tap once on Quick Access Toolbar commands.

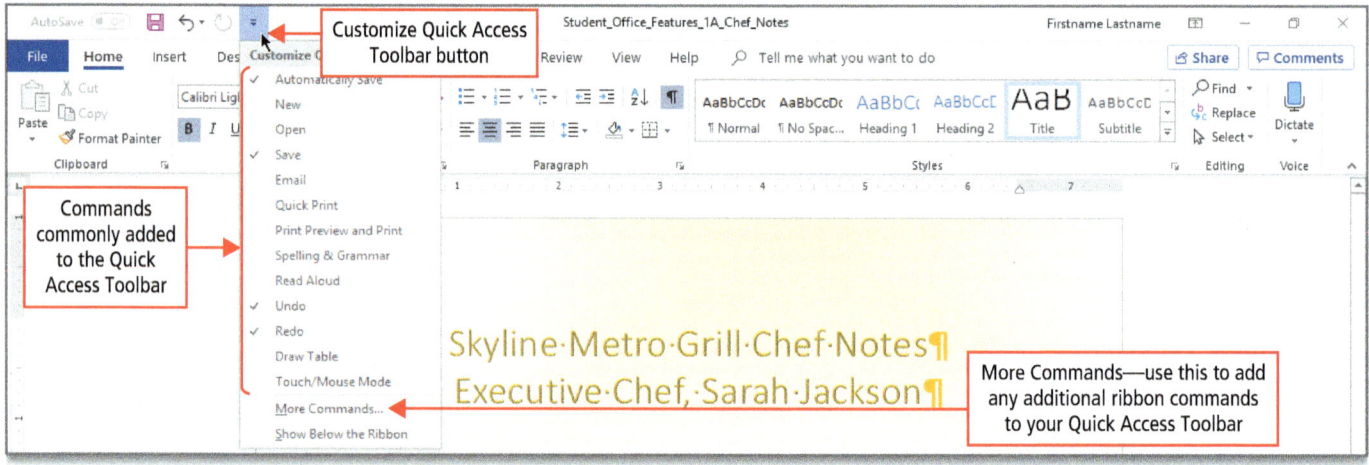

Figure 1.17

3 On the list, click **Print Preview and Print**, and then notice that the icon is added to the **Quick Access Toolbar**. Compare your screen with Figure 1.18.

The icon that represents the Print Preview command displays on the Quick Access Toolbar. Because this is a command that you will use frequently while building Office documents, you might decide to have this command remain on your Quick Access Toolbar.

ANOTHER WAY Right-click any command on the ribbon, and then on the shortcut menu, click Add to Quick Access Toolbar.

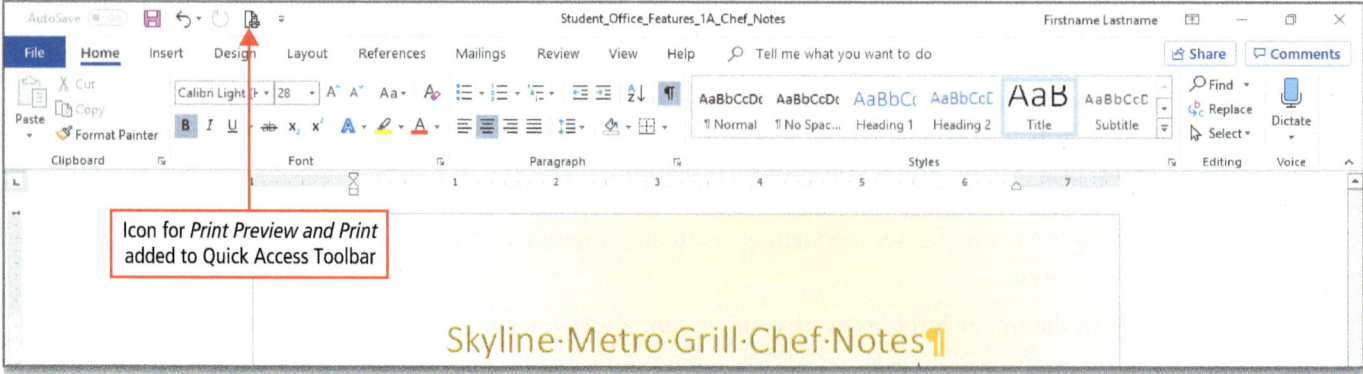

Figure 1.18

Activity 1.08 | Performing Commands from the Ribbon

> **1** In the second line of text, click to place the insertion point to the right of the letter *n* in *Jackson*. Press Enter three times. Compare your screen with Figure 1.19.

Word creates three new blank paragraphs, and no Text Effect is applied.

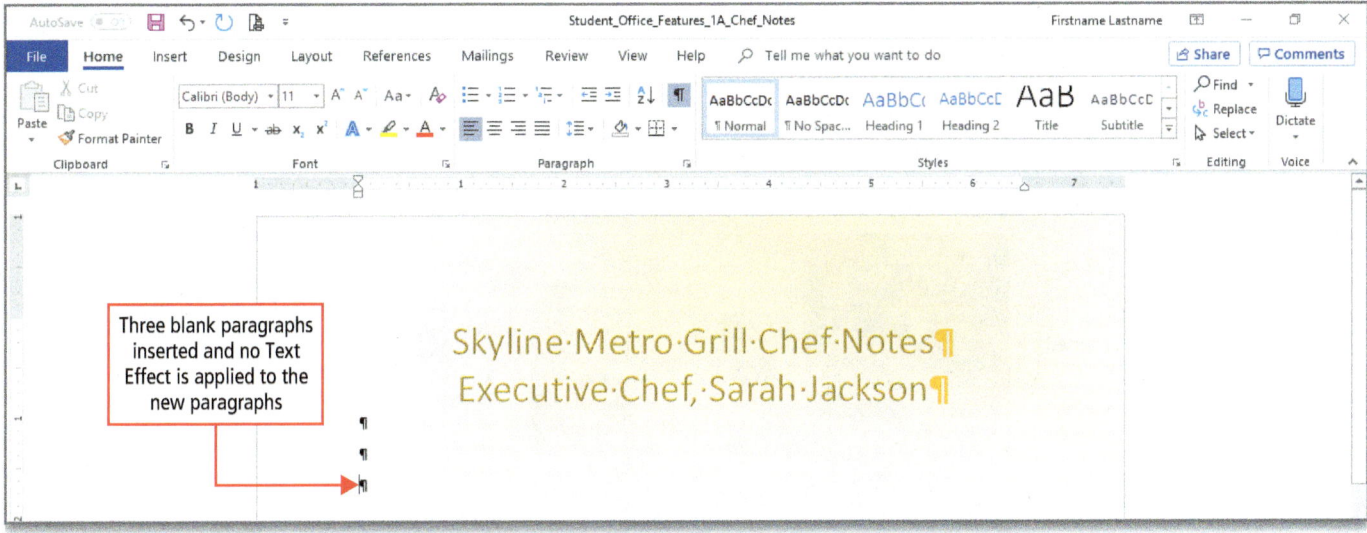

Three blank paragraphs inserted and no Text Effect is applied to the new paragraphs

Skyline·Metro·Grill·Chef·Notes¶
Executive·Chef,·Sarah·Jackson¶

Figure 1.19

> **2** Click to position the insertion point to the left of the **second blank paragraph** that you just inserted. On the ribbon, click the **Insert tab**. In the **Illustrations group**, *point* to **Pictures** to display its ScreenTip.

Many buttons on the ribbon have this type of *enhanced ScreenTip*, which displays useful descriptive information about the command.

> **3** Click **Pictures**. In the **Insert Picture** dialog box, navigate to your **Office Features Chapter 1 folder**, double-click the **of01A_Chefs** picture, and then compare your screen with Figure 1.20.

The picture displays in your Word document.

 MAC TIP Click Picture from File, then navigate to your Office Features Chapter 1 folder.

> **For Non-MyLab Submissions**
> The of01A_Chefs picture is included with this chapter's Student Data Files, which you can obtain from your instructor or by downloading the files from www.pearsonhighered.com/go

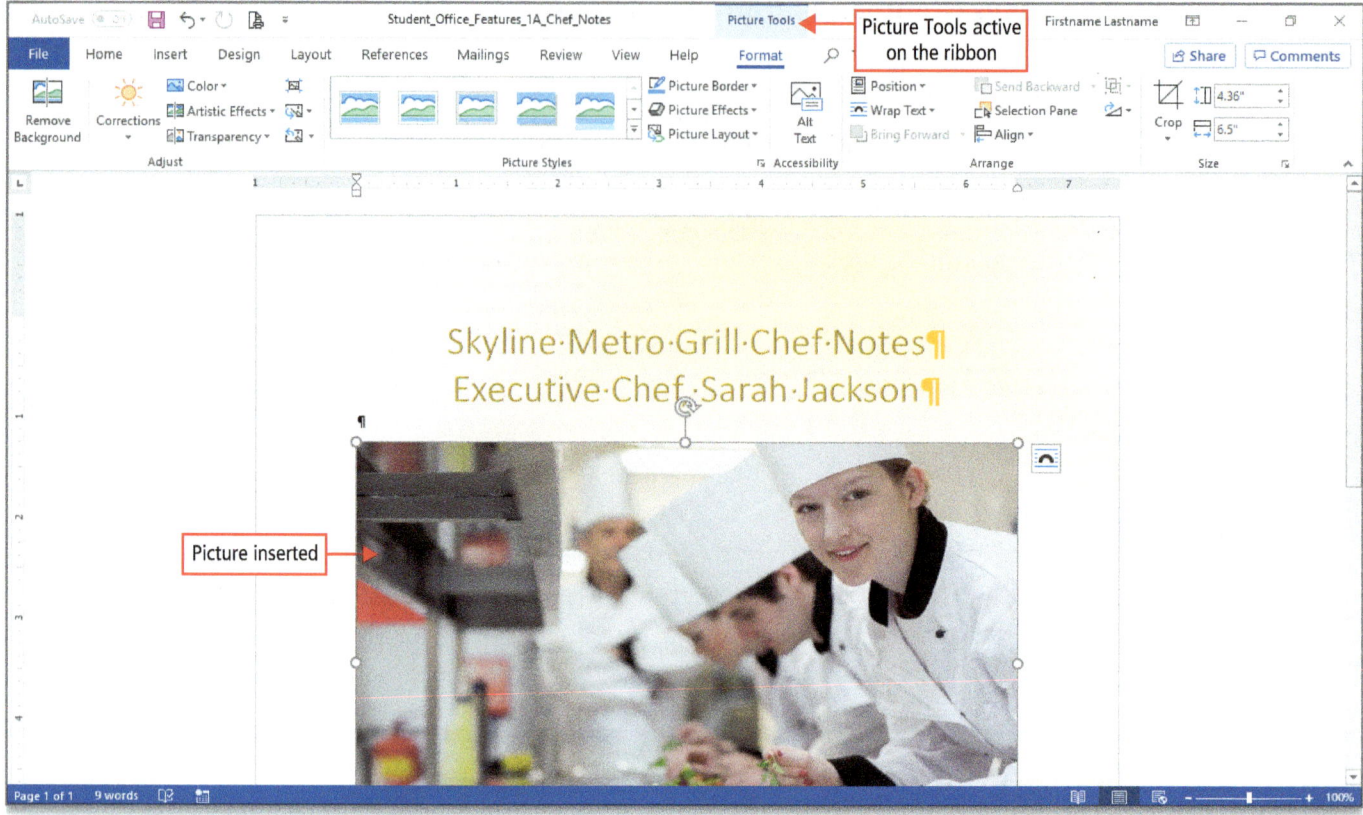

Figure 1.20

4 ▶ In the upper right corner of the picture, point to the **Layout Options** button 🖼 to display its ScreenTip, and then compare your screen with Figure 1.21.

> *Layout Options* enable you to choose how the ***object***—in this instance an inserted picture—interacts with the surrounding text. An object is a picture or other graphic such as a chart or table that you can select and then move and resize.

> When a picture is selected, the Picture Tools become available on the ribbon. Additionally, *sizing handles*—small circles or squares that indicate an object is selected—surround the selected picture.

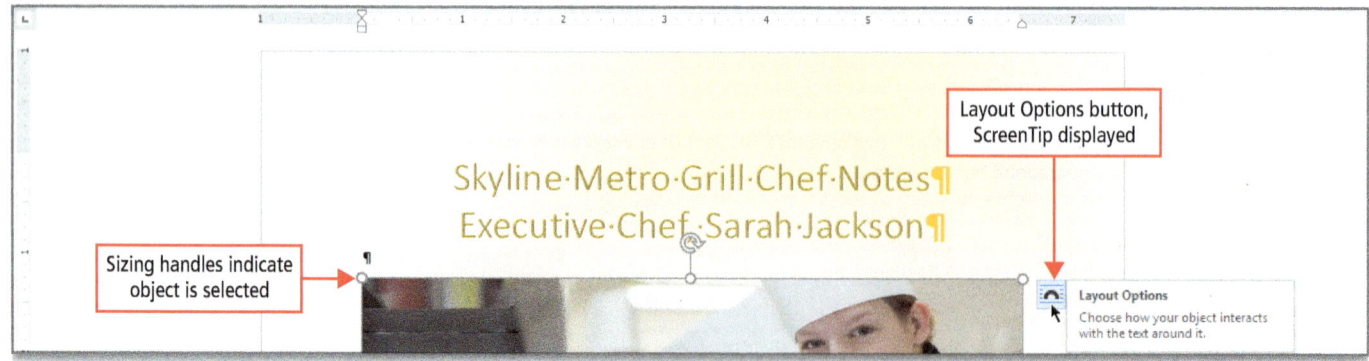

Figure 1.21

5 ▶ With the image selected, click **Layout Options** 🖼, and then under **With Text Wrapping**, in the second row, click the first layout—**Top and Bottom**. In the upper right corner of the Layout Options dialog box, click **Close** ✕.

MAC TIP With the picture selected, on the Picture Format tab, click Wrap text. On the menu, click Top and Bottom.

6 ▶ On the ribbon, with the **Picture Tools Format tab** active, at the right, in the **Size group**, click in the **Shape Height** box ⬦ 0.29" ⬦ to select the existing text. Type **2** and press Enter.

7 ▶ On the **Picture Tools Format tab**, in the **Arrange group**, click **Align**, and then at the bottom of the list, locate **Use Alignment Guides**. If you do not see a checkmark to the left of **Use Alignment Guides**, click the command to enable the guides.

8 ▶ If necessary, click the image again to select it. Point to the image to display the ⬦ pointer, hold down the left mouse button and move your mouse slightly to display a green line at the left margin, and then drag the image to the right and down slightly until a green line displays in the center of the image as shown in Figure 1.22, and then release the left mouse button.

MAC TIP Alignment guides may not be available. On the Picture Format tab, click Align, click Align Center. Be sure two blank paragraphs display above the image.

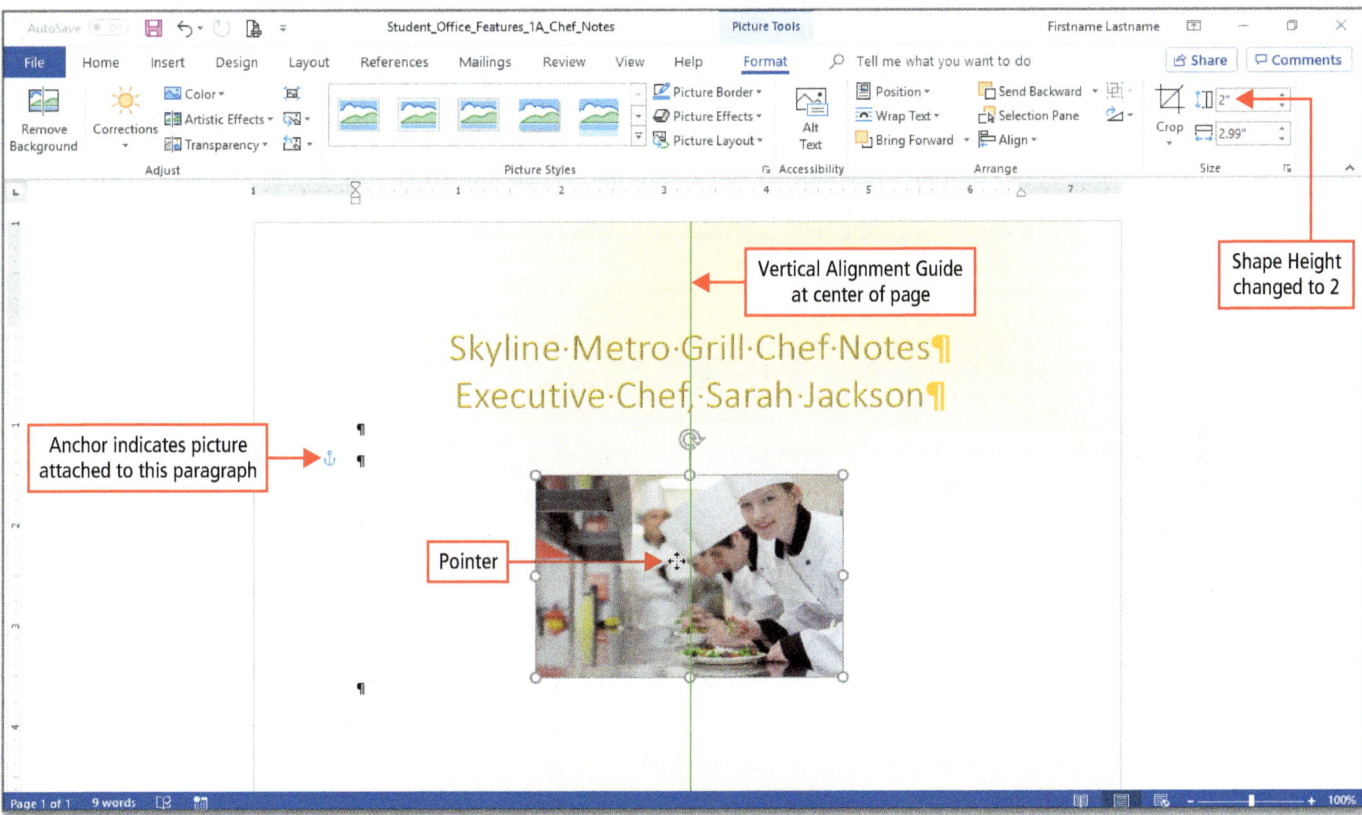

Figure 1.22

9 ▶ Be sure that there are two blank paragraphs above the image and that the anchor symbol is attached to the second blank paragraph mark—if necessary, drag the picture up slightly or down slightly. If you are not satisfied with your result, on the Quick Access Toolbar, click Undo ↶ and begin again.

Alignment guides are green lines that display to help you align objects with margins or at the center of a page.

Inserted pictures anchor—attach to—the paragraph at the insertion point location—as indicated by an anchor symbol.

10 On the ribbon, on the **Picture Tools Format tab**, in the **Picture Styles group**, point to the first style to display the ScreenTip *Simple Frame, White*, and notice that the image displays with a white frame.

🖥 **MAC TIP** Preview may not be available.

NOTE **The Size of Groups on the Ribbon Varies with Screen Resolution**

Your monitor's screen resolution might be set higher than the resolution used to capture the figures in this book. At a higher resolution, the ribbon expands some groups to show more commands that are available with a single click, such as those in the Picture Styles group. Or, the group expands to add descriptive text to some buttons, such as those in the Arrange group. Regardless of your screen resolution, all Office commands are available to you. In higher resolutions, you will have a more robust view of the ribbon commands.

11 Watch the image as you point to the second picture style, and then to the third, and then to the fourth.

Recall that Live Preview shows the result of applying an editing or formatting change as you point to possible results—*before* you actually apply it.

12 In the **Picture Styles group**, click the fourth style—**Drop Shadow Rectangle**. Reposition the picture up or down so that it is anchored to the second blank paragraph above the image, and then click anywhere outside of the image to deselect it. Notice that the Picture Tools no longer display on the ribbon. Compare your screen with Figure 1.23.

Contextual tabs on the ribbon display only when you need them.

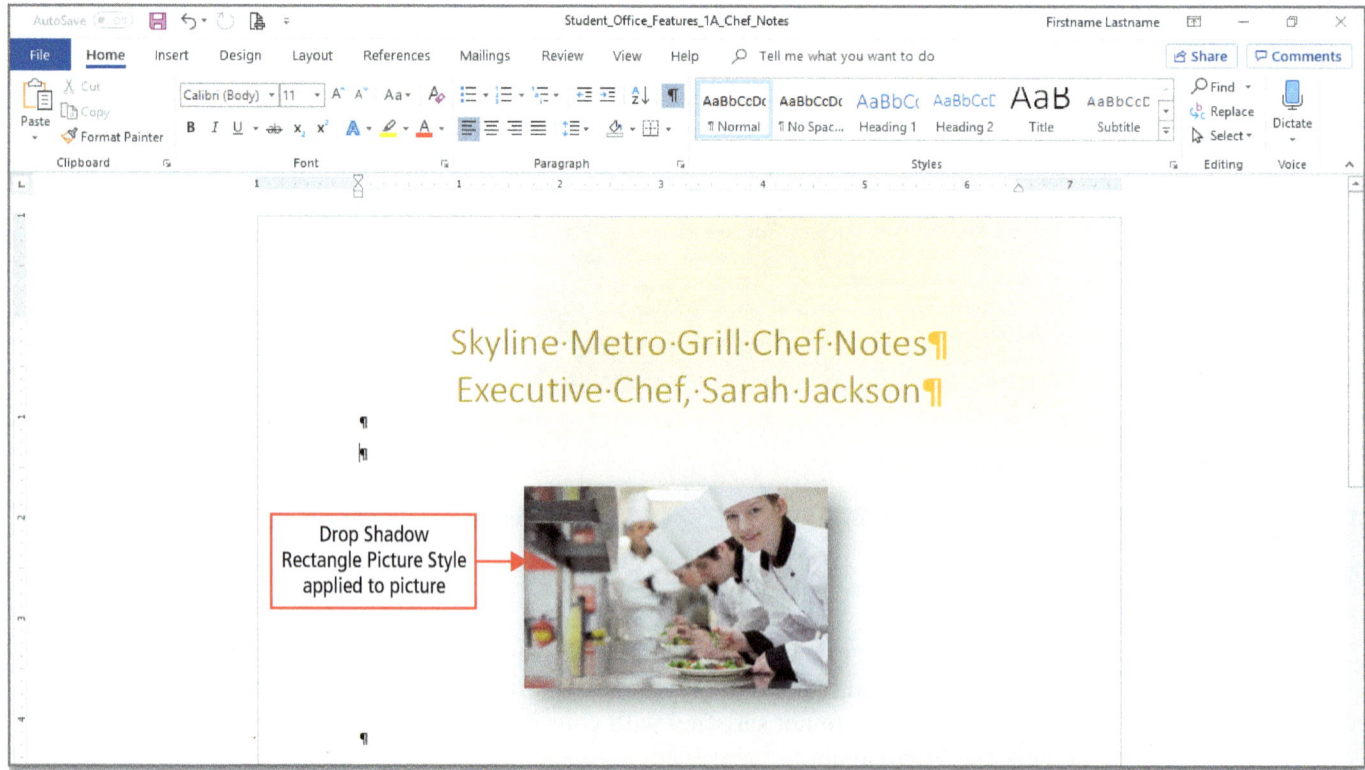

Figure 1.23

13 On the **Quick Access Toolbar**, click **Save** 🖫 to save the changes you have made.

Activity 1.09 | Minimizing the Ribbon

1 ▶ Point to any tab on the ribbon and right-click to display a shortcut menu.

Here you can choose to display the Quick Access Toolbar below the ribbon or collapse the ribbon to maximize screen space. You can also customize the ribbon by adding, removing, renaming, or reordering tabs, groups, and commands, although this is not recommended until you become an expert Word user.

2 ▶ Click **Collapse the Ribbon** and notice that only the ribbon tabs display. Click the **Home tab** to display the commands. Click in the last blank paragraph—or anywhere in the document—and notice that the ribbon goes back to the collapsed display.

 MAC TIP To minimize the ribbon, click the up arrow on the top right of the screen.

3 ▶ Right-click any ribbon tab, and then click **Collapse the Ribbon** again to remove the check mark from this command.

Most expert Office users prefer the full ribbon display.

4 ▶ Point to any tab on the ribbon, and then on your mouse device, roll the mouse wheel. Notice that different tabs become active as you roll the mouse wheel.

You can make a tab active by using this technique, instead of clicking the tab.

MORE KNOWLEDGE | **Displaying KeyTips**

Instead of a mouse, some individuals prefer to navigate the ribbon by using keys on the keyboard. You can do this by activating the *KeyTip* feature where small labels display on the ribbon tabs and also on the individual ribbon commands. Press [Alt] to display the KeyTips on the ribbon tabs, and then press [N] to display KeyTips on the ribbon commands. Press [Esc] to turn the feature off. NOTE: This feature is not yet available on a Mac.

Activity 1.10 | Changing Page Orientation and Zoom Level

MOS
1.2.1

1 ▶ On the ribbon, click the **Layout tab**. In the **Page Setup group**, click **Orientation**, and notice that two orientations display—*Portrait* and *Landscape*. Click **Landscape**.

In ***portrait orientation***, the paper is taller than it is wide. In ***landscape orientation***, the paper is wider than it is tall.

2 ▶ In the lower right corner of the screen, locate the **Zoom slider** .

Recall that to zoom means to increase or decrease the viewing area. You can zoom in to look closely at a section of a document, and then zoom out to see an entire page on the screen. You can also zoom to view multiple pages on the screen.

3 Drag the **Zoom slider** ▬▬|▬▬+ to the left until you have zoomed to approximately *60%*. Compare your screen with Figure 1.24.

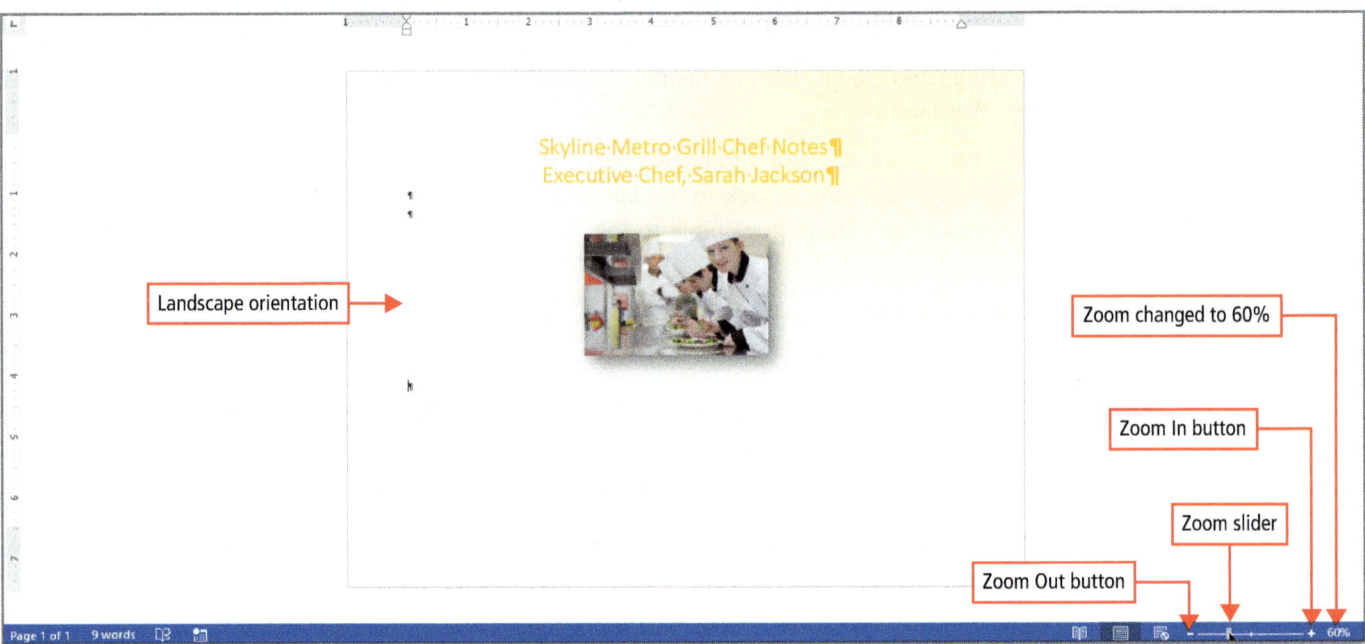

Figure 1.24

🖐 **BY TOUCH**   Drag the Zoom slider with your finger.

4 Use the technique you just practiced to change the **Orientation** back to **Portrait**.

The default orientation in Word is Portrait, which is commonly used for business documents such as letters, reports, and memos.

5 In the lower right corner, click the **Zoom In** button ➕ as many times as necessary to return to the **100%** zoom setting.

Use the zoom feature to adjust the view of your document for editing and for your viewing comfort.

🔄 **ANOTHER WAY**   You can also control Zoom from the ribbon. On the View tab, in the Zoom group, you can control the Zoom level and also zoom to view multiple pages.

6 On the **Quick Access Toolbar**, click **Save** 💾.

MORE KNOWLEDGE   **Zooming to Page Width**

Some Office users prefer *Page Width*, which zooms the document so that the width of the page matches the width of the window. Find this command on the View tab, in the Zoom group.

1 If necessary, on the right edge of your screen, drag the vertical scroll box to the top of the scroll bar. To the left of *Executive Chef, Sarah Jackson*, point in the margin area to display the ⬚ pointer and click one time to select the entire paragraph. Compare your screen with Figure 1.25.

Use this technique to select complete paragraphs from the margin area—drag downward to select multiple-line paragraphs—which is faster and more efficient than dragging through text.

Figure 1.25

2 On the **Home tab**, in the **Font Group**, click **Clear All Formatting** ⬚. Compare your screen with Figure 1.26.

This command removes all formatting from the selection, leaving only the normal, unformatted text.

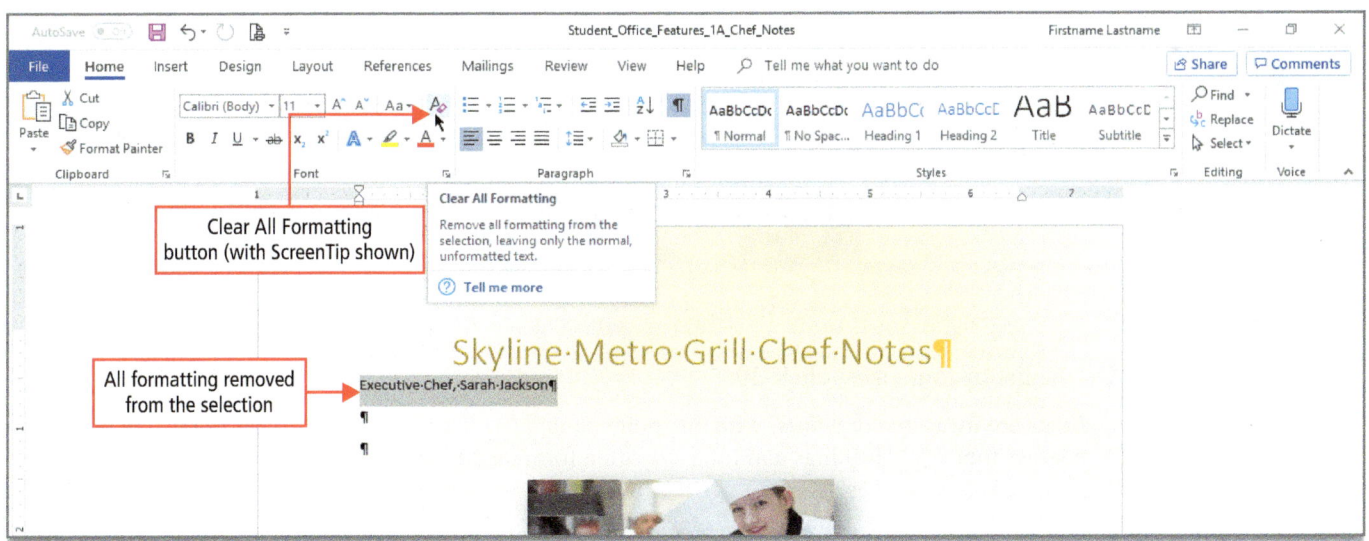

Figure 1.26

3 With the text still selected, on the **Home tab**, in the **Paragraph group**, click **Center** ⬚.

4 With the text still selected, on the **Home tab**, in the **Font group**, click the **Font button arrow** ⬚. On the alphabetical list of font names, scroll down and then locate and *point to* **Cambria**.

A *font* is a set of characters with the same design and shape. The default font in a Word document is Calibri, which is a ***sans serif font***—a font design with no lines or extensions on the ends of characters.

The Cambria font is a ***serif font***—a font design that includes small line extensions on the ends of the letters to guide the eye in reading from left to right.

The list of fonts displays as a gallery showing potential results. For example, in the Font gallery, you can point to see the actual design and format of each font as it would look if applied to text.

5 ▶ Point to several other fonts and observe the effect on the selected text. Then, scroll back to the top of the **Font** gallery. Under **Theme Fonts**, click **Calibri Light**.

A *theme* is a predesigned combination of colors, fonts, line, and fill effects that look good together and is applied to an entire document by a single selection. A theme combines two sets of fonts— one for text and one for headings. In the default Office theme, Calibri Light is the suggested font for headings.

6 ▶ With the paragraph *Executive Chef, Sarah Jackson* still selected, on the **Home tab**, in the **Font group**, click the **Font Size button arrow** 11 ▾, point to **20**, and then notice how Live Preview displays the text in the font size to which you are pointing. Compare your screen with Figure 1.27.

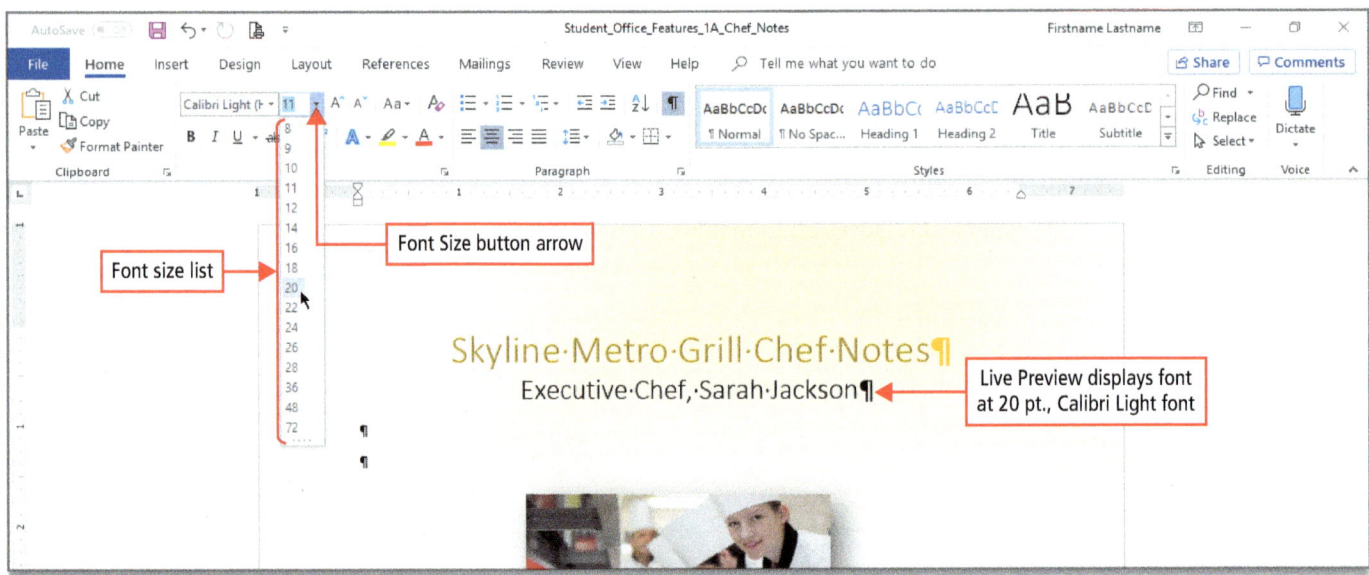

Figure 1.27

7 ▶ On the list of font sizes, click **20**.

Fonts are measured in *points*, with one point equal to 1/72 of an inch. A higher point size indicates a larger font size. Headings and titles are often formatted by using a larger font size. The word *point* is abbreviated as *pt*.

8 ▶ With *Executive Chef, Sarah Jackson* still selected, on the **Home tab**, in the **Font group**, click the **Font Color button arrow** A ▾. Under **Theme Colors**, in the sixth column, click the fifth (next to last) color, and then click in the last blank paragraph to deselect the text.

9 ▶ With your insertion point in the blank paragraph below the picture, type **Rehearsal Dinner Menu Ideas** and then press Enter two times.

10 Type **Appetizers** and press ⌷Enter⌷ two times. Type **Salads** and press ⌷Enter⌷ two times. Type **Main Dishes** and press ⌷Enter⌷ two times.

11 Type **Desserts** and press ⌷Enter⌷ four times. Compare your screen with Figure 1.28.

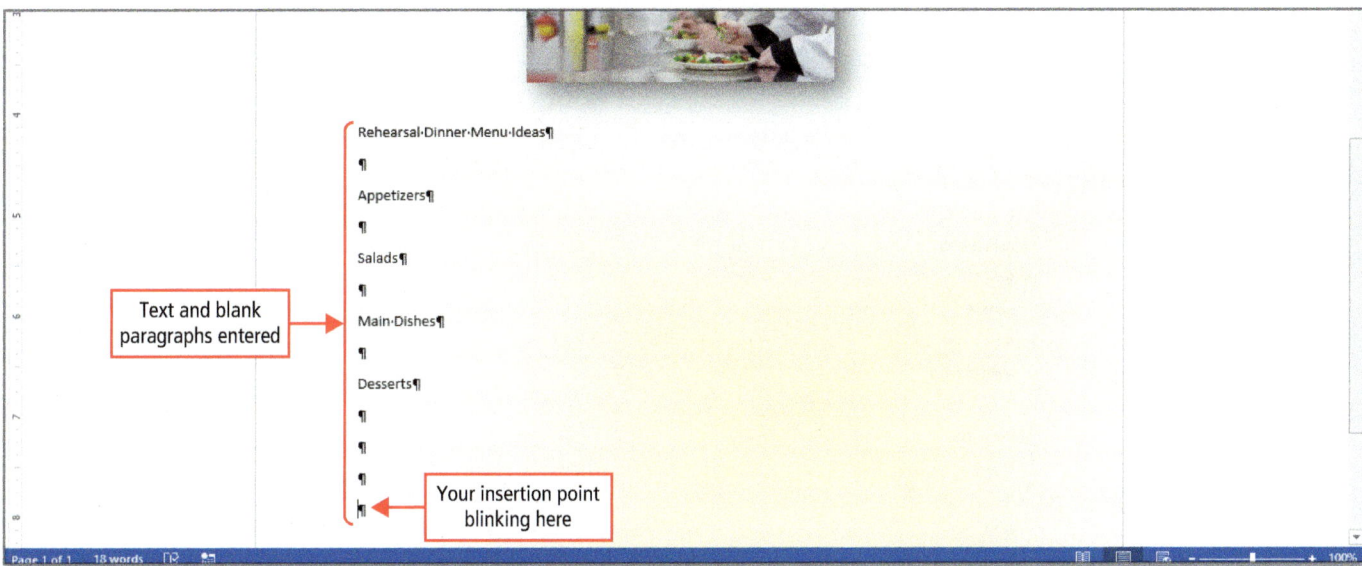

Rehearsal·Dinner·Menu·Ideas¶

¶

Appetizers¶

¶

Salads¶

¶

Text and blank paragraphs entered → Main·Dishes¶

¶

Desserts¶

¶

¶

¶

¶ ← **Your insertion point blinking here**

Page 1 of 1   18 words   ⌷R   ⌷⌷   100%

Figure1.28

12 Click anywhere in the word *Dinner* and then ***triple-click***—click the left mouse button three times—to select the entire paragraph. If the entire paragraph is not selected, click in the paragraph and begin again.

13 With the paragraph selected, on the mini toolbar, click the **Font Color** button ⌷A ⌷⌷, and notice that the text color of the selected paragraph changes.

The font color button retains its most recently used color—the color you used to format *Executive Chef, Sarah Jackson* above. As you progress in your study of Microsoft Office, you will use other commands that behave in this manner; that is, they retain their most recently used format. This is commonly referred to as *MRU*—most recently used.

Recall that the mini toolbar places commands that are commonly used for the selected text or object close by so that you reduce the distance you must move your mouse to access a command. If you are using a touch screen device, most commands that you need are close and easy to touch.

MAC TIP   Use commands on the ribbon, on the Home tab.

14 With the paragraph *Rehearsal Dinner Menu Ideas* still selected and the mini toolbar displayed, on the mini toolbar, click **Bold** ⌷B⌷ and **Italic** ⌷I⌷.

Font styles include bold, italic, and underline. Font styles emphasize text and are a visual cue to draw the reader's eye to important text.

15 On the mini toolbar, click **Italic** $\boxed{I}$ again to turn off the Italic formatting. Click anywhere to deselect, and then compare your screen with Figure 1.29.

A ***toggle button*** is a button that can be turned on by clicking it once, and then turned off by clicking it again.

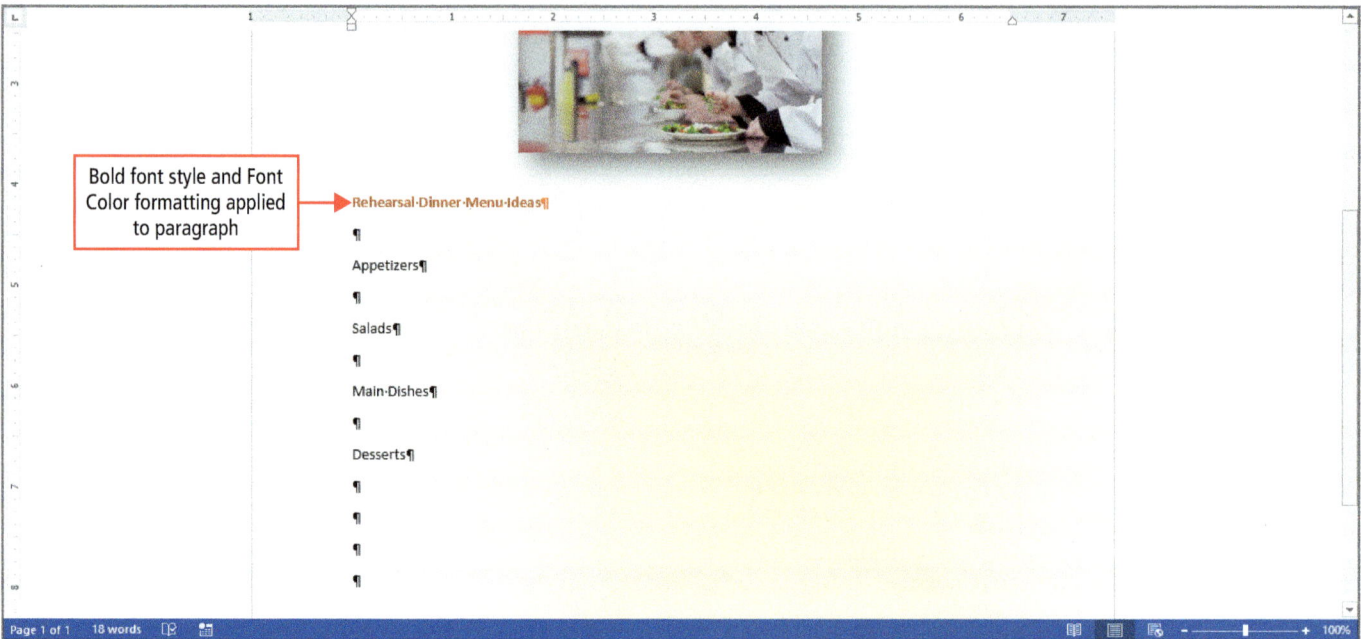

Figure 1.29

Activity 1.12 | Using Format Painter

Use the ***Format Painter*** to copy the formatting of specific text or copy the formatting of a paragraph and then apply it in other locations in your document.

1 To the left of *Rehearsal Dinner Menu Ideas*, point in the left margin to display the $\boxed{\cancel{\mathcal{A}}}$ pointer, and then click one time to select the entire paragraph. Compare your screen with Figure 1.30.

Use this technique to select complete paragraphs from the margin area. This is particularly useful if there are many lines of text in the paragraph. You can hold down the left mouse button and drag downward instead of trying to drag through the text.

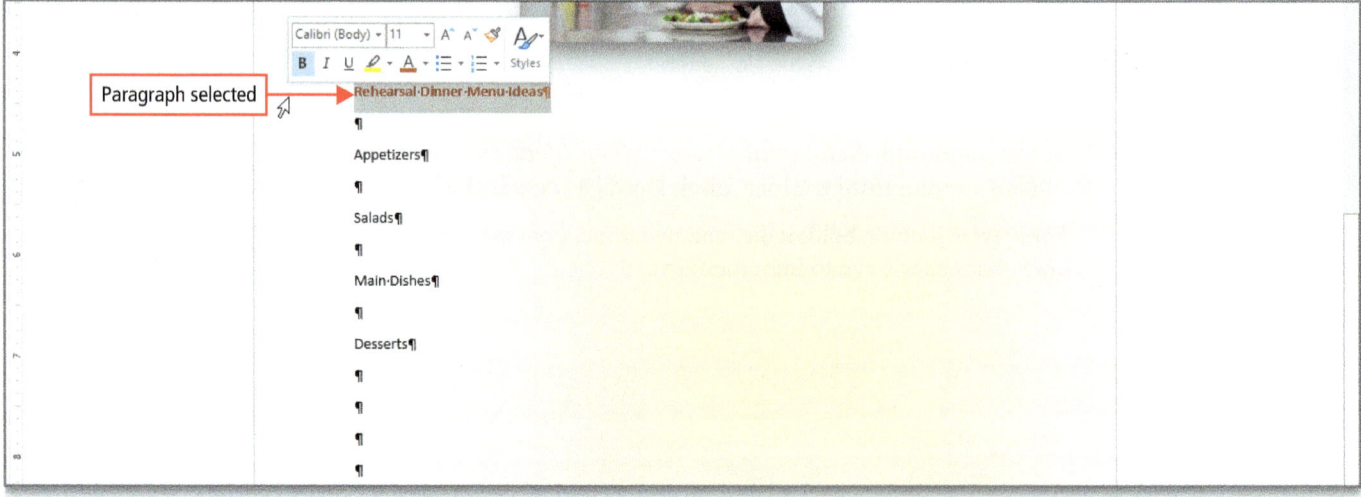

Figure 1.30

2 With *Rehearsal Dinner Menu Ideas* still selected, on the mini toolbar, click **Format Painter** 🖌. Then, move your mouse to the right of the word *Appetizers*, and notice the 🖌I mouse pointer. Compare your screen with Figure 1.31.

> The pointer takes the shape of a paintbrush and contains the formatting information from the paragraph where the insertion point is positioned or from what is selected. Information about the Format Painter and how to turn it off displays in the status bar.

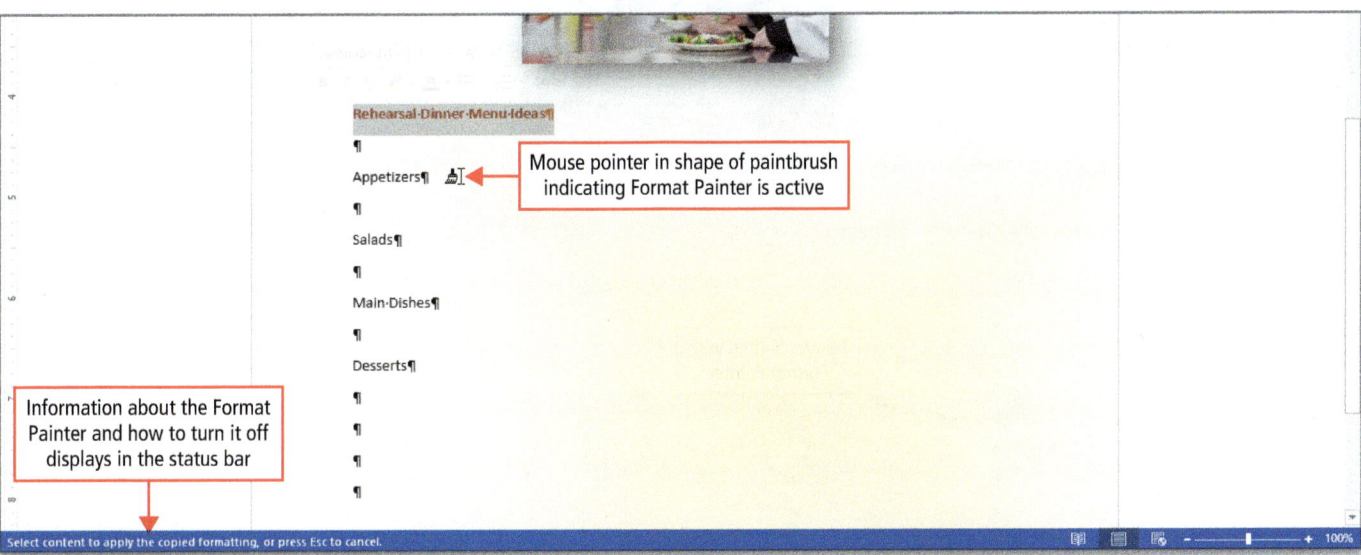

Mouse pointer in shape of paintbrush indicating Format Painter is active

Information about the Format Painter and how to turn it off displays in the status bar

Figure 1.31

3 With the 🖌I pointer, drag to select the paragraph *Appetizers* and notice that the font color and Bold formatting is applied. Then, click anywhere in the word *Appetizers*, right-click to display the mini toolbar, and on the mini toolbar, *double-click* **Format Painter** 🖌.

4 Select the paragraph *Salads* to copy the font color and Bold formatting, and notice that the pointer retains the 🖌I shape. You might have to move the mouse slightly to see the paintbrush shape.

> When you *double-click* the Format Painter button, the Format Painter feature remains active until you either click the Format Painter button again, or press [Esc] to cancel it—as indicated on the status bar.

5 With Format Painter still active, drag to select the paragraph *Main Dishes*, and then on the ribbon, on the **Home tab**, in the **Clipboard group**, notice that **Format Painter** is selected, indicating that it is active. Compare your screen with Figure 1.32.

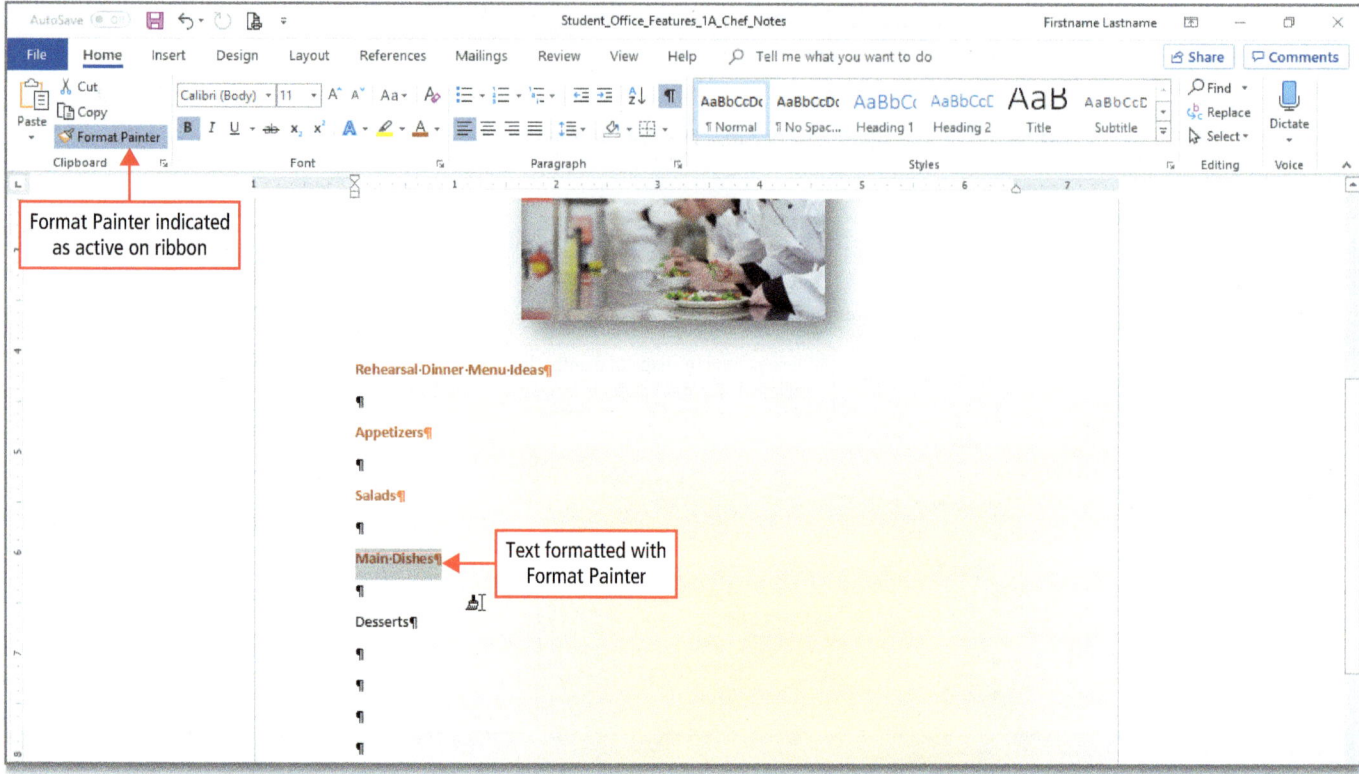

Figure 1.32

6 Select the paragraph *Desserts* to copy the format, and then on the ribbon, click **Format Painter** to turn the command off.

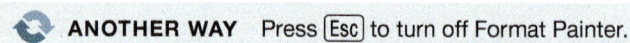
ANOTHER WAY   Press (Esc) to turn off Format Painter.

7 On the **Quick Access Toolbar**, click **Save** to save the changes you have made to your document.

Activity 1.13 | Using Keyboard Shortcuts and Using the Clipboard to Copy, Cut, and Paste

The ***Clipboard*** is a temporary storage area that holds text or graphics that you select and then cut or copy. When you ***copy*** text or graphics, a copy is placed on the Clipboard and the original text or graphic remains in place. When you ***cut*** text or graphics, a copy is placed on the Clipboard, and the original text or graphic is removed—cut—from the document.

After copying or cutting, the contents of the Clipboard are available for you to ***paste***—insert—in a new location in the current document, or into another Office file.

1 On your keyboard, hold down `Ctrl` and press `Home` to move to the beginning of your document, and then take a moment to study the table in Figure 1.33, which describes similar keyboard shortcuts with which you can navigate quickly in a document.

MAC TIP Press `command ⌘` + `fn` + to move to the top of a document.

To Move	On a Windows PC press:	On a Mac press:
To the beginning of a document	`Ctrl` + `Home`	`command ⌘` + `fn` + `←`
To the end of a document	`Ctrl` + `End`	`command ⌘` + `fn` + `→`
To the beginning of a line	`Home`	`command ⌘` + `←`
To the end of a line	`End`	`command ⌘` + `→`
To the beginning of the previous word	`Ctrl` + `←`	`option` + `←`
To the beginning of the next word	`Ctrl` + `→`	`option` + `→`
To the beginning of the current word (if insertion point is in the middle of a word)	`Ctrl` + `←`	`option` + `←`
To the beginning of the previous paragraph	`Ctrl` + `↑`	`command ⌘` + `↑`
To the beginning of the next paragraph	`Ctrl` + `↓`	`command ⌘` + `↓`
To the beginning of the current paragraph (if insertion point is in the middle of a paragraph)	`Ctrl` + `↑`	`command ⌘` + `↑`
Up one screen	`PgUp`	`fn` + `↑`
Down one screen	`PgDn`	`fn` + `↓`

Figure 1.33

2 To the left of *Skyline Metro Grill Chef Notes*, point in the left margin area to display the pointer, and then click one time to select the entire paragraph. On the **Home tab**, in the **Clipboard group**, click **Copy**.

Because anything that you select and then copy—or cut—is placed on the Clipboard, the Copy command and the Cut command display in the Clipboard group of commands on the ribbon. There is no visible indication that your copied selection has been placed on the Clipboard.

ANOTHER WAY Right-click the selection, and then click Copy on the shortcut menu; or, use the keyboard shortcut `Ctrl` + `C`.

MAC TIP Press `command ⌘` + `C` as a keyboard shortcut for the Copy command.

3 On the **Home tab**, in the **Clipboard group**, to the right of the group name *Clipboard*, click the **Dialog Box Launcher** button ⌐, and then compare your screen with Figure 1.34.

> The Clipboard pane displays with your copied text. In any ribbon group, the ***Dialog Box Launcher*** displays either a dialog box or a pane related to the group of commands. It is not necessary to display the Clipboard in this manner, although sometimes it is useful to do so.

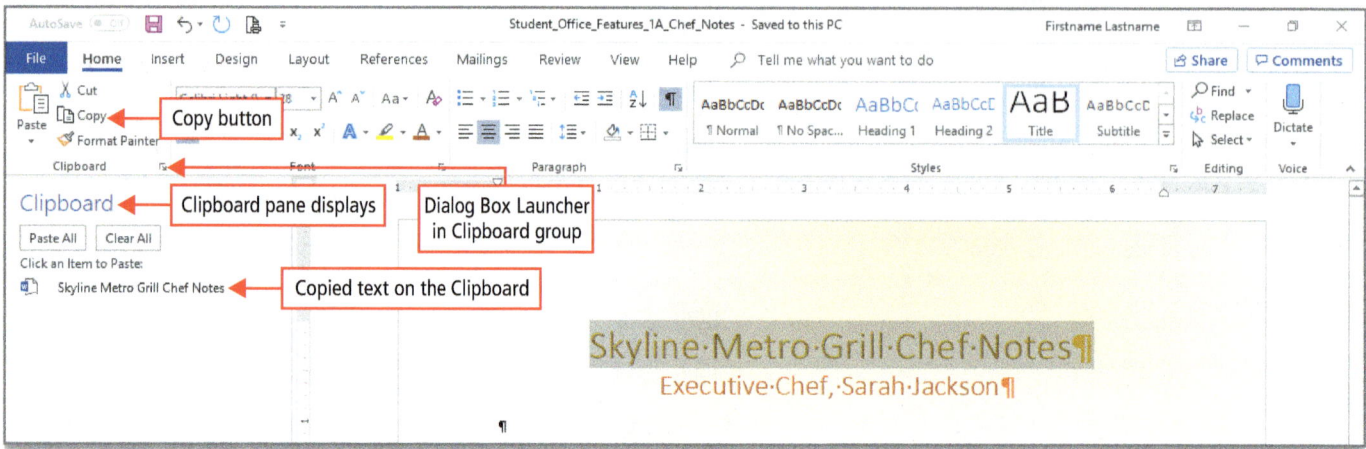

Figure 1.34

4 In the upper right corner of the **Clipboard** pane, click **Close** ☒.

5 Press Ctrl + End to move to the end of your document. On the **Home tab**, in the **Clipboard group**, point to **Paste**, and then click the *upper* portion of this split button.

> The Paste command pastes the most recently copied item on the Clipboard at the insertion point location. If you click the lower portion of the Paste button, a gallery of Paste Options displays. A ***split button*** is divided into two parts; clicking the main part of the button performs a command, and clicking the arrow displays a list or gallery with choices.

6 Below the pasted text, click **Paste Options** 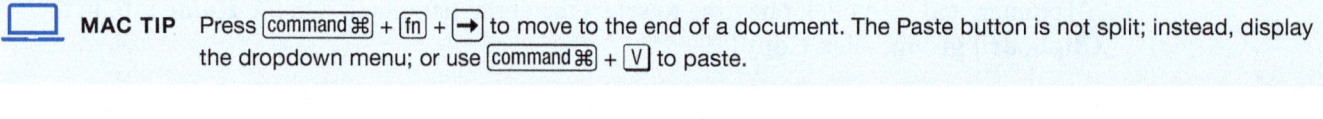 as shown in Figure 1.35.

> Here you can view and apply various formatting options for pasting your copied or cut text. Typically, you will click Paste on the ribbon and paste the item in its original format. If you want some other format for the pasted item, you can choose another format from the ***Paste Options gallery***, which provides a Live Preview of the various options for changing the format of the pasted item with a single click. The Paste Options gallery is available in three places: on the ribbon by clicking the lower portion of the Paste button—the Paste button arrow; from the Paste Options button that displays below the pasted item following the paste operation; or on the shortcut menu if you right-click the pasted item.

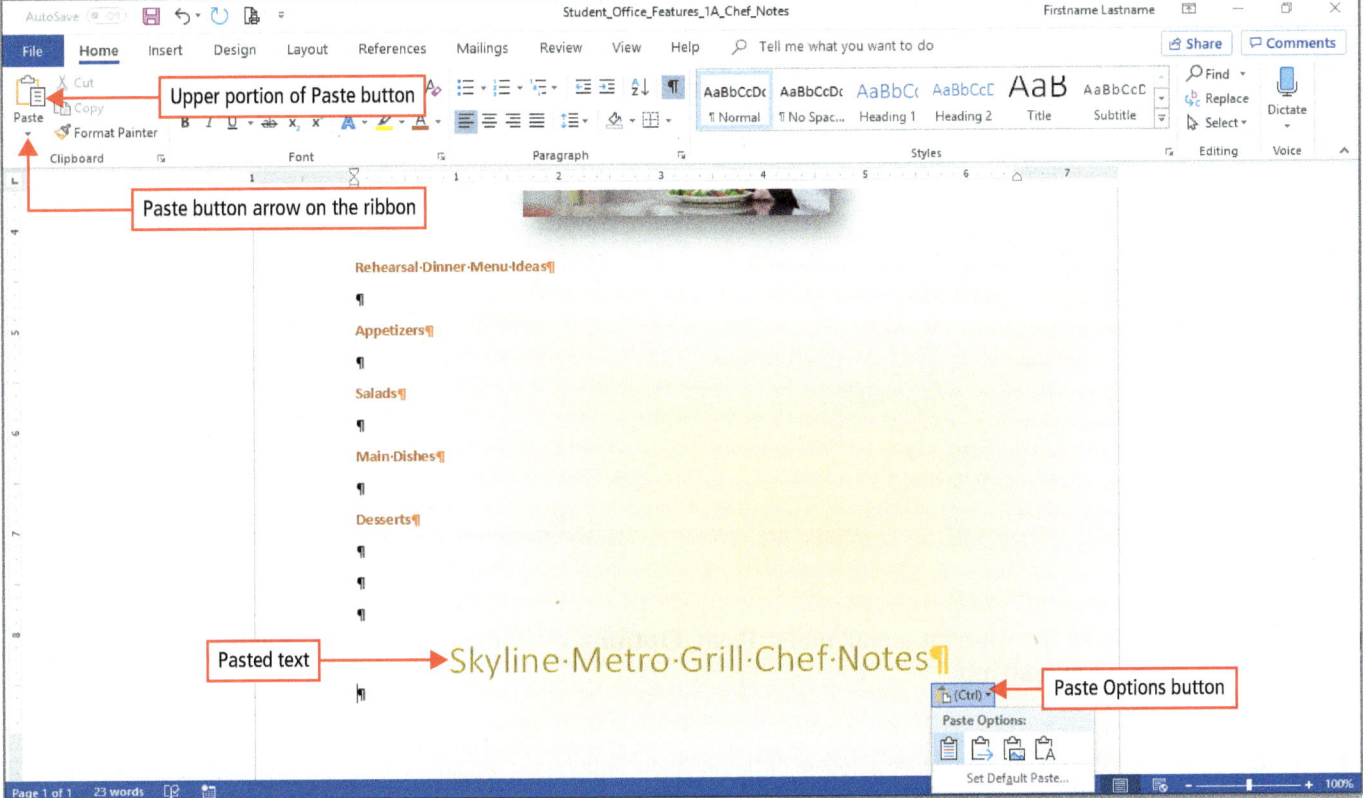

Figure 1.35

> **7** In the **Paste Options** gallery, *point* to each option to see the Live Preview of the format that would be applied if you clicked the button.

> The contents of the Paste Options gallery are contextual; that is, they change based on what you copied and where you are pasting.

> **8** Press Esc to close the gallery; the button will remain displayed until you take some other screen action.

> **9** On your keyboard, press Ctrl + Home to move to the top of the document, and then click the **chefs image** one time to select it. While pointing to the selected image, right-click, and then on the shortcut menu, click **Cut**.

> Recall that the Cut command cuts—removes—the selection from the document and places it on the Clipboard.

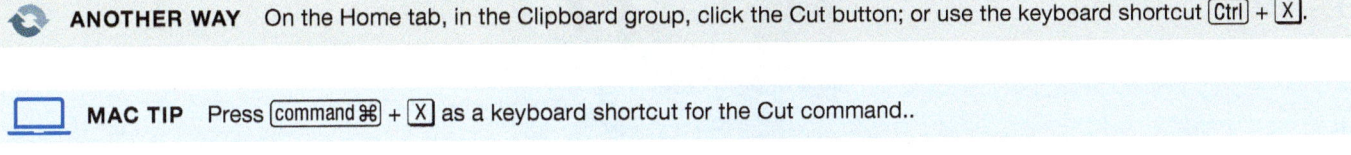

ANOTHER WAY   On the Home tab, in the Clipboard group, click the Cut button; or use the keyboard shortcut Ctrl + X.

MAC TIP   Press command ⌘ + X as a keyboard shortcut for the Cut command..

> **10** Press Ctrl + End to move to the end of the document.

11 With the insertion point blinking in the blank paragraph at the end of the document, right-click, and notice that the **Paste Options** gallery displays on the shortcut menu. Compare your screen with Figure 1.36.

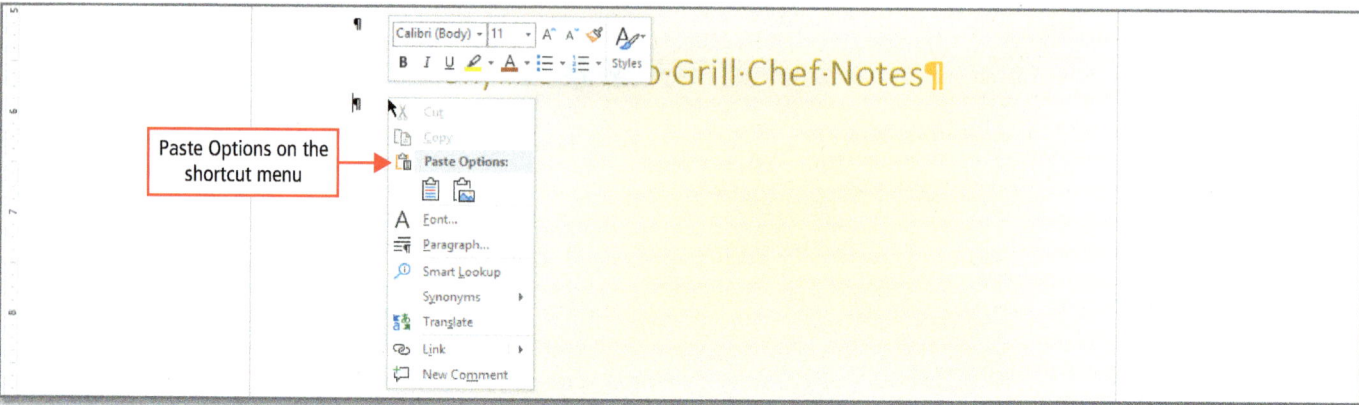

Figure 1.36

12 On the shortcut menu, under **Paste Options**, click the first button—**Keep Source Formatting**.

MAC TIP On the shortcut menu, click Paste, click the Paste Options button, and then click Keep Source Formatting.

13 Point to the picture to display the ⬚ pointer, and then drag to the right until the center green **Alignment Guide** displays and the blank paragraph is above the picture. Release the left mouse button.

MAC TIP In the Arrange group, on the Picture Format tab, click Align, click Align Center.

14 Above the picture, select the text *Chef Notes*, type **Festive Salad** and then compare your screen with Figure 1.37.

Figure 1.37

15 Click **Save** 🖫.

Activity 1.14 | Adding Alternative Text for Accessibility

MOS
5.4.3

1 Point to the **chefs picture** and right-click. On the shortcut menu, click **Edit Alt Text** to display the **Alt Text** pane.

Alternative text helps people using a *screen reader*, which is software that enables visually impaired users to read text on a computer screen to understand the content of pictures. *Alt text* is the term commonly used for this feature.

2 In the **Alt Text** pane, notice that Word generates a suggested description of the picture. Click in the box, select the existing text, and then type **Young chefs making salads in a restaurant kitchen** and then compare your screen with Figure 1.38.

Anyone viewing the document with a screen reader will see the alternative text displayed instead of the picture.

Figure 1.38

3 **Close** ✕ the **Alt Text** pane. Press Ctrl + Home to move to the top of your document. On the Quick Access Toolbar, click **Save** 🖫 to the changes you have made to your document.

Objective 5   Finalize an Office Document

GO! Learn How
Video OF1-5

There are steps you will want to take to finalize your documents. This typically includes inserting a footer for identifying information and adding Document Properties to facilitate searching. Recall that Document Properties—also known as metadata—are details about a file that describe or identify it, such as the title, author name, subject, and keywords that identify the document's topic or contents. You might also want to take some security measures or mark information to find later.

Activity 1.15 | Inserting a Footer, Inserting Document Info, and Adding Document Properties

MOS

1.3.2

1 On the **Insert tab**, in the **Header & Footer group**, click **Footer**. At the bottom of the list, click **Edit Footer**, and then with the **Header & Footer Tools Design tab** active, in the **Insert group**, click **Document Info**. Click **File Name** to add the file name to the footer.

A *footer* is a reserved area for text and graphics that displays at the bottom of each page in a document. It is common in organizations to add the file name to the footer of documents so that documents are easily identified.

MAC TIP   In the Insert group, click Field. In the dialog box, under Categories, click Document Information. Then under Field names, click FileName. Click OK.

2 On the right end of the ribbon, click **Close Header and Footer**.

3 On the **Quick Access Toolbar**, point to the **Print Preview and Print** button 🔳 you placed there, right-click, and then click **Remove from Quick Access Toolbar**.

> If you are working on your own computer and you want to do so, you can leave the icon on the toolbar; in a college lab, you should return the software to its original settings.

4 Click the **File tab** to display **Backstage** view. With the **Info tab** active, in the lower right corner, click **Show All Properties**. Click in the **Tags** box, and then type **rehearsal dinners, menus**

> *Tags*—also referred to as *keywords*—are custom file properties in the form of words that you associate with a document to give an indication of the document's content. Use tags to assist in searching for and organizing files.

> **MAC TIP** On the menu bar, click File, click Properties, click the Summary tab, and then type the tags in the Keywords box. Click OK.

5 Click in the **Subject** box, and then type your course name and number—for example, *CIS 10, #5543*. Under **Related People**, be sure your name displays as the author. (To edit the Author, right-click the name, click Edit Property, type the new name, click in a white area to close the list, and then click OK.)

6 On the left, click **Save** to save your document and return to the Word window.

Activity 1.16 | Inspecting a Document

Word, Excel, and PowerPoint all have the same commands to inspect a file before sharing it.

> **MAC TIP** On the menu bar, click Tools. Here you can click Protect Document and Check Accessibility.

MOS
1.4.1,1.4.2, 1.4.3

1 With your document displayed, click the **File tab**, on the left, if necessary, click **Info**, and then on the right, click **Check for Issues**.

2 On the list, click **Inspect Document**.

> The *Inspect Document* command searches your document for hidden data or personal information that you might not want to share publicly. This information could reveal company details that should not be shared.

3 In the lower right corner of the **Document Inspector** dialog box, click **Inspect**.

> The Document Inspector runs and lists information that was found and that you could choose to remove.

4 In the lower right corner of the dialog box, click **Close**, and then click **Check for Issues** again. On the list, click **Check Accessibility**.

> The *Check Accessibility* command checks the document for content that people with disabilities might find difficult to read. The Accessibility Checker pane displays on the right and lists objects that might require attention.

5 **Close** ☒ the **Accessibility Checker** pane, and then click the **File tab**.

6 Click **Check for Issues**, and then click **Check Compatibility**.

> The *Check Compatibility* command checks for features in your document that may not be supported by earlier versions of the Office program. This is only a concern if you are sharing documents with individuals with older software.

7 Click **OK**. Leave your Word document displayed for the next Activity.

Activity 1.17 | Inserting a Bookmark and a 3D Model

1.1.2, 5.2.6

A *bookmark* identifies a word, section, or place in your document so that you can find it quickly without scrolling. This is especially useful in a long document.

3D models are a new kind of shape that you can insert from an online library of ready-to-use three-dimensional graphics. A 3D model is most powerful in a PowerPoint presentation where you can add transitions and animations during your presentation, but you can also insert a 3D model into a Word document for an impactful image that you can position in various ways.

1 In the paragraph *Rehearsal Dinner Menu Items*, select the word *Menu*.

2 On the **Insert tab**, in the **Links group**, click **Bookmark**.

3 In the **Bookmark** name box, type **menu** and then click **Add**.

4 Press Ctrl + Home to move to the top of your document.

5 On the **Home tab**, at the right end of the ribbon, in the **Editing group**, click the **Find button arrow**, and then click **Go To**.

 ANOTHER WAY   Press Ctrl + G, which is the keyboard shortcut for the Go To command.

MAC TIP   On the menu bar, click Edit, point to Find, click Go To. In the dialog box, click Bookmark.

6 Under **Go to what**, click **Bookmark**, and then with *menu* indicated as the bookmark name, click **Go To**. **Close** the **Find and Replace** dialog box, and notice that your bookmarked text is selected for you.

7 Click to position your insertion point at the end of the word *Desserts*. On the **Insert tab**, in the **Illustrations group**, click the upper portion of the **3D Models button** to open the **Online 3D Models** dialog box.

NOTE   3D Models Not Available?

If the 3D Models command is not available on your system, in the **Illustrations group**, click **Pictures**, and then from the files downloaded with this project, click of01A_Cupcake. Change the Height to .75" and then move to Step 12.

8 In the search box, type **cupcake** and then press Enter.

9 Click the image of the **cupcake in a pink and white striped wrapper**—or select any other cupcake image. At the bottom, click **Insert**.

10 Point to the **3D control** in the center of the image, hold down the left mouse button, and then rotate the image so the top of the cupcake is pointing toward the upper right corner of the page—your rotation need not be exact. Alternatively, in the 3D Model Views group, click the More button ⊡, and then locate and click Above Front Left.

11 With the cupcake image selected, on the **3D Model Tools Format tab**, in the **Size group**, click in the **Height** box, type **.75"** and press Enter.

12 In the **Arrange group**, click **Wrap Text**, and then click **In Front of Text**. Then, in the **Arrange group**, click **Align**, and click **Align Right** to position the cupcake at the right margin.

13 Press Ctrl + Home to move to the top of your document. On the **Quick Access Toolbar**, click **Save** 🖫.

Activity 1.18 | Printing a File and Closing a Desktop App

1 Click the **File tab** to return to **Backstage** view, on the left click **Print**, and then compare your screen with Figure 1.39.

> Here you can select any printer connected to your system and adjust the settings related to how you want to print. On the right, the ***Print Preview*** displays, which is a view of a document as it will appear on paper when you print it. Your page color effect will not display in Print Preview nor will the shading print. This effect appears only to anyone viewing the document on a screen.
>
> At the bottom of the Print Preview area, in the center, the number of pages and page navigation arrows with which you can move among the pages in Print Preview display. On the right, the Zoom slider enables you to shrink or enlarge the Print Preview. ***Zoom*** is the action of increasing or decreasing the viewing area of the screen.

ANOTHER WAY From the document screen, press Ctrl + P or Ctrl + F2 to display Print in Backstage view.

MAC TIP Press command ⌘ + P.

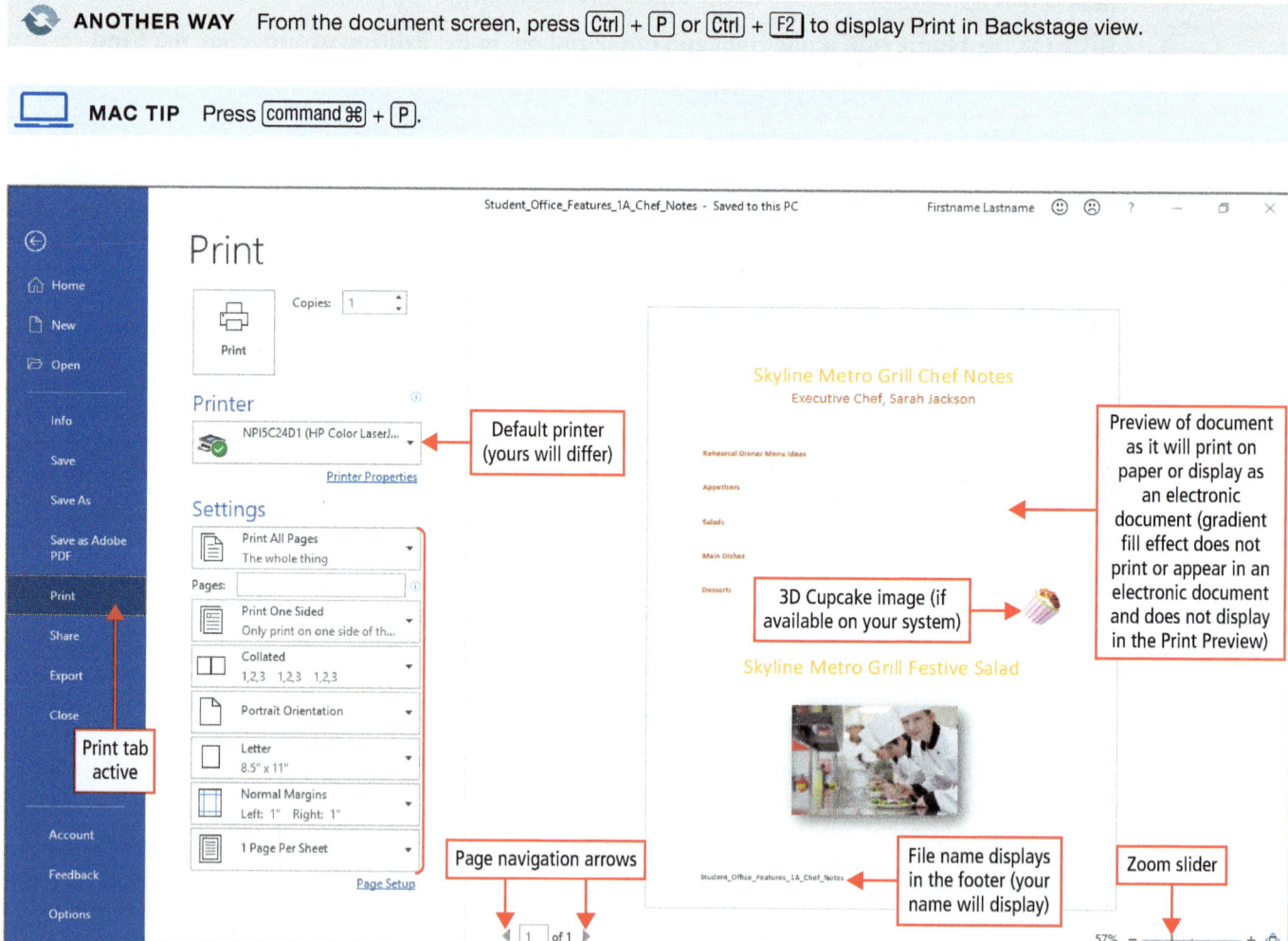

Figure 1.39

2 On the left, click **Save**. In the upper right corner of your screen, click **Close** ☒ to close Word. If a message displays regarding copied items, click No.

MAC TIP On the menu bar, click File, click Close.

For Non-MyLab Submissions: Determine What Your Instructor Requires as Your Submission
As directed by your instructor, submit your completed Word document.

3 In **MyLab IT**, locate and click the Grader Project **Office Features 1A Chef Notes**. In **step 3**, under **Upload Completed Assignment**, click **Choose File**. In the **Open** dialog box, navigate to your **Office Features Chapter 1 folder**, and then click your **Student_Office_Features_1A_ Chef_Notes** file one time to select it. In the lower right corner of the **Open** dialog box, click **Open**.

The name of your selected file displays above the Upload button.

4 To submit your file to **MyLab IT** for grading, click **Upload**, wait a moment for a green **Success!** message, and then in **step 4**, click the blue **Submit for Grading** button. Click **Close Assignment** to return to your list of **Course Materials**.

MORE KNOWLEDGE | **Creating an Electronic Image of Your Document**

You can create an electronic image of your document that looks like a printed document. To do so, in Backstage view, on the left click Export. On the right, click Create PDF/XPS, and then click the Create PDF/XPS button to display the Publish as PDF or XPS dialog box.

PDF stands for *Portable Document Format*, which is a technology that creates an image that preserves the look of your file. This is a popular format for sending documents electronically, because the document will display on most computers. *XPS* stands for *XML Paper Specification*—a Microsoft file format that also creates an image of your document and that opens in the XPS viewer.

ALERT | **The Remaining Activities in This Chapter Are Optional**

The following Activities describing the Office Help features are recommend but are optional to complete.

Objective 6 | **Use the Office Help Features**

GO! Learn How
Video OF1-6

Within each Office program, you will see the *Tell Me* feature at the right end of the ribbon— to the right of the Help tab. This is a search feature for Microsoft Office commands that you activate by typing in the *Tell me what you want to do* box. Another way to use this feature is to point to a command on the ribbon, and then at the bottom of the displayed ScreenTip, click *Tell me more*.

Activity 1.19 | Using Microsoft Office Tell Me, Tell Me More, the Help Tab, and Adding Alt Text to an Excel Chart

MOS
5.3.3

1 Start Excel and open a **Blank workbook**. With cell **A1** active, type **456789** and press [Enter]. Click cell **A1** again to make it the active cell.

2 ▸ At the top of the screen, click in the *Tell me what you want to do* box, and then type **format as currency** In the displayed list, to the right of **Accounting Number Format**, click the ▸ arrow. Compare your screen with Figure 1.40.

As you type, every keystroke refines the results so that you can click the command as soon as it displays. This feature helps you apply the command immediately; it does not explain how to locate the command.

MAC TIP Click the Help tab on the menu bar.

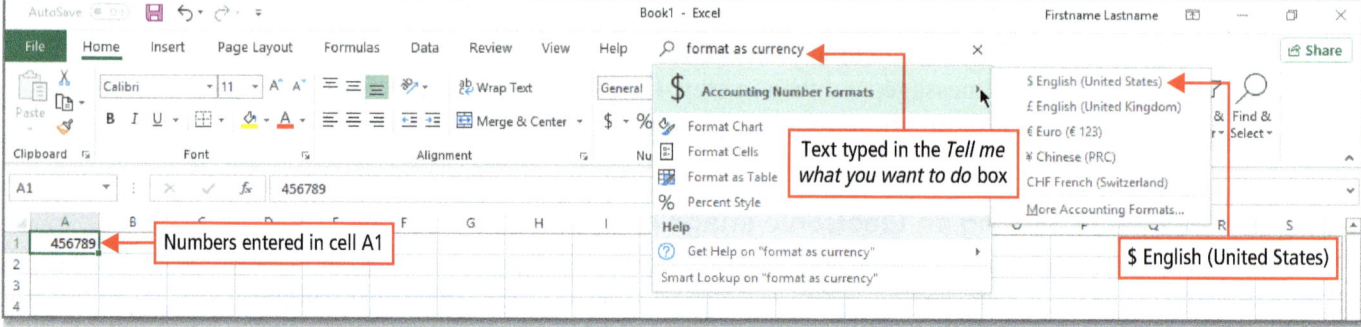

Figure 1.40

3 ▸ Click **$ English (United States)**.

4 ▸ On the **Home tab**, in the **Font group**, *point* to the **Font Color** button <u>A</u>▾ to display its ScreenTip, and then click **Tell me more**.

Tell me more is a prompt within a ScreenTip that opens the Office online Help system with explanations about how to perform the command referenced in the ScreenTip.

5 ▸ In the **Help** pane that displays on the right, if necessary, click **Change the color of text**. Compare your screen with Figure 1.41.

As you scroll down, you will notice that the Help pane displays extensive information about the topic of changing the color of text, including how to apply a custom color.

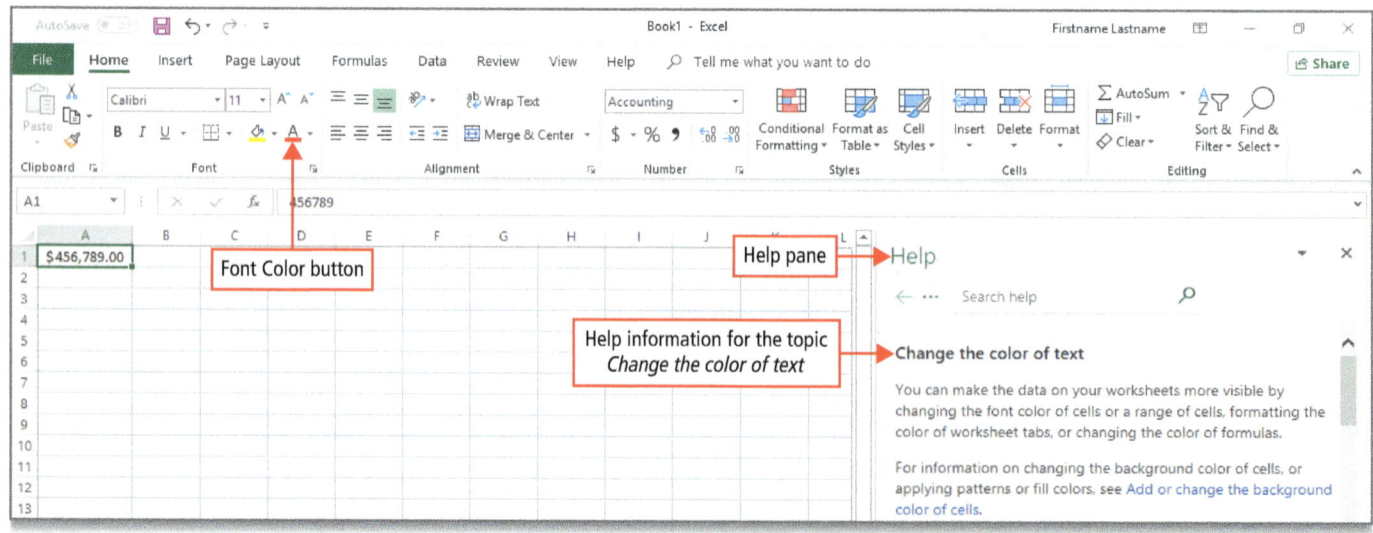

Figure 1.41

6 ▸ **Close** ✕ the **Help** pane.

7 On the ribbon, click the **Help tab**. In the **Help** group, click **Help**. In the **Help** pane, type **3D models** and then click the **Search** button 🔍. Click **Get creative with 3D models**, and then compare your screen with Figure 1.42.

Some Help topics include videos like this one to demonstrate and explain the topic.

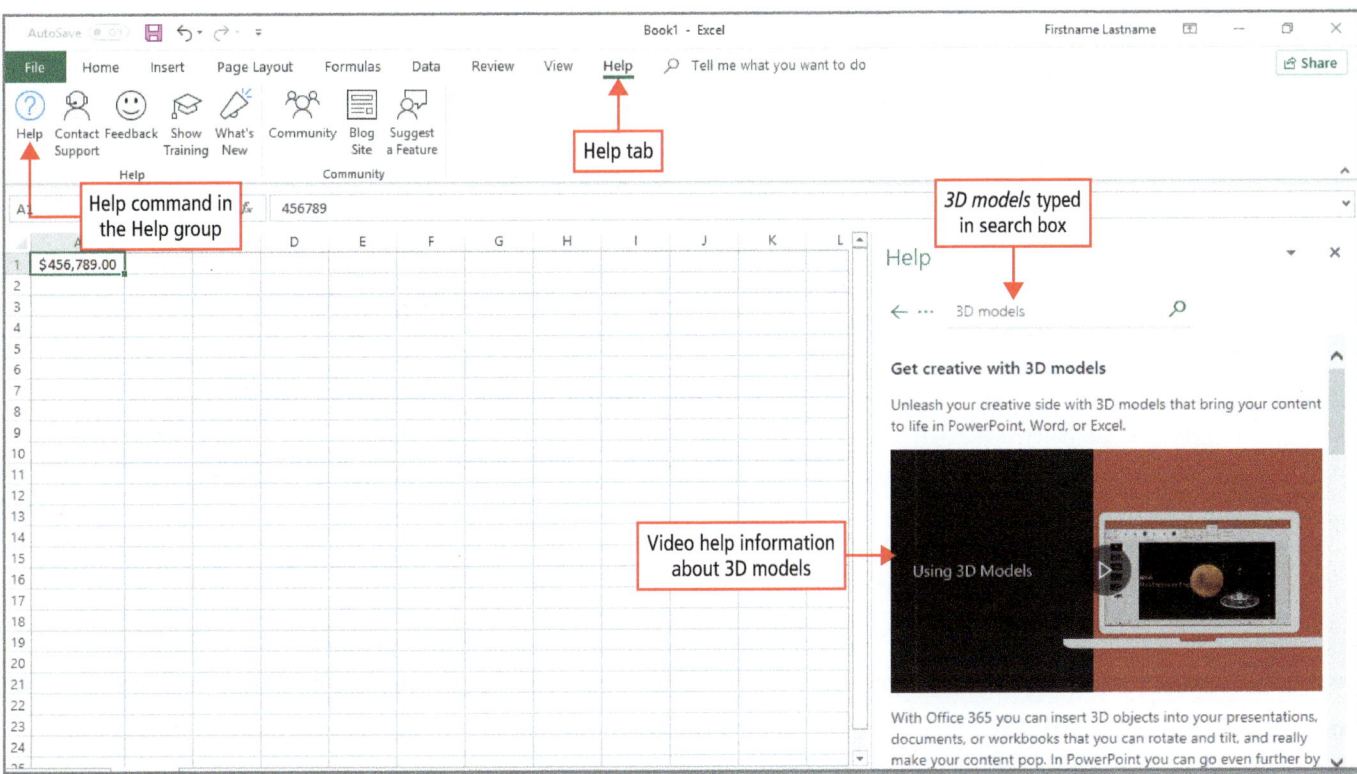

Figure 1.42

8 In the **Help** group and the **Community** group, look at the buttons.

Here you can Contact Support, send Feedback, Show Training developed by Microsoft, and see new features. In the Community group, you can visit the Excel Community, read the Excel Blog, and suggest new features.

9 ▶ Click **Show Training**, and then compare your screen with Figure 1.43.

Here you can view training videos developed by Microsoft.

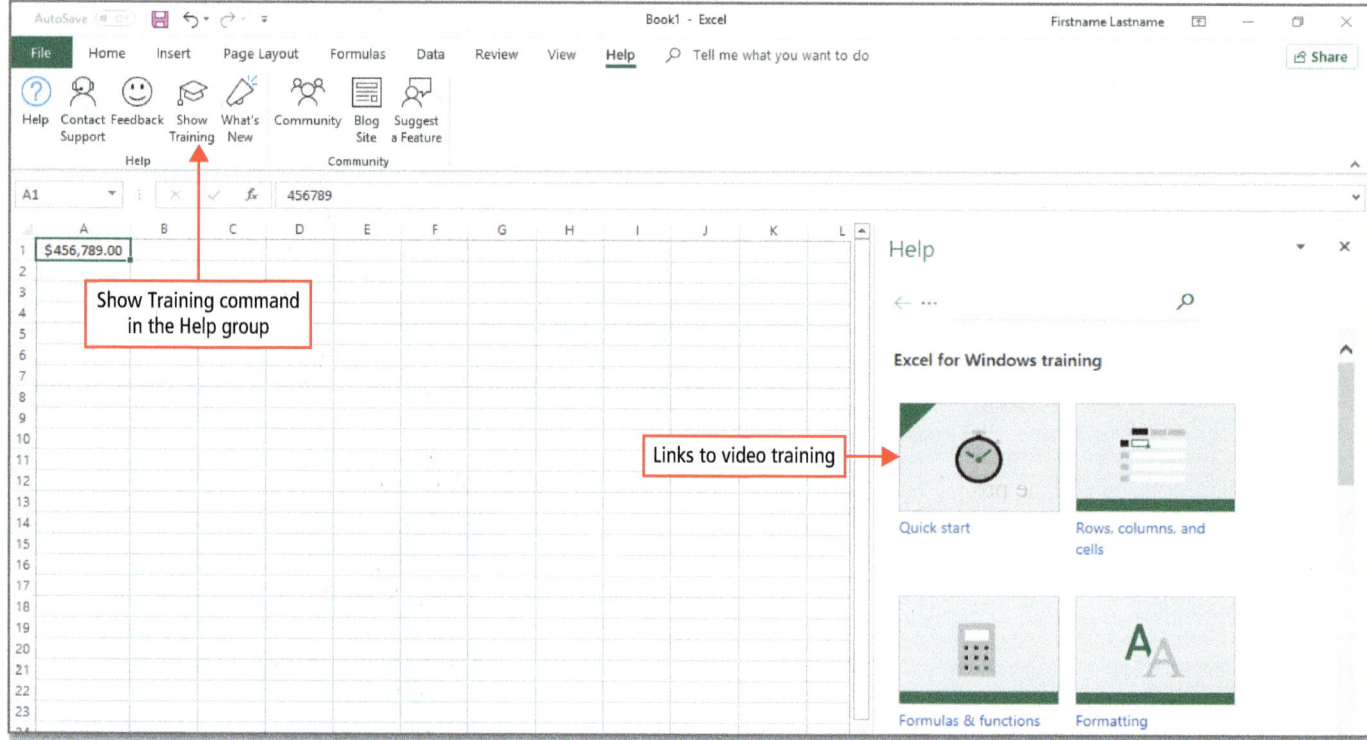

Figure 1.43

10 ▶ Click cell **A1**, and then click the **Insert tab**. In the **Charts group**, click **Recommended Charts**, and then in the **Insert Chart** dialog box, with the first chart selected, click **OK**.

11 ▶ Click the **Chart Tools Format tab**, and then in the **Accessibility group**, click **Alt Text**.

Here you can add text to describe the chart, similar to the Alt Text you added for the chef's image.

12 ▶ **Close** ☒ the **Help** pane, **Close** ☒ the **Alt Text** pane, and then in the upper right corner of the Excel window, click **Close** ☒. Click **Don't Save**.

MORE KNOWLEDGE **Don't Type, Talk! With the New Dictate Feature**

Office 365 subscribers will see the *Dictate* feature in Word, PowerPoint, Outlook, and OneNote for Windows 10. When you enable Dictate, you start talking and as you talk, text appears in your document or slide. Dictate is one of Microsoft's Office Intelligent Services, which adds new cloud-enhanced features to Office. Dictate is especially useful in Outlook when you must write lengthy emails. The Dictate command is on the Home tab in Word and PowerPoint and on the Message tab in Outlook.

You have completed Project 1A **END**

Hotel Files

Project Activities

In Activities 1.20 through 1.38, you will assist Barbara Hewitt and Steven Ramos, who work for the Information Technology Department at the Boston headquarters office of the Bell Orchid Hotels. Barbara and Steven must organize some of the files and folders that comprise the corporation's computer data. As you progress through the project, you will insert screenshots of windows that you create into a PowerPoint presentation with five slides that will look similar to Figure 1.44.

Project Files for **MyLab IT Grader**

For Project 1B, you will start with the Windows 10 desktop displayed, and then learn how to create a folder for your **MyLab IT** files as you work through the project instruction. At the appropriate point in the project, you will be instructed to download your files from your **MyLab IT** course.

Project Results

GO! Project 1B
Where We're Going

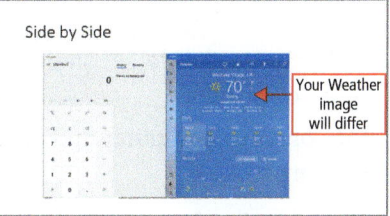

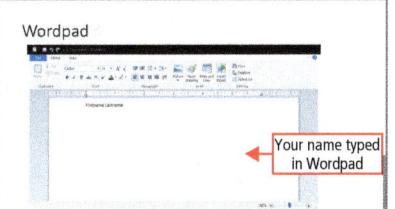

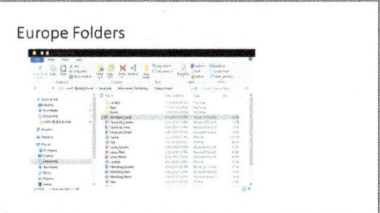

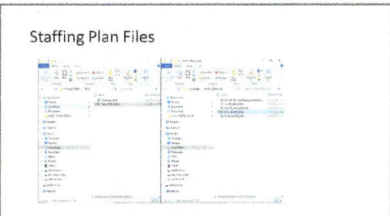

Figure 1.44

For Non-MyLab Submissions Start with the Windows 10 Desktop Displayed

For Project 1B, you will start with the Windows 10 desktop displayed and learn how to create a folder and save a new PowerPoint presentation as you work through the project instruction. Additionally, you will need the Student Data Files **win01_1B_Bell_Orchid** from your instructor or from www.pearsonhighered.com/go.

Objective 7 Explore Windows 10

ALERT Because Windows 10 periodically checks for and then automatically downloads updates, you are assured that your device is up to date with the latest features and security improvements. Therefore, you may encounter some variations in what appears on your screen and what is shown in this instruction. Microsoft Office 365 is fully installed on your PC or Mac; no internet access is necessary to create or edit documents. When you *are* connected to the internet, you will receive monthly upgrades and new features, so you always have the latest versions of Office apps as soon as they are available. Your subscription gives you continuous free access to the latest innovations and refinements.

A *program* is a set of instructions that a computer uses to accomplish a task. A computer program that helps you perform a task for a specific purpose is referred to as an *application*. As an example, there are applications to create a document using word processing software, to play a game, to view the latest weather report, to edit photos or videos, or to manage financial information.

An *operating system* is a specific type of computer program that manages the other programs on a computing device such as a desktop computer, a laptop computer, a smartphone, a tablet computer, or a game console. You need an operating system to:

- Use application programs.
- Coordinate the use of your computer hardware such as a keyboard, mouse, touchpad, touchscreen, game controller, or printer.
- Organize data that you store on your computer and access data that you store on your own computer and in other locations.

Windows 10 is an operating system developed by Microsoft Corporation that works with mobile computing devices and also with traditional desktop and laptop PCs.

The three major tasks of an operating system are to:

- Manage your computer's hardware—the printers, scanners, disk drives, monitors, and other hardware attached to it.
- Manage the application software installed on your computer—programs like those in Microsoft Office and other programs you might install to edit photos and videos, play games, and so on.
- Manage the *data* generated from your application software. Data refers to the documents, worksheets, pictures, songs, and so on that you create and store during the day-to-day use of your computer.

The Windows 10 operating system continues to perform these three tasks, and additionally is optimized for touchscreens; for example, tablets of all sizes and convertible laptop computers. Windows 10 works equally well with any input device, including a mouse, keyboard, touchscreen, and *pen*—a pen-shaped stylus that you tap on a computer screen.

In most instances, when you purchase a computer, the operating system software is already installed. The operating system consists of many smaller programs, stored as system files, which transfer data to and from the disk and transfer data in and out of your computer's memory. Other functions performed by the operating system include hardware-specific tasks such as checking to see if a key has been pressed on the keyboard and, if it has, displaying the appropriate letter or character on the screen.

Windows 10, in the same manner as other operating systems and earlier versions of the Windows operating system, uses a *graphical user interface*—abbreviated as *GUI* and pronounced *GOO-ee*. A graphical user interface uses graphics such as an image of a file folder or wastebasket that you click to activate the item represented. A GUI commonly incorporates the following:

- A *pointer*—any symbol that displays on your screen in response to moving your mouse and with which you can select objects and commands.

- An *insertion point*—a blinking vertical line that indicates where text will be inserted when you type or where an action will take place.

- A *pointing device*, such as a mouse or touchpad, to control the pointer.

- *Icons*—small images that represent commands, files, applications, or other windows.

- A *desktop*—a simulation of a real desk that represents your work area; here you can arrange icons such as shortcuts to programs, files, folders, and various types of documents in the same manner you would arrange physical objects on top of a desk.

In Windows 10, you also have a Start menu with tiles that display when you click the Start button in the lower left corner of your screen. The array of tiles serves as a connected dashboard to all of your important programs, sites, and services. On the Start menu, your view is tailored to your information and activities.

The physical parts of your computer such as the central processing unit (CPU), memory, and any attached devices such as a printer, are collectively known as *resources*. The operating system keeps track of the status of each resource and decides when a resource needs attention and for how long.

Application programs enable you to do work on, and be entertained by, your computer—programs such as Word and Excel found in the Microsoft Office suite of products, Adobe Photoshop, and computer games. No application program, whether a larger desktop app or smaller *Microsoft Store app*—a smaller app that you download from the Store—can run on its own; it must run under the direction of an operating system.

For the everyday use of your computer, the most important and most often used function of the operating system is managing your files and folders—referred to as *data management*. In the same manner that you strive to keep your paper documents and file folders organized so that you can find information when you need it, your goal when organizing your computer files and folders is to group your files so that you can find information easily. Managing your data files so that you can find your information when you need it is one of the most important computing skills you can learn.

Activity 1.20 | Recognizing User Accounts in Windows 10

On a single computer, Windows 10 can have multiple user accounts. This is useful because you can share a computer with other people in your family or organization and each person can have his or her own information and settings—none of which others can see. Each user on a single computer is referred to as a *user account*. Figure 1.45 shows the Settings screen where you can add additional users to your computer.

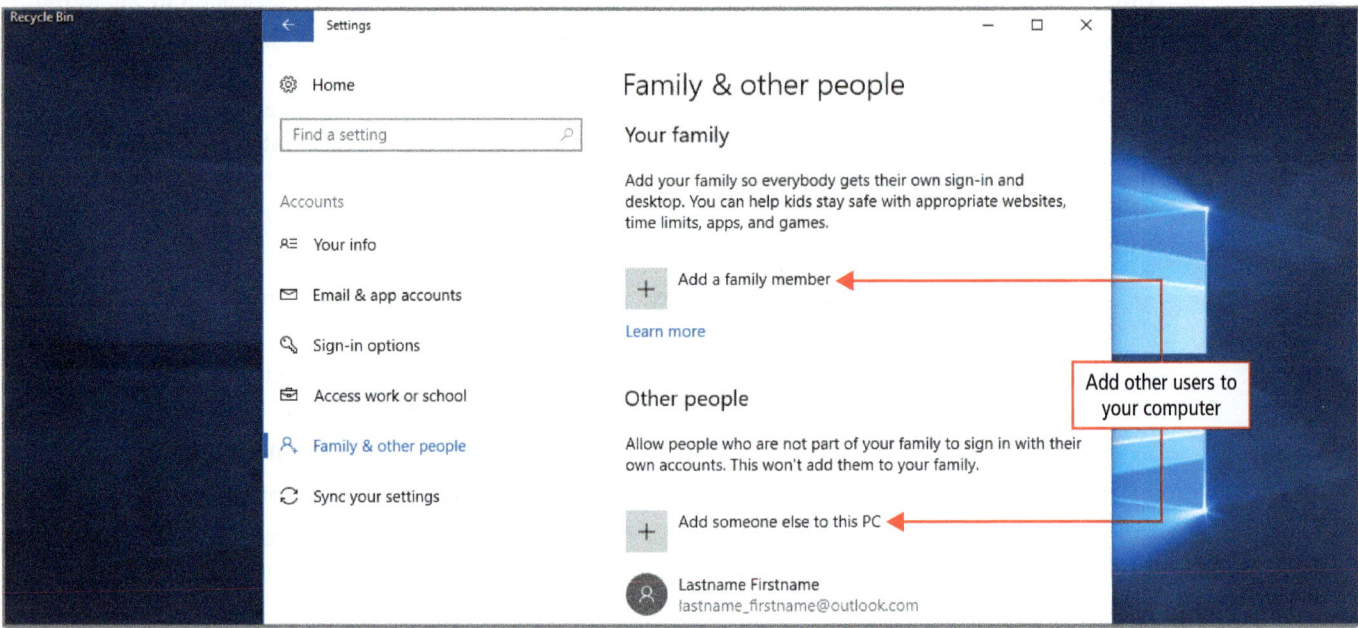

Figure 1.45

NOTE   Comparing Your Screen with the Figures in This Textbook

Your screen will more closely match the figures shown in this textbook if you set your screen resolution to 1280 x 768. At other resolutions, your screen will closely resemble, but not match, the figures shown. To view your screen's resolution, on the desktop, right-click in a blank area, click *Display settings*, and then click the Resolution arrow. To adjust the resolution, select the desired setting, and then click OK.

With Windows 10, you can create a *Microsoft account*, and then use that account to sign in to *any* Windows 10 computer on which you have, or create, a user account. By signing in with a Microsoft account you can:

• Download apps from the Microsoft Store
• Get your online content—email, social network updates, updated news—automatically displayed in an app when you sign in

Optionally, you can create a local account for use only on a specific PC. On your own Windows 10 computer, you must establish and then sign in with either a local account or a Microsoft account. Regardless of which one you select, you must provide an email address to associate with the user account name. If you create and then sign in with a local account, you can still connect to the internet, but you will not have the advantage of having your personal arrangement of apps displayed on your Start menu every time you sign in to that PC. You can use any email address to create a local account—similar to other online services where an email address is your user ID. You can also use any email address to create a Microsoft account.

To enjoy and get the full benefit of Windows 10, Microsoft Office, Skype, and free OneDrive cloud storage, if you have not already done so, create a Microsoft account. To do so, in your preferred web search engine, search for *create a Microsoft account*.

You can create an account using any email address. By signing in with a Microsoft account, your computer becomes your connected device where *you*—not your files—are the center of activity. At your college or place of employment, sign-in requirements will vary, because those computers are controlled by the organization's IT (Information Technology) professionals who are responsible for maintaining a secure computing environment for the entire organization.

Activity 1.21 | **Turning On Your Computer, Signing In, and Exploring the Windows 10 Environment**

Before you begin any computer activity, you must, if necessary, turn on your computer. This process is commonly referred to as ***booting the computer***. Because Windows 10 does not require you to completely shut down your computer except to install or repair a hardware device, in most instances moving the mouse or pressing a key will wake your computer in a few seconds. So, most of the time you will skip the lengthier boot process.

In this Activity, you will turn on your computer and sign in to Windows 10. Within an organization, the sign-in process may differ from that of your own computer.

ALERT   The look and features of Windows 10 will differ between your own PC and a PC you might use at your college or workplace.

The Activities in this project assume that you are working on your own PC and signed in with a Microsoft account, or that you are working on a PC at your college or workplace where you are permitted to sign into Windows 10 with your own Microsoft account.

If you do not have a Microsoft account, or are working at a computer where you are unable to sign in with your Microsoft account, you can still complete the Activities, but some steps will differ.

On your own computer, you created your user account when you installed Windows 10 or when you set up your new computer that came with Windows 10. In a classroom or lab, check with your instructor to see how you will sign in to Windows 10.

NOTE   Create your Microsoft account if you have not already done so.

To benefit from this instruction and understand your own computer, be sure that you know your Microsoft account login and password and use that to set up your user account. If you need to create a Microsoft account, in your preferred web search engine, search for *create a Microsoft account* and click the appropriate link.

1 If necessary, turn on your computer, and then examine Figure 1.46.

The Windows 10 *lock screen* fills your computer screen with a background—this might be a default picture from Microsoft such as one of the ones shown in the Lock screen settings in Figure 1.46 or a picture that you selected if you have personalized your system already. You can also choose to have a slide show of your own photos display on the lock screen.

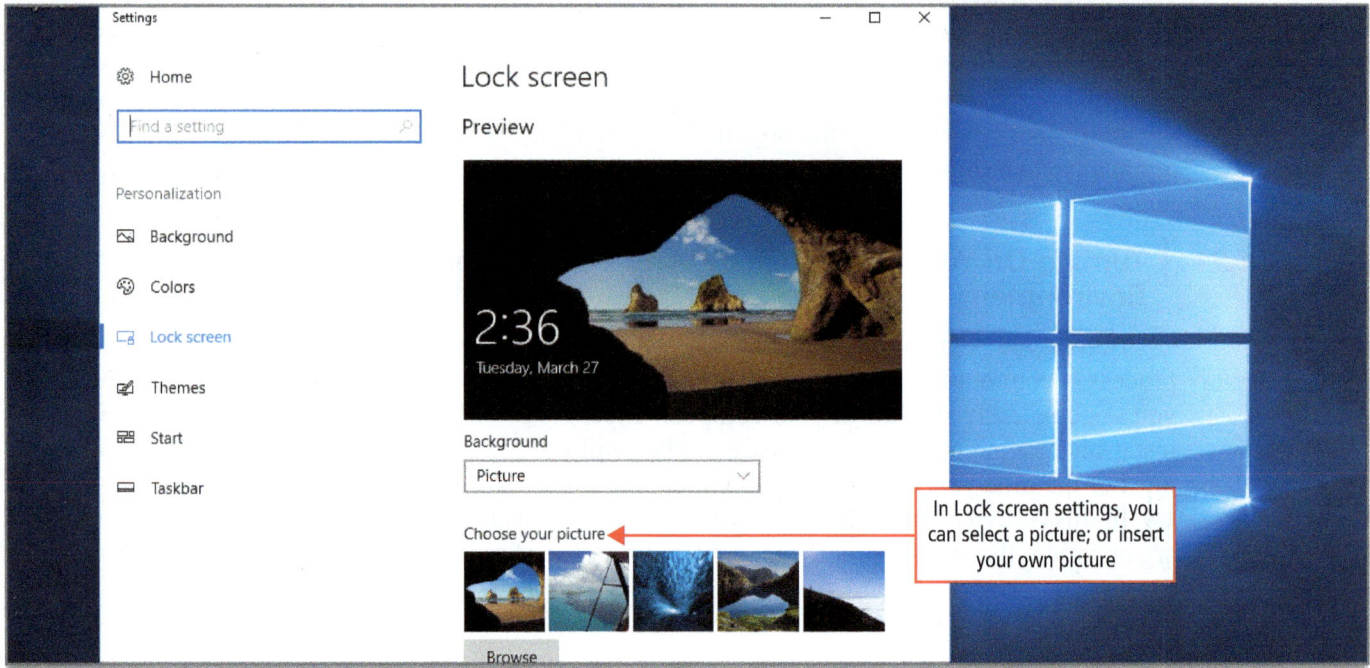

Figure 1.46

2 Determine whether you are working with a mouse and keyboard system or with a touchscreen system. If you are working with a touchscreen, determine whether you will use a stylus pen or the touch of your fingers.

NOTE   This Book Assumes You Are Using a Mouse and Keyboard, but You Can Also Use Touch

This instruction uses terminology that assumes you are using a mouse and keyboard, but you need only touch gestures (described at the beginning of Project 1A in this chapter) to move through the instruction easily using touch. If a touch gesture needs more clarification, a *By Touch* box will assist you in using the correct gesture. Because more precision is needed for desktop operations, touching with a stylus pen may be preferable to touch using your fingers. When working with Microsoft Store apps, finger gestures are usually precise enough.

3 Press [Enter] to display the Windows 10 sign-in screen. If you are already signed in, go to Step 5.

BY TOUCH   On the lock screen, swipe upward to display the sign-in screen. Tap your user image if necessary to display the Password box.

4 If you are the displayed user, type your password (if you have established one) and press [Enter]. If you are not the displayed user, click your user image if it displays or click the Switch user arrow [→] and then click your user image. Type your password.

The Windows 10 desktop displays with a default desktop background, a background you have selected, or perhaps a background set by your college or workplace.

5 ▶ In the lower left corner of your screen, move the mouse pointer over—*point to*—**Start** ⊞ and then *click*—press the left button on your mouse pointing device—to display the **Start menu**. Compare your screen with Figure 1.47, and then take a moment to study the table in Figure 1.48. If your list of programs does not display, in the upper left, click the ☰.

The *mouse pointer* is any symbol that displays on your screen in response to moving your mouse.

The Windows 10 *Start menu* displays a list of installed programs on the left and a customizable group of square and rectangular boxes—referred to as *tiles*—on the right. You can customize the arrangement of tiles from which you can access apps, websites, programs, folders, and tools for using your computer by simply clicking or tapping them.

Think of the right side of the Start menu as your connected *dashboard*—a one-screen view of links to information and programs that matter to *you*—through which you can connect with the people, activities, places, and apps that you care about.

Some tiles are referred to as *live tiles*, because they are constantly updated with fresh information relevant to you—the number of new email messages you have or new sports scores that you are interested in. Live tiles are at the center of your Windows 10 experience.

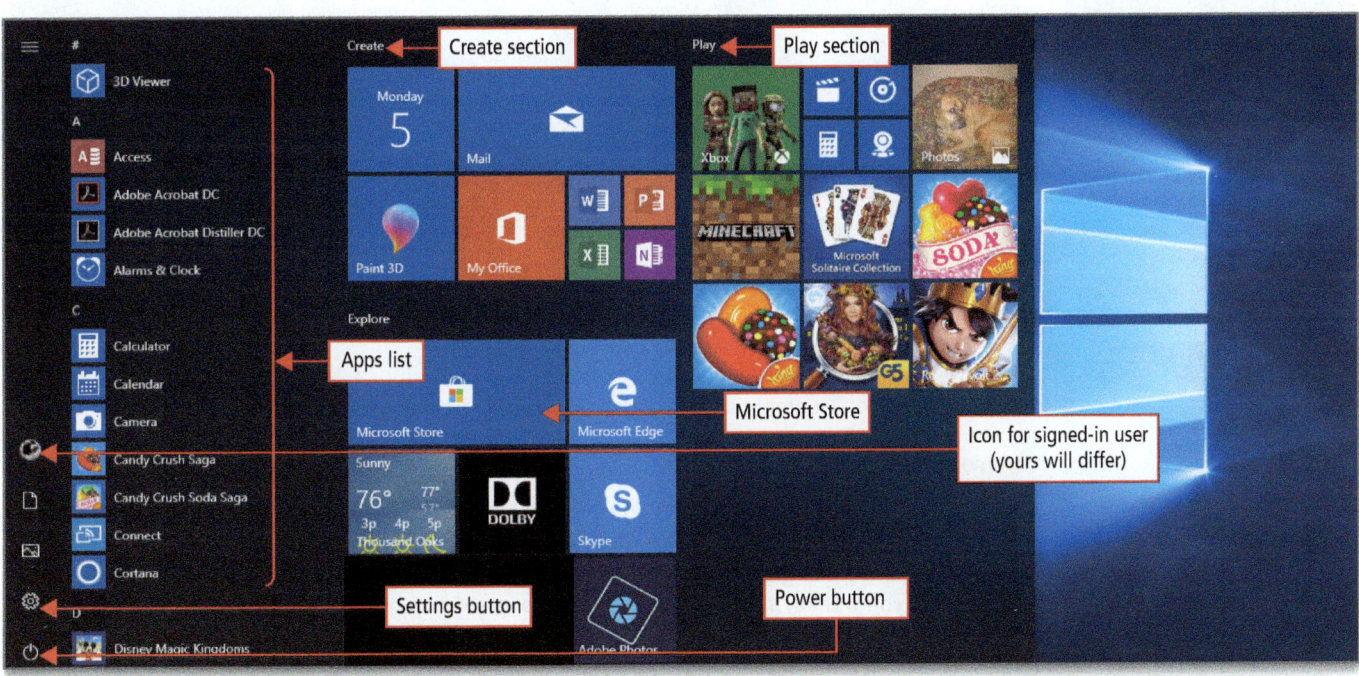

Figure 1.47

Parts of the Windows 10 Start Menu	
Create	Apps pinned to the Start menu that relate to your own information; for example, your Mail, your Calendar, and apps with which you create things; for example, your Office apps.
Apps list	Displays a list of the apps available on your system (yours will differ).
Play and Explore	Apps pinned to the Start menu that relate to games or news apps that you have installed; you can change this heading or delete it.
Power button	Enables you to set your computer to Sleep, Shut down, or Restart.
Settings	Displays the Settings menu to change any Windows 10 setting.
Signed-in User	Displays the icon for the signed-in user.

Figure 1.48

6 ▶ Click **Start** ⊞ again to close the Start menu. Compare your screen with Figure 1.49, and then take a moment to study the parts of the Windows desktop as shown in the table in Figure 1.50.

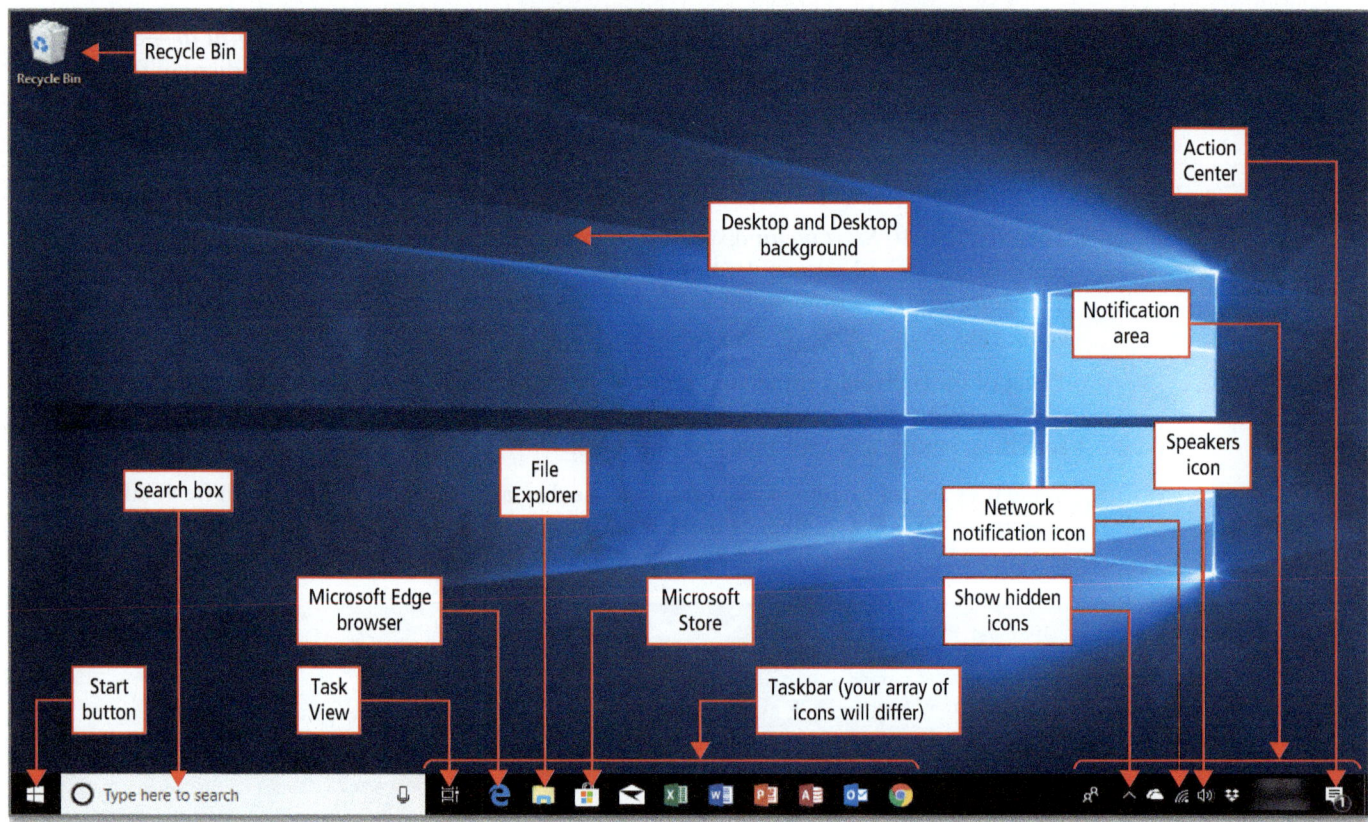

Figure 1.49

Parts of the Windows 10 Desktop	
Action Center	Displays the Action Center in a vertical pane on the right of your screen where you can see notifications—such as new mail or new alerts from social networks—at the top and access commonly used settings at the bottom.
Desktop	Serves as a surface for your work, like the top of an actual desk. Here you can arrange icons—small pictures that represent a file, folder, program, or other object.
Desktop background	Displays the colors and graphics of your desktop; you can change the desktop background to look the way you want it, such as using a picture or a solid color. Also referred to as *wallpaper*.
File Explorer	Launches the File Explorer program, which displays the contents of folders and files on your computer and on connected locations and also enables you to perform tasks related to your files and folders such as copying, moving, and renaming. If your File Explorer icon does not display, search for it, right-click its name in the search results, and then click Pin to taskbar.
Microsoft Edge browser	Launches Microsoft Edge, the web browser program developed by Microsoft that is included with Windows 10.
Microsoft Store	Opens the Microsoft Store where you can select and download Microsoft Store apps.
Network notification icon	Displays the status of your network.
Notification area	Displays notification icons and the system clock and calendar; sometimes referred to as the *system tray*.
Recycle Bin	Contains files and folders that you delete. When you delete a file or folder, it is not actually deleted; it stays in the Recycle Bin if you want it back, until you take an action to empty the Recycle Bin.
Search box	If *Cortana*—Microsoft's intelligent personal assistant—is enabled, a small circle will display on the left edge of the Search box. If Cortana is not enabled, a search icon displays at the left edge.

Parts of the Windows 10 Desktop	
Show hidden icons	Displays additional icons related to your notifications.
Speakers icon	Displays the status of your computer's speakers (if any).
Start button	Displays the Start menu.
Task View	Displays your desktop background with a small image of all open programs and apps. Click once to open, click again to close. May also display the Timeline.
Taskbar	Contains buttons to launch programs and buttons for all open programs; by default, it is located at the bottom of the desktop, but you can move it. You can customize the number and arrangement of buttons.

Figure 1.50

Activity 1.22 │ Pinning a Program to the Taskbar

Snipping Tool is a program within Windows 10 that captures an image of all or part of your computer's screen. A *snip*, as the captured image is called, can be annotated, saved, copied, or shared via email. Any capture of your screen is referred to as a *screenshot*, and there are many other ways to capture your screen in addition to the Snipping Tool.

> **NOTE** Snip & Sketch Offers Improved Snipping Capabilities
>
> Although Snipping Tool will be available for several more years, a newer tool for snipping, called Snip & Sketch, will roll out to Windows 10 users. Find it by typing Snip & Sketch in the search box.

1 In the lower left corner of your screen, click in the **Search box**.

Search relies on *Bing*, Microsoft's search engine, which enables you to conduct a search on your PC, your apps, and the web.

2 With your insertion point in the search box, type **snipping** Compare your screen with Figure 1.51.

> **BY TOUCH** On a touchscreen, tap in the Search box to display the onscreen keyboard, and then begin to type *snipping*.

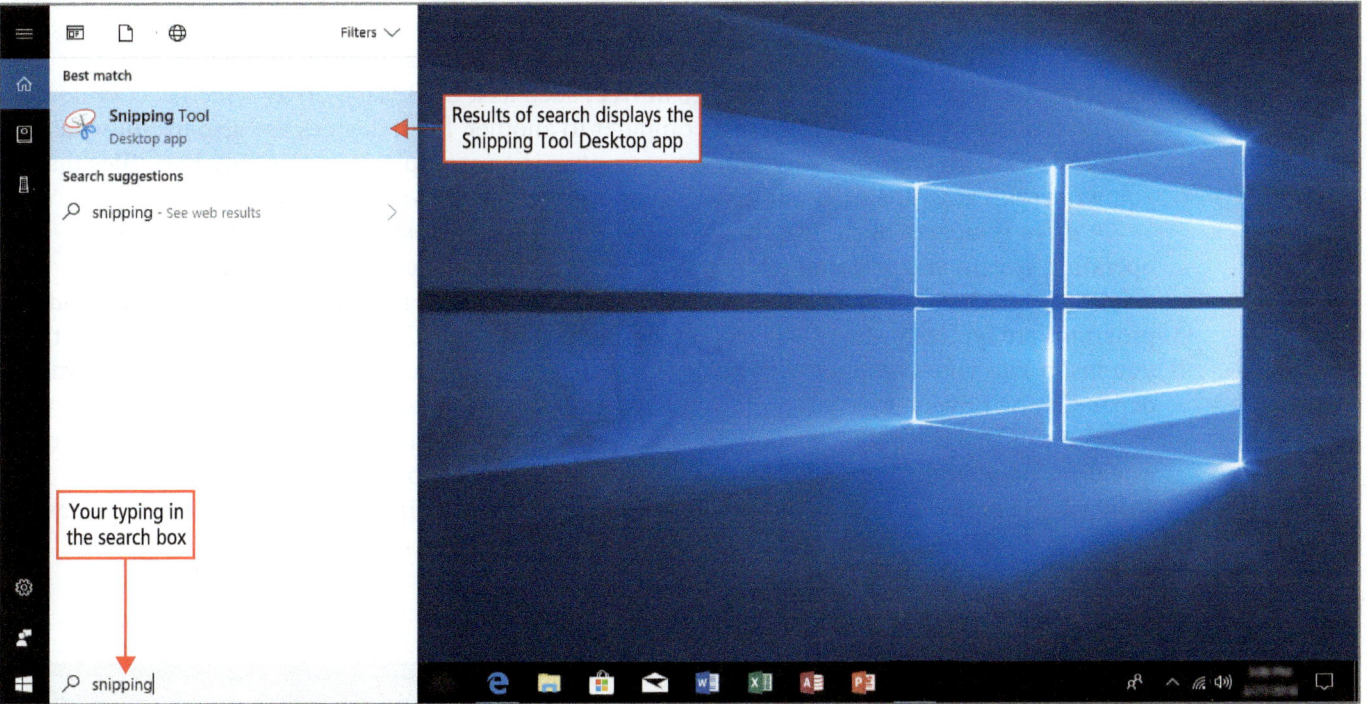

Figure 1.51

3 With the **Snipping Tool Desktop app** shaded and displayed at the top of the search results, press ⏎Enter one time.

> The Snipping Tool program's *dialog box*—a small window that displays options for completing a task—displays on the desktop, and on the taskbar, the Snipping Tool program button displays underlined and framed in a lighter shade to indicate that the program is open.

👉 **BY TOUCH**   In the search results, tap the Snipping Tool app.

4 On the taskbar, point to the **Snipping Tool** button 🖼 and then *right-click*—click the right mouse button one time. On the displayed **Jump List**, click **Pin to taskbar**.

> A *Jump List* displays destinations and tasks from a program's taskbar icon when you right-click the icon.

👉 **BY TOUCH**   On the taskbar, use the *Swipe to select* technique—swipe upward with a short quick movement—to display the Jump List. On the list, tap *Pin to taskbar*.

5 Point to the upper right corner of the **Snipping Tool** dialog box, and then click **Close** ☒.

> Because Snipping Tool is a useful tool, while completing the Projects in this textbook, it is recommended that you leave Snipping Tool pinned to your taskbar.

Objective 8 | Prepare to Work with Folders and Files

A *file* is a collection of information stored on a computer under a single name. Examples of a file include a Word document, an Excel workbook, a picture, a song, or a program. A *folder* is a container in which you store files. Windows 10 organizes and keeps track of your electronic files by letting you create and label electronic folders into which you can place your files.

Activity 1.23 | Creating a New Folder to Store a File

In this Activity, you will create a new folder and save it in a location of your choice. You might decide to use a *removable storage device*, such as a USB flash drive, which is commonly used to transfer information from one computer to another. Such devices are also useful when you want to work with your files on different computers. For example, you probably have files that you work with at your college, at home, and possibly at your workplace.

A *drive* is an area of storage that is formatted with a file system compatible with your operating system and is identified by a drive letter. For example, your computer's *hard disk drive*—the primary storage device located inside your computer where some of your files and programs are typically stored—is usually designated as drive *C*. Removable storage devices that you insert into your computer will be designated with a drive letter—the letter designation varies depending on how many input ports you have on your computer.

You can also use *cloud storage*—storage space on an internet service that can also display as a drive on your computer. When you create a Microsoft account, free cloud storage called *OneDrive* is provided to you. If you are signed in with your Microsoft account, you can access OneDrive from File Explorer.

Increasingly, the use of removable storage devices for file storage is becoming less common, because having your files stored in the cloud where you can retrieve them from any device is more convenient and efficient.

1 ▸ Be sure your Windows desktop is still displayed. If you want to do so, insert your USB flash drive. If necessary, close any messages.

Plugging in a device results in a chime sound—if sound is enabled. You might see a message in the taskbar or on the screen that the device software is being installed.

2 ▸ On your taskbar, check to see if the **File Explorer** icon 📁 displays. If it does, move to Step 3. If not, in the search box, type **file explorer** under **Best match**, point to **File Explorer Desktop app**, right-click, and then click **Pin to taskbar**.

In an enterprise environment such as a college or business, File Explorer may not be pinned to the taskbar by default, so you might have to pin it there each time you use the computer. Windows 10 Home, the version of Windows that comes on most consumer PCs, typically has File Explorer pinned to the taskbar by default.

3 ▸ On the taskbar, click **File Explorer** 📁. If necessary, in the upper right corner of the **File Explorer** window, click Expand the Ribbon ⌄.

File Explorer is the program that displays the contents of locations, folders, and files on your computer and also in your OneDrive and other cloud storage locations.

The *ribbon* is a user interface in Windows 10 that groups commands for performing related tasks on tabs across the upper portion of a window. Commands for common tasks include copying and moving, creating new folders, emailing and zipping items, and changing the view.

Use the *navigation pane*—the area on the left side of File Explorer window—to get to locations—your OneDrive, folders on your PC, devices and drives connected to your PC, and other PCs on your network.

4 On the ribbon at the top of the window, click the **View tab**, and then in the **Layout group**, click **Tiles**. Compare your screen with Figure 1.52, and then take a moment to study the parts of the File Explorer window as shown in the table in Figure 1.53.

NOTE   Does your ribbon show only the tab names? Does your Quick Access toolbar display below the ribbon?

By default, the ribbon is minimized and appears as a menu bar, displaying only the ribbon tabs. If your ribbon displays only tabs, click the Expand the Ribbon arrow ⌄ on the right side to display the full ribbon. If your Quick Access toolbar displays below the ribbon, point to it, right-click, and then click Show Quick Access Toolbar above the Ribbon.

The *File Explorer window* displays with the Quick access area selected by default. A File Explorer window displays the contents of the current location and contains helpful parts so you can *navigate*—explore within the file organizing structure of Windows. A *location* is any disk drive, folder, network, or cloud storage area in which you can store files and folders.

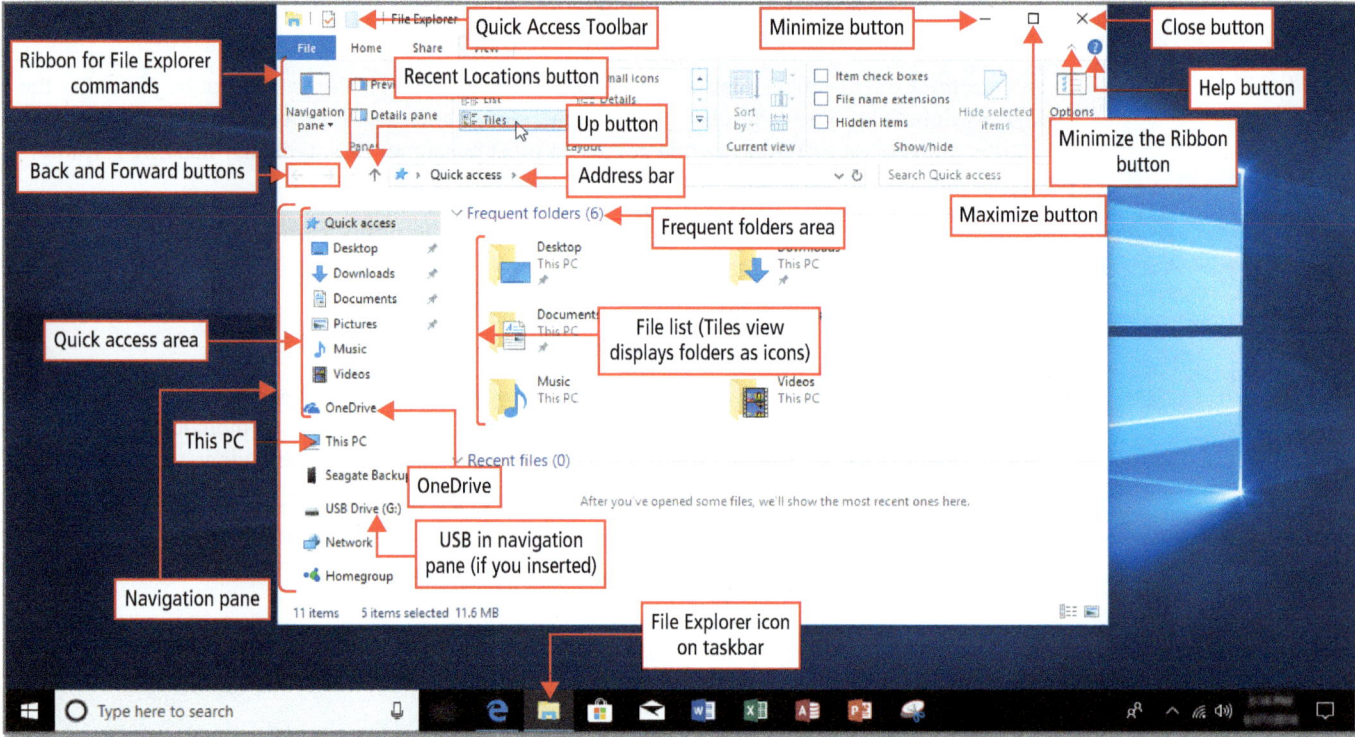

Figure 1.52

Parts of the File Explorer Window

Address bar	Displays your current location in the folder structure as a series of links separated by arrows.
Back and Forward buttons	Provides the ability to navigate to other folders you have already opened without closing the current folder window. These buttons work with the address bar; that is, after you use the address bar to change folders, you can use the Back button to return to the previous folder.
Close button	Closes the window.
File list	Displays the contents of the current folder or location; if you type text into the Search box, only the folders and files that match your search will display here—including files in subfolders.
Frequent folders area	When Quick access is selected in the navigation pane, displays the folders you use frequently.
Help button	Opens a Bing search for Windows 10 help.
Maximize button	Increases the size of a window to fill the entire screen.
Minimize button	Removes the window from the screen without closing it; minimized windows can be reopened by clicking the associated button in the taskbar.

Parts of the File Explorer Window

Minimize the Ribbon button	Collapses the ribbon so that only the tab names display.
Navigation pane	Displays—for the purpose of navigating to locations—the Quick access area, your OneDrive if you have one and are signed in, locations on the PC at which you are working, any connected storage devices, and network locations to which you might be connected.
OneDrive	Provides navigation to your free file storage and file sharing service provided by Microsoft that you get when you sign up for a Microsoft account; this is your personal cloud storage for files.
Quick access area	Displays commonly accessed locations—such as Documents and Desktop—that you want to access quickly.
Quick Access Toolbar	Displays commonly used commands; you can customize this toolbar by adding and deleting commands and by showing it below the ribbon instead of above the ribbon.
Recent Locations button	Displays the path to locations you have visited recently so that you can go back to a previously working directory quickly.
Ribbon for File Explorer commands	Groups common tasks such as copying and moving, creating new folders, emailing and zipping items, and changing views.
Search box	Locates files stored within the current folder when you type a search term.
This PC	Provides navigation to your internal storage and attached storage devices including optical media such as a DVD drive.
Up button	Opens the location where the folder you are viewing is saved—also referred to as the *parent folder*.

Figure 1.53

5 > In the **navigation pane**, click **This PC**. On the right, under **Devices and drives**, locate **Windows (C:)**—or **OS (C:)**—point to the device name to display the ⟨⟩ pointer, and then right-click to display a shortcut menu. Compare your screen with Figure 1.54.

A *shortcut menu* is a context-sensitive menu that displays commands and options relevant to the active object. The Windows logo on the C: drive indicates this is where the Windows 10 operating system is stored.

👉 **BY TOUCH**   Press and hold briefly to display a shaded square and then release.

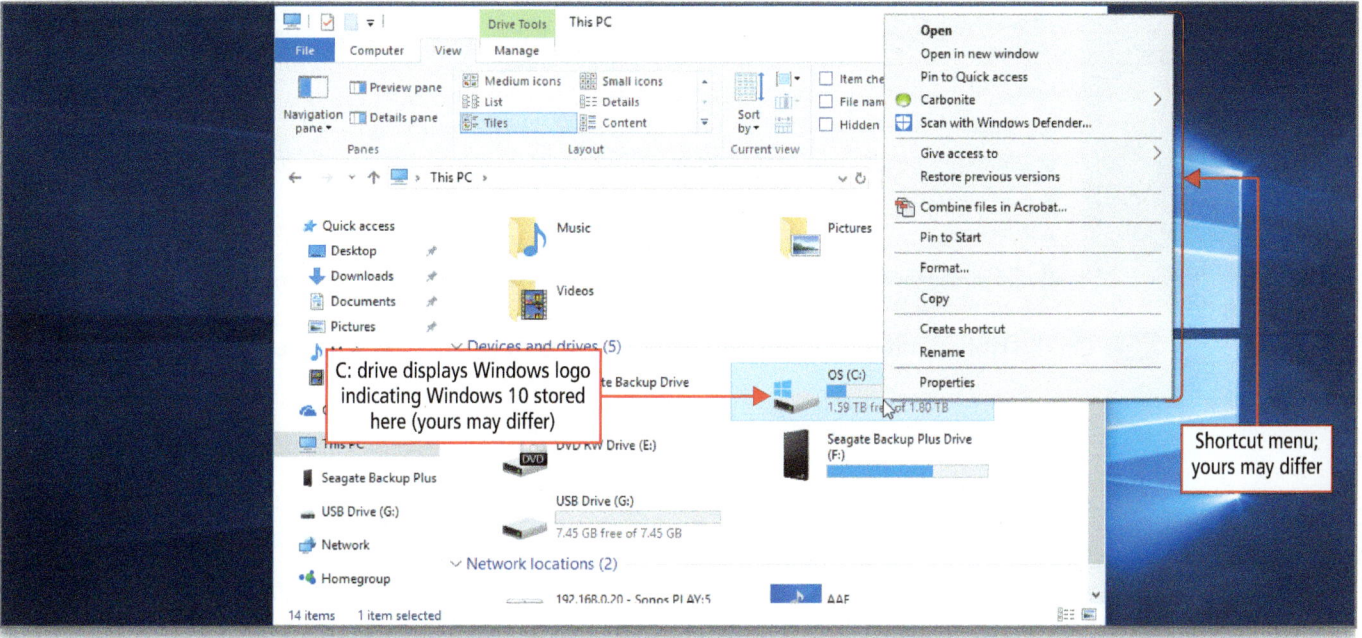

C: drive displays Windows logo indicating Windows 10 stored here (yours may differ)

Shortcut menu; yours may differ

Figure 1.54

6 ❯ On the shortcut menu, click **Open** to display the *file list* for this drive.

A file list displays the contents of the current location. This area is also referred to as the *content pane*. If you enter a search term in the search box, your results will also display here. Here, in the C: drive, Windows 10 stores various files related to your operating system.

ANOTHER WAY Point to the device name and double-click to display the file list for the device.

7 ❯ On the ribbon, notice that the **Drive Tools** tab displays above the **Manage tab**.

This is a *contextual tab*, which is a tab added to the ribbon automatically when a specific object is selected and that contains commands relevant to the selected object.

8 ❯ To the left of the **address bar**, click **Up** ⬆ to move up one level in the drive hierarchy and close the file list.

The *address bar* displays your current location in the folder structure as a series of links separated by arrows. Use the address bar to enter or select a location. You can click a part of the path to go to that level. Or, click at the end of the path to select the path for copying.

9 ❯ Under **Devices and drives**, click your **USB flash drive** to select it—or click the folder or location where you want to store your file for this project—and notice that the drive or folder is highlighted in blue, indicating it is selected. At the top of the window, on the ribbon, click the **Computer tab**, and then in the **Location group**, click **Open**. Compare your screen with Figure 1.55.

The file list for the selected location displays. There may be no files or only a few files in the location you have selected. You can open a location by double-clicking its name, using the shortcut menu, or by using this ribbon command.

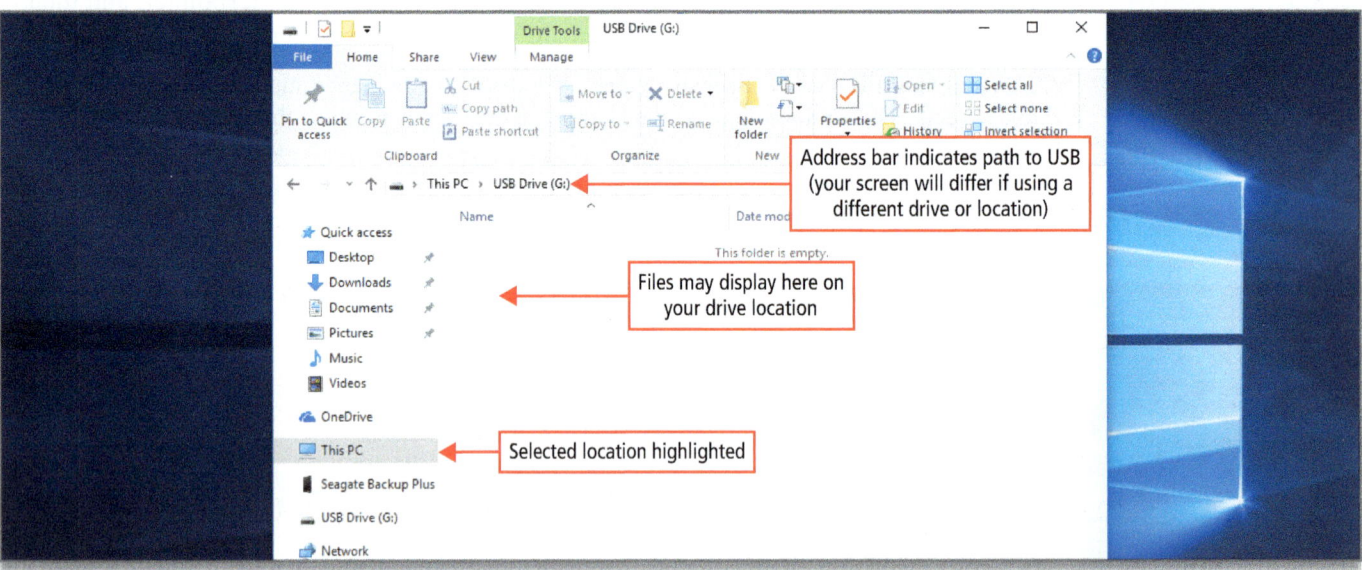

Figure 1.55

10 ❯ On the ribbon, on the **Home tab**, in the **New group**, click **New folder**.

11 With the text *New folder* highlighted, type **Windows 10 Chapter 1** and then press Enter to confirm the folder name and select—highlight—the new folder. With the folder selected, press Enter again to open the File Explorer window for your **Windows 10 Chapter 1** folder. Compare your screen with Figure 1.56.

> Windows creates a new folder in the location you selected. The address bar indicates the *path* from This PC to your folder. A path is a sequence of folders that leads to a specific file or folder.
>
> To *select* means to specify, by highlighting, a block of data or text on the screen with the intent of performing some action on the selection.

BY TOUCH You may have to tap the keyboard icon in the lower right corner of the taskbar to display the onscreen keyboard.

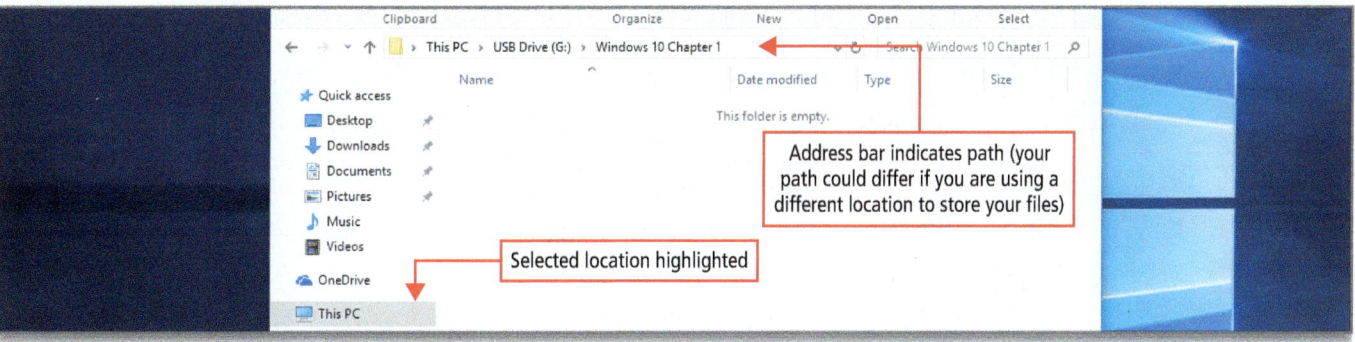

Figure 1.56

MORE KNOWLEDGE **Use OneDrive as Cloud Storage**

OneDrive is Microsoft's *cloud storage* product. Cloud storage means that your data is stored on a remote server that is maintained by a company so that you can access your files from anywhere and from any device. The idea of having all your data on a single device—your desktop or laptop PC—has become old fashioned. Because cloud storage from large companies like Microsoft are secure, many computer users now store their information on cloud services like OneDrive. Anyone with a Microsoft account has a large amount of free storage on OneDrive, and if you have an Office 365 account—free to most college students—you have 1 terabyte or more of OneDrive storage that you can use across all Microsoft products. That amount of storage is probably all you will ever need—even if you store lots of photos on your OneDrive. OneDrive is integrated into the Windows 10 operating system.

Activity 1.24 | Creating and Saving a File

1 In the upper right corner of your **Windows 10 Chapter 1** folder window, click **Close** ☒.

2 In the lower left corner, click **Start** ▦.

Project 1B: Hotel Files | **Office and Windows** 59

3 Point to the right side of the **apps list** to display a **scroll bar**, and then drag the **scroll box** down to view apps listed under **T**. Compare your screen with Figure 1.57.

To *drag* is to move something from one location on the screen to another while holding down the left mouse button; the action of dragging includes releasing the mouse button at the desired time or location.

A vertical *scroll bar* displays on the right side of the menu area. A scroll bar displays when the contents of a window or pane are not completely visible. A scroll bar can be vertical as shown or horizontal and displayed at the bottom of a window.

Within the scroll bar, you can move the *scroll box* to bring the contents of the window into view. The position of the scroll box within the scroll bar indicates your relative position within the window's contents. You can click the *scroll arrow* at either end of the scroll bar to move within the window in small increments.

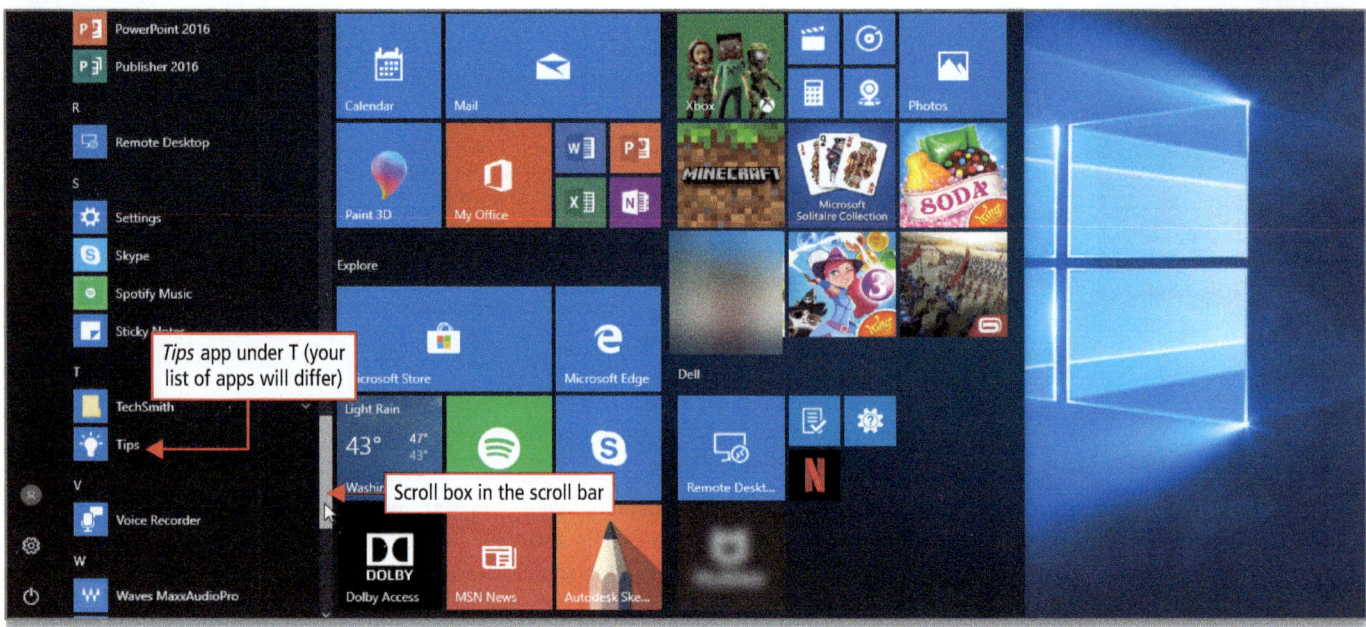

Figure 1.57

MORE KNOWLEDGE **Jump to a Lettered Section of the Apps List Quickly**

To move quickly to an alphabetic section of the apps list, click an alphabetic letter on the list to display an onscreen alphabet, and then click the letter of the alphabet to which you want to jump.

---

4 Click **Tips**. If necessary, in the upper right, click **Maximize** ☐ so that the **Tips** window fills your entire screen. Then, move your mouse pointer to the right edge of the screen to display the **scroll bar**. Compare your screen with Figure 1.58.

In any window, the *Maximize* button will maximize the size of the window to fill the entire screen.

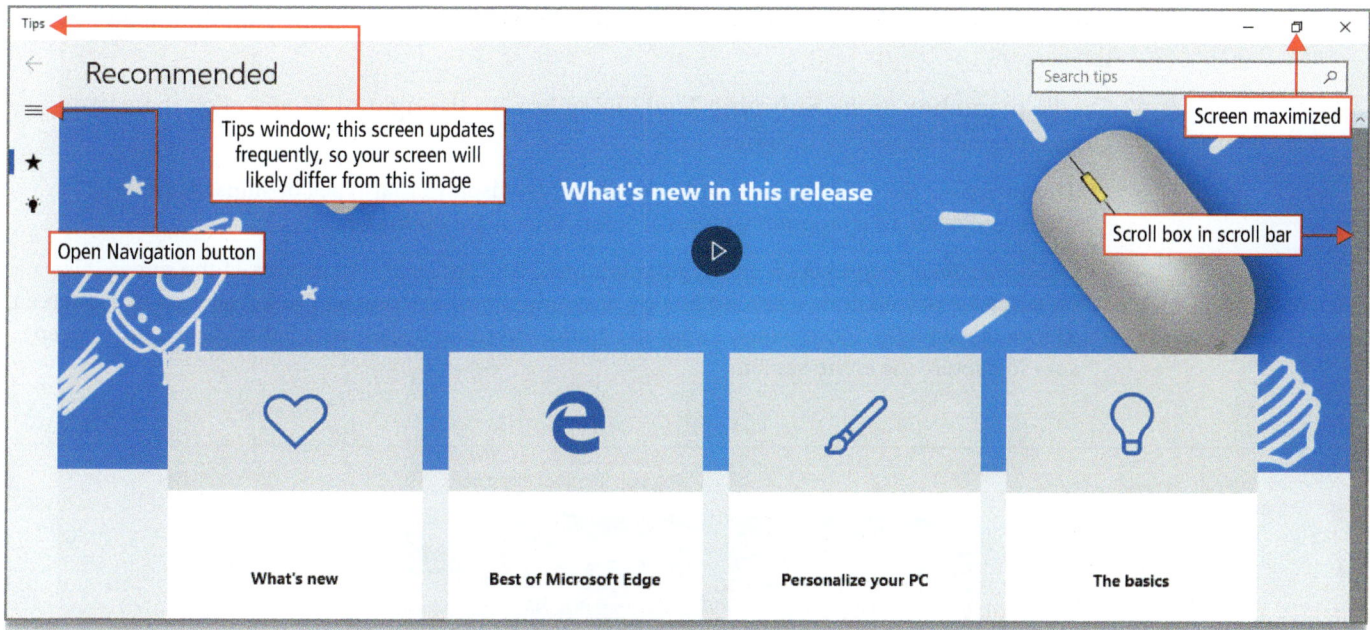

Figure 1.58

5 In the upper left corner, click **Open Navigation** ☰.

This icon is commonly referred to as a *menu icon* or a *hamburger menu* or simply a *hamburger*. The name derives from the three lines that bring to mind a hamburger on a bun. This type of button is commonly used in mobile applications because it is compact to use on smaller screens.

When you click the hamburger icon, a menu expands to identify the icons on the left—Recommended and Collections.

6 Click **Collections**, and then click **Windows**. Click **Get organized**. Move your mouse within the center right side of the screen to display a slideshow arrow ⟩, and then click the arrow until you get to the tip **Snap apps side by side**; if this tip is not available, pause at another interesting tip. Compare your screen with Figure 1.59.

To find interesting new things about Windows, Office, Microsoft Mixed Reality, and other topics, take time to explore the Tips app.

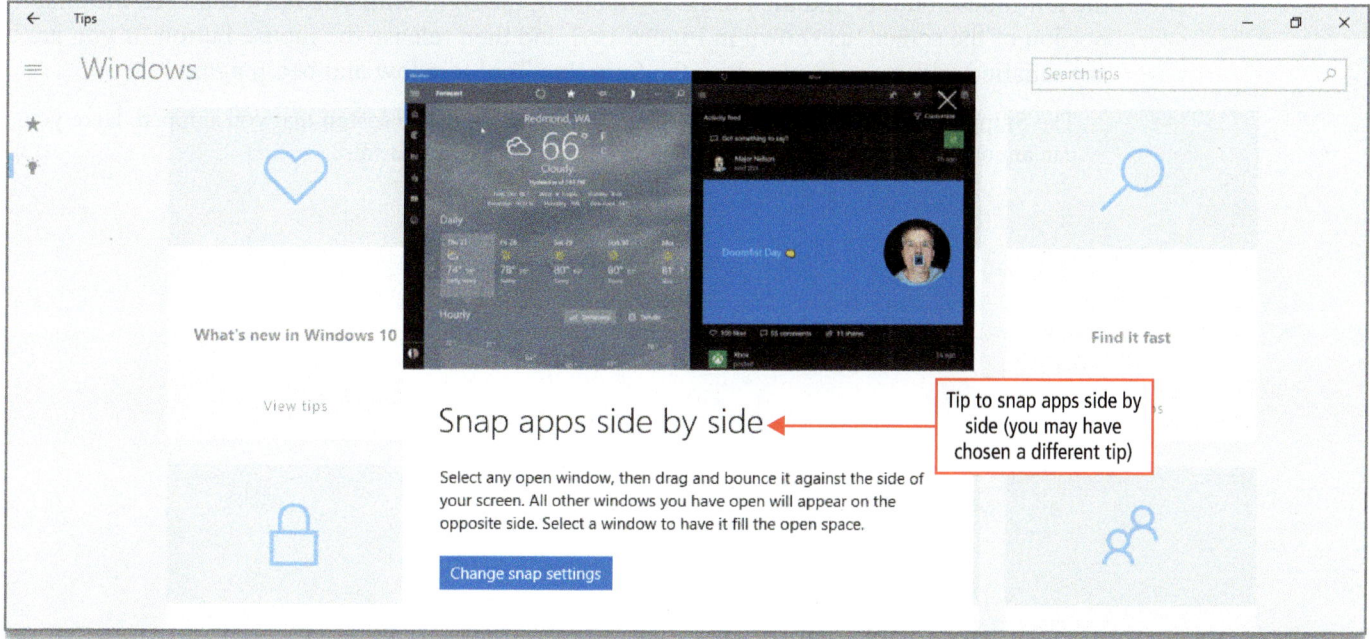

Figure 1.59

7 ▶ On the taskbar, click **Snipping Tool** 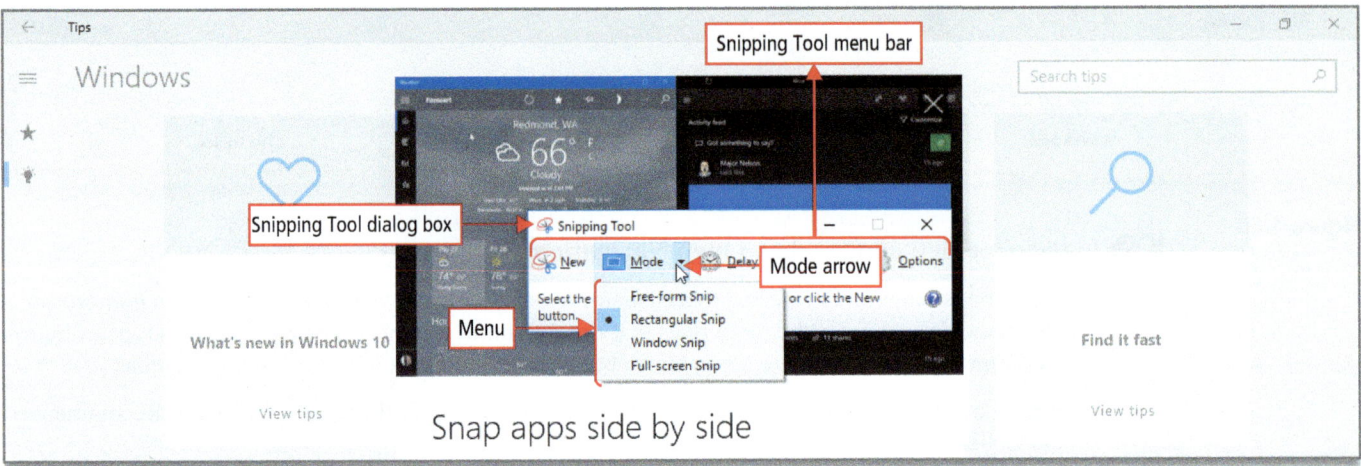 to display the small **Snipping Tool** dialog box over the screen.

8 ▶ On the **menu bar** of the **Snipping Tool** dialog box, to the right of *Mode*, click the **arrow**. Compare your screen with Figure 1.60.

This *menu*—a list of commands within a category—displays four types of snips. A group of menus at the top of a program window is referred to as the *menu bar*.

Use a *free-form snip* to draw an irregular line such as a circle around an area of the screen. Use a *rectangular snip* to draw a precise box by dragging the mouse pointer around an area of the screen to form a rectangle. Use a *window snip* to capture the entire displayed window. Use a *full-screen snip* to capture the entire screen.

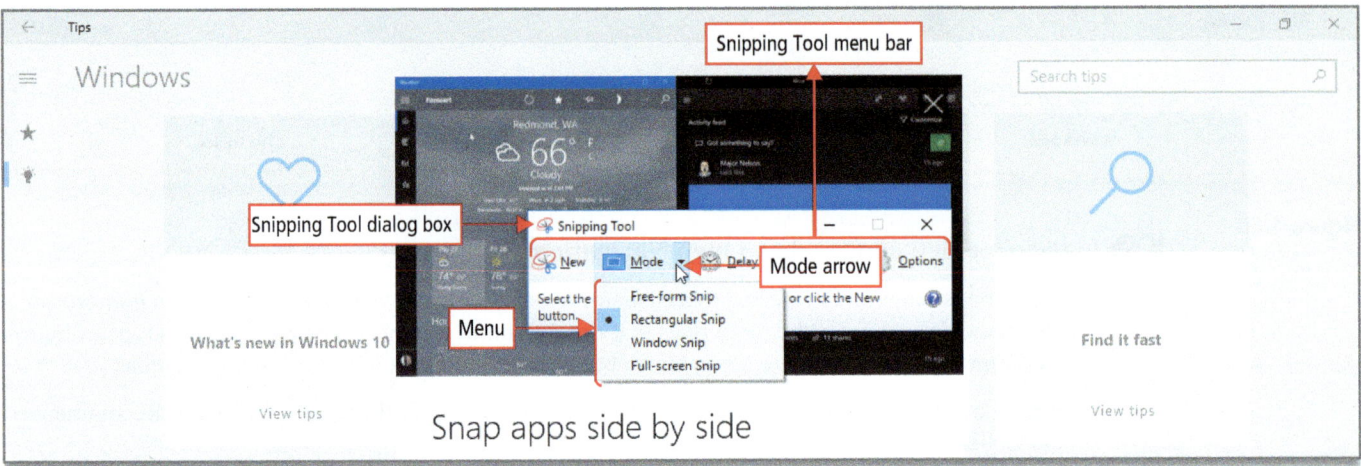

Figure 1.60

9 ▶ On the menu, click **Rectangular Snip**, and move your mouse slightly. Notice that the screen dims and your pointer takes the shape of a plus sign ⊞.

10 ▶ Move the ⊞ pointer to the upper left corner of the slide portion of the screen, hold down the left mouse button, and then drag down and to the right until you have captured the slide portion of the screen, as shown in Figure 1.61 and then release the mouse button. If you are not satisfied with your result, close the Snipping Tool window and begin again.

The Snipping Tool mark-up window displays the portion of the screen that you snipped. Here you can annotate—mark or make notes on—save, copy, or share the snip.

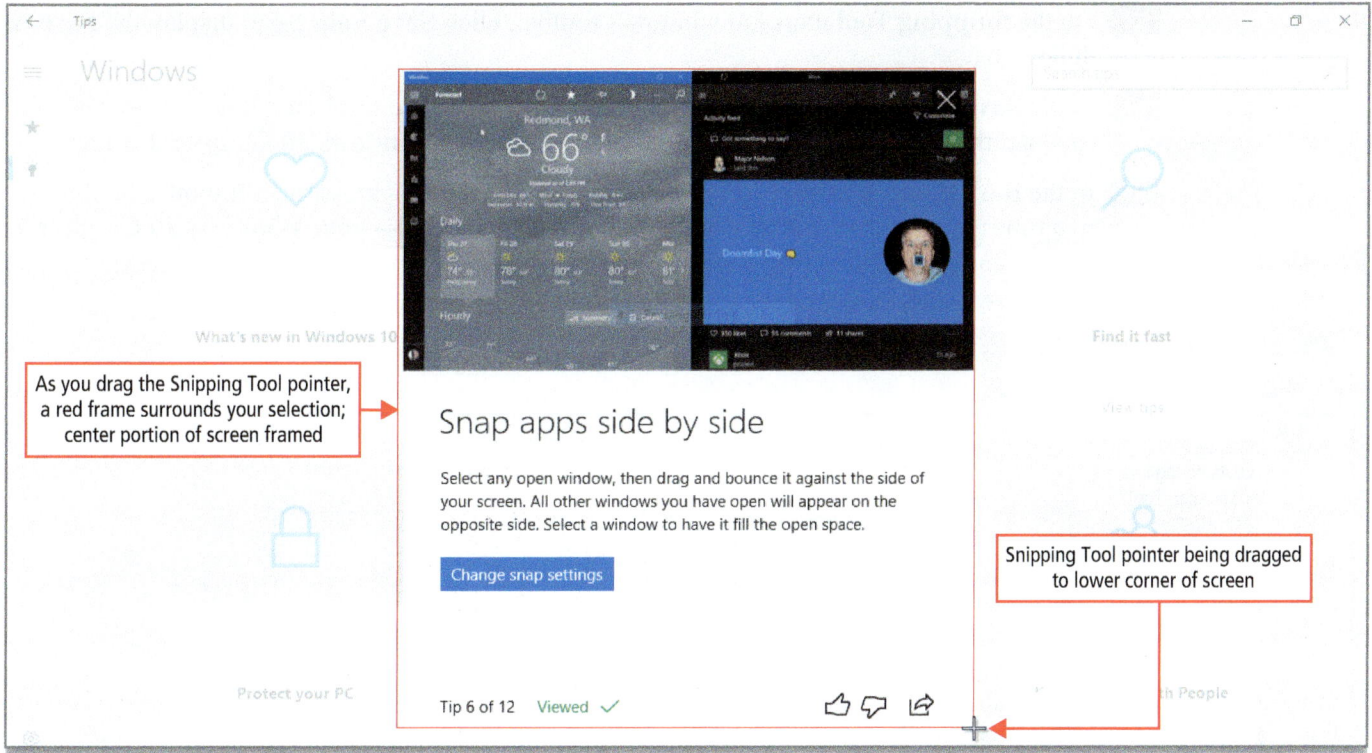

As you drag the Snipping Tool pointer, a red frame surrounds your selection; center portion of screen framed

Snipping Tool pointer being dragged to lower corner of screen

Figure 1.61

11 On the toolbar of the displayed **Snipping Tool** mark-up window, click the **Pen button arrow** 🖊, and then click **Red Pen**. Notice that your mouse pointer displays as a red dot.

12 On the snip—remember that you are now looking at a picture of the portion of the screen you captured—use the red mouse pointer to draw a circle around the text *Snap apps side by side*—or whatever the name of the tip you selected is. The circle need not be precise. If you are not satisfied with your circle, on the toolbar, click the Eraser button 🧹, point anywhere on the red circle, click to erase, and then begin again. Compare your screen with Figure 1.62.

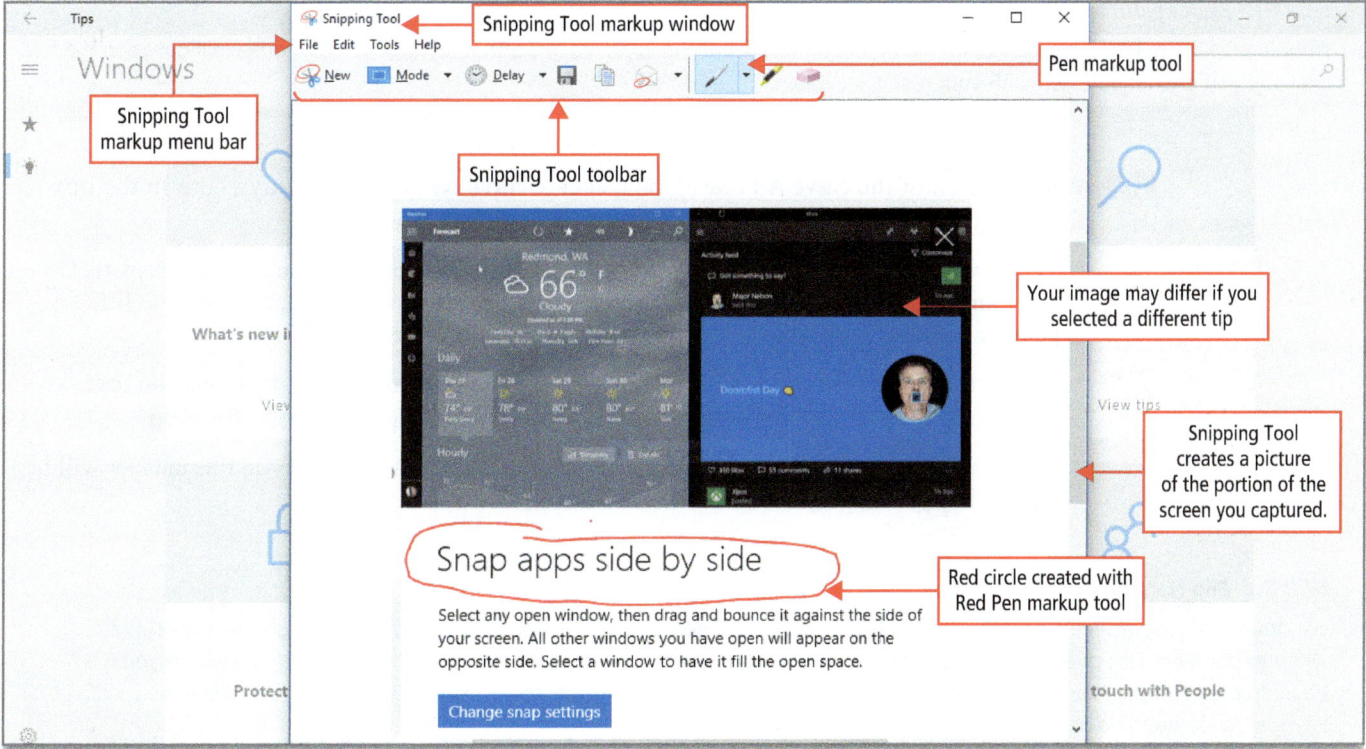

Snipping Tool markup window

Pen markup tool

Snipping Tool markup menu bar

Snipping Tool toolbar

Your image may differ if you selected a different tip

Snipping Tool creates a picture of the portion of the screen you captured.

Red circle created with Red Pen markup tool

Figure 1.62

13 On the **Snipping Tool** mark-up window's toolbar, click **Save Snip** to display the **Save As** dialog box.

14 In the **Save As** dialog box, in the **navigation pane**, drag the scroll box down as necessary to find and then click the location where you created your **Windows 10 Chapter 1** folder.

15 In the **file list**, scroll as necessary, locate and *double-click*—press the left mouse button two times in rapid succession while holding the mouse still—your **Windows 10 Chapter 1** folder. Compare your screen with Figure 1.63.

⟳ **ANOTHER WAY**   Right-click the folder name and click Open.

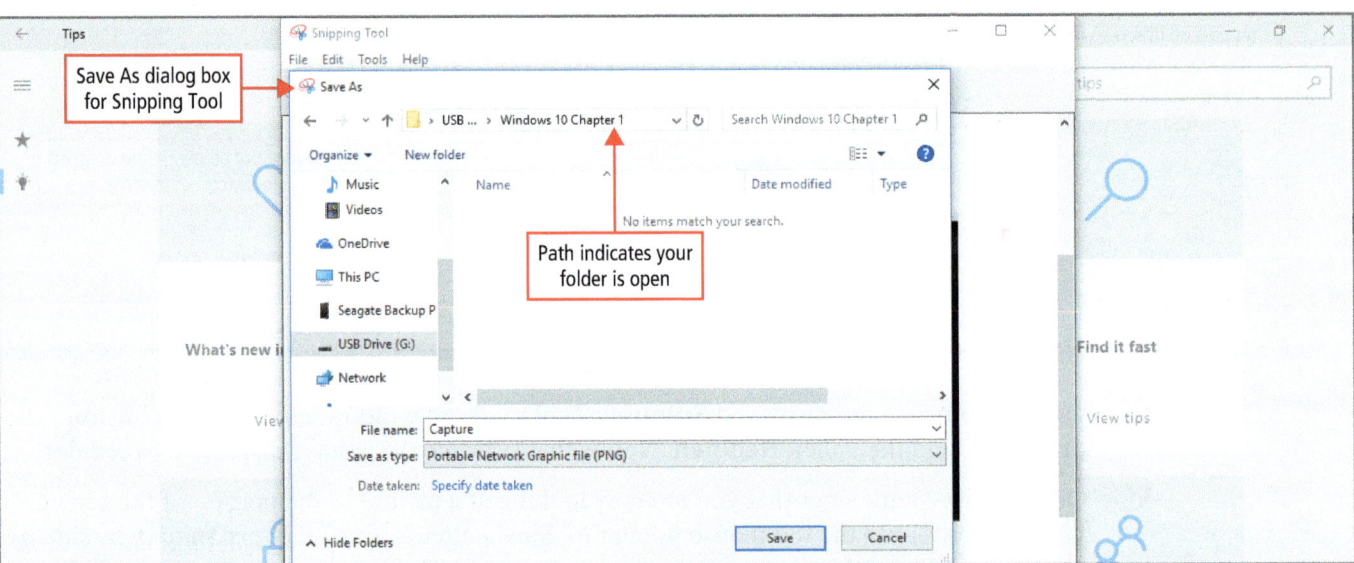

Figure 1.63

NOTE   Successful Double-Clicking Requires a Steady Hand

Double-clicking needs a steady hand. The speed of the two clicks is not as important as holding the mouse still between the two clicks. If you are not satisfied with your result, try again.

---

16 At the bottom of the **Save As** dialog box, locate **Save as type**, click anywhere in the box to display a list, and then on the displayed list click **JPEG file**.

> *JPEG*, which is commonly pronounced *JAY-peg* and stands for Joint Photographic Experts Group, is a common file type used by digital cameras and computers to store digital pictures. JPEG is popular because it can store a high-quality picture in a relatively small file.

17 At the bottom of the **Save As** dialog box, click in the **File name** box to select the text *Capture*, and then using your own name, type **Lastname_Firstname_1B_Tip_Snip**

> Within any Windows-based program, text highlighted in blue—selected—in this manner will be replaced by your typing.

NOTE   File Naming in This Textbook

Windows 10 recognizes file names with spaces. You can use spaces in file names, however, some programs, especially when transferring files over the internet, may insert the extra characters %20 in place of a space. In this instruction you will be instructed to save files using an underscore instead of a space. The underscore key is the shift of the ⎯ key—on most keyboards located two or three keys to the left of ⌫ Backspace .

---

18 In the lower right corner of the window, click **Save**.

19 **Close** ☒ the **Snipping Tool** mark-up window, and then **Close** ☒ the **Tips** window.

20 Close any open windows and display your Windows desktop.

> You have successfully created a folder and saved a file within that folder.

MORE KNOWLEDGE **The Hamburger**

For a brief history of the hamburger icon, visit http://blog.placeit.net/history-of-the-hamburger-icon

---

For Non-MyLab Submissions

Start PowerPoint and click Blank Presentation. Click the File tab, on the left click Save As, click Browse, and then navigate to your Windows 10 Chapter 1 folder. At the bottom of the Save As dialog box, in the File name box, using your own name, name the file **Lastname_Firstname_Windows_10_1B_Hotel_Files** and then click Save. Move to Activity 1.26.

Activity 1.25 | Downloading and Extracting Zipped Files

1 If the Microsoft PowerPoint application is not pinned to your taskbar, use the same technique you used to search for and pin the Snipping Tool application to search for and pin the PowerPoint application to your taskbar.

2 Sign in to your **MyLab IT** course. In your course, locate and click **Windows 10 1B Hotel Files**, click Download Materials, and then click Download All Files. Using the Chrome browser (if you are using a different browser see notes below), use the steps below to extract the zipped folder to your **Windows 10 Chapter 1** (or use your favorite method to download and extract files):

- In the lower left, next to the downloaded zipped folder, click the small **arrow**, and then click **Show in folder**. The zipped folder displays in *File Explorer*—the Windows program that displays the contents of locations, folders, and files on your computer—in the Downloads folder. (Unless you have changed default settings, downloaded files go to the Downloads folder on your computer.)
- With the zipped folder selected, on the ribbon, under **Compressed Folder Tools**, click the **Extract tab**, and then at the right end of the ribbon, click **Extract all**.
- In the displayed **Extract Compressed (Zipped) Folders** dialog box, click **Browse**. In the **Select a destination** dialog box, use the navigation pane on the left to navigate to your **Windows 10 Chapter 1 folder**, and double-click its name to open the folder and display its name in the **Address bar**.
- In the lower right, click **Select Folder**, and then in the lower right, click **Extract**; when complete, a new File Explorer window displays showing the extracted files in your chapter folder. For this Project, you will see a PowerPoint file with your name and another zipped folder named **win01_1B_Bell_Orchid**, which you will extract later, a result file to check against, and an Instruction file. Take a moment to open **Windows_10_1B_Hotel_Files_Instructions**; note any recent updates to the book.
- **Close** ☒ both File Explorer windows, close the Grader download screens, and close any open documents For this Project, you should close MyLab and any other open windows in your browser.

3 From the taskbar, click **File Explorer**, navigate to and reopen your **Windows 10 Chapter 1 folder**, and then double-click the PowerPoint file you downloaded from **MyLab IT** that displays your name—**Student_Windows_10_1B_Hotel_Files**. In your blank PowerPoint presentation, if necessary, at the top click **Enable Editing**.

Activity 1.26 | Locating and Inserting a Saved File Into a PowerPoint Presentation

1 Be sure your PowerPoint presentation with your name is displayed. Then, on the **Home tab,** in the **Slides group**, click **Layout**. In the displayed gallery, click **Title Only**. If necessary, on the right, close the Design Ideas pane. Click anywhere in the text *Click to add title*, and then type **Tip Snip**

2 Click anywhere in the empty space below the title you just typed. Click the **Insert tab**, and then in the **Images group**, click **Pictures**. In the **navigation pane**, click the location of your **Windows 10 Chapter 1** folder, open the folder, and then in the **Insert Picture** dialog box, click one time to select your **Lastname_Firstname_1B_Tip_Snip** file. In the lower right corner of the dialog box, click **Insert**. If necessary, close the Design Ideas pane on the right. If necessary, drag the image to the right so that your slide title *Tip Snip* displays.

3 On the Quick Access Toolbar, click **Save** 🖫, and then in the upper right corner of the PowerPoint window, click **Minimize** ⎯ so that PowerPoint remains open but not displayed on your screen; you will need your PowerPoint presentation as you progress through this project.

4 **Close** ☒ the File Explorer window and close any other open windows.

Activity 1.27 | Using Snap and Task View

Use *Snap* to arrange two or more open windows on your screen so that you can work with multiple screens at the same time.

Snap with the mouse by dragging the *title bar*—the bar across the top of the window that displays the program, file, or app name—of one app to the left until it snaps into place, and then dragging the title bar of another app to the right until it snaps into place.

Snap with the keyboard by selecting the window you want to snap, and then pressing ⊞ + ←. Then select another window and press ⊞ + →. This is an example of a *keyboard shortcut*—a combination of two or more keyboard keys used to perform a task that would otherwise require a mouse.

1 From your desktop, click **Start** ⊞. In the list of apps, click the letter **A** to display the alphabet, and then click **W**. Under **W**, click **Weather**. If necessary, personalize your weather content by typing your zip code into the Search box, selecting your location, and clicking Start.

2 By using the same technique to display the alphabet, click **C**, and then click **Calculator**. On the taskbar, notice that icons display to show that the Weather app and the Calculator app are open. Notice also that on the desktop, the most recently opened app displays on top and is also framed on the taskbar. Compare your screen with Figure 1.64.

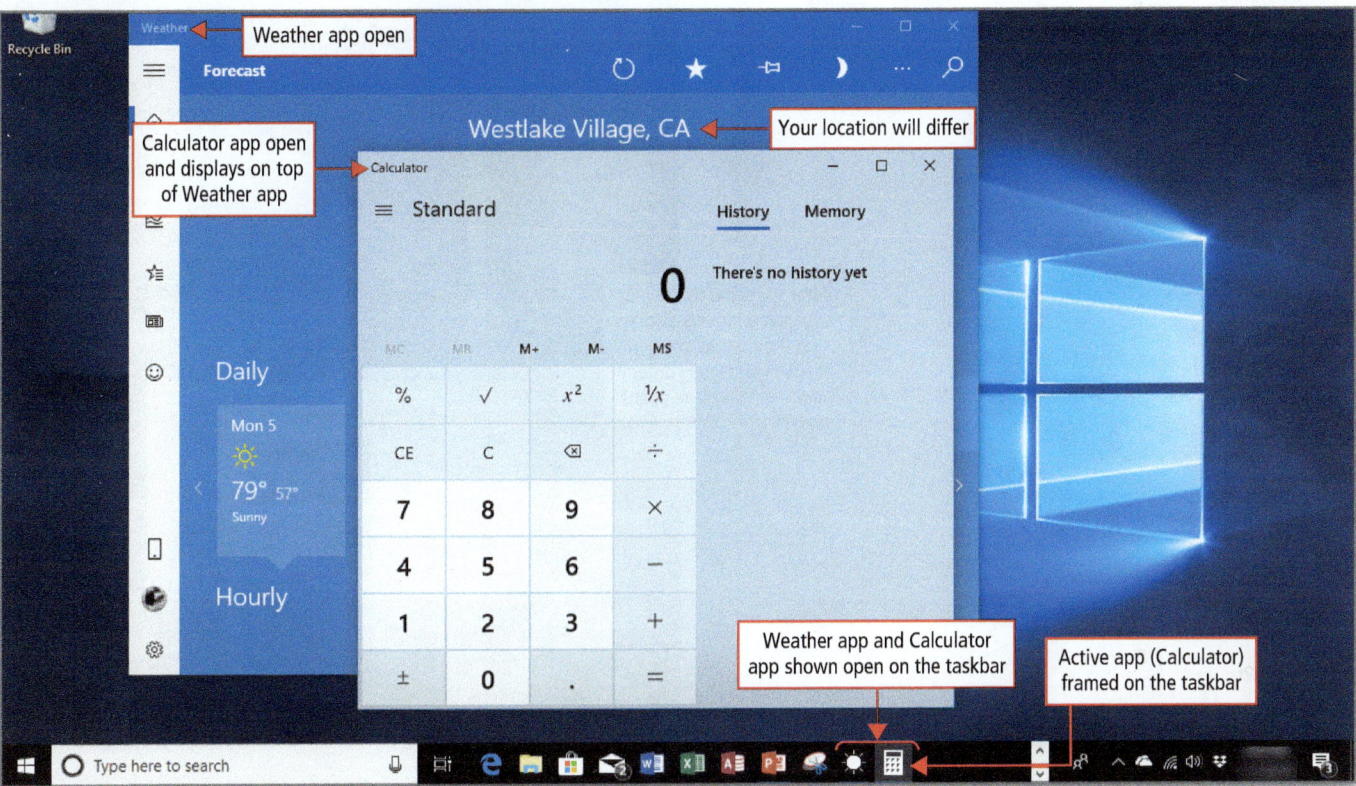

Figure 1.64

3 Point to the word *Calculator* at the top of this open app, hold down your left mouse button, drag your mouse pointer to the left edge of your screen until an outline displays to show where the window will snap, and then release the mouse button. Compare your screen with Figure 1.65.

On the right, all open windows display—your PowerPoint presentation and the Weather app. This feature is *Snap Assist*—after you have snapped a window, all other open windows display as *thumbnails* in the remaining space. A thumbnail is a reduced image of a graphic.

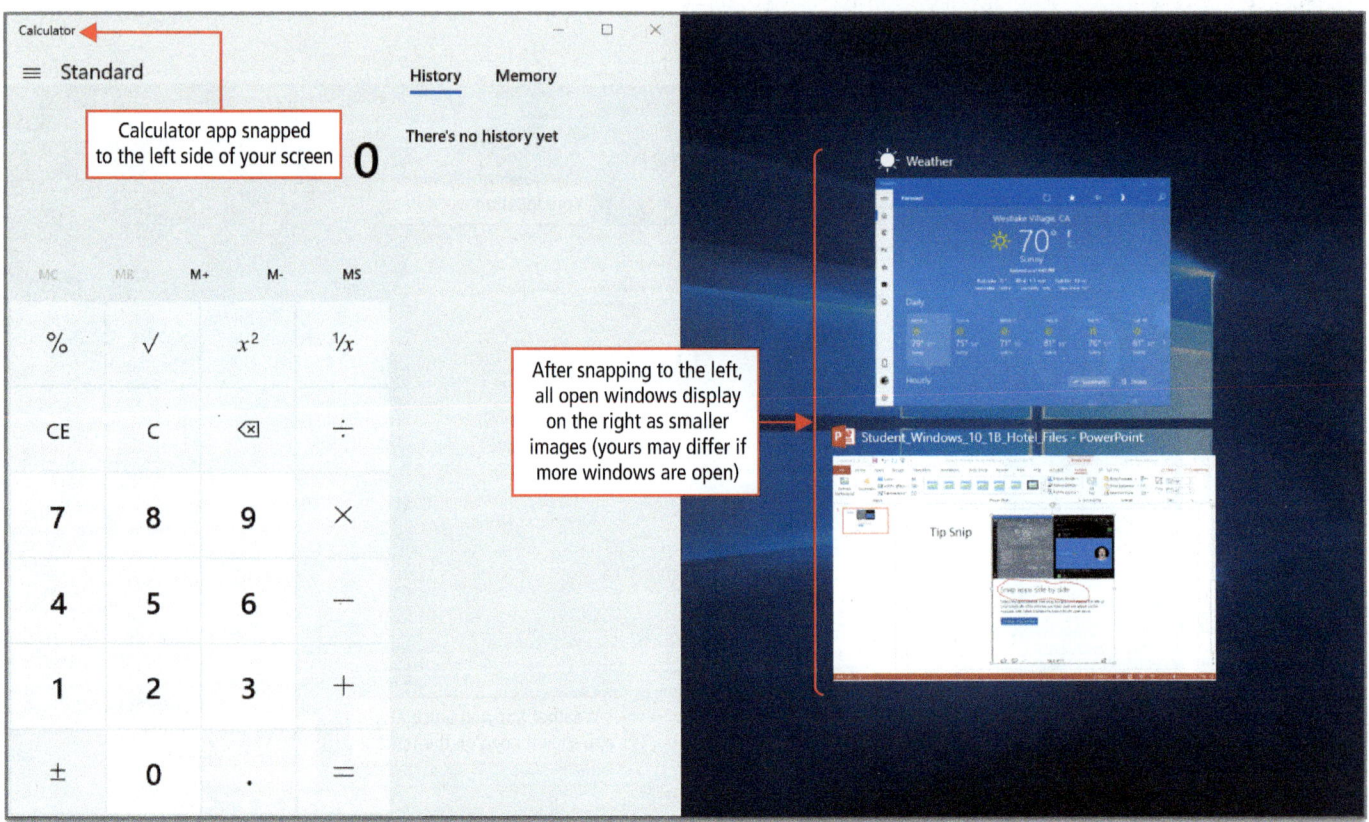

Figure 1.65

4 Click the **Weather** app to have it fill the right half of your screen.

5 In the lower left of your keyboard, press and hold down ▣ and then in upper right of your keyboard, locate and press and release PrintScrn. Notice that your screen dims momentarily.

This is another method to create a screenshot. This screenshot file is automatically stored in the Screenshots folder in the Pictures folder of your hard drive; it is also stored on the Clipboard if you want to copy it immediately.

A screenshot captured in this manner is saved as a *.png* file, which is commonly pronounced PING, and stands for Portable Network Graphic. This is an image file type that can be transferred over the internet.

6 On the taskbar, click **Task View** 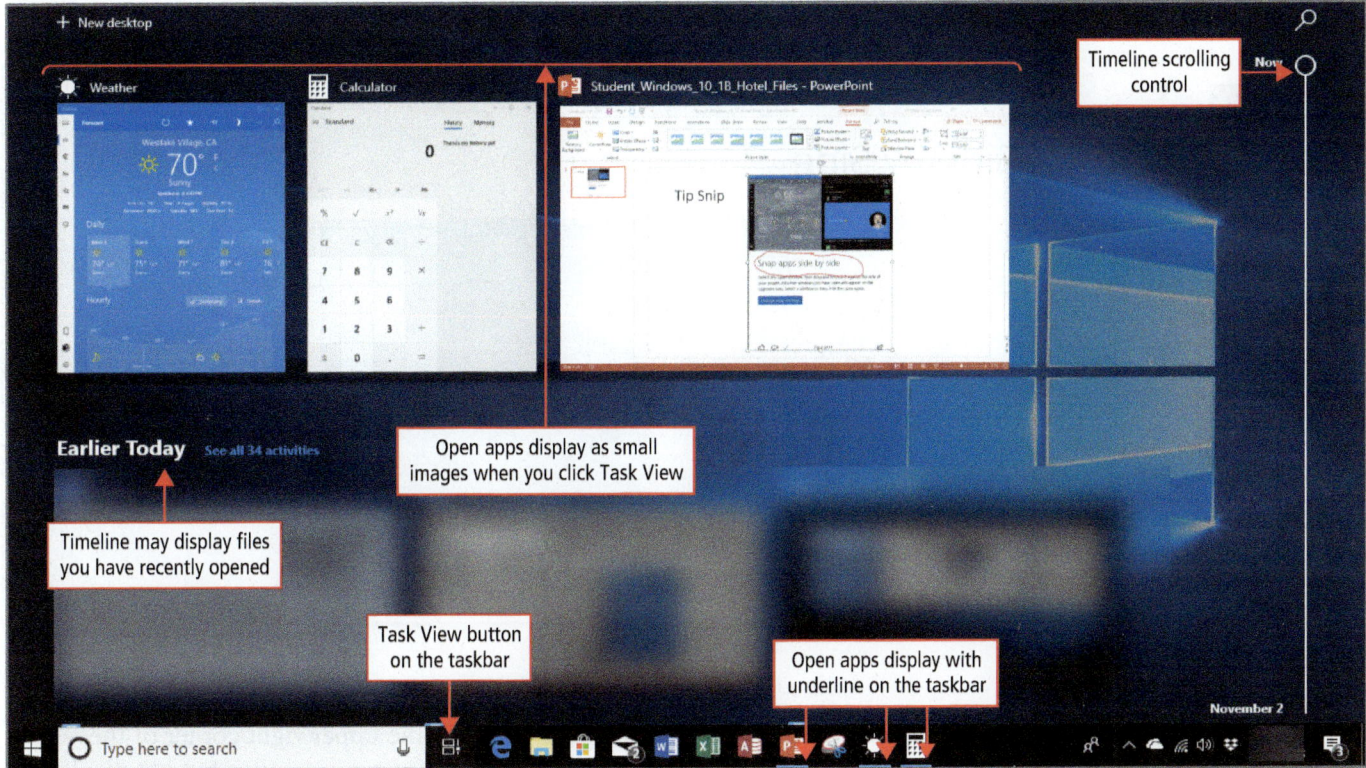, point to one of the open apps, and then compare your screen with Figure 1.66.

Use the *Task View* button on the taskbar to see and switch between open apps—including desktop apps. You may see the Windows 10 feature *Timeline*, with which, when you click the Task View button, you can see your activities and files you have recently worked on across your devices. For example, you can find a document, image, or video you worked on yesterday or a week ago.

Figure 1.66

7 From **Task View**, click your **PowerPoint** window. On the **Home tab**, in the **Slides group**, click the upper portion of the **New Slide** button to insert a new slide in the same layout as your previous slide.

An arrow attached to a button will display a menu when clicked. Such a button is referred to as a *split button*—clicking the main part of the button performs a command and clicking the arrow opens a menu with choices.

8 As the title type **Side by Side** and then click in the blank space below the title. On the ribbon, on the **Home tab**, in the **Clipboard group**, click the upper portion of the **Paste** button to paste your screenshot into the slide.

Recall that by creating a screenshot using the ⊞ + PrintScrn command, a copy was placed on the Clipboard. A permanent copy is also stored in the Screenshots folder of your Pictures folder. This is a convenient way to create a quick screenshot.

9 With the image selected, on the ribbon, under **Picture Tools**, click **Format**. In the **Size group**, click in the **Shape Height** box ⬚ 0.05" ⬍ , type 5 and press Enter. Drag the image down and into the center of the space so that your slide title is visible. Compare your screen with Figure 1.67.

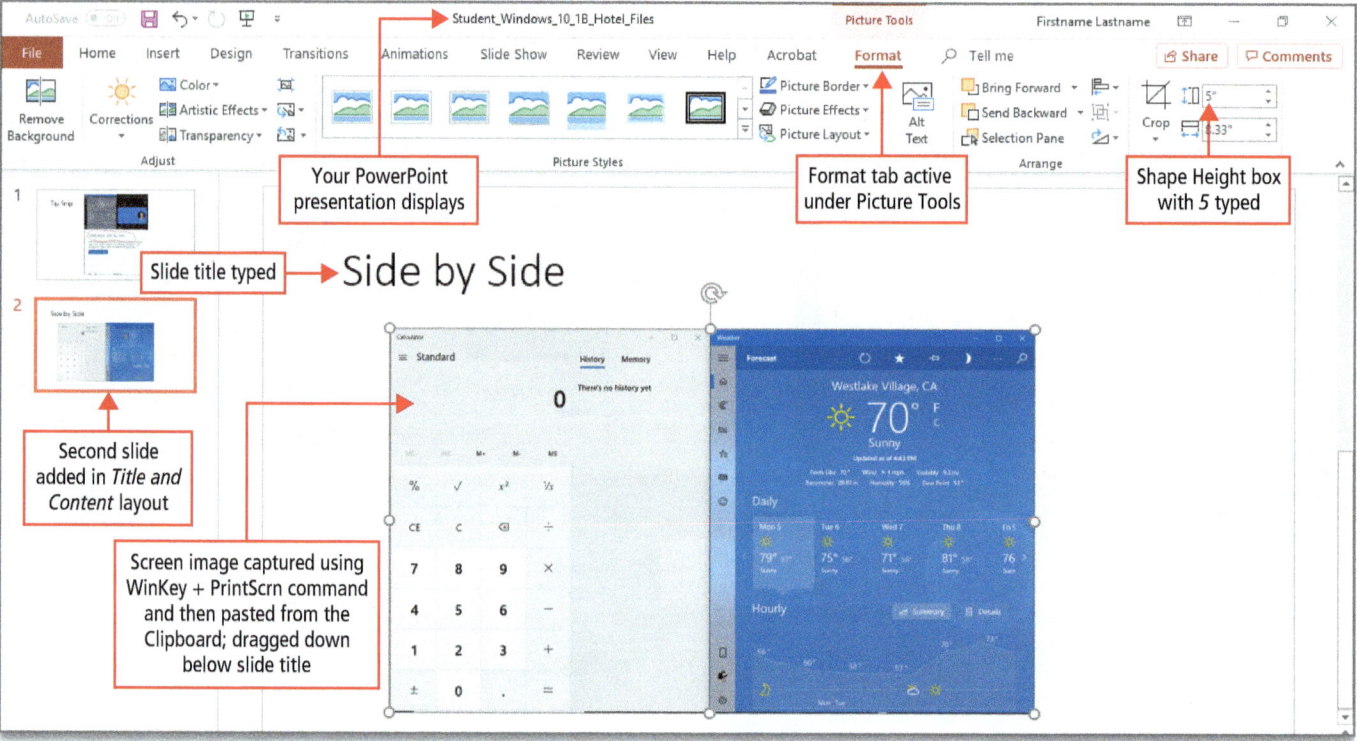

Figure 1.67

10 On the Quick Access Toolbar, click **Save** 🖫, and then in the upper right corner of the PowerPoint window, click **Minimize** ⬚ so that PowerPoint remains open but not displayed on your screen.

11 **Close** ☒ the **Calculator** app and the **Weather** app to display your desktop.

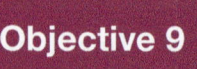 | Use File Explorer to Extract Zipped Files and to Display Locations, Folders, and Files

A file is the fundamental unit of storage that enables Windows 10 to distinguish one set of information from another. A folder is the basic organizing tool for files. In a folder, you can store files that are related to one another. You can also place a folder inside of another folder, which is then referred to as a *subfolder*.

Windows 10 arranges folders in a structure that resembles a *hierarchy*—an arrangement where items are ranked and where each level is lower in rank than the item above it. The hierarchy of folders is referred to as the *folder structure*. A sequence of folders in the folder structure that leads to a specific file or folder is a *path*.

Activity 1.28 | Navigating with File Explorer

Recall that File Explorer is the program that displays the contents of locations, folders, and files on your computer and also in your OneDrive and other cloud storage locations. File Explorer also enables you to perform tasks related to your files and folders such as copying, moving, and renaming. When you open a folder or location, a window displays to show its contents. The design of the window helps you navigate—explore within the file structure so you can find your files and folders—and so that you can save and find your files and folders efficiently.

In this Activity, you will open a folder and examine the parts of its window.

1 With your desktop displayed, on the taskbar, *point to* but do not click **File Explorer** , and notice the ScreenTip *File Explorer*.

> A **ScreenTip** displays useful information when you perform various mouse actions, such as pointing to screen elements.

2 Click **File Explorer** to display the **File Explorer** window.

> File Explorer is at work anytime you are viewing the contents of a location or the contents of a folder stored in a specific location. By default, the File Explorer button on the taskbar opens with the **Quick access** location—a list of files you have been working on and folders you use often—selected in the navigation pane and in the address bar.

> The default list will likely display the Desktop, Downloads, Documents, and Pictures folders, and then folders you worked on recently or work on frequently will be added automatically, although you can change this behavior.

> The benefit of the Quick access list is that you can customize a list of folders that you go to often. To add a folder to the list quickly, you can right-click a folder in the file list and click Pin to Quick Access.

> For example, if you are working on a project, you can pin it—or simply drag it—to the Quick access list. When you are done with the project and not using the folder so often, you can remove it from the list. Removing it from the list does not delete the folder, it simply removes it from the Quick access list.

3 On the left, in the **navigation pane**, scroll down if necessary, and then click **This PC** to display folders, devices, and drives in the **file list** on the right. Compare your screen with Figure 1.68.

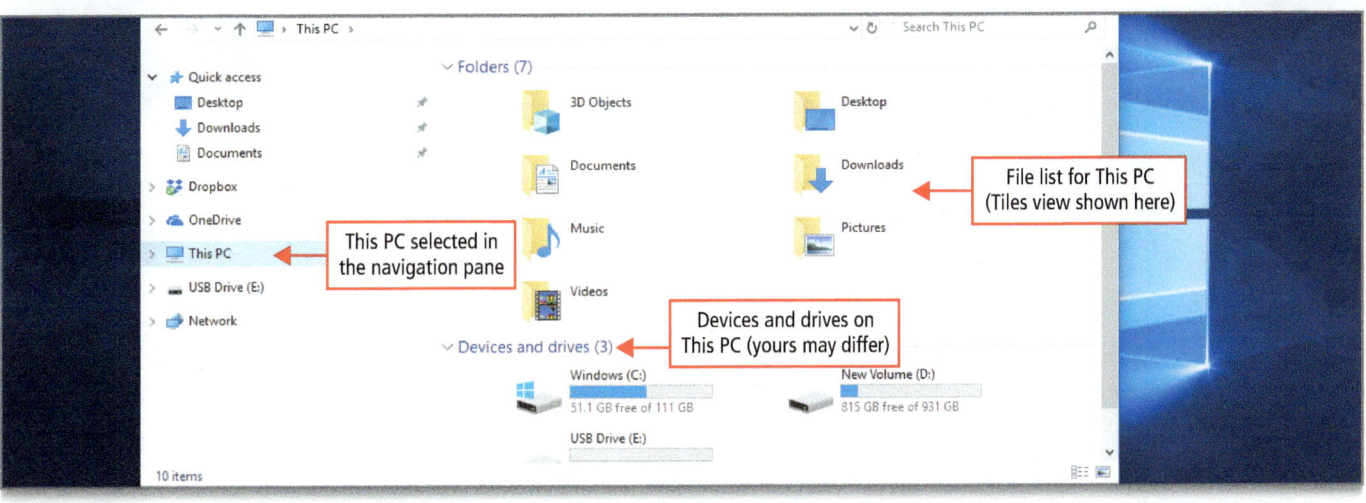

Figure 1.68

4 If necessary, in the upper right corner, click Expand the Ribbon ⊡. In the **file list**, under **Folders**—click **Documents** one time to select it, and then on the ribbon, on the **Computer tab**, in the **Location group**, click **Open**.

5 On the ribbon, click the **View tab**. In the **Show/Hide group**, be sure that **Item check boxes** is selected—select it if necessary, and then in the **Layout group**, if necessary, click **Details**.

The window for the Documents folder displays. You may or may not have files and folders already stored here. Because this window typically displays the file list for a folder, it is also referred to as the *folder window*. Item check boxes make it easier to select items in a file list and also to see which items are selected in a file list.

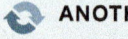 **ANOTHER WAY**   Point to Documents, right-click to display a shortcut menu, and then click Open; or, point to Documents and double-click.

6 Compare your screen with Figure 1.69, and then take a moment to study the parts of the window as described in the table in Figure 1.70.

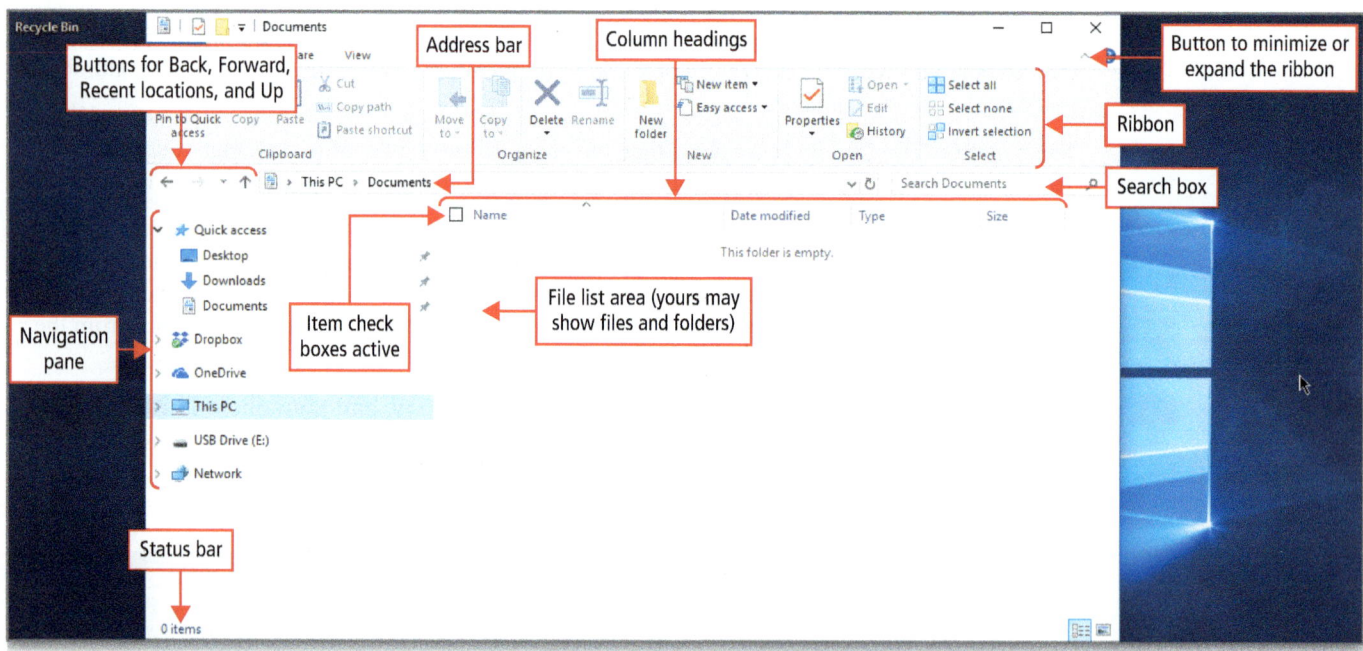

Figure 1.69

Parts of the File Explorer Window	
Window Part	**Function**
Address bar	Displays your current location in the file structure as a series of links separated by arrows. Tap or click a part of the path to go to that level or tap or click at the end to select the path for copying.
Back, Forward, Recent locations, and Up buttons	Enable you to navigate to other folders you have already opened without closing the current window. These buttons work with the address bar; that is, after you use the address bar to change folders, you can use the Back button to return to the previous folder. Use the Up button to open the location where the folder you are viewing is saved—also referred to as the *parent folder*.
Column headings	Identify the columns in Details view. By clicking the column heading name, you can change how the files in the file list are organized; by clicking the arrow on the right, you can select various sort arrangements in the file list. By right-clicking a column heading, you can select other columns to add to the file list.
File list	Displays the contents of the current folder or location. If you type text into the Search box, a search is conducted on the folder or location only, and only the folders and files that match your search will display here—including files in subfolders.
Minimize the Ribbon or Expand the Ribbon button	Changes the display of the ribbon. When minimized, the ribbon shows only the tab names and not the full ribbon.
Navigation pane	Displays locations to which you can navigate; for example, your OneDrive, folders on This PC, devices and drives connected to your PC, folders listed under Quick access, and possibly other PCs on your network. Use Quick access to open your most commonly used folders and searches. If you have a folder that you use frequently, you can drag it to the Quick access area so that it is always available.
Ribbon	Groups common tasks such as copying and moving, creating new folders, emailing and zipping items, and changing views of the items in the file list.
Search box	Enables you to type a word or phrase and then searches for a file or subfolder stored in the current folder that contains matching text. The search begins as soon as you begin typing; for example, if you type *G*, all the file and folder names that start with the letter *G* display in the file list.
Status bar	Displays the total number of items in a location, or the number of selected items and their total size.

Figure 1.70

7 ▶ Move your pointer anywhere into the **navigation pane**, and notice that a downward pointing arrow ˅ displays to the left of *Quick access* to indicate that this item is expanded, and a right-pointing arrow > displays to the left of items that are collapsed.

You can click these arrows to collapse and expand areas in the navigation pane.

Activity 1.29 | Using File Explorer to Extract Zipped Files

> **For Non-MyLab Users**
> From your instructor or from www.pearsonhighered.com/go download the zipped folder **win01_1B_Bell_Orchid** to your **Windows 10 Chapter 1** folder.

1 ▶ In the **navigation pane**, if necessary expand **This PC**, scroll down if necessary, and then click your **USB flash drive** (or the location where you have stored your chapter folder) one time to display its contents in the **file list**. Double-click to open your **Windows 10 Chapter 1 folder** and locate the zipped folder **win01_1B_Bell_Orchid**.

2 ▶ Use the steps below to extract this zipped folder to your **Windows 10 Chapter 1 folder** as follows (or use your favorite method to unzip):

- On the **Home tab**, click **New folder**, and then name the folder **win01_1B_Bell_Orchid**
- Click the zipped folder **win01_1B_Bell_Orchid** one time to select it.

- With the zipped folder selected, on the ribbon, under **Compressed Folder Tools**, click the **Extract tab**, and then at the right end of the ribbon, click **Extract all**.
- In the displayed **Extract Compressed (Zipped) Folders** dialog box, click **Browse**. In the **Select a destination** dialog box, use the navigation pane on the left to navigate to your **Windows 10 Chapter 1 folder**, and then double-click the name of the new folder you just created to open the folder and display its name in the **Address bar**.
- In the lower right, click **Select Folder**, and then in the lower right, click **Extract**. When complete, click the Up button ⬆ one time. You will see the extracted folder and the zipped folder.
- To delete the unneeded zipped version, click it one time to select it, and then on the **Home tab**, in the **Organize group**, click **Delete**. If necessary, click Yes. Now that the files are extracted, you do not need the zipped copy.

3 ▶ **Close** ☒ all File Explorer windows to display your desktop.

Activity 1.30 | Using File Explorer to Display Locations, Folders, and Files

1 ▶ From the taskbar, open **File Explorer** 📁. In the **navigation pane**, if necessary expand **This PC**, scroll down if necessary, and then click your **USB flash drive** (or the location where you have stored your chapter folder) one time to display its contents in the **file list**. In the **file list**, double-click your **Windows 10 Chapter 1 folder** to display its contents. Compare your screen with Figure 1.71.

In the navigation pane, *This PC* displays all of the drive letter locations attached to your computer, including the internal hard drives, CD or DVD drives, and any connected devices such as a USB flash drive.

Your PowerPoint file, your *Tip_Snip* file, and your extracted folder *win01_1B_Bell_Orchid* folder display if this is your storage location.

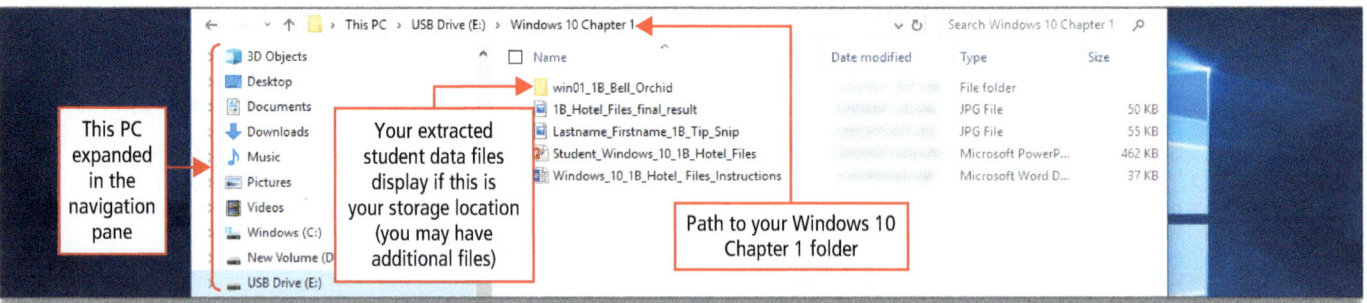

Figure 1.71

2 In the **file list**, double-click the **win01_1B_Bell_Orchid** folder to display the subfolders and files.

Recall that the corporate office of the Bell Orchid Hotels is in Boston. The corporate office maintains subfolders labeled for each of its large hotels in Honolulu, Orlando, San Diego, and Santa Barbara.

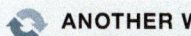 **ANOTHER WAY** Right-click the folder, and then click Open; or, select the folder and then on the ribbon, on the Home tab, in the Open group, click Open.

3 In the **file list**, double-click **Orlando** to display the subfolders, and then look at the **address bar** to view the path. Compare your screen with Figure 1.72.

Within each city's subfolder, there is a structure of subfolders for the Accounting, Engineering, Food and Beverage, Human Resources, Operations, and Sales and Marketing departments.

Because folders can be placed inside of other folders, such an arrangement is common when organizing files on a computer.

In the address bar, the path from the flash drive to the win01_1B_Bell_Orchid folder to the Orlando folder displays as a series of links.

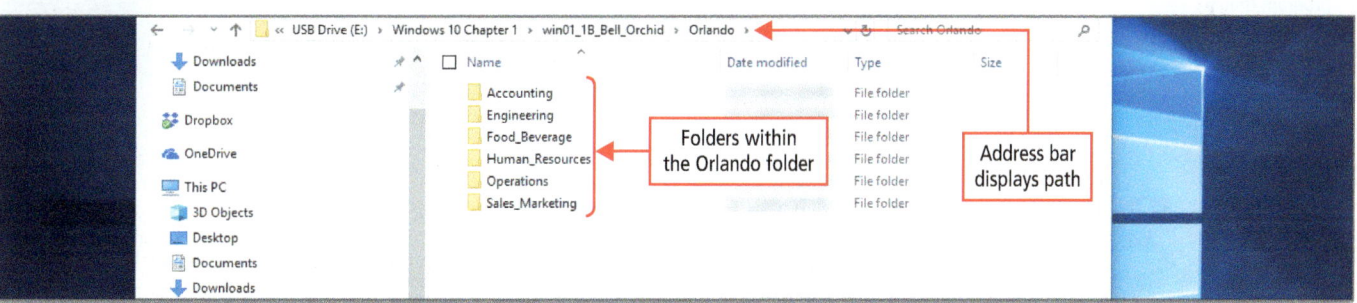

Figure 1.72

4 In the **address bar**, to the right of **win01_1B_Bell_Orchid**, click the ⊳ arrow to display a list of the subfolders in the **win01_1B_Bell_Orchid** folder. On the list that displays, notice that **Orlando** displays in bold, indicating it is open in the file list. Then, on the list, click **Honolulu**.

The subfolders within the Honolulu folder display.

5 In the **address bar**, to the right of **win01_1B_Bell_Orchid**, click the ⊳ arrow again to display the subfolders in that folder. Then, on the **address bar**—not on the list—point to **Honolulu** and notice that the list of subfolders in the **Honolulu** folder displays.

After you display one set of subfolders in the address bar, all of the links are active and you need only point to them to display the list of subfolders.

Clicking an arrow to the right of a folder name in the address bar displays a list of the subfolders in that folder. You can click a subfolder name to display its contents. In this manner, the address bar is not only a path, but it is also an active control with which you can step from the current folder directly to any other folder above it in the folder structure just by clicking a folder name.

6 On the list of subfolders for **Honolulu**, click **Sales_Marketing** to display its contents in the **file list**. On the **View tab**, in the **Layout group**, if necessary, click **Details**. Compare your screen with Figure 1.73.

 ANOTHER WAY In the file list, double-click the Sales_Marketing folder.

The files in the Sales_Marketing folder for Honolulu display in the Details layout. To the left of each file name, an icon indicates the program that created each file. Here, there is one PowerPoint file, one Excel file, one Word file, and four JPEG images.

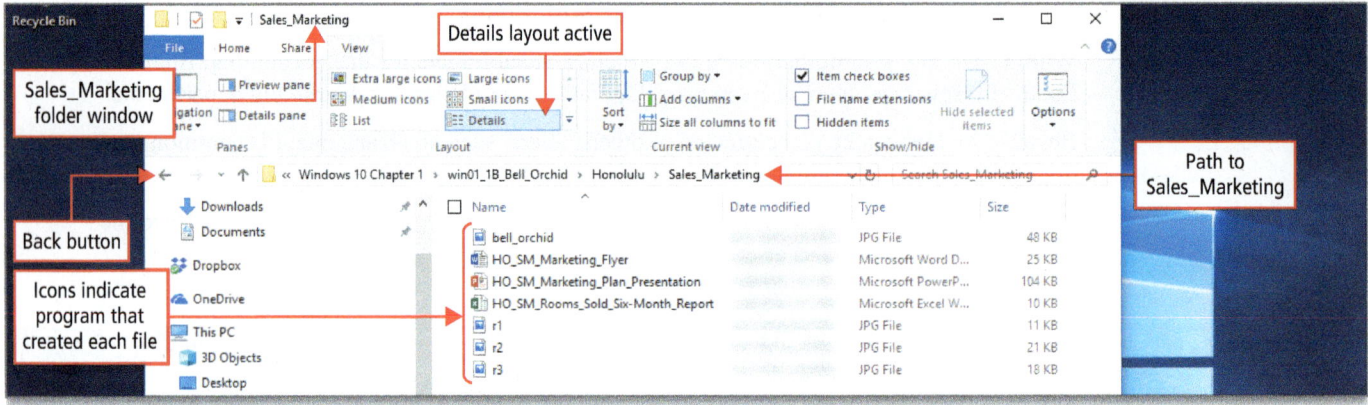

Figure 1.73

7 In the upper left portion of the window, click **Back** ← one time.

The Back button retraces each of your clicks in the same manner as clicking the Back button when you are browsing the internet.

8 In the **file list**, point to the **Human_Resources** folder, and then double-click to open the folder.

9 In the **file list**, click one time to select the PowerPoint file **HO_HR_New_Employee_ Presentation**, and then on the ribbon, click the **View tab**. In the **Panes group**, click **Details pane**, and then compare your screen with Figure 1.74.

The *Details pane* displays the most common *file properties* associated with the selected file. File properties refer to information about a file, such as the author, the date the file was last changed, and any descriptive *tags*—properties that you create to help you find and organize your files.

Additionally, a thumbnail image of the first slide in the presentation displays, and the status bar displays the number of items in the folder.

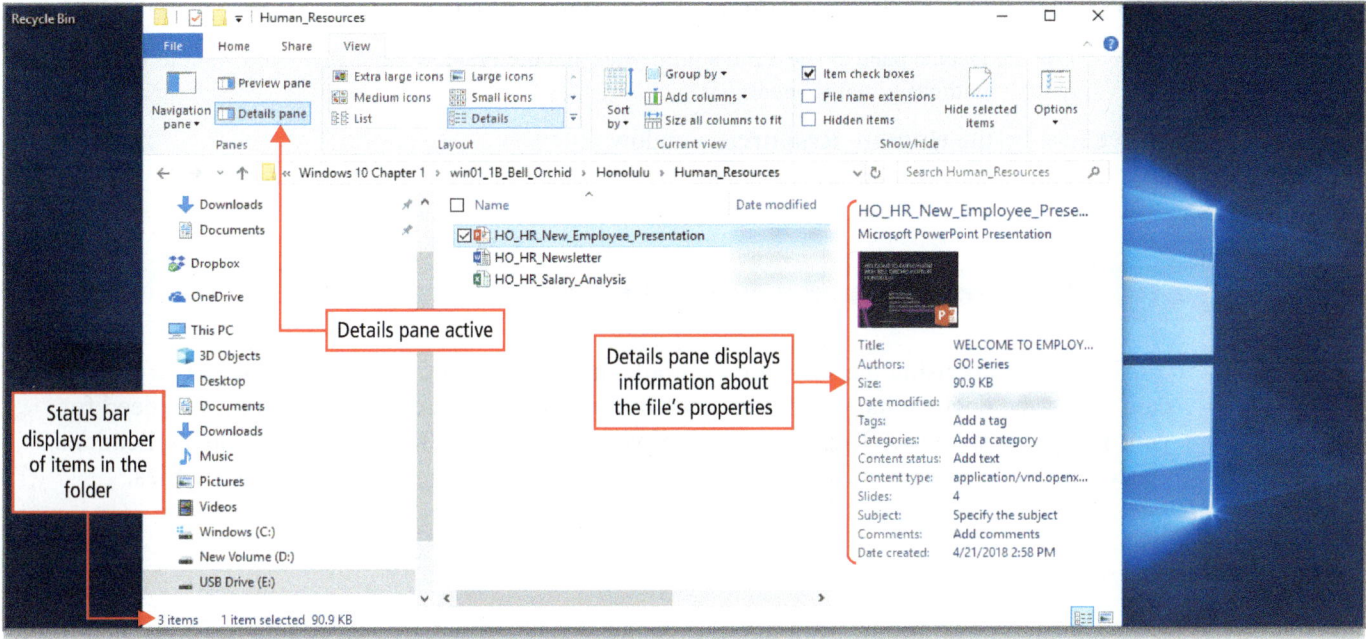

Figure 1.74

10 On the right, in the **Details pane**, click **Add a tag**, type **New Employee meeting** and then at the bottom of the pane click **Save**.

Because you can search for tags, adding tags to files makes them easier to find.

ANOTHER WAY With the file selected, on the Home tab, in the Open group, click Properties to display the Properties dialog box for the file, and then click the Details tab.

11 On the ribbon, on the **View tab**, in the **Panes group**, click **Preview pane** to replace the **Details pane** with the **Preview pane**. Compare your screen with Figure 1.75.

In the Preview pane that displays on the right, you can use the scroll bar to scroll through the slides in the presentation; or, you can click the up or down scroll arrow to view the slides as a miniature presentation.

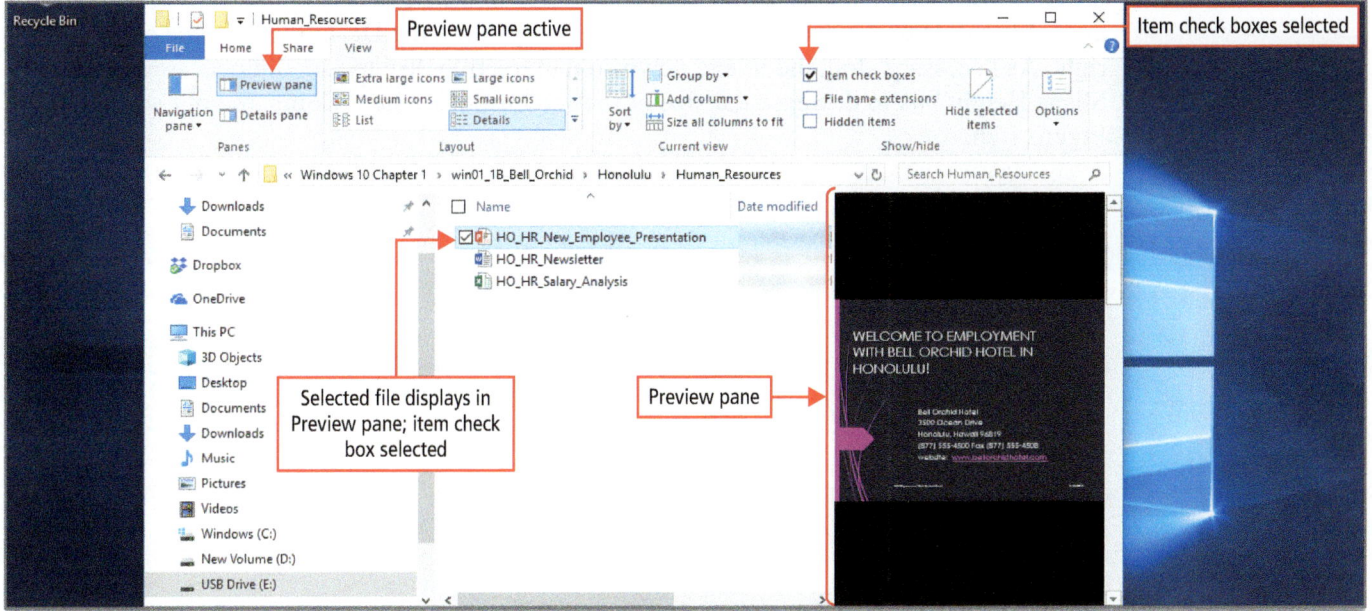

Figure 1.75

12 On the ribbon, click **Preview pane** to close the right pane.

Use the Details pane to see a file's properties and the Preview pane when you want to look at a file quickly without actually opening it.

13 Close ☒ the **Human_Resources** window.

| Objective 10 | Start Programs and Open Data Files |

When you are using the software programs installed on your computer, you create and save data files—the documents, workbooks, databases, songs, pictures, and so on that you need for your job or personal use. Therefore, most of your work with Windows 10 desktop applications is concerned with locating and starting your programs and locating and opening your files.

Activity 1.31 | Starting Programs

You can start programs from the Start menu or from the taskbar by pinning a program to the taskbar. You can open your data files from within the program in which they were created, or you can open a data file from a window in File Explorer, which will simultaneously start the program and open your file.

1 Be sure your desktop displays and that your PowerPoint presentation is still open but minimized on the taskbar. You can point to the PowerPoint icon to have a small image of the active slide display. Click **Start** ⊞ to place the insertion point in the search box, type **wordpad** and then click the **WordPad Desktop app**.

2 With the insertion point blinking in the document window, type your first and last name.

3 From the taskbar, open your PowerPoint presentation. On the **Home tab**, click the upper portion of the **New Slide** button to insert a blank slide in the Title Only layout. Click anywhere in the text *Click to add title*, and then type **Wordpad**

4 Click anywhere in the lower portion of the slide. On the **Insert tab**, in the **Images group**, click **Screenshot**, and then under **Available Windows**, click the image of the WordPad program with your name typed to insert the image in the PowerPoint slide. Click in a blank area of the slide to deselect the image; if necessary, close the Design Ideas pane on the right. As necessary, drag the image down so that the title displays, and if necessary, use the Shape Height box to decrease the size of the screenshot slightly. Compare your screen with Figure 1.76.

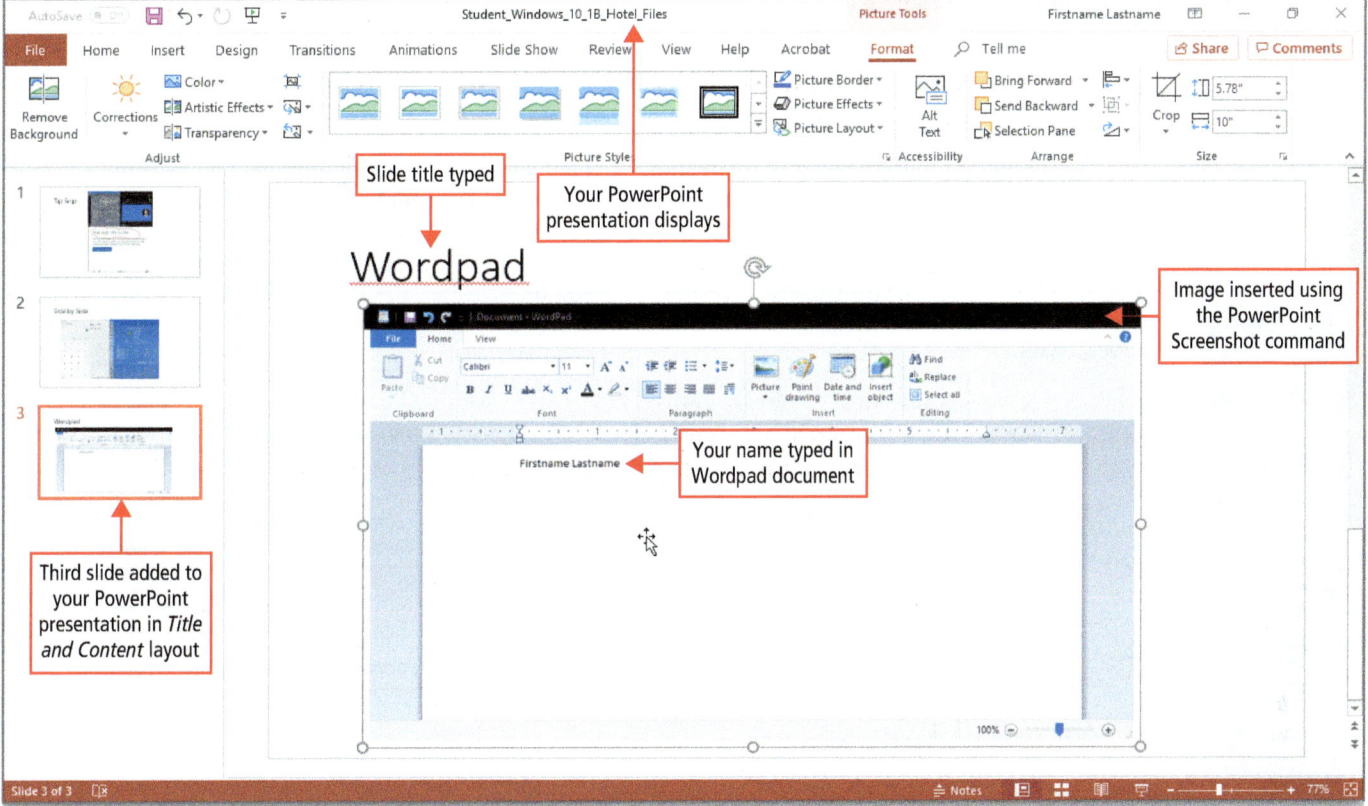

Figure 1.76

5 On the Quick Access toolbar, click **Save** 🖫 and then in the upper right corner of the PowerPoint window, click **Minimize** 〔−〕 so that PowerPoint remains open but not displayed on your screen.

6 **Close** 〔✕〕 **WordPad**, and then click **Don't Save**.

Activity 1.32 | Opening Data Files

1 ▶ Open **Microsoft Word** from your taskbar, or click **Start** ▦, type **Microsoft word** and then open the **Word** desktop app. Compare your screen with Figure 1.77.

The Word program window has features that are common to other programs you have opened; for example, commands are arranged on tabs. When you create and save data in Word, you create a Word document file.

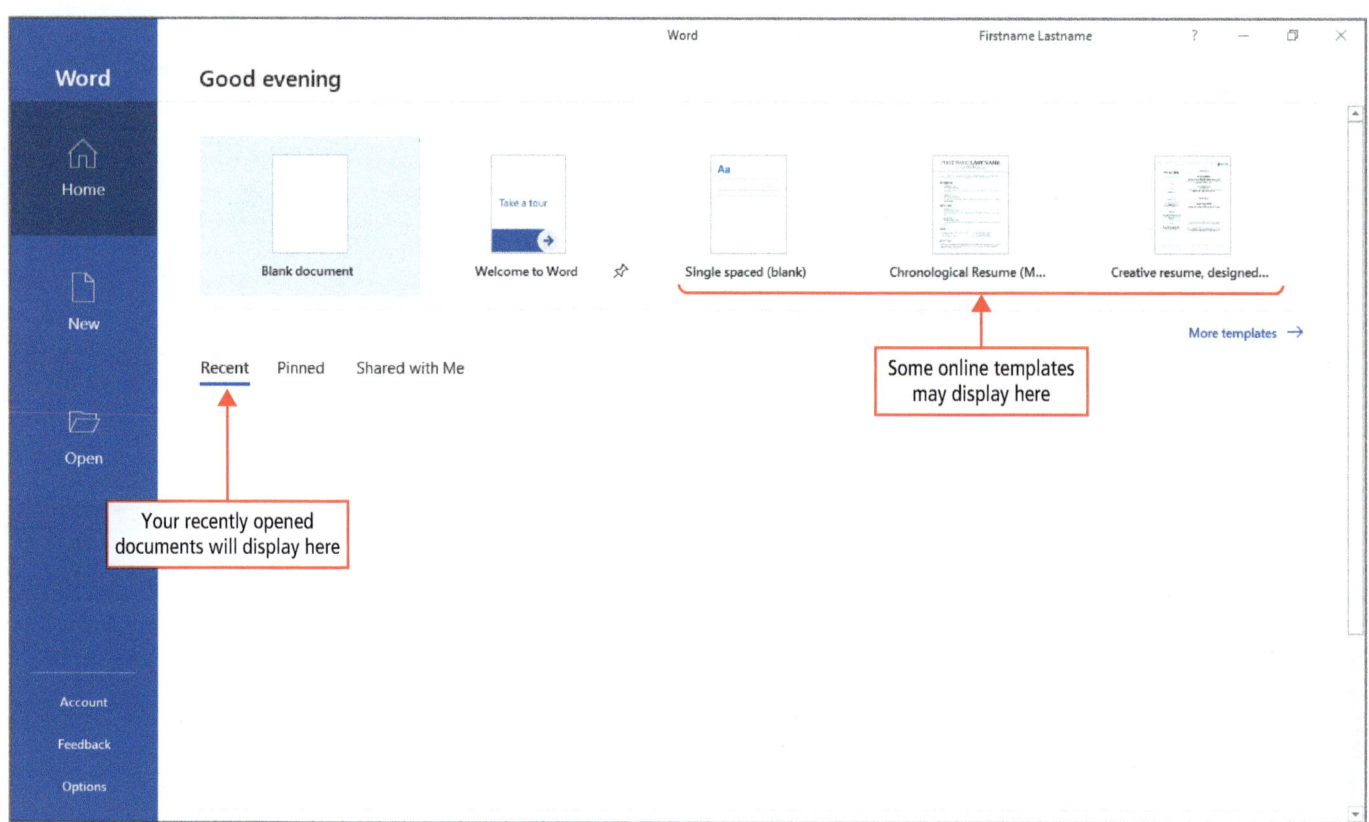

Figure 1.77

2 ▶ On the left, click **Open**. Notice the list of places from which you can open a document, including your OneDrive if you are logged in. Click **Browse** to display the **Open** dialog box. Compare your screen with Figure 1.78, and then take a moment to study the table in Figure 1.79.

Recall that a dialog box is a window containing options for completing a task; the layout of the Open dialog box is similar to that of a File Explorer window. When you are working in a desktop application, use the Open dialog box to locate and open existing files that were created in the desktop application.

When you click Browse, typically the Documents folder on This PC displays. You can use the skills you have practiced to navigate to other locations on your computer, such as your removable USB flash drive.

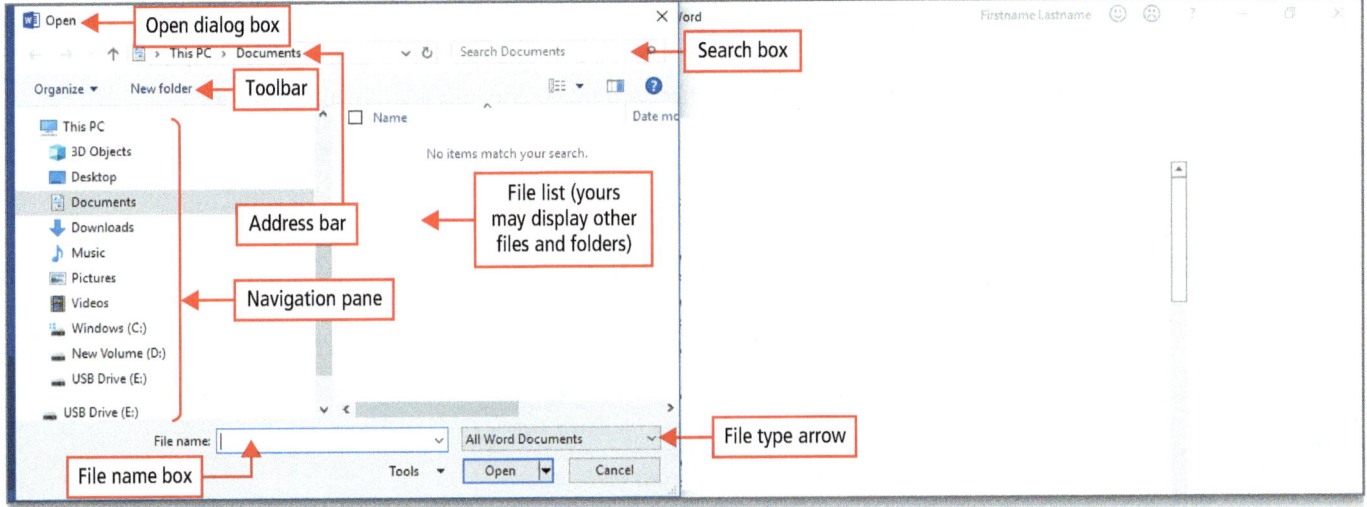

Figure 1.78

Dialog Box Element	Function
Address bar	Displays the path in the folder structure.
File list	Displays the list of files and folders that are available in the folder indicated in the address bar.
File name box	Enables you to type the name of a specific file to locate it—if you know it.
File type arrow	Enables you to restrict the type of files displayed in the file list; for example, the default *All Word Documents* restricts (filters) the type of files displayed to only Word documents. You can click the arrow and adjust the restrictions (filters) to a narrower or wider group of files.
Navigation pane	Navigate to files and folders and get access to Quick access, OneDrive, and This PC.
Search box	Search for files in the current folder. Filters the file list based on text that you type; the search is based on text in the file name (and for files on the hard drive or OneDrive, in the file itself), and on other properties that you can specify. The search takes place in the current folder, as displayed in the address bar, and in any subfolders within that folder.
Toolbar	Displays relevant tasks; for example, creating a new folder.

Figure 1.79

3 In the **navigation pane**, scroll down as necessary, and then under **This PC**, click your **USB flash drive** or whatever location where you have stored your files for this project. In the **file list**, double-click your **win01_1B_Bell_Orchid** folder to open it and display its contents.

4 In the upper right portion of the **Open** dialog box, click the **More options arrow** ▾, and then set the view to **Large icons**. Compare your screen with Figure 1.80.

The Live Preview feature indicates that each folder contains additional subfolders.

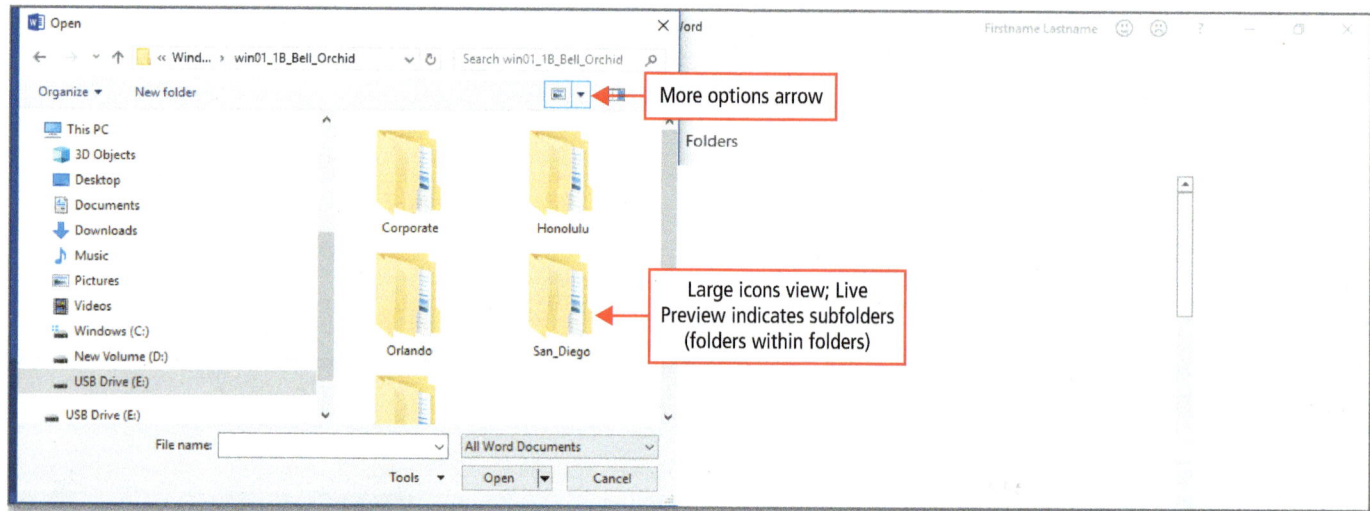

Figure 1.80

5 In the **file list**, double-click the **Corporate** folder, and then double-click the **Accounting** folder.

The view returns to the Details view.

6 In the **file list**, notice that only one document—a Word document—displays. In the lower right corner, locate the **File type** button, and notice that *All Word Documents* displays as the file type. Click the **File type arrow**, and then on the displayed list, click **All Files**. Compare your screen with Figure 1.81.

When you change the file type to *All Files*, you can see that the Word file is not the only file in this folder. By default, the Open dialog box displays only the files created in the active program; however, you can display variations of file types in this manner.

Microsoft Office file types are identified by small icons, which is a convenient way to differentiate one type of file from another. Although you can view all the files in the folder, you can open only the files that were created in the active program, which in this instance is Microsoft Word.

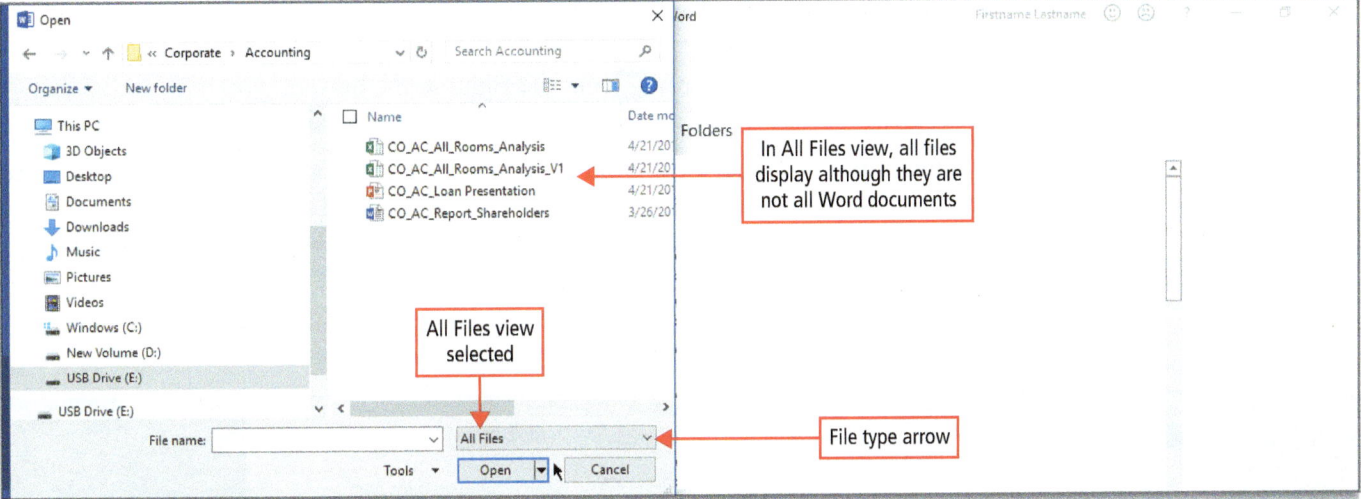

Figure 1.81

7 Change the file type back to **All Word Documents**. Then, in the **file list**, double-click the **CO_AC_Report_Shareholders** Word file to open the document. Take a moment to scroll through the document. If necessary, Maximize □ the window.

8 **Close** ☒ the Word window.

9 Click **Start** ⊞, and then search for **.txt** At the top, click **Filters**, click **Documents**, and then on the list, click **Structure.txt in Future_Hotels**.

The file opens using the Windows 10 *Notepad* desktop app—a basic text-editing program included with Windows 10 that you can use to create simple documents.

In the search box, you can search for files on your computer, and you can search for a file by its *file name extension*—a set of characters at the end of a file name that helps Windows understand what kind of information is in a file and what program should open it. A *.txt file* is a simple file consisting of lines of text with no formatting that almost any computer can open and display.

10 **Close** ☒ the Notepad program.

MORE KNOWLEDGE **Do Not Clutter Your Desktop by Creating Desktop Shortcuts or Storing Files**

On your desktop, you can add or remove *desktop shortcuts*, which are desktop icons that can link to items accessible on your computer such as a program, file, folder, disk drive, printer, or another computer. In previous versions of Windows, many computer users commonly did this.

Now the Start menu is your personal dashboard for all your programs and online activities, and increasingly you will access programs and your own files in the cloud. So do not clutter your desktop with shortcuts—doing so is more confusing than useful. Placing desktop shortcuts for frequently used programs or folders directly on your desktop may seem convenient, but as you add more icons, your desktop becomes cluttered and the shortcuts are not easy to find. A better organizing method is to use the taskbar for shortcuts to programs. For folders and files, the best organizing structure is to create a logical structure of folders within your Documents folder or your cloud-based OneDrive.

You can also drag frequently-used folders to the Quick access area in the navigation pane so that they are available any time you open File Explorer. As you progress in your use of Windows 10, you will discover techniques for using the taskbar and the Quick access area of the navigation pane to streamline your work instead of cluttering your desktop.

Activity 1.33 | Searching, Pinning, Sorting, and Filtering in File Explorer

1 ▶ From the taskbar, open **File Explorer** 📁. On the right, at the bottom, you may notice that under **Recent files**, you can see files that you have recently opened.

2 ▶ In the **navigation pane**, click your **USB flash drive**—or click the location where you have stored your files for this project. Double-click your **Windows 10 Chapter 1 folder** to open it. In the upper right, click in the **Search** box, and then type **pool** Compare your screen with Figure 1.82.

Files that contain the word *pool* in the title display. If you are searching a folder on your hard drive or OneDrive, files that contain the word *pool* within the document will also display. Additionally, Search Tools display on the ribbon.

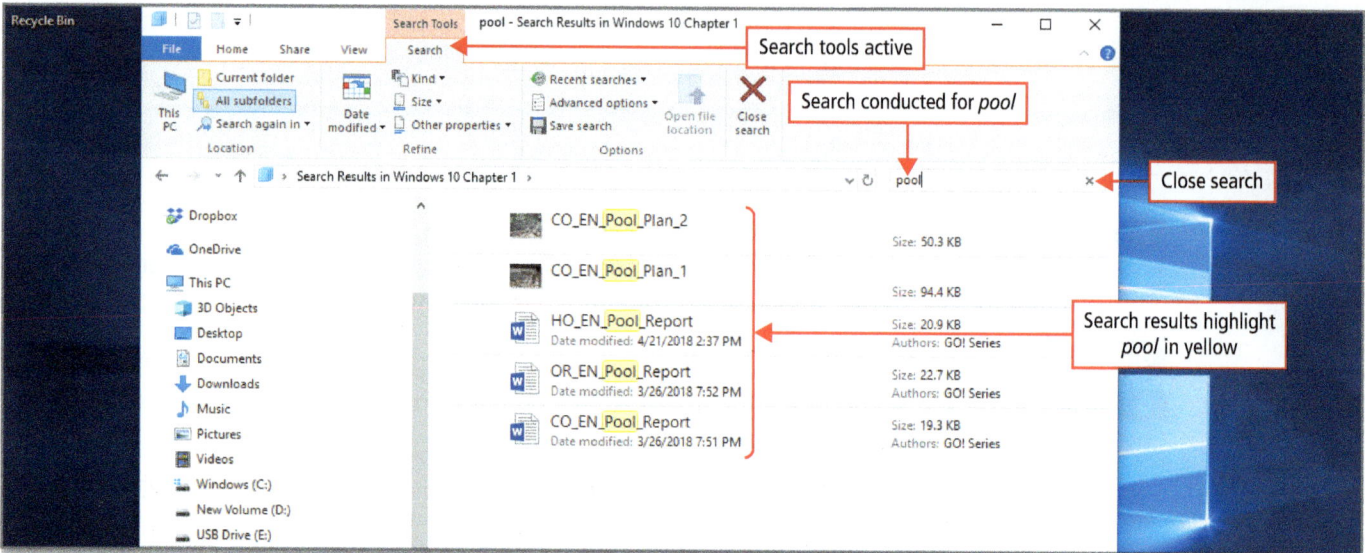

Figure 1.82

3 ▶ In the search box, clear the search by clicking ☒, and then in the search box type **Paris.jpg** Notice that you can also search by using a file extension as part of the search term.

4 ▶ **Clear** ☒ the search. Double-click your **win01_1B_Bell_Orchid** folder to open it.

5 ▶ On the **Home tab**, in the **Clipboard group**, click **Pin to Quick access**. If necessary, scroll up in the navigation pane. Compare your screen with Figure 1.83.

You can pin frequently used folders to the Quick access area, and then unpin them when you no longer need frequent access. Folders that you access frequently will also display in the Quick access area without the pin image. Delete them by right-clicking the name and clicking Unpin from Quick access.

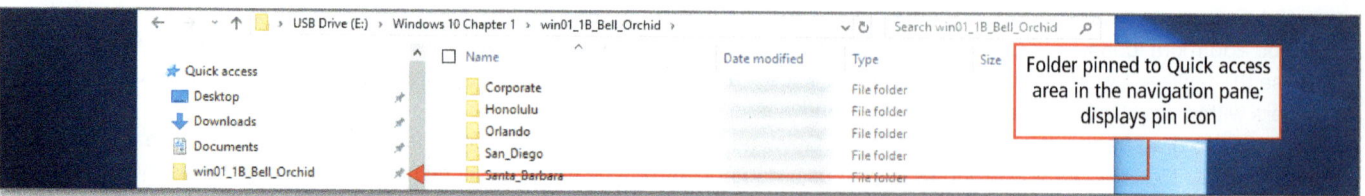

Figure 1.83

🔄 **ANOTHER WAY** In the file list, right-click a folder name, and then click Pin to Quick access; or, drag the folder to the Quick access area in the navigation pain and release the mouse button when the ScreenTip displays Pin to Quick access.

---

6 In the **file list**—double-click the **Corporate** folder and then double-click the **Engineering** folder.

7 On the **View tab**, in the **Current view group**, click **Sort by**, and then click **Type**. Compare your screen with Figure 1.84.

Use this technique to sort files in the file list by type. Here, the JPG files display first, and then the Microsoft Excel files, and so on—in alphabetic order by file type.

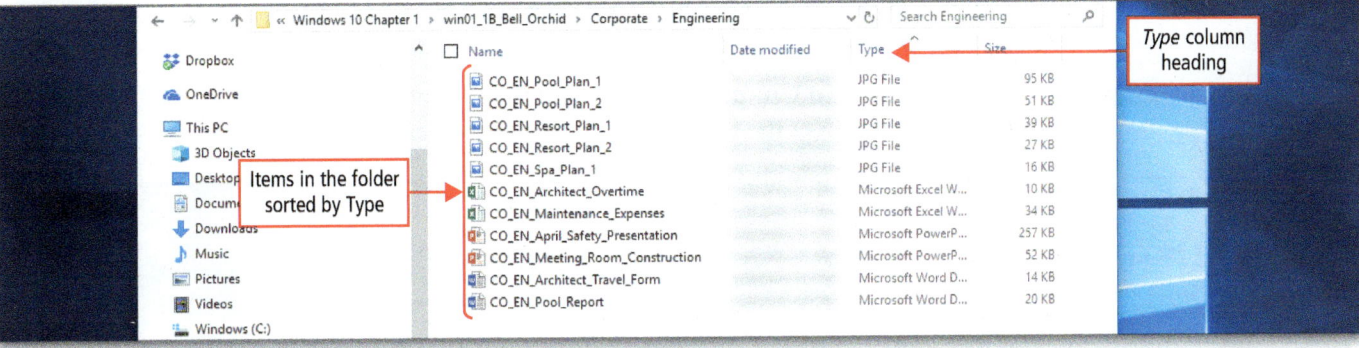

Figure 1.84

8 Point to the column heading **Type**, and then click **^**.

9 Point to the column heading **Type** again, and on the right, click ⌄. On the displayed list, click **Microsoft PowerPoint Presentation**, and notice that the file list is filtered to show only PowerPoint files.

A *filtered list* is a display of files that is limited based on specified criteria.

10 To the right of the **Type** column heading, click the check mark and then click **Microsoft PowerPoint Presentation** again to clear the Microsoft PowerPoint filter and redisplay all of the files.

11 **Close** ☒ the File Explorer window.

ALERT   Allow Time to Complete the Remainder of This Project in One Session

If you are working on a computer that is not your own, for example in a college lab, plan your time to complete the remainder of this project in one working session. Allow 45 to 60 minutes.

Because you will need to store and then delete files on the hard disk drive of the computer at which you are working, it is recommended that you complete this project in one working session—*unless you are working on your own computer or you know that the files will be retained*. In your college lab, files you store on the computer's hard drive will not be retained after you sign off.

Objective 11   Create, Rename, and Copy Files and Folders

File management includes organizing, copying, renaming, moving, and deleting the files and folders you have stored in various locations—both locally and in the cloud.

Activity 1.34 | Copying Files from a Removable Storage Device to the Documents Folder on the Hard Disk Drive

Barbara and Steven have the assignment to transfer and then organize some of the corporation's files to a computer that will be connected to the corporate network. Data on such a computer can be accessed by employees at any of the hotel locations through the use of sharing technologies. For example, *SharePoint* is a Microsoft technology that enables employees in an organization to access information across organizational and geographic boundaries.

1 ▶ Close any open windows, but leave your open PowerPoint presentation minimized on the taskbar.

2 ▶ From the taskbar, open **File Explorer** ▣. In the **navigation pane**, if necessary expand **This PC**, and then click your USB flash drive or the location where you have stored your chapter folder to display its contents in the file list.

> Recall that in the navigation pane, under This PC, you have access to all the storage areas inside your computer, such as your hard disk drives, and to any devices with removable storage, such as CDs, DVDs, or USB flash drives.

3 ▶ Open your **Windows 10 Chapter 1** folder, and then in the **file list**, click **win01_1B_Bell_Orchid** one time to select the folder. Compare your screen with Figure 1.85.

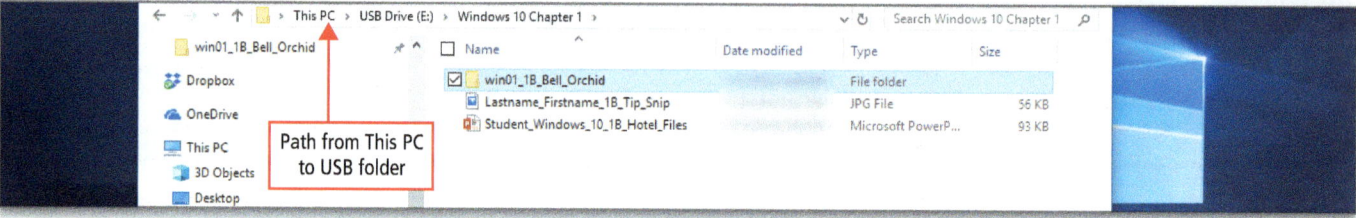

Figure 1.85

4 ▶ With the **win01_1B_Bell_Orchid** folder selected, on the ribbon, on the **Home tab**, in the **Clipboard group**, click **Copy**.

> The Copy command places a copy of your selected file or folder on the *Clipboard* where it will be stored until you use the Paste command to place the copy somewhere else. The Clipboard is a temporary storage area for information that you have copied or moved from one place and plan to use somewhere else.
>
> In Windows 10, the Clipboard can hold only one piece of information at a time. Whenever something is copied to the Clipboard, it replaces whatever was there before. In Windows 10, you cannot view the contents of the Clipboard nor place multiple items there in the manner that you can in Microsoft Word.

🔄 **ANOTHER WAY**   With the item selected in the file list, press [Ctrl] + [C] to copy the item to the clipboard.

5 ▶ To the left of the address bar, click **Up** [↑] two times. In the **file list**, double-click your **Documents** folder to open it, and then on the **Home tab**, in the **Clipboard group**, click **Paste**.

> A *progress bar* displays in a dialog box and also displays on the taskbar button with green shading. A progress bar indicates visually the progress of a task such as a copy process, a download, or a file transfer.
>
> The Documents folder is one of several folders within your *personal folder* stored on the hard disk drive. For each user account—even if there is only one user on the computer—Windows 10 creates a personal folder labeled with the account holder's name.

🔄 **ANOTHER WAY**   With the destination location selected, press [Ctrl] + [V] to paste the item from the clipboard to the selected location. Or, on the Home tab, in the Organize group, click Copy to, find and then click the location to which you want to copy. If the desired location is not on the list, use the Choose location command at the bottom.

6 ▶ **Close** [X] the **Documents** window.

Barbara and Steven can see that various managers have been placing files related to new European hotels in the *Future_Hotels* folder. They can also see that the files have not been organized into a logical structure. For example, files that are related to each other are not in separate folders; instead they are mixed in with other files that are not related to the topic.

In this Activity, you will create, name, and rename folders to begin a logical structure of folders in which to organize the files related to the European hotels project.

1 ▶ From the taskbar, open **File Explorer** 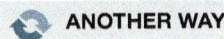, and then use any of the techniques you have practiced to display the contents of the **Documents** folder in the **file list**.

NOTE   Using the Documents Folder and OneDrive Instead of Your USB Drive

In this modern computing era, you should limit your use of USB drives to those times when you want to quickly take some files to another computer without going online. Instead of using a USB drive, use your computer's hard drive, or better yet, your free OneDrive cloud storage that comes with your Microsoft account.

There are two good reasons to stop using USB flash drives. First, searching is limited on a USB drive—search does not look at the content inside a file. When you search files on your hard drive or OneDrive, the search extends to words and phrases actually *inside* the files. Second, if you delete a file or folder from a USB drive, it is gone and cannot be retrieved. Files you delete from your hard drive or OneDrive go to the Recycle Bin where you can retrieve them later.

---

2 ▶ In the **file list**, double-click the **win01_1B_Bell_Orchid** folder, double-click the **Corporate** folder, double-click the **Information_Technology** folder, and then double-click the **Future_Hotels** folder to display its contents in the file list; sometimes this navigation is written as *Documents > win01_1B_Bell_Orchid > Corporate > Information_Technology > Future_Hotels*.

Some computer users prefer to navigate a folder structure by double-clicking in this manner. Others prefer using the address bar as described in the following Another Way box. Use whatever method you prefer—double-clicking in the file list, clicking in the address bar, or expanding files in the Navigation pane.

ANOTHER WAY   In the navigation pane, click Documents, and expand each folder in the navigation pane. Or, In the address bar, to the right of Documents, click >, and then on the list, click win01_1B_Bell_Orchid. To the right of win01_1B_Bell_Orchid, click the > and then click Corporate. To the right of Corporate, click > and then click Information_Technology. To the right of Information_Technology, click >, and then click Future_Hotels.

---

3 ▶ In the **file list**, be sure the items are in alphabetical order by **Name**. If the items are not in alphabetical order, recall that by clicking the small arrow in the column heading name, you can change how the files in the file list are ordered.

4 ▶ On the ribbon, click the **View tab**, and then in the **Layout group**, be sure **Details** is selected.

The *Details view* displays a list of files or folders and their most common properties.

ANOTHER WAY   Right-click in a blank area of the file list, point to View, and then click Details.

---

5 ▶ On the ribbon, click the **Home tab**, and then in the **New group**, click **New folder**. With the text *New folder* selected, type **Paris** and press Enter. Click **New folder** again, type **Venice** and then press Enter. Create a third **New folder** named **London**

In a Windows 10 file list, folders are listed first, in alphabetic order, followed by individual files in alphabetic order.

6 Click the **Venice** folder one time to select it, and then on the ribbon, on the **Home tab**, in the **Organize group**, click **Rename**. Notice that the text *Venice* is selected. Type **Rome** and press Enter.

 ANOTHER WAY   Point to a folder or file name, right-click, and then on the shortcut menu, click Rename.

7 In the **file list**, click one time to select the Word file **Architects**. With the file name selected, click the file name again to select all the text. Click the file name again to place the insertion point within the file name, edit the file name to **Architects_Local** and press Enter. Compare your screen with Figure 1.86.

You can use any of the techniques you just practiced to change the name of a file or folder.

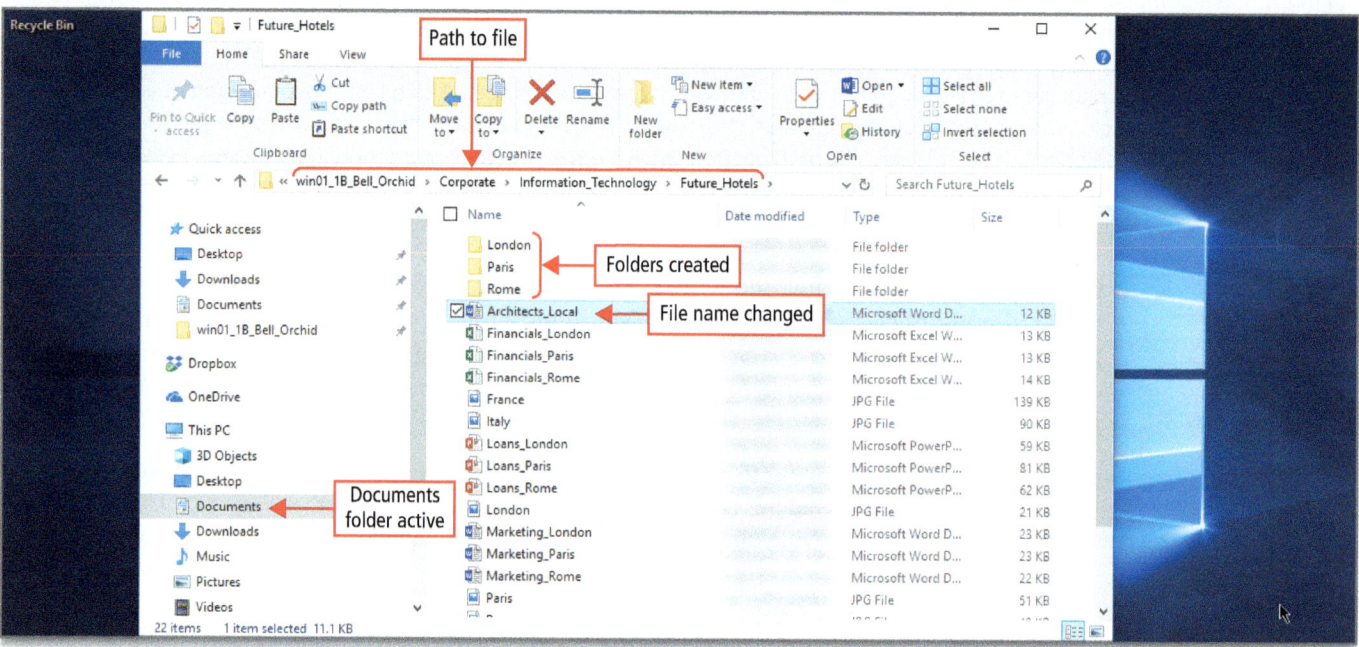

Figure 1.86

8 On the taskbar, click the **PowerPoint** icon to redisplay your **Windows_10_1B_Hotel_Files** presentation, and then on the **Home tab**, click the upper portion of the **New Slide** button to insert a new slide with the Title Only layout.

9 Click anywhere in the text *Click to add title*, type **Europe Folders** and then click anywhere in the empty space below the title.

10 On the **Insert tab**, in the **Images group**, click **Screenshot**, and then under **Available Windows**, click the image of your file list. On the **Picture Tools Format tab**, in the **Size group**, click in the **Shape Height** box, type **5** and then press Enter. As necessary, drag the image down so that the title you typed is visible; your presentation contains four slides.

11 Above the **File tab**, on the Quick Access toolbar, click **Save**, and then in the upper right corner, click **Minimize** so that PowerPoint remains open but not displayed on your screen.

12 **Close** the **Future_Hotels** window.

Activity 1.36 | Copying Files

Copying, moving, renaming, and deleting files and folders comprise the most heavily used features within File Explorer. Probably half or more of the steps you complete in File Explorer relate to these tasks, so mastering these techniques will increase your efficiency.

When you *copy* a file or a folder, you make a duplicate of the original item and then store the duplicate in another location. In this Activity, you will assist Barbara and Steven in making copies of the Staffing_Plan file, and then placing the copies in each of the three folders you created—London, Paris, and Rome.

1 From the taskbar, open **File Explorer** 📁, and then by double-clicking in the file list or following the links in the address bar, navigate to **This PC > Documents > win01_1B_Bell_ Orchid > Corporate > Information_Technology > Future_Hotels**.

2 In the upper right corner, **Maximize** ☐ the window. On the **View tab**, if necessary set the **Layout** to **Details**, and then in the **Current view group**, click **Size all columns to fit** 🔢.

3 In the **file list**, click the file **Staffing_Plan** one time to select it, and then on the **Home tab**, in the **Clipboard group**, click **Copy**.

4 At the top of the **file list**, double-click the **London folder** to open it, and then in the **Clipboard group**, click **Paste**. Notice that the copy of the **Staffing_Plan** file displays. Compare your screen with Figure 1.87.

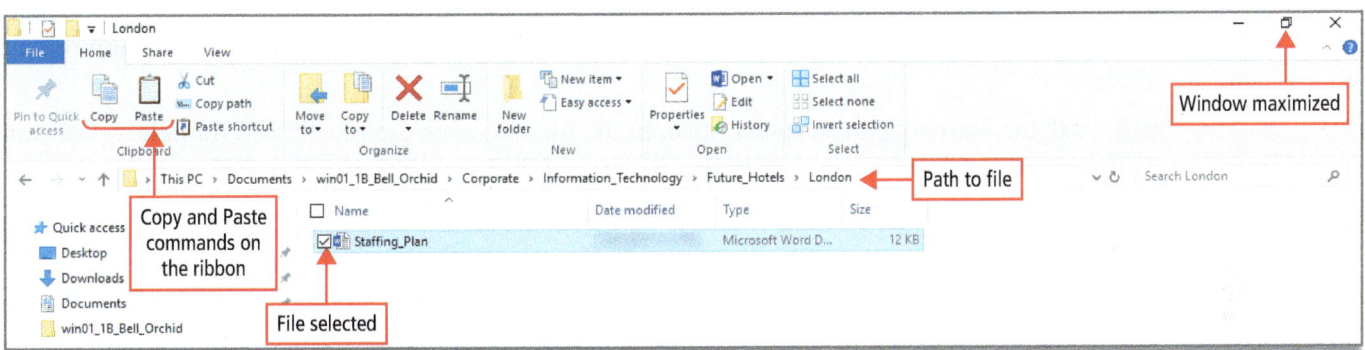

Figure 1.87

🔄 **ANOTHER WAY** Right-click the file you want to copy, and on the menu click Copy. Then right-click the folder into which you want to place the copy, and on the menu click Paste. Or, select the file you want to copy, press Ctrl + C to activate the Copy command, open the folder into which you want to paste the file, and then press Ctrl + V to activate the Paste command.

5 With the **London** window open, by using any of the techniques you have practiced, rename this copy of the **Staffing_Plan** file to **London_Staffing_Plan**

6 To the left of the **address bar**, click **Up** ⬆ to move up one level in the folder structure and to redisplay the **file list** for the **Future_Hotels** folder.

🔄 **ANOTHER WAY** In the address bar, click Future_Hotels to redisplay this window and move up one level in the folder structure.

7 Click the **Staffing_Plan** file one time to select it, hold down Ctrl, and then drag the file upward over the **Paris** folder until the ScreenTip + *Copy to Paris* displays, and then release the mouse button and release Ctrl.

> When dragging a file into a folder, holding down Ctrl engages the Copy command and places a *copy* of the file at the location where you release the mouse button. This is another way to copy a file or copy a folder.

8 Open the **Paris** folder, and then rename the **Staffing_Plan** file **Paris_Staffing_Plan** Then, move up one level in the folder structure to redisplay the **Future_Hotels** window.

9 Double-click the **Rome** folder to open it. With your mouse pointer anywhere in the **file list**, right-click, and then from the shortcut menu click **Paste**.

> A copy of the Staffing_Plan file is copied to the folder. Because a copy of the Staffing_Plan file is still on the Clipboard, you can continue to paste the item until you copy another item on the Clipboard to replace it.

10 Rename the file **Rome_Staffing_Plan**

11 On the **address bar**, click **Future_Hotels** to move up one level and open the **Future_Hotels** window—or click Up ↑ to move up one level. Leave this folder open for the next Activity.

Activity 1.37 | Moving Files

When you *move* a file or folder, you remove it from the original location and store it in a new location. In this Activity, you will move items from the Future_Hotels folder into their appropriate folders.

1 With the **Future_Hotels** folder open, in the **file list**, click the Excel file **Financials_London** one time to select it. On the **Home tab**, in the **Clipboard group**, click **Cut**.

> The file's Excel icon dims. This action places the item on the Clipboard.

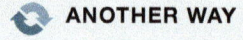 **ANOTHER WAY**   Right-click the file or folder, and then on the shortcut menu, click Cut; or, select the file or folder, and then press Ctrl + X.

2 Double-click the **London** folder to open it, and then on the **Home tab**, in the **Clipboard group**, click **Paste**.

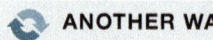 **ANOTHER WAY**   Right-click the folder, and then on the shortcut menu, click Paste; or, select the folder, and then press Ctrl + V.

3 Click **Up** ↑ to move up one level and redisplay the **Future_Hotels** folder window. In the **file list**, point to **Financials_Paris**, hold down the left mouse button, and then drag the file upward over the **Paris** folder until the ScreenTip *Move to Paris* displays, and then release the mouse button.

4 Open the **Paris** folder, and notice that the file was moved to this folder. Click **Up** ↑—or on the address bar, click Future_Hotels to return to that folder.

5 In the **file list**, click **Loans_London** one time to select it. hold down `Ctrl`, and then click the photo image **London** and the Word document **Marketing_London** to select the three files. Release the `Ctrl` key. Compare your screen with Figure 1.88.

Use this technique to select a group of noncontiguous items in a list.

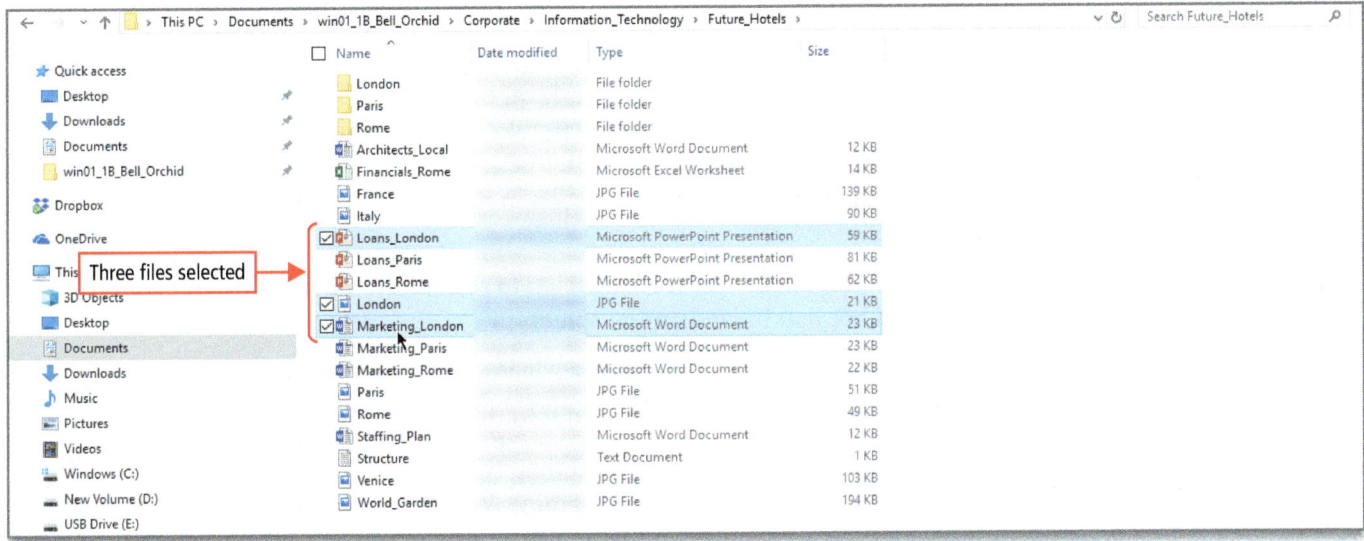

Figure 1.88

6 Point to any of the selected files, hold down the left mouse button, and then drag upward over the **London** folder until the ScreenTip →*Move to London* displays and *3* displays over the files being moved, and then release the mouse button.

You can see that by keeping related files together—for example, all the files that relate to the London hotel—in folders that have an appropriately descriptive name, it will be easier to locate information later.

7 By dragging, move the **Architects_Local** file into the **London** folder.

8 In an empty area of the file list, right-click, and then click **Undo Move**. Leave the **Future_Hotels** window open for the next Activity.

Any action that you make in a file list can be undone in this manner.

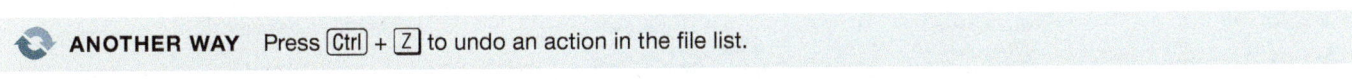

ANOTHER WAY   Press `Ctrl` + `Z` to undo an action in the file list.

MORE KNOWLEDGE   **Using Shift + Click to Select Files**

If a group of files to be selected are contiguous (next to each other in the file list), click the first file to be selected, hold down `Shift` and then click the left mouse button on the last file to select all of the files between the top and bottom file selections.

Activity 1.38 | Copying and Moving Files by Snapping Two Windows

Sometimes you will want to open, in a second window, another instance of a program that you are using; that is, two copies of the program will be running simultaneously. This capability is especially useful in the File Explorer program, because you are frequently moving or copying files from one location to another.

In this Activity, you will open two instances of File Explorer, and then use snap, which you have already practiced in this chapter, to display both instances on your screen.

To copy or move files or folders into a different level of a folder structure, or to a different drive location, the most efficient method is to display two windows side by side and then use drag and drop or copy (or cut) and paste commands.

In this Activity, you will assist Barbara and Steven in making copies of the Staffing_Plan files for the corporate office.

1 In the upper right corner, click **Restore Down** to restore the **Future_Hotels** window to its previous size and not maximized on the screen.

Use the ***Restore Down*** command to resize a window to its previous size.

2 Hold down and press to snap the window so that it occupies the left half of the screen.

3 On the taskbar, *point* to **File Explorer** and then right-click. On the jump list, click **File Explorer** to open another instance of the program. With the new window active, hold down and press to snap the window so that it occupies the right half of the screen.

4 In the window on the right, click in a blank area to make the window active. Then navigate to **Documents > win01_1B_Bell_Orchid > Corporate > Human_Resources**. Compare your screen with Figure 1.89.

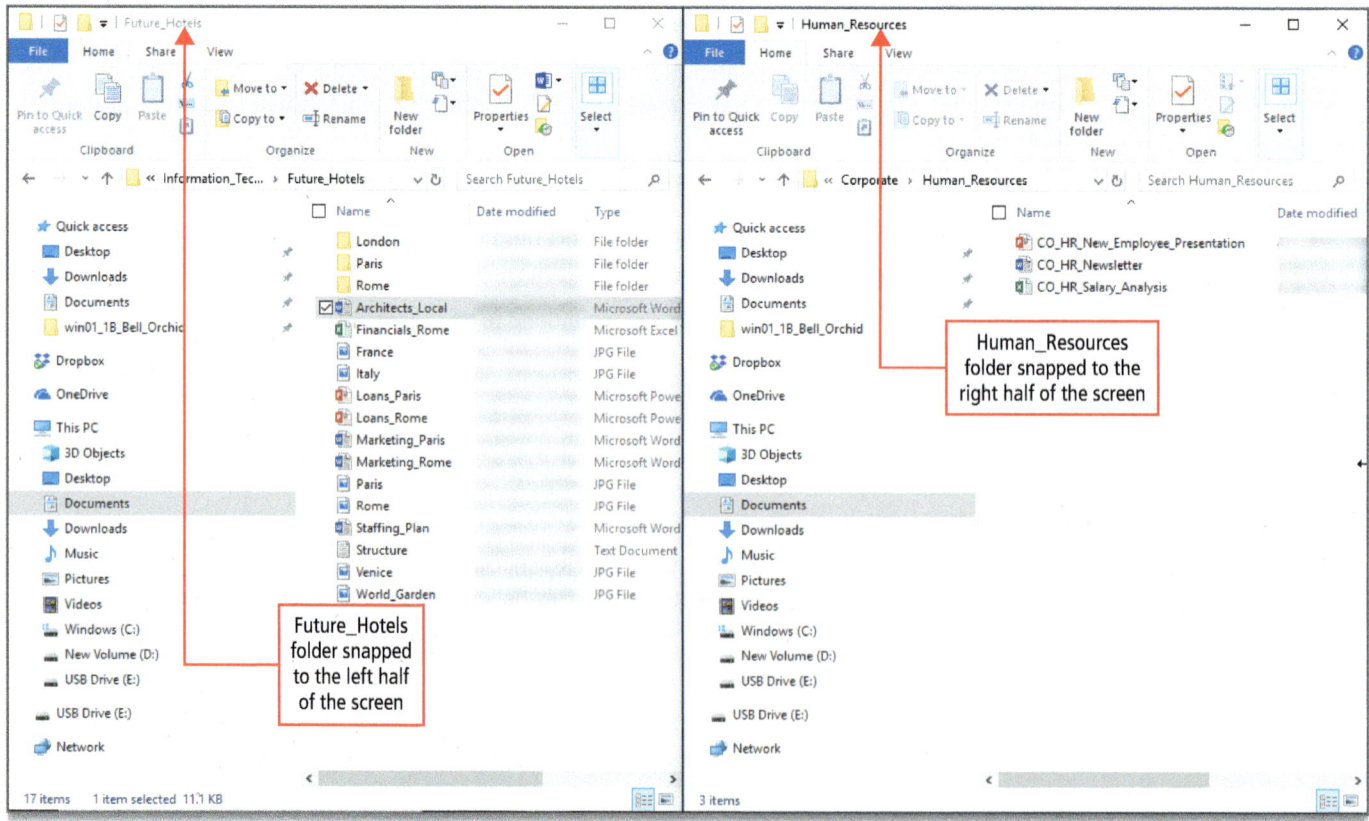

Figure 1.89

5 In the left window, double-click to open the **Rome** folder, and then click one time to select the file **Rome_Staffing_Plan**.

6 Hold down Ctrl, and then drag the file into the right window, into an empty area of the **Human_Resources file list**, until the ScreenTip + *Copy to Human_Resources* displays and then release the mouse button and Ctrl.

7 In the left window, on the **address bar**, click **Future_Hotels** to redisplay that folder. Open the **Paris** folder, point to **Paris_Staffing_Plan** and right-click, and then click **Copy**.

> You can access the Copy command in various ways; for example, from the shortcut menu, on the ribbon, or by using the keyboard shortcut Ctrl + C.

8 In the right window, point anywhere in the **file list**, right-click, and then click **Paste**.

9 On the taskbar, click the PowerPoint icon to redisplay your **Windows_10_1B_Hotel_Files** presentation, and then on the **Home tab**, click the upper portion of the **New Slide** button to insert a new slide with the **Title Only** layout; this will be your fifth slide.

10 Click anywhere in the text *Click to add title*, type **Staffing Plan Files** and then click anywhere in the empty space below the title.

11 On the **Insert tab**, in the **Images group**, click **Screenshot**, and then click **Screen Clipping**. When the dimmed screen displays, move the ⊞ pointer to the upper left corner of the screen, hold down the left mouse button, and drag to the lower right corner but do not include the taskbar. Then release the mouse button.

> Because you have two windows displayed side by side, each window displays under Available Windows. Recall that to capture an entire screen that contains more than one window, use the Screen Clipping tool with which you can capture a snapshot of your screen.

12 If necessary, close the Design Ideas pane on the right. On the **Picture Tools Format tab**, in the **Size group**, click in the **Shape Height** box, type **5** and press Enter. As necessary, drag the image down so that the title you typed is visible.

13 Click outside of the image to deselect it, and then press Ctrl + Home to display the first slide in your presentation; your presentation contains five slides.

14 In the upper right, **Close** ☒ the **PowerPoint** window, and when prompted, click **Save**.

15 **Close** ☒ all open windows.

For Non-MyLab Submissions Determine What Your Instructor Requires for Submission
As directed by your instructor, submit your completed PowerPoint file.

16 In **MyLab IT**, locate and click the Grader Project **Windows 10 1B Hotel Files**. In **step 3**, under **Upload Completed Assignment**, click **Choose File**. In the **Open** dialog box, navigate to your **Windows 10 Chapter 1 folder**, and then click your **Student_Windows_10_1B_Hotel_Files** file one time to select it. In the lower right corner of the **Open** dialog box, click **Open**.

> The name of your selected file displays above the Upload button.

17 To submit your file to **MyLab IT** for grading, click **Upload**, wait a moment for a green **Success!** message, and then in **step 4**, click the blue **Submit for Grading** button. Click **Close Assignment** to return to your list of **Course Materials**.

> **MORE KNOWLEDGE** | **Deleting Files and Using the Recycle Bin**
>
> It is good practice to delete files and folders that you no longer need from your hard disk drive and removable storage devices. Doing so makes it easier to keep your data organized and also frees up storage space.
>
> When you delete a file or folder from any area of your computer's hard disk drive or from OneDrive, the file or folder is not immediately deleted. Instead, the deleted item is stored in the **Recycle Bin** and remains there until the Recycle Bin is emptied. Thus, you can recover an item deleted from your computer's hard disk drive or OneDrive so long as the Recycle Bin has not been emptied. Items deleted from removable storage devices like a USB flash drive and from some network drives are immediately deleted and cannot be recovered from the Recycle Bin.
>
> To permanently delete a file without first moving it to the Recycle Bin, click the item, hold down Shift, and then press Delete. A message will display indicating *Are you sure you want to permanently delete this file?* Use caution when using Shift + Delete to permanently delete a file because this action is not reversible.
>
> You can restore items by dragging them from the file list of the Recycle Bin window to the file list of the folder window in which you want to restore. Or, you can restore them to the location they were deleted from by right-clicking the items in the file list of the Recycle Bin window and selecting Restore.

You have completed Project 1B **END**

wavebreakmedia/Shutterstock, Monkey Business Images/Fotolia, Ivanko80/Shutterstock, Monkey Business Images/Shutterstock

Microsoft Office Specialist (MOS) Skills in This Chapter

Project 1A

Microsoft Word

1.1.1	Search for text
1.2.1	Set up document pages
1.2.4	Configure page background elements
1.2.4	Modify basic document properties
1.3.1	Modify basic document properties
1.4.1	Locate and remove hidden properties and personal information
1.4.2	Locate and correct accessibility issues
1.4.3	Locate and correct compatibility issues
2.2.5	Clear formatting
5.2.6	Format 3D models
5.4.3	Add alternative text to objects for accessibility

Microsoft Excel

5.3.3	Add alternative text to charts for accessibility

Build Your E-Portfolio

An E-Portfolio is a collection of evidence, stored electronically, that showcases what you have accomplished while completing your education. Collecting and then sharing your work products with potential employers reflects your academic and career goals. Your completed documents from the following projects are good examples to show what you have learned: 1A and 1B.

GO! For Job Success

Discussion: Managing Your Computer Files

Your instructor may assign this discussion to your class, and then ask you to think about, or discuss with your classmates, these questions:

g-stockstudio/Shutterstock

Why do you think it is important to follow specific guidelines when naming and organizing your files?

Why is it impractical to store files and shortcuts to programs on your desktop?

How are you making the transition from storing all your files on physical media, such as flash drives or the hard drive of your computer, to storing your files in the cloud where you can access them from any computer with an internet connection?

End of Chapter

Summary

Many Office features and commands, such as accessing the Open and Save As dialog boxes, performing commands from the ribbon and from dialog boxes, and using the Clipboard are the same in all Office desktop apps.

A desktop app is installed on your computer and requires a computer operating system such as Microsoft Windows or Apple's macOS to run. The programs in Microsoft Office 365 and Office 2019 are considered to be desktop apps.

The Windows 10 Start menu is your connected dashboard—this is your one-screen view of information that updates continuously with new information and personal communications that are important to you.

File Explorer is at work anytime you are viewing the contents of a location, a folder, or a file. Use File Explorer to navigate your Windows 10 folder structure that stores and organizes the files you create.

GO! Learn It Online

Review the concepts, key terms, and MOS skills in this chapter by completing these online challenges, which you can find at **MyLab IT**.

Chapter Quiz: Answer matching and multiple-choice questions to test what you have learned in this chapter.

Lessons on the GO!: Learn how to use all the new apps and features as they are introduced by Microsoft.

Quiz: Answer questions to review the MOS skills that you practiced in this chapter.

Monkey Business Images/Fotolia

Glossary

Glossary of Chapter Key Terms

.png file An image file type that can be transferred over the internet, an acronym for Portable Network Graphic.

.txt file A simple file consisting of lines of text with no formatting that almost any computer can open and display.

3D models A new kind of shape that you can insert from an online library of ready-to-use three-dimensional graphics.

Address bar In a File Explorer window, the area that displays your current location in the folder structure as a series of links separated by arrows.

Alignment The placement of text or objects relative to the margins.

Alignment guides Green lines that display when you move an object to assist in alignment.

Alt text Text added to a picture or object that helps people using a screen reader understand what the object is; also called *alternative text*.

Alternative text Text added to a picture or object that helps people using a screen reader understand what the object is; also called *alt text*.

Application A computer program that helps you perform a task for a specific purpose.

AutoSave An Office 365 feature that saves your document every few seconds—if saved on OneDrive, OneDrive for Business, or SharePoint Online—and enables you to share the document with others for real-time co-authoring.

Backstage tabs The area along the left side of Backstage view with tabs to display screens with related groups of commands.

Backstage view A centralized space for file management tasks; for example, opening, saving, printing, publishing, or sharing a file.

Bing Microsoft's search engine.

Bookmark A command that marks a word, section, or place in a document so that you can jump to it quickly without scrolling.

Booting the computer The process of turning on the computer.

Center alignment The alignment of text or objects centered horizontally between the left and right margin.

Check Accessibility A command that checks a document for content that people with disabilities might find difficult to read.

Check Compatibility A command that searches your document for features that may not be supported by older versions of Office.

Click The action of pressing the left button of the mouse pointing device.

Clipboard A temporary storage area that holds text or graphics that you select and then cut or copy.

Cloud computing Applications and services that are accessed over the internet.

Cloud storage Online storage of data so that you can access your data from different places and devices.

Commands An instruction to a computer program that causes an action to be carried out.

Compressed Folder Tools A command available in File Explorer with which you can extract compressed files.

Compressed files Files that have been reduced in size, take up less storage space, and can be transferred to other computers faster than uncompressed files.

Content pane In a File Explorer window, another name for the file list.

Context menus Menus that display commands and options relevant to the selected text or object; also called *shortcut menus*.

Context-sensitive commands Commands that display on a shortcut menu that relate to the object or text that is selected.

Contextual tab A tab added to the ribbon automatically when a specific object is selected and that contains commands relevant to the selected object.

Copy A command that duplicates a selection and places it on the Clipboard.

Cortana Microsoft's intelligent personal assistant in Windows 10 and also available on other devices; named for the intelligent female character in the video game Halo.

Cut A command that removes a selection and places it on the Clipboard.

Dashboard The right side of the Start menu that is a one-screen view of links to information and programs that matter to you.

Data The documents, worksheets, pictures, songs, and so on that you create and store during the day-to-day use of your computer.

Data management The process of managing files and folders.

Default The term that refers to the current selection or setting that is automatically used by a computer program unless you specify otherwise.

Deselect The action of canceling the selection of an object or block of text by clicking outside of the selection.

Desktop A simulation of a real desk that represents your work area; here you can arrange icons such as shortcuts to files, folders, and various types of documents in the same manner you would arrange physical objects on top of a desk.

Desktop app A computer program that is installed on your PC and requires a computer operating system such as Microsoft Windows to run; also known as a *desktop application*.

Desktop application A computer program that is installed on your PC and requires a computer operating system such as Microsoft Windows to run; also known as a *desktop app*.

Desktop shortcuts Desktop icons that can link to items accessible on your computer such as a program, file, folder, disk drive, printer, or another computer.

Details pane When activated in a folder window, displays—on the right—the most common file properties associated with the selected file.

Details view A command that displays a list of files or folders and their most common properties.

Dialog box A small window that displays options for completing a task.

Dictate A feature in Word, PowerPoint, Outlook, and OneNote for Windows 10; when you enable Dictate, you start talking and as you talk, text appears in your document or slide.

Dialog Box Launcher A small icon that displays to the right of some group names on the ribbon and that opens a related dialog box or pane providing additional options and commands related to that group.

Document properties Details about a file that describe or identify it, including the title, author name, subject, and keywords that identify the document's topic or contents; also known as *metadata*.

Double-click The action of pressing the left mouse button two times in rapid succession while holding the mouse still.

Glossary

Download The action of transferring or copying a file from another location—such as a cloud storage location, your college's Learning Management System, or from an internet site—to your computer.

Drag The action of holding down the left mouse button while moving your mouse.

Drive An area of storage that is formatted with a file system compatible with your operating system and is identified by a drive letter.

Edit The process of making changes to text or graphics in an Office file.

Editor A digital writing assistant in Word and Outlook that displays misspellings, grammatical mistakes, and writing style issues.

Ellipsis A set of three dots indicating incompleteness; an ellipsis following a command name indicates that a dialog box will display if you click the command.

Enhanced ScreenTip A ScreenTip that displays useful descriptive information about the command.

Extract To decompress, or pull out, files from a compressed form.

File Information stored on a computer under a single name.

File Explorer The Windows program that displays the contents of locations, folders, and files on your computer.

File Explorer window A window that displays the contents of the current location and contains helpful parts so that you can navigate—explore within the file organizing structure of Windows.

File list In a File Explorer window, the area that displays the contents of the current location.

File name extension A set of characters at the end of a file name that helps Windows understand what kind of information is in a file and what program should open it.

File properties Information about a file, such as the author, the date the file was last changed, and any descriptive tags.

Fill The inside color of an object.

Filtered list A display of files that is limited based on specified criteria.

Folder A container in which you can store files.

Folder structure The hierarchy of folders.

Folder window A window that typically displays the File List for a folder.

Font A set of characters with the same design and shape.

Font styles Formatting emphasis such as bold, italic, and underline.

Footer A reserved area for text or graphics that displays at the bottom of each page in a document.

Format Painter The command to copy the formatting of specific text or to copy the formatting of a paragraph and then apply it in other locations in your document; when active, the pointer takes the shape of a paintbrush.

Formatting The process of applying Office commands to make your documents easy to read and to add visual touches and design elements to make your document inviting to the reader; establishes the overall appearance of text, graphics, and pages in an Office file—for example, in a Word document.

Formatting marks Characters that display on the screen, but do not print, indicating where the Enter key, the Spacebar, and the Tab key were pressed; also called *nonprinting characters*.

Free-form snip From the Snipping Tool, a command that draws an irregular line such as a circle around an area of the screen.

Full-screen snip From the Snipping Tool, a command that captures the entire screen.

Gallery An Office feature that displays a list of potential results.

Gradient fill A fill effect in which one color fades into another.

Graphical user interface Graphics such as an image of a file folder or wastebasket that you click to activate the item represented.

Groups On the Office ribbon, the sets of related commands that you might need for a specific type of task.

GUI An abbreviation of the term graphical user interface.

Hamburger Another name for a hamburger menu.

Hamburger menu Another name for a menu icon, deriving from the three lines that bring to mind a hamburger on a bun.

Hard disk drive The primary storage device located inside your computer where some of your files and programs are typically stored, usually designated as drive C.

Hierarchy An arrangement where items are ranked and where each level is lower in rank than the item above it

Icons Small images that represent commands, files, applications, or other windows.

Info tab The tab in Backstage view that displays information about the current file.

Insertion point A blinking vertical line that indicates where text or graphics will be inserted.

Inspect Document A command that searches your document for hidden data of personal information that you might not want to share publicly.

JPEG An acronym that stands for *Joint Photographic Experts Group* and that is a common file type used by digital cameras and computers to store digital pictures.

Jump List A display of destinations and tasks from a program's taskbar icon when you right-click the icon.

Keyboard shortcut A combination of two or more keyboard keys, used to perform a task that would otherwise require a mouse.

KeyTip The letter that displays on a command in the ribbon and that indicates the key you can press to activate the command when keyboard control of the ribbon is activated.

Keywords Custom file properties in the form of words that you associate with a document to give an indication of the document's content.

Landscape orientation A page orientation in which the paper is wider than it is tall.

Layout Options A button that displays when an object is selected and that has commands to choose how the object interacts with surrounding text.

Live Preview A technology that shows the result of applying an editing or formatting change as you point to possible results—*before* you actually apply it.

Live tiles Tiles that are constantly updated with fresh information.

Location Any disk drive, folder, or other place in which you can store files and folders.

Lock screen A background that fills the computer screen when the computer boots up or wakes up from sleep mode.

Maximize A window control button that will enlarge the size of the window to fill the entire screen.

Menu A list of commands within a category.

Menu bar A group of menus at the top of a program window.

Menu icon A button consisting of three lines that, when clicked, expands a menu; often used in mobile applications because it is compact to use on smaller screens—also referred to a *hamburger menu*.

Glossary

Metadata Details about a file that describe or identify it, including the title, author name, subject, and keywords that identify the document's topic or contents; also known as *document properties*.

Microsoft account A user account with which you can sign in to any Windows 10 computer on which you have, or create, an account.

Microsoft Store app A smaller app that you download from the Microsoft Store.

Mini toolbar A small toolbar containing frequently used formatting commands that displays as a result of selecting text or objects.

Minimize A window control button that will keep a program open but will remove it from screen view.

Move In File Explorer, the action of removing a file or folder from its original location and storing it in a new location.

Mouse pointer Any symbol that displays on the screen in response to moving the mouse.

MRU Acronym for *most recently used*, which refers to the state of some commands that retain the characteristic most recently applied; for example, the Font Color button retains the most recently used color until a new color is chosen.

Navigate A process for exploring within the file organizing structure of Windows.

Navigation pane The area on the left side of the File Explorer window to access your OneDrive, folders on your PC, devices and drives connected to your PC, and other PCs on your network.

Nonprinting characters Characters that display on the screen, but do not print, indicating where the Enter key, the Spacebar, and the Tab key were pressed; also called *formatting marks*.

Notepad A basic text-editing program included with Windows 10 that you can use to create simple documents.

Object A text box, picture, table, or shape that you can select and then move and resize.

Office 365 A version of Microsoft Office to which you subscribe for an annual fee.

OneDrive Microsoft's free cloud storage for anyone with a free Microsoft account.

Operating system A specific type of computer program that manages the other programs on a computing device such as a desktop computer, a laptop computer, a smartphone, a tablet computer, or a game console.

Option button In a dialog box, a round button that enables you to make one choice among two or more options.

Page Width A command that zooms the document so that the width of the page matches the width of the window.

Paragraph symbol The symbol ¶ that represents the end of a paragraph.

Parent folder The location in which the folder you are viewing is saved.

Paste The action of placing text or objects that have been copied or cut from one location to another location.

Paste Options gallery A gallery of buttons that provides a Live Preview of all the Paste options available in the current context.

Path A sequence of folders that leads to a specific file or folder.

PDF The acronym for Portable Document Format, which is a file format that creates an image that preserves the look of your file, but that cannot be easily changed; a popular format for sending documents electronically, because the document will display on most computers.

Pen A pen-shaped stylus that you tap on a computer screen.

Personal folder The folder created on the hard drive for each Windows 10 user account on a computer; for each user account—even if there is only one user on the computer—Windows 10 creates a personal folder labeled with the account holder's name.

Point to The action of moving the mouse pointer over a specific area.

Pointer Any symbol that displays on your screen in response to moving your mouse.

Pointing device A mouse or touchpad used to control the pointer.

Points A measurement of the size of a font; there are 72 points in an inch.

Portable Document Format A file format that creates an image that preserves the look of your file, but that cannot be easily changed; a popular format for sending documents electronically, because the document will display on most computers.

Portrait orientation A page orientation in which the paper is taller than it is wide.

Print Preview A view of a document as it will appear when you print it.

Program A set of instructions that a computer uses to accomplish a task.

Progress bar A bar that displays in a dialog box—and also on the taskbar button—that indicates visually the progress of a task such as a copy process, a download, or a file transfer.

pt The abbreviation for *point* when referring to a font size.

Quick access In the navigation pane in a File Explorer window, a list of files you have been working on and folders you use often.

Real-time co-authoring A process where two or more people work on the same file at the same time and see changes made by others in seconds.

Rectangular snip From the Snipping Tool, a command that draws a precise box by dragging the mouse pointer around an area of the screen to form a rectangle.

Recycle Bin The area where deleted items are stored until you empty the bin; enables you to recover deleted items until the bin is emptied.

Removable storage device A device such as a USB flash drive used to transfer information from one computer to another.

Resources The collection of the physical parts of your computer such as the central processing unit (CPU), memory, and any attached devices such as a printer.

Restore Down A command that resizes a window to its previous size.

Ribbon In Office applications, displays a group of task-oriented tabs that contain the commands, styles, and resources you need to work in an Office desktop app. In a File Explorer window, the area at the top that groups common tasks on tabs. such as copying and moving, creating new folders, emailing and zipping items, and changing the view on related tabs.

Right-click The action of clicking the right mouse button one time.

Sans serif font A font design with no lines or extensions on the ends of characters.

Screen reader Software that enables visually impaired users to read text on a computer screen to understand the content of pictures.

Screenshot Any captured image of your screen.

ScreenTip A small box that displays useful information when you perform various mouse actions such as pointing to screen elements or dragging.

Glossary

Scroll arrow An arrow found at either end of a scroll bar that can be clicked to move within the window in small increments.

Scroll bar A vertical bar that displays when the contents of a window or pane are not completely visible; a scroll bar can be vertical, displayed at the side of the window, or horizontal, displayed at the bottom of a window.

Scroll box Within a scroll bar, a box that you can move to bring the contents of the window into view.

Select To specify, by highlighting, a block of data or text on the screen with the intent of performing some action on the selection.

Selecting Highlighting, by dragging with your mouse, areas of text or data or graphics, so that the selection can be edited, formatted, copied, or moved.

Serif font A font design that includes small line extensions on the ends of the letters to guide the eye in reading from left to right.

SharePoint A Microsoft technology that enables employees in an organization to access information across organizational and geographic boundaries.

Shortcut menu A menu that displays commands and options relevant to the selected text or object; also called a *context menu*.

Sizing handles Small circles or squares that indicate a picture or object is selected.

Snap An action to arrange two or more open windows on your screen so that you can work with multiple screens at the same time.

Snap Assist A feature that displays all other open windows after one window is snapped.

Snip An image captured by the Snipping tool that can be annotated, saved, copied, or shared via email.

Snipping tool A Windows 10 program that captures an image of all or part of your computer's screen.

Split button A button divided into two parts and in which clicking the main part of the button performs a command and clicking the arrow opens a menu with choices.

Start menu A Windows 10 menu that displays as a result of clicking the Start button and that displays a list of installed programs on the left and a customizable group of tiles on the right that can act as a user dashboard.

Style A group of formatting commands, such as font, font size, font color, paragraph alignment, and line spacing that can be applied to a paragraph with one command.

Subfolder The term for a folder placed within another folder.

Synchronization The process of updating computer files that are in two or more locations according to specific rules—also called *syncing*.

Syncing The process of updating computer files that are in two or more locations according to specific rules—also called *synchronization*.

System tray Another term for the notification area on the taskbar that displays notification icons and the system clock and calendar.

Tabs (ribbon) On the Office ribbon, the name of each activity area.

Tags Custom file properties in the form of words that you associate with a document to give an indication of the document's content; used to help find and organize files. Also called keywords.

Task View A taskbar button that displays your desktop background with small images of all open programs and apps and from which you can see and switch between open apps, including desktop apps.

Taskbar The bar at the bottom of your Windows screen that contains buttons to launch programs and buttons for all open apps.

Tell Me A search feature for Microsoft Office commands that you activate by typing what you are looking for in the Tell Me box.

Tell me more A prompt within a ScreenTip that opens the Office online Help system with explanations about how to perform the command referenced in the ScreenTip.

Template A preformatted document that you can use as a starting point and then change to suit your needs.

Theme A predesigned combination of colors, fonts, and effects that look good together and that is applied to an entire document by a single selection.

Timeline A Windows 10 feature that when you click the Task view button, you can see activities you have worked on across your devices; for example, you can find a document, image, or video you worked on yesterday or a week ago.

Thumbnail A reduced image of a graphic.

Tiles A group of square and rectangular boxes that display on the start menu.

Title bar The bar across the top of the window that displays the program, file, or app name.

Toggle button A button that can be turned on by clicking it once and then turned off by clicking it again.

Toolbar A row, column, or block of buttons or icons that displays across the top of a window and that contains commands for tasks you perform with a single click.

Triple-click The action of clicking the left mouse button three times in rapid succession.

Undo On the Quick Access Toolbar, the command that reverses your last action.

Unzip The process of extracting files that have been compressed.

User account A user on a single computer.

Wallpaper Another term for the Desktop background.

Window snip From the Snipping Tool, a command that captures the entire displayed window.

Windows 10 An operating system developed by Microsoft Corporation that works with mobile computing devices and also with traditional desktop and laptop PCs.

XML Paper Specification A Microsoft file format that creates an image of your document and that opens in the XPS viewer.

XPS The acronym for *XML Paper Specification*—a Microsoft file format that creates an image of your document and that opens in the XPS viewer.

Zip The process of compressing files.

Zoom The action of increasing or decreasing the size of the viewing area on the screen.

Introducing Microsoft PowerPoint 2019

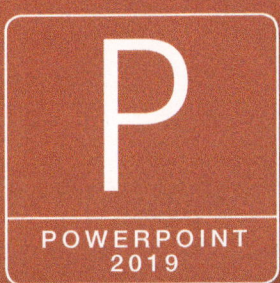

Sunshine Studio/Shutterstock

PowerPoint 2019: Introduction

Introduction to PowerPoint

Communication skills are critical to your success in many careers, and when it comes to communicating *your* ideas, presentation is everything! Whether you are planning to deliver your presentation in person or online—to a large audience or to a small group—Microsoft PowerPoint 2019 is a versatile business tool that will help you create presentations that make a lasting impression. Additionally, collaborating with others to develop a presentation is easy because you can share the slides you create by using your free Microsoft OneDrive cloud storage.

Microsoft PowerPoint 2019 includes a variety of themes that you can apply to a new presentation. Each theme includes several theme variants that coordinate colors, fonts, and effects. The benefit of this approach is that the variations evoke different moods and responses, yet the basic design remains the same. As a result, you can use a similar design within your company to brand your presentations, while still changing the colors to make the presentation appropriate to the audience and topic. You do not have to determine which colors work well together in the theme you choose, because professional designers have already done that for you. So you can concentrate on how best to communicate your message. Focus on creating dynamic, interesting presentations that keep your audience engaged!

Getting Started with Microsoft PowerPoint

1
POWERPOINT
2019

PROJECT 1A

Outcomes
Create a company overview presentation.

Objectives
1. Create a New Presentation
2. Edit a Presentation in Normal View
3. Add Pictures to a Presentation
4. Print and View a Presentation

PROJECT 1B

Outcomes
Create a new product announcement presentation.

Objectives
5. Edit an Existing Presentation
6. Format a Presentation
7. Use Slide Sorter View
8. Apply Slide Transitions

Bety X/Shuttestock

In This Chapter

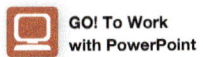
GO! To Work with PowerPoint

In this chapter, you will use Microsoft PowerPoint to study presentation skills, which are among the most important skills you will learn. Good presentation skills enhance your communications—written, electronic, and interpersonal. In this technology-enhanced world, communicating ideas clearly and concisely is a critical personal skill. Microsoft PowerPoint 2019 is presentation software with which you create electronic slide presentations. Use PowerPoint to present information to your audience effectively. You can start with a new, blank presentation and add content, pictures, and themes, or you can collaborate with colleagues by inserting slides that have been saved in other presentations.

The projects in this chapter relate to **Kodiak West Travel**, which is a travel agency with offices in Juneau, Anchorage, and Victoria. Kodiak West Travel works closely with local vendors to provide clients with specialized adventure travel itineraries. The company was established in 2001 in Juneau and built a loyal client base that led to the expansion into Anchorage and Victoria. As a full-service travel agency, Kodiak West Travel agents strive to provide their clients with travel opportunities that exceed their expectations. The company works with all major airlines, cruise lines, hotel chains, and vehicle rental companies as well as with small, specialized, boutique hotels.

PROJECT 1A

Company Overview Presentation

MyLab IT
Project 1A Grader for Instruction
Project 1A Simulation for Training and Review

Project Activities

In Activities 1.01 through 1.16, you will create the first five slides of a new presentation that Kodiak West Travel tour manager Ken Dakano is developing to introduce the tour services that the company offers. Your completed presentation will look similar to Figure 1.1.

Project Files for **MyLab IT** Grader

1. In your storage location, create a folder named **PowerPoint Chapter 1**.
2. In your **MyLab IT** course, locate and click **PowerPoint 1A KWT Overview**, Download Materials, and then Download All Files.
3. Extract the zipped folder to your PowerPoint Chapter 1 folder. Close the Grader download screens.
4. Take a moment to open the downloaded **PowerPoint_1A_KWT_Overview_Instructions**; note any recent updates to the book.

Project Results

GO! Project 1A
Where We're Going

Figure 1.1 Project 1A KWT Overview

For Non-MyLab Submissions

For Project 1A, you will need:
p01A_KWT_Overview
p01A_Bay
p01A_Glacier

In your storage location, create a folder named **PowerPoint Chapter 1**
In your PowerPoint Chapter 1 folder, save your presentation as:
Lastname_Firstname_1A_KWT_Overview

After you have named and saved your presentation, close the file and then, on the next page, begin with Step 1.

NOTE   **If You Are Using a Touch Screen**

Tap an item to click it.

Press and hold for a few seconds to right-click; release when the information or commands display.

Touch the screen with two or more fingers and then pinch together or stretch your fingers apart to zoom in and out.

Slide your finger on the screen to scroll—slide left to scroll right and slide right to scroll left.

Slide to rearrange—similar to dragging with a mouse.

Swipe to select—slide an item a short distance with a quick movement—to select an item and bring up commands, if any.

Objective 1   Create a New Presentation

ALERT   Because Office 365 is a cloud-based subscription service that receives continuous updates, you may encounter some variations in what appears on your screen and what is shown in this instruction. Microsoft Office 365 is fully installed on your PC or Mac; no internet access is necessary to create or edit documents. When you *are* connected to the internet, you will receive monthly upgrades and new features, so you always have the latest versions of Office apps as soon as they are available. Your subscription gives you continuous free access to the latest innovations and refinements.

GO! Learn How
Video P1-1

Microsoft PowerPoint 2019 is software you can use to present information to your audience effectively. You can edit and format a blank presentation by adding text, a presentation theme, and pictures. When you start PowerPoint, presentations you have recently opened, if any, display on the left. On the right you can select either a blank presentation or a *theme*—a set of unified design elements that provides a look for your presentation by applying colors, fonts, and effects. A presentation consists of one or more slides. Similar to a page in a document—a presentation *slide* can contain text, pictures, tables, charts, and other multimedia or graphic objects.

Activity 1.01 | Identifying Parts of the PowerPoint Window

In this Activity, you will start PowerPoint and identify the parts of the PowerPoint window.

1 Start PowerPoint. In the list of templates, click **Facet** to view a preview of the Facet theme and the color variations associated with this theme. If Facet is not visible, use the Search templates box to search for it. Below the theme preview, click either the left- or right-pointing **More Images** ◄ and ► arrows to view how various types of slides in this theme display. To the right of the preview, click each of the color variations. After you have viewed each color, click the original green color.

 MAC TIP   There is no color preview available in the Mac version of PowerPoint.

2 On either the left or right side of the preview window, notice the arrow, and then compare your screen with Figure 1.2. Click the right- or left-pointing arrow several times to view other available themes, and then return to the **Facet** theme.

You can use the arrows to the left and right of the preview window to scroll through the available themes.

MAC TIP Scroll down on the opening screen to view other themes.

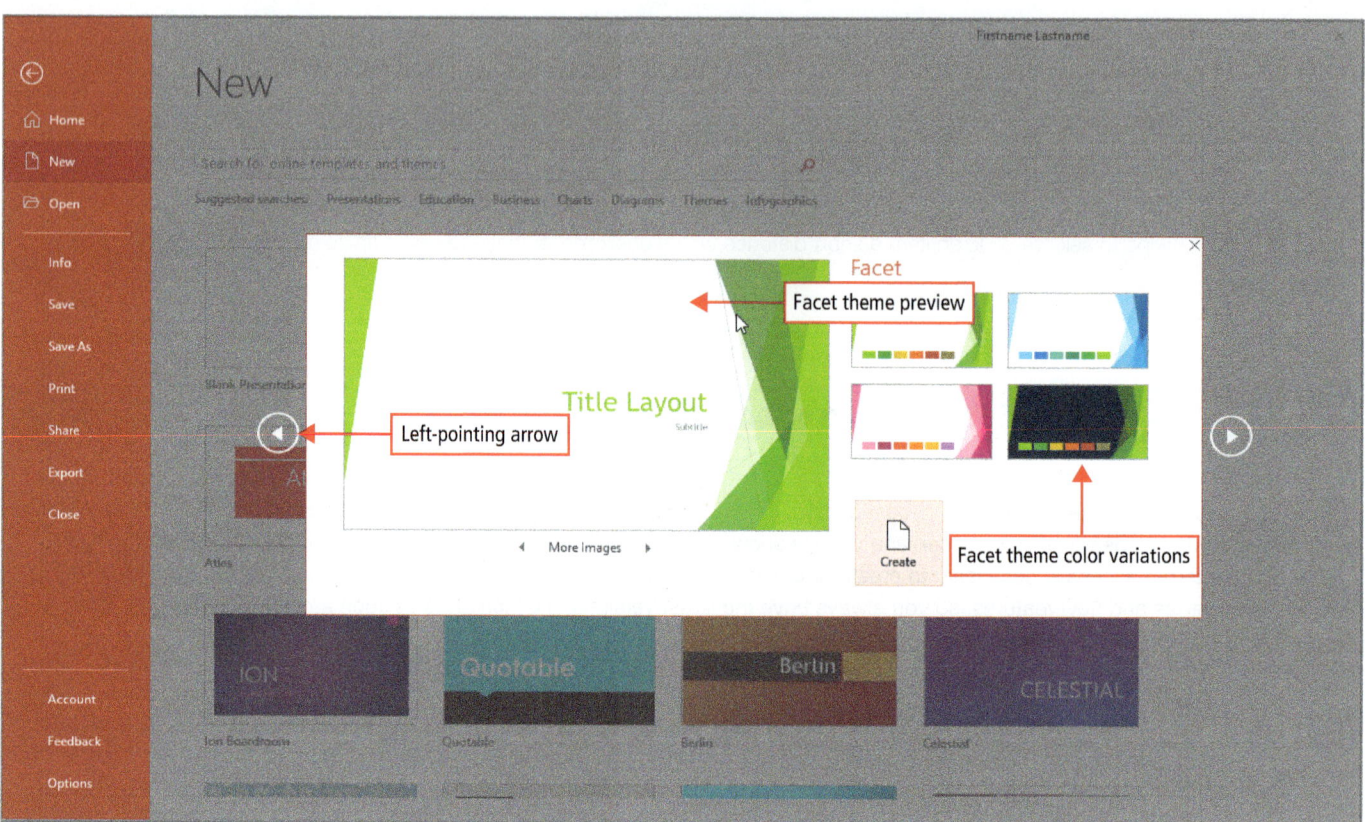

Figure 1.2

3 In the lower right area of the preview window, click **Create** to begin a new presentation using the **Facet** theme.

4 Compare your screen with Figure 1.3, and then take a moment to study the parts of the PowerPoint window described in the table in Figure 1.4.

The presentation displays in *normal view*, which is the primary editing view in PowerPoint where you write and design your presentations. On the left, a pane displays miniature images—*thumbnails*—of the slides in your presentation. On the right, the *Slide pane* displays a larger image of the active slide.

MAC TIP To display group names on the ribbon, display the menu, click PowerPoint, click Preferences, click View, select the Show group titles check box.

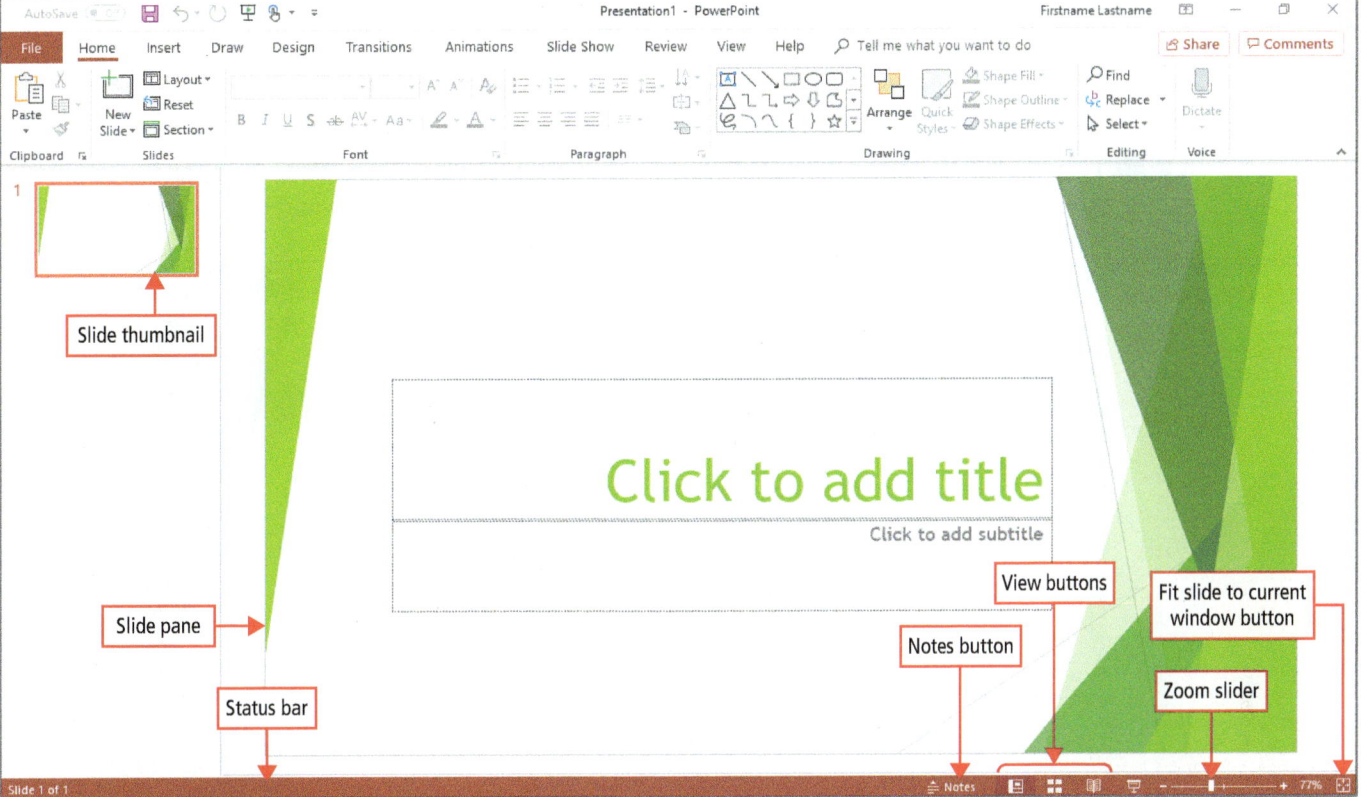

Figure 1.3

Microsoft PowerPoint Screen Elements	
Screen Element	**Description**
Slide pane	Displays a large image of the active slide.
Slide thumbnails	Miniature images of each slide in the presentation. Clicking a slide thumbnail displays the slide in the Slide pane.
Status bar	Displays, in a horizontal bar at the bottom of the presentation window, the current slide number, number of slides in a presentation, Notes button, View buttons, Zoom slider, and Fit slide to current window button; you can customize this area to include additional information.
View buttons	Control the look of the presentation window with a set of commands.
Zoom slider	Zooms the slide displayed in the Slide pane, in and out.
Fit slide to current window button	Fits the active slide to the maximum view in the Slide pane.

Figure 1.4

5 In the upper right corner of your screen, click **Close** ⊠ to close PowerPoint. Do not save your file. Navigate to your **PowerPoint Chapter 1 folder**, and then double-click the PowerPoint file you downloaded from **MyLab IT** that displays your name—**Student_PowerPoint_1A_ KWT_Overview**. In your presentation, if necessary, at the top, click **Enable Editing**.

For Non-MyLab Submissions
Open your saved **Lastname_Firstname_1A_KWT_Overview** presentation.

Activity 1.02 | Entering Presentation Text

When you create a new presentation, PowerPoint displays a new blank presentation with a single slide—a title slide in Normal view. The *title slide* is usually the first slide in a presentation; it introduces the presentation topic.

1 In the **Slide pane**, click in the text *Click to add title*, which is the title placeholder.

A *placeholder* is a box on a slide with dotted or dashed borders that holds title and body text or other content such as charts, tables, and pictures. This slide contains two placeholders, one for the title and one for the subtitle.

2 Type **Kodiak West** and then click in the subtitle placeholder. Type **Your Travel** and then press Enter to create a new line in the subtitle placeholder. Type **Your Way** and then compare your screen with Figure 1.5.

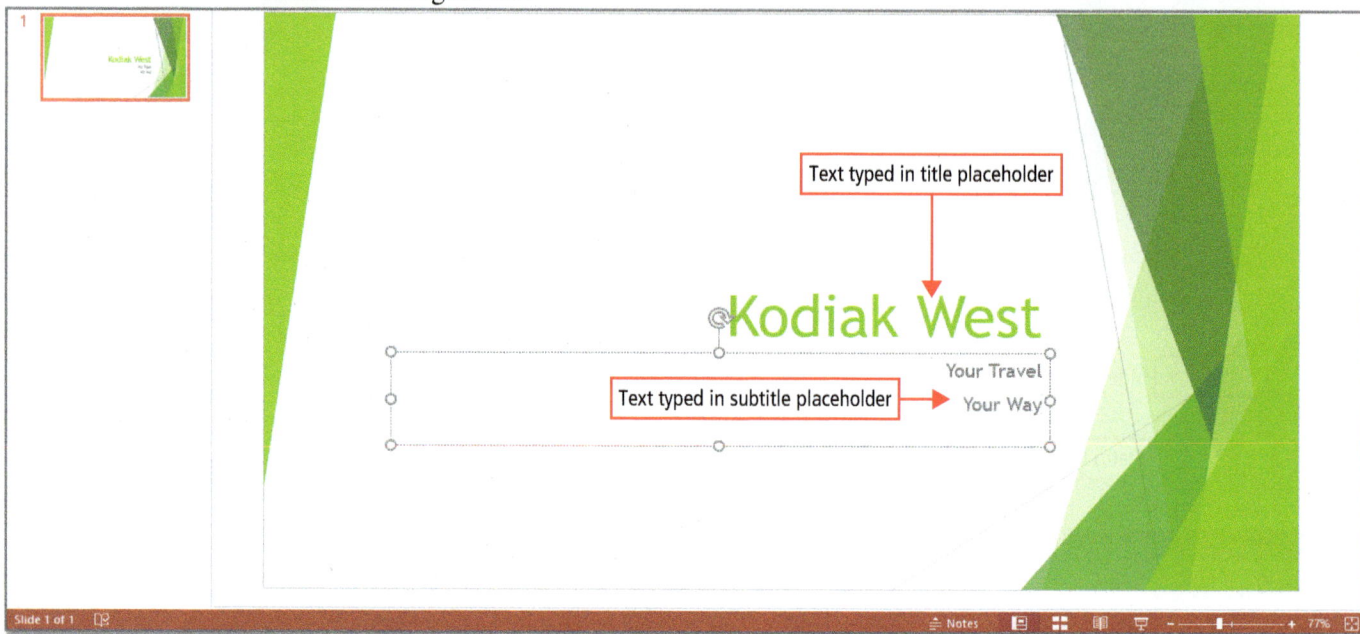

Figure 1.5

3 On the **Quick Access Toolbar**, click **Save** 🖫.

Activity 1.03 | Applying a Presentation Theme

A theme is a set of unified design elements that provides a look for your presentation by applying colors, fonts, and effects. After you create a presentation, you can change the look of your presentation by applying a different theme. Kodiak West Travel wants a theme that evokes a feeling of nature.

1 On the ribbon, click the **Design tab**. In the **Themes group**, click **More** ⯆ to display the **Themes** gallery. Compare your screen with Figure 1.6.

The themes displayed on your system may differ from Figure 1.6.

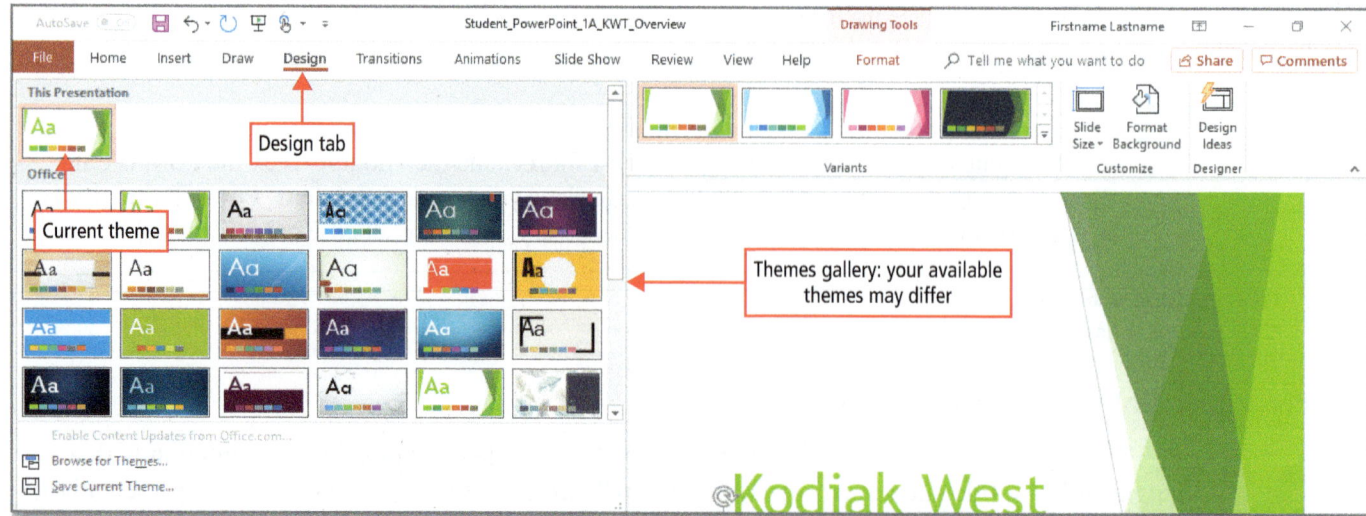

Figure 1.6

2 In the gallery, point to several of the themes and notice that a ScreenTip displays the name of each theme, and the Live Preview feature displays how each theme would look if applied to your presentation.

The first theme that displays is the Office Theme.

MAC TIP Live previews do not display in the Mac version of PowerPoint.

3 Use the ScreenTips to locate the **Organic** theme shown in Figure 1.7.

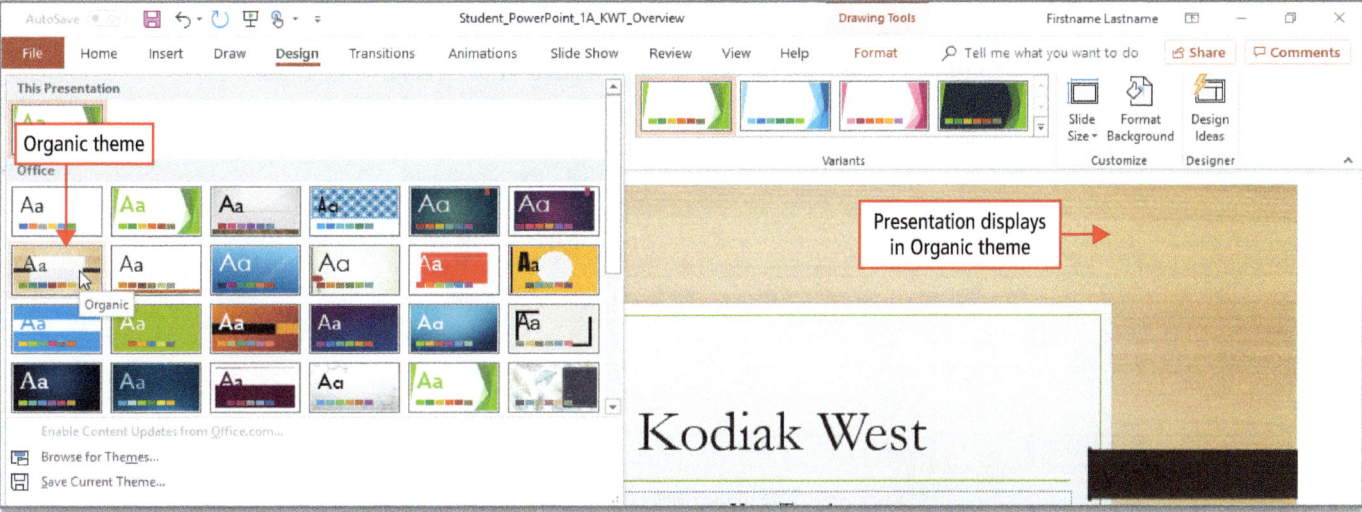

Figure 1.7

4 Click **Organic** to change the presentation theme and then **Save** 💾 your presentation.

ALERT If your system does not have the Organic theme, use the theme file downloaded with your data files from **MyLab IT**. In the themes gallery, click Browse for Themes, navigate to your PowerPoint Chapter 1 folder, locate the Organic.thmx file and click Apply.

Objective 2 Edit a Presentation in Normal View

GO! Learn How
Video P1-2

Editing is the process of modifying a presentation by adding and deleting slides or by changing the contents of individual slides.

Activity 1.04 | Inserting a New Slide

2.1.3

Your presentation consists of a single slide. Most presentations consist of multiple slides. This presentation will highlight the company and consist of five slides when finished.

1 On the **Home tab**, in the **Slides group**, point to the **New Slide arrow**—the lower part of the New Slide button. Compare your screen with Figure 1.8.

The New Slide button is a *split button*—a type of button in which clicking the main part of the button performs a command and clicking the arrow opens a menu, list, or gallery. The upper, main part of the New Slide button, when clicked, inserts a slide without displaying any options. The lower part—the New Slide arrow—when clicked, displays a gallery of slide *layouts*— the arrangement of elements, such as title and subtitle text, lists, pictures, tables, charts, shapes, and movies, on a slide.

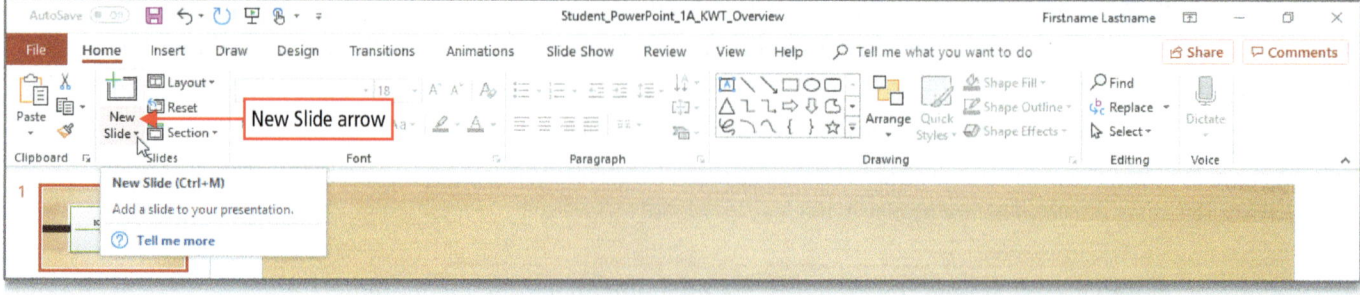

Figure 1.8

> **2** In the **Slides group**, click the lower portion of the **New Slide** button—the **New Slide arrow**—to display the gallery, and then compare your screen with Figure 1.9.

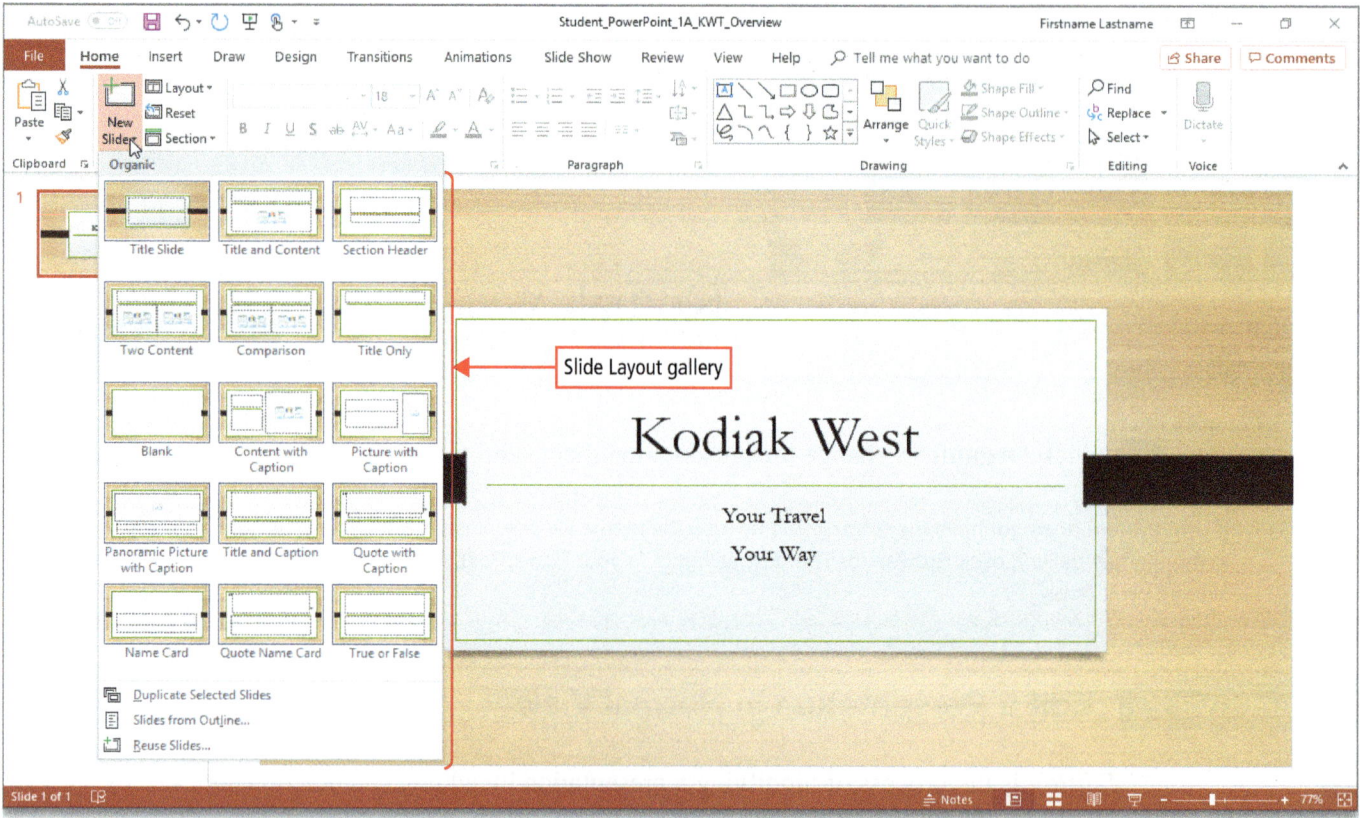

Figure 1.9

> **3** In the gallery, click the **Panoramic Picture with Caption** layout to insert a new slide. Notice that the new blank slide displays in the **Slide pane**, and a slide thumbnail displays at the left. Compare your screen with Figure 1.10.

BY TOUCH In the gallery, tap the desired layout to insert a new slide.

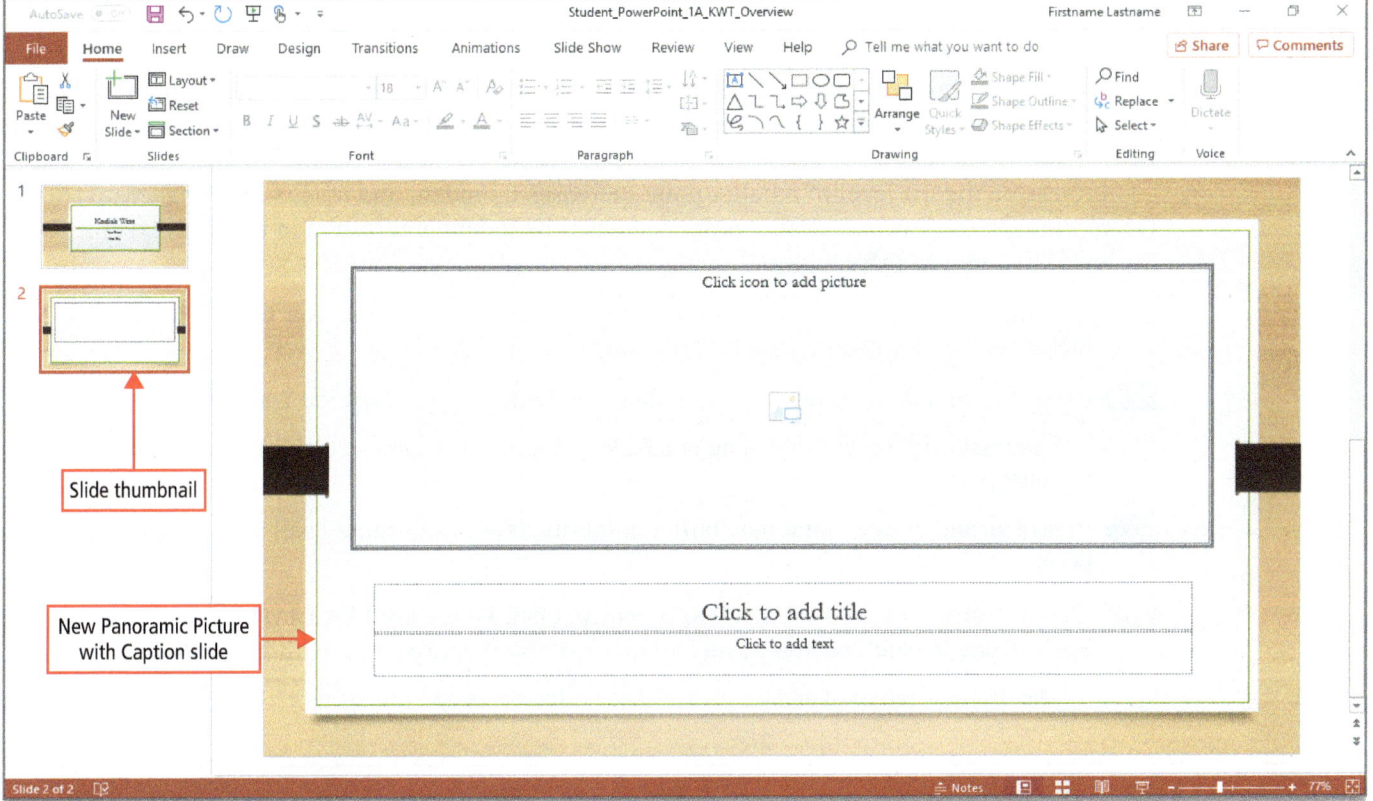

Figure 1.10

4 On the new slide, below the picture placeholder, click the text *Click to add title*, and then type **Your Dreams**

5 Below the title placeholder, click in the text placeholder. Type **Whether you want to trek on a glacier or spend your time in quiet solitude, Kodiak West Travel can make your dream a reality.** Compare your screen with Figure 1.11.

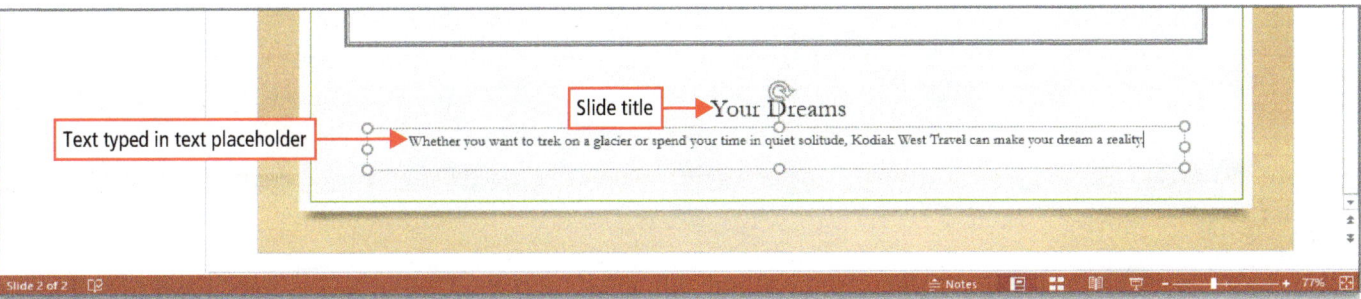

Figure 1.11

6 On the **Home tab**, in the **Slides group**, click the **New Slide arrow** to display the gallery, and then click **Title and Content**. In the title placeholder, type **Our Expertise** and then below the title placeholder, click in the content placeholder. Type **Over 20 years of experience in the travel industry**

7 **Save** 💾 your presentation.

Activity 1.05 | Increasing and Decreasing List Levels

3.1.3

You can organize text in a PowerPoint presentation according to *list levels*. List levels, each represented by a bullet symbol, are similar to outline levels. On a slide, list levels are identified by the bullet style, indentation, and the size of the text. The first level on an individual slide is the title.

Increasing the list level of a bullet point increases its indent and results in a smaller text size. Decreasing the list level of a bullet point decreases its indent and results in a larger text size. Use list levels to organize information.

1 ▶ On **Slide 3**, if necessary, click at the end of the first bullet point after the word *industry*, and then press Enter to insert a new bullet point.

2 ▶ Press Tab, and then notice that the bullet is indented. Type **Certified Travel Associates**

By pressing Tab at the beginning of a bullet point, you can increase the list level and indent the bullet point.

3 ▶ Press Enter and notice that a new bullet point displays at the same level as the previous bullet point.

4 ▶ On the **Home tab**, in the **Paragraph group**, click **Decrease List Level** ⬅️. Type **Specializing in land and sea travel** and then compare your screen with Figure 1.12.

The indent is removed and the size of the text increases.

Figure 1.12

5 ▶ Press Enter, and then on the **Home tab**, click **Increase List Level** ➡️. Type **Pacific Northwest including U.S. and Canada**

You can use the Increase List Level button to indent the bullet point.

6 ▶ Compare your screen with Figure 1.13, and then **Save** 💾 your presentation.

Figure 1.13

Activity 1.06 | **Adding Speaker Notes to a Presentation**

The ***Notes pane*** is an area of the Normal view window that displays below the Slide pane with space to type notes about the active slide. You can refer to these notes while making a presentation, reminding you of the important points that you want to discuss. This will be helpful when employees of Kodiak West give the presentation before new customers.

1 With **Slide 3** displayed, in the **Status bar**, click **Notes** 📑, and then notice that below the Slide pane, the Notes pane displays. Click in the **Notes** pane, and then type **Kodiak West Travel has locations in Juneau, Anchorage, and Victoria.**

The Notes button is a toggle button. Clicking once will display the Notes pane, clicking again will hide it.

2 **Save** 💾 your presentation, and then compare your screen with Figure 1.14.

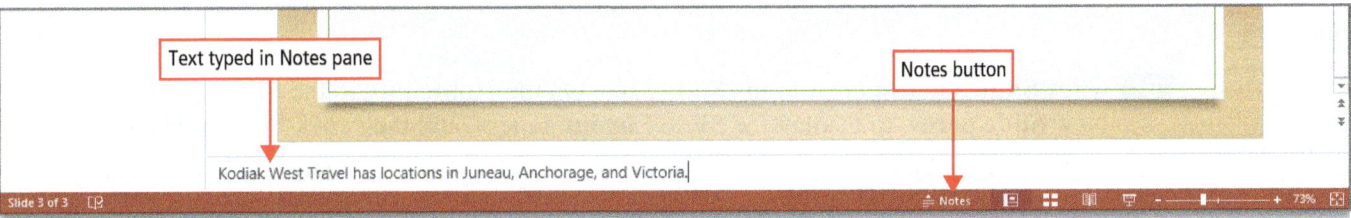

Figure 1.14

Activity 1.07 | **Displaying and Editing Slides in the Slide Pane**

1 On the left side of the PowerPoint window, look at the slide thumbnails, and then notice that the presentation contains three slides. On the right side of the PowerPoint window, in the vertical scroll bar, point to the scroll box, and then hold down the left mouse button to display a ScreenTip indicating the slide number and title.

2 Drag the scroll box up until the ScreenTip displays *Slide: 2 of 3 Your Dreams*. Compare your slide with Figure 1.15, and then release the mouse button to display **Slide 2**.

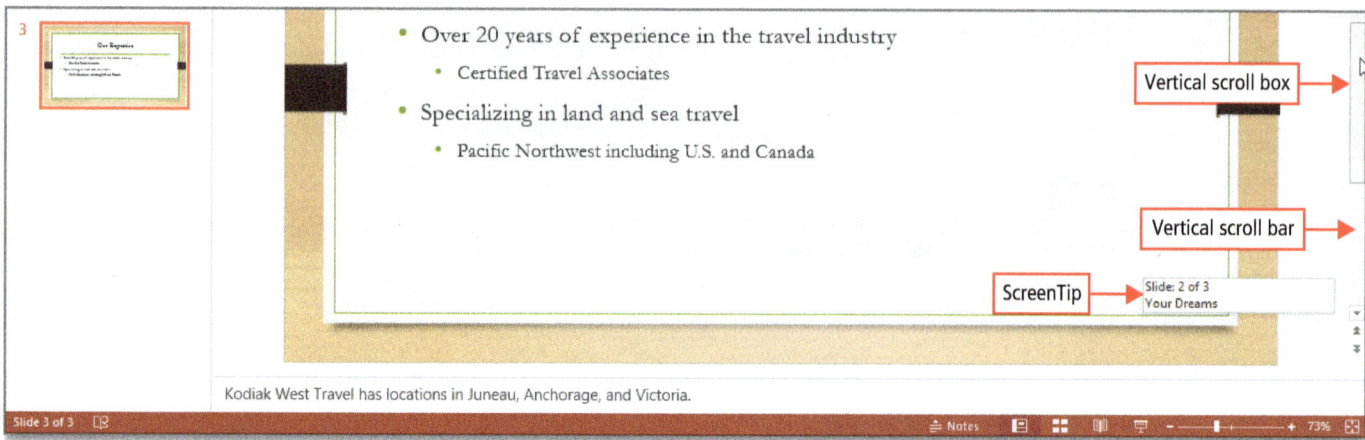

Figure 1.15

3 At the bottom of the slide, in the content placeholder, click at the end of the sentence, after the period. Press Spacebar, and then type **If you can dream it, we can help you get there.**

4 On the left side of the PowerPoint window, in the slide thumbnails, point to **Slide 3**, and then notice that a ScreenTip displays the slide title. Compare your screen with Figure 1.16.

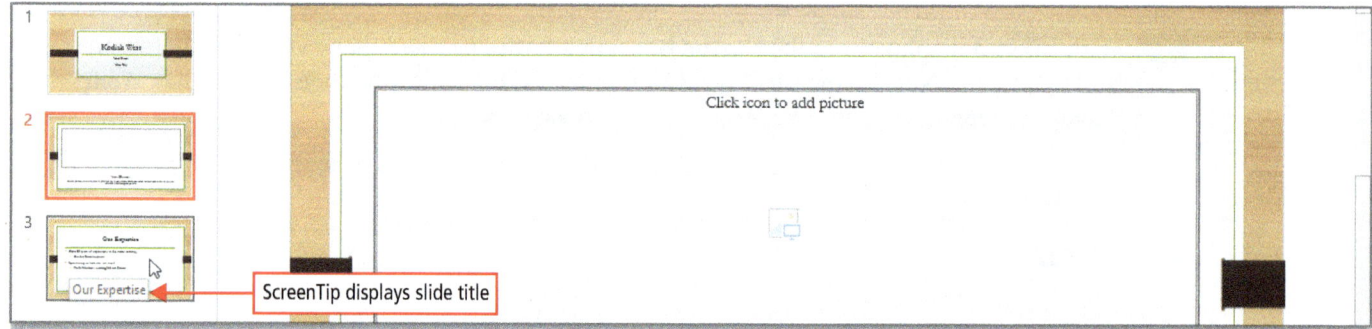

Figure 1.16

5 Click **Slide 3** to display it in the Slide pane. On the **Home tab**, in the **Slides group**, click the **New Slide arrow** to display the **Slide Layout** gallery, and then click **Section Header**.

A *section header* is a type of slide layout that changes the look and flow of a presentation by providing text placeholders that do not contain bullet points.

6 Click in the title placeholder, and then type **About Our Company**

7 Click in the content placeholder below the title, and then type **Kodiak West Travel was established in May of 2001 by Ken Dakona and Mariam Dorner, two Alaska residents whose sense of adventure and commitment to ecotourism is an inherent aspect of their travel itineraries.** Compare your screen with Figure 1.17.

The placeholder text is resized to fit within the placeholder. The AutoFit Options button displays.

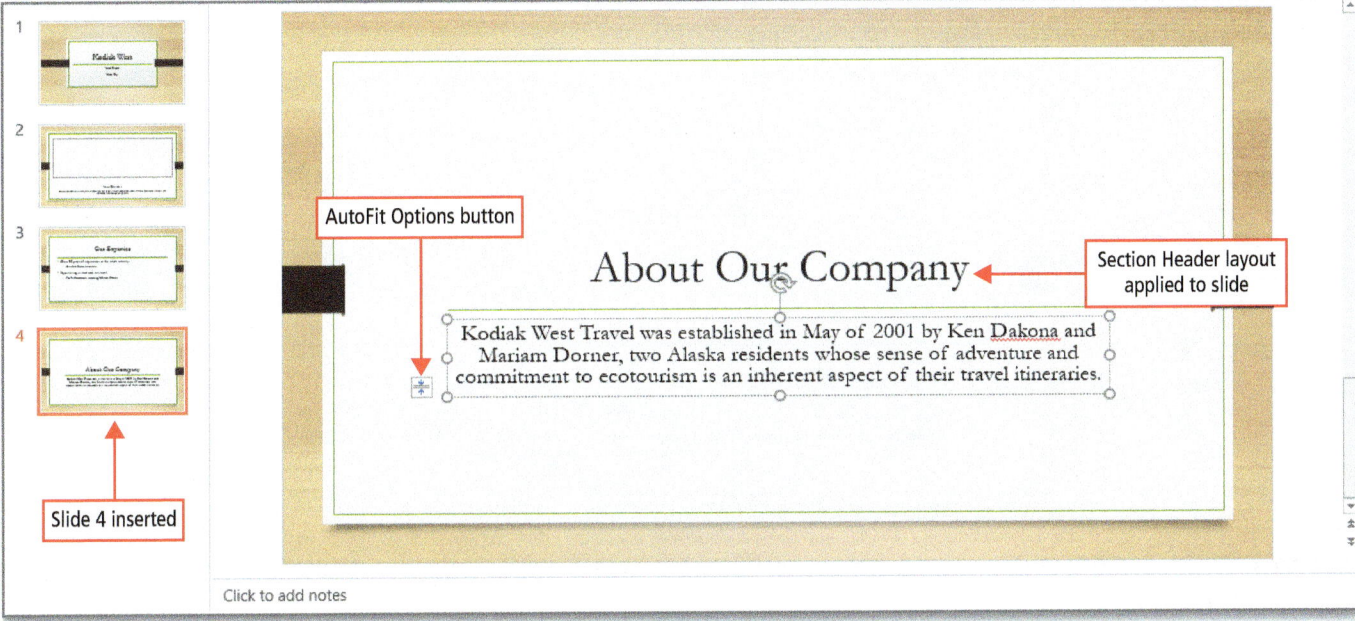

Figure 1.17

8 ▶ Click **AutoFit Options** ⊞, review the AutoFit options and then click outside the menu to close it.

The *AutoFit Text to Placeholder* option keeps the text contained within the placeholder by reducing the size of the text. The *Stop Fitting Text to This Placeholder* option turns off the AutoFit option so that the text can flow beyond the placeholder border; the text size remains unchanged. You can also choose to split the text between two slides, continue on a new slide, or divide the text into two columns.

💻 **MAC TIP** To adjust AutoFit, on the Shape Format tab, click More Formats to open the Format pane. On the Format pane, click Text Options, and click the Text Box tab.

9 ▶ In the slide thumbnails, click **Slide 1** to display it in the Slide pane, and then in the slide title, click at the end of the word *West*. Press `Spacebar`, and then type **Travel**

Clicking a slide thumbnail is the most common method used to display a slide in the Slide pane.

10 ▶ **Save** 🖫 your presentation.

Objective 3 | Add Pictures to a Presentation

GO! Learn How
Video P1-3

Photographic images add impact to a presentation and help the audience visualize your message. Photos can be inserted from files or from online sources, and format and enhance the images using tools built into PowerPoint.

Activity 1.08 | Inserting a Picture from a File

Many slide layouts in PowerPoint accommodate digital picture files so that you can easily add pictures you have stored. The travel agency has a collection of photographs to be inserted in the presentation that highlights the beauty of the region.

1 ▶ Display **Slide 2**, and then compare your screen with Figure 1.18.

In the center of the picture placeholder, the *Pictures* button displays.

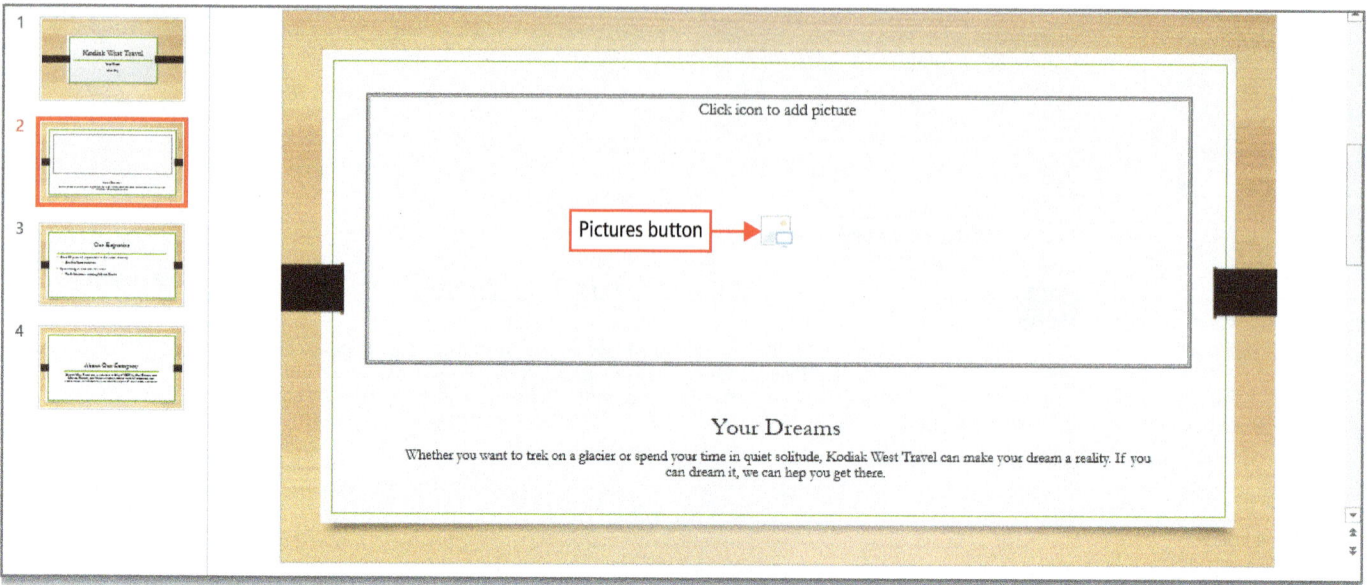

Figure 1.18

> ![2] In the picture placeholder, click **Pictures** 🖼 to open the **Insert Picture** dialog box. Navigate to the data files downloaded with this project, click **p01A_Glacier**, and then click **Insert** to insert the picture in the placeholder. If necessary, close the Design Ideas pane. Compare your screen with Figure 1.19.
>
> > Small circles—*sizing handles*—surround the inserted picture and indicate that the picture is selected and can be modified or formatted. The *rotation handle*—a circular arrow above the picture—provides a way to rotate a selected image. The Picture Tools are added to the ribbon, providing picture formatting commands.

NOTE   Design Ideas Pane

The Design Ideas pane may open each time you insert a picture. The pane includes ideas for ways to format and lay out a slide. In this project you will not use these suggestions, so you can close the pane each time it opens.

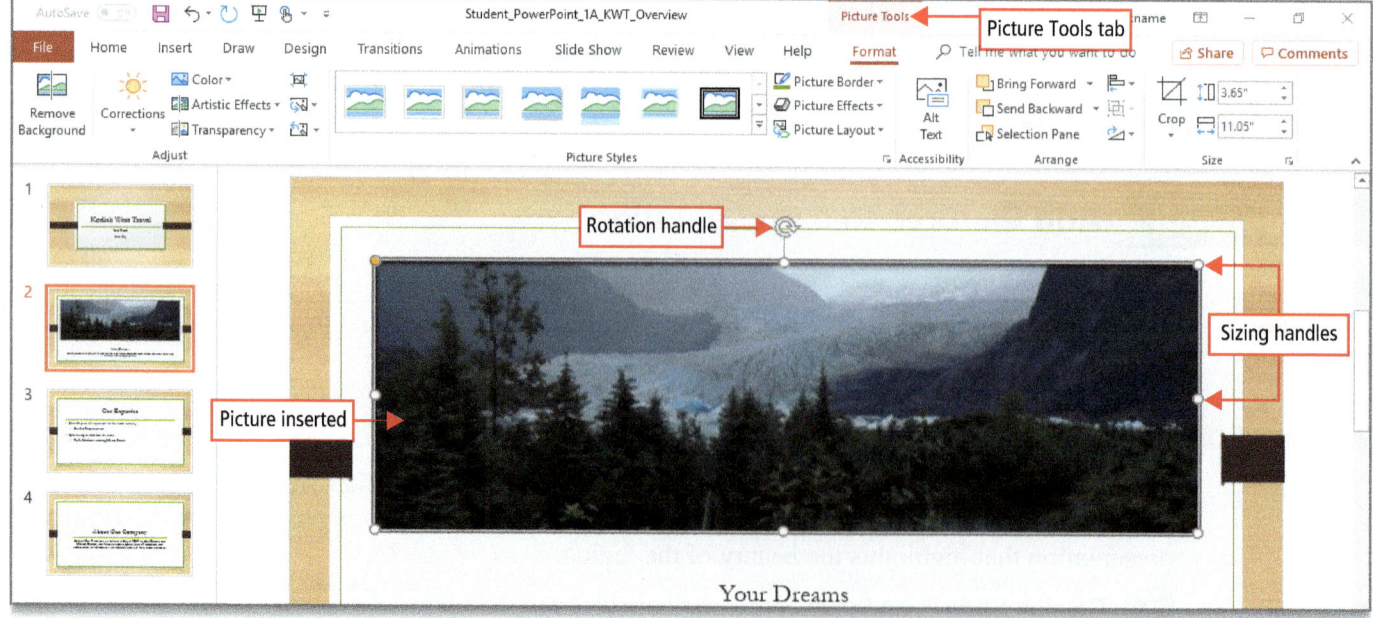

Figure 1.19

3 ▶ Display **Slide 3**. On the **Home tab**, in the **Slides group**, click the **New Slide arrow**, and then click **Title and Content**. In the title placeholder, type **Your Vacation**

4 ▶ In the content placeholder, click **Pictures** 🖼. Navigate to the data files for this project, and then click **p01A_Bay**. Click **Insert**, **Save** 💾 the presentation, and then compare your screen with Figure 1.20.

Figure 1.20

Activity 1.09 | Applying a Style to a Picture

3.3.2

When you select a picture, the Picture Tools display, adding the Format tab to the ribbon. The Format tab provides numerous styles that you can apply to your pictures. A *style* is a collection of formatting options that you can apply to a picture, text, or an object.

1 ▶ With **Slide 4** displayed, if necessary, click the picture to select it. On the ribbon, notice that the *Picture Tools* are active and the *Format* tab displays.

2 ▶ On the **Picture Tools Format tab**, in the **Picture Styles group**, click **More** ⯆ to display the **Picture Styles** gallery, and then compare your screen with Figure 1.21.

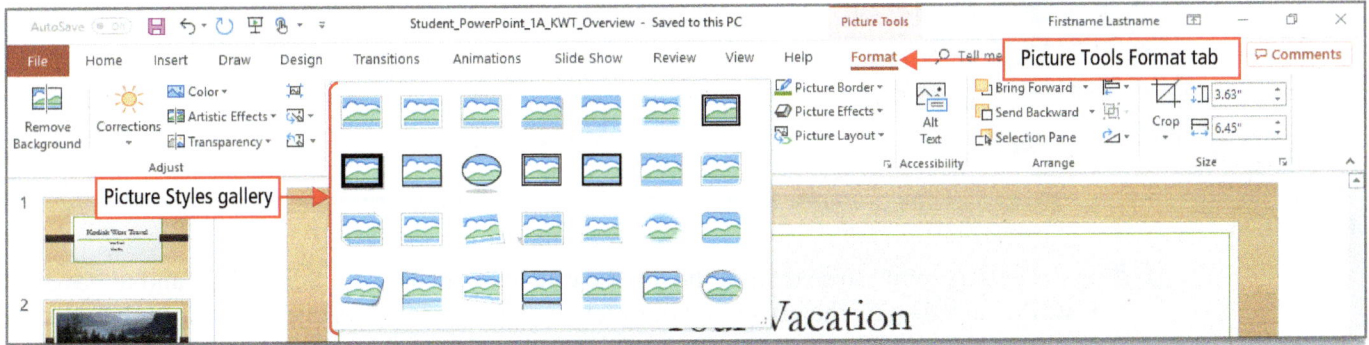

Figure 1.21

3 ▸ In the gallery, point to several of the picture styles to display the ScreenTips and to view the effect on your picture. Point to each style to display a ScreenTip, and then locate and click **Simple Frame, Black**. Click in a blank area of the slide, compare your screen with Figure 1.22, and then **Save** 🖫 the presentation.

Simple Frame, Black style applied to picture

Figure 1.22

Activity 1.10 | Applying and Removing Picture Artistic Effects

MOS
3.3.2

Artistic effects are formats applied to images that make pictures resemble sketches or paintings.

1 ▸ On **Slide 4**, click the picture to select it. On the **Picture Tools Format tab**, in the **Adjust group**, click **Artistic Effects** to display the **Artistic Effects** gallery. Compare your screen with Figure 1.23.

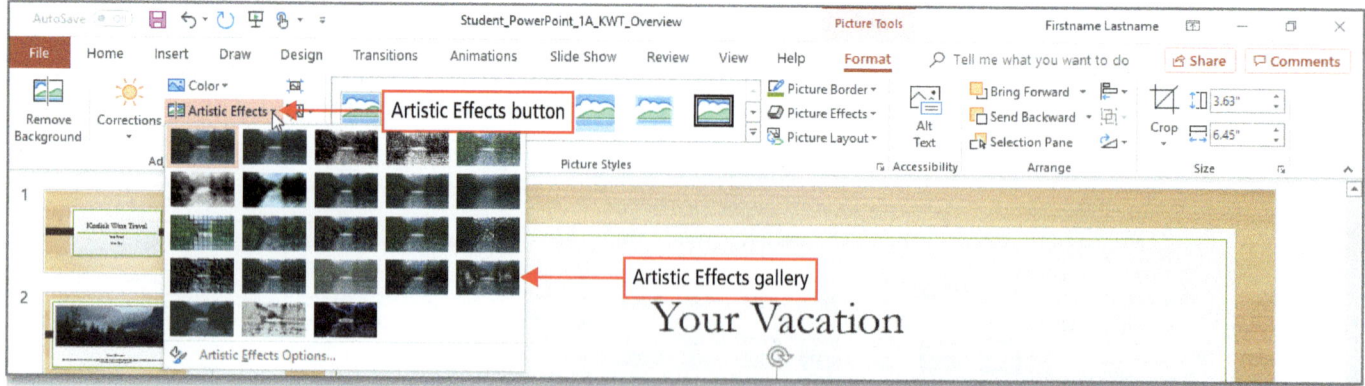

Artistic Effects button

Artistic Effects gallery

Figure 1.23

2 ▸ In the gallery, point to several of the artistic effects to display the ScreenTips and to have Live Preview display the effect on your picture. Then, locate and click the **Glow Diffused** effect.

3 ▸ With the picture still selected, on the **Format tab**, in the **Adjust group**, click **Artistic Effects** again to display the gallery. In the first row, click the first effect—**None**—to remove the effect from the picture and restore the previous formatting. **Save** 🖫 the presentation.

Objective 4 | Print and View a Presentation

GO! Learn How
Video P1-4

There are several print options in PowerPoint. For example, you can print full page images of your slides, presentation handouts to provide your audience with copies of your slides, or Notes pages displaying speaker notes below an image of the slide.

Activity 1.11 | Viewing a Slide Show

1.2.2

When you view a presentation as an electronic slide show, the entire slide fills the computer screen, and an audience can view your presentation if your computer is connected to a projection system.

1 On the ribbon, click the **Slide Show tab**. In the **Start Slide Show group**, click **From Beginning**. Compare your slide with Figure 1.24.

The first slide fills the screen, displaying the presentation as the audience would see it if your computer was connected to a projection system.

ANOTHER WAY Press F5 to start the slide show from the beginning. Or, display the first slide you want to show and click the Slide Show button on the lower right side of the status bar.

MAC TIP On the Slide Show tab click Play from Start.

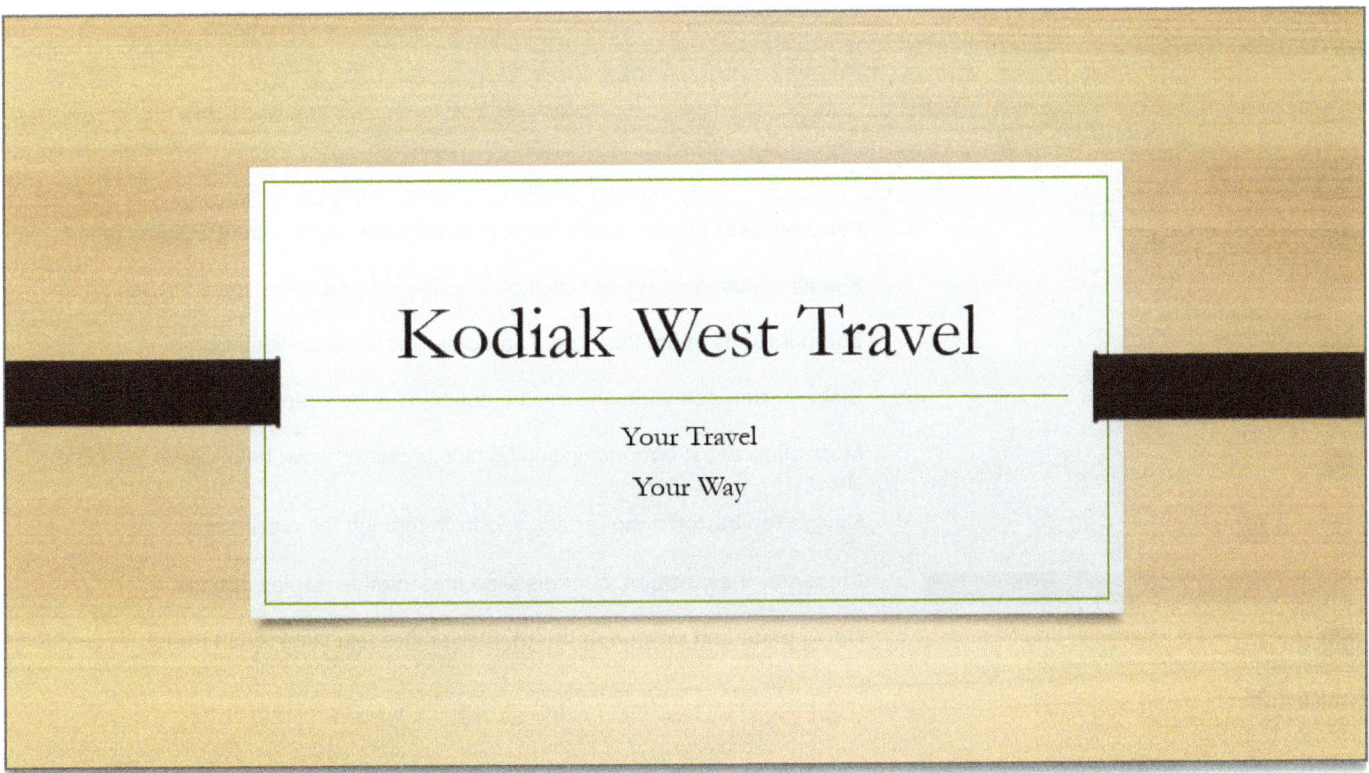

Figure 1.24

2 Click the left mouse button or press Spacebar to advance to the second slide.

3 Continue to click or press Spacebar until the last slide displays, and then click or press Spacebar one more time to display a ***black slide***—a slide that displays after the last slide in a presentation indicating that the presentation is over.

> **4** With the black slide displayed, click the left mouse button to exit the slide show and return to the presentation.

🔄 **ANOTHER WAY** Press [Esc] to exit the slide show.

Activity 1.12 | Using Presenter View

1.4.5

Presenter View shows the full-screen slide show on one monitor or projection screen for the audience to see, while enabling the presenter to view a preview of the next slide, notes, and a timer on another monitor.

> **1** On the **Slide Show tab**, in the **Monitors** group, if necessary, select the Use Presenter View check box. Hold down [Alt] and press [F5]. Take a moment to study the parts of the PowerPoint Presenter View window described in the table in Figure 1.25.

> If you do not have two monitors, you can practice using Presenter View by pressing [Alt] + [F5]. You will see only the presenter's view—not the audience's view—in this mode.

ALERT **Alt + F5 does not open Presenter View**

On a notebook computer, you may need to press the Fn or Function Lock key to override the preassigned function of the F5 key.

💻 **MAC TIP** On the Slide Show tab, click Presenter View. Point to the current slide to display Presenter View tools.

Microsoft PowerPoint Presenter View Elements	
Screen Element	**Description**
`0:00:00 II ↻`	**Timer:** running time, pause timer, and reset timer options
✏️	**Pen and laser pointer tools:** point to or annotate slides during a presentation
🔲	**See all slides:** displays all slides on the screen to easily navigate between them
🔍	**Zoom into the slide:** focus on a part of a slide while presenting
⬛	**Black or unblack slide show:** hide or unhide the presentation
⊙	**More slide show options:** including hide presenter view, help, pause, and end show
◀ and ▶	**Navigation buttons:** move back and forth through the presentation
`SHOW TASKBAR  DISPLAY SETTINGS ▾  END SLIDE SHOW`	**Presenter View ribbon:** controls slide presentation display options
A⁺	**Notes pane text size adjustment:** make notes text larger or smaller

Figure 1.25

> **2** Below the current slide, click the **Advance to the next animation or slide arrow** ⊙ to display **Slide 2**.

👉 **BY TOUCH** Advance to the next slide by swiping the current slide to the left.

3 In the upper right corner of the **Presenter View** window, point to the next slide—*Our Expertise*—and then click. Notice that the notes that you typed on **Slide 3** display. Compare your screen with Figure 1.26.

Clicking the image of the next slide advances the presentation.

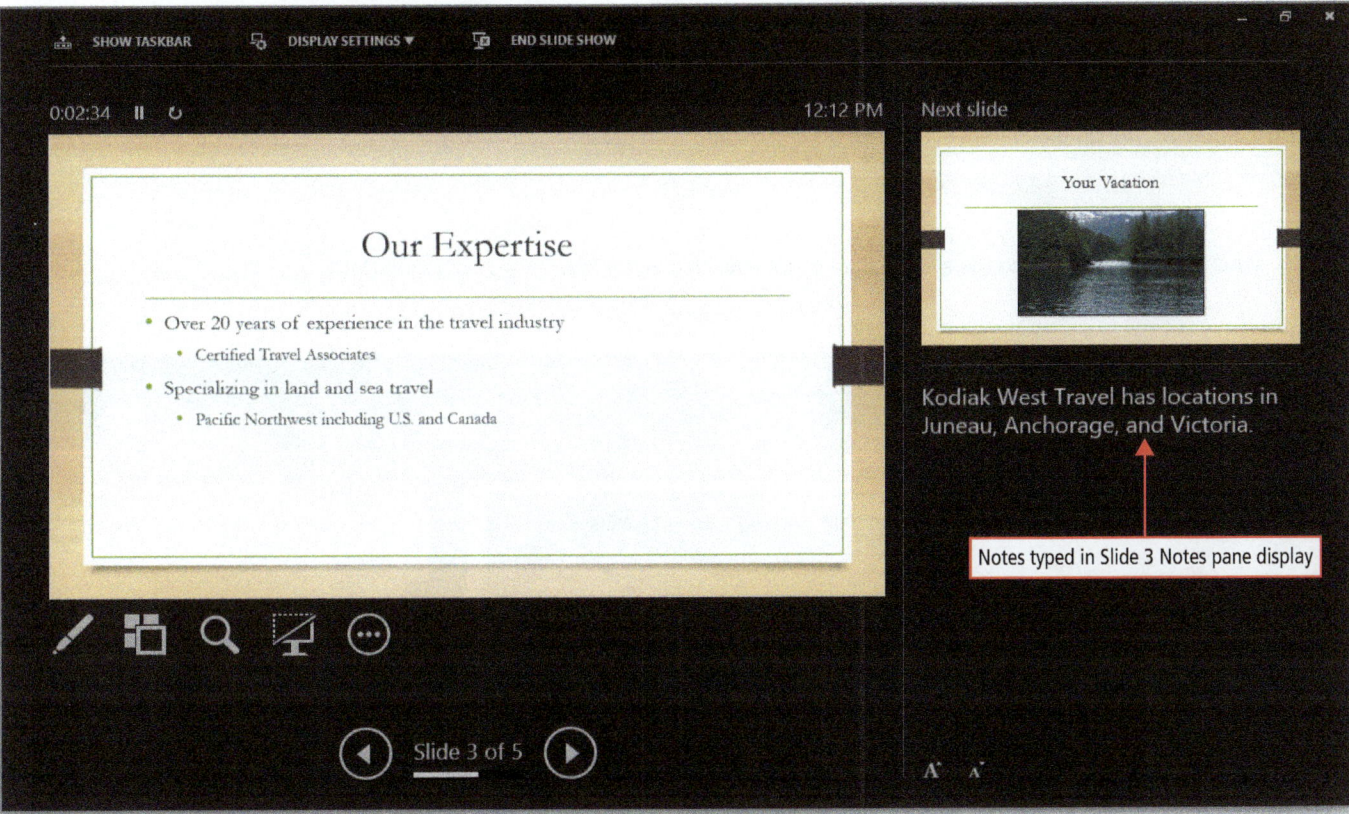

Figure 1.26

4 Below the notes, click **Make the text larger** to increase the font size of the notes in Presenter view to make the notes easier to read.

5 Below the current slide, click the second button—**See all slides**. Compare your screen with Figure 1.27.

A thumbnail view of all of the slides in your presentation displays. Here you can quickly move to another slide, if for example, you want to review a concept or answer a question related to a slide other than the current slide.

MAC TIP All slides are visible below the current slide in Presenter View.

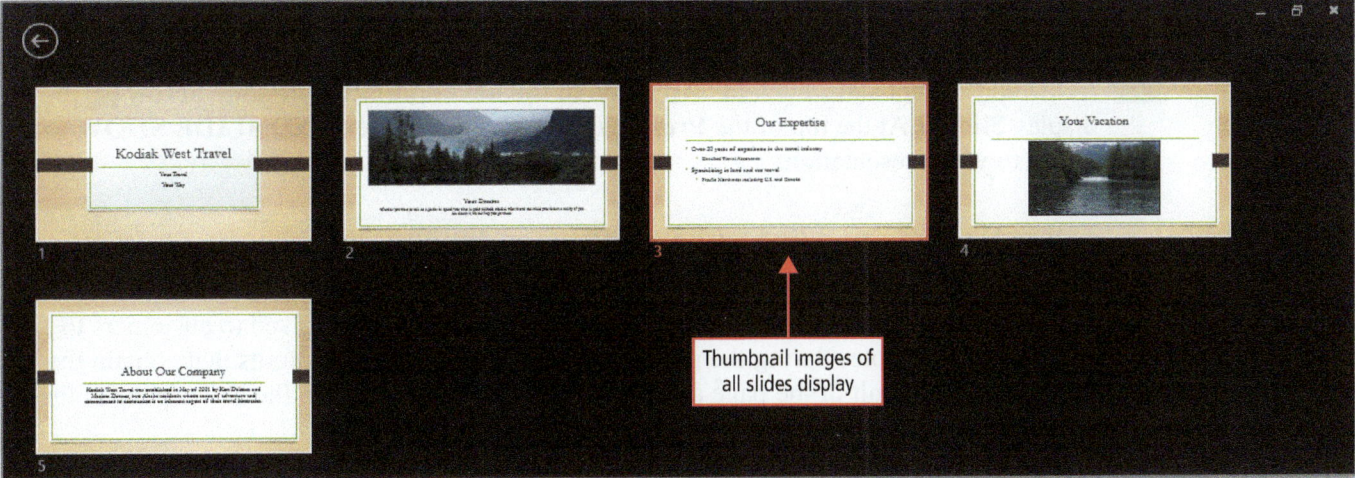

Figure 1.27

6 Click **Slide 4** to make Slide 4 the current slide in Presenter View. Below the current slide, click the third button—**Zoom into the slide** 🔍. Move the 🔍 pointer to the middle of the picture on the current slide, and then click to zoom in on the picture. Notice that the 🖐 pointer displays. Compare your slide with Figure 1.28.

With the 🖐 pointer displayed, you can move the zoomed image to draw close-up attention to a specific part of your slide.

BY TOUCH Touch the current slide with two fingers and then pinch together to zoom in or stretch your fingers apart to zoom out.

MAC TIP The Zoom into the slide feature is not available in the Mac version of PowerPoint.

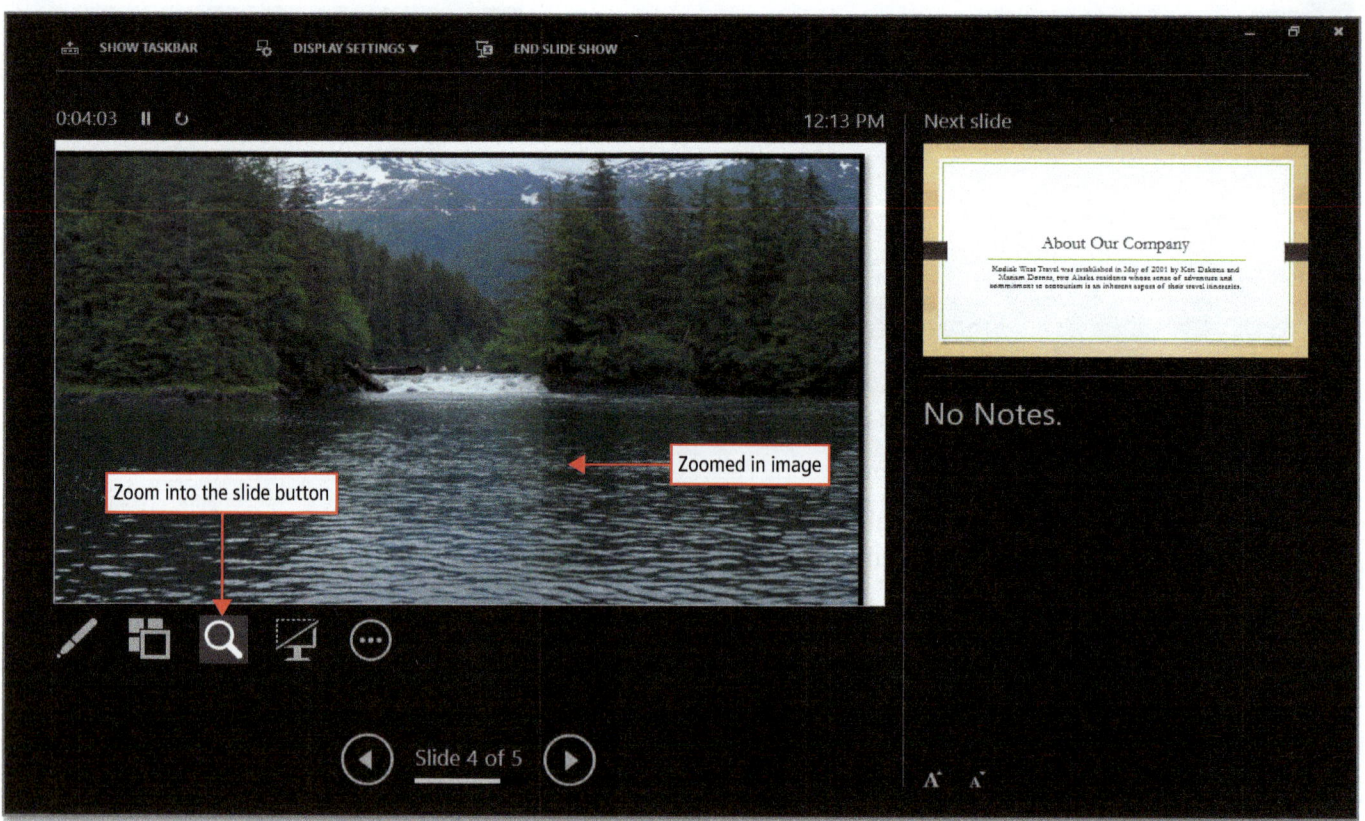

Figure 1.28

7 Below the current slide, click the **Advance to the next animation or slide arrow** 🔘 to display **Slide 5**. At the top of the **Presenter View** window, click **END SLIDE SHOW** to return to your presentation.

Activity 1.13 | Inserting Headers and Footers on Slide Handouts

A *header* is text that prints at the top of each sheet of *slide handouts* or *notes pages*. Slide handouts are printed images of slides on a sheet of paper. These can be given to customers to follow along and take notes during the presentation. Notes pages are printouts that contain the slide image on the top half of the page and notes that you have created in the Notes pane in the lower half of the page.

In addition to headers, you can insert *footers*—text that displays at the bottom of every slide or that prints at the bottom of a sheet of slide handouts or notes pages.

1 ▶ Click the **Insert tab**, in the **Text group**, click **Header & Footer** to display the **Header and Footer** dialog box.

2 ▶ In the **Header and Footer** dialog box, click the **Notes and Handouts tab**. Under **Include on page**, select the **Date and time** check box, and as you do so, watch the Preview box in the upper right corner of the Header and Footer dialog box.

> The two narrow rectangular boxes at the top of the Preview box are placeholders for the header text and date. When you select the Date and time check box, the placeholder in the upper right corner is outlined, indicating the location in which the date will display.

3 ▶ Be sure that the **Update automatically** option button is selected so that the current date prints on the notes and handouts each time the presentation is printed. If it is not selected, click the Update automatically option button.

4 ▶ Verify that the **Page number** check box is selected and select it if it is not. If necessary, clear the Header check box to omit this element. Notice that in the **Preview** box, the corresponding placeholder is not selected.

5 ▶ Select the **Footer** check box, and then click in the **Footer** box. Type **1A_KWT_Overview** so that the file name displays as a footer, and then compare your dialog box with Figure 1.29.

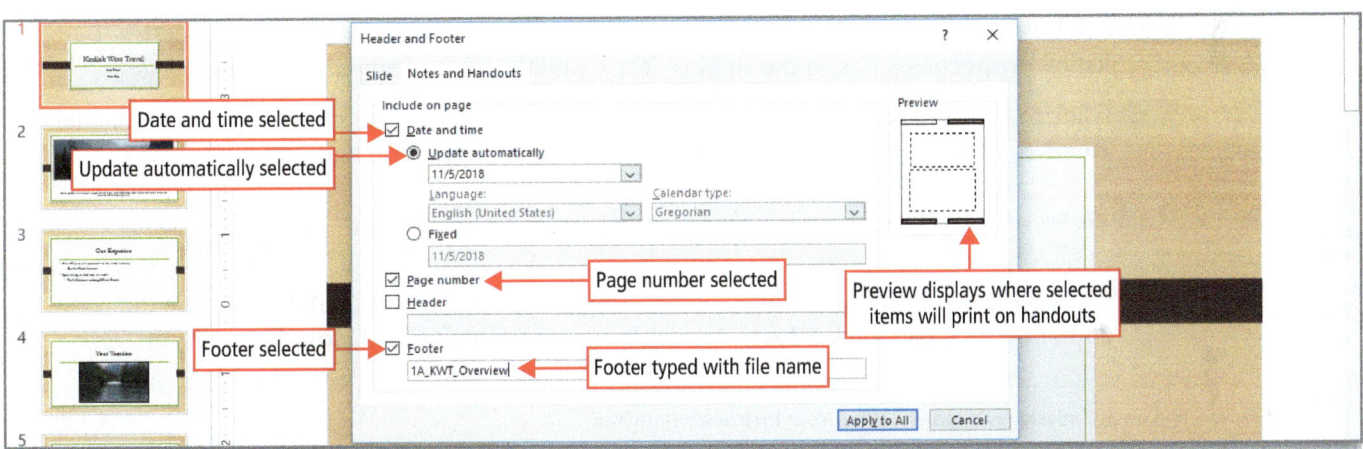

Figure 1.29

6 ▶ In the lower right corner of the dialog box, click **Apply to All**. Save 🔲 your presentation.

Activity 1.14 | Inserting Slide Numbers on Slides

MOS

1.2.3,
2.2.3

In this Activity, you will insert the slide numbers on the presentation slides.

1 ▶ Display **Slide 1**. On the **Insert tab**, in the **Text group**, click **Header & Footer** to display the **Header and Footer** dialog box.

2 ▶ In the **Header and Footer** dialog box, if necessary, click the Slide tab. Under **Include on slide**, select the **Slide number** check box, and then select the **Don't show on title slide** check box. Verify that all other check boxes are cleared, and then compare your screen with Figure 1.30.

> Selecting the *Don't show on title slide* check box omits the slide number from the first slide in a presentation.

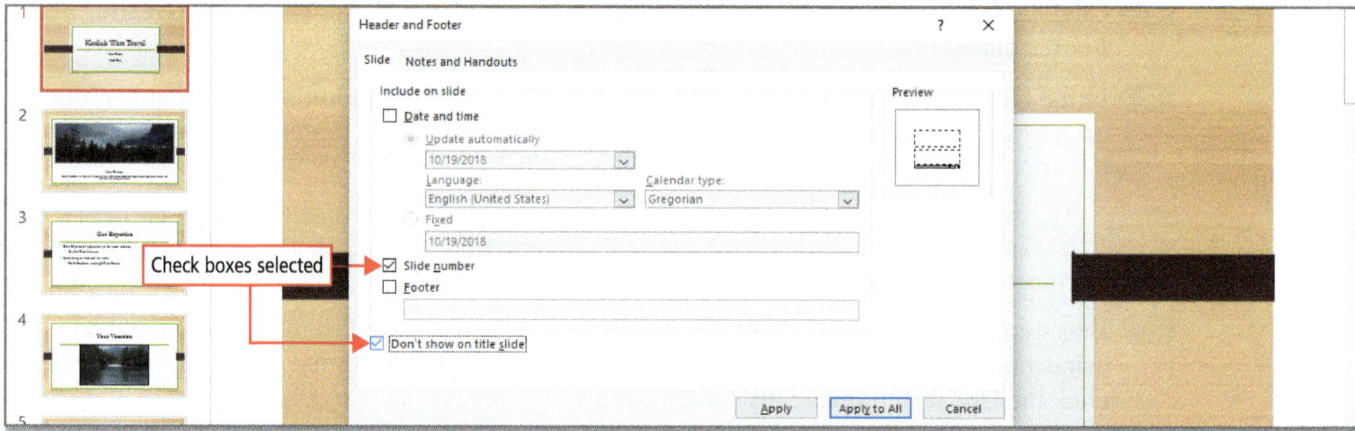

Figure 1.30

3 Click **Apply to All**, and then notice that on the first slide, the slide number does not display.

4 Display **Slide 2**, and then notice that the slide number displays in the lower right area of the slide. Display each slide in the presentation and notice the placement of the slide number.

> The position of the slide number and other header and footer information is determined by the theme applied to the presentation.

5 Click **File** to redisplay **Backstage** view. On the Info tab, click **Show All Properties**. In the list of **Properties**, click to the right of **Tags**, and then type **company overview**

6 Click to the right of **Subject**, and then type your course name and section number. Under **Related People**, be sure that your name displays as the author, and edit if necessary.

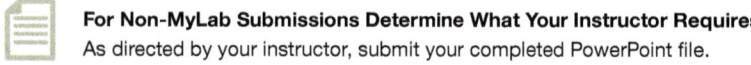

MAC TIP Click the File menu, click Properties, click the Summary tab, and instead of Tags, use the Keywords box.

7 Click **Save** 🖫. If you will not be completing the following optional Activity, on the right end of the title bar, click **Close** ☒ to close the presentation and close PowerPoint.

📄 **For Non-MyLab Submissions Determine What Your Instructor Requires**
As directed by your instructor, submit your completed PowerPoint file.

---

8 In **MyLab IT**, in your **Course Materials**, locate and click the Grader Project **PowerPoint 1A KWT Overview**. In **step 3**, under **Upload Completed Assignment**, click **Choose File**. In the **Open** dialog box, navigate to your **PowerPoint Chapter 1 folder**, and then click your **Student_PowerPoint_1A_KWT_Overview** file one time to select it. In the lower right corner of the **Open** dialog box, click **Open**.

> The name of your selected file displays above the Upload button.

9 To submit your file to **MyLab IT** for grading, click **Upload**, wait a moment for a green **Success!** message, and then in **step 4**, click the blue **Submit for Grading** button. Click **Close Assignment** to return to your list of **Course Materials**.

Activity 1.15 | Printing Presentation Handouts

1.3.3

Use Backstage view to preview the arrangement of slides and to print your presentation.

1 If necessary, open your **Student_PowerPoint_1A_KWT_Overview** presentation. Display **Slide 1**. Click **File** to display **Backstage** view, and then click **Print**.

The Print tab displays the tools you need to select your settings and view a preview of your presentation. On the right, Print Preview displays your presentation exactly as it will print. If your system is not connected to a color printer, your slide may display in black and white.

2 Under **Settings**, click **Full Page Slides**, and then compare your screen with Figure 1.31.

The gallery displays either the default print setting—Full Page Slides—or the most recently selected print setting.

MAC TIP   In the Print window, click Show Details. Under Layout, click Slides.

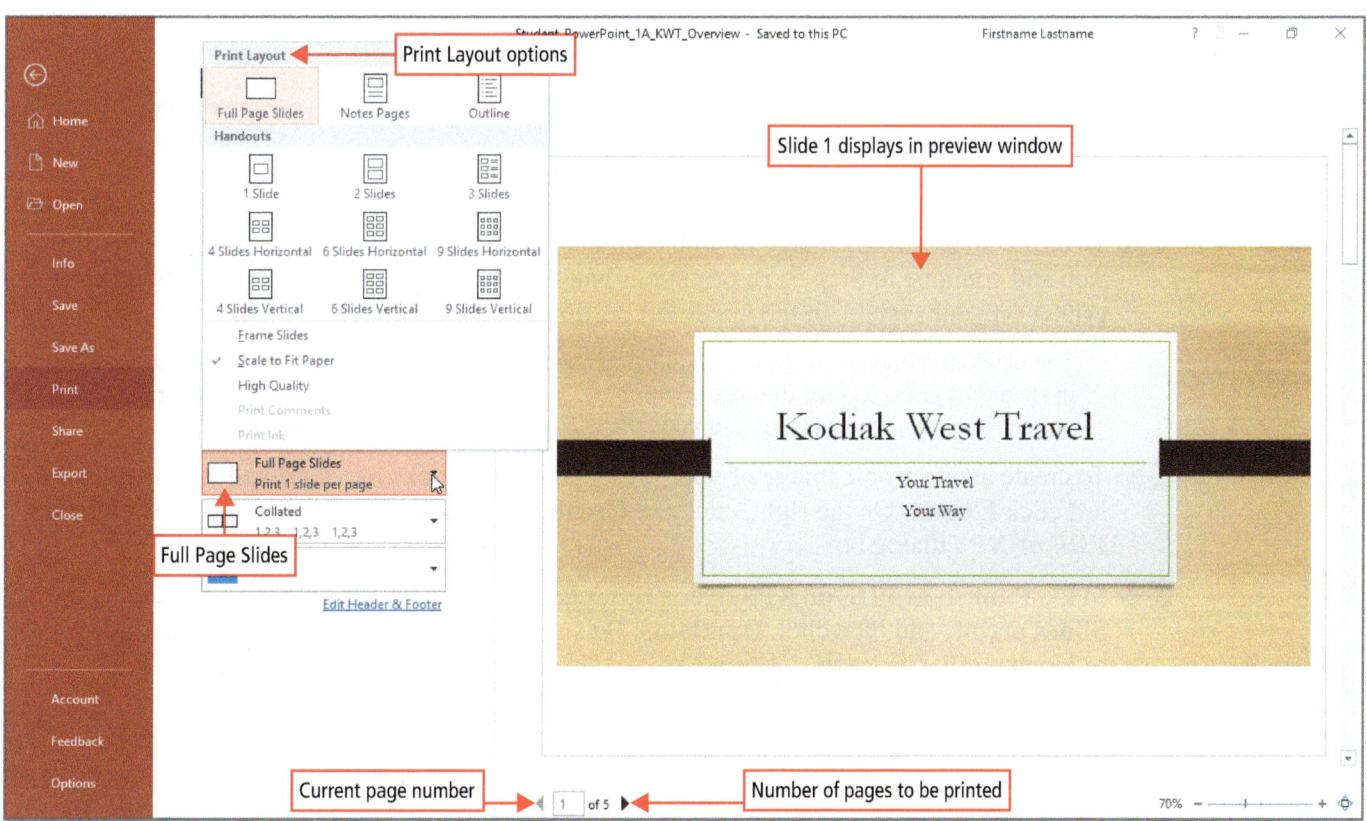

Figure 1.31

3 In the gallery, under **Handouts**, click **6 Slides Horizontal**. Notice that the **Print Preview** on the right displays the slide handout, and that the current date, file name, and page number display in the header and footer. Compare your screen with Figure 1.32.

In the Settings group, the Portrait Orientation option displays; here you can change the print orientation from Portrait to Landscape.

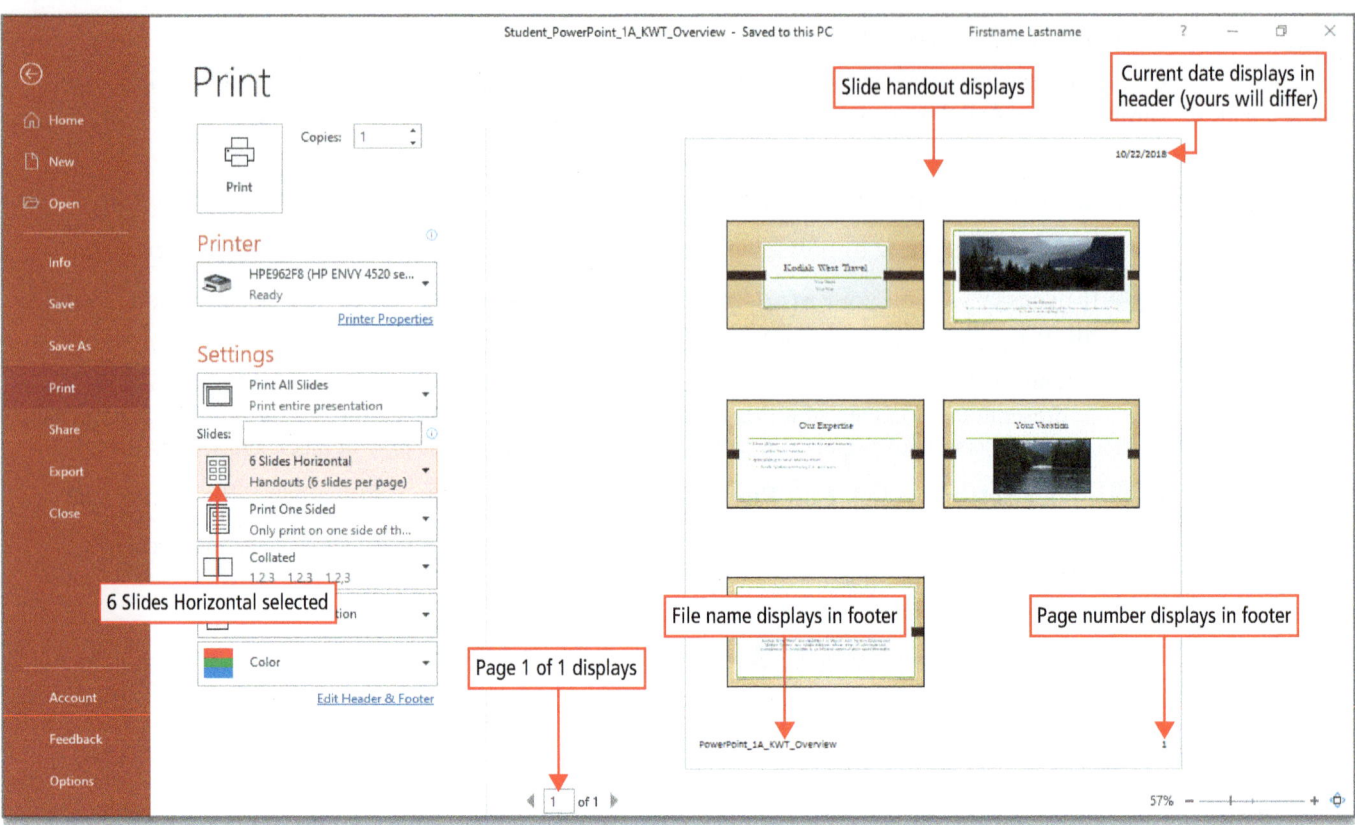

Figure 1.32

4 ▸ To create an electronic image of your handouts that looks like printed handouts, skip this step and continue to Step 5. To print your handout document on paper using the default printer on your system, in the upper left portion of the screen, click **Print**.

> The handout will print on your default printer—on a black and white printer, the colors will print in shades of gray. To save the cost of color ink, you can print in grayscale by clicking the Color button. Backstage view closes and your file redisplays in the PowerPoint window.

5 ▸ To create an electronic image of your presentation that looks like a printed document, on the left click **Export**. On the right, click the **Create PDF/XPS** button to display the **Publish as PDF or XPS** dialog box.

6 ▸ In the **Publish as PDF or XPS** dialog box, click **Options**. Under **Publish what**, click the **Slides arrow**, and then click **Handouts**. Be sure **Slides per page** is set to **6** and **Order** is set to **Horizontal.** Click **OK.**

💻 **MAC TIP** In the Print window, click the PDF arrow, and then click Save as PDF.

7 ▸ Navigate to your **PowerPoint Chapter 1** folder, and then click **Publish**. If your Adobe Acrobat or Reader program displays your PDF, close the PDF file. If your PDF displays in Microsoft Edge, in the upper right corner click Close ☒. Notice that your presentation redisplays in PowerPoint.

Activity 1.16 | Printing Speaker Notes

1.3.2

1 On the **Print tab**, under **Settings**, click **6 Slides Horizontal**, and then under **Print Layout**, click **Notes Pages** to view the presentation notes for **Slide 1**; recall that you created notes for **Slide 3**.

Indicated below the Notes page are the current slide number and the number of pages that will print when Notes Pages is selected. You can use the Next Page and Previous Page arrows to display each Notes page in the presentation.

2 At the bottom of the **Print Preview**, click **Next Page** ▶ two times so that **Page 3** displays. Notice that the notes that you typed for Slide 3 display below the image of the slide. Compare your screen with Figure 1.33.

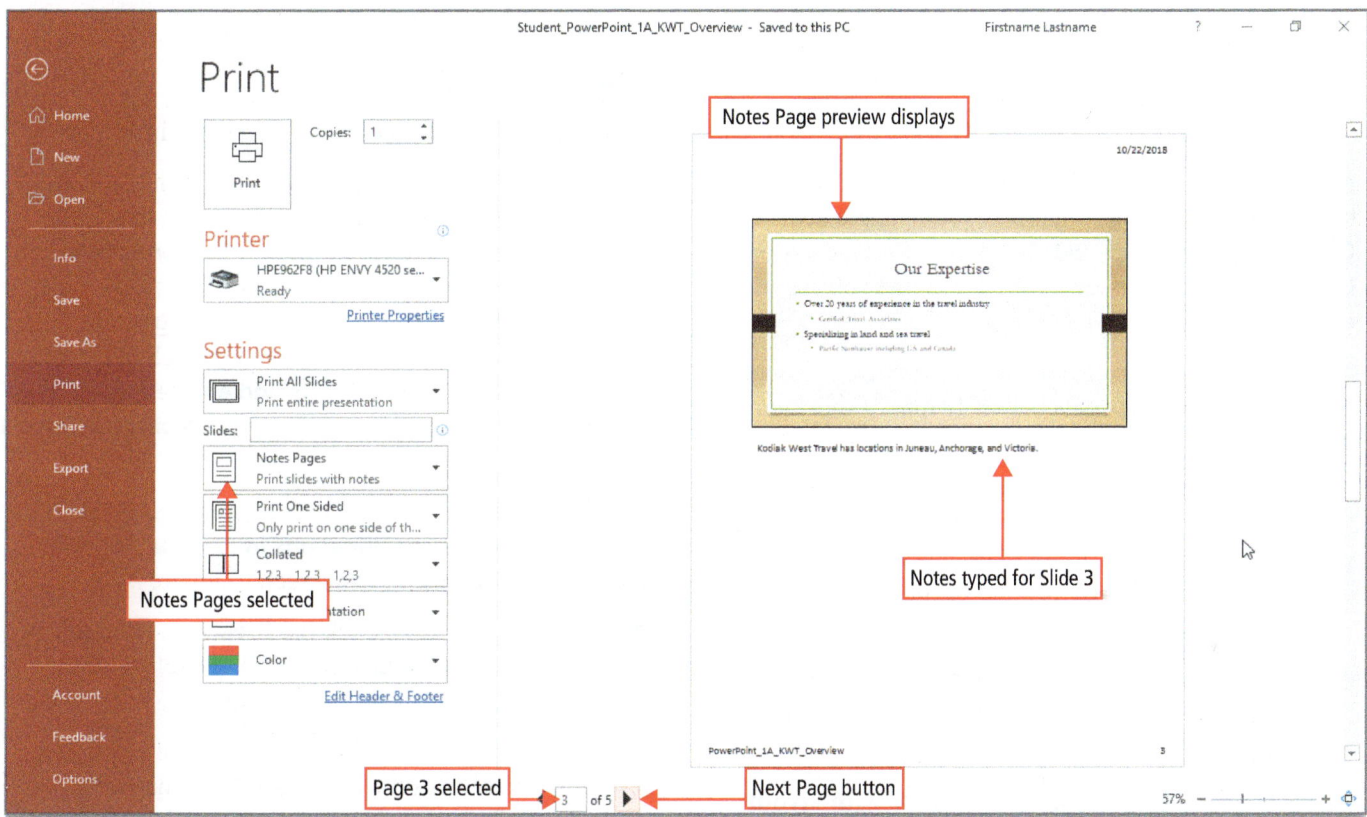

Figure 1.33

3 Under **Settings**, click in the **Slides box**. Type **3** and then click **Notes Pages**. In the lower section, click **Frame Slides**. Under **Printer**, click the printer arrow, click **Microsoft Print to PDF**, and then click **Print** to print your presentation to a PDF file.

Microsoft Print to PDF is an automatically installed printer option in Windows 10, which enables you to create an image that looks like a printed document.

ALERT   No Microsoft Print to PDF Printer Option Available

If you are using Windows 7 or 8, select the Microsoft XPS Document Writer printer instead to print your presentation to the XPS format, a Microsoft file format that also creates an image of your document and that opens in the XPS viewer.

4 Navigate to the location where you store your files for this chapter, name the file **Lastname_Firstname_1A_KWT_Overview_Notes** and then click **Save** 💾. **Close** PowerPoint.

You have completed Project 1A   **END**

»»» GO! With Google

ALERT **Working with Web-Based Applications and Services**

Computer programs and services on the web receive continuous updates and improvements, so the steps to complete this web-based activity may differ from the ones shown. You can often look at the screens and the information presented to determine how to complete the activity.

If you do not already have a Google account, you will need to create one before you begin this activity. Go to http://google.com and in the upper right corner, click Sign in. On the Sign In screen, click Use another account, click Create Account. On the Create your Google Account page, complete the form, read and agree to the Terms of Service and Privacy Policy, and then click Next step. On the Welcome screen, click Get Started.

Activity | Creating a Company Overview Presentation in Google Slides

In this Activity, you will use Google Slides to create a presentation similar to the one you created in Project 1A.

1 From the desktop, open your browser, navigate to **http://google.com**, and sign in to your Google account. Click **Google apps** ⦙⦙⦙ and click Drive ▲. Open your **GO! Web Projects** folder—or click New to create and then open this folder if necessary.

2 In the left pane, click **New**, and then click **Google Slides**. In the **Themes** pane, click **Tropic**. If this theme is not available, select another theme. **Close** the **Themes** pane.

3 At the top of the window, click **Untitled presentation** and then, using your own name, type **Lastname_Firstname_1A_Google_Slides** as the file name and then press Enter.

4 In the title placeholder, type **Kodiak West Travel** and then in the subtitle placeholder type **Your Travel - Your Way**

5 On the **toolbar**, click the **New slide with layout arrow** ⊞, and then click **Caption**.

6 On the **toolbar**, click **Image** 🖼. Click **Upload from computer**. Navigate to your student data files, and then click **p01A_Glacier**. Click **Open**.

7 In the text placeholder, type **Your Dreams**

8 On the **toolbar**, click the **New slide with layout arrow** ⊞, and then click **Title and body**. In the title placeholder, type **Our Expertise**

9 Click in the content placeholder. On the toolbar, if necessary, click More, and click **Bulleted list** ▤. In the placeholder, type **Over 20 years of experience in the travel industry** and then press Enter. Press Tab. Type **Certified Travel Associates** and then press Enter. On toolbar, if necessary, click More, and then click **Decrease indent** ▤. Type **Specializing in land and sea travel** and then press Enter. Press Tab and then type **Pacific Northwest including U.S. and Canada**

10 Below the slide, click in the **Notes** pane. Type **Kodiak West Travel has locations in Juneau, Anchorage, and Victoria.** Compare your screen to Figure A.

11 In the upper right, click the **Present button arrow**, click **Present from beginning**. Click the left mouse button to progress through the presentation. When the last slide displays, press Esc or click **Exit**.

12 Your presentation will be saved automatically. If you are instructed to submit your file, click the File menu, point to Download as, and then click Microsoft PowerPoint, PDF Document, or another format as directed by your instructor. The file will download to your default download folder as determined by your browser settings. Sign out of your Google account and close your browser.

»»» **GO!** With Google continues on next page

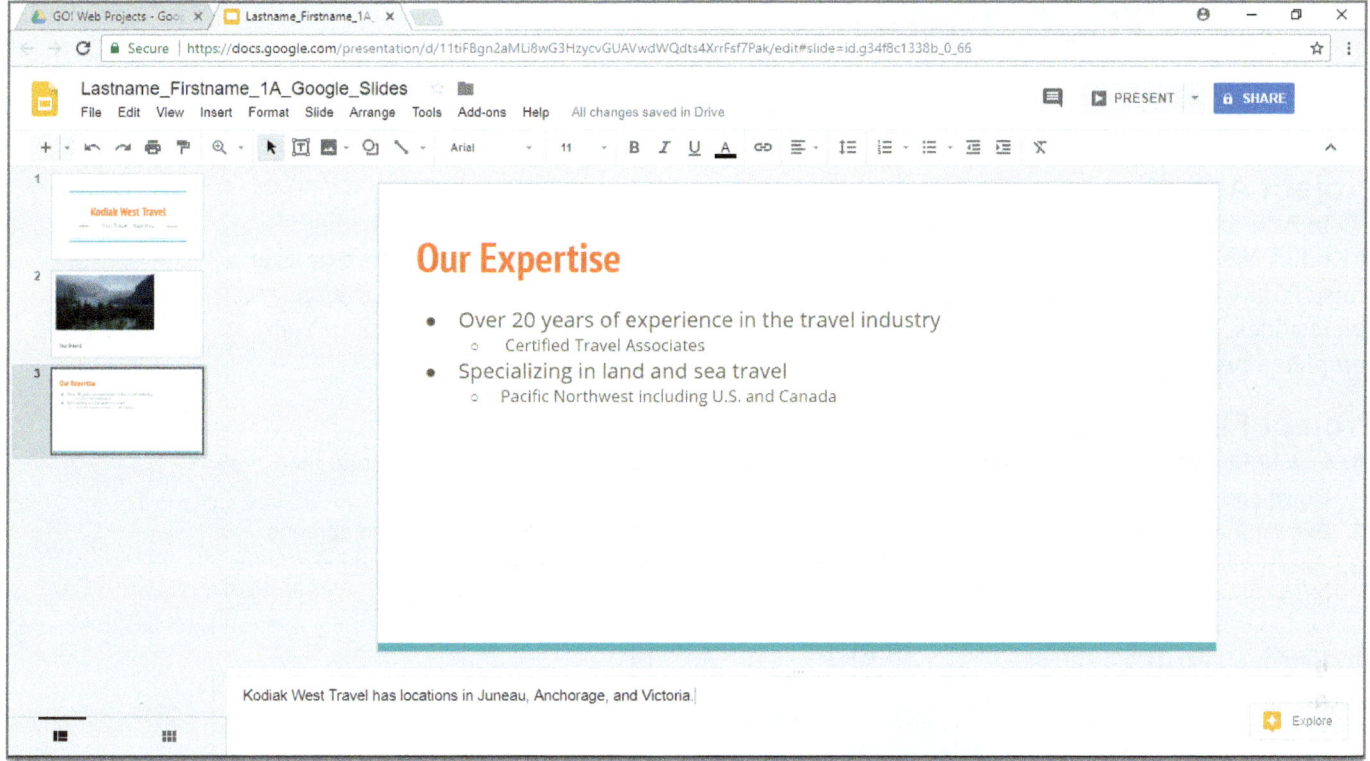

Figure A

PROJECT 1B

Itinerary Presentation

Project Activities

In Activities 1.17 through 1.33, you will combine two presentations that the marketing team at Kodiak West Travel developed describing itinerary ideas when visiting Seattle before or after a cruise. You will insert slides from one presentation into another, and then you will rearrange and delete slides. You will also apply font formatting and slide transitions to the presentation. Your completed presentation will look similar to Figure 1.34.

Project Files for **MyLab IT** Grader

1. In your **MyLab IT** course, locate and click **PowerPoint 1B Seattle**, Download Materials, and then Download All Files.
2. Extract the zipped folder to your PowerPoint Chapter 1 folder. Close the Grader download screens.
3. Take a moment to open the downloaded **PowerPoint_1B_Seattle_Instructions**; note any recent updates to the book.

Project Results

GO! Project 1B
Where We're Going

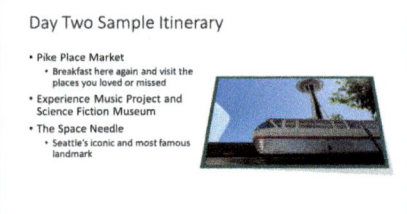

Figure 1.34 Project 1B Seattle

For Non-MyLab Submissions

For Project 1B, you will need: In your PowerPoint Chapter 1 folder, save your presentation as:

p01B_Seattle   **Lastname_Firstname_1B_Seattle**
p01B_Slides

After you have named and saved your presentation, on the next page, begin with Step 2.

Objective 5 Edit an Existing Presentation

GO! Learn How
Video P1-5

Recall that editing refers to the process of adding, deleting, and modifying presentation content. You can edit presentation content in either the Slide pane or in the presentation outline.

Activity 1.17 | Changing Slide Size

MOS
1.2.1

Presentations created with one of the new themes in PowerPoint default to a widescreen format using a 16:9 *aspect ratio*—the ratio of the width of a display to the height of the display. This slide size is similar to most television and computer monitor screens. Previous versions of PowerPoint used a squarer format with a 4:3 aspect ratio.

1 Navigate to your **PowerPoint Chapter 1 folder**, and then double-click the downloaded PowerPoint file that displays your name—**Student_PowerPoint_1B_Seattle**. In your presentation, if necessary, at the top click **Enable Editing**.

2 Notice that **Slide 1** displays in a squarish format.

3 On the **Design tab**, in the **Customize group**, click **Slide Size**, and then click **Widescreen (16:9)**. Compare your screen with Figure 1.35 and notice that the slide fills the slide pane. **Save** 🖫 the presentation.

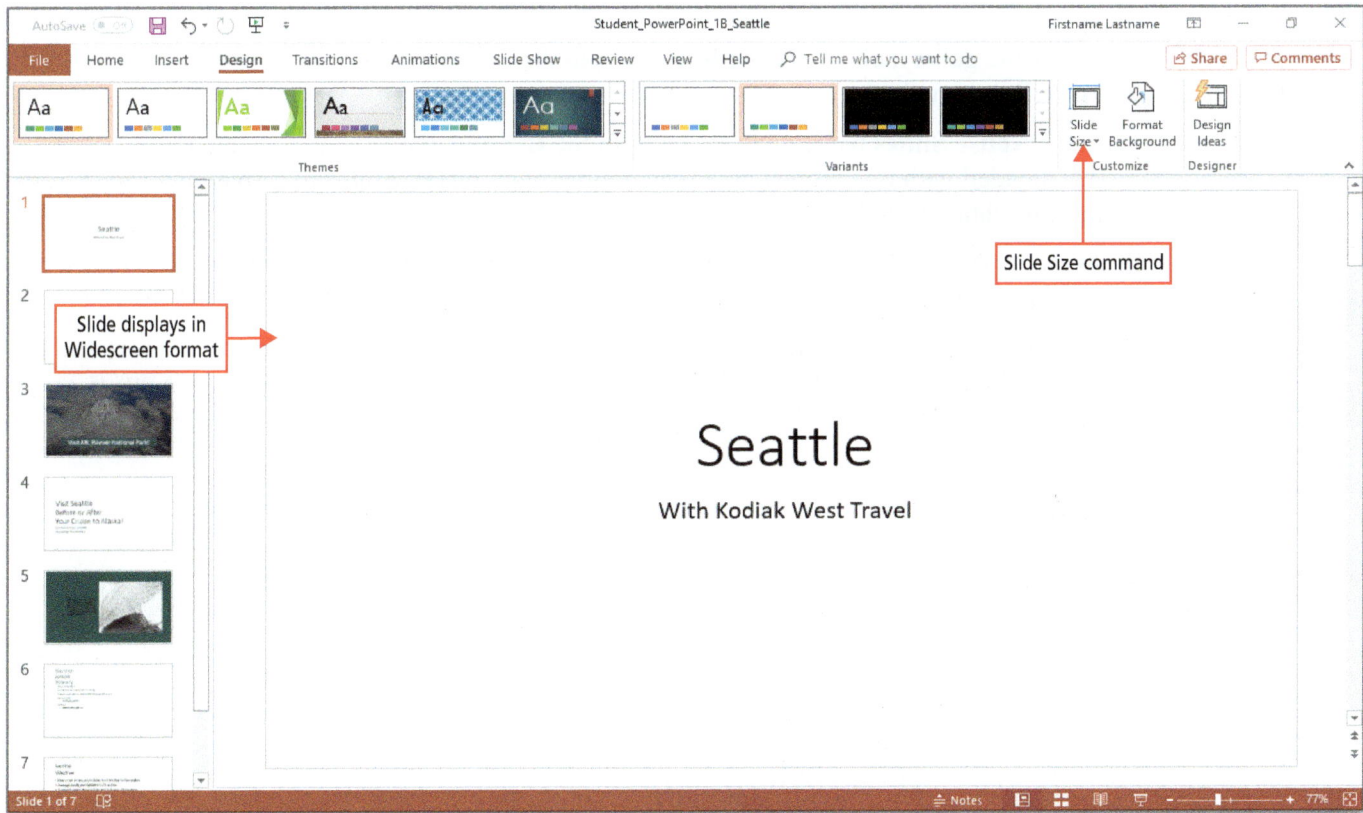

Figure 1.35

Activity 1.18 | Inserting Slides from an Existing Presentation

Presentation content is commonly shared among group members in an organization. Rather than re-creating slides, you can insert slides from an existing presentation into the current presentation. In this Activity, you will insert slides from an existing presentation into your 1B_Seattle presentation.

1 With **Slide 1** displayed, on the **Home tab**, in the **Slides group**, click the **New Slide arrow** to display the **Slide Layout** gallery and additional commands for inserting slides. Compare your screen with Figure 1.36.

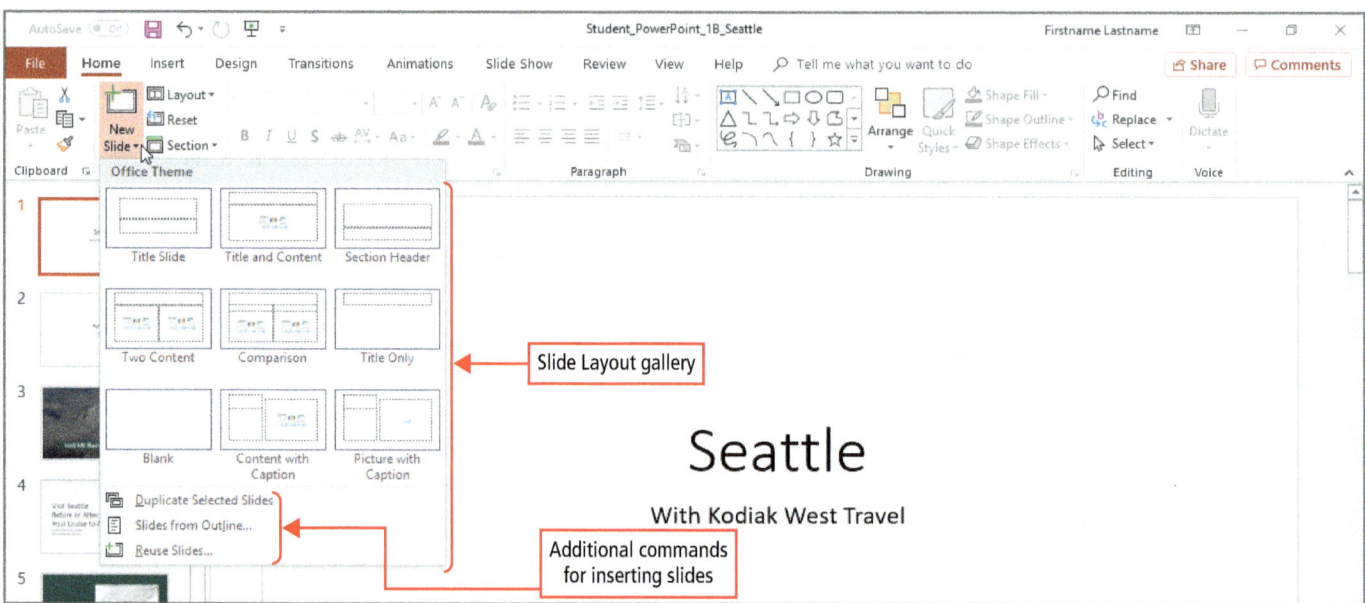

Figure 1.36

2 Below the gallery, click **Reuse Slides** to open the Reuse Slides pane on the right side of the PowerPoint window.

3 In the **Reuse Slides** pane, click **Browse**. In the **Browse** dialog box, navigate to the data files downloaded with this project, and then double-click **p01B_Slides** to display the slides from this presentation in the Reuse Slides pane.

4 At the bottom of the **Reuse Slides** pane, be sure that the **Keep source formatting** check box is *cleared*, and then compare your screen with Figure 1.37.

When the *Keep source formatting* check box is cleared, the theme formatting of the presentation into which the slides are inserted is applied. When the *Keep source formatting* check box is selected, you retain the formatting of the slides when inserted into the presentation.

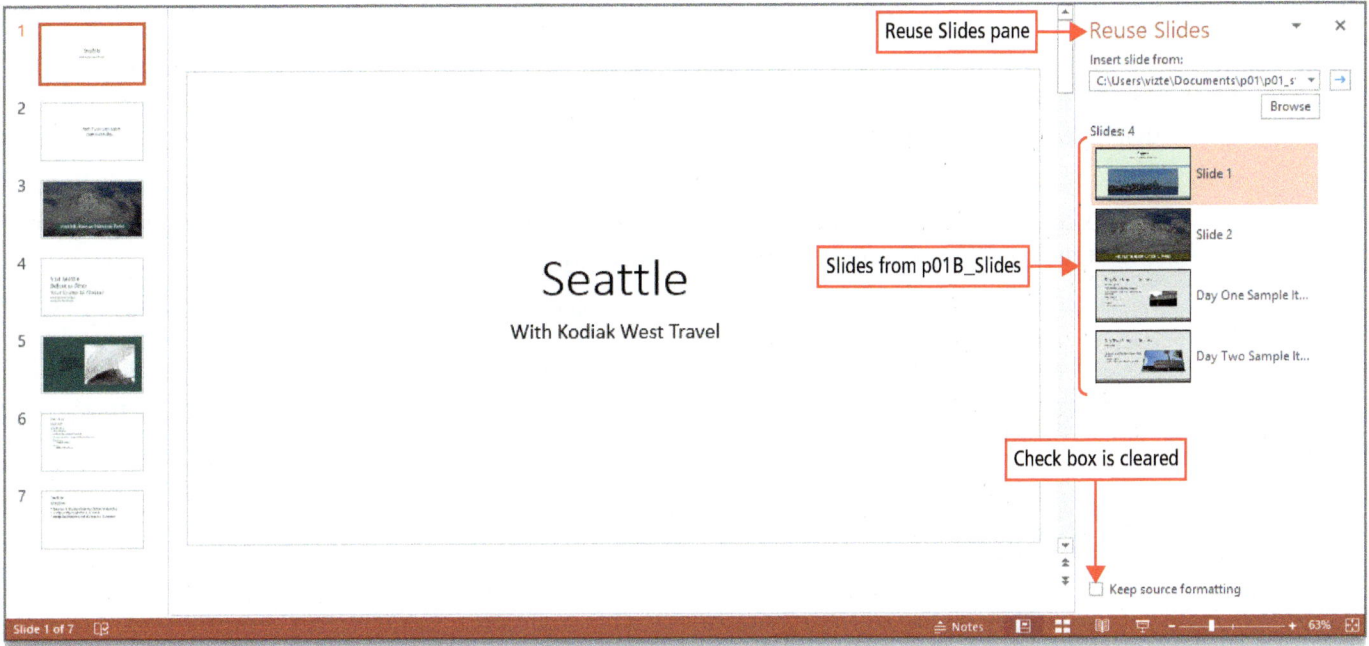

Figure 1.37

5 In the **Reuse Slides** pane, point to each slide to view a ScreenTip displaying the file name and the slide title.

6 In the **Reuse Slides** pane, click the first slide to insert the slide after **Slide 1** in your Seattle presentation. Notice that the inserted slide adopts the color of your Seattle presentation theme.

NOTE   Inserting Slides

You can insert slides into your presentation in any order; remember to display the slide that will come before the slide that you want to insert.

MAC TIP Mac users can only insert all slides from an existing presentation. With Slide 1 selected, on the Home tab, click the New Slide arrow, click Reuse Slides, and navigate to the data files for this project. Double-click p01B_Slides to insert all four slides into your presentation after Slide 1. Select and press delete to delete Slide 3—*Visit Mt. Rainier National Park!* and Slide 4—*Day One Sample Itinerary*. Drag the new Slide 3—*Day Two Sample Itinerary* after the existing Slide 7. Skip to Step 9.

---

7 In your **1B_Seattle** presentation, in the slide thumbnails, click **Slide 7** to display it in the **Slide pane**.

8 In the **Reuse Slides** pane, click the fourth slide, *Day Two Sample Itinerary*, to insert it after **Slide 7**.

Your presentation contains nine slides. When a presentation contains a large number of slides, a scroll box displays to the right of the slide thumbnails so that you can scroll and then select the thumbnails.

9 Close ☒ the **Reuse Slides** pane, and then **Save** 💾 the presentation.

MORE KNOWLEDGE   Inserting All Slides

You can insert all of the slides from an existing presentation into the current presentation at one time. In the Reuse Slides pane, right-click one of the slides that you want to insert, and then click Insert All Slides.

Activity 1.19 | Displaying and Editing the Presentation Outline

Outline View displays the presentation outline to the left of the Slide pane. You can use the outline to edit the presentation text. Changes that you make in the outline are immediately displayed in the Slide pane.

1 To the right of the slide thumbnails, if necessary, drag the scroll box up, and then click **Slide 1** to display it in the Slide pane. On the **View tab**, in the **Presentation Views group**, click **Outline View**. Compare your screen with Figure 1.38.

The outline displays at the left of the PowerPoint window in place of the slide thumbnails. Each slide in the outline displays the slide number, slide icon, and the slide title in bold. Slides that do not display a slide title in the outline use a slide layout that does not include a title, for example, the Blank layout.

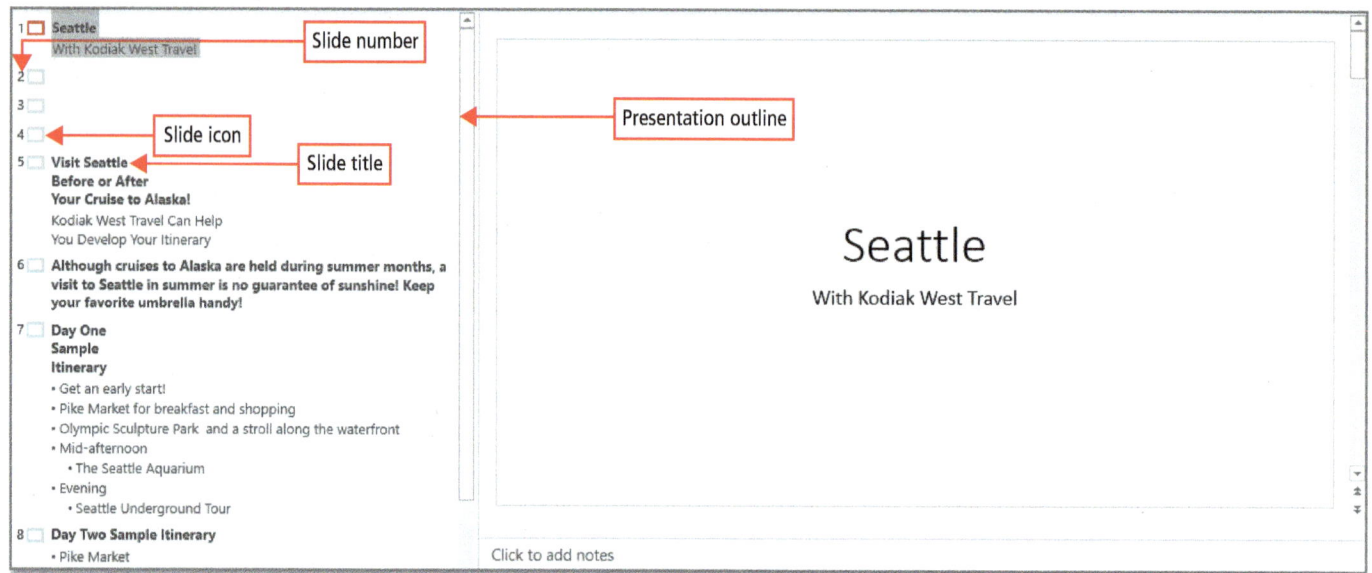

Figure 1.38

2 In the **Outline**, in **Slide 7**, drag to select the text of the second and third bullet points—*Pike Market for breakfast and shopping*, and *Olympic Sculpture Park and a stroll along the waterfront*. Compare your screen with Figure 1.39.

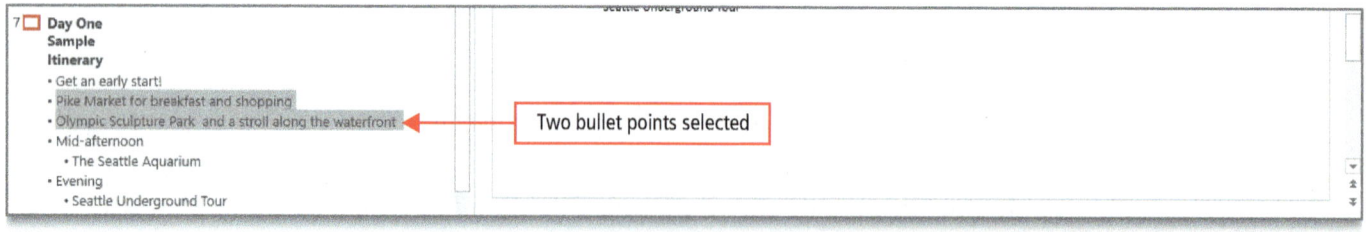

Figure 1.39

3 On the **Home tab**, in the **Paragraph group**, click **Increase List Level** one time to increase the list level of the selected bullet points.

When you type in the outline or change the list level, the changes also display in the Slide pane.

4 In the **Outline**, in **Slide 7**, click at the end of the last bullet point after the word *Tour*. Press Enter to create a new bullet point at the same list level as the previous bullet point. Type **Pike Place Market for dinner** and then compare your screen with Figure 1.40.

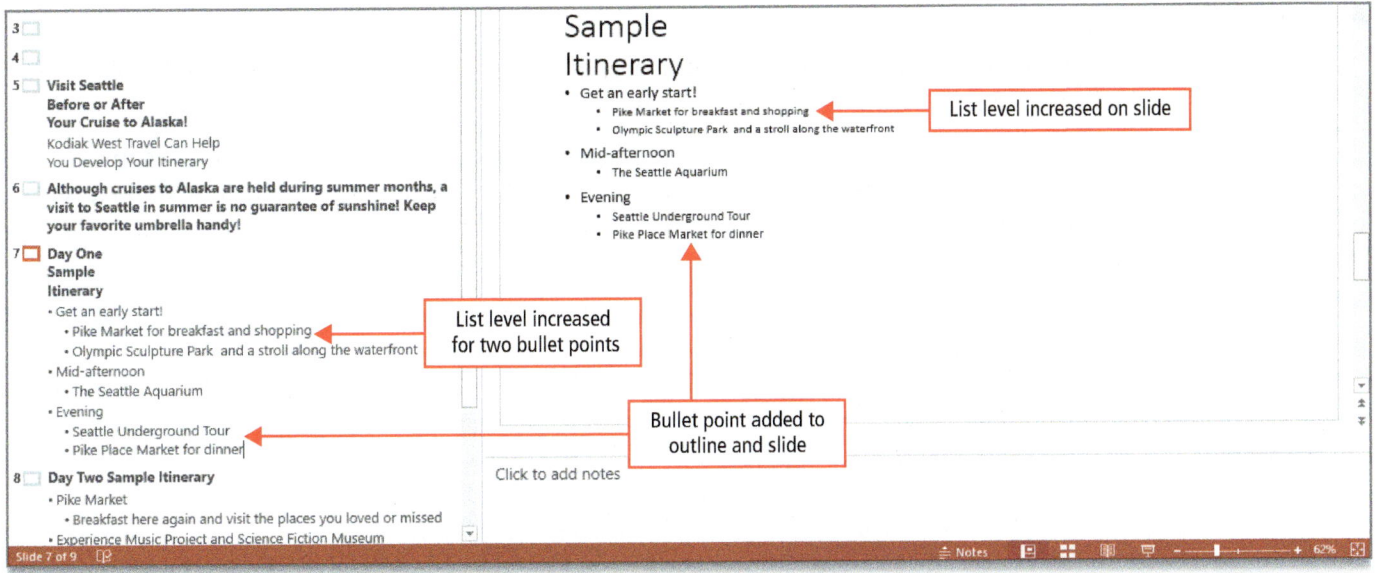

Figure 1.40

MOS
2.3.2

5 In the **Status bar**, click **Normal** 🔲 to close Outline View and redisplay the slide thumbnails. **Save** 🔲 the presentation.

> You can type text in the Slide pane or in the Outline. Displaying the Outline enables you to view the entire flow of the presentation text.

Activity 1.20 | Deleting and Moving a Slide

1 To the right of the slide thumbnails, locate the vertical scroll bar and scroll box. If necessary, drag the scroll box down so that **Slide 9** displays in the slide thumbnails. Click **Slide 9** to display it in the Slide pane. Press Delete to delete the slide from the presentation.

> Your presentation contains eight slides.

2 If necessary, scroll the slide thumbnails so that **Slide 4** displays. Point to **Slide 4**, hold down the left mouse button, and then drag down to position the **Slide 4** thumbnail below the **Slide 8** thumbnail. Release the mouse button, and then compare your screen with Figure 1.41. **Save** 🔲 the presentation.

> You can easily rearrange your slides by dragging a slide thumbnail to a new location in the presentation.

BY TOUCH Use your finger to drag the slide you want to move to a new location in the presentation.

Figure 1.41

Activity 1.21 | Finding and Replacing Text

The Replace command enables you to locate all occurrences of specified text and replace it with alternative text.

1 Display **Slide 1**. On the **Home tab**, in the **Editing group**, click **Replace**. In the **Replace** dialog box, in the **Find what** box, type **Pike Market** and then in the **Replace with** box, type **Pike Place Market** Compare your screen with Figure 1.42.

📘 **MAC TIP** Find and Replace are in the Edit menu.

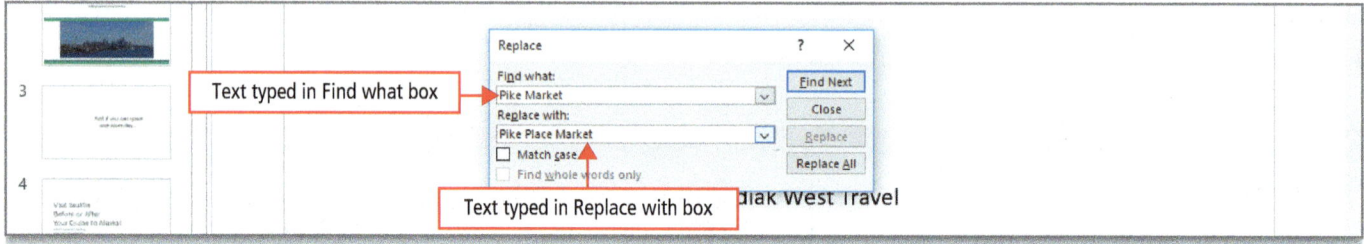

Figure 1.42

2 In the **Replace** dialog box, click **Replace All** to display a message box indicating that two replacements were made.

3 In the message box, click **OK**. **Close** ☒ the **Replace** dialog box, and then click **Save** 🖫.

Objective 6   Format a Presentation

GO! Learn How
Video P1-6

Formatting refers to changing the appearance of the text, layout, and design of a slide. Recall that a theme is a set of unified design elements that provides a look for your presentation by applying colors, fonts, and effects.

Activity 1.22 | Applying a Theme Variant

Each PowerPoint theme includes several *variants*—variations on the theme style and color. The themes and variants that are available on your system may vary.

1 On the **Design tab**, in the **Variants group**, notice that four variants of the current theme display and the second variant is applied.

2 Point to each of the variants to view the change to **Slide 1**.

If you do not see the same variants, refer to the figures for this activity.

3 With **Slide 1** displayed, in the **Variants group**, point to the **third variant**, and then right-click. Compare your screen with Figure 1.43.

The shortcut menu displays options for applying the variant.

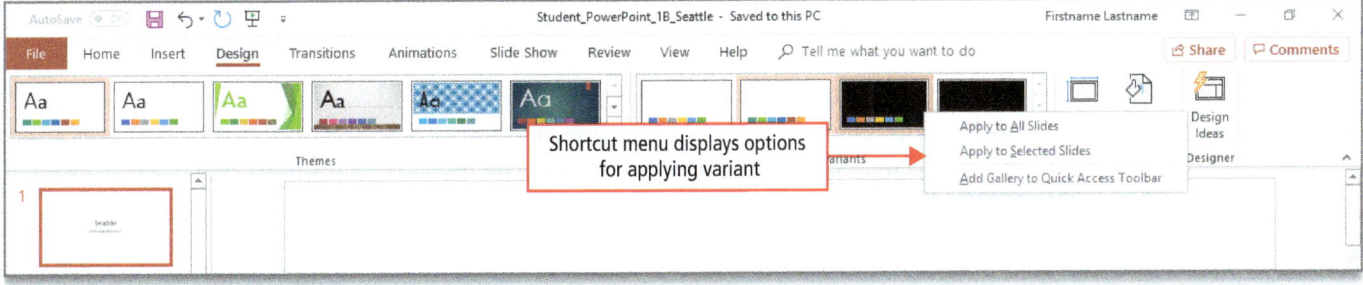

Figure 1.43

> **4** ▸ Click **Apply to Selected Slides** to apply the variant to **Slide 1** only. Compare your screen with Figure 1.44.

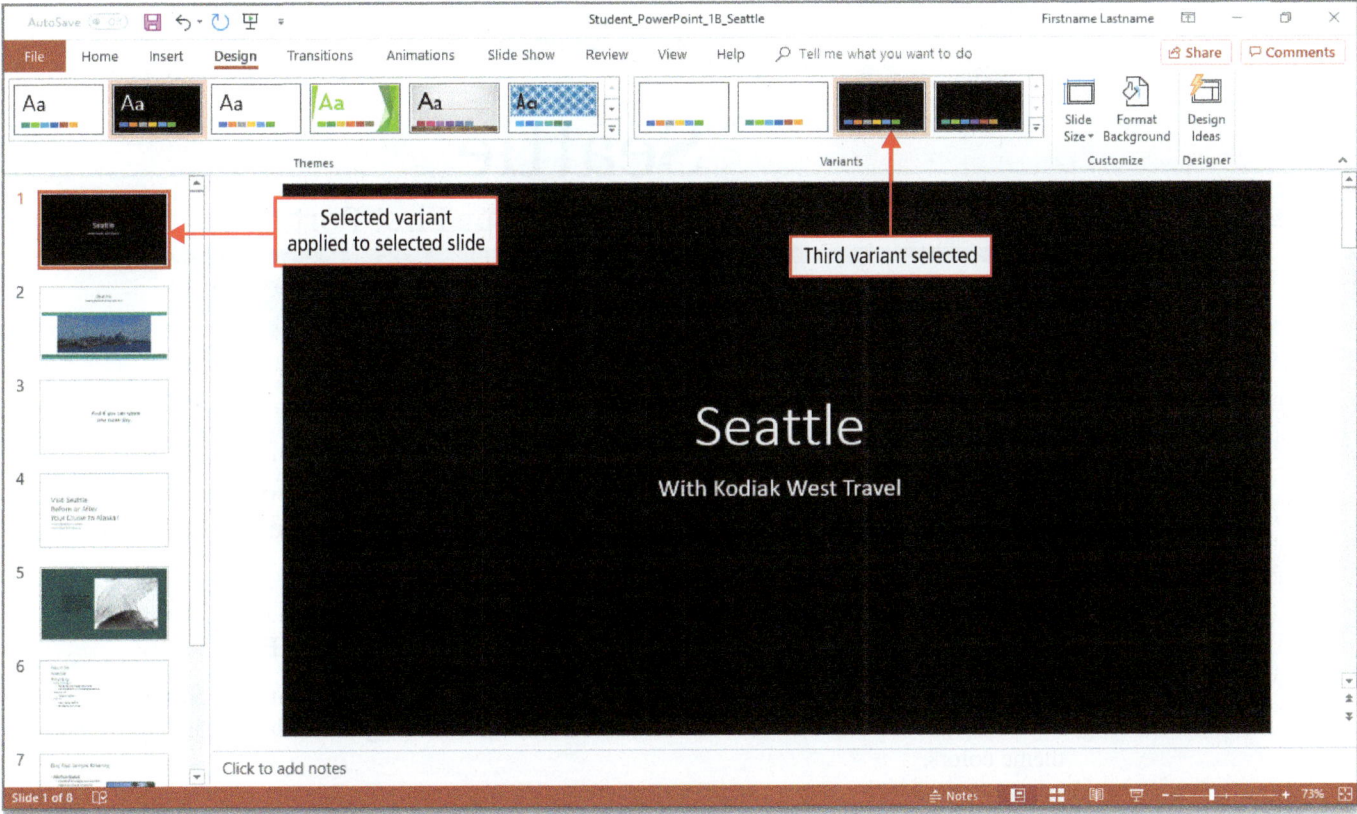

Figure 1.44

> **5** ▸ In the **Variants group**, right-click the **second variant**. On the shortcut menu, click **Apply to All Slides** so that the original variant color is applied to all of the slides in the presentation. **Save** 🔲 your presentation.

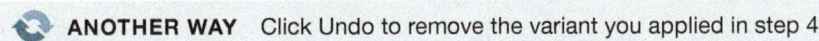

🔄 **ANOTHER WAY** Click Undo to remove the variant you applied in step 4.

Activity 1.23 | Changing Fonts and Font Sizes

A font is a set of characters with the same design and shape and fonts are measured in points. Font styles include bold, italic, and underline, and you can apply any combination of these styles to presentation text. Font styles and font color are useful to provide emphasis and are a visual cue to draw the reader's eye to important text.

> **1** ▸ Display **Slide 2**. Select all of the text in the title placeholder, point to the mini toolbar, and then click the **Font arrow** to display the available fonts. Scroll the font list, and then click **Georgia**.

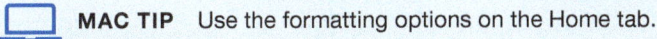

💻 **MAC TIP** Use the formatting options on the Home tab.

2 ▶ Select the first line of the title—*Seattle*. On the mini toolbar, click the **Font Size arrow** and then click **80**.

3 ▶ Select the second line of the title—*Making the Most of Your First Port*. On the **Home tab**, in the **Font group**, click the **Font Size arrow**, and then click **36**. Click in a blank area of the slide to cancel your selection, and then compare your screen with Figure 1.45. **Save** 🖫 your presentation.

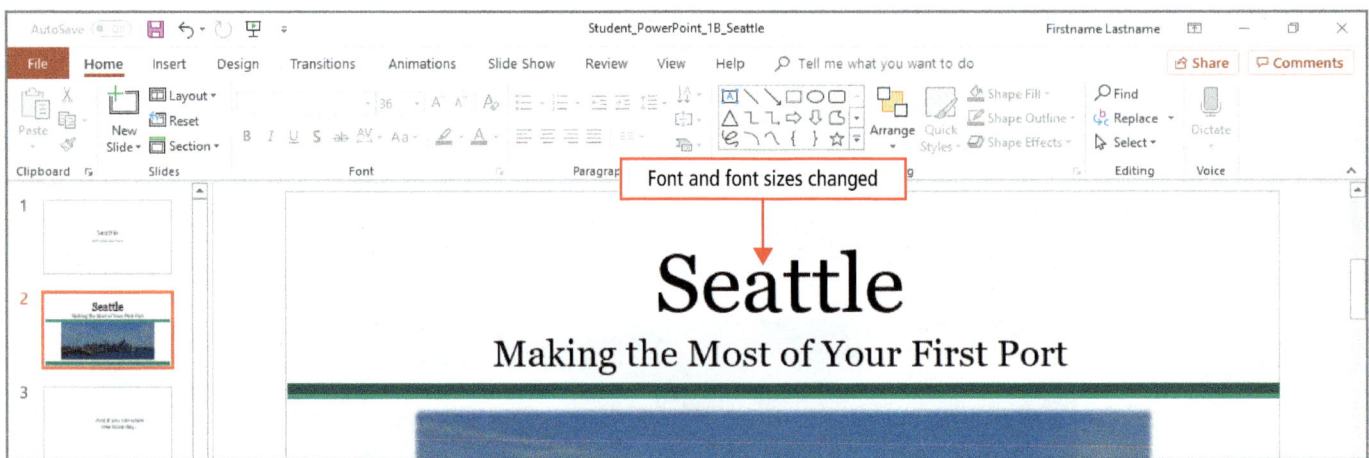

Figure 1.45

Activity 1.24 | Changing Font Styles and Font Colors

Font styles include bold, italic, and underline, and you can apply any combination of these styles to presentation text. Font styles and font color are useful to provide emphasis and are a visual cue to draw the reader's eye to important text.

1 ▶ Display **Slide 3**, and then select both lines of text. On the **Home tab**, in the **Font group**, click the **Font Color arrow** 🅰️ and then compare your screen with Figure 1.46.

The colors in the top row of the color gallery are the colors associated with the presentation theme—*Frame*. The colors in the rows below the first row are light and dark variations of the theme colors.

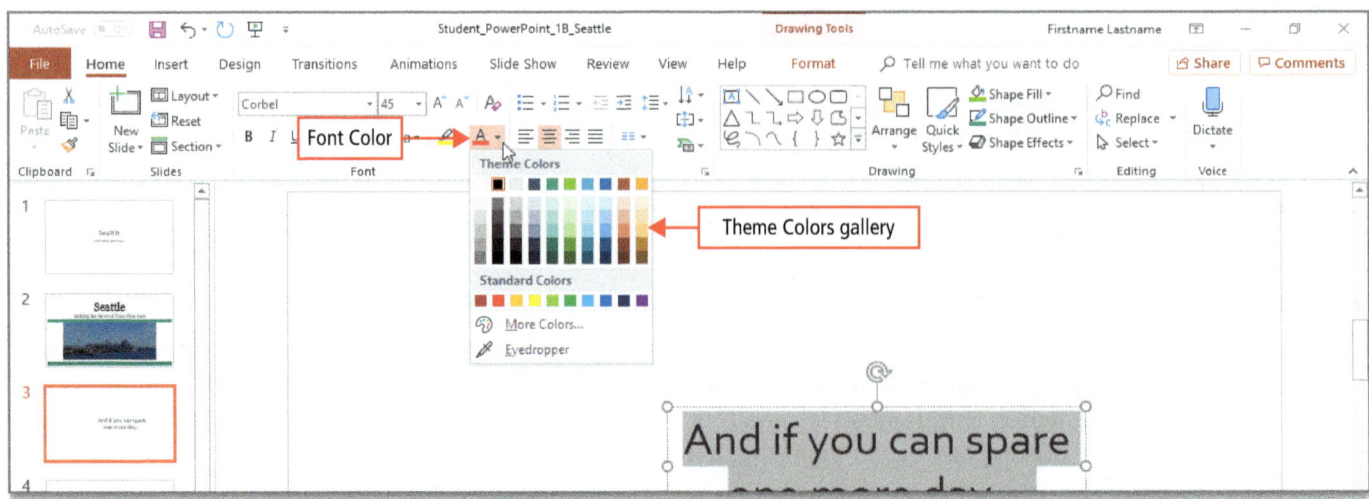

Figure 1.46

2 Point to several of the colors and notice that a ScreenTip displays the color name and Live Preview displays the selected text in the color to which you are pointing.

3 Under Theme Colors, in the fifth column of colors, click the last color to change the font color. Notice that on the **Home tab**, the lower part of the **Font Color** button displays the most recently applied font color.

> When you click the Font Color button instead of the Font Color button arrow, the color displayed in the lower part of the Font Color button is applied to selected text without displaying the color gallery.

4 With the two lines of text still selected, right-click within the selected text to redisplay the mini toolbar, and then from the mini toolbar, apply **Bold** and **Italic**.

5 Display **Slide 4**, and then select the title—*Visit Seattle Before or After Your Cruise to Alaska!* On the mini toolbar, click **Font Color** [A▾] to apply the most recently applied font color to the selection. Select the subtitle—*Kodiak West Travel Can Help You Develop Your Itinerary*—and then change the **Font Color** to most recently applied color. Compare your screen with Figure 1.47. **Save** [💾] your presentation.

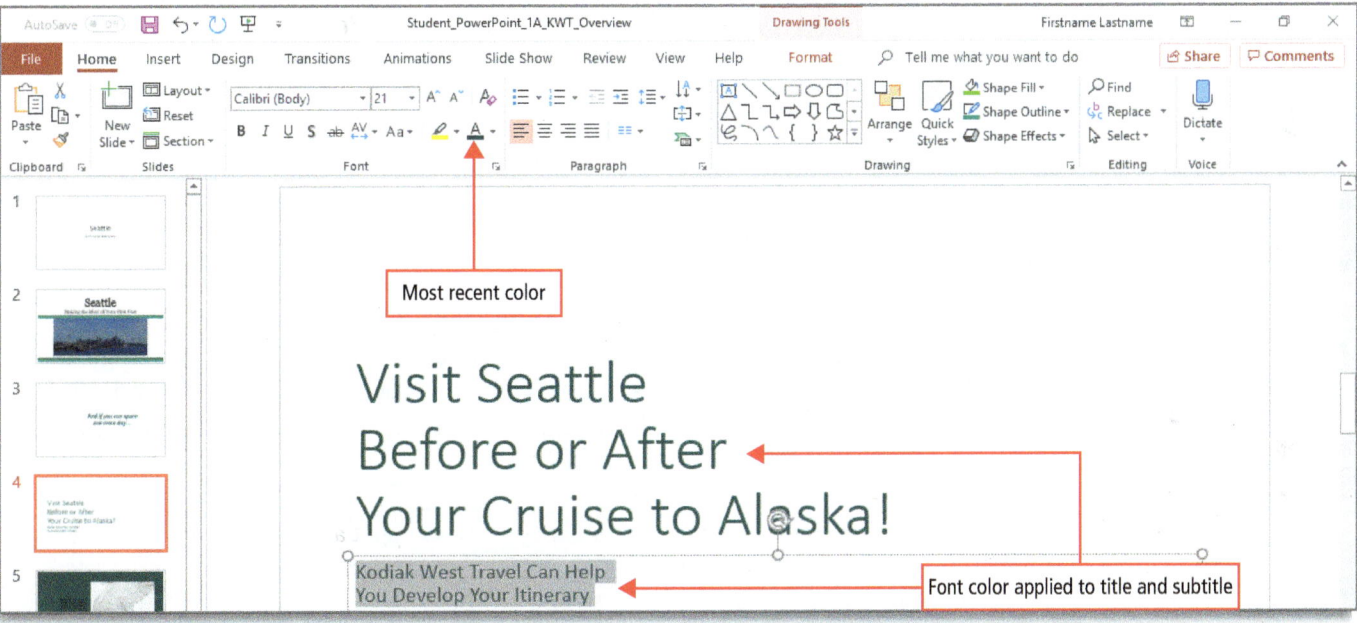

Figure 1.47

Activity 1.25 | Aligning Text

In PowerPoint, *text alignment* refers to the horizontal placement of text within a placeholder. You can align text left, centered, right, or justified.

1 Display **Slide 5**, and then select all of the text in the paragraph. Click the **Font Color arrow** [A▾] and change the font color to the first color in the first column.

2 On the **Home tab**, in the **Paragraph group**, click **Center** [≡] to center the text within the placeholder.

3 Display **Slide 4**, and then click anywhere in the slide title. Press [Ctrl] + [E] to use the keyboard shortcut to center the text.

4 ▸ On **Slide 4**, using one of the methods that you practiced, **Center** the subtitle. Click in a blank area of the slide. Compare your screen with Figure 1.48 and then **Save** 🖫 the presentation.

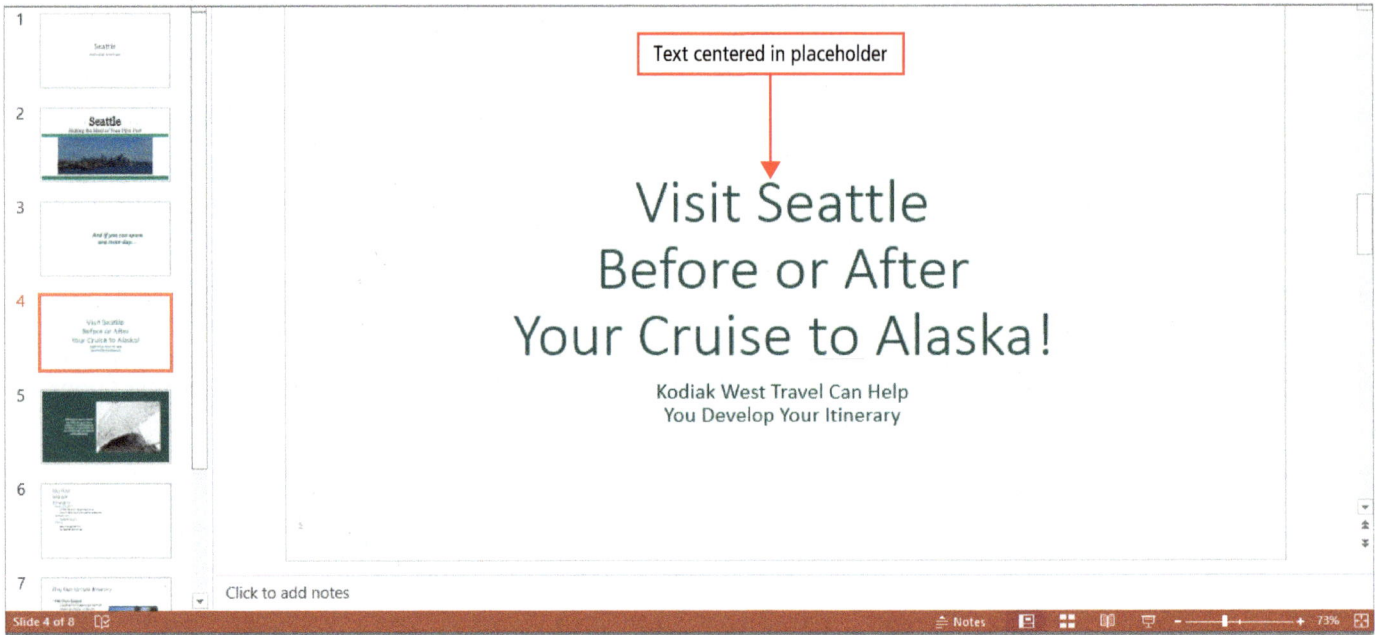

Figure 1.48

Activity 1.26 │ Changing Line Spacing

1 ▸ Display **Slide 5**, and then click anywhere in the paragraph. On the **Home tab**, in the **Paragraph group**, click **Line Spacing** 🔲. In the list, click **2.0** to change from single spacing to double spacing between lines of text. Compare your screen with Figure 1.49.

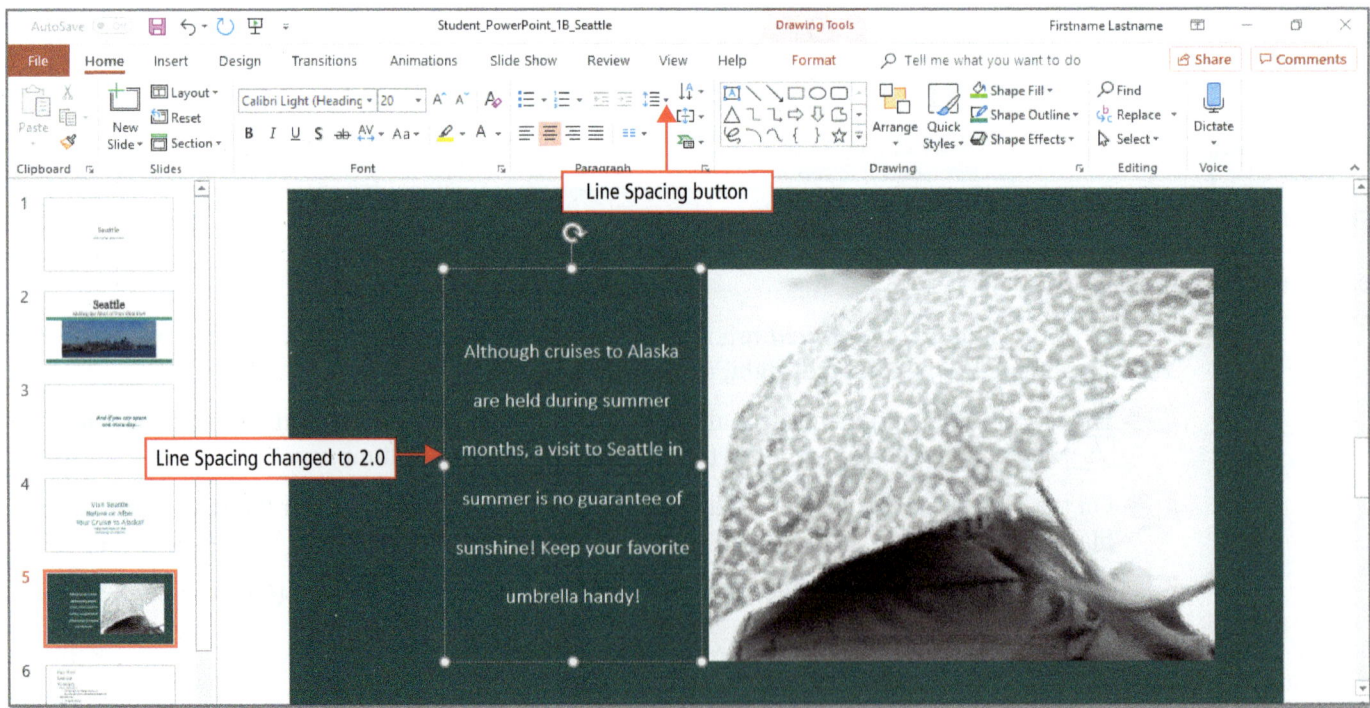

Figure 1.49

2 ▸ **Save** 🖫 your presentation.

Activity 1.27 | Changing the Slide Layout

The slide layout defines the placement of the content placeholders on a slide. PowerPoint includes predefined layouts that you can apply to your slide for arranging slide elements. For example, a Title Slide contains two placeholder elements—the title and the subtitle. When you design your slides, consider the content that you want to include, and then choose a layout with the elements that will display the message you want to convey in the best way.

1 Display **Slide 1**. On the **Home tab**, in the **Slides group**, click **Layout** to display the **Slide Layout** gallery. Notice that *Title Slide* is selected, indicating the layout of the current slide.

2 Click **Section Header** to change the slide layout. Compare your screen with Figure 1.50, and then **Save** your presentation.

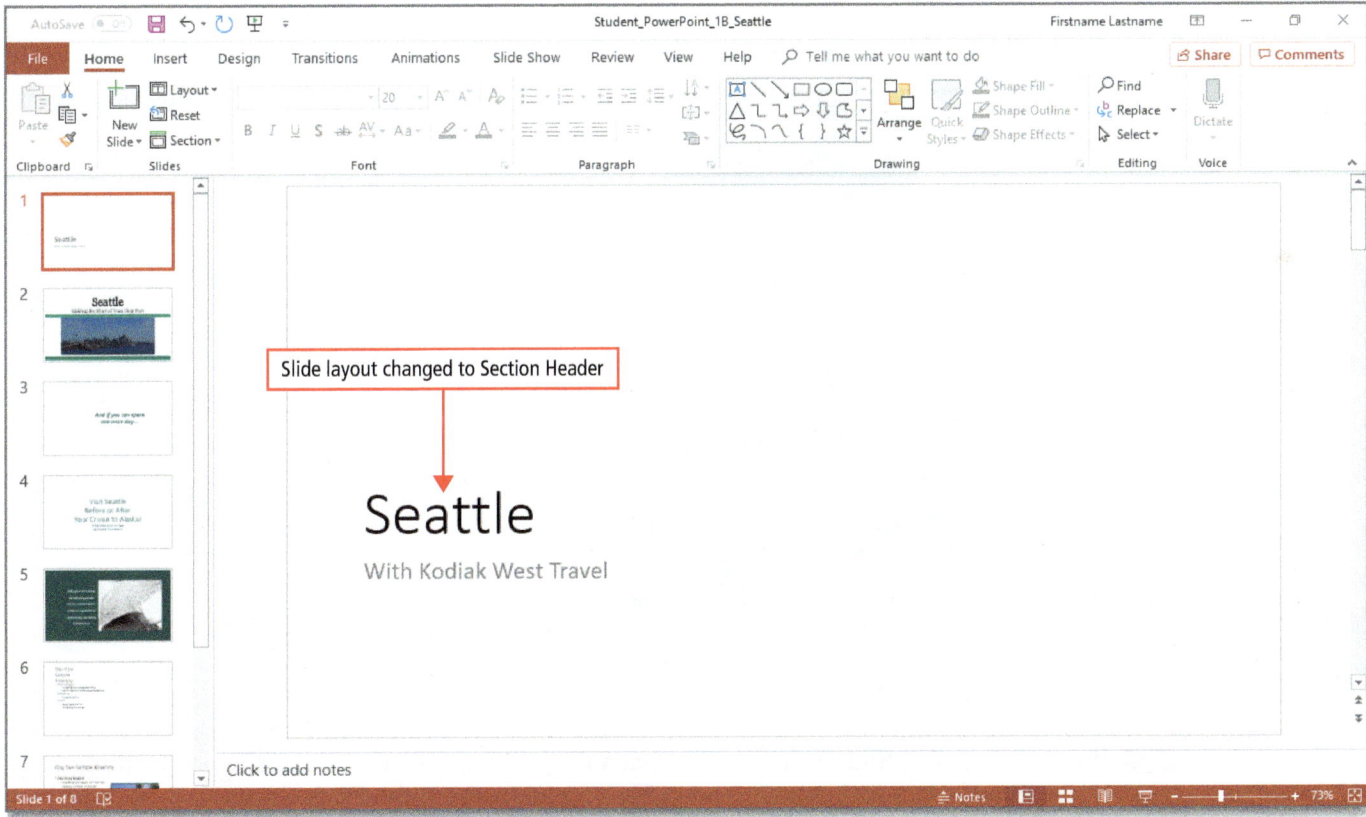

Figure 1.50

Objective 7 Use Slide Sorter View

GO! Learn How
Video P1-7

Slide Sorter view displays thumbnails of all of the slides in a presentation. Use Slide Sorter view to rearrange and delete slides and to apply formatting to multiple slides.

Activity 1.28 | Deleting Slides in Slide Sorter View

1 ⟩ In the lower right corner of the PowerPoint window, click **Slide Sorter** ⊞ to display all of the slide thumbnails. Compare your screen with Figure 1.51.

Your slides may display larger or smaller than those shown in Figure 1.51.

> 🔄 **ANOTHER WAY** On the View tab, in the Presentation Views group, click Slide Sorter.

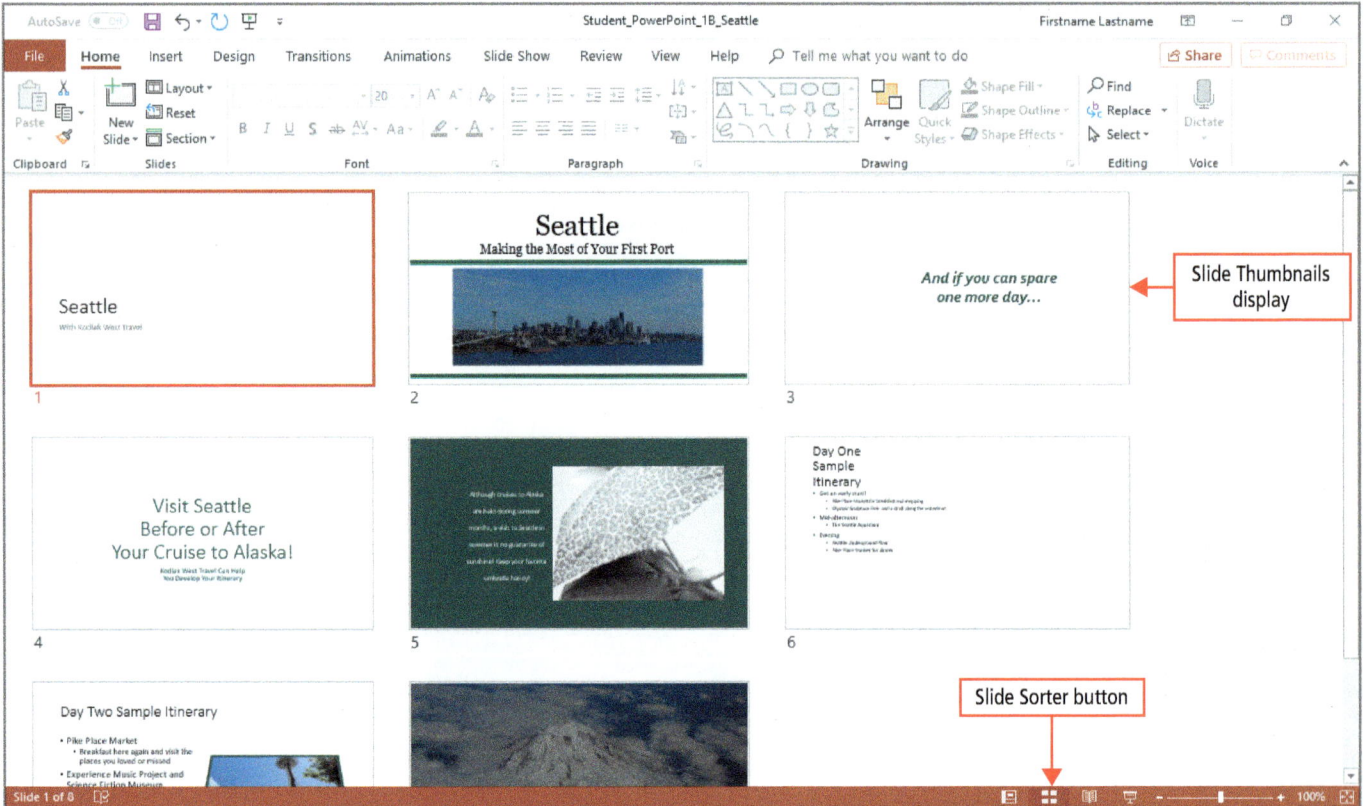

Figure 1.51

2 ⟩ If necessary, click Slide 1, and notice that a thick outline surrounds the slide, indicating that it is selected. On your keyboard, press Delete to delete the slide. Click **Save** 🖫.

Activity 1.29 | Moving a Single Slide in Slide Sorter View

1 ⟩ With the presentation displayed in Slide Sorter view, point to **Slide 2**. Hold down the left mouse button, and then drag to position the slide to the right of **Slide 6**, as shown in Figure 1.52.

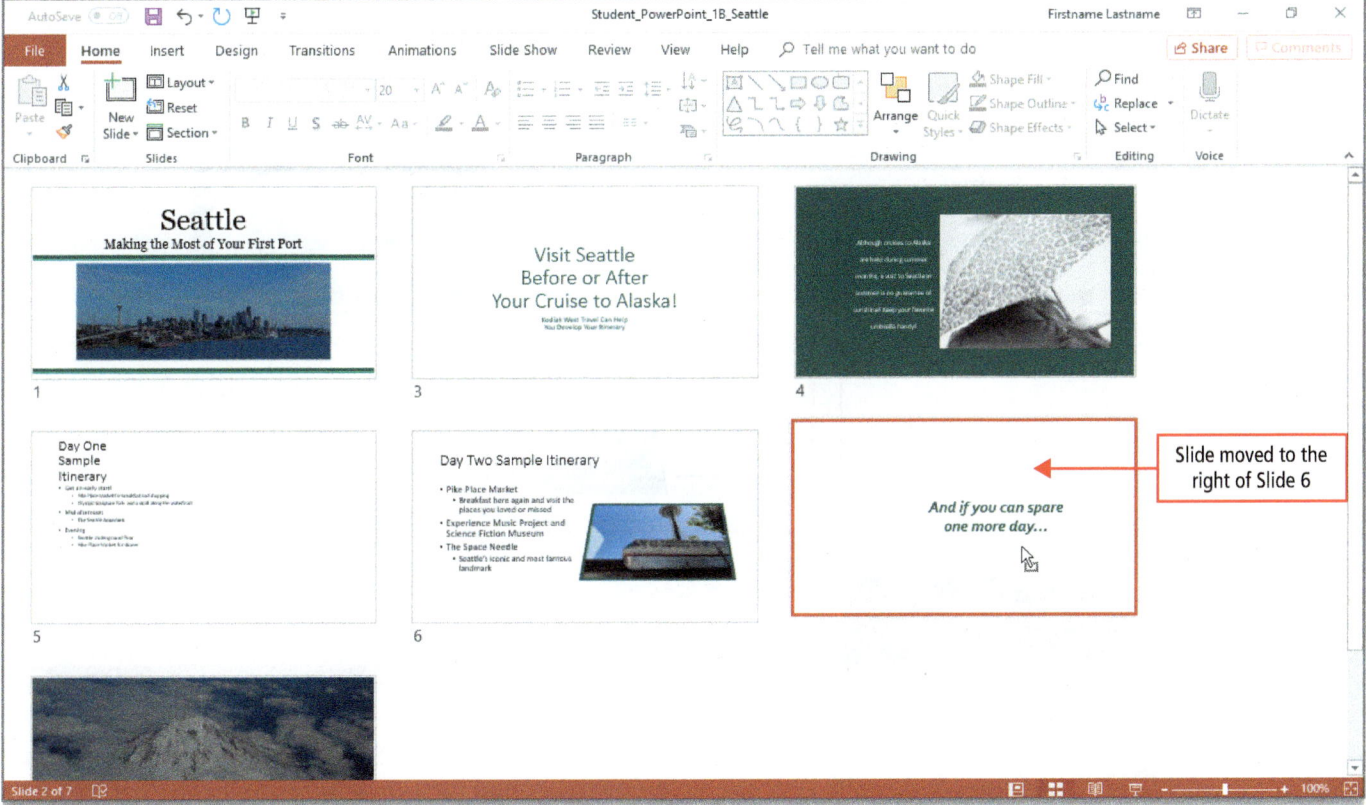

Figure 1.52

2 ▶ Release the mouse button to move the slide to the **Slide 6** position in the presentation. **Save** 🖫 your presentation.

Activity 1.30 | Selecting Contiguous and Noncontiguous Slides and Moving Multiple Slides

2.3.2

Contiguous slides are slides that are adjacent to each other in a presentation. *Noncontiguous slides* are slides that are not adjacent to each other in a presentation.

1 ▶ Click **Slide 2**, hold down Ctrl, click **Slide 4**, release Ctrl. Notice that both slides are selected.

The noncontiguous slides—Slides 2 and 4—are outlined, indicating that both are selected. By holding down Ctrl, you can select noncontiguous slides.

💻 **MAC TIP** Hold down command ⌘ + click.

2 ▶ Click **Slide 3**, so that only Slide 3 is selected. Hold down Shift, click **Slide 5**, and then release Shift. Compare your screen with Figure 1.53.

The contiguous slides—Slides 3, 4, and 5—are outlined, indicating that all three slides are selected. By holding down Shift, you can create a group of contiguous selected slides.

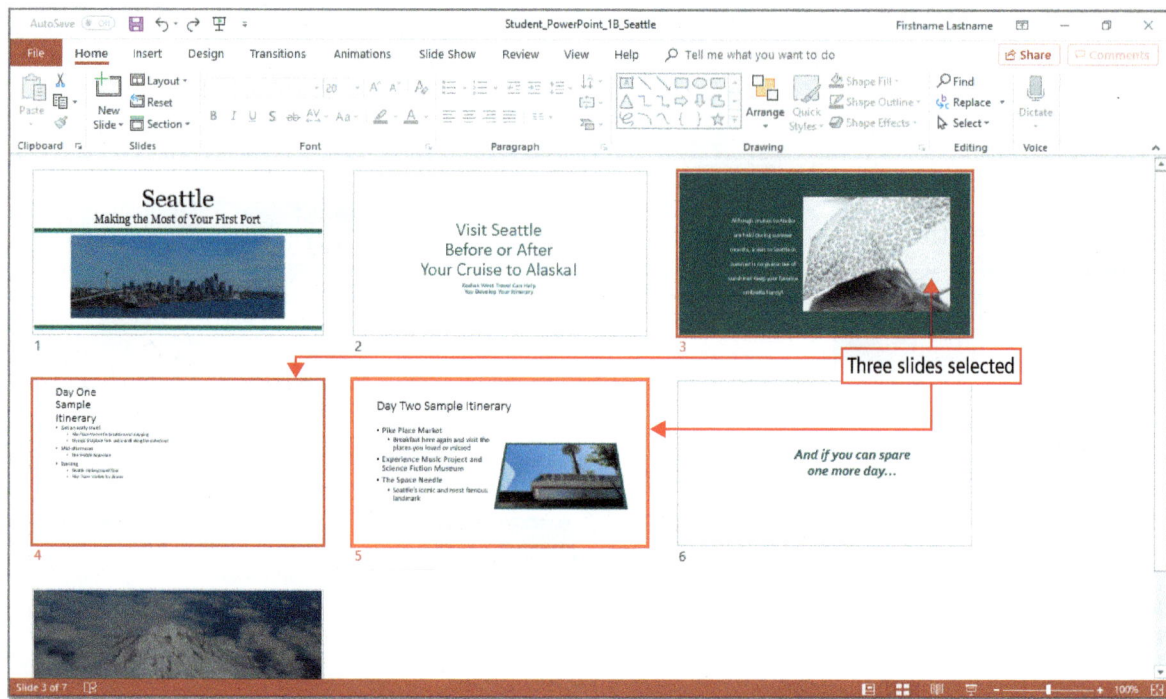

Figure 1.53

3 With **Slides 3, 4,** and **5** selected, hold down $\boxed{\text{Ctrl}}$, and then click **Slide 3**. Notice that only **Slides 4** and **5** are selected.

> With a group of selected slides, you can press $\boxed{\text{Ctrl}}$ and then click a selected slide to *deselect* it.

4 Point to either of the selected slides, hold down the left mouse button, and then drag to position the two slides to the right of **Slide 2**. Compare your screen with Figure 1.54.

> The selected slides are dragged as a group, and the number 2 in the upper left area of the selected slides indicates the number of slides that you are moving.

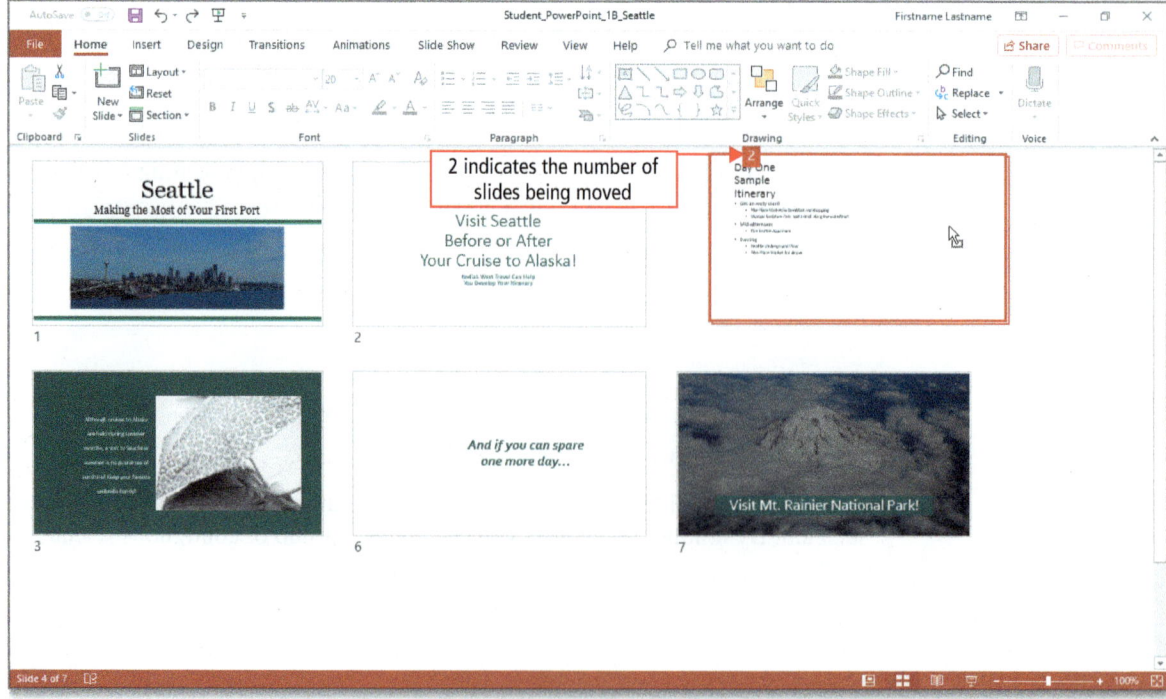

Figure 1.54

5 Release the mouse button to reposition the slides. On the View tab, click **Normal**  to return to Normal view. **Save** 🖫 your presentation.

Objective 8 | Apply Slide Transitions

GO! Learn How

Video P1-8

Slide transitions are the motion effects that occur in Slide Show view when you move from one slide to the next during a presentation. You can choose from a variety of transitions, and you can control the speed and method with which the slides advance.

Activity 1.31 | Applying Slide Transitions to a Presentation

MOS

5.1.1, 5.1.2

In this Activity, you will apply a slide transition to all the slides in the presentation.

1 Display **Slide 1**. On the **Transitions tab**, in the **Transition to This Slide group**, click **More** ⬚ to display the **Transitions** gallery. Compare your screen with Figure 1.55.

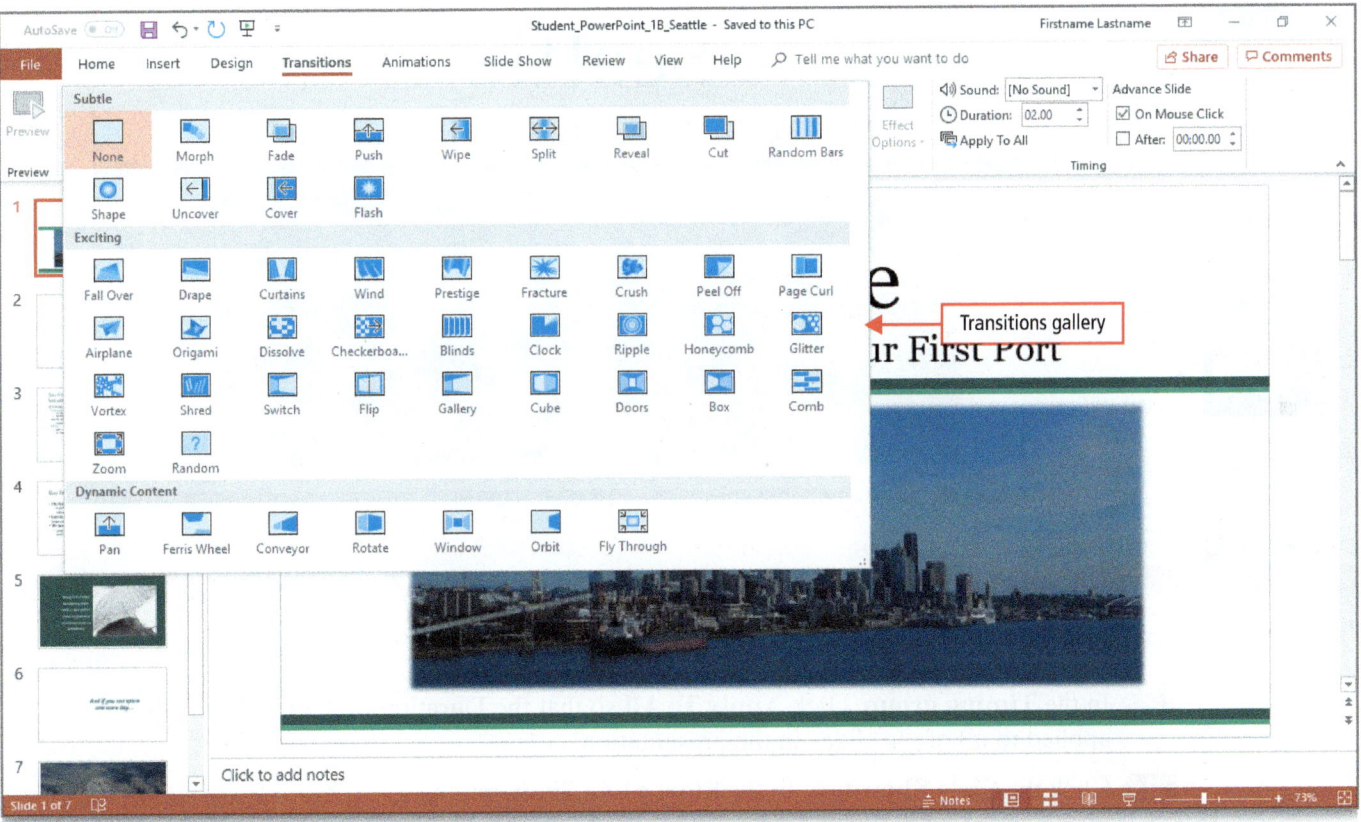

Figure 1.55

2 Under **Subtle**, click **Fade** to apply and view the transition. In the **Transition to This Slide group**, click **Effect Options** to display the way the slide enters the screen. Click **Smoothly**. In the **Timing group**, click **Apply To All** to apply the *Fade, Smoothly* transition to all of the slides in the presentation. **Save** 🖫 your presentation.

The Effect Options vary depending on the selected transition. In the slide thumbnails, a star displays below the slide number providing a visual cue that a transition has been applied to the slide.

Activity 1.32 | Setting Slide Transition Timing Options

In this Activity, you will modify the duration of the transition—the amount of time it takes for the transition to complete.

1 In the **Timing group**, notice that the **Duration** box displays *00.70*, indicating that the transition lasts 0.70 seconds. Click the **Duration up spin arrow** several times until *01.75* displays. Under **Advance Slide**, verify that the **On Mouse Click** check box is selected. Compare your screen with Figure 1.56.

With On Mouse Click selected, the presenter controls when the current slide advances to the next slide by clicking the mouse button or by pressing ⃞Spacebar⃞.

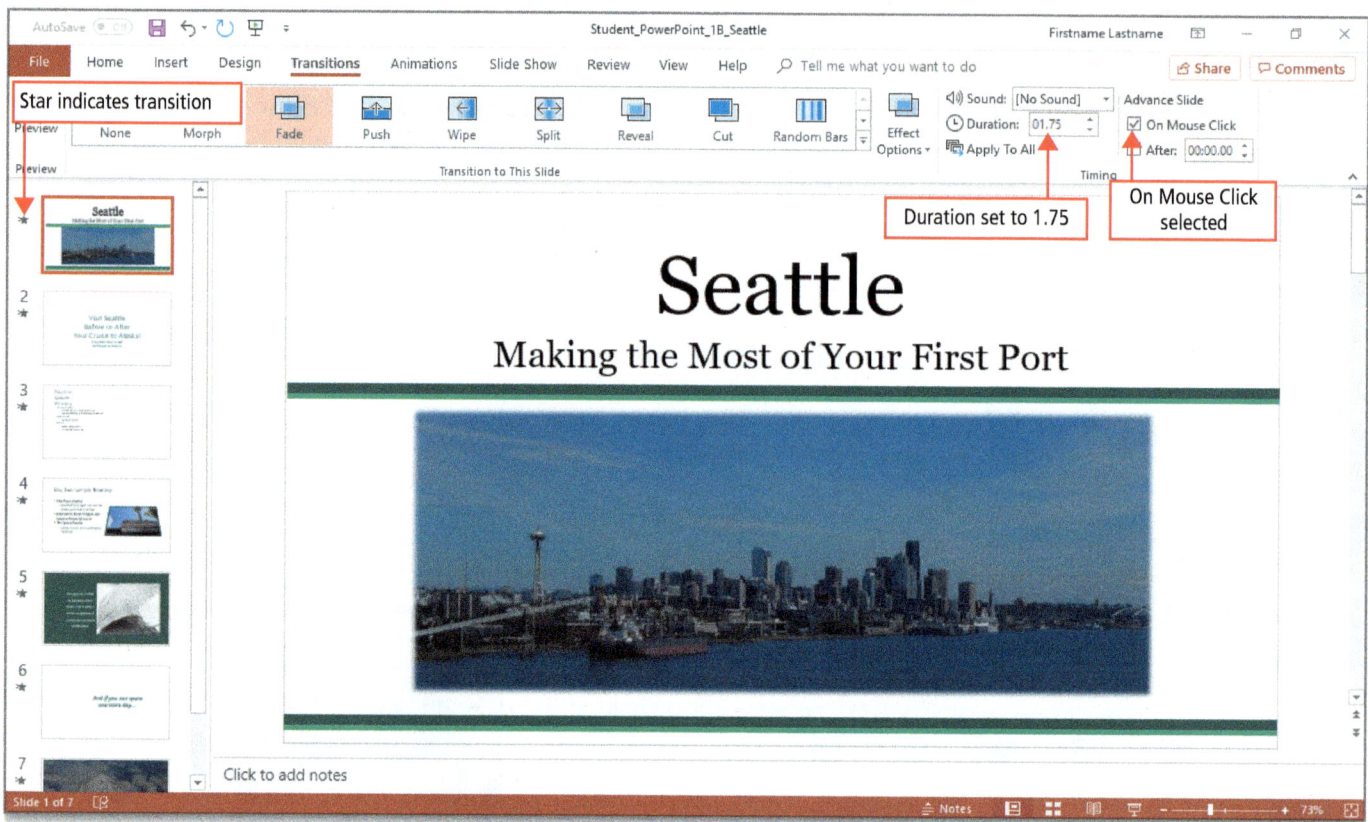

Figure 1.56

2 In the **Timing group**, click **Apply To All** so that the Duration of *1.75* seconds transition is applied to all of the slides in the presentation.

3 Click the **Slide Show tab**. In the **Start Slide Show group**, click **From Beginning**, and then view your presentation, clicking the mouse button to advance through the slides. When the black slide displays, click the mouse button one more time to display the presentation in Normal view. **Save** 🖫 your presentation.

MORE KNOWLEDGE **Applying Multiple Slide Transitions**

You can apply more than one type of transition in your presentation by displaying the slides one at a time, and then clicking the transition that you want to apply instead of clicking Apply To All.

Activity 1.33 | Displaying a Presentation in Reading View

1.2.2, 1.2.3

Organizations frequently conduct online meetings when participants are unable to meet in one location. The *Reading view* in PowerPoint displays a presentation in a manner similar to a slide show but the taskbar, title bar, and status bar remain available in the presentation window. Thus, a presenter can easily facilitate an online conference by switching to another window without closing the slide show. This is useful for Kodiak West Travel because employees are frequently on the road and attend online meetings.

1 ▶ In the lower right corner of the PowerPoint window, click **Reading View** 📖. Compare your screen with Figure 1.57.

> In Reading view, the status bar contains the Next and Previous buttons, which are used to navigate in the presentation, and the Menu button which is used to print, copy, and edit slides.

🔄 **ANOTHER WAY**   On the View tab, in the Presentation Views group, click Reading View.

💻 **MAC TIP**   Reading view is not available in the Mac version of PowerPoint. Skip to Step 4.

PowerPoint Slide Show - Student_PowerPoint_1B_Seattle - PowerPoint

Title bar

Seattle
Making the Most of Your First Port

Menu button

Previous button   Next button

Slide 1 of 7

Figure 1.57

2 ▶ Press Spacebar to display **Slide 2**. Click the left mouse button to display **Slide 3**. In the status bar, click **Previous** ⊲ to display **Slide 2**.

3 ▶ In the status bar, click **Menu** 🗐 to display the Reading view menu, and then click **End Show** to return to Normal view.

POWERPOINT

1

4 ▶ On the **Insert tab**, in the **Text group**, click **Header & Footer**, and then click the **Notes and Handouts tab**. Under **Include on page**, select the **Date and time** check box, and if necessary, select Update automatically. If necessary, select the **Page number** check box and clear the **Header** check box. Select the **Footer** check box, in the **Footer** box, type **1B_Seattle** and then click **Apply to All**.

5 ▶ Display **Backstage** view. On the Info tab, on the right, at the bottom of the **Properties** list, click **Show All Properties**. On the list of properties, click to the right of **Tags**, and then type **Seattle** To the right of **Subject**, type your course name and section number. Under **Related People**, be sure that your name displays as the author; edit if necessary.

6 ▶ On the left, scroll up as necessary, and then click **Save** 🔲.

For Non-MyLab Submissions Determine What Your Instructor Requires
As directed by your instructor, submit your completed PowerPoint presentation.

---

7 ▶ **Close** ☒ PowerPoint.

8 ▶ In **MyLab IT**, in your **Course Materials**, locate and click the Grader Project **PowerPoint 1B Seattle**. In **step 3**, under **Upload Completed Assignment**, click **Choose File**. In the **Open** dialog box, navigate to your **PowerPoint Chapter 1 folder**, and then click your **Student_PowerPoint_1B_Seattle** file one time to select it. In the lower right corner of the **Open** dialog box, click **Open**.

   The name of your selected file displays above the Upload button.

9 ▶ To submit your file to **MyLab IT** for grading, click **Upload**, wait a moment for a green **Success!** message, and then in **step 4**, click the blue **Submit for Grading** button. Click **Close Assignment** to return to your list of **Course Materials**.

You have completed Project 1B   **END**

| **Objective** | **Create an Itinerary Presentation in Google Slides** |

ALERT **Working with Web-Based Applications and Services**

Computer programs and services on the web receive continuous updates and improvements, so the steps to complete this web-based activity may differ from the ones shown. You can often look at the screens and the information presented to determine how to complete the activity.

If you do not already have a Google account, you will need to create one before you begin this activity.

Activity | **Creating an Itinerary Presentation in Google Slides**

In this Activity, you will use Google Slides to create a presentation similar to the one you created in Project 1B.

1 From the desktop, open your browser, navigate to **http://google.com**, and then sign in to your Google account. Click the **Google apps** icon ⊞ and then click **Drive** 🛆.

Open your **GO! Web Projects** folder—or create and then open this folder, if necessary.

2 In the left pane, click **New**, and then click **File upload** 🛅. Navigate to your student data files, click **p01_1B_Google_Slides**, and then click **Open**.

3 Wait a moment for the upload to complete, point to the uploaded file **p01_1B_Google_Slides.pptx**, and then right-click. On the shortcut menu, click **Rename**. Delete the existing text, and then using your own last name and first name, type **Lastname_Firstname_1B_Google_Slides** Click **OK** to rename the file.

4 Right-click the file that you just renamed, point to **Open with**, and then click **Google Slides**.

5 On **Slide 1**, in the Title placeholder, drag to select the two lines of text. On the **toolbar**, click the **Font arrow** ▾, and then click **Georgia**.

6 Select the text *Making the Most of Your First Port*. On the **toolbar**, click the **Font Size arrow** 10, and then click **24**.

7 Click **Slide 2**. Click the **Edit menu**, and then click **Delete** to remove the slide from the presentation.

8 With **Slide 2**—*Seattle Weather*—displayed, press Delete to remove the slide from your presentation. Notice that the presentation contains seven slides.

9 Display **Slide 3**, and then click in the paragraph on the left side of the slide. Drag to select the text, and then on the **toolbar**, click **Text color** 🅰. Under **Theme**,

click the second color—**Theme Color white**. With the paragraph still selected, on the toolbar, click **Bold** 🅱 and **Italic** 🅸. Click **Align** ▤ ▾ and click **Center** ▤. Click anywhere in a blank area of the slide to cancel the selection and view your changes.

10 In the slide thumbnails, point to **Slide 4**, hold down the left mouse button, and then drag up slightly. Notice that a black bar displays above **Slide 4**. Continue to drag up until the black bar displays above **Slide 3**. Release the mouse button to move the slide.

11 Using the technique that you just practiced, move **Slide 5** to position it above **Slide 4**.

12 Display **Slide 6**. Select all three lines of text. Click **Align** ▤ ▾, and then click **Center** ▤. Click anywhere on the slide to cancel the selection. Click **Slide 1** and compare your screen with Figure A.

13 Display **Slide 1**. At the right end of the toolbar, click **Transition** to open the **Animations** pane. On the right, in the Animations pane, click **No transition button**, click **Slide from right**, and then click **Apply to all slides**.

14 To the right of the **menu bar**, click the **Present button arrow**, and then click **Present from beginning**. If necessary, click Allow. Click the left mouse button to progress through the presentation. When the last slide displays, press Esc or in the lower left corner, click **Exit**.

15 Your presentation will be saved automatically. Download as Microsoft PowerPoint, PDF Document, or another format, and submit as directed by your instructor. Sign out of your Google account and close your browser.

»» **GO!** With Google continues on next page

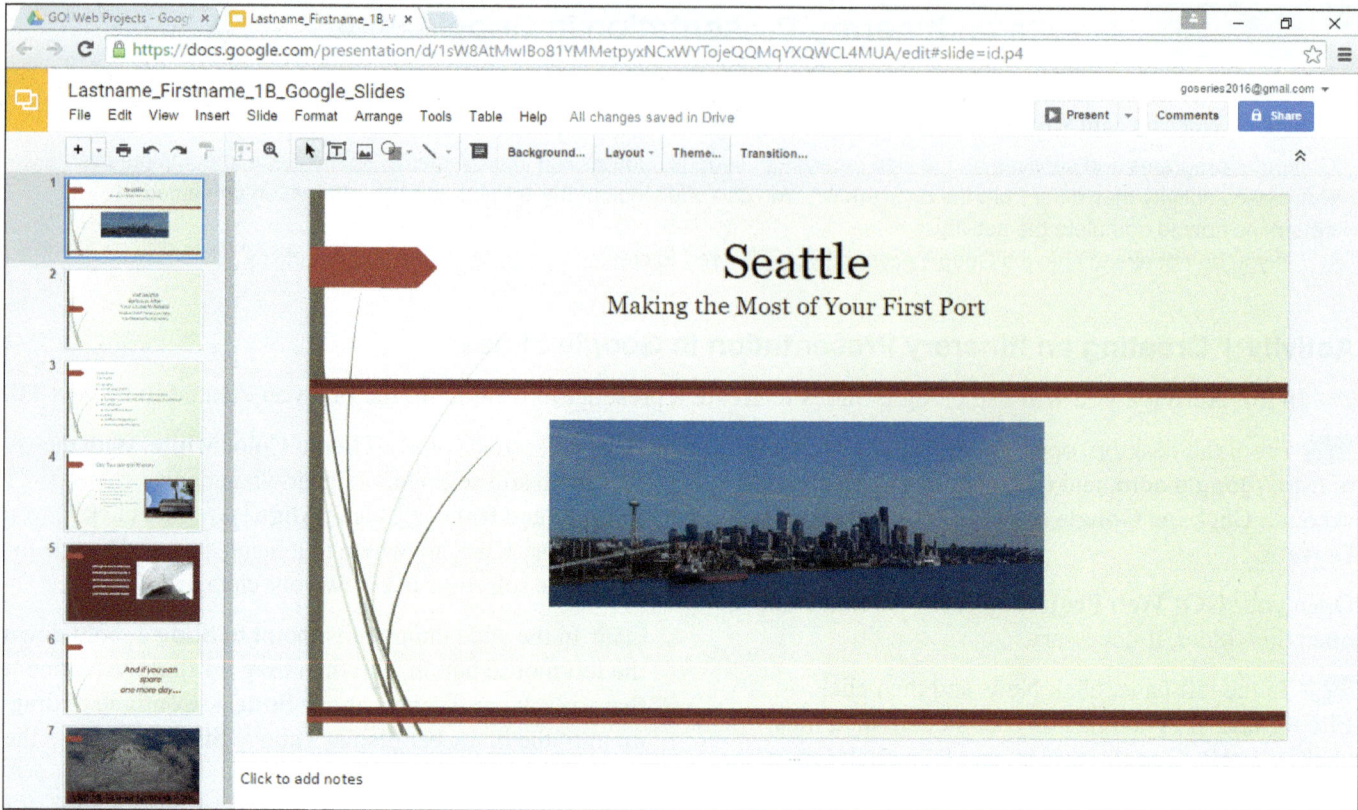

Figure A

wavebreakmedia/Shutterstock, Monkey Business Images/Fotolia, Ivanko80/Shutterstock, Monkey Business Images/Shutterstock

1

POWERPOINT

Microsoft Office Specialist (MOS) Skills in This Chapter

Project 1A	Project 1B
1.2.2 Display presentations in different views	**1.2.1** Change slide size
1.2.3 Set basic file properties	**1.2.2** Display presentations in different views
1.3.2 Print notes pages	**1.2.3** Set basic file properties
1.3.3 Print handouts	**2.1.2** Insert slides from another presentation
1.4.5 Present slide shows by using Presenter View	**2.3.2** Modify slide order
2.1.3 Insert slides and select slide layouts	**5.1.1** Apply basic and 3D slide transitions
2.2.3 Insert slide headers, footers, and page numbers	**5.1.2** Configure transition effects
3.1.3 Create bulleted and numbered lists	**5.3.2** Configure transition start and finish options
3.3.2 Apply built-in styles and effects to images	

Build Your E-Portfolio

An E-Portfolio is a collection of evidence, stored electronically, that showcases what you have accomplished while completing your education. Collecting and then sharing your work products with potential employers reflects your academic and career goals. Your completed documents from the following projects are good examples to show what you have learned: 1G, 1K, and 1L.

GO! For Job Success

Video: Personal Branding

Your instructor may assign this video to your class, and then ask you to think about, or discuss with your classmates, these questions:

g-stockstudio/Shutterstock

How do you suggest job seekers communicate their unique value—their personal brand—to potential employers online?

What are the best ways to network online and offline?

What are some of the biggest pitfalls in using social media to communicate a personal brand?

End of Chapter

Summary

In this chapter, you started a new presentation in PowerPoint. You inserted slides with various layouts, and you entered, edited, and formatted text. You also inserted text from another PowerPoint file.

Use a presentation theme to establish a unified presentation design. You can change the color of the presentation theme by applying one of the predefined variants that are supplied with each theme.

Presentations are often organized in a manner similar to outlines. List levels represent outline levels and are identified by the bullet style, indentation, and text size.

Slide layout defines the placement of content placeholders on a slide. Each presentation theme includes predefined layouts that you can apply to slides for the purpose of arranging slide elements.

GO! Learn It Online

Review the concepts, key terms, and MOS skills in this chapter by completing these online challenges, which you can find at **MyLab IT**.

Chapter Quiz: Answer matching and multiple choice questions to test what you learned in this chapter.

Lessons on the GO!: Learn how to use all the new apps and features as they are introduced by Microsoft.

MOS Prep Quiz: Answer questions to review the MOS skills that you practiced in this chapter.

GO! Collaborative Team Project (Available in Instructor Resource Center)

If your instructor assigns this project to your class, you can expect to work with one or more of your classmates—either in person or by using internet tools—to create work products similar to those that you created in this chapter. A team is a group of workers who work together to solve a problem, make a decision, or create a work product. Collaboration is when you work together with others as a team in an intellectual endeavor to complete a shared task or achieve a shared goal.

Monkey Business Images/Fotolia

Project Guide for PowerPoint Chapter 1

Your instructor will assign Projects from this list to ensure your learning and assess your knowledge.

	Project Guide for PowerPoint Chapter 1		
Project	**Apply Skills from These Chapter Objectives**	**Project Type**	**Project Location**
1A MyLab IT	Objectives 1–4 from Project 1A	**1A Instructional Project (Grader Project)** Instruction Guided instruction to learn the skills in Project A.	In **MyLab IT** and in text
1B MyLab IT	Objectives 5–8 from Project 1B	**1B Instructional Project (Grader Project)** Instruction Guided instruction to learn the skills in Project B.	In **MyLab IT** and in text
1C	Objectives 1–4 from Project 1A	**1C Skills Review (Scorecard Grading)** Review A guided review of the skills from Project 1A.	In text
1D	Objectives 5–8 from Project 1B	**1D Skills Review (Scorecard Grading)** Review A guided review of the skills from Project 1B.	In text
1E MyLab IT	Objectives 1–4 from Project 1A	**1E Mastery (Grader Project)** Mastery and Transfer of Learning A demonstration of your mastery of the skills in Project 1A with extensive decision making.	In **MyLab IT** and in text
1F MyLab IT	Objectives 5–8 from Project 1B	**1F Mastery (Grader Project)** Mastery and Transfer of Learning A demonstration of your mastery of the skills in Project 1B with extensive decision making.	In **MyLab IT** and in text
1G MyLab IT	Objectives 1–8 from Projects 1A and 1B	**1G Mastery (Grader Project)** Mastery and Transfer of Learning A demonstration of your mastery of the skills in Projects 1A and 1B with extensive decision making.	In **MyLab IT** and in text
1H	Combination of Objectives from Projects 1A and 1B	**1H GO! Fix It (Scorecard Grading)** Critical Thinking A demonstration of your mastery of the skills in Projects 1A and 1B by creating a correct result from a document that contains errors you must find.	IRC
1I	Combination of Objectives from Projects 1A and 1B	**1I GO! Make It (Scorecard Grading)** Critical Thinking A demonstration of your mastery of the skills in Projects 1A and 1B by creating a result from a supplied picture.	IRC
1J	Combination of Objectives from Projects 1A and 1B	**1J GO! Solve It (Rubric Grading)** Critical Thinking A demonstration of your mastery of the skills in Projects 1A and 1B, your decision-making skills, and your critical thinking skills. A task-specific rubric helps you self-assess your result.	IRC
1K	Combination of Objectives from Projects 1A and 1B	**1K GO! Solve It (Rubric Grading)** Critical Thinking A demonstration of your mastery of the skills in Projects 1A and 1B, your decision-making skills, and your critical thinking skills. A task-specific rubric helps you self-assess your result.	In text
1L	Combination of Objectives from Projects 1A and 1B	**1L GO! Think (Rubric Grading)** Critical Thinking A demonstration of your understanding of the chapter concepts applied in a manner that you would outside of college. An analytic rubric helps you and your instructor grade the quality of your work by comparing it to the work an expert in the discipline would create.	In text
1M	Combination of Objectives from Projects 1A and 1B	**1M GO! Think (Rubric Grading)** Critical Thinking A demonstration of your understanding of the chapter concepts applied in a manner that you would outside of college. An analytic rubric helps you and your instructor grade the quality of your work by comparing it to the work an expert in the discipline would create.	IRC
1N	Combination of Objectives from Projects 1A and 1B	**1N You and GO! (Rubric Grading)** Critical Thinking A demonstration of your understanding of the chapter concepts applied in a manner that you would in a personal situation. An analytic rubric helps you and your instructor grade the quality of your work.	IRC
1O	Combination of Objectives from Projects 1A and 1B	**1O Collaborative Team Project for PowerPoint Chapter 1** Critical Thinking A demonstration of your understanding of concepts and your ability to work collaboratively in a group role-playing assessment, requiring both collaboration and self-management.	IRC

Glossary

Glossary of Chapter Key Terms

Artistic effects Formats applied to images that make pictures resemble sketches or paintings.

Aspect ratio The ratio of the width of a display to the height of the display.

Black slide A slide that displays after the last slide in a presentation indicating that the presentation is over.

Contiguous slides Slides that are adjacent to each other in a presentation.

Editing The process of modifying a presentation by adding and deleting slides or by changing the contents of individual slides.

Footer Text that displays at the bottom of every slide or that prints at the bottom of a sheet of slide handouts or notes pages.

Formatting The process of changing the appearance of the text, layout, and design of a slide.

Header Text that prints at the top of each sheet of slide handouts or notes pages.

Layout The arrangement of elements, such as title and subtitle text, lists, pictures, tables, charts, shapes, and movies, on a slide.

List level An outline level in a presentation represented by a bullet symbol and identified in a slide by the indentation and the size of the text.

Noncontiguous slides Slides that are not adjacent to each other in a presentation.

Normal view The primary editing view in PowerPoint where you write and design your presentations.

Notes page A printout that contains the slide image on the top half of the page and notes that you have created on the Notes pane in the lower half of the page.

Notes pane An area of the Normal view window that displays below the Slide pane with space to type notes regarding the active slide.

Outline view A PowerPoint view that displays the presentation outline to the left of the Slide pane.

Placeholder A box on a slide with dotted or dashed borders that holds title and body text or other content such as charts, tables, and pictures.

Presenter view A view that shows the full-screen slide show on one monitor or projection screen while enabling the presenter to view a preview of the next slide, notes, and a timer on another monitor.

Reading view A view in PowerPoint that displays a presentation in a manner similar to a slide show but in which the taskbar, title bar, and status bar remain available in the presentation window.

Rotation handle A circular arrow that provides a way to rotate a selected image.

Section header A type of slide layout that changes the look and flow of a presentation by providing text placeholders that do not contain bullet points.

Sizing handles Small circles surrounding a picture that indicate that the picture is selected.

Slide A presentation page that can contain text, pictures, tables, charts, and other multimedia or graphic objects.

Slide handout Printed images of slides on a sheet of paper.

Slide pane A PowerPoint screen element that displays a large image of the active slide.

Slide Sorter view A presentation view that displays thumbnails of all of the slides in a presentation.

Slide transitions Motion effects that occur in Slide Show view when you move from one slide to the next during a presentation.

Split button A type of button in which clicking the main part of the button performs a command and clicking the arrow opens a menu, list, or gallery.

Style A collection of formatting options that you can apply to a picture, text, or an object.

Text alignment The horizontal placement of text within a placeholder.

Theme A set of unified design elements that provides a look for your presentation by applying colors, fonts, and effects.

Thumbnails Miniature images of presentation slides.

Title slide A slide layout—most commonly the first slide in a presentation—that provides an introduction to the presentation topic.

Variant A variation on the presentation theme style and color.

Chapter Review

Skills Review | **Project 1C Glaciers**

In the following Skills Review, you will create a new presentation by inserting content and pictures, adding notes and footers, and applying a presentation theme. Your completed presentation will look similar to Figure 1.58.

Project Files

For Project 1C, you will need:

New blank PowerPoint presentation

p01C_Glacier_Bay

p01C_Ice

p01C_Ship

You will save your presentation as:

Lastname_Firstname_1C_Glaciers

Project Results

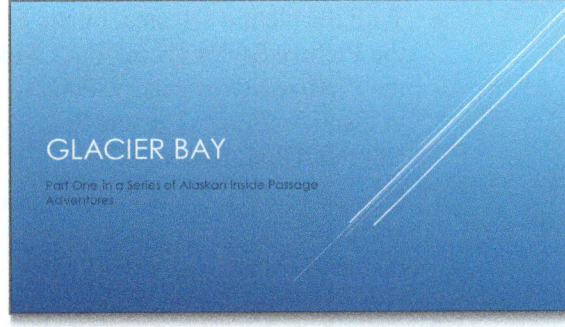
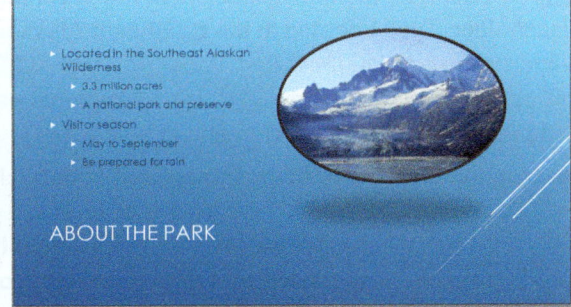

Figure 1.58 Project 1C Glaciers

(continues on next page)

Chapter Review

1 ▶ Start PowerPoint. On the right, if necessary, click Find More, click **Slice**, and then click **Create**. On the **Quick Access Toolbar**, click **Save** 🔲. Under **Save As**, click **Browse**. Navigate to your **PowerPoint Chapter 1** folder. In the **File name** box, using your own name, replace the existing text with **Lastname_Firstname_1C_Glaciers** and then click **Save**. In the **Slide pane**, click in the text *Click to add title*. Type **Glacier Bay** and then click in the subtitle placeholder. Type **Part One in a Series of Alaskan Passage Adventures**

  a. On the **Home tab**, in the **Slides group**, click the **New Slide arrow**, and then in the gallery, click **Two Content**. Click the text *Click to add title*, and then type **About the Park**

2 ▶ On the left side of the slide, click in the content placeholder. Type **Located in the Southeast Alaskan Wilderness** and then press Enter. Press Tab. Type **3.3 million acres** and then press Enter. Type **A national park and preserve** and then press Enter.

  a. On the **Home tab**, in the **Paragraph group**, click **Decrease List Level**. Type **Visitor season** and then press Enter. On the **Home tab**, in the **Paragraph group**, click **Increase List Level**. Type **May to September**

  b. On the **Home tab**, in the **Slides group**, click the **New Slide arrow**, and then in the gallery, click **Panoramic Picture with Caption**. In the lower portion of the slide, click the text *Click to add title*, and then type **Prepare to be Amazed!**

  c. Click in the text placeholder. Type **Before you reach Glacier Bay, walk around your cruise ship to find the best viewing locations. Make sure your camera battery is charged!**

  d. On the **Home tab**, in the **Slides group**, click the **New Slide arrow**, and then in the gallery, click **Content with Caption**. In the title placeholder, type **Learn More!**

  e. Click in the text placeholder on the right, and then type **A national park ranger will board your ship during your visit to Glacier Bay. Check your ship's itinerary for presentation information and locations.**

3 ▶ With **Slide 4** displayed, in the **Status bar**, click **Notes**. Click in the **Notes pane**, and then type **Your cruise ship will spend between 6 and 8 hours in Glacier Bay.**

  a. On the left side of the PowerPoint window, in the slide thumbnails, click **Slide 1**. Click in the subtitle placeholder after the *n* in *Alaskan*. Press Spacebar, and then type **Inside**

  b. In the slide thumbnails, click **Slide 2**, and then click at the end of the last bullet point after the word *September*. Press Enter, and then type **Be prepared for rain**

4 ▶ With **Slide 2** displayed, in the placeholder on the right side of the slide, click **Pictures**. Navigate to your data files for this project, and then click **p01C_Glacier_Bay**. Click **Insert**. If necessary, close the Design Ideas pane.

  a. With the picture selected, on the **Format tab**, in the **Picture Styles group**, click **More** ▼ to display the **Picture Styles** gallery. Point to several styles to display a ScreenTip, and then locate and click **Beveled Oval, Black**.

  b. Display **Slide 3**. In the Picture placeholder, click **Pictures**. Navigate to your student data files, and then click **p01C_Ice**. Click **Insert**.

  c. Display **Slide 4**. In the content placeholder on the left side of the slide, click **Pictures**. Navigate to the data files for this project, and then insert **p01C_Ship**. On the **Format tab**, in the **Picture Styles group**, click **More** ▼ to display the **Picture Styles** gallery. Point to each style to display a ScreenTip, and then locate and click **Soft Edge Rectangle**.

  d. With the picture still selected, on the **Format tab**, in the **Adjust group**, click **Artistic Effects** to display the gallery. Point to each effect to display a ScreenTip, and then locate and click **Crisscross Etching**.

5 ▶ On the **Slide Show tab,** in the **Start Slide Show group**, click **From Beginning**. (Mac users click Play from Start.)

  a. Click the left mouse button or press Spacebar to advance to the second slide. Continue to click or press Spacebar until the last slide displays, and then click or press Spacebar one more time to display a black slide.

  b. With the black slide displayed, click the left mouse button or press Spacebar to exit the slide show and return to the presentation.

(continues on next page)

Chapter Review

6 Click the **Insert tab**, and then in the **Text group**, click **Header & Footer** to display the **Header and Footer** dialog box.

a. In the **Header and Footer** dialog box, click the **Notes and Handouts tab**. Under **Include on page**, select the **Date and time** check box. If necessary, click the Update automatically option button so that the current date prints on the notes and handouts.

b. Select the **Page number** check box. If necessary, clear the Header check box to omit this element. Select the **Footer** check box. In the **Footer** box, type **1C_Glaciers** and then click **Apply to All**.

c. In the upper left corner of your screen, click the **File** tab to display **Backstage** view. On the right, at the bottom of the **Properties list**, click **Show All**

Properties. (Mac users, click the File menu, click Properties, click the Summary tab, and instead of Tags, use the Keywords box.)

d. On the list of Properties, click to the right of **Tags** to display an empty box, and then type **Glacier Bay** Click to the right of **Subject** to display an empty box, and then type your course name and section number. Under **Related People**, be sure that your name displays as the author; edit if necessary.

e. **Save** your presentation. As directed by your instructor, create and submit a paper printout or an electronic image of your presentation that looks like a printed document; or, submit your completed PowerPoint file. **Close** PowerPoint.

You have completed Project 1C | END

Chapter Review

Skills Review	Project 1D Photography

Apply 1B skills from these Objectives:

5. Edit an Existing Presentation
6. Format a Presentation
7. Use Slide Sorter View
8. Apply Slide Transitions

In the following Skills Review, you will edit an existing presentation by inserting slides from another presentation, applying font and slide formatting, and applying slide transitions. Your completed presentation will look similar to Figure 1.59.

Project Files

For Project 1D, you will need:

p01D_Photography

p01D_Photography_Slides

You will save your presentation as:

Lastname_Firstname_1D_Photography

Project Results

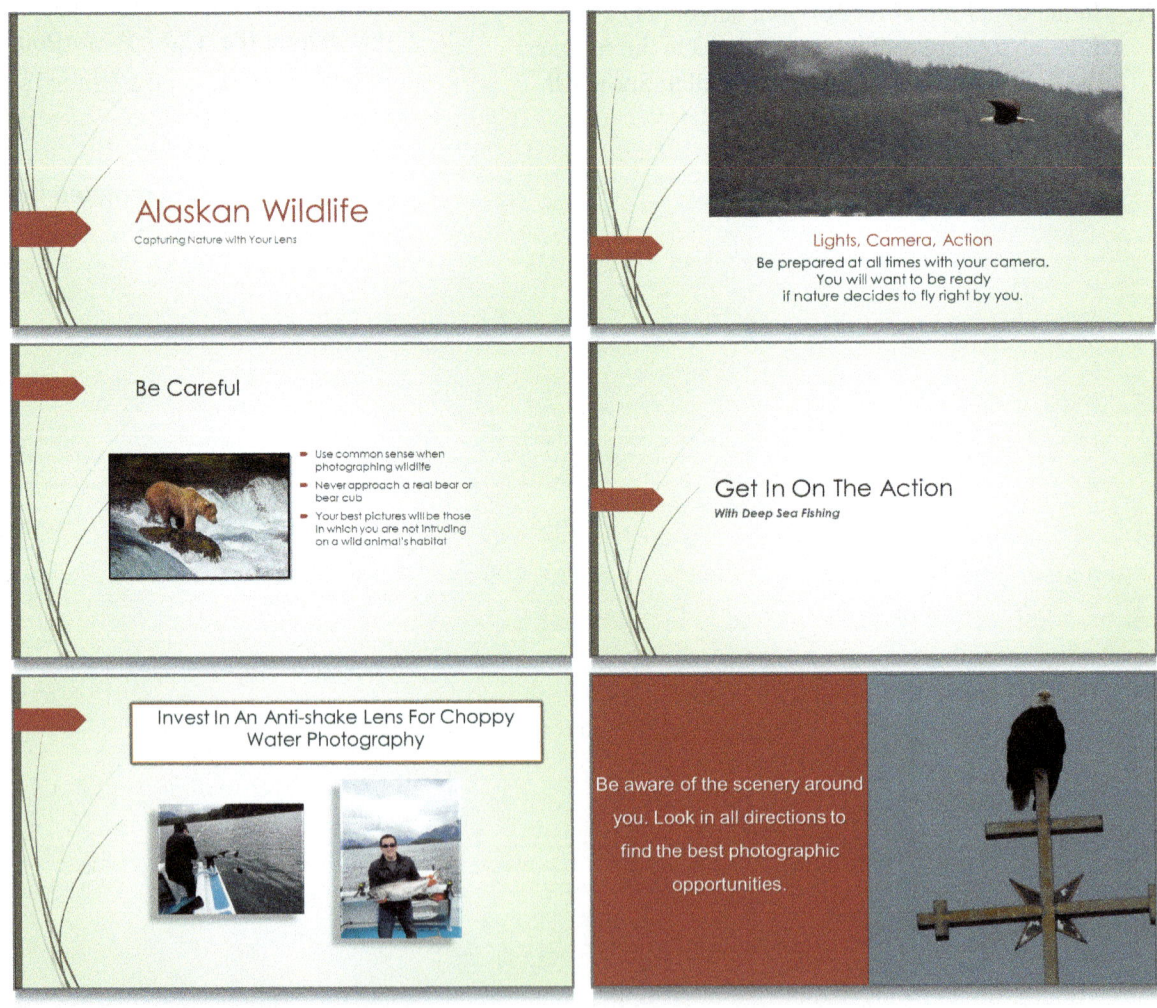

Figure 1.59 Project 1D Photography

(continues on next page)

Chapter Review

Skills Review: Project 1D Photography (continued)

1 From your student data files, double-click **p01D_Photography** to open it. On the **File tab**, click **Save As**, navigate to your **PowerPoint Chapter 1** folder, and then using your own name, save the file as **Lastname_Firstname_1D_Photography**

a. On the **Design tab**, in the **Customize group**, click **Slide Size**, and then click **Widescreen (16:9)**.

b. With **Slide 1** displayed, on the **Home tab**, in the **Slides group**, click the **New Slide arrow**, and then click **Reuse Slides**. In the **Reuse Slides** pane, click **Browse**. In the **Browse** dialog box, navigate to the data files for this project, and then double-click **p01D_Photography_Slides** to display the slides from this presentation in the **Reuse Slides** pane.

c. At the bottom of the **Reuse Slides** pane, be sure that the **Keep source formatting** check box is *cleared*. In the **Reuse Slides** pane, click the first slide—*Alaskan Wildlife*—to insert the slide after Slide 1.

d. At the left of your screen, in the slide thumbnails, click **Slide 6** to display it in the **Slide pane**. In the **Reuse Slides** pane, click the second slide—*Be Careful*—to insert it after **Slide 6**. **Close** the **Reuse Slides** pane. (Mac users click the New Slide arrow, click Reuse Slides, and navigate to the data files for this project. Double-click p01D_Photography_ Slides to insert all four slides into your presentation after Slide 1. Delete Slide 4—*Lights, Camera, Action*—and Slide 5— *Be aware of the scenery.* Drag the new Slide 3—*Be Careful*—after Slide 6.)

2 Display **Slide 1**. On the **View tab**, in the **Presentation Views group**, click **Outline View**.

a. In the **Outline**, in **Slide 7**, drag to select the second and third bullet points—beginning with *Never approach* and ending with *animal's home*.

b. On the **Home tab**, in the **Paragraph group**, click **Decrease List Level** one time.

c. In the **Outline**, in the same slide, click at the end of the first bullet point after the word *sense*. Press Spacebar, and then type **when photographing wildlife**

d. In the **Status bar**, click **Normal** to display the slide thumbnails.

3 Display **Slide 8**, and then press Delete to delete the slide from the presentation.

a. Display **Slide 1**. On the **Home tab**, in the **Editing group**, click **Replace**. In the **Replace** dialog box, in the **Find what** box, type **home** and then in the **Replace with** box, type **habitat**

b. In the **Replace** dialog box, click **Replace All** to display a message box indicating that one replacement was made. In the message box, click **OK**. **Close** the **Replace** dialog box. (Mac users, click the Edit menu, point to Find, and then click Replace.)

c. On the **Design tab**, in the **Variants group**, right-click the first variant. On the shortcut menu, click **Apply to All Slides** so that the variant color is applied to all of the slides in the presentation.

4 Display **Slide 5**. Select all of the text in the placeholder. On the **Home tab**, in the **Font group**, click the **Font arrow**, scroll the font list, and then click **Arial**. Click the **Font Size arrow**, and then click **32**. In the **Paragraph group**, click **Line Spacing**, and then click **1.5**.

a. Display **Slide 2**. On the **Home tab**, in the **Slides group**, click **Layout** to display the **Slide Layout** gallery. Click **Title Slide** to change the slide layout.

b. On **Slide 2**, select the title—*Alaskan Wildlife*. On the **Home tab**, in the **Font group**, click the **Font Color arrow**. In the fifth column, click the first color— **Dark Red, Accent 1**.

c. Display **Slide 3**, and then select the title—*Lights, Camera, Action*. On the mini toolbar, click **Font Color** to apply the font color **Dark Red, Accent 1**.

d. Display **Slide 4**, and then, click anywhere in the text. On the **Home tab**, in the **Paragraph group**, click **Center** to center the text within the placeholder.

e. Display **Slide 6**, and then select the subtitle. From the mini toolbar, apply **Bold** and **Italic**.

f. In the slide thumbnails, point to **Slide 7**, hold down the left mouse button, and then drag up to position the slide between **Slides 3** and **4**.

5 In the lower right corner of the PowerPoint window, click **Slide Sorter** to display all of the slide thumbnails. Click **Slide 1**, so that it is selected. On your keyboard, press Delete to delete the slide.

a. Click **Slide 4**, and then hold down Ctrl and click **Slide 5**. With both slides selected, point to either of the selected slides, hold down the left mouse button, and then drag to position the two slides to the right of **Slide 6**. Release the mouse button to move the two slides. In the status bar, click **Normal** to return to Normal view.

b. Display **Slide 1**. On the **Transitions tab**, in the **Transition to This Slide group**, click **More** ▾ to display the **Transitions** gallery.

(continues on next page)

Chapter Review

c. Under **Exciting**, click **Gallery** to apply and view the transition. In the **Transition to This Slide group**, click **Effect Options**, and then click **From Left**. In the **Timing group**, click **Apply To All** to apply the *Gallery, From Left* transition to all of the slides in the presentation.

d. In the **Timing group**, click the **Duration up spin arrow** so that *01.75* displays. Under **Advance Slide**, verify that the **On Mouse Click** check box is selected; select it if necessary. In the **Timing group**, click **Apply To All**.

e. Click the **Slide Show tab**. In the **Start Slide Show group**, click **From Beginning**, and then view your presentation, clicking the mouse button to advance through the slides. When the black slide displays, click the mouse button one more time to display the presentation in Normal view. (Mac users click Play from Start.)

6 On the **Insert tab**, in the **Text group**, click **Header & Footer** to display the **Header and Footer** dialog box.

a. In the **Header and Footer** dialog box, click the **Notes and Handouts tab**. Under **Include on page**, select the **Date and time** check box. If necessary, click the Update automatically option button so that the current date prints on the notes and handouts.

b. Select the **Page number** check box. If necessary, clear the Header check box to omit this element. Select the **Footer** check box. In the **Footer** box, type **1D_Photography** and then click **Apply to All**.

c. In the upper left corner of your screen, click the **File** tab to display **Backstage** view. On the right, at the bottom of the **Properties list**, click **Show All Properties**.

d. On the list of Properties, click to the right of **Tags**, and then type **photography** Click to the right of **Subject**, and then type your course name and section number. Under **Related People**, be sure that your name displays as the author. If necessary, right-click the author name, click Edit Property, type your name, and click OK. (Mac users, click the File menu, click Properties, click the Summary tab, and instead of tags, use the Keywords box.)

e. **Save** your presentation. As directed by your instructor, create and submit a paper printout or an electronic image of your presentation that looks like a printed document; or, submit your completed PowerPoint file. **Close** the presentation.

You have completed Project 1D | END

1

POWERPOINT

Mastering PowerPoint **Project 1E Juneau**

Apply 1A skills from these Objectives:

1. Create a New Presentation
2. Edit a Presentation in Normal View
3. Add Pictures to a Presentation
4. Print and View a Presentation

In the following Mastering PowerPoint project, you will create a new presentation that Kodiak West Travel will use in their promotional materials to describe activities in the city of Juneau. Your completed presentation will look similar to Figure 1.60.

Project Files for MyLab IT Grader

1. In your **MyLab IT** course, locate and click **PowerPoint 1E Juneau**, Download Materials, and then Download All Files.
2. Extract the zipped folder to your PowerPoint Chapter 1 folder. Close the Grader download screens.
3. Take a moment to open the downloaded **PowerPoint_1E_Juneau_Instructions**; note any recent updates to the book.

Project Results

Figure 1.60 Project 1E Juneau

For Non-MyLab Submissions
For Project 1E, you will need:
p01E_Juneau
p01E_Glacier
p01E_Whale
p01E_Falls

In your PowerPoint Chapter 1 folder, save your presentation as:
Lastname_Firstname_1E_Juneau

After you have named and saved your presentation on the next page, begin with Step 2.
After Step 14, save and submit your file as directed by your instructor.

(continues on next page)

Content-Based Assessments (Mastery and Transfer of Learning)

1 ▶ Navigate to your **PowerPoint Chapter 1 folder** and then double-click the PowerPoint file you downloaded from **MyLab IT** that displays your name—**Student_PowerPoint_1E_Juneau**. If necessary, at the top, click **Enable Editing**.

2 ▶ As the title of this presentation, type **Juneau Alaska** and as the subtitle, type **Kodiak West Travel**

3 ▶ Insert a **New Slide** using the **Content with Caption** layout. In the title placeholder, type **The View from Above**

4 ▶ In the content placeholder on the right side of the slide, from the files downloaded with this project, insert the picture **p01E_Aerial_View**. Format the picture with the **Rotated, White** picture style.

5 ▶ In the text placeholder on the left, type **View a glacial ice field from above by plane or helicopter. If you are more adventurous, try glacier trekking in Juneau where you can land on a glacier and climb an ice wall.**

6 ▶ Insert a **New Slide** using the **Two Content** layout. In the title placeholder, type **On Land and Sea**

7 ▶ In the content placeholder on the right, type the following text, increasing and decreasing the list level as shown below. In this presentation theme, the first level bullet points do not include a bullet symbol.

> **On the water**
> > **Whale watching**
> > **Kayaking**
> **Mount Roberts tramway**
> > **Spectacular views of Juneau**
> > **Recreational hiking trails**

8 ▶ In the content placeholder on the right, from the files downloaded with this project, insert the picture **p01E_Whale**. Apply the **Reflected Rounded Rectangle** picture style.

9 ▶ Insert a new slide with the **Picture with Caption** layout. In the title placeholder, type **Mendenhall Glacier** and then in the picture placeholder, from the files downloaded with this project, insert the picture **p01E_Falls**.

10 ▶ In the text placeholder, type **Walk to Mendenhall Glacier from the Visitor Center to get a close-up view of Nugget Falls.**

11 ▶ In the **Notes pane**, type **Mendenhall Glacier is the most famous glacier in Juneau and in some years is visited by over 400,000 people.**

12 ▶ Insert a **Header & Footer** on the **Notes and Handouts**. Include the **Date and time** updated automatically, the **Page number**, and a **Footer** with the text **1E_Juneau** and apply to all the slides.

13 ▶ Display the **Document Properties**. As the **Tags** type **Juneau** As the **Subject** type your course and section number. Be sure your name is indicated as the Author. (Mac users use the Keywords box.)

14 ▶ **Save** your presentation, and then view the slide show from the beginning. **Close** the presentation and close PowerPoint.

15 ▶ In **MyLab IT**, in your **Course Materials**, locate and click the Grader Project **PowerPoint 1E Juneau**. In **step 3**, under **Upload Completed Assignment**, click **Choose File**. In the **Open** dialog box, navigate to your **PowerPoint Chapter 1 folder**, and then click your **Student_ PowerPoint_1E_Juneau** file one time to select it. In the lower right corner of the **Open** dialog box, click **Open**.

The name of your selected file displays above the Upload button.

16 ▶ To submit your file to **MyLab IT** for grading, click **Upload**, wait a moment for a green **Success!** message, and then in **step 4**, click the blue **Submit for Grading** button. Click **Close Assignment** to return to your list of **Course Materials**.

You have completed Project 1E **END**

Content-Based Assessments (Mastery and Transfer of Learning)

MyLab IT Grader	Mastering PowerPoint	Project 1F Refuge

In the following Mastering PowerPoint project, you will edit a presentation regarding a wildlife refuge where Kodiak West Travel conducts tours. Your completed presentation will look similar to Figure 1.61.

Apply 1B skills from these Objectives:

5. Edit an Existing Presentation
6. Format a Presentation
7. Use Slide Sorter View
8. Apply Slide Transitions

Project Files for MyLab IT Grader

1. In your MyLab IT course, locate and click **PowerPoint 1F Refuge**, Download Materials, and then Download All Files.
2. Extract the zipped folder to your PowerPoint Chapter 1 folder. Close the Grader download screens.
3. Take a moment to open the downloaded **PowerPoint_1F_Refuge_Instructions**; note any recent updates to the book.

Project Results

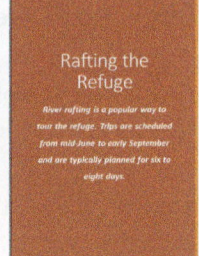

Figure 1.61 Project 1F Refuge

For Non-MyLab Submissions

For Project 1F, you will need:
p01F_Refuge
p01F_Excursions

In your PowerPoint Chapter 1 folder, save your workbook as:
Lastname_Firstname_1F_Refuge

After you have named and saved your presentation on the next page, begin with Step 2.

After Step 14, save and submit your file as directed by your instructor.

(continues on next page)

Content-Based Assessments (Mastery and Transfer of Learning)

1 ▶ Navigate to your **PowerPoint Chapter 1 folder** and then double-click the PowerPoint file you downloaded from **MyLab IT** that displays your name—**Student_PowerPoint_1F_Refuge**. If necessary, at the top, click **Enable Editing**.

2 ▶ Change the **Slide Size** to **Widescreen (16:9)**.

3 ▶ Display the presentation **Outline**. In the **Outline**, on **Slide 2**, increase the list level of the third and the fifth bullet points. Click at the end of the last bullet point after the word *roads*, and then type **or facilities**

4 ▶ Return the presentation to **Normal view**, and then display **Slide 4**. Display the **Reuse Slides** pane. Browse to open from the files downloaded with this project, **p01F_Excursions**. Make sure the **Keep source formatting** check box is *cleared*. With **Slide 4** in your presentation displayed, insert the last two slides from the **Reuse Slides** pane. (Mac users insert all slides and delete Slide 5—*Wildlife and Excursions*.)

5 ▶ Display **Slide 1**, and then change the layout to **Title Slide**.

6 ▶ Select the subtitle—*Experience Alaska with Kodiak West Travel*. Change the **Font** to **Arial**, and the **Font Size** to **28**. Change the **Font Color** to **Black, Text 1**. **Center** the title and the subtitle.

7 ▶ Display **Slide 5**, and then select the paragraph in the content placeholder. Apply **Bold** and **Italic**, and then change the **Font Size** to **16**.

8 ▶ **Center** the paragraph text, and then change the **Line Spacing** to **1.5**. **Center** the slide title.

9 ▶ In **Slide Sorter** view, delete **Slide 3**. Move **Slide 5** to position it after **Slide 2**.

10 ▶ Move **Slide 4** to the end of the presentation.

11 ▶ In **Normal** view, display **Slide 1**. Apply the **Split** transition and change the **Effect Options** to **Horizontal Out**. Change the **Duration** to **1.75** and apply the transition to all of the slides in the presentation. View the slide show from the beginning.

12 ▶ Insert a **Header & Footer** on the **Notes and Handouts**. Include the **Date and time** updated automatically, the **Page number**, and a **Footer** with the text **1F_Refuge**

13 ▶ Display the **Document Properties**. As the **Tags** type **refuge, tours** As the **Subject** type your course and section number. Be sure your name is indicated as the **Author**. (Mac users use the Keywords box.) **Save** your presentation.

14 ▶ In the upper right corner of your screen, click **Close** ⊠ to close PowerPoint.

15 ▶ In **MyLab IT**, in your **Course Materials**, locate and click the Grader Project **PowerPoint 1F Refuge**. In **step 3**, under **Upload Completed Assignment**, click **Choose File**. In the **Open** dialog box, navigate to your **PowerPoint Chapter 1 folder**, and then click your **Student_ PowerPoint_1F_Refuge** file one time to select it. In the lower right corner of the **Open** dialog box, click **Open**.

> The name of your selected file displays above the Upload button.

16 ▶ To submit your file to **MyLab IT** for grading, click **Upload**, wait a moment for a green **Success!** message, and then in **step 4**, click the blue **Submit for Grading** button. Click **Close Assignment** to return to your list of **Course Materials**.

You have completed Project 1F   **END**

Content-Based Assessments (Mastery and Transfer of Learning)

MyLab IT Grader	Mastering PowerPoint	Project 1G Northern Lights

Apply 1A and 1B skills from these Objectives:

1. Create a New Presentation
2. Edit a Presentation in Normal View
3. Add Pictures to a Presentation
4. Print and View a Presentation
5. Edit an Existing Presentation
6. Format a Presentation
7. Use Slide Sorter View
8. Apply Slide Transitions

In the following Mastering PowerPoint project, you will edit an existing presentation that describes the Northern Lights and ideal viewing areas. Your completed presentation will look similar to Figure 1.62.

Project Files for MyLab IT Grader

1. In your **MyLab IT** course, locate and click **PowerPoint 1G Northern Lights**, Download Materials, and then Download All Files.
2. Extract the zipped folder to your PowerPoint Chapter 1 folder. Close the Grader download screens.
3. Take a moment to open the downloaded **PowerPoint_1G_Northern_Lights_Instructions**; note any recent updates to the book.

Project Results

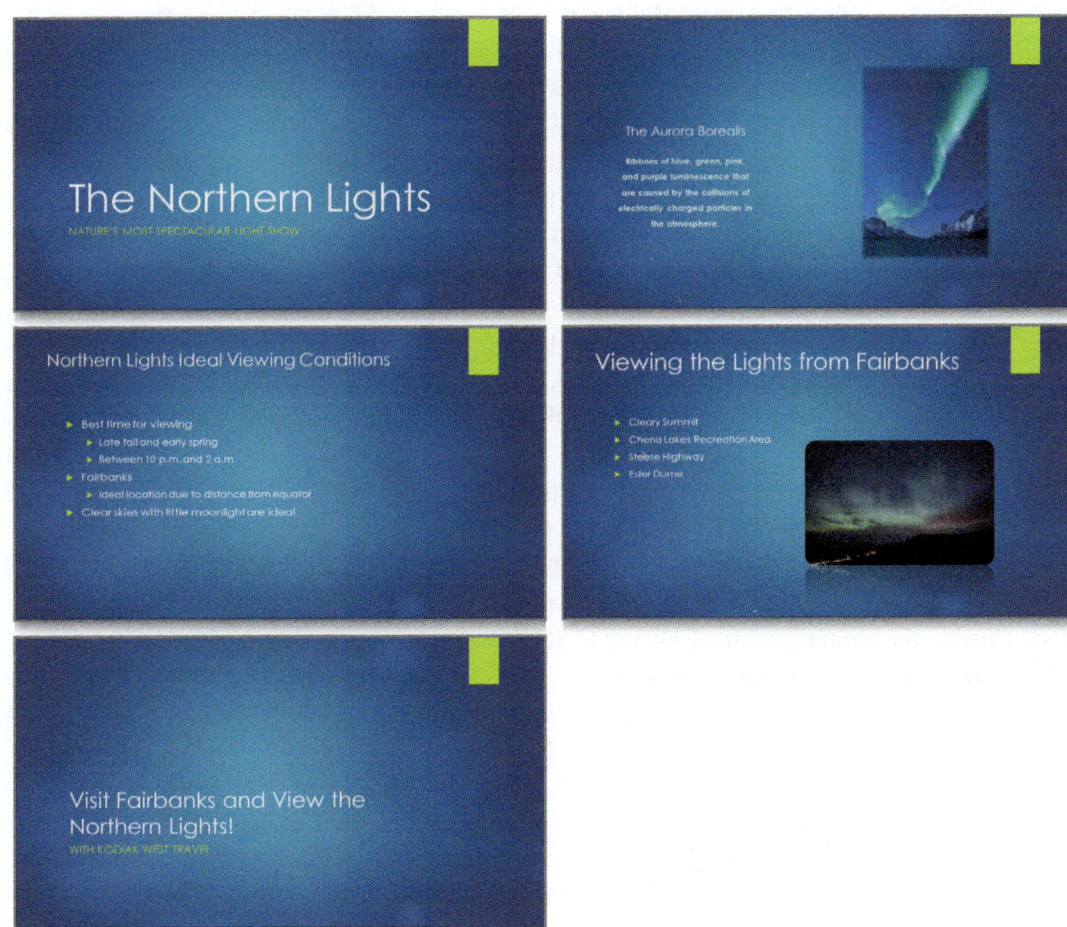

Figure 1.62 Project 1G Northern Lights

For Non-MyLab Submissions

For Project 1G, you will need:
p01G_Northern_Lights
p01G_Lights
p01G_Slides

In your PowerPoint Chapter 1 folder, save your presentation as:
Lastname_Firstname_1G_Northern_Lights

After you have named and saved your presentation on the next page, begin with Step 2.
After Step 17, save and submit your file as directed by your instructor.

Content-Based Assessments (Mastery and Transfer of Learning)

1 Navigate to your **PowerPoint Chapter 1 folder,** and then double-click the PowerPoint file you downloaded from **MyLab IT** that displays your name—**Student_PowerPoint_1G_Northern_Lights**. If necessary, at the top, click **Enable Editing**.

2 Replace all occurrences of the text **North** with **Northern** and then change the layout of **Slide 1** to **Title Slide**.

3 Apply the **Ion** theme, with the second, blue variant option.

4 Change the **Slide Size** to **Widescreen (16:9)**.

5 Display **Slide 2**, open the **Reuse Slides** pane, and then from the files downloaded with this project, browse for and open the presentation **p01G_Slides**. If necessary, clear the Keep source formatting check box, and then insert the last two slides from the **p01G_Slides** file. (Mac users insert all slides and delete Slide 3—*Alaska Slides.)*

6 Display **Slide 2**. In either the slide pane or in the slide outline, click at the end of the first bullet point after the word *time*. Add the words **for viewing** and then in the same slide, increase the list level of the second and third bullet points.

7 With **Slide 2** still displayed, select the title and change the **Font Size** to **32**. In the **Notes pane**, type the following notes: **The lights reach their peak in September and March.**

8 Display **Slide 3**. Select the paragraph of text, and then change the **Font Color** to **Green, Accent 6, Lighter 60%**—in the last column, the third color**.** Change the **Font Size** to **16**, and then apply **Bold**.

9 Change the paragraph **Line Spacing** to **1.5**, and then **Center** the paragraph and the slide title.

10 With **Slide 3** still displayed, format the picture with the **Soft Edge Rectangle** picture style and the **Marker** artistic effect.

11 Display **Slide 4**. In the content placeholder on the right, from your student data files, insert the picture **p01G_Lights**. Apply the **Reflected Rounded Rectangle** picture style.

12 Move **Slide 3** between **Slides 1** and **2**.

13 Display **Slide 4**. Insert a **New Slide** with the **Section Header** layout. In the title placeholder type **Visit Fairbanks and View the Northern Lights!** In the text placeholder, type **With Kodiak West Travel**

14 Apply the **Uncover** transition and change the **Effect Options** to **From Top**. Change the **Timing** by increasing the **Duration** to **01.25**. Apply the transition effect to all of the slides. View the slide show from the beginning.

15 **Insert** a **Header & Footer** on the **Notes and Handouts**. Include the **Date and time** updated automatically, the **Page number**, and a **Footer**, using your own name, with the text **1G_Northern_Lights**

16 Display the **Document Properties**. As the **Tags,** type **northern lights, Fairbanks** As the **Subject,** type your course and section number. Be sure your name is indicated as the Author. (Mac users use the Keywords box.) **Save** your presentation.

17 In the upper right corner of your screen, click **Close** to close PowerPoint.

18 In **MyLab IT**, in your **Course Materials**, locate and click the Grader Project **PowerPoint 1G Refuge**. In **step 3**, under **Upload Completed Assignment**, click **Choose File**. In the **Open** dialog box, navigate to your **PowerPoint Chapter 1 folder**, and then click your **Student_PowerPoint_1G_Refuge** file one time to select it. In the lower right corner of the **Open** dialog box, click **Open**.

The name of your selected file displays above the Upload button.

19 To submit your file to **MyLab IT** for grading, click **Upload**, wait a moment for a green **Success!** message, and then in **step 4**, click the blue **Submit for Grading** button. Click **Close Assignment** to return to your list of **Course Materials**.

You have completed Project 1G   **END**

Content-Based Assessments (Critical Thinking)

Apply a combination of the **1A** and **1B** skills.	**GO! Fix It**	**Project 1H Rain Forest**	IRC
	GO! Make It	**Project 1I Eagles**	IRC
	GO! Solve It	**Project 1J Packrafting**	IRC
	GO! Solve It	**Project 1K Packing**	

Project Files

For Project 1K, you will need:

p01K_Packing

You will save your presentation as:

Lastname_Firstname_1K_Packing

Open the file p01K_Packing and save it as **Lastname_Firstname_1K_Packing** Complete the presentation by applying a theme and changing the variant. Format the presentation attractively by applying appropriate font formatting and by changing text alignment and line spacing. Change the layout of the last slide to an appropriate layout. On Slide 2, insert a picture that you have taken yourself, or use one of the pictures in your student data files that you inserted in other projects in this chapter. Apply a style to the picture. Apply slide transitions to all of the slides in the presentation, and then insert a header and footer that includes the date and time updated automatically, **1K_Packing** in the footer, and the page number. Add your name, your course name and section number, and the tags **packing, weather** to the properties. Save and print or submit as directed by your instructor.

		Performance Level		
		Exemplary	**Proficient**	**Developing**
Performance Criteria	**Apply a theme and a variant**	An appropriate theme and variant were applied to the presentation.	A theme was applied but the variant was not changed.	Neither a theme nor the variant theme were applied.
	Apply font and slide formatting	Font and slide formatting is attractive and appropriate.	Adequately formatted but difficult to read or unattractive.	Inadequate or no formatting.
	Use appropriate pictures and apply styles attractively	An appropriate picture was inserted and a style is applied attractively.	A picture was inserted but a style was not applied.	Picture was not inserted.
	Apply appropriate slide layout to Slide 4	An appropriate layout was applied to the last slide.	The slide layout was changed but is not appropriate for the type of slide.	The slide layout was not changed.

You have completed Project 1K   END

Outcomes-Based Assessments (Critical Thinking)

Rubric

The following outcomes-based assessments are open-ended assessments. That is, there is no specific correct result; your result will depend on your approach to the information provided. Make Professional Quality your goal. Use the following scoring rubric to guide you in how to approach the problem, and then to evaluate how well your approach solves the problem.

The *criteria*—Software Mastery, Content, Format and Layout, and Process—represent the knowledge and skills you have gained that you can apply to solving the problem. The *levels of performance*—Professional Quality, Approaching Professional Quality, or Needs Quality Improvements—help you and your instructor evaluate your result.

	Your completed project is of Professional Quality if you:	Your completed project is Approaching Professional Quality if you:	Your completed project Needs Quality Improvements if you:
1-Software Mastery	Choose and apply the most appropriate skills, tools, and features and identify efficient methods to solve the problem.	Choose and apply some appropriate skills, tools, and features, but not in the most efficient manner.	Choose inappropriate skills, tools, or features, or are inefficient in solving the problem.
2-Content	Construct a solution that is clear and well organized, contains content that is accurate, appropriate to the audience and purpose, and is complete. Provide a solution that contains no errors of spelling, grammar, or style.	Construct a solution in which some components are unclear, poorly organized, inconsistent, or incomplete. Misjudge the needs of the audience. Have some errors in spelling, grammar, or style, but the errors do not detract from comprehension.	Construct a solution that is unclear, incomplete, or poorly organized, contains some inaccurate or inappropriate content, and contains many errors of spelling, grammar, or style. Do not solve the problem.
3-Format and Layout	Format and arrange all elements to communicate information and ideas, clarify function, illustrate relationships, and indicate relative importance.	Apply appropriate format and layout features to some elements, but not others. Overuse features, causing minor distraction.	Apply format and layout that does not communicate information or ideas clearly. Do not use format and layout features to clarify function, illustrate relationships, or indicate relative importance. Use available features excessively, causing distraction.
4-Process	Use an organized approach that integrates planning, development, self-assessment, revision, and reflection.	Demonstrate an organized approach in some areas, but not others; or, use an insufficient process of organization throughout.	Do not use an organized approach to solve the problem.

Content-Based Assessments (Critical Thinking)

Apply a combination of the 1A and 1B skills.

GO! Think	Project 1L Bears

Project Files

For Project 1L, you will need:

New blank PowerPoint presentation
p01L_Bear

You will save your presentation as:

Lastname_Firstname_1L_Bears

Cindy Barrow, Tour Operations Manager for Kodiak West Travel, is developing a presentation describing brown bear viewing travel experiences that the company is developing. In the presentation, Cindy will be describing the brown bear habitat and viewing opportunities.

Kodiak bears are the largest known size of brown bears on record; they can weigh as much as 2,000 pounds and can get as large as polar bears. Kodiak bears are active during the day and are generally solitary creatures. The Kodiak Bear Travel Experience is a small, personalized travel adventure available to only eight participants at a time. It is an opportunity to peer into the life of these majestic mammals.

The adventure takes place on Kodiak Island near a lake with a high concentration of salmon, making it the perfect natural feeding ground for the Kodiak bears. Travelers can view the bears from boats, kayaks, and recently constructed viewing platforms, and guides are available.

This is a true wildlife experience as the area is home to deer, fox, and river otter. Accommodations are available at the Kodiak West Breakfast Inn from mid-June to the end of August. Peak season is early August, and reservations can be made up to one year in advance. The cost is $1,800 per person for one week, and includes all meals, use of watercraft, and guided tours.

Using the preceding information, create a presentation that Cindy can show at a travel fair. The presentation should include four to six slides describing the travel experience. Apply an appropriate theme and use slide layouts that will effectively present the content. Insert at least one picture and apply appropriate picture formatting. You may use your own image file, search for one online, or from your student data files, use the file p01L_Bear. Apply font formatting and slide transitions and modify text alignment and line spacing as necessary.

Save the file as **Lastname_Firstname_1L_Bears** and then insert a header and footer that include the date and time updated automatically, **1L_Bears** in the footer, and the page number. Add your name, your course name and section number, and the tags **bears, tours** to the properties. Save and print or submit as directed by your instructor.

You have completed Project 1L | END

Content-Based Assessments (Critical Thinking)

GO! Think	**Project 1M Sitka**	**IRC**
You and GO!	**Project 1N Travel**	**IRC**
GO! Cumulative Team Project	**Project 1O Bell Orchid Hotels**	**IRC**

Formatting PowerPoint Presentations

2
POWERPOINT
2019

PROJECT 2A

Outcomes
Format a presentation to add visual interest and clarity.

Objectives
1. Format Numbered and Bulleted Lists
2. Insert Online Pictures
3. Insert Text Boxes and Shapes
4. Format Objects

PROJECT 2B

Outcomes
Enhance a presentation with WordArt and SmartArt.

Objectives
5. Remove Picture Backgrounds and Insert WordArt
6. Create and Format a SmartArt Graphic
7. Insert a 3D Object

Antonio V. Oquias/Shutterstock

In This Chapter

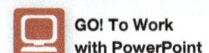 **GO! To Work with PowerPoint**

A well-designed PowerPoint presentation helps the audience understand complex information while keeping them focused on your message. Color is an important element that enhances your slides and draws the audience's interest by creating focus. When designing the background and element colors for your presentation, be sure that the colors you use provide contrast so that the text is visible on the background. Use elements such as images, shapes, and other graphics to enhance your presentation and illustrate your message.

The projects in this chapter relate to **Sensation Park Entertainment Group**, an entertainment company that operates 15 regional theme parks across the United States, Mexico, and Canada. Park types include traditional theme parks, water parks, and animal parks. This year the company will launch three of its new "Sensation Parks" where attractions combine fun and the discovery of math and science information, and where teens and adults enjoy the free Friday night concerts. The company focuses on safe and imaginative attractions that appeal to guests with a variety of entertainment interests, including adventure, science, and the arts.

Employee Training Presentation

MyLab IT
Project 2A Grader for Instruction
Project 2A Simulation for Training and Review

Project Activities

In Activities 2.01 through 2.21, you will format a presentation for Marc Johnson, Director of Operations for Sensation Park Entertainment Group, which describes important safety guidelines for employees. Your completed presentation will look similar to Figure 2.1.

Project Files for **MyLab IT Grader**

1. In your storage location, create a folder named **PowerPoint Chapter 2**.
2. In your **MyLab IT** course, locate and click **PowerPoint 2A Safety**, Download Materials, and then Download All Files.
3. Extract the zipped folder to your PowerPoint Chapter 2 folder. Close the Grader download screens.
4. Take a moment to open the downloaded **PowerPoint_2A_Safety_Instructions**; note any recent updates to the book.

Project Results

GO! Project 2A
Where We're Going

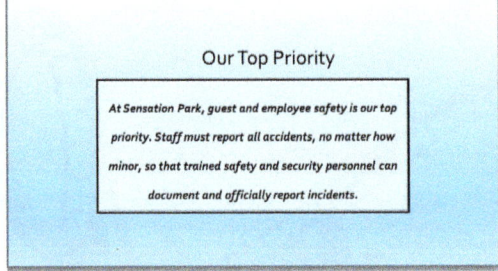
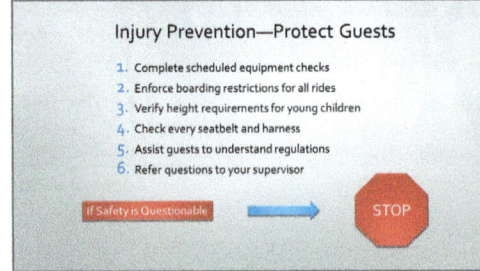
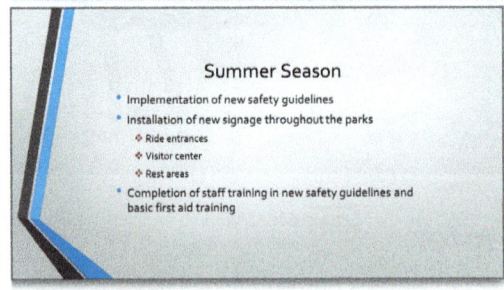
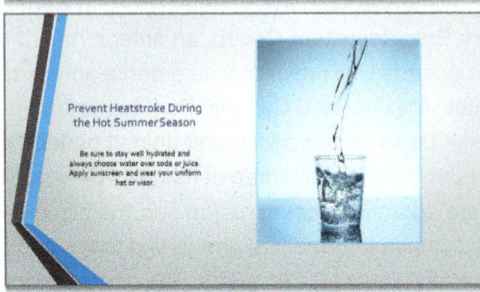
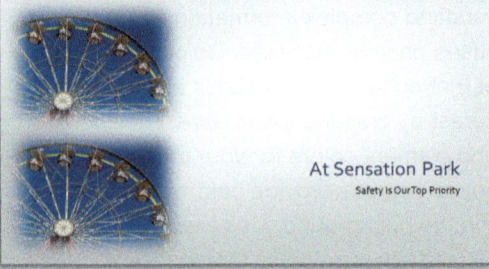

Figure 2.1 Project 2A Safety

For Non-MyLab Submissions
For Project 2A, you will need:

In your storage location, create a folder named **PowerPoint Chapter 2**
In your PowerPoint Chapter 2 folder, save your presentation as:

p02A_Safety

Lastname_Firstname_2A_Safety

After you have named and saved your presentation, on the next page, begin with Step 2.

NOTE	If You Are Using a Touch Screen

Tap an item to click it.

Press and hold for a few seconds to right-click; release when the information or commands display.

Touch the screen with two or more fingers and then pinch together or stretch your fingers apart to zoom in and out.

Slide your finger on the screen to scroll—slide left to scroll right and slide right to scroll left.

Slide to rearrange—similar to dragging with a mouse.

Swipe to select—slide an item a short distance with a quick movement—to select an item and bring up commands, if any.

Objective 1 | Format Numbered and Bulleted Lists

ALERT Because Office 365 is a cloud-based subscription service that receives continuous updates, you may encounter some variations in what appears on your screen and what is shown in this instruction. Microsoft Office 365 is fully installed on your PC or Mac; no internet access is necessary to create or edit documents. When you *are* connected to the internet, you will receive monthly upgrades and new features, so you always have the latest versions of Office apps as soon as they are available. Your subscription gives you continuous free access to the latest innovations and refinements.

GO! Learn How
Video P2-1

The font, color, and style of a numbered or bulleted list are determined by the presentation theme; however, you can format these elements by changing the bulleted and numbered list styles and colors. A ***bulleted list***, sometimes called an unordered list, is a list of items preceded by small dots or other shapes, which do not indicate order or rank. In a ***numbered list***, or ordered list, items are preceded by numbers, which indicate sequence or rank of the items.

Activity 2.01 | Selecting Placeholder Text

A placeholder is a box on a slide with dotted or dashed borders that holds title and body text or other content such as charts, tables, and pictures. You can format placeholder contents by selecting text or by selecting the entire placeholder.

1 Navigate to your **PowerPoint Chapter 2 folder**, and then double-click the PowerPoint file you downloaded from **MyLab IT** that displays your name—**Student_PowerPoint_2A_ Safety**. In your presentation, if necessary, at the top click **Enable Editing**.

2 Display **Slide 2**, and then click anywhere in the content placeholder with the single bullet point.

3 Point to the dashed border surrounding the placeholder to display the 🔲 pointer, and then click one time to display the border as a solid line. Compare your screen with Figure 2.2.

When a placeholder's border displays as a solid line, all of the text in the placeholder is selected, and any formatting changes that you make will be applied to *all* of the text in the placeholder.

 MAC TIP The border may not display as a dashed line; however, clicking the border will select all text in the placeholder.

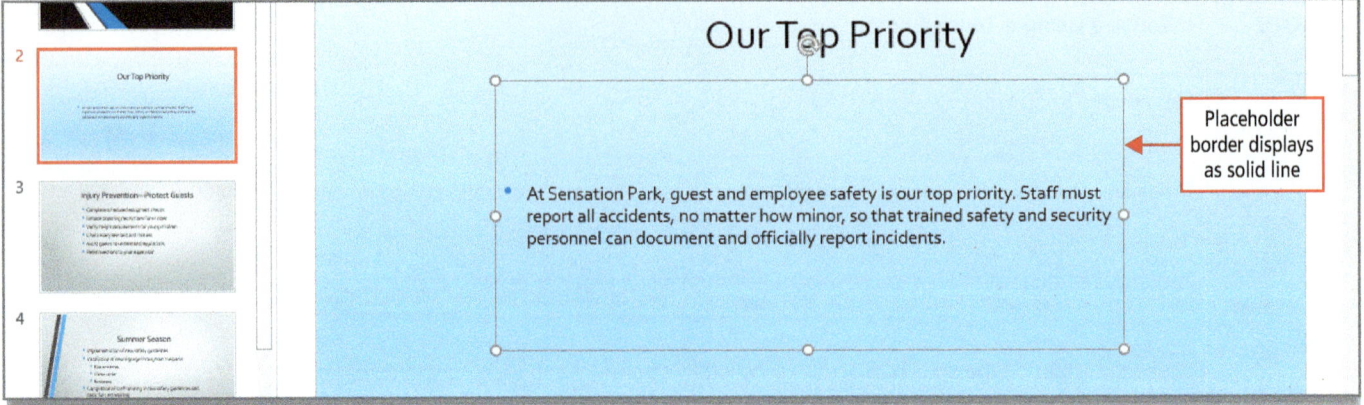

Figure 2.2

> 4 ▸ With the border of the placeholder displaying as a solid line, change the **Font Size** [60 ▾] to **24**. Notice that the font size of *all* of the placeholder text increases.
>
> 5 ▸ **Save** 💾 your presentation.

Activity 2.02 | Changing a Bulleted List to a Numbered List

MOS
3.1.3

You can easily change a bulleted list to a numbered list. In this safety presentation, the list of steps to follow should be a numbered list, such as the rules employees should follow for injury prevention.

> 1 ▸ Display **Slide 3**, and then click anywhere in the bulleted list. Point to the placeholder dashed border to display the ⬚ pointer, and then click one time to display the border as a solid line indicating that all of the text is selected.
>
> 2 ▸ On the **Home tab**, in the **Paragraph group**, click **Numbering** ▤▾ and then compare your slide with Figure 2.3. **Save** 💾 your presentation.

> All of the bullet symbols are converted to numbers. The color of the numbers is determined by the presentation theme.

💻 **MAC TIP** If group names do not display on your ribbon, open PowerPoint. On the menu, click PowerPoint, and then click Preferences. Click View, and then in the View dialog box, select the Show group titles check box. Close the dialog box to display group names on the ribbon.

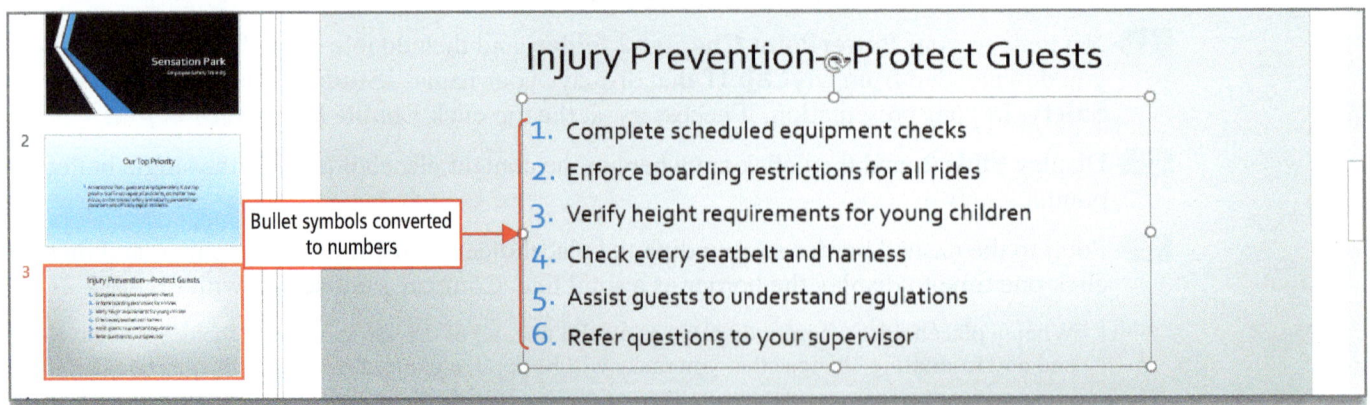

Figure 2.3

Activity 2.03 | Changing the Shape and Color of a Bulleted List Symbol

MOS
3.1.3

The presentation theme includes default styles for the bullet points in content placeholders. You can customize a bullet by changing its style, color, and size. It is good practice to create presentations that use styles, colors, and other formatting that represent the brand of the company.

1 Display **Slide 4**, and then select the three second-level bullet points—*Ride entrances*, *Visitor center*, and *Rest areas*.

2 On the **Home tab**, in the **Paragraph group**, click the **Bullets button arrow** ▤▾ to display the **Bullets** gallery, and then compare your screen with Figure 2.4.

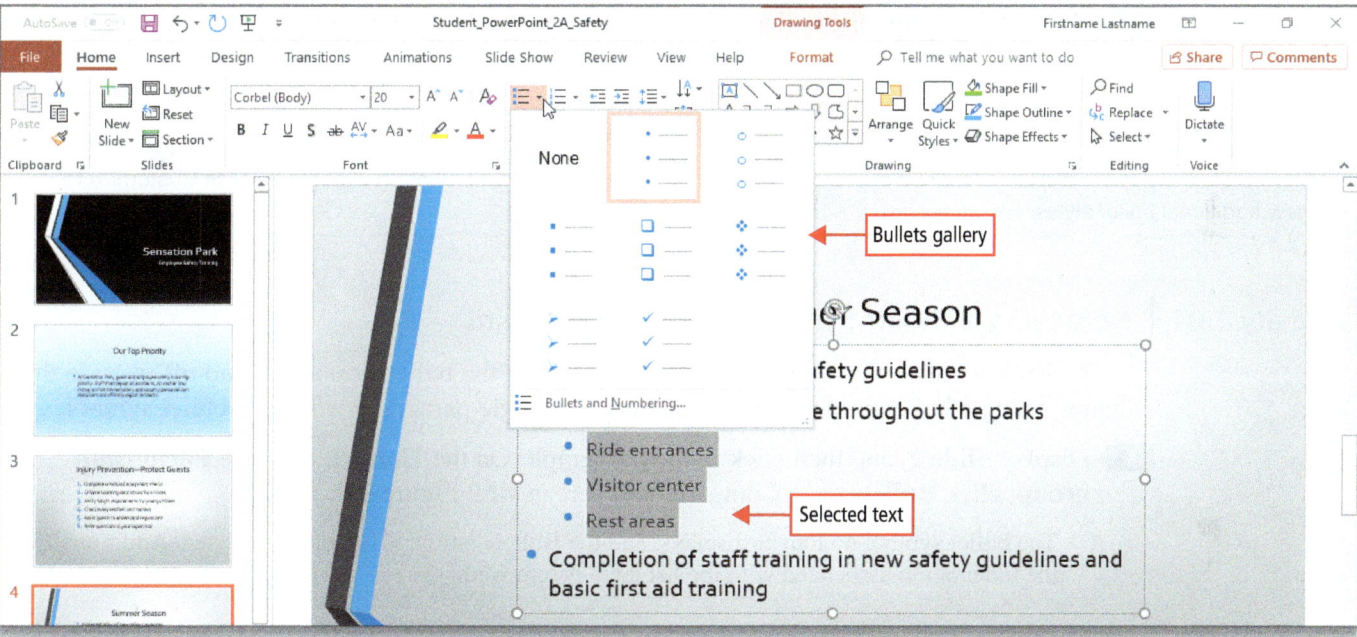

Figure 2.4

3 Below the **Bullets** gallery, click **Bullets and Numbering**. In the **Bullets and Numbering** dialog box, point to several bullet styles to display each ScreenTip. Then, in the second row, click **Star Bullets**. If the Star Bullets are not available, in the second row of bullets, click the second bullet style, and then click the Reset button.

4 Below the gallery, click **Color** 🎨▾. Under **Theme Colors**, in the eighth column, click the last color. In the **Size** box, select the existing number, type **100** and then compare your dialog box with Figure 2.5.

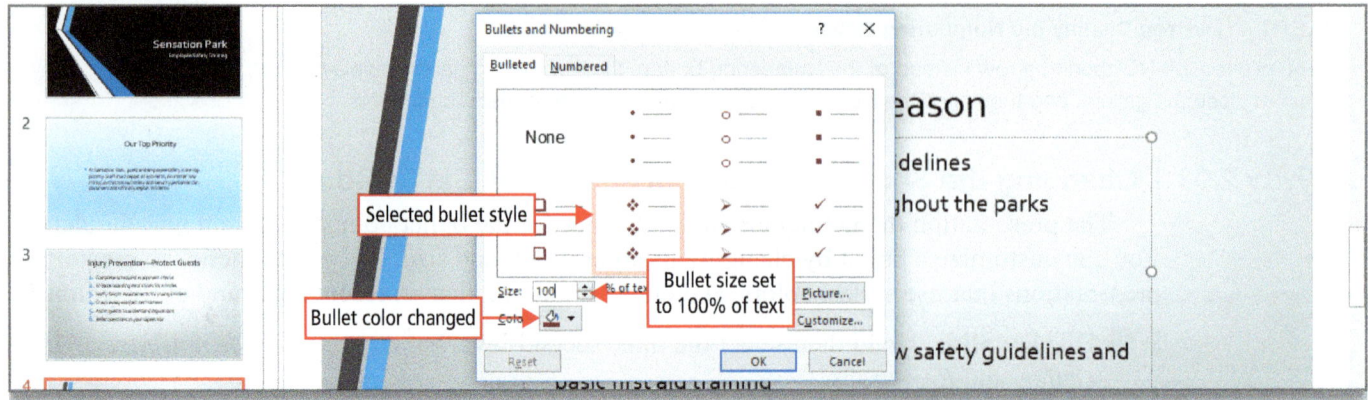

Figure 2.5

5 ▷ Click **OK** to apply the bullet style, and then **Save** 🖫 your presentation.

Activity 2.04 | Removing a Bullet Symbol from a Bullet Point

The Bullets button is a toggle, enabling you to turn the bullet symbol on and off. A slide that contains a single bullet point can be formatted as a single paragraph *without* a bullet symbol.

1 ▷ Display **Slide 2**, and then click in the paragraph. On the **Home tab**, in the **Paragraph group**, click **Bullets** ▤ ▾. Compare your screen with Figure 2.6.

The bullet symbol no longer displays, and the Bullets button is no longer selected. Additionally, the indentation associated with the list level is removed.

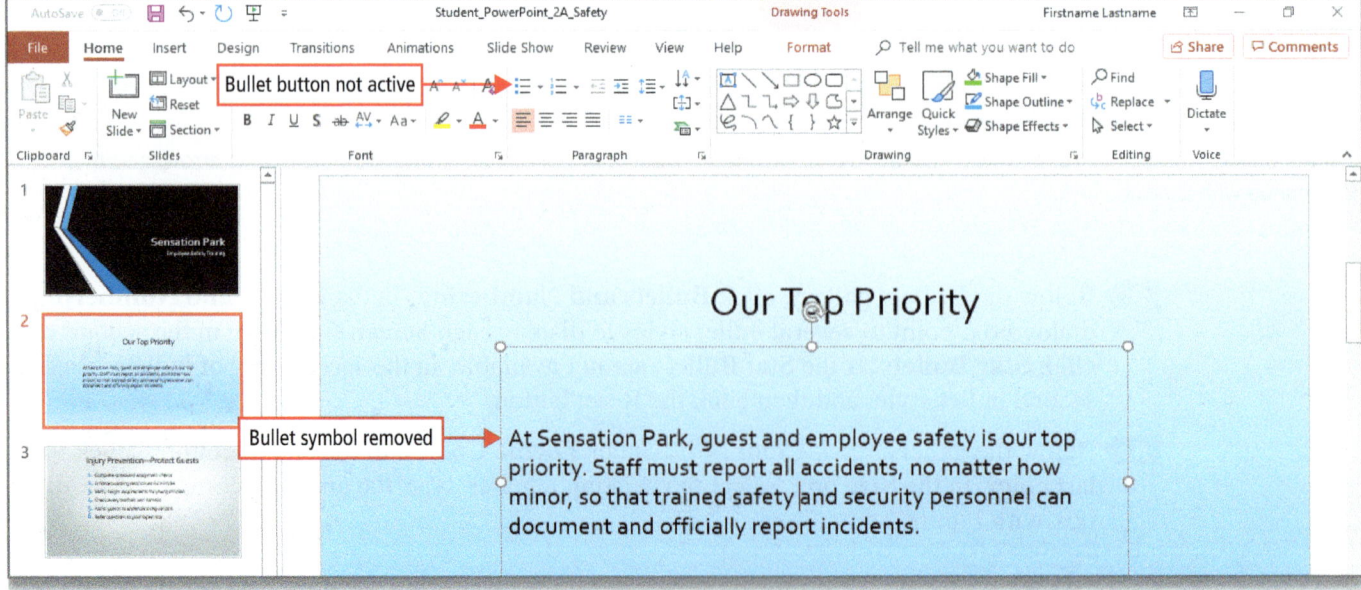

Figure 2.6

2 ▶ Click the dashed border to display the solid border and to select all of the text in the paragraph, and then apply **Bold** [B] and **Italic** [I]. In the **Paragraph group**, click **Line Spacing** [≣▾], and then click **2.0**. **Center** [≣] the paragraph, and then **Save** [💾] your presentation.

Objective 2 | Insert Online Pictures

GO! Learn How
Video P2-2

There are many sources from which you can insert images and other media into a presentation. One type of image that you can insert is a *clip*—a single media file such as art, sound, animation, or a movie.

Activity 2.05 | Inserting Online Pictures in a Content Placeholder

PowerPoint searches Bing when you insert an online picture. You can use various keywords to find online images that are appropriate for your documents.

1 ▶ Display **Slide 5**. In the placeholder on the right side of the slide, click **Online Pictures** [🖼] to display the **Online Pictures** dialog box. With the insertion point in the **Search** box, type **pouring water** Press [Enter] to search for images that contain the keywords *pouring water* and then compare your screen with Figure 2.7.

> 🖥 **MAC TIP**   The Mac version of PowerPoint does not include this feature. Open your browser, navigate to Bing.com, click Images, and search for images that contain the keywords pouring water. Select a vertical image of water being poured, similar to Figure 2.8. Save the file to your computer and use the Insert Picture icon in the content placeholder to insert your downloaded image. For this Activity you can insert the picture p02A_Pouring_Water that is included with the data files for this project.

Figure 2.7

2 ▶ Select a vertical image of water being poured, similar to Figure 2.8.

The results shown indicate the images are licensed under Creative Commons, which, according to www.creativecommons.org is "a nonprofit organization that enables the sharing and use of creativity and knowledge through free legal tools." Creative Commons helps people share and use their photographs, but not allow companies to sell them. For your college assignments, you can use these images so long as you are not profiting by selling the images.
To find out more about Creative Commons, go to *https://creativecommons.org* and watch their video.

> **NOTE   Unable to Locate Similar Image**
>
> If you are unable to locate a suitable image or would prefer to have your project match this text exactly, you can insert the picture p02A_Pouring_Water that is included with the data files for this project.

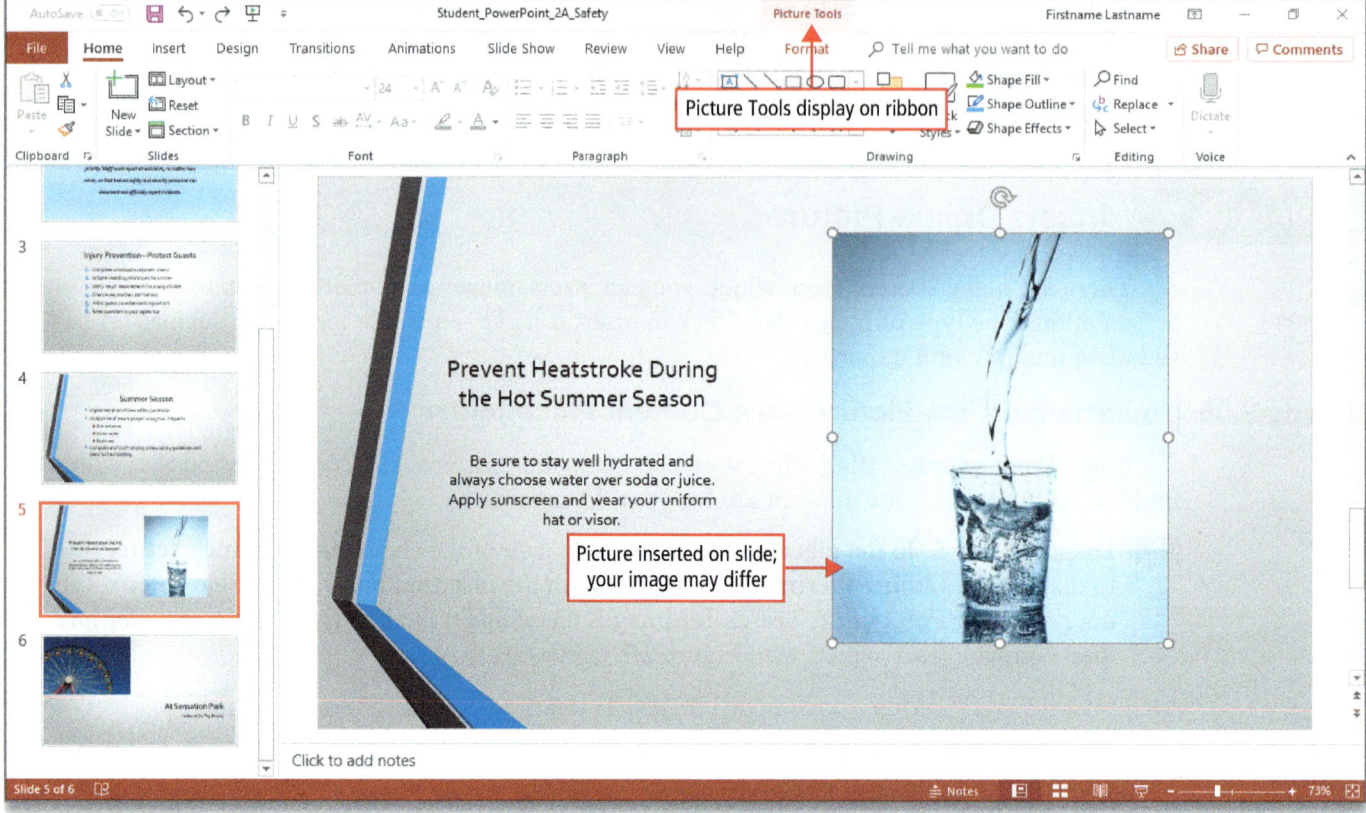

Figure 2.8

> **3** With the water picture selected, click **Insert**. If necessary, close the Design Ideas pane.
>
> On the ribbon, the Picture Tools display, and the pouring water image is surrounded by sizing handles, indicating that it is selected. Your ribbon may also display the Drawing Tools tab.

BY TOUCH   Tap the picture that you want to insert, and then tap Insert.

NOTE   Design Ideas Pane

The Design Ideas pane may open each time you insert a picture. The pane includes ideas for ways to format and layout a slide. In this project you will not use these suggestions, so you can close the pane each time it opens.

NOTE   Credit Line Below Inserted Image

When you insert an online image, PowerPoint may include a credit line below the image. This includes copyright information such as author name and CC (Creative Commons) licenses. When using the work of others, you should appropriately cite your sources. For this exercise, you can delete this information so that your screen will match the figures in this text more closely.

> **4** If necessary, select only the textbox below the inserted image, and then press Delete. **Save** 🖫 your presentation.

Activity 2.06 | Inserting Pictures in Any Location on a Slide

1 Display **Slide 1**. On the **Insert tab**, in the **Images group**, click **Pictures**.

MAC TIP Click Pictures and then click Picture from File.

2 In the **Insert Picture** dialog box, navigate to the data files for this project, click **p02A_Red_Light**, and then click **Insert**. Compare your screen with Figure 2.9. **Save** 🖫 your presentation.

When you insert an image from the ribbon instead of from the button in a content placeholder, PowerPoint inserts the image in the center of the slide.

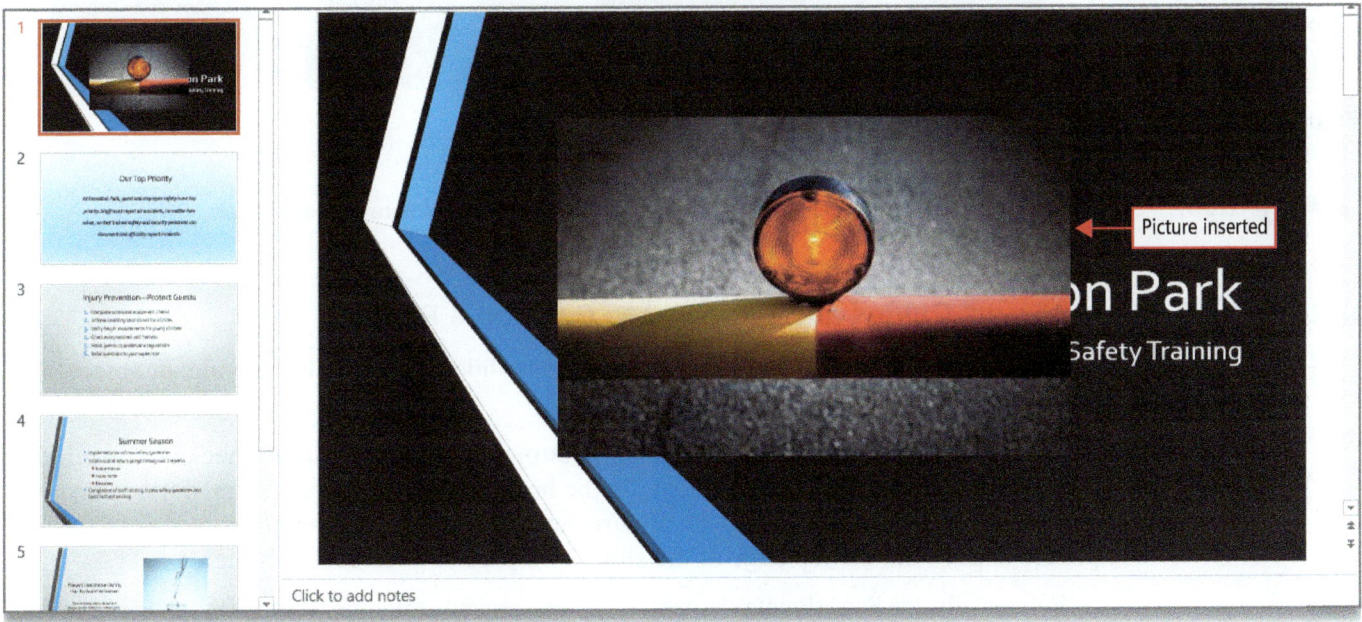

Figure 2.9

Activity 2.07 | Sizing a Picture

3.3.1

A selected image displays sizing handles that you can drag to resize the image. You can also resize an image using the Shape Height and Shape Width boxes on the Format tab.

1 If necessary, select the picture of the red light. On the **Picture Tools Format tab**, in the **Size group**, click in the **Shape Height** box 🔳, and then replace the selected number with **3.5**

2 Press **Enter** to resize the image. Notice that the picture is resized proportionately, and the **Width** box of this image displays *5.26*. Compare your screen with Figure 2.10. **Save** 🖫 your presentation.

When a picture is resized in this manner, the width adjusts in proportion to the picture height.

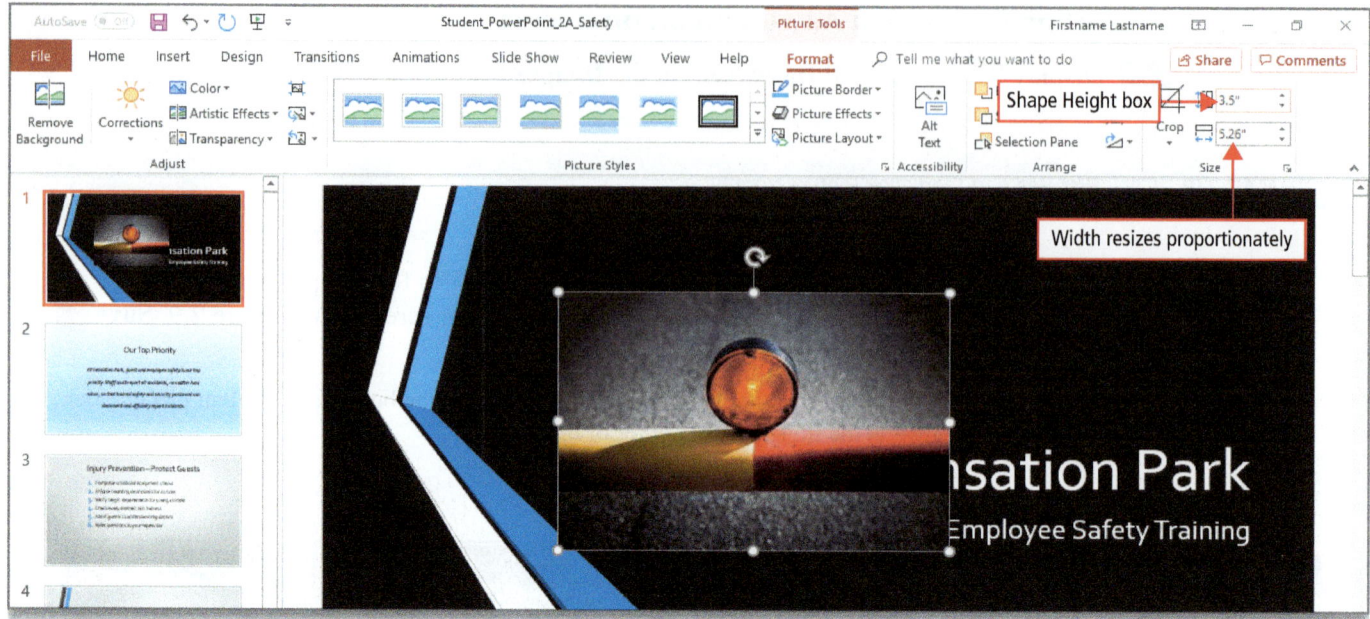

Figure 2.10

👆 **BY TOUCH**   Drag the corner sizing handle with your finger or mouse to resize the picture proportionately.

Activity 2.08 | Using Smart Guides and the Ruler to Position a Picture

MOS
3.5.4

Smart guides are dashed lines that display on your slide when you are moving an object to assist you with alignment.

1 ▶ On **Slide 1**, on the **View tab**, in the **Show group**, verify that the **Ruler** check box is selected and if necessary, select the check box. On the horizontal and vertical rulers, notice that *0* displays in the center. Point to the picture, and then drag up so that the top edge of the picture aligns with the top edge of the slide. Compare your screen with Figure 2.11.

Horizontally, the PowerPoint ruler indicates measurements from the center of the slide *out* to the left and to the right. Vertically, the PowerPoint ruler indicates measurements from the center up and down.

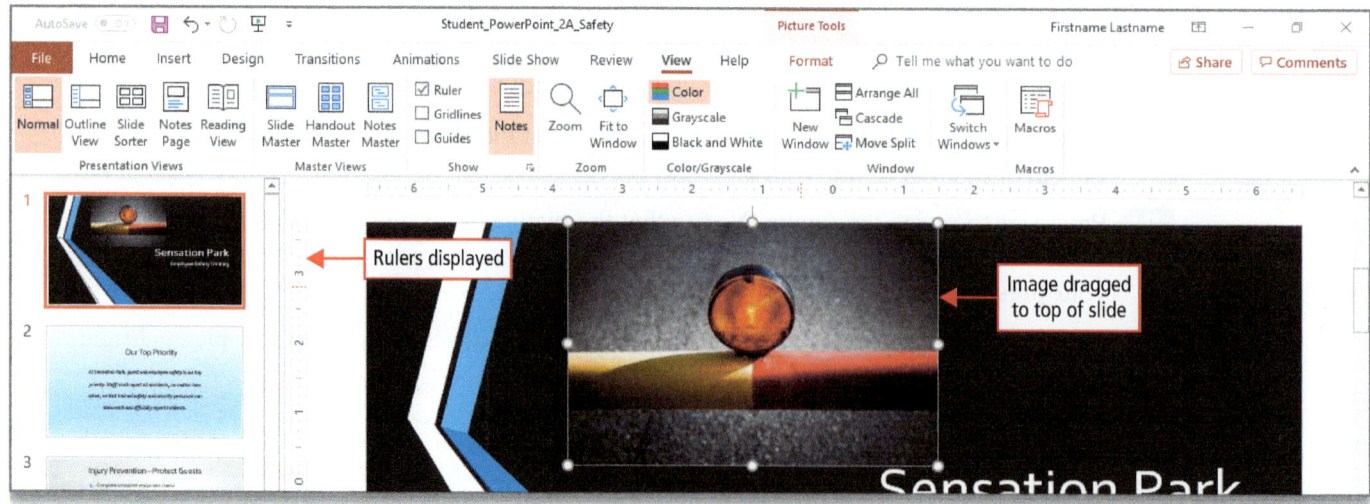

Figure 2.11

2 Point to the picture to display the ⌖ pointer. Hold down [Shift], and then slowly drag the picture to the right and notice that dashed red Smart Guides periodically display along the edges of the picture. When the dashed red Smart Guide displays on the right edge of the picture at approximately **6 inches to the right of zero on the horizontal ruler**, compare your screen with Figure 2.12, and then release the mouse button. **Save** 🖫 the presentation.

Smart Guides display when you move an object and it is aligned with another object on the slide. Here, the Smart Guide displays because the right edge of the picture is aligned with the right edge of the title placeholder. Pressing [Shift] while dragging an object constrains object movement in a straight line either vertically or horizontally. Here, pressing [Shift] maintains the vertical placement of the picture at the top edge of the slide.

Figure 2.12

🔄 **ANOTHER WAY** On the Picture Tools Format tab, in the Size group, click More to open the Format Picture pane. On the Size and Properties tab, and set the position by entering values in the Horizontal position and Vertical position boxes measured from the top left corner or the center of the slide. For this Activity, enter 7.5 in the Horizontal position box and 0 in the Vertical position box.

MORE KNOWLEDGE **Moving an Object by Using the Arrow Keys**

You can use the directional arrow keys on your keyboard to move a picture, shape, or other object in small increments. Select the object so that its outside border displays as a solid line. Then, on your keyboard, press the directional arrow keys to move the selected object in small, precise increments.

Activity 2.09 | Cropping a Picture

3.3.1

When you *crop* a picture, you remove unwanted or unnecessary areas of the picture.

1 Display **Slide 6**, and then select the Ferris wheel picture. On the **Picture Tools Format tab**, in the **Size group**, click the upper portion of the **Crop** button to display the crop handles on the edges of the picture. Compare your screen with Figure 2.13.

Use the *crop handles* like sizing handles to remove unwanted areas of the picture.

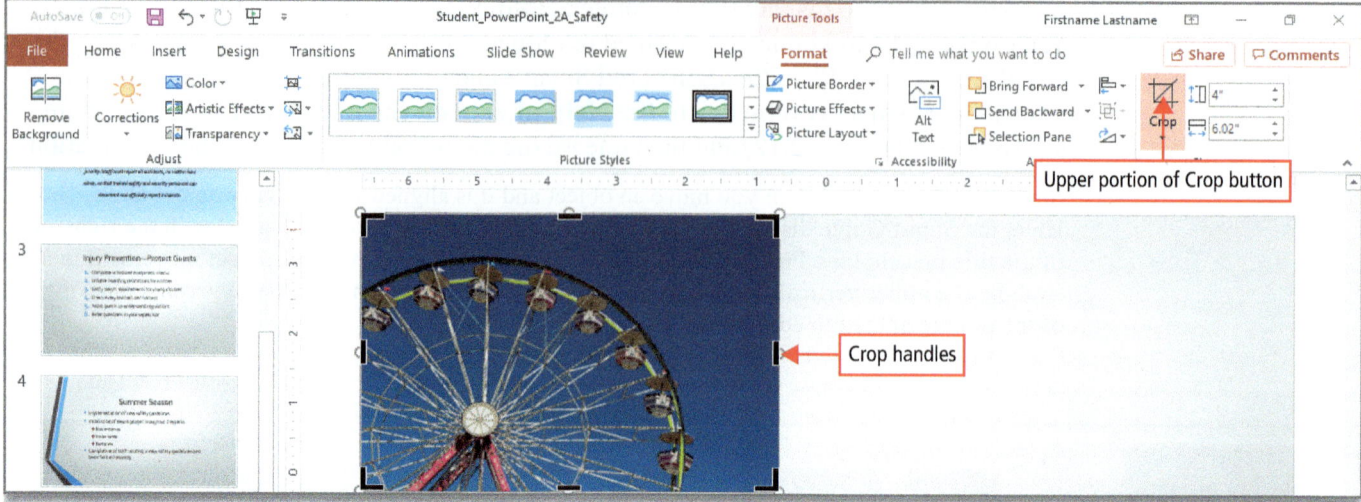

Figure 2.13

> ![2] Point to the center right crop handle to display the crop pointer ⊩. Compare your screen with Figure 2.14.
>
> The ***crop pointer*** is the mouse pointer that displays when cropping areas of a picture.

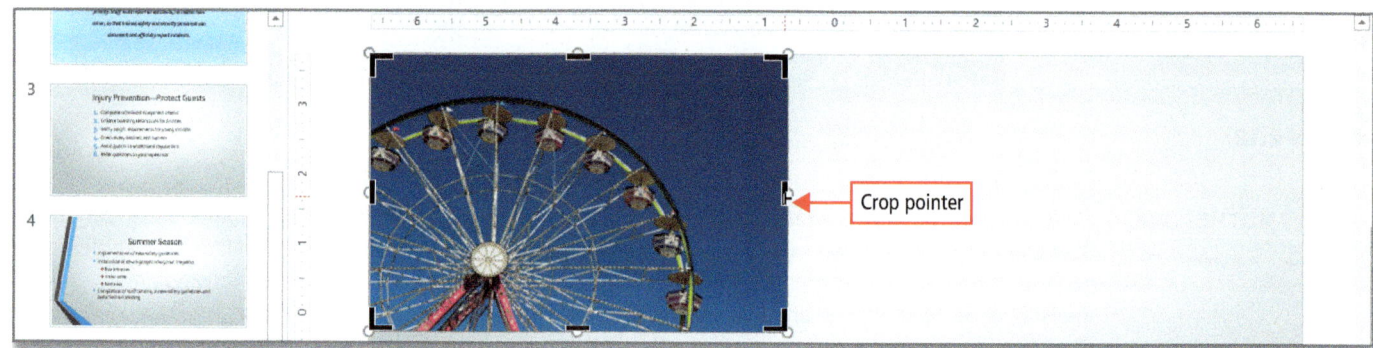

Figure 2.14

> ![3] With the crop pointer displayed, hold down the left mouse button and drag to the left to approximately **1.5 inches to the left of zero on the horizontal ruler**, and then release the mouse button. Compare your screen with Figure 2.15.
>
> The portion of the picture to be removed by the crop displays in gray.

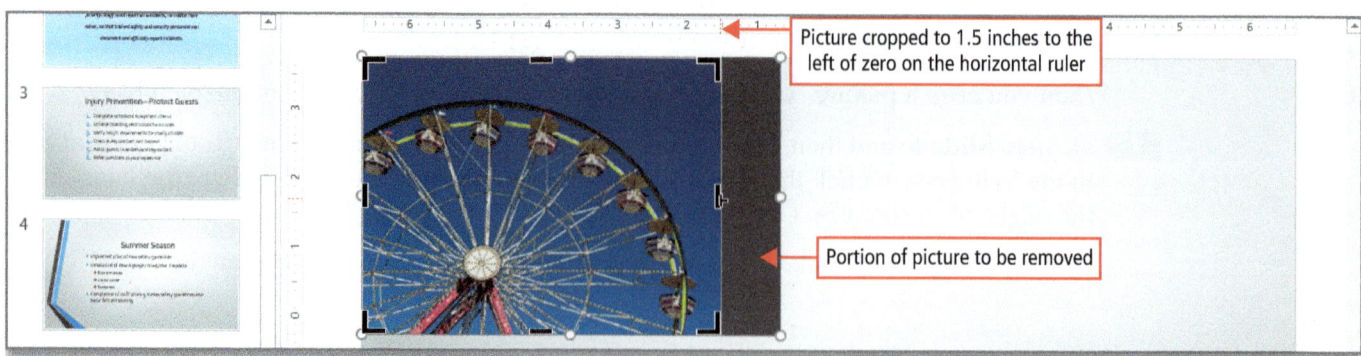

Figure 2.15

4 On the **Picture Tools Format tab**, in the **Size group**, click the upper portion of the **Crop** button to apply the crop, and then **Save** 🖫 your presentation.

ANOTHER WAY Press Enter or click outside the picture to apply the crop.

Activity 2.10 │ Using the Crop to Shape Command to Change the Shape of a Picture

MOS
3.3.1

An inserted picture is typically rectangular in shape; however, you can modify a picture by changing its shape.

1 Display **Slide 1**, and then select the picture. On the **Picture Tools Format tab**, in the **Size group**, click the lower portion of the Crop button—the **Crop arrow**—and then compare your screen with Figure 2.16.

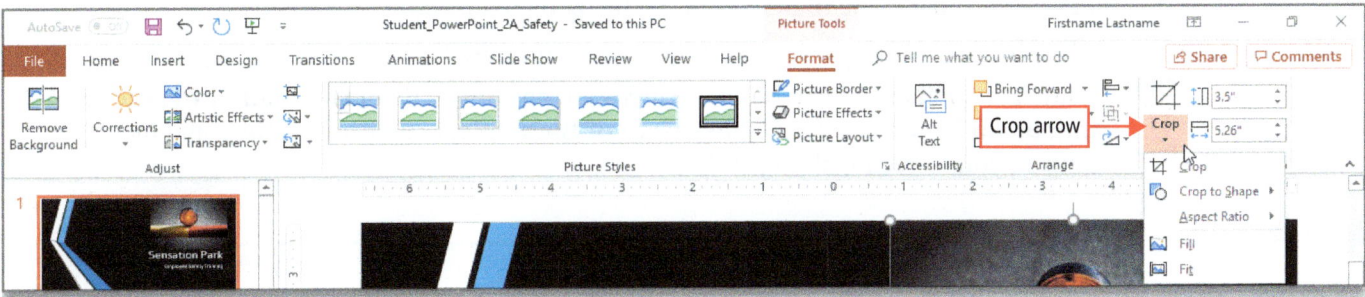

Figure 2.16

2 Point to **Crop to Shape** to display a gallery of shapes. Under **Basic Shapes**, in the first row, click the first shape—**Oval**—to change the picture's shape to an oval. Compare your screen with Figure 2.17.

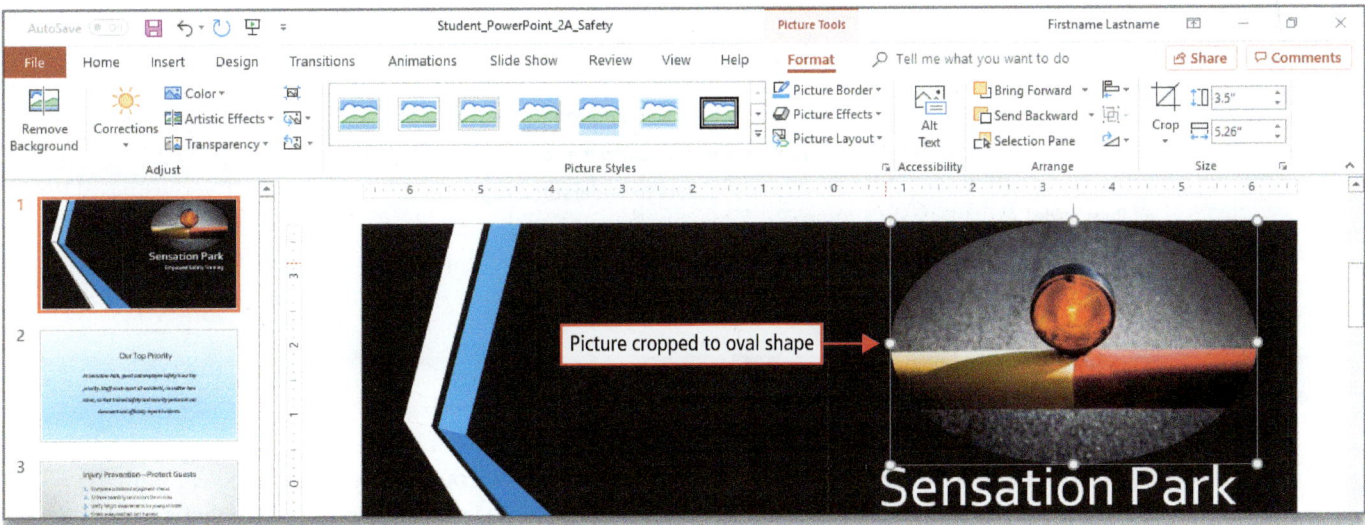

Figure 2.17

3 **Save** 🖫 your presentation.

GO! Learn How

Video P2-3

You can use objects, including text boxes and shapes, to draw attention to important information or to serve as containers for slide text. Many shapes, including lines, arrows, ovals, and rectangles, are available to insert and position anywhere on your slides.

Activity 2.11 | Inserting a Text Box

3.4.3

A *text box* is an object with which you can position text anywhere on a slide.

1 Display **Slide 3** and verify that the rulers display. On the **Insert tab**, in the **Text group**, click **Text Box**.

2 Move the ⬇ pointer to several different places on the slide, and as you do so, in the horizontal and vertical rulers, notice that *ruler guides*—dotted red vertical and horizontal lines that display in the rulers indicating the pointer's position—move also.

Use the ruler guides to help you position objects on a slide.

3 Position the pointer so that the ruler guides are positioned on the **left half of the horizontal ruler at 4.5 inches** and on the **lower half of the vertical ruler at 2 inches**, and then compare your screen with Figure 2.18.

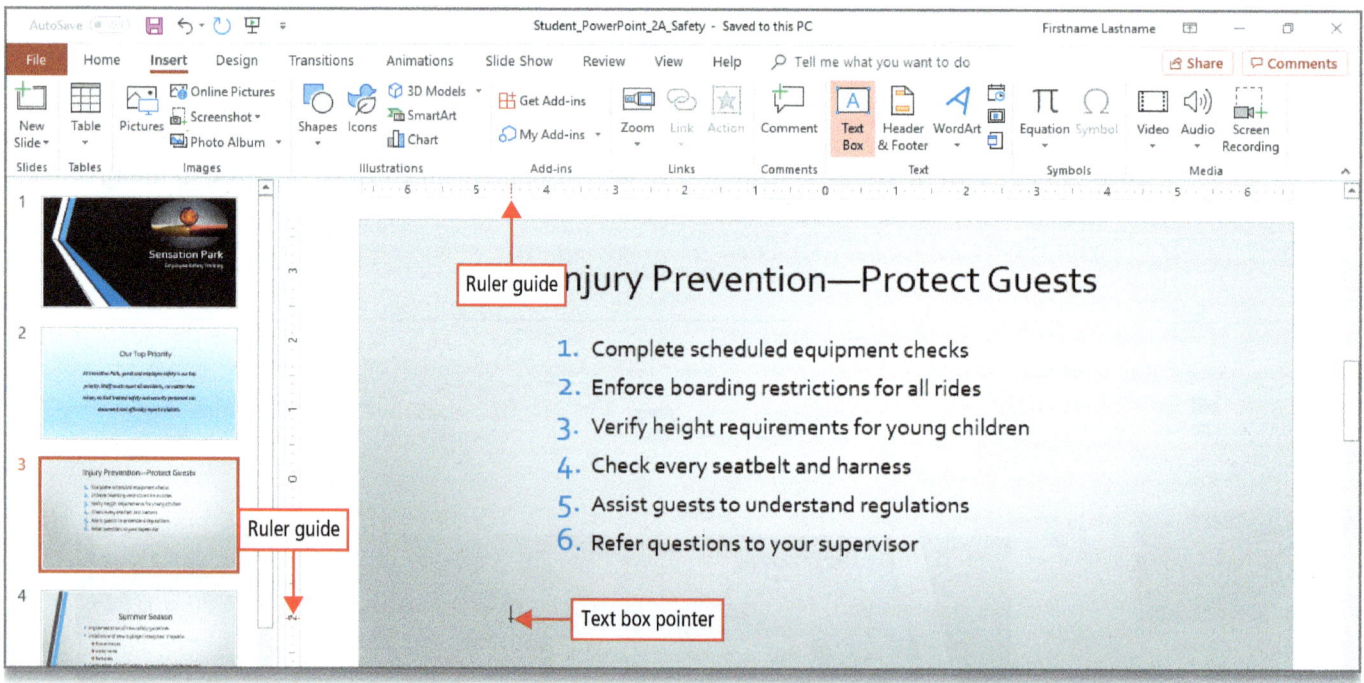

Figure 2.18

4 Click one time to create a narrow rectangular text box surrounded by sizing handles. With the insertion point blinking inside the text box, type **If Safety is Questionable** Notice that as you type, the width of the text box expands to accommodate the text. Compare your screen with Figure 2.19.

Do not be concerned if your textbox is not positioned exactly as shown in the figure.

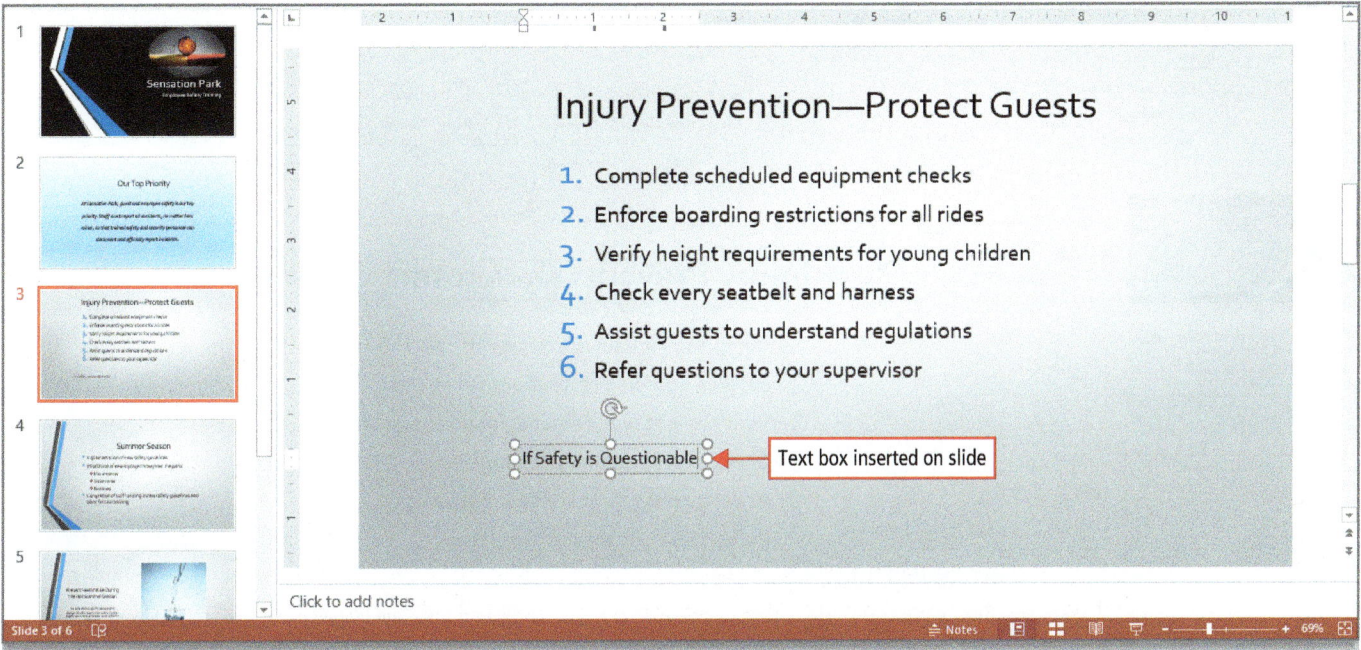

Figure 2.19

5 Select the text that you typed, change the **Font Size** to **24** and then **Save** your presentation.

You can format the text in a text box by using the same techniques that you use to format text in any other placeholder. For example, you can change the font, font style, font size, and font color.

Activity 2.12 | Inserting and Sizing a Shape

3.4.1, 3.4.4

Shapes are slide objects such as lines, arrows, boxes, callouts, and banners. You can size and move a shape using the same techniques that you use to size and move pictures.

1 With **Slide 3** displayed, on the **Insert tab**, in the **Illustrations group**, click **Shapes** to display the **Shapes** gallery. Under **Block Arrows**, click the first shape—**Arrow: Right**. Move the pointer into the slide until the ⊞ pointer—called the *crosshair pointer*—displays, indicating that you can draw a shape.

2 Move the ⊞ pointer to position the ruler guides at approximately **0 on the horizontal ruler** and on the **lower half of the vertical ruler at 2 inches**. Compare your screen with Figure 2.20.

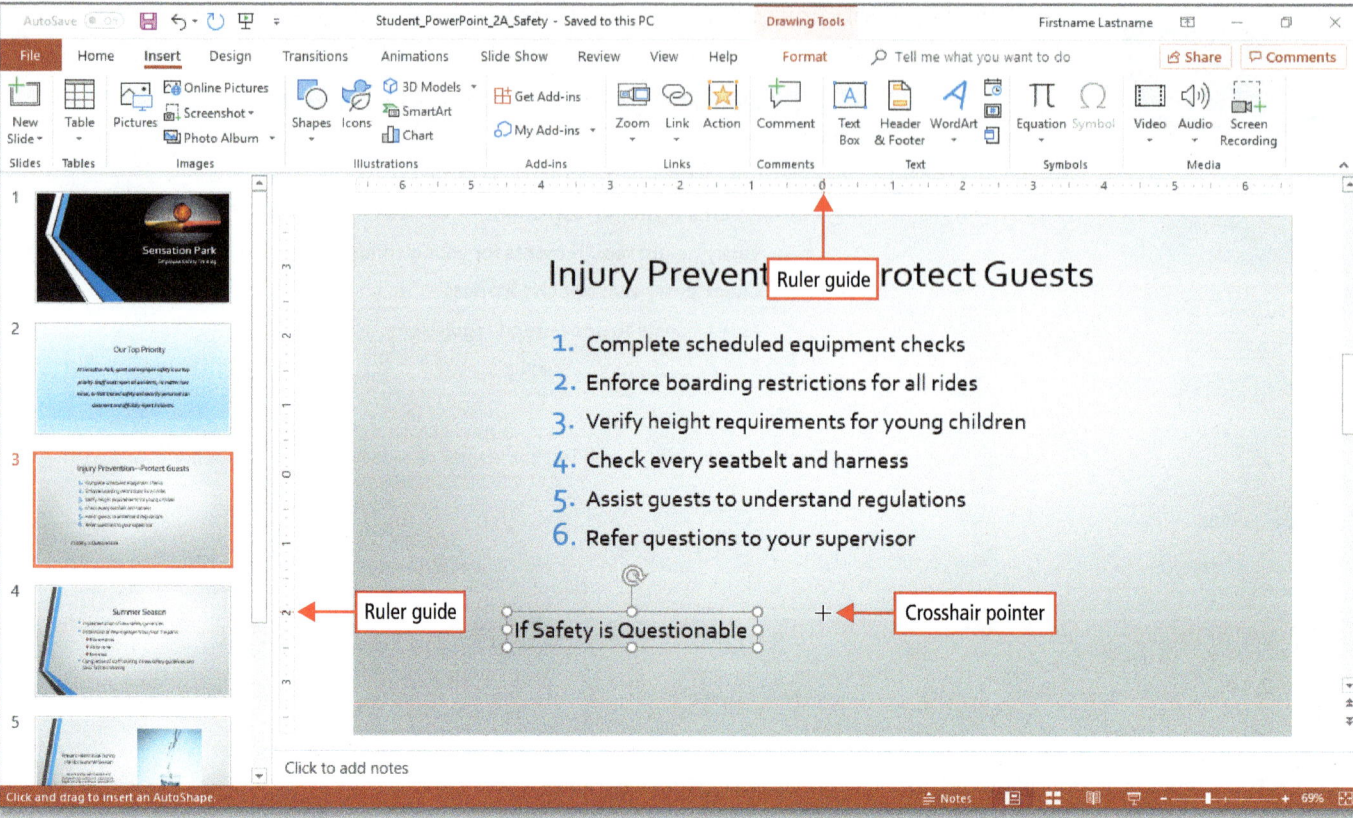

Figure 2.20

3 ▶ Click to insert the arrow. On the **Drawing Tools Format tab,** in the **Size group,** click in the **Shape Height** box 〔Ⅰ〕 to select the number. Type **0.5** click in the **Shape Width** box 〔☷〕. Type **2** and then press 〔Enter〕 to resize the arrow. Compare your screen with Figure 2.21.

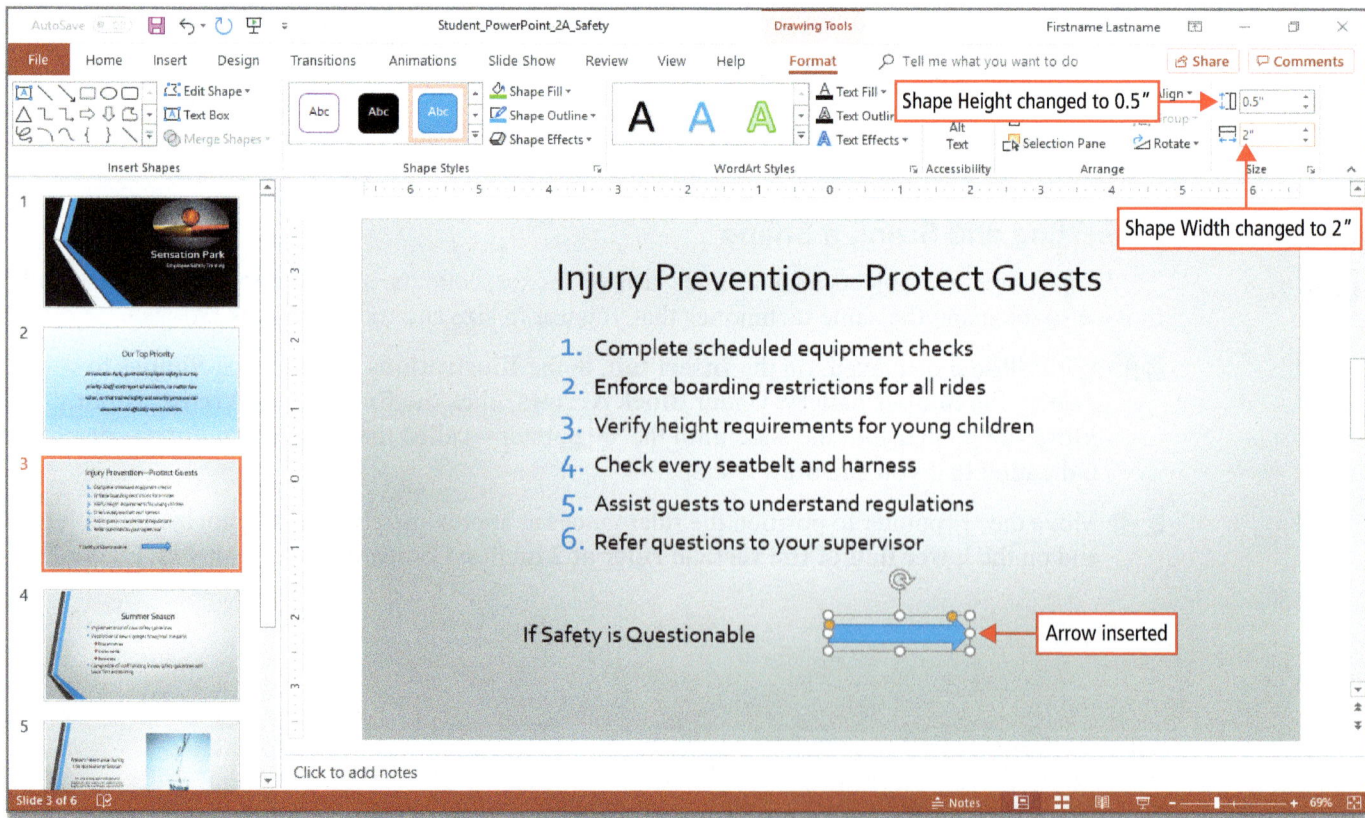

Figure 2.21

4 On the **Drawing Tools Format tab**, in the **Insert Shapes group**, click **More** ▾. In the gallery, under **Basic Shapes**, in the first row, click the second to last shape—**Octagon**.

5 Move the ⊞ pointer to position the ruler guides on the **right half of the horizontal ruler at 3.5 inches** and on the **lower half of the vertical ruler at 1 inch**, and then click one time to insert an octagon.

6 On the **Drawing Tools Format tab**, in the **Size group**, click in the **Shape Height** box ‖↕ to select the number. Type **2** and then click in the **Shape Width** box ▭. Type **2** and then press Enter to resize the octagon. Compare your slide with Figure 2.22.

> Do not be concerned if your shapes are not positioned exactly as shown in the figure. The exact size and location are not important as you will adjust both in a later step.

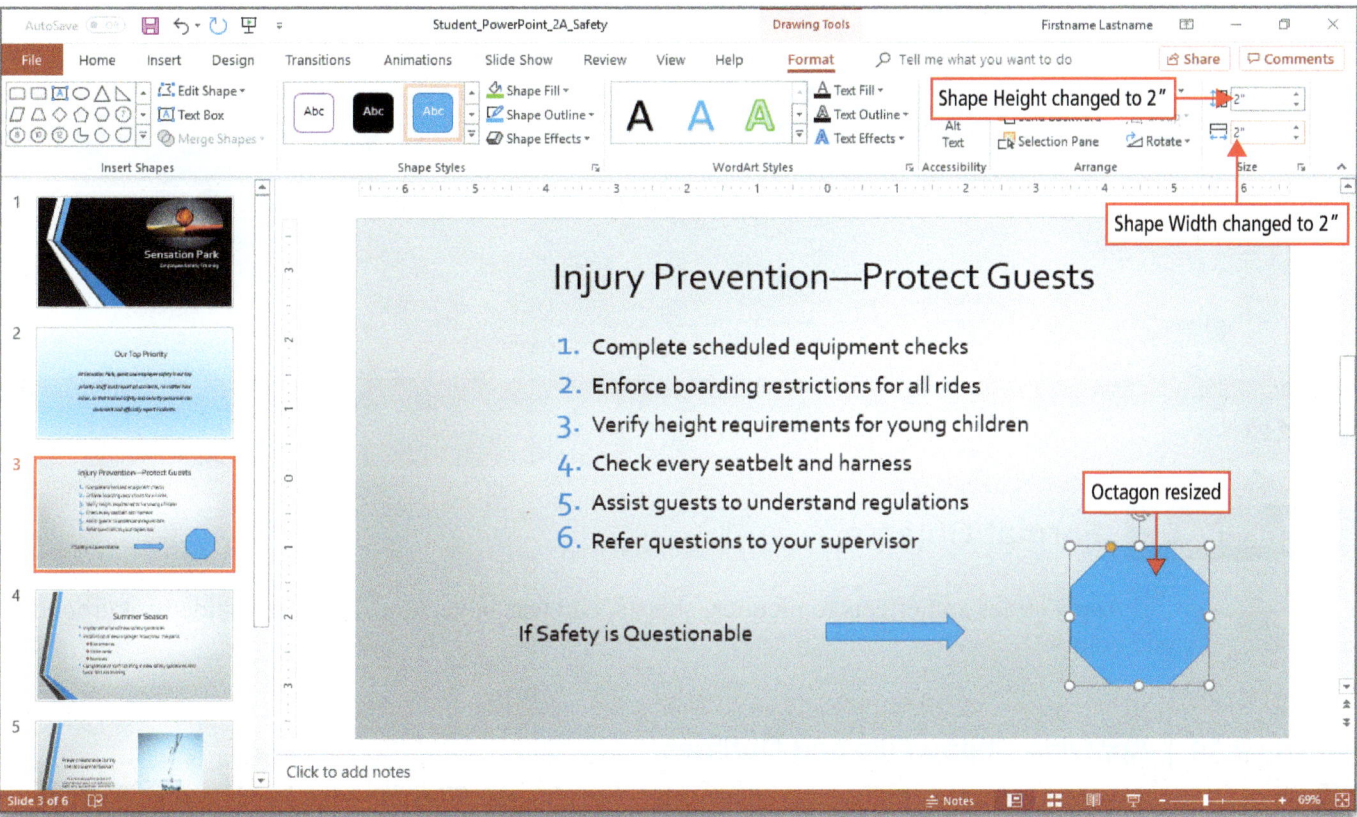

Figure 2.22

7 **Save** 🖫 your presentation.

Activity 2.13 | Adding Text to Shapes

Shapes can serve as a container for text. After you add text to a shape, you can change the font and font size, apply font styles, and change text alignment.

1 On **Slide 3**, if necessary, click the octagon so that it is selected. Type **STOP** and notice that the text is centered within the octagon.

2 Select the text *STOP*, and then change the **Font Size** to **32**.

3 Click in a blank area of the slide to cancel the selection, and then compare your screen with Figure 2.23. **Save** 💾 your presentation.

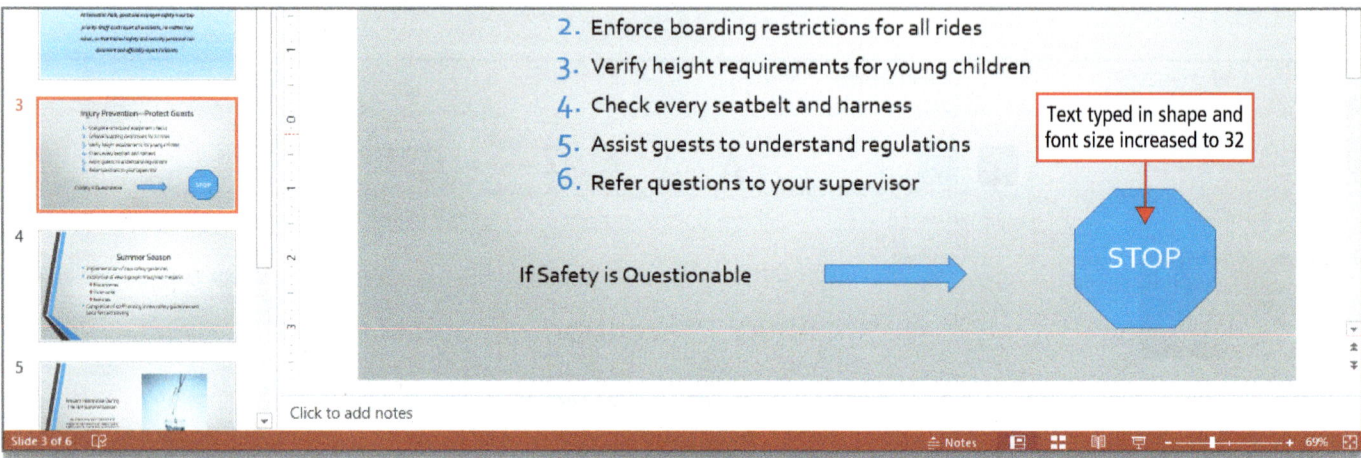

Figure 2.23

Objective 4 | Format Objects

GO! Learn How
Video P 2-4

Apply styles and effects to pictures, shapes, and text boxes to complement slide backgrounds and colors.

Activity 2.14 | Applying Shape Fills and Outlines

3.4.5, 3.4.6

A distinctive way to format a shape is by changing the *fill color*—the inside color of text or of an object—and the outside line color. You can use *shape styles* to apply predefined combinations of these fill and line colors and to apply other effects.

1 Display **Slide 2**, and then click anywhere in the paragraph of text to select the content placeholder.

2 On the **Drawing Tools Format tab**, in the **Shape Styles group**, click the **Shape Fill arrow**. Point to several of the theme colors and watch as Live Preview changes the inside color of the text box. In the fifth column, click the second color.

💻 **MAC TIP** Use the commands on the Shape Format tab.

3 In the **Shape Styles group**, click the **Shape Outline arrow**. Point to **Weight**, click **3 pt**, and notice that a thick outline surrounds the text placeholder. Click in a blank area of the slide so that nothing is selected, and then compare your slide with Figure 2.24. **Save** 💾 your presentation.

You can use combinations of shape fill, outline color, and weight to format an object.

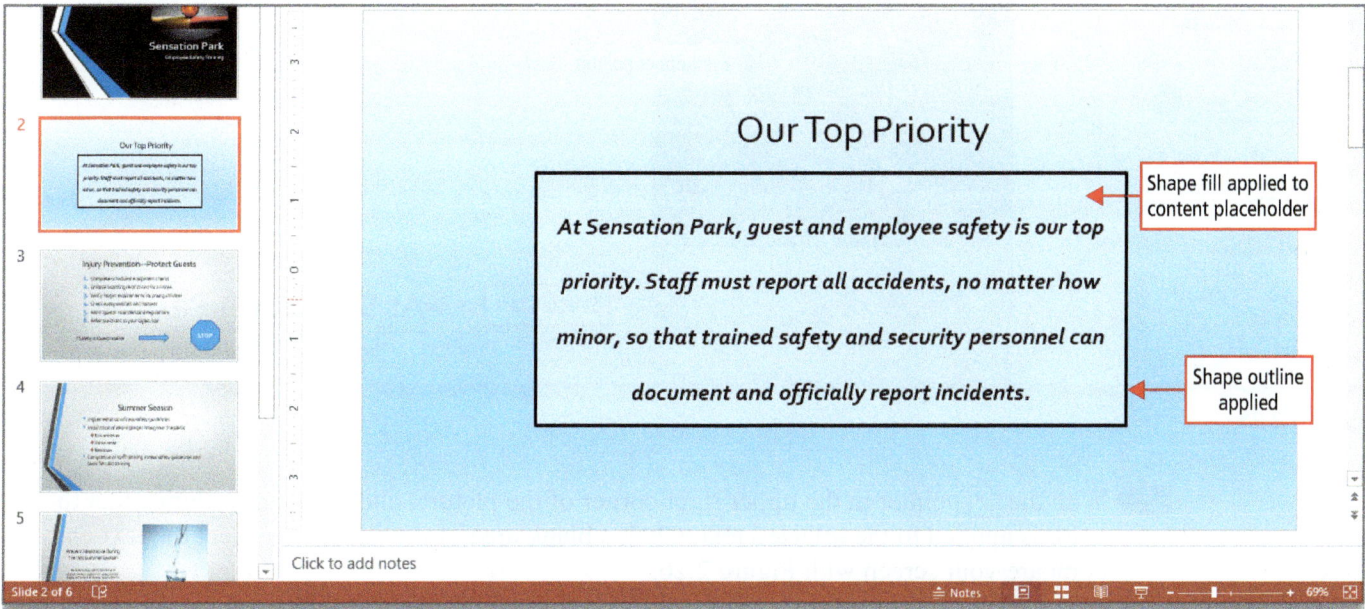

MAC TIP   Click the Shape Outline arrow.

Figure 2.24

Activity 2.15 │ Using the Eyedropper to Change Color

The *eyedropper* is a tool that captures the exact color from an object on your screen and then applies it to any shape, picture, or text. You can use the eyedropper to give your presentation a cohesive look by matching a font color, fill color, border color, or other slide element to any color on any slide.

1 Display **Slide 6**, and then select the title text—*At Sensation Park*.

2 On the **Home tab**, in the **Font group**, click the **Font Color arrow** [A]. Below the gallery, click **Eyedropper**, and then move the [pencil] pointer into the upper right corner of the Ferris wheel picture. Compare your screen with Figure 2.25.

> A small square displays next to the pointer indicating the exact color to which you are pointing. When you hover over a color, it's *RGB* color coordinates display in a ScreenTip, replacing the block of color. RGB is a color model in which the colors red, green, and blue are added together to form another color.

MAC TIP   Click the Font Color arrow and then click More Colors. The Eyedropper is located at the bottom of the Colors dialog box.

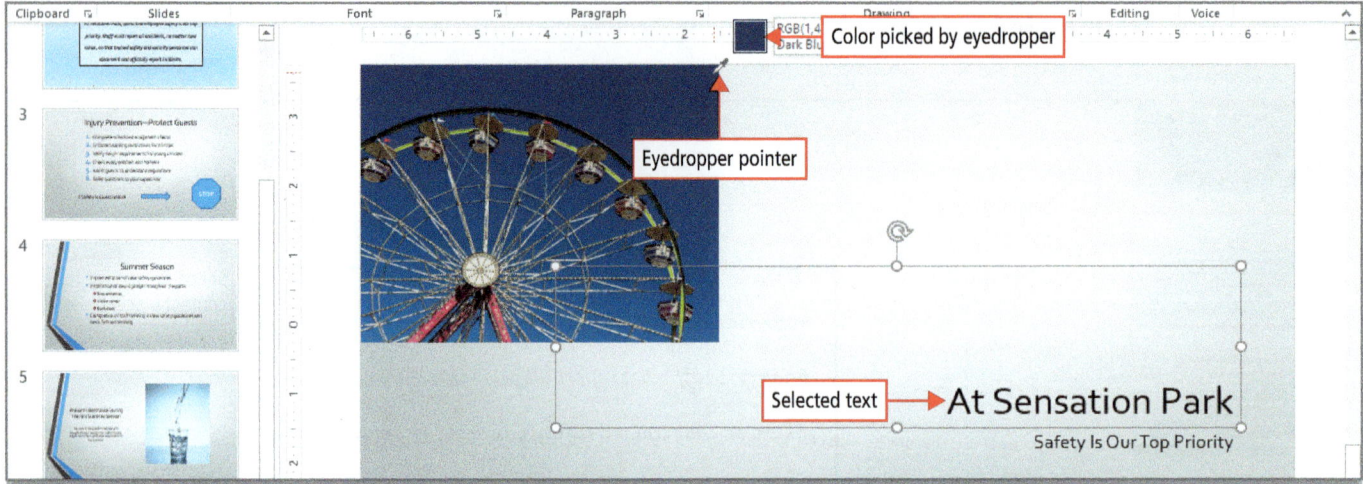

Figure 2.25

3 ▸ With the ✎ pointer in the upper right corner of the picture, click one time. Notice that the color is applied to the selected text. Click a blank area of the slide to deselect the text and compare your screen with Figure 2.26.

Figure 2.26

4 ▸ Display **Slide 5**, and then select the title. On the **Home tab**, click the **Font Color arrow** [A▾]. Under **Recent Colors**, notice that the color you selected with the eyedropper displays. Point to the color to display the ScreenTip—*Dark Blue*. Click **Dark Blue** to apply the color to the selection.

After a color has been selected with the eyedropper, it remains available in the presentation each time the color gallery is displayed. When you use the eyedropper in this manner, you can consistently apply the same color throughout your presentation.

5 ▸ **Save** 🖫 your presentation.

Activity 2.16 | Applying Shape Styles

3.4.6

The default style of the inserted shapes can easily be changed. For example, in this presentation, the octagon shape is blue, but changing it to red will make it stand out and look like a Stop sign.

1 Display **Slide 3**, and then select the **arrow shape**. On the **Drawing Tools Format tab**, in the **Shape Styles group**, click **More** ⬇ to display the **Shape Styles** gallery. Under **Theme Styles**, in the last row, click the second style.

2 Click anywhere in the text *If Safety is Questionable* to select the text box. On the **Drawing Tools Format tab**, in the **Shape Styles group**, click **More** ⬇.

3 Under **Theme Styles**, in the last row, click the fifth style.

4 Select the **octagon shape**, and then apply the same style you applied to the text box.

5 **Save** 💾 your presentation and then compare your screen with Figure 2.27.

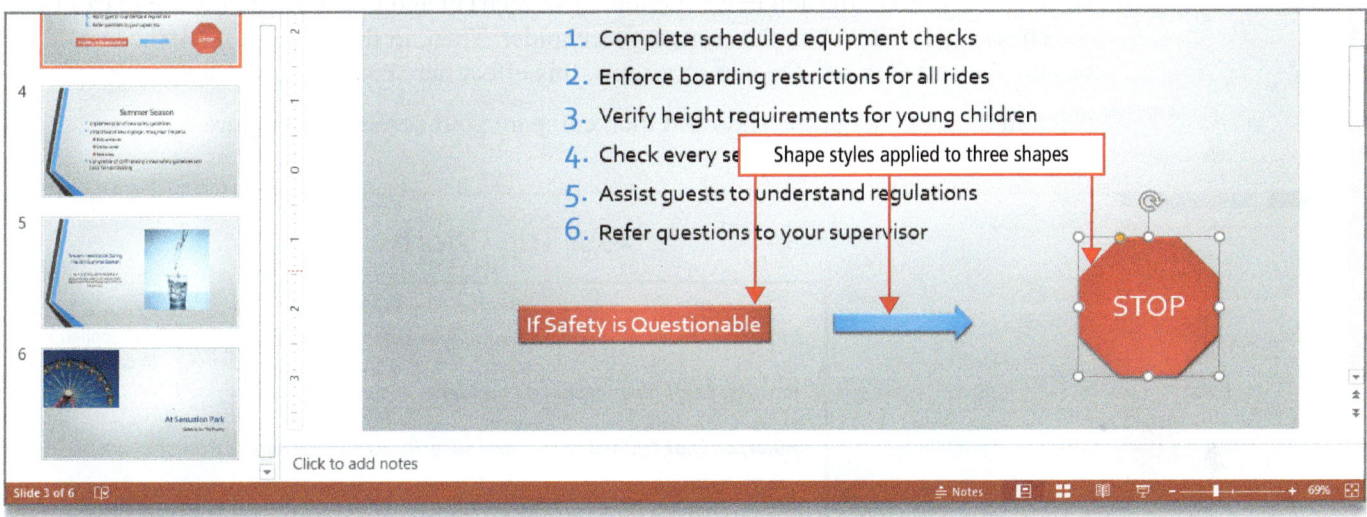

Figure 2.27

Activity 2.17 | Applying Shape and Picture Effects

3.3.2, 3.4.5

1 Display **Slide 1**, and then select the picture. On the **Picture Tools Format tab**, in the **Picture Styles group**, click **Picture Effects**.

A list of effects that you can apply to pictures displays. These effects can also be applied to shapes and text boxes.

2 Point to **Soft Edges**, and then in the **Soft Edges** gallery, point to each style to view its effect on the picture. Click the last **Soft Edges** effect—**50 Point**, and then compare your screen with Figure 2.28.

The soft edges effect softens and blurs the outer edge of the picture so that it blends into the slide background.

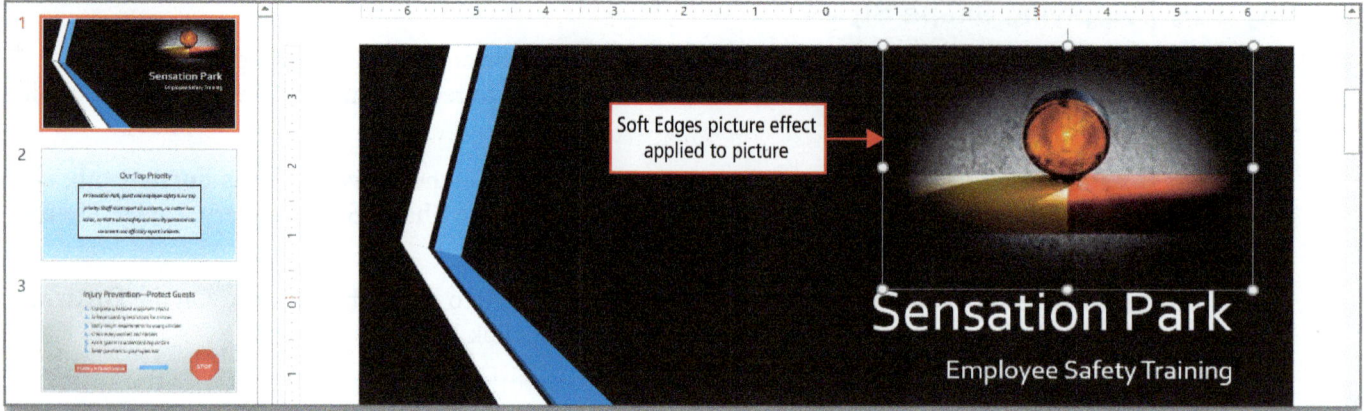

Figure 2.28

3 Display **Slide 2**, and then select the light blue content placeholder. On the **Drawing Tools Format tab**, in the **Shape Styles group**, click **Shape Effects**. Point to **Bevel** to display the **Bevel** gallery. Point to each bevel to view its ScreenTip and to use Live Preview to examine the effect of each bevel on the content placeholder. Then, in the last row, click the last bevel—**Round Convex**. On some systems, this effect may be called Art Deco.

4 Click in a blank area of the slide and then compare your screen with Figure 2.29.

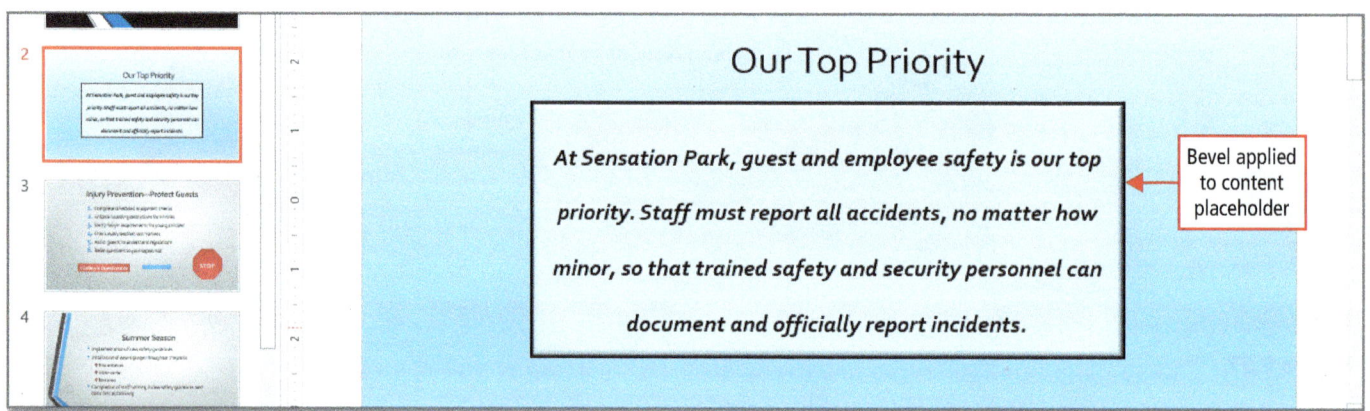

Figure 2.29

5 Display **Slide 5**, and then select the picture. On the **Picture Tools Format tab**, in the **Picture Styles group**, click **Picture Effects**, and then point to **Glow**.

6 Point to several of the effects to view the effect on the picture, and then under **Glow Variations**, in the second row, click the first glow effect—**Glow: 8 point; Blue, Accent color 1**.

The glow effect applies a colored, softly blurred outline to the selected object.

7 **Save** 🖫 your presentation.

Activity 2.18 | Duplicating Objects

1 Display **Slide 6**, and then select the picture.

2 Press and hold down Ctrl, and then press D one time. Release Ctrl.

Ctrl + D is the keyboard shortcut to duplicate an object. A duplicate of the picture overlaps the original picture and the duplicated image is selected.

3 ▶ Compare your screen with Figure 2.30. **Save** 🔲 your presentation.

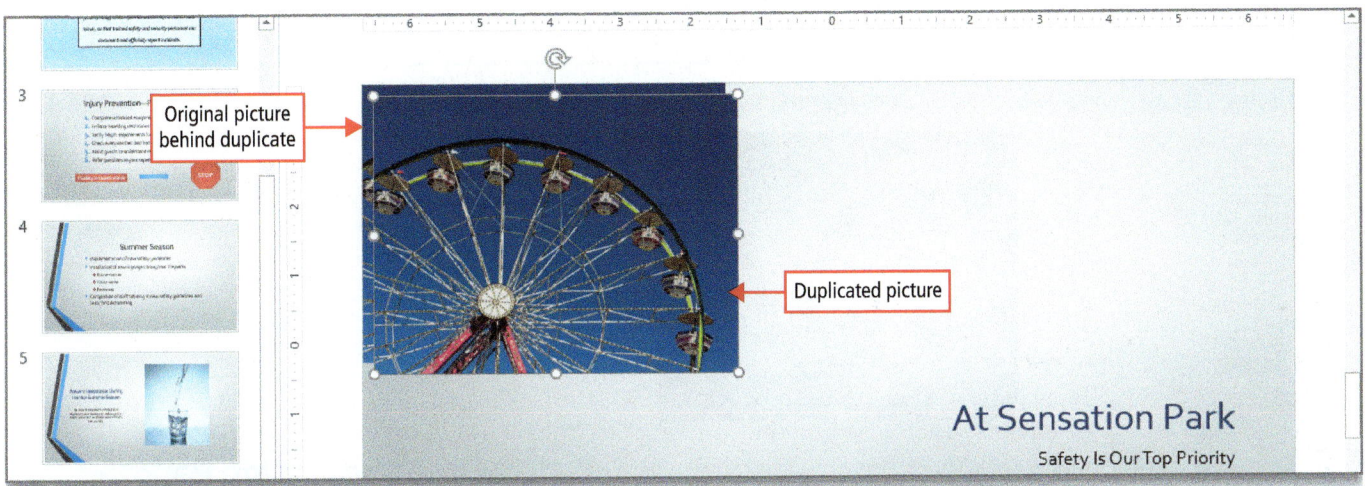

Figure 2.30

Activity 2.19 | Aligning and Distributing Objects Relative to the Slide

You can select multiple slide objects, and then use ribbon commands to align and distribute the objects precisely.

MOS
3.5.2

1 ▶ With **Slide 6** displayed, if necessary click the image in the upper left corner of the slide to select it. Hold down Shift and then click the second image so that both images are selected. Release the Shift key, and then compare your slide with Figure 2.31.

🔄 **ANOTHER WAY**   Position the pointer in the gray area of the Slide pane just outside the upper left corner of the slide to display the ⬚ pointer. Drag down and to the right to draw a transparent, gray, selection rectangle that encloses both pictures.

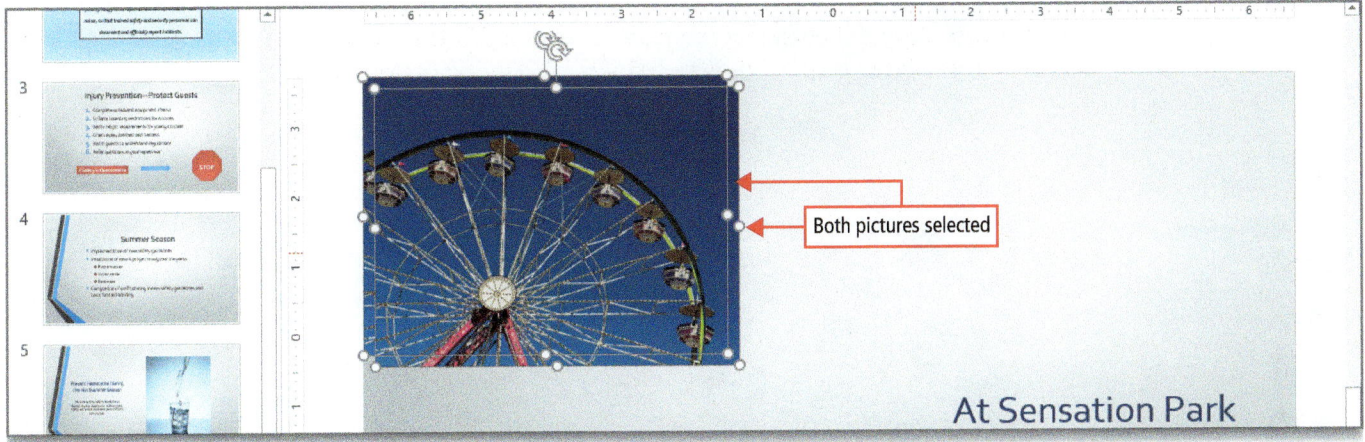

Figure 2.31

2 On the **Picture Tools Format tab**, in the **Arrange group**, click **Align** 📄. At the bottom of the menu, click **Align to Slide** to activate this setting. Click **Align** 📄 again, click **Align Left**, and then compare your screen with Figure 2.32.

The *Align to Slide* setting tells PowerPoint to align each selected object with the slide, rather than with each other. In combination with the Align Left option, this aligns the left edge of each picture with the left edge of the slide.

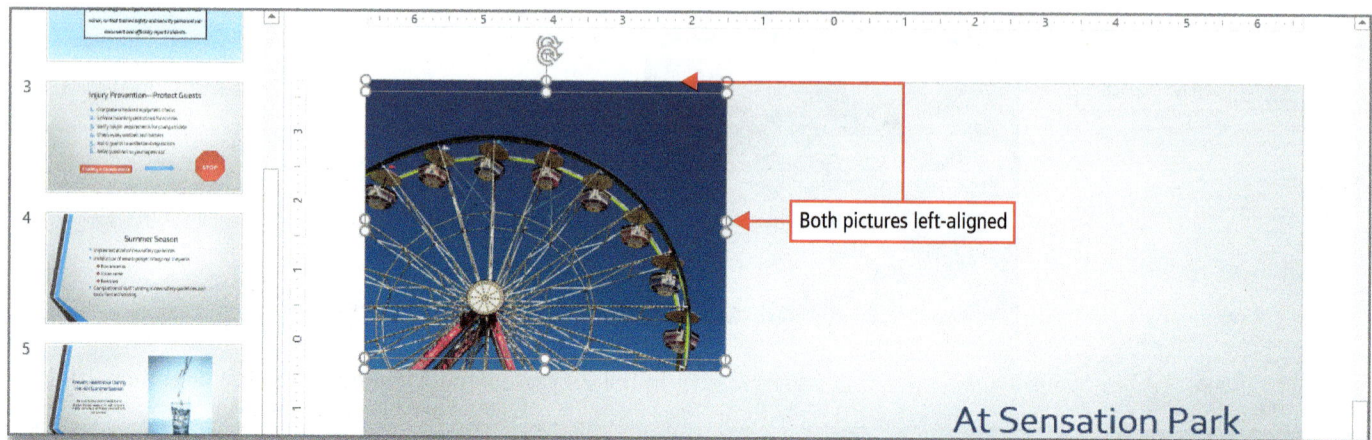

Figure 2.32

3 With both pictures still selected, on the **Picture Tools Format tab**, in the **Arrange group**, click **Align** 📄, and then click **Distribute Vertically**.

The pictures are distributed evenly down the left edge of the slide between the top and bottom edges of the slide.

4 With both pictures selected, on the **Picture Tools Format tab**, in the **Picture Styles group**, click **Picture Effects**. Point to **Soft Edges**, use the ScreenTips to locate and then click **50 Point** to apply the picture effect to both images. Click in a blank area of the slide and compare your screen with Figure 2.33.

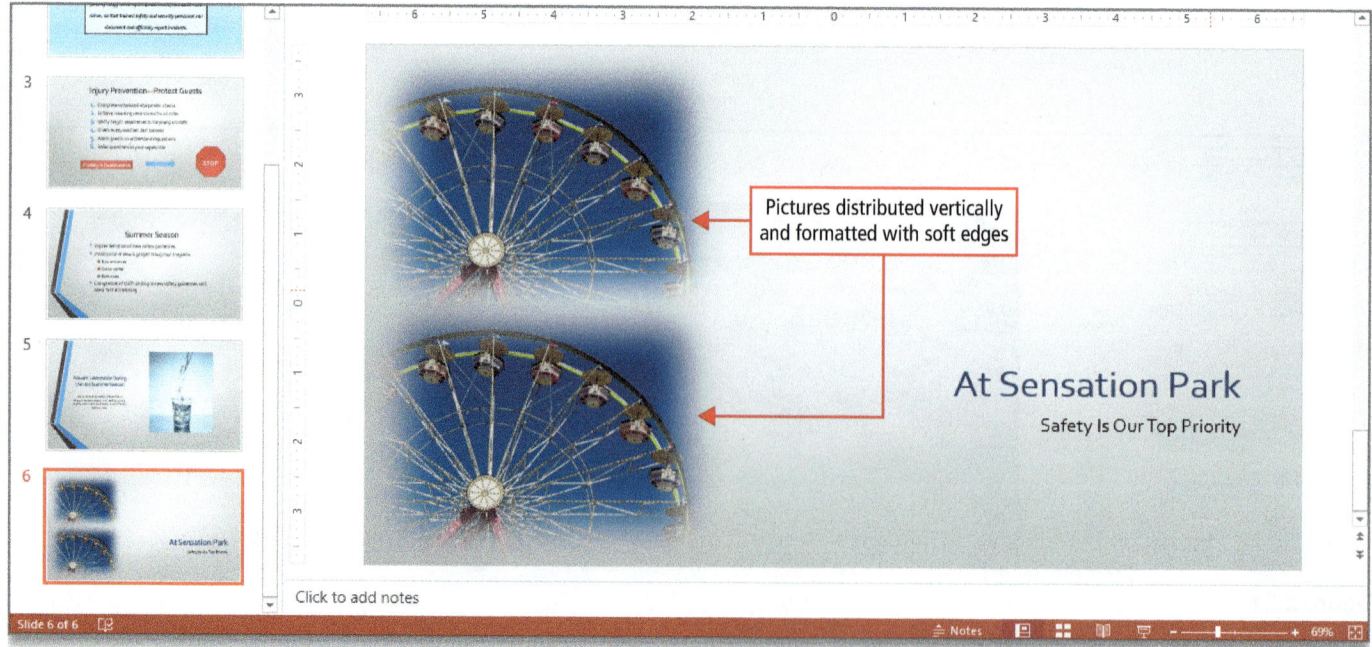

Figure 2.33

5 Save the presentation.

Activity 2.20 | Aligning and Distributing Objects Relative to Each Other

MOS
3.5.2

Using the commands in the Arrange group is a more precise way of aligning objects than positioning the objects manually.

1 Display **Slide 3**, hold down Shift, and then at the bottom of the slide, click the **text box**, the **arrow**, and the **octagon** to select all three objects. Release Shift.

> **BY TOUCH** Tap the text box, hold down Shift, and then tap the arrow and the octagon.

2 With the three objects selected, on the **Drawing Tools Format tab**, in the **Arrange group**, click **Align**. Click **Align Selected Objects**.

The *Align Selected Objects* option will cause the objects that you select to align relative to each other, rather than relative to the edges of the slide.

3 On the **Drawing Tools Format tab**, in the **Arrange group**, click **Align**, and then click **Align Middle**. Click **Align** again, and then click **Distribute Horizontally**.

The midpoint of each object aligns and the three objects are distributed evenly between the left edge of the leftmost object—the text box—and the right edge of the rightmost object—the octagon.

4 Click anywhere on the slide so that none of the objects are selected. Compare your screen with Figure 2.34, and then **Save** the presentation.

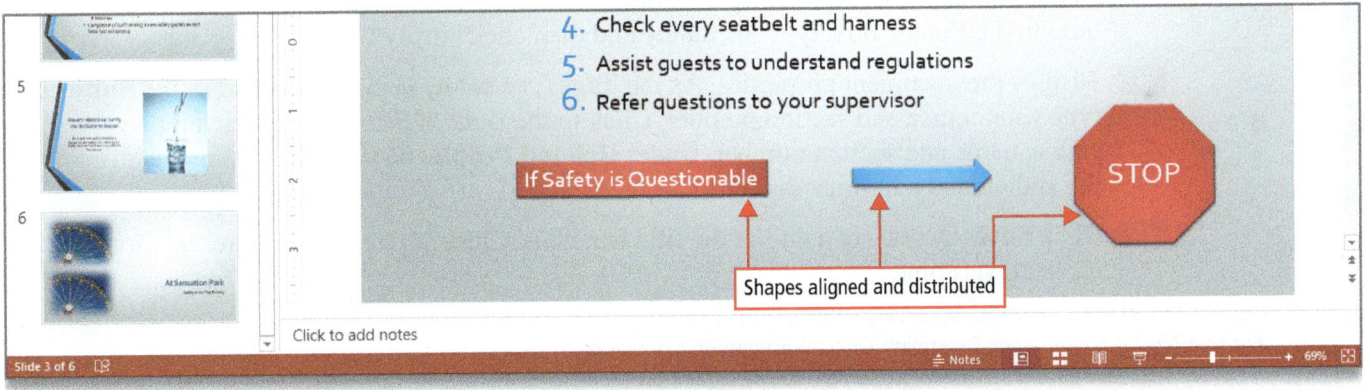

Figure 2.34

Activity 2.21 | Grouping Objects

MOS
3.5.3

You can select multiple objects and group them so that they can be formatted and edited as one object.

1 With **Slide 3** displayed, click the **text box**, hold down Shift, and then click the **arrow** and the **octagon** so that all three objects are selected.

Sizing handles surround each individual object.

2 On the **Drawing Tools Format tab**, in the **Arrange group**, click **Group**, and then click **Group**. Compare your screen with Figure 2.35.

The sizing handles surround all three shapes as one, indicating that the three shapes are grouped into one object. The individual objects are not selected. The grouped object can be formatted, aligned, and moved as one object.

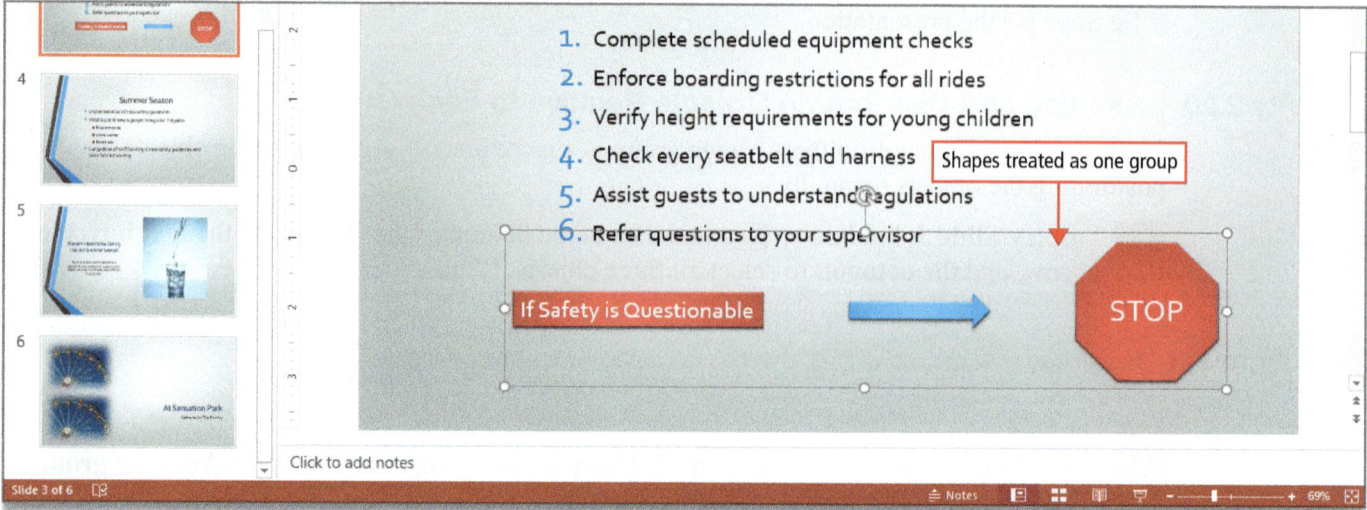

Figure 2.35

3 ▸ On the **Drawing Tools Format tab**, in the **Arrange group**, click **Align**, and then click **Align Center**.

The group is centered horizontally on the slide.

4 ▸ On the **Slide Show tab**, in the **Start Slide Show group**, click **From Beginning**, and then view the slide show. When the black slide displays, press Esc.

5 ▸ On the **Insert tab**, in the **Text group**, click **Header & Footer** to display the **Header and Footer** dialog box. Click the **Notes and Handouts tab**. Under **Include on page**, select the **Date and time** check box, and then select **Update automatically**. Verify the **Header** check box is not selected, and the **Page number** check box is selected. Select the **Footer** check box. In the **Footer** box, type **2A_Safety** and then click **Apply to All**.

6 ▸ Display the document properties. As the **Tags** type **safety presentation** and as the **Subject**, type your course and section number. Click to the right of **Subject**, and then type your course name and section number. Under **Related People**, be sure that your name displays as the author, and edit if necessary.

7 ▸ Click **Save**. On the right end of the title bar, click **Close** ✕ to close the presentation and close PowerPoint.

For Non-MyLab Submissions Determine What Your Instructor Requires
As directed by your instructor, submit your completed PowerPoint file.

8 ▸ In **MyLab IT**, in your **Course Materials**, locate and click the Grader Project **PowerPoint 2A Safety**. In **step 3**, under **Upload Completed Assignment**, click **Choose File**. In the **Open** dialog box, navigate to your **PowerPoint Chapter 2 folder**, and then click your **Student_PowerPoint_2A_Safety** file one time to select it. In the lower right corner of the **Open** dialog box, click **Open**.

The name of your selected file displays above the Upload button.

9 ▸ To submit your file to **MyLab IT** for grading, click **Upload**, wait a moment for a green **Success!** message, and then in **step 4**, click the blue **Submit for Grading** button. Click **Close Assignment** to return to your list of **Course Materials**.

You have completed Project 2A **END**

Objective	Create an Informational Presentation in Google Slides

Activity | Creating an Informational Presentation in Google Slides

In this Activity, you will use Google Slides to create a presentation similar to the one you created in Project 2A.

1 From the desktop, open your browser, navigate to **http://google.com**, and then sign in to your Google account. Click **Google apps** 🔳, and then click **Drive** ▲. Open your **GO! Web Projects** folder—or if necessary, click New to create and then open this folder.

2 In the left pane, click **New**, click **File upload** 🔼, and then in the **Open** dialog box, navigate to your student data files. Select **p02_2A_Google_Slides**. Click **Open**. When the upload is complete and the file name displays in the file list, right-click **p02_2A_Google_Slides**, and then click **Rename**. In the **Rename** dialog box, select and delete the text. Using your own name, as the file name, type **Lastname_Firstname_2A_Google_Slides** and then press Enter. Right-click your file, point to **Open with**, and then click **Google Slides**.

3 Display **Slide 5**. On the **toolbar**, click **Image** 🖼. Click **Search the web**. In the **Search for Google Images** box, type **pouring water** and then press Enter. Select a picture similar to the one that you inserted in Project 2A, and then in the lower left, click **INSERT**. Drag the image to the right and use the sizing handles to position and resize the image so that there is an even amount of space above, below, and to the right of the image. Alternatively, you can insert the picture p02A_Pouring_Water from your student data files.

4 Display **Slide 2**, and then click anywhere in the paragraph. At the right end of the toolbar, if necessary, click More ⋯, and then click **Bulleted list** ☰ to remove the bullet symbol from the paragraph.

5 If necessary, click More. Click **Align** 📑, click **Center** ☰, and then select the entire paragraph. Change the **Font size** to **24** and apply **Bold**.

6 With **Slide 2** displayed and the paragraph selected, on the **toolbar**, click **Fill color** 🎨, and then in the eighth column, select the fifth color—**light blue 1**.

7 Click **Border color** ✏, and then, in the eighth column, select the second color—**blue**. Click **Border weight** ☰, and then click **4px**. Click a blank area of the slide to deselect the text box, and then compare your screen with Figure A.

8 Display **Slide 3**, and then click in the bulleted list. If necessary, click More ⋯, and then click **Numbered list** ☰ to apply numbers to all of the bullet points. It is not necessary to select the text; bullets and numbering are applied to all of the bullet points in a content placeholder.

9 With **Slide 3** displayed, on the **toolbar**, click **Text box** 🔡 to insert a text box in your slide. Click below the content placeholder and drag to create the textbox near the bottom of the slide—the exact size and placement need not be precise.

»» GO! With Google

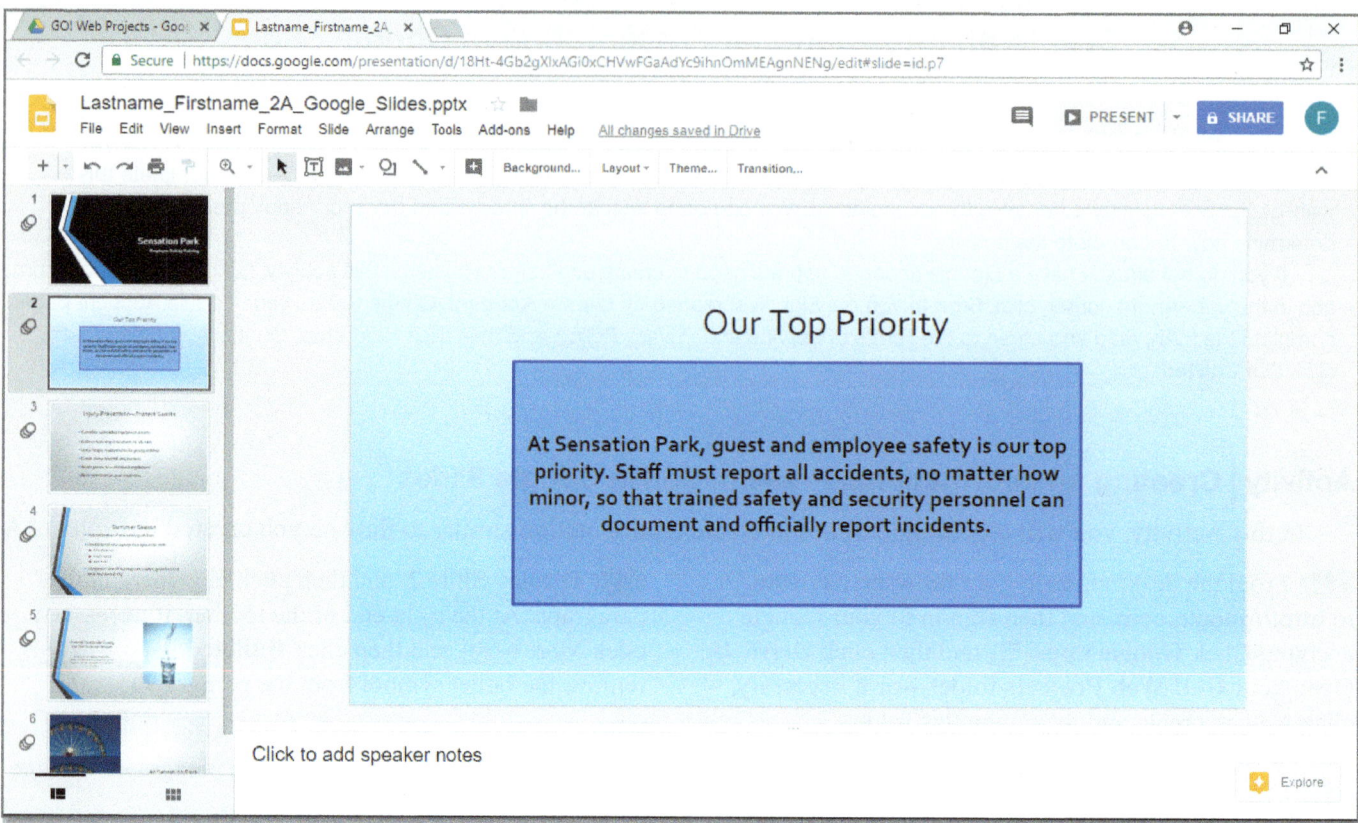

Figure A

10 With the insertion point blinking in the text box, type **If Safety is Questionable** and then on the **toolbar**, click **Fill color** 🖌️. In the first column, click the fourth color—**light red berry 2**. If necessary, drag the sizing handles of the textbox to shorten the text box to fit the text. Click outside the text box to deselect it.

11 On the **toolbar**, click **Shape** 🔲, point to **Arrows**, and then click **Right Arrow**. Position the mouse pointer to the right of the text box and click to insert an arrow in the middle of your slide. Drag the arrow so that it is aligned horizontally with the text box—a red guide will display to assist you—and its left edge aligns with the *y* in *your*. and then on the **toolbar**, click **Fill color** 🖌️. In the eighth column, click the second color—**blue**.

12 On the **toolbar**, click **Shape** 🔲, point to **Shapes**, and then click **Octagon**. Position the mouse pointer to the right of the arrow, and then click to insert an octagon on your slide. Drag the octagon so that its center sizing handle aligns with the arrow point and its left edge aligns with the *s* in *regulations*, and then on the **toolbar**, click **Fill color** 🖌️. In the first column, click the fourth color— **light red berry 2**.

13 Click in the octagon. Type **STOP**, select the text, change the **Font size** to 18, **Align Center**, and then click in a blank area of the slide. Compare your screen with Figure B and make adjustments to the position of the shapes as necessary.

14 Your presentation will be saved automatically. If you are instructed to submit your file, click the File menu, point to Download, and then click PDF or PowerPoint as directed by your instructor. The file will download to your default download folder as determined by your browser settings. Sign out of your Google account.

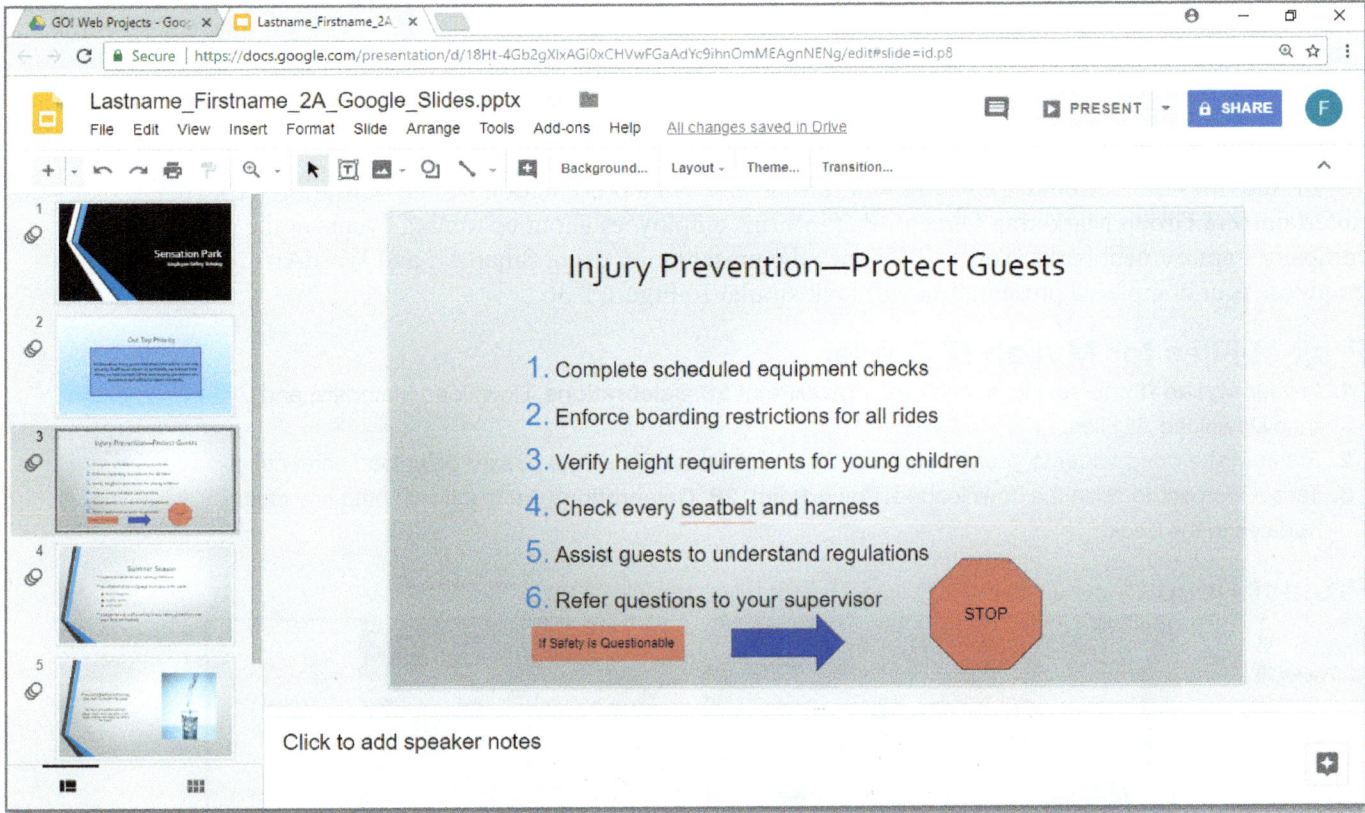

Figure B

Project Activities

In Activities 2.22 through 2.35, you will format slides in a presentation for the Sensation Park Entertainment Group Marketing Director that informs employees about upcoming events at the company's amusement parks. You will enhance the presentation using SmartArt and WordArt graphics. Your completed presentation will look similar to Figure 2.36.

Project Files for MyLab IT Grader

1. In your **MyLab IT** course, locate and click **PowerPoint 2B Celebrations**, Download Materials, and then Download All Files.
2. Extract the zipped folder to your PowerPoint Chapter 2 folder. Close the Grader download screens.
3. Take a moment to open the downloaded **PowerPoint_2B_Celebrations_Instructions**; note any recent updates to the book.

Project Results

GO! Project 2B
Where We're Going

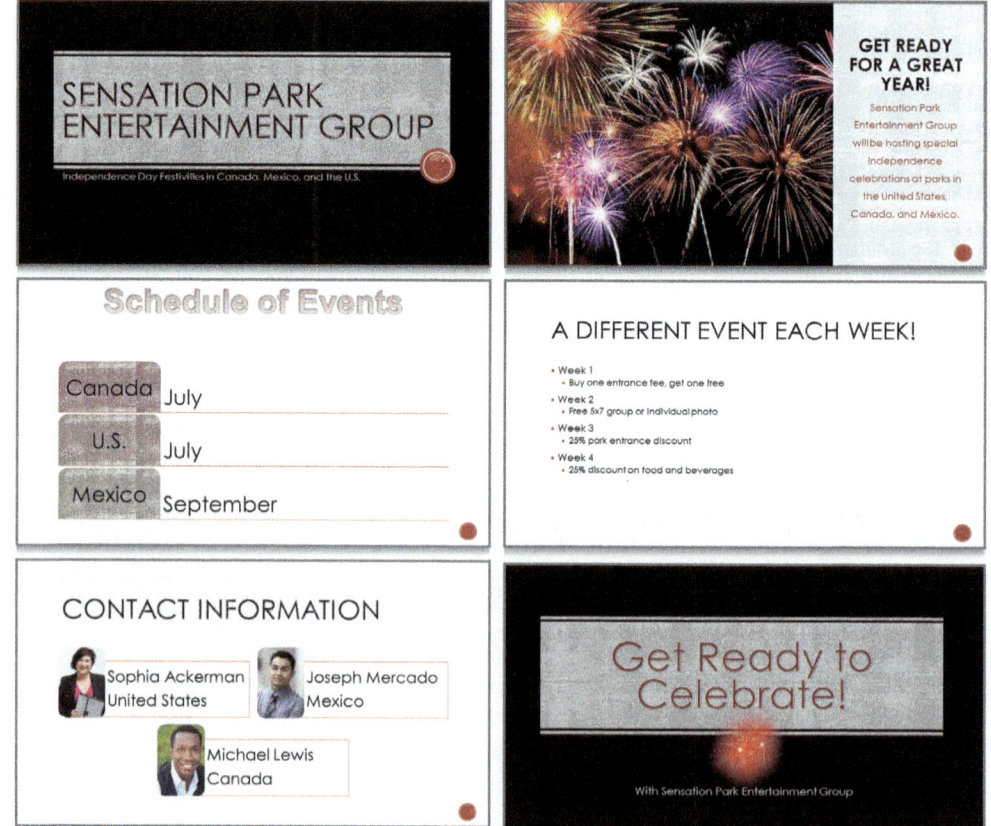

Figure 2.36 Project 2B Celebrations

For Non-MyLab Submissions
For Project 2B, you will need:
p02B_Canada_Contact
p02B_Celebrations
p02B_Mexico_Contact
p02B_US_Contact

In your PowerPoint Chapter 2 folder, save your presentation as:
Lastname_Firstname_2B_Celebrations

After you have named and saved your presentation, on the next page, begin with Step 2.

Objective 5   Remove Picture Backgrounds and Insert WordArt

ALERT   Because Office 365 is a cloud-based subscription service that receives continuous updates, you may encounter some variations in what appears on your screen and what is shown in this instruction. Microsoft Office 365 is fully installed on your PC or Mac; no internet access is necessary to create or edit documents. When you *are* connected to the internet, you will receive monthly upgrades and new features, so you always have the latest versions of Office apps as soon as they are available. Your subscription gives you continuous free access to the latest innovations and refinements.

GO! Learn How
Video P2-5

To avoid the boxy look that results when you insert an image into a presentation, use the ***Background Removal*** command, which removes unwanted portions of a picture so that the picture does not appear as a self-contained rectangle. This enables you to flow a picture into the content of the presentation.

WordArt is a gallery of text styles with which you can create decorative effects, such as shadowed or mirrored text. You can choose from the gallery of WordArt styles to insert a new WordArt object or you can customize existing text by applying WordArt formatting.

Activity 2.22 │ Removing the Background from a Picture and Applying Soft Edge Options

3.3.2

1 Navigate to your **PowerPoint Chapter 2 folder**, and then double-click the downloaded PowerPoint file that displays your name—**Student_PowerPoint_2B_Celebrations**. In your presentation, if necessary, at the top click **Enable Editing**.

2 Display **Slide 6**. Click the fireworks picture to select it, and then on the **Picture Tools Format tab**, in the **Adjust group**, click **Remove Background**. Compare your screen with Figure 2.37.

PowerPoint determines what portion of the picture is the foreground—the portion to keep—and which portion is the background—the portion to remove. The background is overlaid in magenta, leaving the remaining portion of the picture as it will look when the background removal is complete. A rectangular selection area displays that can be moved and sized to select additional areas of the picture. The Background Removal options display in the Refine group on the ribbon.

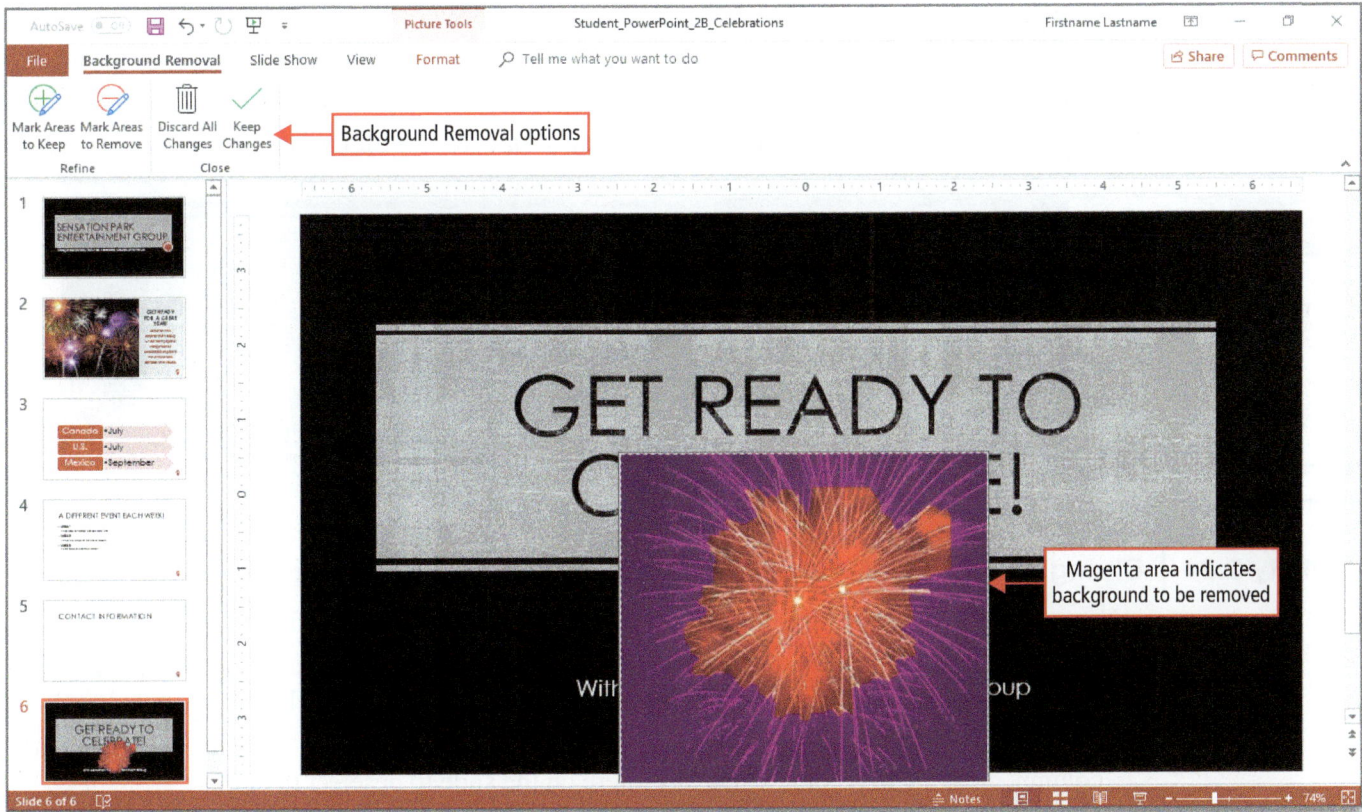

Figure 2.37

3 On the **Background Removal tab**, in the **Close group**, click **Keep Changes** to remove the background.

4 With the picture selected, on the **Picture Tools Format tab**, in the **Picture Styles group**, click **Picture Effects**, point to **Soft Edges**, and then click **50 Point**. **Save** your presentation, and then compare your slide with Figure 2.38.

Figure 2.38

Activity 2.23 | Applying WordArt Styles to Existing Text

MOS
3.1.1

1 On **Slide 6**, click anywhere in the word *Get* to activate the title placeholder, and then select the title—*Get Ready to Celebrate!* Click the **Drawing Tools Format tab**, and then in the **WordArt Styles group**, click **More** to display the WordArt gallery.

2 Point to several WordArt styles to view the change to the slide title. In the first row, click the first style. Click anywhere on the slide outside the title placeholder.

3 **Save** your presentation, and then compare your screen with Figure 2.39.

Figure 2.39

Activity 2.24 | Changing the Text Fill and Text Outline Colors of a WordArt Object

You can modify a WordArt object by changing the colors of the text fill and text outline.

1 On **Slide 6**, select the title. On the **Drawing Tools Format tab**, in the **WordArt Styles group**, click **Text Fill**. Under **Theme Colors**, in the sixth column, click the fifth color.

2 With the text still selected, in the **WordArt Styles group**, click **Text Outline**. In the second column, click the first color. Click anywhere on the slide to deselect the title.

3 **Save** your presentation, and then compare your screen with Figure 2.40.

WordArt text fill and text outline colors changed

Figure 2.40

Activity 2.25 | Inserting and Aligning a WordArt Object

In addition to formatting existing text using WordArt, you can insert a new WordArt object anywhere on a slide.

1 Display **Slide 3**. On the **Insert tab**, in the **Text group**, click **WordArt**. In the gallery, in the second row, click the third WordArt style.

In the center of your slide, a WordArt placeholder displays *Your text here*. Text that you type will replace this text and the placeholder will expand to accommodate the text. The WordArt is surrounded by sizing handles with which you can adjust its size.

2 Type **Schedule of Events** to replace the WordArt placeholder text. Compare your screen with Figure 2.41.

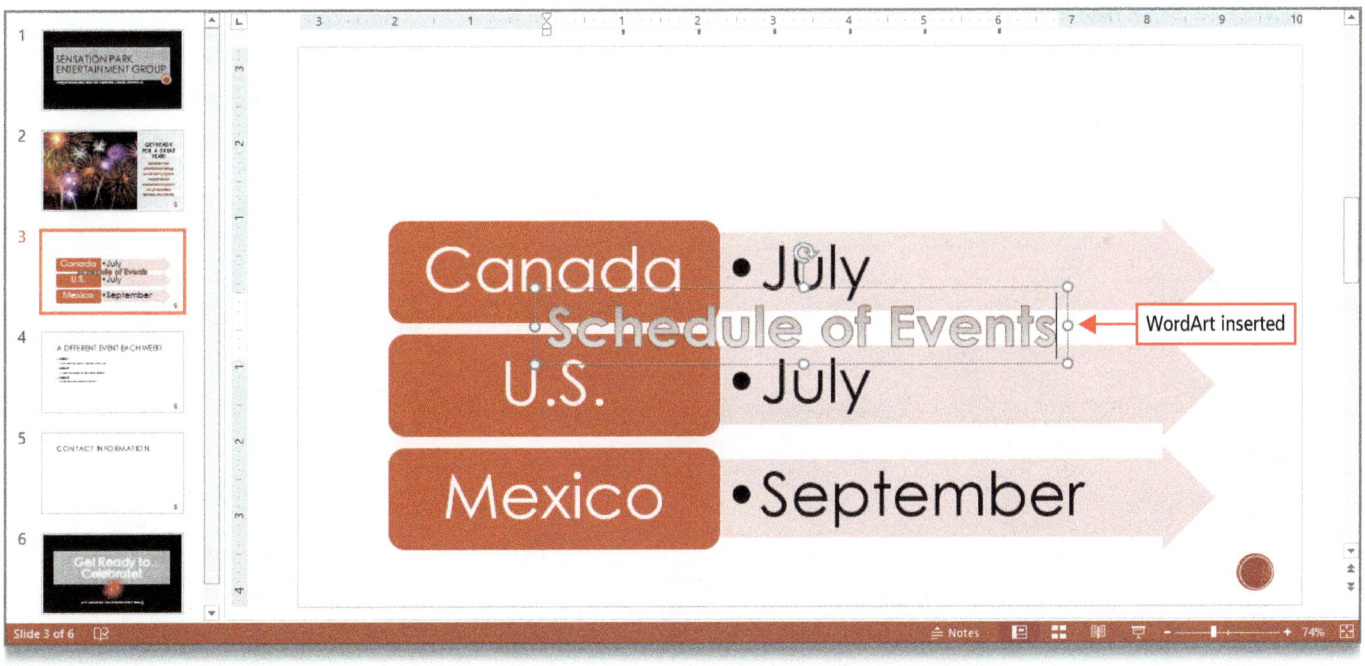

WordArt inserted

Figure 2.41

3 With the WordArt selected, on the **Drawing Tools Format tab**, in the **Arrange group**, click **Align** 🖺, and then click **Align Top** to move the WordArt to the top of the slide.

4 Click in a blank area of the slide, and then compare your screen with Figure 2.42.

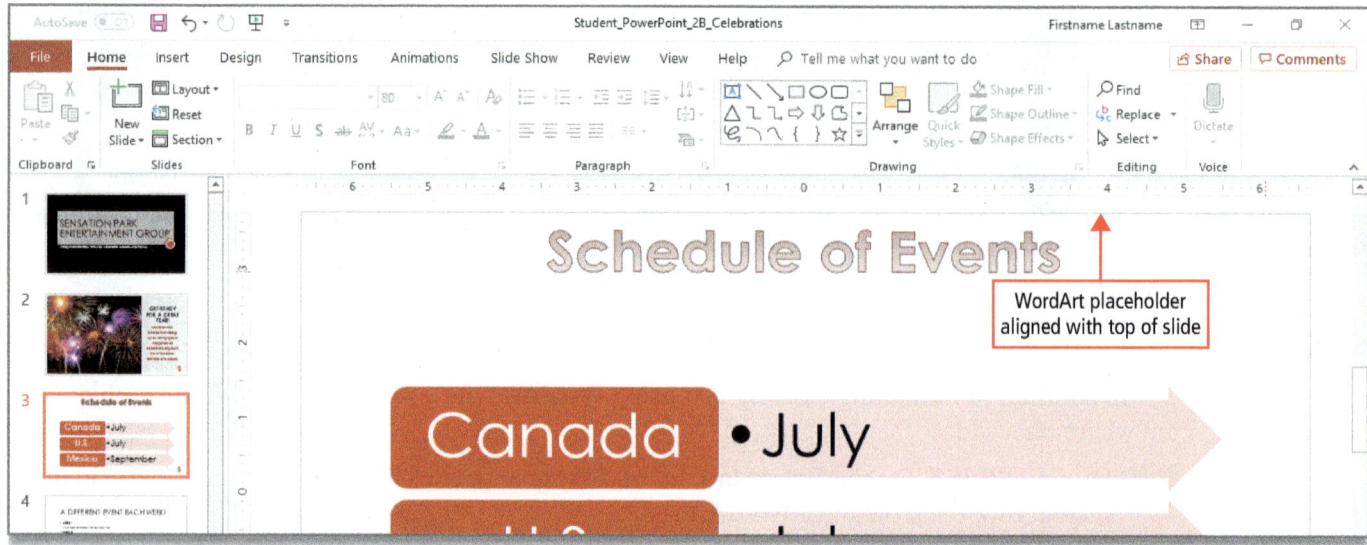

Figure 2.42

> **5** Save 💾 your presentation.

Activity 2.26 | Adding Text Effects to a WordArt

Text effects are formats applied to text that include shadows, reflections, glows, bevels, and 3-D rotations.

> **1** With **Slide 3** displayed, select the **WordArt** text. Change the **Font** to **Arial** and the **Font Size** to **66**.

> **2** On the **Drawing Tools Format tab**, in the **WordArt Styles group**, click **Text Effects**. Point to **Shadow**, and then compare your screen with Figure 2.43.

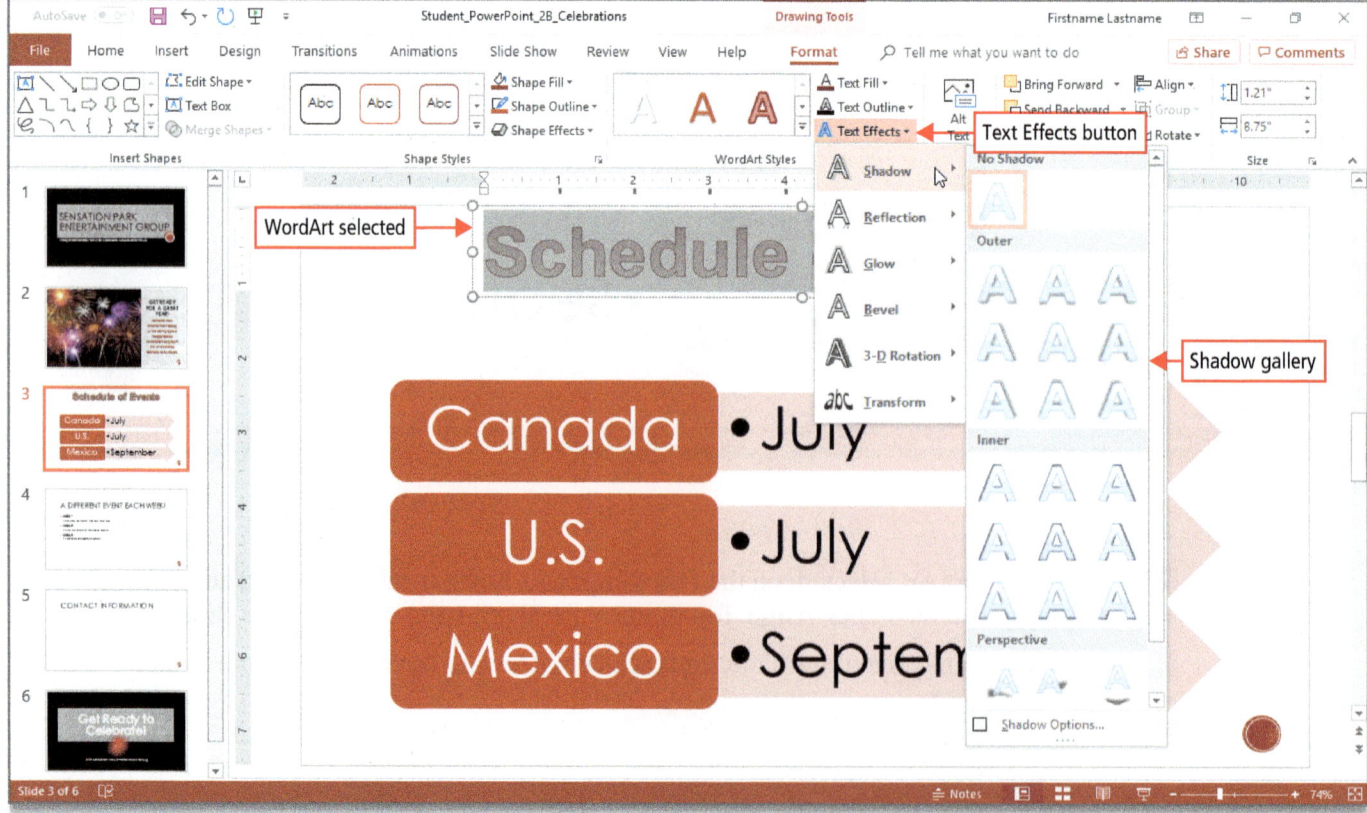

Figure 2.43

3 Under **Outer**, click the last style—**Offset: Top Left**. Click in a blank area of the slide, and then compare your screen with Figure 2.44.

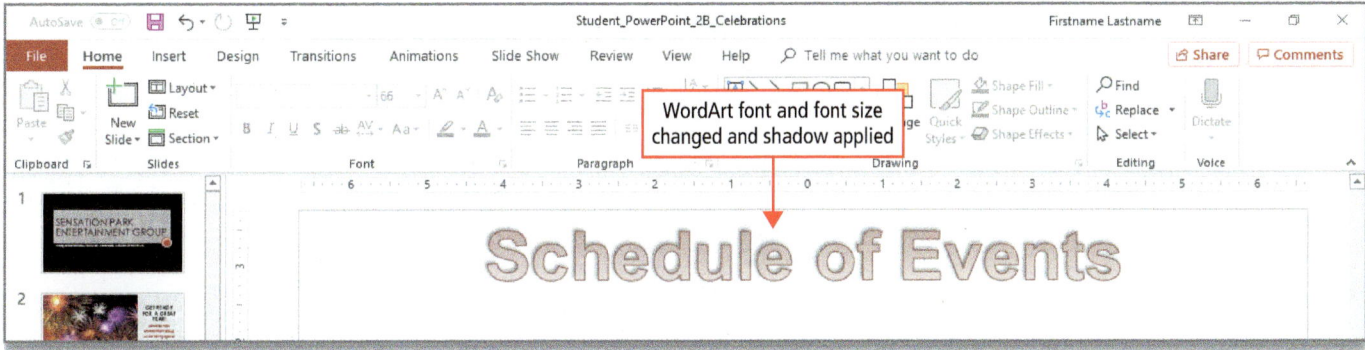

Figure 2.44

4 **Save** 🖫 your presentation.

Objective 6 | Create and Format a SmartArt Graphic

GO! Learn How
Video P2-6

A *SmartArt graphic* is a visual representation of information that you create by choosing from among various layouts to communicate your message or ideas effectively. SmartArt graphics can illustrate processes, hierarchies, cycles, lists, and relationships. You can include text and pictures in a SmartArt graphic, and you can apply colors, effects, and styles that coordinate with the presentation theme.

Activity 2.27 | Creating a SmartArt Graphic from Bulleted Points

MOS
4.3.2

You can convert an existing bulleted list into a SmartArt graphic. When you create a SmartArt graphic, consider the message that you are trying to convey, and then choose an appropriate layout. The table in Figure 2.45 describes types of SmartArt layouts and suggested purposes.

Microsoft PowerPoint SmartArt Graphic Types		
Graphic Type	**Example Layout**	**Purpose of Graphic**
List		Shows non-sequential information
Process		Shows steps in a process or timeline
Cycle		Shows a continual process

Microsoft PowerPoint SmartArt Graphic Types		
Graphic Type	**Example Layout**	**Purpose of Graphic**
Hierarchy	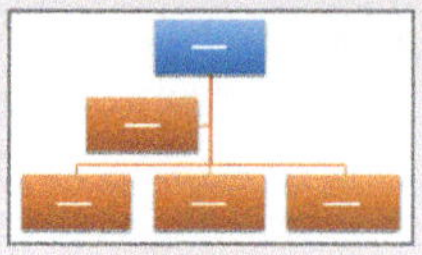	Shows a decision tree or displays an organization chart
Relationship		Illustrates connections
Matrix		Shows how parts relate to a whole
Pyramid	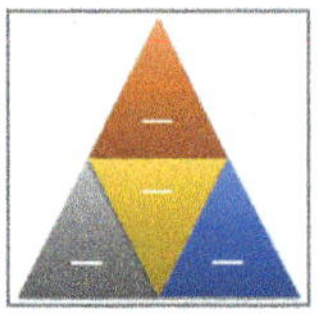	Shows proportional relationships with the largest component on the top or bottom
Picture	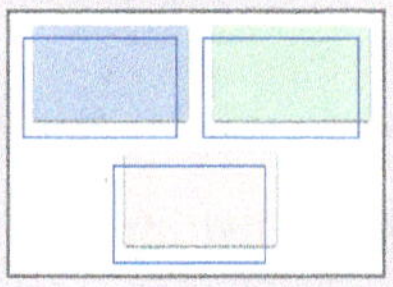	Includes pictures in the layout to communicate messages and ideas
Office.com		Additional layouts available from Office.com

Figure 2.45

1 Display **Slide 4**, and then click anywhere in the bulleted list in the content placeholder. On the **Home tab**, in the **Paragraph group**, click **Convert to SmartArt Graphic** 📊. Below the gallery, click **More SmartArt Graphics**.

> Three sections comprise the Choose a SmartArt Graphic dialog box. The left section lists the SmartArt graphic types. The center section displays the SmartArt layouts according to type. The third section displays the selected SmartArt graphic, its name, and a description of its purpose.

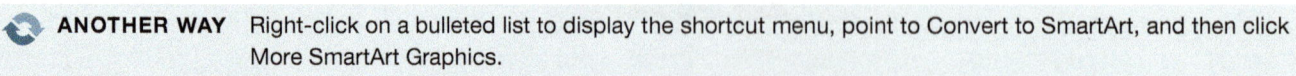 **ANOTHER WAY** Right-click on a bulleted list to display the shortcut menu, point to Convert to SmartArt, and then click More SmartArt Graphics.

2 On the left side of the **Choose a SmartArt Graphic** dialog box, click **List**. Use the ScreenTips to locate and then click **Tab List**. Compare your screen with Figure 2.46.

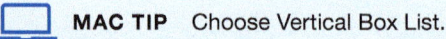 **MAC TIP** Choose Vertical Box List.

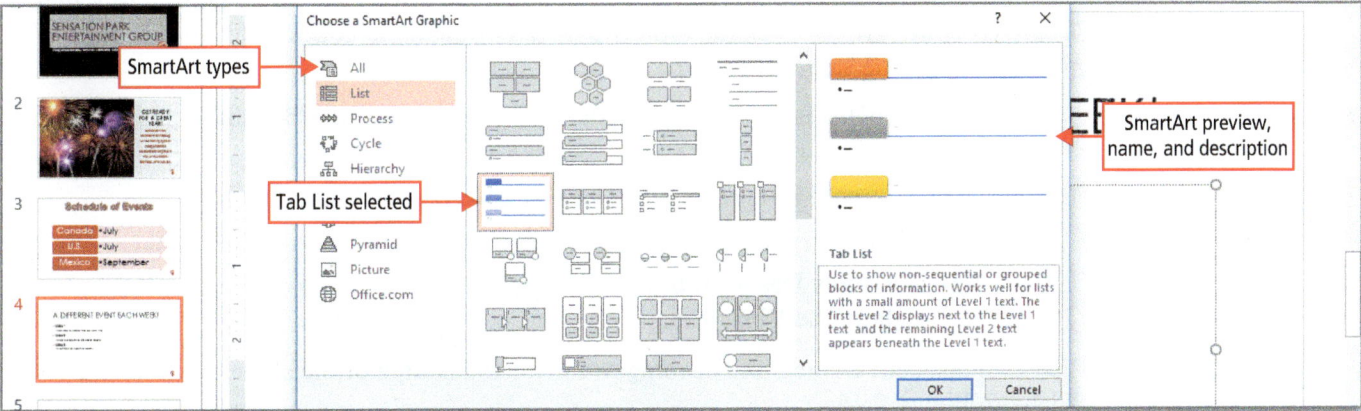

Figure 2.46

3 In the **Choose a SmartArt Graphic** dialog box, click **OK**. If necessary, close the Text pane on the left. **Save** 🖫 your presentation, and then compare your screen with Figure 2.47.

It is not necessary to select all of the text in the list. By clicking in the list, PowerPoint converts all of the bullet points to the selected SmartArt graphic. On the ribbon, the SmartArt contextual tools display two tabs—Design and Format. The thick border surrounding the SmartArt graphic indicates that it is selected and displays the area that the object will cover on the slide.

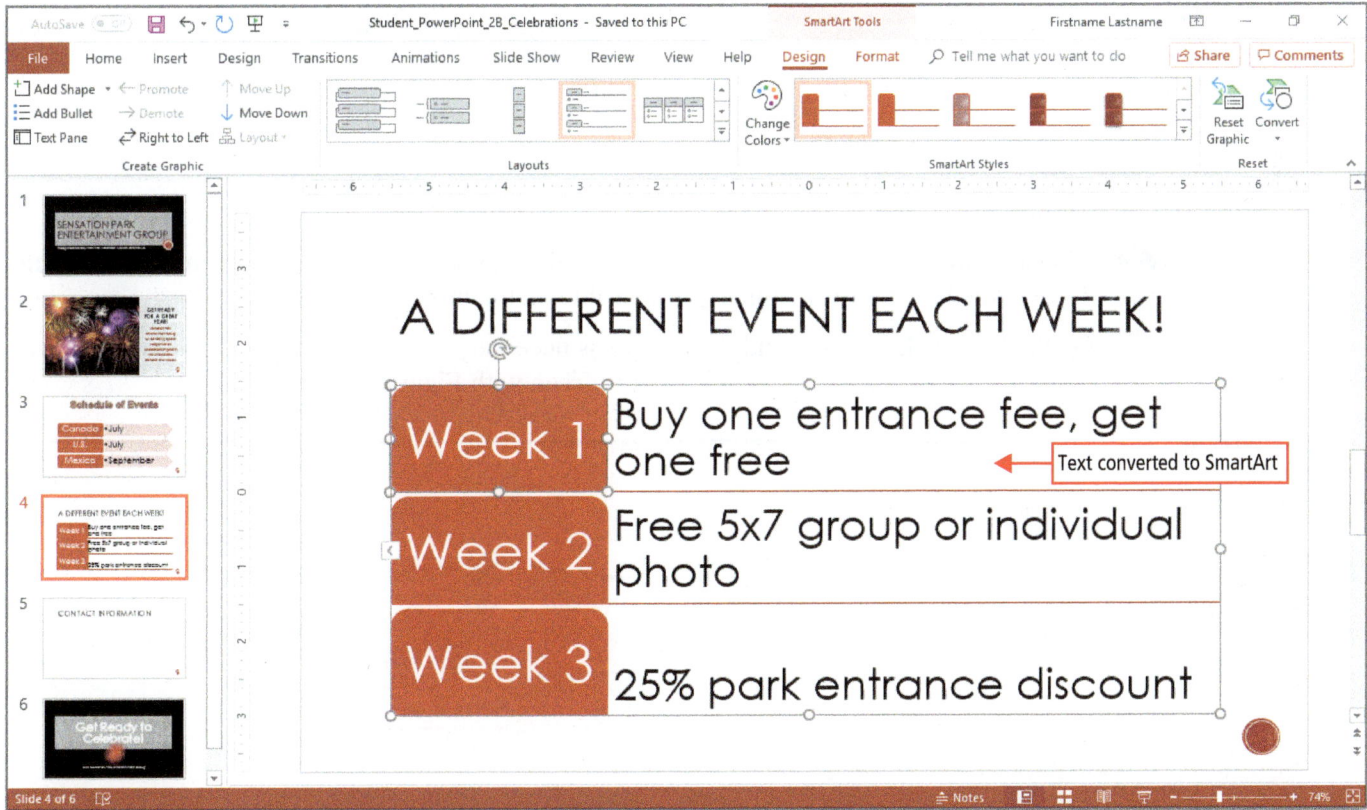

Figure 2.47

Activity 2.28 | Adding Shapes in a SmartArt Graphic

4.3.3

If a SmartArt graphic does not have enough shapes to illustrate a concept or display the relationships, you can add more shapes.

1 Click in the shape that contains the text *Week 3*. On the **SmartArt Tools Design tab**, in the **Create Graphic group**, click the **Add Shape arrow**, and then click **Add Shape After** to insert a shape at the same level. Type **Week 4**

The text in each of the SmartArt shapes resizes to accommodate the added shape.

> **ANOTHER WAY** Right-click the shape, point to Add Shape, and then click Add Shape After.

2 On the **SmartArt Tools Design tab**, in the **Create Graphic group**, click **Add Bullet** to add a bullet to the right of the *Week 4* shape.

3 Type **25% discount on food and beverages** Click a blank area of the slide and compare your slide with Figure 2.48.

Figure 2.48

4 **Save** 🖫 your presentation.

Activity 2.29 | Inserting a SmartArt Graphic Using a Content Layout

4.3.1

1 Display **Slide 5**. In the center of the content placeholder, click **Insert a SmartArt Graphic** 📊 to open the **Choose a SmartArt Graphic** dialog box.

2 On the left, click **Picture**, and then scroll as necessary and use the ScreenTips to locate, and then click **Picture Strips**. Compare your screen with Figure 2.49.

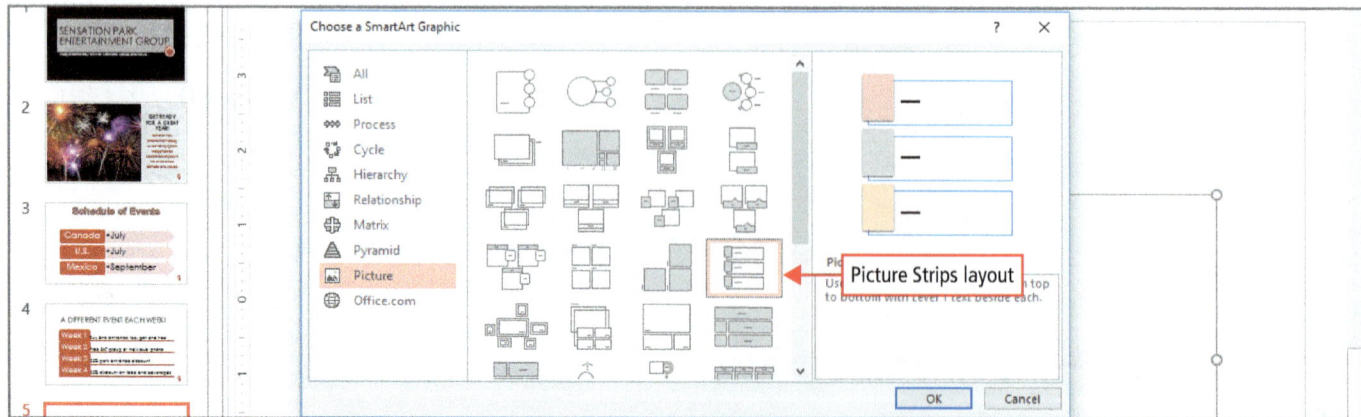

Figure 2.49

3 ▶ Click **OK** to insert the SmartArt graphic.

You can type text directly into the shapes or you can type text in the Text Pane, which may display to the left of your SmartArt graphic. You can toggle the Text Pane display by clicking the Text Pane tab—the small left arrow on the left side of the SmartArt graphic border—or by clicking the Text Pane button in the Create Graphic group.

Activity 2.30 | Inserting Pictures and Text in a SmartArt Graphic

1 ▶ In the SmartArt graphic, in the upper left text rectangle shape, type **Sophia Ackerman** and then press Enter. Type **United States** and then click in the text rectangle on the right. Type **Joseph Mercado** and then press Enter. Type **Mexico** and then click in the lower text rectangle. Type **Michael Lewis** and then press Enter. Type **Canada**

2 ▶ In the top left picture placeholder, click **Insert Picture** 🖼. In the **Insert Pictures** dialog box, click **From a file**. Navigate to your student data files, click **p02B_US_Contact**, and then click **Insert** to insert the picture.

3 ▶ Using the technique you just practiced, in the right picture placeholder, insert **p02B_Mexico_Contact**. In the lower picture placeholder, insert **p02B_Canada_Contact**.

4 ▶ **Save** 💾 your presentation, and then compare your screen with Figure 2.50.

Figure 2.50

Activity 2.31 | Changing the Size and Shape of SmartArt Elements

You can select individual or groups of shapes in a SmartArt graphic and make them larger or smaller, and you can change selected shapes to another type of shape.

1 ▶ With **Slide 5** displayed, click the picture of *Sophia Ackerman*. Hold down Shift, and then click the pictures of *Joseph Mercado* and *Michael Lewis* so that all three pictures are selected. Release Shift.

2 ▶ On the **SmartArt Tools Format tab**, in the **Shapes group**, click **Larger** two times to increase the size of the three pictures.

3 ▶ With the three pictures selected, on the **SmartArt Tools Format tab**, in the **Shapes group**, click **Change Shape**. Under **Rectangles**, click the second shape—**Rectangle: Rounded Corners**.

4 ▶ Click a blank area of the slide, and then compare your screen with Figure 2.51.

Figure 2.51

> **5** ▶ **Save** 🖫 your presentation.

Activity 2.32 | Changing the SmartArt Layout

> **1** ▶ Display **Slide 3**, and then click anywhere in the SmartArt graphic. On the **SmartArt Tools Design tab**, in the **Layouts group**, click **More** ▾, and then click **More Layouts**. In the **Choose a SmartArt Graphic** dialog box, click **List**. Scroll up or down as necessary to locate and then click **Vertical Block List**. Compare your screen with Figure 2.52.

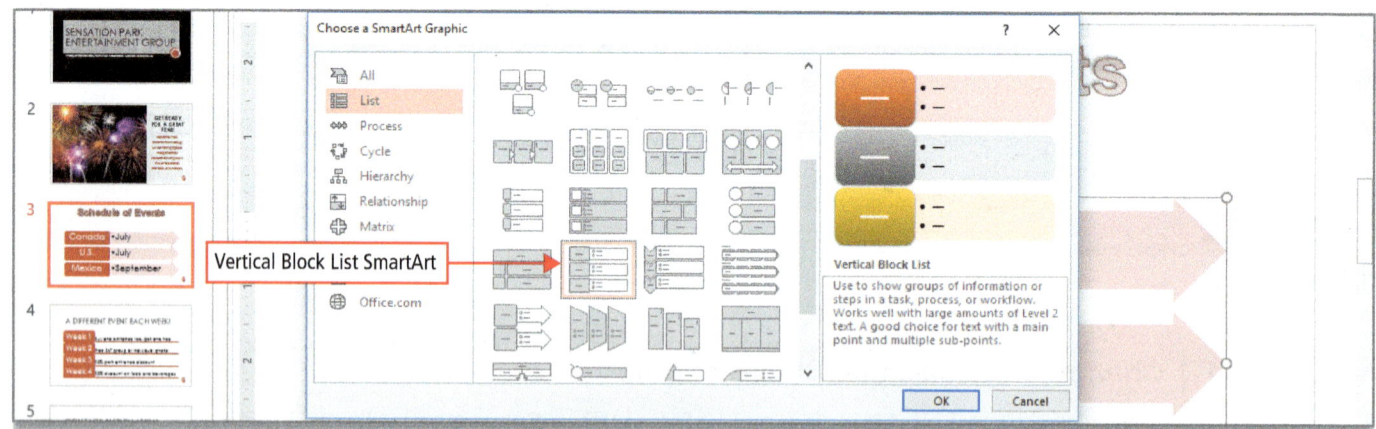

Figure 2.52

> **2** ▶ Click **OK**, and then **Save** 🖫 the presentation.

Activity 2.33 | Changing the Color and Style of a SmartArt Graphic

SmartArt Styles are combinations of formatting effects that you can apply to SmartArt graphics.

> **1** ▶ With **Slide 3** displayed, if necessary, select the SmartArt. On the **SmartArt Tools Design tab**, in the **SmartArt Styles group**, click **Change Colors**. In the color gallery, under **Colorful**, click the second style—**Colorful Range - Accent Colors 2 to 3**—to change the colors.

> **2** ▶ On the **SmartArt Tools Design tab**, in the **SmartArt Styles group**, click **More** ▾ to display the **SmartArt Styles gallery**. Under **Best Matches for Document**, click the third style, **Subtle Effect**. Compare your slide with Figure 2.53.

Figure 2.53

> **3** Save 🖫 your presentation.

Activity 2.34 | Converting a SmartArt to Text

> **1** Display **Slide 4**, and then click anywhere in the SmartArt graphic. On the **SmartArt Tools Design tab**, in the **Reset group**, click **Convert**, and then click **Convert to Text** to convert the SmartArt graphic back to a bulleted list. Compare your screen with Figure 2.54.

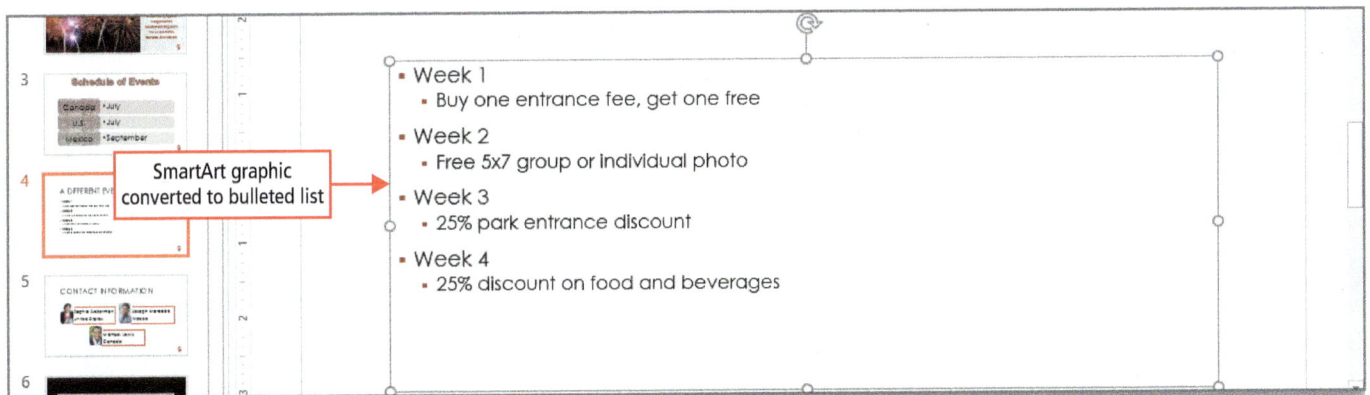

Figure 2.54

> **2** Insert a **Header & Footer** on the **Notes and Handouts**. Include the **Date and time updated automatically**, the **Page number**, and a **Footer** with the text **2B_Celebrations**

> **3** Display the document properties. As the **Tags** type **Independence Day, celebrations** and as the **Subject** type your course and section number. Be sure your name displays as the author, and then **Save** your file. Mac users use the Keywords box for tags.

> **4** View the slide show from the beginning, and then make any necessary adjustments. **Save** 🖫 your presentation.

5 If you will be completing the next optional Activity, leave the presentation open. Otherwise, **Close** ⊠ PowerPoint.

6 In **MyLab IT**, in your **Course Materials**, locate and click the Grader Project **PowerPoint 2B Celebrations**. In **step 3**, under **Upload Completed Assignment**, click **Choose File**. In the **Open** dialog box, navigate to your **PowerPoint Chapter 2 folder**, and then click your **Student_PowerPoint_2B_ Celebrations** file one time to select it. In the lower right corner of the **Open** dialog box, click **Open**.

The name of your selected file displays above the Upload button.

7 To submit your file to **MyLab IT** for grading, click **Upload**, wait a moment for a green **Success!** message, and then in **step 4**, click the blue **Submit for Grading** button. Click **Close Assignment** to return to your list of **Course Materials**.

Objective 7 Insert a 3D Object

ALERT Optional Activity for Non-MyLab IT submissions.

The remaining Activity in this chapter is optional. Check with your instructor to see if you should complete this Activity. This Activity is not available as a **MyLab IT** Grader project or Simulation.

 MAC TIP The Mac version of PowerPoint does not support 3D models. Skip this Activity.

GO! Learn How
Video P2-7

One type of image that you can insert is a 3D object. You can insert a 3D object from a file or download from an online gallery. Microsoft Windows 10 includes Paint 3D, with which you can create your own 3D objects.

Activity 2.35 │ Inserting 3D Objects

4.4.1, 4.4.2

In this Activity, you will insert and position a 3D object from a file.

1 Display **Slide 4**. On the **Insert tab**, in the **Illustrations group**, click the **3D Models arrow**, and then click **From a File**. From your files for this project, insert the 3D model **p02B_Balloon**.

2 If necessary, click the **3D Model Tools Format tab** and compare your screen with Figure 2.55.

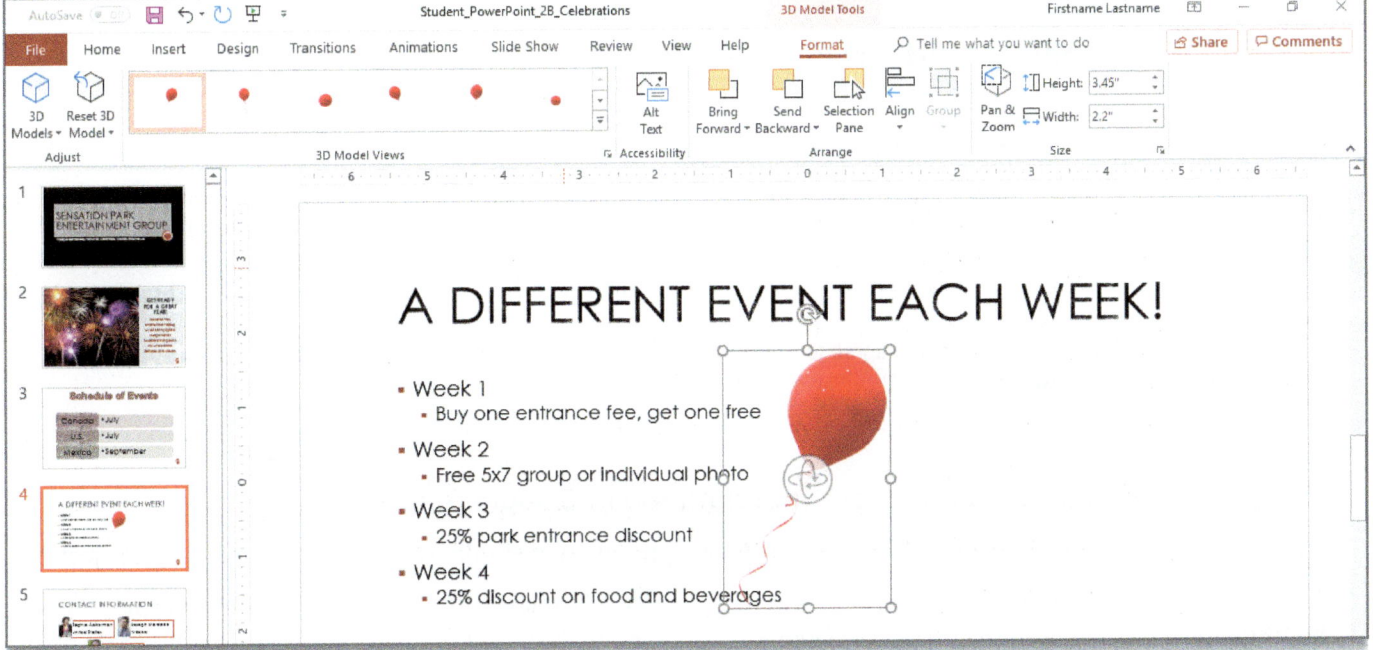

Figure 2.55

3 ▸ Point to the 3D handle in the middle of the balloon object to display the rotation pointer. Click and drag to change the view of the object.

You can rotate a 3D object to view the object from perspective.

4 ▸ Drag the balloon to position it in the white space on the right side of the slide. On the **3D Model Tools Format tab**, in the **3D Model Views group**, click **More**. In the gallery, point to each view to display the ScreenTip. Locate and click **Above Front** to position the balloon.

5 ▸ **Save** 🖫 your presentation and submit as directed by your instructor.

You have completed Project 2B | **END**

»» GO! With Google Slides

Objective | **Create an Advertisement Presentation in Google Slides**

ALERT **Working with Web-Based Applications and Services**

Computer programs and services on the web receive continuous updates and improvements, so the steps to complete this web-based activity may differ from the ones shown. You can often look at the screens and the information presented to determine how to complete the activity.

If you do not already have a Google account, you will need to create one before you begin this activity. Go to http://google.com and in the upper right corner, click **Sign In**. On the Sign In screen, click **Create Account**. On the Create your Google Account page, complete the form, read and agree to the Terms of Service and Privacy Policy, and then click **Next step**. On the Welcome screen, click **Get Started**.

Activity | Creating an Advertisement Presentation in Google Slides

In this Activity, you will use Google Slides to format a presentation similar to the one you created in Project 2B.

1 From the desktop, open your browser, navigate to **http://google.com**, and then sign in to your Google account. Click **Google apps** [icon], and then click **Drive** [icon]. Open your **GO! Web Projects** folder—or create and then open this folder if necessary.

2 On the left, click **New**, and then click **File upload**. Navigate to your student data files, click **p02_2B_Google_Slides**, and then click **Open**. When the upload is complete and file name displays in the file list, right click **p02_2B_Google_Slides**, and then click **Rename**. In the **Rename** dialog box, select and delete the existing text. Using your own name, as the file name, type **Lastname_Firstname_2B_Google_Slides** and then press [Enter]. Right-click the file that you just renamed, point to **Open with**, and then click **Google Slides**.

3 Display **Slide 5**. Click the picture to select it, and then on the **toolbar**, click the **Mask image arrow** [icon], point to **Callouts**, and then click **Explosion 1**.

4 With the picture selected, on the **toolbar**, click **Format options**, and then, under **Adjustments**, drag the **Transparency** slider to **20%**. **Close** the **Format options** pane.

5 Display **Slide 3**. On the **Insert** menu, click **Word art**. In the center of your slide, with your insertion point blinking in the placeholder, type **Schedule of Events** and press [Enter]. The Word art is surrounded by sizing handles with which you can adjust its size.

6 With the **Word art** selected, on the **toolbar**, click **Fill color** [icon], and then in the first column, click the eighth color – **dark red berry 3**. On the **toolbar**, click **Border color** [icon], and then in the first column, click the third color—**light red berry 3**.

7 Drag the **Word art** upward until there is an even amount of white space above and below it. On the menu bar, click **Arrange**, point to **Center on page**, and then click **Horizontally**.

8 With **Slide 3** displayed, select the Word art. On the **toolbar**, change the **Font** to **Georgia**. Compare your screen to Figure A.

9 Your presentation will be saved automatically. Download as a PDF or PowerPoint file and submit as instructed by your instructor. Sign out of your Google account.

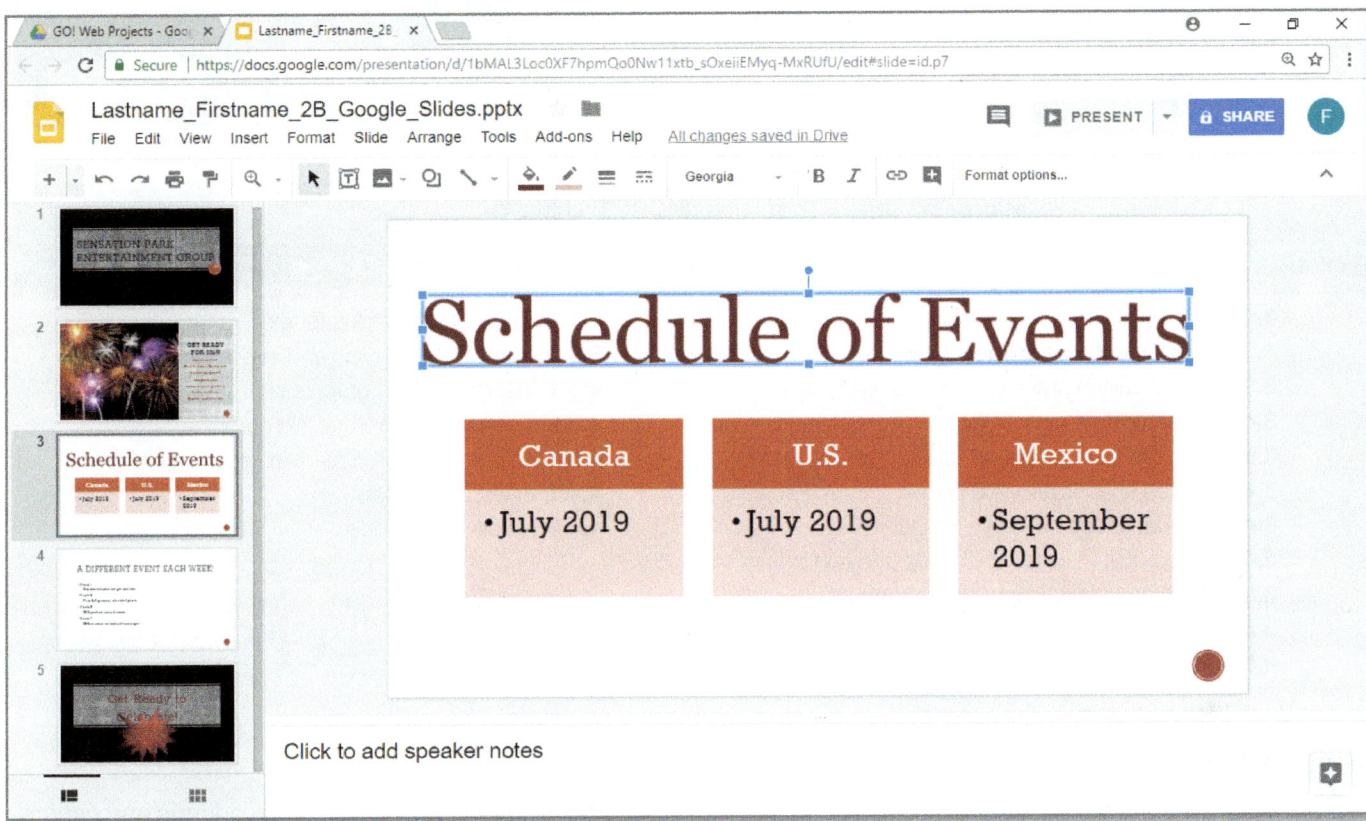

Figure A

»»» GO! To Work

wavebreakmedia/Shutterstock, Monkey Business Images/Fotolia, Ivanko80/Shutterstock, Monkey Business Images/Shutterstock

Microsoft Office Specialist (MOS) Skills in This Chapter	
Project 2A	**Project 2B**
3.1.3 Create bulleted and numbered lists	**3.1.1** Apply built-in styles to text
3.3.1 Resize and crop images	**3.3.2** Apply built-in styles and effects to images
3.3.2 Apply built-in styles and effects to images	**4.3.1** Insert SmartArt graphics
3.4.1 Insert and change shapes	**4.3.2** Convert lists to SmartArt graphics
3.4.3 Add text to shapes and text boxes	**4.3.3** Add and modify SmartArt graphic content
3.4.4 Resize shapes and text boxes	**4.4.1** Insert 3D models
3.4.5 Format shapes and text boxes	**4.4.2** Modify 3D models
3.4.6 Apply built-in styles to shapes and text boxes	
3.5.2 Align shapes, images, and text boxes	
3.5.3 Group shapes and images	
3.5.4 Display alignment tools	

Build Your E-Portfolio

An E-Portfolio is a collection of evidence, stored electronically, that showcases what you have accomplished while completing your education. Collecting and then sharing your work products with potential employers reflects your academic and career goals. Your completed documents from the following projects are good examples to show what you have learned: 2G, 2K, and 2L.

Go! For Job Success

Video: Business Lunch Etiquette

Your instructor may assign this video to your class, and then ask you to think about, or discuss with your classmates, these questions:

g-stockstudio/Shutterstock

In what specific ways did Sara and Jordan demonstrate improper interpersonal communication during their lunch with Karen?

As a manager, did Chris follow the rules of interpersonal communication with his client? Explain your answer.

In what ways did Sara, Jordan, and Theo demonstrate proper or improper *nonverbal* communication skills?

End of Chapter

Summary

Use numbered and bulleted lists in a presentation to focus attention on specific items. The theme that you select includes default styles for bullets, but you can change the shape and color of the symbols.

Use pictures to illustrate an idea. The Online Pictures feature enables you to search the web for images that emphasize important points. Using good keywords is critical to a successful search to find a great picture!

Objects are easily modified in PowerPoint. Removing the picture background and cropping eliminate unnecessary picture parts. Smart guides and alignment options are used to position pictures and shapes.

Use SmartArt graphics to present information to illustrate processes, hierarchies, cycles, lists, and relationships. SmartArt graphics may include text and pictures, and can be formatted with styles and color combinations for maximum impact.

GO! Learn It Online

Review the concepts and key terms, and MOS skills in this chapter by completing these online challenges, which you can find in **MyLab IT**.

Chapter Quiz: Answer matching and multiple choice questions to test what you learned in this chapter.

Lessons on the GO!: Learn how to use all the new apps and features as they are introduced by Microsoft.

MOS Prep Quiz: Answer questions to review the MOS skills that you practiced in this chapter.

GO! Collaborative Team Project (Available in Instructor Resource Center)

If your instructor assigns this project to your class, you can expect to work with one or more of your classmates--either in person or by using Internet tools--to create work products similar to those that you created in this chapter. A team is a group of workers who work together to solve a problem, make a decision, or create a work product. Collaboration is when you work together with others as a team in an intellectual endeavor to complete a shared task or achieve a shared goal.

Monkey Business Images/Fotolia

Project Guide for PowerPoint Chapter 2

Your instructor may assign one or more of these projects to help you review the chapter and assess your mastery and understanding of the chapter.

		Project Guide for PowerPoint Chapter 2	
Project	**Apply Skills from These Chapter Objectives**	**Project Type**	**Project Location**
2A MyLab IT	Objectives 1–4 from Project 2A	**2A Instructional Project (Grader Project)** **Instruction** Guided instruction to learn the skills in Project A.	In **MyLab IT** and in text
2B MyLab IT	Objectives 5–7 from Project 2B	**2B Instructional Project (Grader Project)** **Instruction** Guided instruction to learn the skills in Project B.	In **MyLab IT** and in text
2C	Objectives 1–4 from Project 1A	**2C Skills Review (Scorecard Grading)** **Review** A guided review of the skills from Project 1A.	In text
2D	Objectives 5–7 from Project 1B	**2D Skills Review (Scorecard Grading)** **Review** A guided review of the skills from Project 1B.	In text
2E MyLab IT	Objectives 1–4 from Project 2A	**2E Mastery (Grader Project)** **Mastery and Transfer of Learning** A demonstration of your mastery of the skills in Project 2A with extensive decision making.	In **MyLab IT** and in text
2F MyLab IT	Objectives 5–7 from Project 2B	**2F Mastery (Grader Project)** **Mastery and Transfer of Learning** A demonstration of your mastery of the skills in Project 2B with extensive decision making.	In **MyLab IT** and in text
2G MyLab IT	Objectives 1–7 from Projects 2A and 2B	**2G Mastery (Grader Project)** **Mastery and Transfer of Learning** A demonstration of your mastery of the skills in Projects 2A and 2B with extensive decision making.	In **MyLab IT** and in text
2H	Combination of Objectives from Projects 2A and 2B	**2H GO! Fix It (Scorecard Grading)** **Critical Thinking** A demonstration of your mastery of the skills in Projects 2A and 2B by creating a correct result from a document that contains errors you must find.	IRC
2I	Combination of Objectives from Projects 2A and 2B	**2I GO! Make It (Scorecard Grading)** **Critical Thinking** A demonstration of your mastery of the skills in Projects 2A and 2B by creating a result from a supplied picture.	IRC
2J	Combination of Objectives from Projects 2A and 2B	**2J GO! Solve It (Rubric Grading)** **Critical Thinking** A demonstration of your mastery of the skills in Projects 2A and 2B, your decision-making skills, and your critical thinking skills. A task-specific rubric helps you self-assess your result.	IRC
2K	Combination of Objectives from Projects 2A and 2B	**2K GO! Solve It (Rubric Grading)** **Critical Thinking** A demonstration of your mastery of the skills in Projects 2A and 2B, your decision-making skills, and your critical thinking skills. A task-specific rubric helps you self-assess your result.	In text
2L	Combination of Objectives from Projects 2A and 2B	**2L GO! Think (Rubric Grading)** **Critical Thinking** A demonstration of your understanding of the chapter concepts applied in a manner that you would outside of college. An analytic rubric helps you and your instructor grade the quality of your work by comparing it to the work an expert in the discipline would create.	In text
2M	Combination of Objectives from Projects 2A and 2B	**2M GO! Think (Rubric Grading)** **Critical Thinking** A demonstration of your understanding of the chapter concepts applied in a manner that you would outside of college. An analytic rubric helps you and your instructor grade the quality of your work by comparing it to the work an expert in the discipline would create.	IRC
2N	Combination of Objectives from Projects 2A and 2B	**2N You and GO! (Rubric Grading)** **Critical Thinking** A demonstration of your understanding of the chapter concepts applied in a manner that you would in a personal situation. An analytic rubric helps you and your instructor grade the quality of your work.	IRC
2O	Combination of Objectives from Projects 2A and 2B	**2O Collaborative Team Project for PowerPoint Chapter 2** **Critical Thinking** A demonstration of your understanding of concepts and your ability to work collaboratively in a group role-playing assessment, requiring both collaboration and self-management.	IRC

Glossary

Glossary of Chapter Key Terms

Align to Slide A setting tells PowerPoint to align each selected object with the slide, rather than with each other.

Background Removal A feature that removes unwanted portions of a picture so that the picture does not appear as a self-contained rectangle.

Bulleted list A list of items preceded by small dots or other shapes, which do not indicate order or rank. Sometimes called unordered lists.

Clip A single media file such as art, sound, animation, or a movie.

Crop A command that removes unwanted or unnecessary areas of a picture.

Crop handles Handles used to remove unwanted areas of a picture.

Crop pointer The pointer used to crop areas of a picture.

Crosshair pointer The pointer used to draw a shape.

Eyedropper A tool that captures the exact color from an object on your screen and then applies it to any shape, picture, or text.

Fill color The inside color of text or of an object.

Numbered list A list of items preceded by numbers, which indicate sequence or rank of the items. Sometimes called ordered lists.

RGB A color model in which the colors red, green, and blue are added together to form another color.

Ruler guides Dotted red vertical and horizontal lines that display in the rulers indicating the pointer's position.

Shape A slide object such as a line, arrow, box, callout, or banner.

Shape style Predefined combination of shape fill, line colors, and other effects.

Smart guides Dashed lines that display on your slide when you are moving an object to assist you with alignment.

SmartArt graphic A visual representation of information that you create by choosing from among various layouts to communicate your message or ideas effectively.

SmartArt Styles Combinations of formatting effects that you can apply to SmartArt graphics.

Text box An object with which you can position text anywhere on a slide.

Text effects Formats applied to text that include shadows, reflections, glows, bevels, and 3-D rotations.

WordArt A gallery of text styles with which you can create decorative effects, such as shadowed or mirrored text.

Chapter Review

Skills Review	Project 2C Concerts

Apply 2A skills from these Objectives:

1. Format Numbered and Bulleted Lists
2. Insert Online Pictures
3. Insert Text Boxes and Shapes
4. Format Objects

In the following Skills Review, you will format a presentation that describes annual Concert in the Park events at several Sensation Park Entertainment Group amusement parks. Your completed presentation will look similar to Figure 2.55.

Project Files

For Project 2C, you will need:

p02C_Concerts

p02C_Drums

p02C_Guitar

p02C_Music (optional)

You will save your presentation as:

Lastname_Firstname_2C_Concerts

Project Results

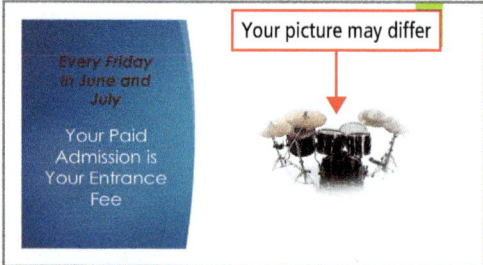

Figure 2.55 Project 2C Concerts

(continues on next page)

Chapter Review

Skills Review: Project 2C Concerts (continued)

1 Start PowerPoint. From the student data files, locate and open **p02C_Concerts**. On the **File tab**, click **Save As**, navigate to your **PowerPoint Chapter 2** folder, and then using your own name, save the file as **Lastname_Firstname_2C_Concerts**

a. If necessary, display the rulers. With **Slide 1** displayed, on the **Insert tab**, in the **Illustrations group**, click **Shapes**, and then under **Basic Shapes**, in the second row, click the fifth shape—**Frame**.

b. Move the pointer to align the ruler guides with the **left half of the horizontal ruler at 3 inches** and with the **upper half of the vertical ruler at 2.5 inches**, and then click to insert the Frame.

c. On the **Format tab**, in the **Size group**, click in the **Shape Height** box to select the number, and then type **1.7** Click in the **Shape Width** box. Replace the selected number with **5.5** and then press Enter to resize the shape.

d. With the frame selected, type **Sensation Park Entertainment Group** and then change the **Font Size** to **28**. Change the **Font Color** to **Light Gray, Background 2**—under Theme Colors, in the third column, the first color. On the **Format tab** in the **Shape Styles group**, click **Shape Fill**, and then under **Theme Colors**, in the third column, click the first color— **Light Gray, Background 2**

2 On the **Insert tab**, in the **Images group**, click **Online Pictures**. In the **Bing Image Search** box, type **sheet music** and then press Enter.

(Mac users, open your browser, navigate to Bing.com, click Images, search for **sheet music** and download an appropriate image. Save the file to your computer and use the Insert Picture icon in the content placeholder to insert your downloaded image. For this Activity you can insert the picture *p02C_Music* that is included with the data files for this project.)

a. Click a horizontal picture of lines of music on a music sheet of your choosing, and then click **Insert**. If necessary, click to select the credit line below the image and press Delete. If you are unable to find a suitable online image or prefer your screen to match the figure for this project, you can insert the picture *p02C_Music* that is included with the data files for this project.

b. On the **Format tab**, in the **Size group**, click in the **Shape Height** box. Replace the selected number with **2.5** and then press Enter to resize the image.

c. Drag the picture down and to the right until intersecting red dashed Smart Guides display, indicating that the picture is center aligned with the title and its top edge aligns with the bottom edge of the title placeholder.

d. With the picture selected, on the **Format tab**, in the **Size group**, click the **Crop arrow**, and then point to **Crop to Shape**. Under **Basic Shapes**, click the first shape—**Oval**. In the **Picture Styles group**, click **Picture Effects**, point to **Soft Edges**, and then click **25 Point**.

e. With the picture selected, hold down Shift, and the click the **frame shape** and the **title placeholder** so that all three objects are selected. On the **Format tab**, in the **Arrange group**, click **Align**, and then click **Align to Slide**. Click **Align** again, and then click **Align Center**. **Save** the presentation.

3 Display **Slide 2**. On the **Insert tab**, in the **Images group**, click **Pictures**. In the **Insert Picture** dialog box, navigate to the data files for this project, click **p02C_Drums**, and then click **Insert**. (Mac users click Pictures and then click Picture from File.)

a. With the picture selected, on the **Format tab**, in the **Size group**, click the **Crop arrow**, and then point to **Crop to Shape**. Under **Basic Shapes**, click the first shape—**Oval**. In the **Picture Styles group**, click **Picture Effects**, point to **Soft Edges**, and then click **50 Point**.

b. Click in the placeholder containing the text *Every Friday in June and July*. On the **Home tab**, in the **Paragraph group**, click **Bullets** to remove the bullet symbol from the title.

c. Select the text *Every Friday in June and July*. On the **Home tab**, in the **Font group**, click the **Font Color button arrow**. Below the gallery, click **Eyedropper**, and then move the eyedropper pointer so that it is pointing to any bright colored area of the drum on the right side of the picture. Click one time to apply the color to the selected text. Apply **Bold** and **Italic** and change the **Font Size** to **32**.

4 Display **Slide 3**, and then select the third and fourth bullet points—*Seating is limited* and *Reserved seating is available*.

a. On the **Home tab**, in the **Paragraph group**, click the **Bullets button arrow**, and then click **Bullets and Numbering**. In the second row, click the first style—**Hollow Square Bullets**. Replace the number in the **Size** box with **90** and then click the **Color arrow**. Under **Recent Colors**, apply the color chosen using the eyedropper on Slide 2. Click **OK**.

(continues on next page)

Chapter Review

   b. Display **Slide 4**, and then click the bulleted list placeholder. Click the dashed border so that it displays as a solid line, and then on the **Home tab**, in the **Paragraph group**, click **Numbering** to change the bullet symbols to numbers.

   c. On the left side of the slide, select the title text, and then on the mini toolbar, click the **Font Color button arrow**. Under **Recent Colors**, apply the color chosen using the eyedropper on Slide 2.

5 Display **Slide 5**. On the **Insert tab**, in the **Images group**, click **Pictures**. In the **Insert Picture** dialog box, navigate to the data files for this project, click **p02C_Guitar**, and then click **Insert**. (Mac users, click Pictures and then click Picture from File.)

   a. Change the picture **Height t**o **5.25** and then drag the picture so that its upper left corner aligns with the upper left corner of the blue area on the slide. On the **Format tab**, in the **Picture Styles group**, click **Picture Effects**, and then point to **Soft Edges**. Click **2.5 Point**.

   b. Press Ctrl + D and then drag the duplicated picture to the right about 1 inch. Press Ctrl + D to insert a third picture.

   c. Point to the third guitar picture that you inserted and then drag to the right so that its upper right corner aligns with the upper right corner of the blue area on the slide.

   d. Hold down Shift and then click the first two guitar pictures so that all three pictures are selected. On the **Format tab**, in the **Arrange group**, click **Align**, and then click **Align to Slide**. Click **Align** again, and then click **Align Middle**.

   e. With the three pictures selected, click **Align**, and then click **Align Selected Objects**. Click **Align** again, and then click **Distribute Horizontally**.

6 With **Slide 5** displayed, on the **Insert tab**, in the **Text group**, click **Text Box**. Move the pointer to align the ruler guides with the **left half of the horizontal ruler at 2 inches** and with the **lower half of the vertical ruler at 2.5 inches**, and then click to insert the text box.

   a. Type **Concerts Begin on June 21!** Select the text and then change the **Font Size** to **32**. On the **Format tab**, in the **Arrange group**, click **Align**, and then click **Align Center**.

   b. Insert a **Header & Footer**, on the **Notes and Handouts tab**. Include the **Date and time updated automatically**, the **Page number,** and a **Footer** with the text **2C_Concerts**

   c. Display the document properties. As the **Tags,** type **concerts** and as the **Subject,** type your course and section number. Be sure your name displays as author, and then **Save** your file.

   d. View the slide show from the beginning. As directed by your instructor, create and submit a paper printout or an electronic image of your presentation that looks like a printed document; or, submit your completed PowerPoint file. **Close** PowerPoint.

You have completed Project 2C   **END**

Chapter Review

Skills Review | Project 2D Corporate Events

Apply 2B skills from these Objectives:

5. Remove Picture Backgrounds and Insert WordArt
6. Create and Format a SmartArt Graphic
7. Insert a 3D Object

In the following Skills Review, you will format a presentation by inserting and formatting WordArt and SmartArt graphics. Your completed presentation will look similar to Figure 2.56.

Project Files

For Project 2D, you will need:

p02D_Corporate_Events

You will save your presentation as:

Lastname_Firstname_2D_Corporate_Events

Project Results

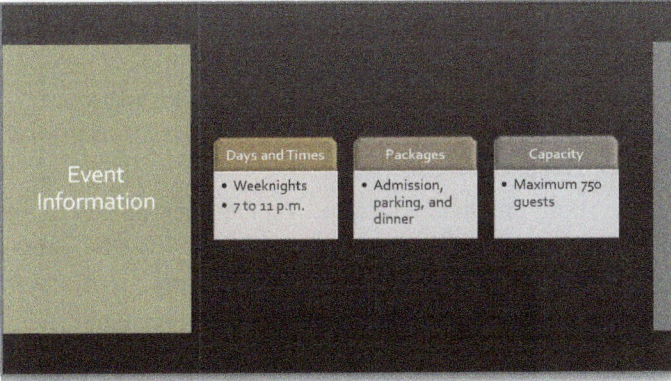
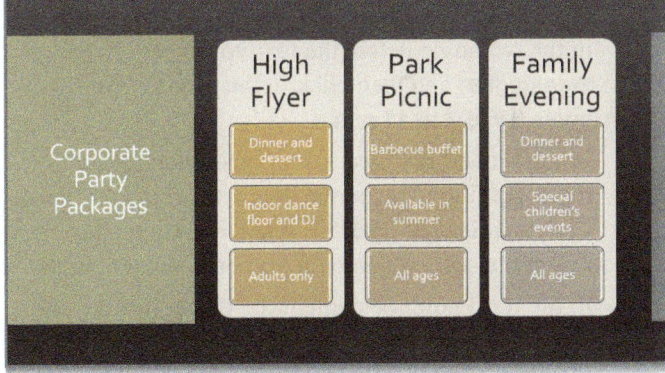
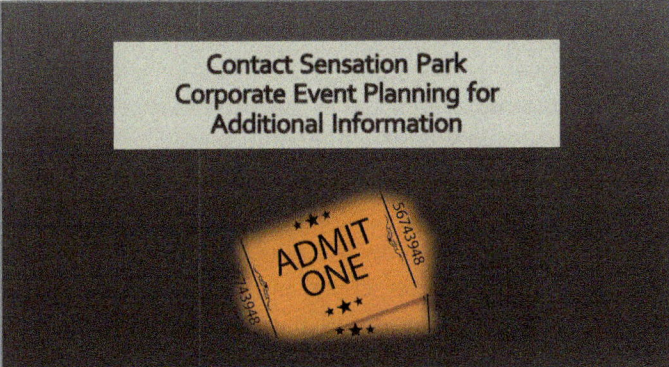

Figure 2.56 Project 2D Corporate Events

(continues on next page)

Chapter Review

1 Start PowerPoint. From your student data files, locate and open **p02D_Corporate_Events**. **Save** the presentation in your **PowerPoint Chapter 2** folder as **Lastname_Firstname_2D_Corporate_Events**

a. With **Slide 1** displayed, select the text *Corporate Event Planning*. On the **Format tab**, in the **WordArt Styles group**, click **More**. In the third row, click the last style—**Fill: Brown, Background color 2; Inner Shadow**. Click outside the placeholder.

b. On the **Insert tab**, in the **Text group**, click **WordArt**. In the **WordArt gallery**, in the first row, click the fourth style—**Fill: White; Outline: Tan, Accent color 5; Shadow**. With the text *Your text here* selected, type **Sensation Park**

c. With the WordArt selected, hold down ⇧Shift, and then click the subtitle. On the **Format tab**, in the **Arrange group**, click **Align**, and then click **Align Selected Objects**. Click **Align** again, and then click **Align Left**.

2 Display **Slide 3**. In the center of the content placeholder, click **Insert a SmartArt Graphic** to open the **Choose a SmartArt Graphic** dialog box. On the left, click **List**, and then scroll as necessary and locate and click **Horizontal Bullet List**. Click **OK**.

a. In the SmartArt graphic, in the first gold rectangle, click **Text**. Type **Days and Times** and then click in the rectangle below the text you typed. Type **Weeknights** and then click in the second bullet point. Type **7 to 11 p.m.**

b. In the second gold rectangle, type **Packages** and then click in the rectangle below the text you typed. Type **Admission, parking, and dinner** and then delete the second text bullet point in the rectangle.

c. In the third gold rectangle, type **Capacity** and then click in the rectangle below the text you typed. Type **Maximum 750 guests** and then delete the second text bullet point in the rectangle.

d. On the **SmartArt Tools Design tab**, in the **SmartArt Styles group**, click **Change Colors**, and then under **Colorful**, click the last style **Colorful Range - Accent Colors 5 to 6**. In the **SmartArt Styles group**, click **More**, and then under **3-D**, in the first row, click the fourth style—**Powder**.

e. Click in the **Days and Times** rectangle, hold down ⇧Shift, and then click the **Packages** and **Capacity** rectangles. On the **SmartArt Tools Format tab**, in the **Shapes group**, click **Change Shape**. Under **Rectangles**, click the fourth shape—**Rectangle: Top Corners Snipped.**

3 Display **Slide 4**, and then click anywhere in the bulleted list. On the **Home tab**, in the **Paragraph group**, click **Convert to SmartArt**. At the bottom of the gallery, click **More SmartArt Graphics**. On the left side of the **Choose a SmartArt Graphic** dialog box, click **List**. Locate and click **Grouped List**, and then click **OK** to convert the list to a SmartArt graphic.

(Mac users, choose the first SmartArt style. On the SmartArt Design tab, below the style gallery, click More. Scroll to List and click Grouped List.)

a. Under **Family Evening**, click in the **Dinner and Dessert** shape, and then on the **SmartArt Tools Design tab**, in the **Create Graphic group**, click **Add Shape**. In the inserted shape, type **Special children's events**

b. With the *Special children's events* shape selected, add another shape, and then type **All ages**

c. On the **SmartArt Tools Design tab**, in the **SmartArt Styles group**, click **Change Colors**. In the **Color** gallery, under **Colorful**, click the last style—**Colorful Range - Accent Colors 5 to 6**.

d. On the **Design tab**, in the **SmartArt Styles group**, click **More** to display the **SmartArt Styles gallery**. Under **3-D**, in the first row, click the third style—**Cartoon**.

4 Display **Slide 5**. Select the picture of the admission tickets, and then on the **Format tab**, in the **Adjust group**, click **Remove Background**. In the **Close group**, click **Keep Changes**.

a. With the picture selected, on the **Format tab**, in the **Picture Styles group**, click **Picture Effects**. Point to **Soft Edges**, and then click **25 Point**.

b. Insert a **Header & Footer** on the **Notes and Handouts**. Include the **Date and time updated automatically**, a **Page number**, and a **Footer** with the text **2D_Corporate_Events**

c. Display the document properties. As the **Tags** type **corporate events** and as the **Subject** type your course and section number. Be sure your name displays as author, and then **Save** your file.

(Mac users, instead of tags, use the Keywords box.)

d. View the slide show from the beginning. As directed by your instructor, create and submit a paper printout or an electronic image of your presentation that looks like a printed document; or, submit your completed PowerPoint file. **Close** PowerPoint.

You have completed Project 2D **END**

Content-Based Assessments (Mastery and Transfer of Learning)

MyLab IT Grader   **Mastering PowerPoint**   **Project 2E Coasters**

Apply **2A** skills from these Objectives:

1. Format Numbered and Bulleted Lists
2. Insert Online Pictures
3. Insert Text Boxes and Shapes
4. Format Objects

In the following Mastering PowerPoint project, you will format a presentation describing new roller coasters being constructed at several Sensation Park Entertainment Group amusement parks. Your completed presentation will look similar to Figure 2.57.

Project Files for **MyLab IT Grader**

1. In your **MyLab IT** course, locate and click **PowerPoint 2E Coasters**, Download Materials, and then Download All Files.
2. Extract the zipped folder to your PowerPoint Chapter 2 folder. Close the Grader download screens.
3. Take a moment to open the downloaded **PowerPoint_2E_Coasters_Instructions**; note any recent updates to the book.

Project Results

Figure 2.57 Project 2E Coasters. (Christian Müller/Fotolia)

For Non-MyLab Submissions

For Project 2E, you will need:

p02E_Coasters

In your PowerPoint Chapter 2 folder, save your presentation as:

Lastname_Firstname_2E_Coasters

After you have named and saved your presentation, on the next page, begin with Step 2.
After Step 13, save and submit your presentation as directed by your instructor.

(continues on next page)

Content-Based Assessments (Mastery and Transfer of Learning)

1 Navigate to your **PowerPoint Chapter 2 folder** and then double-click the PowerPoint file you downloaded from **MyLab IT** that displays your name—**Student_PowerPoint_2E_Coasters**

2 On **Slide 2**, remove the bullet symbol from the paragraph, and then **Center** the paragraph.

3 With the content placeholder selected, display the **Shape Styles** gallery, and then apply the **Subtle Effect – Blue-Gray, Accent 5** style. Apply the **Round Convex** beveled shape effect to the placeholder.

Note—this may be named Art Deco on your system.

4 On **Slide 3**, apply **Numbering** to the first-level bullet points—*Intensity, Hang Time,* and *Last Chance.* Change all of the second-level bullets to **Star Bullets**, and then change the bullet color to the fourth color in the fifth column under Theme Colors.

5 On **Slide 3**, select the title. Using the **Eyedropper**, select the light yellow color of the stripe on the roller coaster car at the right side of the picture and change the font color of the title. On **Slides 1** and **2**, apply the same light yellow color to the slide title on each slide.

6 On **Slide 3**, apply the **Glow: 5 point; Aqua, Accent color 2** picture effect to the picture.

7 Display **Slide 4**. Insert an **Online Picture** by searching for **roller coaster** and then insert a picture of people riding a roller coaster. **Crop** the picture by dragging the crop handles so that it's roughly square in shape.

Note—alternatively, search for an image in a web browser, and then download and insert a relevant image from the results or insert the image *p02E_Roller_Coaster* downloaded with the data files for this project.

8 Align the upper left corner of the picture with the top left corner of the slide, and then change the **Height** to **4.5** Modify the **Picture Effect** by applying a **50 Point Soft Edges** effect.

9 Duplicate the picture, and then use the **Align to Slide** option to align the pictures with the left edge of the slide and to distribute the pictures vertically.

10 Insert a **Text Box** aligned with the **horizontal ruler at 0 inches** and with the **lower half of the vertical ruler at 2.5 inch**. In the text box, type **Starting Summer 2022!** Change the **Font Size** to **28**. Change the **Shape Fill** to the sixth color in the last column under Theme Colors.

11 Select the title and the text box, and then, using the **Align Selected Objects** option, apply **Align Right** alignment.

12 **Insert** a **Header & Footer** on the **Notes and Handouts**. Include the **Date and time updated automatically**, the **Page number**, and a **Footer** with the text **2E_Coasters**

13 Display the document properties. As the **Tags** type **coasters** and as the **Subject** type your course and section. (Mac users enter keywords instead of tags.) Be sure your name displays as author, and then **Save** your file. **Close** PowerPoint.

14 In **MyLab IT**, in your **Course Materials**, locate and click the Grader Project **PowerPoint 2E Coasters**. In **step 3**, under **Upload Completed Assignment**, click **Choose File**. In the **Open** dialog box, navigate to your **PowerPoint Chapter 2 folder**, and then click your **Student_PowerPoint_2E_ Coasters** file one time to select it. In the lower right corner of the **Open** dialog box, click **Open**.

The name of your selected file displays above the Upload button.

15 To submit your file to **MyLab IT** for grading, click **Upload**, wait a moment for a green **Success!** message, and then in **step 4**, click the blue **Submit for Grading** button. Click **Close Assignment** to return to your list of **Course Materials**.

You have completed Project 2E   **END**

MyLab IT Grader

Mastering PowerPoint | **Project 2F Attractions**

Apply 2B skills from these Objectives:

5. Remove Picture Backgrounds and Insert WordArt
6. Create and Format a SmartArt Graphic
7. Insert a 3D Object

In the following Mastering PowerPoint project, you will format a presentation describing new attractions at several of the Sensation Park Entertainment Group amusement parks. Your completed presentation will look similar to Figure 2.58.

Project Files for **MyLab IT** Grader

1. In your **MyLab IT** course, locate and click **PowerPoint 2F Attractions**, Download Materials, and then Download All Files.
2. Extract the zipped folder to your PowerPoint Chapter 2 folder. Close the Grader download screens.
3. Take a moment to open the downloaded **PowerPoint_2F_Attractions_Instructions**; note any recent updates to the book.

Project Results

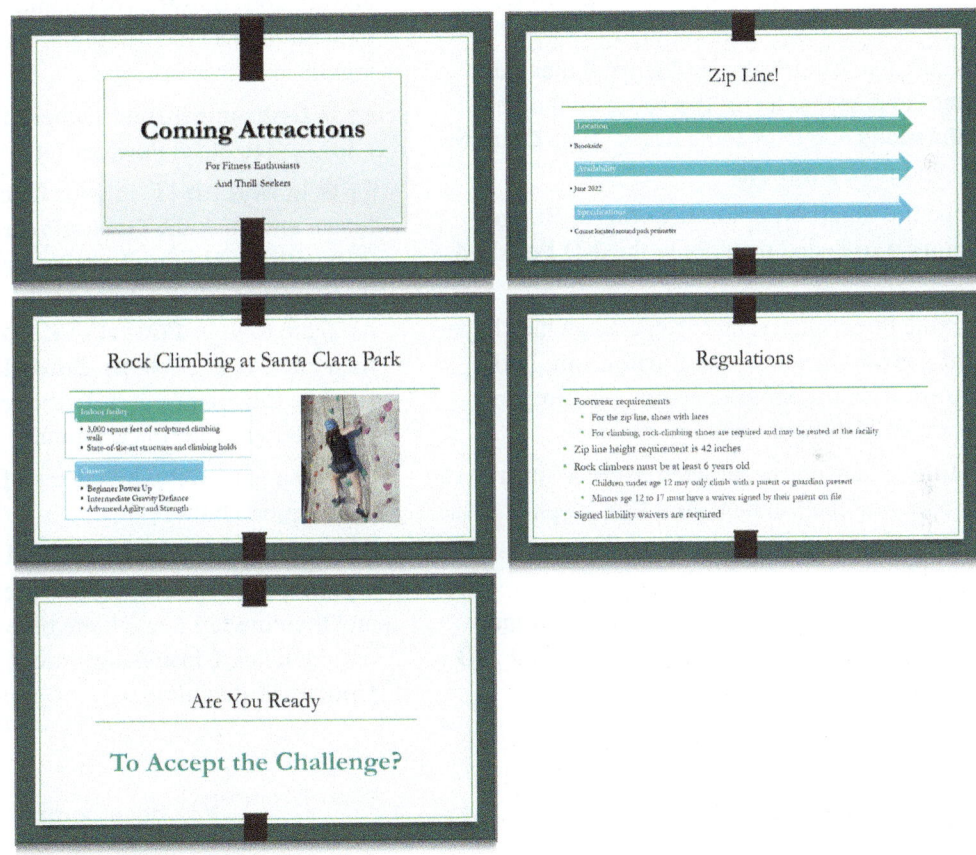

Figure 2.58 Project 2F Attractions

For Non-MyLab Submissions

For Project 2F, you will need:

p02F_Attractions

In your PowerPoint Chapter 2 folder, save your presentation as:

Lastname_Firstname_2F_Attractions

After you have named and saved your presentation, on the next page, begin with Step 2.

After Step 13, save and submit your presentation as directed by your instructor.

(continues on next page)

Content-Based Assessments (Mastery and Transfer of Learning)

1 Navigate to your **PowerPoint Chapter 2 folder** and then double-click the PowerPoint file you downloaded from **MyLab IT** that displays your name—**Student_PowerPoint_2F_Attractions**. If necessary, at the top, click **Enable Editing**.

2 On **Slide 1**, select the title and display the **WordArt** gallery. In the third row, apply the first WordArt style. Change the **Text Outline** by applying under Theme Colors, in the fourth column, the fourth color.

3 On **Slide 2**, in the content placeholder, insert a **List** type **SmartArt** graphic—**Vertical Bullet List**. In the first Text placeholder, type **Location** and then in the bullet point, type **Brookside** In the second placeholder, type **Availability** and then in the bullet point, type **June 2022**

4 Click the *Availability* placeholder, and then add a shape after the placeholder. In the new placeholder, type **Specifications** and then add a bullet. Type **Course located around park perimeter**

5 Change the SmartArt color to **Colorful Range - Accent Colors 4 to 5**, and then apply the **3-D Polished** style.

6 Select the three shapes, and then change the shapes to the **Right Arrow** shape. On the **Format tab**, in the **Shapes group**, click the **Smaller** button one time to decrease the size of the arrows.

7 On **Slide 3**, convert the bulleted list to a **SmartArt** graphic by applying the **Vertical Box List** graphic. (Mac users, convert to Vertical Bullet List and then change to Vertical Box List)

8 Change the SmartArt color to **Colorful Range - Accent Colors 4 to 5**, and then apply the **Polished 3-D** SmartArt style.

9 On **Slide 5**, insert a **WordArt** using the last style in the first row. Replace the WordArt text with **To Accept the Challenge?** Change the **Font Size** to **48**.

10 Drag the WordArt down so that its top edge is positioned on the **lower half of the vertical ruler at 1**. Align center.

11 **Insert** a **Header & Footer** on the **Notes and Handouts**. Include the **Date and time updated automatically**, the **Page number**, and a **Footer** with the text **2F_Attractions**

12 Display the document properties. As the **Tags** type **zip line, rock wall** and as the **Subject,** type your course and section. Be sure your name displays as author, and then **Save** your file. (Mac users enter keywords instead of tags.)

13 In the upper right corner of your screen, click **Close** ☒ to close PowerPoint.

14 In **MyLab IT**, in your **Course Materials**, locate and click the Grader Project **PowerPoint_2F_ Attractions**. In **step 3**, under **Upload Completed Assignment**, click **Choose File**. In the **Open** dialog box, navigate to your **PowerPoint Chapter 2 folder**, and then click your **Student_PowerPoint_2F_ Attractions** file one time to select it. In the lower right corner of the **Open** dialog box, click **Open**.

The name of your selected file displays above the Upload button.

15 To submit your file to **MyLab IT** for grading, click **Upload**, wait a moment for a green **Success!** message, and then in **step 4**, click the blue **Submit for Grading** button. Click **Close Assignment** to return to your list of **Course Materials**.

You have completed Project 2F **END**

| MyLab IT Grader | Mastering PowerPoint | Project 2G Orientation |

Apply 2A and 2B skills from these Objectives:

1. Format Numbered and Bulleted Lists
2. Insert Online Pictures
3. Insert Text Boxes and Shapes
4. Format Objects
5. Remove Picture Backgrounds and Insert WordArt
6. Create and Format a SmartArt Graphic
7. Insert a 3D Object

In the following Mastering PowerPoint project, you will edit an existing presentation that is shown to Sensation Park Entertainment Group employees on their first day of a three-day orientation. Your completed presentation will look similar to Figure 2.59.

Project Files for MyLab IT Grader

1. In your **MyLab IT** course, locate and click **PowerPoint 2G Orientation**, Download Materials, and then Download All Files.
2. Extract the zipped folder to your PowerPoint Chapter 2 folder. Close the Grader download screens.
3. Take a moment to open the downloaded **PowerPoint_2G_Orientation_Instructions**; note any recent updates to the book.

Project Results

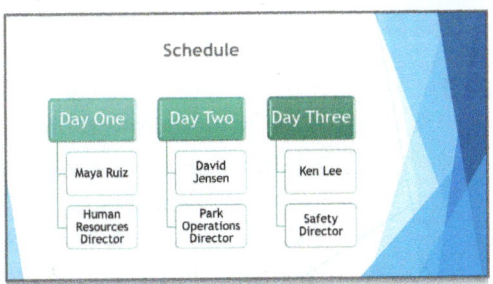
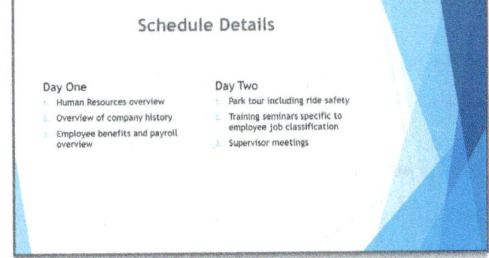
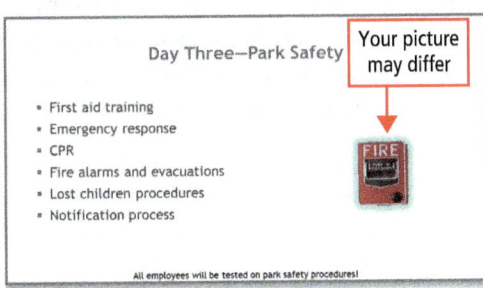

Figure 2.59 Project 2G Orientation

For Non-MyLab Submissions

For Project 2G, you will need:
p02G_Orientation

In your PowerPoint Chapter 2 folder, save your presentation as:
Lastname_Firstname_2G_Orientation

After you have named and saved your presentation, on the next page, begin with Step 2.
After Step 17, save and submit your presentation as directed by your instructor.

(continues on next page)

Content-Based Assessments (Mastery and Transfer of Learning)

1 Navigate to your **PowerPoint Chapter 2 folder** and then double-click the PowerPoint file you downloaded from **MyLab IT** that displays your name—**Student_PowerPoint_2G_Orientation**. If necessary, at the top, click **Enable Editing**.

2 On **Slide 1**, format the subtitle—*New Employee Orientation*—as **WordArt** using the last style in the first row.

3 Select the picture and then **Crop** the image from the left side so that the center-left crop handle aligns with the **left half of the horizontal ruler at 5 inches.**

4 Change the picture **Height** to **3.5** and then apply a **Glow: 8 point; Turquoise, Accent color 1** picture effect to the image. Use the **Align Selected Objects** command to apply **Align Middle** to the title and the picture.

5 On **Slide 2**, remove the bullet symbol from the paragraph, and then change the **Shape Fill** to the second color in the third column under Theme Colors, and the **Shape Outline** to the first color in the second column under Theme Colors.

6 On **Slide 3**, convert the bulleted list to the **Hierarchy** type **SmartArt** graphic—**Hierarchy List**. Change the color to **Colorful Range - Accent Colors 3 to 4**, and then apply the **3-D Inset** style.

7 On **Slide 4**, change the two bulleted lists to **Numbering**.

8 On **Slide 5**, change the bullet symbols to **Filled Square Bullets**, change the **Color** to the fourth color in the third column under Theme Colors, and then change the **Size** to **100**

9 On **Slide 5**, in the placeholder on the right, insert an **Online Picture** by searching for **fire alarm** and then insert a picture of a fire alarm with a background.

Note—alternatively, insert the image *p02G_Alarm* downloaded with the data files for this project.

10 If the option is available, remove the background from the picture, and then apply the **Glow: 18 point, Bright Green, Accent color 3** picture effect.

11 On **Slide 5**, insert a **Text Box** below the content placeholder on the left side of the slide. In the text box, type **All employees will be tested on park safety procedures!** Using the **Align to Slide** option **Align Center** the text box and apply **Align Bottom**.

12 On **Slide 6**, from the **Shapes** gallery, under **Basic Shapes**, insert a **Diamond** of any size anywhere on the slide. Resize the diamond so that its **Shape Height** is **6** and its **Shape Width** is **8**

13 Using the **Align to Slide** option, apply **Align Center**, and **Align Middle** to the diamond shape. Apply the **Moderate Effect – Bright Green, Accent 3** shape style.

14 In the diamond, type **Sensation Park Entertainment Group Welcomes You!** Change the **Font Size** to **28**, and then apply the **Round Convex Bevel** effect to the diamond shape. **Note**—this effect may be called Art Deco on some systems.

15 Insert a **Header & Footer** on the **Notes and Handouts**. Include the **Date and time updated automatically**, the **Page number**, and a **Footer** with the text **2G_Orientation**

16 Display the document properties. As the **Tags** type **orientation** and as the **Subject** type your course and section number. (Mac users use the Keywords box.) Be sure your name displays as author, and then **Save** your file.

17 In the upper right corner of your screen, click **Close** ⊠ to close PowerPoint.

18 In **MyLab IT**, in your **Course Materials**, locate and click the Grader Project **PowerPoint 2G Orientation**. In **step 3**, under **Upload Completed Assignment**, click **Choose File**. In the **Open** dialog box, navigate to your **Excel Chapter 2 folder**, and then click your **Student_PowerPoint_2G_Orientation** file one time to select it. In the lower right corner of the **Open** dialog box, click **Open**.

The name of your selected file displays above the Upload button.

19 To submit your file to **MyLab IT** for grading, click **Upload**, wait a moment for a green **Success!** message, and then in **step 4**, click the blue **Submit for Grading** button. Click **Close Assignment** to return to your list of **Course Materials**.

You have completed Project 2G **END**

Content-Based Assessments (Critical Thinking)

Apply a combination of the **2A** and **2B** skills.

GO! Fix It	**Project 2H Summer Jobs**	IRC
GO! Make It	**Project 2I Renovation Plans**	IRC
GO! Solve It	**Project 2J Business Summary**	IRC
GO! Solve It	**Project 2K Hotel**	

Project Files

For Project 2K, you will need:

p02K_Hotel

You will save your presentation as:

Lastname_Firstname_1K_Packing

Open the file p02K_Hotel and save it in your **PowerPoint Chapter 2** folder as **Lastname_Firstname_2K_Hotel** Complete the presentation by inserting an online picture on the first slide and applying appropriate picture effects. On Slide 2, format the bullet point as a single paragraph and apply a shape style, and then on Slide 3, convert the bulleted list to an appropriate SmartArt graphic. Change the SmartArt color and apply a style. On Slide 4, insert and attractively position a WordArt with the text Save the Date! On the Notes and Handouts, insert a header and footer that includes the date and time updated automatically, the file name in the footer, and the page number. Add your name, your course name and section number, and the tags **hotel, accommodations** to the Properties area. Save your presentation. As directed by your instructor, create and submit a paper printout or an electronic image of your presentation that looks like a printed document; or, submit your completed PowerPoint file.

Performance Criteria		Performance Level		
		Exemplary	**Proficient**	**Developing**
	Insert and format an appropriate online picture	An appropriate online picture was inserted and formatted in the presentation.	An online picture was inserted but was not appropriate for the presentation or was not formatted.	An online picture was not inserted.
	Insert and format appropriate SmartArt graphic	Appropriate SmartArt graphic was inserted and formatted in the presentation.	SmartArt graphic was inserted but was not appropriate for the presentation or was not formatted.	SmartArt graphic was not inserted.
	Insert and format appropriate WordArt	Appropriate WordArt was inserted and formatted in the presentation.	WordArt was inserted but was not appropriate for the presentation or was not formatted.	WordArt was not inserted.
	Remove bullet point and apply appropriate shape style	Bullet point was removed and an appropriate shape style was applied.	Either the bullet point was not removed or the shape style was not applied.	Bullet point was not removed and a shape style was not applied.

You have completed Project 2K | END

Rubric

The following outcomes-based assessments are *open-ended assessments*. That is, there is no specific correct result; your result will depend on your approach to the information provided. Make *Professional Quality* your goal. Use the following scoring rubric to guide you in *how* to approach the problem and then to evaluate *how well* your approach solves the problem.

The *criteria*—Software Mastery, Content, Format and Layout, and Process—represent the knowledge and skills you have gained that you can apply to solving the problem. The *levels of performance*—Professional Quality, Approaching Professional Quality, or Needs Quality Improvements—help you and your instructor evaluate your result.

	Your completed project is of Professional Quality if you:	Your completed project is Approaching Professional Quality if you:	Your completed project Needs Quality Improvements if you:
1-Software Mastery	Choose and apply the most appropriate skills, tools, and features and identify efficient methods to solve the problem.	Choose and apply some appropriate skills, tools, and features, but not in the most efficient manner.	Choose inappropriate skills, tools, or features, or are inefficient in solving the problem.
2-Content	Construct a solution that is clear and well organized, contains content that is accurate, appropriate to the audience and purpose, and is complete. Provide a solution that contains no errors of spelling, grammar, or style.	Construct a solution in which some components are unclear, poorly organized, inconsistent, or incomplete. Misjudge the needs of the audience. Have some errors in spelling, grammar, or style, but the errors do not detract from comprehension.	Construct a solution that is unclear, incomplete, or poorly organized, contains some inaccurate or inappropriate content, and contains many errors of spelling, grammar, or style. Do not solve the problem.
3-Format and Layout	Format and arrange all elements to communicate information and ideas, clarify function, illustrate relationships, and indicate relative importance.	Apply appropriate format and layout features to some elements, but not others. Overuse features, causing minor distraction.	Apply format and layout that does not communicate information or ideas clearly. Do not use format and layout features to clarify function, illustrate relationships, or indicate relative importance. Use available features excessively, causing distraction.
4-Process	Use an organized approach that integrates planning, development, self-assessment, revision, and reflection.	Demonstrate an organized approach in some areas, but not others; or, use an insufficient process of organization throughout.	Do not use an organized approach to solve the problem.

Outcomes-Based Assessments (Critical Thinking)

Apply a combination of the 2A and 2B skills.

GO! Think	Project 2L Interactive Ride

Project Files

For Project 2L, you will need:

New blank PowerPoint presentation

You will save your presentation as:

Lastname_Firstname_2L_Interactive_Ride

As part of its mission to combine fun with the discovery of math and science, Sensation Park Entertainment Group is opening a new, interactive roller coaster at its South Lake Tahoe location. Sensation Park's newest coaster is designed for maximum thrill and minimum risk. In a special interactive exhibit located next to the coaster, riders can learn about the physics behind this powerful coaster and even try their hand at building a coaster.

Guests will begin by selecting the height of the first hill, which determines the coaster's maximum potential energy to complete its journey. Next they will plan the exit path, and build additional hills, loops, and corkscrews. When completed, riders can submit their coaster for a safety inspection to find out whether the ride passes or fails.

Whether the ride passes or fails, riders can take a virtual tour of the ride they created to see the maximum speed achieved, the amount of negative G-forces applied, the length of the track, and the overall thrill factor. They can also see how their coaster compares with other Sensation Park coasters, and they can email the coaster simulation to their friends.

Using the preceding information, create a presentation that Marketing Director, Annette Chosek, will present at a travel fair describing the new attraction. The presentation should include four to six slides with at least one SmartArt graphic and one online picture. Apply an appropriate theme and use slide layouts that will effectively present the content, and use text boxes, shapes, and WordArt if appropriate. Apply font formatting and slide transitions, and modify text alignment and line spacing as necessary. Save the file as **Lastname_Firstname_2L_Interactive_Ride** and then insert a header and footer that includes the date and time updated automatically, the file name in the footer, and the page number. Add your name, your course name and section number, and the tags **roller coaster, new rides** to the Properties area. As directed by your instructor, create and submit a paper printout or an electronic image of your presentation that looks like a printed document; or, submit your completed PowerPoint file.

You have completed Project 2L | END

Outcomes-Based Assessments (Critical Thinking)

GO! Think	Project 2M Research	IRC
You and GO!	Project 2N Theme Park	IRC
GO! Cumulative Team Project	Project 2O Bell Orchid Hotels	IRC

Enhancing a Presentation with Animation, Video, Tables, and Charts

3

POWERPOINT
2019

PROJECT **3A**

Outcomes
Customize a presentation with animation and video

Objectives
1. Customize Slide Backgrounds and Themes
2. Animate a Slide Show
3. Insert a Video

PROJECT **3B**

Outcomes
Create a presentation that includes data in tables and charts

Objectives
4. Create and Modify Tables
5. Create and Modify Charts

fotoGN/Shutterstock

In This Chapter

 GO! To Work with PowerPoint

In this chapter, you will learn how to customize a presentation by modifying the theme, formatting the slide background, and applying animation to slide elements. Additionally, you will learn how to enhance your presentations by inserting tables and charts that help your audience understand numeric data and trends just as pictures and diagrams help illustrate a concept. The data that you present should determine whether a table or a chart would most appropriately display your information. Styles applied to your tables and charts unify these slide elements by complementing your presentation theme.

The projects in this chapter relate to the city of **Pacifica Bay**, a coastal city south of San Francisco. The city's access to major transportation provides both residents and businesses an opportunity to compete in the global marketplace. The city's mission is to create a more beautiful and more economically viable community for its residents. Each year the city welcomes a large number of tourists who enjoy exploring the rocky coastline and seeing the famous landmarks in San Francisco. The city encourages best environmental practices and partners with cities in other countries to promote sound government at the local level.

PROJECT 3A Parks and Trails Presentation

MyLab IT
Project 3A Grader for Instruction
Project 3A Simulation for Training and Review

Project Activities

In Activities 3.01 through 3.17, you will edit and format a presentation that Carol Lehman, Director of Pacifica Bay Parks and Recreation, has created to inform residents about the benefits of using the city's parks and trails. Your completed presentation will look similar to Figure 3.1.

Project Files for MyLab IT Grader

1. In your storage location, create a folder named **PowerPoint Chapter 3**.
2. In to your **MyLab IT** course, locate and click **PowerPoint 3A Trails**, Download Materials, and then Download All Files.
3. Extract the zipped folder to your PowerPoint Chapter 3 folder. Close the Grader download screens.
4. Take a moment to open the downloaded **PowerPoint_3A_Trails_Instructions**; note any recent updates to the book.

Project Results

GO! Project 3A
Where We're Going

Figure 3.1 Project 3A Trails

For Non-MyLab Submissions

For Project 3A, you will need:

p03A_Trails
p03A_Hills
p03A_Video

In your storage location, create a folder named **PowerPoint Chapter 3**
In your PowerPoint Chapter 3 folder, save your presentation as:
Lastname_Firstname_3A_Trails

After you have named and saved your presentation, on the next page, begin with Step 2.

NOTE	If You Are Using a Touch Screen

Tap an item to click it.

Press and hold for a few seconds to right-click; release when the information or commands display.

Touch the screen with two or more fingers and then pinch together or stretch your fingers apart to zoom in and out.

Slide your finger on the screen to scroll—slide left to scroll right and slide right to scroll left.

Slide to rearrange—similar to dragging with a mouse.

Swipe to select—slide an item a short distance with a quick movement—to select an item and bring up commands, if any.

Objective 1 | Customize Slide Backgrounds and Themes

ALERT   Because Office 365 is a cloud-based subscription service that receives continuous updates, you may encounter some variations in what appears on your screen and what is shown in this instruction. Microsoft Office 365 is fully installed on your PC or Mac; no internet access is necessary to create or edit documents. When you *are* connected to the internet, you will receive monthly upgrades and new features, so you always have the latest versions of Office apps as soon as they are available. Your subscription gives you continuous free access to the latest innovations and refinements.

GO! Learn How
Video P3-1

You have practiced customizing presentations by applying themes with unified design elements, backgrounds, and colors that provide a consistent look in your presentation. Additional ways to customize a slide include changing theme fonts and colors, applying a background style, modifying the background color, or inserting a picture on the slide background.

Activity 3.01 | Changing Theme Colors

The presentation theme is a coordinated, predefined set of colors, fonts, lines, and fill effects. In this activity, you will open a presentation in which the Retrospect theme is applied, and then you will change the *theme colors*—a set of coordinating colors that are applied to the backgrounds, objects, and text in a presentation. For this presentation about parks and trails, a green theme is more appropriate than the orange theme.

1 Navigate to your **PowerPoint Chapter 3 folder**, and then double-click the PowerPoint file you downloaded from **MyLab IT** that displays your name—**Student_PowerPoint_3A_ Trails**. In your presentation, if necessary, at the top click **Enable Editing**.

2 Click the **Design tab**, and then in the **Variants group**, click **More**. Point to **Colors** to display the sets of theme colors. Point to several sets and notice the color changes on **Slide 1**.

MAC TIP   To display group names on the ribbon, display the menu, click PowerPoint, click Preferences, click View, and select the Show group titles check box.

MAC TIP   Live Preview is not available in the Mac version of PowerPoint.

3 Click **Green** to change the presentation colors, and then compare your screen with Figure 3.2. **Save** 💾 your presentation.

Changing the colors does not change the overall design of the presentation. In this presentation, the *Retrospect* presentation theme is still applied to the presentation. By modifying the theme colors, you retain the design of the *Retrospect* theme but apply colors that coordinate with the pictures in the presentation, and that are available as text, accent, and background colors.

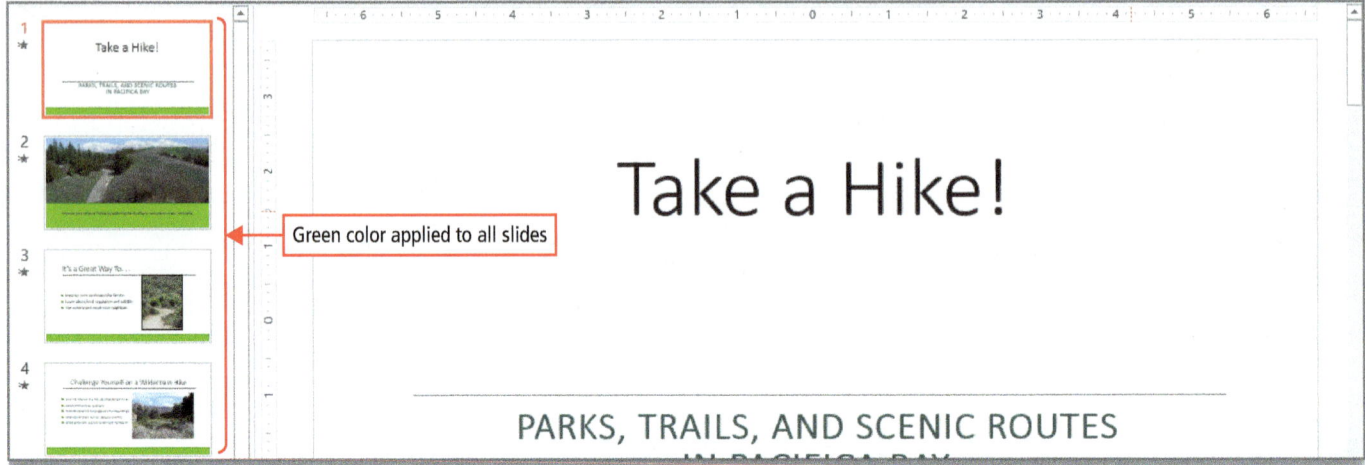

Figure 3.2

Activity 3.02 | Changing Theme Fonts

In addition to theme colors, every presentation theme includes ***theme fonts*** that determine the font to apply to two types of slide text—headings and body. The ***Headings font*** is applied to slide titles and the ***Body font*** is applied to all other text. When you apply a new theme font to the presentation, the text on every slide is updated with the new heading and body fonts.

1 With **Slide 1** displayed, click anywhere in the title placeholder. On the **Home tab**, in the **Font group**, click the **Font arrow**. Notice that at the top of the **Font** list, under **Theme Fonts**, Calibri Light (Headings) and Calibri (Body) display. Compare your screen with Figure 3.3.

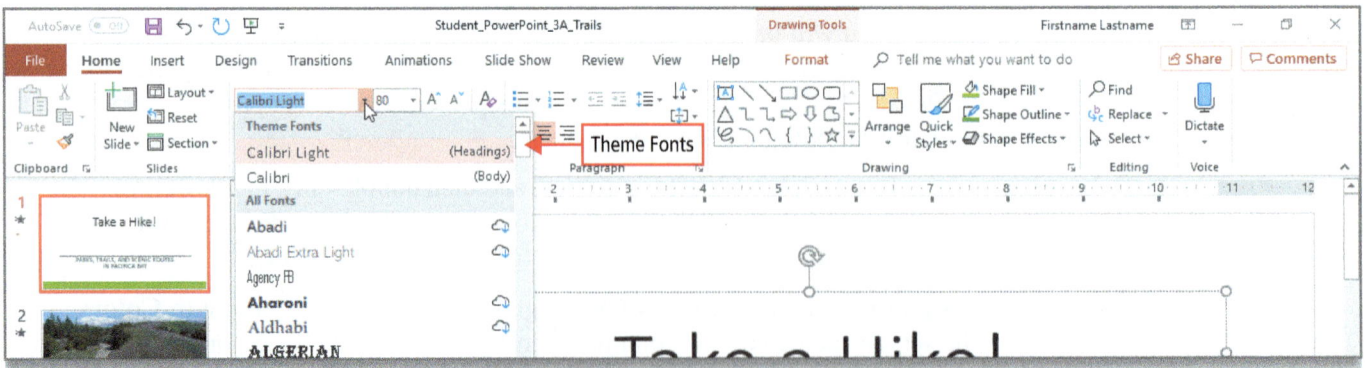

Figure 3.3

2 Click anywhere on the slide to close the Font list. On the **Design tab**, in the **Variants group**, click **More** ⊡. Point to **Fonts**.

> This list displays the name of each theme and the pair of fonts in the theme. The first and larger font in each pair is the Headings font and the second and smaller font in each pair is the Body font.

3 Point to several of the themes and watch as Live Preview changes the title and subtitle text. Scroll to the bottom of the **Fonts** list, and then click **TrebuchetMS**. **Save** 🖫 your presentation and then compare your screen with Figure 3.4.

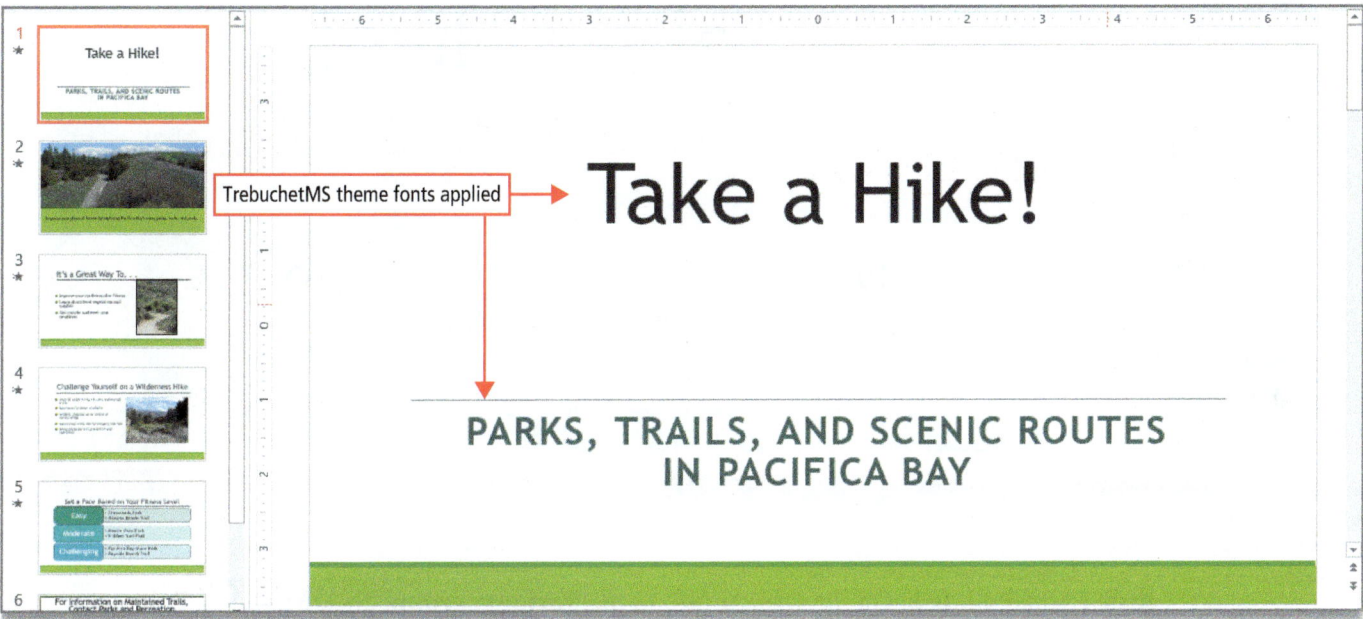

Figure 3.4

Activity 3.03 │ Applying a Background Style

A *background style* is a predefined slide background fill variation that combines theme colors in different intensities or patterns.

1 With **Slide 1** displayed, on the **Design tab**, in the **Variants group**, click **More** ⊡. Point to **Background Styles**, and then compare your screen with Figure 3.5.

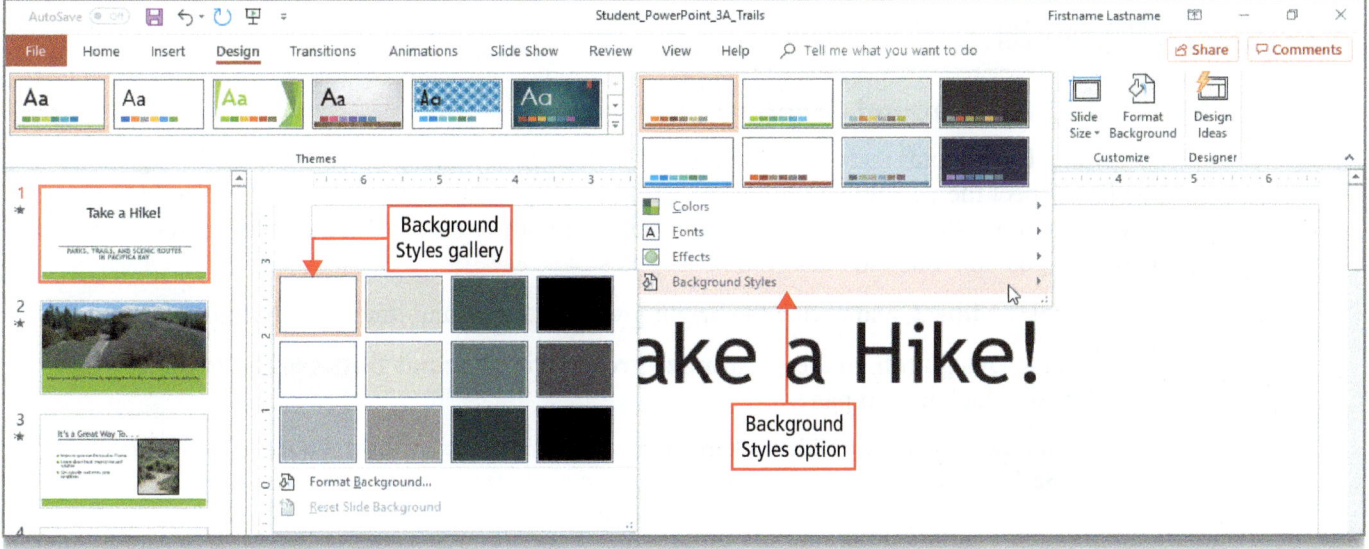

Figure 3.5

2 Point to each of the background styles to view the style on **Slide 1**. Then, in the first row, click **Style 2** Compare your screen with Figure 3.6.

The background style is applied to all the slides in the presentation.

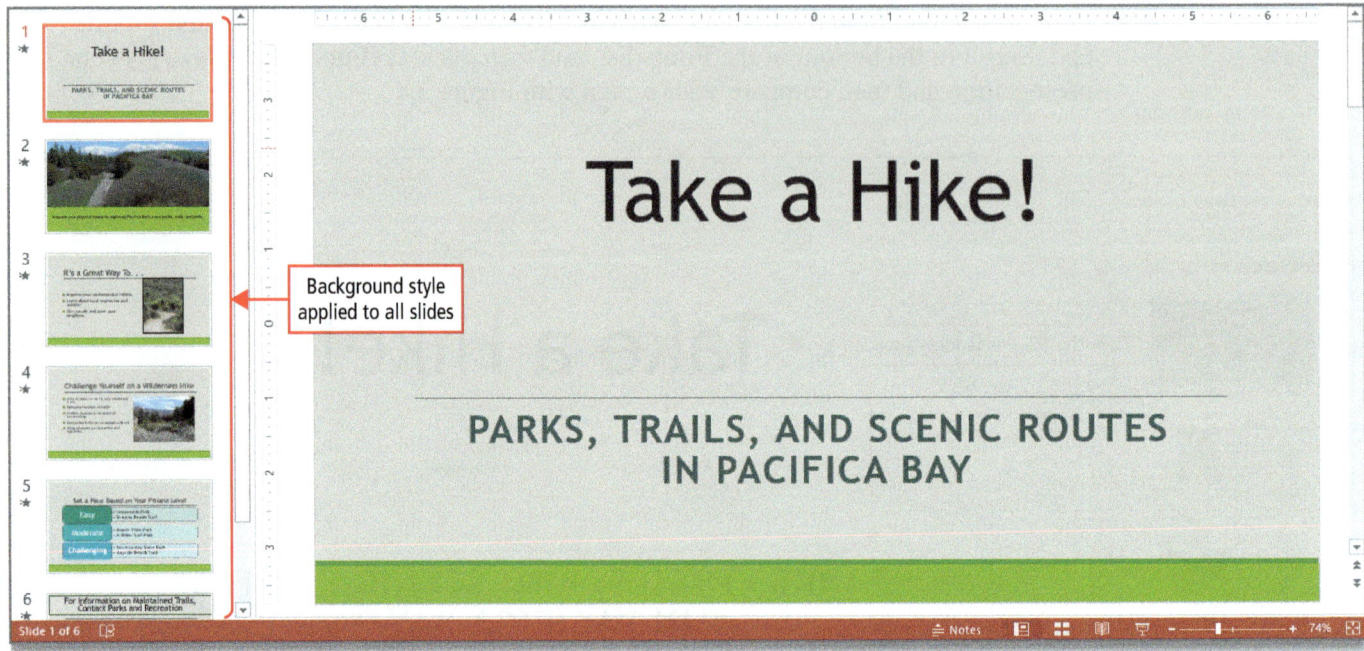

Figure 3.6

3 Display **Slide 5**. On the **Design tab**, in the **Variants group**, click **More** ⬇. Point to **Background Styles**, and then in the third row, right-click the third style—**Style 11**—to display the shortcut menu. On the shortcut menu, click **Apply to Selected Slides** to apply the style to Slide 5.

You can select individual slides to which you apply a background style.

> 💻 **MAC TIP** The Mac version of PowerPoint does not enable you to apply a Background Style to selected slides, but only to the entire presentation. To customize one slide, click Format Background to open the Format Background pane. Apply the solid fill color—Dark Green, Text 2.

4 Save your presentation.

Activity 3.04 | Hiding Background Graphics

MOS
2.2.2

Many PowerPoint themes contain graphic elements that display on the slide background. In the Retrospect theme applied to this presentation, the background includes a rectangle shape and line. Sometimes the background graphics interfere with or clash with the slide content. When this happens, you can hide the background graphics.

1 Display **Slide 2**, and notice the bright green rectangle and line at the bottom of the slide.

2 On the **Design tab**, in the **Customize group**, click **Format Background** to display the Format Background pane.

You can customize a slide background by changing the formatting options in the Format Background pane.

3 In the **Format Background** pane, be sure that under **Fill**, the fill options display, and if necessary, click Fill to display the options. Under **Fill**, select the **Hide Background Graphics** check box. Compare your slide with Figure 3.7.

> The background objects—the rectangle and line below the picture—no longer display.

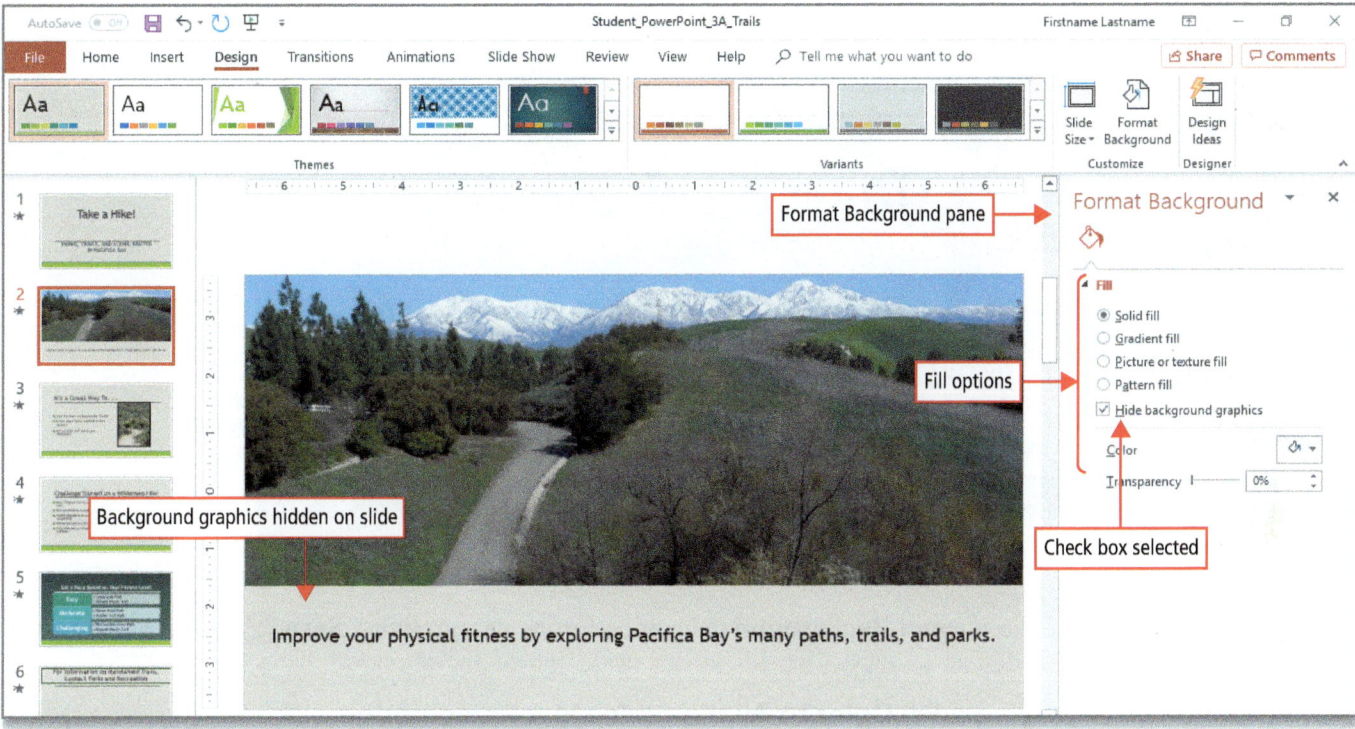

Figure 3.7

4 Leave the Format Background pane open for the next Activity, and then **Save** your presentation.

MORE KNOWLEDGE **Hiding Background Objects from All Slides in a Presentation**

To hide the background objects from all of the slides in a presentation, in the Format Background pane, select the Hide background graphics check box, and then at the bottom of the Format Background pane, click Apply to All.

Activity 3.05 | Applying a Background Fill Color to a Slide

MOS
2.2.2

In addition to applying predefined background styles, you can apply a fill color to one or all of the slides in your presentation.

1 Display **Slide 1**.

2 In the **Format Background** pane, under **Fill**, verify that **Solid fill** is selected, and select it if it is not. To the right of **Color**, click **Fill Color** . Under **Theme Colors**, in the third column, click the second color. Compare your screen with Figure 3.8.

The slightly darker solid fill color is applied to the slide background.

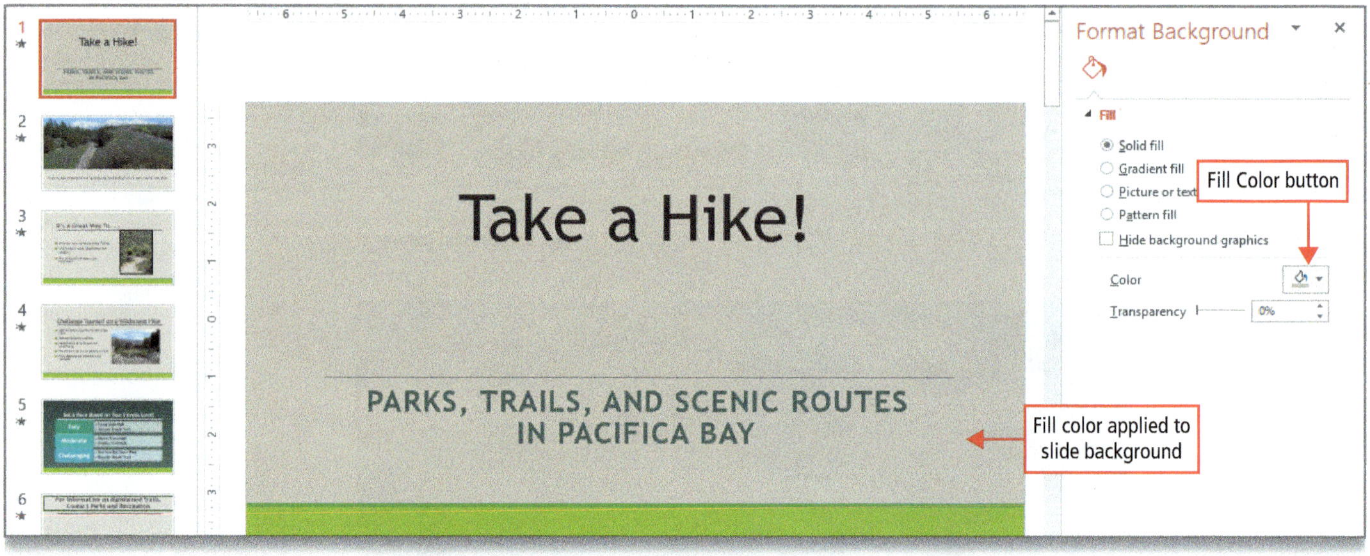

Figure 3.8

3 Leave the **Format Background** pane open for the next Activity. **Save** your presentation.

MORE KNOWLEDGE **Applying a Fill Color to All the Slides in a Presentation**

To apply a fill color to all of the slides in a presentation, in the Format Background pane, select the fill color that you want to apply, and then at the bottom of the Format Background pane, click Apply to All.

MOS 2.2.2

Activity 3.06 | Applying a Background Texture

PowerPoint includes a selection of textures you can use to fill the slide background for visual interest.

1 Display **Slide 2**, hold down Shift and then in the slide thumbnails, click **Slide 4** to select **Slides 2**, **3**, and **4**.

Recall that you can select contiguous slides in this manner.

2 In the **Format Background** pane, under **Fill**, click **Picture or texture fill**.

A background picture that is part of the Retrospect theme may display on the slide background of the three selected slides.

3 Under **Insert picture from**, to the right of **Texture**, click **Texture** . In the **Texture gallery**, in the third row, point to the fourth texture—**Recycled paper**. Compare your screen with Figure 3.9.

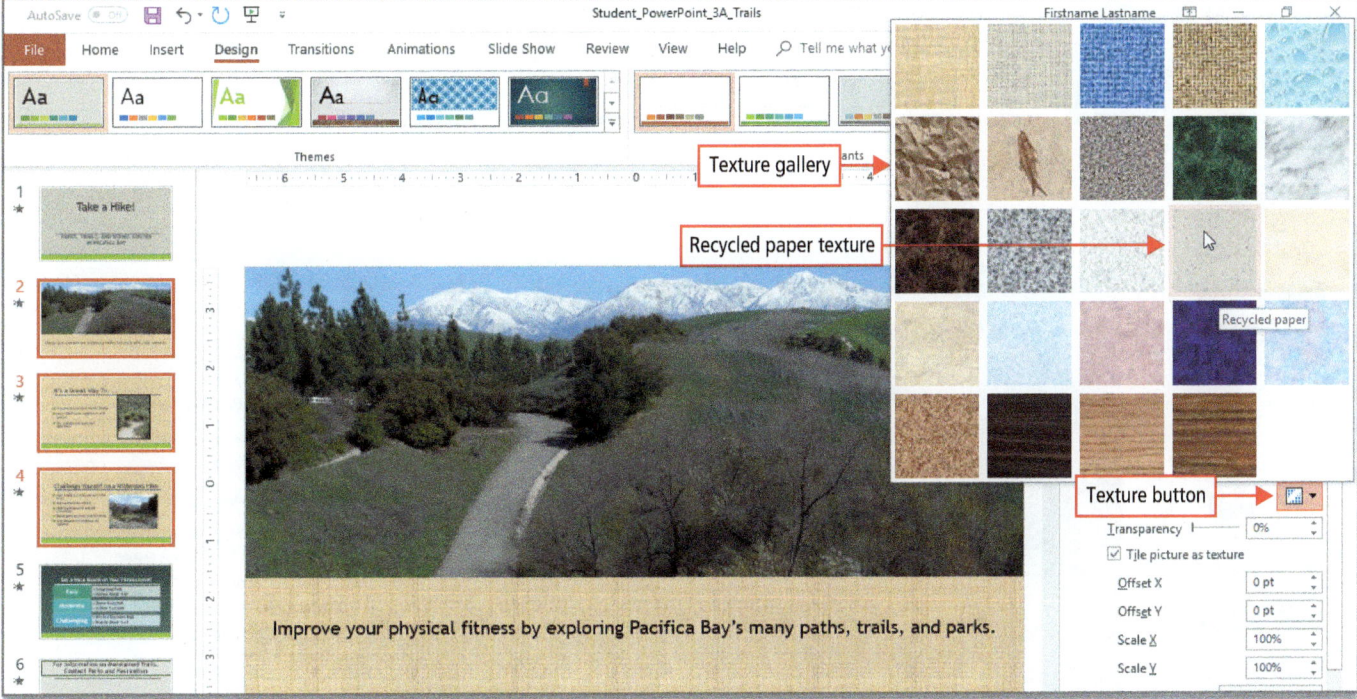

Figure 3.9

4 ▸ Click **Recycled paper** to apply the textured background to the three selected slides.

5 ▸ Leave the **Format Background** pane open for the next Activity, and then **Save** 🖫 your presentation.

Activity 3.07 | **Applying a Picture to the Slide Background and Adjusting Transparency**

MOS
2.2.2

You can insert a picture on a slide background so that the image fills the entire slide.

1 ▸ Display **Slide 6**. In the **Format Background** pane, select the **Hide background graphics** check box.

2 ▸ Under **Fill**, click **Picture or texture fill**. Under **Insert picture from**, click **File**. Navigate to your data files downloaded with this project, click **p03A_Hills**, and then click **Insert**. Compare your slide with Figure 3.10 and notice that the picture displays as the background of Slide 6.

When a picture is applied to a slide background using the Format Background option, the picture is not treated as an object. The picture fills the entire background and you cannot move it or size it.

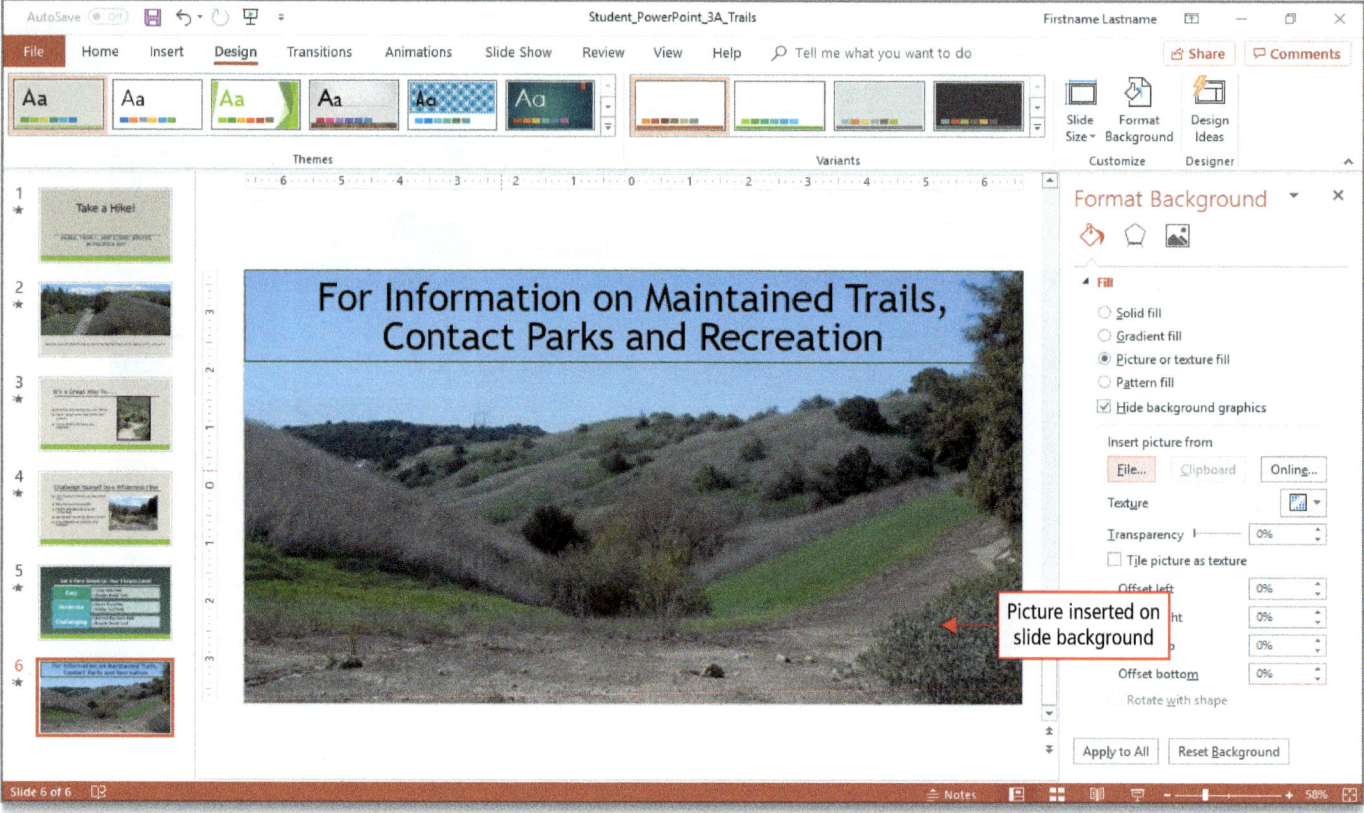

Figure 3.10

3 In the **Format Background** pane, to the right of **Transparency**, notice that *0%* displays, indicating that the picture is inserted in full color. Click in the **Transparency box**, and then replace the number with **50**

> The transparency setting lightens the picture on the slide background. You can use the transparency option when there are other objects on the slide that do not display well against the slide background.

ANOTHER WAY Drag the Transparency slider to the left or right to adjust the transparency figure.

4 Replace the number in the **Transparency box** with **10**

> The 10% transparency setting provides good contrast for the title while still displaying the picture in a vibrant color.

5 Click in the title placeholder. On the **Drawing Tools Format tab**, in the **Shape Styles group**, click **More**. In the fourth row, click the second style. Click anywhere on the slide outside of the title placeholder. Compare your screen with Figure 3.11.

> Adequate contrast between the slide background and slide text is important as it improves slide readability. Use combinations of transparency and text placeholder styles and fills to improve contrast.

Figure 3.11

6 ▸ Leave the **Format Background** pane open for the next Activity. **Save** 🖫 your presentation.

Activity 3.08 | Resetting a Slide Background

1 ▸ Display **Slide 5**. At the bottom of the **Format Background** pane, click **Reset Background**, and then compare your slide with Figure 3.12.

> After making changes to a slide background, you may decide that the original formatting is the best choice for displaying the text and graphics on a slide. The Reset Background feature restores the theme and color theme formatting to a slide.

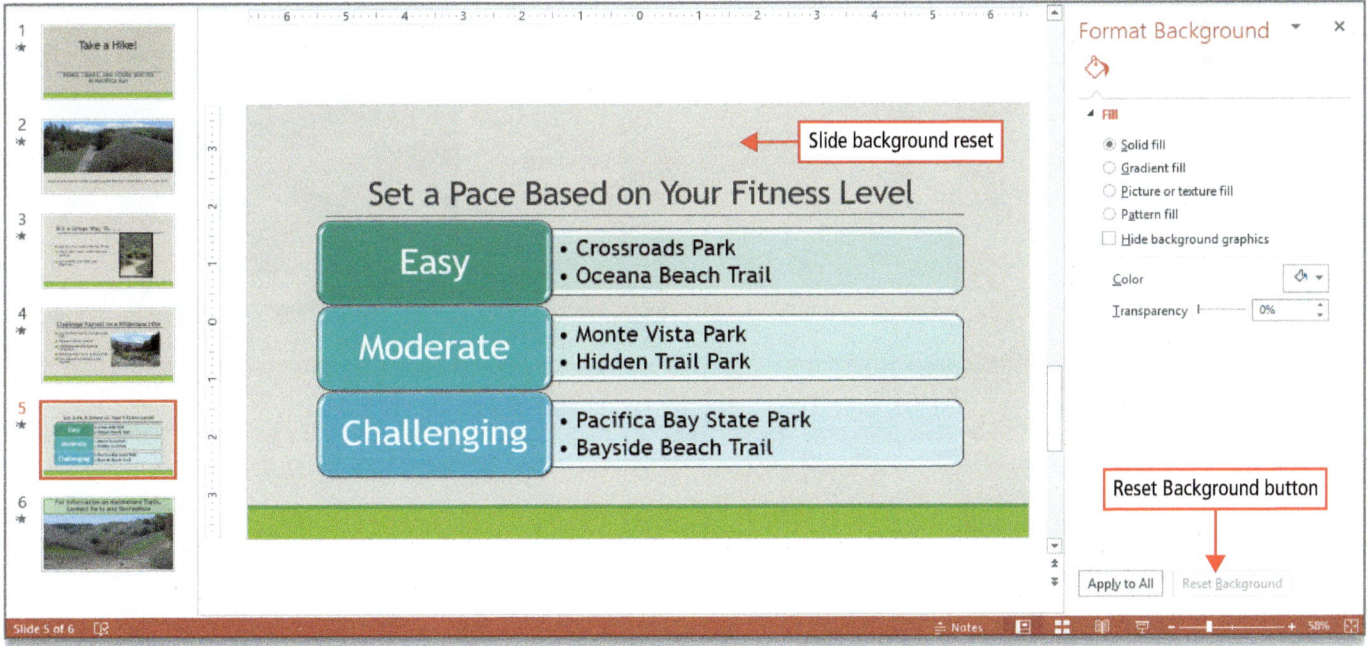

Figure 3.12

2 ▸ **Close** ⊠ the **Format Background** pane, and then **Save** 🖫 your presentation.

GO! Learn How
Video P3-2

Animation is a visual or sound effect added to an object or text on a slide. Use animation to focus the audience's attention, providing the speaker with an opportunity to emphasize important points using the slide element as an effective visual aid.

Activity 3.09 | Applying Animation Entrance Effects and Effect Options

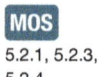

5.2.1, 5.2.3, 5.2.4

Entrance effects are animations that bring a slide element onto the screen. Use the animation Effect Options command to modify an entrance effect.

1 Display **Slide 3**, and then click anywhere in the bulleted list placeholder. On the **Animations tab**, in the **Animation group**, click **More**, and then compare your screen with Figure 3.13.

An entrance effect is animation that brings an object or text onto the screen. An *emphasis effect* is animation that emphasizes an object or text that is already displayed. An *exit effect* is animation that moves an object or text off the screen.

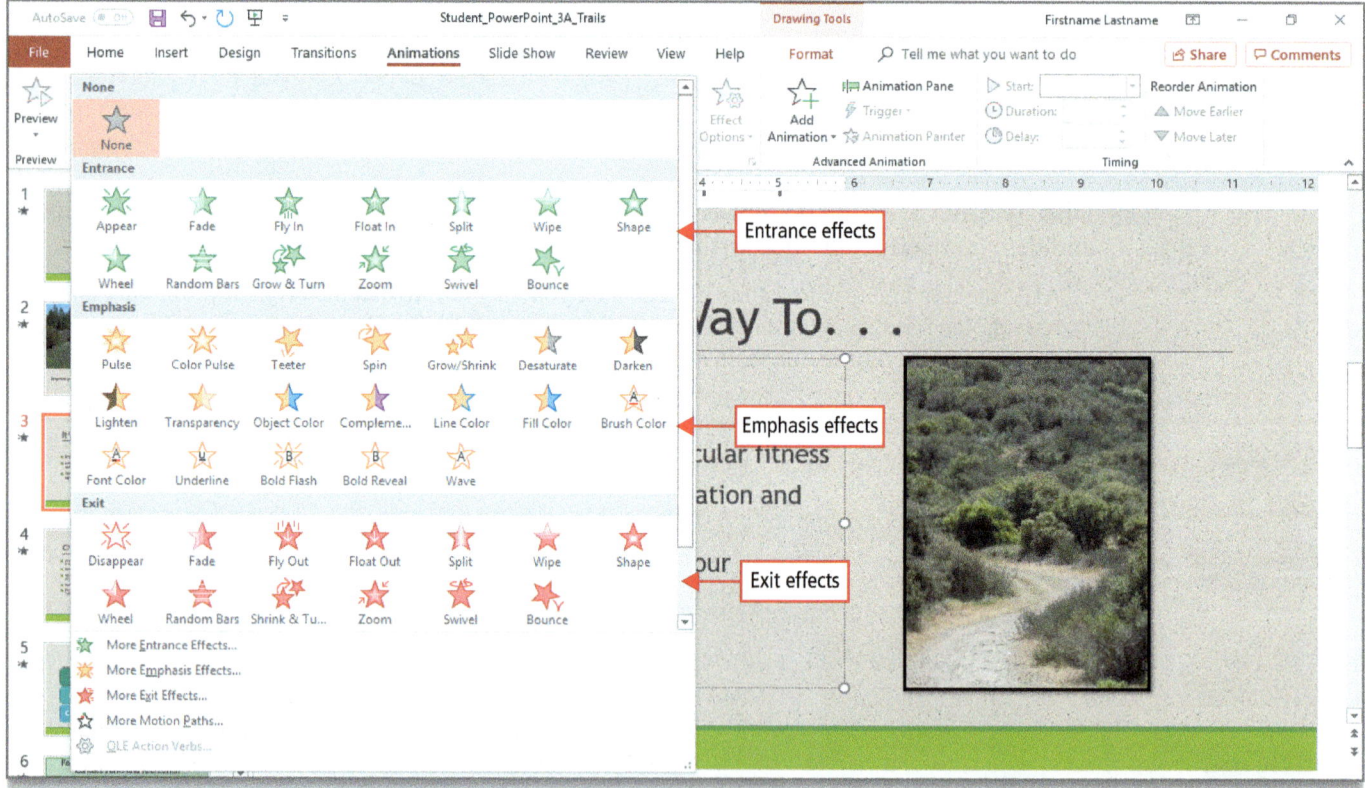

Figure 3.13

2 Under **Entrance**, click **Fly In**, and then notice the animation applied to the list. Compare your screen with Figure 3.14.

The numbers *1, 2,* and *3* display to the left of the bulleted list placeholder, indicating the order in which the bullet points will be animated during the slide show.

MAC TIP The Fly In animation is in the Basic group.

ALERT   Are animation numbers missing?

Make sure to select the Animation tab. If the animation numbers still do not appear on your slide, Save the file to a local drive on your computer, close the file, and reopen it. If the numbers still do not display, continue with the Activity, following along with the figures.

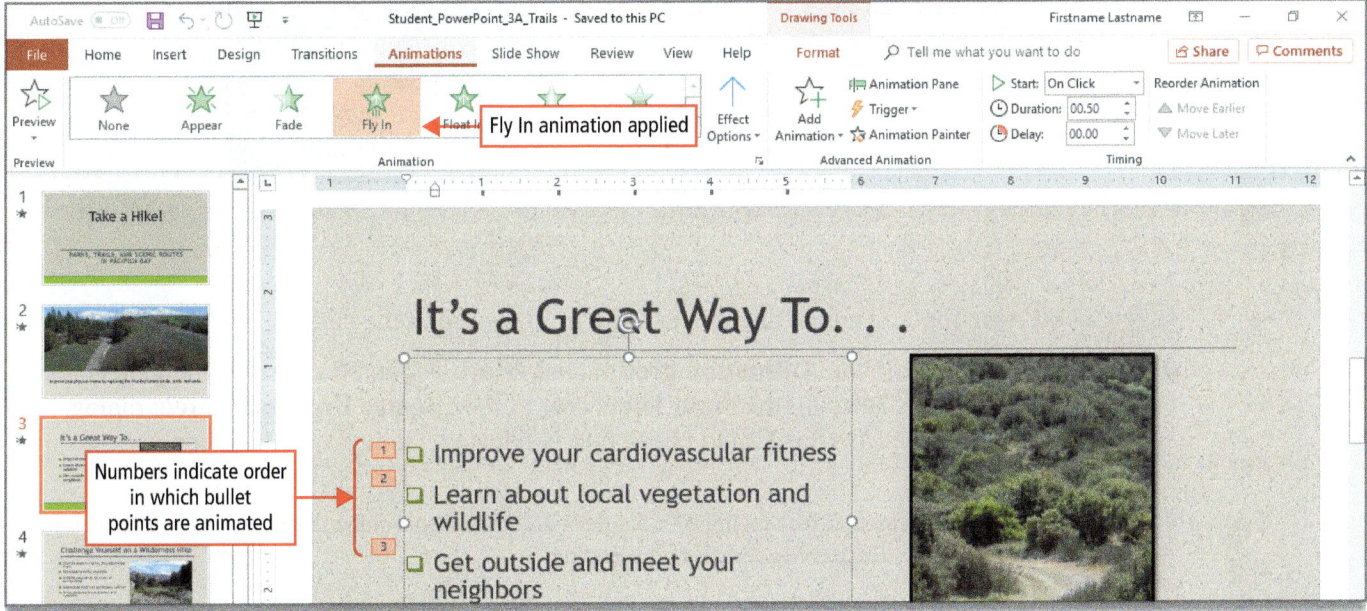

Figure 3.14

3 In the **Animation group**, click **Effect Options**, and then compare your screen with Figure 3.15.

The Effect Options control the direction and sequence in which the animation displays. Additional options may be available with other entrance effects.

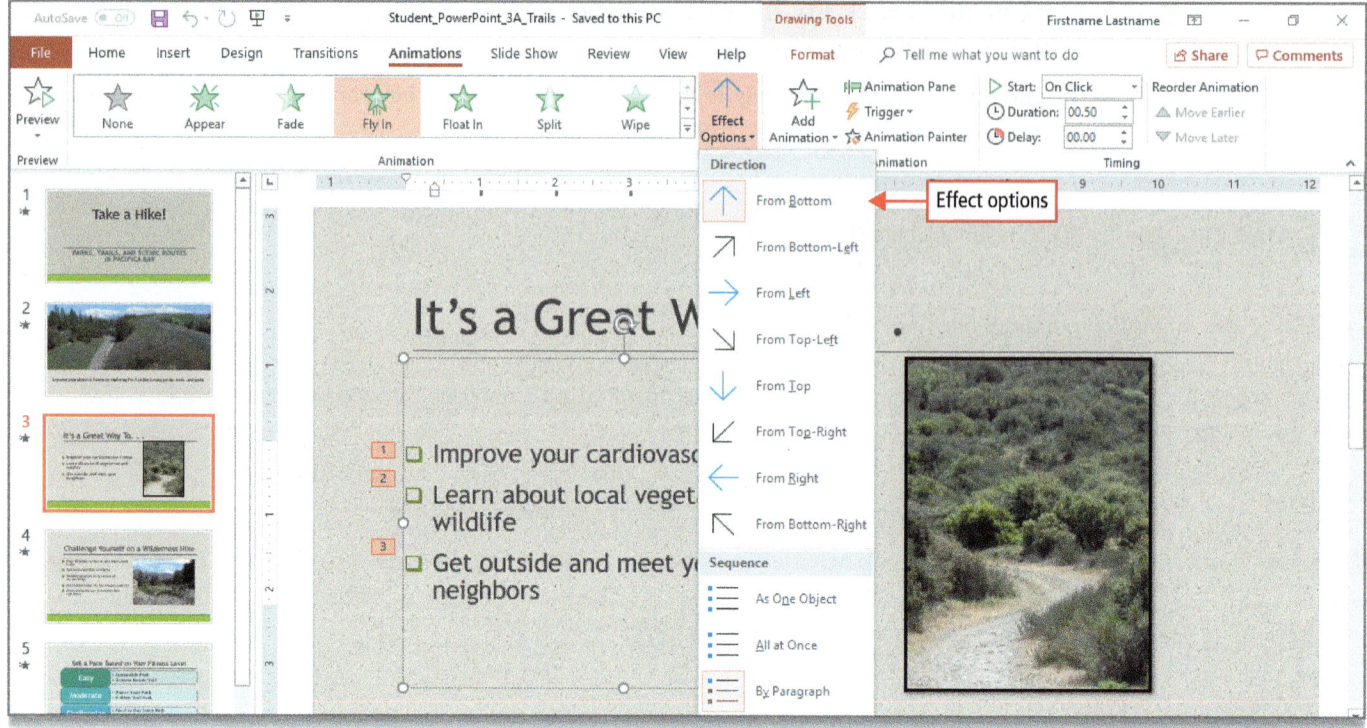

Figure 3.15

4 Click **From Top** and notice the bullets enter from the top of the slide.

5 Select the picture. In the **Animation group**, click **More** ▼ , and then below the gallery, click **More Entrance Effects**. In the lower left corner of the **Change Entrance Effect** dialog box, verify that the **Preview Effect** check box is selected. Compare your screen with Figure 3.16.

The Change Entrance Effect dialog box displays additional entrance effects grouped in four categories: Basic, Subtle, Moderate, and Exciting.

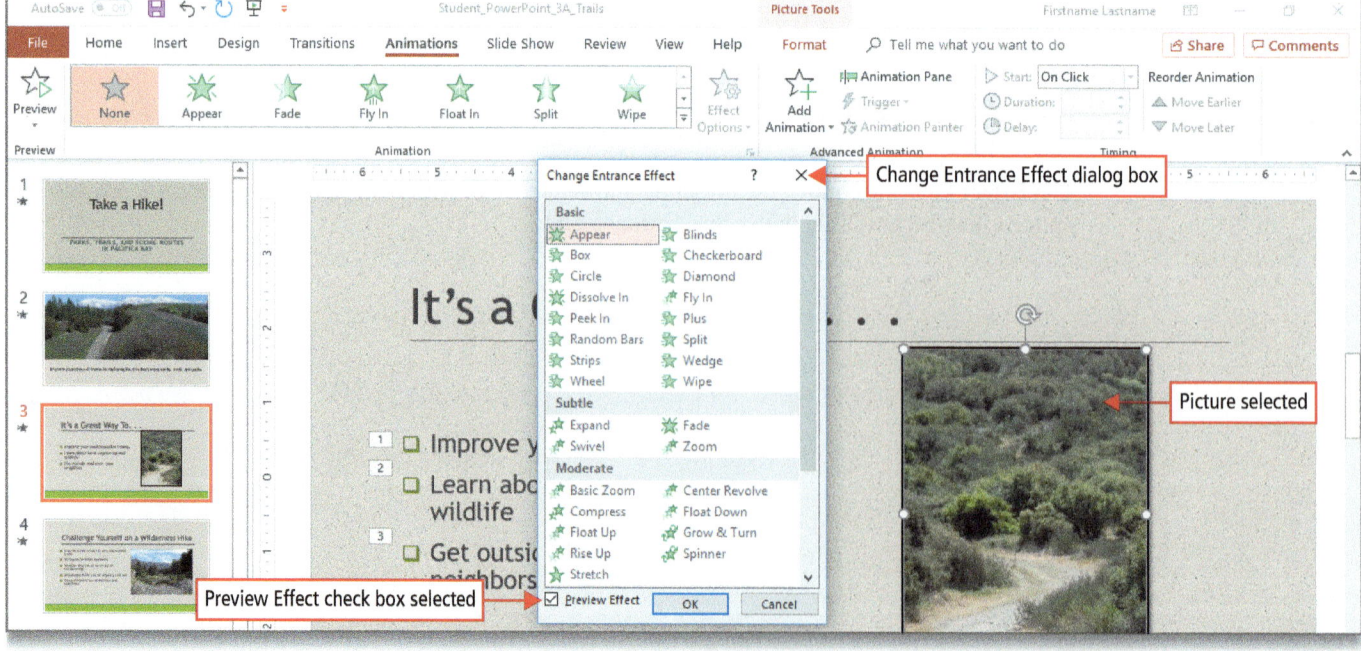

Figure 3.16

6 Under **Subtle**, click **Fade**, and then watch as Live Preview displays the picture with the selected entrance effect. Click **OK**.

The number *4* displays next to the picture, indicating that it is fourth in the slide animation sequence.

7 Click in the title placeholder. On the **Animations tab**, in the **Animation group**, click **More** ⏷, and then under **Entrance**, click **Fade** to apply the animation to the title.

The number 5 displays next to the title, indicating that it is fifth in the slide animation sequence.

8 **Save** 💾 the presentation.

Activity 3.10 | Reordering Animation

5.2.5

1 With **Slide 3** displayed, on the **Animations tab**, in the **Preview group**, click **Preview**.

The list displays first, followed by the picture, and then the title. The order in which animation is applied is the order in which objects display during the slide show.

2 Click in the title placeholder. On the **Animations tab**, in the **Timing group**, under **Reorder Animation**, click **Move Earlier** two times, until the sequence number displays 1, and then compare your screen with Figure 3.17.

> 🖥 **MAC TIP** In the Animations pane, click *5 It's a Great Way to..* and then click the up arrow two times.

To the left of the title placeholder, the number *1* displays. You can use the Reorder Animation buttons to change the order in which text and objects are animated during the slide show.

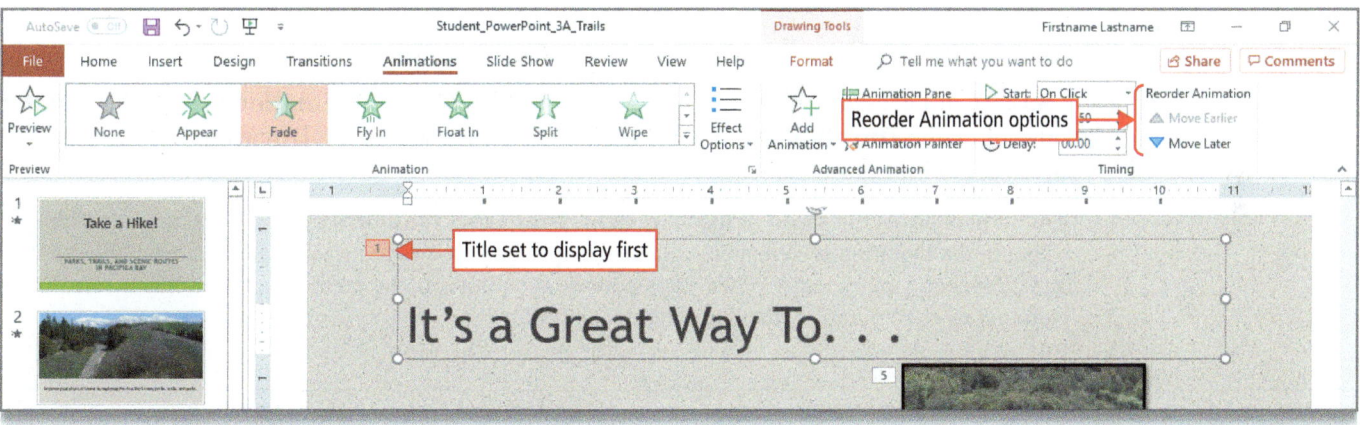

Figure 3.17

Activity 3.11 | Setting Animation Start Options

5.3.2

Timing options control when animated items display in the animation sequence.

1 If necessary, click in the title placeholder. On the **Animations tab**, in the **Timing group**, click the **Start arrow** to display three options—*On Click*, *With Previous*, and *After Previous*. Compare your screen with Figure 3.18.

The ***On Click*** option begins the animation sequence for the selected slide element when the mouse button is clicked or the [Spacebar] is pressed. The ***With Previous*** option begins the animation sequence at the same time as the previous animation or slide transition. The ***After Previous*** option begins the animation sequence for the selected slide element immediately after the completion of the previous animation or slide transition.

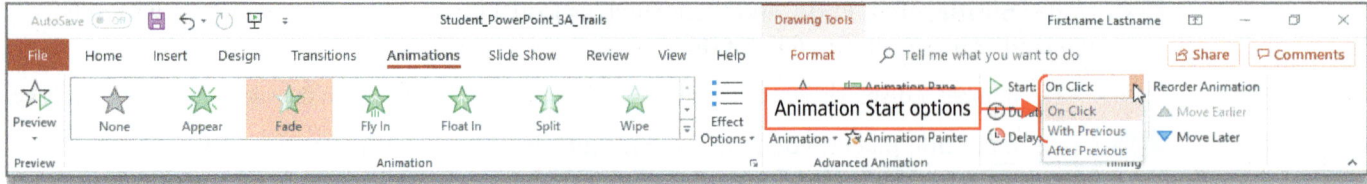

Figure 3.18

2 ▸ Click **After Previous**, and then notice that next to the title, the number *1* is changed to *0*, indicating that the animation will begin immediately after the slide transition; the presenter does not need to click the mouse button or press ⎵Spacebar⎵ to display the title.

3 ▸ Select the picture, and then in the **Timing group**, click the **Start arrow**. Click **With Previous** and notice that the number is changed to *3*, indicating that the animation will begin at the same time as the last bullet in the bulleted list.

4 ▸ On the **Animations tab**, in the **Preview group**, click **Preview** and notice that the title displays first, and that the picture displays at the same time as the last bullet in the bulleted list.

5 ▸ Display **Slide 1**, and then click in the title placeholder. On the **Animations tab**, in the **Animation group**, click the **Entrance** effect **Fly In**, and then click **Effect Options**. Click **From Top**. In the **Timing group**, click the **Start arrow**, and then click **After Previous**.

The number *0* displays to the left of the title indicating that the animation will begin immediately after the slide transition.

6 ▸ **Save** your presentation.

Activity 3.12 | Setting Animation Duration and Delay Timing Options

MOS
5.3.1

1 ▸ On **Slide 1**, if necessary, click in the title placeholder. On the **Animation tab**, in the **Timing group**, click the **Duration up arrow** so that *00.75* displays in the **Duration** box. Compare your screen with Figure 3.19.

Duration controls the speed of the animation. You can set the duration of an animation by typing a value in the Duration box, or you can use the spin box arrows to increase and decrease the duration in 0.25-second increments. When you decrease the duration, the animation speed increases. When you increase the duration, the animation is slowed.

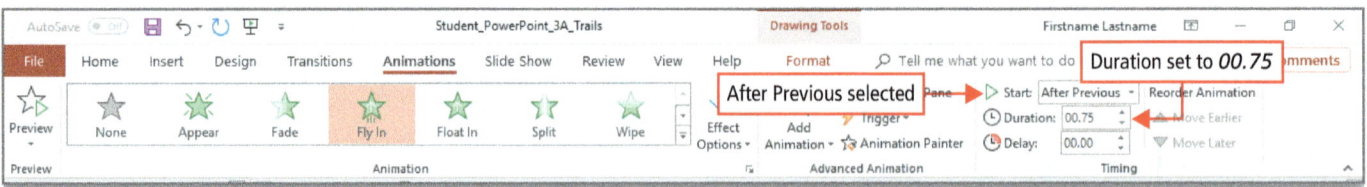

Figure 3.19

2 Click anywhere in the subtitle, and then in the **Animation group**, apply the **Fade** entrance effect. In the **Timing group**, click the **Start arrow**, and then click **After Previous**. In the **Timing group**, select the value in the **Delay** box, type.**50** and then press Enter. Compare your screen with Figure 3.20.

You can use Delay to begin a selected animation after a specified amount of time has elapsed. Here, the animation is delayed by one-half of a second after the completion of the previous animation—the title animation. You can type a value in the Delay or Duration boxes, or you can use the up and down arrows to change the timing.

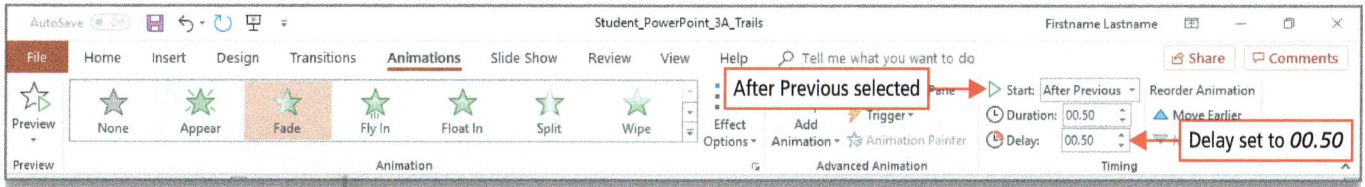

Figure 3.20

3 View the slide show from the beginning and notice the animation on Slides 1 and 3. When the black slide displays, press Esc to return to Normal view, and then **Save** 🖫 your presentation.

Activity 3.13 | Using Animation Painter and Removing Animation

Animation Painter is a feature that copies animation settings from one object to another.

1 Display **Slide 3**, and then click anywhere in the bulleted list. On the **Animations tab**, in the **Advanced Animation group**, click **Animation Painter**. Display **Slide 4**, and then point anywhere in the bulleted list placeholder to display the Animation Painter pointer. Compare your screen with Figure 3.21.

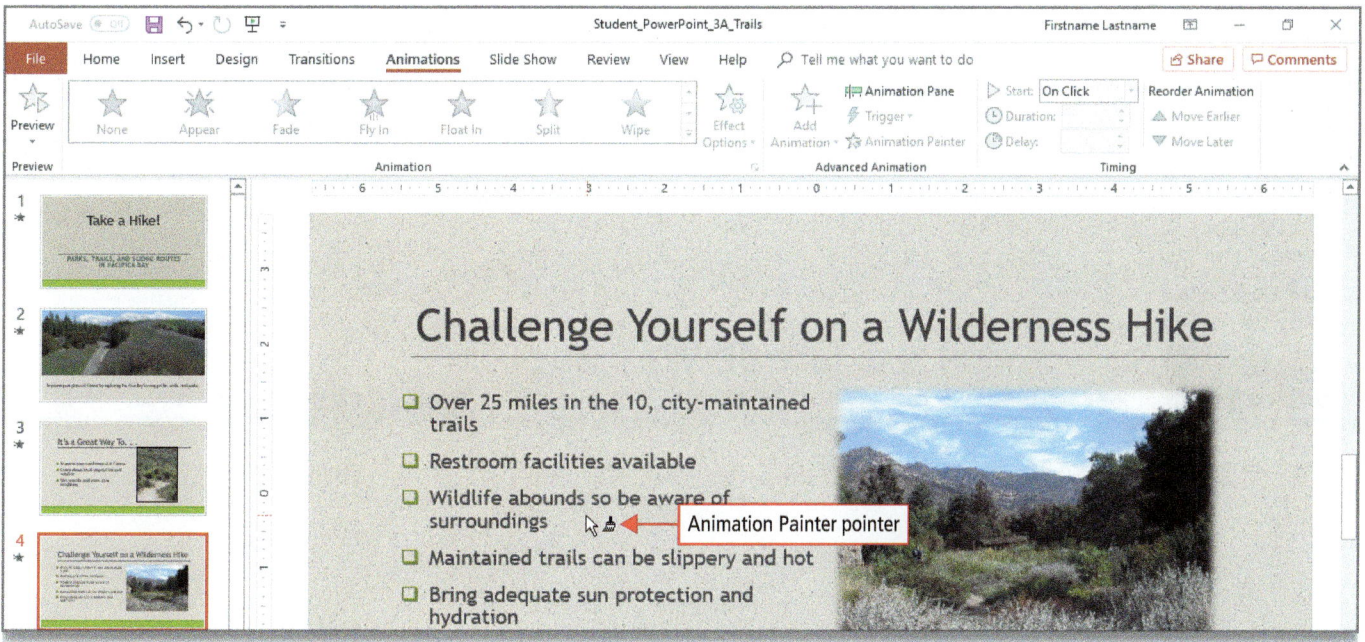

Figure 3.21

2 Click the bulleted list to copy the animation settings from the list on **Slide 3** to the list on **Slide 4.**

3 Display **Slide 3**, and then select the picture. Using the technique that you just practiced, use **Animation Painter** to copy the animation from the picture on **Slide 3** to the picture on **Slide 4**. With **Slide 4** displayed, compare your screen with Figure 3.22.

The numbers displayed to the left of the bulleted list and the picture indicate that animation is applied to the objects.

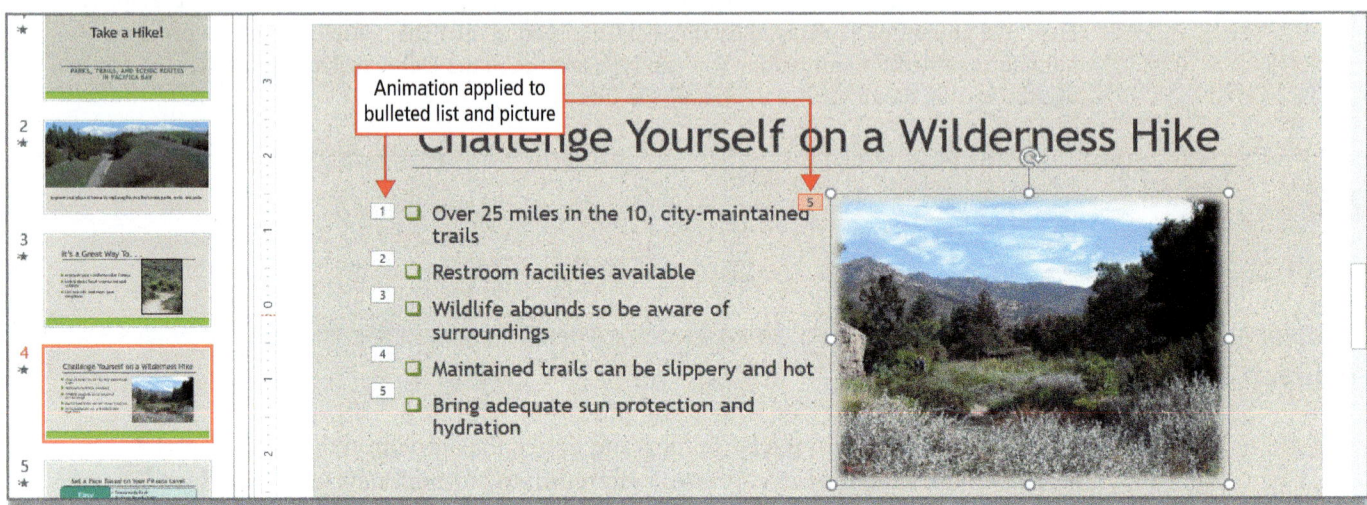

Figure 3.22

4 Display **Slide 3**, and then click in the title placeholder. On the **Animations tab**, in the **Animation group**, click **None** to remove the animation from the title placeholder. Compare your screen with Figure 3.23, and then **Save** your presentation.

MAC TIP In the Animations pane, under ANIMATIONS, select the title and then click the red X to remove the animation.

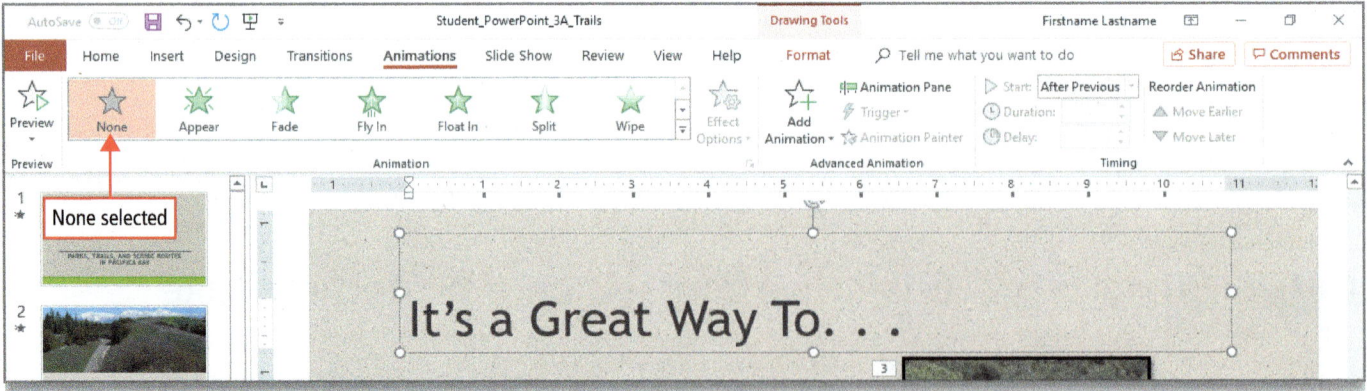

Figure 3.23

GO! Learn How
Video P3-3

You can insert, size, and move videos in a PowerPoint presentation, and you can format videos by applying styles and effects. Video editing features in PowerPoint enable you to trim parts of a video and to compress the video to make the presentation easier to share.

Activity 3.14 | Inserting a Video and Using Media Controls

4.5.1

1 ▶ Display **Slide 1**. On the **Insert tab**, in the **Media group**, click **Video**, and then click **Video on My PC**. In the **Insert Video** dialog box, navigate to the files downloaded with this project, and then click **p03A_Video**. Click **Insert**, and then compare your screen with Figure 3.24.

The video displays in the center of the slide, and media controls display in the control panel below the video.

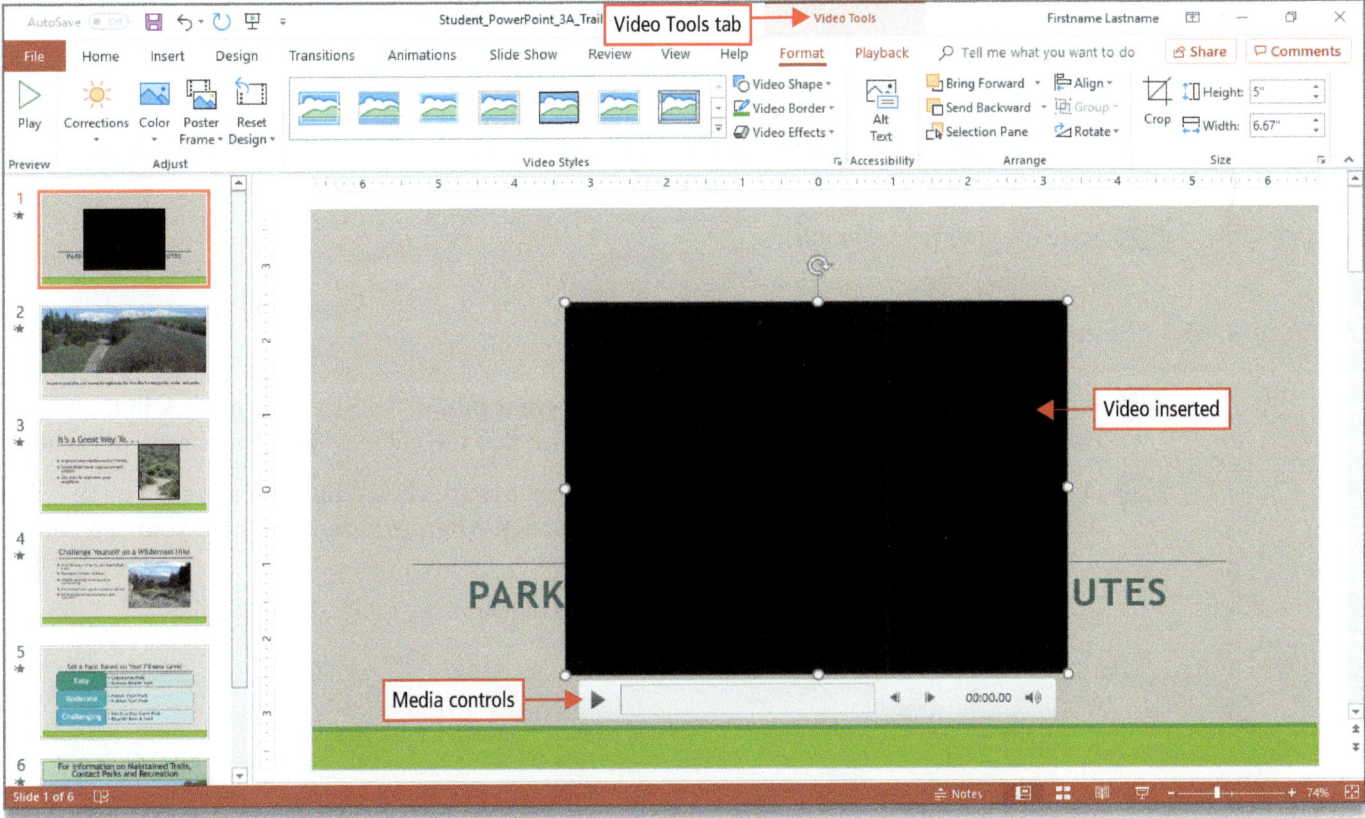

Figure 3.24

2 ▶ Below the video, in the media controls, click **Play/Pause** ▶ to view the video and notice that as the video plays, the media controls display the time that has elapsed since the start of the video.

3 ▶ View the slide show from the beginning. On **Slide 1**, after the subtitle displays, point to the video to display the 🖑 pointer, and then compare your screen with Figure 3.25.

When you point to the video during the slide show, the media controls display.

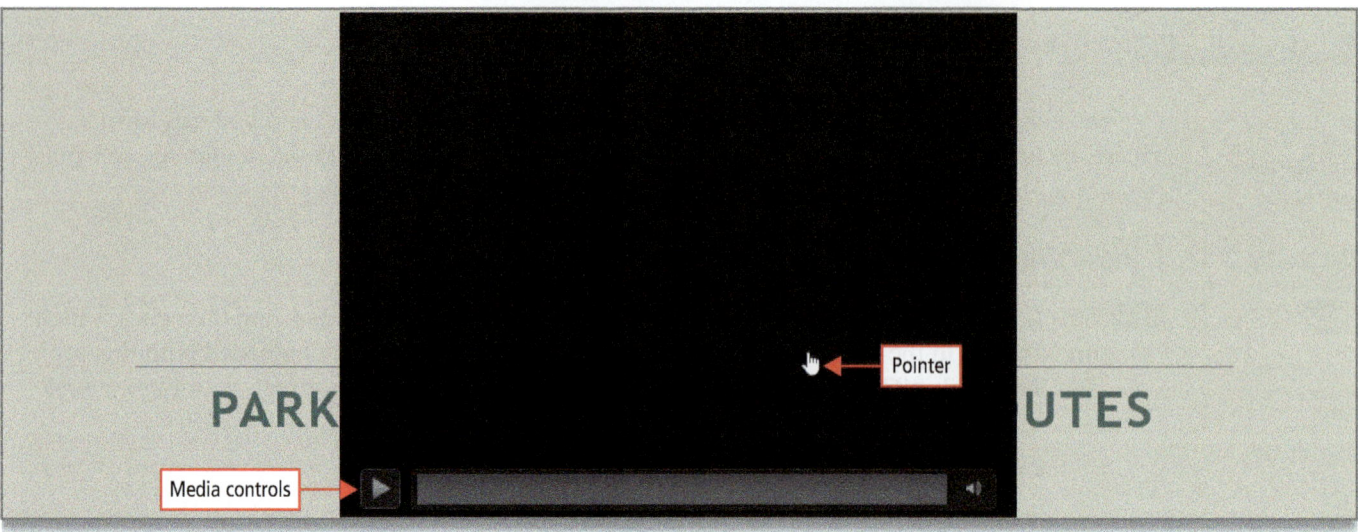

Figure 3.25

4 With the ☝ pointer displayed, click the mouse button to view the video. Move the pointer away from the video and notice that the media controls no longer display. When the video is finished, press Esc to exit the slide show.

5 **Save** 🖫 your presentation.

Activity 3.15 | Sizing and Aligning a Video

1 With the video selected, on the **Video Tools Format tab**, in the **Size group**, click in the **Height** box 🔟. Type **2** and then press Enter. Notice that the video width adjusts proportionately.

2 On the **Video Tools Format tab**, in the **Arrange group**, click **Align** 📐, and then click **Align Center**. Click **Align** 📐 again, and then click **Align Middle**. Compare your screen with Figure 3.26. **Save** 🖫 your presentation.

The video is centered horizontally and vertically on the slide.

Figure 3.26

Activity 3.16 | Changing the Style and Shape of a Video

You can apply styles and effects to a video and change the video shape and border. You can also recolor a video so that it coordinates with the presentation theme.

1 On **Slide 1**, if necessary, select the video. On the **Video Tools Format tab**, in the **Video Styles group**, click **More** [▾] to display the **Video Styles** gallery.

2 Using the ScreenTips to view the style name, under **Subtle**, click the last style—**Drop Shadow Rectangle**. Compare your screen with Figure 3.27.

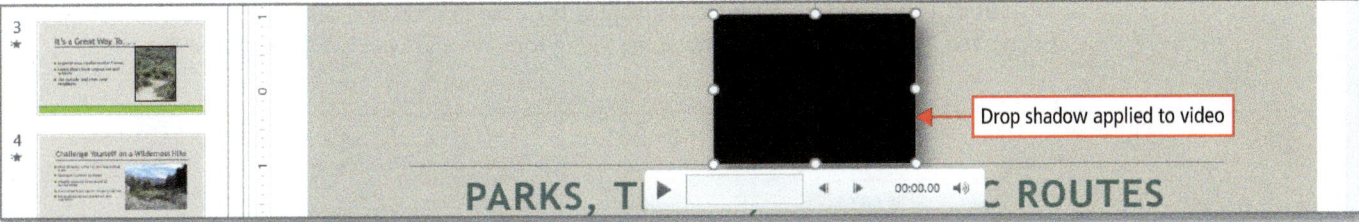

Figure 3.27

3 In the **Video Styles group**, click **Video Shape**, and then under **Rectangles**, click the second shape—**Rectangle: Rounded Corners**. Compare your screen with Figure 3.28.

You can format a video with any combination of styles, shapes, and effects.

MAC TIP Click the Crop arrow, point to Change Shape, and then click Rounded Rectangle.

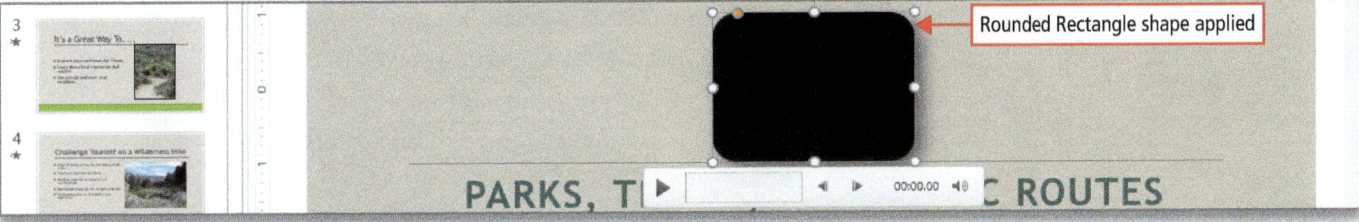

Figure 3.28

Activity 3.17 | Trimming and Compressing a Video and Setting Playback Options

MOS
1.5.5, 4.5.2, 4.5.3

You can *trim*—delete parts of a video to make it shorter—and you can compress a video file to reduce the file size of your PowerPoint presentation. You can trim the video from the beginning and the end.

1 If necessary, select the video. On the **Video Tools Playback tab**, in the **Editing group**, click **Trim Video**, and then compare your screen with Figure 3.29.

At the top of the displayed Trim Video dialog box, the file name and the video duration display. Below the video, a timeline displays with start and end markers indicating the video start and end time. Start Time and End Time boxes display the current start and end of the video. The Previous Frame and Next Frame buttons move the video forward and backward one frame at a time.

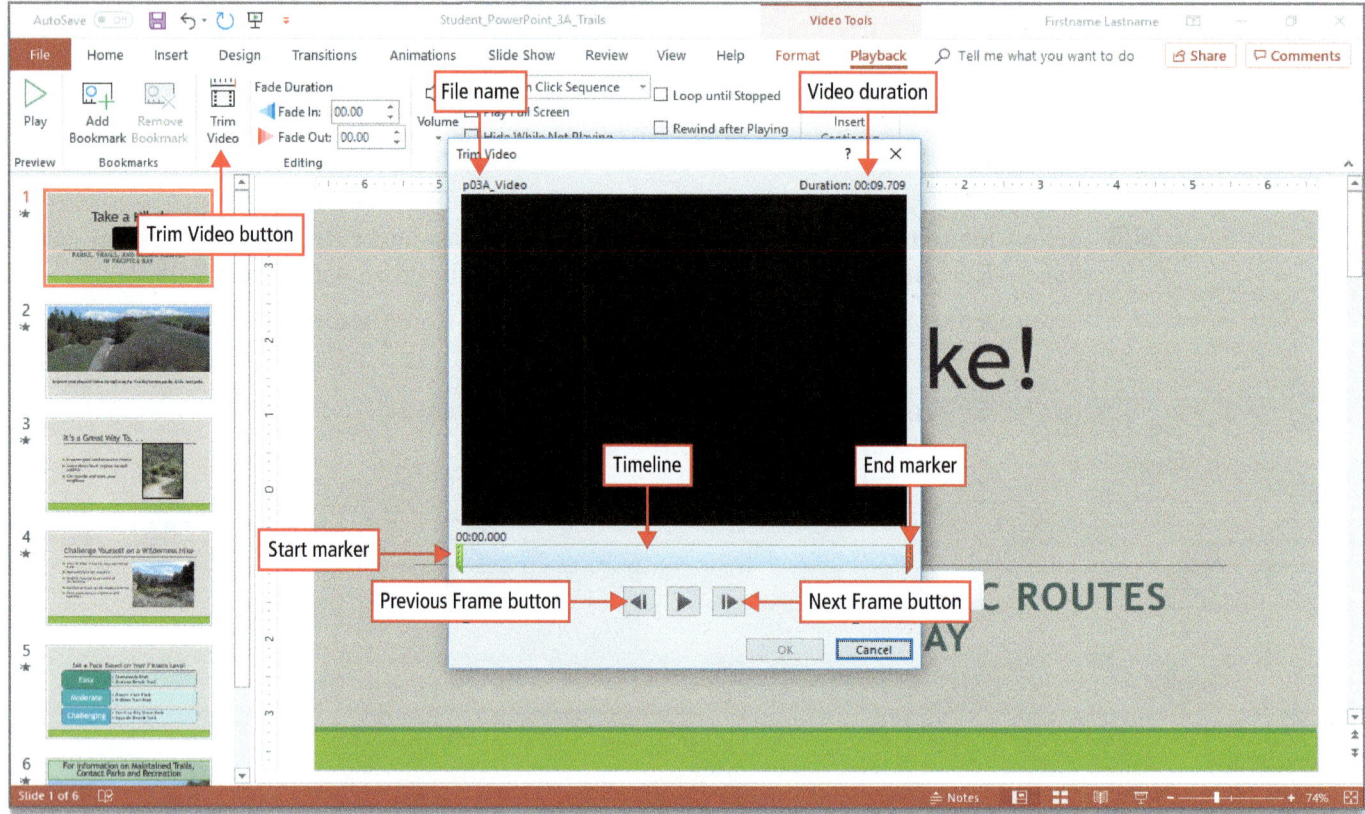

Figure 3.29

2 In the **End Time** box, replace the number with **00:09.425** and then compare your screen with Figure 3.30.

The blue section of the timeline indicates the portion of the video that will play during the slide show. The gray section indicates the portion of the video that is trimmed. The image in the Trim Video dialog box displays the last frame in the video based on the trim setting.

💻 **MAC TIP** Drag the End Trim slider to adjust the duration. The duration counter is above the video preview in the trim window.

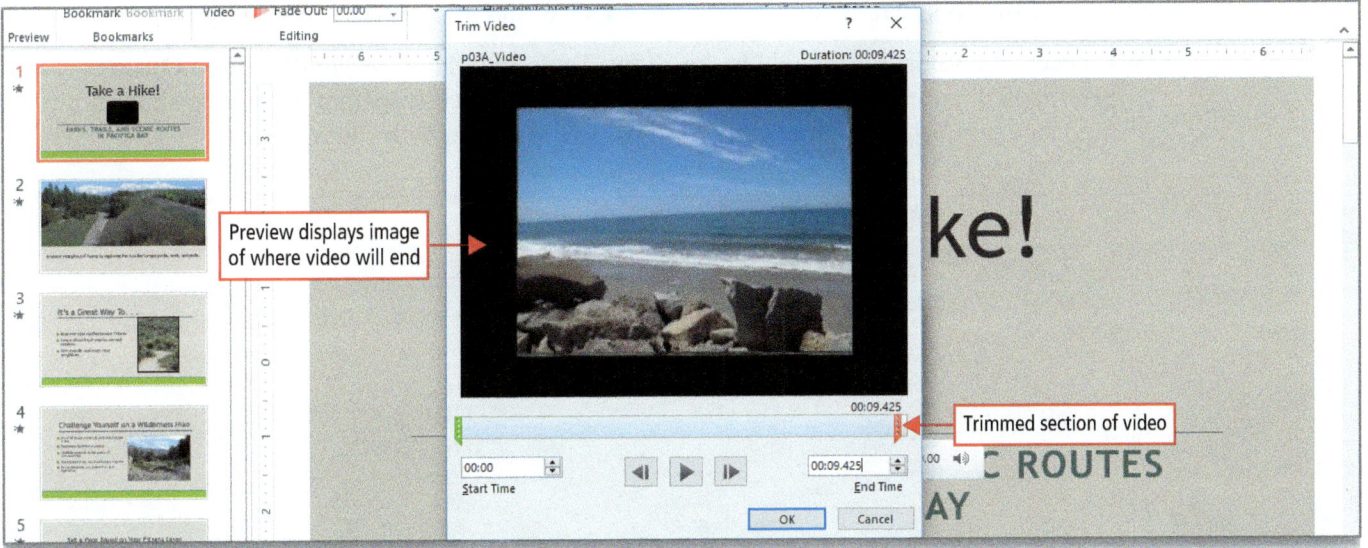

Figure 3.30

3▸ Click **OK** to apply the trim settings.

4▸ Click **File**, and then click **Compress Media**. Read the description of each video quality option, and then click **Standard Quality**. Depending on your system, this may be named Low Quality. Compare your screen with Figure 3.31.

> The Compress Media dialog box displays the slide number on which the selected video is inserted, the video file name, the original size of the video file, and when compression is complete, the amount that the file size was reduced. Because this video is an MP4 video format, which is a compressed format, your dialog box Status may indicate Already Compressed.

💻 **MAC TIP** The Compress Media feature is not available in the Mac version of PowerPoint.

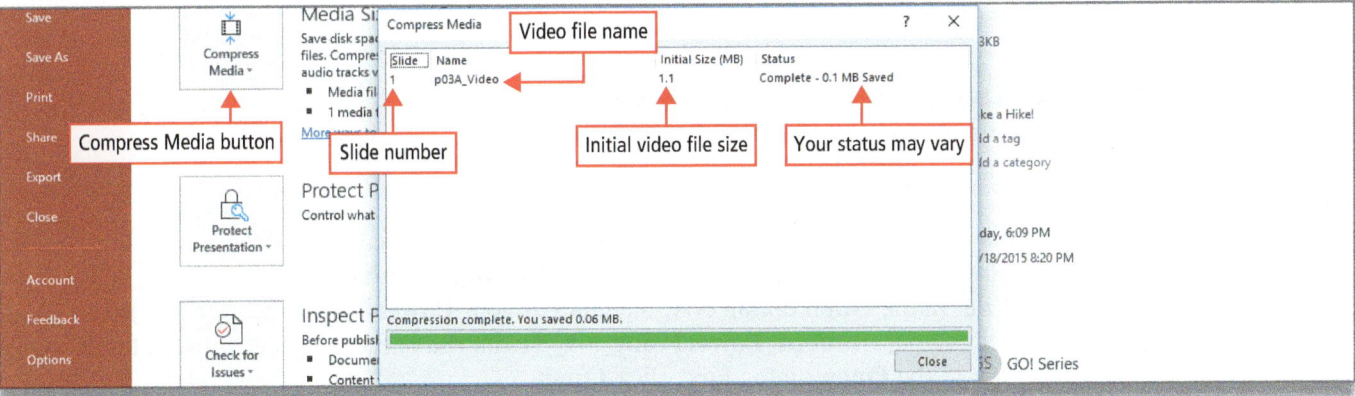

Figure 3.31

5 In the **Compress Media** dialog box, click **Close**, and then on the left, click **Save**.

6 If necessary, select the video. On the **Video Tools Playback tab**, in the **Video Options group**, click the **Start arrow**, and then click **Automatically** so that during the slide show, the video will begin automatically. Compare your screen with Figure 3.32.

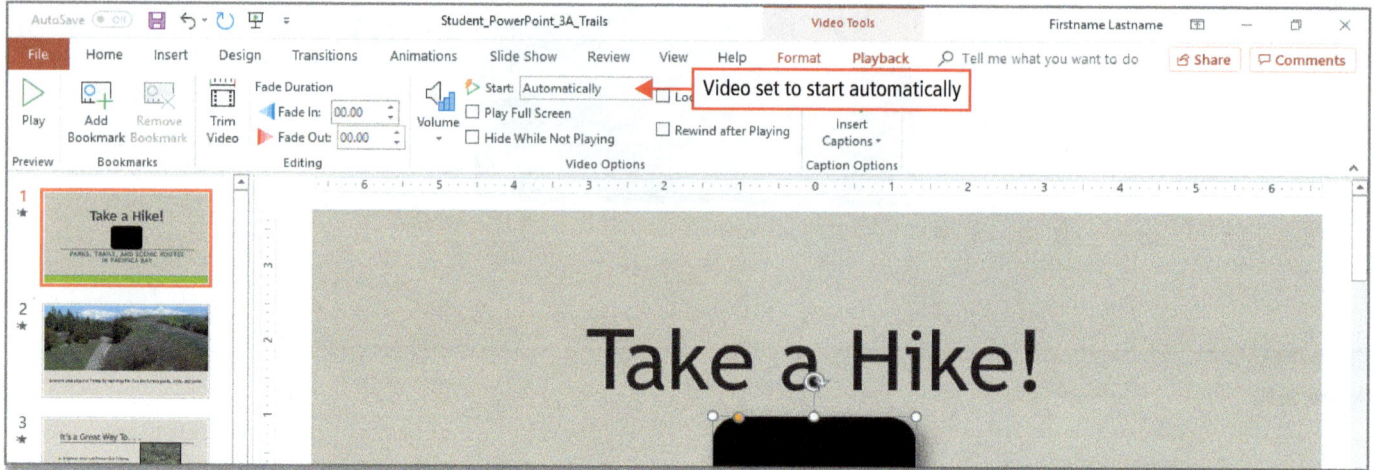

Figure 3.32

7 Click the **Slide Show tab**, in the **Start Slide Show group**, click **From Beginning**, and then view the slide show. Notice that on Slide 1, the video begins playing immediately after the subtitle displays. After you view the video, click the mouse button to advance to the next slide and then continue to view the presentation. Press [Esc] when the black slide displays.

8 Insert a **Header & Footer** on the **Notes and Handouts**. Include the **Date and time** updated automatically, the **Page Number**, and a **Footer**. In the **Footer** box, type **3A_Trails** and then click **Apply to All**.

9 Display the document properties. As the **Tags**, type **walking trails** and as the **Subject**, type your course and section number. Be sure your name displays as author, and then **Save** your file. **Close** PowerPoint.

For Non-MyLab Submissions Determine What Your Instructor Requires
As directed by your instructor, submit your completed PowerPoint presentation.

10 In **MyLab IT**, in your **Course Materials**, locate and click the Grader Project **PowerPoint 3A Trails**. In **step 3**, under **Upload Completed Assignment**, click **Choose File**. In the **Open** dialog box, navigate to your **PowerPoint Chapter 3 folder**, and then click your **Student_PowerPoint_3A_Trails** file one time to select it. In the lower right corner of the **Open** dialog box, click **Open**.

The name of your selected file displays above the Upload button.

11 To submit your file to **MyLab IT** for grading, click **Upload**, wait a moment for a green **Success!** message, and then in **step 4**, click the blue **Submit for Grading** button. Click **Close Assignment** to return to your list of **Course Materials**.

You have completed Project 3A **END**

Objective | **Create an Informational Presentation Using Google Slides**

Activity | **Creating an Informational Presentation in Google Slides**

In this Activity, you will use Google Slides to create a presentation similar to the one you created in Project 3A.

1 From the desktop, open your browser, navigate to **http://google.com**, and then sign in to your Google account. Click **Google apps** [image], and then click **Drive** [image]. Open your **GO! Web Projects** folder—or click New to create and then open this folder, if necessary.

2 In the left pane, click **New**, click **File upload** [image], and then in the **Open** dialog box, navigate to your student data files. Select **p03_3A_Google_Slides**. Click **Open**. When the upload is complete, if necessary, close the Uploads completed message box. Right-click **p03_3A_ Google_Slides**, and then click **Rename**. Using your own name, as the file name, type **Lastname_Firstname_3A_ Google_Slides** and then press Enter. Right-click your file, point to **Open with**, and then click **Google Slides**.

3 On the toolbar, click **Background**, click the **Color arrow**, in the fifth column, click the fourth color—**light green 2**. Click **Done** to apply the light green background to Slide 1.

4 On **Slide 1**, in the title placeholder, select the title text—*Take a Hike!* Click the **Font arrow**, and then click **Georgia**.

5 Display **Slide 2**, and then at the bottom of the slide, click in the text placeholder. On the toolbar, click **Fill color** [image], and then in the fifth column, click the fourth color—**light green 2**. Select the text, and then change the **Font Size** to **36**.

6 With the placeholder selected, point to the center-left sizing handle, and then drag as far to the left as possible without exceeding the left edge of the slide. Repeat this process on the right side of the slide, and then click outside of the placeholder.

7 Display **Slide 3**, and then click anywhere in the bulleted list. On the menu bar click **View**, and then click **Animations** to display the **Animations pane**. On the **Animations pane**, if necessary, click Select an object to animate, click **Add animation**, click the **Fade in arrow**, and then click **Fly in from right**.

8 Click the picture, if necessary, click Select an object to animate, click **Add animation**, click the **Fade in arrow**, and then click **Appear**.

9 Click anywhere in the title text, if necessary, click Select an object to animate, click **Add animation**, click the **Fade in arrow**, and then click **Fly in from top**. Notice the animation sequencing in the Animations pane, which indicates that the title animation Fly in from top will display last. At the bottom of the **Animations pane**, click the **Play** button, and then point to the slide and click the slide four times to preview the animations in sequence.

10 With **Slide 3** displayed, with the title selected, in the **Animations pane**, click the title animation *Fly in from top* and drag it to the top of the list so that it will appear first. At the bottom of the **Animations pane**, click the **Play** button, and then point to the slide and click the slide four times to preview the animations in sequence.

11 Display **Slide 4**, and then click the title. On the **Animations pane**, click **Add animation**, click the **Fade in arrow**, and then click **Fly in from top**.

12 Click the bulleted list. On the **Animations pane**, click **Add animation**, click the **Fade in arrow**, and then click **Fly in from right**.

13 Click the picture, click **Add animation**, click the **Fade in arrow**, and then click **Appear**.

14 Display **Slide 6**, and then click in the title. On the **Animations pane**, click **Add animation**, click the **Fade in arrow**, and then click **Fly in from top**.

15 On the **Animations pane**, if necessary, click ▶ to expand **Slide: No transition**. Click the **No transition arrow**, click **Slide from left**, and then click **Apply to all slides. Close** [×] the **Animations pane**.

»»» **GO!** With Google continues on next page

»» GO! With Google

16 Display **Slide 1**. In the upper right, click the **Present arrow**, click **Present from beginning**. If necessary, click **Allow**. Click the left mouse button to progress through the presentation. When the last slide displays, press (Esc) or click **Exit**.

17 Your presentation will be saved automatically. If you are instructed to submit your file, click the File menu, point to Download as, and then click PDF or PowerPoint as directed by your instructor. The file will download to your default download folder as determined by your browser settings. Sign out of your Google account and close your browser.

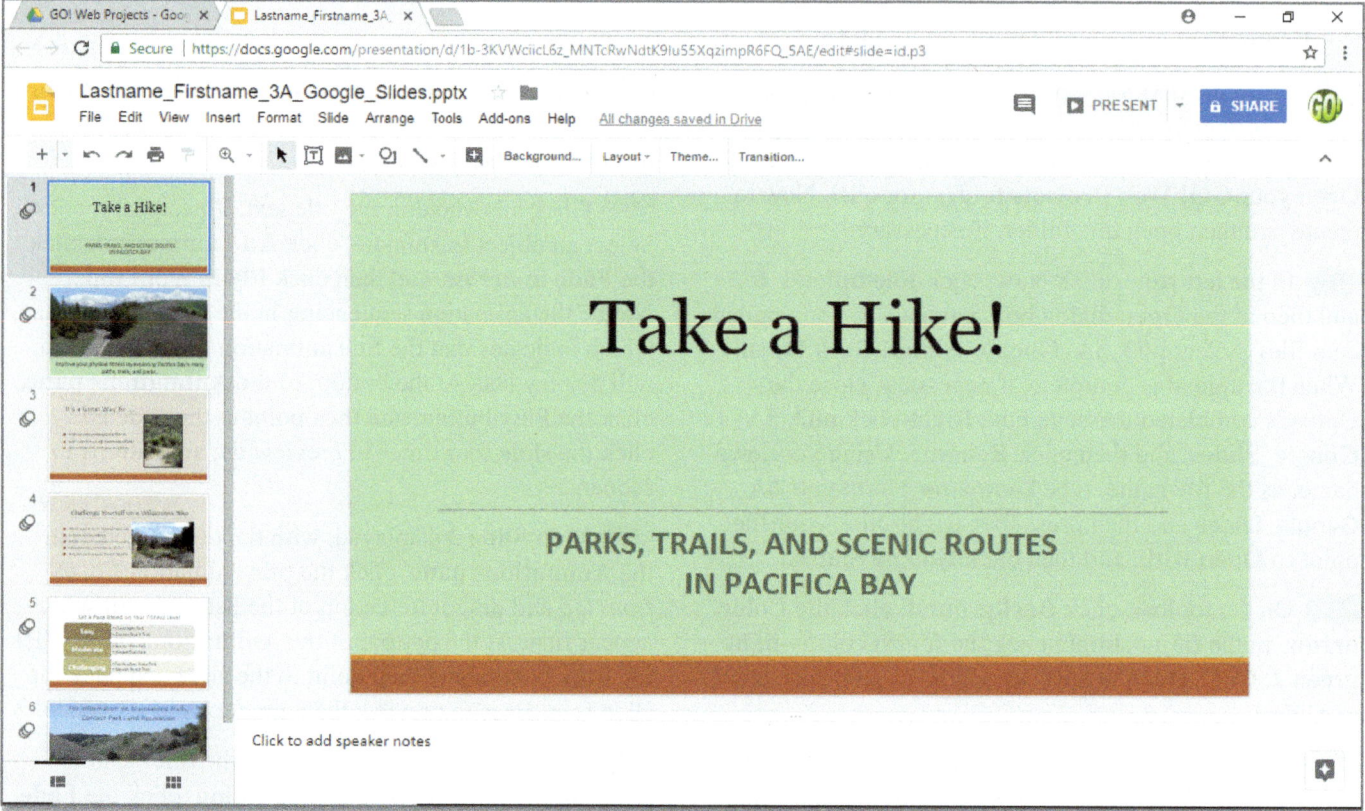

Figure A

PROJECT 3B

Summary and Analysis Presentation

MyLab IT
Project 3B Grader for Instruction
Project 3B Simulation for Training and Review

Project Activities

In Activities 3.18 through 3.30, you will add a table and two charts to a presentation that Mindy Walker, Director of Parks and Recreation, is creating to inform the City Council about enrollment trends in Pacifica Bay recreation programs. Your completed presentation will look similar to Figure 3.33.

Project Files for **MyLab IT** Grader

1. In your **MyLab IT** course, locate and click **PowerPoint 3B Enrollment**, Download Materials, and then Download All Files.
2. Extract the zipped folder to your PowerPoint Chapter 3 folder. Close the Grader download screens.
3. Take a moment to open the downloaded **PowerPoint_3B_Enrollment_Instructions**; note any recent updates to the book.

Project Results

GO! Project 3B
Where We're Going

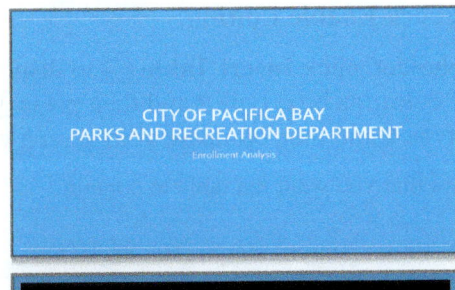
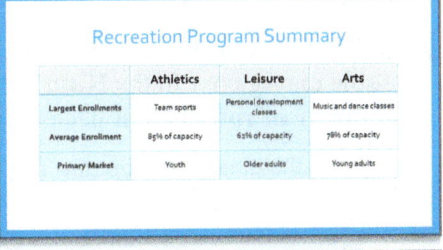
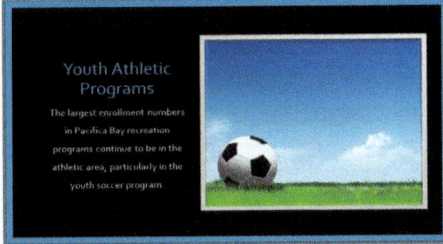

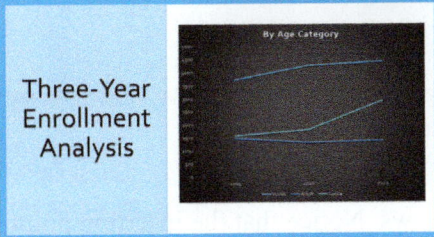
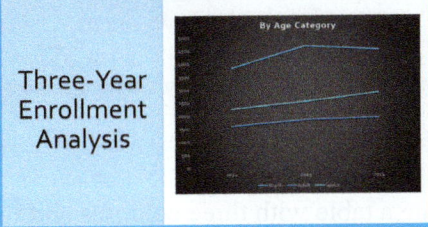

Figure 3.33 Project 3B Enrollment

For Non-MyLab Submissions

For Project 3B, you will need this starting file:
p03B_Enrollment

In your PowerPoint Chapter 3 folder, save your presentation as:
Lastname_Firstname_3B_Enrollment

After you have named and saved your presentation, on the next page, begin with Step 2.

Objective 4 — Create and Modify Tables

ALERT Because Office 365 is a cloud-based subscription service that receives continuous updates, you may encounter some variations in what appears on your screen and what is shown in this instruction. Microsoft Office 365 is fully installed on your PC or Mac; no internet access is necessary to create or edit documents. When you *are* connected to the internet, you will receive monthly upgrades and new features, so you always have the latest versions of Office apps as soon as they are available. Your subscription gives you continuous free access to the latest innovations and refinements.

GO! Learn How
Video P3-4

A *table* is a format for information that organizes and presents text and data in columns and rows. The intersection of a column and row is referred to as a *cell* and is the location in which you type text in a table. Tables are a useful way to organize information.

Activity 3.18 | Creating a Table

MOS
4.1.1

There are several ways to insert a table in a PowerPoint slide. For example, you can insert a slide with a Content Layout and then click the Insert Table button. Or, click the Insert tab and then click Table. In this presentation, a table will be used to summarize the recreation program.

1 Navigate to your **PowerPoint Chapter 3 folder**, and then double-click the downloaded PowerPoint file that displays your name—**Student_PowerPoint_3B_Enrollment**. In your presentation, if necessary, at the top, click **Enable Editing**.

2 Display **Slide 2**. In the content placeholder, click **Insert Table** 🗔 to display the **Insert Table** dialog box. In the **Number of columns** box, type **3** and then press Tab. In the **Number of rows** box, if necessary, type **2** and then compare your screen with Figure 3.34.

Enter the number of columns and rows that you want the table to contain.

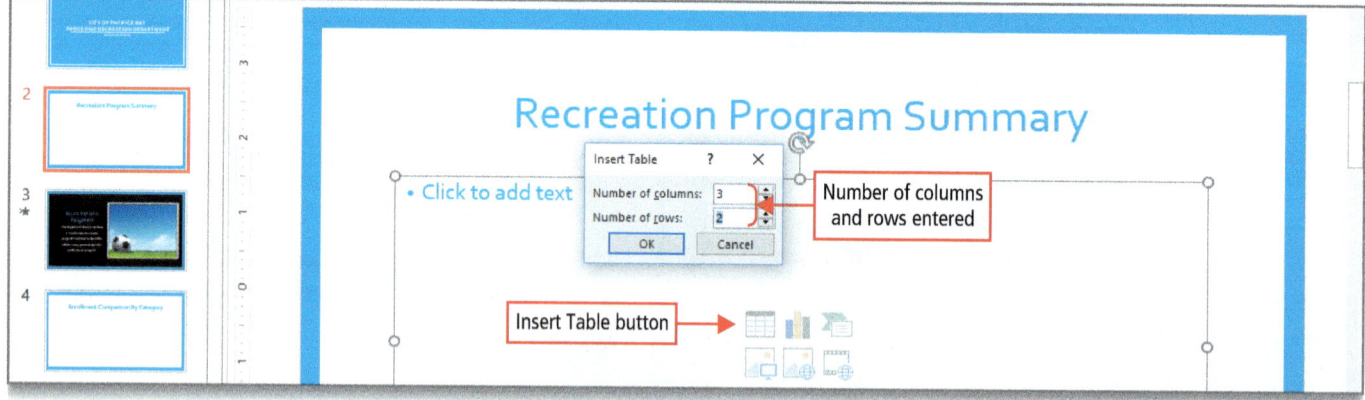

Figure 3.34

3 Click **OK** to create a table with three columns and two rows. Notice that the insertion point is blinking in the upper left cell of the table.

The table extends from the left side of the content placeholder to the right side, and the three columns are equal in width. By default, a style is applied to the table.

ALERT Did You Press Enter instead of Tab?

In a table, pressing Enter creates another line in the same cell. If you press Enter by mistake, you can remove the extra line by pressing Backspace.

4 With the insertion point positioned in the first cell of the table, type **Athletics** and then press Tab.

Pressing Tab moves the insertion point to the next cell in the same row.

5 With the insertion point positioned in the second cell of the first row, type **Leisure** and then press Tab. Type **Arts** and then press Tab to move the insertion point to the first cell in the second row. Compare your table with Figure 3.35.

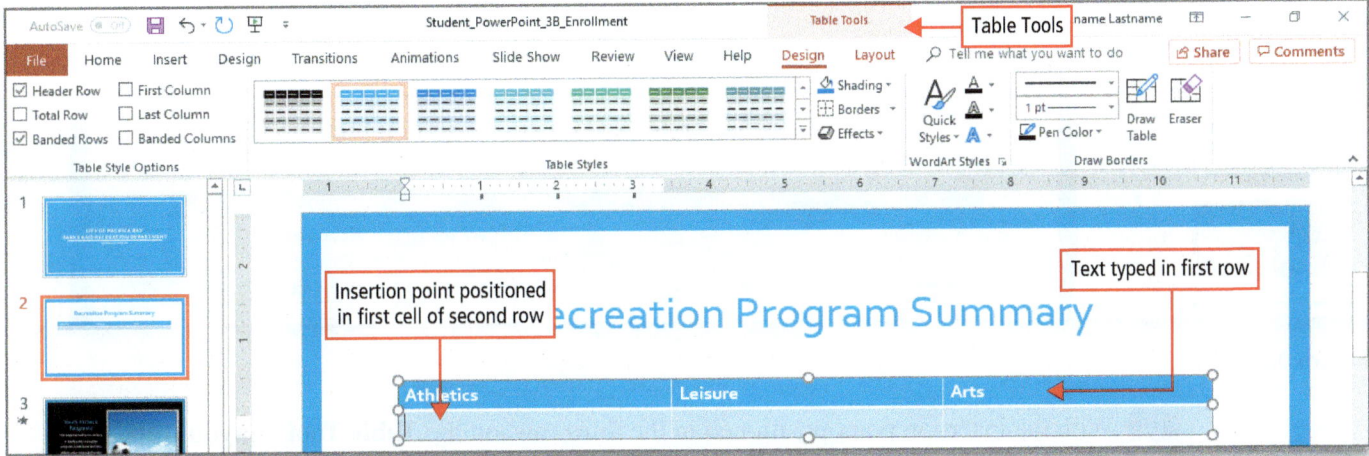

Figure 3.35

6 With the insertion point positioned in the first cell of the second row, type **Team sports** and then press Tab. Type **Personal development classes** and then press Tab. Type **Music and dance classes**

7 Save your presentation.

Activity 3.19 | Inserting Rows and Columns in a Table

MOS
4.1.2

You can modify the layout of a table by inserting or deleting rows and columns.

1 With the insertion point positioned in the last cell of the table, press Tab and notice that a new blank row is inserted.

When the insertion point is positioned in the last cell of a table, pressing Tab inserts a new blank row at the bottom of the table.

2 In the first cell of the third row, type **Youth** and then press Tab. Type **Older adults** and then press Tab. Type **Young adults** and then compare your table with Figure 3.36.

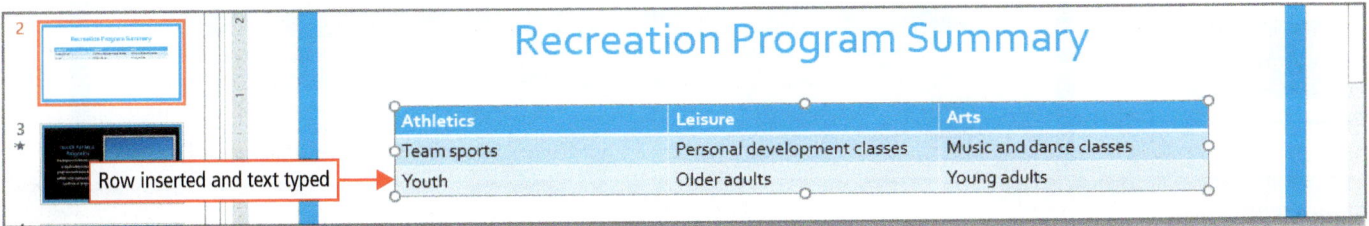

Figure 3.36

ALERT   Did You Add an Extra Row to the Table?

When the insertion point is positioned in the last cell of the table, pressing Tab inserts a new blank row. If you inadvertently inserted a blank row in the table, on the Quick Access Toolbar, click Undo.

3 Click in any cell in the first column, and then click the **Table Tools Layout tab**. In the **Rows & Columns group**, click **Insert Left**.

A new first column is inserted and the width of the columns is adjusted so that all four columns are the same width.

4 In the second row, click in the first cell, and then type **Largest Enrollments**

5 In the third row, click in the first cell, type **Primary Market** and then compare your table with Figure 3.37.

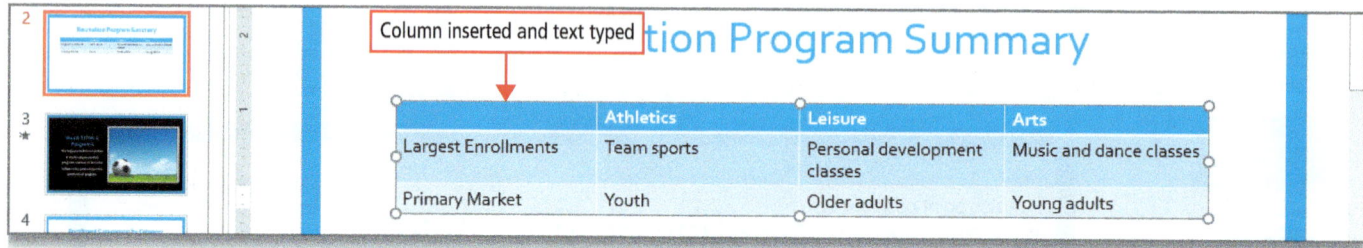

Figure 3.37

6 With the insertion point positioned in the third row, on the **Table Tools Layout tab**, in the **Rows & Columns group**, click **Insert Above** to insert a new third row. In the first cell, type **Average Enrollment** and then press Tab. Type the remaining three entries, pressing Tab to move from cell to cell: **85% of capacity** and **62% of capacity** and **78% of capacity**

7 Save your presentation.

MORE KNOWLEDGE **Deleting Rows and Columns**

To delete a row or column from a table, click in the row or column that you want to delete. Click the Layout tab, and then in the Rows & Columns group, click Delete. In the displayed list, click Delete Columns or Delete Rows.

Activity 3.20 | Sizing a Table

A selected table is surrounded by sizing handles and can be resized in the same manner in which a shape or picture is resized.

1 Point to the bottom, center sizing handle to display the pointer. Compare your screen with Figure 3.38.

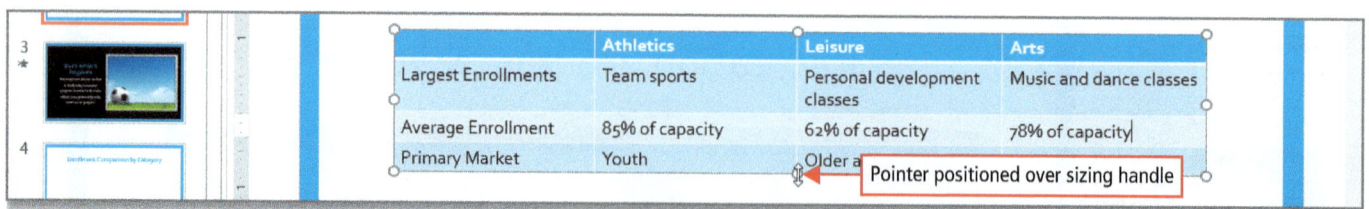

Figure 3.38

2 Hold down the left mouse button, and then drag down until the ruler guide is positioned on the **lower half of the vertical ruler at 2 inches**. Compare your screen with Figure 3.39.

A dim border and the red dotted ruler guides display, indicating the size of the table.

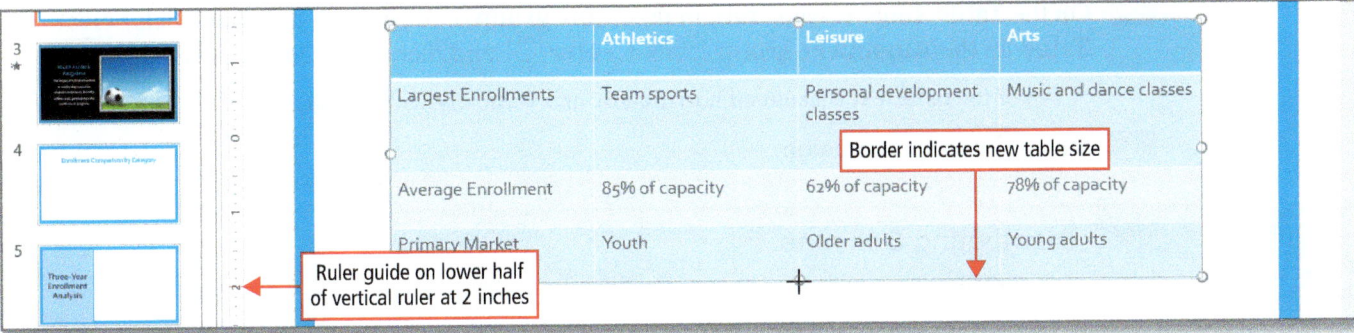

Figure 3.39

3 ▶ Release the mouse button to size the table, and then **Save** 🖫 your presentation.

🔄 **ANOTHER WAY**   On the Layout tab, in the Table Size group, type 3.5 in the Height box.

Activity 3.21 | Distributing Rows and Aligning Table Text

By default, table text is aligned left and the rows adjust as you enter text. This can result in a table with rows of unequal height, which may be visually unappealing or difficult to read. You can adjust the text alignment within the table cells—both horizontally and vertically. You can use the Distribute Rows command so the rows are of equal height.

1 ▶ Click in the first cell of the table. On the **Table Tools Layout tab**, in the **Cell Size group**, click **Distribute Rows**. Compare your table with Figure 3.40.

The Distribute Rows command adjusts the height of the rows in the table so that they are equal.

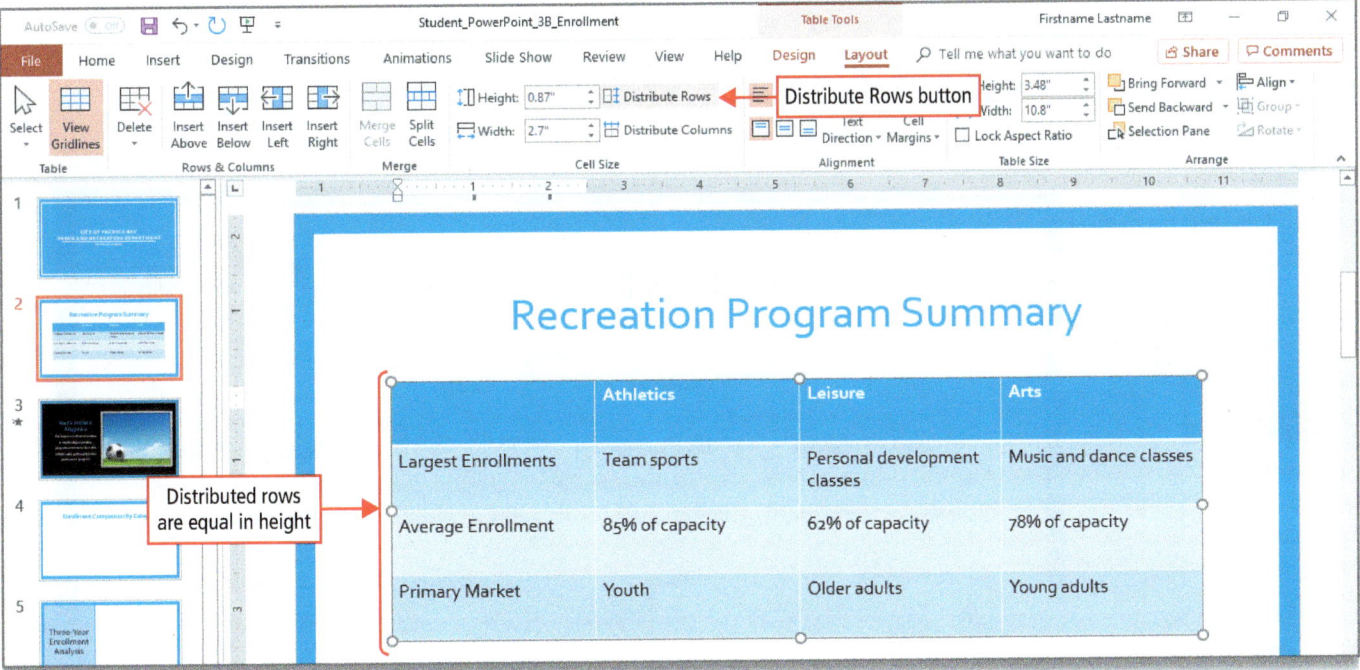

Figure 3.40

2 On the **Table Tools Layout tab**, in the **Table group**, click **Select**, and then click **Select Table**. In the **Alignment group**, click **Center** ▤, and then click **Center Vertically** ▥.

All of the table text is centered horizontally and vertically within the cells.

3 **Save** 🖫 your presentation.

MORE KNOWLEDGE	Distributing Columns

To distribute columns, click anywhere in the table, and then on the Table Tools Layout tab, in the Cell Size group, click Distribute Columns.

Activity 3.22 | Applying and Modifying a Table Style

4.1.3

You can modify the design of a table by applying a *table style*. A table style formats the entire table so that it is consistent with the presentation theme. There are color categories within the table styles—Best Match for Document, Light, Medium, and Dark.

1 Click in any cell in the table. On the **Table Tools Design tab**, in the **Table Styles group**, click **More** ▾. In the **Table Style**s gallery, point to several of the styles to view the Live Preview of the style.

2 Under **Light**, in the third row, click the fourth style—**Light Style 3 – Accent 3**—to apply the style to the table.

3 On the **Table Tools Design tab**, in the **Table Style Options group**, clear the **Banded Rows** check box, and then select the **Banded Columns** check box. Compare your screen with Figure 3.41. **Save** 🖫 the presentation.

The check boxes in the Table Style Options group control where Table Style formatting is applied.

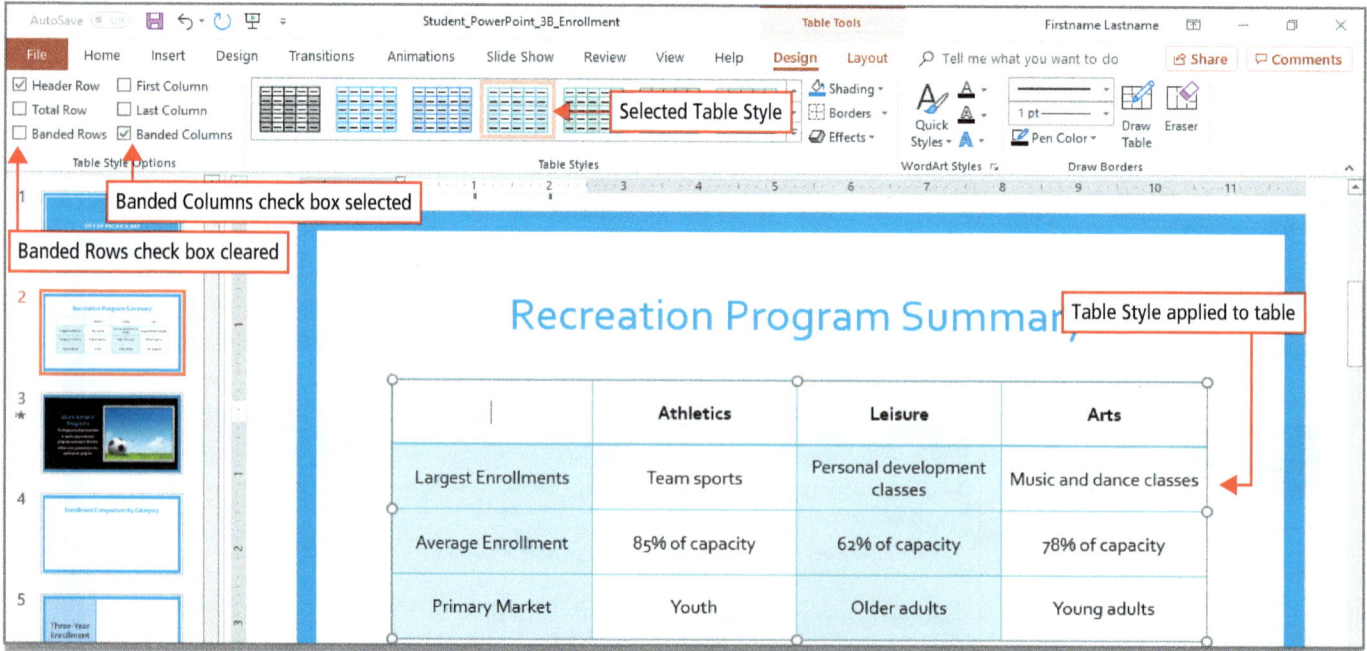

Figure 3.41

Activity 3.23 | Applying Table Effects and Font Formatting

1 Move the pointer outside of the table so that it is positioned to the left of the first row in the table to display the ➡ pointer, as shown in Figure 3.42.

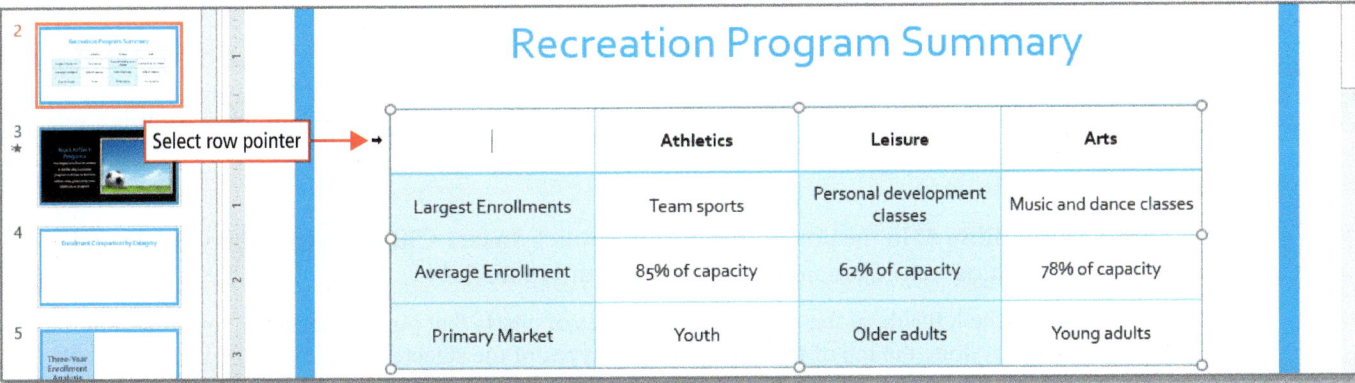

Figure 3.42

2 With the ➡ pointer pointing to the first row in the table, click the mouse button to select the entire row so that you can apply formatting to the selection.

3 With the first row still selected, on the **Table Tools Design tab**, in the **Table Styles group**, click **Effects**. Point to **Cell Bevel**, and then under **Bevel**, click the first bevel—**Round**. Depending on your version of PowerPoint, this may be named *Circle*. With the first table row selected, point to the selection and right-click. On the mini toolbar, change the **Font Size** to **28**.

MAC TIP   Click the Home tab to change the font.

4 Select the first column, and then right-click to display the mini toolbar and shortcut menu. Apply **Bold**.

5 Click in a blank area of the slide, and then compare your slide with Figure 3.43. **Save** 💾 the presentation.

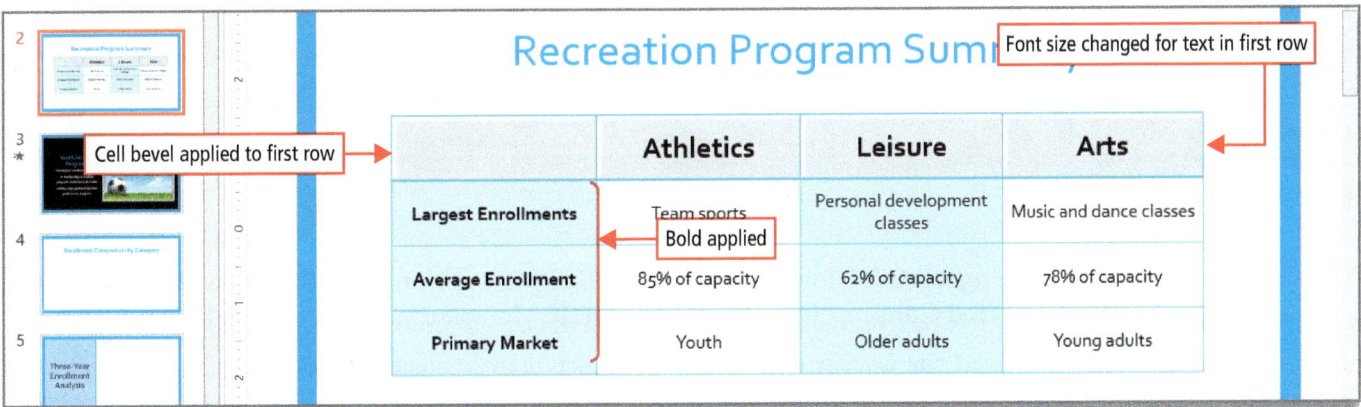

Figure 3.43

GO! Learn How
Video P3-5

A *chart* is a graphic representation of numeric data. Commonly used chart types include bar and column charts, pie charts, and line charts. A chart that you create in PowerPoint is stored in an Excel worksheet that is incorporated into the PowerPoint file.

Activity 3.24 │ Inserting a Column Chart

4.2.1

A *column chart* is useful for illustrating comparisons among related numbers. In this Activity, you will create a column chart that compares enrollment in each category of recreation activities by season.

1 ▶ Display **Slide 4**. In the content placeholder, click **Insert Chart** to display the **Insert Chart** dialog box. Compare your screen with Figure 3.44.

Along the left side of the dialog box, the types of charts that you can insert in your presentation display. Along the top of the dialog box, subtypes of the selected chart type display. By default, Column is selected and a Clustered Column chart displays in the preview area on the right side of the dialog box.

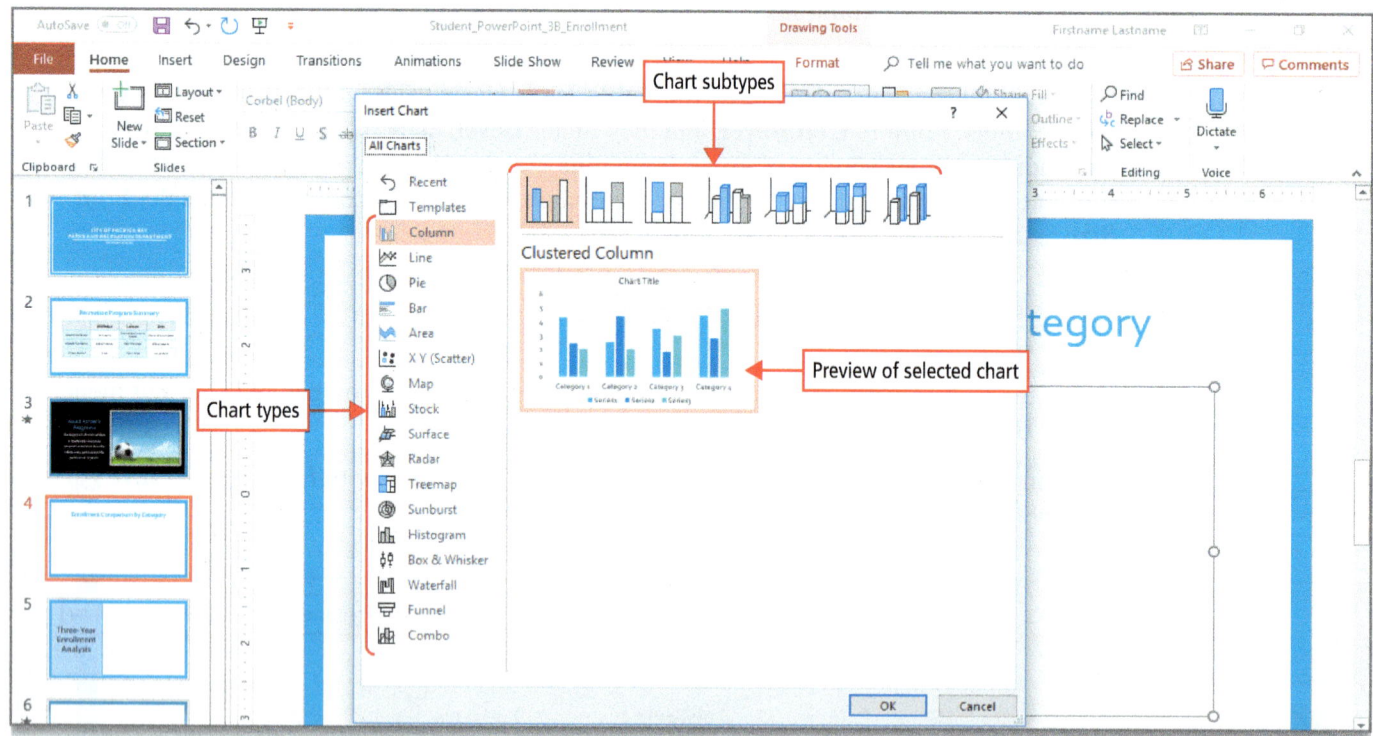

Figure 3.44

2 ▶ Along the top of the dialog box, point to each column chart to view the ScreenTip. Then, with the **Clustered Column** chart selected, click **OK**. Compare your screen with Figure 3.45.

The PowerPoint window displays a column chart in the content placeholder. A *Chart in Microsoft PowerPoint* worksheet window displays with cells, columns, and rows. A cell is identified by the intersecting column letter and row number, forming the *cell reference*.

The worksheet contains sample data from which the chart on the PowerPoint slide is generated. The column headings—*Series 1*, *Series 2*, and *Series 3* display in the chart *legend* and the row headings—*Category 1*, *Category 2*, *Category 3*, and *Category 4*—display as *category labels*. The legend identifies the patterns or colors that are assigned to the data series in the chart. The category labels display along the bottom of the chart to identify the categories of data.

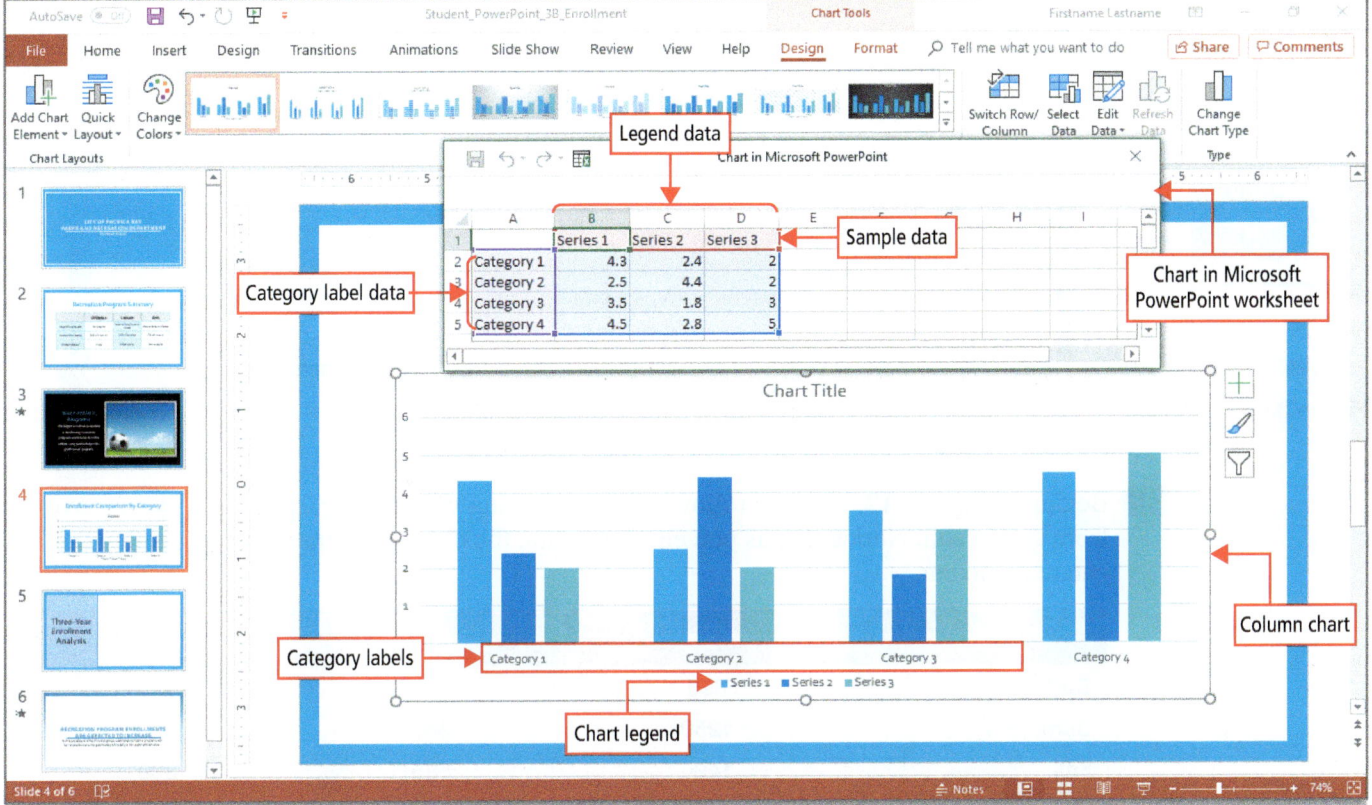

Figure 3.45

Activity 3.25 | Entering Chart Data

1 In the **Chart in Microsoft PowerPoint** worksheet window, in cell **B1**, which contains the text *Series 1,* type **Athletics** and then press Tab to move to cell **C1**.

Below the chart, the chart legend is updated to reflect the change in the Excel worksheet.

2 In cell **C1**, which contains the text *Series 2*, type **Leisure** and then press Tab to move to cell **D1**. Type **Arts** and then press Tab. Notice that cell **A2**, which contains the text *Category 1*, is selected. Compare your screen with Figure 3.46.

The outlined cells define the area in which you are entering data. When you press Tab in the rightmost cell, the first cell in the next row becomes active.

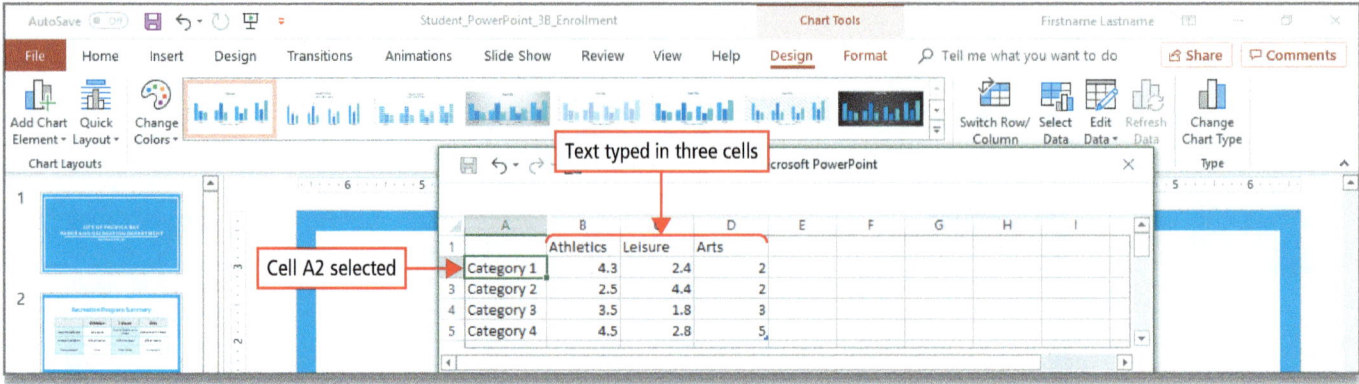

Figure 3.46

3 Beginning in cell **A2**, type the following data (starting with *Spring*), pressing [Tab] to move from cell to cell. Notice that as you enter the data, the chart columns resize to display the entered amounts.

	Athletics	Leisure	Arts
Spring	895	630	720
Summer	1250	350	820
Fall	1490	585	690
Winter	1130	750	

4 In cell **D5**, which contains the value *5*, type **710** and then press [Enter].

Pressing [Enter] in the last cell of the outlined area maintains the existing data range.

ALERT   Did You Press [Tab] After the Last Entry?

If you pressed [Tab] after entering the data in cell D5, you expanded the chart range. In the Chart in Microsoft PowerPoint window, click Undo.

---

5 Compare your worksheet and your chart with Figure 3.47. Correct any typing errors by clicking in the cell that you want to change, and then retype the data.

Each of the 12 cells containing the numeric data that you entered is a ***data point***—a value that originates in a worksheet cell. Each data point is represented in the chart by a ***data marker***—a column, bar, area, dot, pie slice, or other symbol in a chart that represents a single data point. Related data points form a ***data series***; for example, there is a data series for *Athletics*, *Leisure*, and *Arts*. Each data series has a unique color or pattern represented in the chart legend. A placeholder for the chart title displays above the chart.

To the right of the chart, three buttons display. The ***Chart Elements button*** ⊞ enables you to add, remove, or change chart elements such as the title, legend, gridlines, and data labels. The ***Chart Styles button*** 🖌 enables you to set a style and color scheme for your chart. The ***Chart Filters button*** ▽ enables you to change which data displays in the chart.

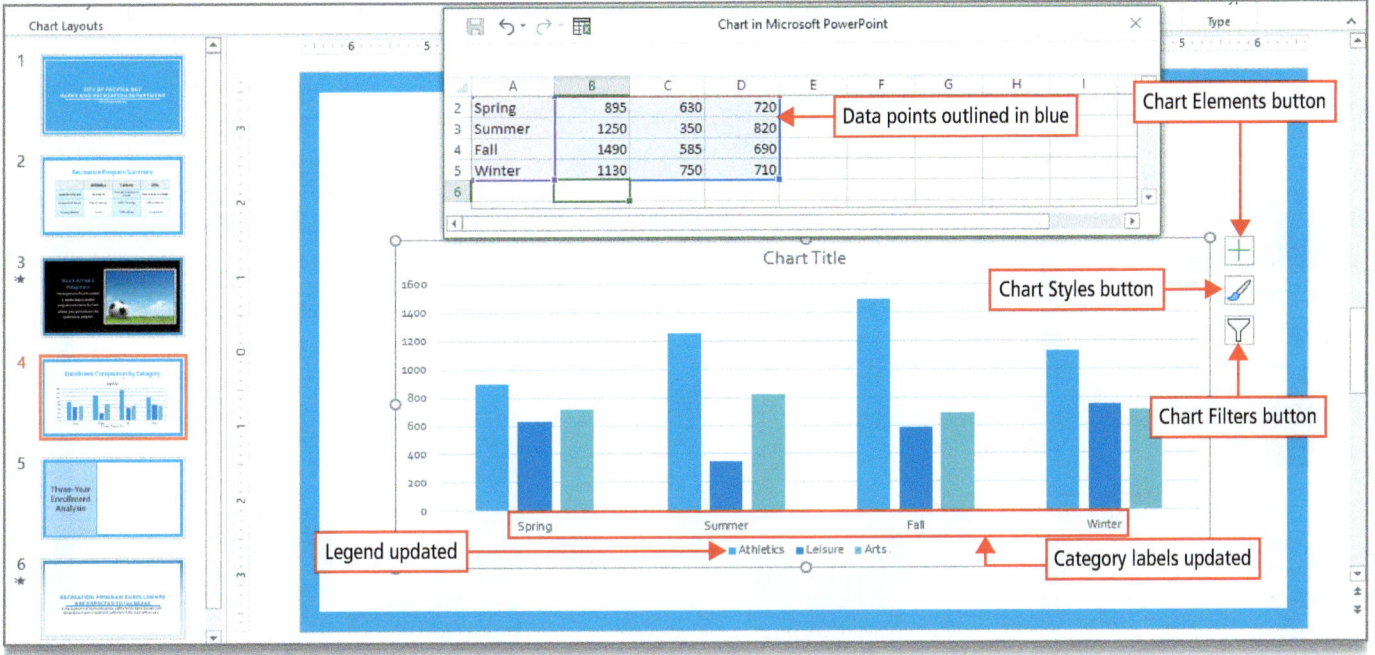

Figure 3.47

> **6** In the upper right corner of the **Chart in Microsoft PowerPoint** worksheet window, click **Close** ⌧. **Save** 🖫 the presentation.
>
> When you save the presentation, the worksheet data is saved with it.

MORE KNOWLEDGE | **Editing the Chart Data After Closing the Worksheet**

You can redisplay the worksheet and make changes to the data after you have closed it. To do so, click the chart to select it, and then on the Chart Tools Design tab in the Data group, click Edit Data.

Activity 3.26 | Applying a Chart Style and Modifying Chart Elements

4.2.2

A ***chart style*** is set of predefined formats applied to a chart, including colors, backgrounds, and effects. ***Chart elements*** are the various components of a chart, including the chart title, axis titles, data series, legend, chart area, and plot area.

> **1** Click the outer edge of the chart, if necessary, to select it. On the **Chart Tools Design tab**, in the **Chart Styles group**, click **More** 🔽 to display the **Chart Styles** gallery.

> **2** In the **Chart Styles** gallery, point to each style to Live Preview the style. Notice that as you point to a chart style, a ScreenTip indicates the chart style number. Click **Style 5**. Compare your screen with Figure 3.48.
>
> This style includes lightly shaded column data markers. Horizontal gridlines display behind the columns.

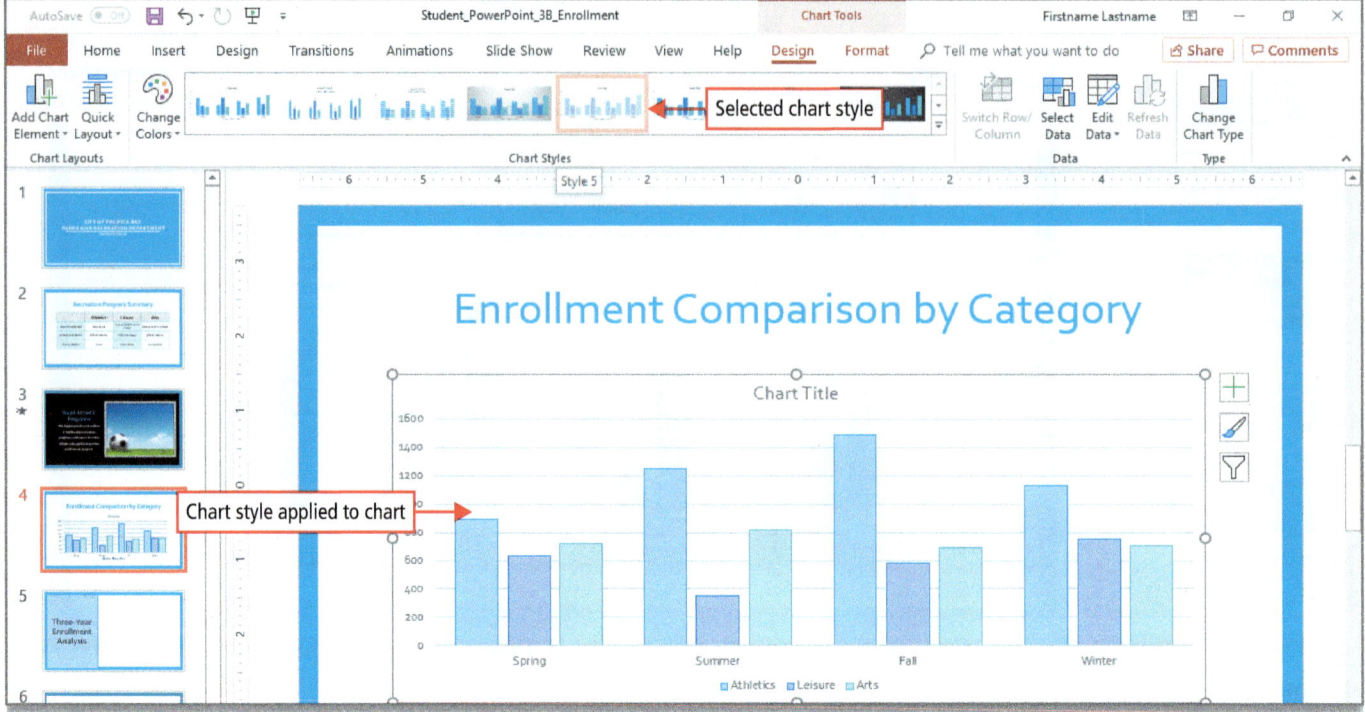

Figure 3.48

> **3** ▶ To the right of the chart, click **Chart Elements** ⊞, and then compare your screen with Figure 3.49.
>
> A list of chart elements displays to the left of the chart. You can select the chart elements that you wish to display in your chart. In this slide, the slide title describes the chart so a chart title is not necessary.

Figure 3.49

> **4** ▶ Under **Chart Elements**, click **Chart Title** to clear the check box and remove the chart title placeholder from the chart. Click **Chart Elements** ⊞ to close the Chart Elements list.

💻 **MAC TIP** On the Chart Design tab, click Add Chart Element.

> **5** ▶ Click in a blank area of the slide, and then compare your screen with Figure 3.50. **Save** 🖫 your presentation.

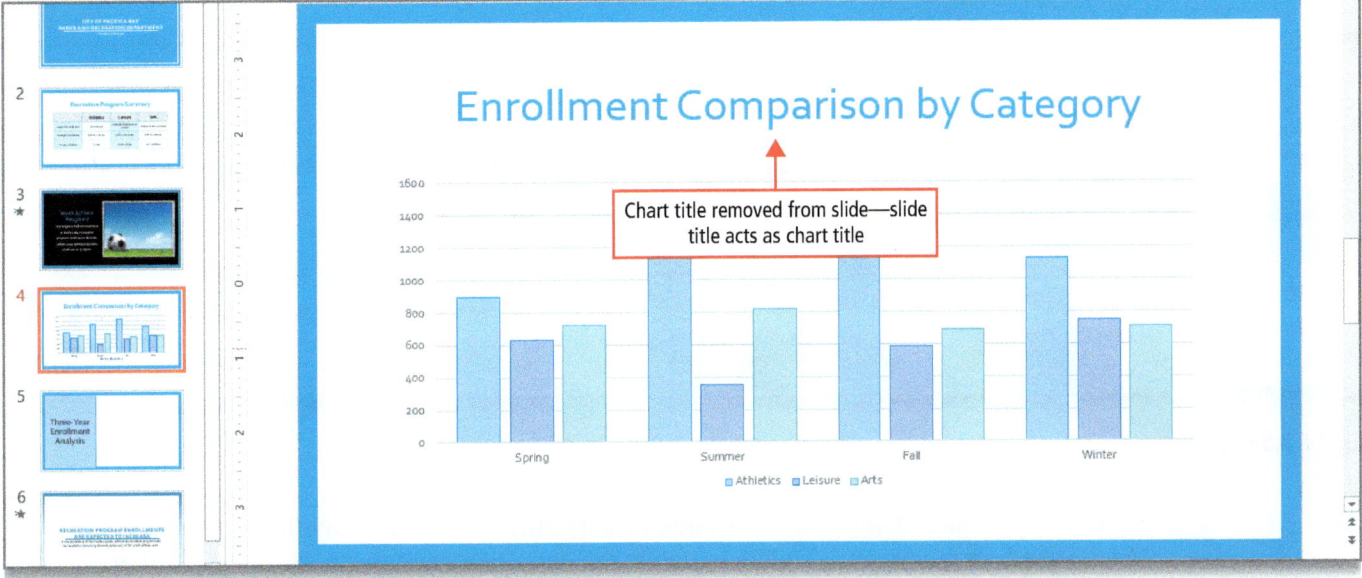

Figure 3.50

Activity 3.27 | Creating a Line Chart and Deleting Chart Data

4.2.1

To analyze and compare annual data over a three-year period, the presentation requires an additional chart. Recall that there are a number of different types of charts that you can insert in a PowerPoint presentation. In this activity, you will create a *line chart*, which is commonly used to illustrate trends over time.

1 Display **Slide 5**. In the content placeholder, click **Insert Chart** ▐▐. On the left side of the **Insert Chart** dialog box, click **Line**, and then on the right, click the fourth chart—**Line with Markers**. Click **OK**.

2 In the worksheet, in cell **B1**, which contains the text *Series 1*, type **Youth** and then press Tab. In cell **C1**, type **Adult** and then press Tab. In cell **D1**, type **Senior** and then press Tab.

3 Beginning in cell **A2**, type the following data, pressing Tab to move from cell to cell. If you make any typing errors, click in the cell that you want to change, and then retype the data.

	Youth	Adult	Senior
2022	3822	1588	2240
2023	4675	1833	2534
2024	4535	1925	2897

4 In the worksheet, position the pointer over **row heading 5** so that the ➡ pointer displays. Compare your screen with Figure 3.51.

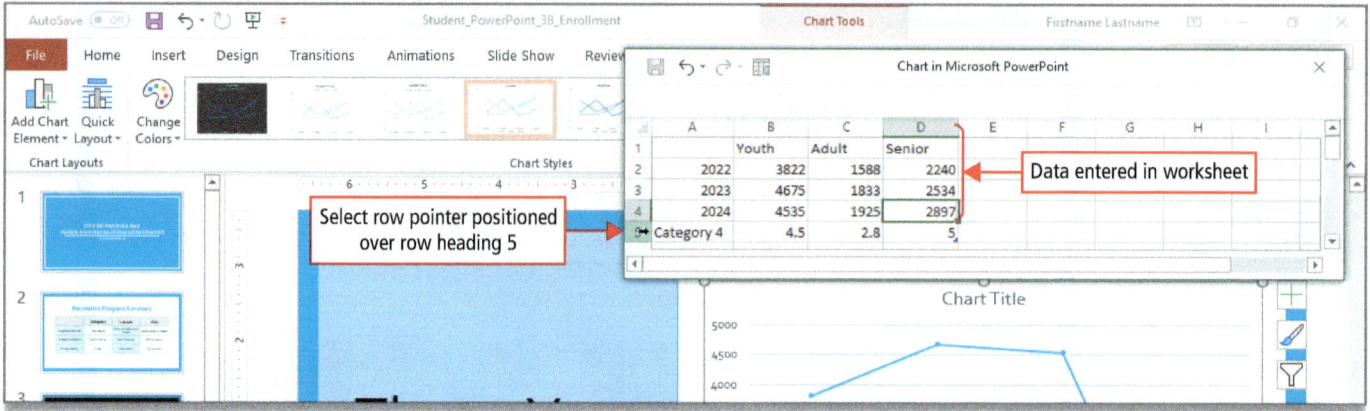

Figure 3.51

5 > With the ➡ pointer displayed, right-click to select the row and display the shortcut menu. On the shortcut menu, click **Delete** to delete the extra row from the worksheet, and then compare your screen with Figure 3.52.

The data in the worksheet contains four columns and four rows, and the outline area defining the chart data range is resized. You must delete columns and rows from the sample worksheet data that you do not want to include in the chart. You can add additional rows and columns by typing column and row headings and then entering additional data. When data is typed in cells adjacent to the chart range, the range is resized to include the new data.

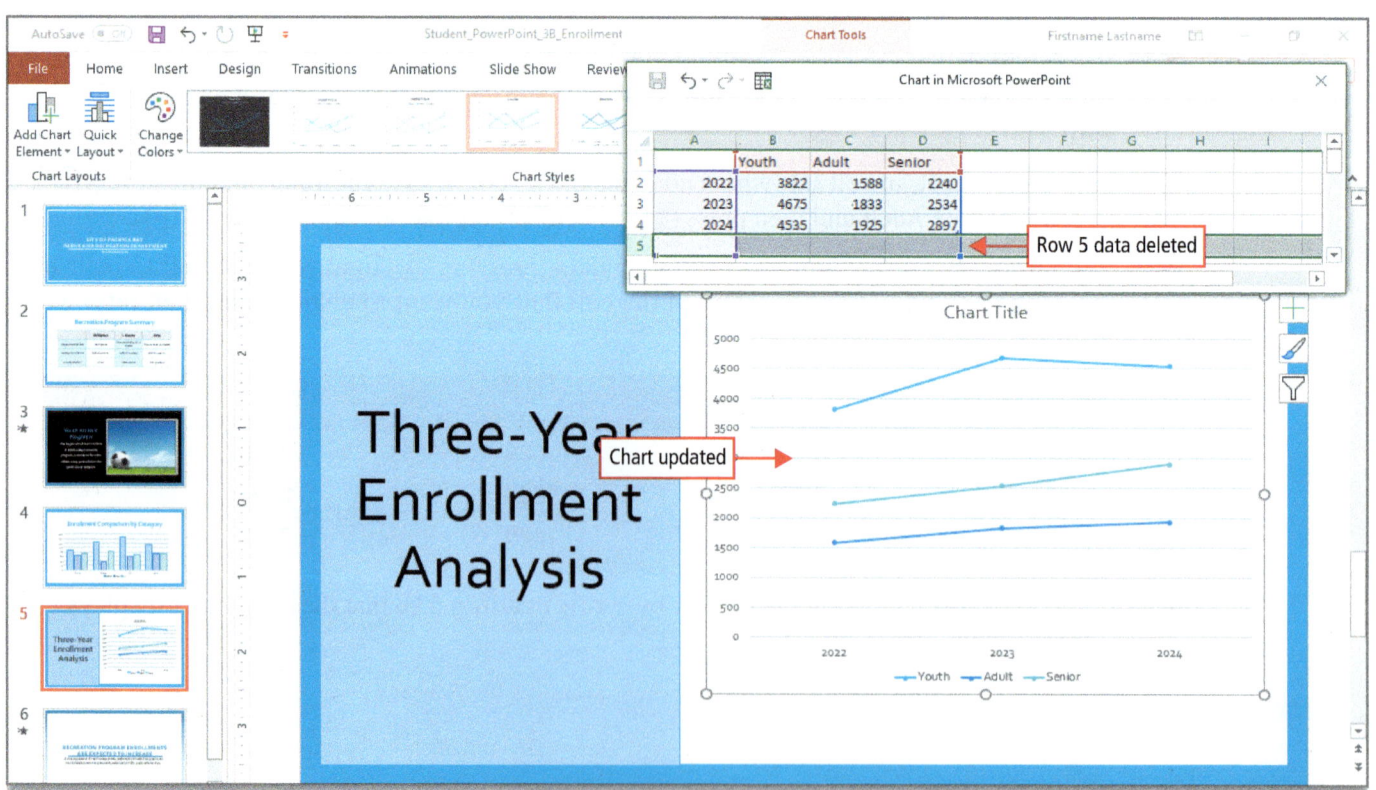

Figure 3.52

Activity 3.28 | Formatting a Line Chart

4.2.2

1 **Close** ☒ the worksheet window. To the right of the chart, click **Chart Styles** ✎. Compare your screen with Figure 3.53.

The Chart Style gallery displays on the left side of the chart and the Style tab is active. The chart styles display in a vertical gallery.

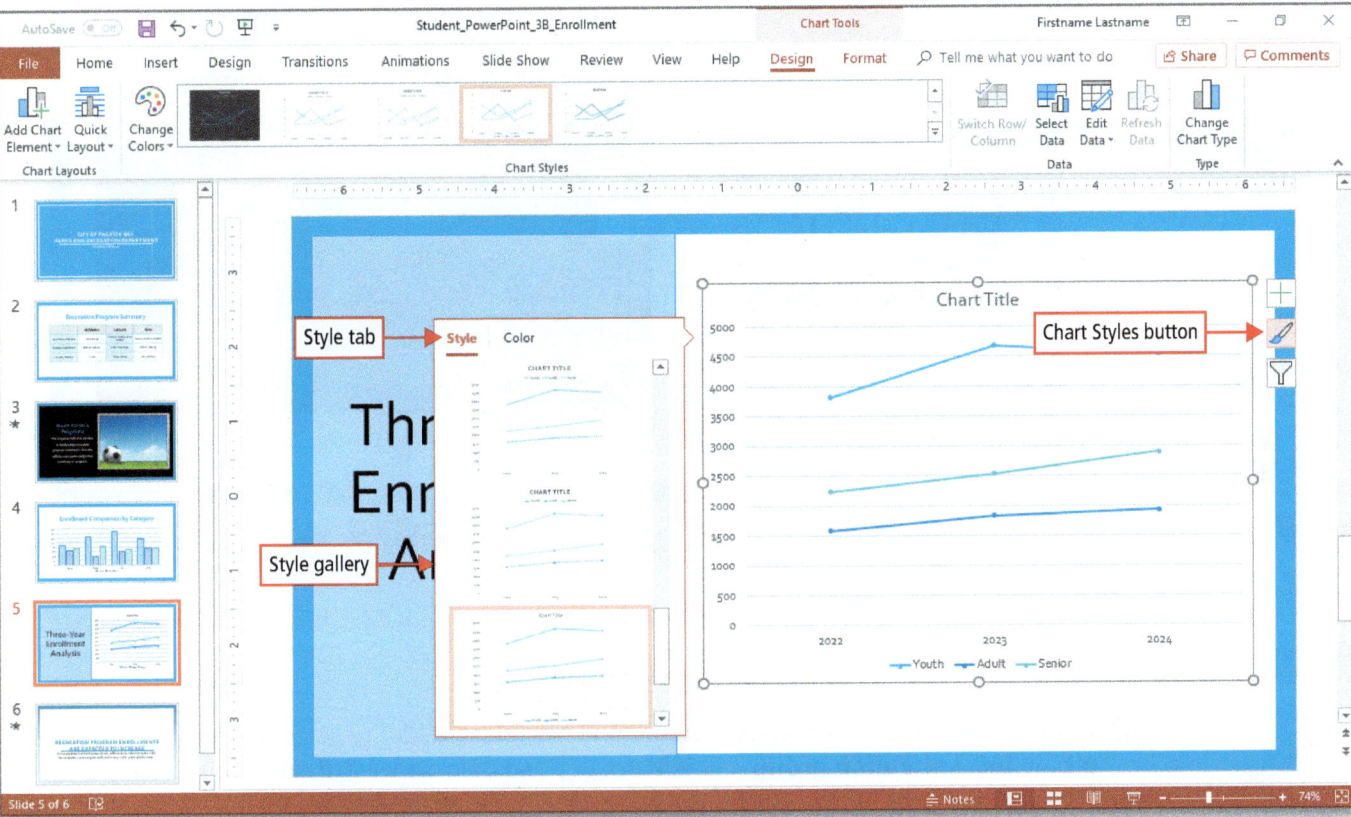

Figure 3.53

2 In the **Chart Style** gallery, be sure that **Style** is selected. Scroll the list, and point to various styles to view the ScreenTips and the effect of the style on the chart. Click **Style 6** and then click anywhere outside of the chart to close the Chart Style gallery.

The styles that display when you click the Chart Styles button are the same as those that display in the Chart Styles gallery on the ribbon. Apply chart styles using the technique that you prefer.

💻 **MAC TIP** On the Chart Design tab, click More.

3 In the chart, click the text **Chart Title**, and then type **By Age Category**

4 Click in a blank area of the slide, and then compare your screen with Figure 3.54. **Save** 💾 your presentation.

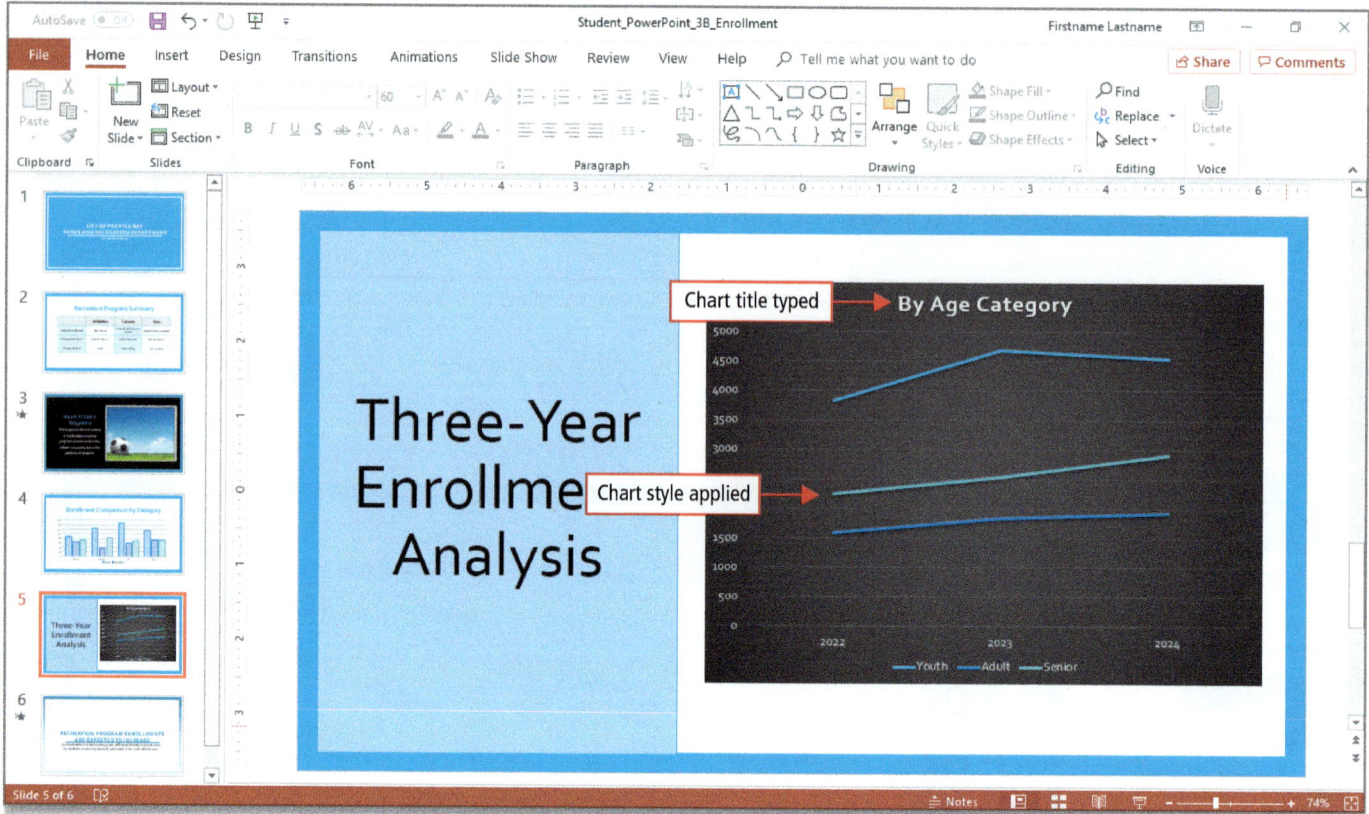

Figure 3.54

Activity 3.29 | Animating a Chart

5.2.1, 5.2.3

1 ▶ Display **Slide 4**, and then click the column chart placeholder to select it. On the **Animations tab**, in the **Animation group**, click **More** ⬇ , and then under **Entrance**, click **Fade**.

2 ▶ In the **Animation group**, click **Effect Options**, and then under **Sequence**, click **By Series**. In the **Preview group**, click **Preview** to preview the By Series effect. On **Slide 4**, notice the chart animation sequence. Compare your screen with Figure 3.55.

> The By Series option displays the chart one data series at a time, and the numbers 1, 2, 3, and 4 to the left of the chart indicate the four parts of the chart animation sequence. The chart animation sequence includes the background, followed by the Athletics data series for each season, and then the Leisure series, and then the Arts series.

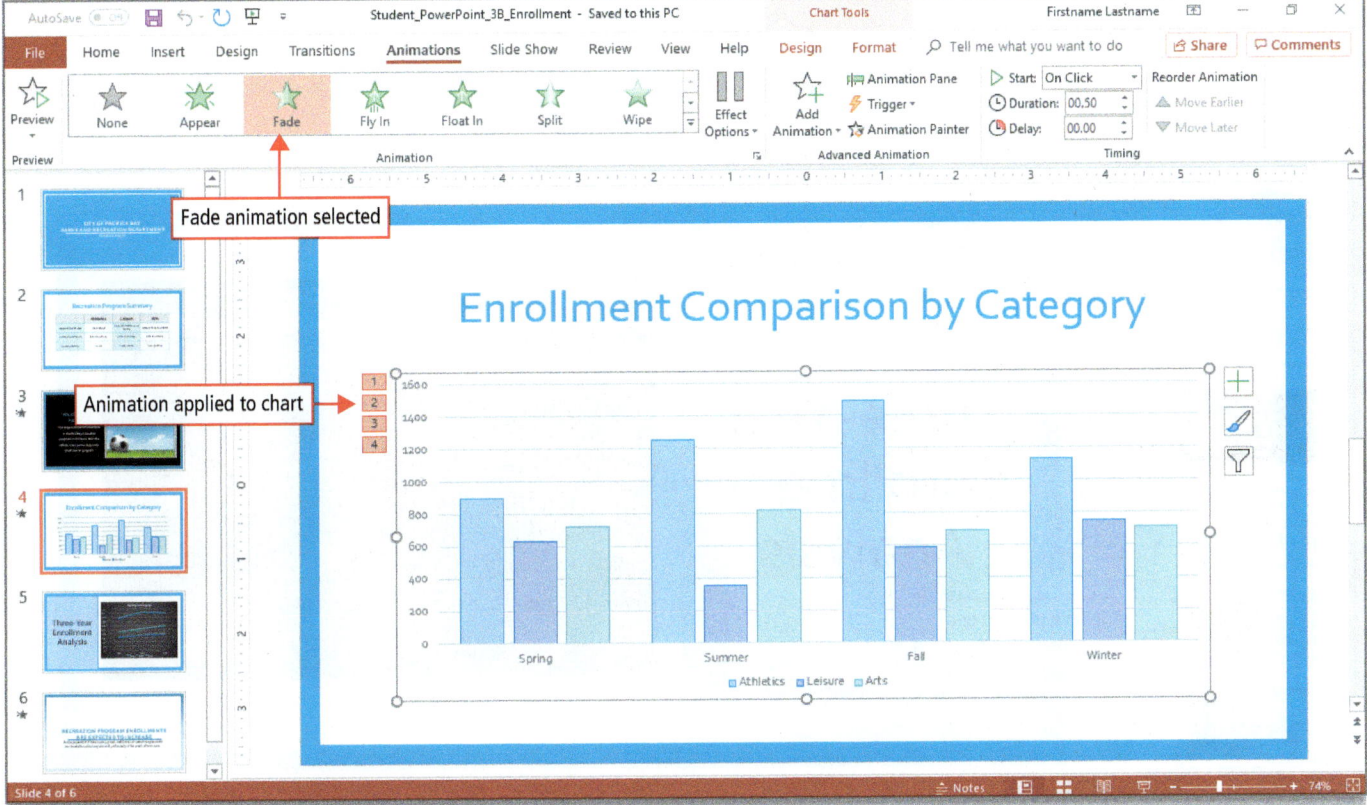

Figure 3.55

> **3** In the **Animation group**, click **Effect Options**, and then under **Sequence**, click **As One Object**. View the slide show from the beginning. On **Slide 4**, notice the chart animation sequence returns to a *1*. Save ⊟ your presentation.

Activity 3.30 | Animating a Chart with the Morph Transition

5.2.1

You have applied animation effects to charts, to make them move in a specified manner as they enter the slide. Another way to animate objects is by making duplicate slides and applying the Morph transition.

> **1** Display **Slide 5**, press Ctrl + D to duplicate the slide.

> **2** On **Slide 5**, click to select the chart. On the **Chart Tools Design tab**, click **Edit Data** to open the **Chart in Microsoft PowerPoint** window. Edit the data in the range **A2:D4** using the following:

2019	3715	1457	1549
2020	4247	1291	1785
2021	4412	1369	2452

> **3** Close the **Chart in Microsoft PowerPoint** window.

> **4** Display **Slide 6**. on the **Transitions tab**, in the **Transition to This Slide group**, point to **Morph**, to display the ScreenTip. Compare your screen with. Figure 3.56

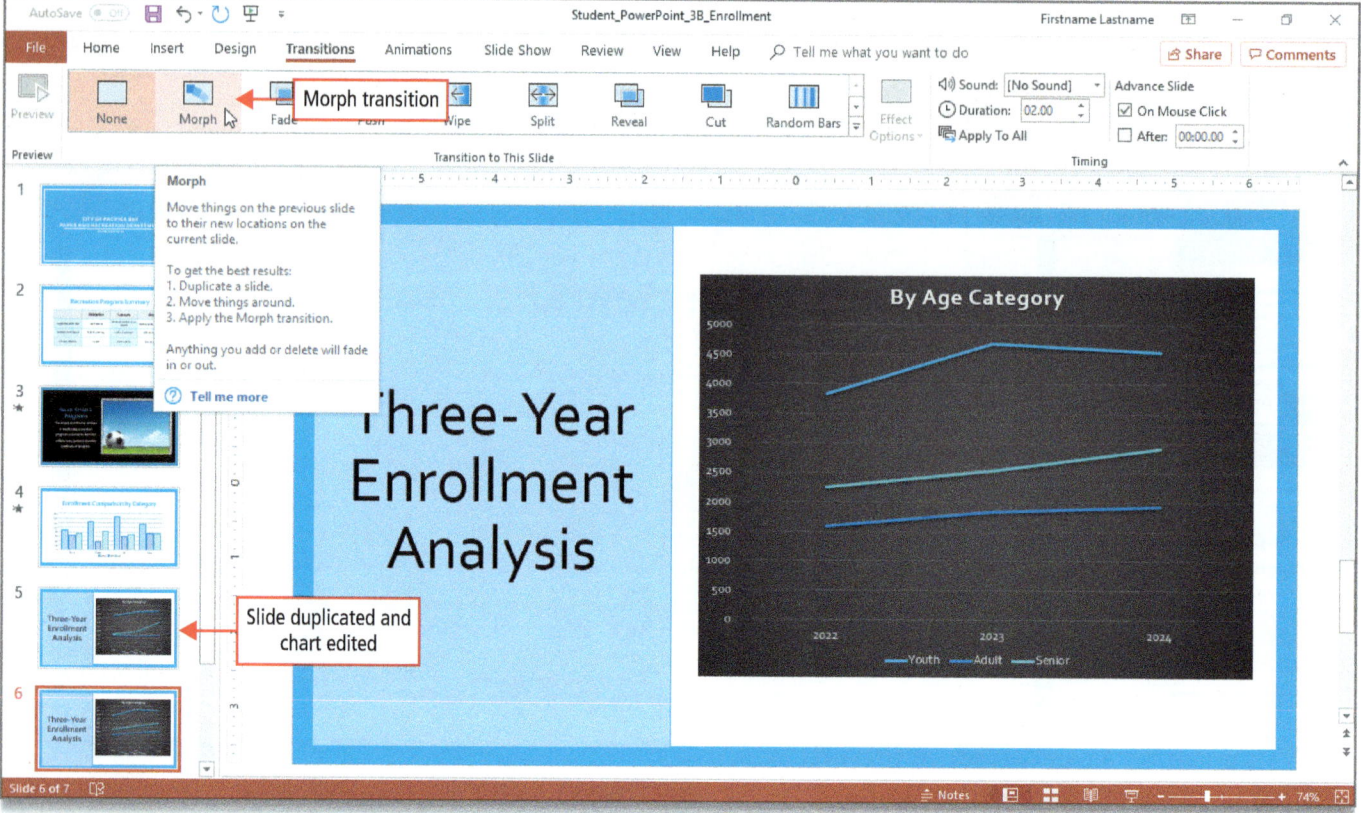

Figure 3.56

5 Click **Morph**. Change the Duration to 1.00.

6 Display **Slide 5**. On the **Slide Show tab**, in the **Start Slide Show group**, click **From Current Slide**. Click to advance to **Slide 6** and notice the morph transition of the graph.

The lines appear to move as you advance the slides.

7 Press Esc to return to your presentation.

8 Insert a **Header & Footer** on the **Notes and Handouts**. Include the **Date and time** updated automatically, the **Page Number**, and a **Footer**. In the Footer box, type **3B_Enrollment** and then click **Apply to All**.

9 Display the document properties. As the **Tags**, type **recreation enrollment** and as the **Subject**, type your course and section number. Be sure your name displays in as author, and then **Save** your file.

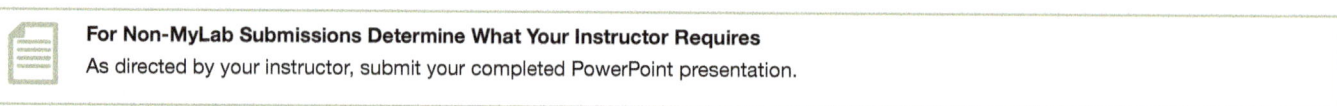

For Non-MyLab Submissions Determine What Your Instructor Requires
As directed by your instructor, submit your completed PowerPoint presentation.

10 Close ☒ PowerPoint.

11 In **MyLab IT**, in your **Course Materials**, locate and click the Grader Project **PowerPoint 3B Enrollment**. In **step 3**, under **Upload Completed Assignment**, click **Choose File**. In the **Open** dialog box, navigate to your **PowerPoint Chapter 3 folder**, and then click your **Student_PowerPoint_3B_ Enrollment** file one time to select it. In the lower right corner of the **Open** dialog box, click **Open**.

The name of your selected file displays above the Upload button.

12 To submit your file to **MyLab IT** for grading, click **Upload**, wait a moment for a green **Success!** message, and then in **step 4**, click the blue **Submit for Grading** button. Click **Close Assignment** to return to your list of **Course Materials**.

You have completed Project 3B | END

»»» GO! With Google

Objective	Create a Summary and Analysis Presentation in Google Slides

ALERT   **Working with Web-Based Applications and Services**

Computer programs and services on the web receive continuous updates and improvements, so the steps to complete this web-based activity may differ from the ones shown. You can often look at the screens and the information presented to determine how to complete the activity.

    If you do not already have a Google account, you will need to create one before beginning this activity.

Activity | Creating a Summary and Analysis Presentation in Google Slides

In this Activity, you will use Google Slides to create a presentation similar to the one you created in Project 3B.

1 From the desktop, open your browser, navigate to **http://google.com**, and then sign in to your Google account. Click **Google apps** ▦ , and then click **Drive** ▲ . Open your **GO! Web Projects** folder—or click New to create and then open this folder if necessary.

2 In the left pane, click **New**, click **File upload**, and then in the **Open** dialog box, navigate to your student data files. Select **p03_3B_Google_Slides**. Click **Open**. When the upload is complete, if necessary, close the Uploads complete message box. Right-click **p03_3B_Google_Slides**, and then click **Rename**. Using your own name, as the file name type **Lastname_Firstname_3B_Googles_Slides** and then press [Enter]. Right-click your file, point to **Open with**, and then click **Google Slides**.

3 Display **Slide 2**. On the menu bar, click **Insert**, point to **Table**, and drag the mouse to the right to highlight four columns and drag down to highlight four rows. Click to insert a 4 X 4 column table. Type the text in Table 1 at the bottom of the page.

4 Display **Slide 4**. On the menu bar, click **Insert**, point to **Chart**, and then click **Column**. In the upper right of the chart, click the link arrow and then click **Open source.** In the Google Sheet, beginning in cell **B1**, type:

	Athletics	Leisure	Arts
Spring	895	630	720
Summer	1250	350	820
Fall	1490	585	690
Winter	1130	750	710

5 In the sheet, double-click the chart to open the **Chart editor** pane. On the **DATA** tab, click **Add Series**. With the **What data?** box displayed, drag to select the range **D1:D5**, the Arts column. Click **OK**. Click the **CUSTOMIZE** tab. Click to open **Chart & axis titles**, and delete the text **Points Scored**.

6 **Close** ☒ the Google Sheet and return to the Google Slide presentation. In the chart, click **UPDATE**. On the menu bar, click **Arrange**, point to **Center on page**, and then click **Horizontally**.

Table 1

	Athletics	Leisure	Arts
Largest Enrollments	Team sports	Personal development classes	Music and dance classes
Average Enrollment	85% of capacity	62% of capacity	78% of capacity
Primary Market	Youth	Older adults	Young adults

»»» **GO!** With Google continues on next page

7 Display **Slide 5**. On the menu bar, click **Insert**, point to **Chart**, and then click **Line**. Click the link arrow and then click **Open source**. In the Google Sheet, beginning in cell **B1**, type the following text:

	Youth	Adult	Senior
2022	3822	1588	2240
2023	4675	1833	2534
2024	4535	1925	2897

8 Double-click the chart to open the **Chart editor**. On the **DATA** tab, change the **Data range** to **A1:D4**. Click the **CUSTOMIZE** tab, click **Chart & axis titles**, and then delete the title text. **Close** ⊠ the Google Sheet and return to the Google Slide presentation. In the chart, click **UPDATE**. Drag the chart to position it in the white area of the slide.

9 Your presentation will be saved automatically. If you are instructed to submit your file, click the File menu, point to Download as, and then click PDF or PowerPoint as directed by your instructor. The file will download to your default download folder as determined by your browser settings. Sign out of your Google account.

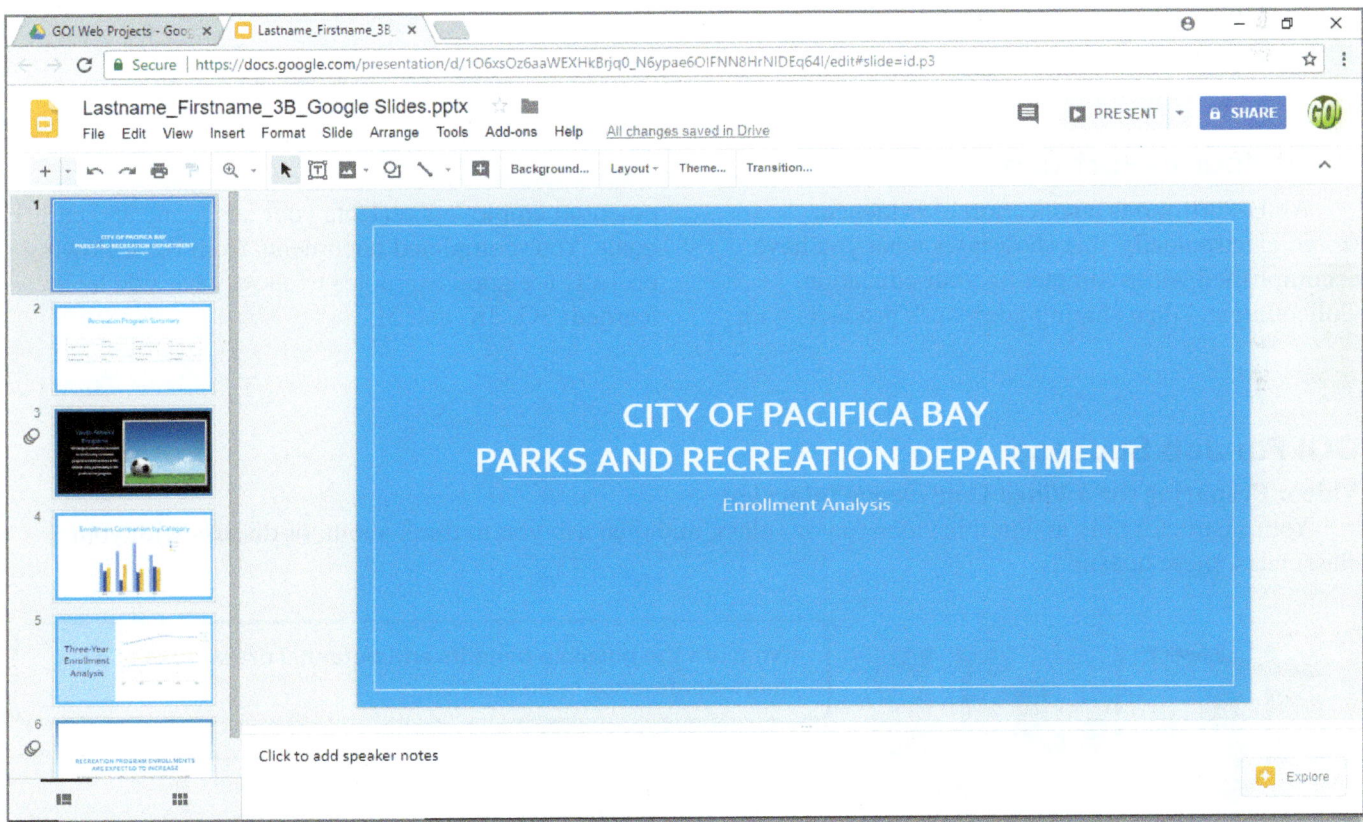

Figure A

»»» GO! To Work

wavebreakmedia/Shutterstock, Monkey Business Images/Fotolia, Ivanko80/Shutterstock, Monkey Business Images/Shutterstock

Microsoft Office Specialist (MOS) Skills in This Chapter

Project 3A	Project 3B
1.5.5 Preserve presentation content	**4.1.1** Create and insert tables
2.2.2 Modify individual slide backgrounds	**4.1.2** Insert and delete table rows and columns
4.5.1 Insert audio and visual clips	**4.1.3** Apply built-in table styles
4.5.2 Create and insert screen recordings	**4.2.1** Create and insert charts
4.5.3 Configure media playback options	**4.2.2** Modify charts
5.2.1 Animate text and graphic elements	**5.2.1** Animate text and graphic elements
5.2.3 Configure animation effects	**5.2.3** Configure animation effects
5.2.4 Configure animation paths	
5.2.5 Reorder animations on a slide	
5.3.1 Set transition effect duration	
5.3.2 Configure transition start and finish options	

Build Your E-Portfolio

An E-Portfolio is a collection of evidence, stored electronically, that showcases what you have accomplished while completing your education. Collecting and then sharing your work products with potential employers reflects your academic and career goals. Your completed documents from the following projects are good examples to show what you have learned: 3G, 3K, and 3L.

GO! For Job Success

Video: Preparing for a Video Conference Interview

Your instructor may assign this video to your class, and then ask you to think about, or discuss with your classmates, these questions:

g-stockstudio/Shutterstock

> What are the possible benefits and potential drawbacks of a video-conference interview?

> What mistakes did Talia make in preparing for this type of interview? What mistakes did she make during the interview itself?

> How would you prepare for a video-conference interview to avoid making those mistakes?

End of Chapter

Summary

There are many ways to modify a presentation theme and customize a presentation. You can apply background styles, insert pictures and textures on slide backgrounds, and change theme fonts and colors.

One way to enhance a presentation and engage an audience is by inserting interesting and informative video. Styles, shapes, and effects can be applied to videos. A video can be trimmed and compressed to make the file size smaller.

Use animation to focus audience attention on a particular slide element in order to draw attention to important points. Apply animation to slide elements in the order in which you want them to display.

Use tables to present information in an organized and attractive manner. Use charts to visually represent data. Apply styles to charts and tables to give your presentations a consistent and informative look.

GO! Learn It Online

Review the concepts and key terms, and MOS skills in this chapter by completing these online challenges, which you can find in **MyLab IT**.

Chapter Quiz: Answer matching and multiple-choice questions to test what you learned in this chapter.

Lessons on the GO!: Learn how to use all the new apps and features as they are introduced by Microsoft.

MOS Prep Quiz: Answer questions to review the MOS skills that you practiced in this chapter.

GO! Collaborative Team Project (Available in Instructor Resource Center)

If your instructor assigns this project to your class, you can expect to work with one or more of your classmates—either in person or by using Internet tools—to create work products similar to those that you created in this chapter. A team is a group of workers who work together to solve a problem, make a decision, or create a work product. Collaboration is when you work together with others as a team in an intellectual endeavor to complete a shared task or achieve a shared goal.

Monkey Business Images/ Fotolia

Project Guide for PowerPoint Chapter 3

Your instructor may assign one or more of these projects to help you review the chapter and assess your mastery and understanding of the chapter.

Project	Apply Skills from These Chapter Objectives	Project Type	Project Location
3A MyLab IT	Objectives 1–3 from Project 3A	**3A Instructional Project (Grader Project)** **Instruction** Guided instruction to learn the skills in Project A.	In **MyLab IT** and in text
3B MyLab IT	Objectives 4–5 from Project 3B	**3B Instructional Project (Grader Project)** **Instruction** Guided instruction to learn the skills in Project B.	In **MyLab IT** and in text
3C	Objectives 1–3 from Project 3A	**3C Skills Review (Scorecard Grading)** **Review** A guided review of the skills from Project 3A.	In text
3D	Objectives 4-5 from Project 3A	**3D Skills Review (Scorecard Grading)** **Review** A guided review of the skills from Project 3B.	In text
3E MyLab IT	Objectives 1–3 from Project 3A	**3E Mastery (Grader Project)** **Mastery and Transfer of Learning** A demonstration of your mastery of the skills in Project 3A with extensive decision making.	In **MyLab IT** and in text
3F MyLab IT	Objectives 4–5 from Project 3A	**3F Mastery (Grader Project)** **Mastery and Transfer of Learning** A demonstration of your mastery of the skills in Project 3B with extensive decision making.	In **MyLab IT** and in text
3G MyLab IT	Combination of Objectives from Projects 3A and 3B	**3G Mastery (Grader Project)** **Mastery and Transfer of Learning** A demonstration of your mastery of the skills in Projects 3A and 3B with extensive decision making.	In **MyLab IT** and in text
3H	Combination of Objectives from Projects 3A and 3B	**3H GO! Fix It (Scorecard Grading)** **Critical Thinking** A demonstration of your mastery of the skills in Projects 3A and 3B by creating a correct result from a document that contains errors you must find.	IRC
3I	Combination of Objectives from Projects 3A and 3B	**3I GO! Make It (Scorecard Grading)** **Critical Thinking** A demonstration of your mastery of the skills in Projects 3A and 3B by creating a result from a supplied picture.	IRC
3J	Combination of Objectives from Projects 3A and 3B	**3J GO! Solve It (Rubric Grading)** **Critical Thinking** A demonstration of your mastery of the skills in Projects 3A and 3B, your decision-making skills, and your critical thinking skills. A task-specific rubric helps you self-assess your result.	IRC
3K	Combination of Objectives from Projects 3A and 3B	**3K GO! Solve It (Rubric Grading)** **Critical Thinking** A demonstration of your mastery of the skills in Projects 3A and 3B, your decision-making skills, and your critical thinking skills. A task-specific rubric helps you self-assess your result.	In text
3L	Combination of Objectives from Projects 3A and 3B	**3L GO! Think (Rubric Grading)** **Critical Thinking** A demonstration of your understanding of the chapter concepts applied in a manner that you would outside of college. An analytic rubric helps you and your instructor grade the quality of your work by comparing it to the work an expert in the discipline would create.	In text
3M	Combination of Objectives from Projects 3A and 3B	**3M GO! Think (Rubric Grading)** **Critical Thinking** A demonstration of your understanding of the chapter concepts applied in a manner that you would outside of college. An analytic rubric helps you and your instructor grade the quality of your work by comparing it to the work an expert in the discipline would create.	IRC
3N	Combination of Objectives from Projects 3A and 3B	**3N You and GO! (Rubric Grading)** **Critical Thinking** A demonstration of your understanding of the chapter concepts applied in a manner that you would in a personal situation. An analytic rubric helps you and your instructor grade the quality of your work.	IRC
3O	Combination of Objectives from Projects 3A and 3B	**3O Collaborative Team Project for PowerPoint Chapter 3** **Critical Thinking** A demonstration of your understanding of concepts and your ability to work collaboratively in a group role-playing assessment, requiring both collaboration and self-management.	IRC
Capstone Project for PowerPoint Chapters 1–3	Combination of Objectives from Projects Chapters 1–3	A demonstration of your mastery of the skills in Chapters 1–3 with extensive decision making. **(Grader Project)**	In **MyLab IT** and IRC

Glossary

Glossary of Chapter Key Terms

After Previous An animation option that begins the animation sequence for the selected slide element immediately after the completion of the previous animation or slide transition.

Animation A visual or sound effect added to an object or text on a slide.

Animation Painter A feature that copies animation settings from one object to another.

Background style A predefined slide background fill variation that combines theme colors in different intensities or patterns.

Body font A font that is applied to all slide text except slide titles.

Category labels Text that displays along the bottom of a chart to identify the categories of data.

Cell The intersection of a column and row in a table.

Cell reference The intersecting column letter and row number that identify a cell.

Chart A graphic representation of numeric data.

Chart elements The various components of a chart, including the chart title, axis titles, data series, legend, chart area, and plot area.

Chart Elements button A button that displays options for adding, removing, or changing chart elements.

Chart Filters button A button that displays options for changing the data displayed in a chart.

Chart style A set of predefined formats applied to a chart, including colors, backgrounds, and effects.

Chart Styles button A button that displays options for setting the style and color scheme for a chart.

Column chart A type of chart used for illustrating comparisons among related numbers.

Data marker A column, bar, area, dot, pie slice, or other symbol in a chart that represents a single data point.

Data point A chart value that originates in a worksheet cell.

Data series A group of related data points.

Emphasis effect Animation that emphasizes an object or text that is already displayed.

Entrance effect Animation that brings a slide element onto the screen.

Exit effect Animation that moves an object or text off the screen.

Headings font A font that is applied to all slide title text.

Legend A chart element that identifies the patterns or colors that are assigned to the data series in the chart.

Line chart A type of chart commonly used to illustrate trends over time.

On Click An animation option that begins the animation sequence for the selected slide element when the mouse button is clicked or the Spacebar is pressed.

Table A format for information that organizes and presents text and data in columns and rows.

Table style A format applied to a table that is consistent with the presentation theme.

Theme colors A set of coordinating colors that are applied to the backgrounds, objects, and text in a presentation.

Theme fonts The fonts that apply to two types of slide text—headings and body.

Timing options Animation options that control when animated items display in the animation sequence.

Trim A command that deletes parts of a video to make it shorter.

With Previous An animation option that begins the animation sequence at the same time as the previous animation or slide transition.

Chapter Review

In the following Skills Review, you will format a presentation by applying slide background styles, colors, pictures, and animation. Your completed presentation will look similar to Figure 3.57.

Apply 3A skills from these Objectives:

1. Customize Slide Backgrounds and Themes
2. Animate a Slide Show
3. Insert a Video

Project Files

For Project 3C, you will need:

p03C_Park
p03C_Park_Scenery
p03C_Park_Video

You will save your presentation as:

Lastname_Firstname_3C_Park

Project Results

Figure 3.57 Project 3C Park

(continues on next page)

Chapter Review

Skills Review: Project 3C Park (continued)

1 ▸ Navigate to your student data files, double-click **p03C_Park**, and then **Save** the presentation in your **PowerPoint Chapter 3** folder as **Lastname_Firstname_3C_Park**

a. On the **Design tab**, in the **Variants group**, click **More**, point to **Colors**, and then click **Orange Red** to change the theme colors.

b. On the **Design tab**, in the **Variants group**, click **More**, point to **Fonts**, and then click **Candara** to change the theme fonts.

c. On the **Design tab**, in the **Customize group**, click **Format Background**. In the **Format Background** pane, under **Fill**, click **Picture or texture fill**. Under **Insert picture from**, to the right of **Texture**, click **Texture**, and then in the third row, click the fourth texture—**Recycled Paper**.

d. **Close** the **Format Background** pane.

2 ▸ Display **Slide 2**. Hold down [Ctrl] and click **Slide 4** so that both **Slides 2** and **4** are selected. On the **Design tab**, in the **Variants group**, click **More**, and then point to **Background Styles**. In the second row, right-click the third style—**Style 7**, and then on the shortcut menu, click **Apply to Selected Slides**. (Mac users, click Slide 2. On the Design tab, in the Customize group, click Format Background. Under Fill, click Solid fill. To the right of Color, click Fill Color, and under theme colors, in the third column click the fifth color—Gray, Background 2, Darker 25%.)

a. Display **Slide 3**. On the **Design tab**, in the **Customize group**, click **Format Background**. Under **Fill**, select the **Hide Background Graphics** check box.

b. In the **Format Background** pane, under **Fill**, click **Picture or texture fill**. Under **Insert picture from**, click **File**, and then navigate to your student data files. Click **p03C_Park_Scenery**, and then click **Insert**.

c. In the **Transparency** box, type **10%**

3 ▸ Display **Slide 5**. If necessary, display the Format Background pane.

a. In the **Format Background** pane, under **Fill**, verify that **Solid Fill** is selected.

b. To the right of **Color**, click **Fill Color**. In the third column, click the first color.

c. **Close** the **Format Background** pane.

4 ▸ With **Slide 5** displayed, on the **Insert tab**, in the **Media group**, click **Video**, and then click **Video on My PC**. Navigate to your student data files, and then click **p03C_Park_Video**. Click **Insert** to insert the video.

a. With the video selected, on the **Format tab**, in the **Size group**, replace the value in the **Height** box with **2.5** and then press [Enter].

b. On the **Format tab**, in the **Arrange group**, click **Align**, and then click **Align Center**. Click **Align** again, and then click **Align Bottom** so that the video is centered and aligned with the lower edge of the slide.

c. With the video selected, on the **Format tab**, in the **Video Styles** group, click **More**, and then under **Subtle**, click the third style—**Soft Edge Rectangle**.

d. In the **Video Styles group**, click **Video Shape**, and then under **Rectangles**, click the second shape—**Rectangle: Rounded Corners**. (Mac users click the Crop arrow, point to Change Shape, and then click Rounded Rectangle.)

e. With the video selected, on the **Playback tab**, in the **Video Options group**, click the **Start arrow**, and then click **Automatically**.

f. On the **Playback tab**, in the **Editing group**, click **Trim Video**. Select the number in the **End Time** box, and then type **00:14** and notice that the video ends with a picture of the park. Click **OK** to apply the trim settings. (Mac users drag the End Trim slider to the left until the Duration counter is roughly 0:14:000, and then click Trim.)

5 ▸ Display **Slide 2**, and then select the text in the bulleted list placeholder. On the **Home tab**, in the **Font group**, click **Font Color**, and then in the second column, click the first color so that the text displays with more contrast against the slide background.

a. With the bulleted list selected, on the **Animations tab**, in the **Animation group**, click **More**, and then under **Entrance**, click **Split**.

b. In the **Animation group**, click **Effect Options**, and then click **Vertical Out**.

c. In the **Timing group**, click the **Start arrow**, and then click **After Previous** so that the list displays after the slide transition.

(continues on next page)

Chapter Review

d. In the **Timing group**, click the **Duration up arrow** two times so that *01.00* displays in the **Duration** box. Click the **Delay up arrow** one time so that *00.25* displays in the **Delay** box. (Mac users, in the Animations pane, click to expand Timing to adjust the **Delay** value.)

6 Display **Slide 3**, and then click in the title placeholder. On the **Animations tab**, in the **Animation group**, click **More**, and then under **Entrance**, click **Wipe**. In the **Timing group**, click the **Start arrow**, and then click **After Previous** so that the title displays immediately after the slide transition.

a. With the title selected, in the **Advanced Animation group**, click **Animation Painter**. Click **Slide 1**, and then click the subtitle—*Remodel Update*—to apply the animation effect to the subtitle.

b. On **Slide 1**, select the title. On the **Animations tab**, in the **Animation group**, click **More**, and then click **None** to remove the animation from the title. (Mac users, in the Animations pane, under ANIMATIONS, select the title and then click the red X to remove the animation.)

c. Insert a **Header & Footer** for the **Notes and Handouts**. Include the **Date and time updated automatically**, the **Page number**, and a **Footer** with the text **3C_Park**

d. On the **Slide Show tab**, in the **Start Slide Show group**, click **From Beginning**, and then view your presentation, clicking the mouse button to advance through the slides. When the video on Slide 5 finishes, press `Esc` to return to the presentation.

7 Click the **File tab**, and then click **Compress Media**. Click **Standard Quality** to make the presentation size smaller and easier to submit. Depending on your system, this may be named Low Quality. When the compression is complete, in the **Compress Media** dialog box, click **Close**. (Mac users, the Compress Media feature is not available in the Mac version of PowerPoint.)

a. Display the document properties. As the **Tags**, type **park remodel** and as the **Subject,** type your course and section number. Be sure your name displays as author, and then **Save** your file.

b. As directed by your instructor, submit your completed PowerPoint presentation. **Close** PowerPoint.

You have completed Project 3C   **END**

Chapter Review

Skills Review | Project 3D Budget

In the following Skills Review, you will format a presentation by inserting and formatting a table, a column chart, and a line chart. Your completed presentation will look similar to Figure 3.58.

Project Files

For Project 3D, you will need:

p03D_Budget

You will save your presentation as:

Lastname_Firstname_3D_Budget

Project Results

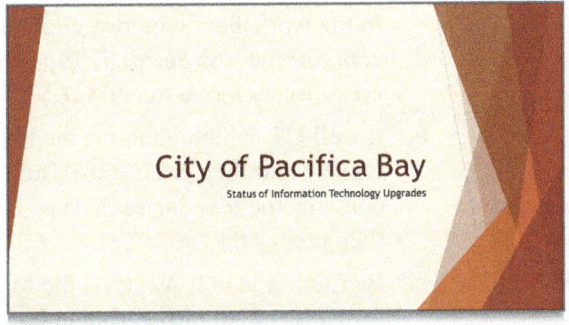
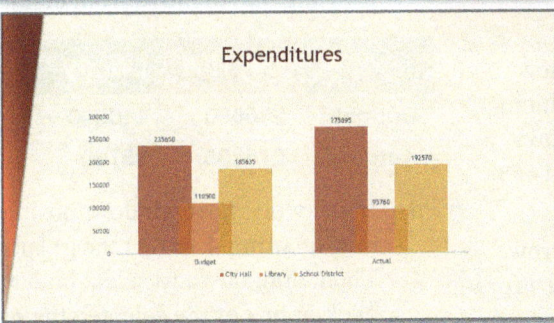
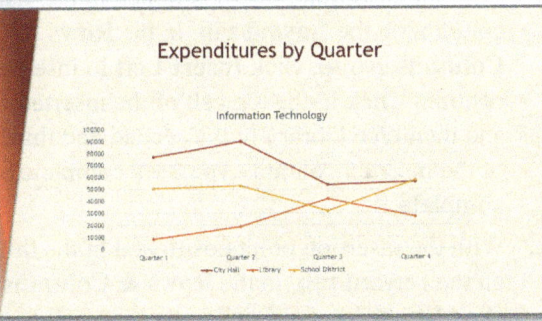

Figure 3.58 Project 3D Budget

(continues on next page)

Chapter Review

1 Navigate to your student data files, double-click **p03D_Budget**, and then **Save** the presentation in your **PowerPoint Chapter 3** folder as **Lastname_Firstname_3D_Budget**

a. Display **Slide 2**. In the content placeholder, click **Insert Table** to display the **Insert Table** dialog box. In the **Number of columns box**, type **3** and then press Tab. In the **Number of rows** box, if necessary, type **2** and then click **OK** to create the table.

b. In the first row of the table, click in the second cell. Type **City Hall** and then press Tab. Type **School District** and then press Tab to move the insertion point to the first cell in the second row.

c. With the insertion point positioned in the first cell of the second row, type **Network Upgrade** and then press Tab. Type **75% complete** and then press Tab. Type **50% complete** and then press Tab to insert a new blank row. In the first cell of the third row, type **Software Training** and then press Tab. Type **50% complete** and then press Tab. Type **20% complete**

d. With the insertion point positioned in the last column, on the **Layout tab**, in the **Rows & Columns group**, click **Insert Left** to insert a new column. Click in the top cell of the inserted column, and then type **Library** In the second and third rows of the inserted column, type **85% complete** and **65% complete**

e. With the insertion point positioned in the third row, on the **Layout tab**, in the **Rows & Columns group**, click **Insert Above**. Click in the first cell of the row you inserted, type **Software Testing** and then press Tab. Type the remaining three entries in the row as follows: **Complete** and **Complete** and **40% complete**

2 At the center of the lower border surrounding the table, point to the sizing handle, and make the table larger by dragging down until the lower edge of the table aligns **on the lower half of the vertical ruler at 2 inches**.

a. Click in the first cell of the table. On the **Layout tab**, in the **Cell Size group**, click **Distribute Rows**.

b. On the **Layout tab**, in the **Table group**, click **Select**, and then click **Select Table**. In the **Alignment group**, click **Center**, and then click **Center Vertically**.

c. On the **Table Tools Design tab**, in the **Table Styles group**, click **More**. Under **Medium**, in the third row, click the second style—**Medium Style 3 – Accent 1**—to apply the style to the table.

d. Move the pointer outside of the table so that it is positioned to the left of the first row in the table to display the → pointer, and then click one time to select the entire row. On the **Design tab**, in the **Table Styles group**, click **Effects**. Point to **Cell Bevel**, and then under **Bevel**, click the first bevel—**Round**. Depending on your version of PowerPoint, this may be named **Circle**. Change the **Font Size** of the text in the first row to **24**.

3 Display **Slide 3**. In the content placeholder, click **Insert Chart** to display the **Insert Chart** dialog box. With the **Clustered Column** chart selected, click **OK**.

a. In the worksheet window, click in cell **B1**, which contains the text *Series 1*. Type **City Hall** and then press Tab to move to cell **C1**.

b. In cell **C1**, which contains the text *Series 2*, type **Library** and then press Tab to move to cell **D1**, which contains the text *Series 3*. Type **School District** and then press Tab.

c. Beginning in cell **A2**, type the following data, pressing Tab to move from cell to cell.

	City Hall	Library	School District
Budget	235650	110500	185635
Actual	275895	95760	192570

d. In the worksheet window, position the pointer over **row heading 4** so that the → pointer displays. Then, drag down to select both **rows 4** and **5**. Right-click in one of the selected the rows to display the shortcut menu. On the shortcut menu, click **Delete**. **Close** the worksheet window. (Mac users press command ⌘ and click.)

e. With the chart selected, on the **Chart Tools Design tab**, in the **Chart Styles group**, click **More**. In the **Chart Styles** gallery, in the second row, click **Style 13** to apply the style to the chart.

f. To the right of the chart, click **Chart Elements**, and then *clear* the **Chart Title** box to remove it from the chart. Select the **Data Labels** box to add the data labels to the chart. (Mac users, on the Chart Design tab, click Add Chart Element, point to Chart Title, and then click None. Click Add Chart Element, point to Data Labels, and then click Outside End.)

(continues on next page)

Chapter Review

Skills Review: Project 3D Budget (continued)

g. With the chart selected, click the **Animations tab**, and then in the **Animation group**, click **More**. Under **Entrance**, click **Split**. In the **Animation group**, click **Effect Options**, and then under **Sequence**, click **By Series**.

4 ▶ Display **Slide 4**. In the content placeholder, click **Insert Chart**. On the left side of the displayed **Insert Chart** dialog box, click **Line**, and then under **Line**, click the fourth chart—**Line with Markers**. Click **OK**.

a. In the worksheet, click in cell **B1**, which contains the text *Series 1*. Type **City Hall** and then press [Tab]. Type **Library** and then press [Tab]. Type **School District**

b. Beginning in cell **A2**, type the following data. After you finish entering the data, close the worksheet window.

	City Hall	Library	School District
Quarter 1	76575	8265	50665
Quarter 2	89670	18675	52830
Quarter 3	53620	41730	31560
Quarter 4	56030	27090	57515

c. Click in the **Chart Title**, and then type **Information Technology**

d. Insert a **Header & Footer** for the **Notes and Handouts**. Include the **Date and time updated automatically**, the **Page number**, and a **Footer** with the file name **3D_Budget**

e. Display the document properties. As the **Tags,** type **technology budget** and as the **Subject,** type your course and section number. Be sure your name displays as author, and then **Save** your file.

f. As directed by your instructor, submit your completed PowerPoint presentation. **Close** PowerPoint.

You have completed Project 3D | **END**

Content-Based Assessments (Mastery and Transfer of Learning)

Apply 3A skills from these Objectives:

1. Customize Slide Backgrounds and Themes
2. Animate a Slide Show
3. Insert a Video

In the following Mastering PowerPoint project, you will format a presentation created by the Pacifica Bay Public Relations department that describes the City of Pacifica Bay Botanical Gardens. Your completed presentation will look similar to Figure 3.59.

Project Files for MyLab IT Grader

1. In your **MyLab IT** course, locate and click **PowerPoint 3E Garden**, Download Materials, and then Download All Files.
2. Extract the zipped folder to your PowerPoint Chapter 3 folder. Close the Grader download screens.
3. Take a moment to open the downloaded **PowerPoint_3E Garden_Instructions**; note any recent updates to the book.

Project Results

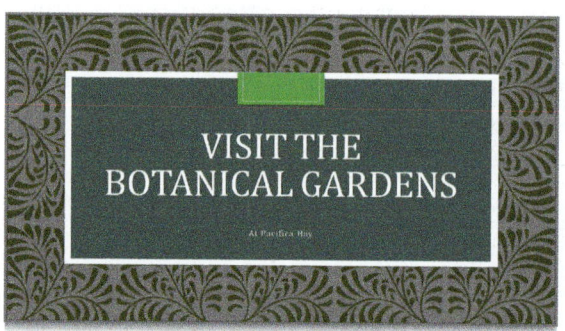

Figure 3.59 Project 3E Garden

For Non-MyLab Submissions

For Project 3E, you will need:

New blank PowerPoint presentation
p03E_Garden
p03E_Flower
p03E_Video

In your PowerPoint Chapter 3 folder, save your presentation as:

Lastname_Firstname_3E_Garden

After you have named and saved your presentation, on the next page, begin with Step 2.
After Step 15, save and submit your presentation as directed by your instructor.

(continues on next page)

Content-Based Assessments (Mastery and Transfer of Learning)

Mastering PowerPoint: Project 3E Gardens (continued)

1 Navigate to your **PowerPoint Chapter 3 folder** and then double-click the PowerPoint file you downloaded from **MyLab IT** that displays your name—**Student_PowerPoint_3E_Garden**

2 Change the **Colors** for the presentation to **Green**, and the **Fonts** to **Cambria**.

3 On **Slide 1**, format the background by changing the **Fill Color** to **Tan, Text 2, Darker 90%**—in the fourth column, the last color.

4 Select **Slides 2** and **3**, and then format the background of the two selected slides with the **Canvas Texture**.

5 On **Slide 2**, select the paragraph on the right side of the slide, and then apply the **Split** entrance effect. Change the **Effect Options** to **Horizontal Out**. Change the **Start** setting to **After Previous**, and then change the **Duration** to **01.00**.

6 Use the **Animation Painter** to apply the same animation from the paragraph on **Slide 2** to the bulleted list on **Slide 3**. Then, on Slide 3, remove the animation from the title.

7 On **Slide 4**, hide the background graphics, and then format the background with a picture from your student data files—**p03E_Flower**. Change the **Transparency** to **50%**.

8 Format the title placeholder with a **Shape Fill** color—in the fifth column, the last color.

9 From your student data files, insert the video **p03E_Video**. Change the **Video Height** to **5**

10 Using the **Align to Slide** option, apply the **Align Center** and **Align Middle** options.

11 Format the video by applying, from the **Video Styles** gallery, a **Moderate** style—**Beveled Oval, Black**.

12 Change the video **Start** setting to **Automatically**, and then trim the video to **00:12** Compress the video using the **Standard Quality** setting or Low Quality depending on your version of PowerPoint. Note— The Compress Media feature is not available in the Mac version of PowerPoint.

13 **Insert** a **Header & Footer** on the **Notes and Handouts**. Include the **Date and time updated automatically**, the **Page number**, and a **Footer** with the text **3E_Garden**

14 Display the document properties. As the **Tags,** type **botanical gardens** and as the **Subject,** type your course and section number. Be sure your name displays in the **Author box**, and then **Save** your file.

15 View the slide show from the beginning. **Close** PowerPoint.

16 In **MyLab IT**, in your **Course Materials**, locate and click the Grader Project **PowerPoint 3E Garden**. In **step 3**, under **Upload Completed Assignment**, click **Choose File**. In the **Open** dialog box, navigate to your **PowerPoint Chapter 3 folder**, and then click your **Student_PowerPoint_3E_Garden** file one time to select it. In the lower right corner of the **Open** dialog box, click **Open**.

The name of your selected file displays above the Upload button.

17 To submit your file to **MyLab IT** for grading, click **Upload**, wait a moment for a green **Success!** message, and then in **step 4**, click the blue **Submit for Grading** button. Click **Close Assignment** to return to your list of **Course Materials**.

You have completed Project 3E **END**

Content-Based Assessments (Mastery and Transfer of Learning)

Apply 3B skills from these Objectives:

4. Create and Modify Tables
5. Create and Modify Charts

In the following Mastering PowerPoint project, you will format several of the slides in a presentation that the City Manager is developing for an upcoming City Council meeting. Your completed presentation will look similar to Figure 3.60.

Project Files for MyLab IT Grader

1. In your **MyLab IT** course, locate and click **PowerPoint 3F Report**, Download Materials, and then Download All Files.
2. Extract the zipped folder to your PowerPoint Chapter 3 folder. Close the Grader download screens.
3. Take a moment to open the downloaded **PowerPoint_3F_Report_Instructions**; note any recent updates to the book.

Project Results

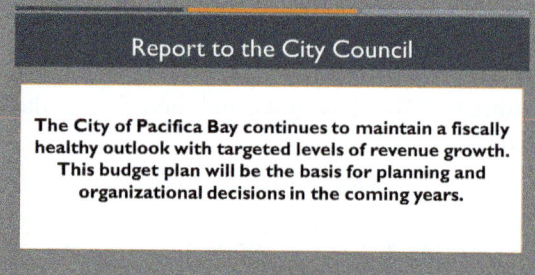

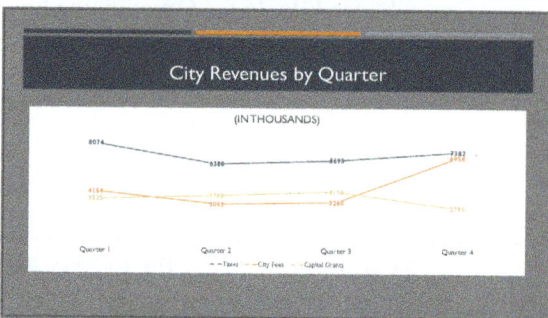

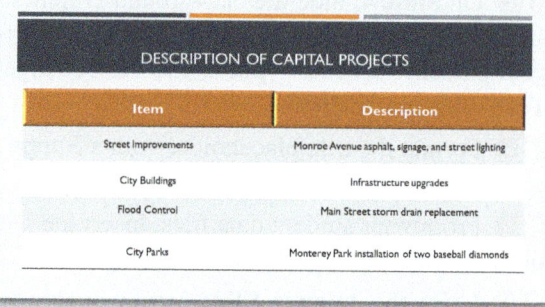

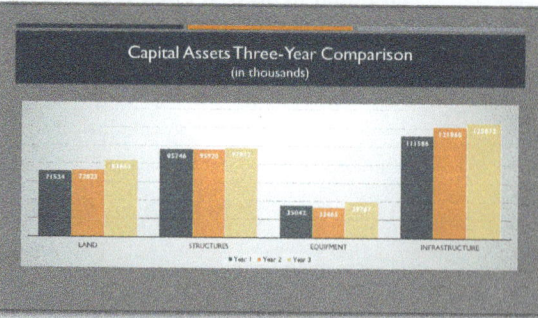

Figure 3.60 Project 3F Report

For Non-MyLab Submissions

For Project 3F, you will need:
p03F_Report

In your PowerPoint Chapter 3 folder, save your presentation as:
Lastname_Firstname_3F_Report

After you have named and saved your presentation, on the next page, begin with Step 2.

After Step 14, save and submit your presentation as directed by your instructor.

(continues on next page)

Mastering PowerPoint: Project 3F Report (continued)

1 Navigate to your **PowerPoint Chapter 3 folder** and then double-click the PowerPoint file you downloaded from **MyLab IT** that displays your name—**Student_PowerPoint_3F_Report**. If necessary, at the top, click **Enable Editing**.

2 On **Slide 3**, in the content placeholder, insert a **Line with Markers** chart. In the worksheet, in cell **B1**, type **Taxes** and then enter the following data:

	Taxes	City Fees	Capital Grants
Quarter 1	8074	4154	3525
Quarter 2	6380	3092	3785
Quarter 3	6695	3260	4150
Quarter 4	7382	6958	2795

3 **Close** the worksheet window. Apply **Chart Style 7**, and then apply the **Wipe** entrance effect to the chart.

4 Including the parentheses, change the **Chart Title** to **(IN THOUSANDS)**

5 On **Slide 4**, in the content placeholder, insert a **Table** with **2 columns** and **5 rows**, and then type the text in **Table 1** at the bottom of the page.

6 Change the height of the table to **4.36"** Align the table text so that it is centered horizontally and vertically within the cells.

7 Apply table style **Medium Style 3 - Accent 2**, and then apply a **Round Bevel** to the first row. Note— Depending on your version of PowerPoint, this may be named Circle Bevel. Change the **Font Size** of the text in the first row to **24**.

8 On **Slide 5**, in the content placeholder, insert a **Clustered Column** chart. In the worksheet, in cell **B1**, type **Year 1** and then enter the following data:

	Year 1	Year 2	Year 3
Land	71534	72823	83653
Structures	95746	95920	97812
Equipment	35042	33465	39767
Infrastructure	111586	121860	125873

9 Apply **Chart Style 4** to the chart, and then remove the **Chart Title** element.

10 Apply the **Wipe** entrance effect to the chart. Change the **Effect Options** so that the animation is applied **By Series**.

11 Change chart animation **Timing** so that the animation starts **After Previous**.

12 Insert a **Header & Footer** on the **Notes and Handouts**. Include the **Date and time updated automatically**, the **Page number**, and a **Footer** with the text **3F_Report**

13 Display the document properties. As the **Tags**, type **city council report** and as the **Subject**, type your course and section number. Be sure your name displays as author, and then **Save** your file.

14 View the slide show from the beginning. **Close** PowerPoint.

15 In **MyLab IT**, in your **Course Materials**, locate and click the Grader Project **PowerPoint 3F Report**. In **step 3**, under **Upload Completed Assignment**, click **Choose File**. In the **Open** dialog box, navigate to your **PowerPoint Chapter 3 folder**, and then click your **Student_PowerPoint_3F_Report** file one time to select it. In the lower right corner of the **Open** dialog box, click **Open**.

The name of your selected file displays above the Upload button.

16 To submit your file to **MyLab IT** for grading, click **Upload**, wait a moment for a green **Success!** message, and then in **step 4**, click the blue **Submit for Grading** button. Click **Close Assignment** to return to your list of **Course Materials**.

Table 1

Item	Description
Street Improvements	Monroe Avenue asphalt, signage, and street lighting
City Buildings	Infrastructure upgrades
Flood Control	Main Street storm drain replacement
City Parks	Monterey Park installation of two baseball diamonds

You have completed Project 3F **END**

MyLab IT Grader

Mastering PowerPoint   **Project 3G Travel**

Apply 3A and 3B skills from these Objectives:

1. Customize Slide Backgrounds and Themes
2. Animate a Slide Show
3. Insert a Video
4. Create and Modify Tables
5. Create and Modify Charts

In the following Mastering PowerPoint project, you will format a presentation that the Pacifica Bay Travel and Tourism Director will show at a conference for California Travel Agents. Your completed presentation will look similar to Figure 3.61.

Project Files for MyLab IT Grader

1. In your **MyLab IT** course, locate and click **PowerPoint 3G Travel**, Download Materials, and then Download All Files.
2. Extract the zipped folder to your Excel Chapter 3 folder. Close the Grader download screens.
3. Take a moment to open the downloaded **PowerPoint_3G_Travel_Instructions**; note any recent updates to the book.

Project Results

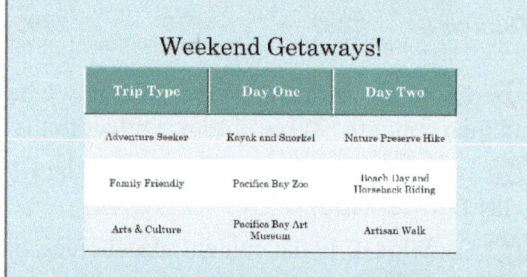

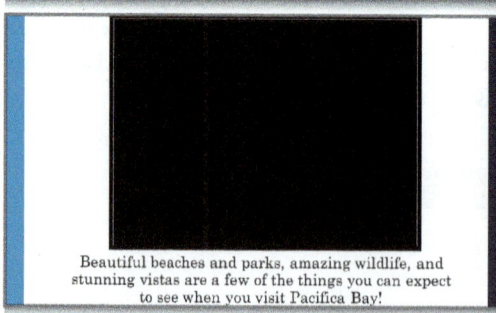

Figure 3.61 Project 3G Travel

For Non-MyLab Submissions

For Project 2G, you will need:

p03G_Travel
p03G_Video
p03G_Background

In your PowerPoint Chapter 3 folder, save your presentation as:

Lastname_Firstname_3G_Travel

After you have named and saved your workbook, open it to launch Excel, and then on the next page, begin with Step 2.

After Step 18, save and submit your presentation as directed by your instructor.

(continues on next page)

Content-Based Assessments (Mastery and Transfer of Learning)

Mastering PowerPoint: Project 3G Travel (continued)

1 Navigate to your **PowerPoint Chapter 3 folder** and then double-click the PowerPoint file you downloaded from **MyLab IT** that displays your name—**Student_PowerPoint_3G_Travel**. If necessary, at the top, click **Enable Editing**.

2 Change the **Colors** for the presentation to **Blue Green**.

3 On **Slide 1**, format the background with the **Water droplets Texture**, and then change the **Transparency** to **50%**.

4 Select **Slides 2 through 4**, and then apply a **Solid fill** to the background of the selected slides—in the second to last column, the third color.

5 On **Slide 2**, hide the background graphics.

6 Insert a **Table** with **3 columns** and **4 rows**. Apply table style **Medium Style 3 - Accent 3**, and then type the information in **Table 1** at the bottom of this page, into the inserted table.

7 Resize the table so that its lower edge extends to **3 inches on the lower half of the vertical ruler (height 4.72")**, and then distribute the table rows. Align the table text so that it is centered horizontally and vertically within the cells.

8 Change the **Font Size** of the first row of the table text to **24**. Apply a **Divot Cell Bevel** to the first row.

9 On **Slide 3**, animate the picture using the **Wipe** entrance effect starting **After Previous**. Change the **Duration** to **01:00**. Apply the **Split** entrance effect to the bulleted list placeholder, and then change the **Effect Options** to **Vertical Out**.

10 On **Slide 4**, insert a **Clustered Column** chart. In the worksheet, in cell **B1**, type **Year 1** and then enter the following data:

	Year 1	Year 2	Year 3
Spring	75600	72300	81460
Summer	105300	128730	143600
Fall	35900	58300	58320
Winter	41600	58430	67300

11 Apply **Chart Style 8** to the chart, and then remove the **Chart Title** element. Apply the **Wipe** entrance effect to the chart and change the **Effect Options** to **By Series**.

12 On **Slide 5**, apply the **Style 1** background style to this slide only. (Mac users, format the background using Solid Fill color White, Background 1.)

13 From your student data files, insert the video **p03G_Video**. Change the **Video Height** to **6** and use the **Align Center** and **Align Top** options to position the video. Apply the **Simple Beveled Rectangle** video style.

14 On the **Playback tab**, change the **Video Options** to **Start** the video **Automatically**. **Trim** the video so that the **End Time** is **00:09** and then compress the media in **Standard Quality** or Low Quality depending on your version of PowerPoint. (Mac users, the Compress Media feature is not available in the Mac version of PowerPoint.)

15 On **Slide 6**, hide the background graphics, and then format the slide background by inserting a picture from your downloaded project files—**p03G_Background**. Set the **Transparency** to **0%**

16 Insert a **Header & Footer** on the **Notes and Handouts**. Include the **Date and time updated automatically**, the **Page number**, and a **Footer** with the text **3G_Travel**

17 Display the document properties. As the **Tags,** type **travel, tourism** and as the **Subject,** type your course and section number. Be sure your name displays as author, and then **Save** your file.

18 View the slide show from the beginning. **Close** PowerPoint.

19 In **MyLab IT**, in your **Course Materials**, locate and click the Grader Project **PowerPoint 3G Travel**. In **step 3**, under **Upload Completed Assignment**, click **Choose File**. In the **Open** dialog box, navigate to your **PowerPoint Chapter 3 folder**, and then click your **Student_PowerPoint_3G_Travel** file one time to select it. In the lower right corner of the **Open** dialog box, click **Open**.

The name of your selected file displays above the Upload button.

20 To submit your file to **MyLab IT** for grading, click **Upload**, wait a moment for a green **Success!** message, and then in **step 4**, click the blue **Submit for Grading** button. Click **Close Assignment** to return to your list of **Course Materials**.

Table 1

Trip Type	Day One	Day Two
Adventure Seeker	Kayak and Snorkel	Nature Preserve Hike
Family-Friendly	Pacifica Bay Zoo	Beach Day and Horseback Riding
Arts & Culture	Pacifica Bay Art Museum	Artisan Walk

You have completed Project 3G **END**

Content-Based Assessments (Critical Thinking)

Apply a combination of the **3A** and **3B** skills.

GO! Fix It	**Project 3H Housing Developments**	**IRC**
GO! Make It	**Project 3I Water Usage**	**IRC**
GO! Solve It	**Project 3J Aquatic Center**	**IRC**
GO! Solve It	**Project 3K Power**	

Project Files

For Project 3K, you will need:

p03K_Power

p03K_Tower

You will save your presentation as:

Lastname_Firstname_3K_Power

Open the file p03K_Power and save it as **Lastname_Firstname_3K_Power** Complete the presentation by applying a theme and then formatting the slide background for the title slide with the picture found in your student data files—p03K_Tower. Adjust the size, position, fill color, and font color on the title slide as necessary so that the title text displays attractively against the background picture. Format the background of at least one other slide using a background style, solid fill color, or texture. On Slide 3, insert a table with the following information:

Power Sources	Percent Used by City
Natural gas	32%
Hydroelectric	17%
Renewables	18%
Coal	23%
Nuclear	10%

On Slide 4, insert and format an appropriate chart to demonstrate the revenue collected from residential power sales over the past three years. Revenue in 2018 was 35.5 million dollars, in 2019 revenue was 42.6 million dollars, and in 2020 revenue was 48.2 million dollars. Apply appropriate animation and slide transitions to the slides. Insert a header and footer that includes the date and time updated automatically, **3K_Power** in the footer, and the page number. Add your name, your course name and section number, and the keywords **power sources, revenue** to the Properties area. Save and then as directed by your instructor, create and submit a paper printout or an electronic image of your presentation that looks like a printed document—either as the Notes and Handouts or as the presentation slides—or, submit your completed PowerPoint file. Close PowerPoint.

Content-Based Assessments (Critical Thinking)

		Performance Level		
		Exemplary	**Proficient**	**Developing**
Performance Elements		You consistently applied the relevant skills	You sometimes, but not always, applied the relevant skills	You rarely or never applied the relevant skills
	Format two slide backgrounds with pictures and styles	Two slide backgrounds were formatted attractively and text displayed with good contrast against backgrounds.	Slide backgrounds were formatted but text did not display well against the chosen background, or only one slide background was formatted.	Slide backgrounds were not formatted with pictures or styles.
	Insert and format appropriate table and chart	Appropriate table and chart were inserted and formatted and the entered data was accurate.	A table and a chart were inserted but were not appropriate for the presentation or either a table or a chart was omitted.	Table and chart were not inserted.
	Apply appropriate animation	Appropriate animation was applied to the presentation.	Animation was applied but was not appropriate for the presentation.	Animation was not applied.

You have completed Project 3K **END**

Outcomes-Based Assessments (Critical Thinking)

Rubric

The following outcomes-based assessments are open-ended assessments. That is, there is no specific correct result; your result will depend on your approach to the information provided. Make Professional Quality your goal. Use the following scoring rubric to guide you in how to approach the problem and then to evaluate how well your approach solves the problem.

The *criteria*—Software Mastery, Content, Format and Layout, and Process—represent the knowledge and skills you have gained that you can apply to solving the problem. The *levels of performance*—Professional Quality, Approaching Professional Quality, or Needs Quality Improvements—help you and your instructor evaluate your result.

	Your completed project is of Professional Quality if you:	Your completed project is Approaching Professional Quality if you:	Your completed project Needs Quality Improvements if you:
1-Software Mastery	Choose and apply the most appropriate skills, tools, and features and identify efficient methods to solve the problem.	Choose and apply some appropriate skills, tools, and features, but not in the most efficient manner.	Choose inappropriate skills, tools, or features, or are inefficient in solving the problem.
2-Content	Construct a solution that is clear and well organized, contains content that is accurate, appropriate to the audience and purpose, and is complete. Provide a solution that contains no errors of spelling, grammar, or style.	Construct a solution in which some components are unclear, poorly organized, inconsistent, or incomplete. Misjudge the needs of the audience. Have some errors in spelling, grammar, or style, but the errors do not detract from comprehension.	Construct a solution that is unclear, incomplete, or poorly organized, contains some inaccurate or inappropriate content, and contains many errors of spelling, grammar, or style. Do not solve the problem.
3-Format and Layout	Format and arrange all elements to communicate information and ideas, clarify function, illustrate relationships, and indicate relative importance.	Apply appropriate format and layout features to some elements, but not others. Overuse features, causing minor distraction.	Apply format and layout that does not communicate information or ideas clearly. Do not use format and layout features to clarify function, illustrate relationships, or indicate relative importance. Use available features excessively, causing distraction.
4-Process	Use an organized approach that integrates planning, development, self-assessment, revision, and reflection.	Demonstrate an organized approach in some areas, but not others; or, use an insufficient process of organization throughout.	Do not use an organized approach to solve the problem.

Outcomes-Based Assessments (Critical Thinking)

Apply a combination of the 3A and 3B skills.

| GO! Think | Project 3L Animal Sanctuary |

Project Files

For Project 3L, you will need:
New blank PowerPoint presentation
You will save your presentation as:
Lastname_Firstname_3L_Animal_Sanctuary

The Pacifica Bay Animal Sanctuary, a nonprofit organization, provides shelter and care for animals in need, including dogs, cats, hamsters, and guinea pigs. The Sanctuary, which celebrates its tenth anniversary in July, has cared for more than 12,000 animals since it opened and is a state-of-the-art facility. Funding for the Sanctuary comes in the form of business sponsorships, individual donations, and pet adoption fees. The following table indicates revenue generated by the Sanctuary during the past three years.

	Fees	Donations	Sponsorships
2018	125,085	215,380	175,684
2019	110,680	256,785	156,842
2020	132,455	314,682	212,648

In addition to shelter services, the Sanctuary offers community service and training programs, veterinarian services, and vaccine clinics. Examples of these services include Canine Obedience classes, microchipping ($25 fee), and the Healthy Pet Hotline (free). Canine Obedience classes are for puppies and adult dogs to improve obedience, socialization, and behavior. Classes last two, three, or four months and cost $150 to $250.

Using the preceding information, create the first five slides of a presentation that the director of the Pacifica Bay Animal Sanctuary will show at an upcoming pet fair. Apply an appropriate theme and use slide layouts that will effectively present the content. Include a line chart with the revenue data, a table with the community service programs information, and at least one slide formatted with a dog or cat on the slide background. Apply styles to the table and chart, apply animation and slide transitions to the slides. Use the techniques that you practiced in this chapter so that your presentation is professional and attractive. Save the file as **Lastname_Firstname_3L_Animal_Sanctuary** and then insert a header and footer that includes the date and time updated automatically, the **3L_Animal_Sanctuary** in the footer, and the page number. Add your name, your course name and section number, and the keywords **animals, pets** to the properties. As directed by your instructor, submit your completed PowerPoint presentation. Close PowerPoint.

You have completed Project 3L | END

Outcomes-Based Assessments (Critical Thinking)

GO! Think	Project 3M Water Sources	IRC
You and GO!	Project 3N Recreation Programs	IRC
GO! Cumulative Team Project	Project 3O Bell Orchid Hotels	IRC

Formatting a Presentation Using Slide Masters, and Reviewing, Comparing, Combining, and Protecting Presentations

4
POWERPOINT
2019

PROJECT 4A

Outcomes
Modify Slide Masters

Objectives
1. Modify Slide Masters
2. Create a Custom Template

PROJECT 4B

Outcomes
Review, Compare, Combine, and Protect Presentations

Objectives
3. Create and Edit Comments
4. Compare and Combine Presentations
5. Prepare a Presentation for Distribution
6. Protect a Presentation

Billion Photos/Shutterstock

In This Chapter

GO! to Work with PowerPoint

PowerPoint provides professionally designed templates to use when creating a new presentation. You can customize a template using slide masters and you can design and create your own templates. You can review and comment on the content of a presentation by inserting and editing comments and compare two versions of a presentation. Before distributing your presentation to others, you can check a presentation for compatibility with other versions, check for accessibility issues, protect the presentation from further editing by marking it as final, and apply password protection to a presentation.

Attorneys at **Thompson Henderson Law Partners** counsel their clients on a wide variety of issues, including contracts, licensing, intellectual property, and taxation, with emphasis on the unique needs of the entertainment and sports industries. Entertainment clients include production companies, publishers, talent agencies, actors, writers, artists—anyone involved in creating or doing business in the entertainment industry. Sports clients include colleges and universities, professional sports teams, and athletes. Increasingly, sports coaches and organizations with concerns about liability are also seeking the firm's counsel.

PROJECT 4A Legal Presentation

Project Activities

In Activities 4.01 through 4.11, you will design a presentation for the Thompson Henderson Law Partners by formatting slide masters. You will save the presentation as a template and use the template to create a new presentation. Your completed presentation will look similar to Figure 4.1.

Project Files for **MyLab IT Grader**

1. In your storage location, create a folder named **PowerPoint Chapter 4**.
2. In your **MyLab IT** course, locate and click **PowerPoint 4A Legal Presentation**, Download Materials, and then Download All Files.
3. Extract the zipped folder to your PowerPoint Chapter 4 folder. Close the Grader download screens.
4. Take a moment to open the downloaded **PowerPoint_4A_Legal_Presentation_Instructions**; note any recent updates to the book.

Project Results

GO! Project 4A
Where We're Going

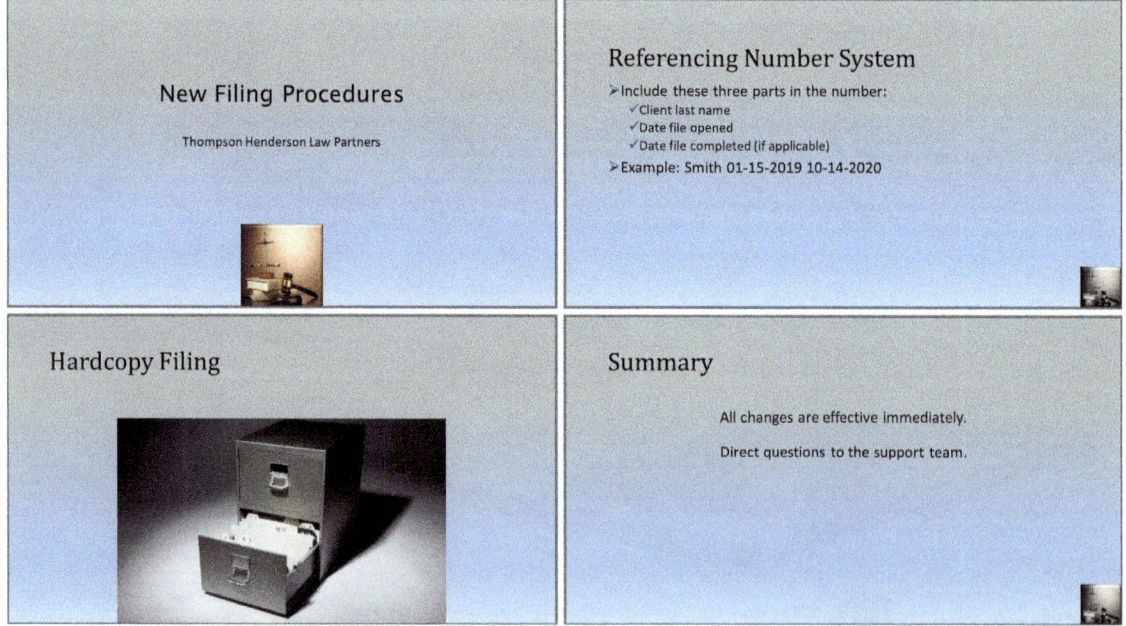

Figure 4.1 Project 4A Legal Presentation

For Non-MyLab Submissions
For Project 4A, you will need:
New blank PowerPoint presentation
p04A_File
p04A_Law1

In your storage location, create a folder named **PowerPoint Chapter 4**
In your PowerPoint Chapter 4 folder, save your presentation as:
Lastname_Firstname_4A_Legal_Presentation

After you have named and saved your presentation, on the next page, begin with Step 2.

NOTE	If You Are Using a Touch Screen

Tap an item to click it.

Press and hold for a few seconds to right-click; release when the information or commands display.

Touch the screen with two or more fingers and then pinch together or stretch your fingers apart to zoom in and out.

Slide your finger on the screen to scroll—slide left to scroll right and slide right to scroll left.

Slide to rearrange—similar to dragging with a mouse.

Swipe to select—slide an item a short distance with a quick movement—to select an item and bring up commands, if any.

Objective 1	Modify Slide Masters

ALERT Because Office 365 is a cloud-based subscription service that receives continuous updates, you may encounter some variations in what appears on your screen and what is shown in this instruction. Microsoft Office 365 is fully installed on your PC or Mac; no internet access is necessary to create or edit documents. When you *are* connected to the internet, you will receive monthly upgrades and new features, so you always have the latest versions of Office apps as soon as they are available. Your subscription gives you continuous free access to the latest innovations and refinements.

GO! Learn How
Video P4-1

When you create a new blank presentation in PowerPoint, the presentation is based on the Office Theme *template*—a file that contains predefined formatting and layout. A *slide master* is part of a template that stores information about the formatting and text that displays on *every* slide in a presentation.

The information stored on the slide master includes such items as the placement and size of text and object placeholders. For example, if your company or organization has a logo that you want to display on *all* the slides in a presentation, you can insert the logo on the slide master. The logo will display in the same location on all slides of the presentation with no further action on your part.

Activity 4.01 | Displaying and Editing Slide Masters

MOS
1.1.1

In this Activity, you will create a new presentation, save it, and then modify the presentation's slide master using the law firm's preferred formatting. The default theme for a new presentation is the Office Theme, so for this presentation you will be modifying the formatting associated with the Office Theme for the slide master. These changes apply only to this presentation—they do not affect the PowerPoint Office theme.

1 Navigate to your **PowerPoint Chapter 4 folder**, and then double-click the PowerPoint file you downloaded from **MyLab IT** that displays your name—**Student_PowerPoint_4A_ Legal_Presentation**. In your presentation, if necessary, at the top click **Enable Editing**.

2 On the **View tab**, in the **Master Views group**, point to, but do not click, **Slide Master**. Read the ScreenTip.

In the Master Views group, there are three views available—Slide Master, Handout Master, and Notes Master.

3 Click **Slide Master**, compare your screen with Figure 4.2, and then take a moment to study the commands in the Edit Master and Master Layout groups described in the table in Figure 4.3.

From the Slide Master tab, you can apply changes such as editing themes, fonts, and colors, customizing backgrounds, and modifying page setup and orientation to specific slide layouts or to the entire theme. For example, if every time you use the Two Content layout in this presentation, the right content placeholder should be narrower than the left, you could make that change in the slide master.

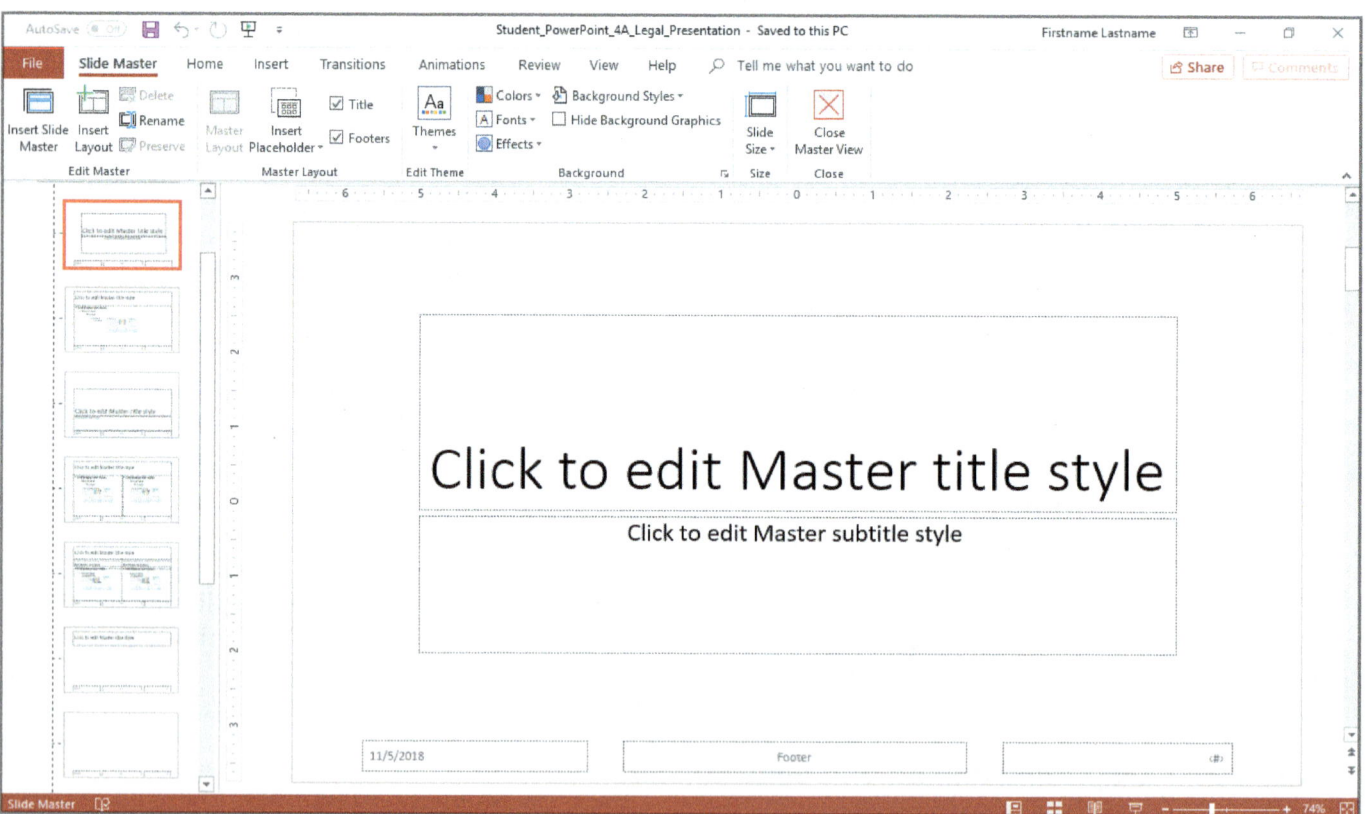

Figure 4.2

Commands on the Slide Master tab	
Screen Element	**Description**
Edit Master group	**Enables you to:**
Insert Slide Master	Add a new slide master to the presentation.
Insert Layout	Add a custom layout to the master slide set.
Delete	Remove this slide master from your presentation.
Rename	Rename your custom layout so you can find it easily in the layout gallery.
Preserve	Preserve the selected master so that it remains with the presentation, even if it is not used.
Master Layout group	**Enables you to:**
Master Layout	Choose the elements to include in the master.
Insert Placeholder	Add a placeholder to the slide layout to hold content, such as a picture, table, media, or text.
Title	Show or hide the title placeholder on this slide.
Footers	Show or hide the footer placeholders.

Figure 4.3

> **4** In the thumbnail pane, scroll up and then point to the first thumbnail to display the ScreenTip—*Office Theme Slide Master: used by slide(s) 1*. Select the **Office Theme Slide Master** and compare your screen with Figure 4.4.

> In Slide Master view, in the thumbnail pane, the larger slide image represents the theme slide master, and the associated layouts are smaller and positioned beneath it.
> The slide master in this presentation is referred to as the Office Theme Slide Master, because a new blank presentation uses the Office Theme. The *Office Theme Slide Master* is the slide master for the Office theme that contains the design, such as the background, that displays on all slide layouts in the presentation. Changes made to the Office Theme Slide Master affect all slide masters in the presentation.

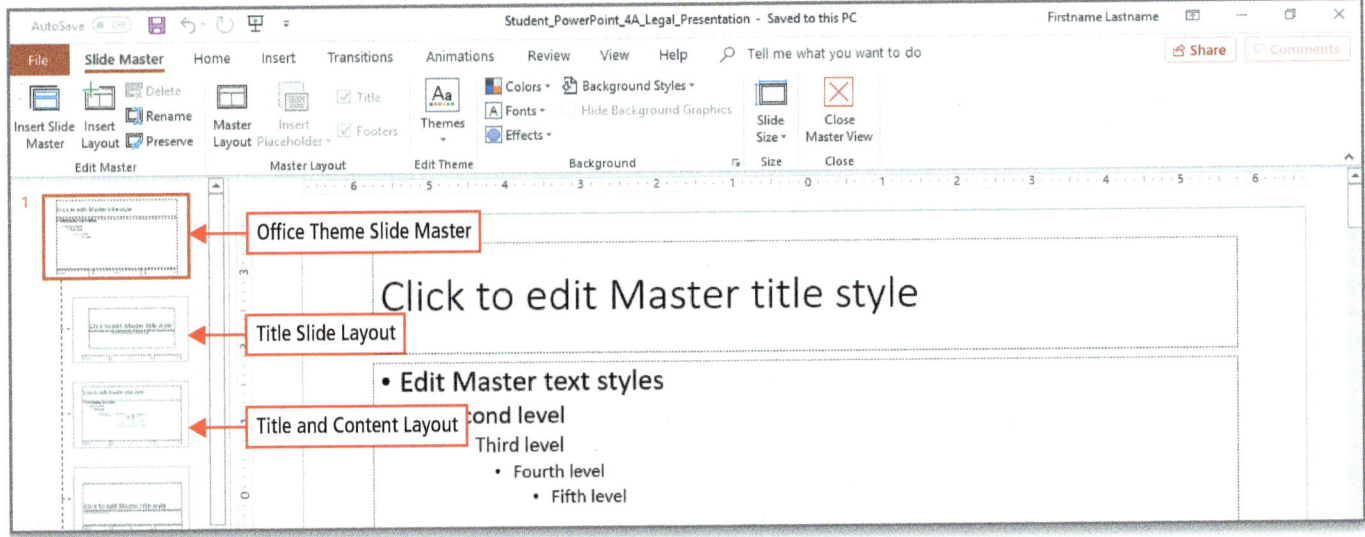

Figure 4.4

> **5** On the **Slide Master tab**, in the **Background group**, click **Fonts**, scroll down as necessary, and then click **Georgia** to change the theme font set.

> Changing the theme font set for the Office Theme Slide Master affects all slide masters in the presentation.

6 Click the second thumbnail—**Title Slide Layout**. On the slide, click anywhere on the dashed border on the Master title style placeholder to display the border as a solid line.

7 On the **Home tab**, in the **Font group**, change the font to **Lucida Sans Unicode**. Change the font size to **40**. **Save** 💾 your presentation and compare your screen with Figure 4.5.

The font and font size changes affect only the Title Slide layout. Each time you select this layout for a slide in this presentation, the font will be Lucida Sans Unicode and the font size will be 40.

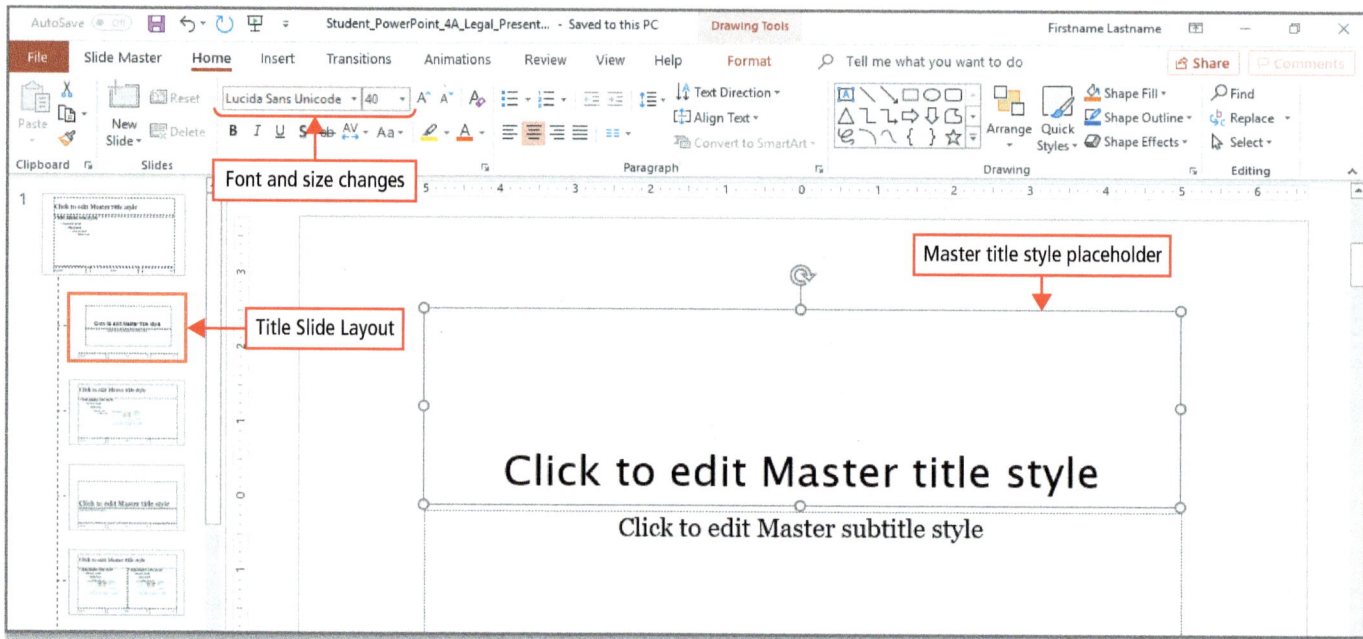

Figure 4.5

 BY TOUCH Tap to select the second thumbnail—Title Slide Layout. On the slide, tap anywhere on the dashed border on the Master title style placeholder to display the border as a solid line. Tap the Home tab. In the Font group, slide the arrow to select the font Lucida Sans Unicode. Tap and slide the arrow to change the font size to 40.

Activity 4.02 | Formatting a Slide Master Background

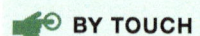
1.1.1

In this Activity, you will customize the slide master background for this presentation by applying a *gradient fill*—a fill effect in which one color fades into another.

1 Click the first thumbnail—**Office Theme Slide Master**. On the **Slide Master tab**, in the **Background group**, click **Background Styles**, and then click **Format Background**. In the **Format Background** pane, under **Fill**, click **Gradient fill**. Click the **Type arrow** to display the list, and then if necessary, click **Linear**.

2 Under **Gradient stops**, point to the first gradient stop on the slider. The ScreenTip *Stop 1 of 4* displays. Drag the selected **gradient stop** slider to the left and then to the right and notice how the background changes on the slide and the percentage of gradation changes in the **Position** box. Position the stop at **25%**.

 ANOTHER WAY You can position the gradient stop by typing the value or using the spin arrows in the Position spin box.

3 ▶ Click the **Color arrow** , and then under **Theme colors**, in the first column, click fourth color. Compare your screen with Figure 4.6.

Applying a gradient stop to the background makes the color vary smoothly from a darker to a lighter shade.

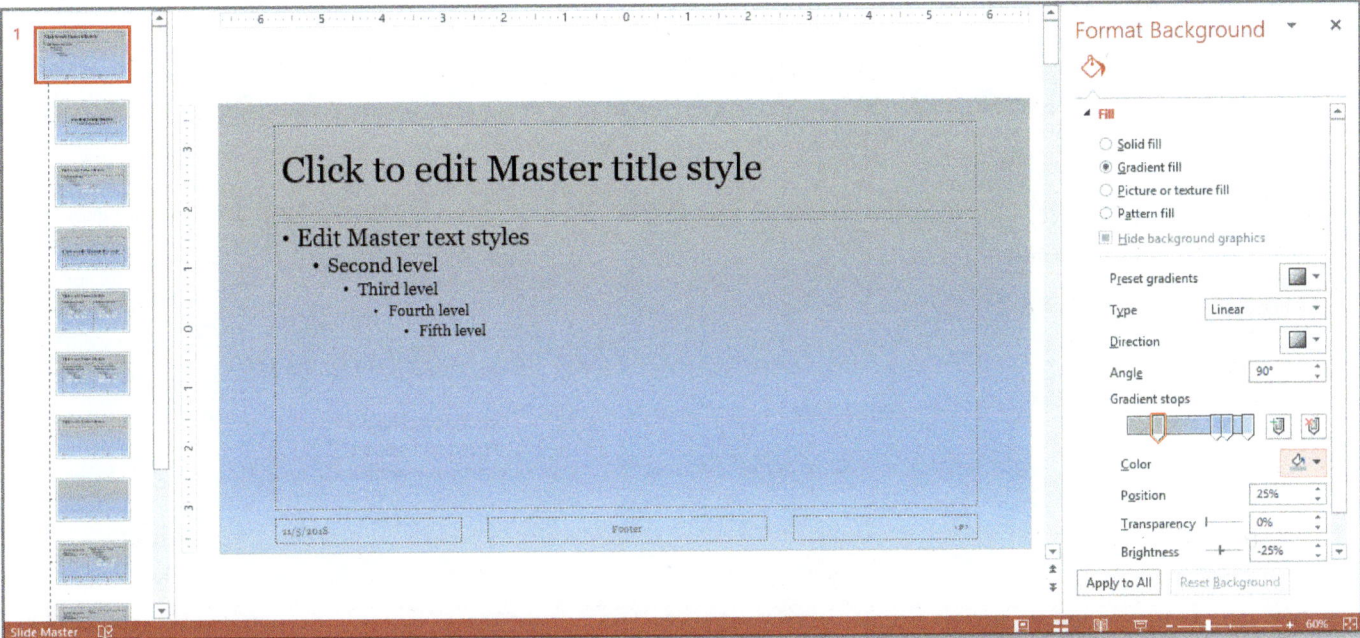

Figure 4.6

4 ▶ At the bottom of the **Format Background** pane, click **Apply to All** and then **Close** ⊠ the pane. **Save** 🖫 your presentation.

Activity 4.03 | Customizing Text Placeholders on a Slide Master

MOS
1.1.2

In this Activity, you will change the size and position of the placeholders on the Title slide master.

1 ▶ Click the **Title Slide Layout** thumbnail to make it the active layout. If necessary, display the ruler. Click the dashed border for the **title placeholder**, and then drag the entire placeholder so the top border is at **3.5 inches on the upper half of the vertical ruler**, using the orange guides that display as you drag to keep the title placeholder aligned with the subtitle placeholder.

2 ▶ Click the dashed border for the **subtitle placeholder**, and then drag the entire placeholder so the top border is at **0.5 inches on the upper half of the vertical ruler**, using the orange guides that display as you drag to keep the placeholders aligned.

Moving a placeholder does not change its size.

3 With the **subtitle placeholder** still selected, drag the **bottom middle sizing handle** to **0.5 inches on the lower half of the vertical ruler** to adjust the size of the placeholder. Compare your screen with Figure 4.7.

Dragging the sizing handle changes the size of the placeholder.

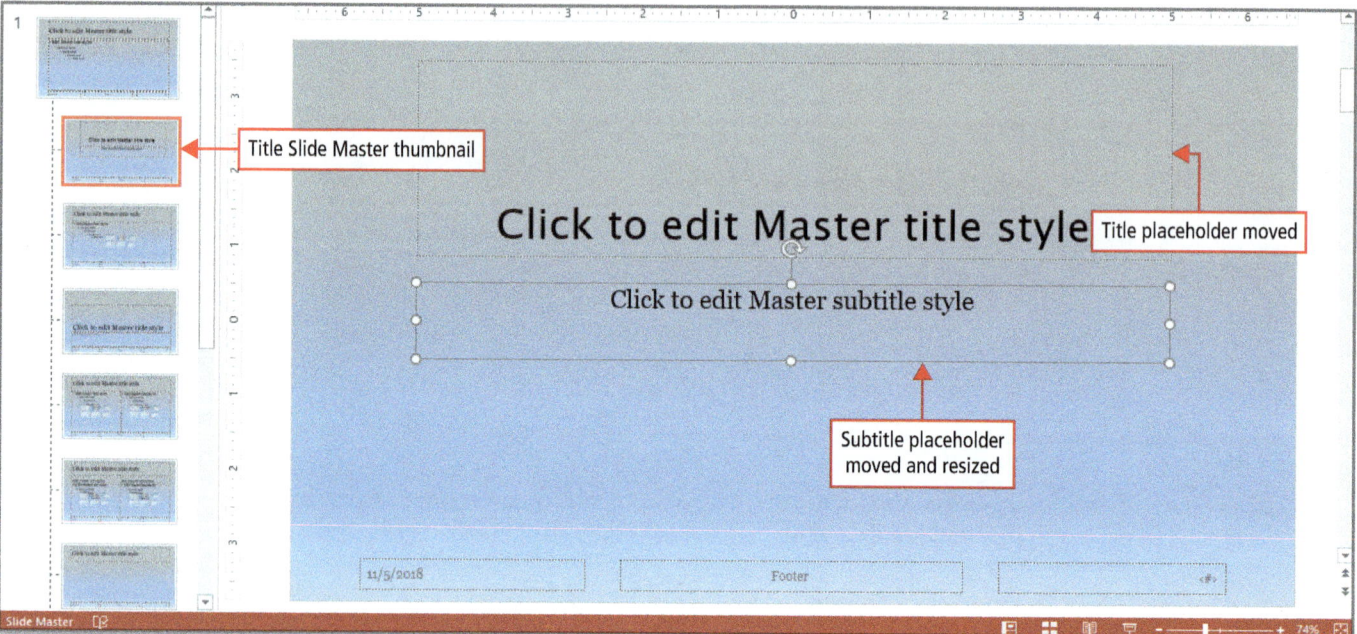

Figure 4.7

4 Click the **Office Theme Slide Master** thumbnail to make it the active slide, and then click anywhere in the first bulleted line. On the **Home tab**, in the **Paragraph group**, click the **Bullets arrow**, and then click **Bullets and Numbering**.

5 In the **Bullets and Numbering** dialog box, on the **Bulleted tab**, click **Arrow Bullets**, and then click the **Color arrow**. Under **Theme Colors**, in the fifth column, click the last color. Compare your screen with Figure 4.8.

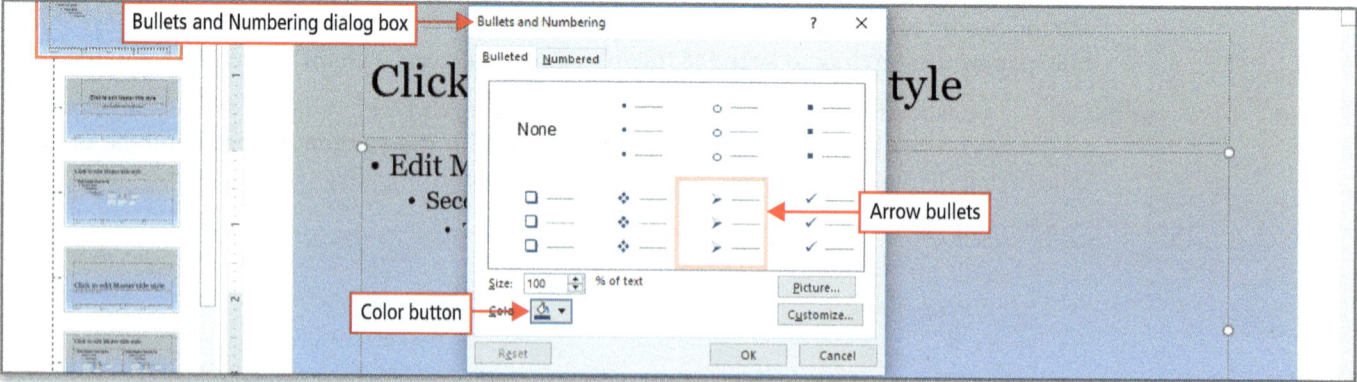

Figure 4.8

6 Click **OK**. Click anywhere in the *Second level* line. Using the technique you practiced for the first bulleted line, change the bullet style to **Filled Square Bullets**, and then change the bullet color to same color as the first level bullets—the last color in the fifth column. Compare your screen with Figure 4.9.

For the first two levels of the bulleted list, all the slides in the presentation will display these custom bullets.

Figure 4.9

7 Save  your presentation.

Activity 4.04 | Formatting Slide Masters by Adding Pictures and Shapes

MOS

1.1.1, 3.4.1, 3.4.4, 3.4.5, 3.4.6

In this Activity, you will add and format a shape, and insert a picture in the shape. Then you will duplicate the shape, move the copied shape to a different slide layout, and resize and recolor the shape.

1 Click the **Title Slide Layout** thumbnail.

2 On the **Insert tab**, in the **Illustrations group**, click **Shapes**. Under **Rectangles**, click the first shape—**Rectangle**. Position the pointer at **2 inches on the right side of the horizontal ruler** and at **3 inches on the upper half of the vertical ruler**, and then click one time to insert the shape.

The rectangle shape displays as a square—the height and width are both the same.

3 With the shape still selected, on the **Drawing Tools Format tab**, in the **Shapes Styles group**, click **Shape Effects**. Point to **Bevel**, and then in the first row, under **Bevel**, click the first effect—**Round**. Depending on your version of PowerPoint, this effect may be named Circle.

4 On the **Drawing Tools Format tab**, in the **Shapes Styles group**, click **Shape Outline**, and then click **No Outline**.

Removing the border softens the appearance of the shape.

5 With the rectangle still selected, on the **Drawing Tools Format tab**, in the **Size group**, change the **Shape Height** to **2"** and the **Shape Width** to **2"**. Compare your screen with Figure 4.10.

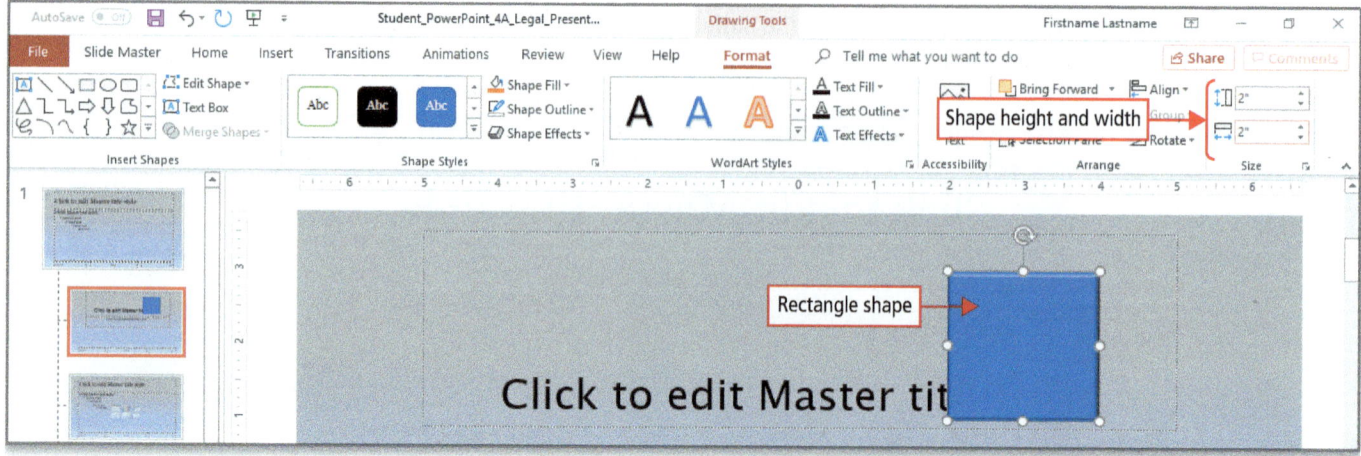

Figure 4.10

6 On the **Drawing Tools Format tab**, in the **Shape Styles group**, click **Shape Fill**, and then click **Picture**.

7 In the **Insert Pictures** dialog box, click **From a file**. Navigate to the downloaded files for this project, click **p04A_Law1**, and then click **Insert**.

The picture fills only the shape.

8 With the shape still selected, on the **Drawing Tools Format tab**, in the **Arrange group**, click **Align**, and then click **Align Center**. Click **Align** again, and then click **Align Bottom**. Compare your screen with Figure 4.11.

The shape with the picture aligns in the horizontal center at the bottom of the slide.

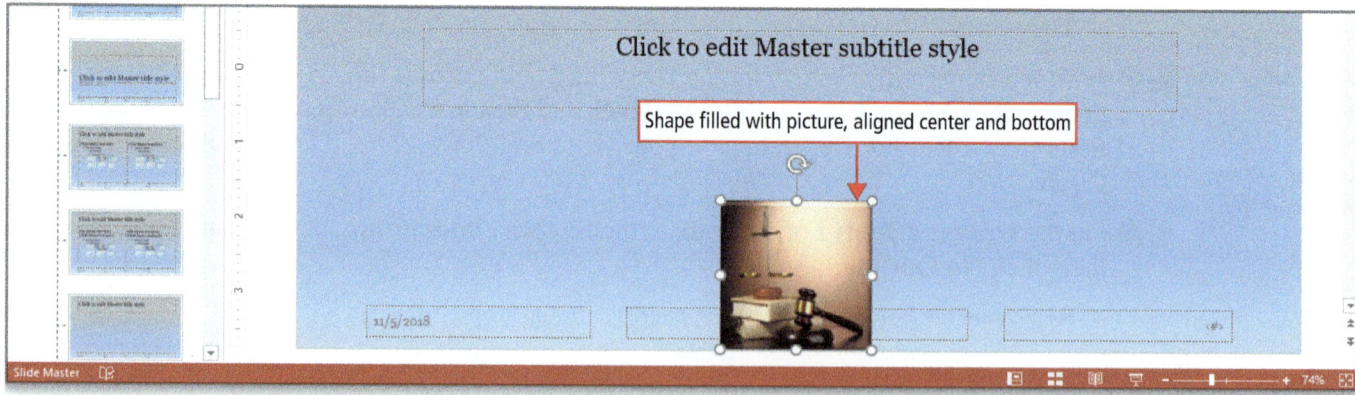

Figure 4.11

9 With the shape still selected, on the **Home tab**, in the **Clipboard group**, click **Copy**. Click the **Title and Content Layout** thumbnail—the third thumbnail. In the **Clipboard group**, click **Paste**.

The copied shape maintains the same format and position.

10 On the **Drawing Tools Format tab**, in the **Size group**, change the **Shape Height** to **1"** and the **Shape Width** to **1"**.

The copied shape is resized for this layout.

11 With the shape still selected, hold down ⌗Shift⌗, and then click on the dashed border of the content placeholder. On the **Drawing Tools Format tab**, in the **Arrange group**, click **Align**, and then click **Align Right**. Click **Align** again, and then click **Align Bottom**.

For this layout, the picture is aligned to the bottom right of the content placeholder.

12 On the **Picture Tools Format tab**, in the **Adjust Group**, click **Color**. Under **Recolor**, in the first row, click the third color—**Sepia**. Compare your screen with Figure 4.12.

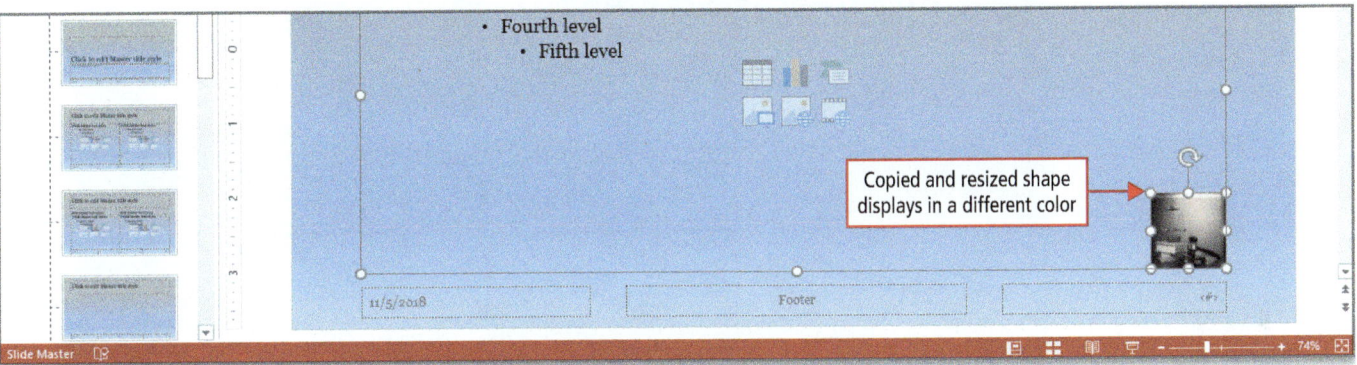

Figure 4.12

13 **Save** your presentation.

Activity 4.05 | Creating a New Slide Layout

MOS

1.1.3

You can create a custom slide layout in Slide Master view. If you need a specific layout of objects on a slide—for example, a brand logo and design—you can create a new slide layout that will be available in the New Slide gallery for this presentation.

1 On the **Slide Master tab**, in the **Edit Master** group, click **Insert Layout**.

2 On the **Slide Master tab**, in the **Master Layout group**, click the **Insert Placeholder arrow**. Compare your screen with Figure 4.13.

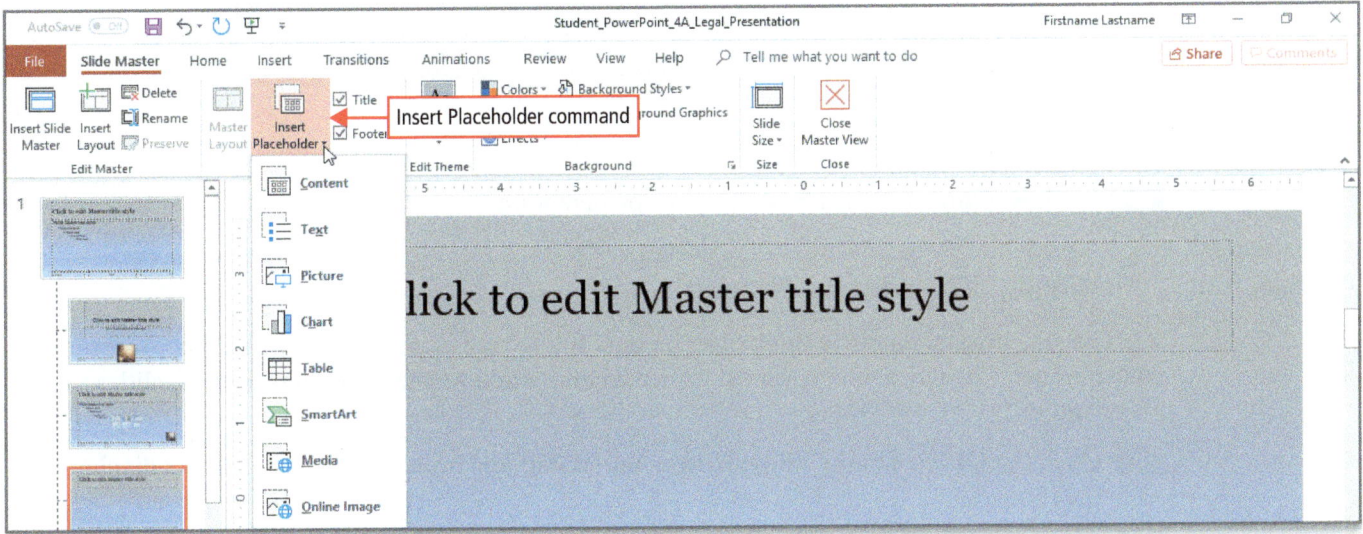

Figure 4.13

3 Click **Picture**. Position the pointer in the approximate center of the slide, and then click one time to insert the picture. On the **Drawing Tools Format tab**, in the **Size** group, change the **Height** of the placeholder to **5"** and change the **Width** of the placeholder to **8"**.

4 On the **Drawing Tools Format tab**, in the **Arrange** group, click **Align**, and then click **Align Center**. Click **Align** again, and then click **Align Bottom**. Compare your screen with Figure 4.14.

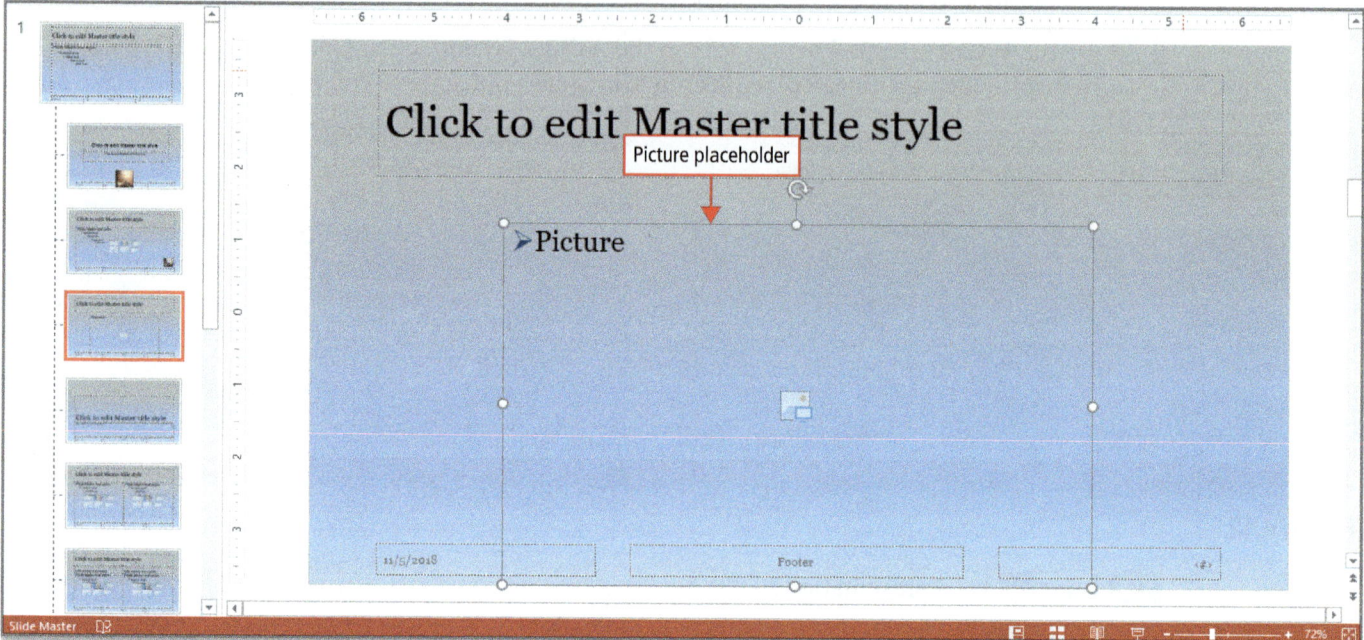

Figure 4.14

5 On the **Slide Master tab**, in the **Edit Master group**, click **Rename**. In the **Rename Layout** dialog box, select and delete the existing text, type **Title and Picture** and then compare your screen with Figure 4.15.

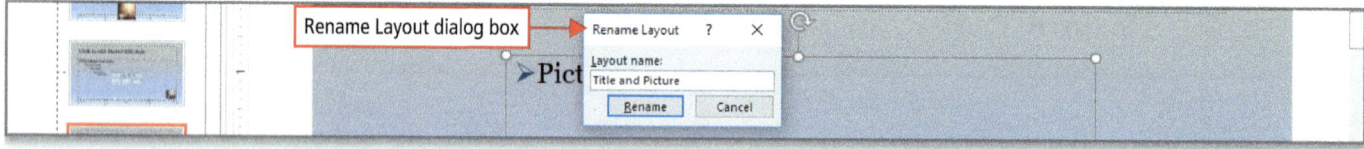

Figure 4.15

6 Click **Rename** and then **Save** your presentation.

Activity 4.06 | Modifying Slide Master Footers

1.1.4

The slide masters include three placeholders in the footer area of the slides: date, footer, and page number. The placeholders on the Office Theme Slide Master will appear on all slides in the presentation.

1 Click the **Office Theme Slide Master** thumbnail and notice three placeholders display in the footer area.

2 Click the **Title Slide Layout** thumbnail, and notice that the image covers the center footer placeholder.

3 Click the dashed border to select the center **Footer** placeholder, and then press Delete. In the same manner, delete the slide number placeholder on the right. Compare your screen with Figure 4.16.

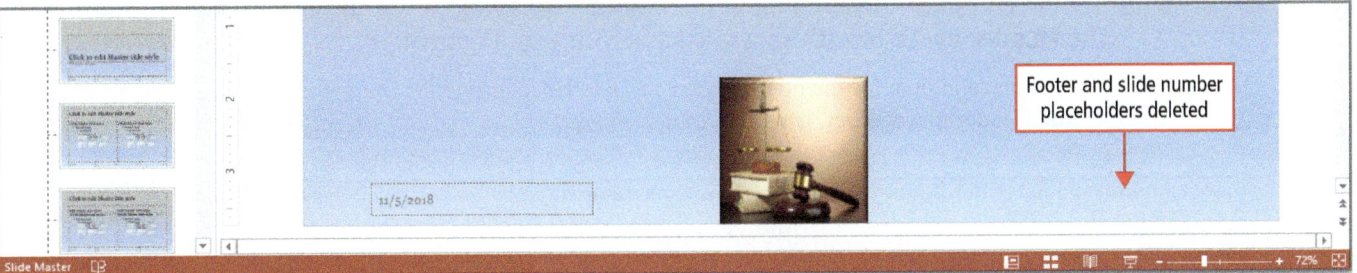

Footer and slide number placeholders deleted

Figure 4.16

4 Click the **Title and Picture Layout** thumbnail—the fourth thumbnail. On the **Slide Master tab**, in the **Master Layout** group, clear the **Footers** check box. Compare your screen with Figure 4.17.

The placeholders are hidden and no longer display in the footer area of this slide layout.

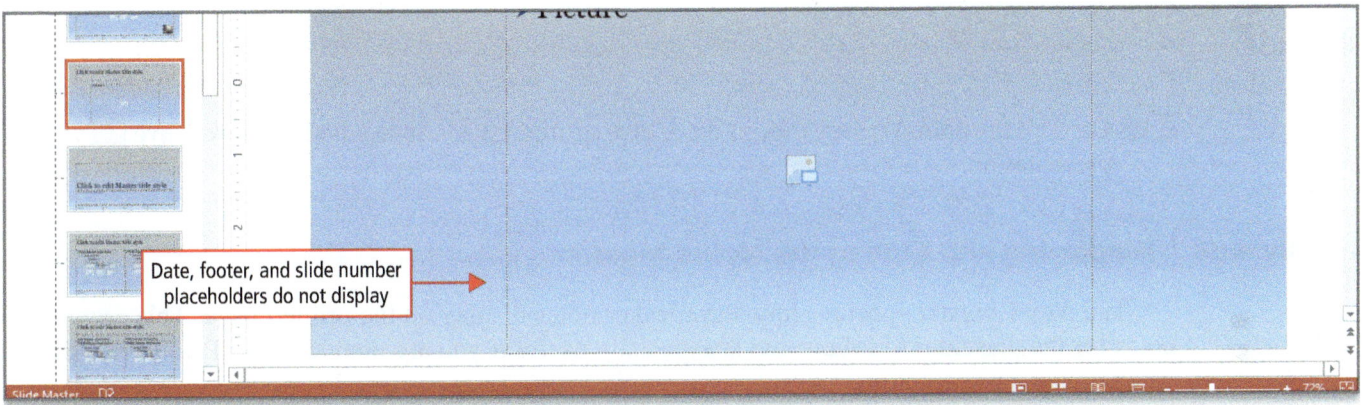

Date, footer, and slide number placeholders do not display

Figure 4.17

5 Save 💾 your presentation.

Activity 4.07 | Displaying and Editing the Handout Master

MOS
1.1.5

In this Activity, you will edit the Handout Master for the meeting template you are building for the Thompson Henderson Law Partners. You can print your presentation in the form of handouts that your audience can use to follow along as you give your presentation or to keep for future reference.

The *Handout Master* specifies the design of presentation handouts for an audience. You can change from landscape to portrait orientations, set the number of slides on a page, and specify whether you want to include the header, footer, date, and page number placeholders.

1 On the **View tab**, in the **Master Views group**, click **Handout Master**. On the **Handout Master tab**, in the **Page Setup group**, click **Handout Orientation**, and then notice that the default orientation is **Portrait**. Click **Slide Size** and notice that the default orientation is **Widescreen**.

2 On the **Handout Master tab**, in the **Page Setup group**, click **Slides Per Page**, and then click **3 Slides**.

You can print the handouts with 1, 2, 3, 4, 6, or 9 slides per page.

3 On the **Handout Master tab**, in the **Page Setup group**, click the **Placeholders group**, clear the **Header** check box. Compare your screen with Figure 4.18.

The placeholders for the notes master include Header, Footer, Date, and Page Number. By clearing the Header placeholder, it will no longer display.

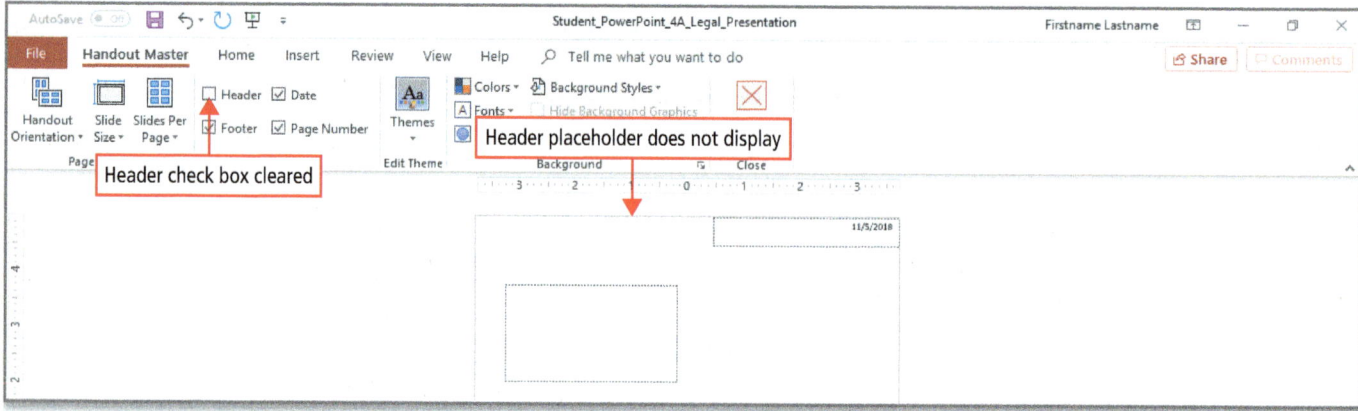

Figure 4.18

4 On the **Handout Master tab**, in the **Close group**, click **Close Master View**. **Save** your presentation.

Activity 4.08 | Displaying and Editing the Notes Master

The *Notes Master* specifies how the speaker notes display on the printed page. This provides notes for the presenter to follow and is especially useful if you are unable to use Presenter View when giving a presentation.

1 On the **View tab**, in the **Master Views group**, click **Notes Master**.

The Notes page displays the slide and speaker notes to assist the speaker when delivering the presentation to a group.

2 On the **Notes Master tab**, in the **Page Setup group**, click **Notes Page Orientation**. Notice that the orientation is set for **Portrait**. Click **Slide Size** and notice that the orientation is set for **Widescreen**.

MOS
1.1.6

3 ▶ On the **Notes Master tab**, in the **Placeholders group**, click to clear the **Header** check box. Compare your screen with Figure 4.19.

> The placeholders for the notes master include Header, Slide Image, Footer, Date, Body, and Page Number. By clearing the Header check box, the placeholder no longer displays.

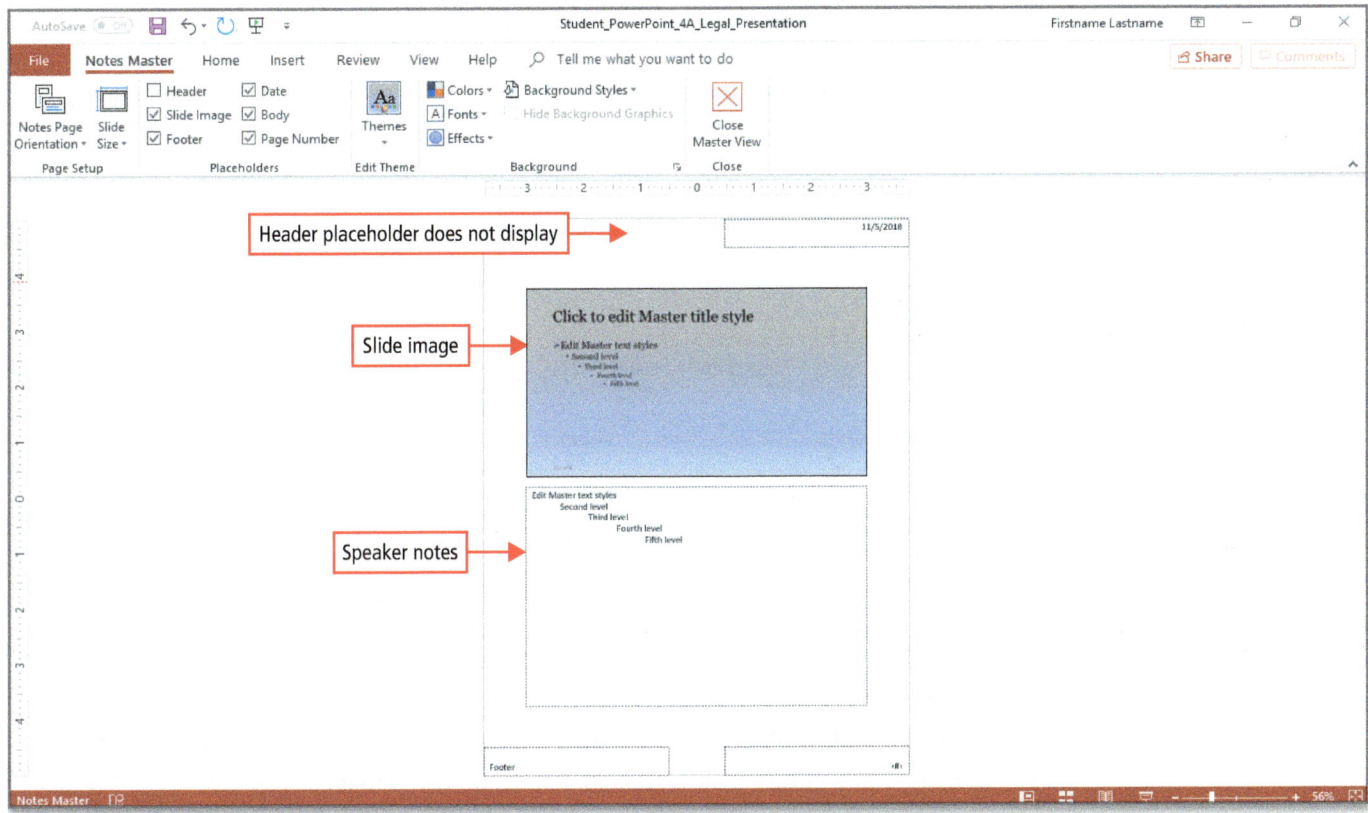

Figure 4.19

4 ▶ On the **Notes Master tab**, in the **Close group**, click **Close Master View**.

5 ▶ On the **Insert tab**, in the **Text group**, click **Header & Footer** to display the **Header and Footer** dialog box, and then click the **Notes and Handouts tab**. Under **Include on page**, select the **Date and time** check box, and then select **Fixed**. If necessary, clear the Header check box, and then select the **Page number** and **Footer** check boxes. In the **Footer** box, type **4A_Meeting_Presentation** and then click **Apply to All**.

6 ▶ Display the document properties. As the **Tags**, type **meeting** and as the **Subject**, type your course and section number. Be sure your name displays as author, and then **Save** 🔲 your file.

Objective 2 | **Create a Custom Template**

GO Learn How
Video P4-2

Use a template to standardize the design of the slides in a presentation. When you want to reuse a presentation design, you can save your presentation as a PowerPoint template. A template is saved as a *.potx* file.

Activity 4.09 | Saving a Presentation as a Template

The law firm wants a standard look for meeting presentations. After you design and create a custom presentation to be used for meeting presentations, save it as a template file. When the firm needs a meeting presentation, they can use the customized template you created. When a template is opened, a new *copy* of the presentation opens, preserving the original template for future use.

1 ▷ Display the **Save As** dialog box. Click the **Save as type arrow**. From the list of file types, click **PowerPoint Template**. Notice the save location changes to the Custom Office Templates folder. Compare your screen with Figure 4.20.

By default, Microsoft PowerPoint saves your templates in the Custom Office Templates folder in your Documents folder. When you create a new PowerPoint presentation, templates saved in the Custom Office Templates folder can be accessed by clicking Custom on the New tab in Backstage view.

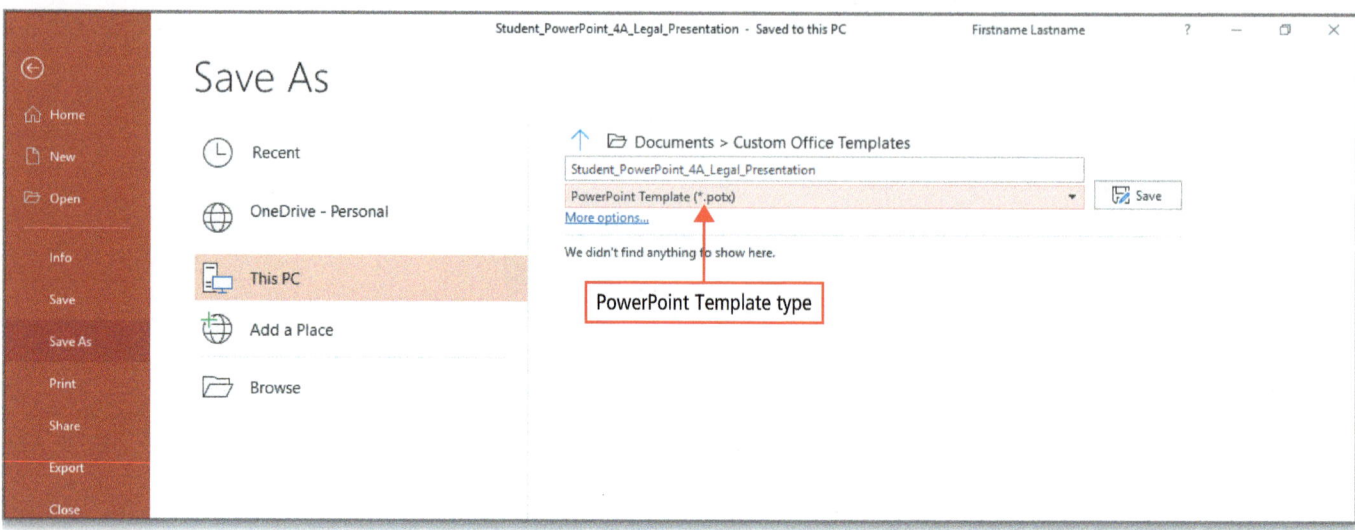

Figure 4.20

2 ▷ Navigate to your **PowerPoint Chapter 4** folder, change the file name to **Student_ PowerPoint_4A_Legal_Template** and then click **Save**. **Close** PowerPoint.

For this Activity, you will save your presentation in your PowerPoint Chapter 4 folder rather than the Custom Office Templates folder, which may be restricted in a lab environment.

3 ▷ On the taskbar, click **File Explorer**. Navigate to your **PowerPoint Chapter 4** folder. If necessary, click the View tab, and in the Layout group, click Details. Widen the **Name** and **Type** columns. Notice there are two files, a *Microsoft PowerPoint Presentation* file and a *Microsoft PowerPoint Template* file. Notice the icons for the two file types are slightly different. Compare your screen with Figure 4.21.

The file extension *.potx* is automatically added to your file name. By default, Windows may not display file extensions, but instead identifies the file type in the Type column. The icon for the template file has a gold bar across the top.

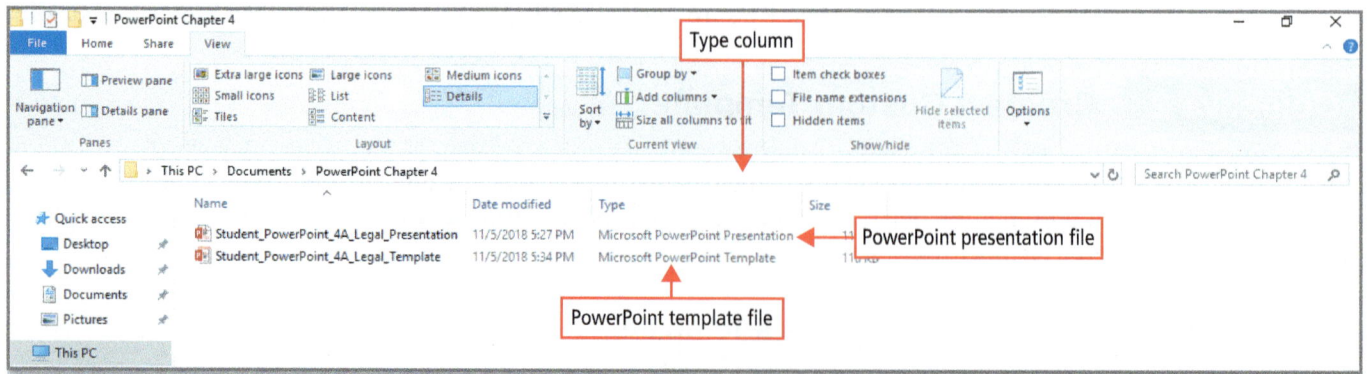

Figure 4.21

Activity 4.10 | Applying a Template to a Presentation

In this Activity, you will use the customized meeting template to create a slide presentation that explains the new filing procedures to the law partners. This presentation will have the standard formatting required by the firm because it will be created using the custom meeting template. Recall that you saved your template in your PowerPoint Chapter 4 folder.

1 In File Explorer, in your **PowerPoint Chapter 4** folder, double-click your **Student_ PowerPoint_4A_Legal_Template** Microsoft PowerPoint Template file. Compare your screen with Figure 4.22.

A new presentation opens from the template. The file name on the title bar displays as Presentation1. Your number may differ.

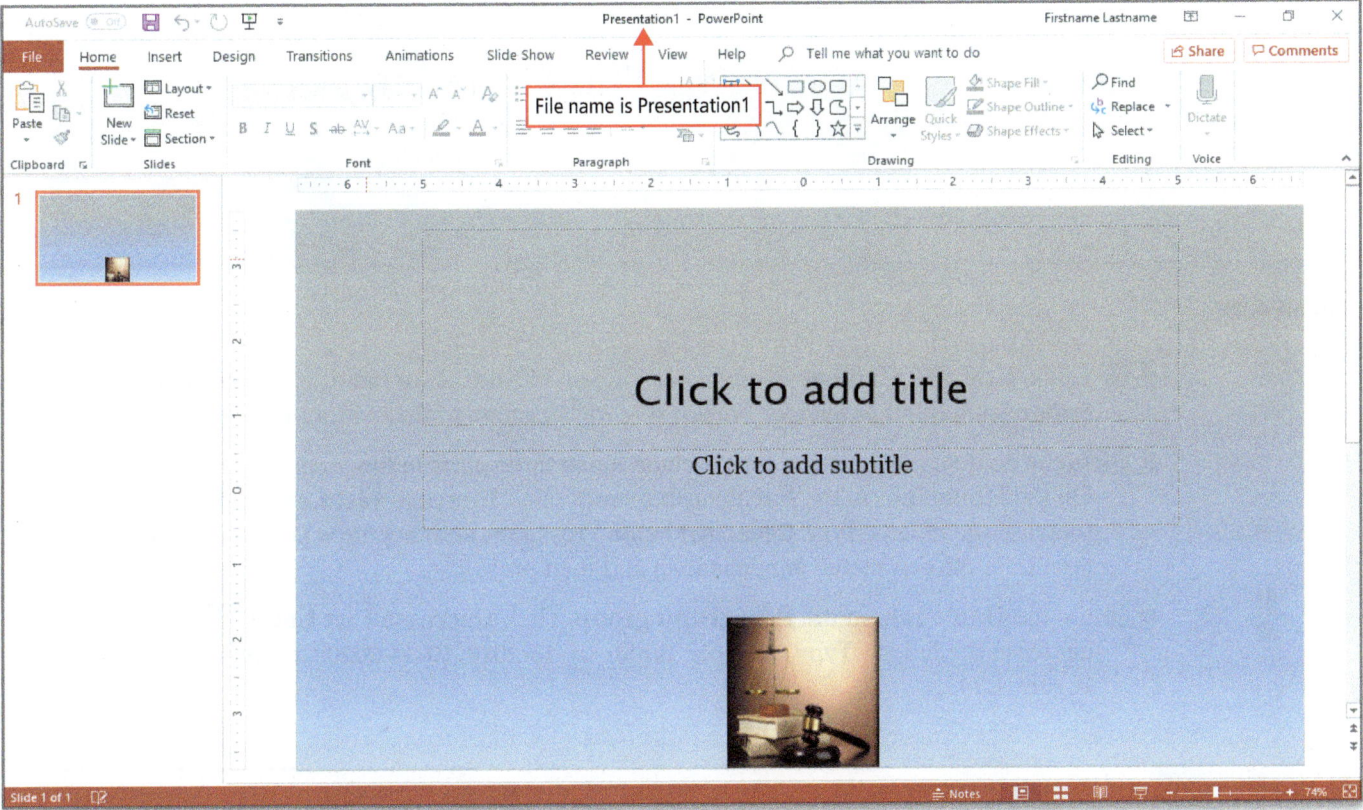

Figure 4.22

2 Display the **Save As** dialog box. If necessary, navigate to the location where you are saving your files. Notice the *Save as type* is **PowerPoint Presentation**, and then save the file as **Lastname_Firstname_PowerPoint_4A_Filing_Procedures**

The file name on the title bar displays as *Lastname_Firstname_PowerPoint_4A_Filing_Procedures*.

3 On **Slide 1**, click the title placeholder, and then type **New Filing Procedures** Click the subtitle placeholder, and then type **Thompson Henderson Law Partners**

4 On the **Home tab**, in the **Slides group**, click the **New Slide arrow**. The gallery displays the customized slide layouts that you created using the slide master. Compare your screen with Figure 4.23.

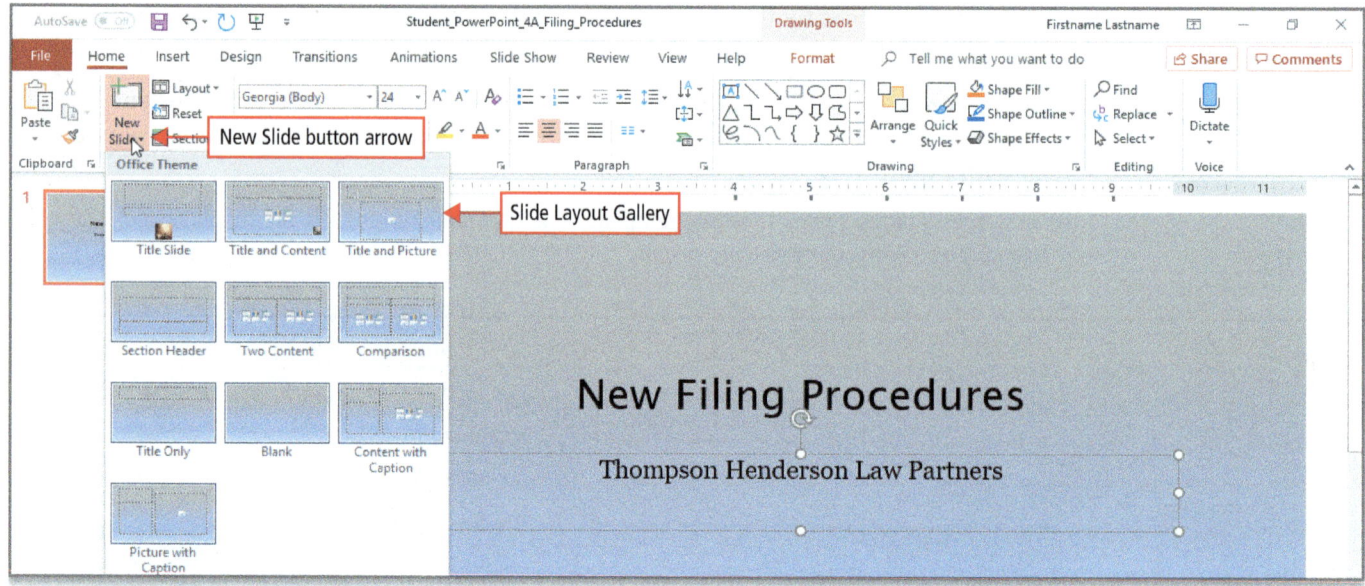

Figure 4.23

5 Click **Title and Content** to add a new slide. On **Slide 2**, in the title placeholder, type **Referencing Number System** Press Ctrl + Enter to move to the content placeholder.

6 In the content placeholder, type **Include these three parts in the number:** and then press Enter. On the **Home tab**, in the **Paragraph group**, click **Increase List Level** [icon] one time to increase the indent. Type **Client last name** Press Enter, and then type **Date file opened** Press Enter, type **Date file completed (if applicable)** and then press Enter.

7 On the **Home tab**, in the **Paragraph group**, click **Decrease List Level** [icon] one time to decrease the indent. Type **Example: Smith_01-15-2019_10-14-2020** Compare your screen with Figure 4.24.

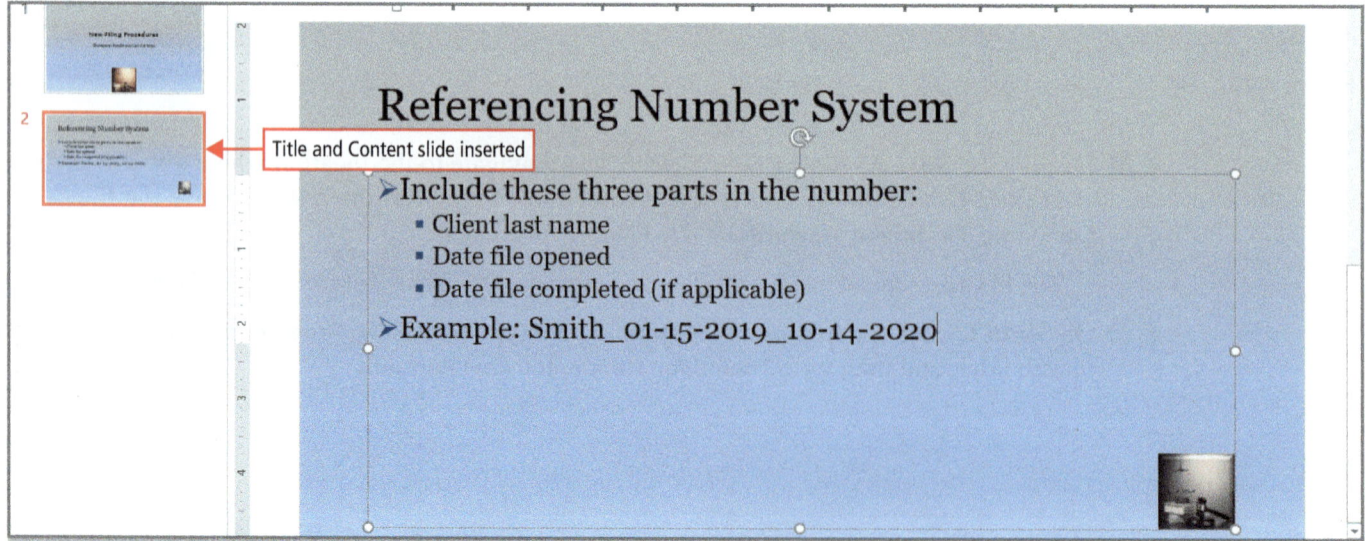

Figure 4.24

8 On the **Home tab**, in the **Slides group**, click the **New Slide arrow**, and then click **Title and Picture** to add the third slide. In the title placeholder, type **Hardcopy Filing**

9 In the content placeholder, click the **Pictures** icon. Navigate to the downloaded files for this project and insert the picture **p04A_File**. If necessary, close the Design Ideas pane.

10 Compare your screen with Figure 4.25.

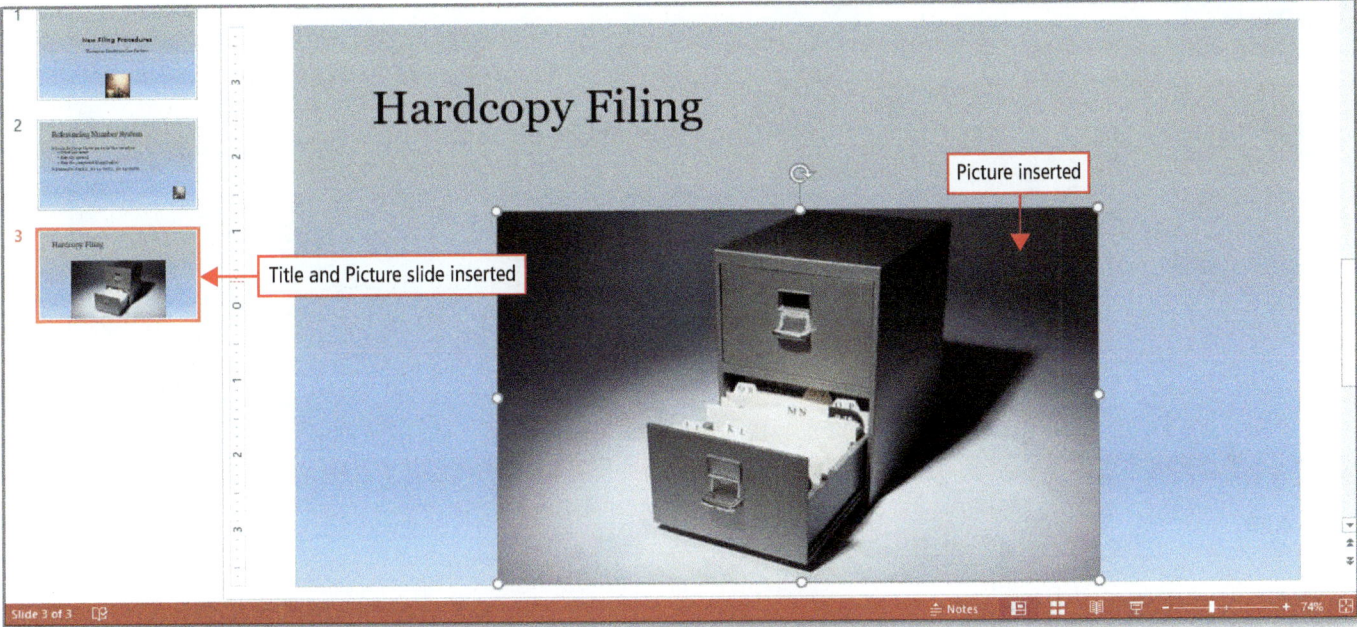

Figure 4.25

11 On the **Home tab**, in the **Slides group**, click the **New Slide arrow**, and then click **Title and Content** to add the fourth slide. In the title placeholder, type **Summary** In the content placeholder, type **All changes are effective immediately.** Press Enter and type **Direct questions to the support team.** Select both lines, and then on the **Home tab**, in the **Paragraph group**, click **Bullets** ≣ ▾ to remove the bullets. In the **Paragraph group**, click **Center**.

12 On the **Home tab**, in the **Paragraph group**, click **Line Spacing**, and then click **1.5**. Click a blank area of the slide and compare your screen with Figure 4.26.

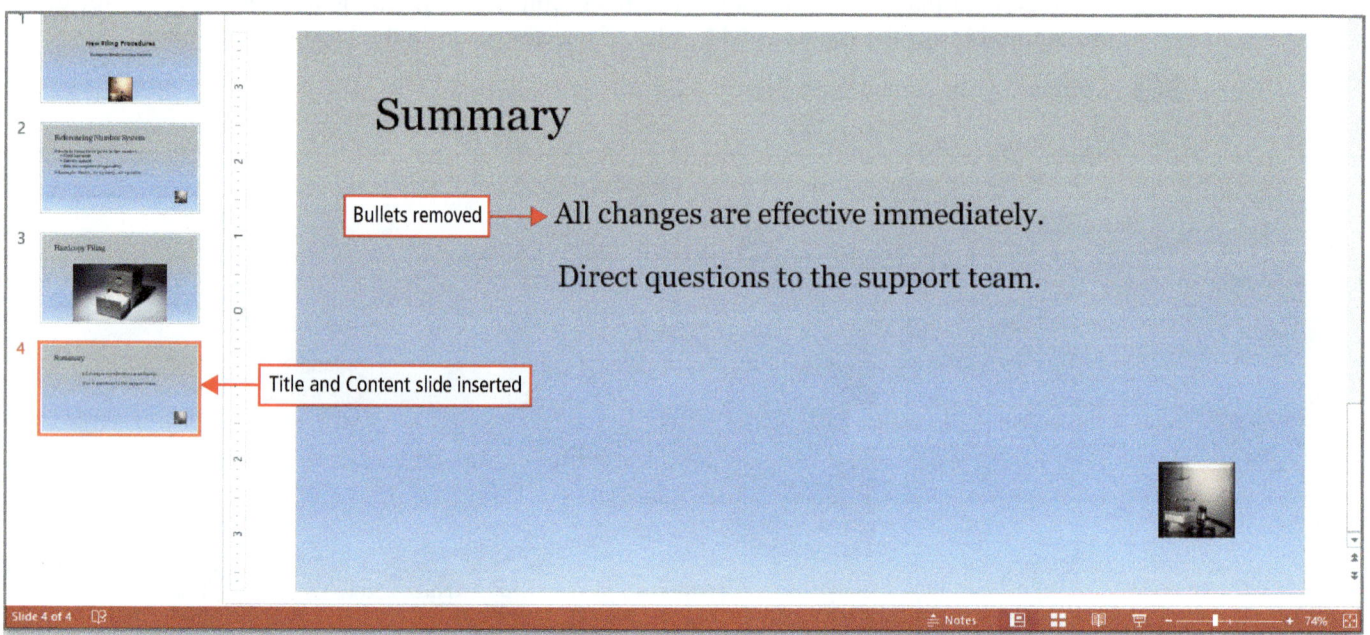

Figure 4.26

13 On the **Insert tab**, in the **Text group**, click **Header & Footer** to display the **Header and Footer** dialog box. Click the **Notes and Handouts tab**. Under **Include on page**, verify that the **Date and time** check box and the **Fixed** option are selected. If necessary, type today's date. If necessary, clear the Header check box, and then select the **Page number** and **Footer** check boxes. In the **Footer** box, type **4A_Filing_Procedures** and then click **Apply to All**.

14 Click the **File tab**, and then in the lower right portion of the screen, click **Show All Properties**. In the **Tags** box, type **filing, number, system** Verify that your course name and section number appear in the **Subject** box and your name appears as author. **Save** 🖫 the presentation.

Activity 4.11 | Editing Slide Masters in an Existing Presentation

1.1.2

You can change the master design for a presentation created from your custom template. In this Activity, you will change the bullet style on the Title and Content Layout slide master. This will change the formatting for this presentation only—it will not affect the meeting template.

1 With your **Lastname_Firstname_PowerPoint_4A_Filing_Procedures** file open, on the **View tab**, in the **Master Views group**, click **Slide Master**.

2 Scroll up as necessary and click the first thumbnail—**Office Theme Slide Master**. On the **Slide Master tab**, in **Background group**, click **Fonts**, and then click **Office 2007-2010**.

The font set for this presentation is changed. The title font is changed to Cambria (Heading).

3 In the content placeholder, click the *Second level* bulleted line. On the **Home tab**, in the **Paragraph group**, click the **Bullets arrow** . Click **Checkmark Bullets**. Compare your screen with Figure 4.27.

> The second-level bullets are displayed as checkmarks. Recall that changes made to the first thumbnail affect all slides in the presentation.

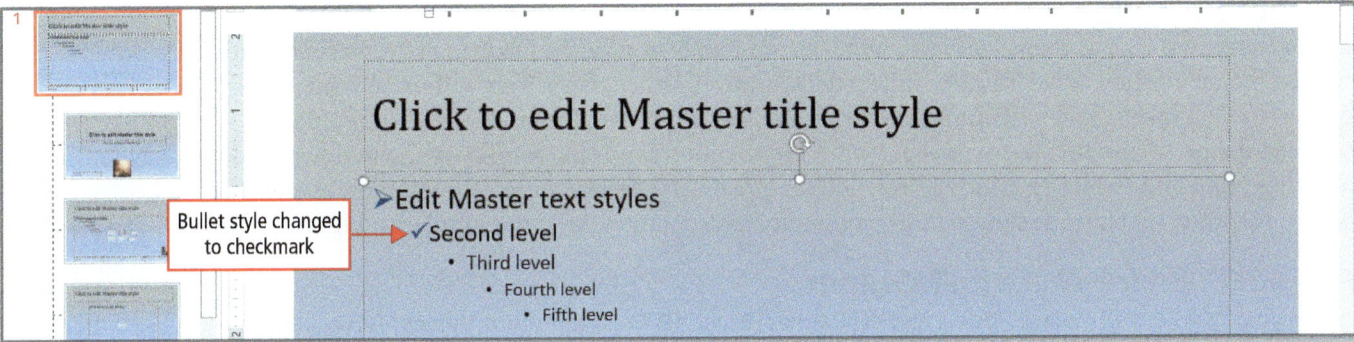

Figure 4.27

4 On the **Slide Master tab**, in the **Close group**, click **Close Master View**. Click **Slide 2** and notice the second-level bullets display as checkmark bullets,

5 On the **Slide Show tab**, in the **Start Slide Show group**, click **From Beginning**. View the entire slide presentation.

6 **Save** your presentation.

7 **Close** PowerPoint and **Close** File Explorer.

For Non-MyLab Submissions Determine What Your Instructor Requires
Print or submit your files electronically as directed by your instructor.
Lastname_Firstname_4A_Legal_Presentation (PowerPoint Presentation),
Lastname_Firstname_4A_Legal_Template (PowerPoint Template), and
Lastname_Firstname_4A_Filing_Procedures (PowerPoint Presentation).

---

8 In **MyLab IT**, in your **Course Materials**, locate and click the Grader Project **PowerPoint 4A Legal Presentation**. In **step 3**, under **Upload Completed Assignment**, click **Choose File**. In the **Open** dialog box, navigate to your **PowerPoint Chapter 4 folder**, and then click your **Lastname_Firstname_PowerPoint_4A_Filing_Procedures** file one time to select it. In the lower right corner of the **Open** dialog box, click **Open**.

> The name of your selected file displays above the Upload button.

9 To submit your file to **MyLab IT** for grading, click **Upload**, wait a moment for a green **Success!** message, and then in **step 4**, click the blue **Submit for Grading** button. Click **Close Assignment** to return to your list of **Course Materials**.

You have completed Project 4A **END**

PROJECT 4B

Entertainment Law Presentation

MyLab IT
Project 4B Grader for Instruction
Project 4B Simulation for Training and Review

Project Activities

In Activities 4.12 through 4.21, you will use comments to provide feedback to a presentation created by a colleague at the Thompson Henderson Law Partners firm. You will use editing tools such as the thesaurus. You will compare two versions of a presentation to view the differences between the presentations. You will check your presentation for compatibility with previous versions of PowerPoint and for accessibility issues, and then mark the presentation as final. Finally, you will password-protect your presentation. Your completed presentation will look similar to Figure 4.28.

Project Files for **MyLab IT Grader**

1. In your **MyLab IT** course, locate and click **PowerPoint 4B Entertainment Basics**, Download Materials, and then Download All Files.
2. Extract the zipped folder to your PowerPoint Chapter 4 folder. Close the Grader download screens.
3. Take a moment to open the downloaded **PowerPoint_4B_Entertainment_Basics_Instructions**; note any recent updates to the book.

Project Results

GO Project 4B
Where We're Going

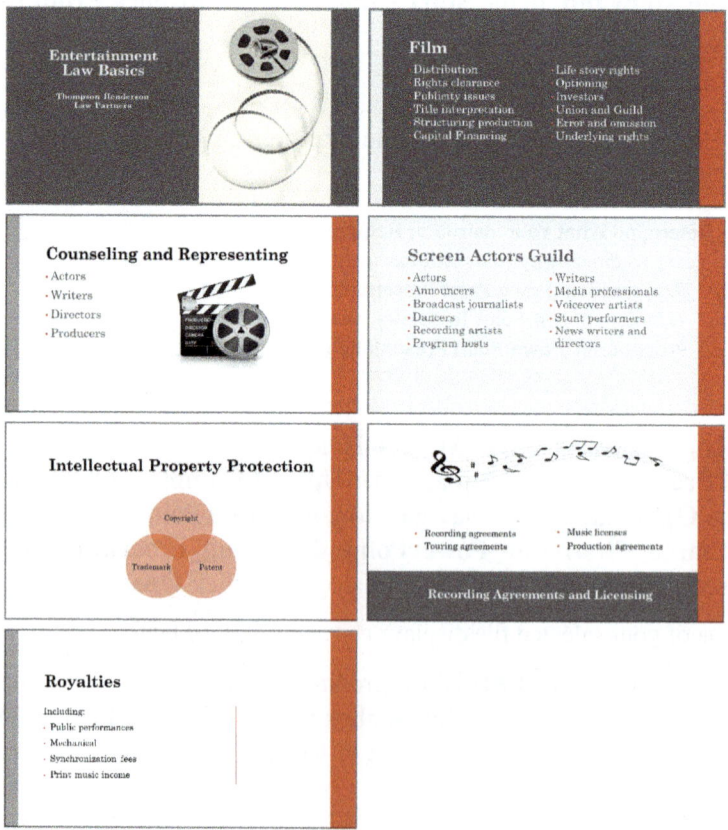

Figure 4.28 Project 4B Entertainment Law Presentation

For Non-MyLab Submissions
For Project 4B, you will need:
p04B_Entertainment_Basics
p04B_Entertainment_Basics2

In your PowerPoint Chapter 4 folder, save your presentation as:
Lastname_Firstname_4B_Entertainment_Basics

After you have named and saved your presentation, on the next page, begin with Step 2.

Objective 3 | Create and Edit Comments

ALERT Because Office 365 is a cloud-based subscription service that receives continuous updates, you may encounter some variations in what appears on your screen and what is shown in this instruction. Microsoft Office 365 is fully installed on your PC or Mac; no internet access is necessary to create or edit documents. When you *are* connected to the internet, you will receive monthly upgrades and new features, so you always have the latest versions of Office apps as soon as they are available. Your subscription gives you continuous free access to the latest innovations and refinements.

GO! Learn How
Video P4-3

A ***comment*** is a note that you can attach to text or objects on a slide, or to an entire slide. Comments provide feedback on a presentation. A ***reviewer*** is someone who adds comments to the presentation to provide feedback. Comments enable you to collaborate on a presentation with others.

Activity 4.12 | Adding Comments

1.5.4

Comments can be added by the person who created the presentation or by reviewers who are invited to provide suggestions. In this Activity, you will review and add comments to a presentation. The Comments pane enables you to view and track comments next to the text being discussed, and to see who replied to a comment and when—similar to a threaded style conversation. Additional participants can reply and join the conversation.

1 Navigate to your **PowerPoint Chapter 4 folder**, and then double-click the downloaded PowerPoint file that displays your name—**Student_PowerPoint_4B_Entertainment_ Basics**. In your presentation, if necessary, at the top click **Enable Editing**.

2 Display **Slide 2**, and then on the **Review tab**, in the **Comments group**, click **New Comment**. In the **Comments pane** on the right, in the comment text box, type **Good job. I think this is a comprehensive list.** Compare your screen with Figure 4.29.

The comment icon displays in the upper left corner of the slide. The comment displays in the Comments pane. The name of the person that entered the comment and the date or time displays in the comment box.

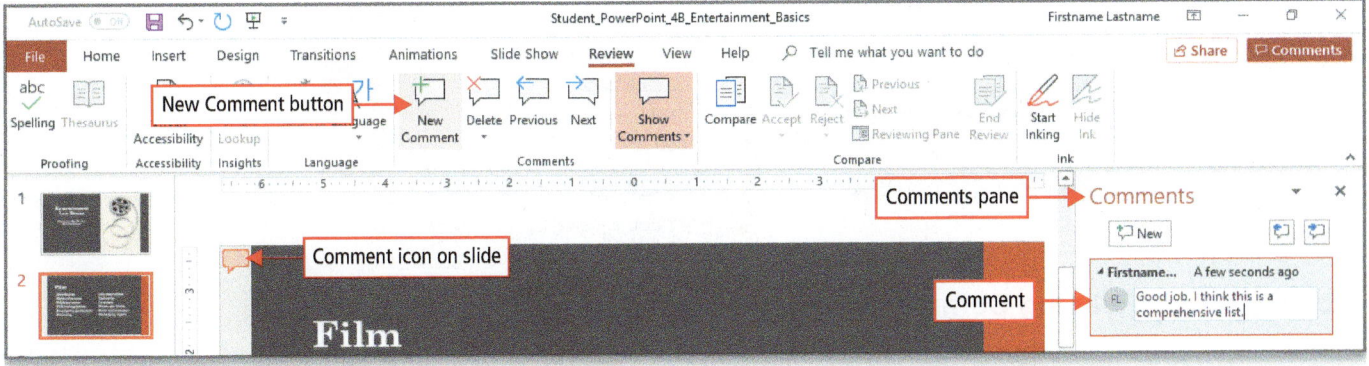

Figure 4.29

3 Display **Slide 3**. Click at the end of the third bulleted item, after *Directors*. In the **Comments** pane, click **New**. Type **What kind of directors?** Click outside the comment pane to deselect it. Compare your screen with Figure 4.30.

The comment icon is located at the insertion point on the slide.

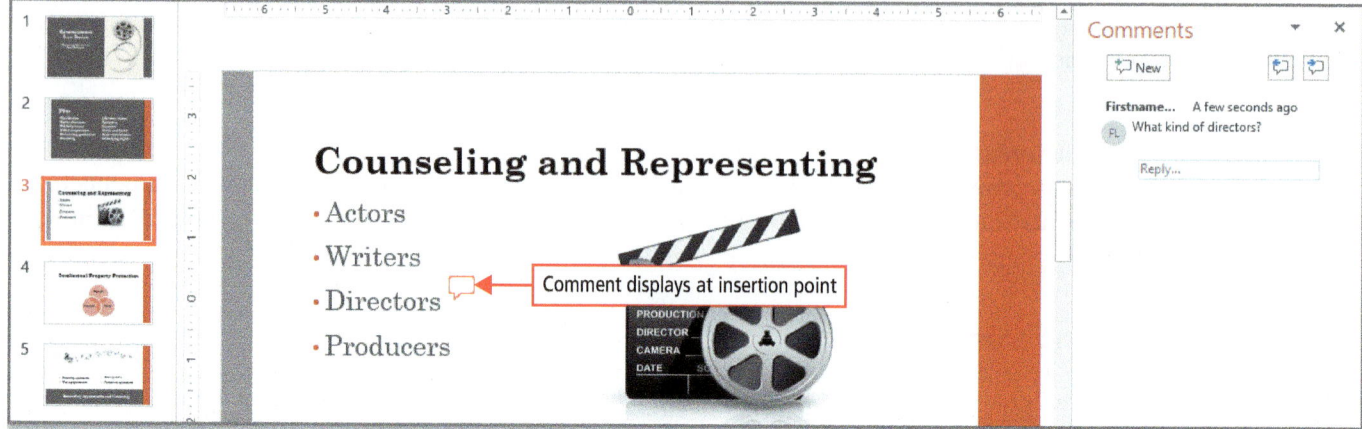

Figure 4.30

4 Display **Slide 5**, and then enter a new comment with the text **Is the word "agreements" necessary?** In the slide, drag the comment icon so it is positioned under the words "*Production agreements.*" Compare your screen with Figure 4.31. **Save** the presentation.

By default, new comments display in the upper left corner of the slide; however, you can drag a comment box to any position on the slide so that it is closer to the relevant text or object.

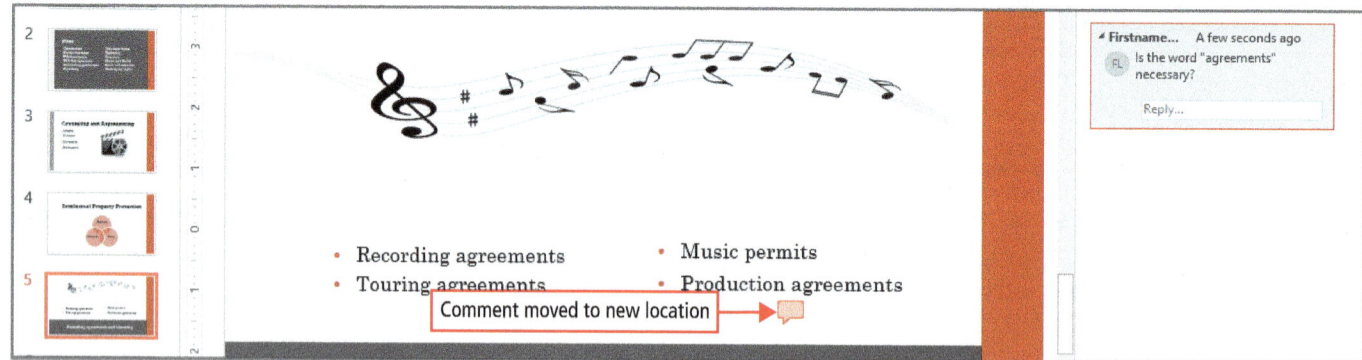

Figure 4.31

Activity 4.13 | Reading Comments

1.5.4

In this Activity, you will navigate among the comments entered in a presentation.

1 Display **Slide 2**. On the **Review tab**, in the **Comments group**, click the **Show Comments arrow**, and then click **Show Markup** to turn the option off. Notice that the comment is no longer displayed and the **Comments** pane closes. Click the **Show Comments arrow**, and then click **Show Markup** again to redisplay the comment on the slide. Click the **Show Comments arrow**, and then click **Comments pane** to redisplay the **Comments pane**.

 ANOTHER WAY You can display the Comments pane by clicking the Comments button on the PowerPoint ribbon, below the Close button.

2 Display **Slide 1**. On the **Review tab**, in the **Comments group**, click **Next**. The first comment displays in the **Comments** pane so you can read it. Click **Next** again to read the second comment, which is on **Slide 3**. Continue clicking **Next** until you see the message *PowerPoint reached the end of the presentation. Do you want to continue from the beginning?* Compare your screen with Figure 4.32.

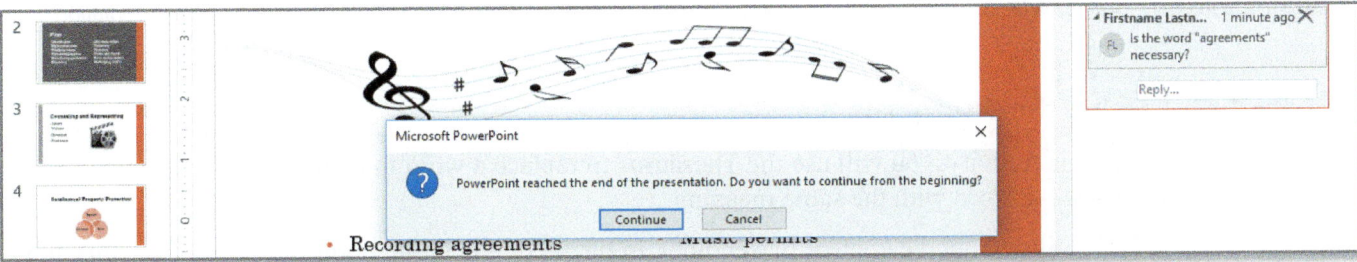

Figure 4.32

3 Click **Cancel** to close the message, and then on the **Review tab** in the **Comments group**, click **Previous** to read the previous comment. Continue clicking **Previous** until you receive this message: *PowerPoint reached the beginning of the presentation. Do you want to continue from the end?* Click **Cancel**.

Use the Next and Previous buttons to read through the comments in your presentation.

MAC TIP   On a Mac, after the last comment is reached, PowerPoint will display the first comment again.

Activity 4.14 | Editing Comments

1.5.4

When a reviewer has entered comments in your presentation, you can read and reply to those comments in the Comments pane. In this Activity, you will reply to a comment and delete a comment.

1 On **Slide 2**, in the **Comments pane**, read the comment. Under the comment, click in the **Reply** box, and then type **Yes, the list is lengthy. I will make a note to allow enough time to cover these during the presentation.** Click outside the comment pane to close the comment. Compare your screen with Figure 4.33.

An additional comment is added in the Comments pane. Two comment icons display at the upper left portion of the slide.

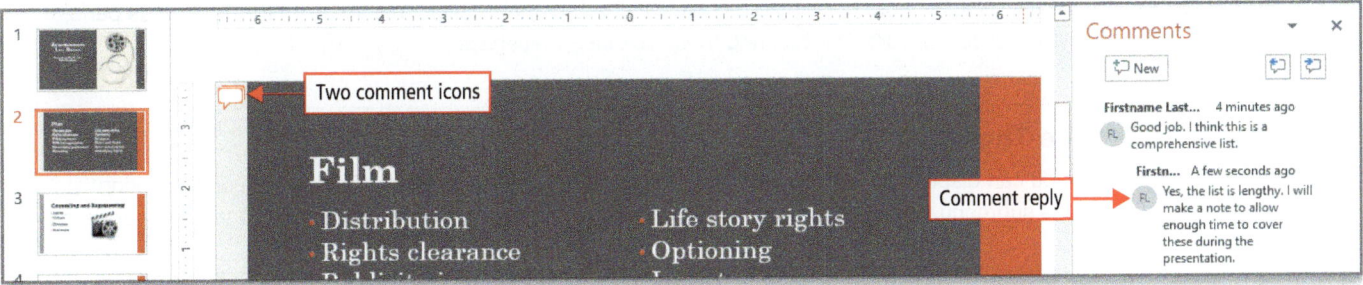

Figure 4.33

2 Click **Next** until you reach the comment on **Slide 5**. On the **Review tab**, in the **Comments group**, click the **Delete arrow**, and then read the three options: *Delete, Delete All Comments on Slide*, and *Delete All Comments in This Presentation*. Click **Delete** to remove this comment.

The comment is deleted.

3 **Close** the **Comments pane** and **Save** 🖫 the presentation.

MORE KNOWLEDGE **Ink**

Ink is markup that can be applied to a slide using a touchscreen or stylus, which enables you to draw, write, or highlight text on a Windows 10 touch screen. If your computer has the capability to add ink, an Ink group will display at the end of the Review tab and the Delete options will include *Delete, Delete All Comments and Ink on This Slide*, and *Delete All Comments and Ink in This Presentation*.

Activity 4.15 | Using the Thesaurus

In this Activity, you will use the Thesaurus to replace a word in a presentation with a *synonym*—a word with the same meaning.

1 On **Slide 5**, in the content placeholder, in the second column, point to the word *permits* and right-click.

2 On the shortcut menu, point to **Synonyms**, and then compare your screen with Figure 4.34.

A list of words with the same meaning as *permits* displays.

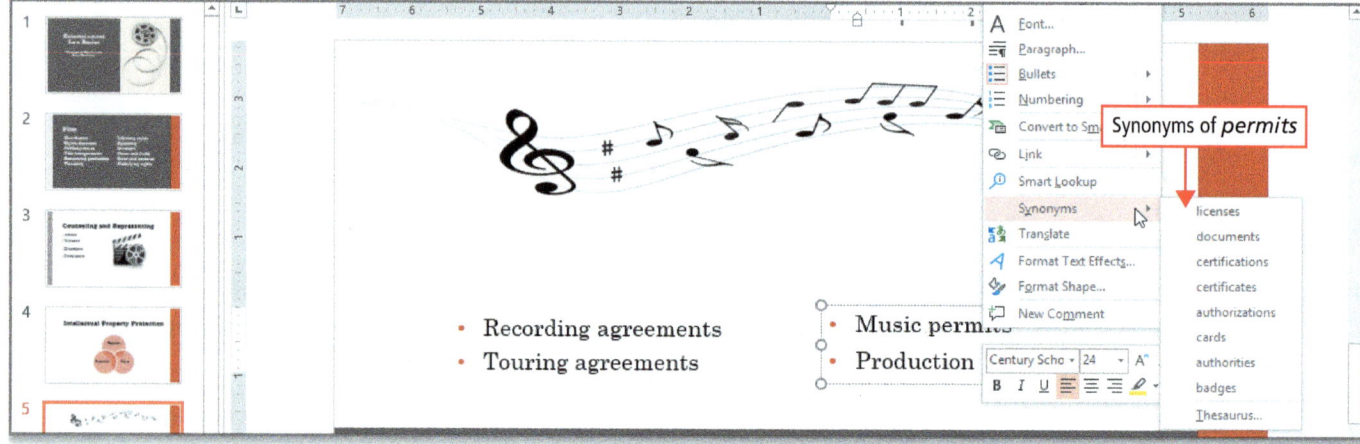

Figure 4.34

3 Click **licenses** to change the word *permits* to *licenses*. **Save** 🖫 your presentation.

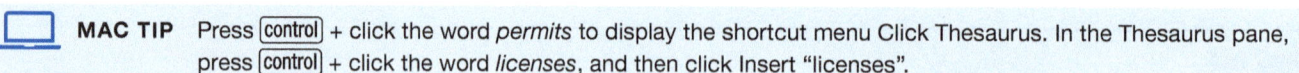

💻 **MAC TIP** Press ⌃ control + click the word *permits* to display the shortcut menu Click Thesaurus. In the Thesaurus pane, press ⌃ control + click the word *licenses*, and then click Insert "licenses".

MORE KNOWLEDGE **The Thesaurus**

When a word is selected, you can display the Thesaurus pane by clicking on Thesaurus on the Review tab, or by clicking Thesaurus on the Synonyms submenu. The Thesaurus pane displays a complete Thesaurus of synonyms and *antonyms*—words with an opposite meaning.

Objective 4 **Compare and Combine Presentations**

GO! Learn How
Video P4-4

PowerPoint enables you to compare and combine presentations by merging them into a single presentation, highlighting and listing the differences. You can review the changes and choose the edits for the final presentation. This feature is useful if you work with others on presentations, or if you just want to see what differences exist between two versions of a presentation.

Activity 4.16 | Comparing and Combining Presentations

In this Activity, you will view two versions of a presentation to compare their differences.

> **MAC TIP** The Compare feature is not available in the Mac version of PowerPoint. Display Slide 3. On the Home tab, click the New Slide arrow, click Reuse Slides, and navigate to the student data files for this project. Double-click MAC_ONLY_p04B_Entertainment_Basics2 to insert the *Screen Actors Guild* slide. Display Slide 2, click before the word *Financing*, type **Capital** and press [spacebar] one time. Skip this Activity and continue with Activity 4.17.

1 ▸ Display **Slide 1**. On the **Review tab**, in the **Compare group**, click **Compare**. In the **Choose File to Merge with Current Presentation** dialog box, navigate to your student data files for this chapter, click **p04B_Entertainment_Basics2**, and then click **Merge**.

The Revisions pane displays on the right side of the slide. Here you can locate all instances in which the two presentations differ.

2 ▸ At the top of the **Revisions pane**, if necessary, click **Details** so that it is selected—displays in orange. Compare your screen with Figure 4.35.

Revision Details displays two sections—Slide Changes and Presentation Changes. The Slide Changes section indicates differences between the two presentations for the active slide. The Presentation Changes section lists entire slides that were added or removed when the two presentations were merged.

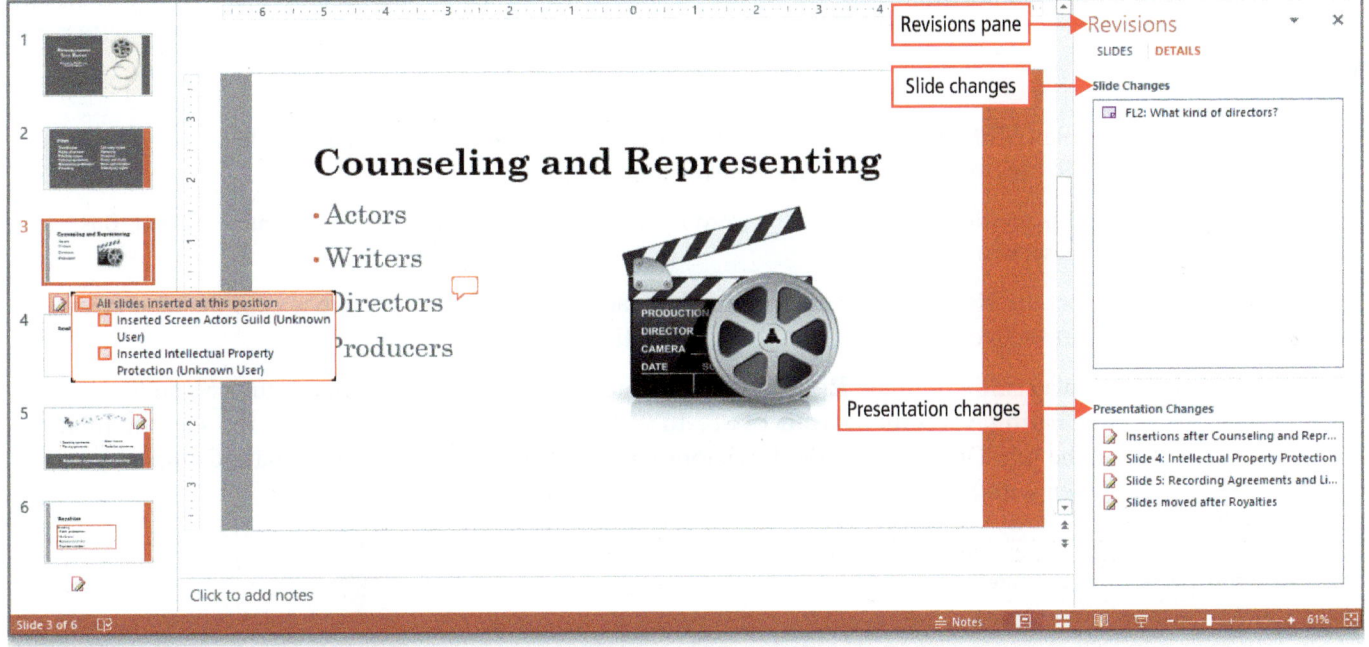

Figure 4.35

3 ▸ In the **Revisions** pane, under **Presentation Changes**, click **Insertions after "Counseling and Rep . . .**

4 In the thumbnails, if necessary, click to expand *All slides inserted in this position*, and then select the **Revisions** check box that indicates *Inserted "Screen Actors Guild"* to accept the revision and insert the slide into your presentation. Display Slide 4 and compare your screen with Figure 4.36.

You can use the Revisions check box to accept or reject the addition of the slide. Your Student_PowerPoint_4B_Entertainment_Basics presentation does not include this suggested revision; the slide is in the p04B_Entertainment_Basics2 presentation.

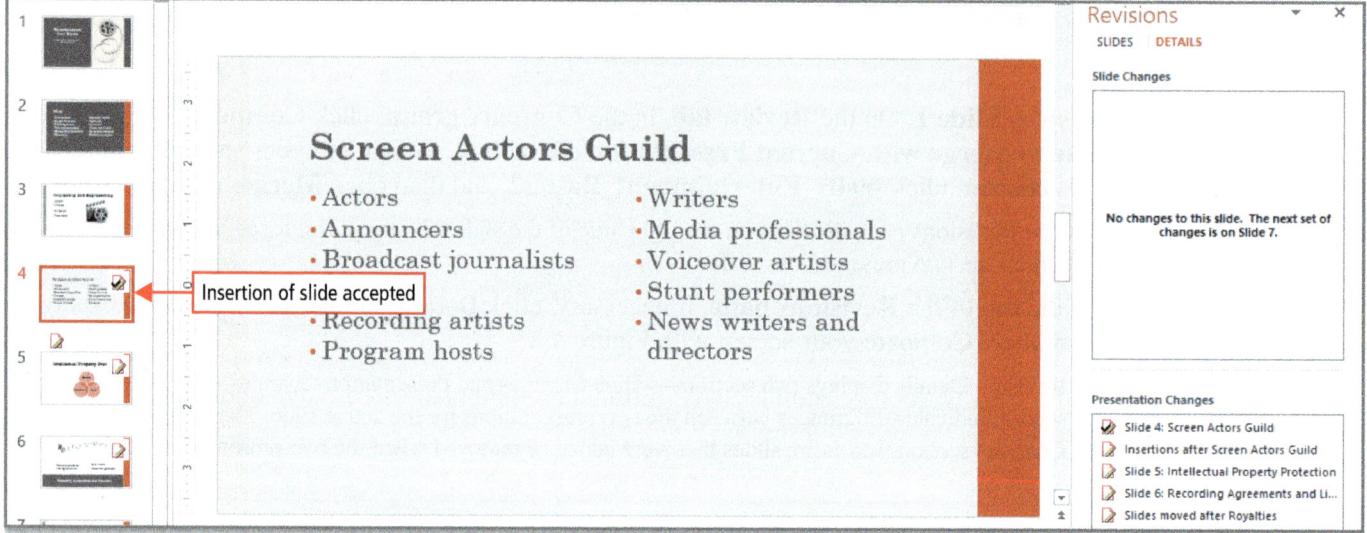

Figure 4.36

5 Display **Slide 2** and notice that a **Revisions** icon displays in the middle of the slide. Click the **Revisions** icon to display the **Revisions** check box.

This revision indicates that the word *Capital* was inserted from the p04B_Entertainment_Basics2 presentation.

6 Select the **Revisions** check box that indicates *Inserted "Capital"* to accept the change and insert the word *Capital* from the presentation.

7 Display **Slide 6**. In the **Revisions pane**, under **Presentation Changes**, click **Slide 6: Recording Agreements and Li . . .** to display a **Revisions** check box in the slide thumbnails on the left. Do *not* select the Revisions check box on the Slide 6 thumbnail. Compare your screen with Figure 4.37.

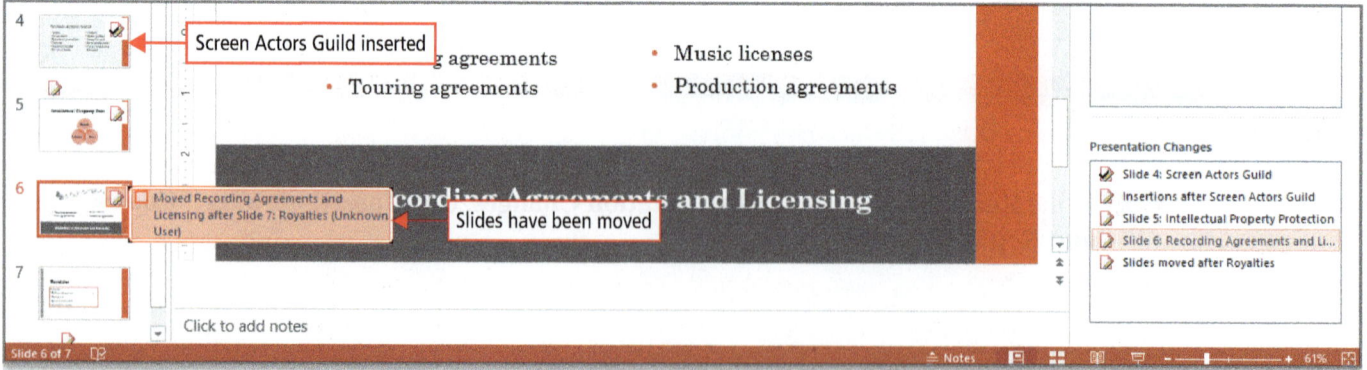

Figure 4.37

8 In the **Revisions pane**, under **Presentation Changes**, click **Slides moved after "Royalties"** to display a **Revisions** check box under **Slide 7** in the slide thumbnails on the left. Do *not* select the **Revisions** check box under the **Slide 7** thumbnail.

9 On the **Review tab,** in the **Compare group**, click **End Review**, and then in the **Microsoft PowerPoint** message box, click **Yes**.

The presentation is now merged with the selected changes, the revisions to Slides 6 and 7 are not included, and the Revisions pane closes. The unapplied changes were discarded.

10 On **Slide 1**, in the **Notes pane**, type **Review complete** and then **Save** 🖫 your presentation.

MORE KNOWLEDGE | **View Multiple Presentations**

You can view two presentations side by side to see the differences between them. On the View tab, in the Window group, click Arrange All. The presentations display side by side on the screen.

Objective 5 | Prepare a Presentation for Distribution

GO! Learn How
Video P4-5

Before distributing a PowerPoint presentation to others, check the presentation for accessibility issues and for compatibility with other versions of PowerPoint. Review the contents of the presentation to ensure that it does not contain sensitive or personal information that you do not want to share with other people. Such information might be stored in the document itself or in the document properties.

Activity 4.17 | Using the Accessibility Checker

MOS
1.5.3

To ensure that a PowerPoint presentation is accessible and can be read by individuals with disabilities, you can run the Accessibility Checker. The *Accessibility Checker* finds any potential accessibility issues and creates a report so that you can resolve the issues to make your file easier for those with disabilities to use. In this Activity, you will run the Accessibility Checker and correct identified problems.

1 From the **File tab**, on the **Info tab**, click **Check for Issues**, and then click **Check Accessibility**. Compare your screen with Figure 4.38.

The Accessibility Checker pane opens, and the Inspection Results display an error on four slides and a warning on four slides that you should address. Errors are more severe than warnings.

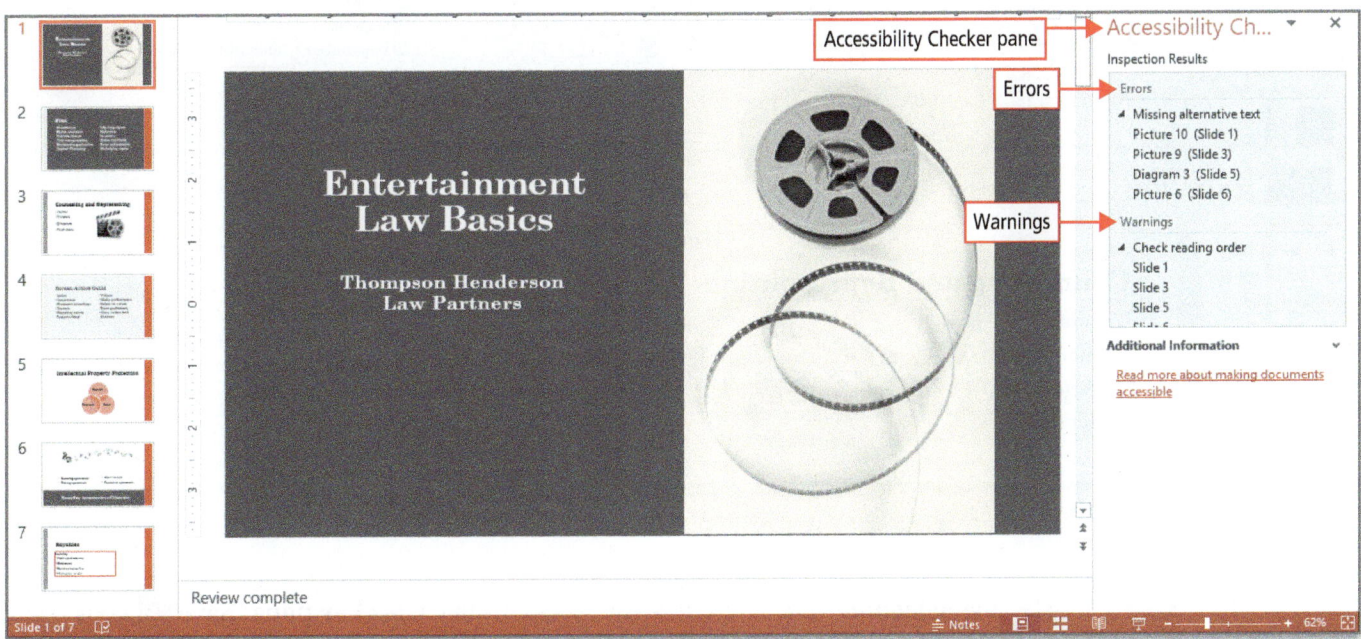

Figure 4.38

2 In the **Accessibility Checker pane**, under **Errors**, click **Picture 10 (Slide 1)**. Under **Additional Information**, read the information under **Why Fix**. Scroll down and read **Steps To Fix**.

Alt text is used in documents and webpages to provide a text description of an image when someone points to the image. Alt text will be read by screen reader software—software that reads aloud the text that displays on the screen.

3 On the slide, point to the image of a film reel, right-click, and then click **Edit Alt Text**. In the box in the **Alt Text** pane, type **film reel** and notice the error no longer displays in the Accessibility Checker pane.

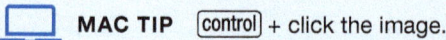 **MAC TIP** `control` + click the image.

4 In the **Accessibility Checker pane**, under **Errors**, click **Picture 9 (Slide 3)**. With the image selected, in the **Alt Text** box, type **movie clapper board**

5 Using the technique you practiced, add the alt text **copyright, trademark, patent** to the diagram on **Slide 5**. Add the alt text **musical notes** to the picture on **Slide 6** and then **Close** ☒ the **Alt Text** pane.

No errors display in the Accessibility Checker pane.

6 In the **Accessibility Checker pane**, under **Warnings**, under **Check Reading Order**, click **Slide 3**. Read the *Why Fix* and *Steps To Fix* sections. On the **Home tab**, in the **Drawing group**, click **Arrange**, and then click **Selection Pane**.

Tips are items you should review to ensure your presentation does not contain content that people with disabilities might find difficult to read.

7 In the **Selection pane**, drag **Title 1** to the first position. Compare your screen with Figure 4.39.

Reading order determines the sequence items will be read using screen reader software.

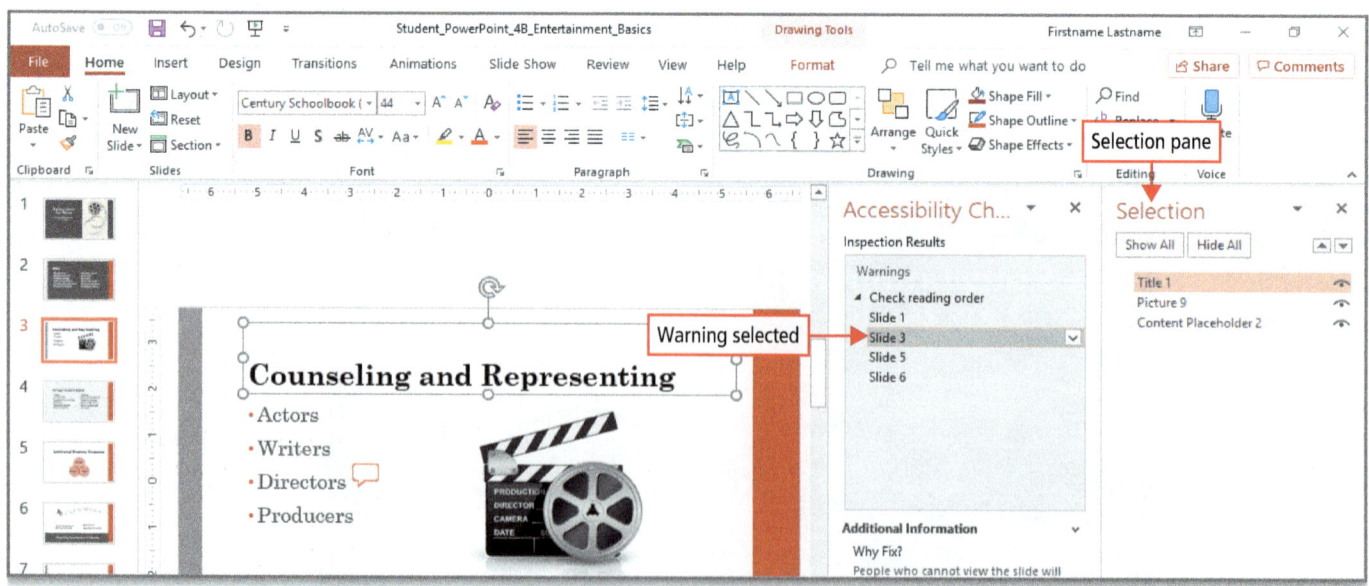

Figure 4.39

8 **Close** ☒ the **Selection pane** and **Close** the **Accessibility Checker pane**. **Save** 🔲 your presentation.

Activity 4.18 | Using the Compatibility Checker

5.2.2

The **Compatibility Checker** locates any potential compatibility issues between PowerPoint 2019 and earlier versions of PowerPoint. The Compatibility Checker creates a report so that you can resolve the issues. PowerPoint 2019 and PowerPoint 365 files are compatible with 2007, 2010, 2013, and 2016 files; however, PowerPoint does not support saving files to PowerPoint 95 or earlier.

MAC TIP The Compatibility Checker is not available in the Mac version of PowerPoint. Skip this Activity and continue with Activity 4.20.

1 Click **File**, click **Check for Issues**, and then click **Check Compatibility**. Compare your screen with Figure 4.40.

The Compatibility Checker summary identifies parts of the presentation that cannot be edited in earlier versions of PowerPoint because those features are not available.

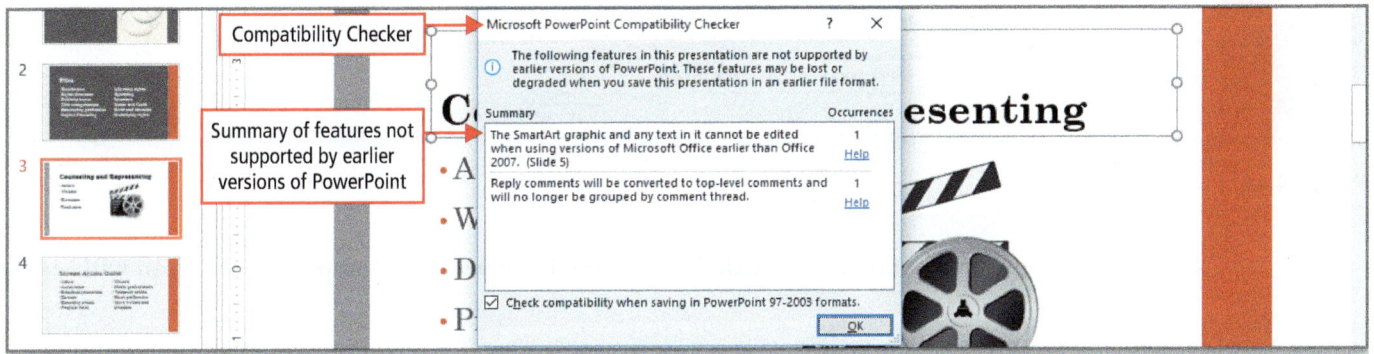

Figure 4.40

2 Click **OK**.

> **MORE KNOWLEDGE** **Compatibility Mode**
>
> If necessary, you can save the presentation in *compatibility mode*, which saves the file as a PowerPoint 97–2003 Presentation. This disables features in PowerPoint that are incompatible with older versions of PowerPoint.

Activity 4.19 | Inspecting a Document

1.5.3

Every presentation file has *properties*, which are details about a file that describe or identify the file, including the title, author name, subject, and tags that identify the file's topic or contents—also known as *metadata*. The **Document Inspector** is a PowerPoint feature that can find and remove hidden properties and personal information in a presentation.

In this Activity, you will inspect the workbook and review the results that the Document Inspector finds to determine what information, if any, should be removed.

MAC TIP The Document Inspector is not available in the Mac version of PowerPoint. Skip this Activity and continue with Activity 4.20.

1 From the **File tab**, click **Check for Issues**, and then click **Inspect Document**. Compare your screen with Figure 4.41.

The Document Inspector dialog box displays and lists the various types of content that will be checked. By default, all the check boxes are selected.

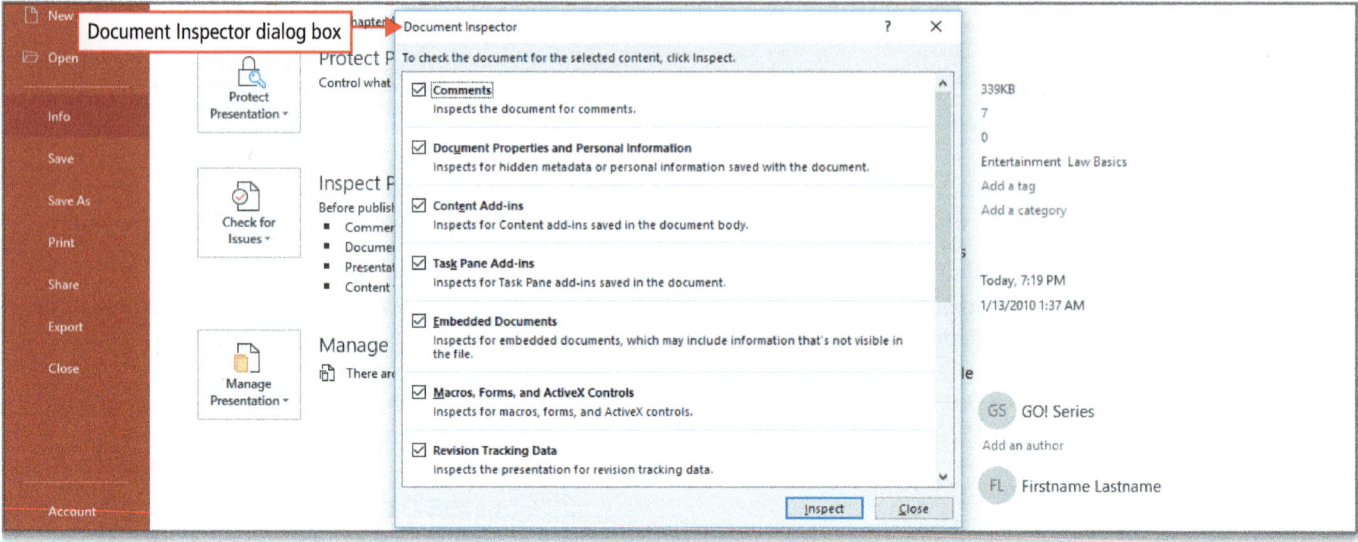

Figure 4.41

2 In the lower right corner of the dialog box, click **Inspect** and compare your screen with Figure 4.42.

The Document Inspector indicates three categories that contain sensitive or personal information. A red exclamation point and a Remove All button display in the inspection results for these three categories. In this presentation, the Document Inspector found comments, document properties, author information, and Presentation Notes.

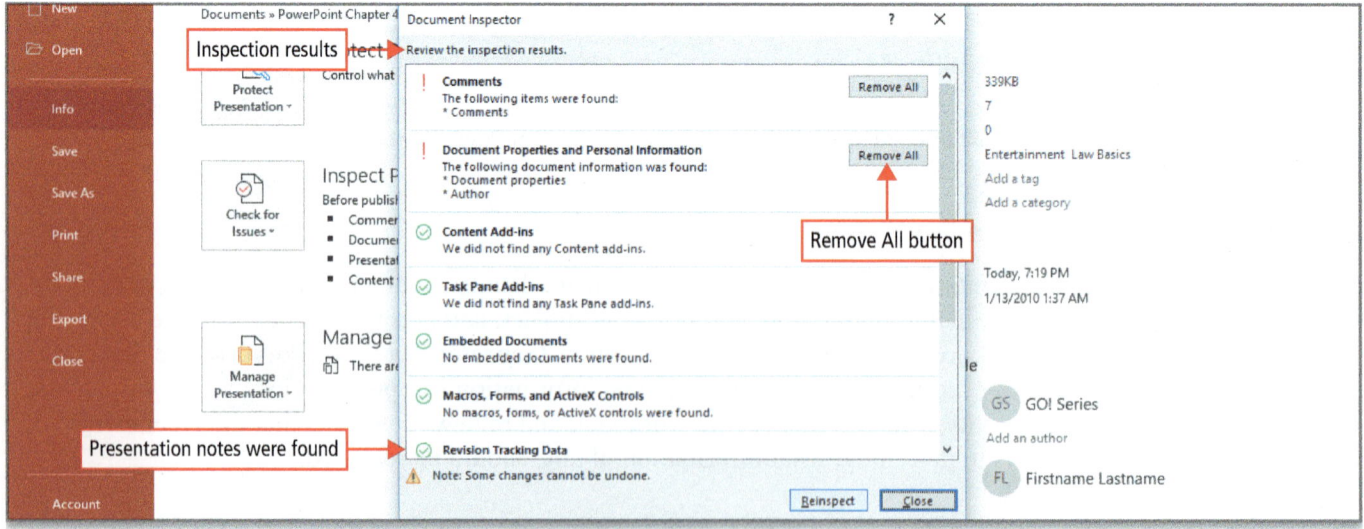

Figure 4.42

3 ▶ Scroll to the bottom of the list, and to the right of **Presentation Notes**, click **Remove All**.

The presentation notes are removed from the file. This information is not needed by the distribution recipients of the presentation.

NOTE   Removing Document Properties and Personal Information

When you remove document properties and personal information using the Document Inspector, it applies a setting that automatically removes properties and personal information whenever you save the document. To add properties such as author or tags to such a file, on the File tab, enter the properties, and then click *Allow this information to be saved in your file.*

---

4 ▶ In the lower right corner of the **Document Inspector** dialog box, click **Close**. **Save**  your presentation.

Objective 6   Protect a Presentation

GO! Learn How
Video P4-6

In the following activities, you will add a password to protect the contents of the presentation and mark your presentation as final.

Activity 4.20 | Encrypting a Presentation

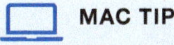
1.5.2

You can provide another level of security for your presentation by adding *encryption*, which is the process by which a file is encoded so that it cannot be opened without the password. Encryption is more than simple password protection—the process digitally obscures information to make it unreadable without a valid key to decode it. Encryption prevents someone from opening the file without the password. Passwords are case sensitive. In this Activity, you will apply encryption to your presentation.

1 ▶ Click **File,** click **Protect Presentation**, and then click **Encrypt with Password**.

💻 **MAC TIP**   Click File, click Passwords, and then select the *Encrypt this presentation and require a password to open* checkbox.

---

2 ▶ In the **Encrypt Document** dialog box, in the **Password** box, type **goseries** and then click **OK**. Compare your screen with Figure 4.43.

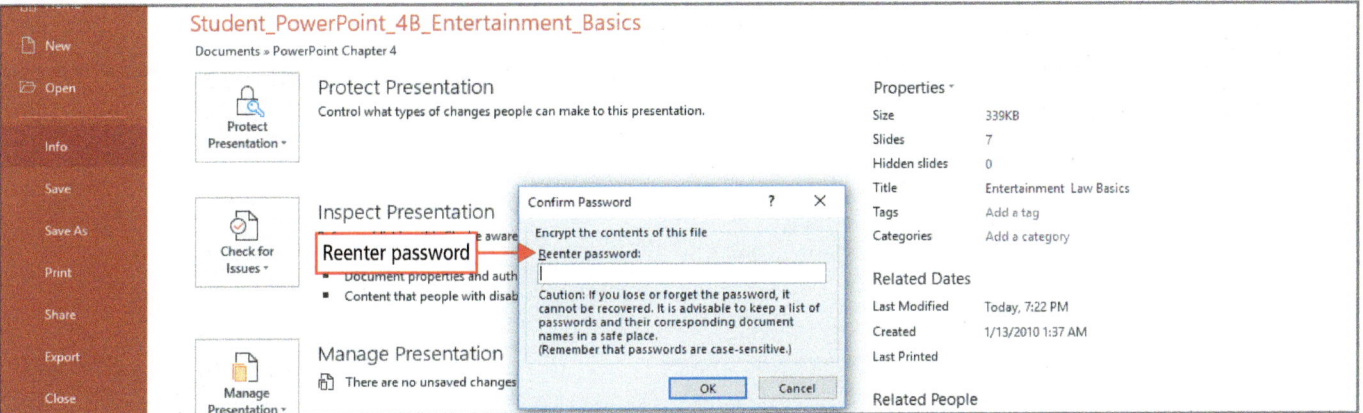

Figure 4.43

3 In the **Confirm Password** dialog box, type **goseries** and then click **OK**. Save and **Close** the file. Leave PowerPoint open.

4 **Open** your **Student_PowerPoint_4B_Entertainment_Basics** file.

The Password dialog box displays.

5 In the Password dialog box, type **goseries** and then click **OK** to open the presentation.

6 If you are submitting this project to the **MyLab IT** grader system, display the Encrypt Document dialog box, highlight the text in the Password box, and then press ⌨Delete or ⌨Backspace to remove the password. Click OK to accept the change.

Activity 4.21 | Marking a Presentation as Final

MOS
1.5.1

Before you share a presentation, you can apply the ***Mark as Final command*** to indicate this is the finished version of the file. The Mark as Final command makes the document read-only, which prevents additional changes to the document and disables typing. This is not a security feature. When someone opens the presentation, he or she will be notified by PowerPoint that the document is marked as final to discourage editing but will be given an option to edit the file anyway.

1 Click **File,** click **Protect Presentation**, and then click **Mark as Final**. Compare your screen with Figure 4.44.

The Microsoft PowerPoint dialog box displays and indicates that the presentation will be marked as final and then saved.

💻 **MAC TIP** The Mark as Final feature is not available in the Mac version of PowerPoint. Skip this Activity.

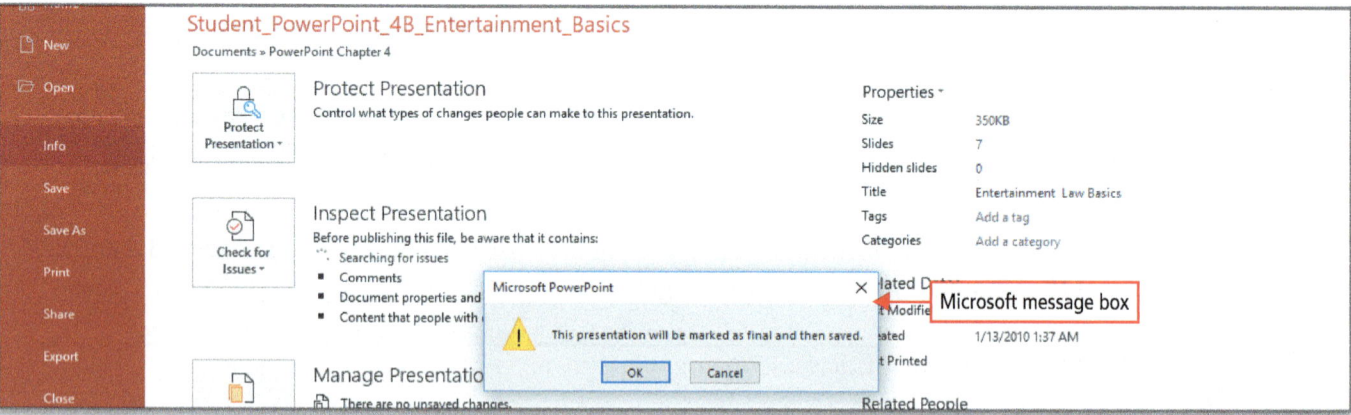

Figure 4.44

2 Click **OK**. Read the message box, and then click **OK**. Compare your screen with Figure 4.45.

The workbook is marked as final. The title bar displays *Read-Only* to indicate the file can be read but not edited. A yellow bar displays below the ribbon tabs, indicating that *An author has marked this presentation as final to discourage editing.* If someone opening the file clicks Edit Anyway, the workbook will no longer be marked as final and will not be a Read-Only file.

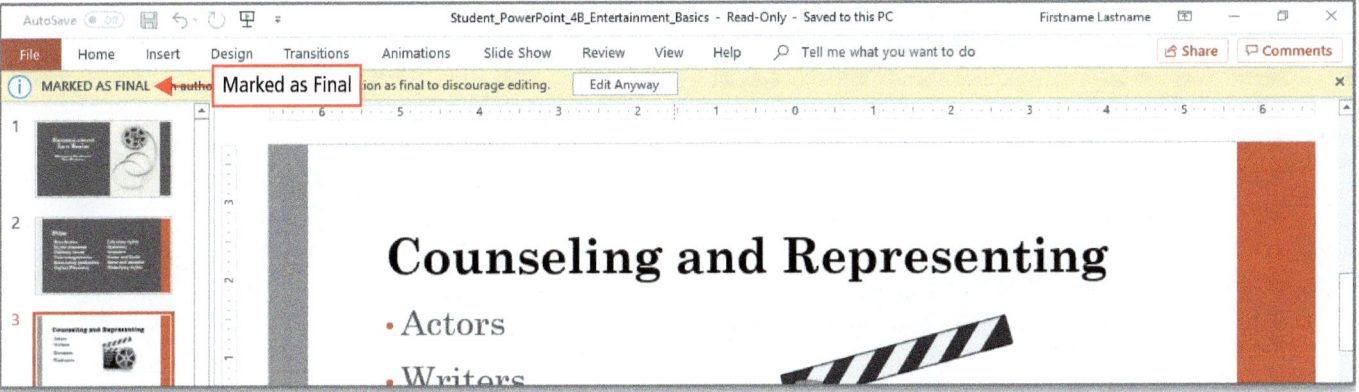

Figure 4.45

3 Click any slide and type text to confirm the presentation cannot be edited.

4 **Close** ⊠ PowerPoint.

> **For Non-MyLab Submissions Determine What Your Instructor Requires**
> As directed by your instructor, submit your completed PowerPoint presentation.

5 In **MyLab IT**, in your **Course Materials**, locate and click the Grader Project **PowerPoint 4B Entertainment Basics**. In **step 3**, under **Upload Completed Assignment**, click **Choose File**. In the **Open** dialog box, navigate to your **PowerPoint Chapter 4 folder**, and then click your **Student_PowerPoint_4B_Entertainment_Basics** file one time to select it. In the lower right corner of the **Open** dialog box, click **Open**.

The name of your selected file displays above the Upload button.

6 To submit your file to **MyLab IT** for grading, click **Upload**, wait a moment for a green **Success!** message, and then in **step 4**, click the blue **Submit for Grading** button. Click **Close Assignment** to return to your list of **Course Materials**.

You have completed Project 4B | **END**

»» GO! To Work

Microsoft Office Specialist (MOS) Skills in this Chapter	
Project 4A	**Project 4B**
1.1.1 Change the slide master theme or background	**1.5.1** Restrict editing
1.1.2 Modify the slide master content	**1.5.2** Protect presentations by using passwords
1.1.3 Create slide layouts	**1.5.3** Inspect presentations for issues
1.1.4 Modify slide layouts	**1.5.4** Add and manage comments
1.1.5 Modify the handout master	**3.4.7** Add alt text to graphic elements for accessibility
1.1.6 Modify the notes master	
3.4.1 Insert and change shapes	
3.4.4 Resize shapes and text boxes	
3.4.5 Format shapes and text boxes	
3.4.6 Apply built-in styles to shapes and text boxes	

Build Your E-Portfolio

An E-Portfolio is a collection of evidence, stored electronically, that showcases what you have accomplished while completing your education. Collecting and then sharing your work products with potential employers reflects your academic and career goals. Your completed documents from the following projects are good examples to show what you have learned: 4G, 4K, and 4L.

Go! For Job Success

Discussion: Cyber Incidents

Your instructor may assign these questions to your class, and then ask you to think about them or discuss with your classmates:

The U.S. Homeland Security Department describes cyber incidents (hacking) as actions where there is an attempt to gain unauthorized access to a system or its data, unwanted disruption to service, unauthorized use of a system, or change to a system without the owner's permission. As companies store and process more and more data at centralized, offsite "cloud" data centers, the opportunities for criminals to hack data are growing. Cyber security is an important part of every organization's information systems protocols, and many companies now employ a senior executive with the title Chief Information Security Officer.

g-stockstudio/Shutterstock

> What cyber incidents have you heard of in the news over the last year?

> What precautions have you taken with your personal data to prevent a hack?

> What would you do if you learned a company you do business with, such as your bank or college, had been the subject of a cyber incident?

End of Chapter

Summary

You designed a PowerPoint template containing formats, shapes, and images on the master pages; you then created a presentation based on this template; and you entered text for a meeting on the presentation.

You added comments into the presentation and practiced navigating through the presentation to read, edit, and delete comments in the presentation. You used the Thesaurus tool to edit your presentation.

You edited Handout and Notes Masters. You compared two versions of a presentation to view the differences between the presentations. You then merged the two presentations into a single presentation.

You prepared a presentation for distribution by checking the compatibility and accessibility and by removing personal information. You marked the presentation as Final and password protected the presentation.

GO! Learn It Online

Review the concepts, key terms, and MOS skills in this chapter by completing these online challenges, which you can find in **MyLab IT**.

Chapter Quiz: Answer matching and multiple choice questions to test what you learned in this chapter.

Lessons on the GO!: Learn how to use all the new apps and features as they are introduced by Microsoft.

MOS Prep Quiz: Answer questions to review the MOS skills that you practiced in this chapter.

Project Guide for Powerpoint Chapter 4

Your instructor will assign Projects from this list to ensure your learning and assess your knowledge.

		Project Guide for PowerPoint Chapter 4		
Project	**Apply Skills from These Chapter Objectives**	**Project Type**		**Project Location**
4A **MyLab IT**	Objectives 1–2 from Project 4A	**4A Instructional Project (Grader Project)** Guided instruction to learn the skills in Project 4A.	**Instruction**	In **MyLab IT** and in text
4B **MyLab IT**	Objectives 3–6 from Project 4B	**4B Instructional Project (Grader Project)** Guided instruction to learn the skills in Project 4B.	**Instruction**	In **MyLab IT** and in text
4C	Objectives 1–2 from Project 4A	**4C Chapter Review (Scorecard Grading)** A guided review of the skills from Project 4A.	**Review**	In text
4D	Objectives 3–6 from Project 4B	**4D Chapter Review (Scorecard Grading)** A guided review of the skills from Project 4B.	**Review**	In text
4E **MyLab IT**	Objectives 1–2 from Project 4A	**4E Mastery (Grader Project)** **Mastery and Transfer of Learning** A demonstration of your mastery of the skills in Project 4A with extensive decision making.		In **MyLab IT** and in text
4F **MyLab IT**	Objectives 3–6 from Project 4B	**4F Mastery (Grader Project)** **Mastery and Transfer of Learning** A demonstration of your mastery of the skills in Project 4B with extensive decision making.		In **MyLab IT** and in text
4G **MyLab IT**	Objectives 1–6 from Projects 4A and 4B	**4G Mastery (Grader Project)** **Mastery and Transfer of Learning** A demonstration of your mastery of the skills in Projects 4A and 4B with extensive decision making.		In **MyLab IT** and in text
4H	Combination of Objectives from Projects 4A and 4B	**4H GO! Fix It (Scorecard Grading)** **Critical Thinking** A demonstration of your mastery of the skills in Projects 4A and 4B by creating a correct result from a document that contains errors you must find.		IRC
4I	Combination of Objectives from Projects 4A and 4B	**4I GO! Make It (Scorecard Grading)** **Critical Thinking** A demonstration of your mastery of the skills in Projects 4A and 4B by creating a result from a supplied picture.		IRC
4J	Combination of Objectives from Projects 4A and 4B	**4J GO! Solve It (Rubric Grading)** **Critical Thinking** A demonstration of your mastery of the skills in Projects 4A and 4B, your decision-making skills, and your critical thinking skills. A task-specific rubric helps you self-assess your result.		IRC
4K	Combination of Objectives from Projects 4A and 4B	**4K GO! Solve It (Rubric Grading)** **Critical Thinking** A demonstration of your mastery of the skills in Projects 4A and 4B, your decision-making skills, and your critical thinking skills. A task-specific rubric helps you self-assess your result.		In text
4L	Combination of Objectives from Projects 4A and 4B	**4L GO! Think (Rubric Grading)** **Critical Thinking** A demonstration of your understanding of the Chapter concepts applied in a manner that you would outside of college. An analytic rubric helps you and your instructor grade the quality of your work by comparing it to the work an expert in the discipline would create.		In text
4M	Combination of Objectives from Projects 4A and 4B	**4M GO! Think (Rubric Grading)** **Critical Thinking** A demonstration of your understanding of the Chapter concepts applied in a manner that you would outside of college. An analytic rubric helps you and your instructor grade the quality of your work by comparing it to the work an expert in the discipline would create.		IRC
4N	Combination of Objectives from Projects 4A and 4B	**4N You and GO! (Rubric Grading)** **Critical Thinking** A demonstration of your understanding of the Chapter concepts applied in a manner that you would in a personal situation. An analytic rubric helps you and your instructor grade the quality of your work.		IRC

Glossary

Glossary of Chapter Key Terms

Accessibility Checker A feature that finds any potential accessibility issues and creates a report so that you can resolve the issues to make your file easier for those with disabilities to use.

Alt text Text used in documents and webpages to provide a text description of an image.

Antonym A word having the opposite meaning of another.

Comment A note that you can attach to text or objects on a slide, or to an entire slide.

Compatibility Checker A feature that locates potential compatibility issues between PowerPoint 2019 and earlier versions of PowerPoint.

Compatibility mode Saving a presentation as a PowerPoint 97–2003 presentation.

Document Inspector A PowerPoint feature that can find and remove hidden properties and personal information in a presentation.

Encryption The process by which a file is encoded so that it cannot be opened without the proper password.

Gradient fill A fill effect in which one color fades into another.

Handout Master The specifications for the design of presentation handouts for an audience.

Mark as Final command Makes a presentation file read-only to prevent changes to the document.

Metadata The details about a file that describe or identify the file, including the title, author name, subject, and tags that identify the file's topic or contents. Also known as properties.

Notes Master The specifications for how the speaker notes display on the printed page.

Office Theme Slide Master The slide master for the Office theme that contains the design, such as the background, that displays on all slide layouts in the presentation.

Properties The details about a file that describe or identify the file, including the title, author name, subject, and tags that identify the file's topic or contents. Also known as metadata.

Reviewer A person who adds comments to a presentation to provide feedback.

Slide Master Part of a template that stores information about the formatting and text that displays on every slide in a presentation.

Synonym A word having the same or nearly the same meaning as another.

Template A file that contains predefined formatting and layout. A template has the file extension .potx.

Chapter Review

| Skills Review | Project 4C Contract |

Apply 4A skills from these Objectives:

1. Modify Slide Masters
2. Create a Custom Template

In the following Skills Review, you will create a template that Thompson Henderson Law Partners will use to prepare presentations for the initial meeting with a client. You will use the template to create a presentation for the musical group Billy and the Night Owls. Your completed presentation will look similar to Figure 4.46.

Project Files

For Project 4C, you will need:

New blank PowerPoint Presentation
p04C_Band
p04C_Contract

You will save your files as:

Lastname_Firstname_4C_Contract_Presentation
Lastname_Firstname_4C_Contract_Template
Lastname_Firstname_4C_Night_Owls

Project Results

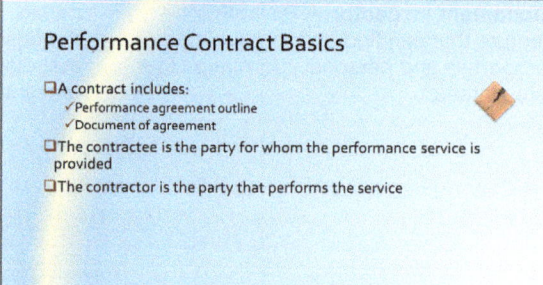
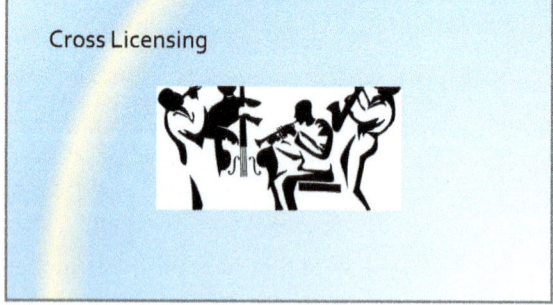
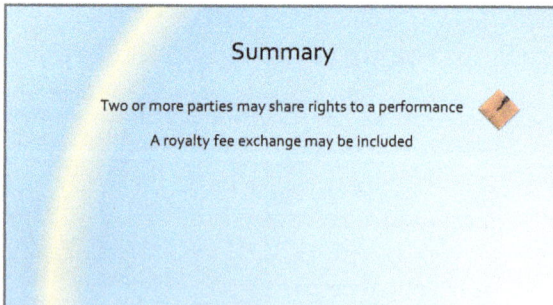

Figure 4.46 Project 4C Contract

(continues on next page)

Chapter Review

Skills Review: Project 4C Contract (continued)

1 ▶ Start PowerPoint, and then click **Blank Presentation**. Display the **Save As** dialog box. Navigate to the location where you are saving your work, using your own name, **Save** the file as **Lastname_Firstname_4C_Contract_Presentation**

2 ▶ On the **View tab,** in the **Master Views group,** click **Slide Master.**

a. On the **Slide Master tab,** in the **Background group,** click **Fonts,** scroll down as necessary, and then click **Corbel.**

b. If necessary, click the second thumbnail—**Title Slide Layout.** On the slide, click anywhere on the dashed border on the Master title style placeholder to display the border as a solid line. On the **Home tab,** in the **Font group,** change the font to **Arial Black.** Change the font size to **48.**

3 ▶ Click the **Office Theme Slide Master** thumbnail.

a. On the **Slide Master tab,** in the **Background group,** click **Background Styles,** and then click **Format Background.** Under **Fill,** click **Gradient fill.** Click the **Type arrow,** and then click **Radial.**

b. Click **Add gradient stop,** and then position the stop at **80%.**

c. Click the **Color arrow,** and then in the eighth column in the second row, click **Gold, Accent 4, Lighter 80%.**

d. Click **Apply to All. Close** the **Format Background** pane.

4 ▶ Click the **Title Slide Layout** thumbnail.

a. Click anywhere on the dashed border for the **title placeholder,** and then drag the entire placeholder so the top border is at **3.5 inches on the upper half of the vertical ruler.**

b. Click anywhere on the dashed border for the **subtitle placeholder,** and then drag the entire placeholder so the top border is at **0.5 inch on the upper half of the vertical ruler.**

c. With the **subtitle placeholder** still selected, drag the bottom middle sizing handle to **0.5 inches on the lower half of the vertical ruler.**

5 ▶ Click the **Office Theme Slide Master** thumbnail, and then click anywhere in the first bulleted line. On the **Home tab,** in the **Paragraph group,** click the **Bullets arrow,** and then click **Bullets and Numbering.**

a. In the **Bullets and Numbering** dialog box, on the **Bulleted tab,** click **Hollow Square Bullets,** and then click the **Color arrow.** Under **Theme Colors,** click **Orange, Accent 2, Darker 50%**—in the sixth column, the last color. Click **OK.**

b. Click anywhere in the *Second level* line. Change the bullet style to **Filled Square Bullets,** and then change the bullet color to **Orange, Accent 2, Darker 50%.**

6 ▶ Click the **Title Slide Layout** thumbnail.

a. From the **Insert tab,** in the **Illustrations group,** click **Shapes.** Under **Basic Shapes,** click the **Diamond** shape. At **2 inches on the right side of the horizontal ruler** and **3 inches on the upper half of the vertical ruler,** click to insert the shape.

b. On the **Drawing Tools Format tab,** in the **Shapes Styles group,** click **Shape Effects,** point to **Preset,** and then click **Preset 2.**

c. With the diamond still selected, in the **Size group,** change the **Shape Height** to **1.5"** and the **Shape Width** to **1.5".**

d. On the **Drawing Tools Format tab,** in the **Shape Styles group,** click **Shape Fill,** and then click **Picture.** Navigate to the location where your data files are stored and select **p04C_Contract.** Click **Insert.**

e. With the shape still selected, on the **Drawing Tools Format tab,** in the **Arrange group,** click **Align.** Click **Align Center.** Click **Align** again, and then click **Align Bottom.**

f. On the **Picture Tools Format tab,** in the **Adjust group,** click **Color.** Under **Recolor,** click the second row, third color—**Orange, Accent color 2 Dark**

g. With the shape still selected, on the **Home tab,** in the **Clipboard group,** click **Copy.** Click the **Title and Content Layout** thumbnail. In the **Clipboard group,** click **Paste.**

h. On the **Drawing Tools Format tab,** in the **Size group,** change the **Shape Height** to **1"** and the **Shape Width** to **1".**

i. With the shape still selected, press the Shift key, and then click the content placeholder. On the **Drawing Tools Format tab,** in the **Arrange group,** click **Align,** and then select **Align Right.** Click **Align,** and then select **Align Top.**

(continues on next page)

Chapter Review

7 ▶ Click the **Slide Master tab**. In the **Edit Master** group, click **Insert Layout**.

a. In the **Master Layout group**, click the **Insert Placeholder arrow**. Click **Picture**. Position the pointer in the approximate center of the slide and then click one time to insert the picture. On the **Drawing Tools Format tab**, in the **Size** group, change the **Height** of the placeholder to **3"** and change the **Width** of the placeholder to **6"**.

b. In the **Arrange** group, click **Align**, and then click **Align Center**. Click **Align** and then click **Align Middle**. On the **Slide Master tab**, in the **Edit Master group**, click **Rename**. In the **Rename Layout** dialog box, select and delete the existing text, type **Title and Picture** Click **Rename.**

8 ▶ Click the **Title Slide Layout** thumbnail.

a. Click the dashed border to select the center **Footer** placeholder, and then press ⌨Delete. In the same manner, delete the slide number placeholder on the right.

b. Click the **Title and Picture Layout** thumbnail—the fourth thumbnail. On the **Slide Master tab**, in the **Master Layout** group, clear the **Footers** check box.

9 ▶ On the **View tab**, in the **Master Views group**, click **Handout Master**. On the **Handout Master tab**, click **Slides Per Page**, and then click **2 Slides**. In the **Placeholders group**, clear the **Header** check box.

10 ▶ On the **View tab**, in the **Master Views group**, click **Notes Master**. [0]On the **Notes Master tab**, in the **Placeholders group**, clear the **Header** check box. **Close** the Master view.

11 ▶ On the **Insert tab**, in the **Text group**, click **Header & Footer** to display the **Header and Footer** dialog box. Click the **Notes and Handouts tab**. Under **Include on page**, select the **Date and time** check box, and then select **Fixed** and confirm today's date. If necessary, clear the Header check box, and then select the **Page number** and **Footer** check boxes. In the **Footer** box, type **4C_ Contract_Presentation** and then click **Apply to All**.

12 ▶ Click the **File tab**, and then display all file properties. In the **Tags** box, type **contract**, **template** and in the **Subject** box type your course name and section number. Be sure your name appears as author. **Save** the presentation. (Mac **users** enter keywords instead of tags.)

13 ▶ Print or submit your **Lastname_Firstname_4C_ Contract_Presentation** file electronically as directed by your instructor.

14 ▶ Display the **Save As** dialog box and then click the **Save as type box arrow**. Click **PowerPoint Template**. Navigate to your **PowerPoint Chapter 4** folder and then **Save** the file as **Lastname_Firstname_4C_Contract_Template**

15 ▶ **Close** PowerPoint. Open **File Explorer.** Navigate to your **PowerPoint Chapter 4** folder. If necessary, click the View tab, and in the **Layout group**, click **Details**. Widen the **Name** and **Type** columns.

a. Double-click your **Lastname_Firstname_4C_ Contract_Template** PowerPoint Template file. Notice *Presentation1* is displayed in the title bar. The number following *Presentation* may vary.

b. Display the **Save As** dialog box. Navigate to the location where you are saving your files and then save the file as **Lastname_Firstname_4C_Night_Owls**

16 ▶ On **Slide 1**, in the title placeholder, type **Billy and the Night Owls** In the subtitle placeholder, type **Thompson Henderson Law Partners**

a. On the **Home tab**, in the **Slides group**, click the **New Slide arrow**, and then click **Title and Content**.

b. On **Slide 2**, in the title placeholder, type **Performance Contract Basics**

c. In the content placeholder, type the following bulleted items, using the **Increase and Decrease List Level** buttons as needed to increase the second and third bulleted lines only:

- **A contract includes:**
  - **Performance agreement outline**
  - **Document of agreement**
- **The contractee is the party for whom the performance service is provided**
- **The contractor is the party that performs the service**

17 ▶ On the **Home tab**, in the **Slides group**, click the **New Slide arrow**, and then click **Title and Picture** to add a third slide.

a. In the title placeholder, type **Cross Licensing**

b. In the content placeholder, click the **Pictures** icon. Navigate to your student data files and insert the image **p04C_Band**.

c. At the bottom of the PowerPoint window, on the status bar, click **Notes**. In the **Notes pane**, type **Cross licensing is a legal agreement.**

(continues on next page)

Chapter Review

Skills Review: Project 4C Contract (continued)

d. On the **Home tab**, in the Slides group, click the **New Slide arrow**, and then click **Title and Content**. In the **title placeholder**, type and center the title **Summary** In the **content placeholder**, type **Two or more parties may share rights to a performance** Press Enter and type **A royalty fee exchange may be included** Select both lines, and then on the **Home tab**, in the **Paragraph group**, click **Bullets** to remove the bullets. In the **Paragraph group**, click **Center**. In the **Paragraph group**, click **Line Spacing**, and then click **1.5**.

18 With your **Lastname_Firstname_4C_Night_Owls** file open, on the **View tab**, in the **Master Views group**, click **Slide Master**.

a. Click the **Office Theme Slide Master** thumbnail. In the content placeholder, click the second bulleted line. On the **Home tab**, in the **Paragraph group**, click the **Bullets button arrow**. Click **Checkmark Bullets**.

b. On the **Slide Master tab**, in the **Close group**, click **Close Master View**.

19 On the **Insert tab**, in the **Text group**, click **Header & Footer** to display the **Header and Footer** dialog box. Click the **Notes and Handouts tab**. Under **Include on page**, verify that the **Date and time** check box and the **Fixed** option are selected. If necessary, type today's date. If necessary, clear the Header check box, and then select the **Page number** and **Footer** check boxes. In the **Footer** box, type **4C_Night_Owls** and then click **Apply to All**.

a. Display the document properties. As the **Tags,** type **royalty, rights** and as the **Subject,** type your course and section number. Be sure your name displays as author, and then **Save** your file.

b. As directed by your instructor, create and submit a paper printout or an electronic image of your presentation that looks like a printed document— either as the Notes and Handouts or as the presentation slides—or, submit your completed PowerPoint file. **Close** PowerPoint.

You have completed Project 4C | **END**

Chapter Review

Skills Review **Project 4D Athlete Taxes**

Apply 4B skills from these Objectives:

3. Create and Edit Comments
4. Compare and Combine Presentations
5. Prepare a Presentation for Distribution
6. Protect a Presentation

In the following Skills Review, you will modify a presentation created by Thompson Henderson Law Partners as a brief overview of taxation issues to present to Finley Davidson, who is a professional football player. You will add comments to the presentation, compare and combine presentations, prepare the document for distribution, and then password-protect it. Your completed presentation will look similar to Figure 4.47.

Project Files

For Project 4D, you will need:

p04D_Athlete_Taxes
p04D_Athlete_Taxes2
You will save your presentation as
Lastname_Firstname_4D_Athlete_Taxes

Project Results

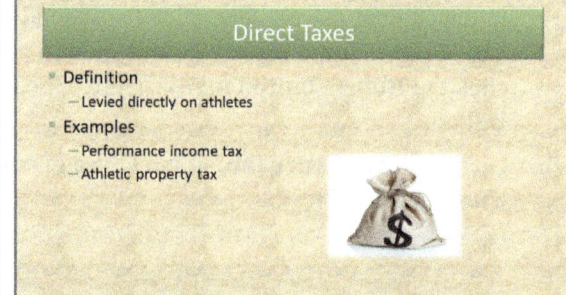
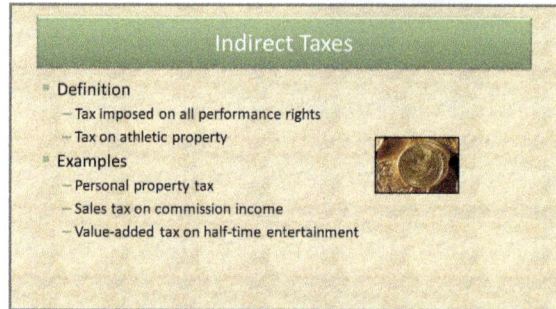
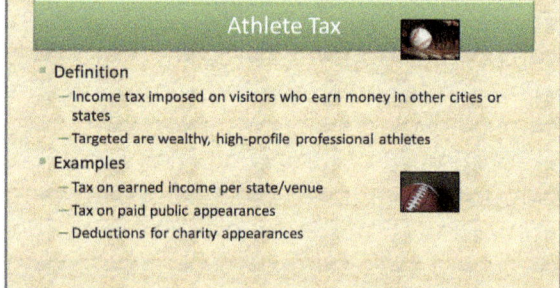
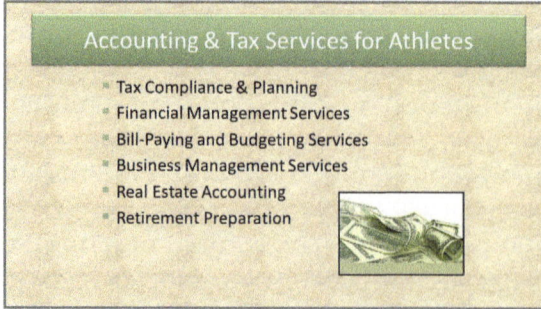

Figure 4.47 Project 4D Athlete Taxes

(continues on next page)

346 **PowerPoint** | Chapter 4: Formatting a Presentation Using Slide Masters, and Reviewing

Chapter Review

Skills Review: Project 4D Athlete Taxes (continued)

1 Navigate to your student data files, and then double-click **p04D_Athlete_Taxes.** In your presentation, if necessary, at the top click **Enable Editing.** On the **File tab,** click **Save As,** navigate to your **PowerPoint Chapter 4 folder,** and then using your own name, save the file as **Lastname_Firstname_4D_Athlete_Taxes**

2 Display **Slide 2,** and then on the **Review tab,** in the **Comments group,** click **New Comment.** In the **Comments pane** in the comment text box, type **It would be a good idea to add a few more examples.**

3 Display **Slide 3.** Click at the end of the bulleted item that ends with *commission income.* In the **Comments pane,** click **New.** Type **I am glad you added this one.** Click outside the comment to deselect it.

4 Display **Slide 4** and then enter a new comment with the text **Is this clear enough for the client to understand?** Click outside the comment. In the slide, drag the comment icon so it is positioned under the word *Deductions.*

5 Display **Slide 2.** In the **Comments** pane, click in the **Reply** box, and then type **Ask sports agents for more examples.**

6 Click **Next** until you reach the comment on **Slide 3.** On the **Review tab,** in the **Comments group,** click **Delete** to remove this comment. **Close** the **Comments** pane.

7 Display **Slide 2.** Right-click *sportspersons,* and then on the shortcut menu, point to **Synonyms.** Click **athletes** to change the word *sportspersons* to *athletes.* (Mac users Press `control` + click the word *sportspersons.* In the shortcut menu, click Thesaurus. In the Thesaurus pane, press `Control` + click the word *athletes,* and then click Insert "*athletes*".)

8 Display **Slide 1.** On the **Review tab,** in the **Compare group,** click **Compare.** In the **Choose File to Merge with Current Presentation** dialog box, navigate to your student data files for this chapter, click **p04D_Athlete_Taxes2,** and then click **Merge.**

9 (Mac users, the Compare feature is not available in the Mac version of PowerPoint. In the slide thumbnails, drag Slide 2 *Indirect Taxes* after Slide 3 *Direct Taxes.* Display Slide 3. Click before *performance rights,* type **all** and then press `Spacebar` one time. Display Slide 4. On the Home tab, click the New Slide arrow, click Reuse Slides, navigate to your data files for this project, and insert MAC_ONLY_p04D_Athlete_Taxes2. Skip to Step 9.)

a. In the **Revisions** pane, under **Presentation Changes,** click **Slide 2: Direct Taxes** to display a **Revisions** check box in the **Slides and Outline pane** on the left. Do *not* select the **Revisions** check box on **Slide 2.**

b. In the **Revisions** pane, under **Presentation Changes,** click **Slides moved after "Indirect Taxes"** to display a **Revisions** check box in the **Slides and Outline** pane on the left. Do *not* select the **Revisions** check box on **Slide 3.**

c. On **Slide 3** notice that a **Revisions** icon displays on the slide. Click the **Revisions** icon to display the **Revisions** check box. Select the **Revisions** check box that indicates *Inserted "all"* to accept the change and insert the word *all.*

d. In the **Revisions** pane, under **Presentation Changes,** click **Insertions after "Athlete Tax"** to display a **Revisions** check box in the **Slides and Outline** pane on the left. Select the **Revisions** check box that indicates *Inserted "Accounting & Tax Services for Athletes"* to accept the change and insert the slide into the presentation

e. On the **Review tab,** in the **Compare group,** click **End Review,** and then click **Yes.**

f. On **Slide 1,** in the **Notes pane,** type **Review complete** and then **Save** your presentation.

10 From the **File tab,** click **Check for Issues,** and then click **Check Accessibility.** (Mac users, on the Review tab, click Accessibility Checker.)

a. In the **Accessibility Checker pane,** under **Errors,** click **Picture 6 (Slide 1).** In the slide, point to the image, right-click, and then click **Edit Alt Text.** In the **Alt Text** box, type **Calculator and money** (Mac users, `control` + click the image.)

b. In the **Accessibility Checker pane,** under **Errors,** click **Picture 2 (Slide 2).** With the image selected, in the **Alt Text** box, type **Money bag**

c. Using the technique you practiced, add the alt text **Pennies** to the image on **Slide 3.** Add the alt text **Baseball** and **Football** to the pictures on **Slide 4** and add the alt text **Money** to the picture on **Slide 5.** **Close** the **Alt Text** pane.

(continues on next page)

Chapter Review

d. In the **Accessibility Checker pane**, under **Warnings**, under **Check Reading Order**, click **Slide 1**. On the **Home tab**, in the **Drawing group**, click **Arrange**, and then click **Selection Pane**.

e. In the **Selection pane**, drag **Picture 6** to the middle position. **Close** the **Selection pane** and **Close** the **Accessibility Checker pane**. **Save** your presentation.

11 Click **File**, click **Check for Issues**, and then click **Check Compatibility**. Click **OK**. (Mac users, the Compatibility Checker is not available in the Mac version of PowerPoint.)

12 From the **File tab**, click **Check for Issues**, and then click **Inspect Document**. In the lower right corner of the dialog box, click **Inspect**. (Mac users, the Document Inspector is not available in the Mac version of PowerPoint.)

a. To the right of **Presentation Notes**, click **Remove All**. In the lower right corner of the **Document Inspector** dialog box, click **Close**. **Save** your presentation.

13 Click **File**. Click **Protect Presentation**, and then click **Encrypt with Password**. (Mac users, click File, click Passwords, and then select the *Encrypt this presentation and require a password to open* checkbox.)

a. In the **Encrypt Document** dialog box, in the **Password** box, type **goseries** and then click **OK**.

b. In the **Confirm Password** dialog box, type **goseries** and then click **OK**. **Save** and **Close** the file. Leave PowerPoint open.

c. **Open** your **Lastname_Firstname_4D_ Athlete_Taxes** file. In the Password dialog box, type **goseries** and then click **OK** to open the presentation.

14 Click **File**. Click **Protect Presentation**, and then click **Mark as Final**. Click **OK**. Read the message box, and then click **OK**. (Mac users, the Mark as Final feature is not available in the Mac version of PowerPoint.)

15 **Close** PowerPoint. Print or submit your presentation electronically as directed by your instructor.

You have completed Project 4D   **END**

4

Mastering PowerPoint | Project 4E Sports Law

In the following Mastering PowerPoint project, you will edit a presentation you already prepared to explain the aspects of Title IX in Collegiate Sports Law and then save it as a template. You will use the template to personalize it for a presentation to Hugh Lopez, who is a college athletic director. Your completed presentation will look similar to Figure 4.48.

Project Files for MyLab IT Grader

1. In your **MyLab IT** course, locate and click **PowerPoint 4E Sports Law**, Download Materials, and then Download All Files.
2. Extract the zipped folder to your PowerPoint Chapter 4 folder. Close the Grader download screens.
3. Take a moment to open the downloaded **PowerPoint_4E_Sports_Law_Instructions**; note any recent updates to the book.

Project Results

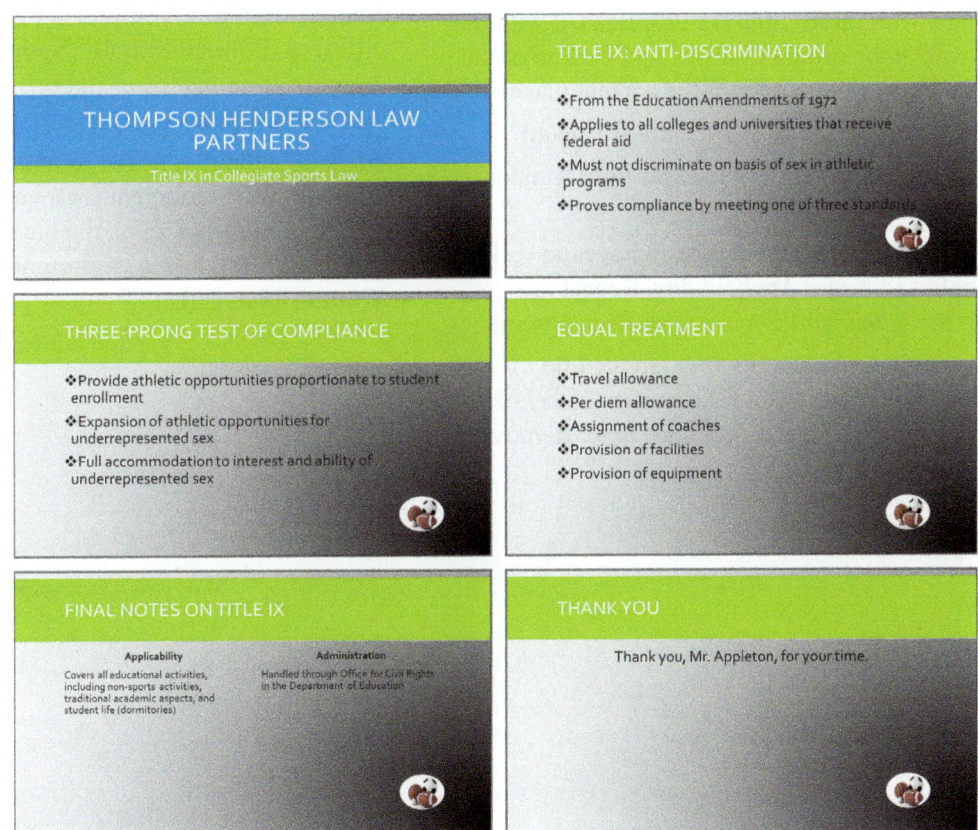

Figure 4.48 Project 4E Sports Law

For Non-MyLab Submissions

For Project 4E, you will need these starting files:
p04E_Sports_Law
p04E_Sports1

In your PowerPoint Chapter 4 folder, save your presentation as:
Lastname_Firstname_4E_Sports_Law

After you have named and saved your presentation, on the next page, begin with Step 2.
After Step 12, save and submit your presentation as directed by your instructor.

(continues on next page)

Content-Based Assessments (Mastery and Transfer of Learning)

1 Navigate to your **PowerPoint Chapter 4 folder** and then double-click the PowerPoint file you downloaded from **MyLab IT** that displays your name—**Student_PowerPoint_4E_Sports_Law**. If necessary, at the top, **click Enable Editing**.

2 Open **Slide Master view**. Scroll up and click the **Banded Slide Master** thumbnail. Apply **Background Style 10**. Format the background with a **Radial Gradient fill**, and then apply it to all slides.

3 On the first bulleted line, change the font size to **32**.

4 On the **Title Slide Layout**, change the Master title style placeholder **font size to 48 pts**. Change the Master subtitle style placeholder **font size to 32 pts**.

5 On the **Title and Content Layout**, insert an **Oval** shape and set the **Height** to **1.0"** and the **Width** to **1.25"**. Fill the shape with **p04E_Sports1** downloaded with this project. Remove the **Shape Outline**, and then align the shape to the lower right corner of the content placeholder.

6 Copy the shape to the **Two Content Layout**.

7 Remove the Header from the **Handout Master**, and then **Close Master View**.

8 On **Slide 5**, in the left column, remove the bullet, and then bold and center *Applicability*. Repeat the formatting for *Administration* in the second column.

9 Add a **Title and Content** slide. In the title placeholder, type **Thank You** In the content placeholder, type **Thank you, Mr. Appleton, for your time.** Remove the bullet and center the text.

10 On the **Title and Content Slide Master**, change the first-level bullets to **Star Bullets**. **Close** the **Master View**.

11 Insert a **Header & Footer** on the **Notes and Handouts**. Include the **Date and time** fixed, the **Page number**, and a **Footer** with the text **4E_Sports_Law** and then click **Apply to All**.

12 Display the document properties. In the **Subject** box, type your course name and section number, and then in the **Tags** box, type **sports, law** Be sure your name appears as author.

13 In **MyLab IT**, in your **Course Materials**, locate and click the Grader Project **PowerPoint 4E Sports Law**. In **step 3**, under **Upload Completed Assignment**, click **Choose File**. In the **Open** dialog box, navigate to your **PowerPoint Chapter 4 folder**, and then click your **Student_PowerPoint_4E_Sports_Law** file one time to select it. In the lower right corner of the **Open** dialog box, click **Open**.

14 To submit your file to **MyLab IT** for grading, click **Upload**, wait a moment for a green **Success!** message, and then in **step 4**, click the blue **Submit for Grading** button. Click **Close Assignment** to return to your list of **Course Materials**.

You have completed Project 4E END

MyLab IT Grader

Mastering PowerPoint | **Project 4F Contract Aspects**

Apply 4B skills from these Objectives:

3. Create and Edit Comments
4. Compare and Combine Presentations
5. Prepare a Presentation for Distribution
6. Protect a Presentation

In the following Mastering PowerPoint project, you will complete a presentation that covers various aspects of contracts in the entertainment industry, including royalties, minors, and advances. You will review the presentation and add comments, and compare and combine presentations before preparing it for distribution. Your completed presentation will look similar to Figure 4.49.

Project Files for **MyLab IT** Grader

1. In your **MyLab IT** course, locate and click **PowerPoint 4F Contract Aspects**, Download Materials, and then Download All Files.
2. Extract the zipped folder to your PowerPoint Chapter 4 folder. Close the Grader download screens.
3. Take a moment to open the downloaded **PowerPoint_4F_Contract_Aspects_Instructions**; note any recent updates to the book.

Project Results

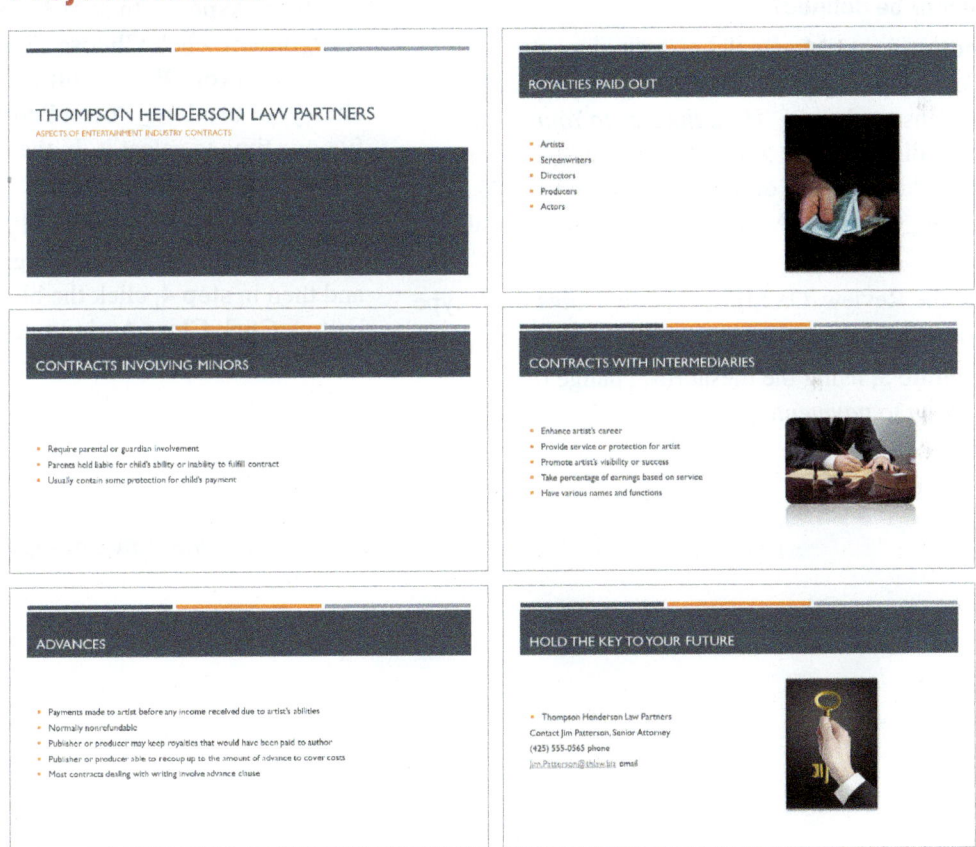

Figure 4.49 Project 4F Contract Aspects

For Non-MyLab Submissions

For Project 4F, you will need:
p04F_Contract_Aspects
p04F_Contract_Aspects2

In your PowerPoint Chapter 4 folder, save your workbook as:
Lastname_Firstname_4F_Contract_Aspects

After you have named and saved your presentation, on the next page, begin with Step 2.
After Step 12, save and submit your presentation as directed by your instructor.

(continues on next page)

Content-Based Assessments (Mastery and Transfer of Learning)

1 Navigate to your **PowerPoint Chapter 4 folder** and then double-click the PowerPoint file you downloaded from **MyLab IT** that displays your name—**Student_PowerPoint_4F_Contract_Aspects**. If necessary, at the top, **click Enable Editing**.

2 Display **Slide 3**. At the end of the last bulleted item, add the comment **Are there any other points that should be added?**

3 On **Slide 4**, select *Intermediaries*, and then add the comment **I think this term needs to be defined.**

4 On **Slide 5**, add the comment **Excellent content!** Drag the comment so it is positioned right after *Advances*.

5 On **Slide 3**, click in the *Reply* box, and then type **Should minor be defined?**

6 **Compare and Merge** the presentation with **p04F_Contract_Aspects2** downloaded with this project. Accept the inserted slide *"Hold the Key to Your Future"*. (Mac users, display Slide 5. Use the Reuse Slides pane to insert the slide at the end of the presentation from MAC_ONLY_p04F_Contract_Aspects2 downloaded with this project.)

7 End the Review. On **Slide 1**, in the **Notes** pane, type **Review complete**

8 On **Slide 3**, using the thesaurus, change the word *compensation* to *payment*.

9 **Run the Accessibility Checker**. Add the **alt text Payments** to the picture on **Slide 2**. Add the **alt text Signature** to the picture on **Slide 4**, and add the **alt text Key** to the picture on **Slide 6**.

10 Insert a **Footer** on **Notes and Handouts** that includes the fixed date and time, page number, and **4F_Contract_Aspects** as the footer.

11 Revise the document properties. In the Tags box, type **royalties, minors, advances** and then in the Subject box, type your course name and section number. Be sure your name appears as author.

12 Save your presentation and close PowerPoint.

13 In **MyLab IT**, in your **Course Materials**, locate and click the Grader Project **PowerPoint 4F Contract Aspects**. In **step 3**, under **Upload Completed Assignment**, click **Choose File**. In the **Open** dialog box, navigate to your **PowerPoint Chapter 4 folder**, and then click your **Student_PowerPoint_4F_Contract_Aspects** file one time to select it. In the lower right corner of the **Open** dialog box, click **Open**.

14 To submit your file to **MyLab IT** for grading, click **Upload**, wait a moment for a green **Success!** message, and then in **step 4**, click the blue **Submit for Grading** button. Click **Close Assignment** to return to your list of **Course Materials**.

You have completed Project 4F **END**

MyLab IT Grader

Mastering PowerPoint | Project 4G Film Production

Apply 4A and 4B skills from these Objectives:

1. Modify Slide Masters
2. Create a Custom Template
3. Create and Edit Comments
4. Compare and Combine Presentations
5. Prepare a Presentation for Distribution
6. Protect a Presentation

In the following Mastering PowerPoint project, you will open a presentation explaining the legal aspects of film production and modify the slide masters. Frequently, Thompson Henderson Law Partners presents this information to college classes, so you will save the presentation as a template. Then you will create a presentation from the template and personalize it for the Film Production course at the local university. Your completed presentation will look similar to Figure 4.50.

Project Files for MyLab IT Grader

1. In your **MyLab IT** course, locate and click **PowerPoint 4G Film Production**, Download Materials, and then Download All Files.
2. Extract the zipped folder to your PowerPoint Chapter 4 folder. Close the Grader download screens.
3. Take a moment to open the downloaded **PowerPoint_4G_Film_Production_Instructions**; note any recent updates to the book.

Project Results

Figure 4.50 Project 4G Film Production

For Non-MyLab Submissions

For Project 4G, you will need:
p04G_Film_Production
p04G_Film

In your PowerPoint Chapter 4 folder, save your presentation as:
Lastname_Firstname_4G_Film_Production

After you have named and saved your presentation, on the next page, begin with Step 2.
After Step 16, save and submit your presentation files as directed by your instructor.

(continues on next page)

Content-Based Assessments (Mastery and Transfer of Learning)

1 Navigate to your **PowerPoint Chapter 4 folder** and then double-click the PowerPoint file you downloaded from **MyLab IT** that displays your name—**Student_ PowerPoint_4G_Film_Production**. If necessary, at the top, click **Enable Editing**. In your **PowerPoint Chapter 4** folder, **Save** the file as a PowerPoint Template with the name **Lastname_Firstname_4G_Film_Template**

2 In **Slide Master view**, on **Basis Slide Master**, change the background to **Style 2**. Format the background with a **Gradient fill**, **Linear type**. Position gradient **Stop 2** at **25%**. Position gradient **Stop 3** at **75%**, set the color to the third color in the eighth column, and then apply to all slides.

3 Change the color of the first bullet to the last color, in the eighth column.

4 Click the **Title and Content Layout** thumbnail. Insert a **Text Box** in the lower left corner of the content placeholder.

5 Inside the text box, type **Thompson Henderson Law Partners** Change the font size to **12 pt** and apply **Bold** and **Center**.

6 Change the **Height** of the text box to **0.5"** and the **Width** to **6.0"**. Use a **Shape Fill** to add **Gradient** with a **Light Variations** of **Linear Down**. **Align** the text box to the **center** and **bottom** of the slide. Hide the footer placeholders on this slide layout.

7 Remove the Header on the **Handout Master**, and then **Close Master View**.

8 Insert the **Header & Footer**. On the **Notes and Handouts tab**, include a **Fixed** date and the **Page number** and **Footer**. In the **Footer** box, type **4G_Film_Production** and then click **Apply to All**.

9 Revise the document properties. In the **Subject** box, type your course name and section number, and then in the **Tags** box, type **film production** Be sure your name displays as author. Close the file.

10 In File Explorer, double-click the template to open a new presentation. Save the presentation as **Lastname_Firstname_4G_Film_Production** On **Slide 1**, after *Presented to,* press Enter, and then type **University Film Production Class**

11 In **Slide Master View**, on the **Title and Content Layout** slide, change first-level bullets to hollow round bullets, and then **Close Master View**.

12 On **Slide 4**, after the third bulleted item, add this comment: **Define Sole Proprietorship.**

13 On **Slide 5**, select *Life rights*, and then add this comment: **Explain how this is intellectual property.**

14 On **Slide 2**, use the Thesaurus to change *payment* to *compensation.*

15 On **Slide 3**, insert the picture file, **p04G_Film**. **Crop to Shape** using the **Rectangle: Diagonal Corners Rounded** under **Rectangles**. (Mac users crop using Round Diagonal Corner Rectangle.) Change the shape **Height** to **2.53"** Align the picture to the right and middle of the content placeholder. **Recolor** the picture to **Grayscale**.

16 Run the **Accessibility Checker** and add the alt text **Contracts** to the picture on **Slide 3**.

17 **Close** PowerPoint.

18 In **MyLab IT**, in your **Course Materials**, locate and click the Grader Project **PowerPoint 4G Refuge**. In **step 3**, under **Upload Completed Assignment**, click **Choose File**. In the **Open** dialog box, navigate to your PowerPoint **Chapter 4 folder**, and then click your **Lastname_Firstname_4G_Film_Production** file one time to select it. In the lower right corner of the **Open** dialog box, click **Open**.

19 To submit your file to **MyLab IT** for grading, click **Upload**, wait a moment for a green **Success!** message, and then in **step 4**, click the blue **Submit for Grading** button. Click **Close Assignment** to return to your list of **Course Materials**.

You have completed Project 4G **END**

Content-Based Assessments (Critical Thinking)

Apply a combination of the **4A** and **4B** skills.

GO! Fix It	Project 4H Labor Issues	IRC
GO! Make It	Project 4I Consignment Contracts	IRC
GO! Solve It	Project 4J Legal Guide	IRC
GO! Solve It	Project 4K Actor Advice	

Project Files

For Project 4K, you will need:

p04K_Actor_Advice
p04K_Cinema

You will save your presentations as:

Lastname_Firstname_4K_Actor_Template
Lastname_Firstname_4K_Actor_Advice

Open **p04K_Actor_Advice** and save it as a template **Lastname_Firstname_4K_Actor_Template** Examine the slide content, and then modify the appropriate slide master with a background style or a theme. Adjust colors and fonts as needed. Insert a shape on the appropriate slide master so the shape displays only on Slide 1, and then insert **p04K_Cinema** in the shape, recolor it, and place it where it is visually pleasing on the slide. Add appropriate alt text to the image. Add additional shape(s) for attractive style and color to the title slide to add interest. Change the bullet style for levels of bullets that are used. On the notes and handouts, insert the fixed date and time, page number, and a footer with the file name. Add your name, your course name and section number, and the tag **template** to the properties.

Create a new presentation based on the template. Personalize the presentation for Julia Simpson. Save the presentation as **Lastname_Firstname_4K_Actor_Advice** On Slide 2, insert a comment. Update the Notes and Handouts footer with **4K_Actor_Advice** and add the tags **contracts, paparazzi, media** and then change the author in the Properties. Mark the presentation as Final and save it. Print or submit electronically as directed by your instructor.

		Performance Level		
		Exemplary	**Proficient**	**Developing**
Performance Criteria	**Customized Office Theme Slide Master with a background or theme and bullet styles.**	Slide master was customized correctly with a background or theme and with bullet styles. Maintained good contrast.	Slide master was not customized with a background or theme and with bullet styles. Customization done on other slide masters.	No slide master customization was completed.
	Inserted a shape with the picture on the Title Slide Layout Master and recolored it. Added alt text.	Shape was inserted on the slide master and was sized, recolored, and placed in an appropriate position. Appropriate alt text added.	The shape was not inserted or recolored on the appropriate slide master. Alt text was not added.	The shape was not inserted or recolored.
	Created and personalized a presentation and marked as final.	Presentation file was created, personalized, included comments, and was marked as final.	Presentation file was created but was not personalized. May or may not have been marked as final.	A presentation file was not created from the template.

You have completed Project 4K | END

Outcomes-Based Assessments (Critical Thinking)

Rubric

The following outcomes-based assessments are *open-ended assessments*. That is, there is no specific correct result; your result will depend on your approach to the information provided. Make *Professional Quality* your goal. Use the following scoring rubric to guide you in *how* to approach the problem and then to evaluate *how well* your approach solves the problem.

The *criteria*—Software Mastery, Content, Format and Layout, and Process—represent the knowledge and skills you have gained that you can apply to solving the problem. The *levels of performance*—Professional Quality, Approaching Professional Quality, or Needs Quality Improvements—help you and your instructor evaluate your result.

	Your completed project is of Professional Quality if you:	Your completed project is Approaching Professional Quality if you:	Your completed project Needs Quality Improvements if you:
1-Software Mastery	Choose and apply the most appropriate skills, tools, and features and identify efficient methods to solve the problem.	Choose and apply some appropriate skills, tools, and features, but not in the most efficient manner.	Choose inappropriate skills, tools, or features, or are inefficient in solving the problem.
2-Content	Construct a solution that is clear and well organized, contains content that is accurate, appropriate to the audience and purpose, and is complete. Provide a solution that contains no errors of spelling, grammar, or style.	Construct a solution in which some components are unclear, poorly organized, inconsistent, or incomplete. Misjudge the needs of the audience. Have some errors in spelling, grammar, or style, but the errors do not detract from comprehension.	Construct a solution that is unclear, incomplete, or poorly organized, contains some inaccurate or inappropriate content, and contains many errors of spelling, grammar, or style. Do not solve the problem.
3-Format and Layout	Format and arrange all elements to communicate information and ideas, clarify function, illustrate relationships, and indicate relative importance.	Apply appropriate format and layout features to some elements, but not others. Overuse features, causing minor distraction.	Apply format and layout that does not communicate information or ideas clearly. Do not use format and layout features to clarify function, illustrate relationships, or indicate relative importance. Use available features excessively, causing distraction.
4-Process	Use an organized approach that integrates planning, development, self-assessment, revision, and reflection.	Demonstrate an organized approach in some areas, but not others; or, use an insufficient process of organization throughout.	Do not use an organized approach to solve the problem.

Outcomes-Based Assessments (Critical Thinking)

Apply a combination of the 4A and 4B skills.

| GO! Think | Project 4L Venue Risks |

Project Files

For Project 4L, you will need:

New blank PowerPoint presentation

You will save your presentation as

Lastname_Firstname_4L_Venue_Template

Lastname_Firstname_4L_Venue_Risks

In this project, you will create a PowerPoint template for Thompson Henderson Law Partners to educate colleges, universities, and other sports venues about safety and security.

Create a template named **Lastname_Firstname_4L_Venue_Template** Customize the slide masters, applying formatting as needed. In the Notes and Handouts, include the fixed date and time, page number, and **4L_Venue** in the footer. Add your name, course name and section number, and the tag **template** to the Properties.

Create a new presentation based on the template that addresses safety and security concerns. Save the presentation as **Lastname_Firstname_4L_Venue_Risks** Add three slides, each using a different layout. Add two comments. Update the Notes and Handouts footer with the new file name. Update your name, course name and section number, and the tags **venue, sports, risk** to the Properties. Mark the PowerPoint presentation as Final. Print or submit electronically as directed by your instructor.

| You have completed Project 4L | END |

| GO! Think | Project 4M Intellectual Property | IRC |

| You and GO! | Project 4N Copyright | IRC |

Applying Advanced Graphic Techniques and Inserting Audio and Video

5

POWERPOINT
2019

PROJECT 5A

Outcomes

Edit and format pictures and add sound to a presentation.

Objectives

1. Apply Picture Corrections
2. Add a Border to a Picture
3. Change the Shape of a Picture
4. Add a Picture to a WordArt Object and Merge Shapes
5. Enhance a Presentation with Audio and Video

PROJECT 5B

Outcomes

Create and edit a presentation using PowerPoint Designer and crop pictures.

Objectives

6. Use PowerPoint Designer
7. Add a Photo Caption and Alt Text
8. Crop a Picture

Pressmaster/Shutterstock

In This Chapter

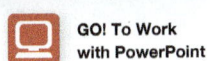

GO! To Work with PowerPoint

PowerPoint includes a variety of methods for formatting and enhancing graphic, video, and audio elements. There are tools for changing the sharpness, brightness, contrast, and shape of a picture; adding a border; and cropping a picture to remove unwanted areas. You can add video clips to your presentations, format the display of the video, trim the size of the clip, and set the video to play automatically or when the mouse is clicked. You can introduce a slide with an audio effect or music, or have an audio effect or music play when the slide or a component on the slide, such as text or a graphic, is clicked.

Cross Oceans Music produces and distributes recordings of innovative musicians from every continent in genres that include Celtic, jazz, New Age, reggae, flamenco, calypso, and unique blends of all styles. Company scouts travel the world attending world music festivals, concerts, performances, shows, and small local venues to find their talented roster of musicians and performers. These artists create new and exciting music using traditional and modern instruments and technologies. Cross Oceans' customers are knowledgeable about music and demand the highest quality digital recordings provided in state-of-the-art formats.

PROJECT 5A

Enhance a Presentation with Graphics and Media

MyLab IT
Project 5A Grader for Instruction
Project 5A Simulation for Training and Review

Project Activities

In Activities 5.01 through 5.12, you will change the sharpness or softness of pictures, and change the brightness and contrast of pictures. You will add borders and change the outline shape of pictures. You will change the shape of a picture, add a WordArt object, and embed a picture and merge shapes. You will insert linked video files and add a trigger to the audio and video. Your completed presentation will look similar to Figure 5.1.

Project Files for **MyLab IT Grader**

1. In your storage location, create a folder named **PowerPoint Chapter 5**.
2. In your **MyLab IT** course, locate and click **PowerPoint 5A Cross Oceans**, Download Materials, and then Download All Files.
3. Extract the zipped folder to your PowerPoint Chapter 5 folder. Close the Grader download screens.
4. Take a moment to open the downloaded **PowerPoint_5A_Cross_Oceans_Instructions**; note any recent updates to the book.

Project Results

GO! Project 5A
Where We're Going

Figure 5.1 Project 5A Cross Oceans Music

For Non-MyLab Submissions

For Project 5A, you will need:

p05A_Cross_Oceans

p05A_Building

p05A_Island

p05A_Drums

p05_Music_Video

p05A_New_Age

p05A_Smooth_Jazz

In your storage location, create a folder named **PowerPoint Chapter 5**
In your PowerPoint Chapter 5 folder, save your presentation as:
Lastname_Firstname_5A_Cross_Oceans

After you have named and saved your presentation, on the next page, begin with Step 2.

Objective 1   Apply Picture Corrections

ALERT   Because Office 365 is a cloud-based subscription service that receives continuous updates, you may encounter some variations in what appears on your screen and what is shown in this instruction. Microsoft Office 365 is fully installed on your PC or Mac; no internet access is necessary to create or edit documents. When you *are* connected to the internet, you will receive monthly upgrades and new features, so you always have the latest versions of Office apps as soon as they are available. Your subscription gives you continuous free access to the latest innovations and refinements.

GO! Learn How
Video P5-1

You can improve the brightness, contrast, or sharpness of pictures. When you *sharpen* an image, the clarity of an image increases. When you *soften* an image, the picture becomes fuzzier. *Brightness* is the perceived radiance or luminosity of an image, and *contrast* is the difference between the darkest and lightest area of a picture.

When you change the overall lightening and darkening of the image, you change the individual *pixels* in an image. *Pixel* is short for *picture element* and represents a single point in a graphic image. *When you recolor* a picture, you change all colors in the image into shades of one color to stylize a picture or make the colors match a background.

Activity 5.01 | Positioning and Ordering Images

3.4.5, 3.5.1, 3.5.4

In this Activity, you will format the objects on a slide to make the slide more visually appealing. Sometimes it is desirable to have text appear on top of an image. In PowerPoint, you can stack objects such as images, shapes, placeholders, and text boxes, on a slide, and use the Send Backward and Bring Forward commands to order the objects in a stack. The Send to Back command will move the object to the bottom of the stack.

You will also use the gridlines to help position an image on the slide.

1 Navigate to your **PowerPoint Chapter 5 folder**, and then double-click the PowerPoint file you downloaded from **MyLab IT** that displays your name—**Student_PowerPoint_5A_ Cross_Oceans**. In your presentation, if necessary, at the top click **Enable Editing**.

  MAC TIP   If group names do not display on your ribbon, on the menu, click PowerPoint, and then click Preferences. Click View, and then in the View dialog box, select the Show group titles check box. Close the dialog box to display group names on the ribbon.

2 On **Slide 1**, click to select the image of the music notes. On the **Picture Tools Format tab**, in the **Arrange group**, click the **Send Backward arrow**, and then click **Send to Back**. Compare your screen with Figure 5.2.

The picture moves behind the slide title.

ANOTHER WAY   To move a picture behind all objects on the slide, right-click the picture, and then click Send to Back.

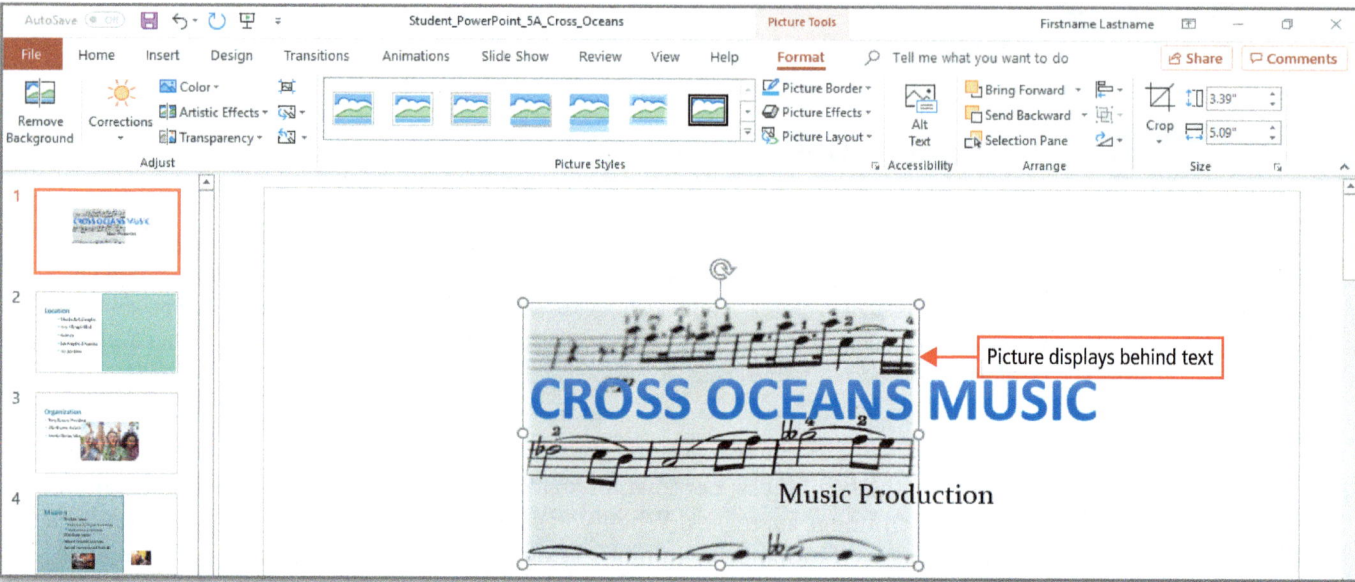

Figure 5.2

3 Display **Slide 2**, and then click the **colored rectangle shape** on the right side of the slide. On the **Drawing Tools Format tab**, in the **Shape Styles group**, click **Shape Fill**, and then click **Picture**. In the **Insert Pictures** dialog box, click **From a file**, navigate to the files downloaded with this this project and then, insert the picture **p05A_Building**. Compare your screen with Figure 5.3.

The picture fills the shape.

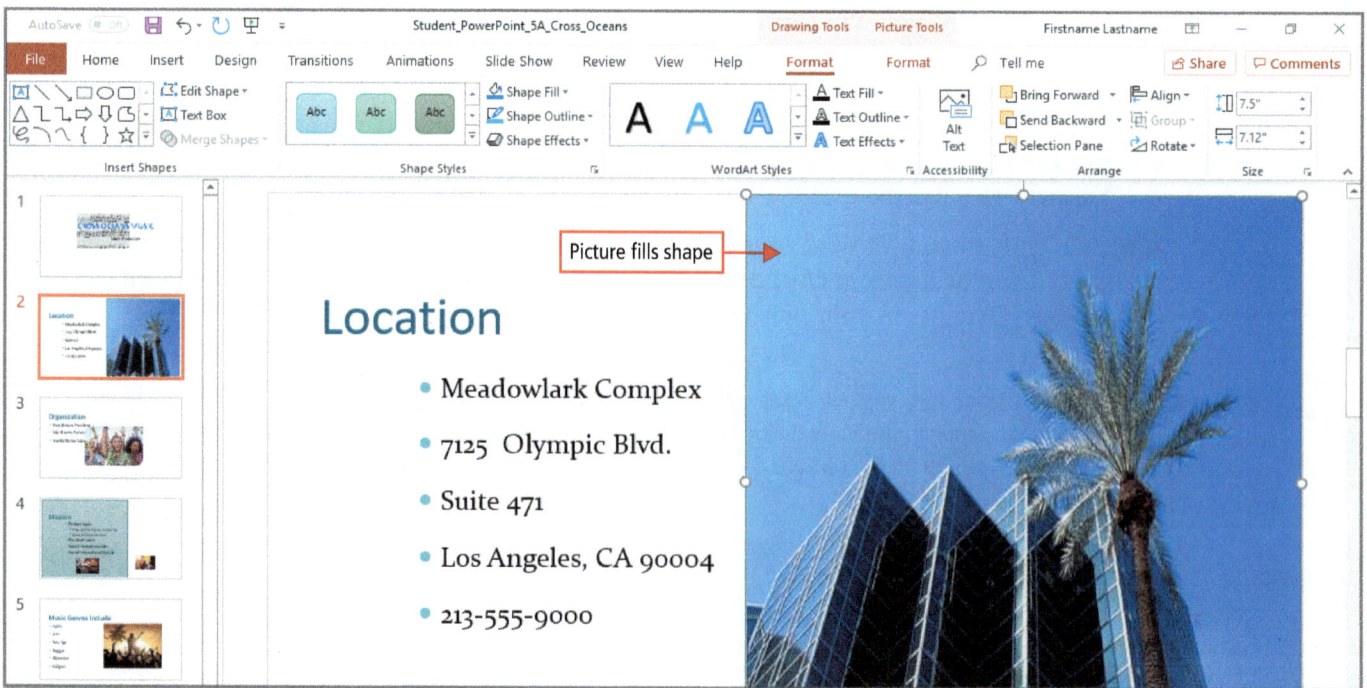

Figure 5.3

4 Display **Slide 3**, and then on the **View tab**, in the **Show group**, select the **Gridlines** check box. If necessary, select the Ruler check box to display the Ruler. Compare your screen with Figure 5.4.

Displaying the gridlines helps you to align objects to the ruler.

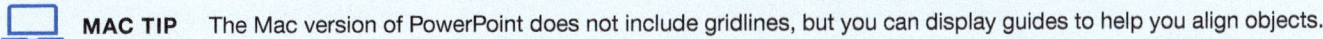

MAC TIP The Mac version of PowerPoint does not include gridlines, but you can display guides to help you align objects.

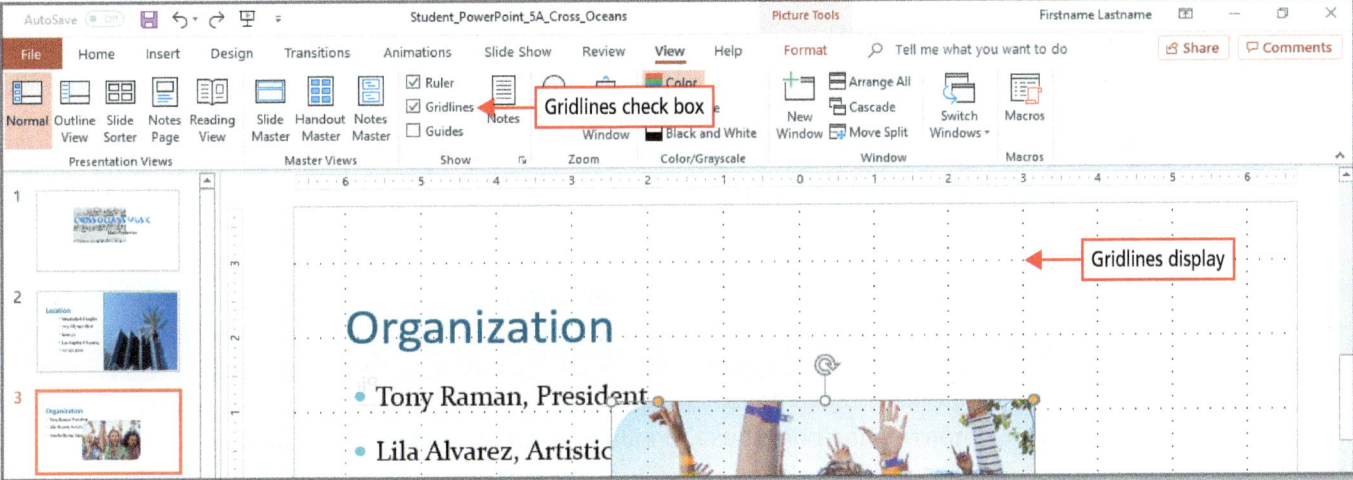

Figure 5.4

5 Click to select the picture. On the **Picture Tools Format tab**, in the **Arrange group**, click the **Send Backward arrow**, and then click **Send to Back**.

6 With the picture selected, on the **Picture Tools Format tab**, in the **Arrange group**, click **Selection Pane**. Compare your screen with Figure 5.5.

The Selection pane displays a list of the objects on the slide.

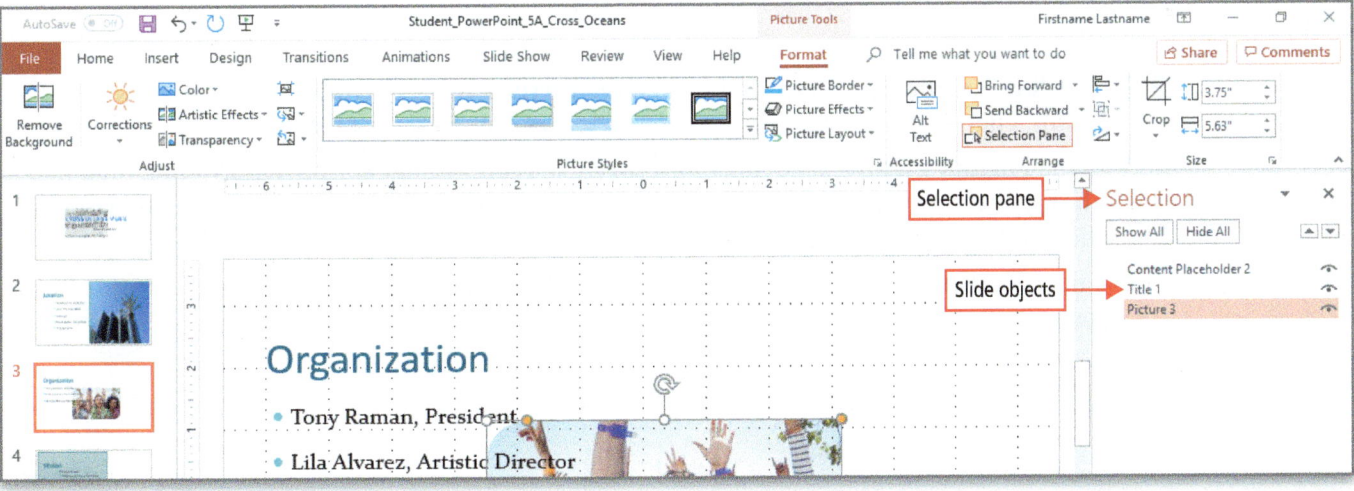

Figure 5.5

7 In the **Selection** pane, click **Content Placeholder 2** to select the content placeholder. Then click **Title 1** to select the title placeholder—*Organization*. Finally, click **Picture 3** to select the picture on the slide.

Use the Selection pane to easily select each object.

8 With the picture selected and using the gridlines as a guide, drag the picture so the right edge of the picture aligns on the **right half of the horizontal ruler at 5 inches** and the bottom edge of the image aligns **on the lower half of the vertical ruler at 3 inches**.

Activity 5.02 | Adjusting Sharpness/Softness of a Picture

In this Activity, you will change the sharpness of a picture so the text on the slide will have greater emphasis. You will use *Presets*— built-in adjustments from a gallery, which enable you to apply one of five standard settings for sharpness.

1 ▶ Take a moment to study the descriptions of the picture adjustment commands, as described in the table in Figure 5.6.

Picture Adjustment Commands	
Command	**Description**
Remove Background	Automatically removes unwanted portions of the picture.
Corrections	Improves the brightness, contrast, or sharpness of the picture.
Color	Changes the color of the picture to improve quality or match document content.
Artistic Effects	Adds an artistic effect to a picture to make it look like a sketch or painting.
Compress Pictures	Compresses pictures in the document to reduce the document file size; also reduces the color format of the image.
Change Picture	Changes to a different picture, preserving the formatting and size of the current picture.
Reset Picture	Discards all formatting changes made to the picture.

Figure 5.6

2 ▶ On **Slide 3**, with the picture selected, on the **Picture Tools Format tab**, in the **Adjust group**, click **Corrections**, and then click **Picture Corrections Options**.

3 ▶ In the **Format Picture** pane, under **Picture Corrections**, under **Sharpen/Soften**, drag the **Sharpness** slider to the left and notice the fuzzy effect on the picture. Drag the **Sharpness** slider to the right and notice the sharpness of the picture.

4 ▶ Under **Sharpen/Soften**, above the slider, click the **Presets arrow** ⊞▾. Compare your screen with Figure 5.7.

Five presets of variable sharp or soft picture corrections display.

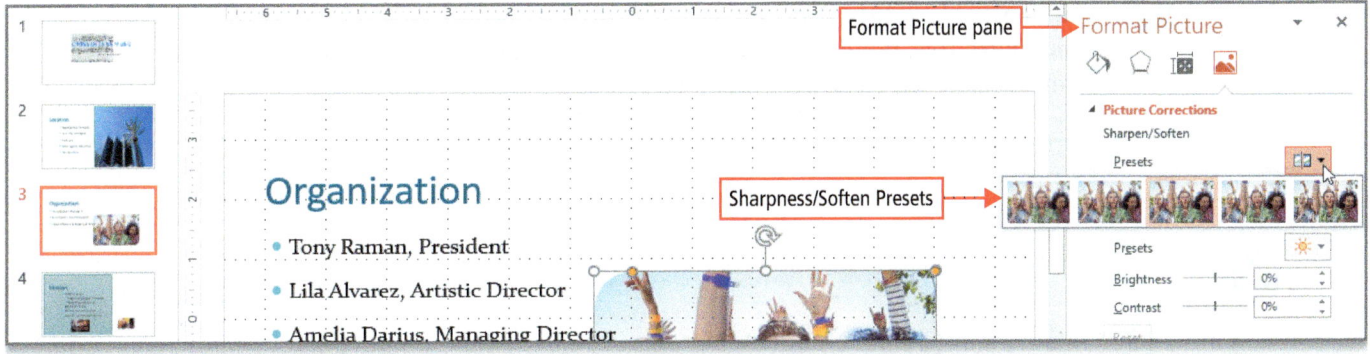

Figure 5.7

5 Click the last option—**Sharpen: 50%**, and then **Save** 🔲 the presentation.

The Sharpness slider is set at 50%.

Activity 5.03 | Changing the Brightness and Contrast of a Picture

In this Activity, you will change the brightness and contrast of a picture. To increase brightness, more light or white is added to the picture by selecting positive percentages. To decrease brightness, more darkness or black is added to the image by selecting negative percentages. Changing the contrast of a picture changes the amount of gray in the image.

1 Display **Slide 1,** and then click to select the picture. At the top of the **Format Picture** pane, click **Picture** 🖼️, and then under **Brightness/Contrast**, drag the **Brightness** slider to the left and then to the right. Notice how the picture brightness changes. In the **Brightness** box, type **-20** and then press ⏎.

2 Under **Brightness/Contrast**, drag the **Contrast** slider to the left and then to the right, and notice how the picture contrast changes. In the **Contrast** box, type **20** and then press ⏎. Compare your screen with Figure 5.8.

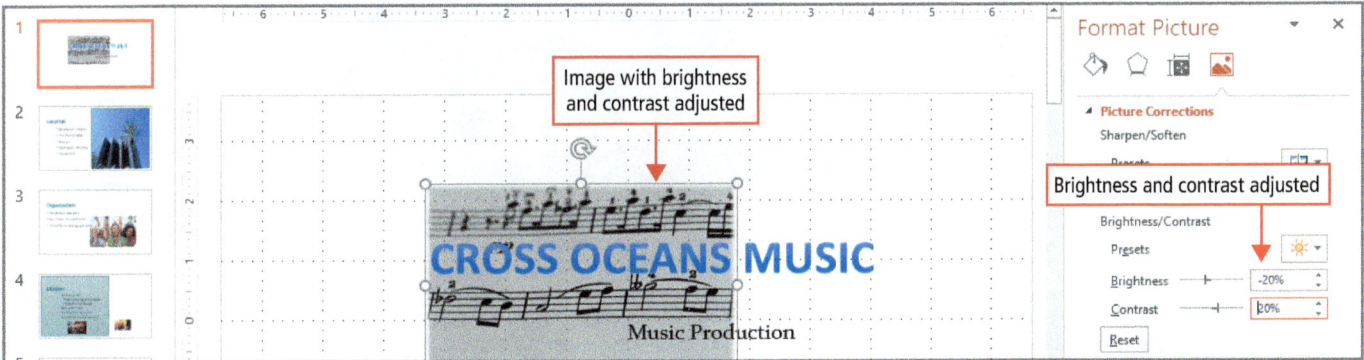

Figure 5.8

3 In the **Format Picture** pane, under **Brightness/Contrast**, click **Presets** ☀️▾. In the gallery, in the fourth row, point to the fourth option—**Brightness: +20% Contrast: +20%**. Compare your screen with Figure 5.9.

Figure 5.9

4 Click **Brightness: +20% Contrast: +20%**.

5 Display **Slide 2**, and then click to select the picture. At the top of the **Format Picture** pane, click **Picture** 🖼️, and then under **Picture Corrections**, set the **Sharpness** to **50%**. **Save** 💾 your presentation and then compare your screen with Figure 5.10.

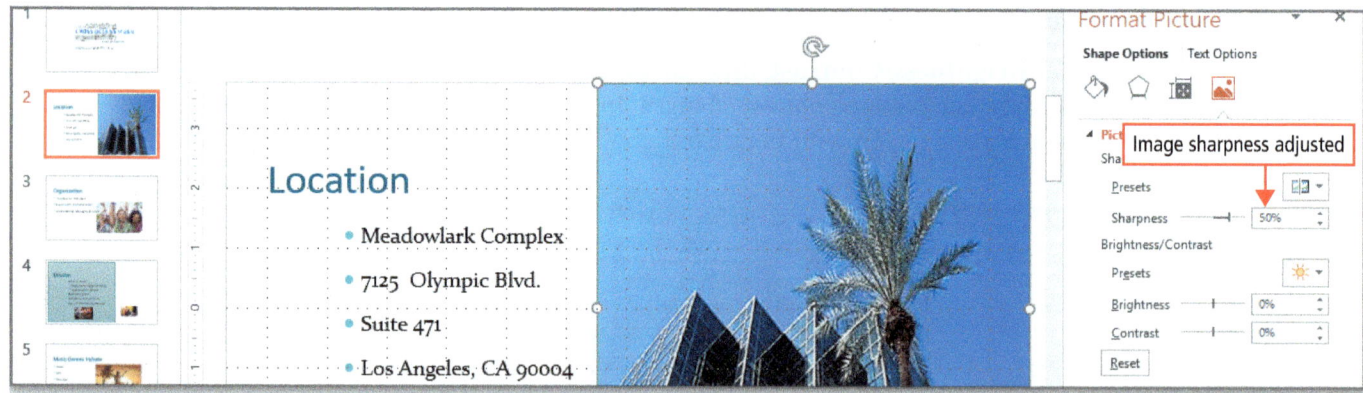

Figure 5.10

<table>
<tr><td>**Objective 2**</td><td>**Add a Border to a Picture**</td></tr>
</table>

GO! Learn How
Video P5-2

You can add a frame—referred to as a **border**—around a picture. You can edit the border color, adjust the **line weight**—the thickness of the line measured in points—and choose how the line displays by using a **line style**, such as a solid line, dots, or dashes.

Activity 5.04 | Adding a Border to a Picture

3.3.2

In this Activity, you will add borders to pictures and then customize those borders by changing the color, line weight, and line style. Borders help define images on a slide.

1 Display **Slide 4**, and then on the right, click the picture of the **guitar player**. In the **Format Picture** pane, click **Size & Properties** 🖼. If necessary, click **Position** to expand the list of commands. In the **Horizontal position** box, type **9.7** and in the **Vertical position** box, type **5.5** and then press Enter.

2 With the picture still selected, on the **Picture Tools Format tab**, in the **Picture Styles group**, click **Picture Border**, and then click in the fifth column, the first color. Click **Picture Border**, point to **Weight**, and then click **2 1/4 pt**. Click **Picture Border**, point to **Dashes**, and then click **Round Dot**—the second style. Click a blank area of the slide to deselect the picture, and then compare your screen with Figure 5.11.

The picture displays with a blue dotted border.

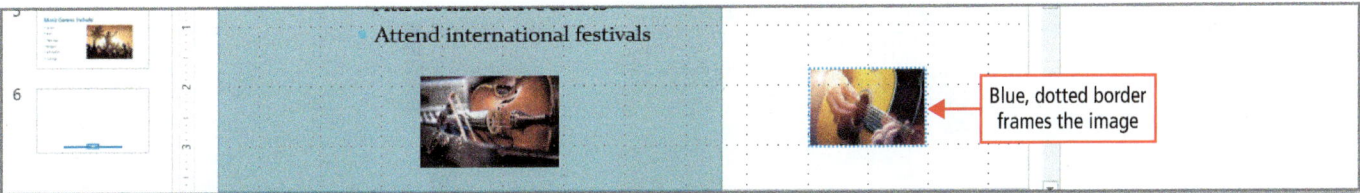

Blue, dotted border frames the image

Figure 5.11

MORE KNOWLEDGE   **Removing a Picture Border**

To remove the border on a picture, click to select the picture. On Picture Tools Format tab, in the Picture Styles group, click Picture Border, and then click No Outline.

---

3 On the left, click the picture of the **violin.** In the **Format Picture** pane, click **Size and Properties** 🖼. In the **Horizontal position** box, type **9.7** and in the **Vertical position** box, type **3** and then press Enter.

4 With the **violin** picture selected, in the **Format Picture** pane, click **Fill & Line** 🖌. If necessary, click **Line** to expand the list of commands. Under **Line**, select **Solid line**. Click the **Color** arrow 🎨, and then under **Standard Colors**, click the fourth color—**Yellow**. Set the **Width** to **4.5** pt and then press Enter. Click a blank area of the slide to deselect the picture.

5 On the **Insert tab**, in the **Images group**, click **Pictures**. From your files downloaded with this project, insert the picture **p05A_Drums**. If necessary, close the Design Ideas pane. In the **Format Picture** pane, click **Size & Properties** 🖼. Under **Size**, set the **Height** to **1.6** and then press Enter.

The picture is sized proportionately.

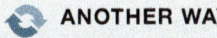 **ANOTHER WAY**   To size a picture proportionately, select the picture, and then drag a corner diagonally to the desired height or width.

---

6 Set the **Horizontal position** to **9.7** and set the **Vertical position** to **0.5** and then press Enter.

7 With the **drums** picture selected, on the **Picture Tools Format tab**, in the **Picture Styles group**, click **Picture Border**, and then under **Theme Colors**, click in the fifth column, the last color.

8 In the **Format Picture** pane, click **Fill & Line** ⬗. Under **Line**, set the **Width** to **9** Scroll down if necessary, click the **Join type arrow**, and then click **Miter**. Compare your screen with Figure 5.12.

A *mitered* border has corners that are square. The default border join has rounded corners.

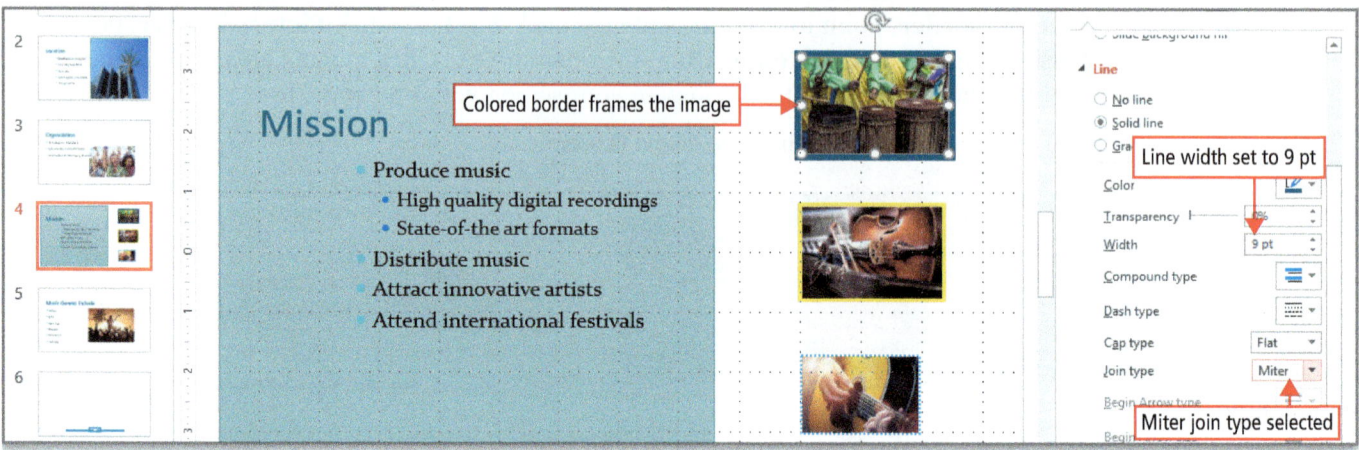

Figure 5.12

9 **Close** ☒ the **Format Picture** pane. With the bordered picture of the **drums** selected, on the **Picture Tools Format tab**, in the **Picture Styles group**, click **Picture Effects**, point to **Reflection**, and then under **Reflection Variations**, click the first variation—**Tight Reflection: Touching**. Click a blank area of the slide to deselect the picture, and then compare your screen with Figure 5.13.

The corners of the border are mitered borders, and a reflection displays below the picture.

Figure 5.13

10 Click the picture of the **drums**, hold down Shift, and then click the other two pictures to select them. Release Shift. On the **Picture Tools Format tab**, in the **Arrange group**, click **Align** ⬚, and then click **Align Center**. Click a blank area of the slide to deselect the pictures, and then compare your screen with Figure 5.14.

🔄 **ANOTHER WAY**   Click and drag to select the three images.

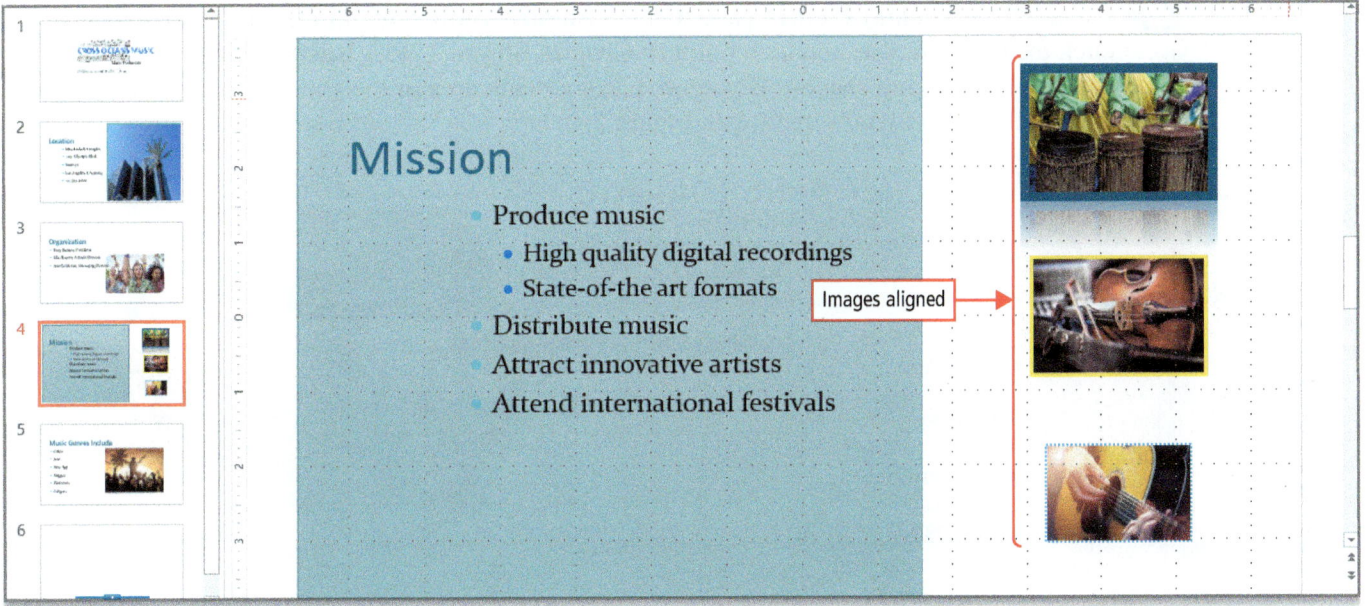

Figure 5.14

11 Display **Slide 5**, and then select the picture. On the **Picture Tools Format tab**, in the **Picture Styles group**, click **Picture Effects**. Point to **Glow**, and then under **Glow Variations**, in the fourth row, click the fifth effect. Compare your screen with Figure 5.15.

The Glow picture effect adds a soft border to the image.

Figure 5.15

12 Save  your presentation.

Objective 3 **Change the Shape of a Picture**

GO! Learn How
Video P5-3

You can change the shape of a picture using the Crop to shape command. You can change the outline shape of an image, with or without a border.

Activity 5.05 | Changing the Shape of a Picture

MOS
3.3.1

In this Activity, you will change a picture on your slide to a shape to make it stand out.

1 On **Slide 5**, right-click the picture, and then click **Size and Position** . Set the **Horizontal position** to **7.1** and set the **Vertical position** to **1.8**.

⬜ **MAC TIP** control + click the picture.

2 ▶ **Close** ⊠ the **Format Picture** pane. On the **Picture Tools Format tab**, in the **Size group**, click the **Crop arrow**, and then point to **Crop to Shape**. Under **Basic Shapes**, in the first row, click the eighth shape—**Hexagon**. Click a blank area of the slide to deselect the picture, and then compare your screen with Figure 5.16.

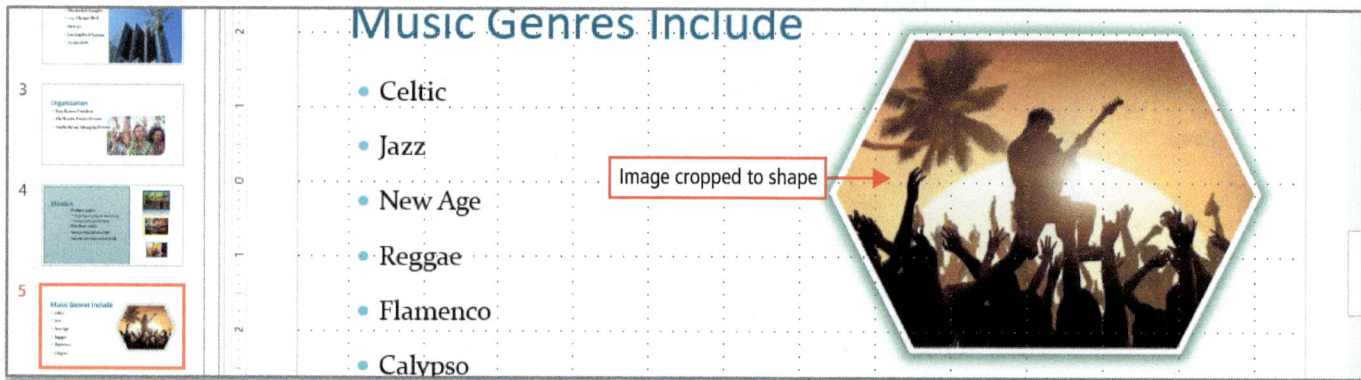

Figure 5.16

3 ▶ On the **View tab**, in the **Show group**, clear the **Gridlines** check box, and then **Save** 🖫 your presentation.

Objective 4	Add a Picture to a WordArt Object and Merge Shapes

GO! Learn How
Video P5-4

A WordArt object can have a picture fill to add interest to a presentation. After adding the WordArt text, insert a picture fill that complements the WordArt message.

Activity 5.06 │ **Adding a WordArt Object with a Picture Background Fill**

In this Activity, you will add a WordArt object as the Cross Oceans logo. Then you will insert a picture as a fill for the WordArt object.

1 ▶ Display **Slide 6**. On the **Insert tab**, in the **Text group**, click **WordArt**. In the third row, click the third style, and then compare your screen with Figure 5.17.

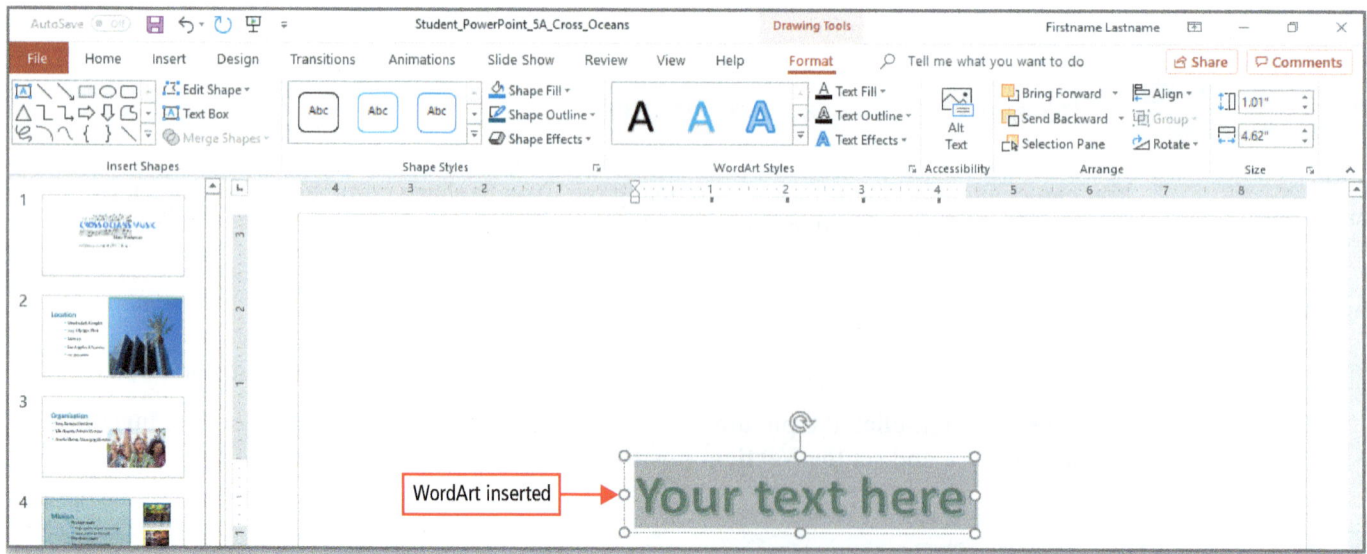

Figure 5.17

2 In the **WordArt** object, with the text selected, type **Cross Oceans** press Enter, and then type **Music** on the second line.

3 On the **Drawing Tools Format tab**, in the **Arrange group**, click **Align** 🔳, and then click **Align Middle**. Click a blank area of the slide to deselect the WordArt, and then compare your screen with Figure 5.18.

The WordArt is aligned horizontally in the middle of the slide.

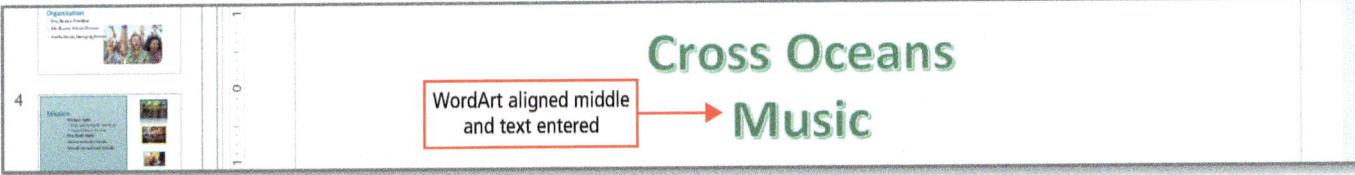

Figure 5.18

4 Click the WordArt to select it again. On the **Drawing Tools Format tab**, in the **Shape Styles group**, click **Shape Fill**, and then click **Picture**. From your files downloaded with this project, insert the picture **p05A_Island**. Compare your screen with Figure 5.19.

Figure 5.19

5 With the WordArt still selected, on the **Picture Tools Format tab**, in the **Adjust group**, click **Color**. Under **Recolor**, in the first row, click the fourth color—**Washout**.

6 Right-click the **WordArt**, and then click **Format Picture**. In the **Format Picture** pane, click **Size & Properties** 🔳. Under **Size**, select the **Lock aspect ratio** check box, set the **Height** to **2.5** and then press Enter. Compare your screen with Figure 5.20.

When *Lock aspect ratio* is selected, you can change one dimension (height or width) of an object, and the other dimension will automatically adjust to maintain the proportion.

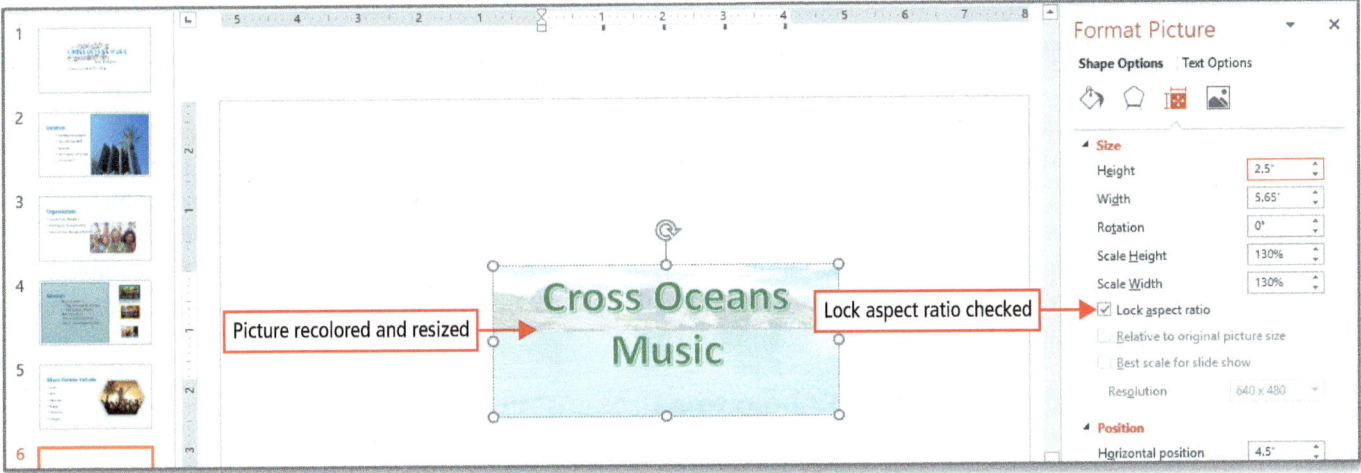

Figure 5.20

7 On the **Picture Tools Format tab**, in the **Arrange group**, click **Align** ▣, and then click **Align Center**. Click in a blank area of the slide to deselect the WordArt.

8 **Save** ▣ your presentation.

Activity 5.07 | Merging Shapes

3.5.3

In this Activity, you will merge three separate shapes into one contiguous shape to create a new shape, move the shape to a new location, and then position the merged shape on the slide.

1 On **Slide 6**, hold down Ctrl and click to select the three blue shapes—a line, a box, and a line.

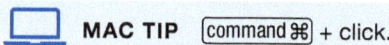

🖥 **MAC TIP** command ⌘ + click.

2 On the **Drawing Tools Format tab**, in the **Insert Shapes group**, click **Merge Shapes**, and then click **Union**.

The three shapes merge into one shape.

3 In the **Format Shape** pane, if necessary, click **Size & Properties** ▣. Under **Position**, in the **Horizontal position** box, type **3** and in the **Vertical position** box, type **6** and then press Enter. **Close** ✕ the **Format Shape** pane, and then compare your screen with Figure 5.21.

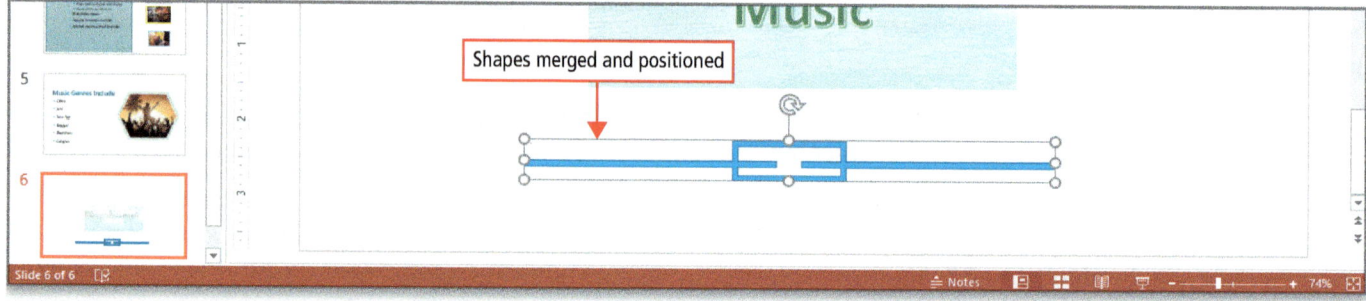

Figure 5.21

4 **Save** ▣ your presentation.

Objective 5 | Enhance a Presentation with Audio and Video

GO! Learn How
Video P5-5

You can add audio and video to enhance a presentation. You can set a file to play one time and then stop, or you can set a file to *loop*—play repeatedly from start to finish until it is stopped manually. A *track*—or song—from a CD can play during a slide show. You can *embed* an audio or video file in a presentation. When you save the presentation, the embedded audio or video file becomes part of the presentation file. When you *link* a file, the audio or video file is saved separately from the presentation. Be sure to obtain permission to link or embed audio and video to a presentation to avoid violating any copyrights.

Activity 5.08 | Adding an Embedded Audio to a Presentation

3.5.1

In this Activity, you will add audio to a presentation by embedding audio files. This will enable the audience to hear the different genres of music presented.

1 ▶ Display **Slide 5**. On the **Insert tab**, in the **Media group**, click **Audio**, and then compare your screen with Figure 5.22.

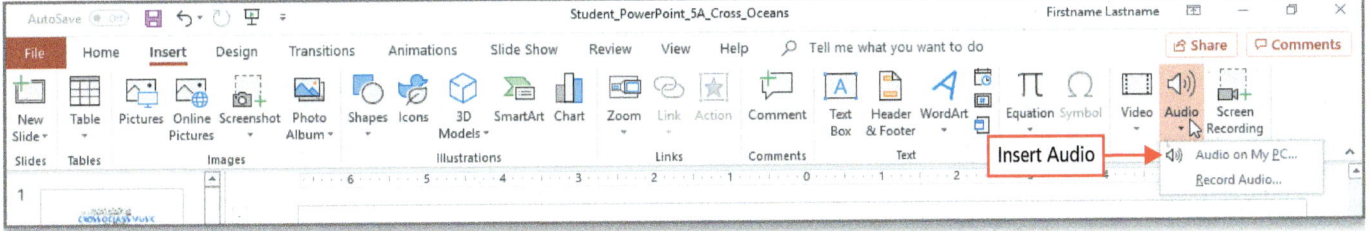

Figure 5.22

2 ▶ Take a moment to study the options available for inserting audio into a presentation, as shown in the table in Figure 5.23.

Sound Options	
Screen Element	**Description**
Audio on My PC	Enables you to insert audio clips such as music, narration, or audio bites from your computer or other computers to which you are connected. Compatible audio file formats include *.mid, .midi, .mp3*, and *.wav*.
Record Audio	Enables you to insert audio by recording the audio through a microphone attached to your computer and then naming and inserting the recorded audio.

Figure 5.23

3 ▶ Click **Audio on My PC**.

💻 **MAC TIP**   Click Audio from file.

4 ▶ In the **Insert Audio** dialog box, click the **Audio Files arrow** to display the audio files supported by PowerPoint, and then compare your screen with Figure 5.24.

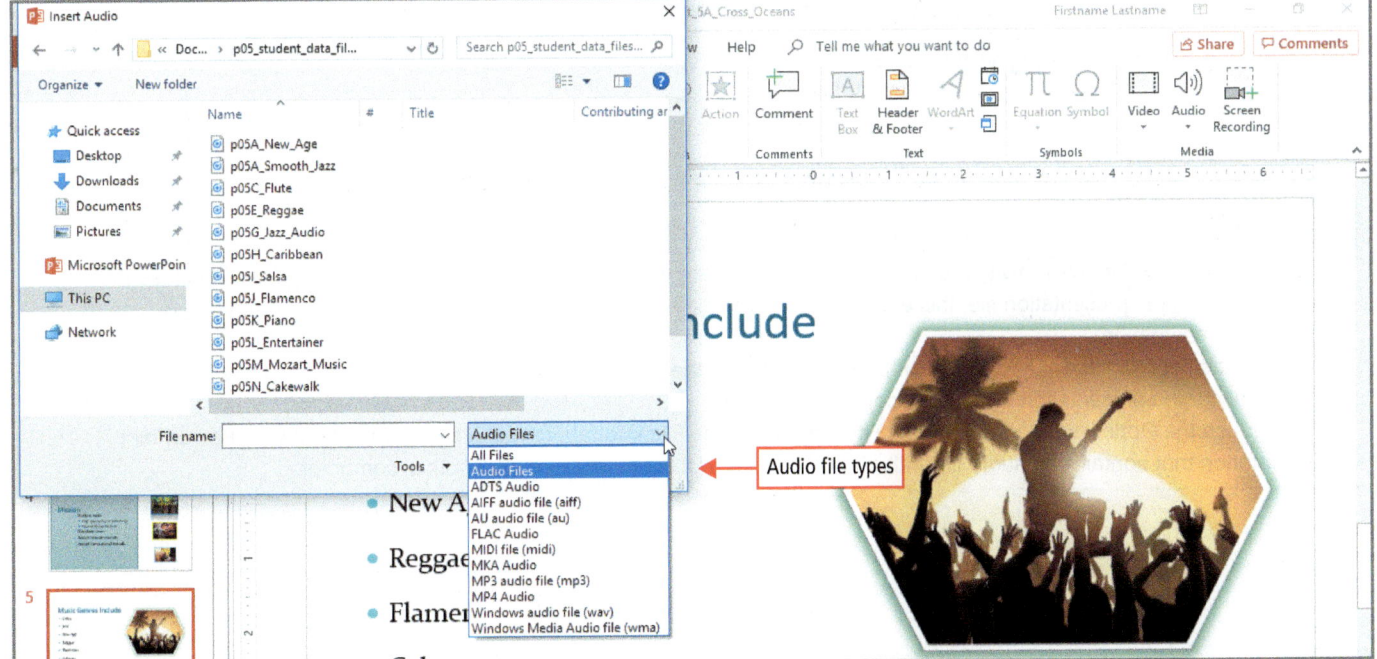

Figure 5.24

5 Take a moment to study the description of the audio file formats supported in PowerPoint, as shown in the table in Figure 5.25.

Audio File Formats Supported in PowerPoint 2019			
File Format	**Extension**	**Description**	**Mac Compatible**
Audio Interchange File Format (AIFF)	.aiff	A legacy uncompressed audio format developed by Apple.	Yes
Audio file (AU)	.au	A legacy audio format developed by Sun Microsystems.	Yes
Musical Instrument Digital Interface (MIDI)	.mid or .midi	A format that contains instructions, not actual sounds. MIDI files are very compact.	No
MPEG-1 or MPEG-2 Audio Layer III (MP3)	.MP3	A common compressed format of digital audio. MP3 files maintain high quality while reducing file size.	Yes
Advanced Audio Coding (MPEG-4)	.m4a, .mp4	A compressed, digital video and audio format.	Yes
Waveform Audio File Format	.wav	An uncompressed audio format found on Windows systems.	Yes
Windows Media Audio file	.wma	A compressed audio format found on Windows systems.	No

Figure 5.25

6 From your files for this project, insert the audio file **p05A_Smooth_Jazz**.

A speaker icon displays on the screen with Playback controls—Play/Pause, Move Back, Move Forward, Time, Mute/Unmute.

7 Display **Slide 1**. On the **Insert tab**, in the **Media group**, click **Audio**. Click **Audio on My PC**. From your project files, insert **p05A_New_Age**.

8 Save 🖫 your presentation.

MORE KNOWLEDGE   **Embedded Sounds versus Linked Sounds**

The audio files used in this Activity are MP3 files. These files are embedded in the PowerPoint presentation. Because the audio is stored within the presentation file, this ensures that the audio will play from any audio-enabled computer that you use to show the presentation.

If your presentation includes linked files, you must copy both the presentation file and the linked files to the same folder if you want to show the presentation on another computer.

You can use the Optimized Media Compatibility feature, on the File Info tab, to make it easier to share your PowerPoint presentation that contains an audio file with others or to show this presentation on another computer.

Activity 5.09 | Configuring Audio Playback Options

4.5.3

In this Activity, you will configure playback options, which determine how the audio will play in the presentation, such as the volume of the audio, and whether it will start automatically or on mouse click.

1 Display **Slide 5**. Click the **Audio** icon 🔊, and then on the **Audio Tools Playback tab**, in the **Audio Options group**, select the **Hide During Show** check box. Click **Volume**, and then click **Medium**. In the **Start** box, click the **arrow**, and then click **Automatically**. Compare your screen with Figure 5.26.

The Hide During Show option hides the audio icon during the slide show.

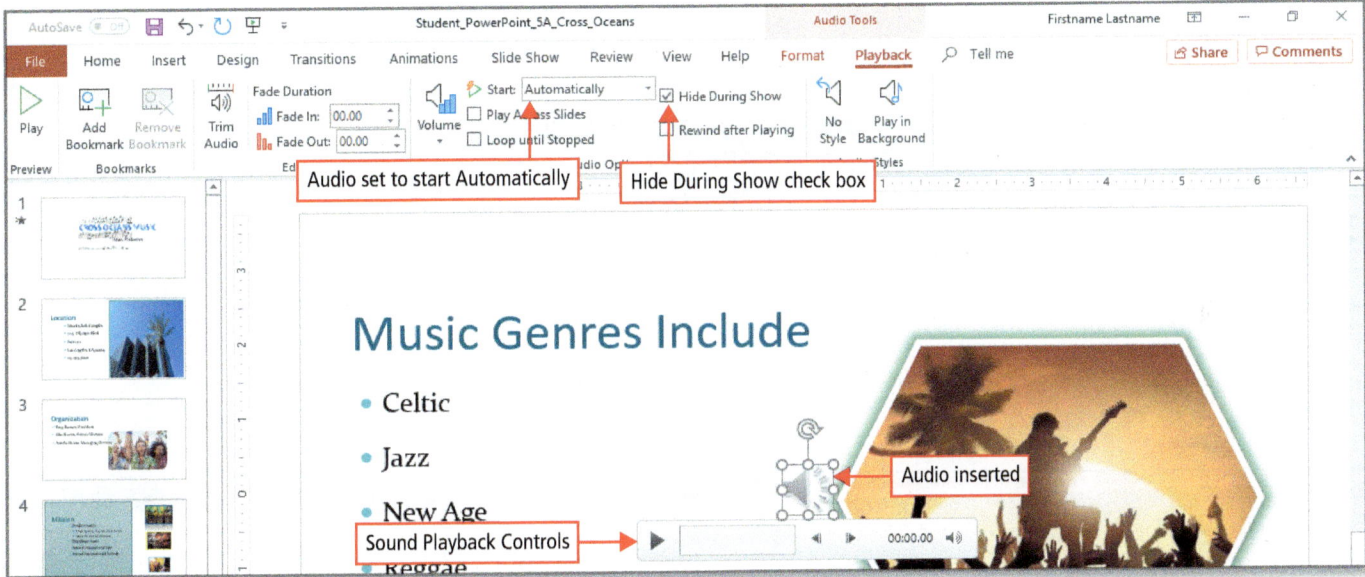

Figure 5.26

MORE KNOWLEDGE **Play an Audio File for the Duration of Your Slide Show**

You can play a song for the duration of your PowerPoint presentation slide show. To do so, on the Audio Tools Playback tab, in the Audio Options group, select the Play Across Slides check box.

---

2 On the **Slide Show tab**, in the **Start Slide Show group**, click **From Current Slide**.

The audio starts automatically when the slide displays. The audio plays one time and then stops.

3 Press ⎋Esc to return to **Normal** view.

4 Display **Slide 1**.

5 In the middle of the slide, right-click the selected **Audio icon** 📢 , and then click **Size and Position** 🔁. If necessary, click **Position** to expand the list of commands. In the **Horizontal position** box, type **9** and in the **Vertical position** box, type **6** and then press Enter. Compare your screen with Figure 5.27.

> This action positions the audio icon away from the main content of the slide so that the icon is easier for the presenter to locate.

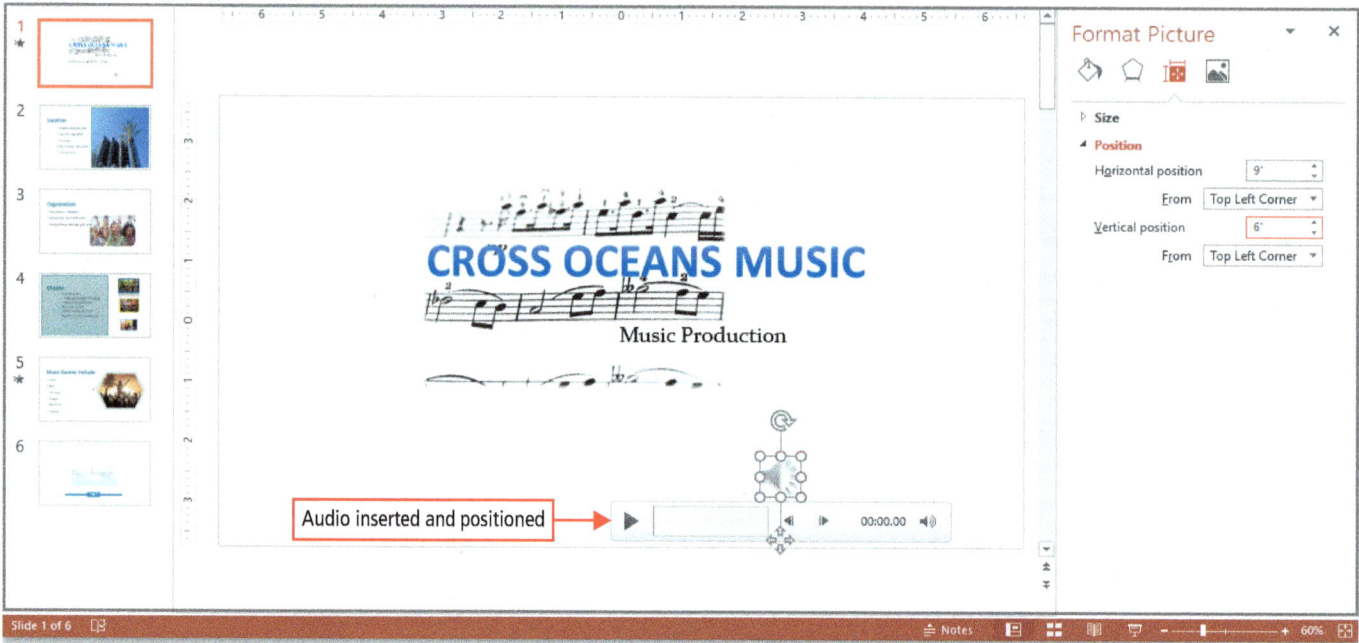

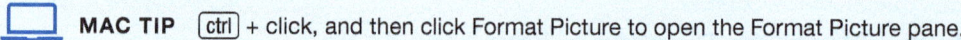

Figure 5.27

6 Close ✕ the **Format Picture** pane.

💻 **MAC TIP** Ctrl + click, and then click Format Picture to open the Format Picture pane.

---

7 On the **Audio Tools Playback tab**, in the **Audio Options group**, to the right of **Start**, if necessary, click **When Clicked On**. On the slide, on the **Sound Playback Controls**, click **Play** ▶ to listen to the audio clip.

8 On the **Audio Tools Playback tab**, in the **Audio Options group**, select the **Hide During Show** check box.

> The audio playback controls will be hidden during the slide show.

9 On the **Slide Show tab**, in the **Start Slide Show group**, click **From Beginning**. Click the slide, and notice that no audio plays; rather the next slide displays.

10 Press Esc to return to **Normal** view, and then display **Slide 1**, and then **Save** 💾 your presentation.

Activity 5.10 | Setting a Trigger for an Embedded Audio in a Presentation

4.5.3

In this Activity, you will set a *trigger*—a portion of text, a graphic, or a picture that, when clicked, causes the audio or video to play. You will use the *Animation Pane* to help you locate the trigger.

MAC TIP The trigger feature is not available in the Mac version of PowerPoint. Skip to Activity 5.11.

1▶ On **Slide 1**, if necessary, click to select the **Audio** icon 🔊 .

2▶ On the **Animations tab**, in the **Advanced Animation group**, click **Animation Pane** to display the **Animation Pane**.

3▶ On the **Animations tab**, in the **Advanced Animation group**, click **Trigger**, and then point to **On Click of**. Compare your screen with Figure 5.28.

The options to select for the trigger display—Picture 8, Title 1, Subtitle 2 or p05A_New_Age.

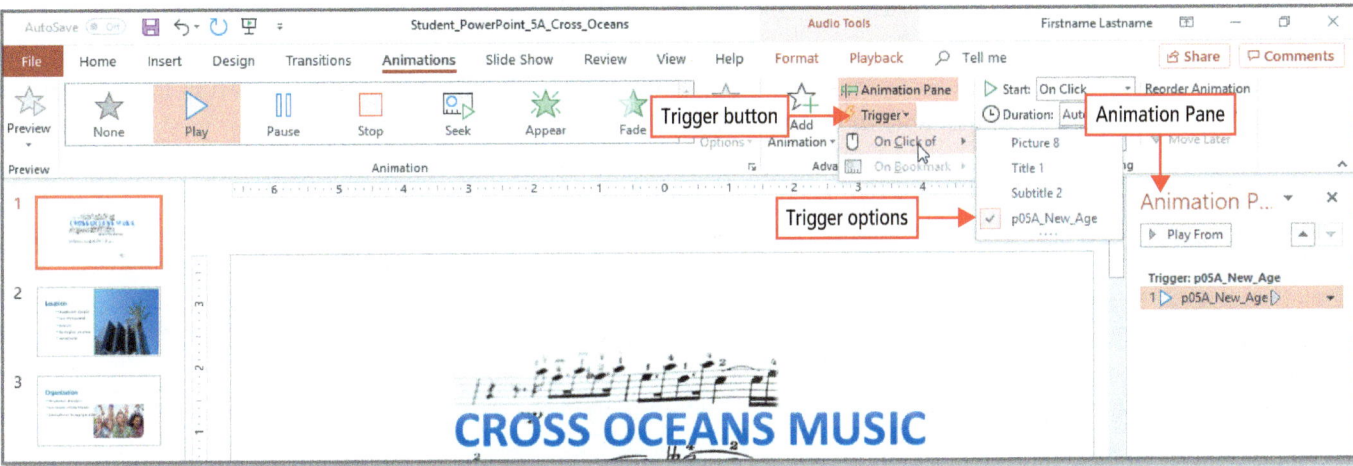

Figure 5.28

4▶ Click **Title 1**. Compare your screen with Figure 5.29.

The Animation Pane identifies the trigger that will cause the audio to play when clicked.

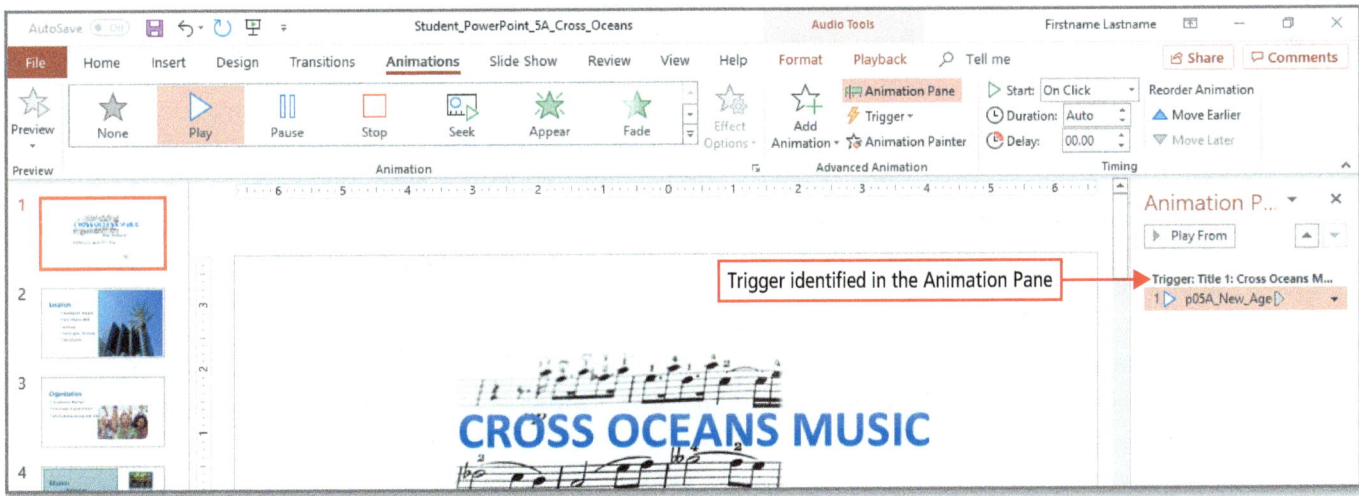

Figure 5.29

5▶ **Close** ✕ the **Animation Pane**.

6▶ On the **Slide Show tab**, in the **Start Slide Show group**, click **From Current Slide**. Point to the title text *Cross Oceans Music* to display the 👆 pointer, and then click to play the audio. Press [Esc] to return to **Normal** view.

7▶ **Save** 💾 your presentation.

Activity 5.11 | Adding a Linked Video to a Presentation

MOS
4.5.1

In this Activity, you will link a video to your presentation. A presentation with a linked video is smaller in file size than a presentation with an embedded video because the video and presentation remain as two separate files. To prevent possible problems with broken links, it is good practice to copy the video into the same folder as your presentation and then link to it there. Both the video file and the presentation file must be available when presenting your slide show.

1 From the taskbar, open **File Explorer**. Navigate to your files downloaded with this project, locate **p05_Music_Video**, copy the video file, and then paste the file into your **PowerPoint Chapter 5** folder. **Close** ✕ **File Explorer** and return to your PowerPoint presentation.

2 Take a moment to study the description of the video file formats supported in PowerPoint, as shown in the table in Figure 5.30.

Video File Formats Supported in PowerPoint 2019			
File Format	**Extension**	**Description**	**Mac Compatible**
Windows Media file— Advanced Systems Format (ASF)	.asf	A Microsoft container for streaming video and audio files. ASF can also contain Digital Rights Management information—a form of copyright protection.	No
Windows Video file— Audio Video Interleaved (AVI)	.avi	A legacy container that combines audio and video into a single file. AVI has been replaced by WMV as the default format on Windows computers.	Maybe, depends on coding format.
MP4 Video file (MP4)	.mp4, .m4v, .mov	A container format that can store video, audio, and subtitle data.	Yes
Movie file—Moving Pictures Experts Group (MPEG)	.mpg or .mpeg	A common compressed video and audio format.	Yes
Adobe Flash Media— Small Web Format (SWF)	.swf	A small animated file that can run in a browser.	No
Windows Media Video file	.wmv	A compressed video format found on Windows systems. The default format on Windows computers.	No

Figure 5.30

3 ▸ Display **Slide 6**. On the **Insert tab**, in the **Media group**, click **Video**, and then click **Video on My PC**. Navigate to your **PowerPoint Chapter 5** folder, and then click **p05_Music_Video** one time. In the lower right corner of the **Insert Video** dialog box, click the **Insert arrow**. Compare your screen with Figure 5.31.

The two options on the Insert list are Insert and Link to File.

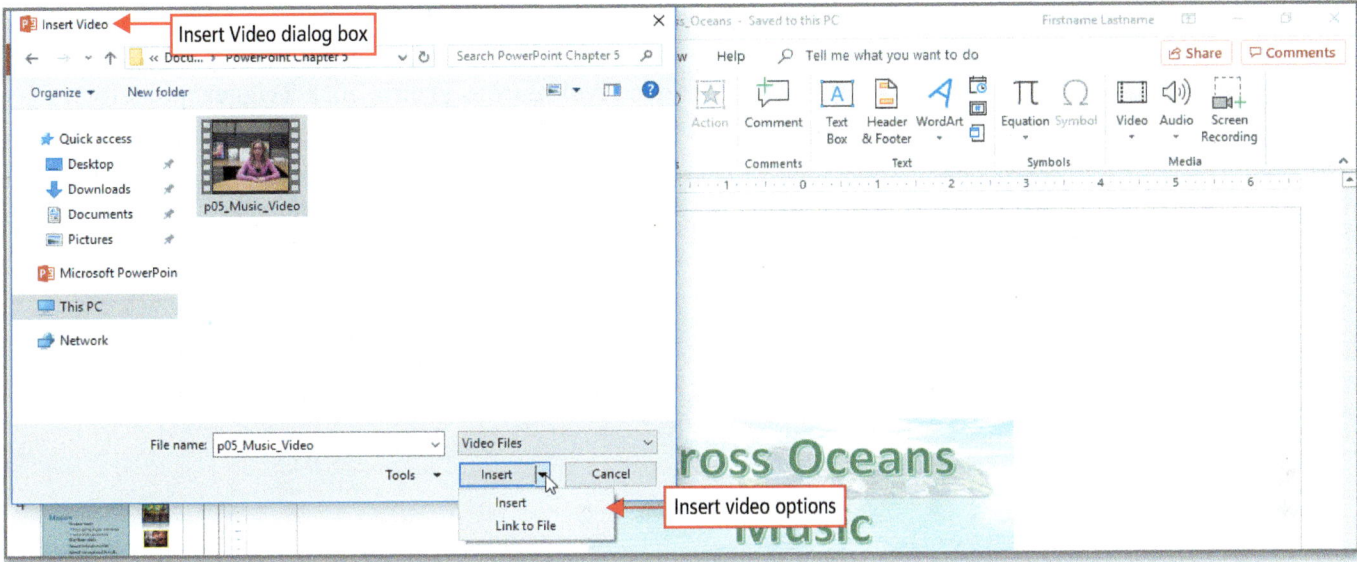

Figure 5.31

4 ▸ Click **Link to File**. With the video selected, on the **Video Tools Format tab**, in the **Size group**, change the **Video Height** to **1.5"**.

🖥 **MAC TIP** Click Movie from File. Locate p05_Music_Video. In the lower left corner of the Choose a Movie dialog box, click Options. Select the Link to file check box, and then click Insert.

5 ▸ Point to the video image in the center of the slide, right-click, and then click **Size and Position** 📐 to display the **Format Video** pane. If necessary, click **Position** to expand the list of commands. In the **Horizontal position** box, type **5.5** and in the **Vertical position** box, type **0.5** and then press Enter. Compare your screen with Figure 5.32.

🖥 **MAC TIP** ctrl + click, and then click Format Video.

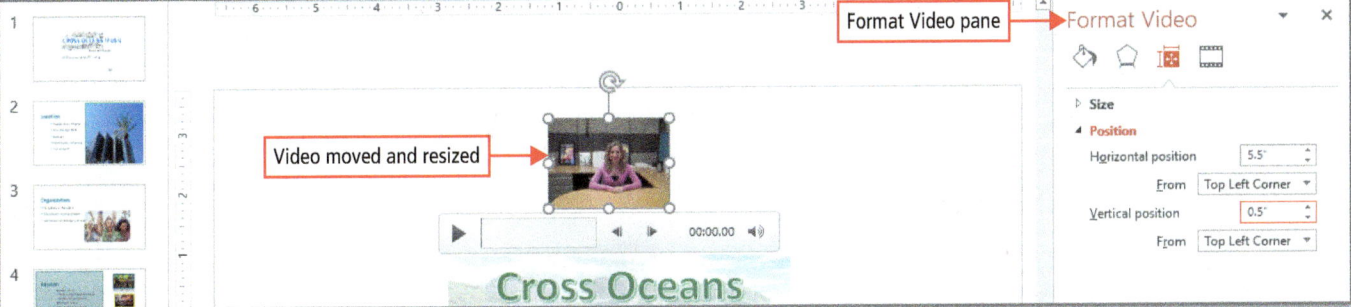

Figure 5.32

6 ▸ **Close** ✕ the **Format Video** pane. **Save** 💾 your presentation.

Activity 5.12 | Changing the Trigger for a Linked Video in a Presentation

MOS
4.5.3

In this Activity, you will use the Animation Pane to change the trigger that will play the video file from the video image to the WordArt shape. You will also set the video to play in full screen.

1 On **Slide 6**, if necessary, click to select the video image.

💻 **MAC TIP** The Mac version of PowerPoint does not include triggers. Skip to Step 4.

2 On the **Animations tab**, in the **Advanced Animations group**, click **Trigger**, point to **On Click of** and then compare your screen with Figure 5.33.

Three options to select for the trigger display— Freeform: Shape 6, Rectangle 1, and p05_Music_Video. Rectangle represents the WordArt shape. The numbers after Freeform and Rectangle may vary.

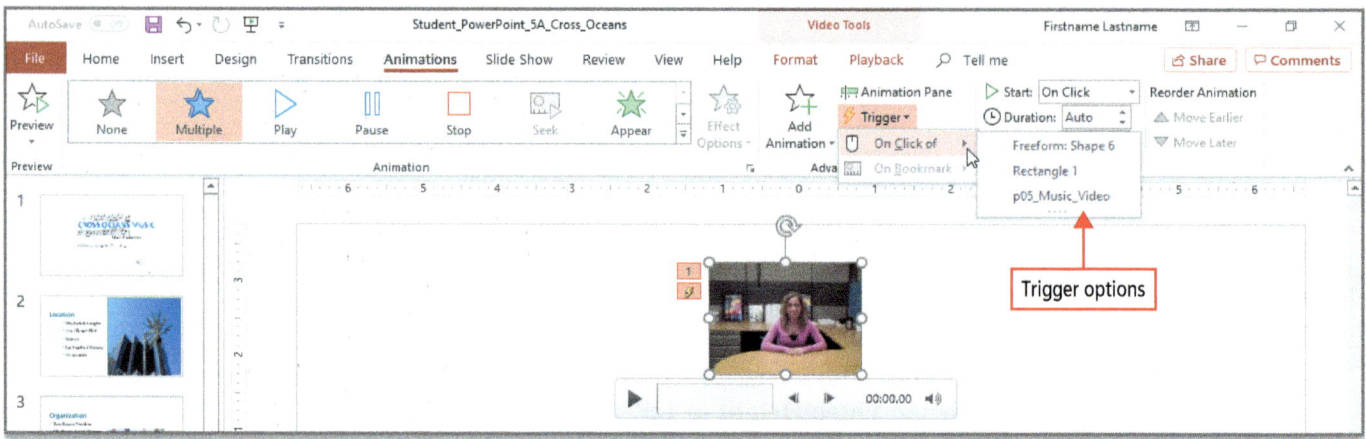

Figure 5.33

3 Click **Rectangle** 1 (the number after Rectangle may vary).

4 On the **Video Tools Playback tab**, in the **Video Options group**, select the **Hide While Not Playing** check box, and then select the **Play Full Screen** check box. Compare your screen with Figure 5.34.

The Hide While Not Playing option hides the video on the slide until you click the trigger to play it.

💻 **MAC TIP** Click Hide During Show.

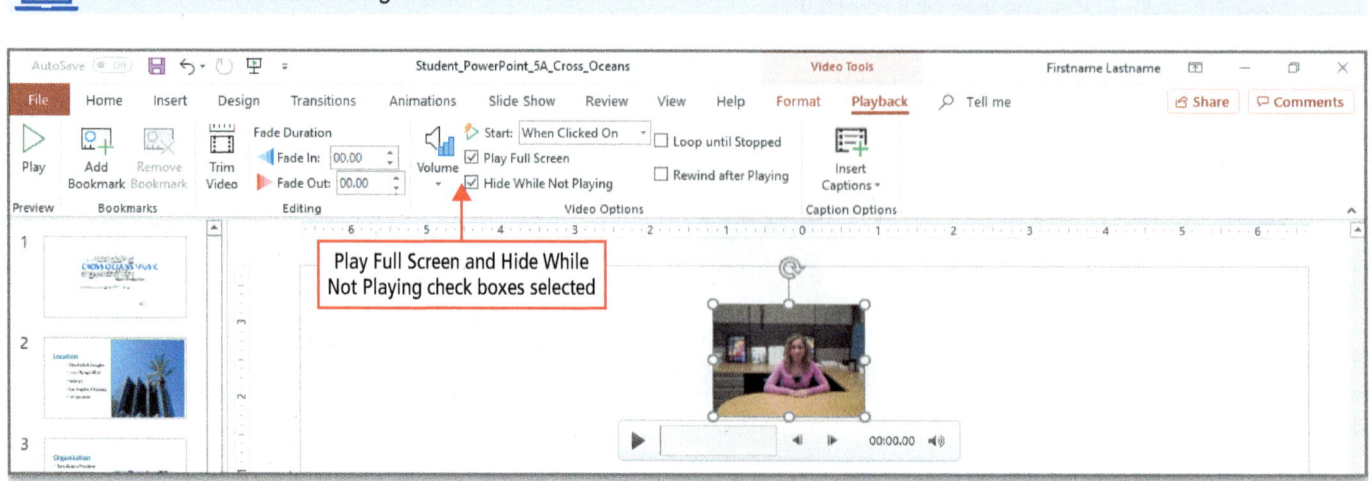

Figure 5.34

5 On the **Slide Show tab**, in the **Start Slide Show group**, click **From Beginning** to view the entire presentation. Click the trigger—the pointer that displays when you point to the title text—on **Slide 1** to hear the audio. When **Slide 6** displays, click the WordArt—where the trigger is now—to view the video. Press Esc to return to Normal view.

6 Open **File Explorer**, and then display the contents of your **PowerPoint Chapter 5** folder. If necessary, on the **View tab**, in the **Layout group**, click **Details**. Notice the size of the presentation file is larger than the size of the video file. Compare your screen with Figure 5.35.

Because the presentation file contains a link to the video file, the video file is not a part of the presentation file size. The video for this presentation is 1,173 KB and the presentation file is 2,263 KB.

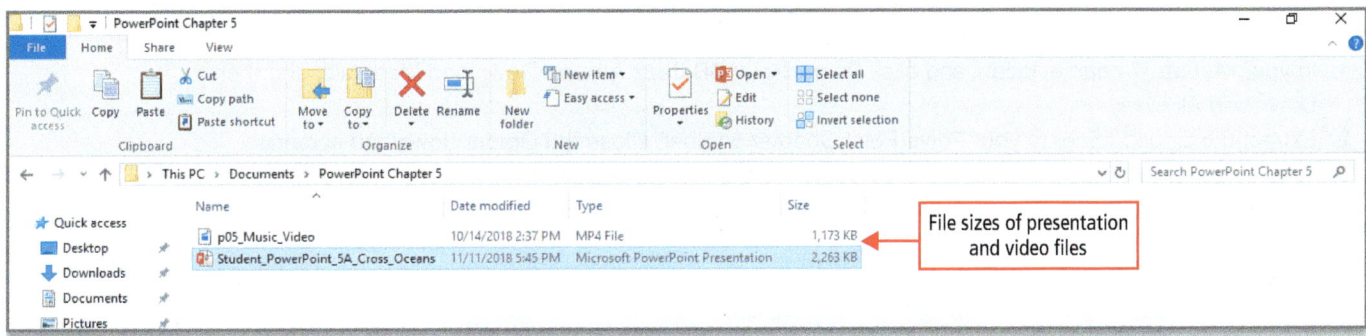

Figure 5.35

7 Close File Explorer.

8 Return to your PowerPoint presentation. On the **Insert tab**, in the **Text group**, click **Header & Footer** to display the **Header and Footer** dialog box. Click the **Notes and Handouts tab**. Under **Include on page**, select the **Date and time** check box, and then select **Fixed**. If necessary, select the **Page number** and **Footer** check boxes. In the **Footer** box, type **5A_Cross_Oceans** and then click **Apply to All**.

9 Display the document properties. As the **Tags**, type **mission, genres** and as the **Subject**, type your course name and section number. Be sure your name appears as author.

10 Close PowerPoint.

For Non-MyLab Submissions

Print or submit your presentation electronically as directed by your instructor.

11 In **MyLab IT**, in your **Course Materials**, locate and click the Grader Project **PowerPoint 5A Cross Oceans**. In **step 3**, under **Upload Completed Assignment**, click **Choose File**. In the **Open** dialog box, navigate to your **PowerPoint Chapter 5 folder**, and then click your **Student_PowerPoint_5A_Cross_Oceans** file one time to select it. In the lower right corner of the **Open** dialog box, click **Open**.

12 To submit your file to **MyLab IT** for grading, click **Upload**, wait a moment for a green **Success!** message, and then in **step 4**, click the blue **Submit for Grading** button. Click **Close Assignment** to return to your list of **Course Materials**.

You have completed Project 5A | END

Jazz Musicians Photo Album

Project Activities

In Activities 5.13 through 5.17, you will create a PowerPoint presentation to display business photos of jazz musicians promoted and recorded by Cross Oceans Music. You will insert photos, and select a layout for each slide using the PowerPoint Design Ideas pane. You will add alt text and captions to photos and crop images. Your completed presentation will look similar to Figure 5.36.

Project Files for MyLab IT Grader

1. In your **MyLab IT** course, locate and click **PowerPoint 5B Jazz Album**, Download Materials, and then Download All Files.
2. Extract the zipped folder to your PowerPoint Chapter 5 folder. Close the Grader download screens.
3. Take a moment to open the downloaded **PowerPoint_5B_Jazz_Album_Instructions**; note any recent updates to the book.

Project Results

GO! Project 5B
Where We're Going

Figure 5.36 Project 5B Jazz Album

For Non-MyLab Submissions

For Project 5B, you will need:
p05B_Jazz_Album
p05B_Jazz1
p05B_Jazz2
p05B_Jazz3
p05B_Jazz4
p05B_Jazz5
p05B_Jazz6

In your PowerPoint Chapter 5 folder, save your presentation as:
Lastname_Firstname_5B_Jazz_Album

After you have named and saved your presentation, on the next page, begin with Step 2.

Objective 6 | Use PowerPoint Designer

ALERT Because Office 365 is a cloud-based subscription service that receives continuous updates, you may encounter some variations in what appears on your screen and what is shown in this instruction. Microsoft Office 365 is fully installed on your PC or Mac; no internet access is necessary to create or edit documents. When you *are* connected to the internet, you will receive monthly upgrades and new features, so you always have the latest versions of Office apps as soon as they are available. Your subscription gives you continuous free access to the latest innovations and refinements.

GO! Learn How
Video P5-6

In the following Activity, you will create a PowerPoint presentation that consists of many photos. *PowerPoint Designer* is a tool that helps you format slides that contain images by suggesting several professionally designed layouts. Designer analyzes the inserted images to determine which layouts to show you.

Activity 5.13 | Using PowerPoint Designer

2.1.3

In this Activity, you will create a presentation to highlight some of the jazz musicians at Cross Oceans Music.

1 Navigate to your **PowerPoint Chapter 5 folder**, and then double-click the downloaded PowerPoint file that displays your name— **Student_PowerPoint_5B_Jazz_Album.** In your presentation, if necessary, at the top click **Enable Editing**.

2 In the Title placeholder type **Jazz Musicians** In the subtitle placeholder, type **Cross Oceans Music** Change the subtitle **Font Size** to **28**, apply **Bold** B . Compare your screen with Figure 5.37.

Figure 5.37

3 ▶ Insert a new **Title and Content** slide. On **Slide 2**, in the content placeholder, click **Pictures**. Navigate to the files downloaded with this project, click **p05B_Jazz1**, and then click **Insert**. If necessary, in the Design Ideas pane, click Turn on. Compare your screen with Figure 5.38.

> The Design Ideas pane opens.

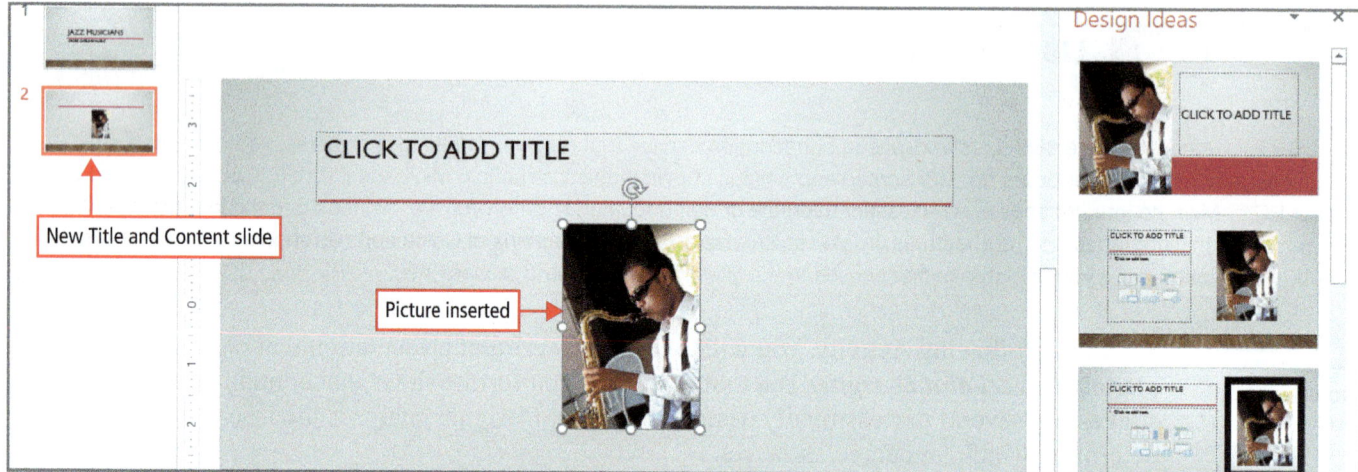

Figure 5.38

4 ▶ Click each idea to preview in the slide pane, and then click the idea layout that most closely matches Figure 5.39—the image on the left and title on the right. In the title placeholder, type **Tenor Saxophone** Compare your screen to Figure 5.39.

> Notice as you edit the slide, the Design pane changes until you have finished typing. The Designer then re-evaluates your slide and makes new suggestions based on your edits.

Figure 5.39

5 ▶ Insert a new **Title and Content** slide. On **Slide 3**, in the content placeholder, click **Pictures**. Navigate to files for this project, click **p05B_Jazz2**, and then click **Insert.** Select the design idea layout that most closely matches Figure 5.40—a full slide view of the image. Compare your screen with Figure 5.40.

Figure 5.40

6 ▶ Insert a new **Two Content** slide. On **Slide 4**, in the image placeholders, insert **p05B_Jazz3** on the left and **p05B_Jazz4** on the right. In the **Design Ideas** pane, click the design idea layout with the title placeholder on the left and two images on the right. In the title placeholder, type **Alto Saxophone Save** 🖫 your presentation and compare your screen with Figure 5.41.

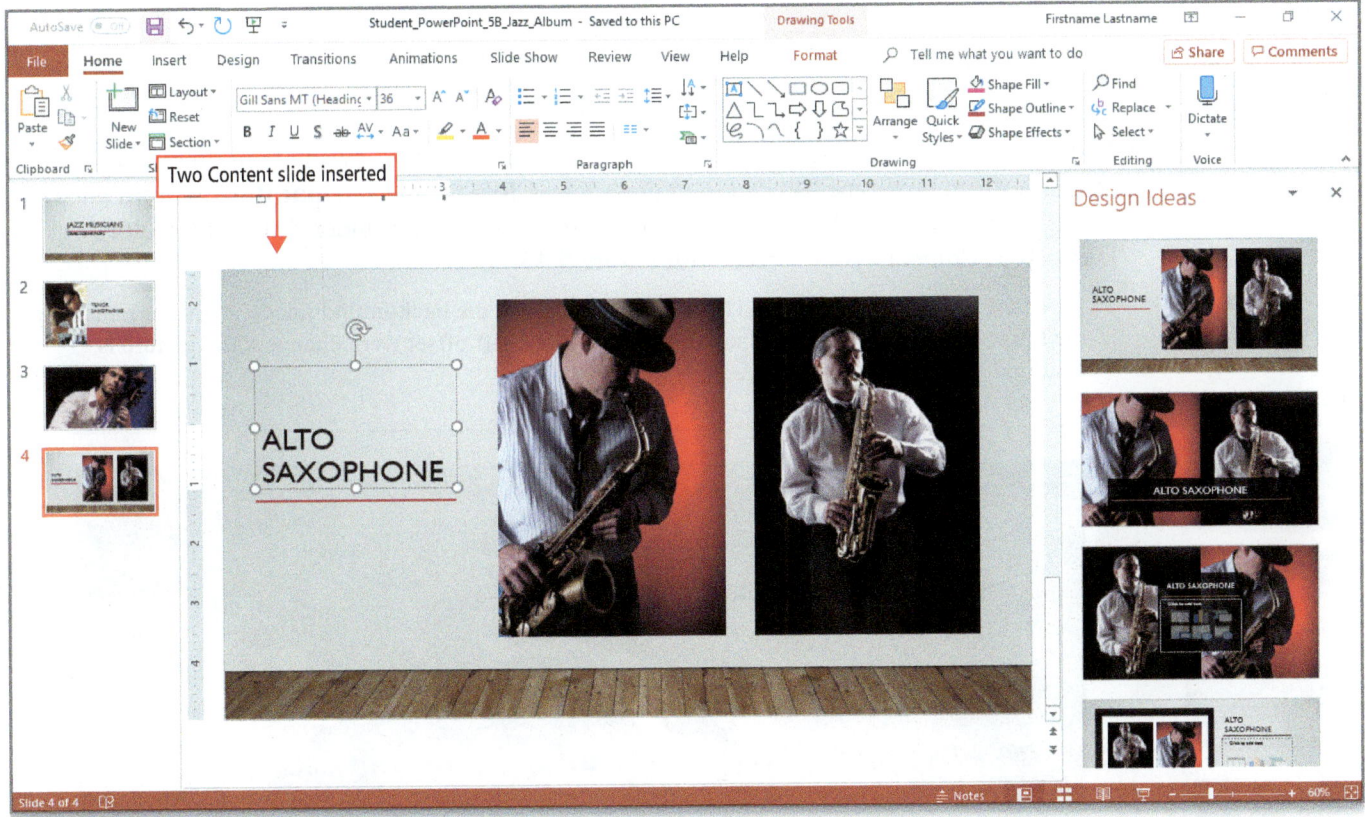

Figure 5.41

Activity 5.14 | Formatting a Slide Background with a Picture

2.2.2, 3.3.1

In this Activity, you will format a slide background with a picture and adjust the way the picture fits the slide.

1 ▶ Display **Slide 1**. **Close** ⊠ the **Design Ideas** pane. On the **Design tab**, click **Format Background**. In the **Format Background** pane, under **Fill**, click **Picture or texture fill**. Select the **Hide Background Graphics** check box.

2 Under **Insert picture from**, click **File**. From your project files, insert **p05B_Jazz5**. Compare your screen with Figure 5.42.

> The picture displays as the background for the title slide. The top of the picture is cut off.

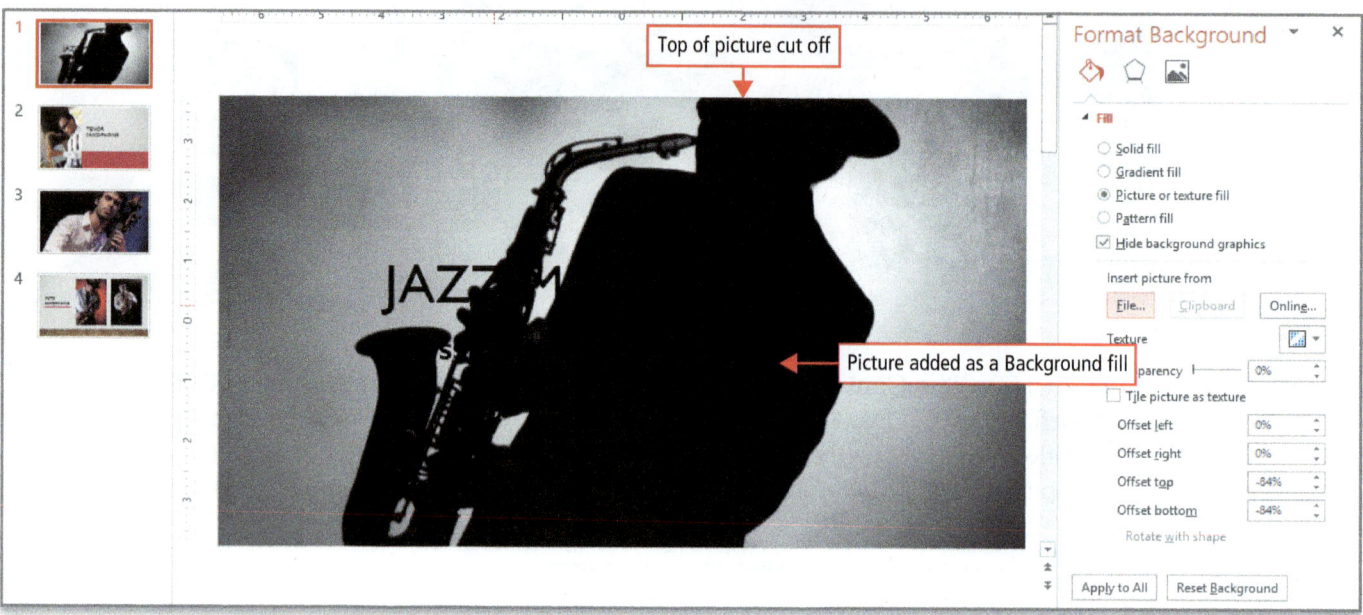

Figure 5.42

3 In the **Format Background** pane, in the **Offset top** box, type **–40** and then press Enter. In the **Offset bottom** box, type **–60** and then press Enter. **Close** × the **Format Background** pane. Change the font color of the title and subtitle to the first color under **Standard Colors— Dark Red**. Compare your screen with Figure 5.43.

> By changing the Offset top and Offset bottom settings, the background image is lowered, making the top visible on the slide. Because only the top and left offset were changed, the picture is distorted, creating an artistic effect.

Figure 5.43

Objective 7 | Add a Photo Caption and Alt Text

GO! Learn How
Video P5-7

Recall that alt text provides a text description of an image, which is used by screen reader software but does not appear on the slide. You can add a *caption*—text that helps to identify or explain a picture or graphic—for each photo, which displays on the slide.

Activity 5.15 | Adding Alt Text

MOS
3.4.7

In this Activity, you will add alt text to images to make them more accessible. Recall the alt text is read by a screen reader and describes an image. Alt text is not visible on the slide.

1 Display **Slide 2**, right-click the image, and then click **Edit Alt Text**.

2 In the **Alt Text** box, type **Tenor Saxophone** and compare your screen with Figure 5.44.

Figure 5.44

Activity 5.16 | Adding a Text Box Caption

MOS
3.4.1, 3.4.3

In this Activity, you will add a text box to caption an image. A caption is visible on the slide.

1 Display **Slide 4**, and close the **Alt Text** pane. On the **Insert tab**, in the **Text group**, click **Text Box**, and then click one time below the picture in the center of the slide. Compare your screen with Figure 5.45.

Figure 5.45

2 ► Type **Our Dynamic Duo of Jazz** On the **Drawing Tool Format tab**, in the **Shape Styles group**, under **Theme Styles**, click the first style. Change the font size to **24.**

3 ► Right-click the text box, click **Format Shape**, and then click **Size & Properties** ▦. Set the **Horizontal** and **Vertical** positions to **6.5.** Close the **Format Shape** pane and compare your screen with Figure 5.46.

Figure 5.46

Objective 8 | Crop a Picture

GO! Learn How
Video P5-8

When you *crop* a picture, you remove unwanted or unnecessary areas of a picture. Images are often cropped to create more emphasis on the primary subject of the image. Recall that the Compress Picture pane provides the option to delete the cropped area of a picture. Deleting the cropped area reduces file size and prevents people from viewing the parts of the picture that you have removed. The *crop handles* are used to remove unwanted areas of a picture and function like sizing handles, and the *Crop tool* is the mouse pointer that displays when removing areas of a picture.

Activity 5.17 | Cropping a Picture and Inserting a Text Box

3.3.1, 3.4.1, 3.5.2

In this Activity, you will crop a picture, add a text box and position the objects on the slide.

1 ► If necessary, display **Slide 4,** and then insert a new **Blank** layout slide. On **Slide 5,** on the **Insert tab**, in the **Images group**, click **Pictures**, and from your project files, insert **p05_Jazz6.** Close the **Design Ideas** pane.

2 ► On the **Picture Tools Format tab**, in the **Size group**, change the picture height to **6.** In the **Arrange group**, click **Align** ▤, and then click **Align Center.** Click **Align** ▤ again, and then click **Align Middle.**

3 ► On the **Picture Tools Format tab**, in the **Size group**, click **Crop.**

4 ► Point to the right middle cropping handle to display the crop pointer ⊢. Compare your screen with Figure 5.47.

The mouse pointer takes the shape of the crop line—in this case, a straight vertical line with a short horizontal line attached.

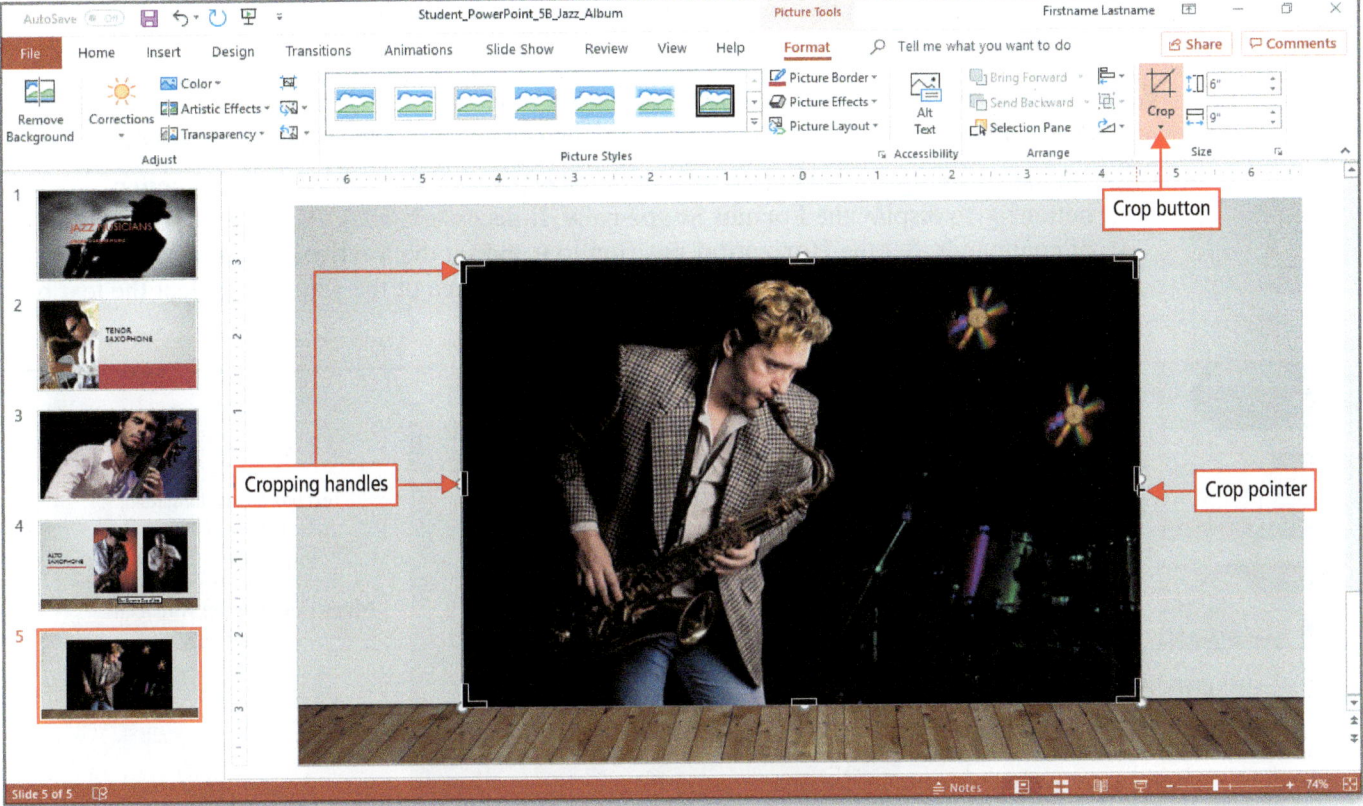

Figure 5.47

5 Drag the pointer to the left until the right edge of the picture aligns with **2 inches to the right of zero** on the **horizontal ruler**, and then release the mouse button. Compare your screen with Figure 5.48.

> The dark area to the right represents the area that will be removed.

Figure 5.48

6 Click in a blank area of the slide to apply the crop.

ANOTHER WAY Click the Crop button to apply the crop.

7 On the **Insert tab**, in the **Text group**, click **Text Box**, and then click one time to the right of the picture.

8 With the text box selected, type **Meet our newest musician** press [Enter], and then type **James Todd** Select both lines of text in the text box, and then change the font size to **24**. **Center** [≡] the text.

9 On the **Drawing Tools Format tab**, in the **Size group**, click the **Dialog Launcher** button [⌐] to display the **Format Shape** pane. If necessary, click **Position** to expand the list of commands. Set the **Horizontal position** to **9** and set the **Vertical position** to **3** **Close** [×] the **Format Shape** pane and click a blank area of the slide to deselect the text box. Compare your screen with Figure 5.49.

Text box added, formatted, and positioned

Meet our newest musician
James Todd

Figure 5.49

10 View the slide show from the beginning, and then return to **Normal** view.

11 On the **Insert tab**, in the **Text group**, click **Header & Footer** to display the **Header and Footer** dialog box. Click the **Notes and Handouts tab**. Under **Include on page**, select the **Date and time** check box, and then select **Fixed**. Insert the footer **5B_Jazz_Album** and **Apply to All**.

12 Display the document properties. As the **Tags**, type **jazz, photo, album** and as the **Subject**, type your course and section number. Be sure your name displays as author, and then **Save** your file.

13 **Close** [×] PowerPoint.

For Non-MyLab Submissions
As directed by your instructor, submit your completed PowerPoint presentation.

14 In **MyLab IT**, in your **Course Materials**, locate and click the Grader Project **PowerPoint 5B Jazz Album**. In **step 3**, under **Upload Completed Assignment**, click **Choose File**. In the **Open** dialog box, navigate to your **PowerPoint Chapter 5 folder**, and then click your **Student_PowerPoint_5B_Jazz_Album** file one time to select it. In the lower right corner of the **Open** dialog box, click **Open**.

15 To submit your file to **MyLab IT** for grading, click **Upload**, wait a moment for a green **Success!** message, and then in **step 4**, click the blue **Submit for Grading** button. Click **Close Assignment** to return to your list of **Course Materials**.

You have completed Project 5B **END**

wavebreakmedia/Shutterstock, Monkey Business Images/Fotolia, Ivanko80/Shutterstock, Monkey Business Images/Shutterstock

5 POWERPOINT

Microsoft Office Specialist (MOS) Skills in This Chapter

Project 5A	Project 5B
3.3.1 Resize and crop images	**2.1.3** Insert slides and select slide layouts
3.3.2 Apply built-in styles and effects to images	**2.2.2** Modify individual slide backgrounds
3.4.5 Format shapes and text boxes	**3.3.1** Resize and crop images
3.5.1 Order shapes, images, and text boxes	**3.4.1** Insert and change shapes
3.5.3 Group shapes and images	**3.4.3** Add text to shapes and text boxes
3.5.4 Display alignment tools	**3.4.7** Add alt text to graphic elements for accessibility
4.5.1 Insert audio and visual clips	**3.5.2** Align shapes, images, and text boxes
4.5.3 Configure media playback options	

Build Your E-Portfolio

An E-Portfolio is a collection of evidence, stored electronically, that showcases what you have accomplished while completing your education. Collecting and then sharing your work products with potential employers reflects your academic and career goals. Your completed documents from the following projects are good examples to show what you have learned: 5G, 5K, and 5L.

Go! For Job Success

Discussion: Free Address System

Your instructor may assign this discussion to your class, and then ask you to think about, or discuss with your classmates, these questions:

Mobile technology, smaller devices, and high-speed internet connections mean that many businesspeople can work anywhere, any time. Because workers no longer need to be at a desk in an office building every day, some companies are designing new workspaces with a free address system. In a free address environment, employees are not assigned a specific desk, cube, or office. Employees who work in the office can move freely from open, collaborative spaces to private, quiet spaces as their work requires. Most companies implement a free address system to save money on real estate costs. Some have found that at any given time, as much as 50% of assigned workspace is empty.

g-stockstudio/Shutterstock

What are some reasons that an employee might not use their assigned office space during the course of a day?

In a true free address system, even top executives do not have assigned offices. What are some activities in a CEO's or vice president's day that would be more difficult in this office setup?

In addition to high-speed internet and cell phones, what are some other technologies that would make it easier for a company to adopt a free address office space?

End of Chapter

Summary

In this chapter, you practiced completing a PowerPoint presentation by inserting and modifying pictures and images, and by changing the sharpness, softness, brightness, and contrast.

Next, you added borders to images. You added a mitered border, a colored border, and a weighted border. You recolored pictures, merged three shapes into one, and added audio and video to a slide show.

You added a WordArt object to the presentation and filled the background with a picture. You changed the method by which audio and video play and created triggers for starting them. You added a video link.

You practiced cropping a picture using the crop tool to remove areas of a picture. You added captions to photos to add clarity.

GO! Learn It Online

Review the concepts, key terms, and MOS skills in this chapter by completing these online challenges, which you can find in **MyLab IT**.

Chapter Quiz: Answer matching and multiple choice questions to test what you learned in this chapter.

Lessons on the GO!: Learn how to use all the new apps and features as they are introduced by Microsoft.

MOS Prep Quiz: Answer questions to review the MOS skills that you practiced in this chapter.

Project Guide for PowerPoint Chapter 5

Your instructor will assign Projects from this list to ensure your learning and assess your knowledge.

	Project Guide for PowerPoint Chapter 5		
Project	**Apply Skills from These Chapter Objectives**	**Project Type**	**Project Location**
5A MyLab IT	Objectives 1–5 from Project 5A	**5A Instructional Project (Grader Project)** Instruction Guided instruction to learn the skills in Project A.	In **MyLab IT** and in text
5B MyLab IT	Objectives 6–8 from Project 5B	**5B Instructional Project (Grader Project)** Instruction Guided instruction to learn the skills in Project B.	In **MyLab IT** and in text
5C	Objectives 1–5 from Project 5A	**5C Skills Review (Scorecard Grading)** Review A guided review of the skills from Project 5A.	In text
5D	Objectives 6–8 from Project 5B	**5D Skills Review (Scorecard Grading)** Review A guided review of the skills from Project 5B.	In text
5E MyLab IT	Objectives 1–5 from Project 5A	**5E Mastery (Grader Project)** Mastery and Transfer of Learning A demonstration of your mastery of the skills in Project 5A with extensive decision making.	In **MyLab IT** and in text
5F MyLab IT	Objectives 6–8 from Project 5A	**5F Mastery (Grader Project)** Mastery and Transfer of Learning A demonstration of your mastery of the skills in Project 5B with extensive decision making.	In **MyLab IT** and in text
5G MyLab IT	Objectives 1–8 from Project 5A	**5G Mastery (Grader Project)** Mastery and Transfer of Learning A demonstration of your mastery of the skills in Projects 5A and 5B with extensive decision making.	In **MyLab IT** and in text
5H	Combination of Objectives from Projects 5A and 5B	**5H GO! Fix It (Scorecard Grading)** Critical Thinking A demonstration of your mastery of the skills in Projects 5A and 5B by creating a correct result from a document that contains errors you must find.	IRC
5I	Combination of Objectives from Projects 5A and 5B	**5I GO! Make It (Scorecard Grading)** Critical Thinking A demonstration of your mastery of the skills in Projects 5A and 5B by creating a result from a supplied picture.	IRC
5J	Combination of Objectives from Projects 5A and 5B	**5J GO! Solve It (Rubric Grading)** Critical Thinking A demonstration of your mastery of the skills in Projects 5A and 5B, your decision-making skills, and your critical thinking skills. A task-specific rubric helps you self-assess your result.	IRC
5K	Combination of Objectives from Projects 5A and 5B	**5K GO! Solve It (Rubric Grading)** Critical Thinking A demonstration of your mastery of the skills in Projects 5A and 5B, your decision-making skills, and your critical thinking skills. A task-specific rubric helps you self-assess your result.	In text
5L	Combination of Objectives from Projects 5A and 5B	**5L GO! Think (Rubric Grading)** Critical Thinking A demonstration of your understanding of the chapter concepts applied in a manner that you would outside of college. An analytic rubric helps you and your instructor grade the quality of your work by comparing it to the work an expert in the discipline would create.	In text
5M	Combination of Objectives from Projects 5A and 5B	**5M GO! Think (Rubric Grading)** Critical Thinking A demonstration of your understanding of the chapter concepts applied in a manner that you would outside of college. An analytic rubric helps you and your instructor grade the quality of your work by comparing it to the work an expert in the discipline would create.	IRC
5N	Combination of Objectives from Projects 5A and 5B	**5N You and GO! (Rubric Grading)** Critical Thinking A demonstration of your understanding of the chapter concepts applied in a manner that you would in a personal situation. An analytic rubric helps you and your instructor grade the quality of your work.	IRC

Glossary

Glossary of Chapter Key Terms

Border A frame around a picture.

Brightness The relative lightness of an image.

Caption Text that helps to identify or explain a picture or a graphic.

Contrast The difference between the light and dark extremes of color in an image.

Crop A command that removes unwanted or unnecessary areas of a picture.

Crop handles Handles used to remove unwanted areas of a picture.

Crop tool The mouse pointer that displays when removing areas of a picture.

Embed Save a file so that the audio or video file becomes part of the presentation file.

Line style How the line displays, such as a solid line, dots, or dashes.

Line weight The thickness of a line measured in points.

Link Save a presentation so that the audio or video file is saved separately from the presentation.

Lock aspect ratio When this option is selected, you can change one dimension (height or width) of an object, such as a picture, and the other dimension will automatically be changed to maintain the proportion.

Loop The audio or video file plays repeatedly from start to finish until it is stopped manually.

Mitered A border with corners that are square.

Pixel Short for picture element, represents a single point in a graphic image.

PowerPoint Designer A tool that helps you format slides that contain images by suggesting several professionally designed layouts.

Presets Built-in adjustments from a gallery.

Recolor To change all the colors in the image to shades of one color.

Sharpen To increase the clarity of an image.

Soften To decrease the clarity of an image or make it fuzzy.

Track A song from a CD.

Trigger A portion of text, a graphic, or a picture that, when clicked, causes the audio or video to play.

Chapter Review

Apply 5A skills from these Objectives:

1. Apply Picture Corrections
2. Add a Border to a Picture
3. Change the Shape of a Picture
4. Add a Picture to a WordArt Object and Merge Shapes
5. Enhance a Presentation with Audio and Video

Skills Review | **Project 5C Celtic Instruments**

In the following Skills Review, you will modify pictures in a presentation about the instruments in the Celtic music genre for the Cross Oceans Music company. You will change the brightness, contrast, and shapes of pictures and add borders to some pictures for emphasis. You will add WordArt and merge a shape. You will add audio files that demonstrate the various instruments played in this type of music and a video file. Your completed presentation will look similar to Figure 5.50.

Project Files

For Project 5C, you will need:

p05C_Celtic_Instruments
p05C_Flute
p05C_Sheet_Music
p05_Music_Video

You will save your presentation as:

Lastname_Firstname_5C_Celtic_Instruments

Project Results

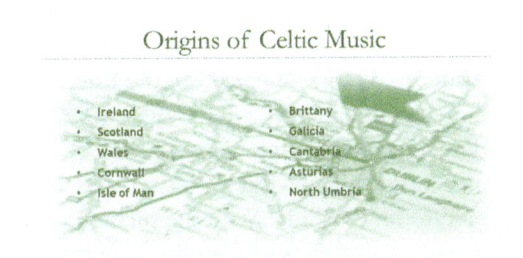
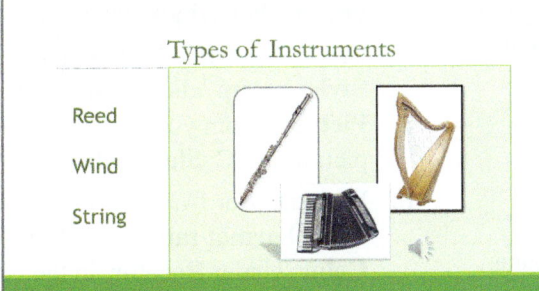

Figure 5.50 Project 5C Celtic Instruments

(continues on next page)

Chapter Review

1 Navigate to your student data files, and then double-click **p05C_Celtic_Instruments.** In your presentation, if necessary, at the top click **Enable Editing.** On the **File tab**, click **Save As,** navigate to your **PowerPoint Chapter 5 folder,** and then using your own name, save the file as **Lastname_Firstname_5C_Celtic_Instruments**

2 On **Slide 1**, click to select the image of the flag.

  a. On the **Picture Tools Format tab**, in the **Arrange group**, click the **Send Backward** arrow, and then click **Send to Back.**

3 Display **Slide 2**, and then click to select the image of the map.

  a. On the **Picture Tools Format tab**, in the **Arrange group**, click the **Send Backward** arrow, and then click **Send to Back.**

4 Click **Slide 1**, and then on the **View tab**, in the **Show group**, select the **Gridlines** check box. (Mac users, select Guides).

  a. On **Slide 1**, click to select the picture.

  b. With the picture selected, on the **Format tab**, in the **Arrange group**, click **Selection Pane.** In the **Selection** pane, click **Title 1** to select the title placeholder. Then, click **Picture 4** to select the picture on the slide. With the picture selected and using the gridlines as a guide, drag the picture so the left edge of the picture aligns on the **left half of the horizontal ruler at 6 inches** and the bottom edge of the image aligns **on the lower half of the vertical ruler at 1 inch. Close** the **Selection** pane. (Mac users, drag the guides to the locations in the step, and then use the guides to position the image.)

  c. On the **Picture Tools Format tab**, in the **Adjust group**, click **Corrections**, and then click **Picture Corrections Options.** In the **Format Picture** pane, under **Brightness/Contrast**, click **Presets**, and then in the first row, third column, click **Brightness: 0% (Normal) Contrast: –40%.**

5 Display **Slide 3**, and then click the picture on the left—the **flute.**

  a. On the **Picture Tools Format tab**, in the **Size group**, click the **Crop arrow**, point to **Crop to Shape**, and then under **Rectangles**, click the second shape— **Rectangle: Rounded Corners.**

  b. In the **Picture Styles group**, click **Picture Border**, under **Theme** colors, click in the first column, the last color. In the **Pictures Styles group**, click **Picture Border**, point to **Weight**, and then click **2 1/4 pt.**

  c. Click the picture in the center—the **accordion.** On the **Format tab**, in the **Picture Styles group**, click the **More arrow**, and then in the third row, click the fourth style—**Perspective Shadow, White.**

  d. In the **Picture Styles group**, click the **Picture Border** button, and then click **No Outline.** In the **Arrange group**, click the **Bring Forward arrow**, and then click **Bring to Front.**

  e. Click the picture of the **harp.** On the **Format tab**, in the **Picture Styles group**, click the **More** arrow, and then in the second row, click the second style—**Simple Frame, Black.**

  f. On the **View tab**, in the **Show group**, clear the **Gridlines** check box.

6 Display **Slide 4.** On the **Insert tab**, in the **Text group**, click **WordArt.** In the second row, click the last style.

  a. In the **WordArt** object, with the text selected, type **Celtic Instruments** Press Enter, type **Presented by** Press Enter, and then type **Cross Oceans Music**

  b. On the **Drawing Tools Format tab**, in the **Arrange group**, click **Align**, and then click **Align Middle.**

  c. On the **Drawing Tools Format tab**, in the **Shape Styles group**, click **Shape Fill**, and then click **Picture.** From your student data files, insert the picture **p05C_Sheet_Music.**

  d. With the WordArt still selected, on the **Picture Tools Format tab**, in the **Adjust group**, click **Color.** Under **Recolor**, in the third row, click the fourth color— **Green, Accent color 3 Light.**

  e. Right-click the **WordArt**, and then click **Format Picture.** (Mac users, press control + click the picture.) In the **Format Picture** pane, click **Size & Properties.** Under **Size**, select the **Lock aspect ratio** check box, set the **Height** to **3** and then press Enter. On the **Picture Tools Format tab**, in the **Arrange group**, click **Align**, and then click **Align Center.**

(continues on next page)

Chapter Review

Skills Review: Project 5C Celtic Instruments (continued)

f. Hold down Control and click to select the four green shapes that make up the shamrock. (Mac users, press command + click.) On the **Drawing Tools Format tab**, in the **Insert Shapes group**, click **Merge Shapes**, and then click **Union**. In the **Format Shape** pane, click **Size & Properties**. Under **Position**, in the **Vertical position** box, type **1** and then press Enter. On the **Drawing Tools Format tab**, in the **Arrange group**, click **Align**, and then click **Align Center**.

7 ▶ Display **Slide 3**. On the **Insert tab**, in the **Media group**, click **Audio**, and then click **Audio on My PC**.

a. In the **Insert Audio** dialog box, click the **Audio Files arrow** (Mac users, click Audio from file.) From your student data files, insert **p05C_Flute**.

b. On the **Audio Tools Playback tab**, in the **Audio Options group**, select the **Hide During Show** check box. In the same ribbon group, click **Volume**, and then click **Medium**. In the **Start** box, click the **arrow**, and then click **Automatically**.

c. In the middle of the slide, right-click the selected **Audio icon**, and then click **Size and Position**. If necessary, click **Position** to expand the list of commands. In the **Horizontal position** box, type **9.7** and in the **Vertical position** box, type **6** and then press Enter. **Close** the **Format Picture** pane.

d. If necessary, click to select the **Audio** icon. (Mac users, the Mac version of PowerPoint does not include triggers. Skip to Step 8.) On the **Animations tab**, in the **Advanced Animation group**, click **Animation Pane** to display the **Animation Pane**.

e. On the ribbon, in the **Advanced Animation group**, click **Trigger**, and then point to **On Click of**. Click **Title 1**. **Close** the **Animation Pane**.

8 ▶ Display **Slide 4**.

a. On the **Insert tab**, in the **Media group**, click **Video**, and then click **Video on My PC**. Navigate to your **PowerPoint Chapter 5** folder, and then click **p05_Music_Video** one time. In the lower right corner of the **Insert Video** dialog box, click the **Insert arrow**. Click **Link to File**. (Mac users, click Movie from File. Locate p05_Music_Video. In the lower left corner of the Choose a Movie dialog box, click Options. Select the Link to file check box, and then click Insert.)

b. With the video selected, on the **Video Tools Format tab**, in the **Size group**, change the **Video Height** to **1.5"**

c. Point to the video image in the center of the slide, right-click, and then click **Size and Position** to display the **Format Video** pane. If necessary, click **Position** to expand the list of commands. In the **Horizontal position** box, type **1** In the **Vertical position** box, type **4.5** and then press Enter. **Close** the **Format Video** pane.

d. If necessary click to select the video image. On the **Animations tab**, in the **Advanced Animations group**, click **Trigger**, point to **On Click of**, and then click **Rectangle 5** (the number after Rectangle may vary). (Mac users, skip this step.)

e. On the **Video Tools Playback tab**, in the **Video Options group**, select the **Hide While Not Playing** check box, and then select the **Play Full Screen** check box.

9 ▶ On the **Slide Show tab**, in the **Start Slide Show group**, click **From Beginning** to view the entire presentation. Click the trigger—the pointer that displays when you point to the title text—on **Slide 3** to hear the audio. When **Slide 4** displays, click the **WordArt** trigger to view the video. Press Esc to return to Normal view.

10 ▶ Return to your PowerPoint presentation. On the **Insert tab**, in the **Text group**, click **Header & Footer** to display the **Header and Footer** dialog box. Click the **Notes and Handouts tab**. Under **Include on page**, select the **Date and time** check box, and then select **Fixed**. In the **Footer** box, type **5C_Celtic_Instruments** and then click **Apply to All**.

11 ▶ Display the document properties. As the **Tags**, type **Celtic, instruments** and as the **Subject,** type your course name and section number. Be sure your name appears as author.

12 ▶ **Save** your presentation. As directed by your instructor, submit your completed PowerPoint presentation. **Close** PowerPoint.

You have completed Project 5C **END**

Chapter Review

Apply **5B** skills from these Objectives:

6. Use PowerPoint Designer
7. Add a Photo Caption and Alt Text
8. Crop a Picture

Skills Review   Project 5D Celtic Album

In the following Skills Review, you will create a photo album for the Cross Oceans Music company. You will insert photos of musicians who record Celtic music and are represented by Cross Oceans. You will add captions and crop unwanted areas of photos. Your completed presentation will look similar to Figure 5.51.

Project Files

For Project 5D, you will need:

p05D_Celtic_Album

p05D_Bagpiper

p05D_Flautist

p05D_Harpist

p05D_Mandolinist

p05D_Violinist

You will save your presentation as:

Lastname_Firstname_5D_Celtic_Album

Project Results

Figure 5.51 Project 5D Celtic Album

(continues on next page)

Chapter Review

Skills Review: Project 5D Celtic Album (continued)

1 Navigate to your student data files, and then double-click **p05D_Celtic_Album.** In your presentation, if necessary, at the top click **Enable Editing.** On the **File tab,** click **Save As,** navigate to your **PowerPoint Chapter 5 folder,** and then using your own name, save the file as **Lastname_Firstname_5D_Celtic_Album**

2 In the Title placeholder type **Celtic Artists** In the subtitle placeholder, type **Cross Oceans Music** Change the **Font Size** to **28,** apply **Bold.**

3 Insert a new **Title and Content** slide. In the content placeholder, click **Pictures.** Navigate to data files for this project, click **p05D_Violinist,** and then click **Insert.** If necessary, in the Design Ideas pane, click Let's Go. If necessary, click Turn on.

4 Click each idea to preview in the slide pane, and then click the idea layout that displays the image on the left and title on the right. In the title placeholder, type **Violinist**

   a. Right-click the image and then click **Edit Alt Text.** In the **Alt Text** box, type **Violinist** and close the **Alt Text** pane.

5 Insert a new **Two Content** slide. In the image placeholders, insert **p05D_Flautist** and **p05D_Mandolinist.** In the **Design Ideas** pane, click the design idea layout with the title placeholder on the right and two images on the left. In the title placeholder, type **Traditional Instruments**

6 Display **Slide 1.** If necessary, **close** the **Design Ideas** pane. On the **Design tab,** click **Format Background.**

   a. In the **Format Background** pane, under **Fill,** click **Picture or texture fill.** Select the **Hide Background Graphics** check box.

   b. Under **Insert picture from,** click **File.** From your student data files, insert **p05D_Harpist.**

   c. In the **Format Background** pane, in the **Offset top** spin box, type **–15** and then press Enter. In the **Offset bottom** spin box, type **–15** and then press Enter. **Close** the **Format Background** pane.

   d. Change the font color of the title and subtitle to the first color under **Theme** colors—**White, Background 1.**

7 Display **Slide 3,** and if necessary, close the **Format Background** pane. On the **Insert tab,** in the **Text group,** click **Text Box,** and then click one time below the picture in the center of the slide.

   a. Type **Flute and Mandolin** On the **Drawing Tools Format tab,** in the **Shape Style group,** under **Theme Styles,** click the second style. Change the font size to **32.**

   b. Right-click the text box, click **Format Shape,** and then click **Size & Properties.** Set the **Horizontal position** to **2.3** and **Vertical position** to **6.5.** Close the **Format Shape** pane.

8 If necessary, display **Slide 3,** and then insert a new **Blank** layout slide. On the **Insert tab,** in the **Images group,** click **Pictures,** and from your project data files, insert **p05D_Bagpiper.** Close the **Design Ideas** pane.

   a. On the **Picture Tools Format tab,** in the **Size group,** click **Crop.**

   b. Drag the right middle cropping handle left until the right edge of the picture aligns with **1.5-inches to the right of zero** on the **horizontal ruler.**

   c. Click in a blank area of the slide to apply the crop.

9 On the **Insert tab,** in the **Text group,** click **Text Box,** and then click one time to the right of the picture. With the text box selected, type **Meet Jake Murphy** Change the font size to **24** and apply **Bold.**

   a. On the **Drawing Tools Format tab,** in the **Size group,** click the **Dialog Launcher** button to display the **Format Shape** pane. If necessary, click Position to expand the list of commands. Set the **Horizontal position** to **8.5** and set the **Vertical position** to **3** Close the **Format Shape** pane and click a blank area of the slide to deselect the text box.

10 On the **Insert tab,** in the **Text group,** click the Header & Footer button to display the **Header and Footer** pane. Click the **Notes and Handouts tab.** Under **Include on page,** select the **Date and time** check box, and then select **Fixed.** Insert the **Footer 5D_Celtic_Album** and then click **Apply to All.**

11 Display the document properties. As the Tags, type **Celtic, music, album** and as the Subject, type your course name and section number. Be sure your name appears as author.

12 **Save** the presentation. As directed by your instructor, submit your completed PowerPoint presentation. **Close** PowerPoint.

You have completed Project 5D   **END**

Content-Based Assessments (Mastery and Transfer of Learning)

Mastering PowerPoint **Project 5E Reggae Music**

Apply 5A skills from these Objectives:

1. Apply Picture Corrections
2. Add a Border to a Picture
3. Change the Shape of a Picture
4. Add a Picture to a WordArt Object and Merge Shapes
5. Enhance a Presentation with Audio and Video

In the following Mastering PowerPoint project, you will modify pictures in a presentation used in educational seminars hosted by Cross Oceans Music. The presentation highlights Reggae music and its roots in jazz and rhythm and blues. You will add WordArt and a merged shape to the presentation. You will add an audio file that represents this genre of music and format it to play across the slides in the slide show. You will add a video file. Your completed presentation will look similar to Figure 5.52.

Project Files for MyLab IT Grader

1. In your **MyLab IT** course, locate and click **PowerPoint 5E Reggae Music**, Download Materials, and then Download All Files.
2. Extract the zipped folder to your PowerPoint Chapter 5 folder. Close the Grader download screens.
3. Take a moment to open the downloaded **PowerPoint_5E_Reggae_Music_Instructions**; note any recent updates to the book.

Project Results

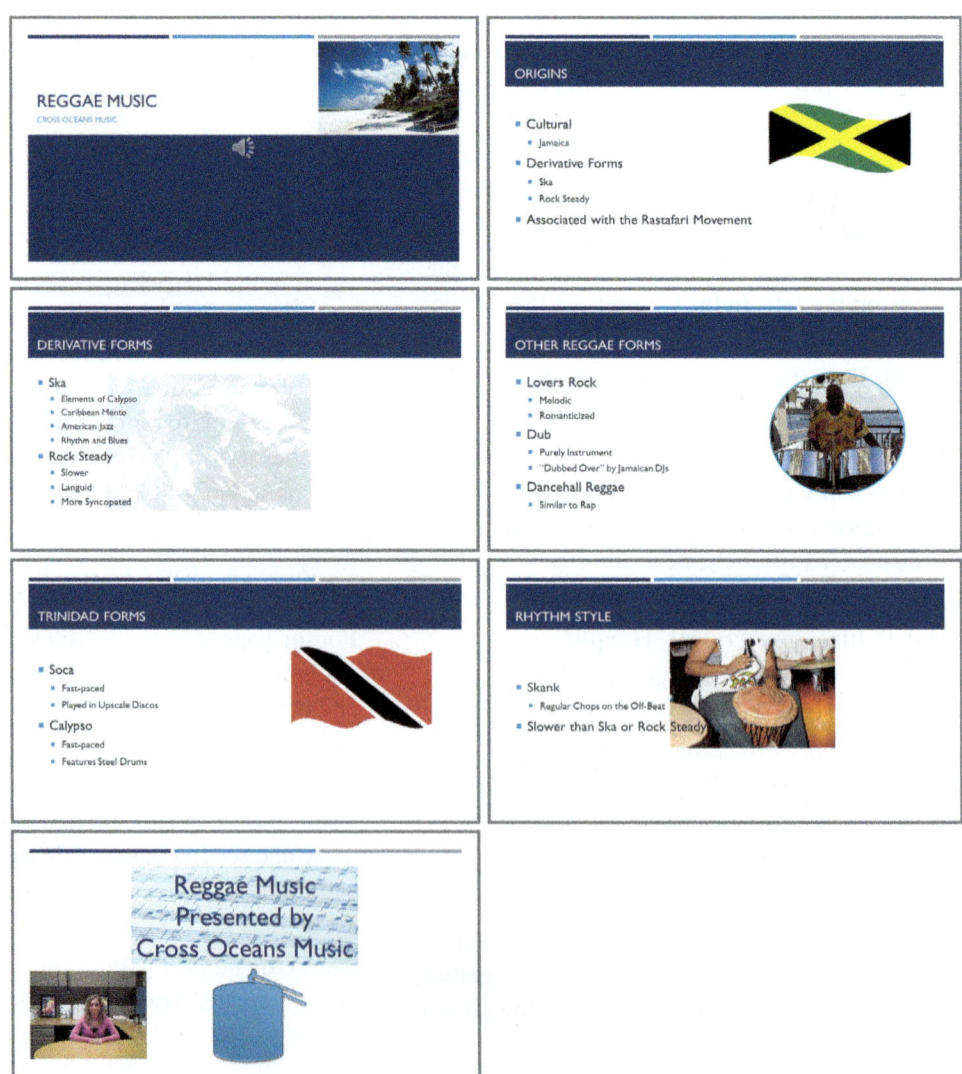

Figure 5.52 Project 5E Reggae Music

(continues on next page)

Mastering PowerPoint: Project 5E Reggae Music (continued)

For Non-MyLab Submissions

For Project 5E, you will need:

p05E_Reggae_Music

p05E_Music

p05E_Reggae

p05_Music_Video

In your PowerPoint Chapter 5 folder, save your presentation as:

Lastname_Firstname_5E_Reggae_Music

After you have named and saved your presentation, on the next page, begin with Step 2.

After Step 16, save and submit your presentation as directed by your instructor.

1 Navigate to your **PowerPoint Chapter 5 folder** and then double-click the PowerPoint file you downloaded from **MyLab IT** that displays your name—**Student_PowerPoint_5E_Reggae_Music**. If necessary, at the top, **click Enable Editing**.

2 On **Slide 1**, from your student data files for this project, insert the audio file **p05E_Reggae**. Set the audio to **Hide During Show** and to start **Automatically**.

3 On **Slide 2**, select the picture, and then **crop** the picture to, under **Stars and Banners**, the **Wave** shape.

4 On **Slide 3**, click the picture, and then send the picture to the back. **Recolor** the picture with the **Washout** color variation.

5 On **Slide 4**, change the picture border to, under Theme Colors, the seventh column, the fifth color. Change the **line weight** to **3pt**. **Crop** the picture to, under **Basic Shapes**, an **Oval** shape.

6 On **Slide 5**, crop the picture to, under **Stars and Banners**, the **Double Wave** shape.

7 On **Slide 6**, select the picture, and then **Send to Back**.

8 On **Slide 7**, insert a **WordArt** using the first style in the second column. Type **Reggae Music** on one line, type **Presented by** on the next line, and then type **Cross Oceans Music** on the third line.

9 Change the **WordArt Horizontal** position to **3.4"** and the **Vertical position** to **1"**.

10 On **Slide 7**, with the **WordArt** selected, use **Shape Fill** to insert the picture **p05E_Music**. **Recolor** the picture using the third style in the third row.

11 On **Slide 7**, insert the video file **p05_Music_Video** as a linked video. Set to **Play Full Screen** and **Hide While Not Playing**.

12 With the video selected, change the **Horizontal** position to **0.5"** and the **Vertical** position to **4"**.

13 Select the three turquoise shapes of the **drum** and **drum sticks**, and merge them into one shape using **Union**.

14 Select the **drum** shape, and then change the **Horizontal position** to **5.5"** and the **Vertical position** to **4"**.

15 Insert a Header and Footer on the Notes and Handouts. Under Include the date and time fixed. Insert the footer **5E_Reggae_Music**

16 Edit the document properties. As the Tags, type **Reggae, music** and as the Subject, type your course name and section number. Be sure your name appears as author.

17 In **MyLab IT**, in your **Course Materials**, locate and click the Grader Project **PowerPoint 5E Reggae Music**. In **step 3**, under **Upload Completed Assignment**, click **Choose File**. In the **Open** dialog box, navigate to your **PowerPoint Chapter 5 folder**, and then click your **Student_PowerPoint_5E_Reggae_Music** file one time to select it. In the lower right corner of the **Open** dialog box, click **Open**.

18 To submit your file to **MyLab IT** for grading, click **Upload**, wait a moment for a green **Success!** message, and then in **step 4**, click the blue **Submit for Grading** button. Click **Close Assignment** to return to your list of **Course Materials**.

You have completed Project 5E | **END**

Content-Based Assessments (Mastery and Transfer of Learning)

Apply 5B skills from these Objectives:

6. Use PowerPoint Designer
7. Add a Photo Caption and Alt Text
8. Crop a Picture

In the following Mastering PowerPoint project, you will create a photo album of pictures of island settings for a CD entitled *Reggae Revisited*. One of these cover designs will be chosen by Cross Oceans Music to be the cover of the soon-to-be-released CD of Reggae and Jamaican music. Your completed presentation will look similar to Figure 5.53.

Project Files for MyLab IT Grader

1. In your **MyLab IT** course, locate and click **PowerPoint 5F CD Cover**, Download Materials, and then Download All Files.
2. Extract the zipped folder to your PowerPoint Chapter 5 folder. Close the Grader download screens.
3. Take a moment to open the downloaded **PowerPoint_5F_CD_Cover_Instructions**; note any recent updates to the book.

Project Results

Figure 5.53 Project 5F CD Cover

For Non-MyLab Submissions

For Project 5F, you will need:

p05F_CD_Cover
p05F_Island2
p05F_Island3

In your PowerPoint Chapter 5 folder, save your workbook as:

Lastname_Firstname_5F_CD_Cover

After you have named and saved your presentation, on the next page, begin with Step 2.

After Step 16, save and submit your presentation as directed by your instructor.

(continues on next page)

Mastering PowerPoint: Project 5F CD Cover (continued)

1 Navigate to your **PowerPoint Chapter 5 folder** and then double-click the PowerPoint file you downloaded from **MyLab IT** that displays your name—**Student_PowerPoint_5F_CD_Cover**. If necessary, at the top, **click Enable Editing**.

2 After **Slide 2**, insert two new **Title and Content** slides.

3 On **Slide 3**, in the content placeholder, from your student data files for this project, insert **p05F_Island2**.

4 On **Slide 4**, in the content placeholder, from your student data files for this project, insert **p05F_Island3**.

5 On **Slide 1**, change the subtitle text to **Cross Oceans Music** Apply **Bold**, and then change the font size to **32**.

6 Delete the title text, *Photo Album*, type **Design Entries for CD Cover** Press Enter, and then type **Reggae & Jamaican Music** Select both lines of the title text, and then change the font size to **44**.

7 On **Slide 2**, add the title **Design 1** Select the picture and change the **Horizontal position** to **1.5"** and the **Vertical position** to **0"**.

8 On **Slide 2**, insert a text box in the blank area to the right of the picture. In the text box, type **Reggae** Press Enter, and then type **Revisited** Change the font of the text in the text box to **Bauhaus 93** and the font size to **72**.

9 On **Slide 2**, select the text box, and then change the **Horizontal position** to **7"** and the **Vertical position** to **3"**.

10 On **Slide 2**, select the picture, and then crop the picture by dragging the left middle cropping handle to align to **4 1/2-inches to the left of zero** on the **horizontal ruler**.

11 On **Slide 3**, add the title **Design 2** Change the height of the picture to **6"** and the **Vertical position** to **0.8"**.

12 On **Slide 3**, insert a text box in the blank area to the right of the picture. Type **Reggae** Press Enter, and then type **Revisited** Change the font of the text in the text box to **Brush Script MT** and the font size to **88**. Apply **Bold**. Change the **Horizontal** position to **1"** and the **Vertical** position to **2.5"**.

13 On **Slide 4**, add the title **Design 3**

14 On **Slide 4**, insert a text box in the blank area to the left of the picture. In the text box, type **Reggae** Press Enter, and then type **Revisited** Change the font of the text in the text box to **Algerian** and the font size to **60**. Apply **Bold**. Change the **Horizontal** position to **1"** and the **Vertical** position to **2.5"**. Change the height of the picture to **6"** and the **Vertical position** to **0.8"**.

15 Review your presentation from the beginning. Insert a footer on the notes and handouts, which includes a fixed date and time, the page number, and the footer **5F_CD_Cover**

16 Display the document properties. As the Tags, type **design, CD, entries** and as the Subject, type your course name and section number. Be sure your name appears as author.

17 In **MyLab IT**, in your **Course Materials**, locate and click the Grader Project **PowerPoint 5F CD Cover**. In **step 3**, under **Upload Completed Assignment**, click **Choose File**. In the **Open** dialog box, navigate to your **PowerPoint Chapter 5 folder**, and then click your **Student_PowerPoint_5F_CD_Cover** file one time to select it. In the lower right corner of the **Open** dialog box, click **Open**.

18 To submit your file to **MyLab IT** for grading, click **Upload**, wait a moment for a green **Success!** message, and then in **step 4**, click the blue **Submit for Grading** button. Click **Close Assignment** to return to your list of **Course Materials**.

You have completed Project 5F | END

Apply 5A and 5B skills from these Objectives:

1. Apply Picture Corrections
2. Add a Border to a Picture
3. Change the Shape of a Picture
4. Add a Picture to a WordArt Object and Merge Shapes
5. Enhance a Presentation with Audio and Video
6. Use PowerPoint Designer
7. Add a Photo Caption and Alt Text
8. Crop a Picture

In the following Mastering PowerPoint project, you will edit a photo album about the origins and elements of jazz by changing the brightness, contrast, and shape of pictures. You will format the presentation to play an audio clip of music. Your completed presentations will look similar to Figure 5.54.

Project Files for **MyLab IT Grader**

1. In your **MyLab IT** course, locate and click **PowerPoint 5G Jazz Origins**, Download Materials, and then Download All Files.
2. Extract the zipped folder to your PowerPoint Chapter 5 folder. Close the Grader download screens.
3. Take a moment to open the downloaded **PowerPoint_5G_Jazz_Origins_Instructions**; note any recent updates to the book.

Project Results

Figure 5.54 Project 5G Jazz Origins

For Non-MyLab Submissions

For Project 5G, you will need:
p05G_Jazz_Origins
p05G_Jazz_Audio
p05G_Jazz2
p05G_Jazz3
p05G_Jazz4

In your PowerPoint Chapter 5 folder, save your presentation as:
Lastname_Firstname_5G_Jazz_Origins

After you have named and saved your presentation, on the next page, begin with Step 2.
After Step 16, save and submit your presentation as directed by your instructor.

(continues on next page)

Content-Based Assessments (Mastery and Transfer of Learning)

Mastering PowerPoint: Project 5G Jazz Origins and Percussion Album (continued)

1 Navigate to your **PowerPoint Chapter 5 folder** and then double-click the PowerPoint file you downloaded from **MyLab IT** that displays your name—**Student_PowerPoint_5G_Jazz_Origins**. If necessary, at the top, **click Enable Editing**.

2 After **Slide 2**, insert two new **Title and Content** slides.

3 On **Slide 3**, in the content placeholder, from your student data files for this project, insert **p05G_Jazz2**. Use the **Design Ideas** pane to change the layout to one that displays the image on the left, and the title on the right.

4 On **Slide 4**, in the content placeholder, from your student data files for this project, insert **p05G_Jazz3**. Use the **Design Ideas** pane to change the layout to one that displays the image on the left, and the title on the right.

5 On **Slide 1**, format the title font standard color red, and the font size **72**. In the subtitle placeholder, type **Origins & Elements** Format the subtitle red, and the font size **48**. Format the background with picture fill, insert **p05G_Jazz4** from your student data files. Set the top offset to **-20%**.

6 On **Slide 2**, set the **Horizontal** position of the picture to **5** and **Vertical** position to **0**. Set the Brightness to **20%**.

7 Insert a text box to the left of the image. In the text box, type **Origin** Press Enter and type **Late 19th Century** Press Enter and type **New Orleans, Louisiana** Change the font size to **32**. Position the text box horizontally at **0.5"** and vertically at **2"**.

8 On **Slide 3**, type the title **Musical Origins** Change the picture **Color** to, under **Color Tone, Temperature: 4700 K**. Change the **Picture Effects** to **Soft Edges, 25 Point**.

9 Insert a text box to the right of the image, above the title. In the text box, type the following list, pressing Enter after each:

Work songs
Hymns
Sorrow songs
Spirituals

10 Change the font size to **28**. Position the text box horizontally at **7"** and vertically at **2"**.

11 On **Slide 4**, type the title **Elements** To the picture, apply **+30% Brightness**. Change the picture shape to **Flowchart: Alternate Process**. Add a picture border, under Theme Colors, in the third column, last row. Set the line weight to **4 1/2 pt**.

12 Insert a text box to the right of the image. In the text box, type the following list, pressing Enter after each:

Blue notes
Swing
Polyrhythm
Syncopation

13 Change the font size to **28**. Position the text box horizontally at **6.5"** and vertically at **1.5"**.

14 On **Slide 1**, insert the audio **p05G_Jazz_Audio**. Position the Audio icon horizontally at **11"** and vertically at **6"**. Change to **Start Automatically** and **Hide During Show**.

15 Review your presentation from the beginning. Insert a footer on the notes and handouts, which includes a fixed date and time, the page number, and the footer **5G_Jazz_Origins**

16 Display the document properties. As the Tags, type **jazz, origins** and as the Subject, type your course name and section number. Be sure your name appears as author.

17 In **MyLab IT**, in your **Course Materials**, locate and click the Grader Project **PowerPoint 5G Jazz Origins**. In **step 3**, under **Upload Completed Assignment**, click **Choose File**. In the **Open** dialog box, navigate to your **PowerPoint Chapter 5 folder**, and then click your **Student_PowerPoint_5G_Jazz_Origins** file one time to select it. In the lower right corner of the **Open** dialog box, click **Open**.

18 To submit your file to **MyLab IT** for grading, click **Upload**, wait a moment for a green **Success!** message, and then in **step 4**, click the blue **Submit for Grading** button. Click **Close Assignment** to return to your list of **Course Materials**.

You have completed Project 5G | **END**

Content-Based Assessments (Critical Thinking)

<table>
<tr><td rowspan="7">Apply a combination of the 5A and 5B skills.</td></tr>
<tr><td>GO! Fix It</td><td>Project 5H Caribbean Music and Strings Album</td><td>IRC</td></tr>
<tr><td>GO! Make It</td><td>Project 5I Salsa Music and Latin Album</td><td>IRC</td></tr>
<tr><td>GO! Solve It</td><td>Project 5J Flamenco Music and Brass Album</td><td>IRC</td></tr>
<tr><td>GO! Solve It</td><td>Project 5K New Age Music and Asian Album</td><td></td></tr>
</table>

Project Files

For Project 5K, you will need:

p05K_NewAge_Music

p05K_Piano

p05_Music_Video

You will save your presentation as:

Lastname_Firstname_5K_NewAge_Music

In this project, you will modify a short presentation that describes the elements of New Age music.

Open **p05K_NewAge_Music**, and then save it as **Lastname_Firstname_5K_NewAge_Music** Improve the presentation by modifying the photos in the slides using the Design Ideas pane. Add the provided audio and video files and set the playback options.

Insert a header and footer on the Notes and Handouts that includes the fixed date and time, the page number, and the footer **5K_NewAge_Music** Add your name, course name and section number, and appropriate tags to the Properties. Submit as directed by your instructor.

<table>
<tr><td rowspan="2" colspan="2"></td><td colspan="3" align="center">Performance Level</td></tr>
<tr><td align="center">Exemplary:</td><td align="center">Proficient:</td><td align="center">Developing:</td></tr>
<tr><td rowspan="2">Performance Criteria</td><td>Modified photos in NewAge_Music.</td><td>Used a variety of picture corrections, shapes, borders and layouts that enhanced the presentation.</td><td>Used some picture corrections, shapes, borders and layouts to enhance the presentation.</td><td>Used few or no picture corrections, shapes, borders and layouts to enhance the presentation.</td></tr>
<tr><td>Added audio and video files and applied playback options.</td><td>Inserted audio and video files in appropriate places and applied playback options. Both played correctly.</td><td>Inserted the audio, but either the playback options were not set or the audio did not play back correctly.</td><td>Inserted the audio, but the playback options were not set and the audio did not play back correctly.</td></tr>
</table>

You have completed Project 5K | END

Outcomes-Based Assessments (Critical Thinking)

Rubric

The following outcomes-based assessments are *open-ended assessments*. That is, there is no specific correct result; your result will depend on your approach to the information provided. Make *Professional Quality* your goal. Use the following scoring rubric to guide you in *how* to approach the problem and then to evaluate *how well* your approach solves the problem.

- The *criteria*—Software Mastery, Content, Format and Layout, and Process—represent the knowledge and skills you have gained that you can apply to solving the problem. The *levels of performance*—Professional Quality, Approaching Professional Quality, or Needs Quality Improvements—help you and your instructor evaluate your result.

	Your completed project is of Professional Quality if you:	Your completed project is Approaching Professional Quality if you:	Your completed project Needs Quality Improvements if you:
1-Software Mastery	Choose and apply the most appropriate skills, tools, and features and identify efficient methods to solve the problem.	Choose and apply some appropriate skills, tools, and features, but not in the most efficient manner.	Choose inappropriate skills, tools, or features, or are inefficient in solving the problem.
2-Content	Construct a solution that is clear and well organized, contains content that is accurate, appropriate to the audience and purpose, and is complete. Provide a solution that contains no errors of spelling, grammar, or style.	Construct a solution in which some components are unclear, poorly organized, inconsistent, or incomplete. Misjudge the needs of the audience. Have some errors in spelling, grammar, or style, but the errors do not detract from comprehension.	Construct a solution that is unclear, incomplete, or poorly organized, contains some inaccurate or inappropriate content, and contains many errors of spelling, grammar, or style. Do not solve the problem.
3-Format and Layout	Format and arrange all elements to communicate information and ideas, clarify function, illustrate relationships, and indicate relative importance.	Apply appropriate format and layout features to some elements, but not others. Overuse features, causing minor distraction.	Apply format and layout that does not communicate information or ideas clearly. Do not use format and layout features to clarify function, illustrate relationships, or indicate relative importance. Use available features excessively, causing distraction.
4-Process	Use an organized approach that integrates planning, development, self-assessment, revision, and reflection.	Demonstrate an organized approach in some areas, but not others; or, use an insufficient process of organization throughout.	Do not use an organized approach to solve the problem.

Outcomes-Based Assessments (Critical Thinking)

Apply a combination of the 5A and 5B skills.

GO! Think	Project 5L Ragtime and Woodwinds Music

Project Files

For Project 5L, you will need:

p05L_Ragtime_Music
p05_Music_Video
p05L_Entertainer

You will save your presentation as:
Lastname_Firstname_5L_Ragtime_Music

In this project, you will edit a presentation about the history and structure of Ragtime music. Open **p05L_Ragtime_Music** and save it as **Lastname_Firstname_5L_Ragtime_Music** Modify the images on the slides. Add audio and video to the presentation. Set the audio file to start automatically and play across slides. Set the video to trigger On Click of Title.

Insert appropriate header and footer, and then update the Properties on the file. Submit your files as directed.

	You have completed Project 5L	END

GO! Think	Project 5M Classical Music and Renaissance Album	IRC

You and GO!	Project 5N Swing Origins	IRC

Delivering a Presentation

6
POWERPOINT
2019

PROJECT 6A

Outcomes
Apply slide transitions and custom animation effects.

Objectives
1. Apply and Modify Slide Transitions
2. Apply Custom Animation Effects
3. Modify Animation Effects

PROJECT 6B

Outcomes
Insert hyperlinks, create custom slide shows, and view presentations.

Objectives
4. Insert Hyperlinks
5. Create Custom Slide Shows
6. Present and View a Slide Presentation

lzf/Shutterstock

In This Chapter

 **GO! To Work with PowerPoint**

Microsoft PowerPoint includes tools that can turn a lackluster presentation into one that captivates the attention of the audience. You can apply animation to individual slides, to a slide master, or to a custom slide layout. You can also apply transitions and other animation effects to all the slides in a presentation or only to selected slides. In addition, you can insert hyperlinks into a presentation to quickly link to a webpage, to another slide, or to a document. You can create a custom show composed of selected slides. PowerPoint includes an annotation tool that enables you to write or draw on slides during your presentation.

Penn Liberty Motors has one of eastern Pennsylvania's largest inventories of popular new car brands, sport utility vehicles, hybrid cars, and motorcycles. Its sales, service, and finance staff are all highly trained and knowledgeable about Penn Liberty's products, and the company takes pride in its consistently high customer satisfaction ratings. Penn Liberty also offers extensive customization options for all types of vehicles through its accessories division. Custom wheels, bike and ski racks, car covers, and chrome accessories are just a few of the ways Penn Liberty customers make personal statements with their cars.

PROJECT
6A Penn Liberty Motors

MyLab IT
Project 6A Grader for Instruction
Project 6A Simulation for Training and Review

Project Activities

In Activities 6.01 through 6.05, you will add slide transitions and animation effects to a presentation that outlines the organizational structure and location of Penn Liberty Motors. Your completed presentation will look similar to Figure 6.1.

Project Files for MyLab IT Grader

1. In your storage location, create a folder named **PowerPoint Chapter 6**.
2. In your **MyLab IT** course, locate and click **PowerPoint 6A Penn Liberty**, Download Materials, and then Download All Files. Close the Grader download screens.
3. Extract the zipped folder to your PowerPoint Chapter 6 folder.
4. Take a moment to open the downloaded **PowerPoint_6A_Penn_Liberty_Instructions**; note any recent updates to the book.

Project Results

GO! Project 6A
Where We're Going

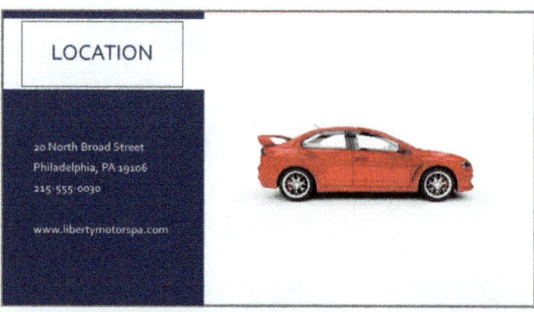

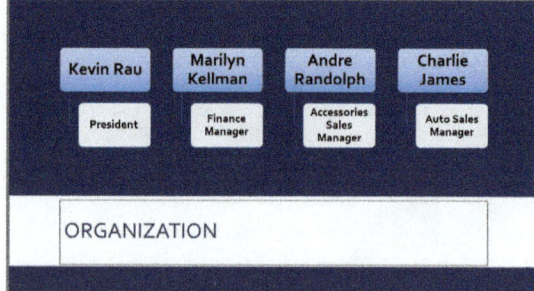

Figure 6.1 Project 6A Penn Liberty Motors

For Non-MyLab Submissions

For Project 6A, you will need:
p06A_Penn_Liberty

In your storage location, create a folder named **PowerPoint Chapter 6**
In your PowerPoint Chapter 6 folder, save your presentation as:
Lastname_Firstname_6A_Penn_Liberty

After you have named and saved your presentation, on the next page, begin with Step 2.

---

410 **PowerPoint** | Chapter 6: Delivering a Presentation

Objective 1 Apply and Modify Slide Transitions

ALERT   Because Office 365 is a cloud-based subscription service that receives continuous updates, you may encounter some variations in what appears on your screen and what is shown in this instruction. Microsoft Office 365 is fully installed on your PC or Mac; no internet access is necessary to create or edit documents. When you *are* connected to the internet, you will receive monthly upgrades and new features, so you always have the latest versions of Office apps as soon as they are available. Your subscription gives you continuous free access to the latest innovations and refinements.

GO! Learn How
Video P6-1

Transitions are motion effects that occur between slides in Slide Show view. A transition adds visual interest as you reveal the content in each slide in your presentation. Different transitions can be applied to selected slides, or the same transition can be applied to all slides. When referring to transitions, *animation* is the motion or movement that occurs as the presentation moves from slide to slide. Animation is also a special effect that is added to text or an object. When applying transitions or animations to a presentation, consider your audience. A presentation that overuses these features will not look professional. Use them only when they enhance the content of the presentation or suit the audience.

You can modify transitions by changing the ***transition speed***—the timing of the transition between all slides or between the previous slide and the current slide. You can set the presentation to display each slide in response to the presenter clicking the mouse button or pressing the Enter key. Or, you can configure the slide show so that the slides advance automatically after a specified amount of time.

Activity 6.01 | Applying and Modifying Slide Transitions

MOS
5.1.1, 5.1.2, 5.3.1

In this Activity, you will apply slide transitions and modify them by changing the transition speed.

1 Navigate to your **PowerPoint Chapter 6 folder**, and then double-click the PowerPoint file you downloaded from **MyLab IT** that displays your name—**Student_PowerPoint_6A_ Penn_Liberty**. In your presentation, if necessary, at the top click **Enable Editing**.

2 On **Slide 1**, on the **Transitions tab**, in the **Transition to This Slide group**, click **More** ▾ to display the **Transitions** gallery, and then compare your screen with Figure 6.2.

The Transitions gallery includes the three categories of slide transitions: Subtle, Exciting, and Dynamic Content. Subtle transitions are the simplest transitions between slides. Exciting transitions add more motion and visual interest but may not be appropriate for professional presentations. Dynamic transitions are a good way to transition between slides that use the same layout—by animating only the placeholders and not the slide background.

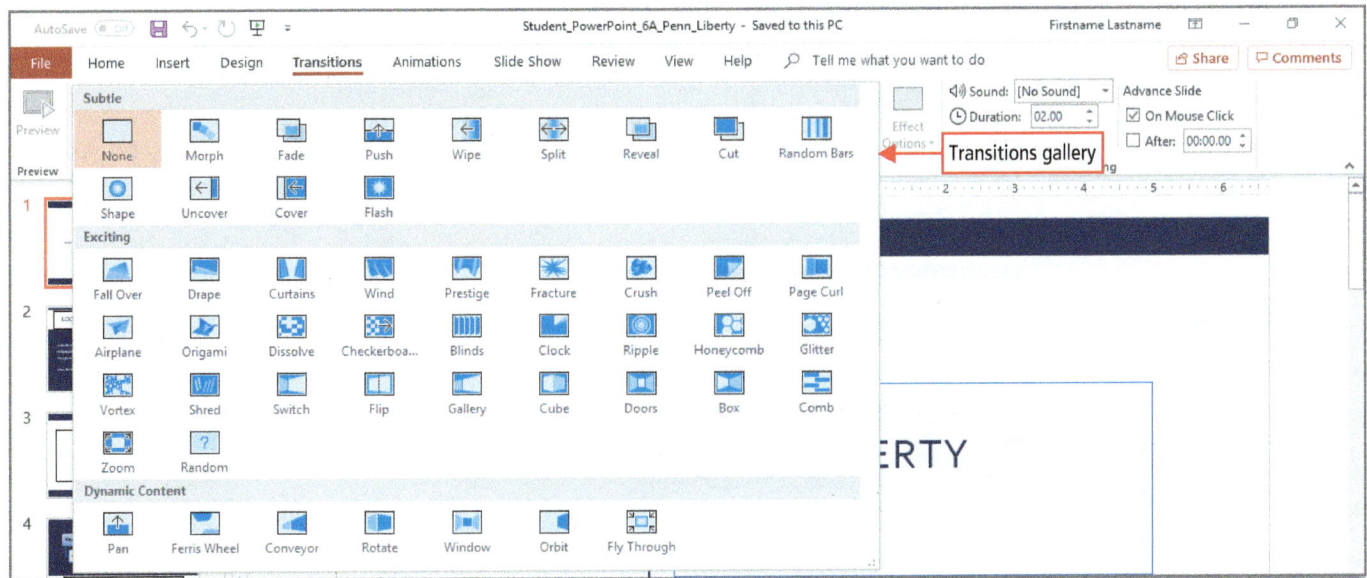

Figure 6.2

3 Under **Subtle**, click the fourth transition—**Push**.

The preview of the Push transition plays on Slide 1.

4 In the **Timing group**, click **Apply To All**. On the **Transitions tab**, in the **Preview group**, click **Preview** and notice the transition preview for Slide 1 plays. Compare your screen with Figure 6.3.

In the slide thumbnails, a Play Animations icon displays under each slide number.

ANOTHER WAY   To preview a slide transition, in the Slide pane, click the Play Animations icon that displays to the left of the slide thumbnail.

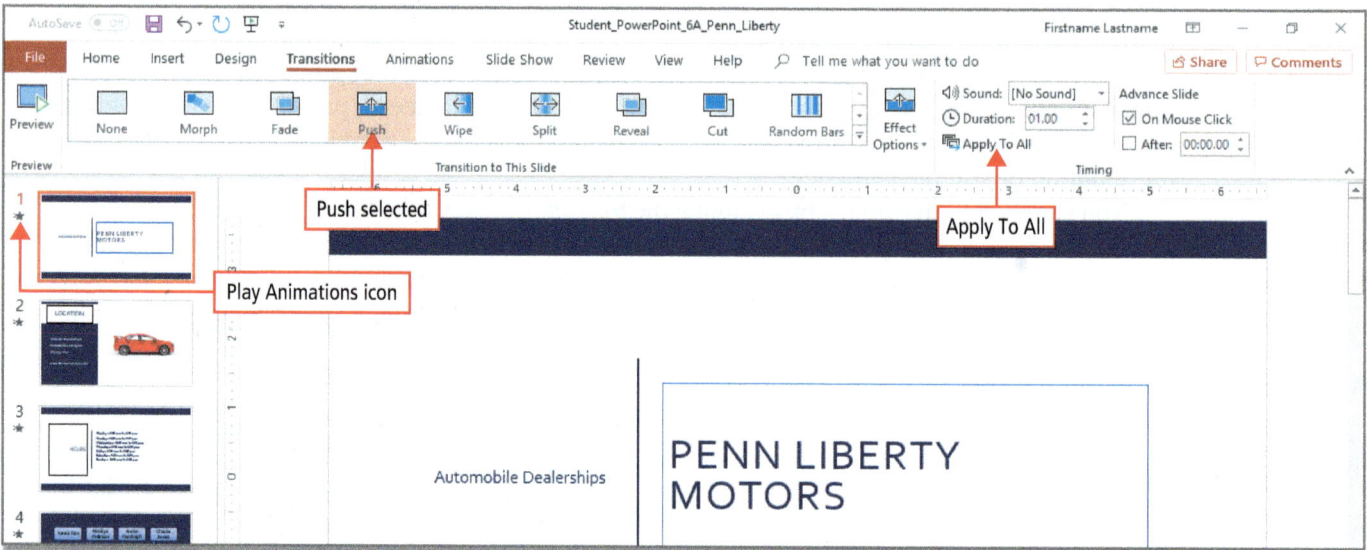

Figure 6.3

5 On the **Slide Show tab**, in the **Start Slide Show group**, click **From Beginning**. View the entire slide show, and then press Enter or Esc to return to **Normal** view.

The Push transition occurs between each slide.

6 Display **Slide 2**. On the **Transitions tab**, in the **Transition to This Slide group**, click the third transition, **Fade**. Compare your screen with Figure 6.4.

The Fade transition is applied to Slide 2 only.

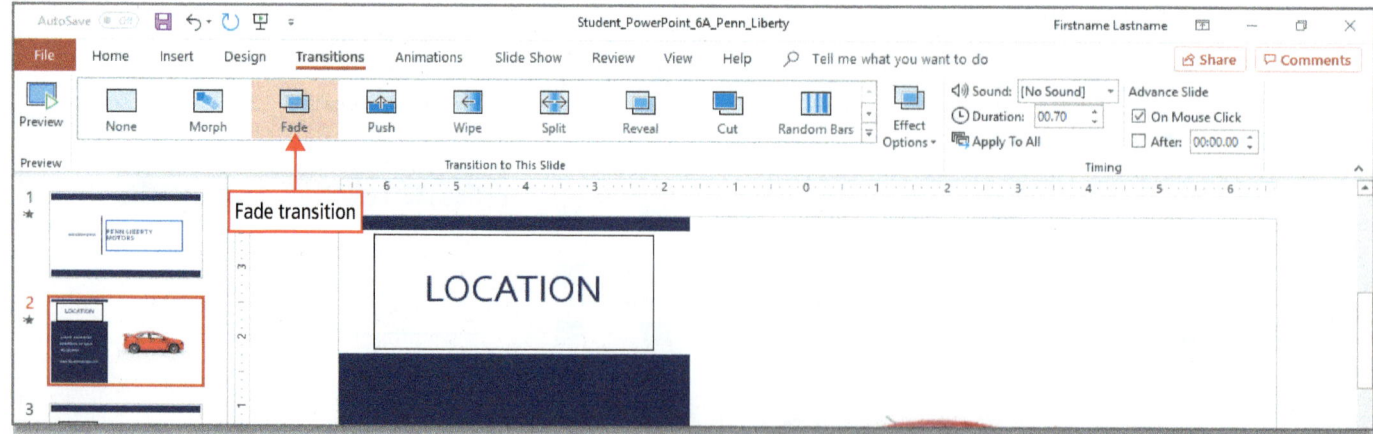

Figure 6.4

7 ▸ View the slide show **From Beginning** and return to **Normal** view.

The Fade transition occurs between Slide 1 and Slide 2. The transition between all the other slides remains set to Push.

👉 **BY TOUCH**   Tap to select the Slide Show tab. In the Start Slide Show group, tap From Beginning.

8 ▸ Display **Slide 5**. On the **Transitions tab**, in the **Timing group**, change the **Duration** to **05.00**. Compare your screen with Figure 6.5.

The transition duration from Slide 4 to Slide 5 is set to five seconds.

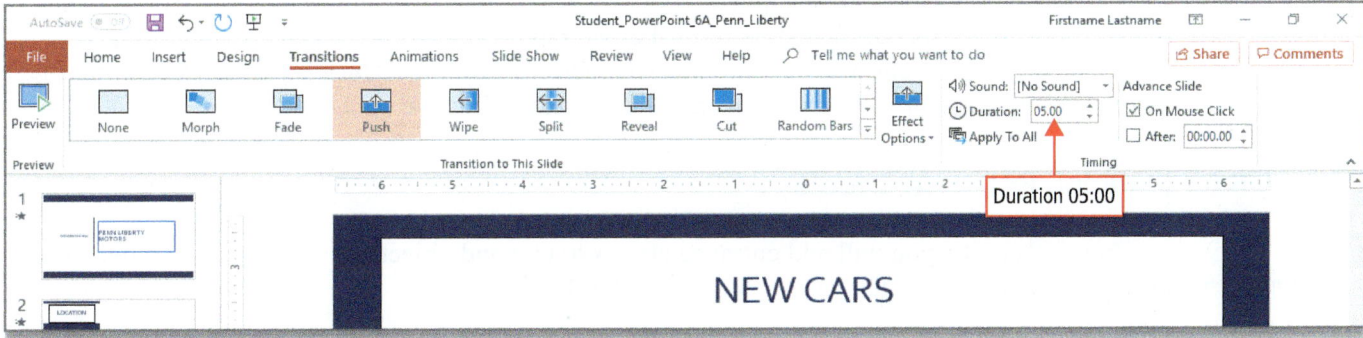

Figure 6.5

9 ▸ View the slide show **From Beginning** and return to **Normal** view. **Save** the presentation.

Slide 5 moves slowly up on the screen.

Activity 6.02 | Advancing Slides Automatically

In this Activity, you will customize a slide show by changing the Advance Slide method to advance slides automatically after a specified number of seconds.

1 ▸ Display **Slide 2**. On the **Transitions tab**, in the **Timing group**, under **Advance Slide**, clear the **On Mouse Click** check box.

2 ▸ In the **Timing group**, under **Advance Slide**, change the **After box** to **00:05.00**. Compare your screen with Figure 6.6.

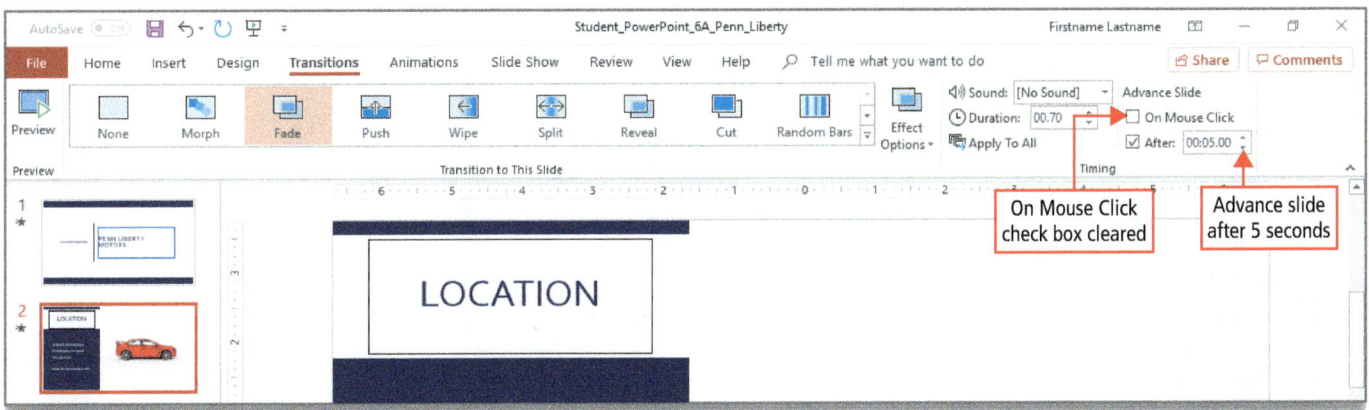

Figure 6.6

3 ▸ View the slide show **From Beginning**—press Enter one time to advance the slide show to **Slide 2**. When **Slide 2** displays, wait 5 seconds for the third slide to display. When **Slide 3** displays, return to **Normal** view.

4 ▸ **Save** the presentation.

Objective 2 | Apply Custom Animation Effects

GO! Learn How
Video P6-2

Like other effects that you can customize in PowerPoint, you can customize animation effects. In this context, *animation* refers to a special effect or sound added to text or to an object. You can add animation to bulleted items, text, or other objects such as charts, graphics, or SmartArt graphics.

Animation can be applied as an ***Entrance effect***, which brings a slide element onto the screen. Animation can also take the form of an ***Emphasis effect***, which emphasizes an object or text that is already displayed. For example, an object can shrink or grow in size, change color, or spin on its center. Or, animation can be applied as an ***Exit effect***, which occurs as the text or object leaves the slide or disappears during a slide show. For example, bulleted items can fly into, or move into, a slide and then fade away. Animation can take the form of a ***Motion Paths effect***, which determines how and in what direction an object or text will move on a slide.

Activity 6.03 | Adding Entrance Effects

MOS
5.2.1, 5.2.3, 5.2.4

In this Activity, you will add entrance effects to text and objects by making them move in a specified manner as the text or graphic enters the slide.

1 Display **Slide 3**, and then click to select the content placeholder with the days and hours of operation. On the **Animations tab**, in the **Advanced Animation group**, click **Add Animation**. Compare your screen with Figure 6.7, and then take a moment to study the animation effects described in the table in Figure 6.8.

💻 **MAC TIP** The Add Animations button is not available in the Mac version of PowerPoint. Use the Gallery instead.

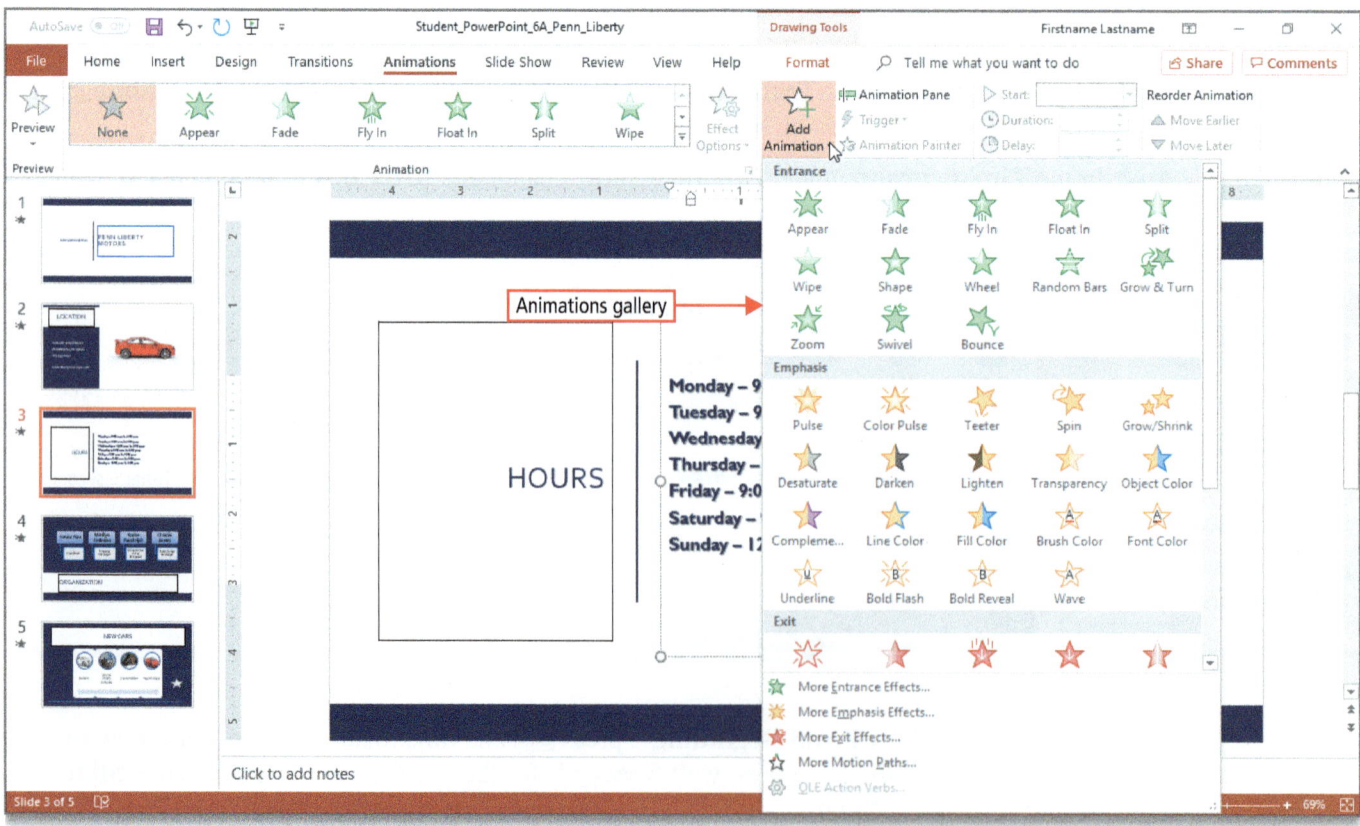

Figure 6.7

Animation Effects	
Effects	**Examples**
Entrance	The object or text fades gradually into focus, flies onto the slide from an edge, or bounces into view.
Emphasis	The object or text shrinks or grows in size, changes color, or spins on its center.
Exit	The object or text flies off the slide, disappears from view, or spirals off the slide.
Motion Paths	The object or text moves up or down, left or right, or in a star or circular pattern.

Figure 6.8

2 ▶ Under **Entrance**, click **Fade**.

3 ▶ On the **Animations tab**, in the **Advanced Animation group**, if necessary, click **Animation Pane**. Compare your screen with Figure 6.9.

The Animation Pane displays the animation you applied on Slide 3.

ALERT   Are animation numbers missing?

Make sure to select the Animation tab. If the animation numbers still do not appear on your slide, Save the file to a local drive, close the file, and reopen it. If the numbers still do not display, continue with the Activity, following along with the figures.

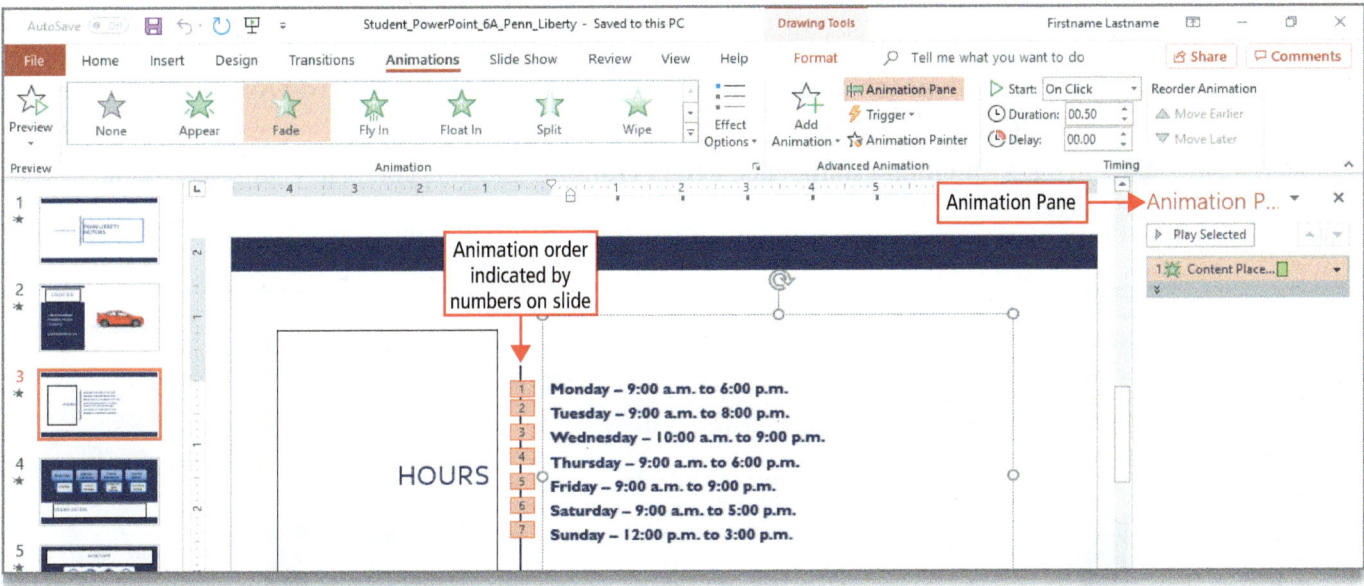

Figure 6.9

4 In the **Animation Pane** on the right side of your screen, under *Content Placeholder*, click ⌄, and then compare your screen with Figure 6.10.

The objects in the content placeholder are listed in the Animation Pane.

MAC TIP Click the expand arrow to the left of Content Placeholder 2.

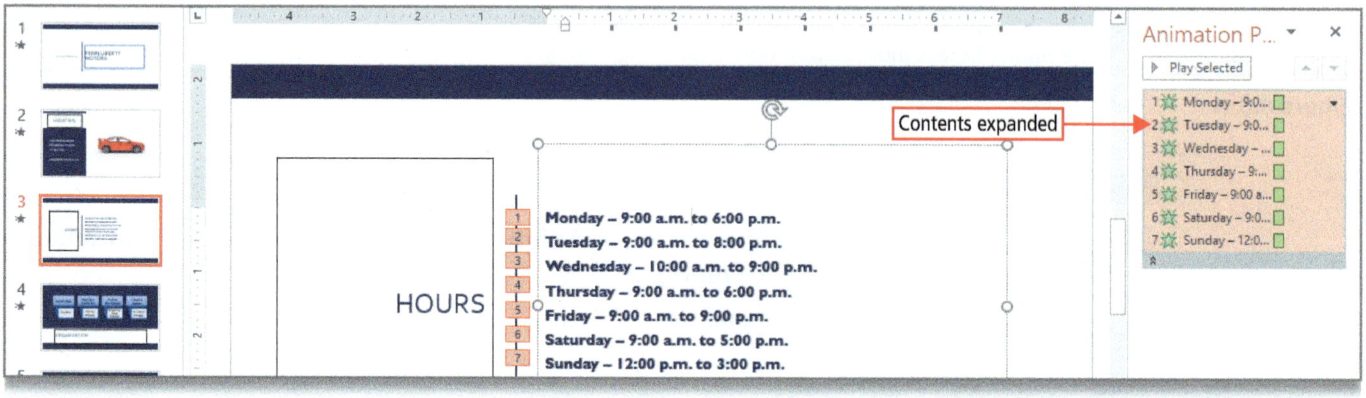

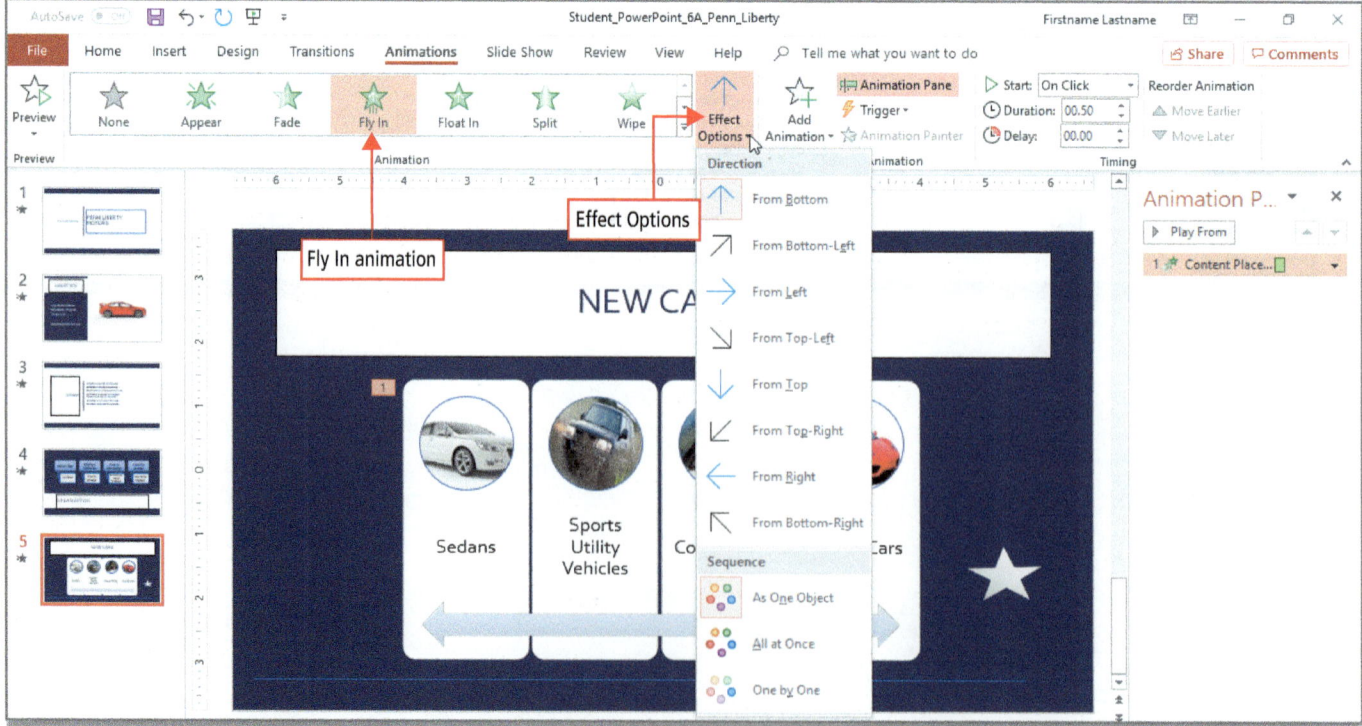

Figure 6.10

5 In the **Animation Pane**, click **1**—the **first entrance effect** for the content placeholder—and then at the top of the **Animation Pane**, click **Play From** to test the animation.

At the bottom of the Animation Pane, a *timeline* displays the number of seconds the animation takes to complete.

6 Display **Slide 5**. Click the **SmartArt graphic** containing the car photos and names. On the **Animations tab**, in the **Advanced Animation group**, click **Add Animation**. Under **Entrance**, click **Fly In**.

7 In the **Animation group**, click **Effect Options**, and then compare your screen with Figure 6.11.

The sequence options are As One Object, All at Once, or One by One.

Figure 6.11

8 Under **Sequence**, click **One by One**.

The shapes in the SmartArt graphic on Slide 5 display one at a time.

9 In the **Animation Pane**, below *Content Placeholder*, click ⯆ to expand the contents, and then compare your screen with Figure 6.12.

Five animations display in the Animation Pane.

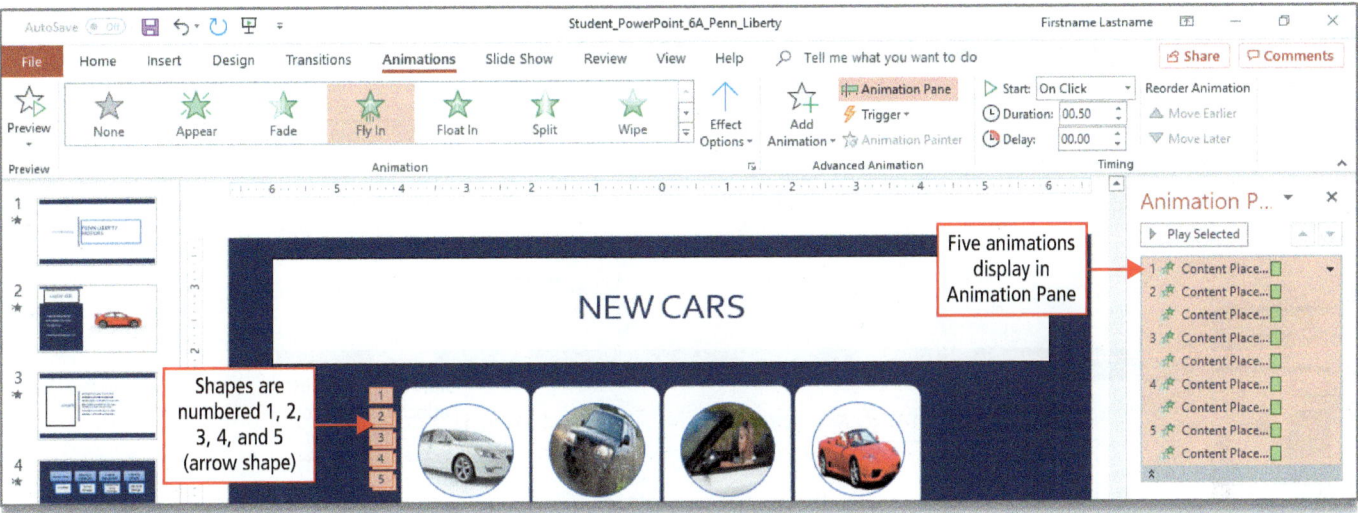

Figure 6.12

10 View the presentation from the beginning, and then return to **Normal** view. **Save** 💾 your presentation.

Each SmartArt shape moves onto the slide individually.

MORE KNOWLEDGE **Effects**

Entrance, Emphasis, Exit, and Motion Paths effects can be selected from the Add Animation gallery or from the Add Effect dialog boxes. The Add Effect dialog box, specific to each type of effect, contains additional effects categorized as Basic, Subtle, Moderate, and Exciting. Motion Paths can also be applied to graphics. Built-in Motion Paths enable you to make text or a graphic move in a particular pattern, or you can design your own pattern of movement.

Objective 3 | Modify Animation Effects

GO! Learn How Video P6-3

You can modify or customize entrance effects, emphasis effects, exit effects, and motion paths by changing how they start, the speed at which they occur, and their direction. Effect settings such as timing delays and the number of times an effect is repeated can also be added. Effects can be set to start after a previous effect or simultaneously.

On Click enables you to start an animation when you click the slide or a trigger—such as an image or button, or by pressing Enter or Spacebar. Changing an animation start method to *After Previous* enables the animation effect to begin immediately after the completion of the previous animation or slide transition. Changing the start method to *With Previous* begins the animation sequence at the same time as the previous animation or slide transition.

Activity 6.04 | Modifying Animation Effects

MOS
5.2.3

In this Activity, you will modify the start method of some of the animation effects you added. You will also modify the speed and timing of the animation effects.

1 Display **Slide 3**, and then click to select the content placeholder.

2 In the **Animation Pane**, click the animation item in the list—**Monday**—to select it, and then right-click **Monday**. Compare your screen with Figure 6.13, and then take a moment to review the Start Options described in the table in Figure 6.14.

ANOTHER WAY   Click the down arrow next to Monday.

MAC TIP   In the Animations pane, click Timing.

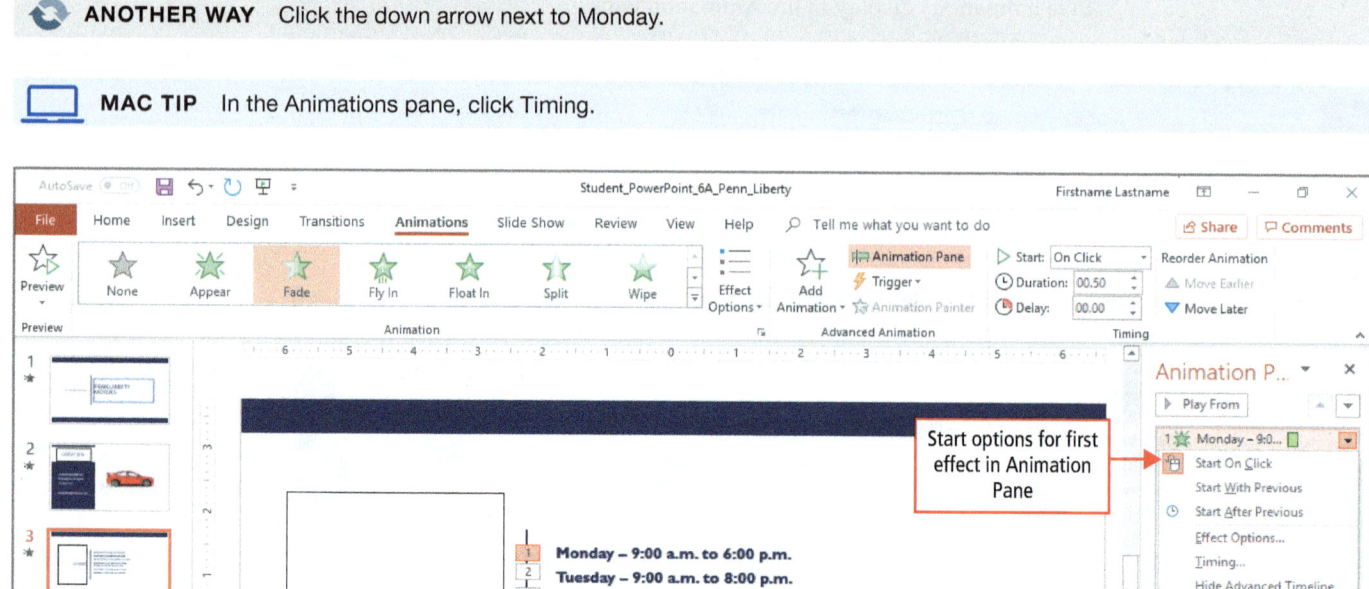

Figure 6.13

Animation Start Options	
Option	**How The Animation Will Begin**
Start On Click	Animation begins when the slide is clicked.
Start With Previous	Animation begins at the same time as the previous effect. One click executes all animation effects applied to the object.
Start After Previous	Animation begins after the previous effect in the list finishes. No additional click is needed. One click executes all animation effects applied to the object.

Figure 6.14

3 Click **Start After Previous**. View the slide show **From Current Slide**, and click seven times to display all items. When **Slide 4** displays, press Esc to return to **Normal** view.

By changing *On Click* to *After Previous*, the first animation displays without having to click the mouse.

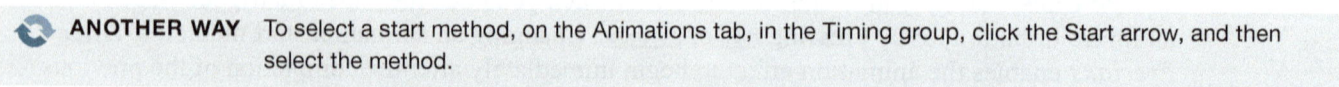

ANOTHER WAY   To select a start method, on the Animations tab, in the Timing group, click the Start arrow, and then select the method.

4 On **Slide 3**, in the **Animation Pane**, click ⊼ to collapse the list. In the **Animation Pane**, right-click the entrance effect for the **Content Placeholder**, and then click **Effect Options** to display the **Fade** dialog box.

5 In the **Fade** dialog box, click the **Timing tab**, click the **Start arrow**, and then click **After Previous**.

6 Click the **Duration arrow**, and then select **1 seconds (Fast)**. Compare your screen with Figure 6.15.

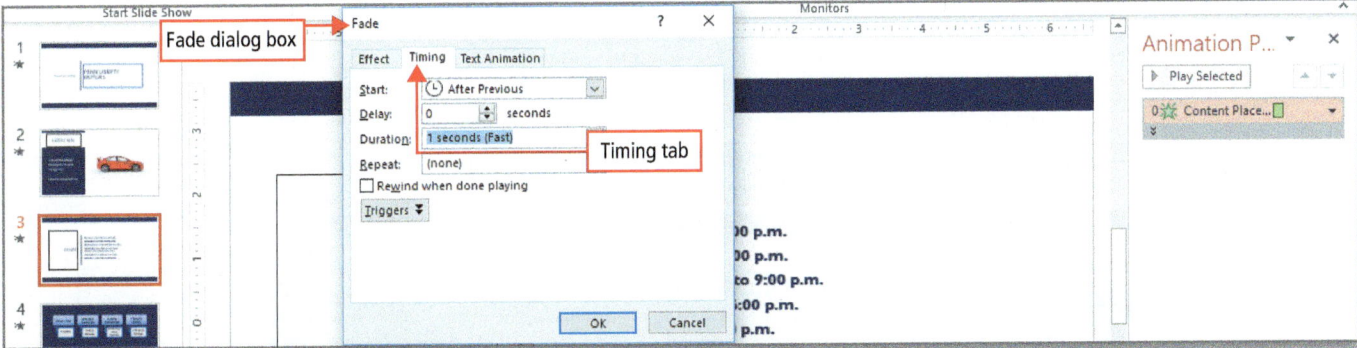

Figure 6.15

7 Click **OK**. View the slide show **From Current Slide** and return to **Normal** view.

8 **Save** 💾 your presentation.

Activity 6.05 | Setting Effect Options

5.2.3

In this Activity, you will set effect options that include having an animation disappear from the slide after the animation effect, and animating text.

1 On **Slide 3**, in the **Animation Pane**, right-click the entrance effect for the **Content Placeholder**, and then click **Effect Options** to display the **Fade** dialog box.

2 In the **Fade** dialog box, on the **Effect tab**, under **Enhancements**, click the **After animation arrow**. Compare your screen with Figure 6.16.

Here you can apply a color change to the animated text or object.

💻 **MAC TIP** In the Animations pane, use Effect Options.

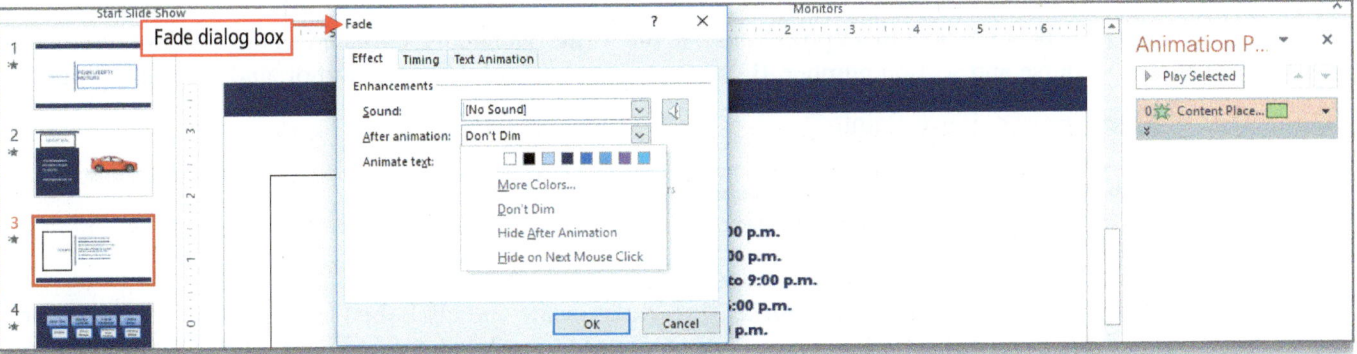

Figure 6.16

3 In the row of colors, click the third color. Click **OK**. Notice that the text for each day displays in light blue as it appears.

The animation changes display automatically one at a time.

4 Display **Slide 5**, and then click to select the SmartArt object.

5 On the **Animations tab**, in the **Animation group**, click **Effect Options**, and then compare your screen with Figure 6.17.

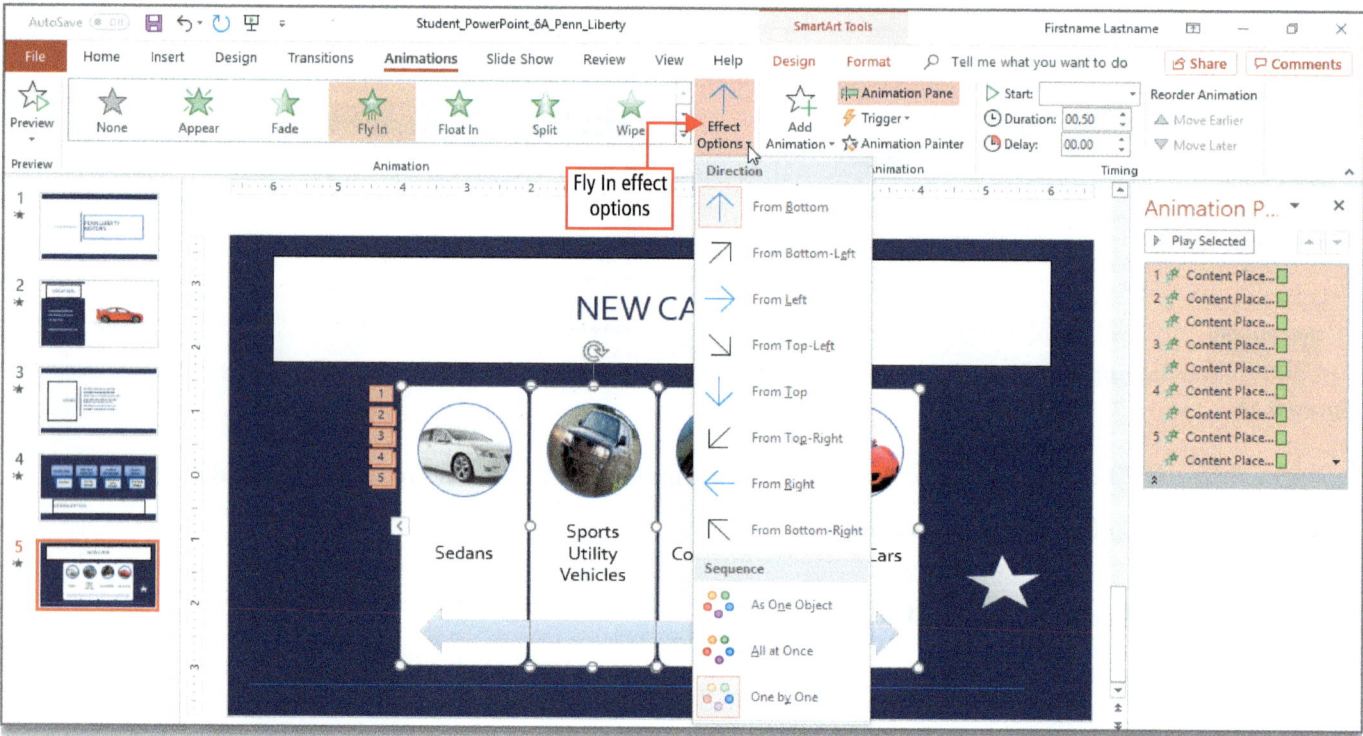

Figure 6.17

6 Click **From Bottom-Left**. In the **Animation Pane**, click **Play Selected**.

Each of the shapes in the SmartArt enters the slide from the lower left corner of the screen—the From Bottom-Left effect.

7 View the slide show **From Beginning**, and then return to **Normal** view. Close the **Animation** pane.

8 Insert a **Header & Footer** on the **Notes and Handouts**. Include the **Date and time** fixed, the **Page Number**, and a **Footer 6A_Penn_Liberty** and then click **Apply to All**.

9 Display the document properties. As the **Tags**, type **hours, cars** and as the **Subject**, type your course and section number. Be sure your name displays as the author, and then **Save** your file.

10 **Close** ☒ PowerPoint.

For Non-MyLab Submissions Determine What Your Instructor Requires
Print or submit your presentation electronically as directed by your instructor.

11 In **MyLab IT**, in your **Course Materials**, locate and click the Grader Project **PowerPoint 6A Penn Liberty**. In **step 3**, under **Upload Completed Assignment**, click **Choose File**. In the **Open** dialog box, navigate to your **PowerPoint Chapter 6 folder**, and then click your **Student_PowerPoint_6A_Penn_Liberty** file one time to select it. In the lower right corner of the **Open** dialog box, click **Open**.

12 To submit your file to **MyLab IT** for grading, click **Upload**, wait a moment for a green **Success!** message, and then in **step 4**, click the blue **Submit for Grading** button. Click **Close Assignment** to return to your list of **Course Materials**.

You have completed Project 6A **END**

PROJECT 6B — Penn Liberty Motors Advertisement

MyLab IT
Project 6B Grader for Instruction
Project 6B Simulation for Training and Review

Project Activities

In Activities 6.06 through 6.16, you will insert hyperlinks into a presentation created by Penn Liberty Motors as an advertisement for the company. The focus of the ad is the location of Penn Liberty Motors in Philadelphia. You will create two custom slide shows from a single presentation to appeal to two different audiences. You will also annotate the presentation. Finally, you will organize your slides into sections and print selections from a presentation. Your completed presentation will look similar to Figure 6.18.

Project Files for **MyLab IT Grader**

1. In your **MyLab IT** course, locate and click **PowerPoint 6B Advertisement**, Download Materials, and then Download All Files. Close the Grader download screens.
2. Extract the zipped folder to your PowerPoint Chapter 6 folder.
3. Take a moment to open the downloaded **PowerPoint_6B _Advertisement_Instructions**; note any recent updates to the book.

Project Results

GO! Project 6B
Where We're Going

Figure 6.18 Project 6B Penn Liberty Motors

For Non-MyLab Submissions
For Project 6B, you will need:
p06B_Advertisement
p06B_Blue_Car
p06B_Penn_Liberty

In your PowerPoint Chapter 6 folder, save your presentation as:
Lastname_Firstname_6B_Advertisement
Lastname_Firstname_6B_Print

After you have named and saved your presentation, on the next page, begin with Step 2.

ALERT   Because Office 365 is a cloud-based subscription service that receives continuous updates, you may encounter some variations in what appears on your screen and what is shown in this instruction. Microsoft Office 365 is fully installed on your PC or Mac; no internet access is necessary to create or edit documents. When you *are* connected to the internet, you will receive monthly upgrades and new features, so you always have the latest versions of Office apps as soon as they are available. Your subscription gives you continuous free access to the latest innovations and refinements.

GO! Learn How
Video P6-4

When giving a presentation, there may be times when you want to display different content. For example, you might have a standard sales presentation to show clients but have a special sale going on at the time of the presentation that you want to highlight. Rather than editing the standard sales presentation, you can link to a sales flyer, webpage, or another presentation from within the standard sales presentation. You can insert *hyperlinks*—navigation elements that, when clicked, will take you to another location, such as a webpage, an email address, another document, or a place within the same document. In a PowerPoint presentation, hyperlinks can link to:

- a webpage
- an email address
- another document or file
- a slide in the presentation
- a slide in a different presentation
- a custom slide show

Activity 6.06 | Inserting a Hyperlink to a Webpage

3.2.1

In this Activity, you will insert a hyperlink into a slide that will link to a webpage.

1 Navigate to your **PowerPoint Chapter 6 folder**, and then double-click the PowerPoint file you downloaded from **MyLab IT** that displays your name—**Student_PowerPoint_6B_ Advertisement**. In your presentation, if necessary, at the top click **Enable Editing**.

2 Display **Slide 4**. Click to select the text box containing the website address *www.philadelphiazoo.org*, and then select the web address text. On the **Insert tab**, in the **Links group**, click **Link** to display the **Insert Hyperlink** dialog box. If necessary, under **Link to**, click **Existing File or Web Page**. Compare your screen with Figure 6.19.

You can link to an Existing File or Web Page, a Place in This Document, Create New Document, or link to an E-mail Address.

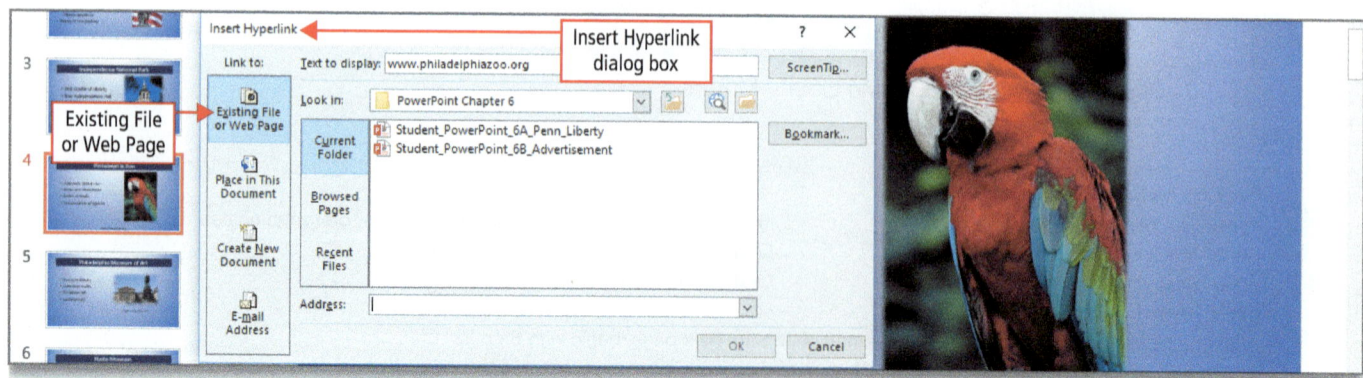

Figure 6.19

3 ▸ In the upper right, click **ScreenTip**. In the **Set Hyperlink ScreenTip** dialog box, in the ScreenTip text box, type **Philadelphia Zoo** and then compare your screen with Figure 6.20.

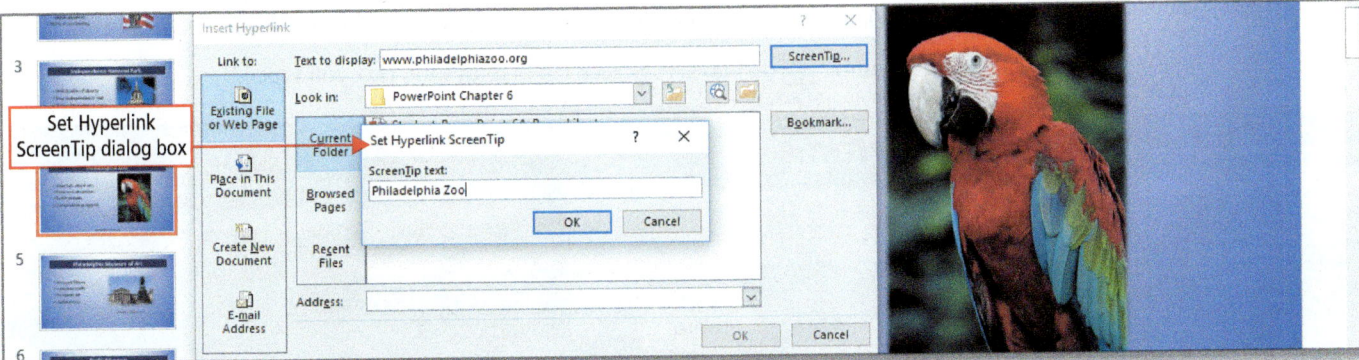

Figure 6.20

4 ▸ Click **OK**. In the **Address** box, type **http://www.philadelphiazoo.org** Compare your screen with Figure 6.21.

The text you typed is a *URL*, or *Uniform Resource Locator*—the address of a website.

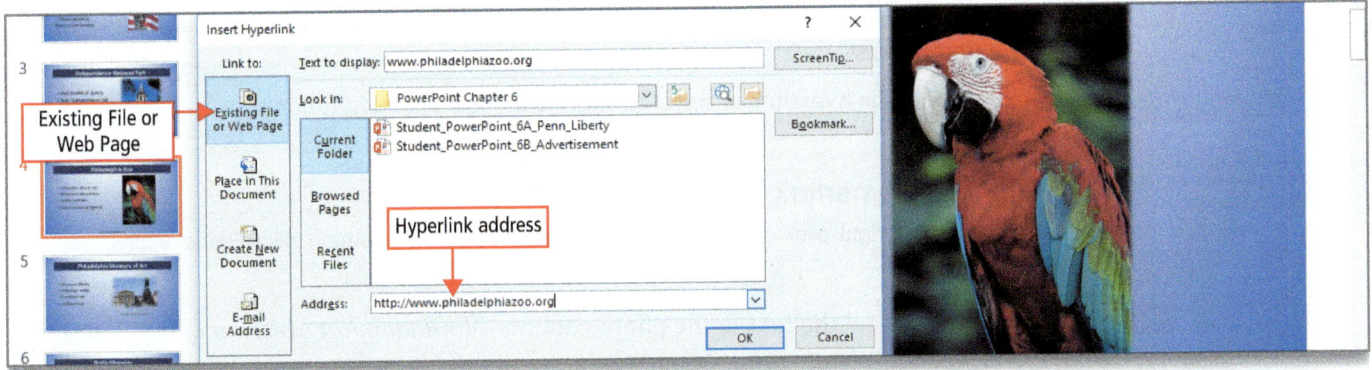

Figure 6.21

MORE KNOWLEDGE   **Understanding Uniform Resource Locators**

A URL consists of the protocol and the IP address or domain name. The URL *http://www.philadelphiazoo.org* begins with ***http—Hypertext Transfer Protocol***—the internet standard protocol that defines the exchange of information on the web. HTTP is the set of communication rules used by your computer to connect to servers on the Web, and tells your computer what type of page you are looking at. A ***protocol*** is a set of rules for communication between devices that determine how data is formatted, transmitted, received, and acknowledged. The most common protocol on the internet is http. Other common protocols are https, which is a secure webpage, or ftp, which stands for File Transfer Protocol. Because most websites use the http protocol, you need not type it as part of the address.

Following the protocol is the ***domain name***, which is sometimes called the second-level domain. In this example, *www. philadelphiazoo.org* is the domain name. The domain name represents a company, organization, or product name and makes it easy for users to remember the address. It is an organization's unique name on the internet, which consists of a chosen name (philadelphiazoo) combined with a ***top-level domain (TLD)*** such as .com, .org, or .gov. The *www* represents the computer on the *philadelphiazoo* domain. It is common to name the computer *www*, so this part of the URL is also often omitted.

At the end of the domain name is the *.org* suffix, which is known as the top-level domain (TLD). The TLD indicates the type of website you are visiting. Common TLDs are *.com* for commercial, *.edu* for U.S. educational, and *.gov* for U.S. government. Websites outside the United States often have a country code TLD, such as *.ca* for Canada or *.uk* for the United Kingdom.

5 Click **OK**. Click a blank area of the slide to deselect the textbox.

The webpage address font displays in purple with an underline indicating it is a hyperlink.

6 Start the slide show **From Current Slide**. On **Slide 4**, without clicking, point to the address *www.philadelphiazoo.org*, and then compare your screen with Figure 6.22.

The Link Select pointer ⬚ displays. A ScreenTip displays the text you typed.

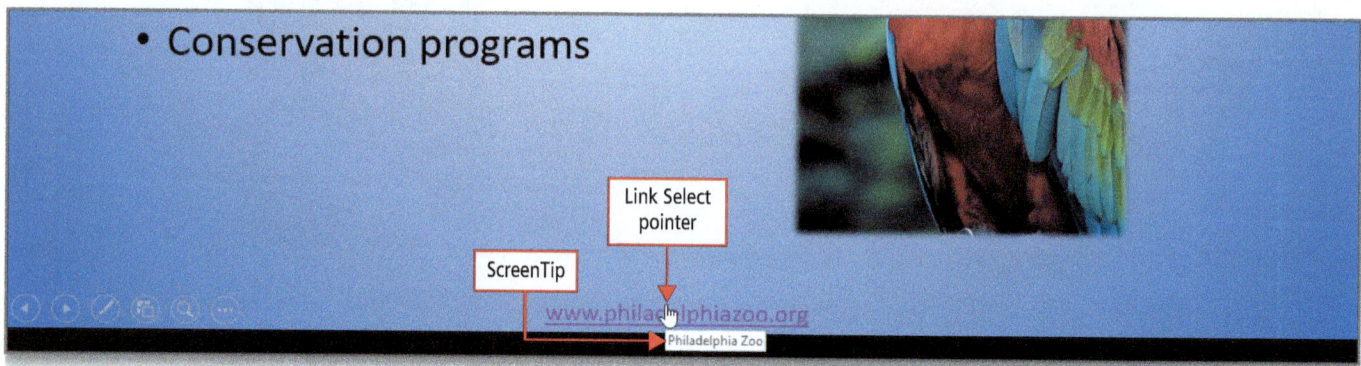

Figure 6.22

7 With the **Link Select** pointer ⬚, click the **hyperlink**.

The webpage displays in your default web browser if you are connected to the internet.

8 **Close** the webpage, and notice that the font color of the hyperlink has changed. Press Esc to return to **Normal** view.

The font color of the hyperlink changes to indicate the link has been followed.

MORE KNOWLEDGE **To Remove a Hyperlink**

Click the text box that contains the hyperlink, right-click on the URL, and then from the shortcut menu, click Remove Link.

---

9 Display **Slide 5**. Select the text in the photo caption—*Philadelphia Museum of Art*. On the **Insert tab**, in the **Links group**, click **Link**.

10 To the right of the **Look in** box, click **Browse the Web** ⬚.

Internet Explorer, or your default browser opens.

⬚ **MAC TIP** Open your browser and proceed with Step 11.

---

11 In your browser address bar, type **www.philamuseum.org** and then press Enter.

12 On the Windows taskbar at the bottom of your screen, click **PowerPoint**. Compare your screen with Figure 6.23.

The website address displays in the Insert Hyperlink dialog box Address box.

ALERT   **No Address Appears in PowerPoint?**

If you are not using Internet Explorer, this step may not work correctly. In that case, copy the URL from your browser address bar and paste it into the Insert Hyperlink dialog box.

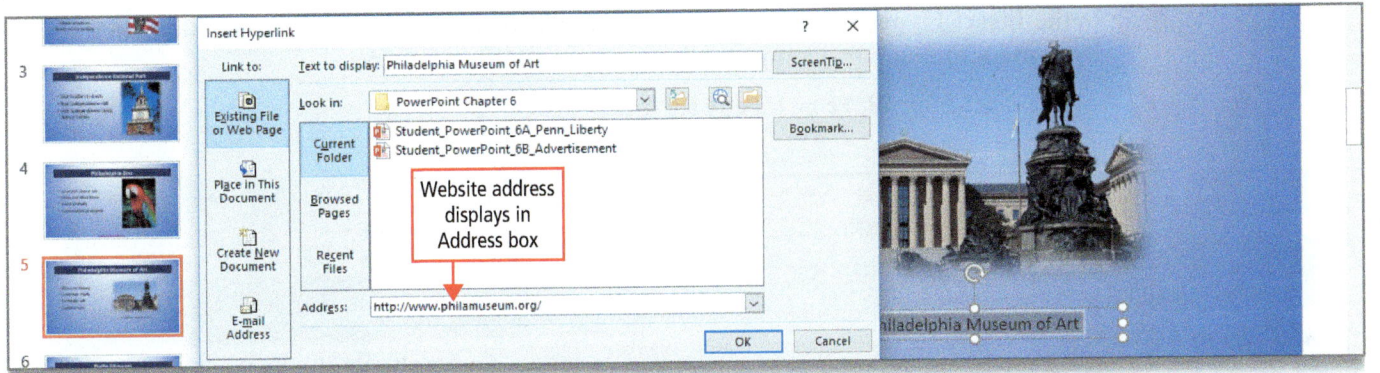
Figure 6.23

> **13** Click **OK**.
>
>> The caption displays as a hyperlink.
>
> **14** View the slide show **From Current Slide**. Point to the caption—*Philadelphia Museum of Art*.
>
>> It is not necessary to format the webpage hyperlink text on the slide in URL format so long as it is linked correctly to the webpage address. Any text or object can serve as a hyperlink.
>
> **15** Click to test the hyperlink. When you are finished, **Close** the webpage and return to PowerPoint. Return to **Normal** view and **Save** 💾 your presentation.

Activity 6.07 | Inserting a Hyperlink to Link to a Slide in Another Presentation

MOS
3.2.1, 3.2.2

In this Activity, you will insert a hyperlink that will link to a slide in another presentation.

> **1** Display **Slide 9**. Select the text in the picture caption—*Penn Liberty Motors New Car Selections*. On the **Insert tab**, in the **Links group**, click **Link** to display the **Insert Hyperlink** dialog box.
>
> **2** In the **Insert Hyperlink** dialog box, if necessary, under **Link to**, click **Existing File or Web Page**. If necessary, click the **Look in arrow**, navigate to your files downloaded with this project and then click **p06B_Penn_Liberty**. Compare your screen with Figure 6.24.

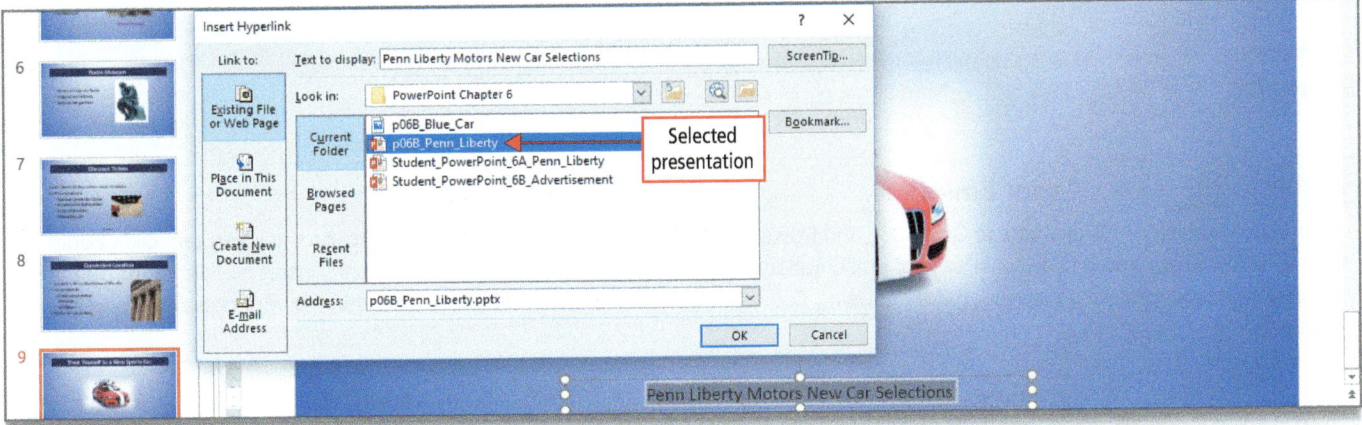
Figure 6.24

3 In the **Insert Hyperlink** dialog box, click **Bookmark** to display the **Select Place in Document** dialog box. Compare your screen with Figure 6.25.

The slides from 6B_Penn_Liberty are listed.

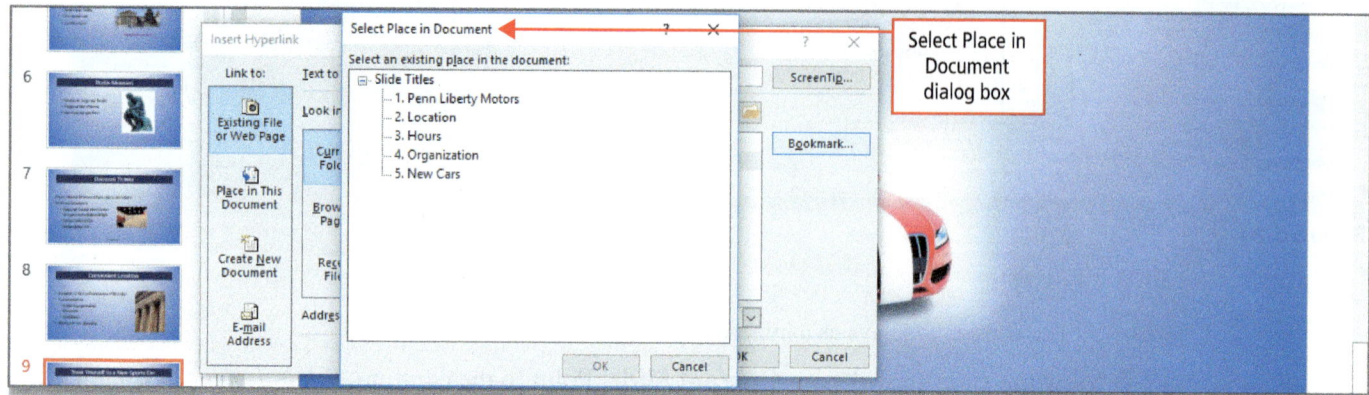

Figure 6.25

4 In the **Select Place in Document** dialog box, click the fifth slide—*New Cars*—and then click **OK**. Compare your screen with Figure 6.26.

The Address box contains the name of the presentation and the number and title of the slide.

MAC TIP In the address box, after the file name, do not press the spacebar, and then type #5 to link to the fifth slide.

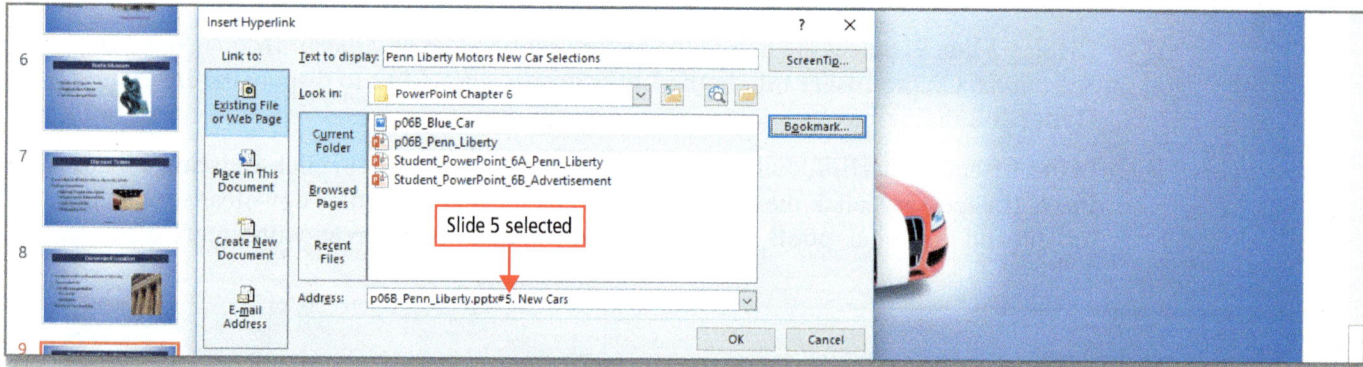

Figure 6.26

> **MORE KNOWLEDGE** **Zoom Links**
>
> Zoom for PowerPoint is available in Office 365 and PowerPoint 2019 for Windows. To add a Zoom, on the Insert tab, click Zoom. Insert a Summary Zoom to summarize your presentation on one slide. To show selected slides only, insert a Slide Zoom. To show a single section only, insert a Section Zoom. Using Zoom links, you can move to slides and sections of your presentation in any order.

5 Click **OK**. On the **Slide Show tab**, in the **Set Up group**, click **Set Up Slide Show**. If necessary, in the **Set Up Show** dialog box, under **Show type**, click **Presented by a speaker (full screen)**. Under **Advance slides**, click **Manually**, and then compare your screen with Figure 6.27.

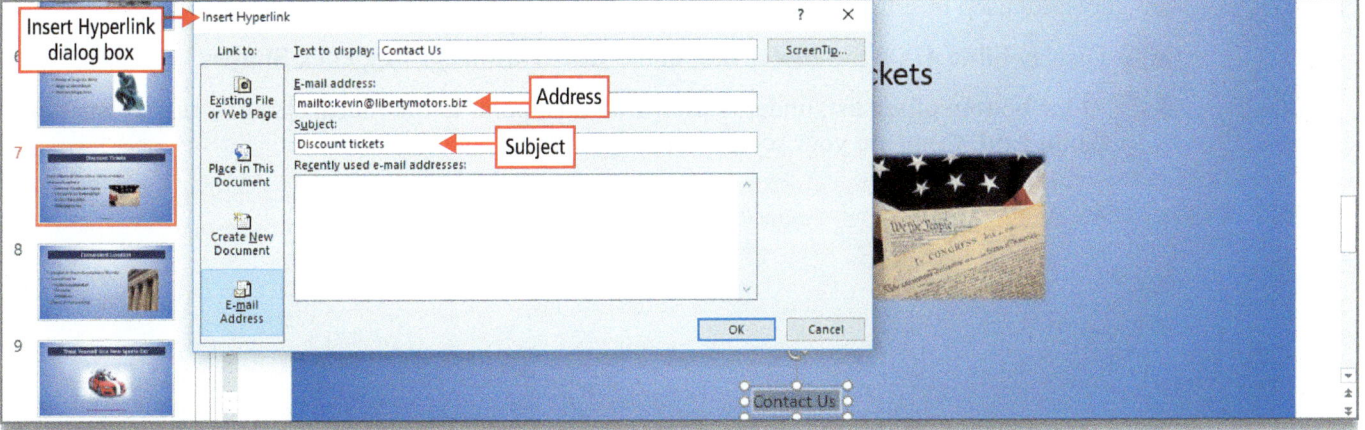

Figure 6.27

6 ▶ Click **OK.** Start the slide show **From Current Slide**, and then click the hyperlink. Press `Enter` five times to display the animation on Slide 5 of the linked *p06B_Penn_Liberty* presentation. Press `Esc` to return to your *Student_6B_Advertisement* presentation, and then press `Esc` to return to **Normal** view.

7 ▶ **Save** 🖫 your presentation.

Activity 6.08 | Inserting a Hyperlink to an Email Address

3.2.1

In this Activity, you will insert a hyperlink that will open an email client and insert the recipient's email address and subject.

1 ▶ Display **Slide 7**. Select the text *Contact Us*, and then on the **Insert tab**, in the **Links group**, click **Link**.

2 ▶ In the **Insert Hyperlink** dialog box, under **Link to**, click **E-mail Address**.

3 ▶ In the **E-mail address** box, type **kevin@libertymotors.biz**

4 ▶ In the **Subject** box, type **Discount tickets** and then compare your screen with Figure 6.28.

The word *mailto:* displays before the email address. This is an *HTML* attribute that identifies this text as an email address. ***HTML—HyperText Markup Language***—is the authoring language that defines the structure of a webpage.

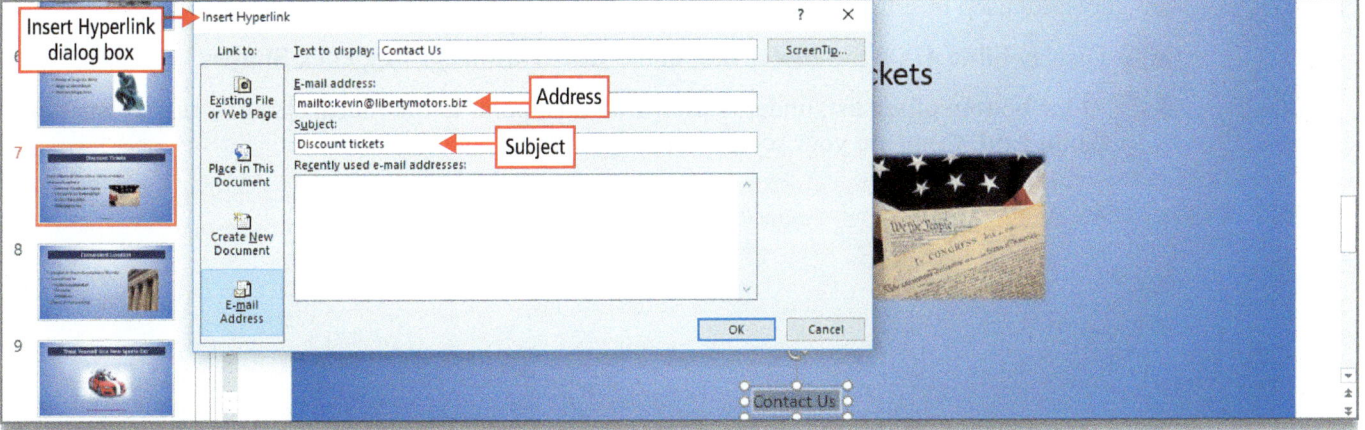

Figure 6.28

5 Click **OK**.

6 Start the slide show **From Current Slide**, and when the slide show displays, click the hyperlink. Compare your screen with Figure 6.29.

If you have an email program configured, your email program opens a new message with the email address you typed in the To box and the subject Discount tickets.

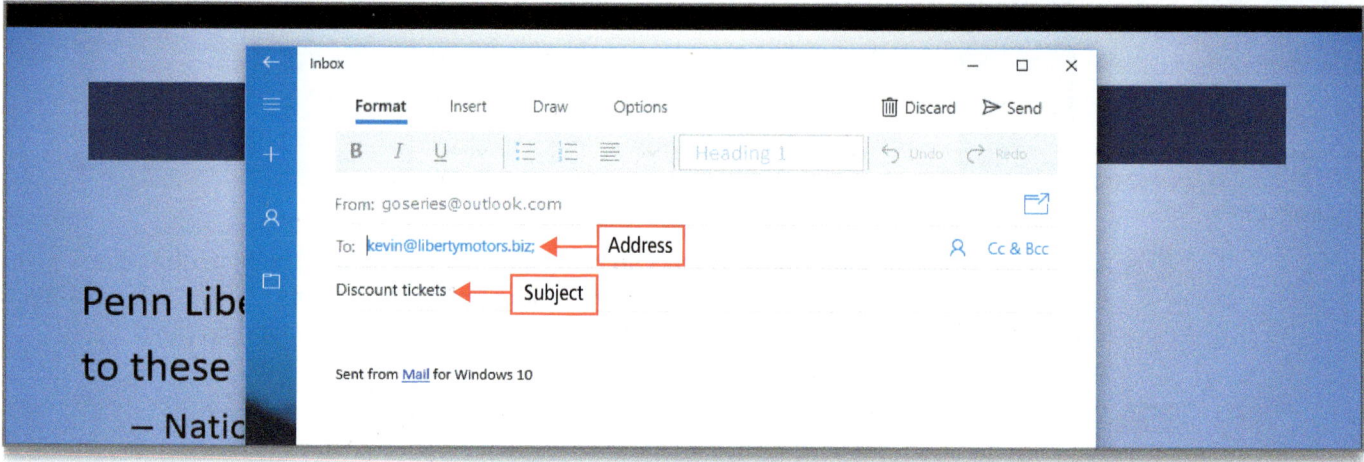

Figure 6.29

ALERT   No email program?

If you do not have an email program configured on your computer, you may see the message *How do you want to open this?* Click outside the message, return to Normal view, save your work, and continue to the next Activity.

7 **Close** the email program without saving changes to the email message, and then return to **Normal** view.

8 **Save** 🖫 the presentation.

Activity 6.09 | Creating an Action Button

An *action button* is a special type of shape that you can add to your presentation and to which you can assign an action. Action buttons have built-in actions or links associated with them and are generally used in self-running slide shows.

1 Display **Slide 4**. On the **Insert tab**, in the **Illustrations group**, click **Shapes**.

2 At the bottom of the list, under **Action Buttons**, point to the fourth shape—**Action Button: Go to End**. Compare your screen with Figure 6.30.

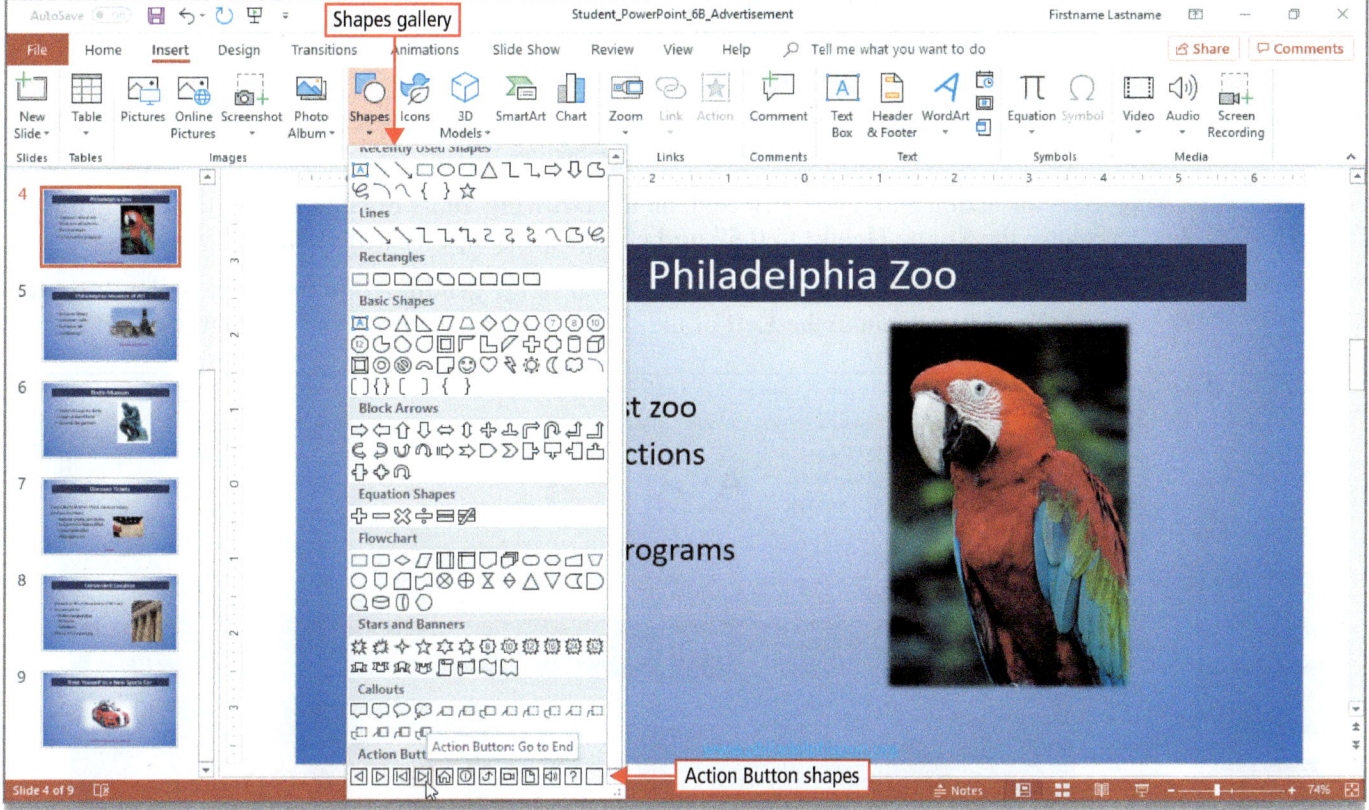

Figure 6.30

3 Click **Action Button: Go to End**, position the ⊞ pointer in the lower left corner of the slide, and then click one time to display the **Action Settings** dialog box. Compare your screen with Figure 6.31.

> The Action Settings dialog box displays. Because the action associated with the Go to End button is to link to the last slide in the presentation, *Last Slide* displays in the Hyperlink to: box.

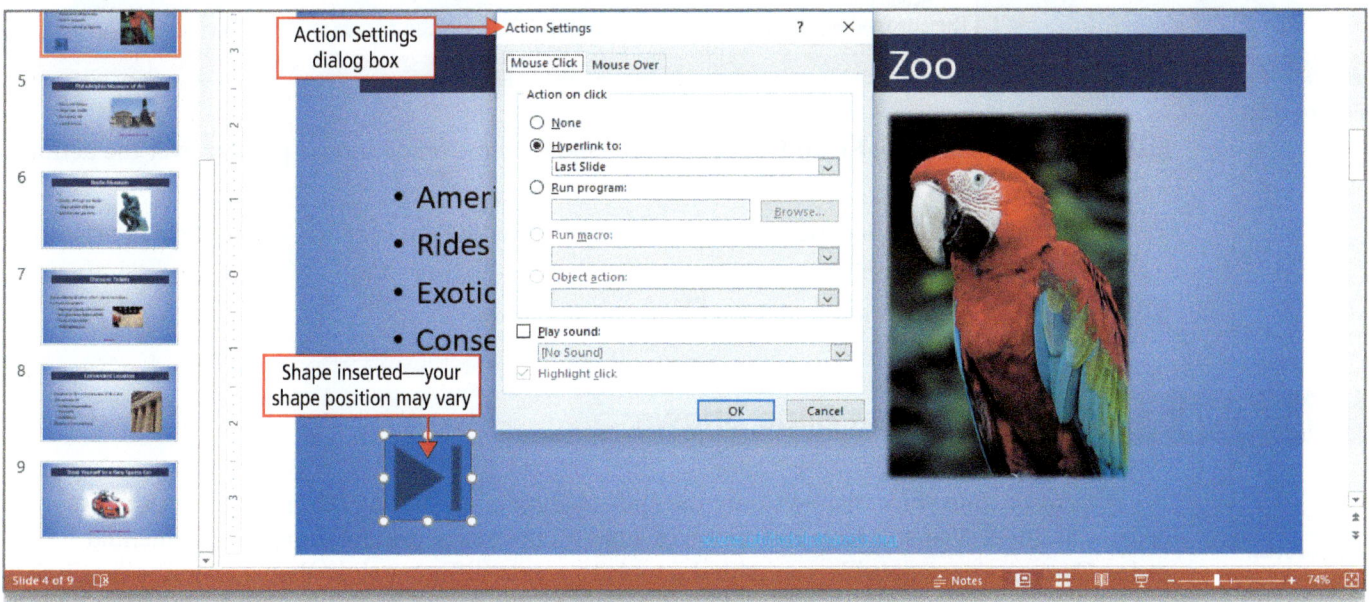

Figure 6.31

4 On the **Mouse Over tab**, if necessary, select **Hyperlink to:**, click the **Hyperlink to: arrow**, and then, click **Last Slide**. Select the **Play sound** check box, click the **Play sound arrow**, scroll as necessary, and then click **Chime**. Click **OK.**

> You can set the action to occur on a Mouse Click or *Mouse Over*; the action will occur when the presenter points to—hovers over—the action button.

5 With the action button still selected, on the **Drawing Tools Format tab**, in the **Size group**, change the **Shape Height** to **0.5"** and change the **Shape Width** to **0.5"**.

6 On the **Drawing Tools Format tab**, in the **Arrange group**, **Align** the shape to the **Bottom** and then **Align** again to the **Left** of the slide. Compare your screen with Figure 6.32.

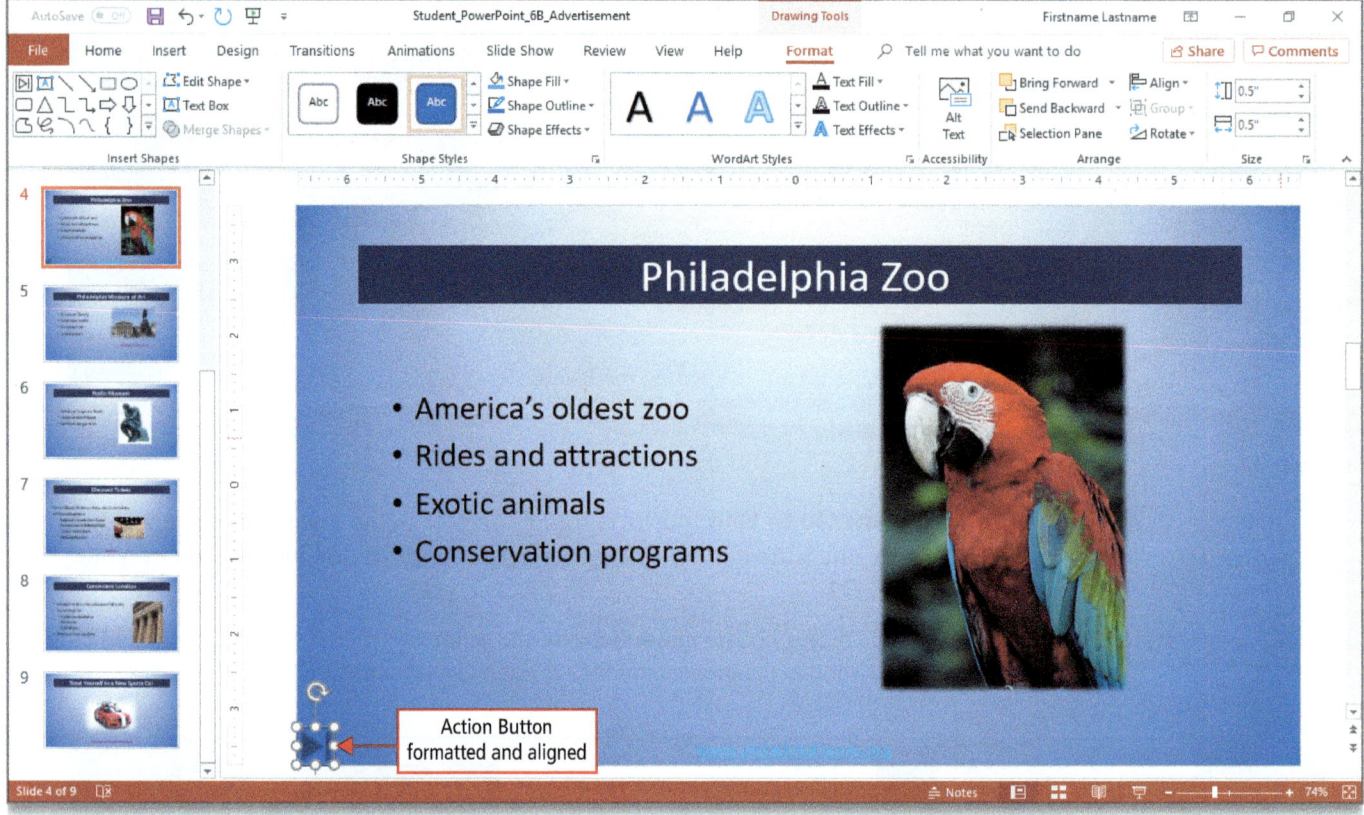

Figure 6.32

7 View the slide show **From Current Slide**, and then move the mouse pointer over the action button.

> The chime effect plays when the mouse pointer is over the action button, and then the last slide in the presentation displays.

8 Return to **Normal** view and **Save** the presentation.

Objective 5 Create Custom Slide Shows

GO! Learn How
Video P6-5

A ***custom slide show*** displays only the slides you want to display to an audience in the order you select. You still have the option of running the entire presentation in its sequential order. Custom shows provide you with the tools to create different slide shows from the original presentation to appeal to different audiences.

There are two types of custom shows—basic and hyperlinked. A ***basic custom slide show*** is a separate presentation saved with its own title containing a subset of the slides from the original presentation. A ***hyperlinked custom slide show*** is a quick way to navigate to a separate slide show from within the original presentation. For example, if your audience wants to know more about a topic, you could have hyperlinks to slides that you could quickly access when necessary.

Activity 6.10 | Creating a Basic Custom Slide Show

1.4.1

In this Activity, you will create a basic custom slide show from an existing presentation.

1 ▶ Display **Slide 1**. On the **Slide Show tab**, in the **Start Slide Show group**, click **Custom Slide Show**, and then click **Custom Shows** to display the **Custom Shows** dialog box.

2 ▶ In the **Custom Shows** dialog box, click **New**. In the **Define Custom Show** dialog box, in the **Slide show name** box, delete the existing text, type **Historic** and then compare your screen with Figure 6.33.

From the Define Custom Show dialog box, you can name a custom slide show and select the slides that will be included in the slide show. All the slides in the current presentation display in the *Slides in presentation* box.

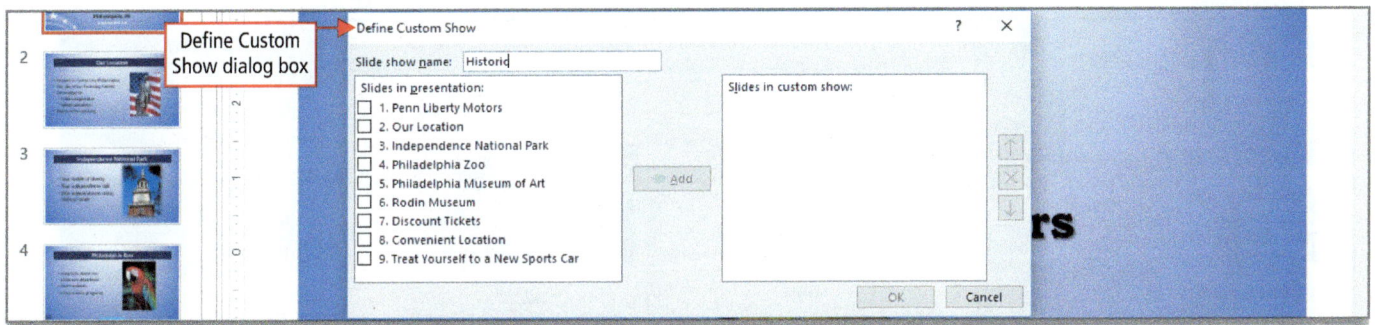

Figure 6.33

3 ▶ Under **Slides in presentation**, select slides **3, 4, 5, 6,** and **7** by clicking in the check boxes, and then click **Add**. Compare your screen with Figure 6.34.

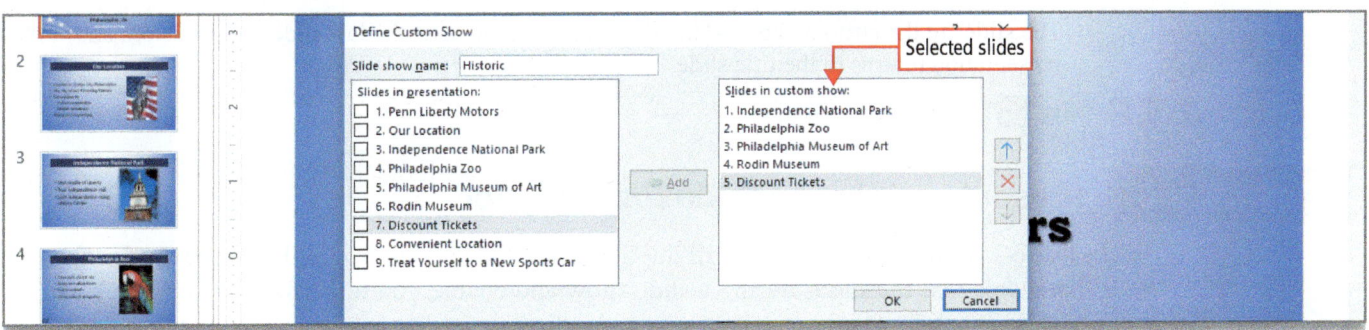

Figure 6.34

4 ▶ Click **OK**. In the **Custom Shows** dialog box, click **Show** to preview your custom show. Click through the slides and return to **Normal** view.

The Historic custom slide show included only five slides.

5 ▶ Save your presentation.

🔄 **ANOTHER WAY**   On the Slide Show tab, in the Start Slide Show group, click Custom Slide Show arrow. Click Historic to view the slide show. When you are finished viewing the slide show, return to Normal view.

Activity 6.11 | Creating a Hyperlinked Custom Slide Show

In this Activity, you will create a hyperlinked custom slide show from an existing presentation by selecting the slides that will be shown in the custom show. These slides can be hyperlinked to the original presentation.

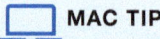 **MAC TIP** In the Links group, click Action. On the Mouse Click tab, select Hyperlink to, and then select Custom Show. Select *Historic,* and check the Show and return box. Click OK and skip to Step 4.

1 On **Slide 1**, click the picture of the **car**.

2 On the **Insert tab**, in the **Links group**, click **Link**. In the **Insert Hyperlink** dialog box, under **Link to:**, click **Place in This Document**.

3 In the **Insert Hyperlink** dialog box, under **Select a place in this document:**, scroll down to display the **Custom Shows**, and then click **Historic**. On the right, under **Slide preview**, select the **Show and return** check box. Compare your screen with Figure 6.35.

When you click Show and return, the Historic show will play and then close, returning you to Slide 1 in your Student_PowerPoint_6B_Advertisement presentation.

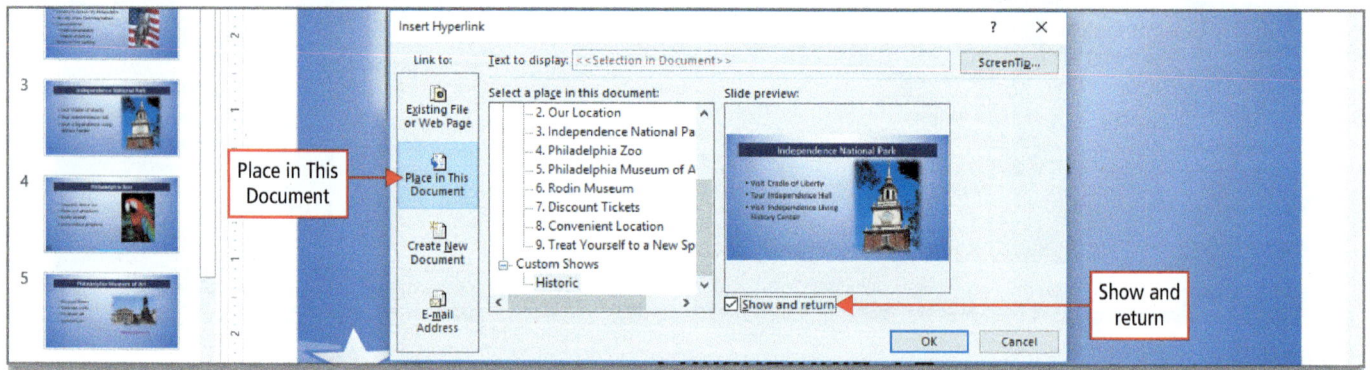

Figure 6.35

4 Click **OK**. Begin to view the slide show from the beginning, and then when the first slide displays, click the picture of the **car** on **Slide 1**. Notice that the custom presentation displays. View the custom slide show and return to **Slide 1** of your presentation. Return to **Normal** view.

The slides in the custom show—Historic—display, and after the last slide in the custom show, the presentation returns to the title slide.

5 Save  your presentation.

Objective 6 | Present and View a Slide Presentation

In the following Activities, you will duplicate and hide slides. You will use the *navigation tools* that display on the slides during a slide show and enable you to perform actions such as move to the next slide, display the previous slide, display the last viewed slide, or move to the end of the slide show. Additionally, you will add an *annotation*—a note or a highlight that can be saved or discarded.

Activity 6.12 | Duplicating and Hiding a Slide

In this Activity, you will duplicate one slide at the end of the presentation. You will hide two slides so that they do not display during the slide show, and you will unhide one slide. You can hide or unhide slides to modify a presentation to be given to different audiences.

1 Display **Slide 9**. On the **Home tab**, in the **Slides group**, click the **New Slide arrow**, and then click **Duplicate Selected Slides**. Compare your screen with Figure 6.36.

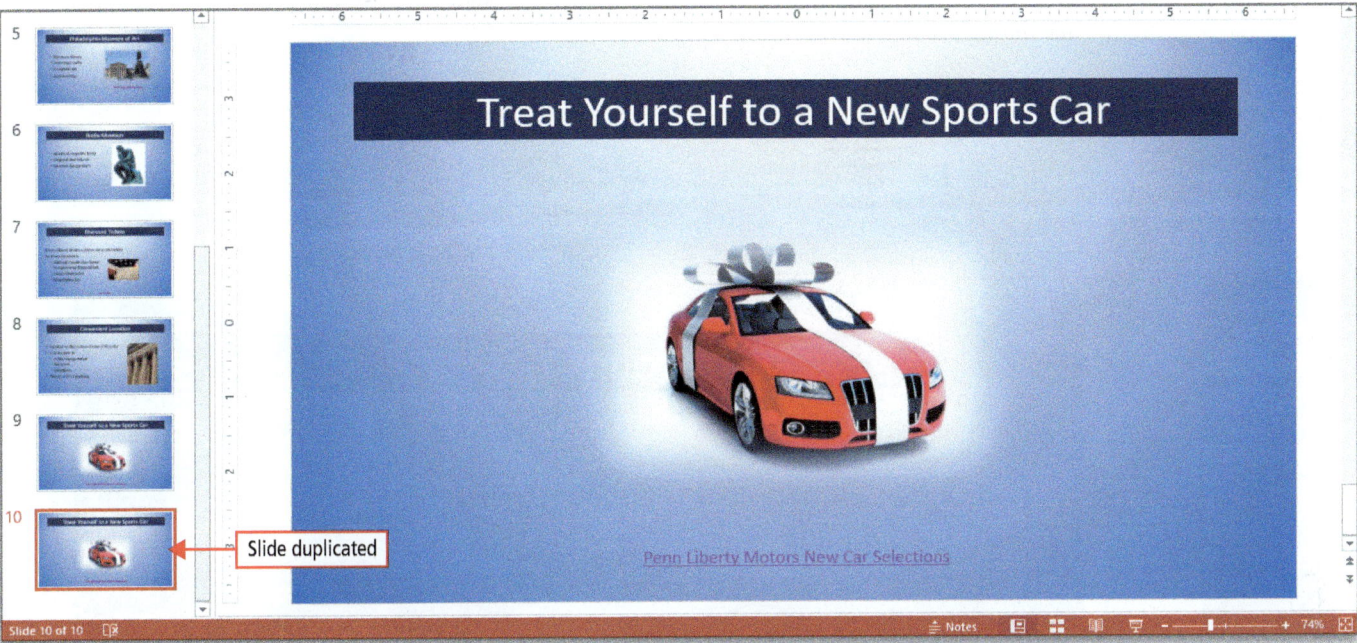

Figure 6.36

🔄 **ANOTHER WAY** Right-click Slide 9, and then click Duplicate Slide.

2 With **Slide 10** selected, point to the picture of the car and right-click, point to **Change Picture,** and then click **From a File**. From your files downloaded with this project, insert the file **p06B_Blue_Car**. In the slide title placeholder, select the words *New Sports Car*, and then type **Sedan** Compare your screen with Figure 6.37.

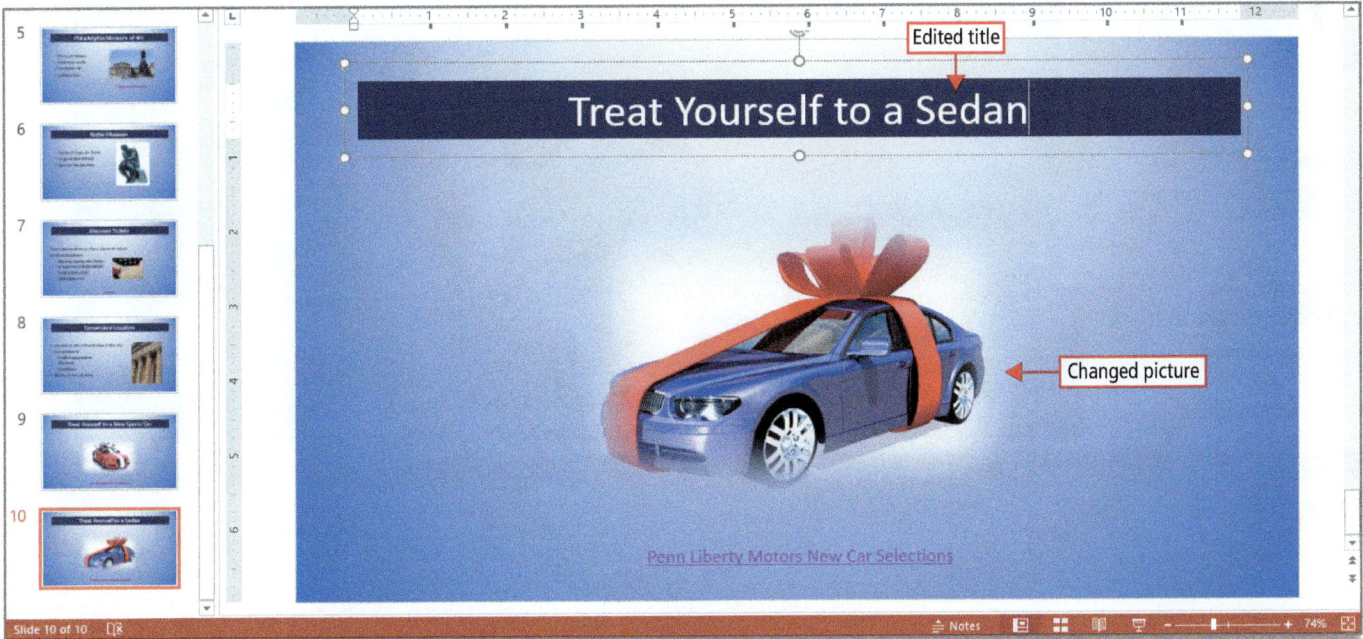

Figure 6.37

3 Display **Slide 7**. On the **Slide Show tab**, in the **Set Up group**, click **Hide Slide**. Compare your screen with Figure 6.38.

In the slide thumbnails pane, the number displayed to the left of the slide thumbnail has a diagonal line through it.

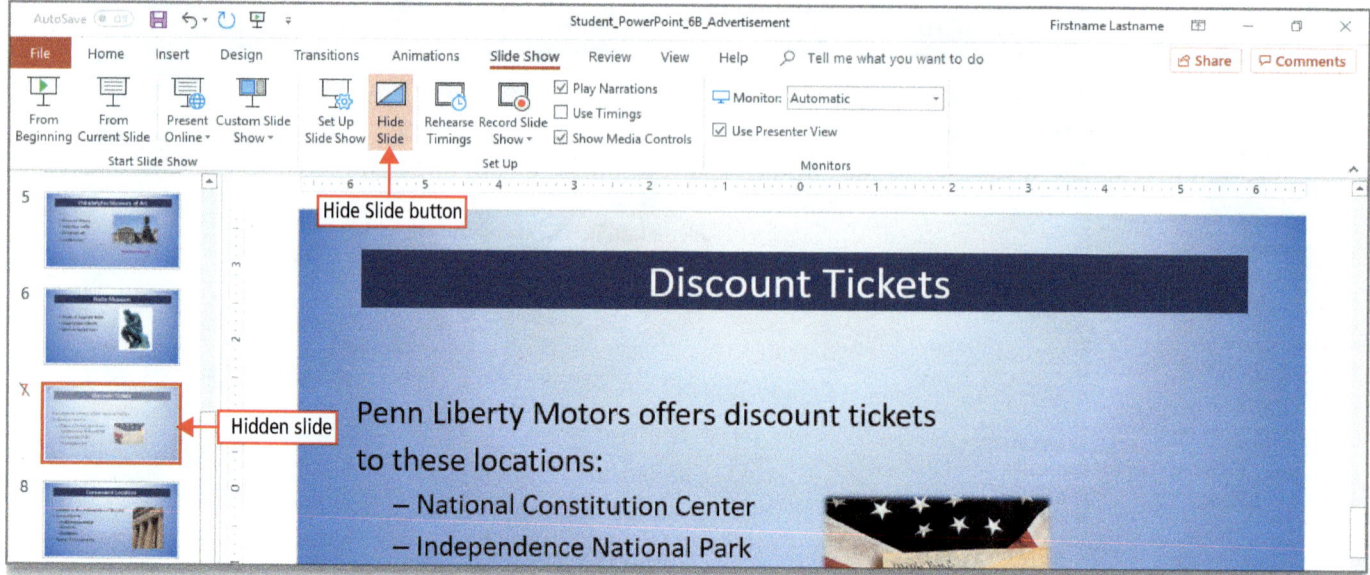

Figure 6.38

4 In the slide thumbnails, right-click the thumbnail for **Slide 9** to display a shortcut menu, and then compare your screen with Figure 6.39.

You can hide a slide from the shortcut menu. In the slides pane, hidden slides are visible but dimmed.

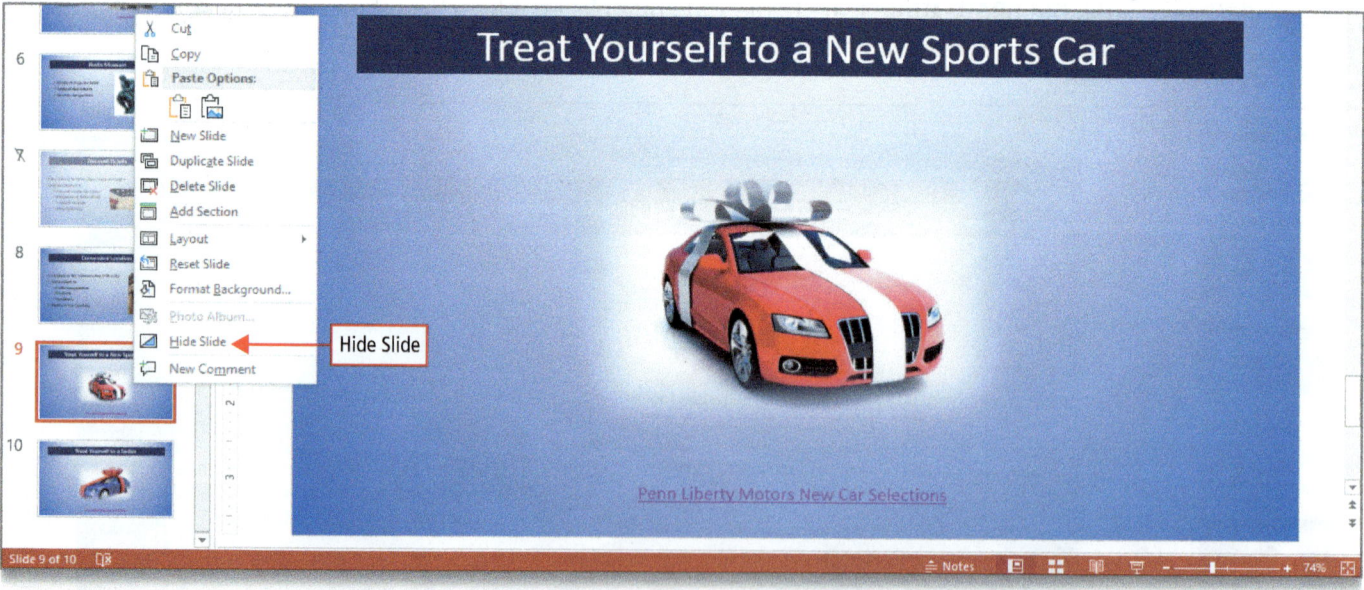

Figure 6.39

5 Click **Hide Slide**.

6 Right-click the **Slide 7** thumbnail to display the shortcut menu, and then click **Hide Slide** to unhide **Slide 7**.

> Slide 7 displays without dimming. Only one slide is hidden—Slide 9.

7 **Save** 🖫 the presentation.

Activity 6.13 | Using the Onscreen Navigation Tools

MOS
1.4.5

In this Activity, you will use the onscreen navigation tools and the slide shortcut menu to navigate to a desired slide in the slide show.

1 On the **Slide Show tab**, in the **Start Slide Show group**, click **From Beginning**. Move the mouse pointer anywhere in the slide, and notice that six buttons display in the lower left corner of the screen. Compare your screen with Figure 6.40.

> Six buttons display when you move the mouse pointer ⬚ on the screen or when you point to the buttons.

Figure 6.40

2 Click **Advance to the next slide** ⊙, and then click **Return to the previous slide** ⊙.

> The slide advances from Slide 1 to Slide 2; then the slide returns from Slide 2 to Slide 1.

3 Click the fourth button—**See all slides** 🔘. Compare your screen with Figure 6.41.

All slides display on the screen. Slide 9, the hidden slide, is dimmed, and the number 9 has a line through it.

MAC TIP This feature is not available in the Mac version of PowerPoint. You can click the third icon to display the menu, and then point to By Title to see a list of all slides, including any hidden slides.

Figure 6.41

MORE KNOWLEDGE **Zoom Slider**

The Zoom Slider in the lower right corner of the screen enables you to change the zoom level so you can change the number of slides that are visible on the screen at one time.

4 Click **Slide 5** to return to the slide show. Right-click anywhere on the slide, point to **Custom Show**, and then click **Historic**. Click to view each of the slides in the custom show. When the slide show is finished, return to **Normal** view.

You can start the custom slide show from any slide in the presentation.

5 On the **Slide Show tab**, in the **Start Slide Show group**, click **From Beginning**. In the lower left corner of the screen, click **More slide show options** ⬭, and then compare your screen with Figure 6.42.

Figure 6.42

6 Click **Show Presenter View**. In **Presenter View**, below the large slide, click **Black or unblack slide show** 🖥. Compare your screen with Figure 6.43.

The large slide changes to black in *Presenter View*—a view that shows the full-screen slide show on one monitor or projection screen while enabling the presenter to view a preview of the next slide, notes, and a timer on another monitor. This is useful when you do not want your presentation to display; for example, before your presentation begins.

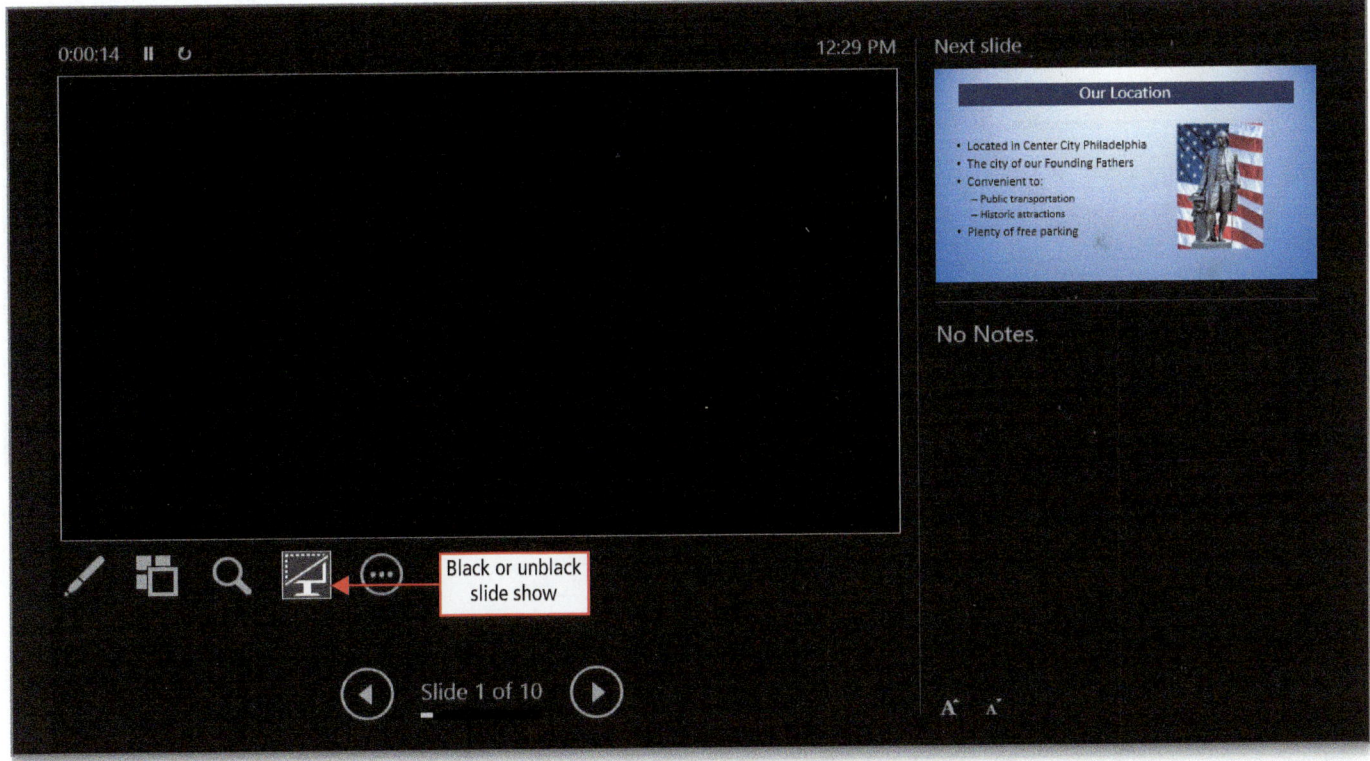

Figure 6.43

7 ▸ Click **Black or unblack slide show** ▣ to make the large slide visible again.

💻 **MAC TIP**   Click the menu icon and point to Screen.

🔄 **ANOTHER WAY**   Click the slide to make the large slide visible again.

8 ▸ Below the large slide, click **More slide show options** ⊙, and then click **Hide Presenter View** to return to the slide show.

MORE KNOWLEDGE   **Presenter View**

Presenter View enables you to project to a second screen. The Swap Presentation View and Slide Show commands are located in the Display Settings, which enable you to swap the screens on which the presentation displays. The Duplicate Slide Show display setting enables you to display a slide show on more than one monitor.

Activity 6.14 | Using the Annotation Tool

In this Activity, you will use the pen and laser tools to highlight and annotate information on a slide.

MOS
3.4.2

1 ▸ In the lower left corner of the screen, click the third button—**Pen and laser tools** ✐. Compare your screen with Figure 6.44. Take a moment to review the Pen and Laser Pointer Tool options, as described in the table shown in Figure 6.45.

Figure 6.44

Pen and Laser Pointer Tools	
Annotation Tool	**Description**
Laser Pointer	Changes your mouse pointer into a laser pointer
Pen	Enables you to write or circle items on the slide
Highlighter	Enables you to emphasize parts of the slide
Eraser	Removes areas of an annotation
Erase All Ink on Slide	Removes all annotations on a slide
Ink Color	Displays a selection of colors for highlighting or writing with the pen

Figure 6.45

2 ❯ Click **Laser Pointer**, and then move your mouse around the screen.

The mouse pointer displays as a large red dot.

3 ❯ Click **Pen and laser tools**, and then click **Laser Pointer** to turn off the laser pointer.

4 ❯ Click the **Advance to next slide** button to advance to **Slide 2**. At the lower left corner of the screen, click **Pen and laser tools**, and then click **Highlighter**.

The mouse pointer displays as a yellow rectangle.

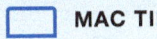 **MAC TIP** The highlighter is not available in the Mac version of PowerPoint. Use the pen instead and change the color to yellow.

5 ❯ Place the highlighter pointer to the left of the *P* in *Public*, and then drag across the text *Public Transportation*. Compare your screen with Figure 6.46.

Our Location

- Located in Center City Philadelphia
- The city of our Founding Fathers
- Convenient to:
  - Public transportation ← [Highlighted text]
  - Historic attractions
- Plenty of free parking

Figure 6.46

6 ❯ Click **Pen and laser tools**. At the bottom of the list, click the fourth color—**Red**. Click **Pen and laser tools**, and then click **Pen**.

The Pen and laser tool displays as a small red dot.

7 ▶ Point above the word *Parking*, and then drag to draw a circle around the word *Parking*. Compare your screen with Figure 6.47.

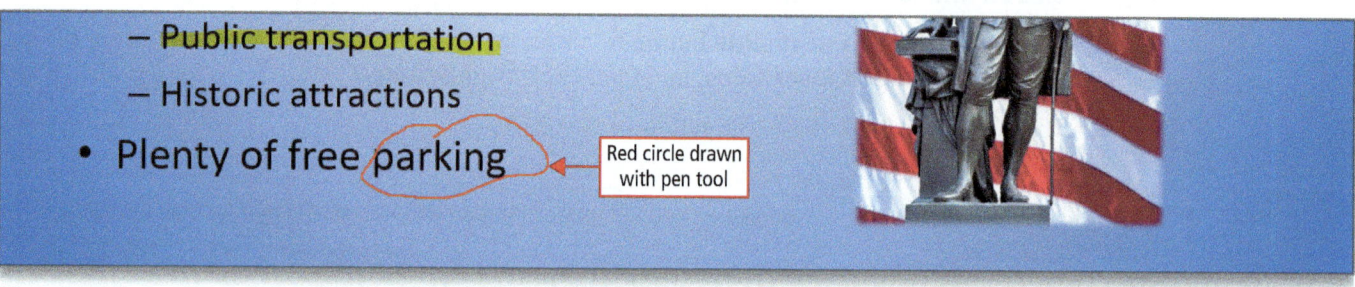

Figure 6.47

8 ▶ Click the **Pen and laser tools** button, and then click **Eraser**. Click one time on the circle to remove the circle.

It is not necessary to drag the eraser.

9 ▶ Click **Pen and laser tools**, and then click **Pen**. Using the technique you practiced, draw a circle around the word *Free*.

10 ▶ Press Esc two times. In the displayed dialog box, click **Keep**.

🖥️ **MAC TIP** The Mac version of PowerPoint does not include the ability to save annotations.

11 ▶ Save 🖫 the presentation.

Activity 6.15 | Creating a Self-Running Presentation

MOS
1.4.2, 1.4.3, 1.4.4

A self-running presentation can run without a presenter, perhaps in a *kiosk*—a booth that includes a computer and a monitor that may have a touchscreen. Kiosks are often located in a location such as a hotel lobby, a trade show, or a convention—places that are frequented by many people. In this Activity, you will set up a presentation to run with no one present to run the slide show. The slides will advance automatically at a set interval.

1 ▶ Display **Slide 1**. On the **Slide Show tab**, in the **Set Up group**, click **Rehearse Timings**. Compare your screen with Figure 6.48.

The presentation slide show begins, the Recording toolbar displays, and the Slide Time box begins timing the presentation.

Figure 6.48

2 When the **Slide Time** box displays **10 (seconds)**, click **Next** 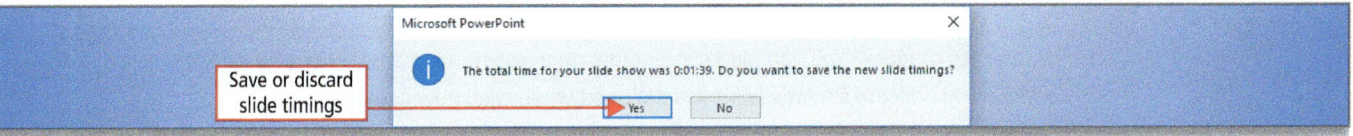. Repeat this step for each slide. After the last slide displays, compare your screen with Figure 6.49.

When you click Next, the slide advances and the slide timing is set for the slide. After you set the time for the last slide, a dialog box displays with the total time for the slide show and prompts you to save the slide timings or discard them.

Save or discard slide timings

Microsoft PowerPoint

The total time for your slide show was 0:01:39. Do you want to save the new slide timings?

Yes   No

Figure 6.49

3 Click **Yes** to save the new slide timings.

4 On the PowerPoint **status bar,** click **Slide Sorter** . With the slides displayed, drag the **Zoom slider** to **70%**. Compare your screen with Figure 6.50.

Slide Sorter view displays with the time of each slide in the presentation. There is a delay between the click and the actual time, so your slide times may not be timed at exactly 10 seconds.

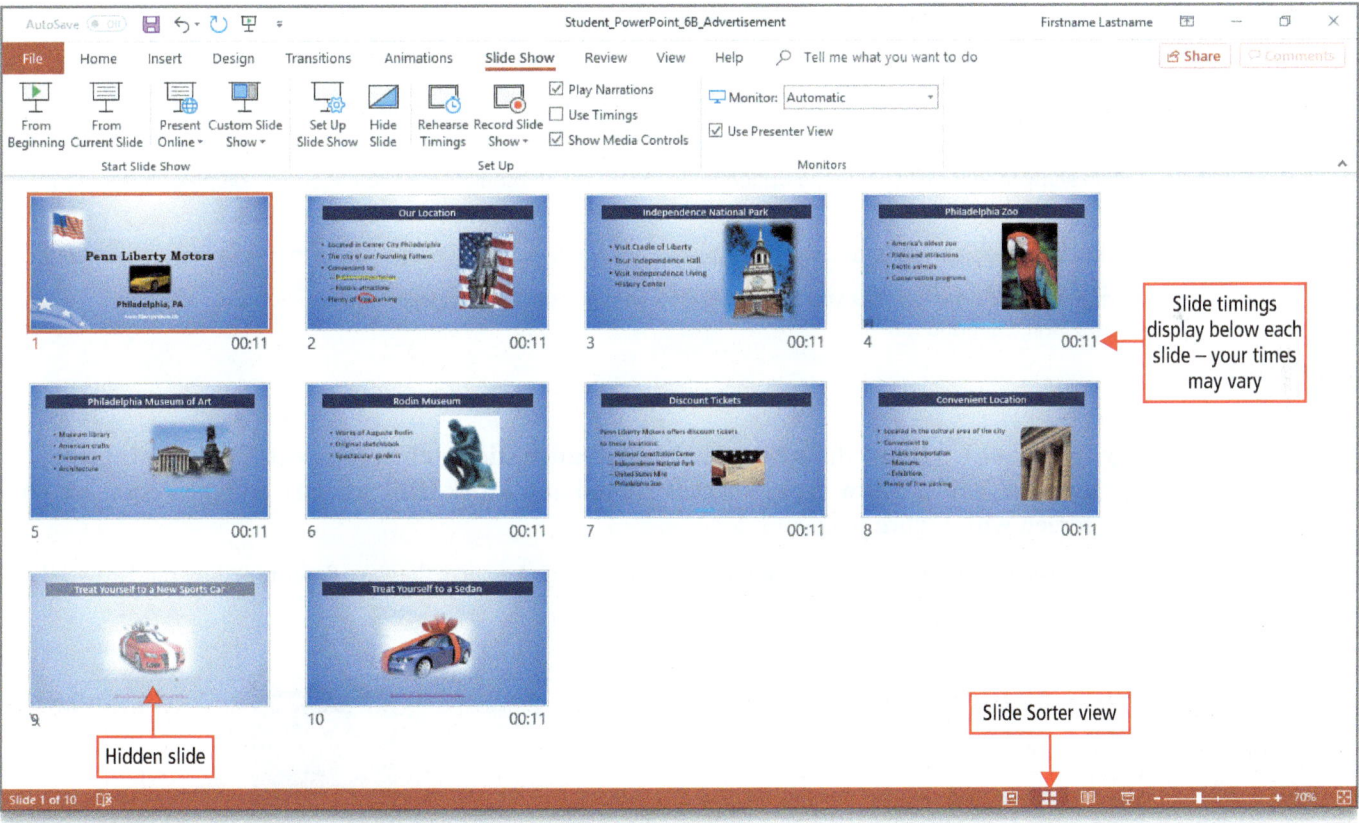

Figure 6.50

5 On the **Slide Show tab**, in the **Set Up group**, click **Set Up Slide Show**. Take a moment to review the options in the **Set Up Show** dialog box described in the table in Figure 6.51.

Set Up Show Options	
	Description
Show type	*Presented by a speaker (full screen)* is used to present to a live audience.
	Browsed by an individual (window) enables your audience to view the presentation from a hard drive, CD, or the internet.
	Browsed at a kiosk (full screen) delivers a self-running show that can run without a presenter in an unattended booth or kiosk. You can also send someone a self-running presentation on a CD.
Show options	*Loop continuously until the Esc key is pressed* is used when the show is unattended.
	Show without narration suppresses any recorded audio in the presentation.
	Show without animation suppresses the animation in the presentation.
	Disable hardware graphics acceleration is used if your video configuration is causing display problems.
	Pen color enables you to select a pen color for the slide show.
	Laser pointer color enables you to select a laser pointer color for the slide show.
Show slides	*All:* Shows all of the slides.
	From: Selects a range of slides to view.
	Custom show: Shows a custom show.
Advance slides	*Manually* lets you advance the slides yourself.
	Using timings, if present, activates the timings you set for each slide.
Multiple monitors	If your computer supports using multiple monitors, a PowerPoint presentation can be delivered on two monitors.
	Slide show monitor gives you the option to select on which monitor the slide show will display, or you can let PowerPoint select the monitor automatically.
	Resolution enables you to use the current resolution or select another resolution that your monitor supports.
	Use Presenter View enables you to run the PowerPoint presentation from one monitor while the audience views it on a second monitor.

Figure 6.51

6 > In the **Set Up Show** dialog box, under **Advance slides**, click to select **Using timings, if present**. Under **Show type**, select **Browsed at a kiosk (full screen)**, and then compare your screen with Figure 6.52.

The advanced options are not available to change because they are determined by the Browsed at a kiosk show settings.

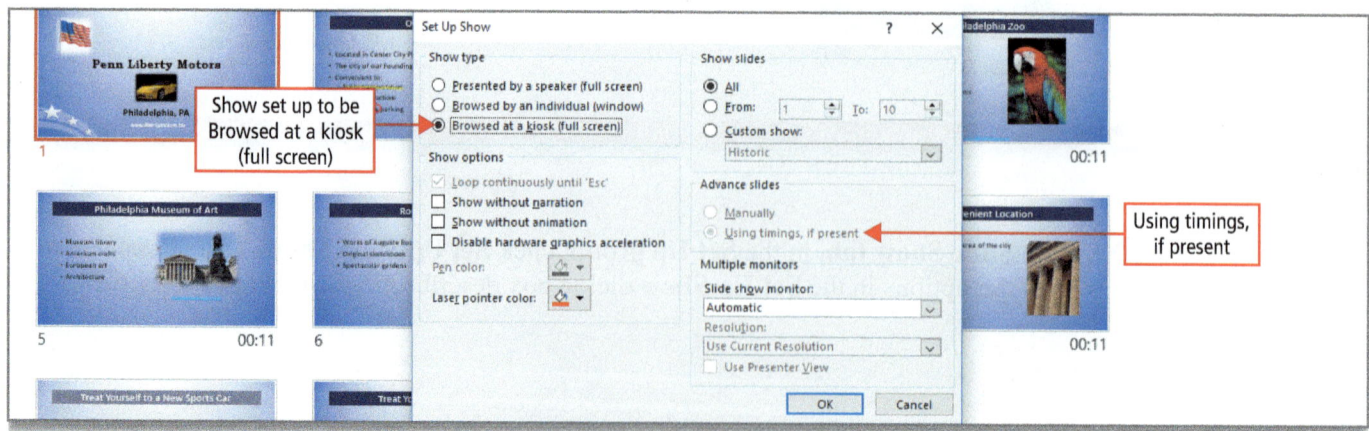

Figure 6.52

7 Click **OK**. Start the slide show **From Beginning**. Wait 10 seconds per slide, and then view a few slides. Press [Esc].

8 On the **Slide Show tab**, in the **Set Up group**, click **Set Up Slide Show**. Under **Show type**, select **Presented by a speaker (full screen)**. Under **Advance slides**, click **Manually**. Click **OK**.

9 Save [🖫] the presentation.

Activity 6.16 | Printing Selections from a Presentation

1.3.1

In this Activity, you will print selections from a presentation. You will select three slides to print.

1 On the status bar, click **Normal** [▣]. Hold down [Ctrl], and then click the thumbnails to select **Slides 1, 2**, and **8**.

2 On the **File tab**, click **Print**. Under Printer, click the Printer arrow, and then click Microsoft Print to PDF. Under **Settings**, click the **Print All Slides arrow**, and then click **Print Selection** Compare your screen with Figure 6.53.

The Print Preview indicates 3 slides will print.

🖥️ **MAC TIP**   In the Printer dialog box, click PDF.

🔄 **ANOTHER WAY**   To print selected files, on the File tab, click Print, and then under Setting, in the Slides box, type the numbers of the slides that you want to print.

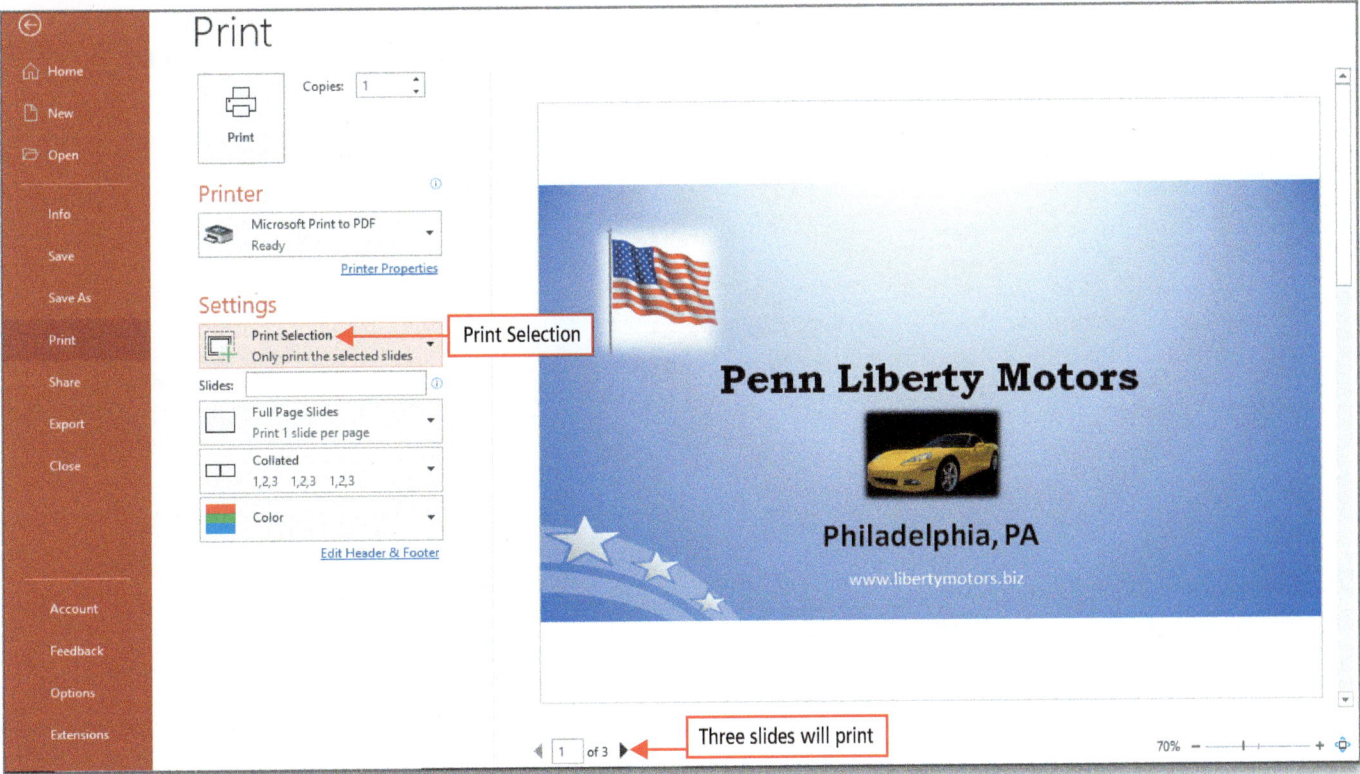

Figure 6.53

3 Click **Print** and save the PDF in your **PowerPoint Chapter 6** folder **as Lastname_Firstname_6B_Print** If the file opens in Microsoft Edge or another PDF reader, close the file. Note: **MyLab IT** users will not submit this file.

4 Insert a **Header & Footer** on the **Notes and Handouts**. Include the **Date and time** fixed, the page number, the footer **6B_Advertisement** and **Apply to All**.

5 Display the document properties. As the **Tags**, type **discount, tourist, attractions** and as the **Subject**, type your course and section number. Be sure your name displays as author, and then **Save** your file.

6 **Close** ☒ PowerPoint.

For Non-MyLab Submissions Determine What Your Instructor Requires
As directed by your instructor, submit your completed PowerPoint presentation and PDF print.

---

7 In **MyLab IT**, in your **Course Materials**, locate and click the Grader Project **PowerPoint 6B Advertisement**. In **step 3**, under **Upload Completed Assignment**, click **Choose File**. In the **Open** dialog box, navigate to your **PowerPoint Chapter 6 folder**, and then click your **Student_PowerPoint_6B_Advertisement** file one time to select it. In the lower right corner of the **Open** dialog box, click **Open**.

8 To submit your file to **MyLab IT** for grading, click **Upload**, wait a moment for a green **Success!** message, and then in **step 4**, click the blue **Submit for Grading** button. Click **Close Assignment** to return to your list of **Course Materials**.

You have completed Project 6B | **END**

wavebreakmedia/Shutterstock, Monkey Business Images/Fotolia, Ivanko80/Shutterstock, Monkey Business Images/Shutterstock

Microsoft Office Specialist (MOS) Skills in This Chapter	
Project 6A	**Project 6B**
5.1.1 Apply basic and 3D slide transitions	**1.3.1** Print all or part of a presentation
5.1.2 Configure transition effects	**1.4.1** Create custom slide shows
5.2.1 Animate text and graphic elements	**1.4.2** Configure slide show options
5.2.3 Configure animation effects	**1.4.3** Rehearse slide show timing
5.2.4 Configure animation paths	**1.4.5** Present slide shows by using Presenter View
5.3.1 Set transition effect duration	**2.1.5** Duplicate slides
5.3.2 Configure transition start and finish options	**2.2.1** Hide and unhide slides
	3.2.1 Insert hyperlinks
	3.2.2 Insert Section Zoom links and Slide Zoom links
	3.4.2 Draw by using digital ink

Build Your E-Portfolio

An E-Portfolio is a collection of evidence, stored electronically, that showcases what you have accomplished while completing your education. Collecting and then sharing your work products with potential employers reflects your academic and career goals. Your completed documents from the following projects are good examples to show what you have learned: 6G, 6K, and 6L.

GO! For Job Success

Discussion: Search Engine Optimization

Your instructor may assign this discussion to your class, and then ask you to think about, or discuss with your classmates, these questions:

Although many website names are well known and company and product pages are easy to find with sites like Facebook and Twitter, most visits to websites—referred to as *traffic*—result from searches on search engines like Google and Bing. Search engines crawl the internet looking for new sites and generating keywords to match searches to sites. To make sure a website is in the top results, site owners use tools called search engine optimization, abbreviated as *SEO*. SEO focuses on creating keywords relevant to the site, noting what other sites link to a site, and examining website structure and design to help ensure that a website is displayed in the first few search results.

Many internet marketing firms specialize in helping site owners enhance SEO by analyzing website data; for example, the number of hits, what site users viewed immediately before landing at the site, search terms used, and the geographic location of the searcher.

g-stockstudio/Shutterstock

Think about a website you use often, like a news, streaming video, or shopping site—what are some keywords that would help others find this site if they were searching on Google or Bing?

What kind of information would be helpful to the site's owner to make sure the site was a top search result?

Major search engines provide some basic analytic and SEO tools for free. What kinds of sites would benefit most from these free or low-cost tools?

End of Chapter

Summary

You used techniques to view and present a slide show by adding and modifying slide transitions and various animation effects, such as entrance, exit, emphasis effects, and motion paths.

Within a slide show, you inserted hyperlinks to quickly link to a webpage, an email address, another document or file, another area of the same document, and other slides within a slide show.

You practiced hiding slides and creating a basic custom slide show and a hyperlinked custom slide show. You created action buttons, assigned an action to the buttons, and used the onscreen navigation tools.

You practiced using annotation tools that enabled you to write or draw on slides during a presentation. You used Presenter view and created a self-running slide show that runs in a loop.

GO! Learn It Online

Review the concepts, key terms, and MOS skills in this chapter by completing these online challenges, which you can find in **MyLab IT**.

Chapter Quiz: Answer matching and multiple choice questions to test what you learned in this chapter.

Lessons on the GO!: Learn how to use all the new apps and features as they are introduced by Microsoft.

MOS Prep Quiz: Answer questions to review the MOS skills that you practiced in this chapter.

Project Guide for PowerPoint Chapter 6

Your instructor will assign Projects from this list to ensure your learning and assess your knowledge.

	Project Guide for PowerPoint Chapter 6		
Project	**Apply Skills from These Chapter Objectives**	**Project Type**	**Project Location**
6A MyLab IT	Objectives 1–3 from Project 6A	**6A Instructional Project (Grader Project)** **Instruction** Guided instruction to learn the skills in Project A.	In **MyLab IT** and in text
6B MyLab IT	Objectives 4–6 from Project 6B	**6B Instructional Project (Grader Project)** **Instruction** Guided instruction to learn the skills in Project B.	In **MyLab IT** and in text
6C	Objectives 1–3 from Project 6A	**6C Skills Review (Scorecard Grading)** **Review** A guided review of the skills from Project 6A.	In text
6D	Objectives 4–6 from Project 6B	**6D Skills Review (Scorecard Grading)** **Review** A guided review of the skills from Project 6B.	In text
6E MyLab IT	Objectives 1–3 from Project 6A	**6E Mastery (Grader Project)** **Mastery and Transfer of Learning** A demonstration of your mastery of the skills in Project 6A with extensive decision making.	In **MyLab IT** and in text
6F MyLab IT	Objectives 4–6 from Project 6B	**6F Mastery (Grader Project)** **Mastery and Transfer of Learning** A demonstration of your mastery of the skills in Project 6B with extensive decision making.	In **MyLab IT** and in text
6G MyLab IT	Objectives 1–6 from Project 6A and 6B	**6G Mastery (Grader Project)** **Mastery and Transfer of Learning** A demonstration of your mastery of the skills in Projects 6A and 6B with extensive decision making.	In **MyLab IT** and in text
6H	Combination of Objectives from Projects 6A and 6B	**6H GO! Fix It (Scorecard Grading)** **Critical Thinking** A demonstration of your mastery of the skills in Projects 6A and 6B by creating a correct result from a document that contains errors you must find.	IRC
6I	Combination of Objectives from Projects 6A and 6B	**6I GO! Make It (Scorecard Grading)** **Critical Thinking** A demonstration of your mastery of the skills in Projects 6A and 6B by creating a result from a supplied picture.	IRC
6J	Combination of Objectives from Projects 6A and 6B	**6J GO! Solve It (Rubric Grading)** **Critical Thinking** A demonstration of your mastery of the skills in Projects 6A and 6B, your decision-making skills, and your critical thinking skills. A task-specific rubric helps you self-assess your result.	IRC
6K	Combination of Objectives from Projects 6A and 6B	**6K GO! Solve It (Rubric Grading)** **Critical Thinking** A demonstration of your mastery of the skills in Projects 6A and 6B, your decision-making skills, and your critical thinking skills. A task-specific rubric helps you self-assess your result.	In text
6L	Combination of Objectives from Projects 6A and 6B	**6L GO! Think (Rubric Grading)** **Critical Thinking** A demonstration of your understanding of the chapter concepts applied in a manner that you would outside of college. An analytic rubric helps you and your instructor grade the quality of your work by comparing it to the work an expert in the discipline would create.	In text
6M	Combination of Objectives from Projects 6A and 6B	**6M GO! Think (Rubric Grading)** **Critical Thinking** A demonstration of your understanding of the chapter concepts applied in a manner that you would outside of college. An analytic rubric helps you and your instructor grade the quality of your work by comparing it to the work an expert in the discipline would create.	IRC
6N	Combination of Objectives from Projects 6A and 6B	**6N You and GO! (Rubric Grading)** **Critical Thinking** A demonstration of your understanding of the chapter concepts applied in a manner that you would in a personal situation. An analytic rubric helps you and your instructor grade the quality of your work.	IRC

Glossary

Glossary of Chapter Key Terms

Action button A special type of shape that you can add to your presentation and to which you can assign an action.

After Previous An animation option that begins the animation sequence for the selected slide element immediately after the completion of the previous animation or slide transition.

Animation 1. The motion or movement that occurs as the presentation moves from slide to slide. 2. A visual or sound effect added to an object or text on a slide.

Annotation A note or a highlight that can be saved or discarded.

Basic custom slide show A separate presentation saved with its own title containing a subset of the slides from the original presentation.

Custom slide show Displays only the slides you want to display to an audience in the order you select.

Domain name Sometimes called the second-level domain. The part of a URL, such as www.philadelphiazoo.org, that represents a company or product name and makes it easy for users to remember the address. An organization's unique name on the internet, which consists of a chosen name (phildelphiazoo) combined with a top level domain such as .com, .org, or .gov.

Emphasis effect Animation that emphasizes an object or text that is already displayed.

Entrance effect Animation that brings a slide element onto the screen.

Exit effect Animation that moves an object or text off the screen.

Hyperlink A navigation element that, when clicked, will take you to another location, such as a webpage, an email address, another document, or a place within the same document. In a PowerPoint presentation, hyperlinks can also be used to link to a slide in the presentation, to a slide in a different presentation, or to a custom slide show.

Hyperlinked custom slide show A quick way to navigate to a separate slide show from within the original presentation.

HyperText Markup Language (HTML) The authoring language that defines the structure of a webpage.

HyperText Transfer Protocol (HTTP) The internet standard protocol that defines the exchange of information on the web. The set of communication rules used by your computer to connect to servers on the Web.

Kiosk A booth that includes a computer and a monitor that may have a touchscreen.

Motion Paths effect An animation effect that determines how and in what direction text or objects will move on a slide.

Mouse Over An action will occur when the presenter points to, or hovers over, the associated object.

Navigation tools Buttons that display on the slides during a slide show that enable you to perform actions such as moving to the next slide, the previous slide, the last viewed slide, or the end of the slide show.

On Click An animation option that begins the animation sequence for the selected slide element when the mouse button is clicked.

Presenter View A view that shows the full-screen slide show on one monitor or projection screen while enabling the presenter to view a preview of the next slide, notes, and a timer on another monitor.

Protocol A set of rules for communication between devices that determines how data is formatted, transmitted, received, and acknowledged.

Timeline A graphical representation that displays the number of seconds the animation takes to complete.

Top-level domain (TLD) The suffix, such as .com or .edu, that follows the domain name in a URL and represents the type of website you're visiting.

Transition A motion effect that occurs between slides in Slide Show view.

Transition speed The timing of the transition between all slides or between the previous slide and the current slide.

Uniform Resource Locator (URL) The address of a website.

With Previous An animation option that begins the animation sequence at the same time as the previous animation or slide transition.

Chapter Review

Skills Review | Project 6C Vintage Car

Apply 6A skills from these Objectives:

1. Apply and Modify Slide Transitions
2. Apply Custom Animation Effects
3. Modify Animation Effects

In the following Skills Review, you will modify a PowerPoint presentation advertising the annual Vintage Car Event hosted by Penn Liberty Motors. You will apply slide transitions and custom animation effects to the slide show to generate interest in the event. Your completed presentation will look similar to Figure 6.54.

Project Files

For Project 6C, you will need:

p06C_Vintage_Cars

You will save your presentation as:

Lastname_Firstname_6C_Vintage_Cars

Project Results

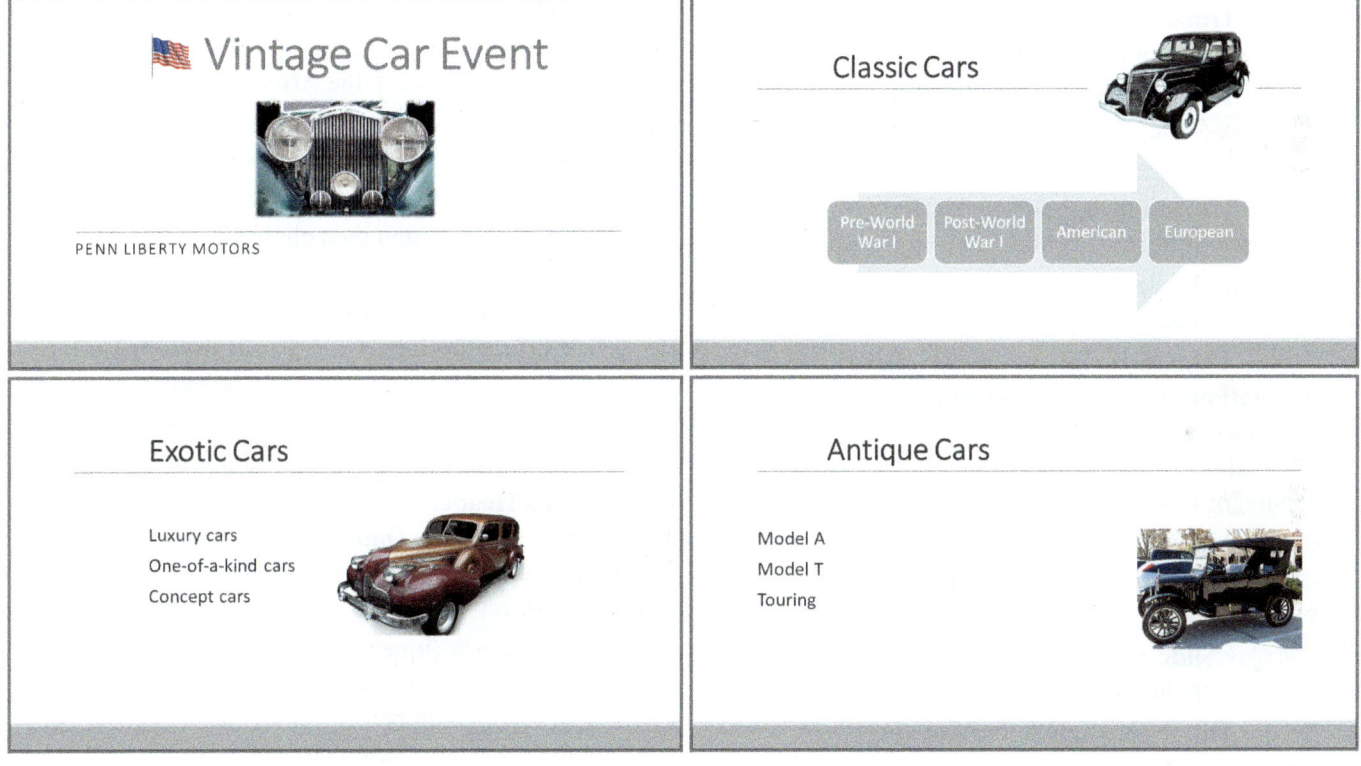

Figure 6.54 Project 6C Vintage Car

(continues on next page)

Chapter Review

1 Navigate to your student data files, and then double-click **p06C_Vintage_Cars**. Using your own name, save the file as **Lastname_Firstname_6C_Vintage_Cars** in your PowerPoint Chapter 6 folder.

2 On **Slide 1**, click the **Transitions tab**.

a. In the **Transition to This Slide group**, click **More** ▼ to display the **Transitions** gallery. Under **Subtle**, in first row, click **Shape**.

b. In the **Timing group**, click **Apply To All**.

3 Display **Slide 2**.

a. On the **Transitions tab**, in the **Transition to This Slide group**, click the fourth transition, **Push**.

b. On the **Transitions tab**, in the **Timing group**, change the Duration to **02.00**.

c. On the **Transitions tab**, in the **Timing group**, under **Advance Slide**, clear the **On Mouse Click** check box.

d. On the **Transitions tab**, in the **Timing group**, under **Advance Slide**, change the **After** box to **00:03.00**.

4 On **Slide 2**, click the **SmartArt** graphic containing the classic car eras.

a. On the **Animations tab**, in the **Advanced Animation group**, click **Add Animation**. Under **Entrance**, click **Fly In**. (Mac users, the Add Animations button is not available in the Mac version of PowerPoint. Use the Gallery instead.)

b. On the **Animations tab**, in the **Animation group**, click **Effect Options**. Under **Sequence**, click **One by One**.

5 Display **Slide 3**, and then click to select the content placeholder with the types of cars.

a. On the **Animations tab**, in the **Advanced Animation group**, click **Add Animation**. Under **Entrance**, click **Fade**.

b. On the **Animations tab**, in the **Advanced Animation group**, click **Animation Pane**.

c. In the **Animation Pane** on the right side of your screen, under **Content Placeholder**, click to expand the animations. Click **1**—the first entrance effect for the content placeholder—and then at the top of the **Animation Pane**, click **Play From** to test the animation.

6 On **Slide 3**, click to select the content placeholder.

a. In the **Animation Pane**, click the first item in the list—**Luxury Cars**—to select it, and then right-click **Luxury Cars**.

b. Click **Start After Previous**.

c. In the **Animation Pane**, click to collapse the list, and then right-click the entrance effect for the **Content Placeholder**. Click **Effect Options**. (Mac users, in the Animations pane, click Timing.)

d. In the **Fade** dialog box, click the **Timing tab**, click the **Start arrow**, and then click **After Previous**. Click the **Duration arrow**, and then select **1 seconds (Fast)**.

e. In the **Fade** dialog box, on the **Effect tab**, under **Enhancements**, click the **After animation arrow**.

f. In the row of colors, click the second color—**Black**. Click **OK**. (Mac users, in the Animations pane, use Effect Options.)

7 Display **Slide 2**, and then click to select the **SmartArt** object.

a. On the **Animations tab**, in the **Animation group**, click **Effect Options**. Click **From Bottom-Left**. In the **Animation Pane**, click **Play Selected**.

8 View the slide show **From Beginning**, and then return to **Normal** view. Close the **Animation pane**.

9 Insert a **Header & Footer** on the **Notes and Handouts**. Include the **Date and time** fixed, the **Page Number**, and a **Footer 6C_Vintage_Cars** and then click **Apply to All**.

10 Display the document properties. As the **Tags**, type **vintage cars, Penn Liberty** and as the **Subject**, type your course and section number. Be sure your name displays as the author, and then **Save** your file.

11 As directed by your instructor, submit your completed PowerPoint file. **Close** PowerPoint.

You have completed Project 6C | END

Chapter Review

Apply 6B skills from these Objectives:

4. Insert Hyperlinks
5. Create Custom Slide Shows
6. Present and View a Slide Presentation

Skills Review **Project 6D Safety**

In the following Skills Review, you will modify a PowerPoint presentation that showcases safety features of the cars sold by Penn Liberty Motors. You will insert hyperlinks to a webpage and the email address of the company's safety director. You will also create custom slide shows of standard safety features available on all vehicles and custom safety features available on select vehicles. You will annotate the slide show and then create a self-running version of the presentation for use in a kiosk. Your completed presentation will look similar to Figure 6.55.

Project Files

For Project 6D, you will need:

p06D_Safety

p06D_Customer_Service

p06D_Advertisement

You will save your files as:

Lastname_Firstname_6D_Safety

Project Results

Figure 6.55 Project 6D Safety

(continues on next page)

Chapter Review

1 Navigate to your student data files, and then double-click **p06D_Safety**. Navigate to your **PowerPoint Chapter 6** folder, and then **Save** the file as **Lastname_Firstname_6D_Safety**

2 Display **Slide 1**.

a. Click to select the picture of the **car**.

b. On the **Insert tab**, in the **Links group**, click **Link** to display the **Insert Hyperlink** dialog box. If necessary, under **Link to**, click **Existing File or Web Page**.

c. In the **Address** box, type **www.nhtsa.dot.gov**

d. Click **ScreenTip**. In the **Set Hyperlink ScreenTip** dialog box, type **National Highway Traffic Safety Administration** Click **OK**. Click **OK** again.

3 With **Slide 1** active, select the subtitle text— *Safety Features*.

a. On the **Insert tab**, in the **Links group**, click **Link**.

b. Under **Link to**, click **Place in This Document**. Scroll down, click **13. Penn Liberty Motors Safety Team**, and then click **OK**.

4 Display **Slide 13**.

a. Select the text *Email Your Concerns*. On the **Insert tab**, in the **Links group**, click **Link**. Under **Link to**, click **E-mail Address**. In the **E-mail address** box, type **safetyteam@libertymotors.biz** In the **Subject** box, type **Safety first** Click **OK**.

b. Select the second bulleted item—*Available to Customers*. On the **Insert tab**, in the **Links group**, click **Link**. In the **Insert Hyperlink** dialog box, under **Link to**, click **Existing File or Web Page**, if necessary, click the **Look in arrow** and navigate to your student data files for this project, and then click **p06D_Advertisement**. Click **OK**.

c. View the slide show **From Current Slide**. Click the hyperlinks to test them.

5 In **Normal** view, Display **Slide 7**.

a. On the **Insert tab**, in the **Illustrations group**, click **Shapes**.

b. At the bottom of the list, under **Action Buttons**, click the third shape— **Action Button: Go to Beginning**.

c. Position the pointer in the lower left corner of the slide, and then click one time to display the **Action Settings** dialog box.

d. On the **Mouse Over tab**, select **Hyperlink to:**, click the **Hyperlink to: arrow**, and then click **First Slide**. Select the **Play sound check box**, click the **Play sound arrow**, scroll as necessary, and then click **Chime**. Click **OK**. (Mac users, in the Links group, click Action. On the Mouse Click tab, select Hyperlink to, and then select Custom Show. Select Historic, and check the Show and return box. Click OK.)

e. With the action button still selected, on the **Drawing Tools Format tab**, in the **Size group**, change the **Shape Height** to **0.5"** and change the **Shape Width** to **0.5"**.

f. On the **Drawing Tools Format tab**, in the **Arrange group**, **Align** the shape to the **Bottom** and then **Align** again to the **Left** of the slide.

g. View the slide show **From Current Slide**, and then move the mouse pointer over the action button. Return to **Normal** view.

6 Display **Slide 1**.

a. On the **Slide Show tab**, in the **Start Slide Show group**, click **Custom Slide Show**, and then click **Custom Shows** to display the **Custom Shows** dialog box.

b. In the **Custom Shows** dialog box, click **New**. In the **Define Custom Show** dialog box, in the **Slide show name** box, delete the existing text, and then type **Standard Safety Features**

c. Under **Slides in presentation**, select slides **3**, **4**, and **5** by clicking in the check boxes, and then click **Add**. Click **OK**.

d. In the **Custom Shows** dialog box, click **Show** to preview your custom show. Click through the slides and return to **Normal** view.

7 In **Normal** view, in the slide thumbnails, on **Slide 1**, click the picture of the **flag**.

a. On the **Insert tab**, in the **Links group**, click **Link**. In the **Insert Hyperlink** dialog box, under **Link to:**, click **Place in This Document**.

b. In the **Insert Hyperlink** dialog box, under **Select a place in this document**, scroll down to display the **Custom Shows**, and then click **Standard Safety Features**. On the right, under **Slide preview**, select the **Show and return** check box. Click **OK**.

(continues on next page)

Chapter Review

Skills Review: Project 6D Safety (continued)

c. Begin to view the slide show **From Beginning**, and then when the first slide displays, click the picture of the **flag** on **Slide 1**. View the custom slide show and return to **Slide 1** of your presentation. Return to **Normal** view.

8 Display **Slide 13**.

a. On the **Home tab**, in the **Slides group**, click the **New Slide arrow**, and then click **Duplicate Selected Slides**.

b. With **Slide 14** selected, point to the picture of the **safety team** and right-click, and then click **Change Picture**. In the **Insert Pictures** dialog box, on the right of **From a File**. From your student data files, insert the file **p06D_Customer_Service**.

c. In the slide title placeholder at the bottom of the slide, select the words *Safety Team* and then type **Customer Service Place**

9 Display **Slide 6**.

a. On the **Slide Show tab**, in the **Set Up group**, click **Hide Slide**.

b. In the slide thumbnails, right-click the thumbnail for **Slide 13** to display a shortcut menu, and then click **Hide Slide**.

10 On the **Slide Show tab**, in the **Start Slide Show group**, click **From Beginning**. Move the mouse pointer anywhere in the slide, and notice that six buttons display in the lower left corner of the screen.

a. Click **Advance to the next slide**, and then click **Return to the previous slide**.

b. Click the fourth button— **See all slides**. (Mac users, this feature is not available in the Mac version of PowerPoint. You can click the third icon to display the menu, and then point to By Title to see a list of all slides, including any hidden slides.)

11 Click **Slide 5** to return to the slide show. Right-click anywhere on the slide, point to **Custom Show**, and then click **Standard Safety Features**. Click to view each of the slides in the custom show. When the slide show is finished, return to **Normal** view.

12 With **Slide 8** active, on the **Slide Show tab**, in the **Start Slide Show group**, click **From Current Slide**. In the lower left corner of the screen, click **More slide show options**, and then click **Show Presenter View**.

a. In **Presenter View**, below the large slide, click **Black or unblack slide show**. Click **Black or unblack slide show** to make the large slide visible again. (Mac users, click the menu icon and point to Screen.)

b. Below the large slide, click **More slide show options**, and then click **Hide Presenter View** to return to the slide show.

13 In the lower left corner of the screen, click the third button— **Pen and laser tools**.

a. Click **Laser Pointer**, and then move your mouse around the screen.

b. Click **Pen and laser tools**, and then click **Laser Pointer** to turn off the laser pointer.

c. Click **Pen and laser tools**, and then click **Highlighter**. (Mac users, the highlighter is not available in the Mac version of PowerPoint. Use the pen instead and change the color to yellow.)

d. Place the highlighter pointer to the left of the *S* in *Seat belt*, and then click and drag to the right to highlight *Seat belt use*.

e. Click **Pen and laser pointer tools**, and then click **Pen**. Circle the first bulleted item—*Built-in sensors detect*.

f. Press [Esc] two times. In the displayed dialog box, click **Keep**. (Mac users, the Mac version of PowerPoint does not include the ability to save annotations.)

14 Display **Slide 1**, click the **Slide Show tab**, and then in the **Set Up group**, click **Rehearse Timings**.

a. When the **Slide Time** box displays **4 (seconds)**, click **Next**. Repeat this step for each slide. After the last slide displays, click **Yes** to save the new slide timings.

b. On the PowerPoint **status bar,** click **Slide Sorter**. With the slides displayed, drag the **Zoom slider** to **70%**.

c. On the **Slide Show tab**, in the **Set Up group**, click **Set Up Slide Show**. In the **Set Up Show** dialog box, under **Advance slides**, click to select **Using timings, if present**. Under **Show type**, select **Browsed at a kiosk (full screen)**, and then click **OK**.

d. Start the slide show **From Beginning**. Wait about 5 seconds per slide, and then view a few slides. Press [Esc].

e. On the **Slide Show tab**, in the **Set Up group**, click **Set Up Slide Show**. Under **Show type**, select **Presented by a speaker (full screen)**. Under **Advance slides**, click **Manually**. Click **OK**.

(continues on next page)

Chapter Review

15 On the status bar, click **Normal**. Hold down Ctrl, and then click the thumbnails to select **Slides 1, 2**, and **8**.

  a. On the **File tab**, click **Print**. To create an electronic printed file, under Printer, click the **Printer arrow**, and then click **Microsoft Print to PDF**. Under **Settings**, click the **Print All Slides arrow**, and then click **Print Selection**. (Mac users, in the Printer dialog box, click PDF.) As directed by your instructor, create and submit a paper printout or an electronic image of your selected slides that looks like a printed document.

16 Insert a **Header & Footer** on the **Notes and Handouts**. Include the **Date and time** fixed, the **Page Number**, and a **Footer 6D_Safety** and then click **Apply to All**.

17 Display the document properties. As the **Tags**, type **safety, seat belts** and as the **Subject**, type your course and section number. Be sure your name displays as the author, and then **Save** your file.

18 As directed by your instructor, submit your completed PowerPoint file. **Close** PowerPoint.

You have completed Project 6D   **END**

MyLab IT Grader | Mastering PowerPoint | Project 6E Race Car

Apply 6A skills from these Objectives:

1. Apply and Modify Slide Transitions
2. Apply Custom Animation Effects
3. Modify Animation Effects

In the following Mastering PowerPoint project, you will modify a PowerPoint presentation advertising the Annual Race Car Rally hosted by Penn Liberty Motors. You will apply slide transitions and custom animation effects to the slide show to make the slide show more dynamic. The purpose is to appeal to race car enthusiasts. Your completed presentation will look similar to Figure 6.56.

Project Files for MyLab IT Grader

1. In your **MyLab IT** course, locate and click **PowerPoint 6E Race Car,** Download Materials, and then Download All Files.
2. Extract the zipped folder to your PowerPoint Chapter 6 folder. Close the Grader download screens.
3. Take a moment to open the downloaded **PowerPoint_6E_Race_Car_Instruction;** note any recent updates to the book.

Project Results

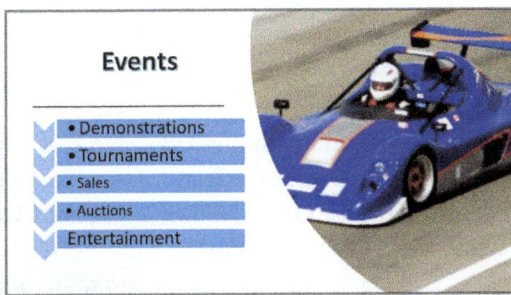
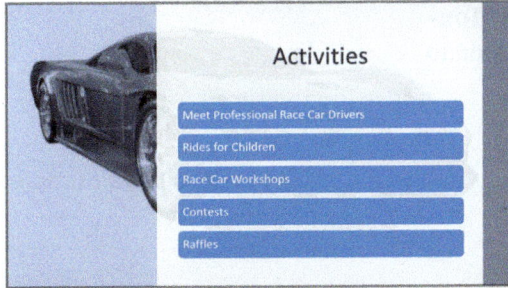
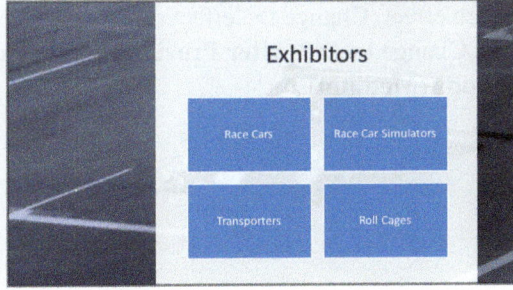
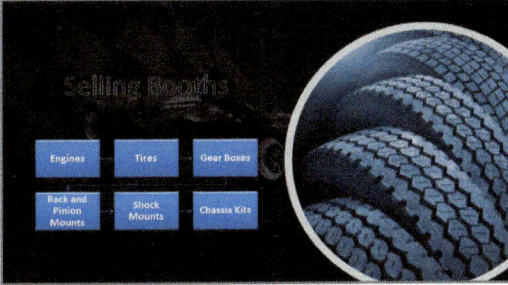

Figure 6.56 Project 6E Race Car

For Non-MyLab Submissions

For Project 6E, you will need:
p06E_Race_Car

In your PowerPoint Chapter 6 folder, save your presentation as:
Lastname_Firstname_6E_Race_Car

After you have named and saved your presentation, on the next page, begin with Step 2.
After Step 10, save and submit your presentation as directed by your instructor.

(continues on next page)

Content-Based Assessments (Mastery and Transfer of Learning)

1 Navigate to your **PowerPoint Chapter 6 folder** and then double-click the PowerPoint file you downloaded from **MyLab IT** that displays your name—**Student_PowerPoint_6E_Race_Car**.

2 On **Slide 1**, apply the **Fade** transition. Set the **Duration** to **1.50**, and apply to all slides.

3 On **Slide 2**, apply the **Push** transition, clear the **On Mouse Click** check box and set the slide to advance after **5** seconds.

4 On **Slide 2**, to the **SmartArt** graphic, apply the **Fly In** entrance animation. Apply the sequence effect option **Level at Once**. Change the entrance effect direction for content placeholder to **From Left**. Set the Duration to **1 seconds (Fast)**.

5 On **Slide 2**, to the **car** image, apply the **Fly In** entrance effect. Change the direction to **From Top-Left**, set the duration to **2 seconds (Medium)**, and then set to start **After Previous**.

6 On **Slide 3**, to the **SmartArt** graphic, apply the **Fly In** entrance animation effect. Change the effect sequence to **One by One, the** direction **From Top**, and the duration to **1 seconds (Fast)**.

7 On **Slide 3**, to the **car** picture, apply the **Fly In** entrance effect. Change the effect direction to **From Top-Right**. Change to start **After Previous** and the duration to **2 seconds (Medium)**.

8 On **Slide 1**, to the **title** placeholder, click **Blinds**—under **More Entrance Effects**, under **Basic**. Set to start **With Previous** and the duration to **1 seconds (Fast)**.

9 Insert a **Header and Footer** on the **Notes and Handouts**. Include the date and time fixed. Insert the footer **6E_Race_Car**

10 Display the document properties. As the **Tags**, type **race, exhibition, event** and as the **Subject**, type your course and section number. Be sure your name displays as the author, and then save your file.

11 In **MyLab IT,** in your **Course Materials**, locate and click the Grader Project **PowerPoint 6E Race Car**. In **step 3**, under **Upload Completed Assignment**, click **Choose File**. In the **Open** dialog box, navigate to your **PowerPoint Chapter 6 folder**, and then click your **Student_PowerPoint_6E_Race_Car** file one time to select it. In the lower right corner of the **Open** dialog box, click **Open**.

12 To submit your file to **MyLab IT** for grading, click **Upload**, wait a moment for a green **Success!** message, and then in **step 4**, click the blue **Submit for Grading** button. Click **Close Assignment** to return to your list of **Course Materials**.

You have completed Project 6E | **END**

MyLab IT Grader

Mastering PowerPoint | **Project 6F Custom Detail Aspects**

Apply 6B skills from these Objectives:

4. Insert Hyperlinks
5. Create Custom Slide Shows
6. Present and View a Slide Presentation

In the following Mastering PowerPoint project, you will modify a PowerPoint presentation listing many of the customization services available at Penn Liberty Motors to give a vehicle a unique appearance. You will insert hyperlinks and create custom slide shows of interior detailing. You will create a self-running version of the presentation for use in the automobile dealership. Your completed presentation will look similar to Figure 6.57.

Project Files for MyLab IT Grader

1. In your **MyLab IT** course, locate and click **PowerPoint 6F Custom Detail**, Download Materials, and then Download All Files.
2. Extract the zipped folder to your PowerPoint Chapter 6 folder. Close the Grader download screens.
3. Take a moment to open the downloaded **PowerPoint_6F_Custom_Detail_Instruction**; note any recent updates to the book.

Project Results

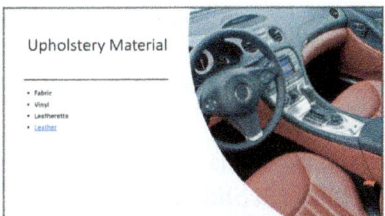
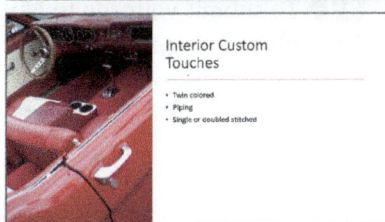

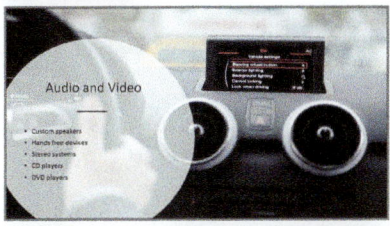
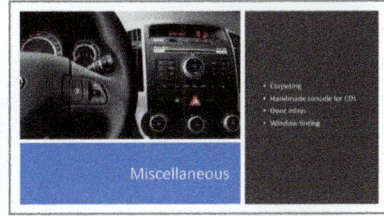
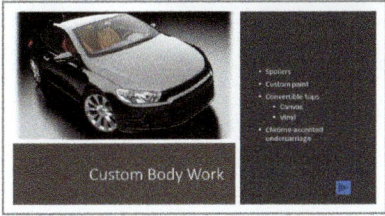
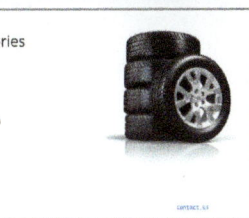

Figure 6.57 Project 6F Custom Detail Aspects

For Non-MyLab Submissions

For Project 6F, you will need: In your PowerPoint Chapter 6 folder, save your workbook as:

p06F_Custom_Detail   **Lastname_Firstname_6F_Custom_Detail**

After you have named and saved your presentation, on the next page, begin with Step 2.

After Step 11, save and submit your presentation as directed by your instructor.

(continues on next page)

Content-Based Assessments (Mastery and Transfer of Learning)

1 Navigate to your **PowerPoint Chapter 6 folder** and then double-click the PowerPoint file you downloaded from **MyLab IT** that displays your name—**Student_PowerPoint_6F_Custom_Detail**

2 On **Slide 1**, select the picture of the **flag**, insert the hyperlink to the webpage **www.dmv.pa.gov** and the **ScreenTip Pennsylvania Driver Vehicle Services**

3 On **Slide 7**, at the lower right corner of the slide, insert an **Action Button: Go Forward or Next** that, on mouse click, links to the next slide. Size the button **0.5″** wide and high.

4 On **Slide 2**, select *Leather*, insert a hyperlink to **Place in This Document**, and link to **3. Interior Custom Touches.**

5 On **Slide 8**, select *Contact Us*, and then add a hyperlink to the email address **customteam@libertymotors.biz** and include the Subject **Customization inquiry**

6 Create a new custom slide show named **Interior Customization**. Add **Slide 3** through **Slide 6** (in that order).

7 On **Slide 1**, select the subtitle *Customization* and insert a hyperlink to the custom show **Interior Customization**. Select the **Show and return** check box.

8 Hide **Slide 5**.

9 Set each slide to display for **5 seconds**. Set the presentation to be **Browsed at a kiosk (full screen)** and advanced using the timings.

10 Review your presentation from the beginning. Insert a footer on the Notes and Handouts, which includes a fixed date and time, the page number, and **6F_Custom_Detail**

11 Display the document properties. As the **Tags**, type **custom, accessories** and as the **Subject**, type your course and section number. Be sure your name displays as the author, and then save your file.

12 In **MyLab IT**, in your **Course Materials**, locate and click the Grader Project **6F Custom Detail**. In **step 3**, under **Upload Completed Assignment**, click **Choose File**. In the **Open** dialog box, navigate to your **PowerPoint Chapter 6 folder**, and then click your **Student_PowerPoint_6F_Custom_Detail** file one time to select it. In the lower right corner of the **Open** dialog box, click **Open**.

13 To submit your file to **MyLab IT** for grading, click **Upload**, wait a moment for a green **Success!**.

You have completed Project 6F | END

MyLab IT Grader

Mastering PowerPoint   Project 6G Repairs

Apply 6A and 6B skills from these Objectives:

1. Apply and Modify Slide Transitions
2. Apply Custom Animation Effects
3. Modify Animation Effects
4. Insert Hyperlinks
5. Create Custom Slide Shows
6. Present and View a Slide Presentation

In the following Mastering PowerPoint project, you will modify a PowerPoint presentation that advertises Penn Liberty Motors' Repair Department and lists the types of repairs performed and the goodwill customer services available. You will apply slide transitions and custom animation effects, insert hyperlinks, and create custom slide shows. Your completed presentation will look similar to Figure 6.58.

Project Files for MyLab IT Grader

1. In your **MyLab IT** course, locate and click **PowerPoint 6G Repairs**, Download Materials, and then Download All Files.
2. Extract the zipped folder to your PowerPoint Chapter 6 folder. Close the Grader download screens.
3. Take a moment to open the downloaded **PowerPoint_6G_Repairs_Instructions**; note any recent updates to the book.

Project Results

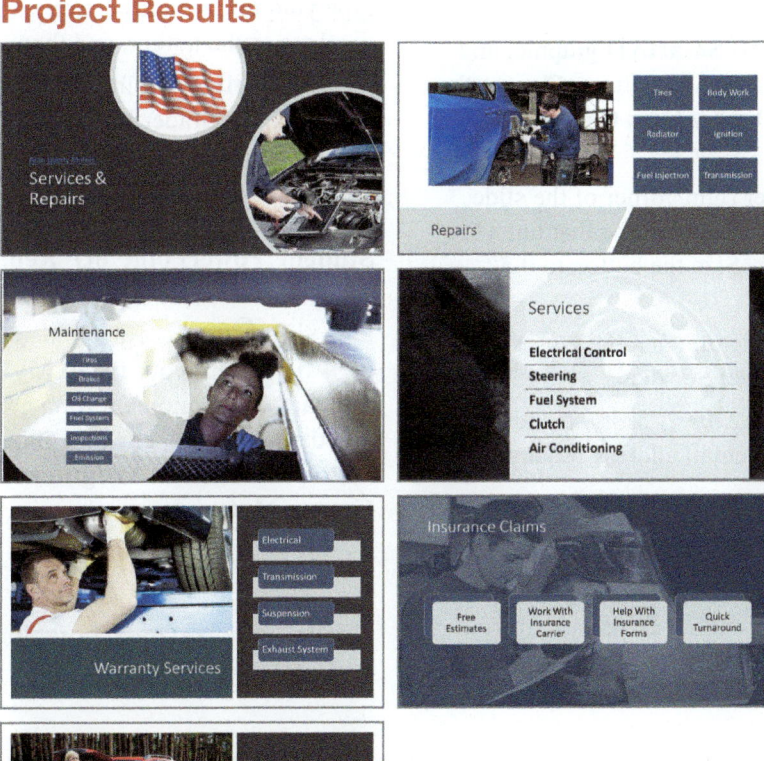

Figure 6.58 Project 6G Repairs

For Non-MyLab Submissions

For Project 6G, you will need: In your PowerPoint Chapter 6 folder, save your presentation as:
p06G_Repairs   **Lastname_Firstname_6G_Repairs**

After you have named and saved your presentation, on the next page, begin with Step 2.

After Step 12, save and submit your presentation as directed by your instructor.

(continues on next page)

Content-Based Assessments (Mastery and Transfer of Learning)

1 Navigate to your **PowerPoint Chapter 6 folder** and then double-click the PowerPoint file you downloaded from **MyLab IT** that displays your name—**Student_PowerPoint_6G_Repairs**

2 Apply a **Push** transition to all slides.

3 On **Slide 2**, select the **SmartArt** graphic. Add the **Fly In** entrance effect, set the effect sequence option to **One by One**, and then set to start **After Previous**. Set the effect direction to **From Left**, and then change the duration to **2 seconds (Medium)**.

4 On **Slide 3**, select the **SmartArt** graphic. Apply the **Fly In** entrance effect, set the effect sequence option to **All at Once**, and then change the direction to **From Left** and the duration to **2 seconds (Medium)**.

5 On **Slide 4**, select the list **SmartArt** graphic, and then add the **Fade** entrance animation effect. Change the effect sequence options to **One by One**. Change the start to **After Previous**.

6 On **Slide 7**, at the lower right corner of the slide, insert an **Action Button: Go Home** shape that links to the first slide on mouse click. Size the button to **0.5″** wide and high.

7 On **Slide 5**, select the picture, and then insert a hyperlink to **Slide 7. Customer Service**.

8 On **Slide 1**. Select *Penn Liberty Motors*, and then insert a hyperlink to the email address **repairs@ libertymotors.biz**

9 Set up a new custom slide show named **Warranty and Maintenance** Add **Slides 1, 3, 4,** and **5** to the custom slide show. Set up a second custom slide show named **Insurance Claims** Add **Slide 6** and **Slide 7** to the custom slide show.

10 On **Slide 2**, select the picture and insert a hyperlink to the custom show **Insurance Claims**. Select the **Show and return** check box.

11 Insert a **Header & Footer** on the **Notes and Handouts**. Include the Date and time fixed, the **Page Number**, and a Footer **6G_Repairs**

12 Display the document properties. As the Tags, type **insurance, maintenance, warranty** and as the Subject, type your course and section number. Be sure your name displays as the author, and then save your file.

13 In **MyLab IT,** in your **Course Materials**, locate and click the Grader Project **PowerPoint 6G Repairs**. In **step 3**, under **Upload Completed Assignment**, click **Choose File**. In the **Open** dialog box, navigate to your **PowerPoint Chapter 6 folder**, and then click your **Student_PowerPoint_6G_Repairs** file one time to select it. In the lower right corner of the **Open** dialog box, click **Open**.

14 To submit your file to **MyLab IT** for grading, click **Upload**, wait a moment for a green **Success!** message, and then in **step 4**, click the blue **Submit for Grading** button. Click **Close Assignment** to return to your list of **Course Materials**.

You have completed Project 6G | **END**

Apply a combination of the **6A** and **6B** skills.

GO! Fix It	**Project 6H Staff**	IRC
GO! Make It	**Project 6I Auto Show**	IRC
GO! Solve It	**Project 6J Leasing**	IRC
GO! Solve It	**Project 6K Special Orders**	

Project Files

For Project 6K, you will need:

p06K_Special_Orders

You will save your presentation as:

Lastname_Firstname_6K_Special_Orders

In this project, you will customize a slide show highlighting special-order vehicles, such as limousines, motorcycles, and race cars, available at Penn Liberty Motors. You will apply transitions and entrance and exit animation effects.

Open **p06K_Special_Orders**, and then save it as **Lastname_Firstname_6K_Special_Orders** Apply transitions and add entrance and exit animation effects. Insert a hyperlink to the Specialized Inventory text for the email address **custom@libertymotors.biz**

Use hyperlinks to link the picture of a vehicle to its features. Create at least two basic custom shows to appeal to two different vehicle enthusiasts, and then insert a hyperlink to one of the custom shows. Create an action button.

Insert a Header & Footer on the Notes and Handouts Handouts that includes the date and time fixed, the page number, and a footer **6K_Special_Orders** In the Properties, add your name, course name and section number for the subject, and the tags **classic, limousines** Save your presentation. Print or submit electronically as directed by your instructor.

	Performance Element	Performance Level		
		Exemplary	**Proficient**	**Developing**
Performance Criteria	**Formatted slide show with a variety of transitions and effects.**	Slide show included relevant transitions and effects.	Slide show included a variety of transitions and effects, but they were not appropriate for the presentation.	Slide show contained no transitions and effects.
	Inserted hyperlinks to website, to email address, and to place in the slide show.	All hyperlinks worked correctly.	One of the hyperlinks did not work correctly.	Hyperlinks were not created, or they did not work correctly.
	Created two custom slide shows and linked one of them.	Created two custom shows and one was linked correctly.	Created one custom show and did not link.	No custom slide shows were created.
	Created an action button.	The action button produced the intended result.	Action button was created but did not work properly.	No action button was created.

You have completed Project 6K | END

Content-Based Assessments (Critical Thinking)

Rubric

The following outcomes-based assessments are *open-ended assessments*. That is, there is no specific correct result; your result will depend on your approach to the information provided. Make *Professional Quality* your goal. Use the following scoring rubric to guide you in *how* to approach the problem and then to evaluate *how well* your approach solves the problem.

The *criteria*—Software Mastery, Content, Format and Layout, and Process—represent the knowledge and skills you have gained that you can apply to solving the problem. The *levels of performance*—Professional Quality, Approaching Professional Quality, or Needs Quality Improvements—help you and your instructor evaluate your result.

	Your completed project is of Professional Quality if you:	Your completed project is Approaching Professional Quality if you:	Your completed project Needs Quality Improvements if you:
1-Software Mastery	Choose and apply the most appropriate skills, tools, and features and identify efficient methods to solve the problem.	Choose and apply some appropriate skills, tools, and features, but not in the most efficient manner.	Choose inappropriate skills, tools, or features, or are inefficient in solving the problem.
2-Content	Construct a solution that is clear and well organized, contains content that is accurate, appropriate to the audience and purpose, and is complete. Provide a solution that contains no errors of spelling, grammar, or style.	Construct a solution in which some components are unclear, poorly organized, inconsistent, or incomplete. Misjudge the needs of the audience. Have some errors in spelling, grammar, or style, but the errors do not detract from comprehension.	Construct a solution that is unclear, incomplete, or poorly organized, contains some inaccurate or inappropriate content, and contains many errors of spelling, grammar, or style. Do not solve the problem.
3-Format and Layout	Format and arrange all elements to communicate information and ideas, clarify function, illustrate relationships, and indicate relative importance.	Apply appropriate format and layout features to some elements, but not others. Overuse features, causing minor distraction.	Apply format and layout that does not communicate information or ideas clearly. Do not use format and layout features to clarify function, illustrate relationships, or indicate relative importance. Use available features excessively, causing distraction.
4-Process	Use an organized approach that integrates planning, development, self-assessment, revision, and reflection.	Demonstrate an organized approach in some areas, but not others; or, use an insufficient process of organization throughout.	Do not use an organized approach to solve the problem.

6

Apply a combination of the 6A and 6B skills.

GO! Think — Project 6L Car Purchase

Project Files

For Project 6L, you will need:

New blank PowerPoint presentation
p06L_Off_Lease

You will save your presentation as:

Lastname_Firstname_6L_Car_Purchase

Penn Liberty Motors has launched a new sales initiative to sell used cars. In this project, you will create a presentation with a minimum of six slides comparing the benefits of buying a new car versus buying a used car. In addition, certified lease cars should be part of the presentation. Include transitions and custom animation effects in the presentation. Create a self-running slide show. Information to be included in your presentation is provided in the file p06L_Off_Lease.

Insert a Header & Footer on the Notes and Handouts that includes the date and time fixed, the page number, and a footer **6L_Car_Purchase** In Properties, add your name and course information and the tags **certification, lease** Save your presentation. Print Handouts 6 slides per page, or submit electronically as directed by your instructor.

You have completed Project 6L | **END**

GO! Think — Project 6M Security — IRC

You and GO! — Project 6N Digital Sound — IRC

Presentations Using Tables and Pie Charts

PROJECT 7A

Outcomes
Create, position, and modify a table in a PowerPoint presentation. Insert a section to organize a presentation.

Objectives
1. Add a Table to a Presentation
2. Add or Delete Table Rows, Columns, and Cells
3. Modify a Table
4. Insert a Section

PROJECT 7B

Outcomes
Create pie charts and customize charts in a PowerPoint presentation.

Objectives
5. Create Pie Charts
6. Modify Charts
7. Change a Chart Type

Phawat/Shutterstock

In This Chapter

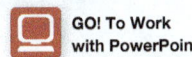

GO! To Work with PowerPoint

A table is useful for displaying information in a PowerPoint presentation. You can create a table directly in PowerPoint. You can also use tables created in Microsoft Word or Excel by copying and pasting them into PowerPoint. You can also create a table by opening an Excel spreadsheet from within PowerPoint. You can modify a table by sizing the table; adding and removing rows, columns, and cells; and splitting and merging cells. You can format a table by applying built-in table styles or changing the border color, line, or weight.

Pie charts show how different parts of something relate to the whole. You can create professional-looking charts by applying predefined layouts, styles, and animation.

The **Seattle–Tacoma Job Fair** is a nonprofit organization that brings employers and job seekers together in the greater Seattle–Tacoma metropolitan area. Each year, the organization holds a number of targeted job fairs, such as the annual Greater Seattle Job Fair, which draws 2,000 employers in more than 70 industries and registers more than 5,000 candidates. Candidate registration is free; employers pay a nominal fee to display and present at the fairs. Candidate resumes and employer postings are managed by a new database system, allowing participants quick and accurate access to job data and candidate qualifications.

PROJECT

7A Job Database

MyLab IT
Project 7A Grader for Instruction
Project 7A Simulation for Training and Review

Project Activities

In Activities 7.01 through 7.10, you will create, copy, and modify tables and add section headers in a PowerPoint presentation that will be used by the database administrator of the Seattle–Tacoma Job Fair organization for an in-house presentation. The presentation will use tables to visually organize the data about the companies that have participated or might participate in the job fair. Your completed presentation will look similar to Figure 7.1.

Project Files

Project Files for MyLab IT Grader

1. In your storage location, create a folder named **PowerPoint Chapter 7**.
2. In your **MyLab IT** course, locate and click **PowerPoint 7A Job Database**, Download Materials, and then Download All Files.
3. Extract the zipped folder to your PowerPoint Chapter 7 folder. Close the Grader download screens.
4. Take a moment to open the downloaded **PowerPoint_7A_Job_Database_Instructions**; note any recent updates to the book.

Project Results

GO! Project 7A
Where We're Going

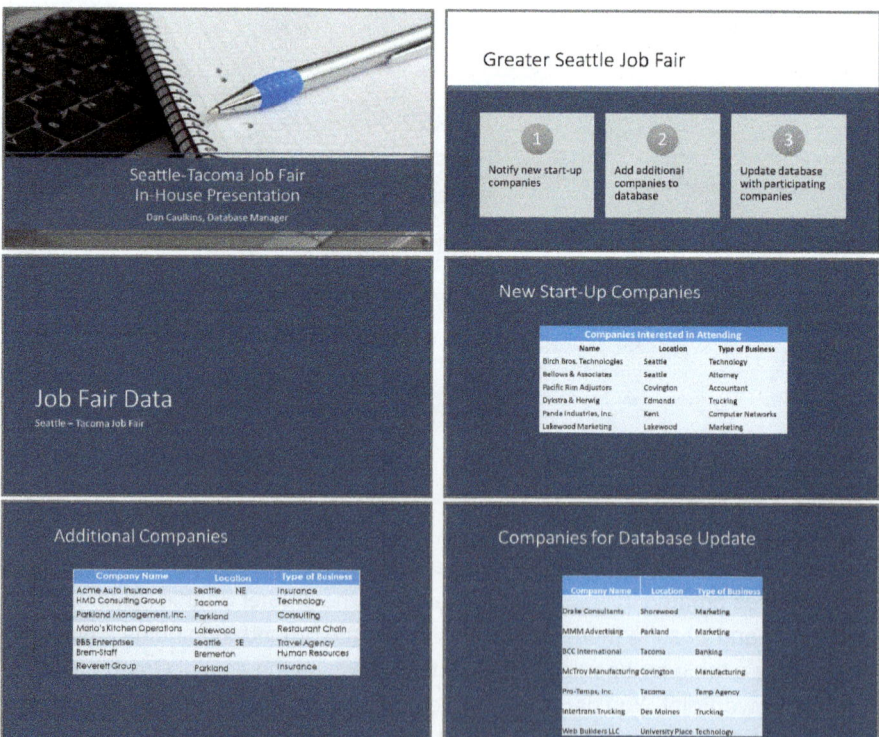

Figure 7.1 Project 7A Job Database

For Non-MyLab Submissions
For Project 7A, you will need:
p07A_Job_Database
p07A_Additional_Companies
p07A_Recent_Participants

In your storage location, create a folder named **PowerPoint Chapter 7**
In your PowerPoint Chapter 7 folder, save your presentation as:
Lastname_Firstname_7A_Job_Database

After you have named and saved your presentation, on the next page, begin with Step 2.

7

POWERPOINT

ALERT   Because Office 365 is a cloud-based subscription service that receives continuous updates, you may encounter some variations in what appears on your screen and what is shown in this instruction. Microsoft Office 365 is fully installed on your PC or Mac; no internet access is necessary to create or edit documents. When you *are* connected to the internet, you will receive monthly upgrades and new features, so you always have the latest versions of Office apps as soon as they are available. Your subscription gives you continuous free access to the latest innovations and refinements.

GO! Learn How
Video P7-1

You can use a *table*—a grid of rows and columns—to present information in a PowerPoint presentation. Tables are a good way to present text and numerical information. You can create a table within PowerPoint and copy and paste tables from Microsoft Word and Excel into a PowerPoint presentation. When you create a table in PowerPoint, it becomes an *embedded* object—an object that is saved with, and becomes part of, the PowerPoint file. Likewise, when you copy information, or an object contained in another file, such as Word or Excel—referred to as the *source file*, and then paste it into the PowerPoint presentation—referred to as the *destination file*, the object becomes part of the destination file. Any changes you make to the embedded object are reflected only in the destination file.

NOTE   **Table Design Variations**

In this project, you will insert tables using various methods, styles, and formatting. When creating your own presentations, however, you should maintain a uniform style or theme.

Activity 7.01 | Creating a Table in PowerPoint

MOS
4.1.1

In this Activity, you will create a table in PowerPoint that describes the companies to be added to the database of the Seattle–Tacoma Job Fair. You will enter data that includes the company name, location, and type of business.

1   Navigate to your **PowerPoint Chapter 7 folder**, and then double-click the PowerPoint file you downloaded from **MyLab IT** that displays your name—**Student_PowerPoint_7A_Job_Database**. In your presentation, if necessary, at the top click **Enable Editing**.

2   Display **Slide 3**. On the **Insert tab**, in the **Tables group**, click **Table** to display the **Insert Table** menu. Compare your screen with Figure 7.2, and then take a moment to study the **Insert Table** commands described in Figure 7.3.

Here, the grid structure resembles a table.

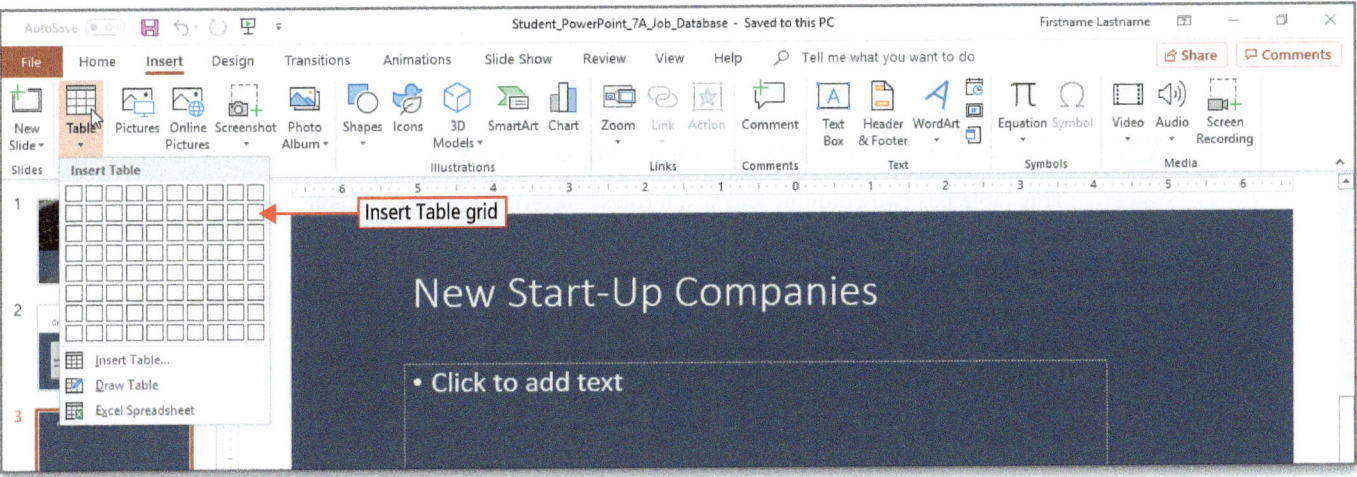

Figure 7.2

Insert Table Commands	
Menu Selection	**Description and Usage**
Table Grid	Enables you to select the number of rows and columns for the table by pointing to the individual cells. Live Preview displays the rows and columns on the slide before you click your selection.
Insert Table	Displays the Insert Table dialog box where you can select the number of columns and number of rows by using a spin box.
Draw Table	Enables you to create a custom table by first drawing the outside boundaries of the table, and then creating rows and columns within the table borders.
Excel Spreadsheet	Opens an Excel worksheet for data entry.

Figure 7.3

3 In the **Table grid**, in the first row, *point* to, but do not click, the second cell, and above the grid, notice that *2×1 Table* displays.

4 In the seventh row, point to the second cell, and then compare your screen with Figure 7.4.

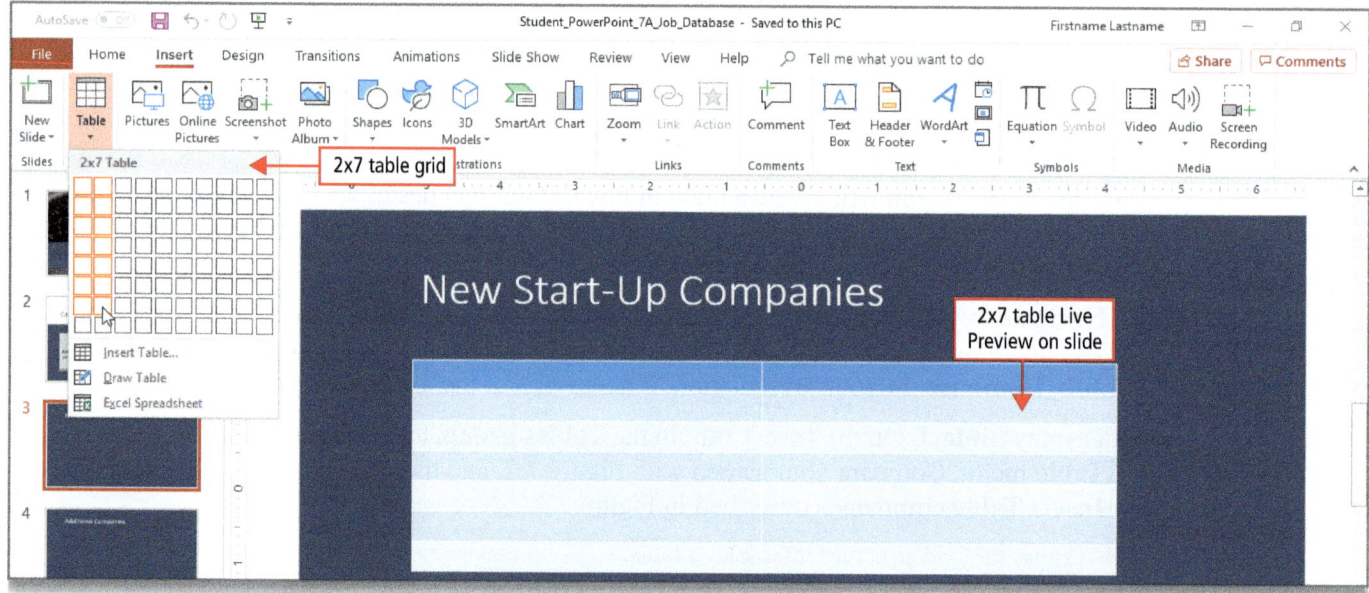

Figure 7.4

5 Click to create the 2×7 table, and then compare your screen with Figure 7.5.

This table has two columns and seven rows—referred to as a 2×7 table. The Table Tools contextual tabs display on the ribbon.

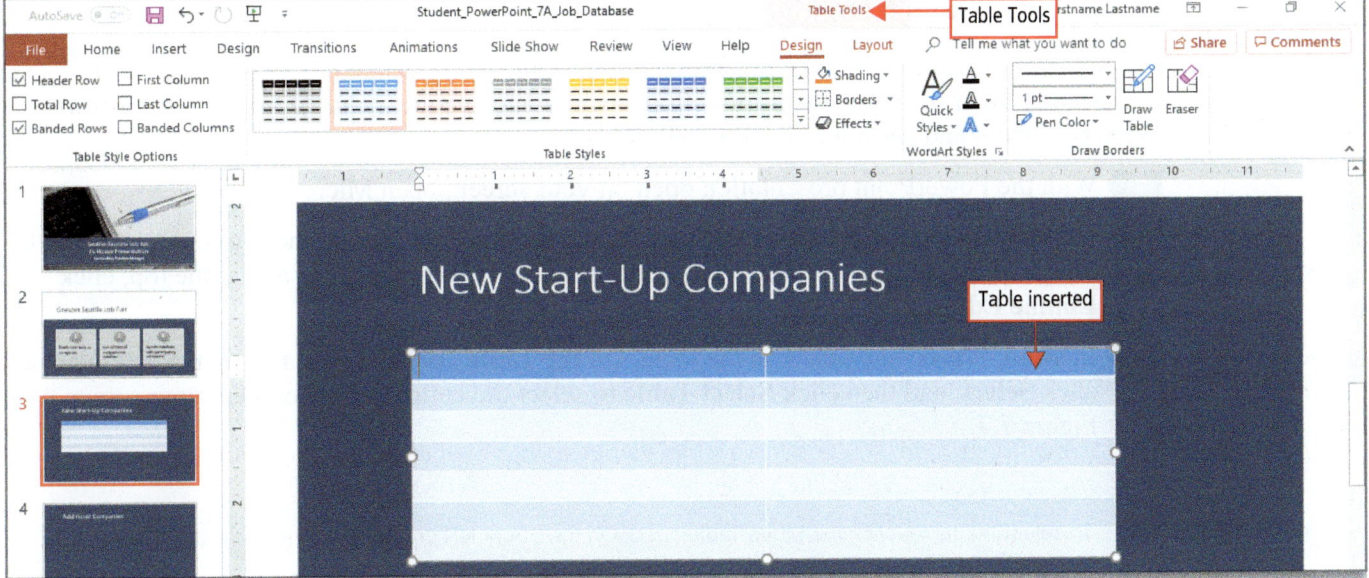

Figure 7.5

6 ▶ With the insertion point blinking in the first cell, type **Name** and then press Tab to move to the second cell in the first row of the table.

7 ▶ With the insertion point in the second cell, type **Location**

This row is referred to as the *header row*—the top row of the table that is formatted differently from the rows containing data.

8 ▶ Press Tab to move to the first cell in the second row. Type the following information in the cells, pressing Tab after each entry except the last entry:

Birch Bros. Technologies	**Seattle**
Bellows & Associates	**Seattle**
Pacific Rim Adjustors	**Covington**
Dykstra & Herwig	**Edmonds**
Panda Industries, Inc.	**Kent**
Lakewood Marketing	**Lakewood**

9 ▶ Click in a blank area of the slide to deselect the table, and then compare your screen with Figure 7.6.

Figure 7.6

10 ▶ **Save** 🖫 your presentation.

Activity 7.02 | Copying a Table from Microsoft Word

MOS
4.1.1

Some of the data needed for this presentation is already formatted in a table in a Word document. Rather than type the information again, you can copy the table from the Microsoft Word document and paste it into a PowerPoint slide.

1 With the PowerPoint presentation open on your screen, open Microsoft Word.

2 On Word's opening screen, click **Open**. Click **Browse**, navigate to the files downloaded with this project, and then open **p07A_Additional_Companies**. If necessary, at the top, click **Enable Editing**.

3 In Word, if necessary, click in the table. On the **Table Tools Layout tab**, in the **Table group**, click **Select**, and then click **Select Table** to select the entire table. Compare your screen with Figure 7.7.

> **ANOTHER WAY** To select the table, click the Move Table handle in the upper left corner of the table.

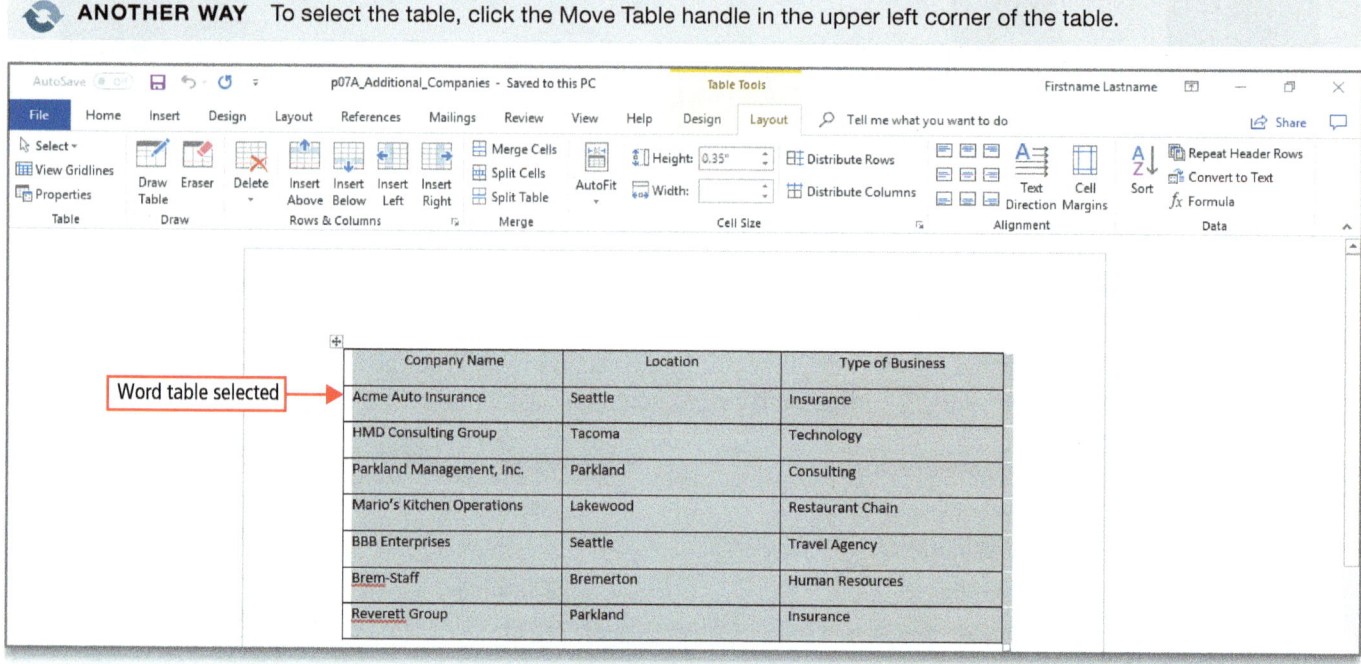

Figure 7.7

4 On the **Home tab**, in the **Clipboard group**, click **Copy** 📋 to copy the table to the Office Clipboard.

5 On the Windows taskbar, click **PowerPoint**. Display **Slide 4**. On the **Home tab**, in the **Clipboard group**, click the **Paste arrow** 📋.

> **ANOTHER WAY** To copy selected text or data, right-click in the selection and click Copy. To paste, right-click in the destination and click Paste. You can also use keyboard shortcuts Ctrl + C to Copy and Ctrl + V to Paste.

6 Point to the first option under **Paste Options** to display the ScreenTip. Click **Use Destination Styles (S)**. If necessary, close the Design Ideas pane. Compare your screen with Figure 7.8.

> The table from the Word document displays on the slide and is formatted with the destination style—the theme that was applied to the presentation. The Paste Options icon displays at the bottom of the table.

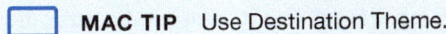 **MAC TIP** Use Destination Theme.

Figure 7.8

7 Click the **Table Tools Design tab**, and then in the **Table Style Options group**, clear the **First Column** check box. Compare your screen with Figure 7.9.

> This action removes the shading from the first column.

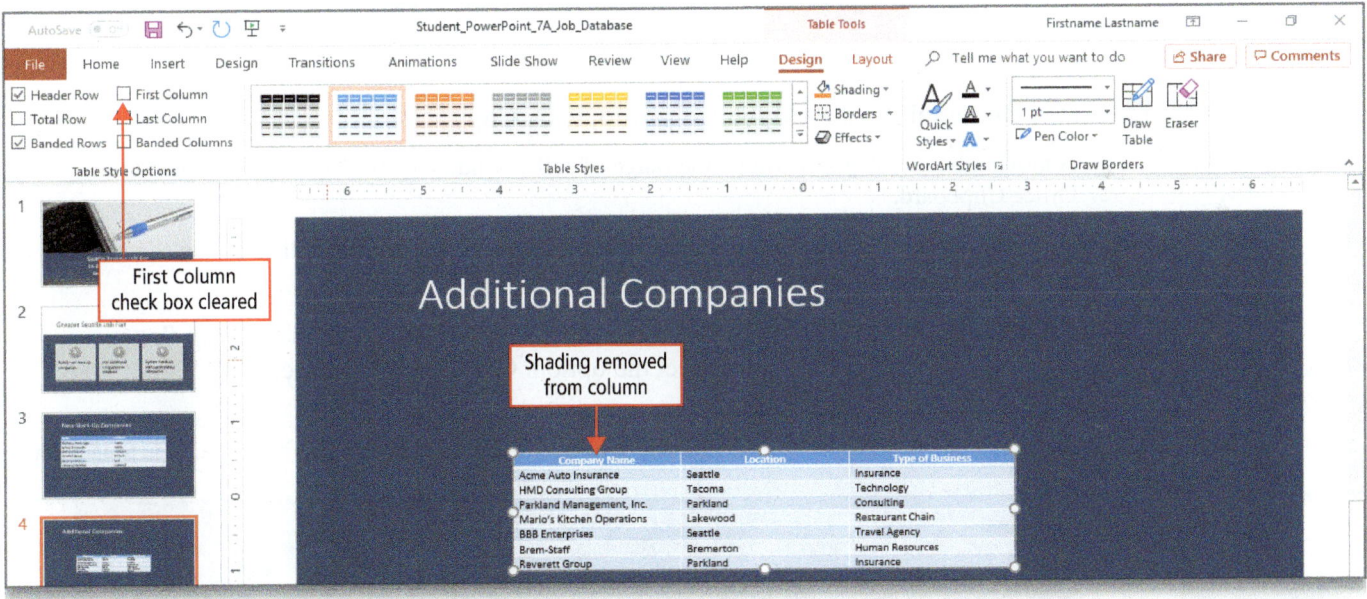

Figure 7.9

8 From the taskbar, return to Word, and then **Close** ✕ Word. If a message displays to save your file, do not save any changes. With your PowerPoint window redisplayed, **Save** 🖫 your presentation.

Activity 7.03 | Copying a Table from Microsoft Excel

3.1.4

Excel is often used to organize information. In this Activity, you will copy information about recent job fair participants located in an Excel worksheet and paste it into your presentation. Because a worksheet is organized in columns and rows like a table, the data will be pasted as a table in PowerPoint.

1 With your PowerPoint presentation displayed, open Microsoft Excel.

2 On Excel's opening screen, click **Open**. Click **Browse**, navigate to the files downloaded with this project, and then open **p07A_Recent_Participants**. If necessary, at the top, click **Enable Editing**.

3 In Excel, with cell **A1** active, hold down ⇧Shift, and then click cell **D8** to select the entire range of cells that contain data. Release ⇧Shift. Compare your screen with Figure 7.10.

A **range** is two or more selected cells on a worksheet that are adjacent or nonadjacent; because the range is treated as a single unit, you can make the same changes or combination of changes to more than one cell at a time.

ANOTHER WAY   To select all the cells in a range, click the first cell, and then drag the mouse to the last cell.

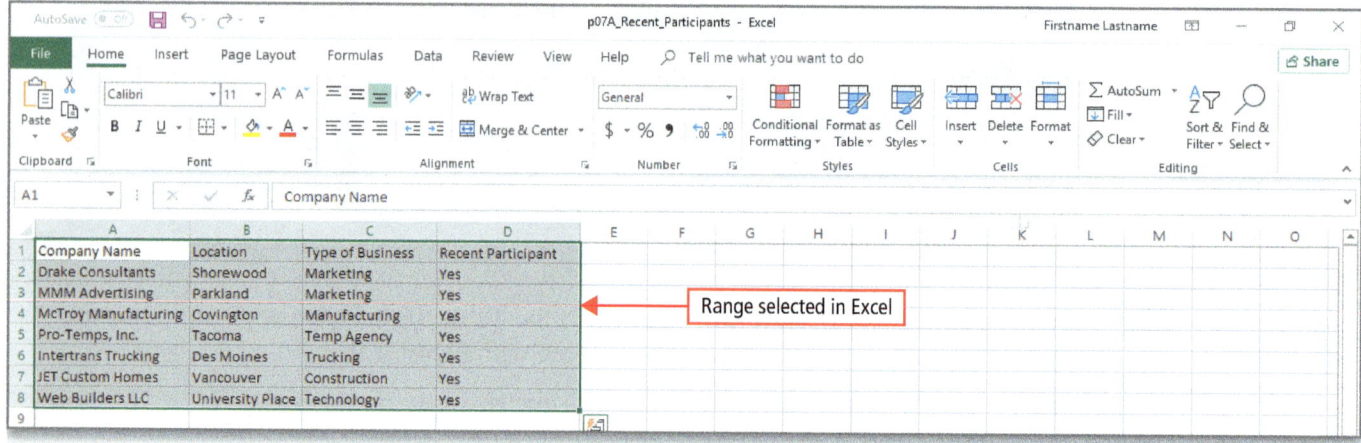

Figure 7.10

4 On the **Home tab**, in the **Clipboard group**, click **Copy** 📋.

A moving border displays around the range of cells to indicate that the range is copied to the Office Clipboard.

5 From the taskbar, redisplay your PowerPoint presentation. Display **Slide 5**. On the **Home tab**, in the **Clipboard group**, click the **Paste arrow** 📋.

6 Under **Paste Options**, *point* to the second option to display the ScreenTip *Keep Source Formatting (K)*, and then click to select the option. Compare your screen with Figure 7.11.

This action retains the formatting of the source—the Excel worksheet. The text is formatted in Calibri 11 pt, which is the default font and font size in Excel, and the table background is transparent.

Figure 7.11

7 From the taskbar, return to **Excel,** and then **Close** ✕ Excel. If a message displays to save your file, do not save any changes.

8 On **Slide 5**, if necessary, select the table. Change the font size to **16**, click in a blank area of the slide to deselect the table. **Save** 🖫 your presentation.

> **MORE KNOWLEDGE** **Inserting a Table by Using the Excel Spreadsheet Command in PowerPoint**
>
> To take advantage of the advanced functionality of Microsoft Excel, you can use Excel to create a table from within PowerPoint. In PowerPoint, on the Insert tab, in the Tables group, click Table, and then click Excel Spreadsheet. An Excel worksheet window opens within PowerPoint. In PowerPoint, the spreadsheet becomes an OLE embedded object. OLE—Object Linking and Embedding—is the program-integration technology used to share information between Office programs. Integration means that Microsoft Office programs support sharing information through linked or embedded objects.

Objective 2   Add or Delete Table Rows, Columns, and Cells

GO! Learn How
Video P7-2

In PowerPoint, you can *merge*—combine—two or more cells into a single cell, and you can also *split*—divide—a cell into two or more cells to add cells to a table. A cell can be merged or split horizontally or vertically. A useful feature in PowerPoint when working with tables is *table gridlines*—nonprinting lines that display between columns and rows in a table. Table gridlines differ from the slide gridlines, which are used to position slide elements.

Activity 7.04 │ Adding and Deleting Table Rows

4.1.2

You can modify a table to accommodate more or less information by adding or deleting rows or columns. In this Activity, you will delete a company name and information from the table by deleting a row, and then add new company information by adding a row to the table.

1 On **Slide 5**, click in the cell that contains *JET Custom Homes* to display the insertion point in the cell. On the **Table Tools Layout tab**, in the **Rows & Columns group**, click **Delete**. Compare your screen with Figure 7.12.

Three delete commands display. From here you can delete columns, rows, or the entire table.

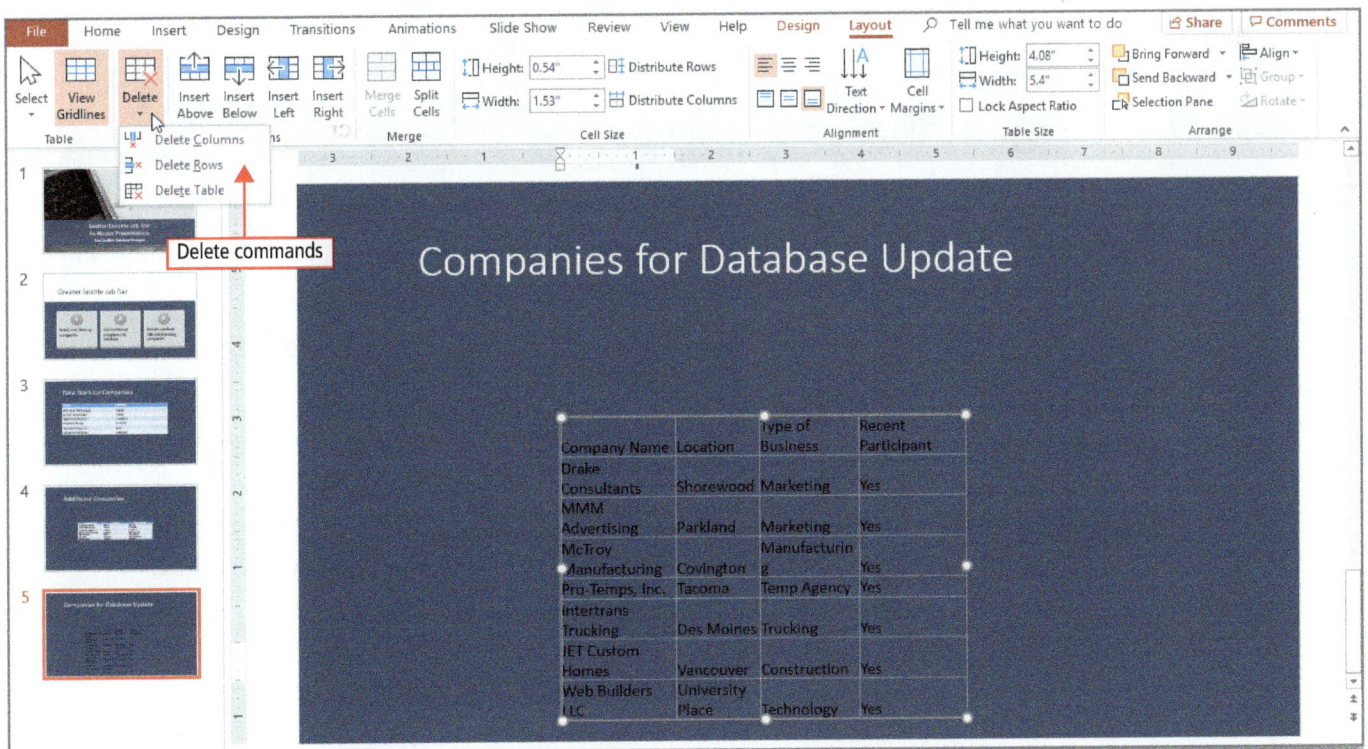

Figure 7.12

2 Click **Delete Rows** to delete the row.

3 Click in the cell that contains *McTroy Manufacturing* to display the insertion point in the cell. On the **Table Tools Layout tab**, in the **Rows & Columns group**, *point* to **Insert Above** and notice the ScreenTip.

> You can insert rows above or below the selected row. You can also insert columns to the left or right of the selected column.

4 Click **Insert Above** to insert a new, blank row above the row.

5 Click to position the insertion point in the new blank row, and then type the following information, pressing ⭾Tab after each entry:

BCC International	Tacoma	Banking	No

6 Save 🖫 your presentation.

Activity 7.05 | Adding and Deleting Table Columns

MOS
4.1.2

The last column of data in the table that you pasted from Excel is not needed for this presentation. Because the table is embedded in your presentation, deleting the column in PowerPoint will not affect the information in the Excel file. To keep the tables in your presentation consistent, you need to add a column to the table on Slide 3 that contains the type of business.

1 On **Slide 5**, point above the column header *Recent Participant*, outside of the table, to display the column select ⬇ pointer. Compare your screen with Figure 7.13.

> Use the column select pointer to select an entire table column.

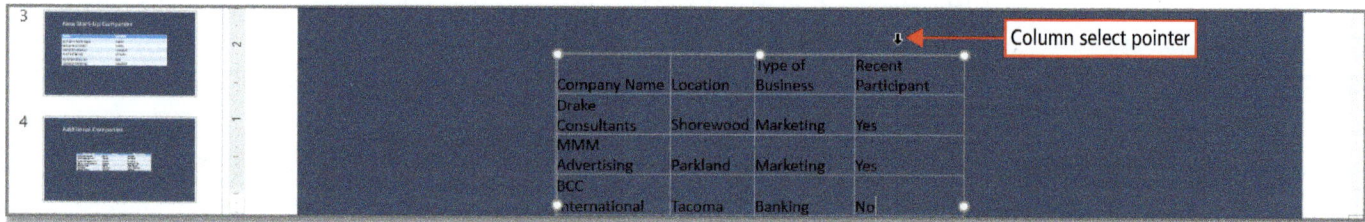

Figure 7.13

2 Right-click to select the column and display the shortcut menu and the mini toolbar. On the mini toolbar, click **Delete**, and then click **Delete Columns**.

> This action removes the column; the table resizes to fit the remaining content.

 MAC TIP To display a shortcut menu, ⟨control⟩ + click, or configure your Mac trackpad or mouse to use right-clicks in System Preferences, by enabling the Secondary click option.

3 Display **Slide 3**. Point to the cell *Location,* and then right-click to display the mini toolbar. On the **mini toolbar**, click **Insert**, and then click **Insert Columns to the Right**.

> This action inserts a new column to the right of the active column and adjusts the width of columns 1 and 2.

4 In the new column, type the following information, press ⬇ to move to the next cell:

Type of Business
Technology
Attorney
Accountant
Trucking
Computer Networks
Marketing

5 **Save** 🖫 your presentation, and then compare your screen with Figure 7.14.

Figure 7.14

Activity 7.06 | Merging and Splitting Table Cells

MOS
4.1.2

You can merge the cells in a row to span multiple columns. A header row that spans multiple columns and contains the table title is often included in a table. Within a table, you can split cells to better organize specific information within the table.

1 On **Slide 3** in the header row, point to any cell and right-click. On the mini toolbar, click **Insert**, and then click **Insert Rows Above**.

2 To the left of the new row, point to display the row select ➡ pointer. Compare your screen with Figure 7.15.

A new header row is inserted in the table. The previous header row adopts the formatting of the other rows in the table.

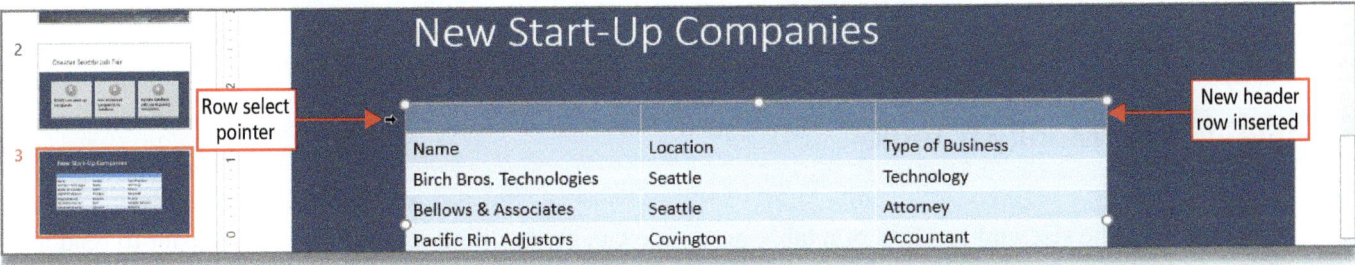

Figure 7.15

3 ▶ Right-click, and then click **Merge Cells**.

The cells in the header row are merged into one large cell.

> **ANOTHER WAY**   Select the cells you want to merge. On the Table Tools Layout tab, in the Merge group, click Merge Cells.

4 ▶ In the new header row, type **Companies Interested in Attending** and then **Center** ☰ the text.

5 ▶ Display **Slide 4**. In **row 2**, in the second column, point to *Seattle* and right-click. Click **Split Cells** to display the **Split Cells** dialog box. Compare your screen with Figure 7.16.

The Split Cells dialog box displays with the number *2* in the *Number of columns* box—the number of cells that will result when the cell is split, or divided, vertically.

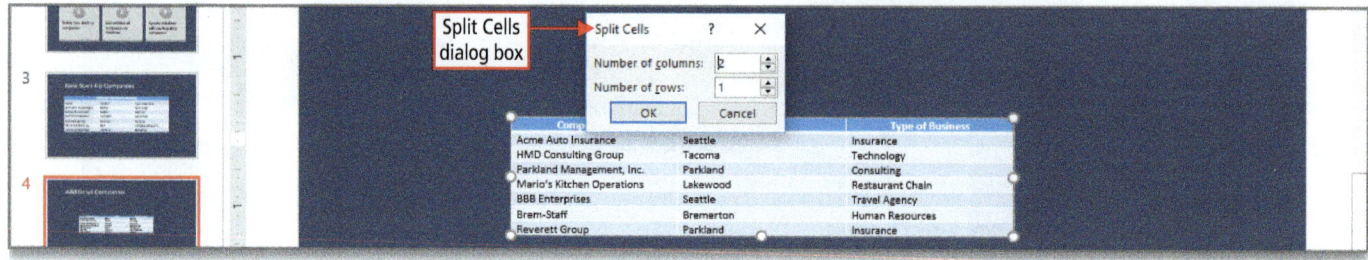

Figure 7.16

6 ▶ Click **OK** to split the cell into two cells that are side by side in the same row.

7 ▶ To the right of the *Seattle* cell, click in the new empty cell, and then type **NE** to indicate that the company is located in the northeast section of Seattle.

8 ▶ In **row 6**, point to *Seattle*, and then by using the technique you just practiced, split the cell into two cells. In the new empty cell, type **SE** to indicate that the company is located in the southeast section of Seattle. Click a blank area of the slide to deselect the table, and then compare your screen with Figure 7.17.

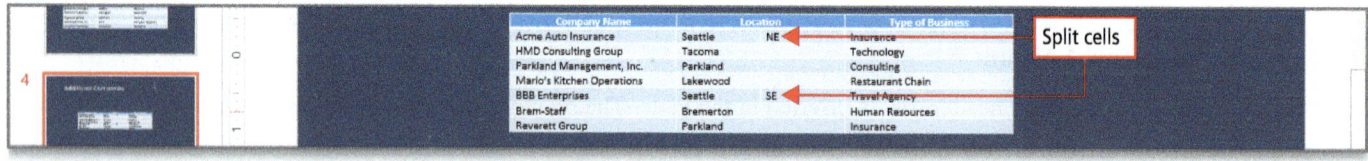

Figure 7.17

9 ▶ **Save** 🖫 your presentation.

Objective 3   Modify a Table

GO! Learn How
Video P7-3

The size and location of a table on a slide can be modified to make the table easier to read and better fit the intention and design of a presentation. You can move and resize a table, and you can change the size of table columns and rows.

You can apply a built-in table style; modify an existing style; and apply borders, color, shading, and texture to emphasize the content of the cells within a table. You can make the table easier to read by applying ***banded rows***—odd and even rows of a table are formatted differently— or ***banded columns***—odd and even columns formatted differently. Banding guides the eye across rows or down columns, making it easier to read the information in a table.

Activity 7.07 | Moving a Table

1 Display **Slide 3**, and then click anywhere in the table.

The table is selected and displays sizing handles.

2 Point to the top edge of the table to display the move horizontal ⚐ pointer. Compare your screen with Figure 7.18.

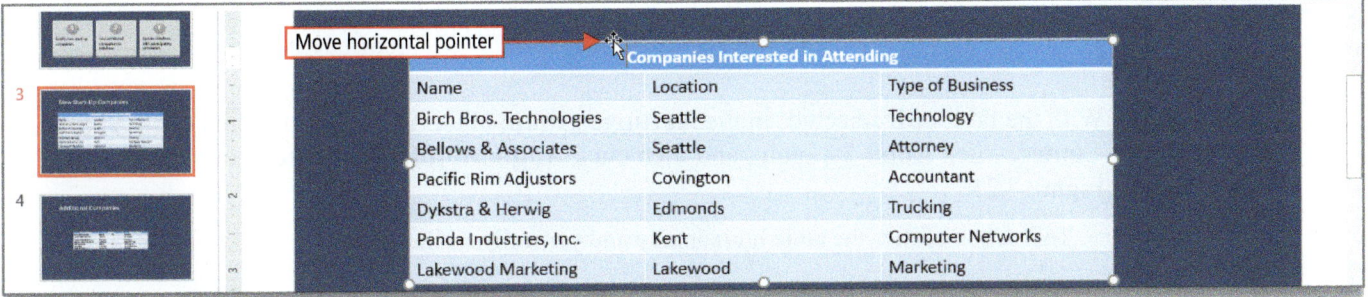

Figure 7.18

3 Hold down Shift, and then drag the table downward until the top of the table aligns on the **upper half of the vertical ruler at 1.5 inches**.

Holding the Shift key maintains the table alignment on the slide.

4 **Save** 🖫 your presentation.

Activity 7.08 | Sizing a Table

The tables on Slides 4 and 5 are small, making the text difficult to read, and the columns are not evenly spaced. You can resize the entire table, adjust column widths, adjust individual row heights, and increase the font size to improve the readability of the slide content.

1 Display **Slide 4**. In **row 1**, point to the cell border between **column 1** and **column 2** to display the ⟺ pointer. Compare your screen with Figure 7.19.

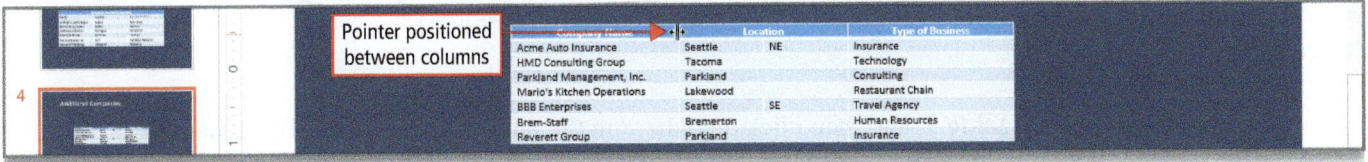

Figure 7.19

2 Double-click the cell border between **column 1** and **column 2** to resize the column.

Double-clicking the border between two columns applies the *AutoFit* command, which resizes a column to accommodate the largest entry.

3 Point to the border between **row 1** and **row 2** to display the ⇕ pointer. Drag the border down until the displayed dotted line aligns with the border between **row 2** and **row 3**, as shown in Figure 7.20.

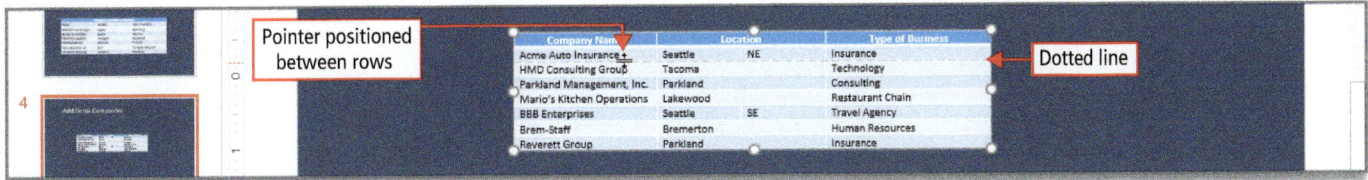

Figure 7.20

4 Release the left mouse button.

The height of row 1—the header row—is doubled.

5 On the **Table Tools Layout tab**, in the **Table Size group**, select the **Lock Aspect Ratio** check box. In the **Table Size group**, set the **Width** to **7.5"**.

When *Lock Aspect Ratio* is selected, you can change one dimension (height or width) of the table, and the other dimension will automatically be changed to maintain the proportion.

MAC TIP The Lock Aspect Ration check box connects the Height and Width boxes.

6 With the table still selected, in the **Arrange group**, click **Align** , and then click **Align Center**. Click **Align** again, and then click **Align Middle**. Compare your screen with Figure 7.21.

This action centers the table horizontally and vertically on the slide.

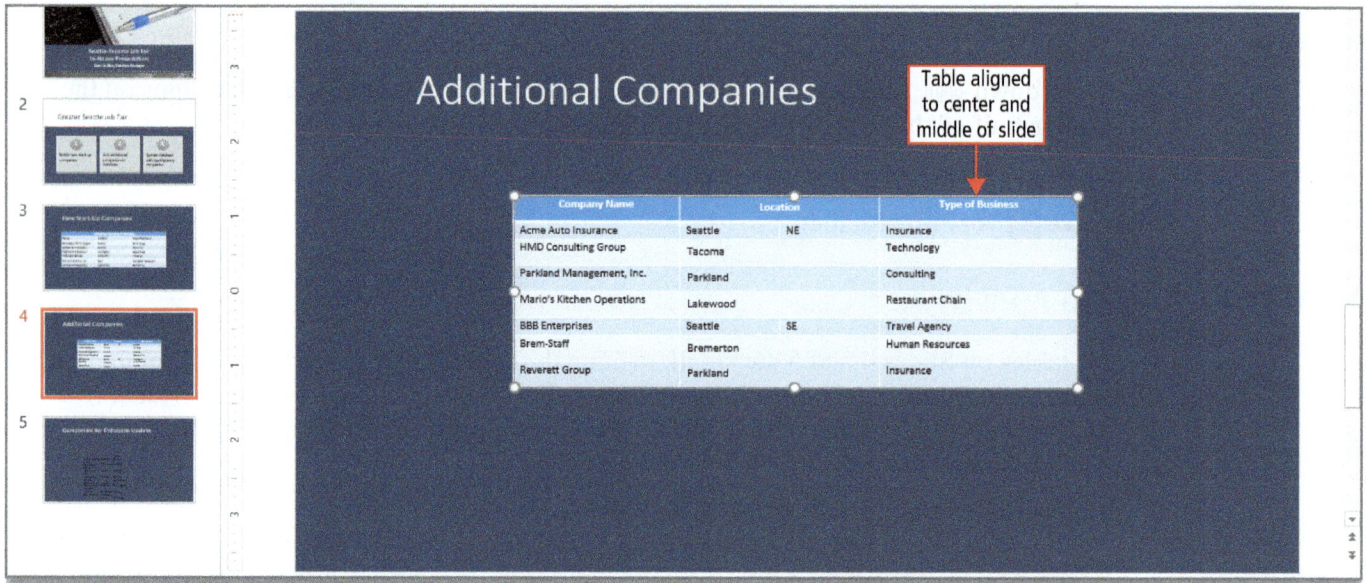

Figure 7.21

7 Display **Slide 5**, and then click anywhere in the table. On the **Table Tools Layout tab**, in the **Table group**, if necessary, click View Gridlines to display the gridlines in the table. The feature is active when the button is shaded.

Because there is no formatting on the table that you copied from Excel, activating the View Gridlines command inserts nonprinting gridlines that visually define the cells. Displaying these nonprinting gridlines makes it easier to work with the cells.

8 In the upper right corner of the table, point to the sizing handle to display the pointer . Using the ruler guides, drag the pointer up and to the right so that the top edge of the table aligns on the **upper half of the vertical ruler at 1.5 inches** and the right edge aligns on the **right half of the horizontal ruler at 3 inches**.

9 ▶ In the **Arrange group**, click **Align** 🖼, and then click **Align Center**. Compare your screen with Figure 7.22.

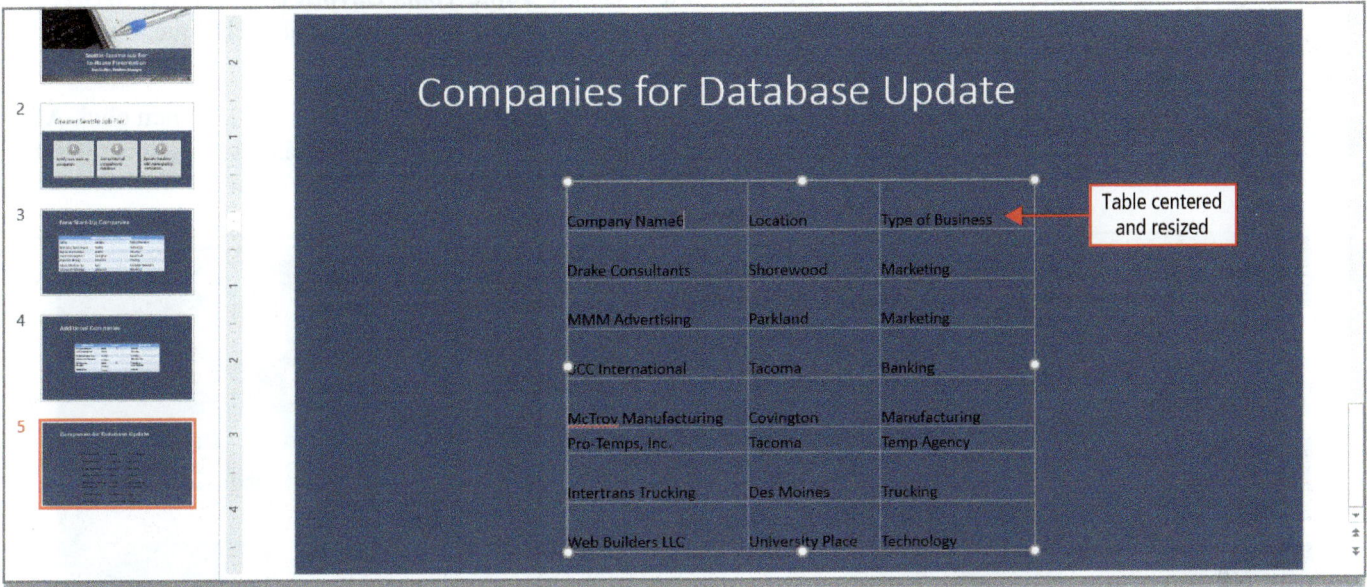

Figure 7.22

10 ▶ On the **Table Tools Layout tab**, in the **Table group**, click **View Gridlines** to turn off the gridlines. **Save** 💾 your presentation.

Activity 7.09 │ Applying Table Styles

4.1.3

PowerPoint includes many predesigned table styles that you can apply and modify. The default table style for this presentation has a darker blue header row, and lighter blue banded table rows. This style is applied to the tables on slides 3 and 4.

1 ▶ Display **Slide 3**, and then click anywhere in the table. On the **Table Tools Design tab**, in the **Table Style Options group**, clear the **Banded Rows** check box.

The banding is removed from the table rows.

2 ▶ On the left side of the table, point to **row 2** to display the ➡ pointer. Right-click to select the row, and then on the mini toolbar, click **Bold** B. If necessary, right click to display the mini tool bar again, and then click **Center** ☰. Click in a blank area of the slide to deselect the table, and then compare your screen with Figure 7.23.

The text in row 2 is centered and displayed in bold.

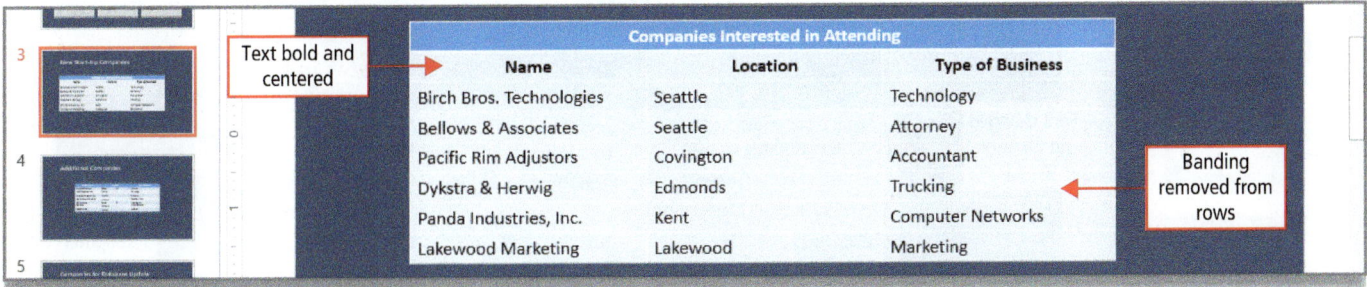

Figure 7.23

3 On the left side of the table, point to **row 1** to display the → pointer. Right-click, and then on the mini toolbar, change the **Font Size** to **24**.

4 In **column 2**, click in the cell *Location*. On the **Table Tools Layout tab**, in the **Cell Size group**, change the **Width** to **2"** to resize the column. Using the same technique, change the width of **column 3** to **2.5"**.

5 On the **Table Tools Layout tab**, in the **Arrange group**, click **Align** 📑, and then click **Align Center** to center the table on the slide. Click in a blank area of the slide to deselect the table, and then compare your screen with Figure 7.24.

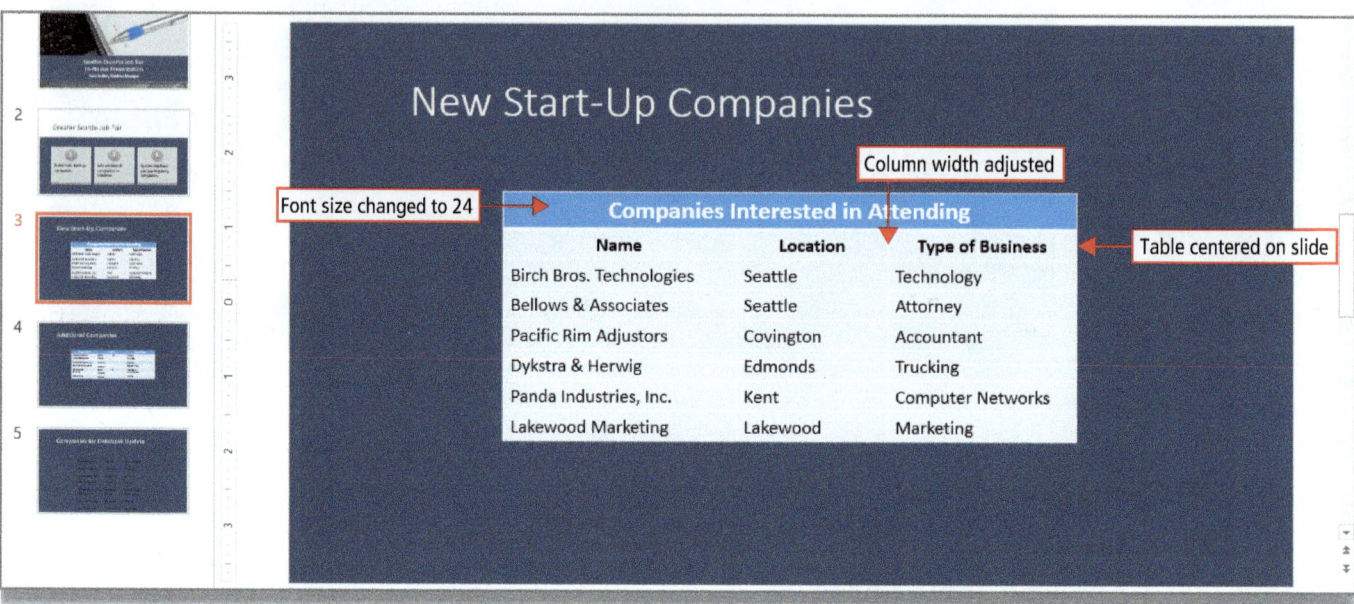

Figure 7.24

6 Display **Slide 4**. Right-click anywhere in the table, and then click **Select Table**. On the **Home tab**, in the **Font group**, change the **Font** to **Century Gothic** and change the **Font Size** to **18**. Change the **Font Size** of **row 1** to **20**.

7 Position the ╫ pointer on the right border of **column 1**, and then double-click to **AutoFit** the contents.

8 On the **Table Tools Layout tab**, in the **Arrange group**, click **Align** 📑, and then click **Align Center**. Click **Align** 📑 again, and then click **Align Middle**. Click in a blank area of the slide to deselect the table, and then compare your screen with Figure 7.25.

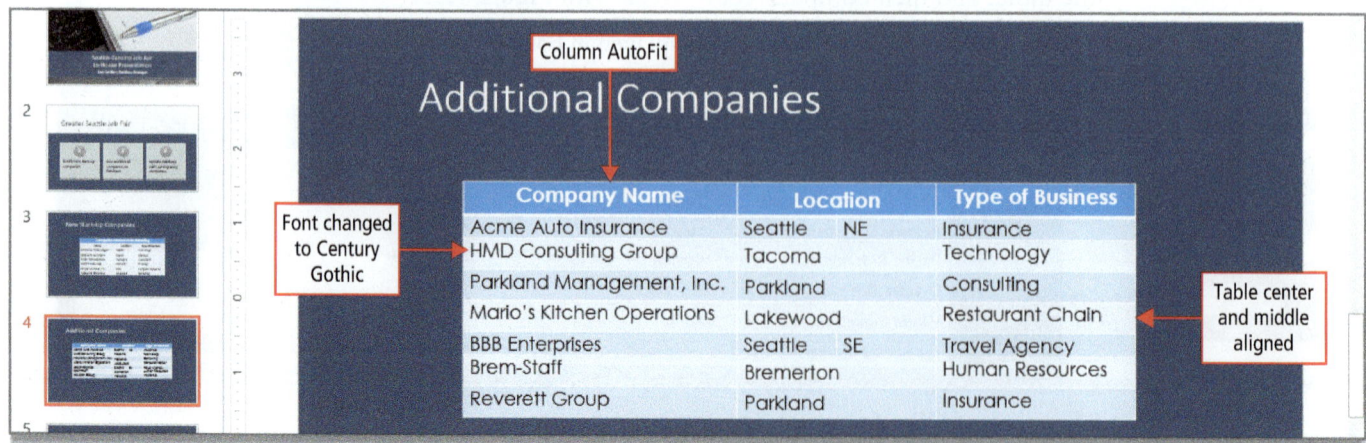

Figure 7.25

9 Display **Slide 5**. Click anywhere in the table. On the **Table Tools Design tab**, in the **Table Styles group**, click **More** ▾ to display the **Table Styles** gallery. Under **Medium**, in the second row, click the second style—**Medium Style 2 – Accent 1**.

10 On the **Table Tools Design tab**, in the **Table Styles Options group,** select the **Header Row** check box and select the **Banded Rows** check box. Compare your screen with Figure 7.26.

The table adopts the same formatting that is used for the tables on Slides 3 and 4.

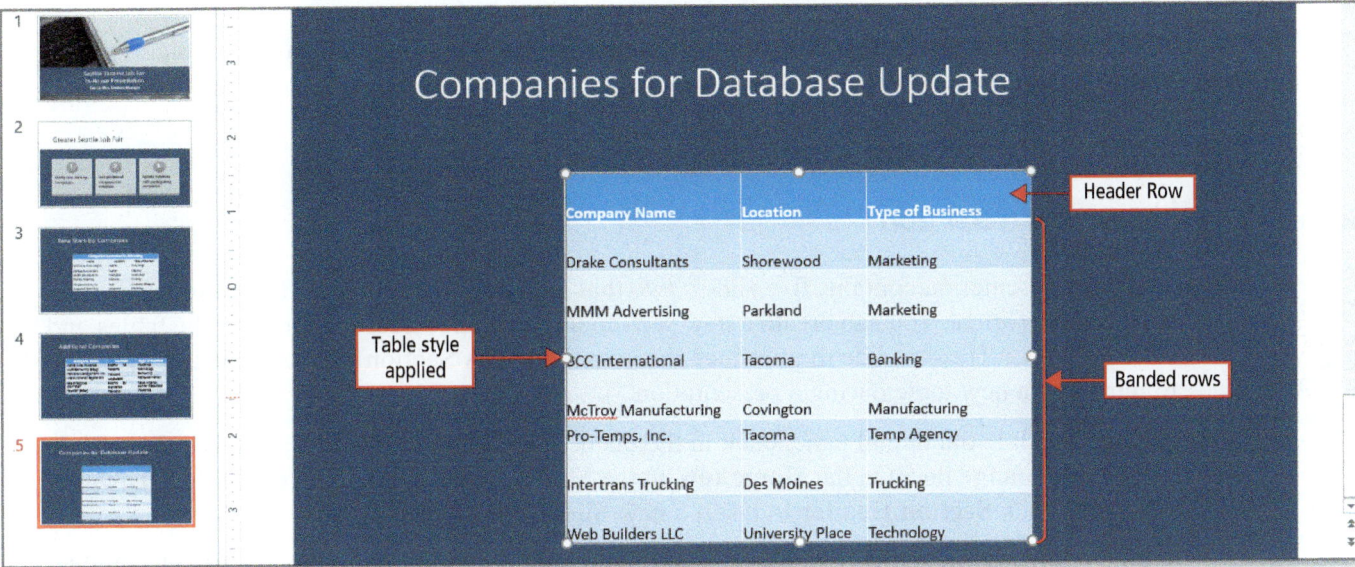

Figure 7.26

11 In **row 1**, change the **Font Size** to **20**, and then **Center** ☰ the text. **AutoFit** the three columns. If necessary, AutoFit rows 5 and 8.

12 **Align** the table to the slide by applying the **Align Center** command. If necessary, if the table is not fully on the slide, drag the table up to make it fit on the slide. Compare your screen with Figure 7.27.

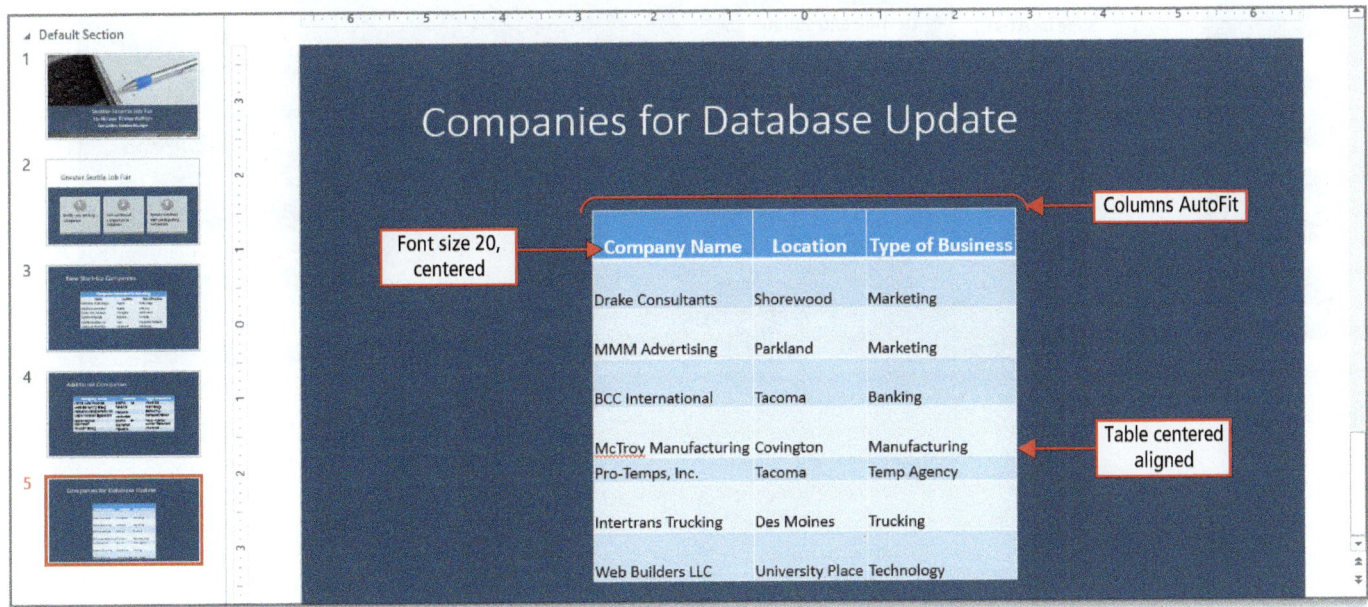

Figure 7.27

13 **Save** 🖫 your presentation.

GO! Learn How

Video P7-4

The slides in a PowerPoint presentation can be grouped using *sections*—a feature to organize your slides similar to using folders to organize your files. You can create sections to outline topics, assign slide ownership while collaborating with others, and organize the slides in your presentation. You can name sections, making them a useful way to locate groups of slides. This is especially helpful in large presentation with many slides and topics.

Use a *section header*—a slide layout that changes the look and flow of a presentation by providing text placeholders that do not contain bullet points—to give the presenter a place to pause and shift topics and break a large presentation into smaller chunks.

Activity 7.10 | Inserting a Section

1.2.2, 2.3.1, 2.3.3

Your presentation contains five slides: two that introduce the topic and three that present the data in table format. You can create a new section to group the slides that contain the tables and insert a Section Header slide to introduce the new section. A Section Header slide is a helpful tool to introduce a new topic during a presentation.

1 ▶ In the slide thumbnail pane, click in the blank space between **Slide 2** and **Slide 3** to display a thin orange line. On the **Home tab**, in the **Slides group**, click the **New Slide arrow**, and then click **Section Header** to insert a new **Slide 3**.

2 ▶ On **Slide 3**, in the title placeholder, type **Job Fair Data** and then, in the subtitle placeholder, type **Seattle-Tacoma Job Fair** Compare your screen with Figure 7.28.

The Section Header slide precedes the slides that contain the tables.

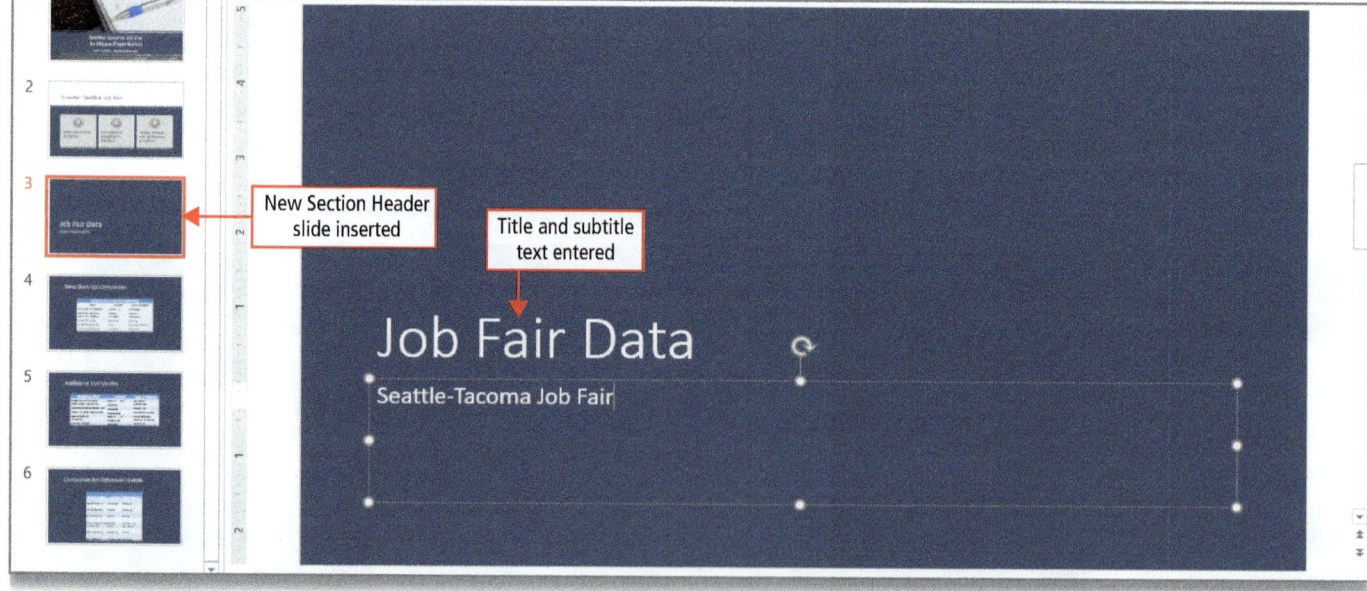

Figure 7.28

3 In the slide thumbnail pane, click in the blank area between **Slide 2** and **Slide 3** to display a thin orange line. On the **Home tab**, in the **Slides group**, click **Section**, and then click **Add Section**. Compare your screen with Figure 7.29.

Untitled Section displays above Slide 3. The slides that follow the new section are all selected, indicating they belong to the new section. *Default Section* displays above Slide 1. Slides that are not part of the new section belong to the default section.

ANOTHER WAY Right-click between the Slide 2 and Slide 3 thumbnails, and then click Add Section.

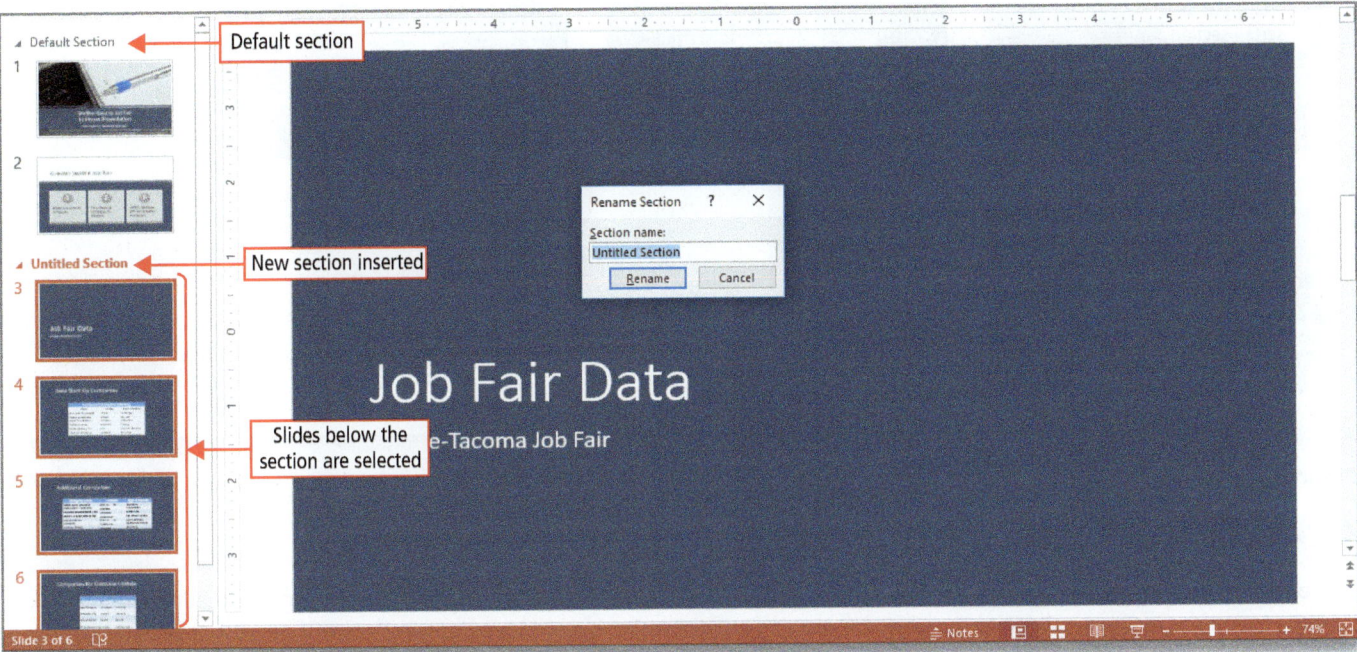

Figure 7.29

4 In the **Rename Section** dialog box, under **Section name**, with *Untitled Section* text selected, type **Job Fair Data**

Use a meaningful section name to identify the purpose of the slides in the section.

5 Click **Rename**. Compare your screen with Figure 7.30.

The renamed section, *Job Fair Data*, displays above the Slide 3 thumbnail.

Figure 7.30

6 ▶ On the **View tab**, in the **Presentation Views group**, click **Slide Sorter**. Notice *the Job Fair Data* section in **Slide Sorter View**. Click the **Default Section arrow**, and then compare your screen with Figure 7.31.

The Default Section collapses. Clicking a section arrow collapses and expands the section to hide or display the slides in the section. You can collapse the section and then drag the section name to reorder sections in a presentation, rather than moving individual slides.

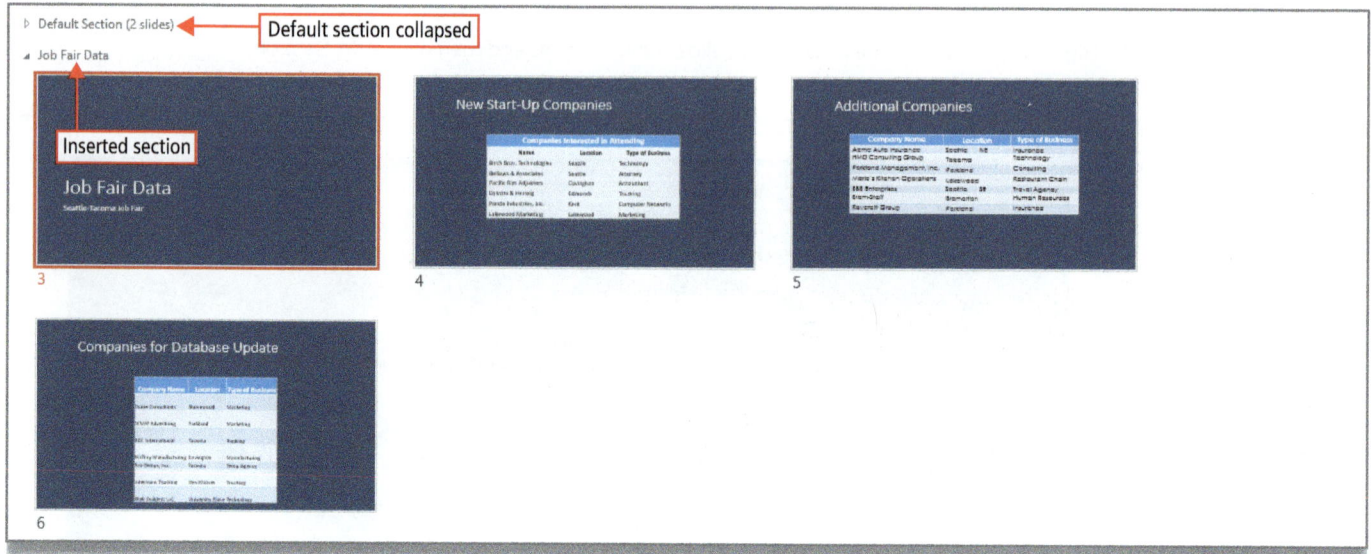

Figure 7.31

MORE KNOWLEDGE   **Move or Remove a Section**

To move a section to a new location, in the slide thumbnails area, drag the section to the new location. Alternatively, right-click the section name that you want to move, and then click Move Section Up or Move Section Down. To remove a section, right-click the section name that you want to remove, and then click Remove Section.

---

7 ▶ On the **View tab**, in the **Presentation Views group**, click **Normal**.

8 ▶ Insert a **Header & Footer** on the **Notes and Handouts**. Include the **Date and time** updated automatically, the page number, and the footer **7A_Job_Database**

9 ▶ Display the document properties. As the **Tags**, type **database, job fair** and as the **Subject**, type your course and section number. Be sure your name displays as author, and then **Save** your file.

10 ▶ **Close** ⊠ PowerPoint.

 For Non-MyLab Submissions Determine What Your Instructor Requires
Print or submit your presentation electronically as directed by your instructor.

---

11 ▶ In **MyLab IT**, in your **Course Materials**, locate and click the Grader Project **PowerPoint 7A Job Database**. In **step 3**, under **Upload Completed Assignment**, click **Choose File**. In the **Open** dialog box, navigate to your **PowerPoint Chapter 7 folder**, and then click your **Student_PowerPoint_7A_Job_Database** file one time to select it. In the lower right corner of the **Open** dialog box, click **Open**.

12 ▶ To submit your file to **MyLab IT** for grading, click **Upload**, wait a moment for a green **Success!** message, and then in **step 4**, click the blue **Submit for Grading** button. Click **Close Assignment** to return to your list of **Course Materials**.

You have completed Project 7A   **END**

<table>
<tr><td>

PROJECT

7B

</td><td>

Fair Demographics

</td><td>

MyLab IT
Project 7B Grader for Instruction
Project 7B Simulation for Training and Review

</td></tr>
</table>

Project Activities

In Activities 7.11 through 7.14, you will add pie charts to a presentation describing the demographics of the attendees at the Seattle–Tacoma Job Fair. You will modify the pie charts and view a chart in grayscale, and you will apply animation to a chart. Your completed presentation will look similar to Figure 7.32.

Project Files for **MyLab IT Grader**

1. In your **MyLab IT** course, locate and click **PowerPoint 7B Fair Demographics**, Download Materials, and then Download All Files. Close the Grader download screens.
2. Extract the zipped folder to your PowerPoint Chapter 7 folder.
3. Take a moment to open the downloaded **PowerPoint_7B_Fair_Demographics_Instructions**; note any recent updates to the book.

Project Results

GO! Project 7B
Where We're Going

Figure 7.32 Project 7B Fair Demographics

For Non-MyLab Submissions

For Project 7B, you will need:

p07B_Fair_Demographics
p07B_Event_Statistics

In your PowerPoint Chapter 7 folder, save your presentation as:

Lastname_Firstname_7B_Fair_Demographics

After you have named and saved your presentation, on the next page, begin with Step 2.

ALERT Because Office 365 is a cloud-based subscription service that receives continuous updates, you may encounter some variations in what appears on your screen and what is shown in this instruction. Microsoft Office 365 is fully installed on your PC or Mac; no internet access is necessary to create or edit documents. When you *are* connected to the internet, you will receive monthly upgrades and new features, so you always have the latest versions of Office apps as soon as they are available. Your subscription gives you continuous free access to the latest innovations and refinements.

GO! Learn How
Video P7-5

A *pie chart* shows the relationship of parts to a whole and plots a single *data series*—a group of related data points or chart values that originates in a worksheet cell. Categories, or *slices*, in a pie chart represent the contribution of each value to the total. The categories on a pie chart should not be negative or zero values.

NOTE Chart Design Variations

In this Project, you will insert charts using various methods, styles, and formatting. When creating your own presentations, you should maintain a uniform style or theme.

Activity 7.11 | Creating a 3-D Pie Chart

4.2.1, 4.2.2

In this Activity, you will create a pie chart to show the age of the attendees at the Seattle–Tacoma Job Fair.

1 Navigate to your **PowerPoint Chapter 7 folder**, and then double-click the PowerPoint file you downloaded from **MyLab IT** that displays your name—**Student_PowerPoint_7B_Fair_Demographics**. In your presentation, if necessary, at the top click **Enable Editing**.

2 Display **Slide 4**. In the content placeholder, click **Insert Chart** [icon].

3 In the **Insert Chart** dialog box, on the left, click **Pie**. At the top right, click the second pie chart type—**3-D Pie**. Compare your screen with Figure 7.33.

The Insert Chart dialog box displays a sample 3-D Pie chart.

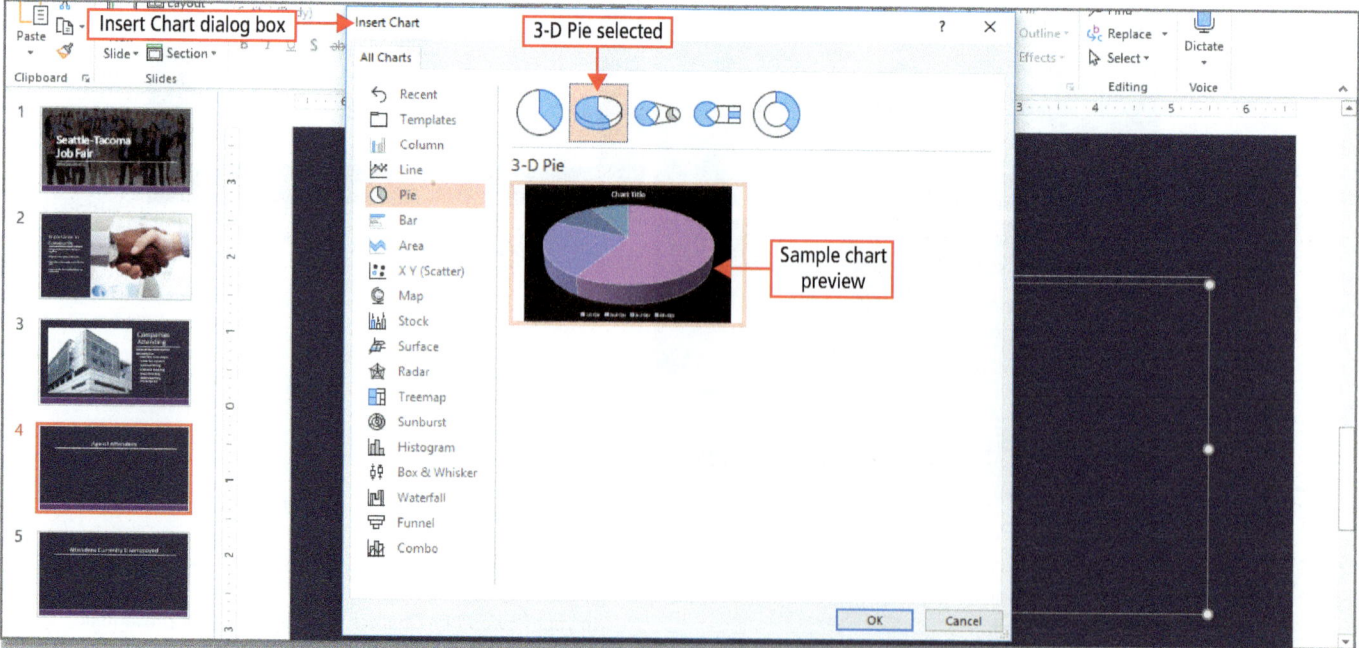

Figure 7.33

4 ▶ Click **OK**.

A *Chart in Microsoft PowerPoint* worksheet window displays. The worksheet contains sample data from which the chart on the PowerPoint slide is generated. Cells A2 through A5 display a purple border, and the data in these cells form the chart legend below the pie chart. Cell B1 displays a red border; this cell contains the chart title. Cells B2 though B5 display a blue border, and these cells contain the data series that is plotted in the chart.

5 ▶ In the **Chart in Microsoft PowerPoint** worksheet window, click in cell **B1**, which contains the text *Sales* as sample data, type **Age of Attendees** and then press Tab.

On the chart, *Age of Attendees* replaces the word *Sales* as the Chart Title.

6 ▶ In cell **A2**, type **24 or Younger** and then press Enter. In cell **A3**, type **25 to 49** and then press Enter. In cell **A4**, type **50 or Older** and then press Enter.

As you type the new data in the worksheet, the pie chart on the slide adjusts to reflect your data.

7 ▶ Position the ⊞ pointer on the border between **column A** and **column B**, and then double-click to **AutoFit column A**. Using the same technique, **AutoFit column B**.

Resizing the columns helps you see the data in the worksheet but has no effect on the chart created in PowerPoint.

8 ▶ Point to cell **A5**, right-click, point to **Delete**, and then point to **Table Rows**. Compare your screen with Figure 7.34.

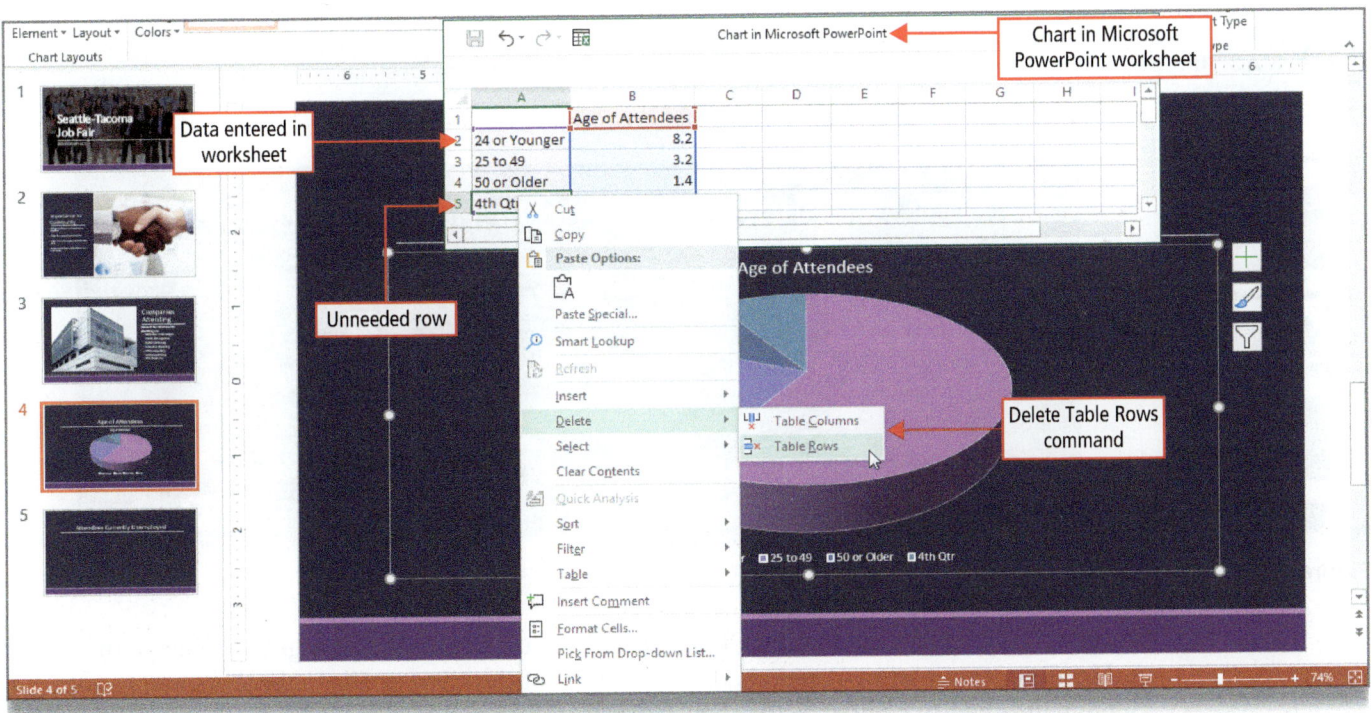

Figure 7.34

9 ▶ Click **Table Rows** to delete the unneeded row.

This action removes the sample data in cell A5, which is not part of your chart. The worksheet range adjusts to include cells A1 through B4, and the chart on the slide also adjusts to display three pie slices.

10 ▶ In cell **B2** type **32%** in cell **B3** type **57%** in cell **B4** type **11%** and then press Enter.

11 ▶ **Close** ✕ the *Chart in Microsoft PowerPoint* worksheet window to return to PowerPoint. **Save** 💾 your presentation.

Activity 7.12 | Importing a Chart

MOS
4.2.1

In this Activity, you will import a chart from Excel that graphically represents the categories of unemployed attendees at the fair. The chart is a ***Bar of Pie chart***, which emphasizes one slice of the pie by representing the slice as a bar showing how the data in the slice are further divided. A similar chart type, ***Pie of Pie chart***, displays the emphasized data as a pie instead of a bar.

1 Display **Slide 5**.

2 With the PowerPoint presentation open on your screen, open Microsoft Excel.

3 On Excel's opening screen, on the left, click **Open**. Click **Browse**, navigate to the files downloaded with this project, and then open **p07B_Event_Statistics**. If necessary, at the top, click **Enable Editing**.

4 In Excel, click the border of the chart to select it. On the **Home tab**, in the **Clipboard group**, click **Copy**.

5 On the Windows taskbar, click the **PowerPoint** program icon to redisplay the PowerPoint window. With **Slide 5** active, right-click in the center of the slide to display **Paste Options** and then click the first option—**Use Destination Theme & Embed Workbook (H)**. If necessary, close the Design Ideas pane. Compare your screen with Figure 7.35.

> The chart is embedded in and displays the theme formatting of the presentation. The chart is divided into five slices. The slice used for the Bar of Pie represents the three categories with the lowest values—Trucking, Professional, and Medical—and these are broken out into a small bar chart.

MAC TIP Select Excel Chart (entire workbook) to embed the chart and select Use Destination Theme.

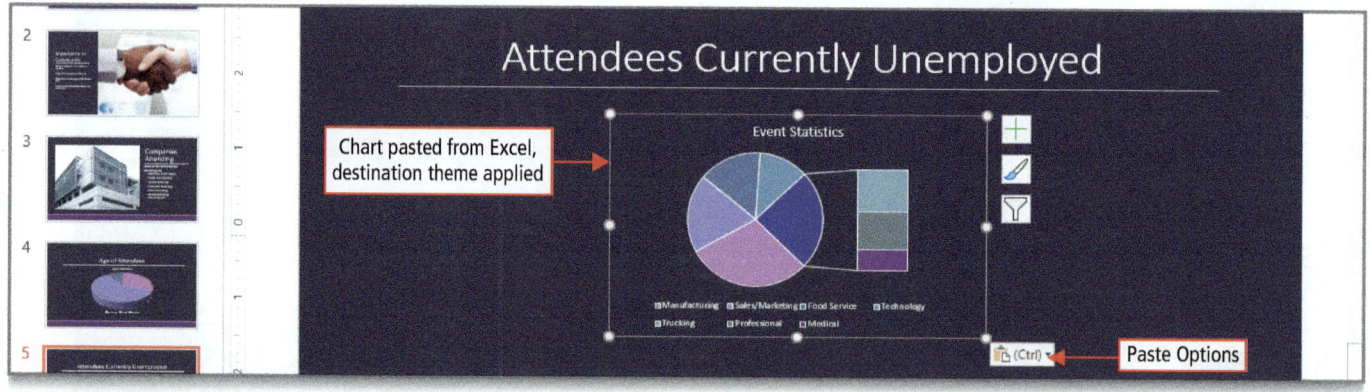

Figure 7.35

6 With the chart selected, on the **Chart Tools Format tab**, in the **Size group**, change the **Height** of the chart to **4"** and change the **Width** of the chart to **6"**. In the **Arrange group**, align the chart to **Center** of the slide. **Save** your presentation.

7 **Close** Excel without saving changes.

MORE KNOWLEDGE | **Import Charts from External Sources**

You can link or embed a chart created in Excel into a PowerPoint presentation, or you can paste the chart as a picture. If you paste the chart as a picture, you will not be able to edit the chart data. You can copy and paste charts created in Word documents but cannot link to the data in the Word document.

Objective 6   Modify Charts

GO! Learn How
Video P7-6

One way to format a chart is by using a *chart style*—a set of predefined formats applied to a chart, including colors, backgrounds, and effects. A *chart layout* determines the placement and display of chart elements such as the chart title, legend, and data labels.

To emphasize a slice of the pie, you can manually *explode*—pull out—the slice so that it stands away from the pie. There is also a pie chart type known as an *exploded pie chart*, which displays all of the slices disconnected, or exploded, from each other.

Activity 7.13 | Modifying a Pie Chart

4.2.2

In this Activity, you will customize a chart by applying a chart style and chart layout. You will highlight the number of attendees of the fair that are 50 or older by exploding the slice in the pie chart.

1 Display **Slide 4**. Just above the colored pie slices, click to the left of *Age of Attendees*, to select the **Chart Area**. On the **Chart Tools Design tab**, in the **Chart Styles group**, click **More** ⬇. In the **Chart Styles** gallery, in the first row, click the third style—**Style 3**.

2 On the **Chart Tools Design tab**, in the **Chart Layouts group**, click the **Quick Layout arrow**, and then click the second layout—**Layout 2**.

3 On the **Chart Tools Design tab**, in the **Chart Layouts group**, click **Add Chart Element**, point to **Data Labels**, and then click **Outside End**. Compare your screen with Figure 7.36.

The data labels display outside of the pie chart next to each slice.

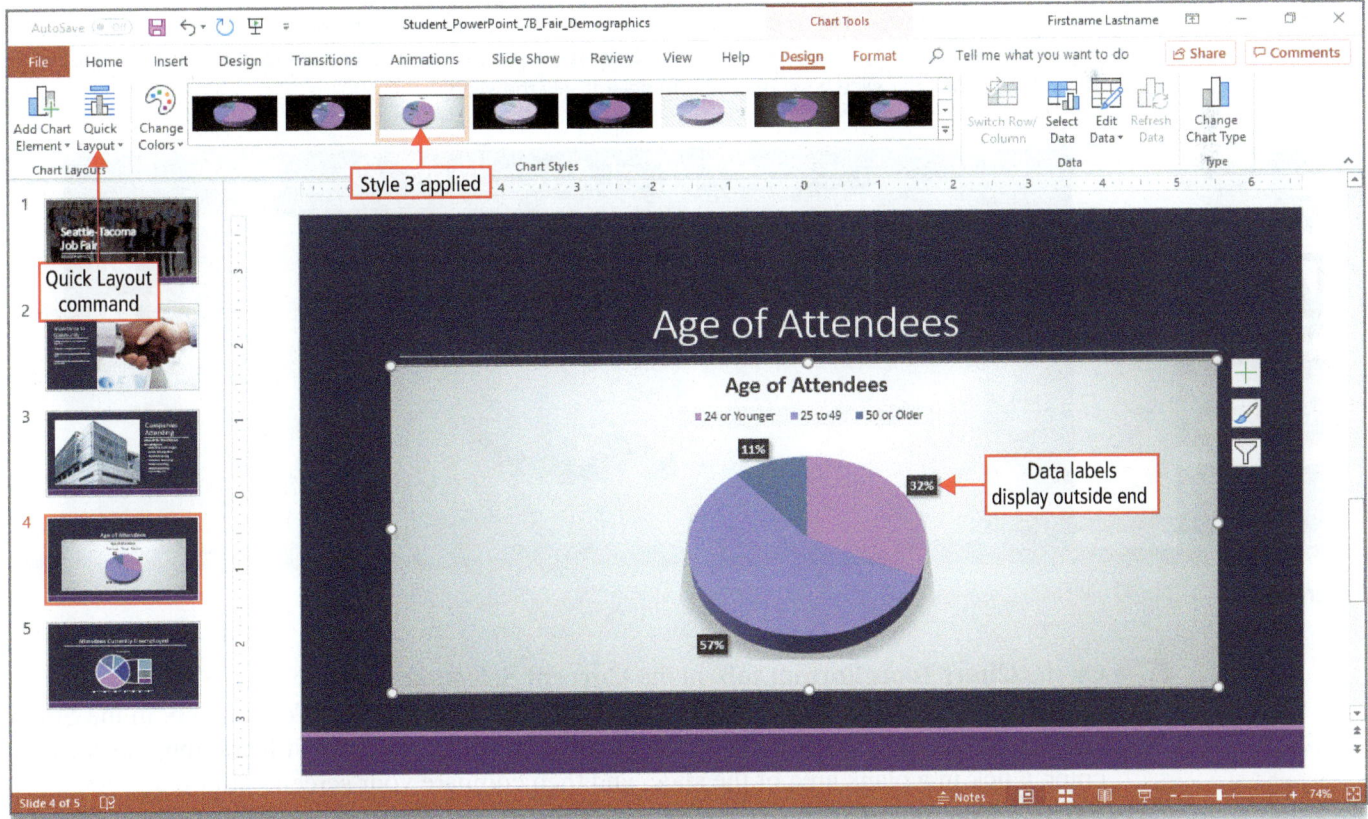

Figure 7.36

4 In the **Chart Layouts group**, click **Add Chart Element**, point to **Chart Title**, and then click **None**.

Because the chart title is already displayed in the slide title, you do not need a chart title to display.

ANOTHER WAY Click in the chart, on the right side of the chart, click Chart Elements ⊞, and then clear the Chart Title check box.

5 Click the pie slice labeled *11%* one time to select the chart, and then click the slice a second time to select only the slice.

6 Right-click the selected slice and then click **Format Data Point**. In the **Format Data Point pane**, set the **Point Explosion** to **25%**. **Close** ⊠ the **Format Data Point pane**. Compare your screen with Figure 7.37.

The Format Data Point pane enables you to precisely position the exploded slice. The selected pie slice is exploded—moved away from—the pie, and the entire pie is resized.

ANOTHER WAY Click the pie slice labeled 11% one time to select the chart, and then click the slice a second time to select only the slice. When the ⬉ pointer displays, drag the slice up and away from the pie, and then release the mouse.

ALERT   Why Did the Format Data Series Pane Display?

If you double-click the pie slice, you will display the Format Data Series pane. This pane is different from the Format Data Point pane, which only modifies the individual pie slice. The Format Data Series pane modifies the entire pie chart. In the Format Data Series pane, you can change the Pie Explosion, but all the pie slices will explode instead of exploding a single pie slice. If you did not intend to use the Format Data Series pane, click Close and try selecting the pie slice again. Be sure to click the slice one time to select the chart, pause, and then click the slice a second time to select only the slice.

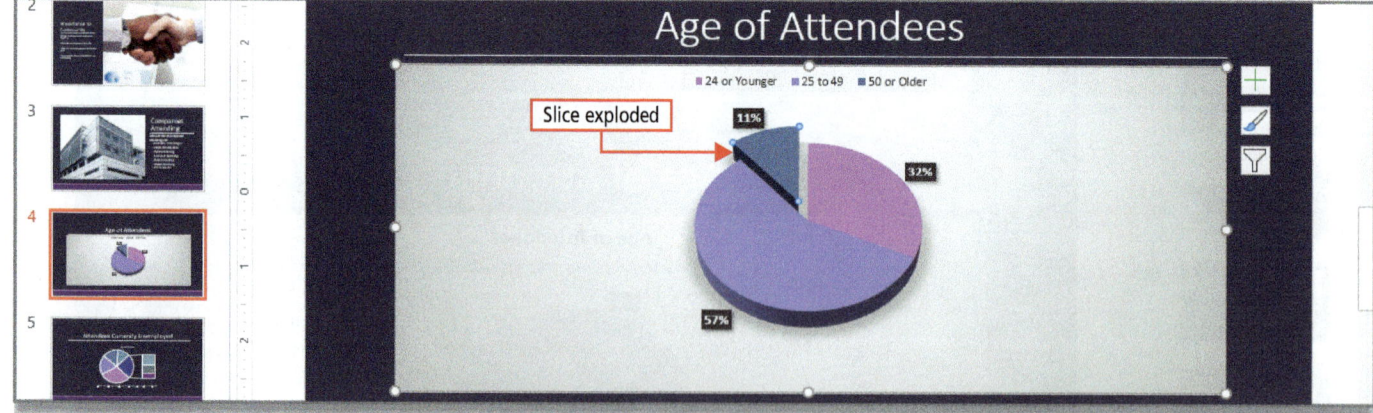

Figure 7.37

7 On the **Chart Tools Format tab**, in the **Current Selection group**, click the **Chart Elements arrow**, and then click **Chart Area**. On the **Chart Tools Format tab**, in the **Shape Styles group**, click **Shape Fill**. Under **Theme Colors**, click in the fifth column, the second color. Click in a blank area of the slide, and then compare your screen with Figure 7.38. **Save** 💾 your presentation.

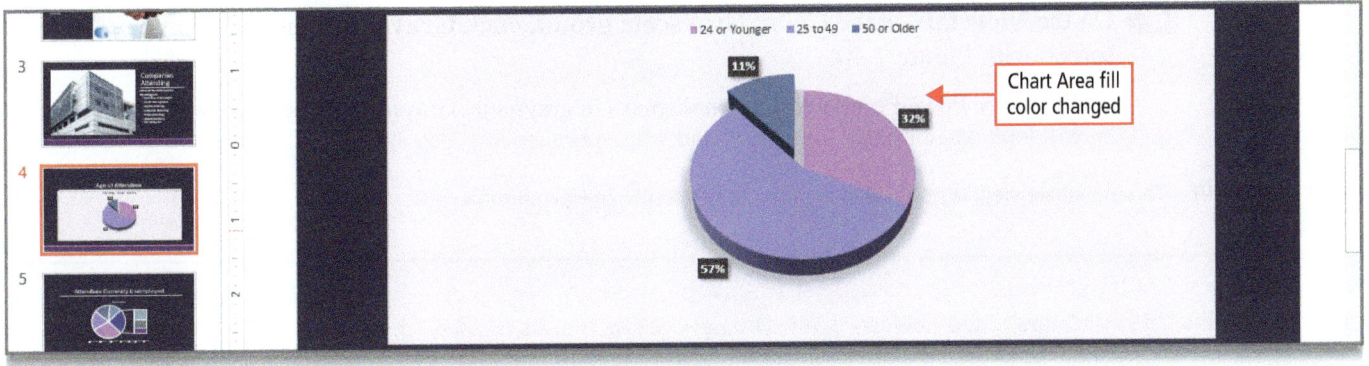

Figure 7.38

<table>
<tr><td>**Objective 7**</td><td>**Change a Chart Type**</td></tr>
</table>

GO! Learn How
Video P7-7

A ***bar chart*** is a chart in which the data is arranged in horizontal bars, which is useful for illustrating comparisons among items. Like a pie chart, a bar chart can compare data points in one data series, but it can also be used to compare multiple data series. A ***clustered bar chart*** compares values across categories.

Activity 7.14 | Changing a Chart Type

1.2.2, 4.2.2

The Bar of Pie chart type on Slide 5 does not adequately illustrate the data it presents. In this Activity, you will change the chart type to a clustered bar chart, which will better compare the industries represented by the fair attendees.

> **1** ▶ Display **Slide 5**. Click anywhere in the chart area to select the chart.

> **2** ▶ On the **Chart Tools Design tab**, in the **Type group**, click **Change Chart Type**.

> **3** ▶ On the left, under **All Charts**, click **Bar**, and then compare your screen with Figure 7.39.

MAC TIP   Point to Column and scroll down to display 2-D bar charts.

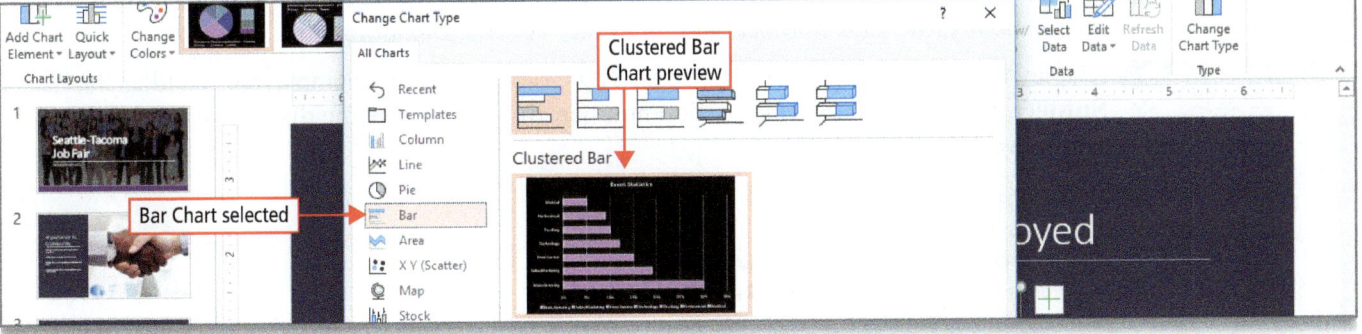

Figure 7.39

> **4** ▶ Click **OK** to insert a **Clustered Bar Chart**.

The Bar of Pie chart changes to a bar chart.

> **5** ▶ On the **Chart Tools Design tab**, in the **Chart Layouts group**, click **Add Chart Element**. Point to **Legend**, and then click **None**.

The legend no longer displays below the chart. Because the axis labels identify the data, a legend is unnecessary.

6 On the **View tab**, in the **Color/Grayscale group**, click **Grayscale**, and then compare your screen with Figure 7.40.

The entire PowerPoint presentation displays in grayscale. Grayscale is useful to see how a chart will look when printed on a black and white printer.

MAC TIP The grayscale view is not available in the Mac version of PowerPoint.

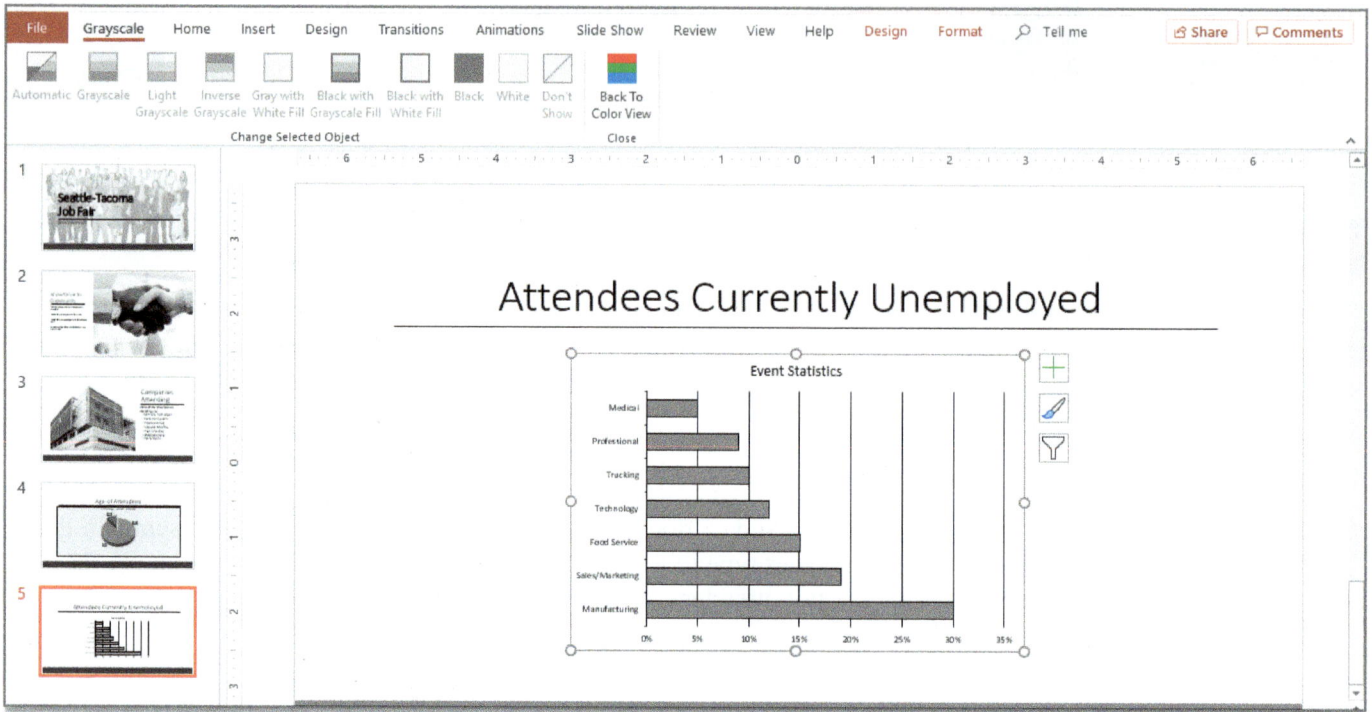

Figure 7.40

7 On the **Grayscale tab**, in the **Close group**, click **Back to Color View**.

8 Insert a **Header & Footer** on the **Notes and Handouts**. Include the **Date and time** updated automatically, the page number, and the footer **7B_Fair_Demographics**

9 Display the document properties. As the **Tags**, type **attendee, unemployment** and as the **Subject**, type your course and section number. Be sure your name displays as author, and then **Save** your file.

10 Close ⊠ PowerPoint.

For Non-MyLab Submissions Determine What Your Instructor Requires
As directed by your instructor, submit your completed PowerPointpresentation.

11 In **MyLab IT**, in your **Course Materials**, locate and click the Grader Project **PowerPoint 7B Fair Demographics**. In **step 3**, under **Upload Completed Assignment**, click **Choose File**. In the **Open** dialog box, navigate to your **PowerPoint Chapter 7 folder**, and then click your **Student_PowerPoint_7B_Fair_Demographics** file one time to select it. In the lower right corner of the **Open** dialog box, click **Open**.

12 To submit your file to **MyLab IT** for grading, click **Upload**, wait a moment for a green **Success!** message, and then in **step 4**, click the blue **Submit for Grading** button. Click **Close Assignment** to return to your list of **Course Materials**.

You have completed Project 7B **END**

wavebreakmedia/Shutterstock, Monkey Business Images/Fotolia, Ivanko80/Shutterstock, Monkey Business Images/Shutterstock

Microsoft Office Specialist (MOS) Skills in This Chapter

Project 7A	Project 7B
1.2.2 Display presentations in different views	**1.2.2** Display presentations in different views
2.3.1 Create sections	**4.2.1** Create and insert charts
2.3.3 Rename sections	**4.2.2** Modify charts
4.1.1 Create and insert tables	
4.1.2 Insert and delete table rows and columns	
4.1.3 Apply built-in table styles	

Build Your E-Portfolio

An E-Portfolio is a collection of evidence, stored electronically, that showcases what you have accomplished while completing your education. Collecting and then sharing your work products with potential employers reflects your academic and career goals. Your completed documents from the following projects are good examples to show what you have learned: 7G, 7K, and 7L.

GO! For Job Success

Discussion: Workplace Mentoring

Your instructor may assign this discussion to your class, and then ask you to think about, or discuss with your classmates, these questions:

Mentors in the workplace have always played an important role in individual career development and organization success. Mentors provide guidance and coaching on skills, business etiquette, organization dynamics, and play the role of trusted advisor for both peers and less-experienced colleagues. Mentoring is a low-cost benefit to the organization that reduces training costs, enhances cross-functional relationships, and provides knowledge transfer from experienced staff to newer employees.

Workers entering the workforce today have lived with mobile technology and social media for most or all of their lives, so some companies now encourage "reverse mentoring." In reverse mentoring, younger workers who have a valuable perspective on technology, emerging markets, and trends work with executives to enhance their ability to stay up to date on changing cultures and demographics. Surveys have shown that these younger mentors express high job satisfaction. Mentors are not limited to those in the same company. Business networking sites like LinkedIn and IMDB provide opportunities for introductions to influential people in any field, and it's not uncommon for them to receive unsolicited requests for advice and mentorship.

g-stockstudio/Shutterstock

In what ways do you think a reverse mentoring relationship would be valuable to a younger worker, and why would they perceive greater job satisfaction?

Do you think it is good business etiquette to reach out to someone you don't know via a networking site?

How would you conduct research to find a common connection to the person you want to meet?

End of Chapter

Summary

You practiced adding tables to a Microsoft PowerPoint presentation using several different methods. You created a table and copied tables from other applications, including Word and Excel.

You practiced moving and sizing tables, merging and splitting table cells, and adding and removing table columns and rows. You added and renamed a slide section.

You used pie charts to show how different categories relate to the whole. You created professional-looking charts by applying a predefined layout and style.

You added visual interest to tables by applying predefined styles, fill color, and chart elements. You imported a chart from an Excel worksheet and changed the chart type.

GO! Learn It Online

Review the concepts, key terms, and MOS skills in this chapter by completing these online challenges, which you can find in **MyLab IT**.

Chapter Quiz: Answer matching and multiple choice questions to test what you learned in this chapter.

Lessons on the GO!: Learn how to use all the new apps and features as they are introduced by Microsoft.

MOS Prep Quiz: Answer questions to review the MOS skills that you practiced in this chapter.

Your instructor will assign Projects from this list to ensure your learning and assess your knowledge.

	Project Guide for PowerPoint Chapter 7		
Project	**Apply Skills from These Chapter Objectives**	**Project Type**	**Project Location**
7A MyLab IT	Objectives 1–4 from Project 7A	**7A Instructional Project (Grader Project)** Instruction Guided instruction to learn the skills in Project A.	In **MyLab IT** and in text
7B MyLab IT	Objectives 5–7 from Project 7B	**7B Instructional Project (Grader Project)** Instruction Guided instruction to learn the skills in Project B.	In **MyLab IT** and in text
7C	Objectives 1–4 from Project 7A	**7C Skills Review (Scorecard Grading)** Review A guided review of the skills from Project 7A.	In text
7D	Objectives 5–7 from Project 7B	**7D Skills Review (Scorecard Grading)** Review A guided review of the skills from Project 7B.	In text
7E MyLab IT	Objectives 1–4 from Project 7A	**7E Mastery (Grader Project)** Mastery and Transfer of Learning A demonstration of your mastery of the skills in Project 7A with extensive decision making.	In **MyLab IT** and in text
7F MyLab IT	Objectives 5–7 from Project 7B	**7F Mastery (Grader Project)** Mastery and Transfer of Learning A demonstration of your mastery of the skills in Project 7B with extensive decision making.	In **MyLab IT** and in text
7G MyLab IT	Objectives 1–7 from Project 7A and 7B	**7G Mastery (Grader Project)** Mastery and Transfer of Learning A demonstration of your mastery of the skills in Projects 7A and 7B with extensive decision making.	In **MyLab IT** and in text
7H	Combination of Objectives from Projects 7A and 7B	**7H GO! Fix It (Scorecard Grading)** Critical Thinking A demonstration of your mastery of the skills in Projects 7A and 7B by creating a correct result from a document that contains errors you must find.	IRC
7I	Combination of Objectives from Projects 7A and 7B	**7I GO! Make It (Scorecard Grading)** Critical Thinking A demonstration of your mastery of the skills in Projects 7A and 7B by creating a result from a supplied picture.	IRC
7J	Combination of Objectives from Projects 7A and 7B	**7J GO! Solve It (Rubric Grading)** Critical Thinking A demonstration of your mastery of the skills in Projects 7A and 7B, your decision-making skills, and your critical thinking skills. A task-specific rubric helps you self-assess your result.	IRC
7K	Combination of Objectives from Projects 7A and 7B	**7K GO! Solve It (Rubric Grading)** Critical Thinking A demonstration of your mastery of the skills in Projects 7A and 7B, your decision-making skills, and your critical thinking skills. A task-specific rubric helps you self-assess your result.	In text
7L	Combination of Objectives from Projects 7A and 7B	**7L GO! Think (Rubric Grading)** Critical Thinking A demonstration of your understanding of the chapter concepts applied in a manner that you would outside of college. An analytic rubric helps you and your instructor grade the quality of your work by comparing it to the work an expert in the discipline would create.	In text
7M	Combination of Objectives from Projects 7A and 7B	**7M GO! Think (Rubric Grading)** Critical Thinking A demonstration of your understanding of the chapter concepts applied in a manner that you would outside of college. An analytic rubric helps you and your instructor grade the quality of your work by comparing it to the work an expert in the discipline would create.	IRC
7N	Combination of Objectives from Projects 7A and 7B	**7N You and GO! (Rubric Grading)** Critical Thinking A demonstration of your understanding of the chapter concepts applied in a manner that you would in a personal situation. An analytic rubric helps you and your instructor grade the quality of your work.	IRC

Glossary

Glossary of Chapter Key Terms

AutoFit A command that resizes a column to accommodate the largest entry.

Banded columns A table setting that enables you to format even columns differently from odd columns to make the table easier to read.

Banded rows A table setting that enables you to format even rows differently from odd rows to make the table easier to read.

Bar chart A chart in which the data is arranged in horizontal bars and that is useful for showing comparisons among items.

Bar of Pie chart A type of pie chart that emphasizes one slice of the pie by representing the slice as a bar showing how the data in the slice are further divided.

Chart layout Determines the placement and display of chart elements such as the chart title, legend, and data.

Chart style A set of predefined formats applied to a chart, including colors, backgrounds, and effects.

Clustered bar chart A bar chart that compares values across categories.

Data series A group of related data points or chart values that originates in a worksheet cell.

Destination file The file into which information or an object is copied.

Embedded A type of object that is saved with, and becomes a part of, a PowerPoint file.

Explode To pull out a slice of a pie chart so that it stands away from the pie in order to emphasize it.

Exploded pie chart A type of pie chart that displays all of the slices disconnected from each other. The slices cannot be manipulated individually.

Header row The top row of the table that is formatted differently from the rows containing data.

Lock Aspect Ratio When this option is selected, you can change one dimension (height or width) of an object, such as a picture or table, and the other dimension will automatically change to maintain the proportion.

Merge To combine two or more cells into a single cell.

Pie chart A chart type that shows the relationship of parts to a whole and plots a single data series.

Pie of Pie chart A type of pie chart that emphasizes one slice of the pie by representing the slice as another pie showing how the data in the slice are further divided.

Range Two or more selected cells on a worksheet that are adjacent or nonadjacent; because the range is treated as a single unit, you can make the same changes or combination of changes to more than one cell at a time.

Section A feature to organize your slides similar to using folders to organize your files.

Section header A slide layout that changes the look and flow of a presentation by providing text placeholders that do not contain bullet points.

Slices Categories in a pie chart that represent parts of the whole and show the contribution of each value to the total.

Source file A file from which information or an object is copied.

Split To divide a cell into two or more cells.

Table A grid of rows and columns.

Table gridlines Nonprinting lines that display between columns and rows in a table.

Chapter Review

Apply 7A skills from these Objectives:

1. Add a Table to a Presentation
2. Add or Delete Table Rows, Columns, and Cells
3. Modify a Table
4. Insert a Section

Skills Review **Project 7C Job Fairs**

In the following Skills Review, you will complete a PowerPoint presentation that includes the various job fairs that the organizers of the Seattle–Tacoma Job Fair will attend in the coming year. You will create a table and insert tables from Microsoft Word and Microsoft Excel. Your completed presentation will look similar to Figure 7.41.

Project Files

For Project 7C, you will need:

p07C_Job_Fairs
p07C_Locations_Dates
p07C_Registration

You will save your presentation as:

Lastname_Firstname_7C_Job_Fairs

Project Results

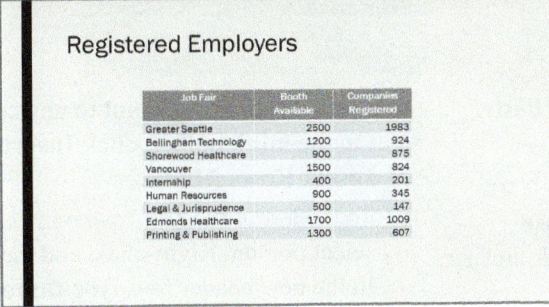

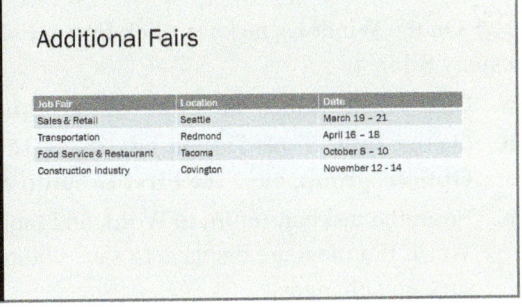

Figure 7.41 Project 7C Job Fairs

(continues on next page)

Chapter Review

1 Locate and open the file **p07C_Job_Fairs**. If necessary, click **Enable Editing**. Navigate to your **PowerPoint Chapter 7** folder, and then save the file as **Lastname_Firstname_7C_Job_Fairs**

2 Display **Slide 5**.

a. On the **Insert tab**, in the **Tables group**, click **Table**.

b. In the **Table** grid, in the fifth row, point to the third cell. Click one time to create a 3×5 table.

c. With the insertion point in the first cell, type **Job Fair** Press Tab. In the second cell, type **Location** and then press Tab. In the third cell, type **Date** and then press Tab.

d. At the beginning of **row 2**, type the following information, pressing Tab after each entry except the last entry:

Sales & Retail	Seattle	March 19–21
Transportation	Redmond	April 16–18
Food Service & Restaurant	Tacoma	October 8–10
Construction Industry	Covington	November 12–14

3 With the PowerPoint presentation open on your screen, open Microsoft Word.

a. On Word's opening screen, click **Open Other Documents**. Navigate to your data files for this project, and then open **p07C_Registration**.

b. In Word, if necessary, click **Enable Editing**. If necessary, click in the table. On the **Table Tools Layout tab**, in the **Table group**, click **Select**, and then click **Select Table** to select the entire table.

c. On the **Home tab**, in the **Clipboard group**, click **Copy**.

4 On the Windows taskbar, click **PowerPoint**. Display **Slide 4**.

a. On the **Home tab**, in the **Clipboard group**, click **Paste**.

b. On the **Table Tools Design tab**, in the **Table Style Options group**, clear the **First Column** check box.

c. From the taskbar, return to Word, and then **Close** Word. If a message displays to save your file, do not save any changes.

5 With the PowerPoint presentation displayed, open Microsoft Excel.

a. On Excel's opening screen, click **Open Other Workbooks**. Navigate to your data files for this project, and then open **p07C_Locations_Dates**. If necessary, click **Enable Editing**.

b. In Excel, with cell **A1** active, hold down Shift, and then click cell **C8**.

c. On the **Home tab**, in the **Clipboard group**, click **Copy**.

6 From the taskbar, redisplay your PowerPoint presentation. Display **Slide 3**.

a. On the **Home tab**, in the **Clipboard group**, click the **Paste arrow**.

b. Below **Paste Options**, click the second option, **Keep Source Formatting (K)**.

c. **Close** Excel without saving any changes.

7 If necessary, display **Slide 3** and click in the table.

a. On the **Table Tools Layout tab**, in the **Table group**, if necessary, click **View Gridlines** to display the table gridlines.

b. Click in the cell that contains *Dayton Technology* to display the insertion point in the cell. On the **Table Tools Layout tab**, in the **Rows & Columns group**, click **Delete**, and then click **Delete Rows**.

c. Point to the cell *Job Fair*, and then right-click to display the mini toolbar. On the mini toolbar, click **Insert**, and then click **Insert Columns to the Right**.

d. In the new column beginning in **row 1**, type the following, pressing ↓ after each entry except the last entry:

Location
Seattle
Shorewood
University Place
Parkland
Edmonds
Bellevue

e. In the header row, point to any cell and right-click. On the mini toolbar, click **Insert**, and then click **Insert Rows Above**.

f. To the left of the new row, point to display the row select pointer. Right-click, and then click **Merge Cells**. In the new header row, type **Currently Scheduled**

g. Right-click the text you just typed. On the Mini toolbar, click **Center**.

h. Right-click in the cell containing *Seattle*.

i. Click **Split Cells**, accept the default of **2** columns, and then click **OK**.

(continues on next page)

Chapter Review

Skills Review: Project 7C Job Fairs (continued)

j. In the new cell, type **SE**

k. Point to the bottom border of **row 1**—*Currently Scheduled*—and then drag the border down until the Move Horizontal pointer is between **row 2** and **row 3**.

l. Point above the column header *Alternative Date*, outside of the table, to display the column select pointer. Use the column select pointer to select an entire table column. Right-click to select the column and display the shortcut menu and the mini toolbar. Note, this will also select the first row because it is merged. On the mini toolbar, click **Delete**, and then click **Delete Columns**.

8 ▸ Display **Slide 4**.

a. In **column 2**, click in the cell *Booth Available*. On the **Table Tools Layout tab**, in the **Cell Size group**, change the **Width** to **2"** to resize the column. Change the width of **column 3** to **2"**.

b. Right-click anywhere in the table, and then click **Select Table**.

c. In upper right corner of the table, point to the sizing handle to display the Diagonal Resize pointer. Hold down Ctrl and drag so the top edge of the table aligns on the **upper half of the vertical ruler at 1 inch** and on the **right half of the horizontal ruler at 3 inches**.

d. With the table still selected, on the **Home tab**, in the **Font group**, change the **Font Size** to **18**.

e. **AutoFit column 1**.

f. Drag the entire table so the top is aligned at **1.5 inches on the upper half of the vertical ruler**. On the **Table Tools Layout tab**, in the **Arrange group**, click **Align** and then click **Align Center** to center the table on the slide.

9 ▸ Display **Slide 3**.

a. Click anywhere in the table.

b. On the Table **Tools Design tab**, in the **Table Styles group**, click **More** ▾ to display the **Table Styles** gallery. Under **Medium**, in the first row, click the second style—**Medium Style 1 – Accent 1**.

c. On the **Table Tools Design tab**, in the **Table Styles Options group**, select the **Header Row** check box and select the **Banded Rows** check box.

d. On the **Table Tools Layout tab**, in the **Table Size group**, select the **Lock Aspect Ratio** check box. In the **Table Size group**, set the **Width** to **7"**.

e. With the table still selected, on the **Home tab**, in the **Font group**, if necessary, change the **Font Size** to **18**. On the **Table Tools Layout tab**, in the **Arrange group**, click **Align**, and then click **Align Center**. Click **Align** again, and then click **Align Middle**.

f. Position the Select Row pointer to the left of **row 1**, and then right-click to select the row. Change the **Font Size** to **24**. On the **Table Tools Layout tab**, in the **Alignment group**, click **Center Vertically**. Using the Select Row pointer, select **row 2**, right-click, and then on the mini toolbar, click **Bold**.

10 ▸ In the slide thumbnails, click in the blank space between **Slide 2** and **Slide 3** to display a thin orange line.

a. On the **Home tab**, in the **Slides group**, click the **New Slide arrow**, and then click **Section Header** to insert a new Slide 3.

b. On **Slide 3**, in the title placeholder, type **Job Fair Data** and then, in the subtitle placeholder, type **Seattle-Tacoma Job Fair**

c. In the slide thumbnails, click in the blank space between **Slide 2** and **Slide 3** to display a thin orange line. On the **Home tab**, in the **Slides group**, click **Section**, and then click **Add Section**.

d. With *Untitled Section* displayed in the slide thumbnails. In the **Rename Section** dialog box, under **Section name**, with *Untitled Section* text selected, type **Job Fair Data** Click **Rename**.

e. On the **View tab**, in the **Presentation Views**, click **Slide Sorter**. Notice *the Job Fair Data* section in **Slide Sorter View**. On the **View tab**, in the **Presentation Views**, click **Normal**.

11 ▸ Insert a **Header & Footer** on the **Notes and Handouts**. Include the **Date and time** updated automatically, the **Page number**, and a **Footer**. In the **Footer** box, type **7C_Job_Fairs** and then click **Apply to All**.

12 ▸ Display the document properties. As the **Tags**, type **job, fair, Seattle** and as the **Subject**, type your course and section number. Be sure your name displays as author, and then **Save** your file.

13 ▸ As directed by your instructor, create and submit a paper printout or an electronic image of your presentation that looks like a printed document—either as the Notes and Handouts or as the presentation slides—or, submit your completed PowerPoint file.

You have completed Project 7C **END**

Chapter Review

Apply 7B skills from these Objectives:

5. Create Pie Charts
6. Modify Charts
7. Change a Chart Type

Skills Review **Project 7D Attendee Survey**

In the following Skills Review, you will complete a PowerPoint presentation regarding a recent Seattle–Tacoma Job Fair and those who attended. The survey represents both unemployed and underemployed individuals who are looking for a position. You will add pie charts to emphasize the data collected. You will modify the pie charts and view a chart in grayscale. Your completed presentation will look similar to Figure 7.42.

Project Files

For Project 7D, you will need:

p07D_Attendee_Survey
p07D_Fair_Attendees
You will save your presentation as:
Lastname_Firstname_7D_Attendee_Survey

Project Results

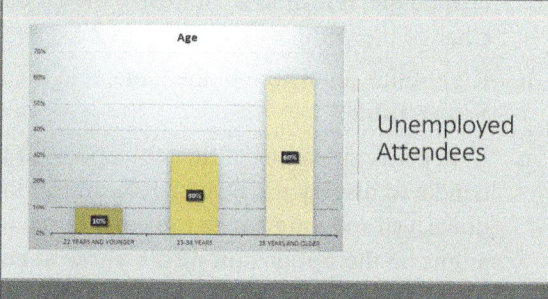
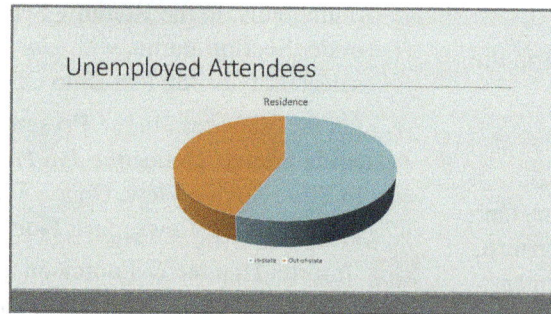
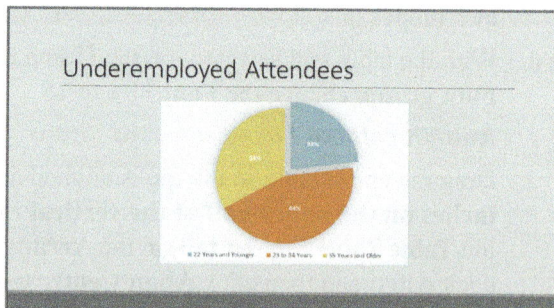

Figure 7.42 Project 7D Attendee Survey

(continues on next page)

Chapter Review

Skills Review: Project 7D Attendee Survey (continued)

1 From your student data files, open the file **p07D_Attendee_Survey**. If necessary, click **Enable Editing**. Navigate to your **PowerPoint Chapter 7** folder, and then using your own name, save the file as **Lastname_Firstname_7D_Attendee_Survey**

2 Display **Slide 3**.

a. In the content placeholder, click **Insert Chart**, and then in the **Insert Chart** dialog box, on the left, click **Pie**. At the top right, click the second pie chart type—**3-D Pie**, and then click **OK**.

b. In the **Chart in Microsoft PowerPoint** worksheet window, click in cell **B1**, type **Residence** In cell **A2**, type **In-state** In cell **A3**, type **Out-of-state**

c. In cell **B2**, type **56%** In cell **B3**, type **44%**

d. Click to select cell **A4**, and then drag to select cell **A5**. With cells **A4** and **A5** selected, right-click and from the shortcut menu, point to **Delete**, and then click **Table Rows**.

e. **Close** the *Chart in Microsoft PowerPoint* worksheet window to return to PowerPoint.

3 With the PowerPoint presentation open on your screen, open Microsoft Excel. On Excel's opening screen, click **Open Other Workbooks**. Navigate to your data files for this project, and then open **p07D_Fair_Attendees**.

a. In Excel, if necessary, click **Enable Editing**. Click the border of the chart to select it. On the **Home tab**, in the **Clipboard group**, click **Copy**. On the Windows taskbar, click the PowerPoint program icon to redisplay the PowerPoint window.

b. Display **Slide 4**. On the **Home tab**, in the **Clipboard group**, click the **Paste arrow**. In the **Paste Options**, click the first option—**Use Destination Theme & Embed Workbook (H)**. Close Excel without saving changes. (Mac users select Excel Chart (entire workbook) to embed the chart and select Use Destination Theme.)

c. With the chart selected, on the **Chart Tools Format tab**, in the **Size group**, change the **Height** of the chart to **4"** and change the **Width** of the chart to **6"**. In the **Arrange group**, align the chart to **Center** of the slide.

d. With the chart selected, on the **Chart Tools Design tab**, in the **Chart Layouts group**, click the **Quick**

Layout arrow, and then click the third layout—**Layout 3**.

e. With the chart selected, on the **Chart Tools Design tab**, in the **Chart Styles group**, click **More**. In the **Chart Styles** gallery, click **Style 11**.

f. On the **Chart Tools Design tab**, in the **Chart Layouts group**, click **Add Chart Element**, point to **Data Labels**, and then click **Center**.

g. Click the pie slice labeled *23%* one time to select the chart, and then click the slice a second time to select only the slice. Drag the slice out slightly up and away from the pie, and then release the mouse. Right-click the exploded slice, click **Format Data Point**. In the **Format Data Point** pane, adjust the **Point Explosion** to **12%**. Close the **Format Data Point** pane.

4 Display **Slide 2**. Click anywhere in the chart area to select the chart.

a. On the **Chart Tools Design tab**, in the **Type group**, click **Change Chart Type**.

b. On the left, under **All Charts**, click **Column**. Click **OK**.

c. On the **Chart Tools Design tab**, in the **Chart Layouts group**, click **Add Chart Element**. Point to **Legend**, and then click **None**.

5 On the **View tab**, in the **Color/Grayscale group**, click **Grayscale** to view the presentation as shown when printing in black and white. On the **Grayscale tab**, in the **Close group**, click **Back To Color View**.

6 Insert a **Header & Footer** on the **Notes and Handouts**. Include the **Date and time** updated automatically, the **Page number**, and a **Footer**. In the Footer box, type **Lastname_Firstname_7D_Attendee_Survey** and then click **Apply to All**.

7 Display the document properties. As the **Tags**, type **attendees, unemployed** and as the **Subject**, type your course and section number. Be sure your name displays as author, and then **Save** your file.

8 As directed by your instructor, create and submit a paper printout or an electronic image of your presentation that looks like a printed document—either as the Notes and Handouts or as the presentation slides—or, submit your completed PowerPoint file.

You have completed Project 7D | **END**

Content-Based Assessments (Mastery and Transfer of Learning)

Mastering PowerPoint   **Project 7E Surveys**

In the following Mastering PowerPoint project, you will complete a PowerPoint presentation by creating and inserting tables of data that have been collected. The Seattle–Tacoma Job Fair organization is conducting surveys in preparation for the upcoming job fairs. Your completed presentation will look similar to Figure 7.43.

Project Files for MyLab IT Grader

1. In your **MyLab IT** course, locate and click **PowerPoint 7E Surveys**, Download Materials, and then Download All Files.
2. Extract the zipped folder to your PowerPoint Chapter 6 folder. Close the Grader download screens.
3. Take a moment to open the downloaded **PowerPoint_7E_Surveys_Instructions**; note any recent updates to the book.

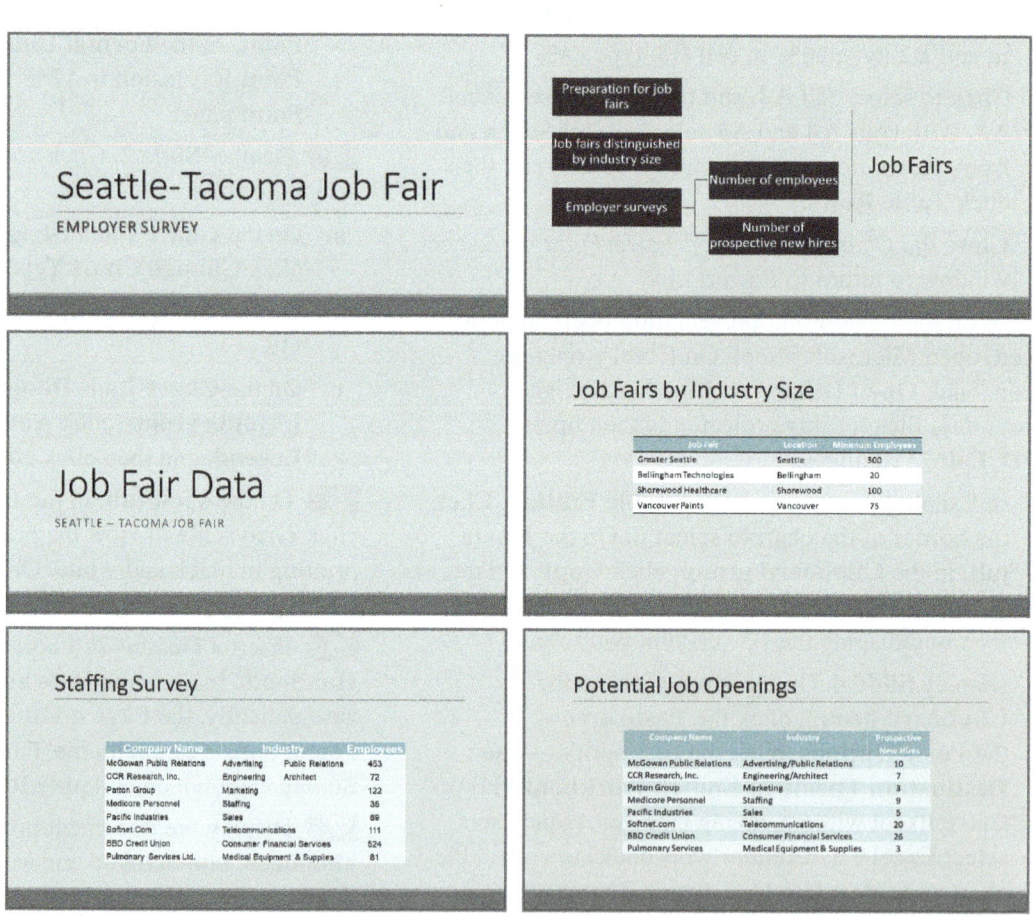

Figure 7.43 Project 7E Surveys

(continues on next page)

Content-Based Assessments (Mastery and Transfer of Learning)

Project Results

1 Navigate to your **PowerPoint Chapter 7 folder** and then double-click the PowerPoint file you downloaded from MyLab IT that displays your name—**Student_PowerPoint_7E_Surveys**. If necessary, click **Enable Editing**.

2 On **Slide 3**, insert a 3 × 5 table. In **row 1**, type the following text:

Job Fair	Location	Minimum Employees

3 Type the following information, beginning in **row 2**:

Greater Seattle	Seattle	500
Bellingham Technology	Bellingham	20
Shorewood Healthcare	Shorewood	100
Vancouver Paints	Vancouver	75

4 Center the text in the **Header Row**.

5 Apply the **Medium Style 3 – Accent 1** design to the table.

6 AutoFit column 2. Set the width of **column 3** to **2.5"**. Center the text in **column 3**.

7 Set the table alignment on the slide to **Align Center** and **Align Middle**.

8 In Excel, open **p07E_Staffing_Survey**. Copy the Excel cell range **A1:D9**, and then paste it on **Slide 4**, using destination styles.

9 In the table on **Slide 4**, delete **column 4. Lock Aspect Ratio** and change the table width to **8"**.

10 Move the table up so it is aligned on the **upper half of the vertical ruler at 0.75 inch**. Set the alignment to **Align Center**.

11 Select the **Header Row** check box.

12 Split the *Advertising/Public Relations* cell into two columns. In the new cell, type **Public Relations** In the original cell, delete */Public Relations*.

13 Split the *Engineering/Architect* cell into two columns. In the new cell, type **Architect** In the original cell, delete*/Architect*

14 Select the table, and then change the Font to Arial and Font Size to 16. Center the text in column 3. Center the text in row 1, and then increase the Font Size of the text in row 1 to 20.

15 In Word, open **p07E_New_Hires**. Copy the table, and then paste it on **Slide 5,** using destination styles.

16 Delete the *Location* column. With aspect ratio locked, increase the table width to **7.5"**. Change the font size of the table text to **18. AutoFit column 1** and **column 2. Center** the text in **column 3**.

17 Move the table up so it is aligned on the **upper half of the vertical ruler at 1 inch**. Set the alignment to **Align Center**.

18 Remove the shading from the first column.

19 Add a **Section Header slide** between **Slides 2** and **3**. On the new **Slide 3**, enter the title **Job Fair Data** and the subtitle **Seattle-Tacoma Job Fair**

20 Add a **Section** between **Slides 2** and **3** and rename it **Job Fair Data**

21 Insert a footer on the notes and handouts that includes a fixed date and time, the page number, and **7E_Surveys**

22 Display the document properties. As the **Tags**, type **survey, industry** and as the **Subject**, type your course and section number. Be sure your name displays as author, and then **Save** your file.

23 In MyLab IT, in your **Course Materials**, locate and click the Grader Project **PowerPoint 7E Surveys**. In **step 3**, under **Upload Completed Assignment**, click **Choose File**. In the **Open** dialog box, navigate to your **PowerPoint Chapter 7 folder**, and then click your **Student_PowerPoint_7E_Surveys** file one time to select it. In the lower right corner of the **Open** dialog box, click **Open**.

24 To submit your file to MyLab IT for grading, click **Upload**, wait a moment for a green **Success!** message, and then in **step 4**, click the blue **Submit for Grading** button. Click **Close Assignment** to return to your list of **Course Materials**.

You have completed Project 7E | **END**

Content-Based Assessments (Mastery and Transfer of Learning)

MyLab IT Grader

Mastering PowerPoint | **Project 7F Statistics**

Apply 7B skills from these Objectives:

5. Create Pie Charts
6. Modify Charts
7. Change a Chart Type

In the following Mastering PowerPoint project, you will complete a PowerPoint presentation by modifying a pie chart showing the statistics of the people who attended the Seattle–Tacoma Job Fair. The presentation also highlights the five largest represented employment areas by industry type. Your completed presentation will look similar to Figure 7.44.

Project Files for **MyLab IT** Grader

1. In your **MyLab IT** course, locate and click **PowerPoint 7F Statistics**, Download Materials, and then Download All Files.
2. Extract the zipped folder to your PowerPoint Chapter 7 folder. Close the Grader download screens.
3. Take a moment to open the downloaded **PowerPoint_7F_Statistics_Instructions**; note any recent updates to the book.

Project Results

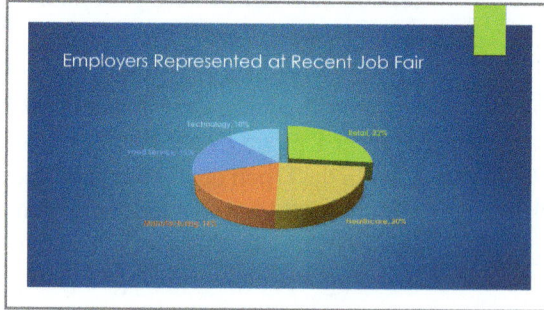
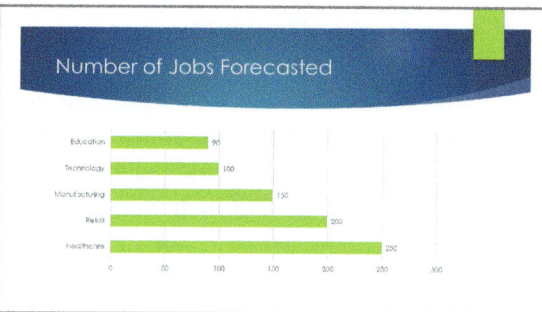

Figure 7.44 Project 7F Statistics

For Non-MyLab Submissions

For Project 7F, you will need: In your PowerPoint Chapter 7 folder, save your workbook as:

p07F_Statistics   **Lastname_Firstname_7F_Statistics**

After you have named and saved your presentation, on the next page, begin with Step 2.

After Step 14, save and submit your presentation as directed by your instructor.

(continues on next page)

1 Navigate to your **PowerPoint Chapter 7 folder** and then double-click the PowerPoint file you downloaded from **MyLab IT** that displays your name—**Student_PowerPoint_7F_Statistics**.

2 On **Slide 3**, remove the **Chart Title**.

3 Set the **Data Labels** to display as **Outside End**.

4 Apply **Chart Style 8**.

5 **Explode** the pie slice labeled *22%* by **15%**.

6 On **Slide 2** insert a new pie chart.

7 In cell **B1**, type **Residence** In cell **A2**, type **In-state** and in then cell **A3**, type **Out-of-state**

8 In cell **B2**, type **72%** and then in cell **B3**, type **28%**

9 In the worksheet, delete **row 4** and **row 5**.

10 Add a new **Title and Content** slide as **Slide 4**. Insert a **Pie of Pie** chart. In the worksheet, beginning in cell **A2**, type the following information:

Healthcare	250
Retail	200
Manufacturing	150
Technology	100
Education	90

11 On **Slide 4**, as the title of the slide, type **Number of Jobs Forecasted**

12 Change the chart type to **Bar**. Delete the chart title and the legend. Set the **Data Labels** to display as **Outside End**.

13 Insert a footer on the notes and handouts that includes a fixed date and time, the page number, and **7F_Statistics**

14 As the **Tags**, type **employers, job, fair** and as the **Subject**, type your course and section number. Be sure your name displays as author, and then **Save** your file.

15 In **MyLab IT**, in your **Course Materials**, locate and click the Grader Project **PowerPoint 7F Statistics**. In **step 3**, under **Upload Completed Assignment**, click **Choose File**. In the **Open** dialog box, navigate to your **PowerPoint Chapter 7 folder**, and then click your **Student_PowerPoint_7F_Statistics** file one time to select it. In the lower right corner of the **Open** dialog box, click **Open**.

16 To submit your file to **MyLab IT** for grading, click **Upload**, wait a moment for a green **Success!**

You have completed Project 7F | END

Content-Based Assessments (Mastery and Transfer of Learning)

Mastering PowerPoint   Project 7G Fair Types

Apply **7A** and **7B** skills from these Objectives:

1. Add a Table to a Presentation
2. Add or Delete Table Rows, Columns, and Cells
3. Modify a Table
4. Insert a Section
5. Create Pie Charts
6. Modify Charts
7. Change a Chart Type

In the following Mastering PowerPoint project, you will modify a presentation by adding pie charts and tables highlighting the many job fairs in the state and the local industries that are participating in the Seattle–Tacoma Job Fair. Your completed presentation will look similar to Figure 7.45.

Project Files for **MyLab IT Grader**

1. In your **MyLab IT** course, locate and click **PowerPoint 7G Fair Types**, Download Materials, and then Download All Files.
2. Extract the zipped folder to your PowerPoint Chapter 7 folder. Close the Grader download screens.
3. Take a moment to open the downloaded **PowerPoint_7G_Fair_Types_Instructions**; note any recent updates to the book.

Project Results

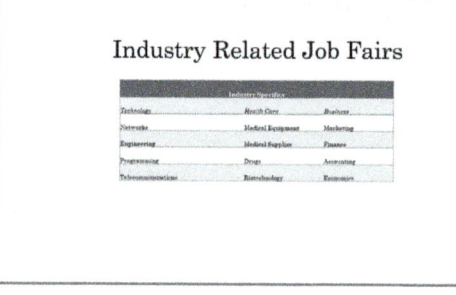

Figure 7.45 Project 7G Fair Types

For Non-MyLab Submissions

For Project 7G, you will need:
p07G_Fair_Types
p07G_Industry_Specifics

In your PowerPoint Chapter 7 folder, save your presentation as:
Lastname_Firstname_7G_Fair_Types

After you have named and saved your presentation, on the next page, begin with Step 2.

After Step 20, save and submit your presentation as directed by your instructor.

(continues on next page)

Content-Based Assessments (Mastery and Transfer of Learning)

Mastering PowerPoint: Project 7G Fair Types (continued)

1 Navigate to your **PowerPoint Chapter 7 folder** and then double-click the PowerPoint file you downloaded from **MyLab IT** that displays your name—**Student_PowerPoint_7G_Fair_Types**.

2 Display **Slide 2**. Insert a **2×2** table.

3 Insert a new row at the bottom of the table.

4 Beginning in the first row, type the following data:

Antioch University	Seattle
University of Puget Sound	Tacoma
University of Washington	Seattle

5 On **Slide 2**, remove the **Header Row** formatting from the table. Apply the style—**Medium Style 1** to the table.

6 With **Lock Aspect Ratio** checked, size the table width to **6.5"**. Set the table alignment on the slide to **Align Center** and **Align Middle**.

7 **AutoFit column 1** and **set the width of column 2 to 2"**.

8 Open the Excel workbook **p07G_Industry_Specifics**, copy the range **A1:D6,** and then paste it on **Slide 3**.

9 Delete the last column.

10 On **Slide 3**, merge the cells in the first row. Apply bold formatting and center the text in the first row. Apply italic formatting to **row 2**.

11 On **Slide 3**, **AutoFit column 2**. Set the width of **column 3 to 1.1"**. Display **Header Row** and **Banded Rows.** Apply the **Table Style** to **Medium Style 1 – Accent 1**.

12 On **Slide 3**, resize the table so the top edge aligns on the **1.5-inch mark above 0 on the vertical ruler** and the right edge aligns at the **3.5-inch mark to the right of 0 on the horizontal ruler**.

13 On **Slide 3**, set the table alignment to **Align Center**.

14 On **Slide 4**, insert a pie chart.

Type the following data in the worksheet, beginning in cell **A2**:

College	35
Industry	20
Professional	18

15 Delete row 5 in the worksheet. Add data labels in the chart that display on the **Inside End** of the slices. Remove the title from the chart.

16 **Explode** the *Industry* slice by **10%**.

17 Add a **Section Header slide** between **Slide 3** and **Slide 4**. Add the title **Job Fair Data** and the subtitle **Seattle-Tacoma Job Fairs**

18 Add a **Section** between **Slide 3** and **Slide 4** and rename it **Job Fair Data** View the presentation in **Slide Sorter View**, and then return to **Normal View**.

19 Insert a footer on the notes and handouts that includes a fixed date and time, the page number, **and 7G_Industry_Specifics**

20 As the **Tags**, type **college, industry, job** and as the **Subject**, type your course and section number. Be sure your name displays as author, and then **Save** your file.

21 In **MyLab IT**, in your **Course Materials**, locate and click the Grader Project **PowerPoint 7G Fair Types** In **step 3**, under **Upload Completed Assignment**, click **Choose File**. In the **Open** dialog box, navigate to your **PowerPoint Chapter 7 folder**, and then click your **Student_PowerPoint_7G_Fair_Types** file one time to select it. In the lower right corner of the **Open** dialog box, click **Open**.

22 To submit your file to **MyLab IT** for grading, click **Upload**, wait a moment for a green **Success!** message, and then in **step 4**, click the blue **Submit for Grading** button. Click **Close Assignment** to return to your list of **Course Materials**.

You have completed Project 7G **END**

Content-Based Assessments (Critical Thinking)

GO! Fix It	Project 7H Job Portfolio	IRC
GO! Make It	Project 7I Interview Primer	IRC
GO! Solve It	Project 7J Richards Consulting	IRC
GO! Solve It	Project 7K Career Development	

Project Files

For Project 7K, you will need:

New blank PowerPoint presentation
p07K_Values

You will save your presentation as:

Lastname_Firstname_7K_Career_Development

In this project, you will create a presentation to present at the next Greater Seattle Job Fair as part of a Career Development Workshop. The purpose is to highlight the importance of career development, whether the job applicant is a recent graduate or a seasoned professional. The presentation is to have an attractive format and an appropriate theme to keep the audience interested.

Create a presentation and save the file as **Lastname_Firstname_7K_Career_Development** Create a presentation with a minimum of six slides, adding tables and charts on at least three slides. Insert the table in the Excel file **p07K_Values** into one of the slides. Use data of your choice and create two pie charts. Include coverage on topics such as workshop goals, breakout sessions, education requirements, available jobs by industry, or others of your choice.

Insert a header and footer that includes the date and time updated automatically, the file name in the footer, and the page number. Add your name, your course name and section number, and the tags **career, education to the properties** Save and print or submit as directed by your instructor.

		Performance Level		
		Exemplary	**Proficient**	**Developing**
	Performance Element	You consistently applied the relevant skills. (5 points)	You sometimes, but not always, applied the relevant skills. (3 points)	You rarely or never applied the relevant skills. (0 or 1 point)
Performance Elements	*Formatted tables*	Tables are accurate and professionally formatted. Inserted Excel table content onto one of the slides.	Tables require additional formatting.	Tables were not completed.
	Inserted two pie charts	Pie charts completed, and data given are correct. Charts are easy to read, and all sections show.	Pie charts are present, but information is inaccurate or difficult to read.	Only one pie chart was created and it is incomplete and the data are inaccurate.
	Maintained a professional appearance	Presentation is free from spelling and grammar errors, and contains an appropriate amount of text per slide.	Presentation includes five slides. Few spelling and grammar errors, and slides contain an appropriate amount of information per slide.	Presentation includes four or fewer slides. Spelling and grammar errors exist, and there is too much information on each slide
	Added required elements	Notes and Handouts footer and Document Properties are completed correctly.	Completed all required items but one.	Failed to complete two or more required items correctly.

You have completed Project 7K | END

Outcomes-Based Assessments (Critical Thinking)

Rubric

The following outcomes-based assessments are open-ended assessments. That is, there is no specific correct result; your result will depend on your approach to the information provided. Make Professional Quality your goal. Use the following scoring rubric to guide you in how to approach the problem and then to evaluate how well your approach solves the problem.

The *criteria*—Software Mastery, Content, Format and Layout, and Process—represent the knowledge and skills you have gained that you can apply to solving the problem. The *levels of performance*—Professional Quality, Approaching Professional Quality, or Needs Quality Improvements—help you and your instructor evaluate your result.

	Your completed project is of Professional Quality if you:	Your completed project is Approaching Professional Quality if you:	Your completed project Needs Quality Improvements if you:
1-Software Mastery	Choose and apply the most appropriate skills, tools, and features and identify efficient methods to solve the problem.	Choose and apply some appropriate skills, tools, and features, but not in the most efficient manner.	Choose inappropriate skills, tools, or features, or are inefficient in solving the problem.
2-Content	Construct a solution that is clear and well organized, contains content that is accurate, appropriate to the audience and purpose, and is complete. Provide a solution that contains no errors of spelling, grammar, or style.	Construct a solution in which some components are unclear, poorly organized, inconsistent, or incomplete. Misjudge the needs of the audience. Have some errors in spelling, grammar, or style, but the errors do not detract from comprehension.	Construct a solution that is unclear, incomplete, or poorly organized, contains some inaccurate or inappropriate content, and contains many errors of spelling, grammar, or style. Do not solve the problem.
3-Format and Layout	Format and arrange all elements to communicate information and ideas, clarify function, illustrate relationships, and indicate relative importance.	Apply appropriate format and layout features to some elements, but not others. Overuse features, causing minor distraction.	Apply format and layout that does not communicate information or ideas clearly. Do not use format and layout features to clarify function, illustrate relationships, or indicate relative importance. Use available features excessively, causing distraction.
4-Process	Use an organized approach that integrates planning, development, self-assessment, revision, and reflection.	Demonstrate an organized approach in some areas, but not others; or, use an insufficient process of organization throughout.	Do not use an organized approach to solve the problem.

Outcomes-Based Assessments (Critical Thinking)

Apply a combination of the **7A** and **7B** skills.

GO! Think	Project 7L Advertising Strategy

Project Files

For Project 7L, you will need:

New blank PowerPoint presentation

p07L_Recommendations

You will save your presentation as:

Lastname_Firstname_7L_Advertising_Strategy

In this project, you will create a presentation of at least four slides that details the new advertising campaign being developed by the Seattle–Tacoma Job Fair organization to reach a wider audience for the upcoming job fairs. Items you should bring into your presentation include identifying the specific audience and determining where to advertise.

Create a table with popular job categories that includes seven areas such as government, retail, healthcare, and information technology. Insert the Excel file **p07L_Recommendations**, which lists various promotional media recommendations from advertising agencies, as a table. Select an attractive theme, and then format the slides appropriately. Create a slide with a pie chart, and format appropriately. Change the pie chart to view in grayscale and then change it back to view in color.

Update the Notes and Handouts footer with the new file name and the author name in the Properties. Save the presentation. Print or submit electronically as directed by your instructor.

	You have completed Project 7L	END

GO! Think	Project 7M Security Jobs	IRC
You and GO!	Project 7N IT Salaries	IRC

Publishing Presentations and Using Sway

8
POWERPOINT
2019

Rawpixel.com/Shutterstock

In This Chapter

 GO! to Work with PowerPoint

Before sharing a presentation, you should proof it to ensure there are no errors and that your message is clear. You can distribute a presentation in several formats depending on the audience and location for the presentation. You can create a video of your presentation or save your presentation in other formats such Picture, Show, or Outline.

Another option is to use Sway—an online tool that Microsoft describes as an app that "lets you create and share interactive reports, presentations, personal stories, newsletters, vacation memories, school and work projects, and more." You can begin a Sway from an existing PowerPoint or Word outline; or, you can create a Sway from scratch. Sways can be viewed using only a web browser.

Laurel County Community College (LCCC) is located in eastern Pennsylvania and serves urban, suburban, and rural populations. The college offers this diverse area a broad range of academic and vocational programs, including associate degrees, certificate programs, and noncredit continuing education and personal development courses. LCCC makes positive contributions to the community through cultural and athletic programs and partnerships with businesses and nonprofit organizations. The college also provides industry-specific training programs for local businesses through its Workforce and Economic Development Center.

PROJECT

8A Demographics

MyLab IT
Project 8A Grader for Instruction
Project 8A Simulation for Training and Review

Project Activities

In Activities 8.01 through 8.09, you will edit a presentation created by the Office of Institutional Research at Laurel County Community College. You will insert slides from an outline created in Word, proof and format the presentation, and then export your presentation in several formats. Your completed results will look similar to Figure 8.1.

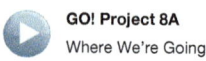 ## Project Files for **MyLab IT Grader**

1. In your storage location, create a folder named **PowerPoint Chapter 8**.
2. In your **MyLab IT** course, locate and click **PowerPoint 8A Demographics**, Download Materials, and then Download All Files. Close the Grader download screens.
3. Extract the zipped folder to your PowerPoint Chapter 8 folder.
4. Take a moment to open the downloaded **PowerPoint_8A_Demographics_Instructions**; note any recent updates to the book.

Project Results

GO! Project 8A
Where We're Going

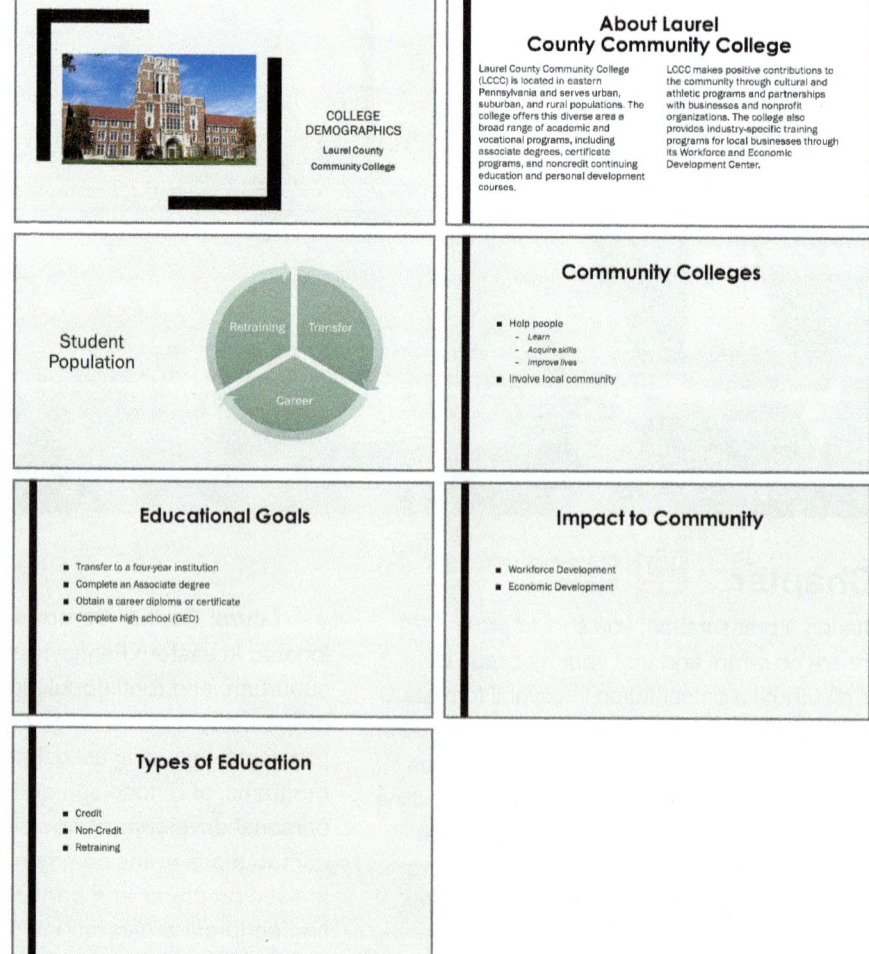

Figure 8.1 Project 8A Demographics

For Non-MyLab Submissions

For Project 8A, you will need:

p08A_Demographics (PowerPoint presentation)
p08A_Educational_Importance (Word document)
p08A_Workforce_Value (Word document)

In your storage location, create a folder named **PowerPoint Chapter 8**
In your PowerPoint Chapter 8 folder, save your presentation as:

Lastname_Firstname_8A_Demographics
Lastname_Firstname_8A_Handouts (Word document)
Lastname_Firstname_8A_Outline (Outline/RTF file)
Lastname_Firstname_8A_Picture (JPG file)
Lastname_Firstname_8A_Show (PowerPoint Slide Show file)
Lastname_Firstname_8A_Video (MP4 file)

After you have named and saved your presentation, begin with Step 2.

Objective 1	**Insert Outline Text from Another Program into a PowerPoint Presentation**

ALERT   Because Office 365 is a cloud-based subscription service that receives continuous updates, you may encounter some variations in what appears on your screen and what is shown in this instruction. Microsoft Office 365 is fully installed on your PC or Mac; no internet access is necessary to create or edit documents. When you *are* connected to the internet, you will receive monthly upgrades and new features, so you always have the latest versions of Office apps as soon as they are available. Your subscription gives you continuous free access to the latest innovations and refinements.

GO! Learn How
Video P8-1

You can bring content created in another program into PowerPoint instead of retyping all of the information. For example, you can use an outline from a Microsoft Word document, a basic text file, or a ***Rich Text Format (RTF) file***—a non-application-specific file format used to transfer formatted text documents between applications—to create slides. The Mac version of PowerPoint only supports RTF files.

A ***heading style*** is a set of formatting characteristics, such as font name, size, color, paragraph alignment, and spacing that is saved and used to quickly format selected text. If the source file—the document from which the outline is obtained—contains heading styles, the slides will be created using the headings present in the file. If the source file contains no heading styles, PowerPoint will create an outline based on ***paragraphs***. A paragraph is any text that has a ***hard return***—pressing Enter to start a new line—after it. PowerPoint will treat each item in a bulleted or numbered list, a title, and a subtitle as a paragraph. Each Level 1 paragraph is treated as a title on a separate slide when the file is inserted into PowerPoint.

Activity 8.01 | Inserting Outline Text from Another Program into a PowerPoint Presentation

MOS
2.1.1

The Office of Institutional Research at Laurel County Community College is developing a presentation that displays the college demographics, and most of the information is already in Word documents in the form of an outline. In this Activity, you will create slides by inserting the outlines created in Microsoft Word into your presentation.

1 ▶ Navigate to your **PowerPoint Chapter 8 folder**, and then double-click the PowerPoint file you downloaded from **MyLab IT** that displays your name—**Student_PowerPoint_8A_ Demographics**. In your presentation, if necessary, at the top click **Enable Editing**.

2 ▶ With the PowerPoint presentation open on your screen, open Microsoft Word. On Word's opening screen, click **Open**. Click **Browse**, navigate to the files downloaded with this project, and then open **p08A_Educational_Importance**. If necessary, click **Enable Editing**.

3 In Word, on the **View tab**, in the **Show group**, if necessary, select the **Navigation Pane** check box. In the **Views group**, click **Outline**, and then compare your screen with Figure 8.2.

Outline view is a document view in Microsoft Word that distinguishes the importance of data by the heading styles that are applied.

MAC TIP Save the file as an RTF file in your PowerPoint Chapter 8 folder.

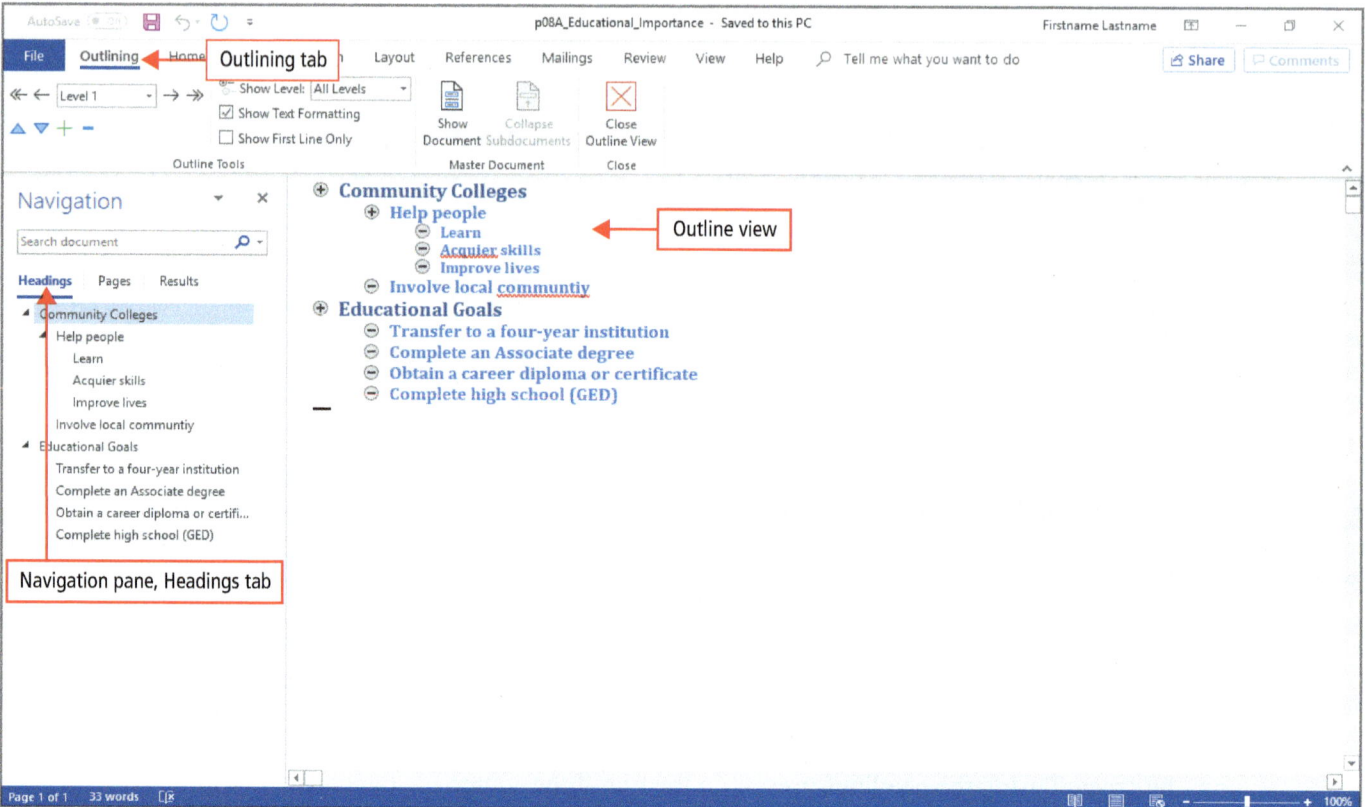

Figure 8.2

4 Examine the data in the file. Click the **File tab**, and then **Close** ✕ the Word document, but leave Word open.

The outline file must be closed to insert the outline into PowerPoint.

5 Return to PowerPoint. Display **Slide 3**. On the **Home tab**, in the **Slides group**, click the **New Slide arrow**, and then click **Slides from Outline**.

6 In the **Insert Outline** dialog box, navigate to your files downloaded with this project, click **p08A_Educational_Importance**, and then click **Insert**.

MAC TIP The Mac version of PowerPoint does not support importing .docx files, instead use the .rtf you saved in Step 3.

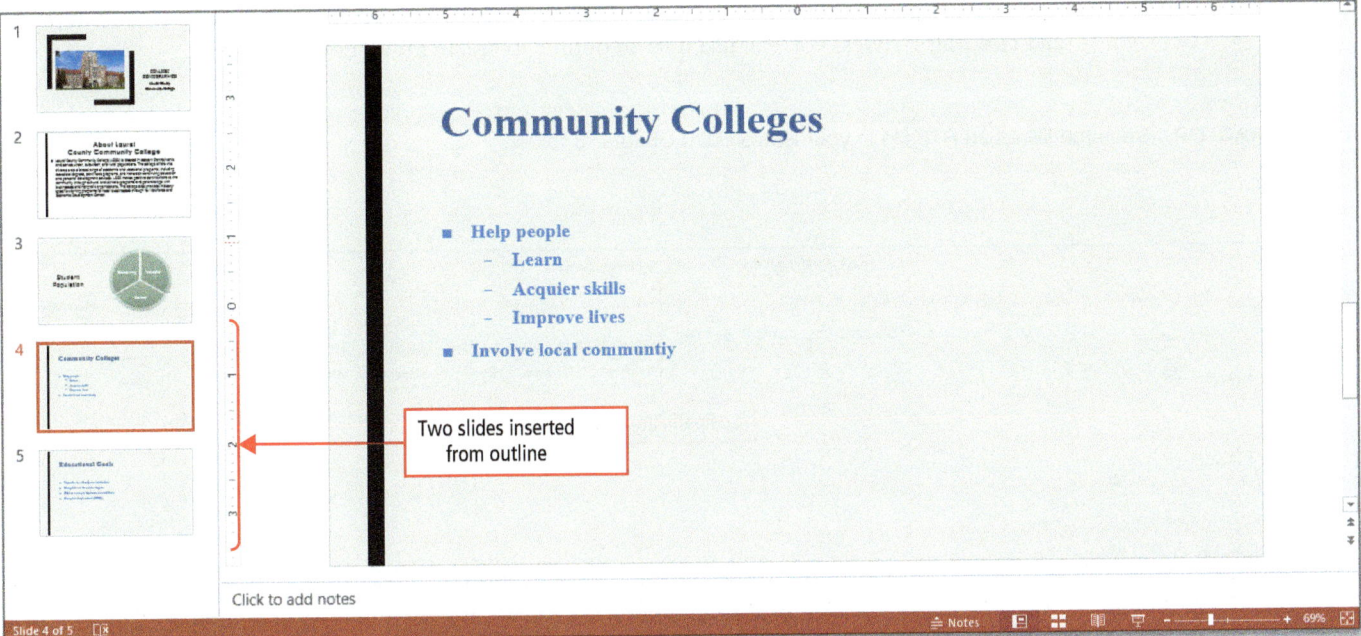

7 Display **Slide 4**, and then compare your screen with Figure 8.3.

After you insert the outline, PowerPoint creates two new slides because there are two Level 1 items in the outline.

Figure 8.3

8 Click the Word icon on the taskbar to return to Word.

9 In Word, from your data files for this project, open **p08A_Workforce_Value**. If necessary, click **Enable Editing**.

This file is a Word 97-2003 Document. On the Word title bar, after the file name, *Compatibility Mode* displays. To ensure that people who are using previous versions of Word will have full editing capabilities, you can save a file as a Word 97-2003 document, or you can save the file as a Word document and select Maintain compatibility with previous versions of Word. The file extension of a Word 97-2003 document is .doc, the file extension of a Word document for versions of Word later than 2003 is .docx.

10 On the **View tab**, in the **Show group**, if necessary, select the **Navigation Pane** check box. On the **Home tab**, in the **Styles group**, notice that the **Heading 1** style is active, indicating that the text *Impact to Community* is formatted as Heading 1. Compare your screen with Figure 8.4.

The Word document displays in Print Layout view. Paragraphs 1 and 4 are formatted as Heading 1. The remaining paragraphs are formatted as Heading 2. Because this Word file contains Heading 1 and Heading 2 styles, you can use it as an outline to create PowerPoint slides.

MAC TIP   Save the file as an RTF file in your PowerPoint Chapter 8 folder.

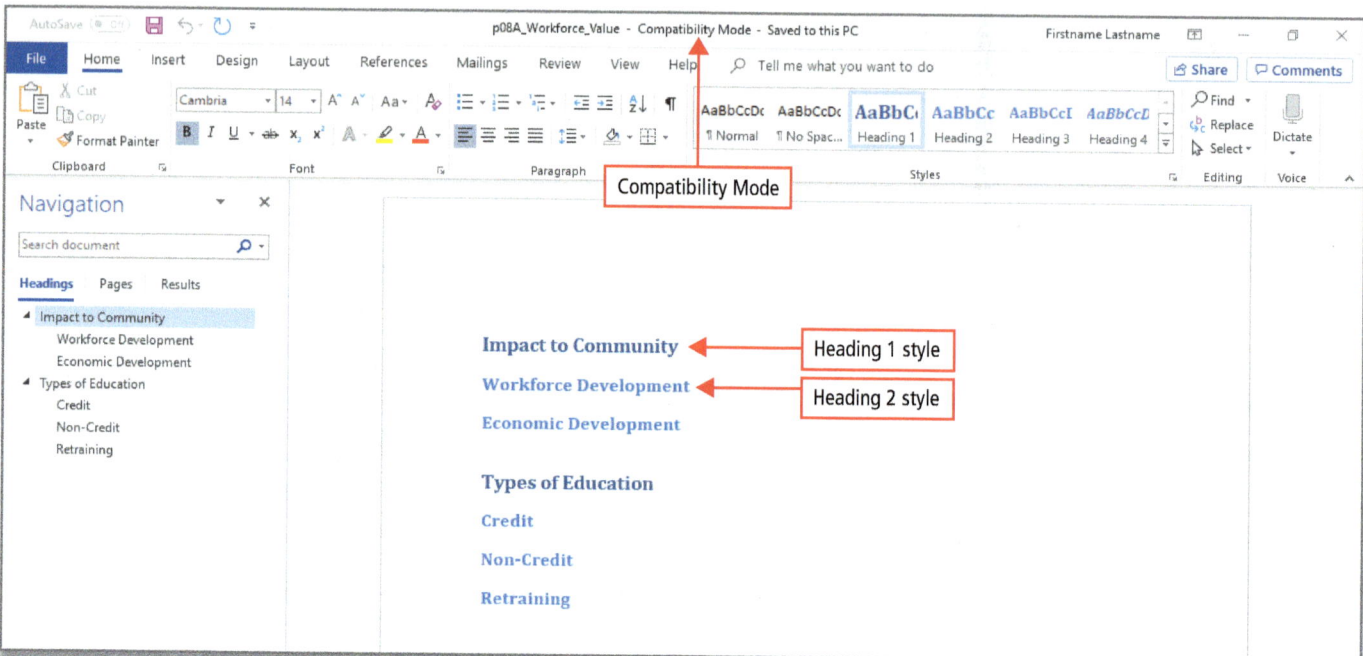

Figure 8.4

11 **Close** ☒ Word. Display **Slide 5**. On the **Home tab**, in the **Slides group**, click the **New Slide arrow**, and then click **Slides from Outline**.

12 In the **Insert Outline** dialog box, from your student data files, insert the file **p08A_Workforce_Value**.

PowerPoint inserts two new slides—Slide 6 and Slide 7—that use the Title and Text layout. The formatting is based on the heading styles of the source document.

MAC TIP   Insert the RTF file you saved in Step 10.

13 Display **Slide 7**. **Save** 💾 your presentation and then compare your screen with Figure 8.5.

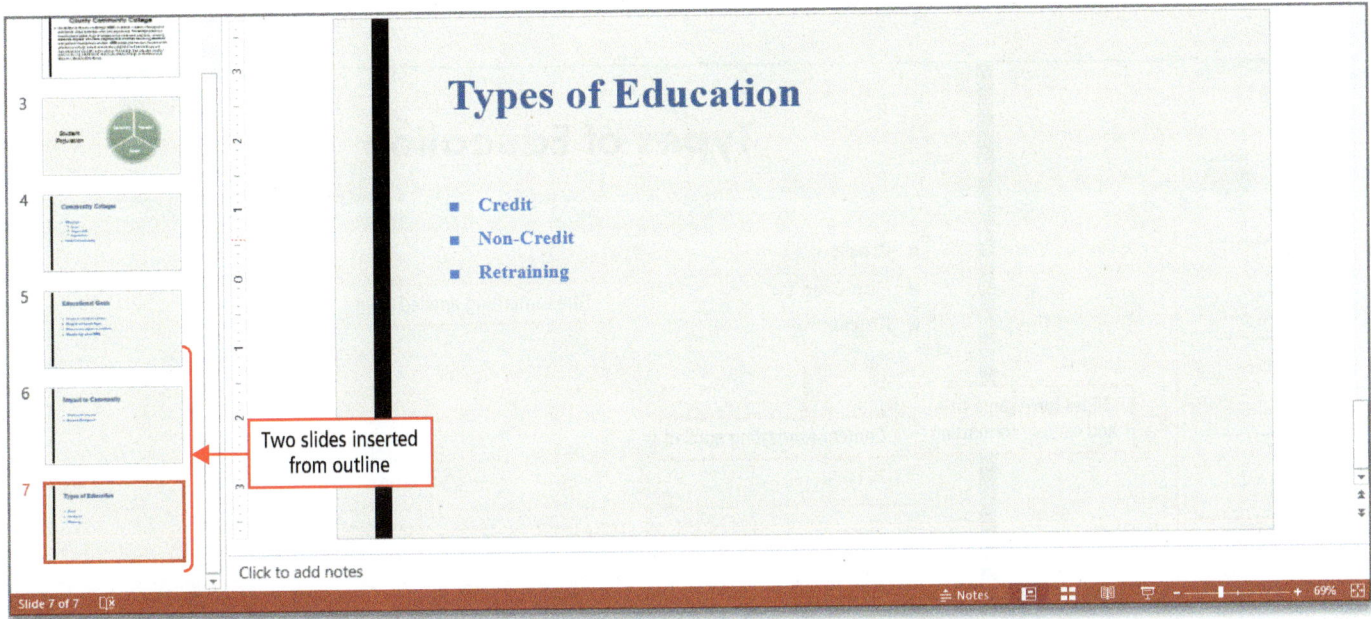

Figure 8.5

Activity 8.02 | Using the Format Painter

The Format Painter enables you to easily copy formatting to text and objects to ensure consistency in the presentation. When bringing in content from other sources, adjust the formatting so that all slides have the same look.

1 Display **Slide 2**. Click in the title placeholder, and then click to display a solid border. On the **Home tab**, in the **Clipboard group**, double-click **Format Painter** 🖌. Compare your screen with Figure 8.6

When you double-click the Format Painter, it remains active until you turn it off.

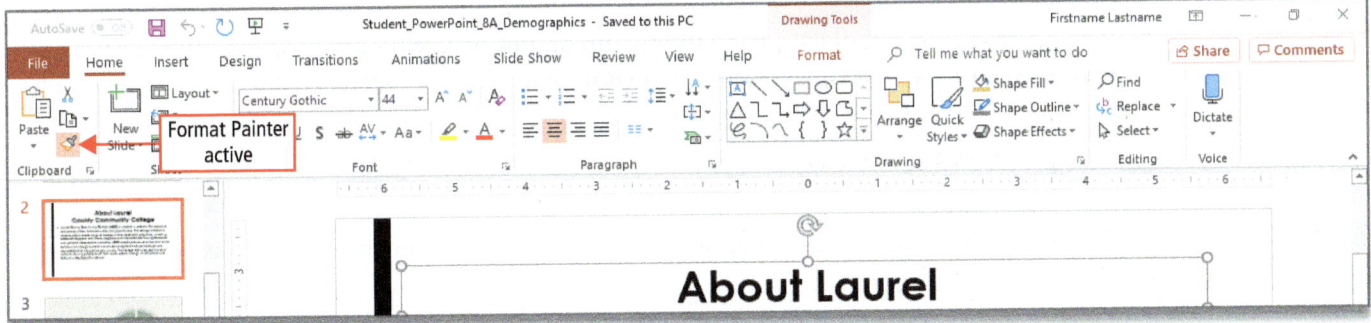

Figure 8.6

2 Display **Slide 4**, and then click in the title placeholder to apply the formatting.

3 Display **Slide 5**, and then click in the title placeholder. Using the same technique, apply the title formatting to the titles on **Slides 6** and **7**. Press Esc to turn off the Format Painter.

The formatting in the title placeholders on Slides 4–7 matches the formatting on Slide 2.

4 Using the technique you practiced, copy the formatting of the content placeholder on **Slide 2**, to the content placeholders on **Slides 4** through **7**. Press Esc to turn off the Format Painter.

5 **Save** 🖫 your presentation and then compare your screen with Figure 8.7.

All slides are formatted with the Franklin Gothic Book font.

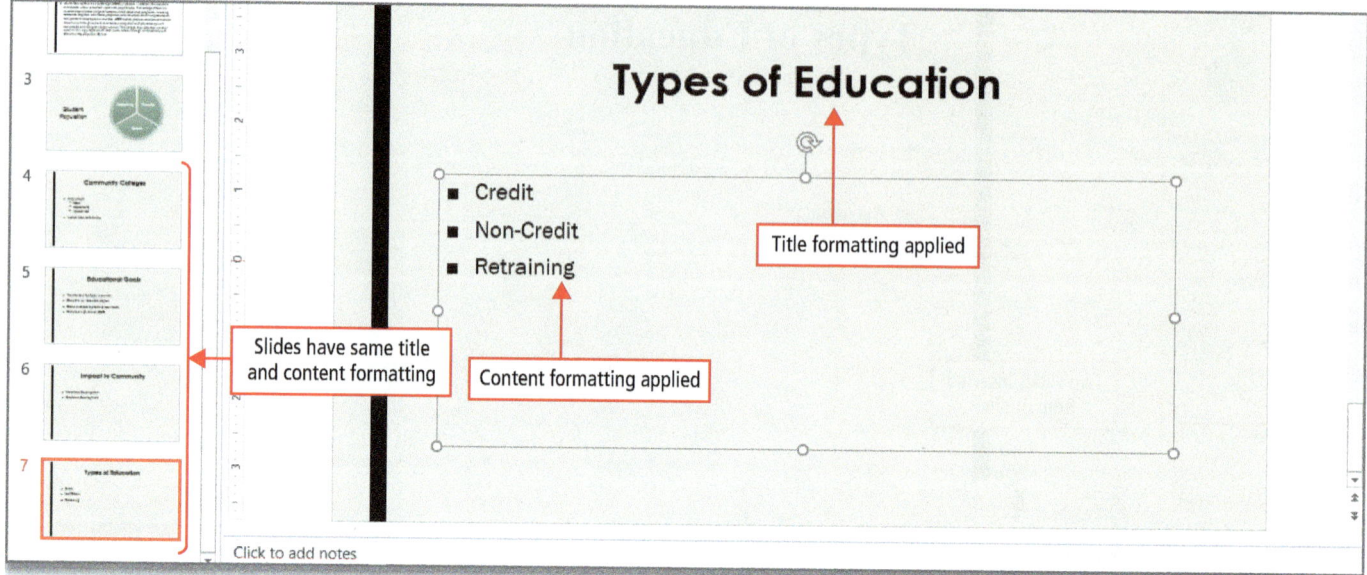

Figure 8.7

Proof a Presentation

GO! Learn How
Video P8-2

Before a presentation is considered finished, it should be checked for errors. A presentation with spelling errors looks unprofessional and draws attention away from your message. PowerPoint includes a spelling checker that compares the words in your presentation to the built-in dictionary. You can also add words to a custom dictionary, such as your last name or industry-specific terms and acronyms.

Activity 8.03 | **Checking Spelling and Using Smart Lookup**

The ***Smart Lookup*** tool uses Bing to look up definitions, Wiki articles, and related searches from the web. You can use Smart Lookup to verify a definition, locate a synonym, or research a term to add more content to your presentation.

1 Display **Slide 2**. In the content placeholder, notice the wavy red lines under *vocotional* and *bussinesses*.

PowerPoint checks your spelling and flags words that are not in its dictionary as possible errors.

2 Right-click *vocotional*, and then compare your screen with Figure 8.8.

Figure 8.8

3 ▸ Click *vocational* to correct the spelling. Using the technique you practiced, change *bussinesses* to *businesses*.

4 ▸ On the **Review tab**, in the **Proofing group**, click **Spelling**, and then compare your screen with Figure 8.9.

The Spelling pane enables you to ignore or change the spelling of the flagged word. Suggested replacements display in the upper section of the pane. The lower section of the pane displays synonyms of the selected word. Next to the word, you can click the speaker icon to hear the word pronounced.

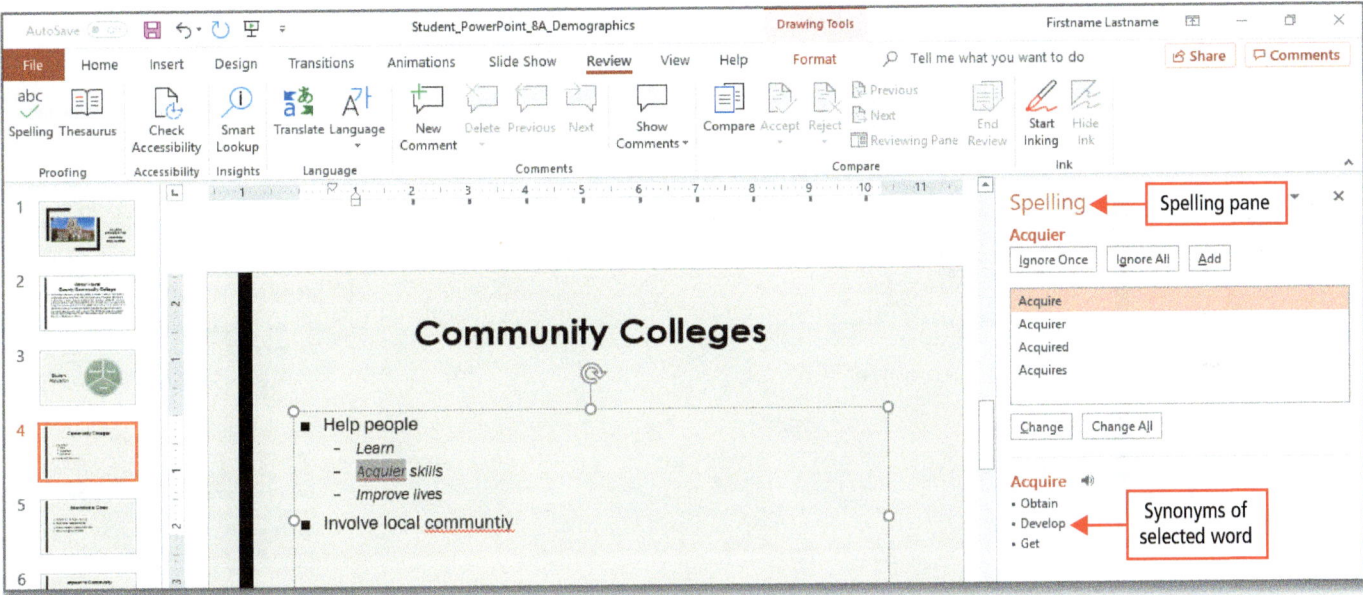

Figure 8.9

5 ▸ With *Acquire* selected in the **Spelling** pane, click **Change**. With *community* selected in the **Spelling** pane, click **Change**.

The spell check is complete, and the Spelling pane closes.

6 ▸ In the Microsoft PowerPoint message, click **OK**.

7 ▸ On **Slide 4**, click in the word *Acquire*. On the **Review tab**, in the **Insights group**, click **Smart Lookup** to display the **Smart Lookup** pane.

The ***Smart Lookup pane*** has two tabs: Explore, which displays synonyms and web results, and Define, which displays a definition, synonyms, and word origin.

 ANOTHER WAY   Right-click the word you want to review, and then click Smart Lookup.

ALERT   Privacy Notice

The first time you click Smart Lookup, a privacy notice may display. Read the message and the privacy statement, and then click Got it.

8 On the **Smart Lookup** pane, click the **Define tab**, read the definition of the selected word, and then compare your screen with Figure 8.10.

The definition and other information in the Smart Lookup pane is more in-depth than what displays in the Spelling pane.

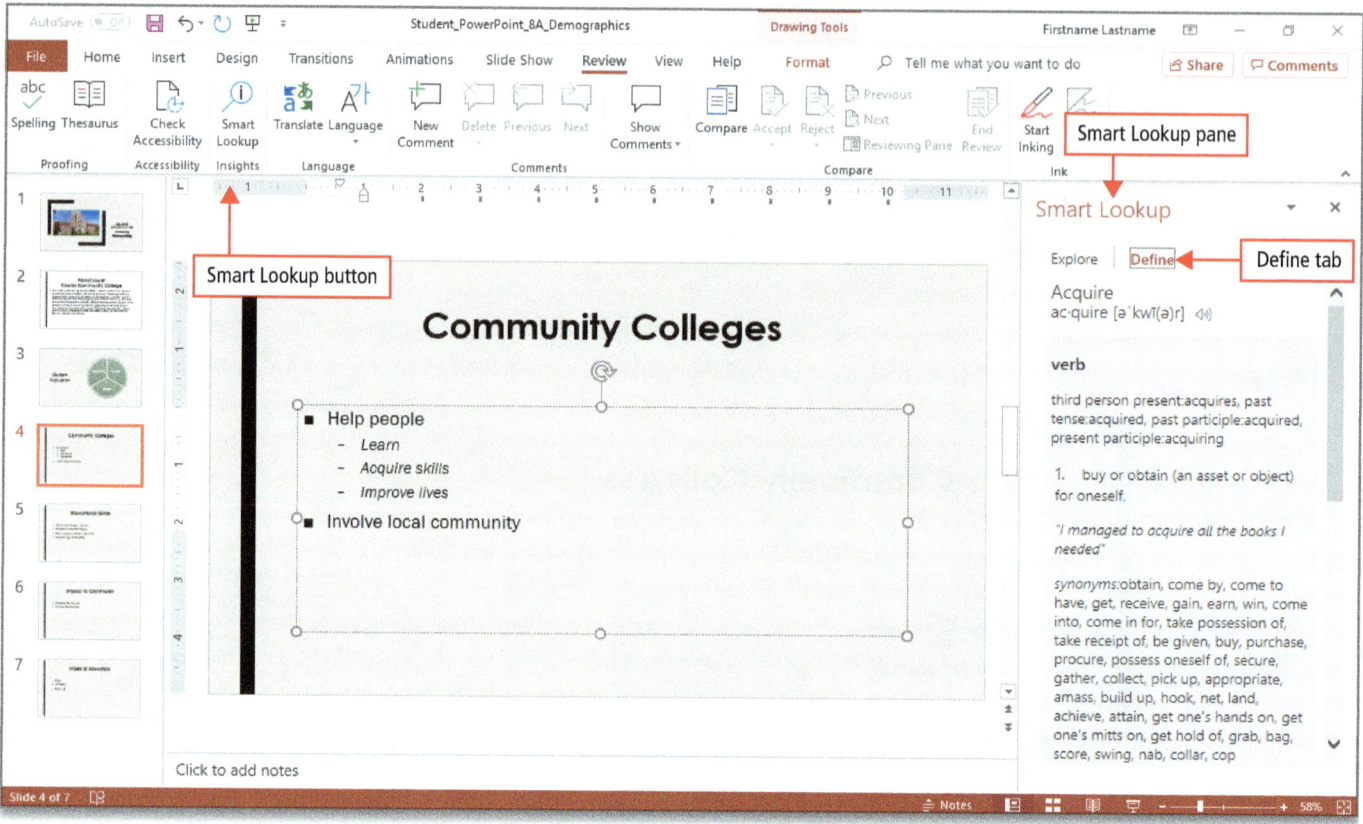

Figure 8.10

9 **Close** × the **Smart Lookup** pane, and then **Save** 🖫 your presentation.

Objective 3 | **Format Text as Columns**

GO! Learn How
Video P8-3

To make large paragraphs of text easier to read, use bullets, divide text into multiple slides, or format the text as columns. Good design follows a 7x7 rule—a maximum of seven lines, with no more than seven words each, whenever possible.

Activity 8.04 | Formatting Text as Columns

3.2.1

In this presentation, the text in the content placeholder on Slide 2 is lengthy and difficult to read, so you will format the text into two columns.

1 Display **Slide 2**. Notice that the text on this slide is one long bullet point.

2 Click in the content placeholder. On the **Home tab**, in the **Paragraph group**, click **Bullets** ≔ ▾ to remove the bullet in the placeholder.

3 On the **Home tab**, in the **Paragraph group**, click **Add or Remove Columns** ≣ ▾, and then compare your screen with Figure 8.11.

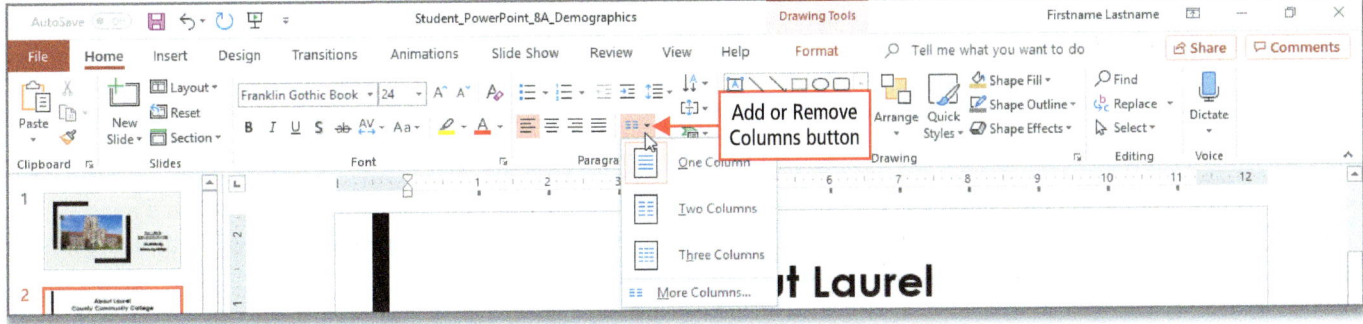

Figure 8.11

4 ► Click **More Columns**. In the **Columns** dialog box, set the **Number** to **2**, change the **Spacing** to **0.5"**, and then click **OK**.

5 ► Near the bottom of the left column, click to position the insertion point to the left of *LCCC makes positive*, and then press [Enter] to move the sentence to the top of the second column. Save your presentation and compare your screen with Figure 8.12.

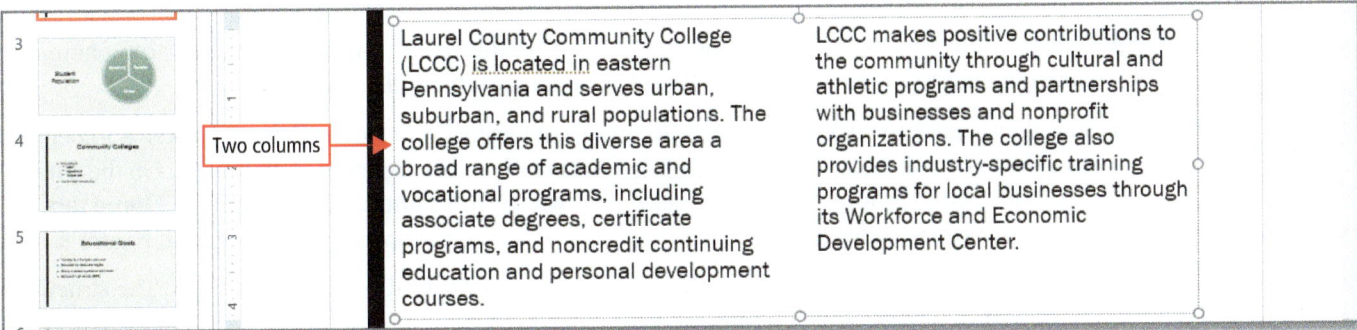

Figure 8.12

6 ► Insert a **Header & Footer** on the **Notes and Handouts**. Include the **Date and time** updated automatically, the **Page number**, and a **Footer**. In the **Footer** box, type **8A_Demographics** and then click **Apply to All**.

7 ► Display the document properties. As the **Tags**, type **education, demographics** and as the **Subject**, type your course and section number. Be sure your name displays as author, and then **Save** your file. If directed by your instructor to complete the next activity, leave your presentation open for the next Activity, otherwise, close PowerPoint.

For Non-MyLab Submissions Determine What Your Instructor Requires

Print or submit your presentation electronically as directed by your instructor.

---

8 ► In **MyLab IT**, in your **Course Materials**, locate and click the Grader Project **PowerPoint 8A Demographics**. In **step 3**, under **Upload Completed Assignment**, click **Choose File**. In the **Open** dialog box, navigate to your **PowerPoint Chapter 8 folder**, and then click your **Student_PowerPoint_8A_Demographics** file one time to select it. In the lower right corner of the **Open** dialog box, click **Open**.

9 ► To submit your file to **MyLab IT** for grading, click **Upload,** wait a moment for a green **Success!** message, and then in **step 4**, click the blue **Submit for Grading** button. Click **Close Assignment** to return to your list of **Course Materials**.

ALERT   The remaining Activities in Project 8A are optional activities and are not available in the **MyLab IT** grader system. Complete these activities and submit as directed by your instructor.

GO! Learn How
Video P8-4

You can export a PowerPoint presentation into different formats for distribution. These formats enable someone to view the presentation, or part of the presentation, without using PowerPoint or being able to edit the presentation.

Activity 8.05 | Saving a Presentation as an Outline

1.5.6

You can export a PowerPoint presentation to a Word outline. When you do so, in the Word outline, slide titles will be formatted with the Heading 1 style and bulleted text will be formatted with the Heading 2 style. Objects such as pictures, charts, SmartArt, and shapes do not display when a PowerPoint file is saved as an outline. The outline is useful for reviewing the organization of the *text* of the presentation.

1 With your **Student_PowerPoint_8A_Demographics** presentation open, display the **Save As** dialog box. If necessary, navigate to your **PowerPoint Chapter 8** folder.

 MAC TIP   Click File, click Export, and then change File Format to RTF.

2 Click the **Save as type arrow**, and then click **Outline/RTF**. In the **File name** box, change the file name to **Student_PowerPoint_8A_Outline** and then click **Save**.

3 Start Word and then click **Open**. Click **Browse**, navigate to your **PowerPoint Chapter 8** folder, and then click your **Student_PowerPoint_8A_Outline** file. Click **Open** to view the file. On the **View tab**, in the **Show group**, if necessary, select the **Navigation Pane** check box. On the **Home tab**, in the **Styles group**, notice that the **Heading 1** style is active. Compare your screen with Figure 8.13.

The Word document text is formatted using the font and font size from PowerPoint. The structure displays in the Navigation pane.

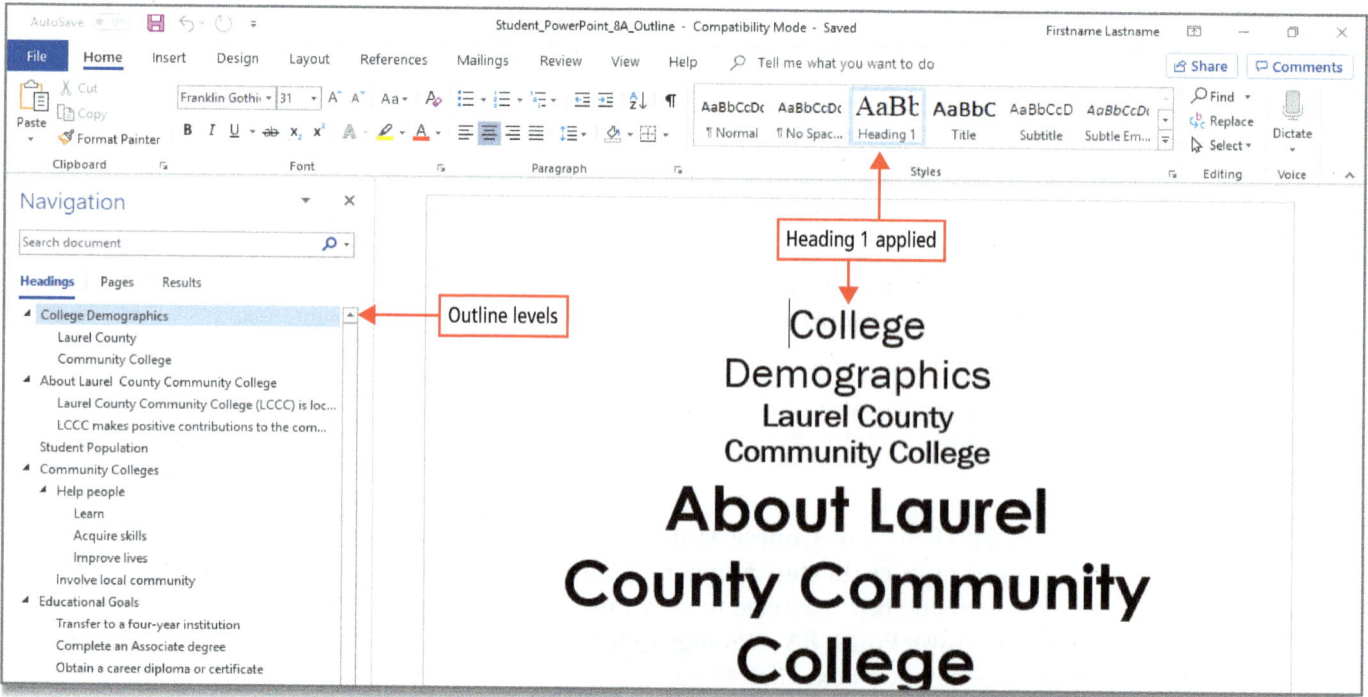

Figure 8.13

4 **Close** ☒ Word without saving.

Activity 8.06 | Saving the Presentation as a Show

When the college distributes a presentation to high school guidance counselors, they save the presentation as a Show. Doing so enables the counselors to double-click to open the presentation in Slide Show view, rather than starting the slide show from Normal view. Because the counselors do not need to edit the presentation, this saves time and makes the presentation look more professional. When the slide show ends, the presentation is closed, rather than returning to the PowerPoint screen. A presentation saved as a show has the file extension .ppsx. To edit a presentation saved as a Show, open the file from PowerPoint.

1 ▸ With your **Student_PowerPoint_8A_Demographics** presentation open, display the **Save As** dialog box. If necessary, navigate to your **PowerPoint Chapter 8** folder. Click the **Save as type arrow**, and then point to **PowerPoint Show**. Compare your screen with Figure 8.14.

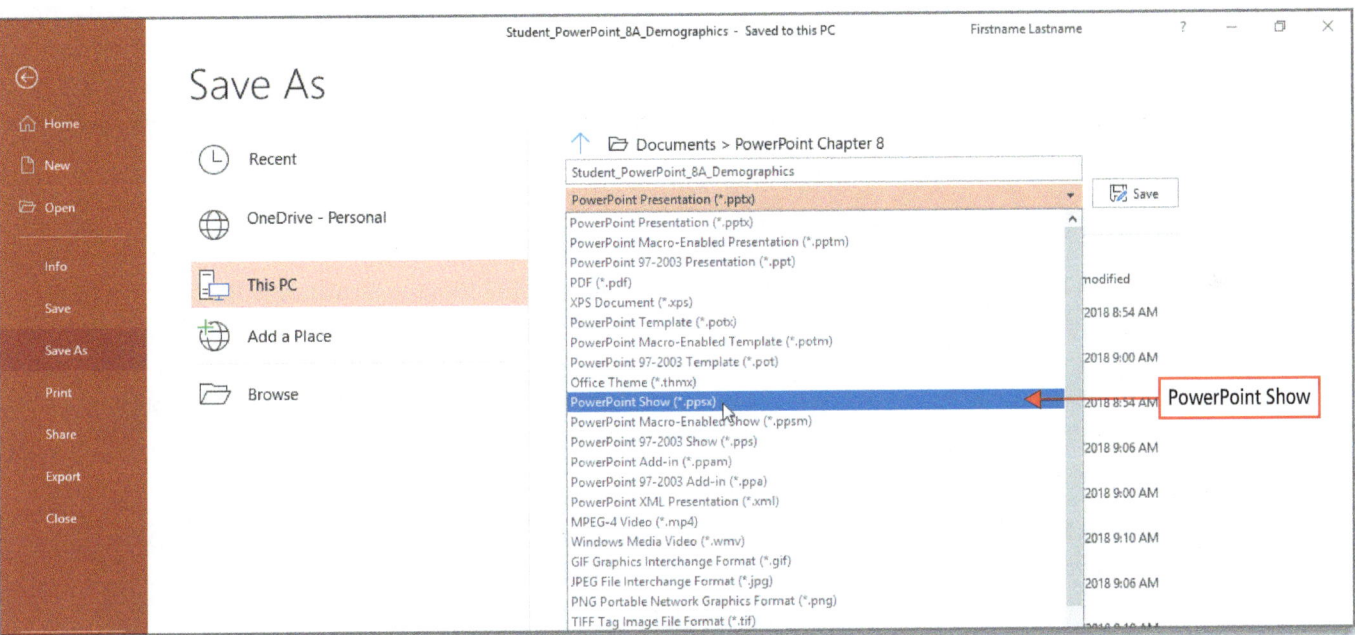

Figure 8.14

2 ▸ Click **PowerPoint Show**. Change the file name to **Student_PowerPoint_8A_Show** and then click **Save**.

3 ▸ **Close** ⊠ the presentation.

4 ▸ Open **File Explorer**, navigate to your **PowerPoint Chapter 8** folder, and then double-click your **Student_PowerPoint_8A_Show** file.

The presentation opens in Slide Show view.

5 ▸ View the presentation and then, press Esc to close the presentation.

Activity 8.07 | Saving a Slide as a Picture

You can save a single slide, or all sides, as image files. A popular image format that you can use is *Joint Photographic Experts Group*—a file format used for photos with the .jpg and .jpeg extensions. This is commonly pronounced JAY-PEG. From the SmartArt graphic on Slide 3, the college wants to make a poster to hang on the office door.

1 Open your **Student_PowerPoint_8A_Demographics** file. Display **Slide 3**.

2 Display the **Save As** dialog box, and then, if necessary, navigate to your **PowerPoint Chapter 8** folder. Click the **Save as type arrow**, and then click **JPEG File Interchange Format**.

MAC TIP   Click File, click Export, and then change File Format to JPG.

3 Change the **File name** to **Student_PowerPoint_8A_Picture** and then click **Save**. Compare your screen with Figure 8.15.

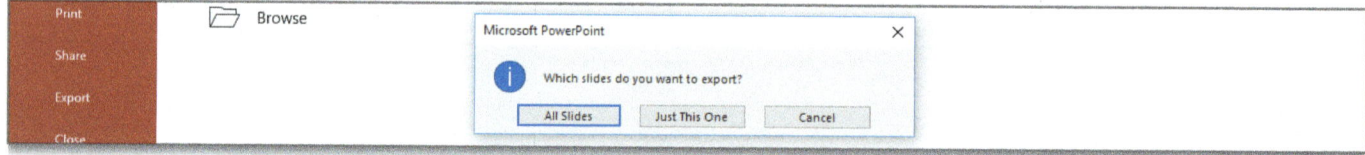

Figure 8.15

4 In the message box, click **Just This One**.

The All Slides option creates a folder containing JPEG files for each slide in the presentation. The Just This One option creates a JPEG file of the displayed slide.

MAC TIP   The Mac version of PowerPoint does not include the option to save only one slide, but creates a folder containing JPEG files for each slide in the presentation.

5 In **File Explorer**, navigate to your **PowerPoint Chapter 8** folder, and then double-click your **Student_PowerPoint_8A_Picture** file.

The image file opens in your default image viewer.

6 **Close** ⊠ the image file and **Close** ⊠ File Explorer.

Activity 8.08 | Creating a Video

MOS
1.5.6

You can create a video from your presentation, which you can distribute by using a disc, flash drive, the web, or email. The video can include recorded timings, narrations, and laser pointer gestures. The video includes all slides not hidden in the slide show and preserves animations, transitions, and media. The viewer does not need to have PowerPoint installed to view the presentation but does need a video player installed. In this Activity, you will create a video of a presentation, and then save the video as a *MP4 video file (.mp4)*—the default file type when saving a video in PowerPoint.

1 In PowerPoint, with your **Student_PowerPoint_8A_Demographics** presentation displayed, click the **File tab**, and then click **Export**. Under **Export**, click **Create a Video**. Compare your screen with Figure 8.16.

Notice this presentation does not have timings or narrations recorded.

MAC TIP   Click File, click Export, and then change File Format to MP4.

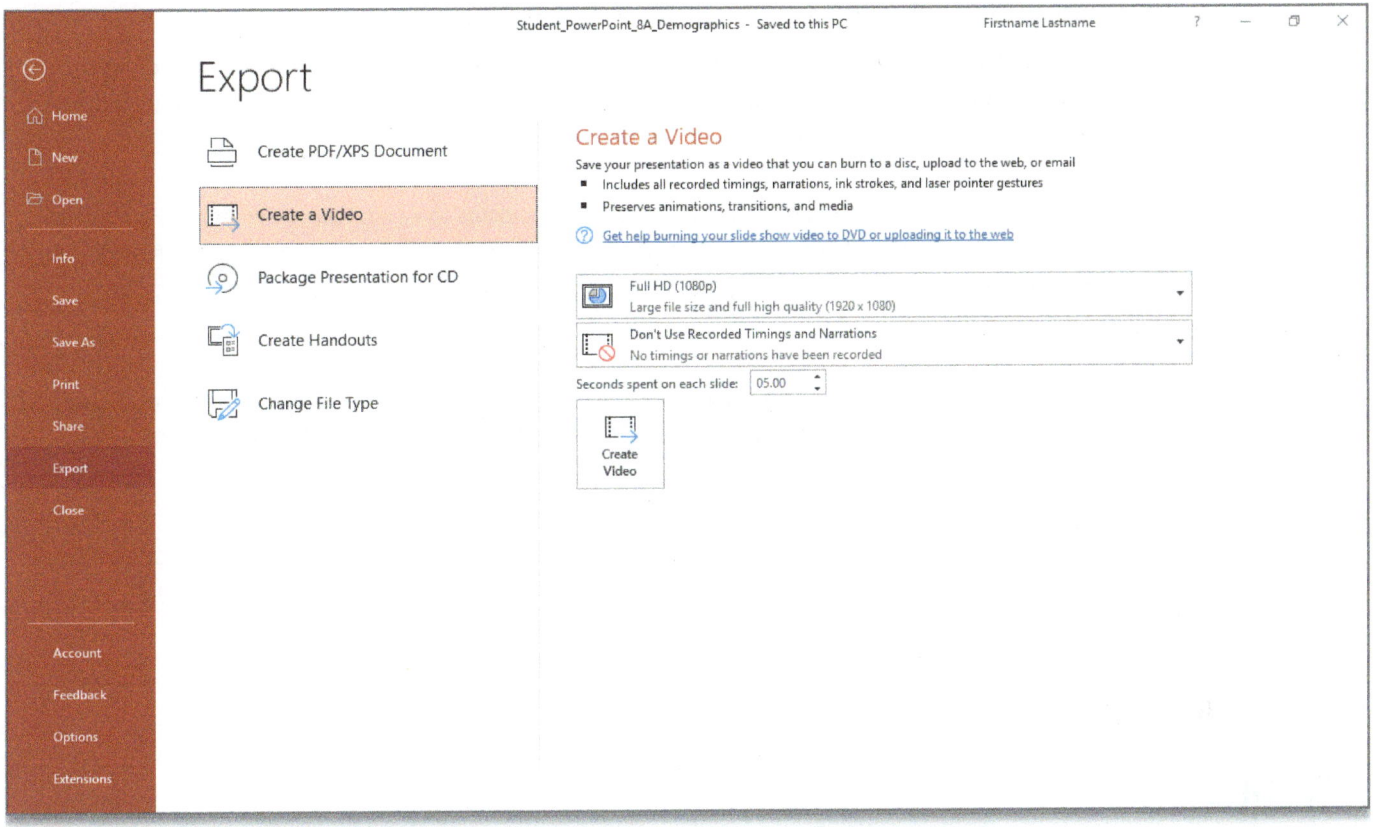

Figure 8.16

2 ▸ To the right of **Seconds spent on each slide**, change the number of seconds to **3.00**, and then click **Create Video**. In the **Save As** dialog box, in your **PowerPoint Chapter 8** folder, save the file as **Student_PowerPoint_8A_Video**

A message displays on the PowerPoint status bar indicating *Creating Student_PowerPoint_8A_Video.mp4*, which shows that the presentation is being exported to video.

3 ▸ When the *Creating video Lastname_Firstname_8A_Video.mp4* message no longer displays in the status bar, in **File Explorer**, display your **PowerPoint Chapter 8** folder. Double-click your **Student_PowerPoint_8A_Video** file to start the video—this may take a few seconds to begin.

The video opens in your default video player.

4 ▸ When the video is finished, close the video player, and then return to **PowerPoint**.

Because the slides were set for 3 seconds per slide, the slide show displays each slide for 3 seconds before advancing to the next slide.

MORE KNOWLEDGE   **Using the Package Presentation for CD Option**

A PowerPoint feature known as *Package Presentation for CD* creates a package of a presentation and related files on a CD. It can also be used to copy and save your presentation on a *network drive*, a *local drive*, or a *flash drive*. A network drive is a shared drive on another computer, such as a server, that is available to others working on the network. A local drive is a drive on your computer, such as the C: drive. A flash drive is a compact removable drive that plugs into the USB port of the computer. When you use Package Presentation for CD, the PowerPoint presentation, including all embedded and linked items—such as fonts, videos, sounds, Excel spreadsheets, and charts—are copied.

Activity 8.09 | Creating Word Handouts

When giving a presentation, you may want to distribute handouts to your audience, so they can take notes and follow along. You can print handouts from PowerPoint or create handouts as a Word document. You can edit and format the handouts in Word.

> **MAC TIP** The Mac version of PowerPoint does not support exporting handouts to Word. You can create PDF or printed handouts using the Print dialog box. Click File, click Print, and then click Show Details. Change the Layout to Handouts (3 slides per page). Click the PDF arrow and click Save as PDF. Save your file as **Student_ PowerPoint_8A_Handouts** and skip the rest of this Activity.

1 In PowerPoint, with your **Student_PowerPoint_8A_Demographics** presentation displayed, click the **File tab**, and then click **Export**. Under **Export**, click **Create Handouts**.

2 On the right, click **Create Handouts**. Compare your screen with Figure 8.17.

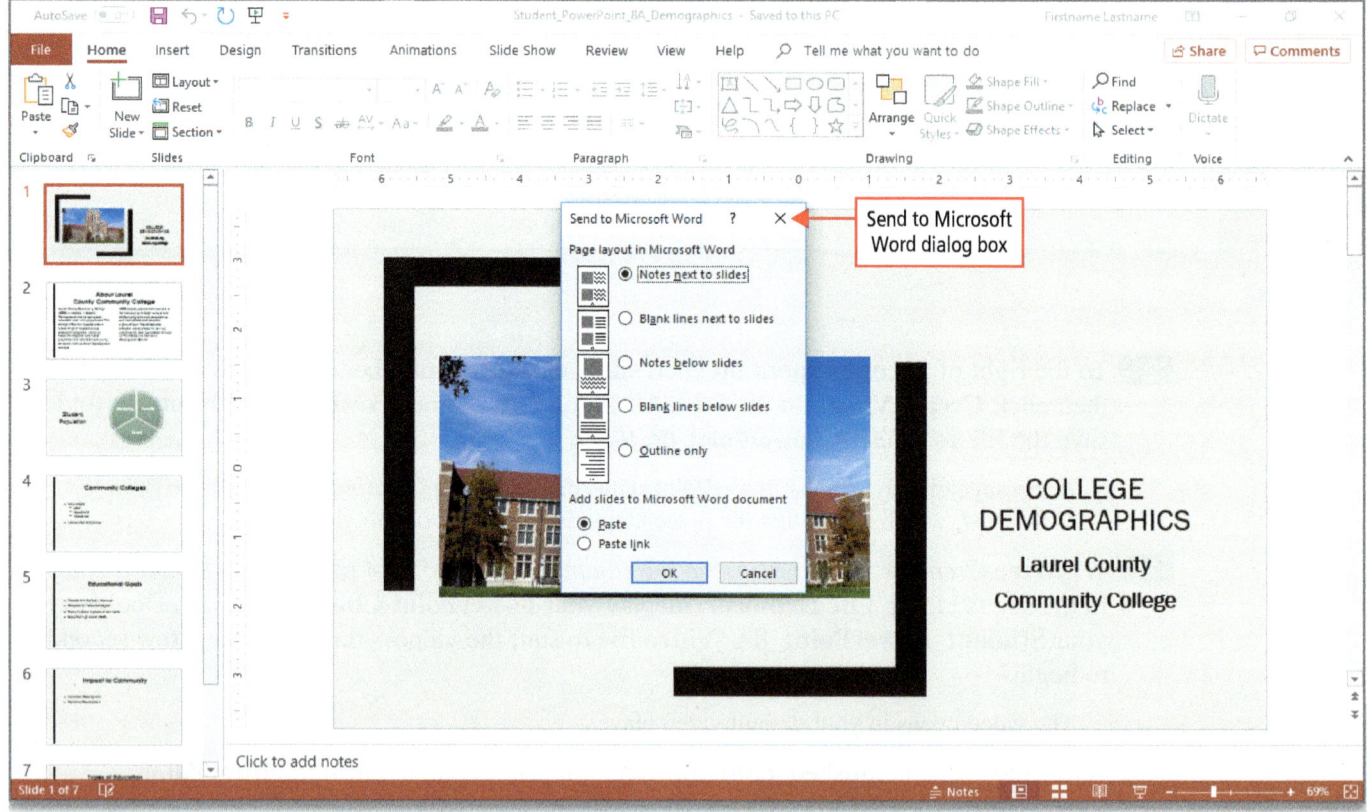

Figure 8.17

3 In the **Send to Microsoft Word** dialog box, click **Blank lines next to slides**. Under **Add slides to Microsoft Word document**, make sure **Paste** is selected, and then click **OK**.

4 On the taskbar, click the icon to switch to Word. If necessary, close the Navigation pane and scroll to the top of the document. Compare your screen with Figure 8.18.

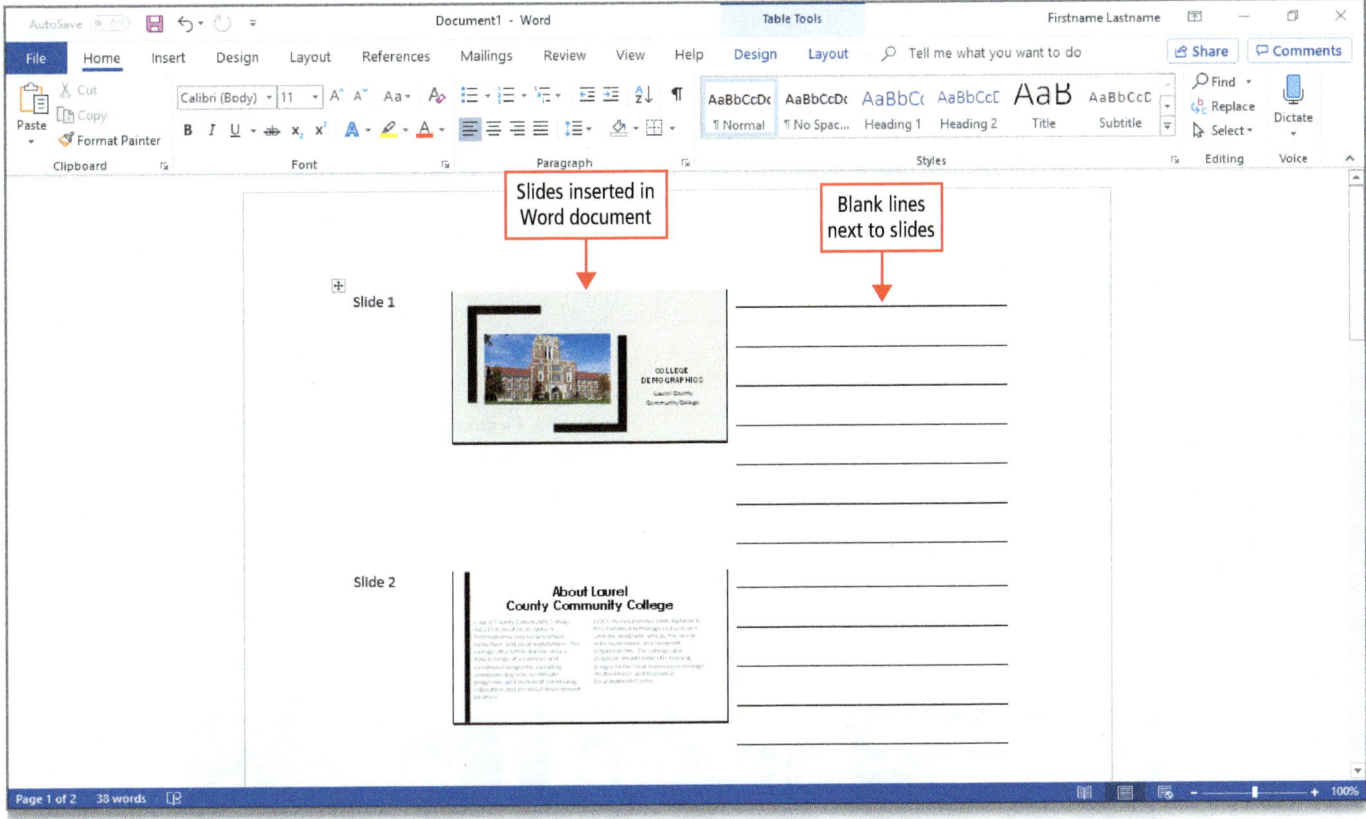

Figure 8.18

5 **Save** the Word file in your **PowerPoint Chapter 8 folder** as **Student_PowerPoint_8A_Handouts** and then **Close** ☒ Word.

6 **Close** PowerPoint. As directed by your instructor, print or submit your files electronically.

You have completed Project 8A **END**

Prospective Students

This Project is not available as a **MyLab IT** grader project and is not available as a **MyLab IT** simulation.

Project Activities

In Activities 8.10 through 8.15, you will use Sway to create an online presentation for Prospective Students from the Office of Admissions at Laurel County Community College. Your completed results will look similar to Figure 8.19.

Project Files

For Project 8B, you will need:

p08B_Campus_Tour (MP4 file)
p08B_Grads (JPG file)
p08B_Prospective_Students (Word document)
p08B_Sports01 (JPG file) p08B_Sports02 (JPG file)
p08B_Sports03 (JPG file)
p08B_Sports04 (JPG file)
p08B_Student01 (JPG file)

You will save your Sways as:

Lastname_Firstname_8B_Prospective_Students
Lastname_Firstname_8B_Remix

Project Results

GO! Project 8B
Where We're Going

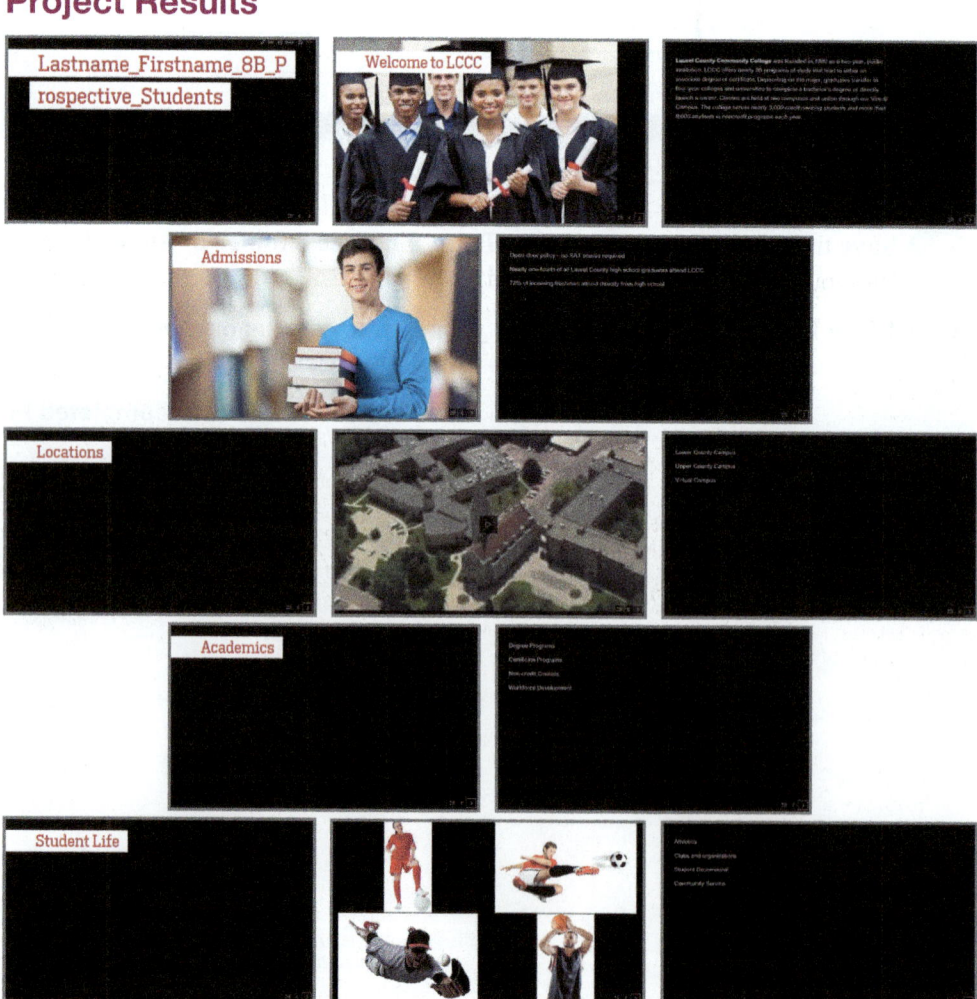

Figure 8.19 Project 8B Prospective Students

Objective 5	Create a Sway Presentation

GO! Learn How
Video P8-5

Microsoft Sway is a free presentation tool that you can use to create and share interactive reports and presentations. Sway uses cards to organize your content—text, images, and videos. There is a web-based version, and an app version for various platforms.

NOTE   Create Your Microsoft Account if You Have Not Already Done So

To benefit from this instruction and understand your own computer, be sure that you know your Microsoft account login and password and use that to set up your user account. If you need to create a Microsoft account, go to account.microsoft.com and click Create a free Microsoft account.

Activity 8.10 | Creating a Sway from a Word Outline

ALERT   Working with Web-Based Applications and Services

Computer programs and services on the web receive continuous updates and improvements, so the steps to complete this web-based activity may differ from the ones shown. You can often look at the screens and the information presented to determine how to complete the activity.

You can create a Sway from scratch, from an existing PowerPoint presentation, or from an outline in Word. For this Sway, the content is already in a Word outline.

1 Open your browser and go to **sway.office.com**. Click **Sign in** and then, if necessary, sign in with your Microsoft account. Compare your screen with Figure 8.20.

Your My Sways page may display Sways that you have created, templates, and tutorials. The Sways on your screen may vary from those in the figure.

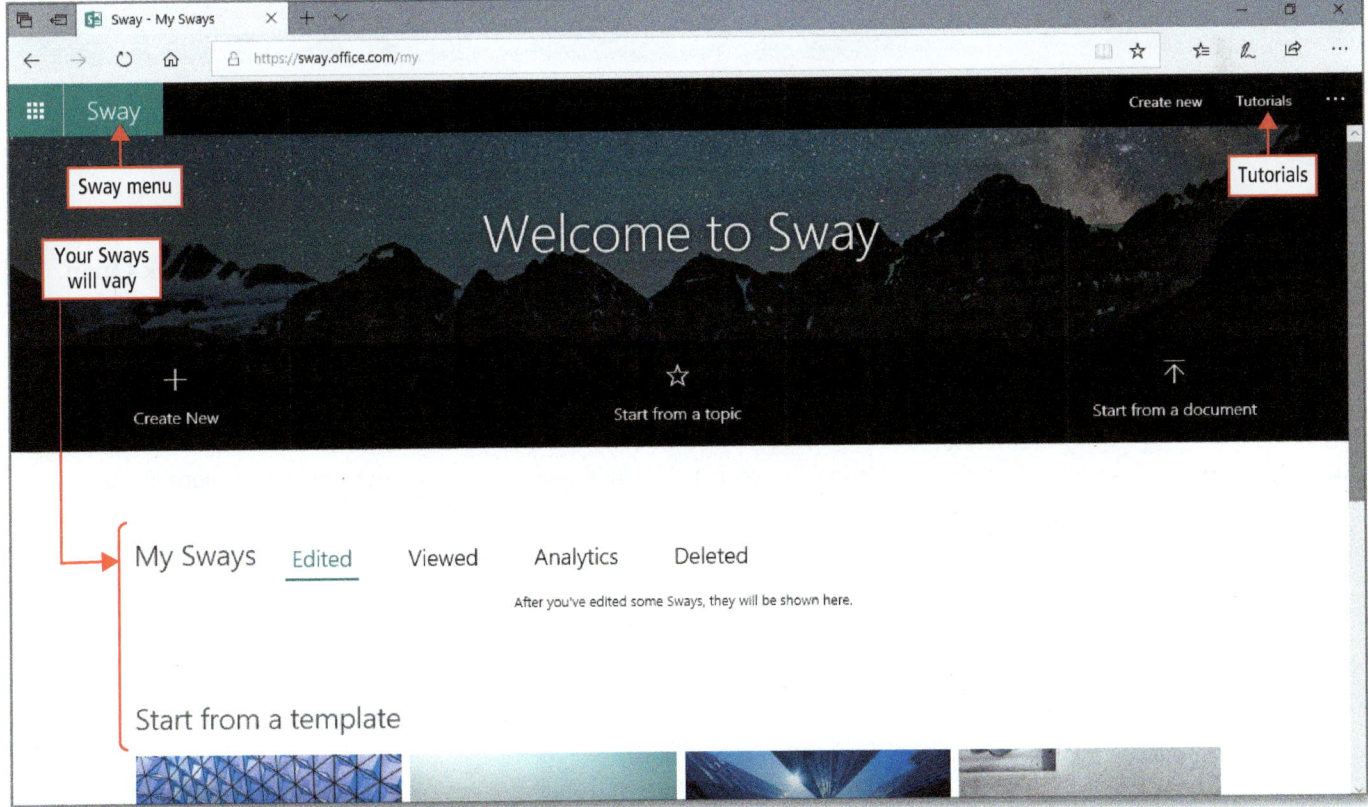

Figure 8.20

2 Start Word, navigate to the data files for this project, and then open the Word file **p08B_Prospective_Students**. If necessary, click **Enable Editing**. Compare your screen with Figure 8.21.

The Word file is formatted as an outline, using the Heading 1 style.

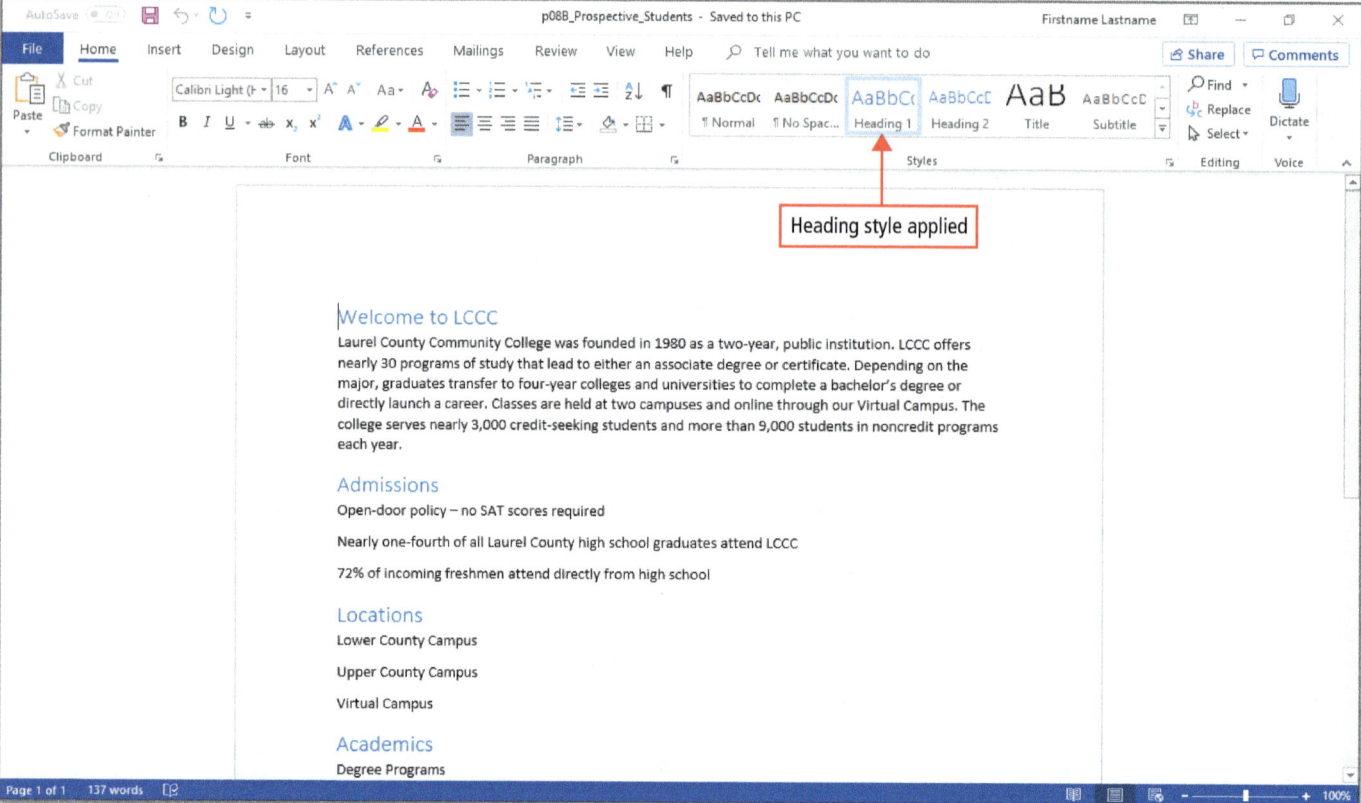

Figure 8.21

3 **Close** ☒ Word to return to your browser.

4 On the My Sways page, click **Start from a document**. In the **Open** dialog box, navigate to the data files for this project, click **p08B_Prospective_Students**, and then click **Open**. Compare your screen with Figure 8.22, and then take a moment to study the parts of the Sway window in the table in Figure 8.23.

A new Sway is created using the content from the Word file.

ALERT Sway applies various formatting styles to your presentation; thus your screens may not match the images in this text exactly.

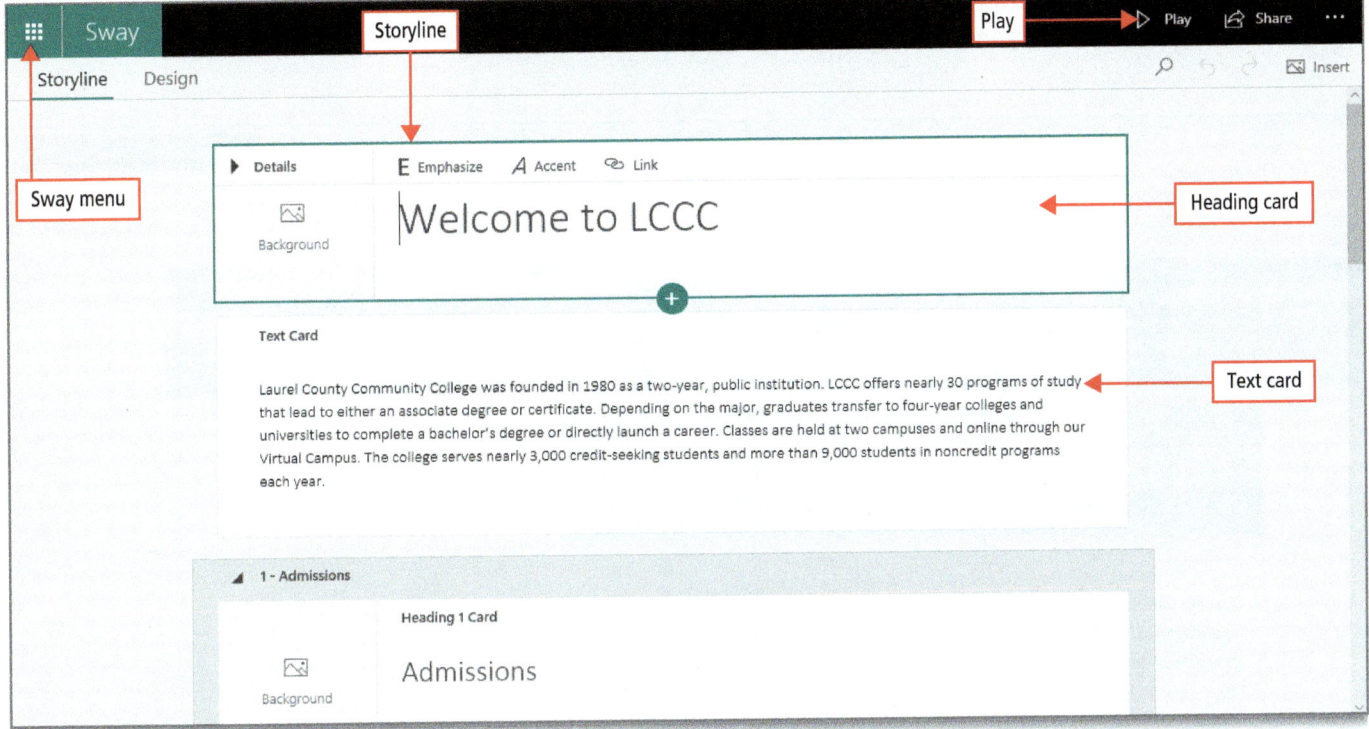

Figure 8.22

Screen Element	Description
Sway menu bar	Contains commands to create and format a Sway.
Storyline	Displays the cards that make up a Sway. Here you can insert, edit, and format your content.
Card	A content element that includes the type of content and commands and settings to work with the content.
Insert button	Displays content source menu to insert different types of content into a Sway.
Design tab	Enables you to preview the way a Sway looks and behaves, and apply themes and style, change fonts, and change layouts.
Play button	Preview how your Sway will appear when you share it.
Share button	Enables you to share your Sway with others.

Figure 8.23 Microsoft Sway Screen Elements

> **5** In the Sway **Storyline**, click in the first card that contains the title *Welcome to LCCC*, and then using your own name, change the title to **Lastname_Firstname_8B_Prospective_Students**

6 On the right side of the screen, click **Play** to view your Sway, and then compare your screen with Figure 8.24.

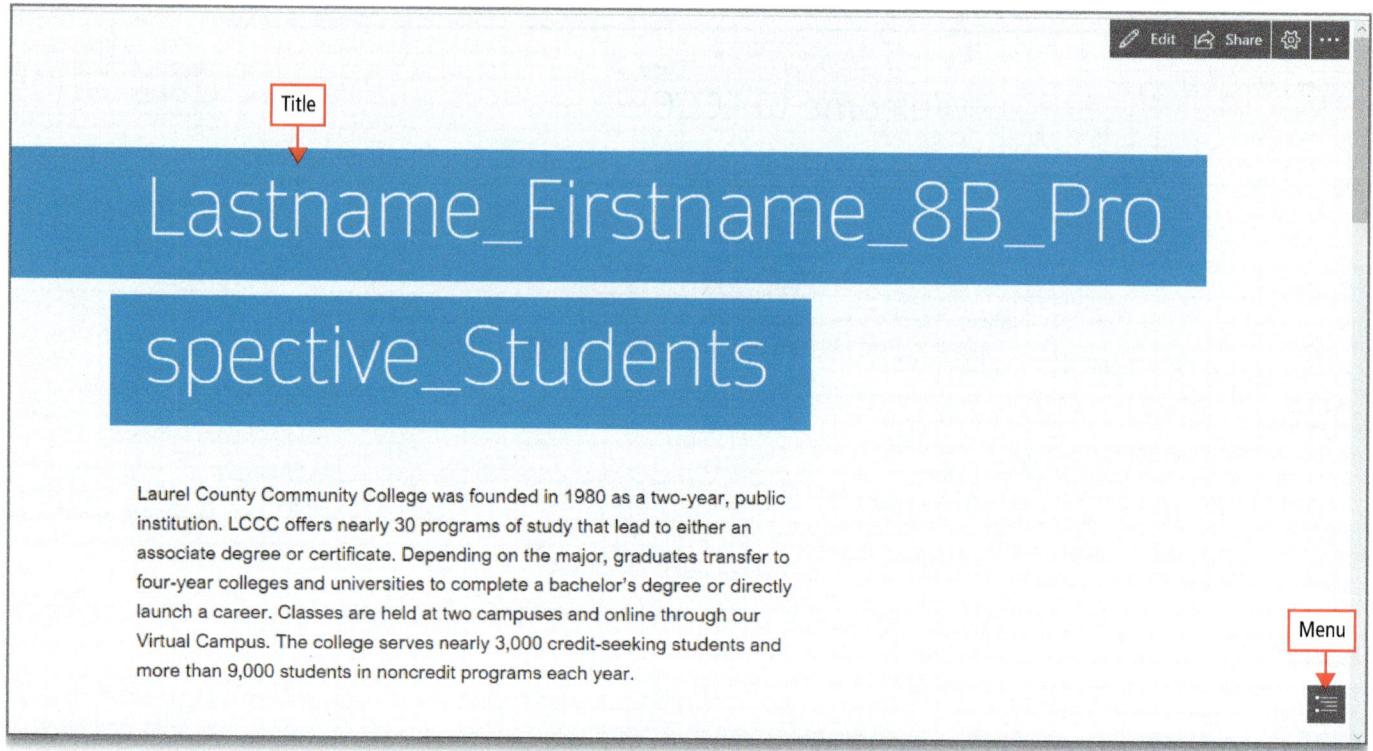

Figure 8.24

7 Use the scroll bar to view the entire Sway, and then in the upper right, click **Edit** to return to your storyline.

| Objective 6 | Add Content to a Sway Presentation |

GO! Learn How
Video P8-6

A Sway can contain different types of content, including text, images, and videos. Like PowerPoint, use visual elements to enhance your presentation.

Activity 8.11 | Adding Images

A Sway can contain different types of content, however the outline you used to create this Sway contains only text. Typically, you will want to add photos and video to enhance your Sway.

1 **In the Storyline**, with the Title card selected, click the **Insert Content button** and compare your screen with Figure 8.25.

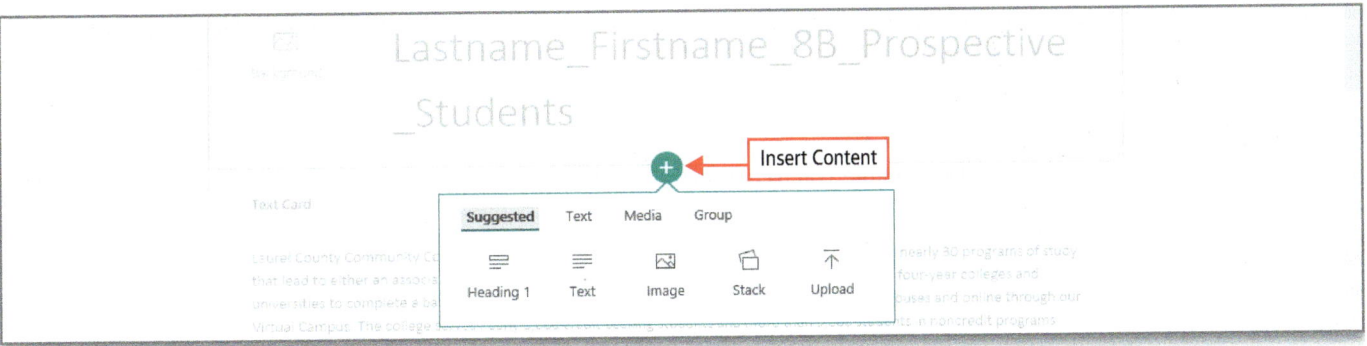

Figure 8.25

2 ▸ Click **Heading 1** to insert a Heading 1 card. In the **Add a first-level heading** box, type **Welcome to LCCC** Notice above the card the words *Welcome to LCCC* display.

The heading card followed by text card display together and are treated as a *Group*—objects that are displayed together on the screen.

3 ▸ On the **Heading card**, click **Background**. On the right, notice that **Suggested** is selected, Scroll to the bottom of the Suggested menu and then compare your screen with Figure 8.26.

You can insert an image from many sources, including your OneDrive storage, social media accounts, and files stored on your computer. When you insert media such as pictures or videos, the Sway Suggested menu displays, showing options that include your OneDrive and popular social media sites. In the Suggested pane, media clips display, based on a Bing search using the terms in your Sway.

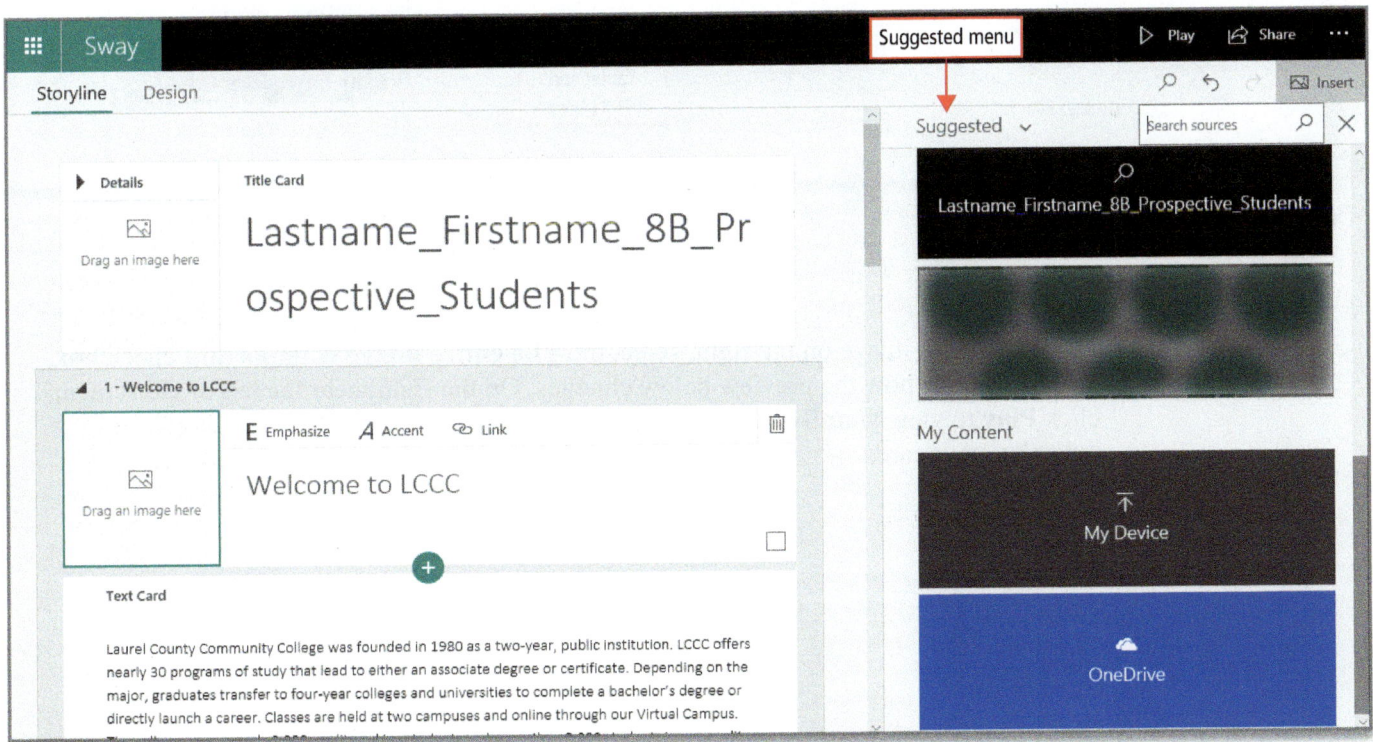

Figure 8.26

4 At the bottom of the **Suggested** menu, click **My Device**. In the **Open** dialog box, navigate to your data files for this project, and then double-click **p08B_Grads**. If necessary, close the Suggested pane. Scroll so the **Heading card** is near the top of your screen. In the **Heading card**, click the image, click **Focus Points**, and then compare your screen with Figure 8.27.

Focus Points enable you to define the parts of an image that are important to display. The preview on the lower left shows how the image will display on mobile devices such as a cell phone or tablet; the preview on the right shows how the image will display in a browser.

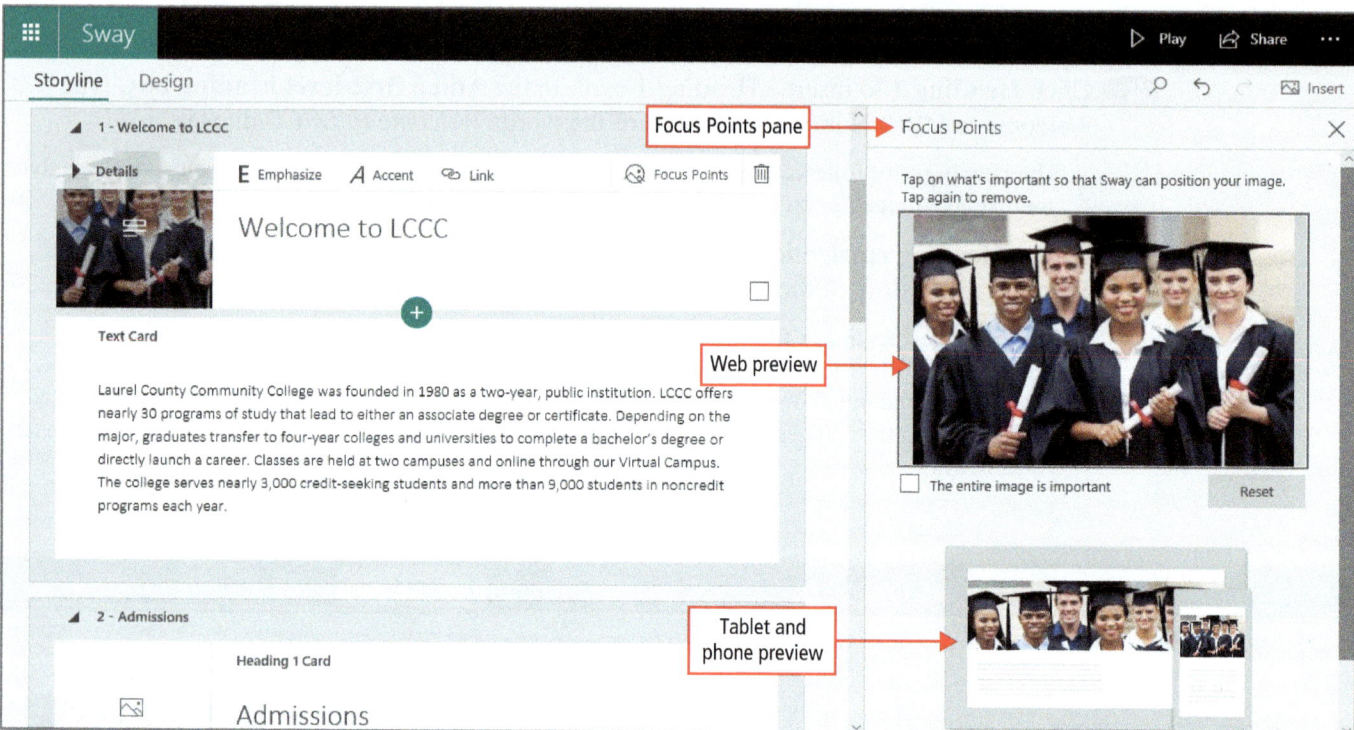

Figure 8.27

5 Under the large image on the right, select the **The entire image is important** check box, and then notice how the preview below changes. On the right, near the top of the screen, click **Play** to view your Sway in your browser. Then in the upper right, click **edit** to redisplay your cards.

6 Using the technique you just practiced, insert the image **p08B_Student01** as the background for the *Admissions* **Heading card**. On the *Admissions* **Heading card**, if necessary, click the image, and then click **Focus Points**.

7 In the large preview image, click the top of the student's head to set the first focus point. Click the top of the stack of books to set the second focus point. Notice how the preview images change as you set the focus points of the image. Compare your screen with Figure 8.28.

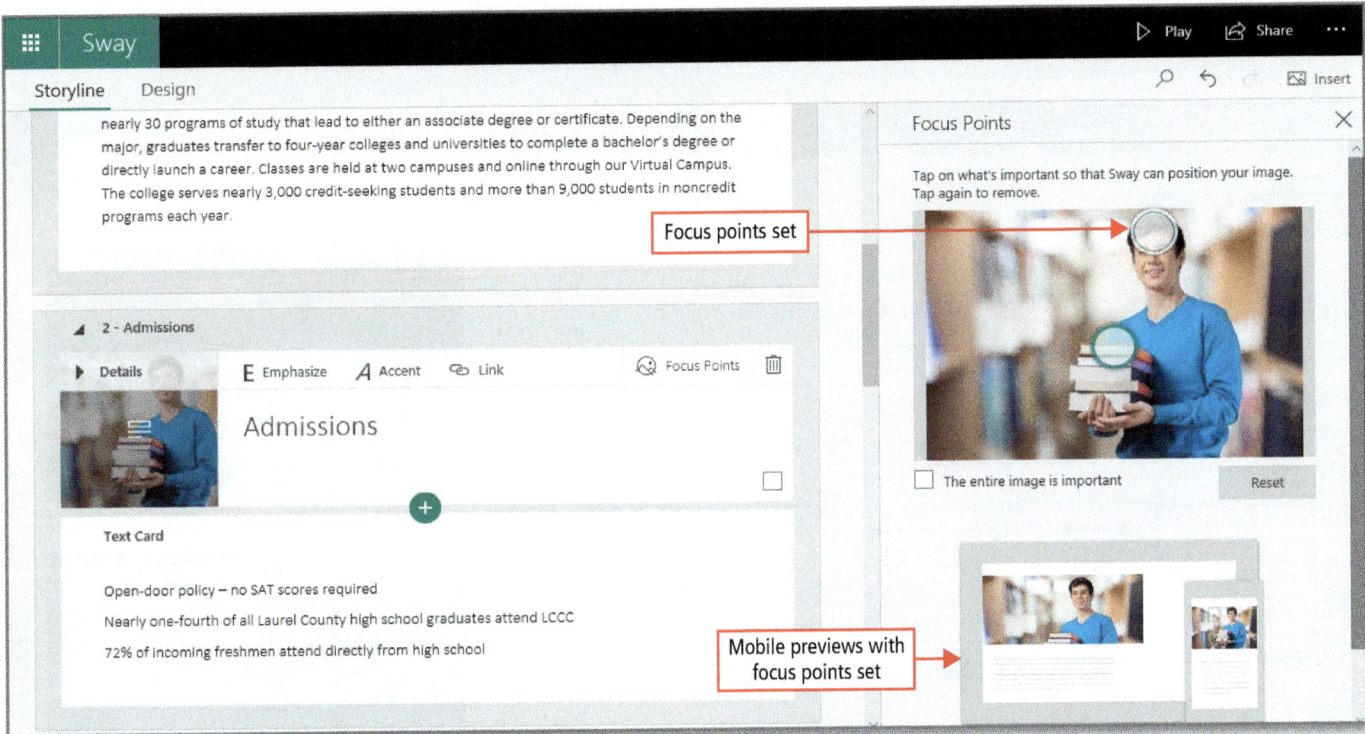

Figure 8.28

8 Click **Play** to preview your Sway so far, and then click **Edit** to return to the storyline. **Close** the **Focus Points** pane.

Activity 8.12 | Adding an Image Group

You can group cards in a Sway to display objects on the same screen. You can group images in three ways: grid, stack, or slide show.

1 In the **Storyline**, scroll down to display the *Student Life* **Heading card**. Click in the text *Student Life* to select it, and then click the **Insert Content button**.

2 Click **Media**, and then click **Image** to add an image card below the *Student Life* **Heading card**. Scroll to the bottom of the **Suggested** pane and compare your screen with Figure 8.29.

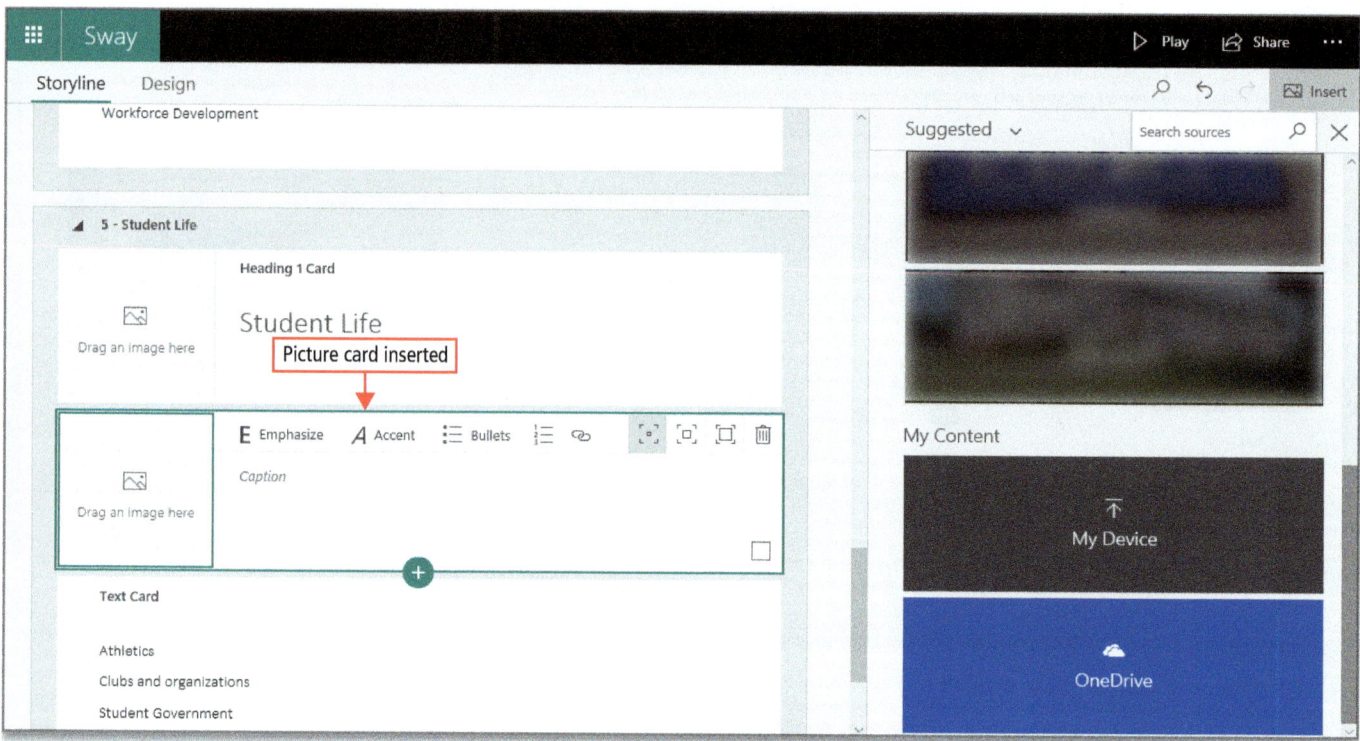

Figure 8.29

3 In the **Suggested** pane, click **My Device**.

4 If necessary, navigate to your student data files for this project. In the **Open** dialog box, click **p08B_Sports01**, press and hold Shift, and then click **p08B_Sports_04** to select four pictures. Release Shift, and then click **Open**.

5 **Close** the **Suggested** pane. If necessary, click to select the check box for each picture, and then compare your screen with Figure 8.30.

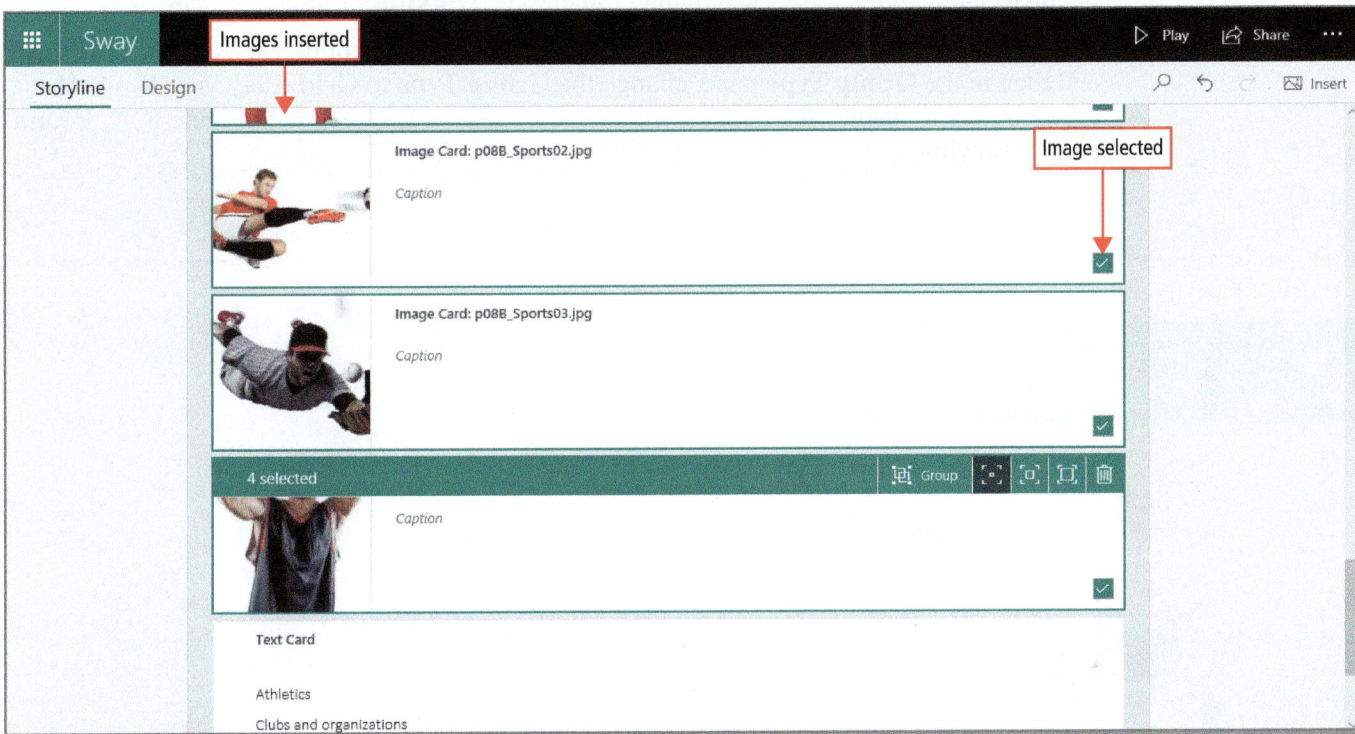

Figure 8.30

6 On the green *4 selected* bar, click **Group**. On the **Group Type** pane, click **Stack**. **Play** your Sway, scroll to the **Student Life** stack and click **Tap to flip through this stack to** view the images. Return to the storyline.

> The images are grouped and the Group Type pane displays on the left. In the Stack layout, all images are resized to the same size and displayed in a pile. This layout does not work well for the images selected.

7 Click the first image of the student wearing a red uniform, and then at the top of the card, click **Focus Points**. Select the **The entire image is important** check box. In the same manner, set the focus points for each of the remaining images to **The entire image is important**.

8 Click the top of the **Image card Group: Stack** to display the commands, click **Group Type**, and then in the **Group Type** pane, change the **Group Type** to **Grid**. **Play** your Sway. Use the scroll bar to display the images, and then compare your screen with Figure 8.31. Return to the **Storyline**.

Figure 8.31

Activity 8.13 | Adding Video

The Engineering Club has created an aerial video of the campus, shot with the quadrotor drone they built. You can insert this video into your Sway.

1 In the **Storyline**, scroll up to the **Locations** group. Click in the *Locations* **Heading card**, and then at the bottom of the card, click **Insert Content**.

2 Under **Media**, click **Video**. In the **Suggested** pane, scroll down and then click **My Device**.

3 If necessary, navigate to your data files for this project. In the **Open** dialog box, click **p08B_Campus_Tour**, and then click **Open**. **Close** the **Suggested** pane, and then compare your screen with Figure 8.32.

The video is inserted into the Sway, and a thumbnail preview displays on the card in the Storyline.

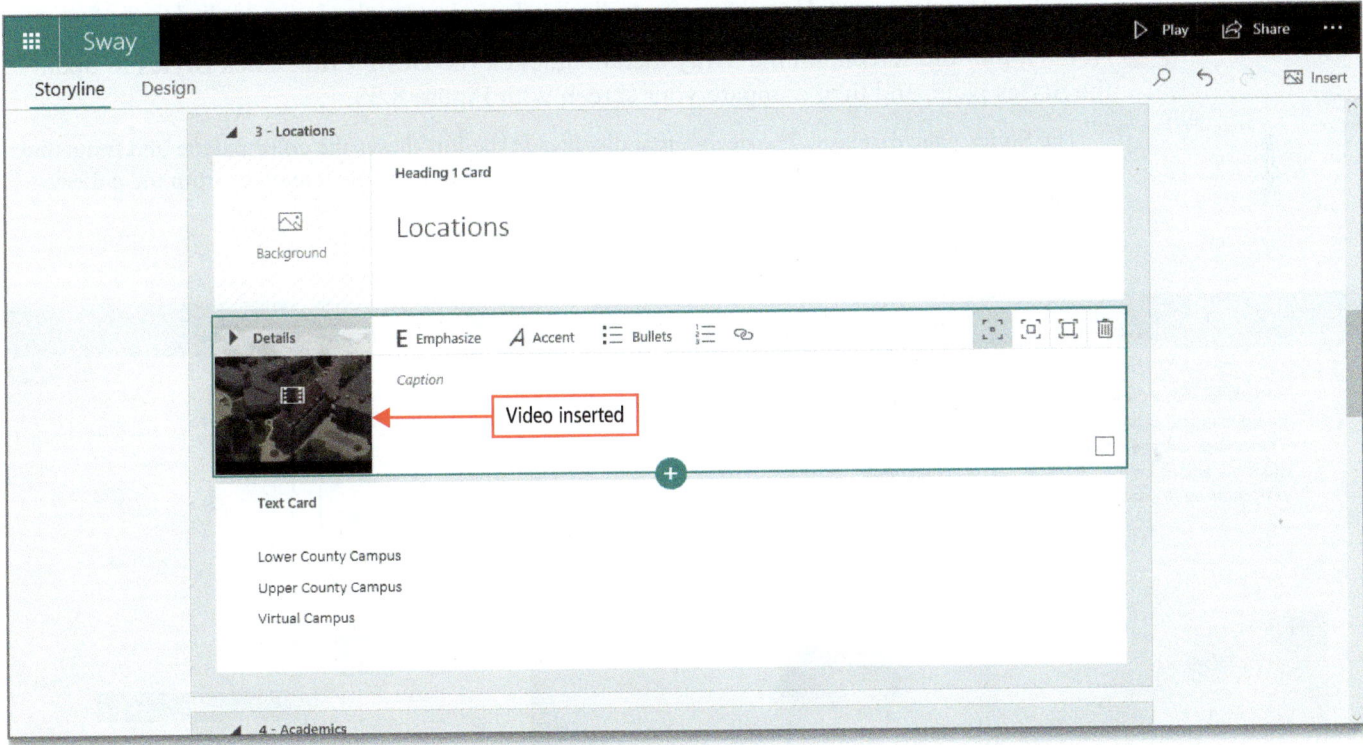

Figure 8.32

4 **Play** your Sway, and then return to the storyline.

Objective 7 | Format a Sway Presentation

GO! Learn How
Video P8-7

You can format your Sway using built-in color palettes and layouts, and you can customize your Sway to match your design needs.

Activity 8.14 | Formatting a Sway

The college colors are red and black, so you will format this Sway using an appropriate color palette and fonts to match the college brand.

1 In the **Storyline**, scroll to display and then click the **Welcome to LCCC** group. On the **Text card**, select the text *Laurel County Community College*, and then click **Emphasize**. Select the last sentence, and then click **Accent**.

By clicking Emphasis, which is similar to bold, or Accent, which is similar to italics, you can apply font styles to text. How these effects display depends upon the design applied to the Sway.

2 At the top of the screen, on the Sway menu bar, click the **Design tab**. Click **Styles** to open the **Styles** pane, and then compare your screen with Figure 8.33.

The Styles pane displays. The design that displays at the top shows the color palette and fonts that have been applied to the Sway. You can customize this design or select another from the gallery below.

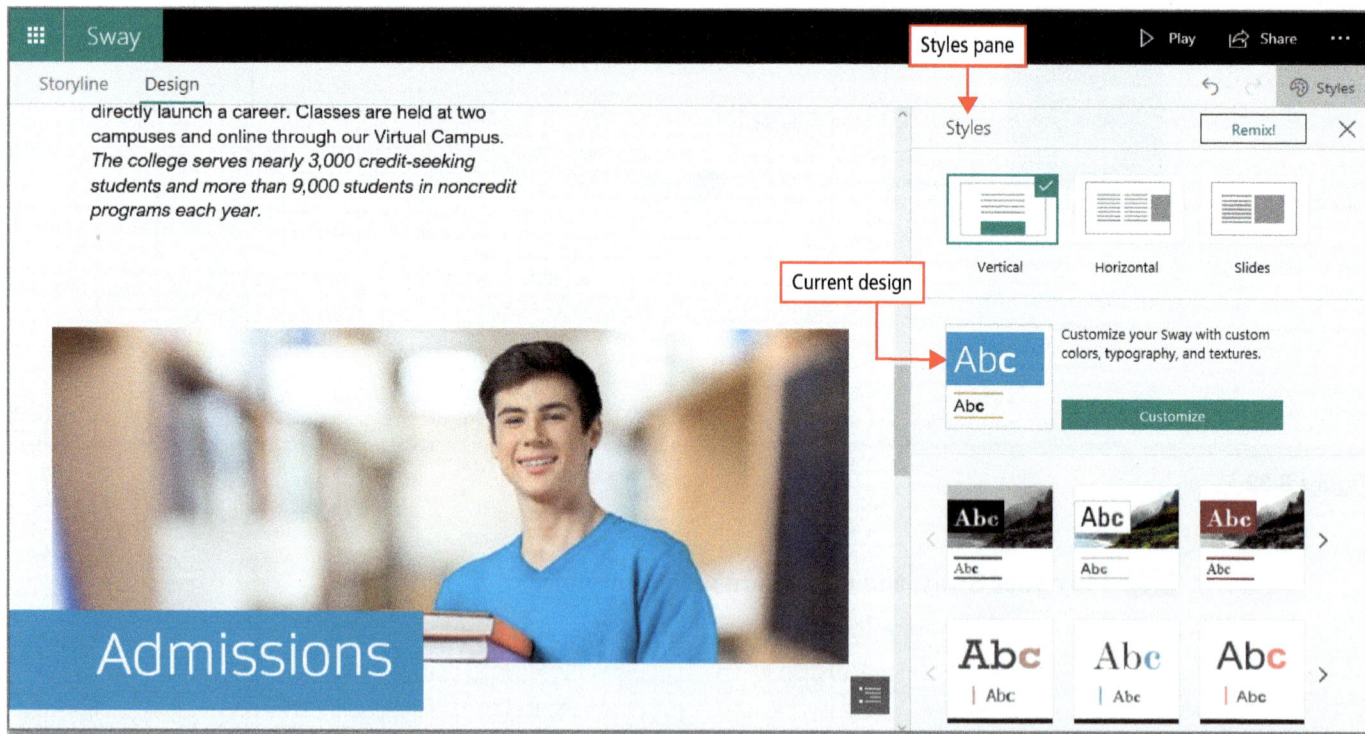

Figure 8.33

3 Click several different options in the gallery and view the Preview to see them applied. Then, click **Customize**. Under **Color inspiration**, notice that the images that you have inserted in the Sway display. If necessary, click the > to scroll to display **Color Option:3**, the picture of the student standing with a white ball, and then click the image.

4 Under **Color palettes**, several new color palettes display, based on the colors in the selected image. Click the first palette, and then compare your screen with Figure 8.34.

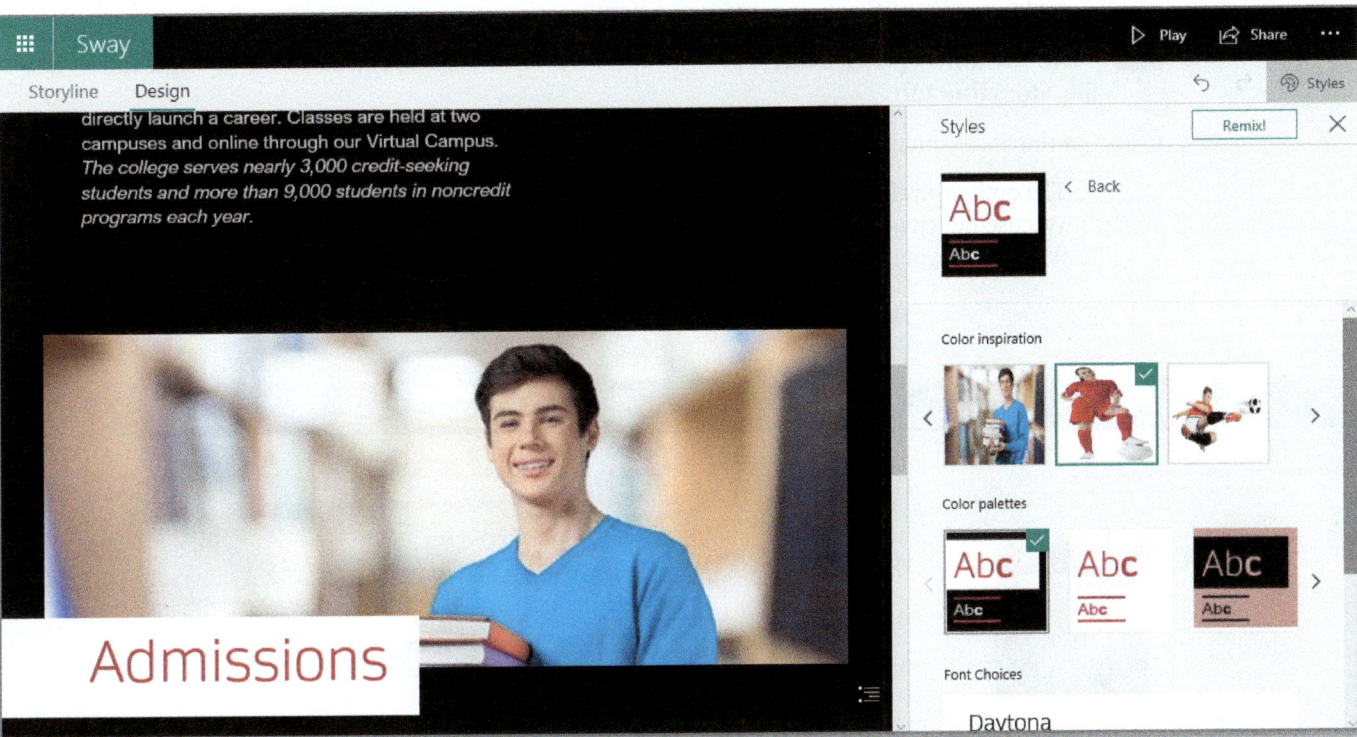

Figure 8.34

5 If necessary, scroll down to display the **Font Choices**. Click the **Font Choices arrow**, locate and then click **Heron Arial Nova**. **Close** the **Styles** pane, play your Sway, and then return to the storyline.

6 Open the **Styles** pane. At the top of the **Styles** pane, notice the three layout options: Vertical, Horizontal, and Slides.

There are three options for layout, which refers to how the Sway will display on the screen. Your Sway can scroll vertically, like a web page; scroll horizontally, left to right, more like a book; or you can set the layout to Slides— optimized for presentation, which displays content more like a traditional PowerPoint, one screen at a time.

7 Click the third option, **Slides**, play your Sway, click **Edit** to return to the **Design tab**. Click the **Storyline tab**.

8 On the Sway menu bar, click **Share**. Compare your screen with Figure 8.35.

The options available to share your Sway may vary, depending upon the type of Microsoft account you used to create the Sway. You can share on Docs.com, popular social media sites, or by sharing the URL of your Sway on Sway.com.

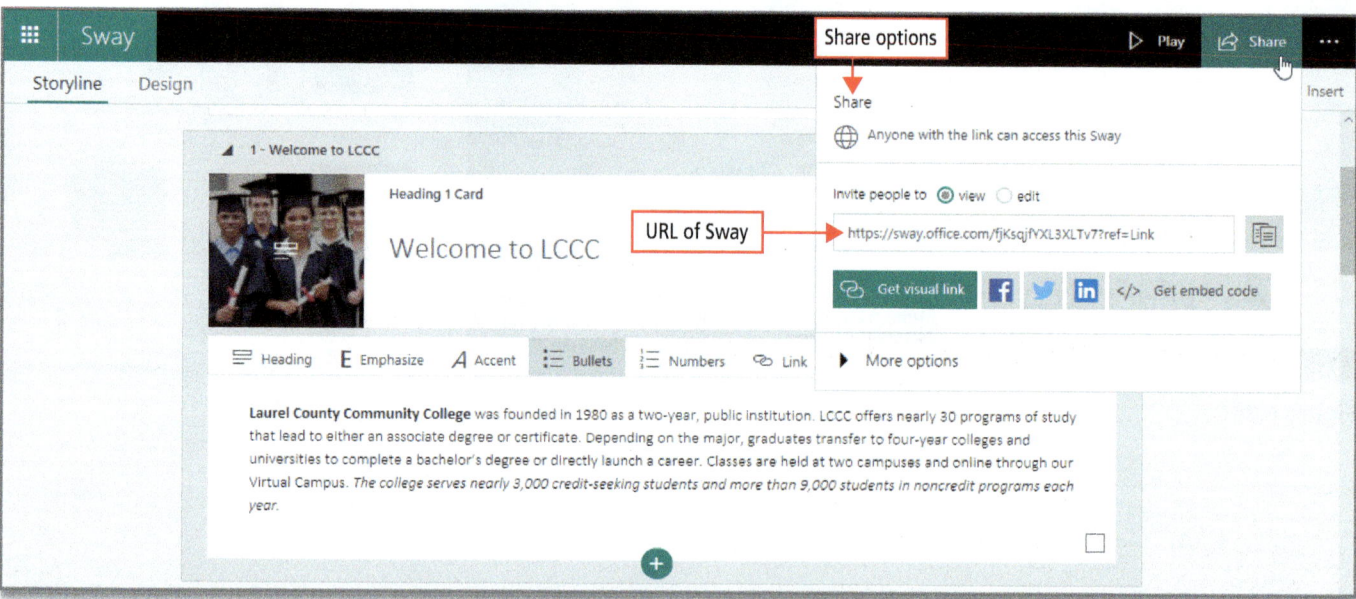

Figure 8.35

9 As directed by your instructor, Share your Sway link with your instructor.

10 On the Sway menu bar, on the right, click **Discover more available options** ![icon], and then click **Export.**

11 In the **Export your Sway** dialog box, click **PDF**. Save the PDF file in your **PowerPoint Chapter 8** folder and submit as directed by your instructor.

Activity 8.15 | Remixing Your Sway

You can customize and design the layout and other elements of a Sway, or you can use the professionally designed options included in Sway. To try out some additional features in Sway, the college will duplicate the Sway so they can continue editing one copy, while keeping the original unchanged.

1 On the Sway menu bar, on the right, click **Discover more available options** ▪▪▪, and then click **Duplicate this Sway**. In the **Duplicate this Sway** dialog box, change the name to **Lastname_Firstname_8B_Remix** and then compare your screen with Figure 8.36.

Duplicate this Sway

We'll create a copy of this Sway and add it to your My Sways page. You can rename it first if you want.

Lastname_Firstname_8B_Remix

Duplicate

Figure 8.36

2 Click **Duplicate**. When the Sway is duplicated, click **Go to My Sways**, and then compare your screen with Figure 8.37.

Two copies of your Sway display.

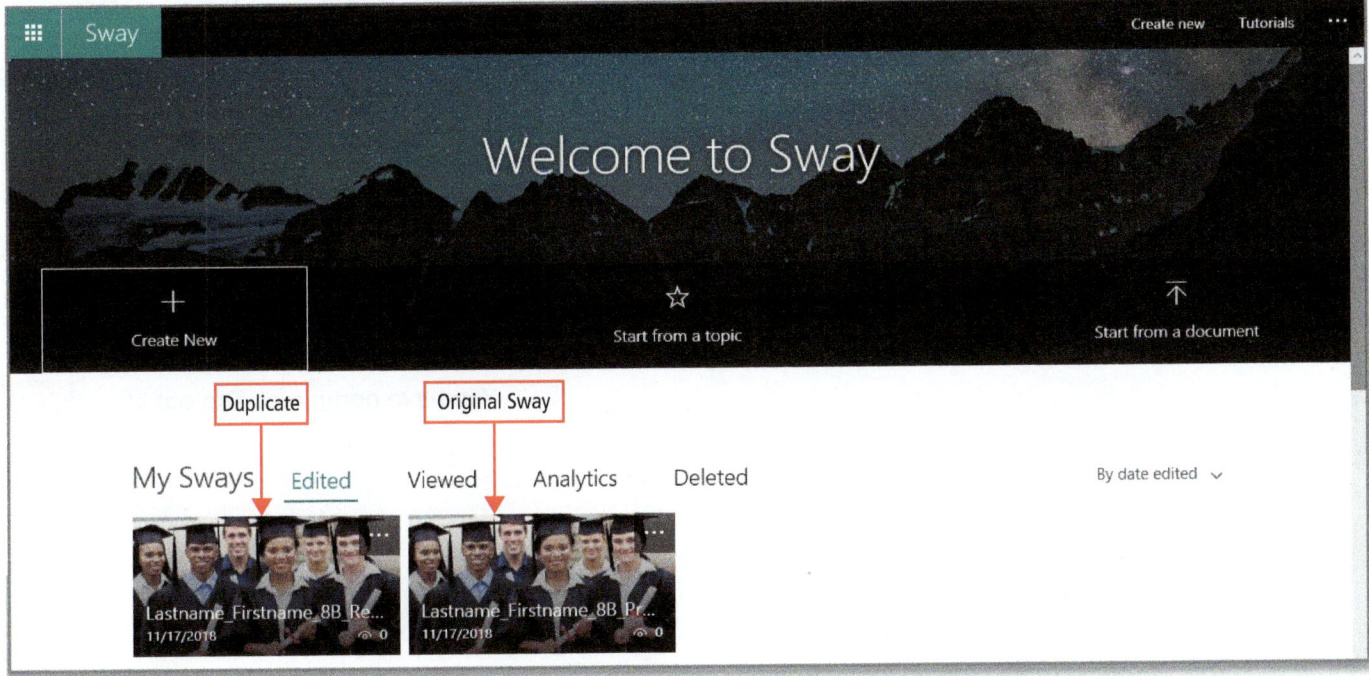

Figure 8.37

3 Click your **Lastname_Firstname_8B_Remix** Sway to open it. Click the **Design tab**, click **Styles**, and then click **Remix!** Compare your screen with Figure 8.38 . Your design may differ.

Remix applies a new design to the Sway. The design applied is randomly selected, and includes color palette, fonts, and navigation changes.

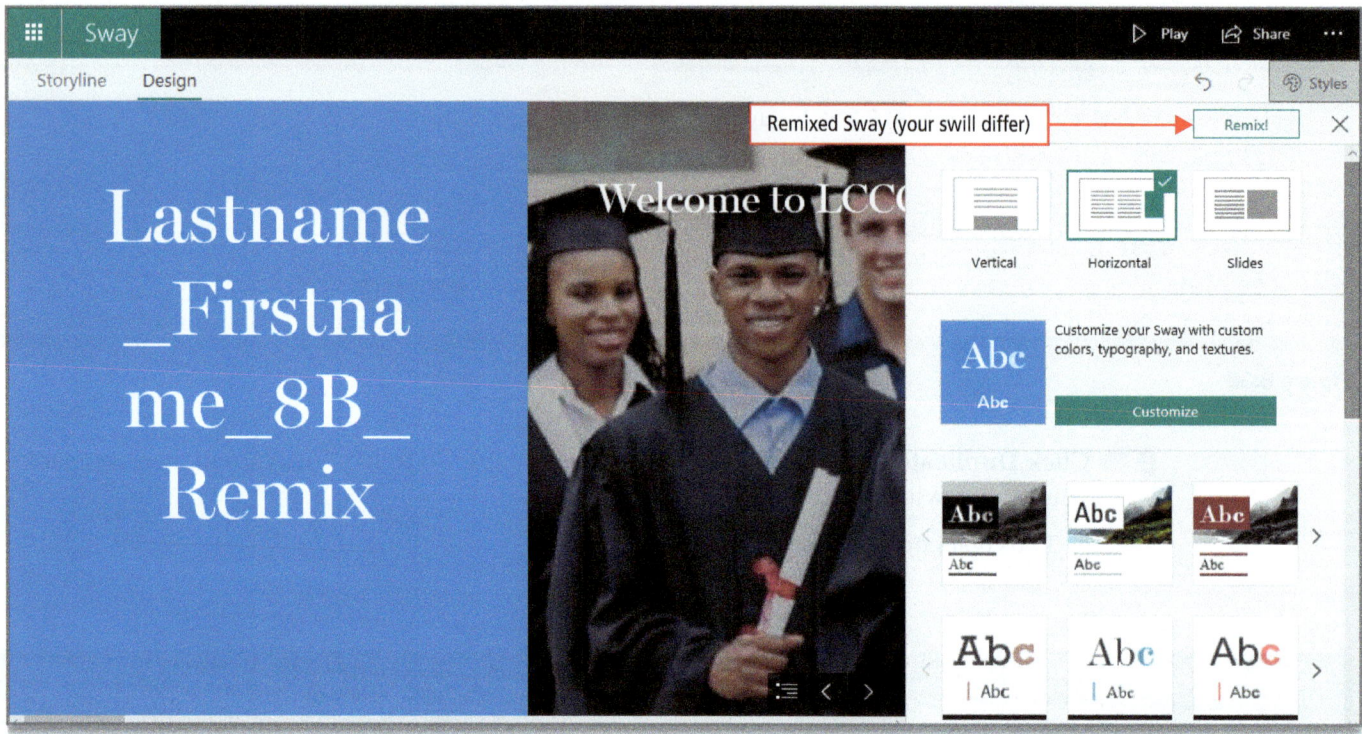

Figure 8.38

4 On the Sway command bar, click **Remix!** several times until you find a design that you like.

5 As directed by your instructor, export or share your Sway. Sign out of Sway and close your browser.

You have completed Project 8B **END**

wavebreakmedia/Shutterstock, Monkey Business Images/Fotolia, Ivanko80/Shutterstock, Monkey Business Images/Shutterstock

8

POWERPOINT

Microsoft Office Specialist (MOS) Skills In This Chapter		
Project 8A		

1.5.6 Export presentations to other formats
2.1.1 Import Word document outlines
3.1.2 Format text in multiple columns

Build Your E-Portfolio

An E-Portfolio is a collection of evidence, stored electronically, that showcases what you have accomplished while completing your education. Collecting and then sharing your work products with potential employers reflects your academic and career goals. Your completed documents from the following projects are good examples to show what you have learned: 8G, 8K, and 8L.

GO! For Job Success

Discussion: Internship

Your instructor may assign this discussion to your class, and then ask you to think about, or discuss with your classmates, these questions:

The demand for experienced employees has made internships a fact of life for many college students. The experience gained during an internship is so valuable in gaining regular employment that some recent graduates will take an unpaid internship to gain entry to a good company. At some companies, the competition for internships is as intense as for a full-time job.

Internships provide an opportunity for students to try out an industry or job before committing to full-time employment. Employers benefit by seeing a possible future employee in a real-world job setting, not just on a resume and interview. The value of internships to the student raises the question of whether and how much an intern should be paid. Employers may feel that the experience and opportunities for full-time jobs they provide are valuable enough that they do not need to provide pay, too. Students, on the other hand, are working and providing value to the company while gaining experience, so they often feel they deserve to be paid. Laws governing when an internship can be unpaid or must be paid can be vague.

g-stockstudio/Shutterstock

What do you think are some other benefits to interns and employers?

Would you consider taking an unpaid internship? What value would you expect to receive in return for your work?

Do you think employers always have an obligation to pay interns, or are there benefits that outweigh payment?

End of Chapter

Summary

You can create a PowerPoint presentation using content from other files. Importing a Word document formatted using Heading styles creates a new slide from each line formatted as Heading 1.

To make large paragraphs of text easier to read, use bullets, divide text into multiple slides, or format the text as columns. Good design follows a 7x7 rule—a maximum of seven lines, with no more than seven words each.

To ensure a professional impression, make sure to proof your presentation. Use the spelling check and Smart Lookup tool to open the Smart Lookup pane to verify spelling and correct word usage.

Sway is an online storytelling, presentation tool that you can use to create presentations that display in a browser. You can start with an existing PowerPoint or Word document or create a Sway from scratch.

GO! Learn It Online

Review the concepts, key terms, and MOS skills in this chapter by completing these online challenges, which you can find in **MyLab IT**.

Chapter Quiz: Answer matching and multiple choice questions to test what you learned in this chapter.

Lessons on the GO!: Learn how to use all the new apps and features as they are introduced by Microsoft.

MOS Prep Quiz: Answer questions to review the MOS skills that you practiced in this chapter.

Project Guide for PowerPoint Chapter 8

Your instructor will assign Projects from this list to ensure your learning and assess your knowledge.

Project	Apply Skills from These Chapter Objectives	Project Type	Project Location
8A **MyLab IT**	Objectives 1–4 from Project 8A	**8A Instructional Project (Grader Project)** Guided instruction to learn the skills in Project 8A.	In **MyLab IT** and in text
8B	Objectives 5–7 from Project 8B	**8B Instructional Project (Grader Project)** Guided instruction to learn the skills in Project 8B.	In text
8C	Objectives 1–4 from Project 8A	**8C Skills Review (Scorecard Grading)** A guided review of the skills from Project 8A.	In text
8D	Objectives 5–7 from Project 8B	**8D Skills Review (Scorecard Grading)** A guided review of the skills from Project 8B.	In text
8E **MyLab IT**	Objectives 1–4 from Project 8A	**8E Mastery (Grader Project)** **Mastery and Transfer of Learning** A demonstration of your mastery of the skills in Project 8A with extensive decision making.	In **MyLab IT** and in text
8F	Objectives 5–7 from Project 8B	**8F Mastery (Grader Project)** **Mastery and Transfer of Learning** A demonstration of your mastery of the skills in Project 8B with extensive decision making.	In text
8G **MyLab IT**	Objectives 1–4 from Project 8A	**8G Mastery (Grader Project)** **Mastery and Transfer of Learning** A demonstration of your mastery of the skills in Project 8A with extensive decision making.	In **MyLab IT** and in text
8H	Objectives 1–4 from Project 8A	**8H GO! Fix It (Scorecard Grading)** **Critical Thinking** A demonstration of your mastery of the skills in Project 8A by creating a correct result from a document that contains errors you must find.	IRC
8I	Objectives 1–4 from Project 8A	**8I GO! Make It (Scorecard Grading)** **Critical Thinking** A demonstration of your mastery of the skills in Project 8A by creating a result from a supplied picture.	IRC
8J	Combination of Objectives from Projects 8A and 8B	**8J GO! Solve It (Rubric Grading)** **Critical Thinking** A demonstration of your mastery of the skills in Projects 8A and 8B, your decision-making skills, and your critical thinking skills. A task-specific rubric helps you self-assess your result.	IRC
8K	Combination of Objectives from Projects 8A and 8B	**8K GO! Solve It (Rubric Grading)** **Critical Thinking** A demonstration of your mastery of the skills in Projects 8A and 8B, your decision-making skills, and your critical thinking skills. A task-specific rubric helps you self-assess your result.	In text
8L	Combination of Objectives from Projects 8A and 8B	**8L GO! Think (Rubric Grading)** **Critical Thinking** A demonstration of your understanding of the chapter concepts applied in a manner that you would outside of college. An analytic rubric helps you and your instructor grade the quality of your work by comparing it to the work an expert in the discipline would create.	In text
8M	Combination of Objectives from Project 8A	**8M GO! Think (Rubric Grading)** **Critical Thinking** A demonstration of your understanding of the chapter concepts applied in a manner that you would outside of college. An analytic rubric helps you and your instructor grade the quality of your work by comparing it to the work an expert in the discipline would create.	IRC
8N from scratch	Combination of Objectives from Project 8A	**8N You and GO! (Rubric Grading)** **Critical Thinking** A demonstration of your understanding of the chapter concepts applied in a manner that you would in a personal situation. An analytic rubric helps you and your instructor grade the quality of your work.	IRC

Glossary

Glossary of Chapter Key Terms

Card A Sway content element that includes the type of content and commands and settings to work with the content.

Flash drive A compact removable drive that plugs into the USB port of the computer.

Focus Points Enable you to define the parts of an image that are important to display.

Group Objects that are displayed together on the screen in a Sway.

Hard return Created by pressing the Enter key to start a new line.

Heading style A set of formatting characteristics, such as font name, size, color, paragraph alignment, and spacing, which is used to quickly format selected text.

Joint Photographic Experts Group A file format used for photos with the .jpg and .jpeg extensions.

Local drive A drive on your computer, such as the C: drive.

Microsoft Sway A free presentation tool that you can use to create and share interactive reports and presentations.

MP4 video file (.mp4) The default file type when saving a video in PowerPoint 2016.

Network drive A shared drive on another computer, usually a server, that is available to others working on the network.

Outline view A document view in Microsoft Word that distinguishes the importance of data by the heading styles that have been applied.

Package Presentation for CD A PowerPoint feature that creates a package of a presentation and related files on a CD for ease of distribution.

Paragraph Any text that has a hard return at the end of it.

Preview Enables you to preview the way a Sway looks and behaves.

Rich Text Format (RTF) file A file format used to transfer formatted text documents between applications.

Smart Lookup A command that uses Bing to look up definitions, Wiki articles, and related searches from the web.

Smart Lookup pane A PowerPoint feature that has two tabs: Explore, which displays synonyms and web results, and Define, which displays a definition, synonyms, and word origin.

Storyline Displays the cards that make up a Sway.

Sway menu bar Contains commands to create and format a Sway.

Chapter Review

| Skills Review | Project 8C Academics |

In the following Skills Review, you will complete a PowerPoint presentation for the Laurel County Community College that gives an overview of programs and academics. You will create slides from outlines created in Word. You will format text as columns, proof your presentation for errors, and save the presentation as an outline, as a show, as a video, and as a picture. The completed presentation will look similar to Figure 8.38.

Project Files

For Project 8C, you will need:

p08C_Academic_Departments (Word document)
p08C_Academics (PowerPoint presentation)
p08C_Educational_Opportunities (Word document)
You will save your files as:
Lastname_Firstname_8C_Academics
Lastname_Firstname_8C_Handouts (Word document)
Lastname_Firstname_8C_Outline (Outline/RTF file)
Lastname_Firstname_8C_Picture (JPG file)
Lastname_Firstname_8C_Show (PowerPoint Slide Show file)
Lastname_Firstname_8C_Video (MP4 file)

Project Results

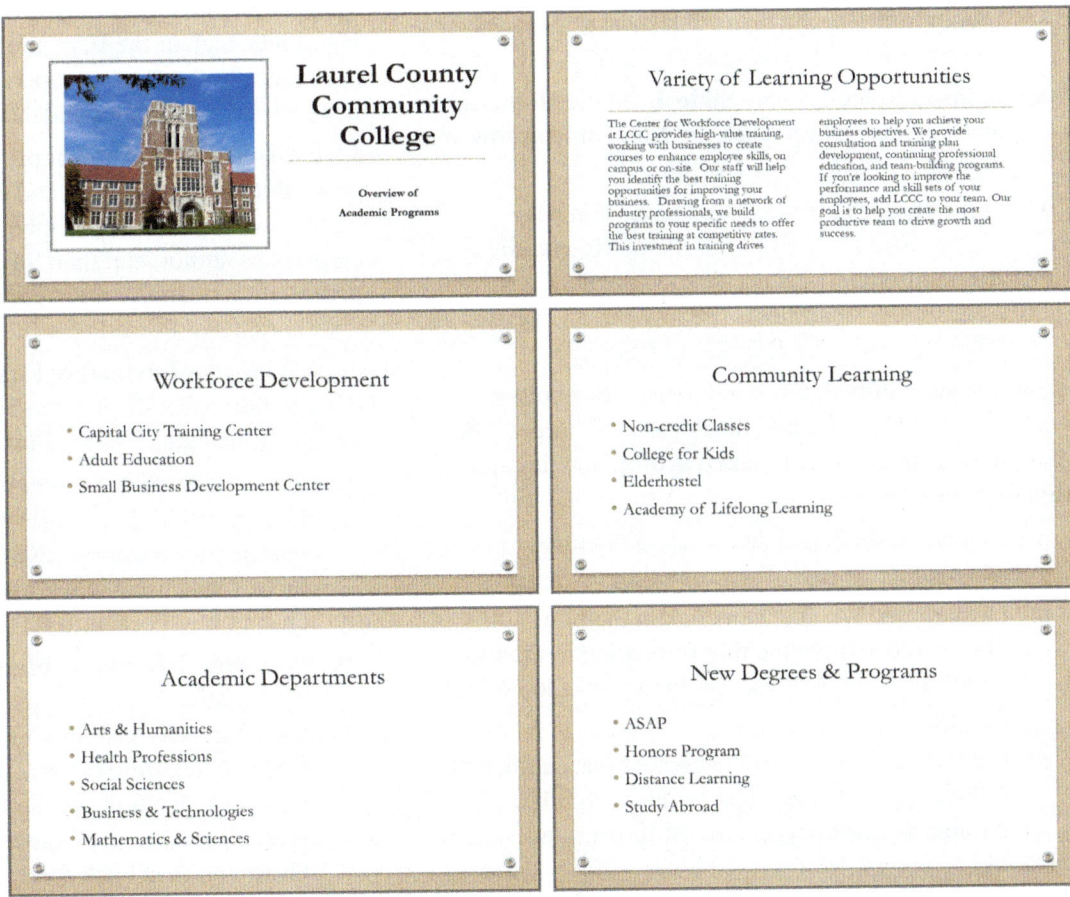

Figure 8.38, Project 8C Academics

(continues on next page)

Chapter Review

1 From the data files for this project, open the file **p08C_Academics**. In your **PowerPoint Chapter 8** folder, using your own name, save the file as **Lastname_Firstname_8C_Academics**

2 With the PowerPoint presentation open on your screen, open Microsoft Word 2019. On Word's opening screen, click **Open Other Documents**. Navigate to your student data files for this chapter, and then open **p08C_Educational_Opportunities**.

  a. In Word, on the **View tab**, in the **Show group**, if necessary, select the **Navigation Pane** check box. In the **Views group**, if necessary, click **Outline**. (Mac users, save the file as an RTF file in your PowerPoint Chapter 8 folder.)

  b. Examine the data in the file, and then **Close** Word.

3 Return to PowerPoint. Display **Slide 2**. On the **Home tab**, in the **Slides group**, click the **New Slide arrow**, and then click **Slides from Outline**.

  a. In the **Insert Outline** dialog box, navigate to your data files for this project, click **p08C_Educational_Opportunities**, and then click **Insert**. (Mac users, insert the RTF file you saved in the previous step.)

  b. In PowerPoint, Display **Slide 4**. On the **Home tab**, in the **Slides group**, click the **New Slide arrow**, and then click **Slides from Outline**.

  c. In the **Insert Outline** dialog box, from your student data files, insert the file **p08C_Academic_Departments**. (Mac users, open the p08C_Academic_Departments file in Word and save as an RTF file. Insert the RTF file in this step).

4 Display **Slide 2**. Click in the title placeholder, and then click the border to display a solid border. On the **Home tab**, in the **Clipboard group**, double-click **Format Painter**.

  a. Display **Slide 3**, and then click in the title placeholder to apply the formatting.

  b. Display **Slide 4**, and then click in the title placeholder. Apply the title formatting to the titles on **Slides 5** and **6**. Press [Esc] to turn off the Format Painter.

  c. Copy the formatting of the content placeholder on **Slide 2**, to the content placeholders on **Slides 3** through **6**. Press [Esc] to turn off the Format Painter.

5 Display **Slide 5**.

  a. In the content placeholder, right-click *Humanitites*, and then click *Humanities* to correct the spelling.

  b. On the **Review tab**, in the **Proofing group**, click **Spelling**. With *Technologies* selected in the **Spelling** pane, click **Change**. Correct the remaining three spelling errors.

6 On **Slide 3**, click in the word *Workforce*.

  a. On the **Review tab**, in the **Insights group**, click **Smart Lookup** to display the **Smart Lookup** pane.

  b. On the **Smart Lookup** pane, click the **Define tab**. Review the definition and then **Close** the **Smart Lookup** pane.

7 Display **Slide 2**. Notice that the text on this slide is one long bullet point.

  a. Click in the content placeholder. On the **Home tab**, in the **Paragraph group**, click **Bullets** to remove the bullet in the placeholder.

  b. On the **Home tab**, in the **Paragraph group**, click **Add or Remove Columns**, and then click **More Columns**. In the **Columns** dialog box, set the **Number** to **2**, change the **Spacing** to **0.5"**, and then click **OK**.

8 Insert a **Header & Footer** on the **Notes and Handouts**. Include the **Date and time** updated automatically, the **Page number**, and a **Footer**. In the **Footer** box, type **8C_Academics** and then click **Apply to All**.

9 Display the document properties. As the **Tags**, type **education, programs** and as the **Subject**, type your course and section number. Be sure your name displays as author, and then **Save** your file. Leave your presentation open. As directed by your instructor, submit your completed PowerPoint file.

10 With your **Lastname_Firstname_8C_Academics** presentation open, display the **Save As** dialog box. If necessary, navigate to your **PowerPoint Chapter 8** folder.

  a. Click the **Save as type arrow**, and then click **Outline/RTF**. In the **File name** box, type **Lastname_Firstname_8C_Outline** and then click **Save**. (Mac users, click File, click Export, and then change File Format to RTF.)

  b. With your **Lastname_Firstname_8C_Academics** presentation open, display the **Save As** dialog box. If necessary, navigate to your **PowerPoint Chapter 8** folder. Click the **Save as type arrow**, and then click **PowerPoint Show**. In the **File name** box, using your own name, type **Lastname_Firstname_8C_Show** and then click **Save**. Close the file.

(continues on next page)

Chapter Review

Skills Review: 8C Academics (continued)

c. Open your **Lastname_Firstname_8C_Academics** presentation. Display **Slide 3**. Display the **Save As** dialog box, and then, if necessary, navigate to your **PowerPoint Chapter 8** folder. Click the **Save as type arrow**, and then click **JPEG File Interchange Format**. Using your own name, change the **File name** to **Lastname_Firstname_8C_Picture** and then click **Save**. In the message box, click **Just This One**. (Mac users, click File, click Export, and then change File Format to JPG. The Mac version of PowerPoint does not include the option to save only one slide, but creates a folder containing JPEG files for each slide in the presentation.)

11 In PowerPoint, with your **Lastname_Firstname_8C_Academics** presentation displayed, click the **File tab**, and then click **Export**.

a. Under **Export**, click **Create a Video**. To the right of **Seconds spent on each slide**, change the number of seconds to **3.00**, and then click **Create Video**. In the **Save As** dialog box, in your **PowerPoint Chapter 8** folder, save the file as **Lastname_Firstname_8C_Video** (Mac users, click File, click Export, and then change File Format to MP4.)

b. In PowerPoint, with your **Lastname_Firstname_8C_Academics** presentation displayed, click the **File tab**, and then click **Export**. Under **Export**, click **Create Handouts**. On the right, click **Create Handouts**. In the **Send to Microsoft Word** dialog box, click **Blank lines next to slides**. Under **Add slides to Microsoft Word document**, make sure **Paste** is selected, and then click **OK**. On the taskbar, click the icon to switch to Word. **Save** the Word file in your **PowerPoint Chapter 8 folder** as **Lastname_Firstname_8C_Handouts** and then **Close** Word. (Mac users, the Mac version of PowerPoint does not support exporting handouts to Word. You can create PDF or printed handouts using the Print dialog box. Click File, click Print, and then click Show Details. Change the Layout to Handouts (3 slides per page). Click the PDF arrow and click Save as PDF.

12 Close PowerPoint. As directed by your instructor, print or submit your files electronically.

You have completed Project 8C | END

Chapter Review

Apply 8B skills from these Objectives:

5. Create a Sway Presentation
6. Add Content to a Sway Presentation
7. Format a Sway Presentation

In the following Skills Review, you will use Sway to create an online presentation for Laurel County Community College that gives an overview of student life at the college. The completed presentation will look similar to Figure 8.39.

Project Files

For Project 8D, you will need:

p08D_Books (JPG file)
p08D_Campus_Tour (MP4 file)
p08D_Student_Life (Word document)
p08D_Student01 (JPG file)
p08D_Student02 (JPG file)
p08D_Student03 (JPG file)
p08D_Student04 (JPG file)
You will save your files as:

Lastname_Firstname_8D_Student_Life
Lastname_Firstname_8D_Remix

Project Results

Figure 8.39, Project 8D Student Life

(continues on next page)

Chapter Review

Skills Review: Project 8D Student Life (continued)

1 Open your browser and go to **sway.com**. Click **Get Started**, and then sign in with your Microsoft account.

a. Click **Start from a document**.

b. In the **Open** dialog box, navigate to the student data files for this chapter, and then open the Word file **p08D_Student_Life**.

c. In the Sway **Storyline**, click in the first card that contains the title *Welcome to LCCC*, and then using your own name, change the title to **Lastname_Firstname_8D_Student_Life**

d. On the right side of the screen, click **Play** to view your Sway. Scroll to view the entire Sway, and then in the upper right, click **Edit** to return to your storyline.

2 In the **Storyline**, with the Title card selected, click the **Insert Content button**. Click **Heading** to insert a Heading 1 card. In the **Add a first-level heading** box, type **Welcome to LCCC** In the **Storyline**, scroll down until the *Welcome to LCCC* **Heading card** is near the top of your screen.

a. On the **Heading card**, click **Background**.

b. At the bottom of the **Suggested** menu, click **My Device**. In the **Open** dialog box, navigate to your data files for this project, and then double-click **p08D_Books**. In the **Heading card**, click the image, and then click **Focus Points.**

c. Under the large image on the right, click **The entire image is important** check box. Click **Play** to view your Sway in your browser. Then click **Edit** to return to your storyline.

3 Insert the image **p08D_Student01** as the background for the *Clubs and Organizations* **Heading card**.

a. On the *Clubs and Organizations* **Heading card**, click the image, and then click **Focus Points**.

b. In the large image, click the top of the tallest student's head to set the first focus point. Click the same student's book to set the second focus point.

c. **Play** your Sway, and then return to the storyline.

4 In the **Storyline**, scroll to display the *Student Life* **Heading card**.

a. Click in the text *Student Life* to select it, and then click the **Insert Content button**.

b. Click **Media**, and then click **Image** to add an image card below the *Student Life* **Heading card**. In the **Suggested** pane, scroll down and click **My Device**.

c. If necessary, navigate to your data files for this project. In the **Open** dialog box, click **p08D_Student02**, press and hold [Shift], and then click **p08D_Student_04** to select three pictures. Release [Shift], and then click **Open**. **Close** the **Suggested** pane. If necessary, click to select the check box for each picture

d. On the green *3 selected* bar, click **Group**. On the **Group Type** pane, click **Slideshow**. **Play** your Sway, scroll to the **Student Life** stack and click **Tap to flip through this stack to** view the images. Return to the storyline.

e. Click the first image of the three students sitting on the grass, and then at the top of the card, click **Focus Points**. Click **The entire image is important**. Set the focus points for each of the remaining images to **The entire image is important**.

5 In the **Storyline**, scroll to the **Campus Tour** group.

a. Click in the *Campus Tour* **Heading card**, and then at the bottom of the card, click **Insert Content**.

b. Under **Media**, click **Video**. In the **Suggested** pane, scroll down and then click **My Device**.

c. If necessary, navigate to your data files for this project. In the **Open** dialog box, click **p08D_ Campus Tour**, and then click **Open**. **Close** the **Suggested** pane.

6 In the **Storyline**, scroll to display and then click the **Welcome to LCCC** group.

a. On the **Text card**, select the text *Laurel County Community College*, and then click **Emphasize**. Select the last sentence, and then click **Accent**.

7 At the top of the screen, on the Sway menu bar, click **Design**.

a. Click **Styles** to open the **Styles** pane. Click **Customize**. Under **Color inspiration**, if necessary, click the > to scroll to display the three students sitting on the grass, and then click the image.

b. Under **Color palettes**, click the third palette—**Color Palette: 3**.

c. If necessary, scroll down to display the **Font Choices**. Click the **Font Choices arrow**, locate and then click **Bodoni**. **Close** the **Design** pane, preview your Sway, and then return to the **Storyline**.

(continues on next page)

Chapter Review

8 ▶ Open the **Styles** pane. At the top of the **Styles** pane, click the third option, **Slides.**

a. Play your Sway, click **Edit** to return to the **Design tab**. Click the **Storyline tab.**

b. On the **Sway menu bar**, click **Share**. As directed by your instructor, **Share** your Sway link with your instructor

c. On the **Sway menu bar**, on the right, click **More options**, and then click **Export.** In the **Export your Sway** dialog box, click **PDF**. Save the PDF file in your **PowerPoint Chapter 8** folder and submit as directed by your instructor.

9 ▶ On the **Sway menu bar**, on the right, click **More options**, and then click **Duplicate this Sway**.

a. In the **Duplicate this Sway** dialog box, change the name to **Lastname_Firstname_8D_Remix**

b. Click **Duplicate**. When the Sway is duplicated, click **Go to My Sways.**

c. Click your **Lastname_Firstname_8D_Remix** Sway to open it. On the Sway menu bar, click **Remix!** Play the Sway.

d. On the Sway command bar, click Design, click Styles, and then click **Remix!** several times until you find a design that you like.

e. As directed by your instructor, share or export your Sway.

f. Sign out of Sway and close your browser.

You have completed Project 8D   **END**

Mastering PowerPoint   Project 8E LCCC Staffing

In the following Mastering PowerPoint project, you will complete a PowerPoint presentation by adding slides from outlines created in Microsoft Word and proofing the file. Your completed presentation will look similar to Figure 8.40.

Project Files for MyLab IT Grader

1. In your **MyLab IT** course, locate and click **PowerPoint 8E LCCC Staffing**, Download Materials, and then Download All Files.
2. Extract the zipped folder to your PowerPoint Chapter 8 folder. Close the Grader download screens.
3. Take a moment to open the downloaded **PowerPoint_8E_LCCC_Staffing_Instructions**; note any recent updates to the book.

Project Results

Figure 8.40   Project 8E LCCC Staffing

For Non-MyLab Submissions

For Project 8E, you will need:

p08E_LCCC_Staffing

p08E_Staff_Positions (Word document)

In your PowerPoint Chapter 8 folder, save your presentation as:

Lastname_Firstname_8E_LCCC_Staffing

After you have named and saved your presentation, on the next page, begin with Step 2.

After Step 8, save and submit your presentation as directed by your instructor.

(continues on next page)

Content-Based Assessments (Mastery and Transfer of Learning)

1 Navigate to your **PowerPoint Chapter 8** folder you created, and then double-click the PowerPoint file you downloaded from **MyLab IT** that displays your name—**Student_PowerPoint_8E_LCCC_Staffing**. If necessary, click **Enable Editing**.

2 On **Slide 3**, display the **New Slide** gallery, and then insert **Slides from Outline** using the file **p08E_Staff_Positions**. (Mac users, convert the Word file to RTF before inserting into PowerPoint).

3 Use the **Format Painter** to copy the formatting from the title placeholder on **Slide 3** to the title placeholders on **Slides 4**, **5**, and **6**.

4 Use the **Format Painter** to copy the formatting from the content placeholder on **Slide 3** to the content placeholders on **Slides 4**, **5**, and **6**.

5 Remove the bullet on **Slide 3**. Format the text as two-columns, with 0.5" spacing between the columns. Move the insertion point before the word *Our* and press Enter to move the text to the top of the second column.

6 Correct the spelling errors on all slide (there should be three corrections).

7 Insert a header and footer on the notes and handouts, which includes the date and time updated automatically, the page number, and the footer **8E_LCCC_Staffing**

8 Modify the **Properties**. As the **Tags**, type **faculty, staffing** as the **Subject**, type your course name and section number. Make sure your name displays as author. **Save** the presentation.

9 In **MyLab IT**, in your **Course Materials**, locate and click the Grader Project **PowerPoint 8E LCCC Staffing**. In **step 3**, under **Upload Completed Assignment**, click **Choose File**. In the **Open** dialog box, navigate to your **PowerPoint Chapter 8 folder**, and then click your **Student_PowerPoint_8E_LCCC_Staffing** file one time to select it. In the lower right corner of the **Open** dialog box, click **Open**.

10 To submit your file to **MyLab IT** for grading, click **Upload**, wait a moment for a green **Success!** message, and then in **step 4**, click the blue **Submit for Grading** button. Click **Close Assignment** to return to your list of **Course Materials**.

You have completed Project 8E | **END**

Apply **8B** skills from these Objectives:

5. Create a Sway Presentation
6. Add Content to a Sway Presentation
7. Format a Sway Presentation

Mastering PowerPoint | Project 8F Student Clubs

In the following Mastering PowerPoint project, you will create a Sway by importing an outline created in Microsoft Word. You will add images and format the Sway. Your completed Sway will look similar to Figure 8.41.

ALERT This Project is not available as a **MyLab IT** grader project.

Project Files

For Project 8F, you will need:

p08F_LCCC_Clubs (Word outline)
p08F_Chemistry (JPG file)
p08F_Garden1 (JPG file)
p08F_Garden2 (JPG file)
p08F_Garden3 (JPG file)
p08F_Garden4 (JPG file)
p08F_Jazz (JPG file)

You will save your files as:

Lastname_Firstname_8F_LCCC_Clubs

Project Results

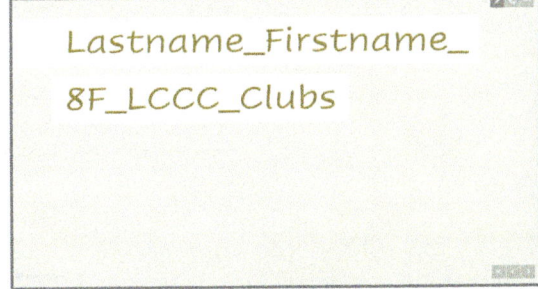

Figure 8.41 Project 8F Student Clubs

(continues on next page)

Content-Based Assessments (Mastery and Transfer of Learning)

1 Open your browser and go to **sway.office.com**.

2 Create a new Sway by importing the Word file **p08F_LCCC_Clubs**. Using your name, rename the Sway **Lastname_Firstname_8F_LCCC_Clubs**

3 After the title card, insert a new **Heading 1** card. In the Add a first-level heading box, type **Agriculture Club** As the background, insert the image **p08F_Garden1**. Set focus points to indicate the entire image is important.

4 Below the **Agriculture Club** card, insert the images **p08F_Garden2**, **p08F_Garden3**, and **p08F_Garden4**. Group the images as a stack.

5 Set the background of the **Chemistry Club** card to the image **p08F_Chemistry**. Set focus points to indicate the entire image is important.

6 Set the background image of the **French Club** card by searching for an online image using the **Suggested** pane. Set focus points as appropriate.

7 Set the **Jazz Club** background as **p08F_Jazz**. Set the focus points so that all of the words are visible.

8 Set the navigation of the Sway to **Scrolls horizontally**.

9 Use the inserted **Chemistry** image as the inspiration image and select an appropriate palette.

10 Change the font set to **Cavolini**.

11 As directed by your instructor, share or export your Sway.

You have completed Project 8F | END

MyLab IT Grader | **Mastering PowerPoint** | **Project 8G Student Clubs**

Apply 8A skills from these Objectives:

1. Insert Outline Text from Another Program into a PowerPoint Presentation
2. Proof a Presentation
3. Format Text as Columns
4. Save a Presentation in Other Formats

In the following Mastering PowerPoint project, you will create a PowerPoint presentation highlighting the various student clubs at Laurel County Community College. Your completed presentation will look similar to Figure 8.42.

Project Files for MyLab IT Grader

1. In your **MyLab IT** course, locate and click **PowerPoint 8G Student Clubs**, Download Materials, and then Download All Files.
2. Extract the zipped folder to your PowerPoint Chapter 8 folder. Close the Grader download screens.
3. Take a moment to open the downloaded **PowerPoint_8G_Student_Clubs_Instructions**; note any recent updates to the book.

Project Results

Figure 8.42   Project 8G Student Clubs

For Non-MyLab Submissions

For Project 8G, you will need:
p08G_Student_Clubs
p08G_Club_Sponsors (Word file)
p08G_LCCC_Clubs (Word file)

In your PowerPoint Chapter 8 folder, save your presentation as:
Lastname_Firstname_8G_Student_Clubs

After you have named and saved your presentation, on the next page, begin with Step 2.
After Step 9, save and submit your presentation as directed by your instructor.

(continues on next page)

Content-Based Assessments (Mastery and Transfer of Learning)

1 Navigate to your **PowerPoint Chapter 8** folder, and then double-click the PowerPoint file you downloaded from **MyLab IT** that displays your name—**Student_PowerPoint_8G_Student_Clubs.**

2 Insert **p08G_LCCC_Clubs** as slides from an outline. (Mac users, convert the Word file to RTF before inserting into PowerPoint).

3 On **Slide 2**, select the title placeholder, and then change the **Font Color** to **Black, Text 1**—the first color in the second column.

4 On **Slide 2**, select the content, and then change the **Font Color** to **Brown, Text 2**—the first color in the fourth column.

5 After **Slide 2**, insert **p08G_Club_Sponsors** as **Slides from Outline**. (Mac users, convert the Word file to RTF before inserting into PowerPoint).

6 Use the **Format Painter** to copy the formatting from the title placeholder on **Slide 2** to the title placeholder on **Slide 3**. Copy the formatting from the content placeholder on **Slide 2** to the content placeholder on **Slide 3.**

7 Remove the bullets from **Slide 3.**

8 Correct the spelling errors on **Slide 2** (there should be two corrections). Ignore any other spelling errors.

9 Insert a header and footer on the notes and handouts, which includes the date and time updated automatically, the page number, and the footer **8G_Student_Clubs** Add the **Tags student, clubs** as the **Subject**, type your course name and section number. Make sure your name displays as author. **Save** the presentation.

10 In **MyLab IT**, in your **Course Materials**, locate and click the Grader Project **PowerPoint 8G Student Club** In **step 3**, under **Upload Completed Assignment**, click **Choose File**. In the **Open** dialog box, navigate to your **PowerPoint Chapter 8 folder**, and then click your **Student_PowerPoint_8G_Student_Clubs** file one time to select it. In the lower right corner of the **Open** dialog box, click **Open.**

11 To submit your file to **MyLab IT** for grading, click **Upload**, wait a moment for a green **Success!** message, and then in **step 4**, click the blue **Submit for Grading** button. Click **Close Assignment** to return to your list of **Course Materials**.

You have completed Project 8G | **END**

Content-Based Assessments (Critical Thinking)

Apply a combination of the 8A and 8B skills.

GO! Fix It	**Project 8H Service Learning**	**IRC**
GO! Make It	**Project 8I Enrollment Trends**	**IRC**
GO! Solve It	**Project 8J Distance Learning**	**IRC**
GO! Solve It	**Project 8K Curriculum Enrollment**	

Project Files

For Project 8K, you will need:

p08K_Curriculum_Areas (Word file)

p08K_Enrollment

You will save your files as:

Lastname_Firstname_8K_Enrollment

Lastname_Firstname_8K_Handout (Word file)

Lastname_Firstname_8K_Picture (JPG file)

Lastname_Firstname_8K_Sway

In this project, you will create a presentation for Laurel County Community College to use to justify hiring more full-time faculty in the programs with the highest enrollments. Open the file **p08K_Enrollment** and save the presentation as **Lastname_Firstname_8K_Enrollment** Add the outline, **p08K_Curriculum_Areas**, to the presentation after the title slide. Format and proof the presentation.

Insert a Header & Footer on the Notes and Handouts, which includes the date and time fixed, the page number, and a footer **8K_Enrollment** In the properties, add your name and course information and the tags **students, enrollment**

Create a handout file named **Lastname_Firstname_8K_Handout**

Save one slide as a Picture—JPEG named **Lastname_Firstname_8K_Picture**

Create a Sway by importing the PowerPoint file. Name the Sway **Lastname_Firstname_8K_Sway** and export or share the Sway as directed by your instructor.

Save your presentation. Print or submit electronically as directed by your instructor.

		Performance Level		
		Exemplary	**Proficient**	**Developing**
Performance Criteria	**Inserted slide from outline**	Text from Word document appears on the slide and is formatted correctly.	Text from Word document appears on the slide but is not formatted correctly.	Slides from outline are not visible.
	Created Handouts	Handouts are created.		Handouts are not created.
	Maintained a professional appearance	Presentation is free from spelling and grammar errors.	Presentation has few spelling and grammar errors.	Spelling and grammar errors exist.
	Sway created from presentation.	Sway created using the correct content.	Sway created using the incorrect content.	Sway not created.
	Added the required elements	Completed all items correctly: file name, fixed date, page number, handouts, footer, and tags.	Completed all required items but one.	Failed to complete two or more required elements correctly.

You have completed Project 8K **END**

Outcomes-Based Assessments (Critical Thinking)

Rubric

The following outcomes-based assessments are *open-ended assessments*. That is, there is no specific correct result; your result will depend on your approach to the information provided. Make *Professional Quality* your goal. Use the following scoring rubric to guide you in *how* to approach the problem and then to evaluate *how well* your approach solves the problem.

The *criteria*—Software Mastery, Content, Format and Layout, and Process—represent the knowledge and skills you have gained that you can apply to solving the problem. The *levels of performance*—Professional Quality, Approaching Professional Quality, or Needs Quality Improvements—help you and your instructor evaluate your result.

	Your completed project is of Professional Quality if you:	Your completed project is Approaching Professional Quality if you:	Your completed project Needs Quality Improvements if you:
1-Software Mastery	Choose and apply the most appropriate skills, tools, and features and identify efficient methods to solve the problem.	Choose and apply some appropriate skills, tools, and features, but not in the most efficient manner.	Choose inappropriate skills, tools, or features, or are inefficient in solving the problem.
2-Content	Construct a solution that is clear and well organized, contains content that is accurate, appropriate to the audience and purpose, and is complete. Provide a solution that contains no errors of spelling, grammar, or style.	Construct a solution in which some components are unclear, poorly organized, inconsistent, or incomplete. Misjudge the needs of the audience. Have some errors in spelling, grammar, or style, but the errors do not detract from comprehension.	Construct a solution that is unclear, incomplete, or poorly organized, contains some inaccurate or inappropriate content, and contains many errors of spelling, grammar, or style. Do not solve the problem.
3-Format and Layout	Format and arrange all elements to communicate information and ideas, clarify function, illustrate relationships, and indicate relative importance.	Apply appropriate format and layout features to some elements, but not others. Overuse features, causing minor distraction.	Apply format and layout that does not communicate information or ideas clearly. Do not use format and layout features to clarify function, illustrate relationships, or indicate relative importance. Use available features excessively, causing distraction.
4-Process	Use an organized approach that integrates planning, development, self-assessment, revision, and reflection.	Demonstrate an organized approach in some areas, but not others; or, use an insufficient process of organization throughout.	Do not use an organized approach to solve the problem.

Outcomes-Based Assessments (Critical Thinking)

Apply a combination of the 8A and 8B skills.

| GO! Think | Project 8L Faculty |

Project Files

For Project 8L, you will need:

New blank PowerPoint presentation
p08L_Programs (Word file)
p08L_Degrees (Word file)
You will save your files as:
Lastname_Firstname_8L_Faculty
Lastname_Firstname_8L_Faculty_Show (Show)
Lastname_Firstname_8L_Sway

In this project, you will create a presentation showing the levels of education of the full-time faculty teaching at Laurel County Communication College.

Insert the files **p08L_Programs** and **p08L_Degrees** near the beginning of the presentation. This presentation should include at least four slides. The presentation is to be professional and appealing to the audience.

Save the presentation as **Lastname_Firstname_8L_Faculty** Check the presentation for spelling and grammar errors, and then save any changes.

Update the Notes and Handouts footer with the new file name. Add the tags **faculty, degrees,** your course information, and the author name in the properties. Save the presentation. Create a PowerPoint Show and Sway of the presentation.

Print or submit electronically as directed by your instructor.

You have completed Project 8L | END

| Project 8M | Anticipated Openings | IRC |
| You and GO! | Project 8N LCCC Faculty | IRC |

Appendix

MICROSOFT OFFICE SPECIALIST POWERPOINT 2019			
Obj Number	**Objective text**	**GO! Activity**	**Page Number**
1.0 Manage Presentations			
1.1	**Modify slide masters, handout masters, and notes masters**		
1.1.1	Change the slide master theme or background	4.01, 4.02, 4.04	305, 308, 311
1.1.2	Modify the slide master content	4.03, 4.11	309, 322
1.1.3	Create slide layouts	4.05	313
1.1.4	Modify slide layouts	4.06	314
1.1.5	Modify the handout master	4.07	315
1.1.6	Modify the notes master	4.08	316
1.2	**Change presentation options and views**		
1.2.1	Change slide size	1.17	131
1.2.2	Display presentations in different views	1.11, 1.19, 1.28, 1.33, 7.10, 7.14	119, 134, 142, 147, 482, 491
1.2.3	Set basic file properties	1.14, 1.33	123, 147
1.3	**Configure print settings for presentations**		
1.3.1	Print all or part of a presentation	6.16	443
1.3.2	Print notes pages	1.16	127
1.3.3	Print handouts	1.15	125
1.3.4	Print in color, grayscale, or black and white		
1.4	**Configure and present slide shows**		
1.4.1	Create custom slide shows	6.10	431
1.4.2	Configure slide show options	6.15	440
1.4.3	Rehearse slide show timing	6.15	440
1.4.4	Set up slide show recording options	Online Supplemental	
1.4.5	Present slide shows by using Presenter View	1.12, 6.13	120, 435
1.5	**Prepare presentations for collaboration**		
1.5.1	Restrict editing	4.21	336
1.5.2	Protect presentations by using passwords	4.20	335
1.5.3	Inspect presentations for issues	4.17, 4.18, 4.19	331, 333, 333
1.5.4	Add and manage comments	4.12, 4.13, 4.14	325, 326, 327
1.5.5	Preserve presentation content	3.17	256
1.5.6	Export presentations to other formats	8.05, 8.06, 8.07, 8.08, 8.09	522, 523, 523, 524, 526
2.0 Manage Slides			
2.1	**Insert slides**		
2.1.1	Import Word document outlines	8.01	513
2.1.2	Insert slides from another presentation	1.18	132

MICROSOFT OFFICE SPECIALIST POWERPOINT 2019			
Obj Number	**Objective text**	**GO! Activity**	**Page Number**
2.1.3	Insert slides and select slide layouts	1.04, 5.13	109, 383
2.1.4	Insert Summary Zoom slides	Online Supplemental	
2.1.5	Duplicate slides	6.12	432
2.2	**Modify slides**		
2.2.1	Hide and unhide slides	6.12	432
2.2.2	Modify individual slide backgrounds	3.03, 3.04, 3.05, 3.06, 3.07, 5.14	239, 240, 241, 242, 243, 385
2.2.3	Insert slide headers, footers, and page numbers	1.14	123
2.3	**Order and group slides**		
2.3.1	Create sections	7.10	482
2.3.2	Modify slide order	1.20, 1.29, 1.30	135, 142, 143
2.3.3	Rename sections	7.10	482
3.0 Insert and Format Text, Shapes, and Images			
3.1	**Format text**		
3.1.1	Apply built-in styles to text	2.23	202
3.1.2	Format text in multiple columns	8.04	520
3.1.3	Create bulleted and numbered lists	1.05, 2.02, 2.03	112, 174, 175
3.2	**Insert links**		
3.2.1	Insert hyperlinks	6.06, 6.07, 6.08, 6.11	422, 425, 427, 432
3.2.2	Insert Section Zoom links and Slide Zoom links	6.07	425
3.3	**Insert and format images**		
3.3.1	Resize and crop images	2.07, 2.09, 2.10, 5.05, 5.14, 5.17	179, 181, 183, 369, 385, 388
3.3.2	Apply built-in styles and effects to images	1.09, 1.10, 2.17, 2.22, 5.04	117, 118, 191, 201, 366
3.3.3	Insert screenshots and screen clippings	Online Supplemental	
3.4	**Insert and format graphic elements**		
3.4.1	Insert and change shapes	2.12, 4.04, 5.16, 5.17	185, 311, 387, 388
3.4.2	Draw by using digital ink	6.14	438
3.4.3	Add text to shapes and text boxes	2.11, 5.16	184, 387
3.4.4	Resize shapes and text boxes	2.12, 4.04	185, 311
3.4.5	Format shapes and text boxes	2.14, 2.17, 4.04, 5.01	188, 191, 311, 361
3.4.6	Apply built-in styles to shapes and text boxes	2.14, 2.16, 4.04	188, 191, 311
3.4.7	Add alt text to graphic elements for accessibility	4.17, 5.15	331, 387
3.5	**Order and group objects on slides**		
3.5.1	Order shapes, images, and text boxes	5.01	361
3.5.2	Align shapes, images, and text boxes	2.19, 2.20, 5.17	193, 195, 388

MICROSOFT OFFICE SPECIALIST POWERPOINT 2019			
Obj Number	**Objective text**	**GO! Activity**	**Page Number**
3.5.3	Group shapes and images	2.21, 5.07	195, 372
3.5.4	Display alignment tools	2.08, 5.01	180, 361
4.0 Insert Tables, Charts, SmartArt, 3D Models, and Media			
4.1	**Insert and format tables**		
4.1.1	Create and insert tables	3.18, 7.01, 7.02, 7.03	262, 467, 470, 471
4.1.2	Insert and delete table rows and columns	3.19, 7.04, 7.05, 7.06	263, 473, 474, 475
4.1.3	Apply built-in table styles	3.22, 7.09	266, 479
4.2	**Insert and modify charts**		
4.2.1	Create and insert charts	3.24, 3.27, 7.11, 7.12	268, 273, 486, 488
4.2.2	Modify charts	3.26, 3.28, 7.11, 7.13, 7.14	271, 275, 486, 489, 491
4.3	**Insert and format SmartArt graphics**		
4.3.1	Insert SmartArt graphics	2.29	208
4.3.2	Convert lists to SmartArt graphics	2.27	205
4.3.3	Add and modify SmartArt graphic content	2.28, 2.30	208, 209
4.4	**Insert and modify 3D models**		
4.4.1	Insert 3D models	2.35	212
4.4.2	Modify 3D models	2.35	212
4.5	**Insert and manage media**		
4.5.1	Insert audio and visual clips	3.14, 5.08, 5.11	253, 372, 378
4.5.2	Create and insert screen recordings	3.17	256
4.5.3	Configure media playback options	3.17, 5.09, 5.10, 5.12	256, 375, 376, 380
5.0 Apply Transitions and Animations			
5.1	**Apply and configure slide transitions**		
5.1.1	Apply basic and 3D slide transitions	1.31, 6.01	145, 411
5.1.2	Configure transition effects	1.31, 6.01	145, 411
5.2	**Animate slide content**		
5.2.1	Animate text and graphic elements	3.09, 3.29, 3.30, 6.03	246, 276, 277, 414
5.2.2	Animate 3D models	Online Supplemental	
5.2.3	Configure animation effects	3.09, 3.29, 6.03, 6.04, 6.05	246, 276, 414, 417, 419
5.2.4	Configure animation paths	3.09, 6.03	246, 414
5.2.5	Reorder animations on a slide	3.10	249
5.3	**Set timing for transitions and animations**		
5.3.1	Set transition effect duration	3.12, 6.01	250, 411
5.3.2	Configure transition start and finish options	1.32, 3.11, 6.02	146, 249, 413

Glossary

Artistic effects Formats applied to images that make pictures resemble sketches or paintings.

Accessibility Checker A feature that finds any potential accessibility issues and creates a report so that you can resolve the issues to make your file easier for those with disabilities to use.

Action button A special type of shape that you can add to your presentation and to which you can assign an action.

After Previous An animation option that begins the animation sequence for the selected slide element immediately after the completion of the previous animation or slide transition.

Alt text Text used in documents and webpages to provide a text description of an image.

Animation 1. The motion or movement that occurs as the presentation moves from slide to slide. 2. A visual or sound effect added to an object or text on a slide.

Animation Painter A feature that copies animation settings from one object to another.

Annotation A note or a highlight that can be saved or discarded.

Antonym A word that has the opposite meaning of another.

Aspect ratio The ratio of the width of a display to the height of the display.

AutoFit A command that resizes a column to accommodate the largest entry.

Background Removal A feature that removes unwanted portions of a picture so that the picture does not appear as a self-contained rectangle.

Background style A predefined slide background fill variation that combines theme colors in different intensities or patterns.

Banded columns A table setting that enables you to format even columns differently from odd columns to make the table easier to read.

Banded rows A table setting that enables you to format even rows differently from odd rows to make the table easier to read.

Bar chart A chart in which the data is arranged in horizontal bars and that is useful for showing comparisons among items.

Bar of Pie chart A type of pie chart that emphasizes one slice of the pie by representing the slice as a bar showing how the data in the slice are further divided.

Basic custom slide show A separate presentation saved with its own title containing a subset of the slides from the original presentation.

Black slide A slide that displays after the last slide in a presentation indicating that the presentation is over.

Body font A font that is applied to all slide text except slide titles.

Border A frame around a picture.

Brightness The relative lightness of an image.

Bulleted list A list of items preceded by small dots or other shapes, which do not indicate order or rank. Sometimes called unordered lists.

Caption Text that helps to identify or explain a picture or a graphic.

Card A Sway content element that includes the type of content and commands and settings to work with the content.

Category labels Text that displays along the bottom of the chart to identify the categories of data.

Cell The intersection of a column and row in a table.

Cell reference The intersecting column letter and row number that identify a cell.

Chart A graphic representation of numeric data.

Chart elements The various components of a chart, including the chart title, axis titles, data series, legend, chart area, and plot area.

Chart Elements button A button that displays options for adding, removing, or changing chart elements.

Chart Filters button A button that displays options for changing the data displayed in a chart.

Chart layout Determines the placement and display of chart elements such as the chart title, legend, and data.

Chart style A set of predefined formats applied to a chart, including colors, backgrounds, and effects.

Chart Styles button A button that displays options for setting the style and color scheme for a chart.

Clip A single media file such as art, sound, animation, or a movie.

Clustered bar chart A bar chart that compares values across categories.

Column chart A type of chart used for illustrating comparisons among related numbers.

Comment A note that you can attach to text or objects on a slide, or to an entire slide.

Compatibility Checker A feature that locates potential compatibility issues between PowerPoint 2019 and earlier versions of PowerPoint.

Compatibility mode Saving a presentation as a PowerPoint 97–2003 presentation.

Contiguous slides Slides that are adjacent to each other in a presentation.

Contrast The difference between the light and dark extremes of color in an image.

Crop A command that removes unwanted or unnecessary areas of a picture.

Crop handles Handles used to remove unwanted areas of a picture.

Crop pointer The pointer used to crop areas of a picture.

Crop tool The mouse pointer that displays when removing areas of a picture.

Crosshair pointer The pointer used to draw a shape.

Custom slide show Displays only the slides you want to display to an audience in the order you select.

Data marker A column, bar, area, dot, pie slice, or other symbol in a chart that represents a single data point.

Data point A chart value that originates in a worksheet cell.

Data series A group of related data points or chart values that originates in a worksheet cell.

Destination file The file into which information or an object is copied.

Document Inspector A PowerPoint feature that can find and remove hidden properties and personal information in a presentation.

Domain name Sometimes called the second-level domain. The part of a URL, such as www .philadelphiazoo.org, that represents a company or product name and makes it easy for users to remember the address. An organization's unique name on the Internet, which consists of a chosen name (phildelphiazoo) combined with a top level domain such as .com, .org, or .gov.

Editing The process of modifying a presentation by adding and deleting slides or by changing the contents of individual slides.

Embed Save a file so that the audio or video file becomes part of the presentation file.

Embedded A type of object that is saved with, and becomes a part of, a PowerPoint file.

Emphasis effect Animation that emphasizes an object or text that is already displayed.

Encryption The process by which a file is encoded so that it cannot be opened without the proper password.

Entrance effect Animation that brings a slide element onto the screen.

Exit effect Animation that moves an object or text off the screen.

Explode To pull out a slice of a pie chart so that it stands away from the pie in order to emphasize it.

Exploded pie chart A type of pie chart that displays all of the slices disconnected from each other. The slices cannot be manipulated individually.

Eyedropper A tool that captures the exact color from an object on your screen and then applies it to any shape, picture, or text.

Fill color The inside color of text or of an object.

Flash drive A compact removable drive that plugs into the USB port of the computer.

Focus Points Enable you to define the parts of an image that are important to display.

Footer Text that displays at the bottom of every slide or that prints at the bottom of a sheet of slide handouts or notes pages.

Formatting The process of changing the appearance of the text, layout, and design of a slide.

Gradient fill A fill effect in which one color fades into another.

Group Objects that are displayed together on the screen in a Sway.

Handout Master The specifications for the design of presentation handouts for an audience.

Hard return Created by pressing the Enter key to start a new line.

Header row The top row of the table that is formatted differently from the rows containing data.

Header Text that prints at the top of each sheet of slide handouts or notes pages.

Heading style A set of formatting characteristics, such as font name, size, color, paragraph alignment, and spacing, which is used to quickly format selected text.

Headings font A font that is applied to all slide title text.

Hyperlink A navigation element that, when clicked, will take you to another location, such as a webpage, an email address, another document, or a place within the same document. In a PowerPoint presentation, hyperlinks can also be used to link to a slide in the presentation, to a slide in a different presentation, or to a custom slide show.

Hyperlinked custom slide show A quick way to navigate to a separate slide show from within the original presentation

HyperText Markup Language (HTML) The authoring language that defines the structure of a webpage.

HyperText Transfer Protocol (HTTP) The Internet standard protocol that defines the exchange of information on the web. The set of communication rules used by your computer to connect to servers on the Web.

Joint Photographic Experts Group A file format used for photos with the .jpg and .jpeg extensions.

Kiosk A booth that includes a computer and a monitor that may have a touchscreen.

Layout The arrangement of elements, such as title and subtitle text, lists, pictures, tables, charts, shapes, and movies, on a slide.

Legend A chart element that identifies the patterns or colors that are assigned to the data series in the chart.

Line chart A type of chart commonly used to illustrate trends over time.

Line style How the line displays, such as a solid line, dots, or dashes.

Line weight The thickness of a line measured in points.

Link Save a presentation so that the audio or video file is saved separately from the presentation.

List level An outline level in a presentation represented by a bullet symbol and identified in a slide by the indentation and the size of the text.

Local drive A drive on your computer, such as the C: drive.

Lock aspect ratio When this option is selected, you can change one dimension (height or width) of an object, such as a picture, and the other dimension will automatically be changed to maintain the proportion.

Loop The audio or video file plays repeatedly from start to finish until it is stopped manually.

Mark as Final command Makes a presentation file read-only to prevent changes to the document.

Merge To combine two or more cells into a single cell.

Metadata The details about a file that describe or identify the file, including the title, author name, subject, and tags that identify the file's topic or contents. Also known as properties.

Microsoft Sway A free presentation tool that you can use to create and share interactive reports and presentations.

Mitered A border with corners that are square.

Motion Paths effect Animation effect that determines how and in what direction an object or text will move on a slide.

Mouse Over An action will occur when the presenter points to, or hovers over, the associated object.

MP4 video file (.mp4) The default file type when saving a video in PowerPoint 2019.

Navigation tools Buttons that display on the slides during a slide show that enable you to perform actions such as move to the next slide, display the previous slide, display the last viewed slide, or move to the end of the slide show.

Network drive A common drive on another computer, usually a server, that is available to others working on the network.

Noncontiguous slides Slides that are not adjacent to each other in a presentation.

Normal view The primary editing view in PowerPoint where you write and design your presentations.

Notes Master The specifications for the design of speaker's notes.

Notes page A printout that contains the slide image on the top half of the page and notes that you have created on the Notes pane in the lower half of the page.

Notes pane An area of the Normal view window that displays below the Slide pane with space to type notes regarding the active slide.

Numbered list A list of items preceded by numbers, which indicate sequence or rank of the items. Sometimes called ordered lists.

Office Theme Slide Master The slide master for the Office theme that contains the design, such as the background, that displays on all slide layouts in the presentation.

On Click An animation option that begins the animation sequence for the selected slide element when the mouse button is clicked or the spacebar is pressed.

Outline view A PowerPoint view that displays the presentation outline to the left of the Slide pane.

Outline view A document view in Microsoft Word that distinguishes the importance of data by the heading styles that have been applied.

Package Presentation for CD A PowerPoint feature that creates a package of a presentation and related files on a CD for ease of distribution.

Paragraph Any text that has a hard return at the end of it.

Pie chart A chart type that shows the relationship of parts to a whole and plots a single data series.

Pie of Pie chart A type of pie chart that emphasizes one slice of the pie by representing the slice as another pie showing how the data in the slice are further divided.

Pixel Short for picture element, represents a single point in a graphic image.

Placeholder A box on a slide with dotted or dashed borders that holds title and body text or other content such as charts, tables, and pictures.

Play Enables you to preview the way a Sway looks and behaves.

PowerPoint Designer A tool that helps you format slides that contain images by suggesting several professionally designed layouts.

Presenter View A view that shows the full-screen slide show on one monitor or projection screen while enabling the presenter to view a preview of the next slide, notes, and a timer on another monitor.

Presets Built-in adjustments from a gallery.

Properties The details about a file that describe or identify the file, including the title, author name, subject, and tags that identify the file's topic or contents. Also known as metadata.

Protocol A set of rules for communication between devices that determines how data is formatted, transmitted, received, and acknowledged.

Range Two or more selected cells on a worksheet that are adjacent or nonadjacent; because the range is treated as a single unit, you can make the same changes or combination of changes to more than one cell at a time.

Reading view A view in PowerPoint that displays a presentation in a manner similar to a slide show but in which the taskbar, title bar, and status bar remain available in the presentation window.

Recolor To change all the colors in the image to shades of one color.

Reviewer A person who adds comments to a presentation to provide feedback.

RGB A color model in which the colors red, green, and blue are added together to form another color.

Rich Text Format (RTF) file A non-application-specific file format used to transfer formatted text documents between applications.

Rotation handle A circular arrow that provides a way to rotate a selected image.

Ruler guides Dotted red vertical and horizontal lines that display in the rulers indicating the pointer's position.

Section A feature to organize your slides similar to using folders to organize your files.

Section header A type of slide layout that changes the look and flow of a presentation by providing text placeholders that do not contain bullet points.

Shape A slide object such as a line, arrow, box, callout, or banner.

Sharpen To increase the clarity of an image.

Sizing handles Small circles surrounding a picture that indicate that the picture is selected.

Slices Categories in a pie chart that represent parts of the whole and show the contribution of each value to the total.

Slide A presentation page that can contain text, pictures, tables, charts, and other multimedia or graphic objects.

Slide handout Printed images of slides on a sheet of paper.

Slide Master Part of a template that stores information about the formatting and text that displays on every slide in a presentation.

Slide pane A PowerPoint screen element that displays a large image of the active slide.

Slide Sorter view A presentation view that displays thumbnails of all of the slides in a presentation.

Slide transitions Motion effects that occur in Slide Show view when you move from one slide to the next during a presentation.

Smart guides Dashed lines that display on your slide when you are moving an object to assist you with alignment.

Smart Lookup A command that uses Bing to look up definitions, Wiki articles, and related searches from the web.

Smart Lookup pane A PowerPoint feature that has two tabs: Explore, which displays synonyms and web results, and Define, which displays a definition, synonyms, and word origin.

SmartArt graphic A visual representation of information that you create by choosing from among various layouts to communicate your message or ideas effectively.

SmartArt Styles Combinations of formatting effects that you can apply to SmartArt graphics.

Soften To decrease the clarity of an image or make it fuzzy.

Source file A file from which information or an object is copied.

Split To divide a cell into two or more cells.

Split button A type of button in which clicking the main part of the button performs a command and clicking the arrow opens a menu, list, or gallery.

Storyline Displays the cards that make up a Sway.

Style A collection of formatting options that you can apply to a picture, text, or an object.

Sway menu bar Contains commands to create and format a Sway.

Synonym A word that has the same or nearly the same meaning as another.

Table A format for information that organizes and presents text and data in columns and rows.

Table gridlines Nonprinting lines that display between columns and rows in a table.

Table style A format applied to a table that is consistent with the presentation theme.

Template A file that contains predefined formatting and layout. A template has the file extension .potx.

Text alignment The horizontal placement of text within a placeholder.

Text box An object with which you can position text anywhere on a slide.

Text effects Formats applied to text that include shadows, reflections, glows, bevels, and 3-D rotations.

Theme A set of unified design elements that provides a look for your presentation by applying colors, fonts, and effects.

Theme colors A set of coordinating colors that are applied to the backgrounds, objects, and text in a presentation.

Theme fonts The fonts that apply to two types of slide text—headings and body.

Thumbnails Miniature images of presentation slides.

Timeline A graphical representation that displays the number of seconds the animation takes to complete.

Timing options Animation options that control when animated items display in the animation sequence.

Title slide A slide layout—most commonly the first slide in a presentation—that introduces the presentation topic.

Top-level domain (TLD) The suffix, such as .com or .edu, that follows the domain name in a URL and represents the type of website you're visiting.

Track A song from a CD.

Transition A motion effect that occurs between slides in Slide Show view.

Transition speed The timing of the transition between all slides or between the previous slide and the current slide.

Trigger A portion of text, a graphic, or a picture that, when clicked, causes the audio or video to play.

Trim A command that deletes parts of a video to make it shorter.

Uniform Resource Locator (URL) The address of a website.

Variant A variation on the presentation theme style and color.

With Previous An animation option that begins the animation sequence at the same time as the previous animation or slide transition.

WordArt A gallery of text styles with which you can create decorative effects, such as shadowed or mirrored text.

Index

changing text fill and text outline colors, 202

defining, 201

inserting and aligning, 203

text effects in, 204–205

WordArt Styles

applying to existing text, 202

WordPad Desktop app, 78

worksheets

copying tables from, 471–473

editing chart data after closing, 271

wrapping text, 22

X

XML Paper Specification, 41

XPS files, 41, 126

Z

zip, 10

zipped files

downloading and extracting, 11–14, 65–66

extracting with File Explorer, 73–74

zipped folders, 65

zoom, 25

zoom levels

changing, 25–26

Page Width, 25–26

Zoom links, 426

Zoom slider, 25–26, 436, 441